THE OXFORD HANDBOOK OF

URBAN POLITICS

THE OXFORD HANDBOOK OF

URBAN POLITICS

Edited by

KAREN MOSSBERGER,
SUSAN E. CLARKE, AND
PETER JOHN

OXFORD
UNIVERSITY PRESS

OXFORD
UNIVERSITY PRESS

Oxford University Press, Inc., publishes works that further
Oxford University's objective of excellence
in research, scholarship, and education.

Oxford New York
Auckland Cape Town Dar es Salaam Hong Kong Karachi
Kuala Lumpur Madrid Melbourne Mexico City Nairobi
New Delhi Shanghai Taipei Toronto

With offices in
Argentina Austria Brazil Chile Czech Republic France Greece
Guatemala Hungary Italy Japan Poland Portugal Singapore
South Korea Switzerland Thailand Turkey Ukraine Vietnam

Published by Oxford University Press, Inc.
198 Madison Avenue, New York, New York 10016

www.oup.com

Library of Congress Cataloging-in-Publication Data
The Oxford handbook of urban politics / edited by
Karen Mossberger, Susan E. Clarke, and Peter John.
p. cm.
ISBN 978-0-19-536786-7 (acid-free paper)
1. Municipal government. 2. Metropolitan government.
3. Sociology, Urban. 4. Urban policy. I. Mossberger, Karen.
II. Clarke, Susan E., 1945– III. John, Peter, 1960–
JS78.O94 2011
320.8'5—dc23 2011022187

Contents

Contributors

Rob Atkinson is Professor and Urban Research Director, University of the West of England.

Harald Baldersheim is Professor of Political Science, University of Oslo.

Talja Blokland is Professor of Urban and Regional Sociology at the Institute of Social Sciences, Humboldt University of Berlin and research associate at the OTB Institute for Housing, Mobility and Urban Studies at Delft University.

Sophie Body-Gendrot is a Professor of Political Science and of American Studies and the Director of the Center of Urban Studies at the University of the Sorbonne–Paris IV.

Julie-Anne Boudreau is Associate Professor of Urban Studies at the Institut National de la Recherche Scientifique (INRS) in Montreal, Canada.

Michael Brown is Professor of Geography at the University of Washington.

Heather Campbell is Professor of Town and Regional Planning at the University of Sheffield.

Alistair Clark is Lecturer in Politics in the School of Geography, Politics, and Sociology at the University of Newcastle.

Susan E. Clarke is Professor of Political Science at the University of Colorado, Boulder.

Colin Copus is Professor of Local Politics at De Montfort University, Leicester, England.

Jonathan S. Davies is Professor of Critical Policy Studies at De Montfort University, Leicester, UK.

Keith Dowding is Professor of Political Science and Director of Research CASS at the Australian National University.

Niels Ejersbo is Associate Professor of Political Science and Public Management at University of Southern Denmark.

Susan S. Fainstein is Professor of Urban Planning at the Graduate School of Design, Harvard University.

Richard Feiock is Augustus B. Turnbull Professor of Public Administration and Policy at Florida State University.

Romain Garbaye is Professor of British Studies at the Université Sorbonne Nouvelle-Paris III (Sorbonne Paris Cité).

Marisol Garcia is Professor of Sociology at the University of Barcelona.

Mike Goldsmith is Emeritus Professor of Government and Politics at the University of Salford.

Hubert Heinelt is Professor of Public Administration, Public Policy, and Urban Research at Darmstadt University of Technology.

Rodney E. Hero is Professor of Political Science at the University of California, Berkeley.

Martin Horak is Director of the Local Government Program and Associate Professor of Political Science at the University of Western Ontario.

Peter John is Professor of Political Science and Public Policy, School of Public Policy, University College London.

Bryan D. Jones is the J.J. "Jake" Pickles Regents Chair in Congressional Studies at the University of Texas at Austin.

Dennis R. Judd is Interim Director of the Great Cities Institute and Professor of Political Science, the University of Illinois at Chicago.

Paul Kantor is Professor Emeritus of Political Science, Fordham University, New York City.

Roger Keil is Director of the City Institute at York University, Toronto.

Norbert Kersting is Professor and Chair of Local and Regional Government at the Institute for Political Science, University of Muenster.

Timothy B. Krebs is Associate Professor in the Department of Political Science at the University of New Mexico.

Daniel Kübler is Associate Professor of Political Science at the University of Zurich.

Christian Lefèvre is Director of the French Institute of Urban Affairs and Professor of Urban Government at the University of Paris Est Marne la Vallee.

Melissa Marschall is Associate Professor of Political Science at Rice University.

Margit Mayer is Professor of Political Science at the Freie Universität Berlin.

Evan McKenzie is Associate Professor of Political Science at the University of Illinois at Chicago.

John Mollenkopf is Professor of Political Science and Sociology, and the Director of the Center for Urban Research at City University, New York.

Karen Mossberger is Professor and Head of Public Administration at the University of Illinois at Chicago.

Eric Oliver is Professor of Political Science at the University of Chicago.

Marion Orr is the Fred Lippitt Professor of Public Policy and Professor of Political Science at Brown University.

Michael A. Pagano is Dean of the College of Urban Planning and Public Affairs and Professor of Public Administration at the University of Illinois at Chicago.

B. Guy Peters is the Maurice Falk Professor of American Government at the University of Pittsburgh.

Jon Pierre is Professor of Political Science, University of Gothenburg and Adjunct Professor, University of Nordland, Norway.

Herwig Reynaert is Professor of Political Science, Director of the Center for Local Politics and Dean of the Faculty of Political and Social Sciences at Ghent University.

Joshua Sapotichne is Assistant Professor of Political Science at Michigan State University.

H. V. Savitch is the Brown and Williamson Distinguished Research Professor at the University of Louisville.

Paru Shah is Assistant Professor of Political Science at the University of Wisconsin–Milwaukee.

Elaine B. Sharp is Professor of Political Science at the University of Kansas.

Kristof Steyvers is Lecturer of Political Science, Ghent University.

Clarence N. Stone is Research Professor of Public Policy and Political Science at George Washington University.

Richard Stren is Emeritus Professor of Political Science, and Senior Advisor, Cities Centre at the University of Toronto.

James H. Svara is Professor in the School of Public Affairs at Arizona State University.

Todd Swanstrom is the E. Desmond Lee Endowed Professor of Community Collaboration and Public Policy Administration at the University of Missouri, St. Louis.

Kurt Thurmaier is Professor and Director, Division of Public Administration, Northern Illinois University.

Jessica Trounstine is Assistant Professor of Political Science at the University of California, Merced.

Ivan Turok is Deputy Executive Director at the Human Sciences Research Council, South Africa, and Honorary Professor at the Universities of Glasgow and Cape Town.

Margaret Weir is Professor of Political Science and Sociology at the University of California, Berkeley.

Mark Whitehead is a Reader in Human Geography, Institute of Geography and Earth Sciences, Aberystwyth University.

Melvin Wingfield is Senior Research Fellow in the Local Governance Research Unit, Department of Politics and Public Policy, De Montfort University.

Hellmut Wollmann is Emeritus Professor of Public Administration at Humboldt University.

Harold Wolman is Professor of Political Science, Public Policy and Public Administration and Director of the George Washington Institute of Public Policy at the George Washington University.

THE OXFORD HANDBOOK OF

URBAN POLITICS

CHAPTER 1

STUDYING POLITICS IN AN URBAN WORLD: RESEARCH TRADITIONS AND NEW DIRECTIONS

KAREN MOSSBERGER,
SUSAN E. CLARKE, AND PETER JOHN

Why study urban politics? One reason is that the study of urban politics captures the rich experience of the urbanized areas in which the majority of the world's population now lives (United Nations 2010). So studying urban decision-making covers the subject matter of much of political science. Yet, this begs the larger question of what knowledge can be gained from examining *urban* politics rather than politics in general? After all, it might make sense to study public policy as it is implemented in urban areas, such as education, housing, urban renewal, and culture; or to analyze political participation more generally, as most votes are cast in cities, and protest and even revolutions start in urban centers—witness Egypt in 2011. Why should we study urban politics across countries, as we advocate here, when cities are embedded in different national political systems? Surely, the main variations that interest political scientists occur across states rather than within them?

In contrast to these arguments, we view urban political research as making an essential contribution to understanding political phenomena more generally, as well as to the specific context of local politics and urban environments. That is, we need to conceptualize and understand local/urban political processes, public problems, and forms of decision-making in relationship to a particular space or location, rather than just analyze the subareas of voting, policymaking, and social movements. Urban political scholars examine the politics of local areas as a set of linked processes, which vary considerably within the nation-state. These variations are tied to the specific constraints and traditions of particular places, which provide cases of political representation and policymaking. In this way, national politics is built from and is constituted by varied and complex subsystems in urban areas. Urban politics is both a field in its own right, with particular dynamics and constraints that vary from place to place; and an area of research that tells political scientists and other scholars much about politics more generally, whether at the local, national, or supranational level. Moreover, the existence of subnational areas across countries provides a unique research opportunity to extend the range of generalization, as scholars can observe variations both across and within countries. Today, the politics of urbanized areas reflect the ways in which societies deal with issues such as social and economic change, and how they attempt to realize their visions of democracy, inclusion, and justice. The study of urban politics offers a view of globalization and the diffusion of policy ideas in an age when urban areas and societies are ever more connected through an international economy, a shared environment, increased immigration, and more advanced information technology networks. Thus, it is no surprise to find urban scholars pursuing comparative research.[1]

With these opportunities in mind, the *Oxford Handbook of Urban Politics* has several goals: to present the diverse approaches to urban politics that populate the field today; to showcase new directions and emerging agendas; and to advocate a comparative perspective for urban analyses. The unique contribution of this volume is to provide a cross-national outlook on issues and research approaches across many different topics in urban politics.

Dialogue across countries necessitates a common conceptual language. While there are different traditions, with most European researchers referring to local politics, and North American scholars using the urban nomenclature, the various chapters show there is a basis for common agreement. At its most straightforward, urban politics is about authoritative decision-making at a smaller scale than national units—the politics of the subnational level, which is something that scholars from Europe, North America, and the rest of the world can agree about. Additionally, understanding the breadth of urban politics in the twenty-first century increasingly draws on a metropolitan perspective, including those who live in urbanized areas as well as the central cities (see Stoker 1998, 120 in Britain; and the Brookings Institution 2010 in the U.S.). Similarly, we construe the concept of urban politics broadly, as related to local governance as well as local government in urbanized areas.

1. Examples of attention to comparative research in urban politics in recent years include Sellers (2002), Kantor and Savitch (2002), Pierre (2005), Denters and Mossberger (2006), John (2001), DiGaetano and Strom (2003), Denters and Rose (2005) to name just a few.

While we have encouraged authors to connect their work to main currents in political science when possible, we have also urged them to discuss what is distinctively urban or local, and the contribution that an urban viewpoint makes. For example, the local character of urban politics also carries special significance in democratic societies. John Stuart Mill wrote that local governments are "schools of democracy" that afford greater participatory opportunities than other levels of government. Reality may sometimes be far from this ideal, as the Clark and Krebs chapter on local elections points out. Yet, urban politics has always the potential to be more participatory because local issues are also immediate, affecting the quality of life for residents in ways that are often readily apparent. At the same time that some forms of participation, such as voting, are declining on the local level, urban politics may yield new models for civic participation, that take advantage of the smaller scale and potential for greater interaction. Grassroots participation and representation are central concerns in urban politics, as discussed in the chapter on neighborhoods by Blokland and Horak and on social movements by Mayer and Boudreau. The concept of social capital has permeated nearly every area of social science, but it has special resonance in local politics, as Hero and Orr show in their chapter. Certainly, the study of urban politics provides a window into important questions and problems in democracy at the level closest to the citizen.

1. Comparative Thinking and a Bold Experiment

The contributions in this *Handbook* present a critical assessment of the state of theory and research on each topic, including methods, debates, and questions for future research. For this volume, however, we challenged authors to go a step further, and to bring a comparative perspective to their observations. The aims of this volume are comparative, but in the sense that we asked authors to assess research from multiple scholarly communities rather than to conduct cross-national research. In doing so, we hoped to move beyond a U.S.-centric volume and encompass the work of urban scholars in the UK, Canada, Europe, and elsewhere. Taking a comparative perspective allows us to compare empirical findings across studies in different countries, such as whether structural differences in local elections affect policy responsiveness. Theoretically, we can ask whether concepts such as "the just city" have different meanings across borders; or whether we can usefully compare local cultural conflicts in Europe and the U.S. Cross-national research on issues can also illuminate trends. Local government reforms have swept across countries, but does this represent convergence? A comparative approach allows us to consider evidence on interdependence, convergence, or persistent differences in urban political phenomena, as well as the implications of these trends for policy, politics, and scholarship.

To do this most effectively, we tried to stimulate a cross-national dialogue even where little had existed. Many contributions are written by paired authors from different sides of the Atlantic, chosen by the coeditors. Some had worked together before, but most had not. We matched junior scholars with senior colleagues when possible, and included authors from geography, sociology, and other social sciences. While the development of similar literatures or explicitly cross-national research differs across topics, we found many scholars doing related research across countries.

The comparative lens in this volume mainly reflects a North American and European focus. Restricting the scope primarily to these societies is intended to avoid comparing too broadly across widely varied contexts, where concept-stretching and theory become problematic (Sartori 1991, Collier and Levitsky 1997). Still, several chapters do acknowledge the growth of research on urban politics in developing countries. Goldsmith's chapter on intergovernmental relations examines trends in developing nations, and the Mayer and Boudreau chapter includes social movements in the global south. In the emerging agendas section, Stren considers critical issues for current and future research in these increasingly urban societies.

2. Innovation and Diversity in Urban Politics

In the following pages, we showcase "agenda-setting" work that is shaping the field. Readers will recognize familiar core themes of urban politics such as community power, growth and decline, poverty, and race. But, many chapters offer new insights based on contemporary trends. For example, Marschall and Shah indicate a need to study the politics of race and ethnicity in smaller cities in the U.S. because of the demographic change that has occurred in such communities. The chapter on local agendas is coauthored by scholars who have challenged urban political scientists to pay more attention to general theories of politics such as punctuated equilibria (Sapotichne, Jones, and Wolf 2007). Other chapters reflect the evolution of urban research in the last decades, addressing topics such as wired cities, sustainable cities, and the just city.

The first section of the volume introduces urban theory and research related to power and participation. The authors in this section demonstrate the diversity of theoretical approaches employed in studying urban politics, including institutionalism, rational choice, governance, and electoral behavior. While these theoretical frameworks are applied outside the urban context as well, the local vantage point yields important advantages, such as the ability to study interactions within systems of multilevel governance.

The second section addresses institutions and democratic practices within cities. The contributions range from research on the informal practices in neighborhoods and social movements to the changing formal structures and bureaucratic reforms that have characterized local government and intergovernmental relations in many countries.

The third section explores "Politics and the Changing Social Organization of Cities," including issues such as social capital, cultural conflicts, polarization and enclaves, race, ethnicity, immigration, and poverty. The diversity of cities makes them the ideal place to study these important issues and their implications for politics.

The fourth section on urban policy emphasizes the particular processes and politics of urban policy. Authors discuss what cities do across countries (the policy role that they play), and agenda-setting at the local level. Rather than trying to cover the many different substantive domains that are important for urban policy, chapters focus on selected areas of policy. These are issues that have animated the urban literature in recent decades (such as growth and decline, and economic competition) or that currently have special significance in the urban setting (such as security and environmental sustainability).

The concluding section, "Emerging Research Agendas," represents recent trends in urban politics and new issues that are likely to influence research and theory in the future. These include a recognition of the changing context of "the urban," in the suburbs and metropolitan regions of more developed countries, and the rapidly urbanizing centers of the developing world. Chapters examine the impact of technology on democracy and governance, and normative questions about social justice and urban politics. In the conclusion, Clarke provides an overview of themes that appear throughout the volume. Overall, the contributions in this *Handbook* demonstrate the many ways in which the policy-oriented and contextually grounded research typical of urban politics strengthens and extends our understanding of contemporary political and social dynamics.

REFERENCES

Brookings Institution Metropolitan Policy Program. 2010. *State of Metropolitan America: On the Front Lines of Demographic Transformation.* Available at http://www.brookings.edu/~/media/Files/Programs/Metro/state_of_metro_america/metro_america_report.pdf. Accessed March 20, 2011.

Collier, David, and Steven Levitsky. 1997. Democracy with Adjectives: Conceptual Innovation in Comparative Research. *World Politics* 49(3): 430–51.

Denters, Bas, and Karen Mossberger. 2006. Building Blocks for a Methodology for Comparative Political Research. *Urban Affairs Review* 41(4): 550–71.

Denters, Bas, and Lawrence E. Rose, eds. 2005. *Comparing Local Governance: Trends and Developments.* Houndmills, Basingtoke, Hampshire: Palgrave Macmillan.

DiGaetano, Alan, and Elizabeth Strom. 2003. Comparative Urban Governance: An Integrated Aproach. *Urban Affairs Review* 38(3): 356–95.

John, Peter. 2001. *Local Governance in Western Europe.* London: Sage Publications.

Kantor, Paul, and H. V. Savitch. 2002. *Cities in the International Marketplace: The Political Economy of Urban Development in North America and Western Europe.* Princeton, NJ: Princeton University Press.

Pierre, Jon. 2005. Comparative Urban Governance: Uncovering Complex Causalities. *Urban Affairs Review* 40(4): 446–62.

Sapotichne, Joshua, Bryan D. Jones, and Michelle Wolf. 2007. Is Urban Politics a Black Hole? Analyzing the Boundary between Political Science and Urban Politics. *Urban Affairs Review* 43(1): 76–106.

Sartori, Giovanni. 1991. Comparing and Miscomparing. *Journal of Theoretical Politics* 3(3): 243–57.

Sellers, Jefferey M. 2002. *Governing from Below: Urban Regions and the Global Economy.* Cambridge: Cambridge University Press.

Stoker, Gerry. 1998. Theory and Urban Politics. *International Political Science Review* 19(2): 119–29.

United Nations. 2010. *2009 Revision of World Urbanization Prospects.* Available at http://esa.un.org/unpd/wup/Documents/WUP2009_Press-Release_Final_Rev1.pdf. Accessed March 20, 2011.

PART I

POWER AND PARTICIPATION IN URBAN POLITICS

CHAPTER 2

POWER

CLARENCE N. STONE

For a period beginning in the 1950s and running through much of the 1970s, power was a central topic in political science, both in urban politics and more generally. The 2006 Annual Meeting of the American Political Science Association brought a brief return to prominence with "Power Reconsidered" as its theme. Notably, however, Richard Vallely's introductory essay to the program commented that after those opening years the topic of power "lost much of its fizz." He did suggest that there are signs of a cautious resurgence of interest, reflecting not so much a shift in fashion as a reality that, when all is said and done, much of political science is about power, even when treated, as often it is, obliquely.

One way of approaching this important but elusive concept is through a window of city politics, or what is commonly called community power. Alan Harding, for example, links power and place-shaping policy. In his examination of the urban arena, Harding allows ample room for political agency but without ignoring structural inequalities that form its context (2009).

1. Power in Context

The complexity of the urban setting illustrates why power can be a matter of wide-ranging debate. Start with a basic conception. Power can be broadly understood as the capacity to make things happen that otherwise would not happen. It is a significant form of causation, but can come in various forms. In the Max Weber tradition, Robert Dahl emphasizes conflict between intentional actors—A

This chapter draws on an earlier conference paper coauthored by Peter John.

has power over B to the extent that she can get B to do something B would not otherwise do (1957: 202–3). This basic scenario assumes that preferences are set and power is that which determines the outcome in a straightforward instance of clashing wills.

A different school of thought de-emphasizes individual actors in favor of power as a feature of a collectivity (Boulding 1989; cf. Hartsock 1983). Relations within the collectivity are crucial. The individual preferences of members of the collectivity may be malleable instead of firmly set, and they can vary in intensity. If the collectivity is able to act cohesively and effectively in pursuit of its chosen aims, then it is powerful. If unable to do so, it is weak. With this backdrop, consider how governing alliances form and evolve. While participation in an alliance may provide an opportunity to pursue policy aims, it may also require resource commitments and tacit obligations to become part of the alliance.

Think beyond the question of who prevails when A and B, with their fixed preferences, clash. A wider range of possibilities is at issue, and one lens for viewing them is asking who is and is not part of a governing alliance at a particular moment in time and why. Questions about alliance formation are a first step for moving past the question of "who governs," and it can be taken without letting go of inquiry into the role of choice-making agents. Asking simply "who governs" tends to reduce power study to a question of which body of individuals governs when political scientists in reality are interested in the choices key actors make within structures and constraints, and in the light of the leanings and choices of other actors.

Focusing on a body of individuals is an understandable misstep. Everybody who has carried out a study of policy leadership in the city inevitably dwells on the handful of people who seem to run the city whether it is old party bosses or a group of powerful business members, not least because those interviewed often talk in such terms. It is not easy to avoid a reduction to "which individuals." Transporting the analysis away from finding a group of powerful individuals may seem like a search for amorphous and depoliticized structures. It can lead to terms like "power structure" or the third face of power (Lukes 2005), which may be appealing but in the end get rid of politics. It also creates an entity that is very hard to study and that makes difficult the testing of hypotheses in a manner that is consistent with practice in mainstream political science.

The empirical dead-end that the debate about community power reached in the 1970s was partly a result of reification. In reality, the operation of power is embedded in a body of relationships that are far from static. Attention needs to go to both the operation of power and the field of relationships within which it occurs. In short, both agency and context matter. Community power then is not something to be distilled from actions and attributed to individuals, but rather is a body of relationships over which political agents engage in ongoing struggle. So where to begin? Alan Harding's recent essay offers a particularly useful springboard (2009).

2. Alan Harding and Agency

Harding's strategy is to build selectively on the old to move toward something new. He offers a brief history of the concept of community power, emphasizing that choice-making agents are at its core. His approach is thus compatible with (but not identical to) a rational-choice approach. In Harding's account, the community-power debate in its origins rescued human agency from an early urban sociology tied too closely to "blind imperatives" derived from a structural logic (2009: 29). Pluralists (who thought power was dispersed in the government structure) and their critics (who saw the governing process as not open and inclusive) alike found that there was not a single elite of wealth and status who governs a city, but that there were issues, debates, and political struggles. For his part Harding gives power a context by writing about community (urban) power as opposed to something abstract and context-free. The latter approach, Harding argues, is inescapably beset with unresolved questions about the nature and measurement of power in some essential sense. Harding thus stays clear of many esoteric and fine-grained theories of power and instead seeks to illuminate major features of the political landscape as they bear on the urban condition. He embraces a political-economy perspective (perhaps thereby underplaying the roles of race and gender), but he nevertheless puts us on a path toward recognizing the central place that power holds in urban political analysis.

Harding reminds us that the power debate came about, not from a dispute over generic qualities of power, but from inquiry into the workings of representative democracy in the local arena. Floyd Hunter (1953), thought of as a leading voice in an elitist school of politics, challenged the textbook version of democracy on the grounds that a civic and largely business-centered elite controlled agenda-setting in Atlanta. He also charted a path of reform that he believed would bring practice nearer to the ideal of inclusive representation. Robert Dahl, the iconic pluralist, presented New Haven (1961) as a realistic version of representative democracy, but one that in Dahl's case emphasized the political skill of an entrepreneurial mayor in building support for an ambitious redevelopment agenda despite the presence of strong centrifugal forces. Harding presents both sides of the community-power debate as concerned with "collective, place-shaping choices" and how they were made (2009: 32).

Framed in this way, the power debate is not about an unanchored query into the abstract nature of power, but instead is a concrete inquiry into how the politics of place-shaping constitutes itself. Indeed, Harding believes that the earlier unbounded debate about power lost appeal as it took a de-urbanized form and became more and more a conceptual argument (2009: 31). Grounding in the global and intergovernmental setting is relevant and, one could argue, today it is even essential. Yet Harding views this grounding, not as a matter of imposing an external logic, but as simply providing a context in which policy is forged through the "struggles and bargains between different groups and interests" (2009: 35).

By implication, power is inclusion in the process of making place-shaping decisions, and powerlessness is exclusion from that process. We should not think of this as a refined operationalization but only as a useful starting place in marking the political landscape and exploring its major features. Later in the discussion I offer a way of thinking about the exercise of power that is less conventional than what is suggested by the phrase "struggles and bargains."

Harding is clearly more in the camp of Floyd Hunter (rightly understood) than Robert Dahl. Although Harding does not go very far in laying out the specifics of how "collective place-shaping" takes place, he draws two closely related conclusions from past work. He notes that the community-power debate thoroughly demolishes the notion that the politics of place-shaping consists of anything so simple as elected officials translating the desires of citizens into policies that embody those desires. Instead he underscores a business bias: "the capacity of business groups and business 'needs' to shape policy agendas and decisions" (32). Harding quotes Charles Lindblom's *Politics and Markets* (1977): "business executives come to be admitted to circles of explicit negotiation, bargaining, and reciprocal persuasion, for which ordinary citizens are excluded" (quoted by Harding 2009: 34; p. 179 of Lindblom). In short, not only does business enjoy a special position because of its control of investment capital, but also its resources and position give it an inside post against which outsiders ("ordinary citizens") are little able to contend.

Harding focuses very much on the entrepreneurial city (see Harding et al. 1994), and thus argues that concerns and issues do not spring up in a vacuum; they arise and get filtered through ongoing connections and capacities to act. This does not mean that established relationships are beyond challenge. Indeed some national policies are launched with the aim of altering embedded local relationships, whether it be President Lyndon Johnson's Great Society or Prime Minister Margaret Thatcher's neoliberal remaking of Britain. But, as Harding argues, bounded human agency is an integral part of the process. Nationally backed efforts to remake relationships encounter inertia and resistance. National policymakers face unresponsive institutions and they also suffer from a lack of information in the center about local challenges. This of course may increase the salience of power relationships within local authorities and reduce the extent to which excluded local actors can draw on groups outside the locality to fight on their behalf.

Harding offers little elaboration of the struggles and bargains that constitute human political agency, but he clearly sees much more than decisional power at work. For attention to broader aspects of power, we need to look further afield and reconsider the faces of power, while adhering to Harding's insistence on agency and its applicability to the urban (that is, the collective, place-shaping) arena of policy.

3. The Faces of Power Reconsidered

There was a time when every student of politics was introduced to the different dimensions of power, summed up in an essay by Lukes (1974, 2005). On one side were the pluralists who focused on observable conflict and decisions; the second side was about the way in which powerful interests ensured that some issues were not on the agenda—nondecisions. Added to the two faces of power was the third dimension: ideology and political consciousness were among the terms used. Instead of pursuing shades of difference among these and related terms, below I employ "the faces of power" as a rough composite and steer clear of the more esoteric aspects of power as a phenomenon. Instead I adhere to Harding's call for a simpler line of inquiry.

My concern is to shift the emphasis from particular decisions and short-term outcomes to that of policy direction. Any mobilization may be a precursor to change in durable relationships, but that is a matter to be determined by research not by assumption. Durable relationships are the bedrock on which community power is exercised, and exclusion from those networks is a source of powerlessness. In bringing agency to light, I propose that such relationships, not particular individuals, be the main objects to keep in mind. Political agency does not mean action by disconnected individuals. Choices are made in a social context, and how relationships pervade the pursuit and foreclosing of choices is at the heart of the study of urban politics.

Consider an example that demonstrates the difficulty of exercising power for the excluded. In a study of gentrification along Chicago's Lakefront, sociologist Mary Pattillo widens the lens to include race and class (2007). Tracing the experience of public housing tenants in high-rise buildings and the many assurances they were given about no displacement from the old until the new was available, Pattillo concludes that "promises are political acts" (256). She elaborates:

> Over time, [promises] are pronounced, manipulated, retracted, and denied within a context of unequal abilities to define the situation. Public housing residents were from the very beginning fearful that the announced plans to rehabilitate the Lakefront Properties were nothing more than a front for actual designs to reclaim now prime lakefront land for the wealthy.... Their fears were dismissed as paranoid, and they were placated with promises of renovated buildings to which they would have the first opportunity to move back. But public housing residents seemed to be the only people whose memories endured through successive CHA, HUD, mayoral, aldermanic, and civic administrations. When they tried to commit their memory to paper in the form of contractual accords and agreements, they were still foiled by mercurial arrangements and porous legal mechanisms. (256)

Pattillo concludes: "the marginalization of poor citizens from the social networks of power allows public actors to define and redefine situations to further their own interests" (256).

At another point Pattillo assesses the situation this way: "Public housing residents did not have access to powerful networks. They were unable to hold institutions accountable. They could not define the terms of the debate. And because of their poverty, their claim on cultural, moral, or civic legitimacy was constantly called into question" (225). They lacked a place in the kinds of networks (relationships) that facilitate participation in the governing process.

Pattillo's analysis shifts the spotlight from those in a position to be an effective part of authoritative collective decision-making to those left outside. "Marginalization" is the key term she applies to those who are essentially excluded from the governing process. To her study, we can add many others about the poor and excluded in a long line of urban research from the 1960s to the present day (e.g. Gaventa 1980).

It is important to move from the easy cases of lack of power to the more ambiguous ones. Marginalization is rarely absolute (Cohen 1999). It is subject to change and can operate as a matter of degree, but is still a factor that counters the notion of a neutral playing field. In an earlier study of school desegregation in the 1960s, Robert Crain had found that the issue was never addressed on a blank political slate (1968). Civic and political relationships in place largely determined how responsive localities were to compliance with orders to desegregate. Where cosmopolitan elites had an established role in the education arena, as in Atlanta and Baltimore, peaceful desegregation was more likely to take place. Where they lacked such a role, as in New Orleans and Boston, turmoil and even violence were more likely to occur. Issues surface in a context of relationships already established. These relationships can be modified, but doing so is likely to be slow and difficult unless backed by substantial resources and by actors in a position to give change a sense of urgency. But sometimes a powerless group can get a break if their concerns fit a topic that catches on in the local agenda or if another group embraces their cause. As Dowding (1996) argues, that does not make them systemically powerful. But it does highlight the importance of contingency, opportunity, and political skill and timing.

A number of elements need to be taken into account in a relational understanding of power. Guideposts include:

3.1. Policy Direction

The evidence to be considered does not come from isolated decisions here and there, but rather from a flow of decisions, actions, and inactions over time. Because any given decision is subject to reversal or modification with a slight shift in circumstances, multiple observations are better than one or even a few. The aim is to understand a policy direction, not a given outcome at some particular point. Moreover, because power is not static, it is the trajectory that is important. And this means that shifts or modifications in direction are among the things to be examined closely.

3.2. Scope of Agency

Agency in collective, place-shaping choices comes in varying scopes. Some efforts may be responses to specific, short-term problems; but others may be part of a priority agenda. Though it might seem to some that the political landscape favors narrow, ad hoc decisions because they require less broad and less sustained action, the experience of Pattillo's public housing tenants suggest otherwise. Ad hoc concessions often prove not to be lasting. They are subject to significant crosscurrents. In some instances actors see the need for broad, long-term policy responses to problems and challenges, and they may set in motion courses of action that run counter to various ad hoc responses guided by unrelated considerations. To the extent that they succeed initially in their pursuits, ad hoc efforts inconsistent with broad and substantially supported aims are likely to be overrun or thrust aside, as was the case for public housing tenants seeking to retain space on Chicago's Lakefront. Though agendas themselves can be altered or replaced, they, not isolated decisions, are the major landmarks for policy direction.

3.3. Decision Processes

With scope of policy in mind, we can see why political activity is not confined to substantive issues. Especially for those with ample resources, efforts may go into developing or defending a favorable decision process, as portrayed in the second face of power. Think of it as investing in production as opposed to spending on retail goods (Stone 1982). Though calling for an investment up front, it is generally more efficient to expend resources on a process likely to yield favorable decisions than it is to influence decisions one by one. Consider how, for example, New Haven's Mayor Lee created a redevelopment process insulated from the city's board of aldermen and kept it closely tied to the office of mayor. In a similar move, Atlanta's governing coalition placed that city's redevelopment process with the Atlanta Housing Authority, an independent agency well insulated from popular pressures by virtue of a board of commissioners appointed for long, staggered terms of office. The faces-of-power issue thus calls for determining who is in a position to invest in (shape) the decision process and can bring together the resources to do so and who, like Chicago's tenants of public housing, lacks such a capacity.

3.4. Coalition-Building

In devising processes and pursuing place-shaping goals, actors in the collective decision process are not only potential rivals, they are also potential allies. A key part of the urban political scene revolves around the formation of policy coalitions and the emergence of some as usually able to control the agenda-setting process. Coalitions may be built pragmatically over time, hence developed in stages. Effective coalitions are not necessarily composed of like-minded members or members with similar value commitments (contrast Sabatier and Jenkins-Smith 1999). For example, a remarkable feature of Atlanta's long-running biracial coalition is that its members do not share a common ideology (Stone 1989). Instead this coalition consists of black political and business leaders who came together with white business and political leaders around an agenda framed by the slogan "the city too busy to hate." This slogan joined together the economic-growth goals of Atlanta's white business leaders with the racial-change goals of the city's black community. Framing, of course, does not stand alone, but can be combined with the distribution of selective incentives and the accommodation of sundry small-scale policy aims (Stone 1989). Although lines of cooperation are not predetermined, some connections, as Lindblom recognizes (1977), are more easily made than others (see also Stone 1980). And, as both Lindblom and Pattillo make clear from quite different perspectives, the making and maintenance of contacts is a valuable asset for building trust and facilitating alliances. Those without such contacts are greatly disadvantaged.

3.5. Choice in a Multilevel Setting

Though hardly formed on a neutral playing field, creative choices in a multilevel setting are part of the picture and potential sources of change. Thus it should also be borne in mind that relationship building at the local level does not operate in isolation. As Harding notes, cities are not "self-contained and independent entities" (2009: 32). Central government can alter the terms of local interaction by putting resources into the picture for designated purposes or altering rules of operation. For instance, Savitch and Kantor found in their cross-national study that the intergovernmental system can greatly affect place-shaping choices (2002; see also Sellers 2002). The Chicago example illustrates the impact of fiscal decentralization in creating incentives for real estate development on the agenda of American cities, although the extent and manner of pursuing those incentives is by no means a foregone conclusion. Countries differ in the degree to which they operate in an integrated manner across levels and also in the degree to which they make use of policies such as fiscal equalization. In addition, entities such as the European Union can bring still another layer of actors into play.

3.6. Policies in Complex Bundles

Real-world policy choices often are not simple and clear cut. Policy alternatives may come in complex bundles, and so another consideration is the matter of trade-offs (Jones 1994). Preferences in the abstract are one thing; preferences in reality are a different matter. Most choices involve opportunity costs. Pursuing one preference may mean foregoing another. Finally, achieving an intended aim may not be the end of the story. A given policy goal achieved may turn out to have unanticipated consequences.

One might be tempted to assume that the preferences of actors involved in collective choice-making are based on self-interests, and let it go at that. Such interests are undeniably a strong factor. However, they are not self-defining. We human beings are creatures of bounded rationality (Simon 1956; Jones 2001). We have limited understanding of the world around us and an incomplete repertoire of experiences to draw on. Because we do not know some aspects of complicated issues, discovery is a potential part of preference formation (Cohen and March 1986).

Another factor is feasibility (Chong 1991). Each of us discounts some preferences as being unrealistic. We give them little weight because we see them as infeasible, but circumstances and understandings can change perceptions.

Consider, for example, a group of city business executives concerned with place-shaping. They may prefer low property taxes and a high-performance education system. They may realize that to some degree these are contradictory preferences. Amply financed schools are more likely to be high performance. But a preference to sacrifice low taxes for better schools may depend on several calculations. One is whether the executives believe greater funding will in the particular circumstances actually convert into better schools. Or it might depend on whether local education funding generates greater intergovernmental support for education. Details can tilt a preference one way or another. There is also the question of intensity of preference. A corporate executive expecting a transfer to another city may for that reason become less committed to any given local issue. If the general pattern of corporate assignments is one of high geographic mobility, then place-shaping may diminish as a goal. A mix of factors can come into play to elevate some preferences and lessen the importance of others. Against this background coalition formation is not fully predictable without highly detailed information.

3.7. Complexity and Coalitions in Place-Shaping

Place-shaping does not occupy a narrow span of policy. It involves more than specific economic development initiatives. The above hypothetical example links education with place-shaping. Similar links occur with social peace or crime-control and other policy arenas. Moreover, as the economy continues to evolve the nature of the players also changes. In the U.S. today there is growing interest in the "ed and med" sector as many cities come to see their economic future tied to universities, hospitals, and related institutions (Perry and Wiewel 2005; Rodin 2007). Security costs, land needed for expansion, and a desire for responsible and constructive relations with surroundings residents are among the considerations that can come into play from a variety of actors, including community foundations and others from the philanthropic sector. With such a complex of factors at work and such a range of advocates in play, there is much leeway in how interests are defined and combined into policy agendas.

3.8. Preemption

Classic works on the "faces of power" often assume a political setting in which those in established governing arrangements seek to limit the scope of decision-making by heading off or weakening challenges. As put at one point, "those in a position of domination lay particularly heavy stress upon preventing the disaffected from raising issues..." (Bachrach and Baratz 1970: 105). Suppression is the focal activity (cf. Moore 1978). However, important as suppression may be, it is only part of the picture. It assumes that the push for change is from below, and resources along with advantaged positions are used to weaken that attempt. But significant energy for change may come from the top, and it sometimes takes the form of well-resourced players modifying arrangements so that they can obtain an inside advantage and pursue their favored agenda. Those in the lower ranks of society may find themselves politically isolated. Preemption rather than suppression may be the operative process (Stone 1988). No direct act of suppression may be involved.

3.9. Powerlessness Brought About by Social Change

Some elements of the community may simply be left out of consideration as broad, impersonal changes unfold. Without adequate resources, they are powerless to respond to profound sources of change. Consider, for example, the extraordinary case of Chicago's 1995 heat wave in which over 500 people died from heat-related causes. Sociologist Eric Klinenberg did a "social autopsy" that puts the event in context and shows the consequences of extreme marginalization (2002). The crux of the disaster was the "rise of an aging population of urban residents who live alone" (230). Klinenberg points to a changing society in which old-style neighborhoods with many social connections and forms of mutual, family-, and church-based assistance are becoming rare. This new "individuating" society is characterized by a spatial concentration that heightens the social distance between those who are affluent and those who are impoverished. As put by Klinenberg, "concentrated deprivation and abandonment compounds the risks of crime, disease, violence and isolation for the poor while putting impoverished people and regions out of sight" (231).

At the time of the heat wave, the city had embarked on efforts to "reinvent government" and contracted out a number of services. The city employed a language of empowerment of the citizen as a consumer; however, critics of this approach talked of "abandonment and vulnerability" (157). Klinenberg pictured a mismatch "between service delivery programs that demand activist clients and an increasingly elderly population whose isolation and frailty hinder their capacity to claim the assistance they need" (158).

Large impersonal forces such as individualization can have consequences for which some groups possess little capacity to respond. Powerlessness leads to neglect, as in the case of Chicago's elderly poor. In some cases large impersonal forces trigger a struggle over space, as in the case of gentrification spurred by globalization (Hyra 2008). In such instances, struggle makes the condition of powerlessness manifest. But the intricacy of the urban situation and the resulting complexity of coalition formation may leave many categories of residents without the allies needed to have a voice in responding to change. Their powerlessness is evident, not in the battles they lose nor in the acts of suppression they have experienced, but simply because they lack the *power to* engage effectively in the process of governing. We can understand this condition only by paying close heed to relationships that are not formed as well as those that are.

4. Relationships: Moving beyond *Who Governs?*

Not only is it important to see particular decisions in a policy-direction context, it is also important to move beyond who governs in an immediate sense and consider the question of how actors are related when collective decisions are made. We therefore need to be more attentive to what relationships political leaders (agents) work on and how they align and realign them, that is, how they form a collective *power to* act (Stone 1989, 227–29). Actors exercise power by shaping and entering arrangements among collectivities. Such a move may involve no direct clash of wills, but it may have long-term consequences for lines of conflict. In short, actors vary in capacity to shape and enter "power to" arrangements, and they all face limitations in this capacity.

To illustrate this point, we propose to reexamine the executive-centered coalition formed by Mayor Richard Lee in New Haven. The purpose in returning to this important feature in Dahl's classic work is to show why the relational dimension is a fundamental part of agency. A leader like Mayor Lee does not simply pursue a policy goal; Lee had to reshape relationships in order to pursue that goal. However, those reshaped relationships could not be used freely to pursue a range of other goals. Sets of relationships are not neutral means to pursue just any aim, and each set is better suited to pursue some aims than others. Thus it is less important to say that Mayor Lee governed than to understand how he governed and the constraints surrounding his leadership in that process.

Before reexamining Lee's leadership, we need to put him in broad context and acknowledge the wide difference between U.S. cities and their European counterparts (ignoring for now intra-European differences). Because the U.S. is less state-centered than are most European countries and because place-shaping governance in the U.S. has long been more decentralized than in most European countries, U.S. cities display a more complicated but less formal institutional architecture related to governance. Consider the basic point that electoral politics in U.S. cities is not organized around programmatic parties with strong local-national ties. For example, Atlanta's city elections are nonpartisan; those in New Haven are partisan, but patronage plays a major role. Overall the elements for governing are less formalized in the U.S., and the role of policy and managerial professionals is more modest.[1] In addition, the U.S. intergovernmental system allows for a more wide-ranging degree of local experiences. Even with decentralization in Europe, U.S. cities are generally less integrated into national programs and policies. With a less formalized structure of governance, in U.S. cities "candidate politics" is more pronounced than in Europe.

1. Change is occurring and transatlantic differences may be lessening (see John 2001), but the base points in an earlier time are quite divergent.

Relationships are less embedded in the governmental sector, and the governmental sector in the U.S. is less tightly organized for a governing role. While change puts generalizations at risk, it is nevertheless the case that, in the early days of the community-power debate, local civic and political relationships in U.S. cities took a decidedly less state-centered form.[2]

In his study of New Haven (1961), Dahl offers no explicit answer to his question of who actually governs, but two things stand out in his analysis. One is the central importance he attaches to elections as the mechanism that links leader actions to popular preferences. In Dahl's pluralism, the electoral connection is the crucial relationship. The second factor that Dahl emphasizes is the role of the gifted political entrepreneur, of which he sees Mayor Richard Lee as a prime example (see also Wolfinger 1974; Rae 2003). In Dahl's account, Lee was able to make a go of a large and complex redevelopment agenda where others had failed or not even made a sustained effort (for a less mayor-centric view, see Domhoff 1978). Dahl's interpretation is that Lee had the right combination of skills and resources along with a sense of how to stay within the bounds of an initially latent but loosely defined popular consensus.

Dahl's core analysis runs as follows:

> *Popular consensus + leadership skill in activating support → ambitious redevelopment.*

Alternatively, however, one can see a highly complex process in which the orchestration of relationships, not consensus, is the central element. Moreover, Lee's accomplishment in creating an executive-centered coalition is more limited than Dahl understood, writing, as he did, somewhat early in Lee's mayoral career.

What contextual relations does Dahl underplay? (1) The city's business leadership was distrustful of the city's largely patronage-based political organization—an organization by no means inclined to be subservient to the mayor; and (2) the city's black population was on the rise in numbers but lacking in ability to overcome its standing as a marginal group. The importance of this second point is enlarged by the fact that the civil rights movement put into place heightening expectations that made relegation to marginality highly frustrating.[3]

2. Note the observation of sociologist Robert Crain in his classic study of the politics of school desegregation: "one of the most complex issues in the study of American local government [is] the phenomenon of the businessmen and others who, without holding formal office, make up a civic elite that influences the government's actions" (1968: 356). Note also that, throughout much of the twentieth century, education was a policy arena in which career specialists played a very far-reaching role, closer to the European experience than was the case for most other policy arenas.

3. It should be acknowledged that Dahl's understanding of New Haven was based on research completed before the turbulent 1960s came to the forefront. Note, however, that recent research on the early years of Lee's mayoralty indicates that cross-racial consensus was weak even during the relatively quiet 1950s (Williams 2008).

With regard to business-city relations, Lee's challenge was not activating consensus; it was instead achieving an accommodation between business and city political arrangements. Lee did this first of all by creating a redevelopment agency tied to the mayor's office but largely disconnected from the city's ward-based city council.[4] Lee was able to do this by relying heavily on federal and intergovernmental funds along with foundation grants, thus bypassing legislative control of the budget. He secured the support of business and other weighty elements of the community through the use of a Citizens Action Commission (CAC), an advisory group appointed on grounds quite divergent from the city's patronage politics. Lee described the group this way:

> We've got the biggest muscles in New Haven on the top C.A.C.... They're muscular because they control wealth, they're muscular because they control industries, represent banks. They're muscular because they head up labor. They're muscular because they represent the intellectual portions of the community. They're muscular because they are articulate, because they're respectable, because of financial power, and because of the accumulation of prestige which they have built up over the years as individuals in all kinds of causes, whether United Fund, Red Cross or whatever. (Quoted in Dahl 1961: 130)

Was CAC window dressing? Perhaps in the sense of a voice in detailed decisions, but it placed the redevelopment program in a body of relationships in which business could keep an eye on the general character of the redevelopment program. A purpose of CAC was to reassure business especially, but others as well, that the city's redevelopment initiative was not a patronage operation. Significantly it was also an incompletely representative body, providing no voice for neighborhood groups.

The CAC played a part, an unsuccessful part as it turned out, in another major issue. Mayor Lee sought to formalize the position of the executive-centered coalition by proposing a new city charter that would enhance the authority of the mayor's office. Though the CAC endorsed the mayor's move, the charter lost in a referendum because the city's party organizations opposed it. Employing the CAC helped Mayor Lee align the city's "biggest muscles" with a largely externally funded redevelopment agenda and that mattered. When Lee moved to a different agenda, that alignment no longer carried great weight and Lee lost the referendum even though he himself had been recently reelected by a wide margin.

Writing before the racial turmoil of the 1960s, Dahl understandably did not foresee imminent changes in black politics in the city. New Haven's African American population of the 1950s was small though growing and, in Dahl's analysis, it was content to play the city's patronage game. At the same time, in pursuing redevelopment Mayor Lee came to see a need for an extensive social-policy agenda (Murphy 1971; Marris and Rein 1982). But his efforts in that vein generated controversy. The

4. In his study of New Haven Douglas Rae reports that the redevelopment agency was called "the Kremlin" in apparent recognition of its inaccessibility to much of the populace (2003: 318).

city attempted to pursue this aim through an independent and initially foundation-funded organization, Community Progress Incorporated. It was headed by a board created somewhat in the mold of CAC, but it needed to cultivate a much different constituency. It was formally independent of the mayor's office but de facto closely tied to it. That proved to be an unsuccessful approach, out of line with growing demands for greater community engagement. With external funding, the city's social agencies could increase services offered, but proved unable to solve the puzzle of how to align constructively with a marginal population, many members of which were highly frustrated but possessed limited resources and on their own lacked empowering relationships.

Discontent spilled over into the urban renewal program, and New Haven was one of the cities hit by civil disorder in 1967. That same year, when a federal Commission on Urban Problems held hearings in New Haven, city officials were so uneasy about maintaining order they positioned police throughout the hall to contain a feared outbreak of disruptive protest. As it was, by one account the hearing revealed "seething discontent" (Rae 2003: 350).

From Dahl's tabulation of successful initiatives and effective vetoes, Mayor Richard Lee was the central figure in governing New Haven. That he also won a succession of reelections underscores a continuing capacity to garner popular support. There is no question but that he was a large figure on the scene. But a close look at New Haven during the Lee mayoralty points to a pattern of governance in which Lee's capacity to govern was not a personal phenomenon but something contingent on an ability to work within a context and construct a particular supporting body of relationships while containing sources of discontent. That Lee was a key actor in governing seems a less apt description of his role than that that his early success in promoting redevelopment could not be extended to other important areas of policy. Even pursuit of redevelopment hit rough spots as the 1960s unfolded.

When we put Richard Lee's mayoralty in a trajectory of action and choice over time, it no longer seems apt to describe the mayor as an entrepreneurial leader governing by activating a consensus. As something vague, elusive, and tenuous, New Haven's consensus proves to be a poor tracking concept. Instead it seems more realistic to consider the spotty efforts by the mayor to orchestrate supportive relationships to bring about various policy outcomes and ask why the record is spotty. The important question would seem to be, not the mayor's record itself, but how and why various efforts had the outcome they did. In this way Mayor Lee becomes a less central figure in answering the question of who governs.[5]

Dahl's emphasis on New Haven's elected mayor as a central figure carries with it the implication that the path to empowerment is electoral mobilization in order to influence the mayor. Treating the mayor's record as a trajectory points up a weakness in this strategy. The mayor's office was important only as it linked with a broader body of relationships. Addressing a wide range of relationships rather than relying mainly on electoral mobilization appears a truer path to empowerment.

5. Consider a later view from the mayor's office, as offered in Rae (2003).

In the analysis of power, Dahl's "initiations and vetoes" and rankings on reputational lists by others have equally failed an adequacy test. Power is not a generic substance; it is highly situational. It is manifested in the formation of a durable relationship behind a policy direction. Just as the link between relationship and policy informs us that Mayor Lee's leadership in New Haven was only selectively effective, the inability of the British government to mandate local government-business partnerships tells us how difficult it is to spark a power relationship (Davies 2001). What Daniel Bell once called "enacted change" as an instance of power is beyond any simple metric (1961, 346–47), but a focus on a trajectory of policy-linked relationships enables us to examine political agency at work.

5. Conclusion

In writing *Community Power Structure*, Floyd Hunter sought to present a relational understanding of power.[6] He saw Atlanta as characterized by an arrangement that contradicted the ideals of representative government by elevating the concerns of some segments of society over others. His book, however, has seldom been treated on those terms. Though Hunter's identification of forty power figures (ten in four sectors) was only an interim step in a more complex form of analysis, that step proved to be one that invited misunderstanding. His term power structure has often been interpreted as referring to a specific body of actors (a "who") rather than as an overall arrangement of relationships in governing.

The temptation to play down relationships in favor of individual actors is strong. Actors are more easily observed than are their relationships. Dahl, for example, traces the evolution of power relationships in New Haven in large part by identifying the social background of individual occupants of the office of mayor. As employed here, being empowered consists of being part of a governing alliance and thereby having a voice in governing decisions. Empowerment is closely akin to what Browning, Marshall, and Tabb call political incorporation (1984). Of course, the simple matter of being or not being part of a governing alliance can and should be refined by considering how members of the alliance are connected in ways less superficial than membership in an official body. Hence it is vital that research go beyond the question of which individual actors "govern"' and examine the relationships on which a governing alliance is constructed, the strength of the alliance itself, and the policy scope of the alliance's agenda.

6. Significantly the term "relational power" has come to be strongly embraced by the Industrial Areas Foundation, the network of community organizations built on the early work of famed organizer Saul Alinsky. Relational power represents a shift from central reliance on confrontation to a realization that getting things done often hinges on the ability of people to establish a cooperative relationship (Cortés 1993: 20).

The challenge is to treat power as involving human agents making choices collectively while taking into account the importance of context. Clarissa Hayward thus encourages us not to concentrate on those who seem powerful and their political mechanisms but instead on the ways that relationships are defined by "practices and institutions" in order to question how they might be modified so as to bring about a more inclusive context in which collective decisions are made (2000: 176).

Robert Dahl treated contested election as the key context for empowerment, and Richard Valelly (2006) reminds us that, for some members of the discipline, this view remains basic to their understanding of power. We suggest that a much wider look at relationships is needed. Floyd Hunter started out by calling for a reexamination of the associational life of urban communities and how it empowers and disempowers. That message became lost, but could usefully be rediscovered.

As Hunter understood, the mere existence of an association does not guarantee a significant voice in place-shaping politics; the experience of Chicago's public housing residents does, however, reveal the consequences of being organizationally weak and disconnected. Nevertheless, a group can be highly organized and yet excluded from the inner networks of governing. Still there are clear examples of neighborhood and advocacy groups able to gain connections with the governmental sector and thereby become empowered as part of the collective decision process of governing the locality (Medoff and Sklar 1994).

Power is not an all-or-nothing phenomenon. Groups unable to establish a priority agenda may nonetheless be able to negotiate significant concessions from those who can. Hence some neighborhoods, environmental organizations, and working-class groups of color have learned to frame demands in such a way as to achieve significant gains (Altshuler and Luberoff 2003). In some cases these are embodied in formal documents called "community benefits agreements," and, in contrast with Pattillo's Lakefront public housing tenants, they sometimes achieve lasting concessions. These are matters to be weighed with relation to their scope and durability. Though not determining overall policy direction, concession can modify the impact on vulnerable populations. The nature of such benefits usually depends on who the major players are and the terms on which they are related to vulnerable populations and whether these populations have an active and ongoing say or not.

Sharp clashes of interest of the kind that often occurred between development-minded businesses and poor neighborhoods have not disappeared nor have their consequences—in many places "the ghost of urban renewal is always present" (Pattillo 2007: 8). Big universities and hospitals are also among the players often feared and mistrusted, but change is possible. In some instances entities in the "ed and med" sector have come to see that their well-being is in significant ways interlocked with the nonaffluent residents around them and have built new relationships accordingly (Rodin 2007). The scope and durability of these relationships are matters well worth inquiry, and it is research that can be informed by employing power as a framework of analysis.

Community power can become a user-friendly lens through which we can gain a much enhanced understanding of urban governance. By examining the flow of policy over time and probing the relationships that direct this flow, we can see that power is far from a static phenomenon. A past in which downtown business excluded poor neighborhoods or distant technocrats lacked connections to nonaffluent urban residents serves as an unreliable guide to the future. New players and potentially newly understood relationships open up possible fresh power configurations. To examine such a complex interplay between continuity and change requires a more detailed and more contextually informed analysis than what comes from a quick study of officeholders and civic elites. And even in-depth investigations need a wide lens if they are to be truly *community* power studies.

REFERENCES

Altshuler, Alan. and David Luberoff. 2003. *Mega-projects: The changing politics of urban public investment*. Washington, DC: Brookings Institution Press.

Bachrach, Peter, and Morton S. Baratz. 1970. *Power and poverty*. New York: Oxford Univ. Press.

Bell, Daniel. 1961. *The end of ideology*. New York: Collier Books.

Browning, Rufus P., Dale R. Marshall, and David H. Tabb. 1984. *Protest is not enough*. Berkeley. Univ. of California Press.

Boulding, Kenneth E. 1989. *Three faces of power*. London: Sage.

Chong, Dennis. 1991. *Collective action and the civil rights movement*. Chicago: Univ. of Chicago Press.

Cohen, Cathy J. 1999. *The boundaries of blackness*. Chicago: Univ. of Chicago Press.

Cohen, Michael D., and James G. March. 1986. *Leadership and ambiguity*, 2nd ed. Boston: Harvard Business School Press.

Cortés, Ernesto, Jr. 1993. "Reweaving the fabric." *Interwoven destinies*, ed. Henry G. Cisneros, 294–310. New York: Norton.

Crain, Robert L. 1968. *The politics of school desegregation*. Chicago: Aldine Publishing Company.

Dahl, Robert A. 1957. "The concept of power." *Behavioral Science* 2 (July): 201–15.

———. 1961. *Who governs?* New Haven, CT: Yale Univ. Press.

Davies, Jonathan S. 2001. *Partnerships and regimes*. Aldershot: Ashgate.

Domhoff, G. William. 1978. *Who really rules?* New Brunswick, NJ: Transaction Press.

Dowding, Keith. 1996. *Power*. Minneapolis: Univ. of Minnesota Press.

Gaventa, John. 1980. *Power and powerlessness*. Urbana: Univ. of Illinois Press.

Harding, Alan. 2009. "The history of community power," *Theories of urban politics*, 2nd ed., ed. Jonathan S. Davies and David L. Imbroscio, 27–39. London: Sage.

Harding, Alan, J. Dawson, R. Evans, and M. Parkinson, eds. 1994. *European cities towards 2000*. Manchester: Manchester Univ. Press.

Hartsock, Nancy C. M. 1983. *Money, sex, and power*. Boston: Northeastern Univ. Press.

Hayward, Clarissa R. 2000. *De-facing power*. New York: Cambridge Univ. Press.

Hunter, Floyd. 1953. *Community power structure*. Chapel Hill: Univ. of North Carolina Press.

Hyra, Derek S. 2008. *The new urban renewal*. Chicago: Univ. of Chicago Press.

Jones, Bryan D. 1994. *Reconceiving decision-making in democratic politics*. Chicago: Univ. of Chicago Press.

———. 2001. *The architecture of choice*. Chicago: Univ. of Chicago Press.

Klinenberg, Eric. *Heat wave*. Chicago: Univ. of Chicago Press, 2002.
Lindblom, Charles E. 1977. *Politics and markets*. New York: Basic Books.
Lukes, Steven. 1974. *Power: A radical view*. New York: Macmillan.
———. 2005. *Power: A radical view*, 2nd ed. New York: Palgrave Macmillan.
Marris, Peter, and Martin Rein. 1982. *Dilemmas of social reform*. 2nd ed. Chicago: Univ. of Chicago Press.
Medoff, P., and H. Sklar. 1994. *Streets of hope*. Boston: South End Press.
Moore, Barrington. 1978. *Injustice: The social bases of obedience and revolt*. London: Macmillan Press.
Murphy, Russell D. 1971. *Political entrepreneurs and urban poverty*. Lexington, MA: Heath Lexington Books.
Pattillo, Mary. 2007. *Black on the block*. Chicago: Univ. of Chicago Press.
Perry, David C., and Wim Wiewel. 2005. *The university as urban developer*. Armonk, NY: M.E. Sharpe.
Rae, Douglas W. 2003 *City: Urbanism and its end*. New Haven, CT: Yale Univ. Press.
Rodin, Judith. 2007. *The university and urban revival*. Philadelphia: Univ. of Pennsylvania Press.
Sabatier, Paul A., and Hank C. Jenkins-Smith. 1999. "The advocacy coalition framework." *Theories of the policy process*, ed. Paul A. Sabatier, 117–66. Boulder, CO: Westview Press.
Savitch, H. V., and Paul Kantor. 2002. *Cities in the international marketplace*. Princeton, NJ: Princeton Univ. Press.
Sellers, Jeffrey. 2002. *Governing from below*. Cambridge: Cambridge Univ. Press.
Soss, Joe. 1999. "Lessons of welfare." *American Political Science Review* 93, 2 (June): 363–80.
Stone, Clarence N. 1980. "Systemic power in community decision making," *American Political Science Review* 74, 4 (December): 978–90.
———. 1982. "Social stratification, nondecision-making, and the study of community power." *American Politics Quarterly* 10 (July): 275–302.
———. 1988. "Preemptive power: Floyd Hunter's 'Community power structure' reconsidered." *American Journal of Political Science* 32 (February): 82–104.
——— 1989. *Regime politics*. Lawrence: Univ. Press of Kansas.
Valelly, Richard M. 2006. "Power reconsidered." Originally published in *The Chronicle Review*, issue dated August 11, vol. 52, issue 49. http://chronicle.com
Williams, Yohuru. 2008. *Black politics/white power*. Malden, MA: Blackwell Publishing
Wolfinger, Raymond E. *The politics of progress*. Englewood Cliffs, NJ: Prentice-Hall, 1974.

CHAPTER 3

INTRALOCAL COMPETITION AND COOPERATION

KEITH DOWDING AND RICHARD FEIOCK

1. Introduction

The broad theme running through this chapter is given by its title—the relationship between competition and cooperation at the local level. Some people believe that the best way of organizing the public services provided by urban governments is to induce competition between providers. Using private markets as an analogy, the idea is that competition provides better and cheaper services than central planning. Others believe that competition for public services induces inefficiencies. The central argument for that view is that public services are exactly those types of goods for which markets fail and governments need to intervene. We review the technical argument for these positions in section 2. To some extent these debates mirror a more general debate in the urban literature over the optimal number and relevant size of urban jurisdictions. Some believe that urban governments are best organized into large units based around metropolitan areas or cities and large rural districts or counties (the terms vary across nations). Others believe that large numbers of small jurisdictions are preferable. Thus, another prominent theme is consolidation versus fragmentation. Orthogonal to these debates is also an account of how "rationalist" should be the organization of urban government. Should we try to design the best system of government based on technical and normative criteria or should the state be allowed to evolve organically to provide the kinds of service that people want? Do we want hierarchically ordered systems with command or organically grown systems of cooperation? Which is more efficient? Which provide the greater equality?

Cooperation is the theme in Section 4, since complex fragmented governments do pose coordination and collective action problems and we examine the myriad ways that local governments and agencies attempt to solve these problems. We begin by asking what the role of local government is and some of the problems that make answering questions about efficiency and welfare so difficult to answer.

2. Public Services and their Measurement

2.1. Why Provide Services?

The history of urban government in the developed world at least begins with citizens making demands for certain types of services. Initially these included general protections such as local defense, "law and order," and the rights to make local bylaws; but even early on in the process some welfare services were demanded. By the mid to late nineteenth century with a growing middle class further demands were made and so urban government developed by providing some goods and services where markets failed or partially failed, such as streetlights, sewerage, and waste collection and disposal, education, and other amenities (Prest 1990; Monkkonen 1988). In the developed world urban governments grew further in the period after World War II by providing more general welfare services involving explicitly redistributive policies.

Market failure occurs where goods and services display a high degree of "publicness." A public good is conventionally defined by two conditions: (1) a good is "jointly supplied" (or "nonrival") if one person's consumption does not reduce the amount available to others. For example, litter collection from a park affects all park users equally and one person's enjoyment of a park does not reduce others' pleasure. (2) A good is "nonexcludable" if the consumption of one person makes it available to other group members. If I sweep the snow and ice away from the front of my house so I do not slip, I enable others not to slip when they walk by my house. A pure private good is rival + excludable; a pure public good is nonrival + nonexcludable. So if we have a group with i members and a good x where the total amount of the good x available is X, then the consumption feasibility constraint is: if x is a private good then $\sum X_i \leq X$. If x is a public good then $x_i \leq X$. If $i = 2$ (it is a group of two members) and $X = x_1 + \alpha x_2$ (the first expression is what one person consumes, the second what the other consumes). So if $\alpha = 1$ then we have a private good. If $\alpha = 0$ then we have a public good. And if $0 < \alpha < 1$ then we have a mixed good. The degree of publicness affects the quality of demand signals.

The demand problem for collective goods is that if they are paid for at the point of delivery, unlike private goods, individuals have an incentive to underspecify their true demand, giving the wrong signal to suppliers and resulting in allocatively inefficient supply (Samuelson 1954; 1955; 1958), and the standard welfarist response to such issues is that such market failure requires government intervention. Neither degree of jointness nor nonexcludability is a static concept, and both technical and economic advances enable goods to become more or less private over time (for example, TV signals are now excludable where once this was technically infeasible; rich clientele might make a park economically excludable). One aspect of the changing nature of urban governance has been the general advance in wealth of the median voter who is prepared to reveal true preferences for excludable varieties of goods such as education enabling more vibrant markets. Since the later 1970s as voters exclude themselves from standard urban services, pressure for reducing their public supply and cutting tax has increased.

Not only do goods differ in degree of "publicness" but many services provided by governments are private goods and the decision for government intervention is based not on poor market signals but rather considerations of equity. Universal education, universal health schemes, housing, and many other welfare services are justified not by Samuelsonian considerations but because the political community has decided that these should be provided (what Savas [1987] calls "worthy goods"). So two important normative issues enter into consideration of the organization of the state: technical features driving efficient allocations and political commitments driving universalist equal welfare distributions.

The greatest extension of urban services occurred during the 1960s and early 1970s when the welfare state grew in the developed world following the strengthening of universalist and egalitarian principles. During this expansion local governments in Europe and the U.S. grew enormously both in terms of personnel but also in the forms of services they provided, both through their own initiatives but also as the point of delivery for state and central government service-provision.

2.2. Efficiency

Theoretical debates surrounding the best way of organizing local government often turn both on the interpretation of key normative values and on how those normative values are measured in empirical analysis: none more so than that of "efficiency."

One state of the world is said to be Pareto preferred to another state if there is at least one person who prefers the first state to the second and there is no person who prefers the second to the first. When utilized in public policy terms the strict conditions are relaxed and two components of efficiency emerge: technical (or productive) efficiency and allocative efficiency. Technical efficiency is the relationship between inputs and outputs. The higher the output of some productive process relative to the input the more technically efficient that process is. Thus at any given level of input citizens should all be better off the more technically efficient the production. Allocative efficiency is a relationship between demand and supply. It is generally considered that the more people who receive the type and level of service they want the more allocatively efficient the distribution.

Most tests of the efficiency of consolidated versus fragmented government tend to look only at either technical efficiency or allocative efficiency; rarely do they consider both simultaneously. Furthermore the measures of technical and allocative efficiency vary. All too often technical efficiency is measured by examining costs only without considering variations in the output. So writers will use data showing that fragmented (or consolidated) government spends less on a given service as though this fact in itself demonstrates productive efficiency. But of course productive efficiency requires that the same level of service is provided at lower cost. Spending cuts do not necessarily result in efficiency gains. Competition can mean a race to the bottom if the governments feel that reelection chances are determined by tax rates rather than service quality. It might be argued that the fact that tax rates determine reelection prospects demonstrates that poorer services at lower costs are preferred by the median voter who can stand as the test of allocative efficiency. However, given low rates of turnout in local elections the median voter need not represent the median citizen especially given the social and economic status (SES)-driven nature of the propensity to vote.

Allocative efficiency is usually measured by examining satisfaction as revealed through citizen surveys. However, interpretation of stated preferences in this manner often lacks theoretical justification. It has long been recognized that citizens tend to be more satisfied with services they use than with questions about their satisfaction with services more generally (Appleby and Alvarez-Rosete 2003; Goodsell 1990) and there are relationships between SES and stated satisfaction (Stipak 1979; Lyons et al. 1992; Dowding and John 2008). It is also recognized that levels of perceived satisfaction often do not correlate with objective performance indicators (Brown and Coulter 1983; DeHoog et al. 1990; Lyons et al. 1992; Parks 1983; Stipak 1980; Van Ryzin 2004; Van Ryzin et al. 2004; Link and Oldendick 2000; James 2009) and it is usually considered that the objective indicators are poorly specified or simply provide targets for councils to hit rather than useful measures of actual performance (Boyne 1997; Boyne 2002; Boyne et al. 2002; McLean et al. 2007).

One of the major problems with the satisfaction literature is that it is not clear where satisfaction comes from. While we expect there to be some relationship between satisfaction and actual levels of quality a number of factors can intervene to make comparative analysis problematic. For example, experimentally it is known that framing affects expectations, which in turn affect stated satisfaction (Kahneman 1999; Kahneman and Tversky 2000; Kahneman and Snell 1990) and there is a growing literature examining how expectations can affect stated satisfaction in this area (Roch and Poister 2006; Van Ryzin et al. 2004; James 2009). Where a service does better than expected (positive disconfirmation) satisfaction will result; where it falls short of expectations (negative disconfirmation) the consumer is likely to be dissatisfied (Spreng et al. 1996; Anderson 1973; Westbrook and Reilly 1983). Thus improving services from a low base might lead to greater stated satisfaction than maintaining services at a higher overall level. We can see therefore that there are considerable empirical problems encountered in attempting to measure the efficiency of different organizational structures.

3. Competition

3.1. Theory

Competition between providers of services is justified on both intrinsic and instrumental grounds. In recent years "choice" has been thought to be justified in its own right, allowing people more control of their lives. Whatever the efficiency of introducing choice, people gain process utility from feeling in more control and being able to pick and choose their service-providers (Le Grand 2007)—though any such gains might be outweighed by the costs of choice (Schwartz 2004; Dowding and John 2009). More generally, a multiplicity of rival service-providers is thought to enhance both allocative and productive efficiency—the former by enabling heterogeneity of services, the latter through competitive processes that drive down costs and mitigate the excesses of public-monopoly-induced rent-seeking. The earliest model of such competition was Tiebout (1956) who suggested that fragmented governments in large metropolitan areas could provide competition by inducing households to locate in those jurisdictions that provide them with the optimal tax-service packages. Allocative and productive efficiency would occur if the signals provided by such geographical mobility were strong enough to induce policy change.

Evidence for Tiebout mobility has been found (Dowding et al. 1994; John et al. 1995; Percy and Hawkins 1992; Teske et al. 1993; Bickers and Stein 1998; Stein 1987), though it is doubtful that the signals provided are strong enough to induce major policy change through such mobility alone (Dowding and Mergoupis 2003; Dowding 2008) and without this, along with matching conditions for people and communities, there is no guarantee of an equilibrium or that any equilibrium will be Pareto efficient (Atkinson and Stiglitz 1980, 538–51).

The exit mechanism can also work for businesses (Tiebout 1957) and Oates and Schwab (1991) suggest that tax competition can be applied to mobile capital, offering tax incentives to firms to locate in certain jurisdictions. This can lead to lower business taxes all round and a distribution from households to businesses as jurisdictions find themselves in a prisoners' dilemma situation. Exit should also operate within the context of politics or voice (Hirschman 1970) and politics might soften any exit effects. Hendrick et al. (2007) suggest that some tax policies—such as property taxes—are more conducive to voice processes, and others to exit—such as sales taxes, for example, may induce exiting one tax area to shop in another, obviously with far lower costs than moving house. Empirically examining the interaction between exit and voice is problematic (Dowding et al. 2000); the best extant attempt finds only weak effects of the one upon the other (Dowding and John 2012).

Nevertheless, proponents of fragmentation argue that the mere fact that governments do not have a clear local monopoly and can learn from successes and failures of nearby jurisdictions improves tax-service quality overall. In the leviathan hypothesis local governments are compared to private sector monopolies and seek to maximize revenue providing resources to rent-seek and provide bureaucratic slack (Brennan and Buchanan 1980; Oates 1985; Heil 1991; Chicoine and Walzer 1985; Moesen and Cauwenberge 2000). Where there is interjurisdictional competition across a metropolitan area the monopoly opportunities are restricted (Schneider 1989); hence where there is higher interjurisdictional competition the leviathan hypothesis states local taxes and expenditure should be higher. Some find evidence for the hypothesis (Martin and Wagner 1978; Shapiro and Sonstelie 1982; Sjoquist 1982; Nelson 1987, Zax 1988; 1989; Eberts and Gronberg 1990; Craw 2008) others evidence contradicting it (Palumbo 1983; Forbes and Zampelli 1989; Dolan 1990; Turnbull and Djoundourian 1993), with others finding mixed results (DiLorenzo 1983; Campbell 2004).

But fragmentation is not the only possible driver of expenditure. Higher expenditures in mayor-council communities might be a response to greater rent-seeking opportunities than in council-manager communities (see below) for which some evidence has been documented (Lyons 1978; Stumm and Corrigon 1998), though some studies reject this claim (Morgan and Pelissero 1980; Farnham 1990; Deno and Mehay 1987; Hayes and Chang 1990) with others giving mixed results (Farnham 1987; Ruhil 2003; Jung 2006). One recent study examines both leviathan and institutional effects together, suggesting there is some evidence of this institutional mediation of the competition effect (Craw 2008).

3.2. Organization for Competition

Within the political economy approach two broad theories of state organization operate with rather different principles. In what we call the "rationalist" school, tiers of government with technically specified demarcated spheres of responsibility are envisaged. This branch is strongly associated with ideas of "fiscal federalism" (Oates 1972; 1988; Blackorby and Brett 2000; Breton 1996). While competition exists horizontally across tiers, coordination and cooperation are mandated vertically by higher tiers. The stronger statist tradition in Europe and countries with European colonial ties has led to a more rationalist system in those countries.

The "irrationalist" school sees a more complex set of interlocking and overlapping jurisdictions created by evolution or "spontaneous order," which Hayek (1982) argues produces efficient markets. It is particularly associated with polycentric government (defended notably by the "Bloomington School" [Bish 1971; Bish and Ostrom 1973; McGinnis ed. 1999; Oakerson 1999; Ostrom et al. 1988]) and "marble cake" federalism (Ostrom 1987). Strong in the United States, polycentrist institutions in more "rationalist" countries have also been overlain with increasing complexity in the past fifteen to twenty years.

Fiscal federalism specifies a normative framework for the assignment of functions at different tiers of government with appropriate fiscal instruments for implementing those functions (Oates 1999). The principles are rationally defended in terms of efficiency largely determined by the principles of fiscal equivalence and the internalization of externalities (Olson 1969). Decision-making is dispersed across different and competing units with bundles of competencies. At the lowest levels there can be multiple competing jurisdictions. Citizen-consumers (or households) can choose to locate in the local jurisdictions that supply the best tax-service package for them (Tiebout 1956). The competition can drive allocative and productive efficiency allowing for both heterogeneity and competition over salient issues. Higher tiers provide coordination across the lower tiers, ensure economies of large scale for certain services and enable greater redistribution to enhance equality across different classes or groups of citizens who will be heterogenously distributed across the lower-level jurisdictions. There would be no overlap between jurisdictions at each level nor dual competencies across tiers. Such systems are rationalistic, as they are designed using the principles of fiscal equivalence and efficient production. Since reform would be costly and time-consuming they are meant to be stable and enduring.

The problems associated with fiscal federalism include the variable nature of goods and services. What might rationally be provided at one tier given technical and economic feasibility constraints at one time will not necessarily remain so over the long term as technical possibilities and new demand and supply conditions obtain. New demands for new types of services need to be slotted in while rent-seeking activity might cause irrationalities and pathologies to develop. While the lowest tiers might have discretionary powers to provide services not offered by other jurisdictions, the only response a household does have when certain demands are not met is to geographically relocate and such exit is costly. Standard public finance suggests that cross-subsidies from higher tiers to lower tiers will stimulate local demand at the same rate as tax cuts; while matching grants will do so at a lower cost to the donor tier (Cullis and Jones 1992, 312–14). However, empirical evidence suggests this is not the case. Gramlich and Galper (1973) estimate that each $1 of additional unconditional grant to state and local governments induces a $0.43 increase in local spending, while Gramlich's (1977) review suggests that lump-sum grants stimulate greater lower-tier spending than would tax cuts by as much eight to ten times as much. The so-called flypaper effect (money sticks to the sector it hits) is explained by "fiscal illusion" (voters think the real price of the service is the cost to the lower tier [Oates 1979; 1988]); budget maximizing (Niskanen 1971; King 1984); or Romer and Rosenthal's (1980) setter model where agencies offer a straight choice of reversionary budgets with lower utility to the median voter than the suggested budget with excess expenditure.

Polycentric government is composed of sets of single and multipurpose agencies with overlapping jurisdictions. Extending the idea, Frey and Eichenberger (1996a; 1996b; 1999) describe functional, overlapping, and competing jurisdictions (FOCJ), which are units defined over the tasks they do (functions), that may geographically overlap, and which directly compete with each other in the sense that individuals and organizations may choose which unit to belong to. They are jurisdictions in the sense they have enforcement power and can levy taxes. In effect FOCJ applies a Buchanan (1965) club analysis to local provision. Clubs form when like-minded people gather for welfare or other reasons. What happens in FOCJ is that similarly minded households and organization use the same service-providers as they have similar demands. Frey and Eichenberger see both U.S. special districts (i.e. ones created to provide a particular service) (Mehay 1984; Zax 1988, ACIR 1987; Foster 1997) and aspects of Swiss cantons as potential progenitors. Intersecting membership allows household exit without any need for geographical mobility.

The advantages of this type of governance structure include great flexibility for policy entrepreneurs to respond to demands, and citizens having an ever wider choice of agencies to deliver services in an age of greater complexity and faster technical change. Even in the more rationalistic systems of Europe, ad hoc problem-driven agencies, task forces, and interagency, interregional, and intermunicipal commissions have developed to try to deal with perceived problems. Single-purpose agencies might allow for more obvious accountability for the functions they provide than occurs with bundled services. The "irrationality" is defended by neoclassicists as it reflects an evolution of demands, which are met at equilibrium with entrepreneurial suppliers.

Problems that occur with the irrationalist system include difficulties in recognizing rent-seeking activities of so many units; costly search as households face a massive array of potential suppliers; and second-order coordination problems. As the number of jurisdictions multiply the problem of coordinating activities increases. We discuss some of these coordination problems in our discussion of cooperation below. Furthermore in a remarkable book Reifschneider (2006) demonstrates that the efficiency of FOCJ arrangements requires several restrictions: (1) there must be competition in all types of local public goods—if there is a monopoly supplier of just one public good all the gains from increased competition in other types can be lost, (2) efficiency requires discriminatory prices—largely so that higher costs of further-flung households will not be subsidized, (3) weak competition with low geographical mobility can drive out some units, (4) cooperation and collusion between FOCJ units, while bringing benefits that might emerge for specific goods, will drive out inefficiencies of competition overall. Once again, we see that the number of issues involved in urban governance regimes is such that it is difficult to provide a rationalized system.

Reifschneider (2006) proves that cooperation between units will reduce the efficiency of competitive processes. In that sense cooperation and competition are incompatible. However, cooperation might enhance welfare if it can reduce negative externalities and reduce production costs. It can also reduce spillover effects.

Furthermore, outside of pure theory, a system of some competition and cooperation might provide certain benefits. It is also the case the organically grown irrationalist processes cannot ensure efficiency, evolution cannot take one step back to go two steps forward. But human intellect can. Local politicians and administrators, and local people can see gains in cooperation between functionally distinct and jurisdictional different units. In the next section we examine the development of institutionally developed collective action especially in the most irrationalist systems in the United States.

4. Cooperation

4.1. Theory

Local government is increasingly taking on an "irrationalist" or polycentric character not only in the U.S. but around the world. Recent work has begun to explore collaborative intergovernmental arrangements as alternatives to centralized governmental provision of services. Competitive efficiencies need to be supported as diseconomies in public good production and interjurisdictional externalities bring obvious inefficiencies.

Institutional collective action (ICA) problems arise directly from the delegation of service responsibilities to a multitude of local governments and authorities. Fragmentation creates diseconomies of scale, positive and negative externalities, and common property resource problems. Independent service-provision decisions made by jurisdictions acting alone may hinder the ability of government officials to take advantage of opportunities to reduce the average cost of public services to their residents.

Formal and informal interlocal cooperation emerges through dynamic political contracting between or among local authorities. Cooperation results from bargaining and negotiation among the officials of affected jurisdictions. Leaders in each community weigh the utility that they expect to receive cooperatively with the utility that they gain when acting noncooperatively, but cooperative exchanges are not without transaction costs. The joint gains produced by collaborative arrangements may not be sufficient to stimulate the collective action necessary for local actors to create these mechanisms.

Consolidation of governmental authority may mitigate the ICA dilemma by eliminating independent authorities but this comes at a high cost. The costs of centralization include: creating great uncertainties about the balance of authority between levels of government, disrupting ongoing governance activities, and transforming the ICA dilemma into an intraorganizational dilemma that may be no easier to resolve (see Brierly 2004).

The ICA framework applies theories of individual-level collective action (Olson 1965) to institutional actors such as cities, counties, and government agencies (Feiock 2009; Feiock and Scholz 2010). Intergovernmental exchange relationships are embedded in larger social, political, and economic structures. Thus, agency and social network theories provide a basis for identifying benefits and transaction costs of collaboration (Lubell et al. 2002; Schneider et al. 2003; Feiock and Scholz 2009). If we assume that institutional actors act self-interestedly by selecting the available strategy that most enhances their short-term interests, then absent collaborative institutions, the collective action problem dictates that the outcomes of individual decisions will at times lead to collectively inefficient decisions.

Production efficiencies are lost if local authorities are too small to efficiently produce on their own a service each government wishes to provide. In addition, production of the service by small fragmented units produces externalities that spill across jurisdiction boundaries. The extent to which these ICA problems obtain depends on the specific policy arena, the governmental units affected, and the nature of the collective problems they face.

A policy arena is composed of formal policymaking venues with statutory authority to make policy decisions enforceable by the government, formal rules about participation and decision processes in each venue, and policy actors who are concerned with these policies. Externally imposed rules combine with the underlying collective problem to determine the specific incentives facing each actor.

The study of urban politics has traditionally focused on regional or central authorities as the mechanism for solving collective action problems. Instead, we argue that there are an array of mechanisms that vary in the extent to which self-organization is evident in their creation and use. The next section outlines the tools of regional governance and classifies them by their focus on collective or network relationships and the autonomy retained by local government units.

4.2. Organization for Cooperation

Feiock and Scholz (2009) suggest that the range of institutions that have emerged to mitigate ICA problems can be best understood according to the degree of autonomy the mechanisms afford local actors. Feiock (2009) argues that in regional governance these tools vary with regard to whether they focus on collective multilateral relationships or on individual bilateral exchange in networks. We extend this framework here to examine intergovernmental collaboration more generally by defining a formal taxonomy of collaborative institutions and arraying them according to whether the coordination mechanism relies primarily on political authority, legal or contractual arrangements, or social embeddedness and the extent to which the terms of a governance arrangement are subject to bargaining by individual members.

Centralized authority, mutually binding contracts or agreements, and network embeddedness provide three general mechanisms available to integrate decision-making across local government units in a metropolitan area (Feiock 2004; 2009).

Under centralized authority a new governmental unit is created or a higher-level government intervenes to consolidate authority and internalize ICAs. Under contracting, fragmented governments legally bind themselves to mutual action. Under embedded relations, agreements among local units are coordinated and enforced through a network of social, economic, and political relationships rather than formal authority (Feiock 2009). These mechanisms are not mutually exclusive and can complement each other (Feiock and Scholz 2009). The nature of these mechanisms makes them more or less costly for individual governments to exit the collaboration. Exit is most difficult with collaborative arrangements mandated through governmental authority, and easiest with cooperation based on voluntary relationships and social constraints.

4.2.1. *Centralized Authority*

Higher-level governments often have the authority to resolve collective problems due to fragmentation by expanding the geographic or functional jurisdiction of government to "internalize" the externalities resulting from fragmentation. For example, the political consolidation of general purpose local government unites multiple governments into a consolidated metropolitan government entity. Higher-level governments can also design and mandate special districts or networks to internalize unconsidered impacts over a broad geographic area for specific functions.

The political and administrative costs of relying on centralized authority as a regional integration mechanism limit the scope of its use. Existing government units generally resist their loss of autonomy, and production efficiencies are achieved at the cost of reducing the ability of local units to vary the provision of services to reflect different local preferences. Thus allocative efficiency is traded off for technical efficiency.

4.2.2. *Mutually Binding Agreements*

Contracts and regional organizations require the consent of those involved, so this institutional system preserves the autonomy of local actors while providing a more formalized mechanism for resolving externality issues of concern to all parties. To the extent that enabling legislation minimizes the transaction costs involved in developing, negotiating, and enforcing agreements, the Coase (1960; 1988) theorem suggests that contracting can resolve many of the diverse externality problems.

The ability to make legally binding agreements can be very flexible, involving bilateral agreements between two governments, or in other cases setting up a voluntary organization that binds the local governments to some degree, but relies on mutual consent. These arrangements are formally constituted, but voluntary in the sense that members participate at will and must approve activities. These institutions generally have limited authority to force members to do what they do not want to do, and the forces of both cooperation and competition remain within the arrangements (Gerber and Gibson 2006).

4.2.3. *Network Embeddedness*

Embeddedness relies on social, economic, and political relationships rather than formal authority. Self-organizing policy networks that rely on this mechanism offer several potential advantages over more formal solutions. By preserving the autonomy of the actors in a given dilemma, self-governing institutions avoid the inevitable political conflicts involved in revoking existing authority from local governments or specialized agencies. By generally requiring consent of all members, self-governing institutions enhance the search for mutually advantageous resolution of ICA and reduce the conflicts involved when majorities can impose solutions on unwilling minorities. By ensuring sufficient flexibility for rules, procedures, and exchanges to be decided locally, self-governing institutions can customize these rules to best fit the local conditions and specific ICA situations. To the extent that self-governing institutions contribute to local social capital, the resolution of one ICA can provide the basis for resolving unrelated ICAs in the same region as well.

Informal policy network structures emerge unplanned from interactions among institutional actors. Informal networks coordinate complex decisions within the formal structure. They preserve full local autonomy and require no formal authority, although federal and state programs can influence their development (Schneider et al. 2003). Policy networks can also complement central authority or contracts. The formal authority structures in political systems rely on informal, self-organized relationships among authorities for performance and stability to buffer the system from changing demands. Network interactions that tie responses to actions in one area to those in other policy areas or across time help members identify partners who are less likely to defect and build an enforcement structure to reduce transaction costs.

Cooperative arrangements also differ in the extent to which the terms of a governance arrangement are uniformly applied to all participants in a collective arrangement or are subject to bargaining by individual members. Figure 3.1 depicts nine general categories of cooperative service arrangements classified by whether the focus is on the extent to which terms are negotiated and whether the coordination mechanism allows individual units to act autonomously to enter or exit relationships. The upper row of the vertical dimension reflects relationships that are defined exogenously with decisions made collectively to bind all actors. The bottom row reflects relationships that are networks of individual choices by local units endogenously created through bilateral bargaining by individual members. The center row encompasses mechanisms that are somewhat standardized but subject to some influence by individual participants. The horizontal dimension captures the nature of the regional coordination mechanism. Forms to the left rely on the exogenous resources and authority of higher-level governments or other exogenous organizations. To the middle along this dimension, local units delegate some level of authority by voluntarily entering into organizations or contractual arrangements that bind themselves to some degree, but rely on mutual consent. To the right side,

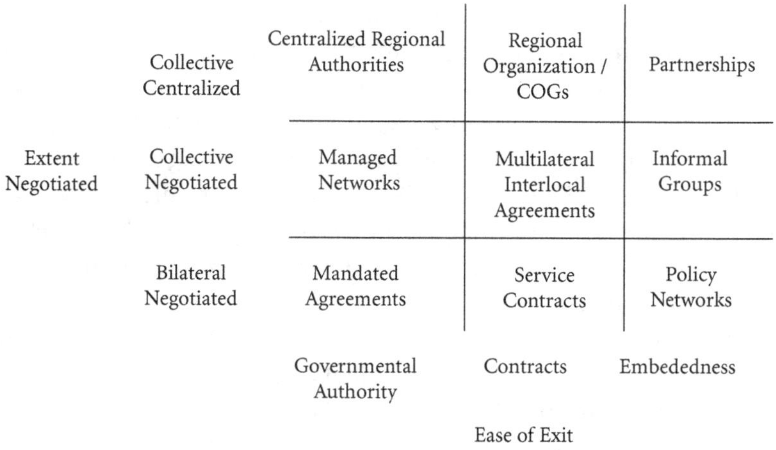

Figure 3.1. Collaborative Service Arrangement

relationships are informal and coordination is enforced by embedded social, economic, and political relationships rather than formal authority.

The types of collaborative institutions vary from centralizing governmental authorities in the upper-left quadrant that resolve the ICA problem by centralizing decision authority over the involved area, to informal policy networks in the lower-right quadrant that rely exclusively on self-organization and social embeddedness to coordinate decisions while preserving the autonomy of the involved policy actors.

Centralized regional authorities with sufficient functional and geographic scope can "internalize" the externality and scale problems as argued in fiscal federalist approaches. One example is the uniting of multiple local governments into a consolidated metropolitan general purpose government. Special districts provide a less obtrusive means of internalizing unconsidered impacts over a broad geographic area for a specific function. Regional authorities can be created and imposed by higher-level governments. For example, many states use regional level special districts to mitigate the horizontal problem of metropolitan service-provision for geographic consolidation of services like planning, resource management, schools, or emergency services (Mullin 2010; Andrew 2010).

Despite this efficiency rationale, efforts at city-county consolidation in the U.S. have been mostly unsuccessful. The failures of consolidation efforts can be attributed to political conflict and the availability of alternative, less costly coordination mechanisms (Carr and Feiock 2004). The political and administrative costs of creating regional governments limit the scope of consolidation and special district solutions to a narrow range of ICA problems. Existing agencies and government units generally resist any loss of authority. The larger units gain efficiencies in production, but frequently at the cost of reducing the ability of local units to vary the provision of services to reflect heterogeneous local preferences.

Managed networks encompass a set of mechanisms designed or coordinated by third parties such as higher-level government. In a managed network a higher-level government provides funds and incentives for collaborative service arrangements. Typically a higher-level government designates a lead organization with responsibility for developing, managing, and coordinating intergovernmental service-provision (Provan and Kenis 2008). An extensive literature focused on these managed service implementation networks has developed (Bardach 1998; Milward and Provan 2000; Mandell 2001; Meier and O'Toole 2001; Agranoff and McGuire 2003; Graddy and Chen 2006).

Mandated agreements require two governments—often a city and county or school district—to enter into service agreements. They specify the nature scope and some of the terms of agreements. In a managed network a higher-level government may provide funding but mandates the formation of collaborative relations among specified local governmental actors.

Regional organizations (RGO) are focused on collective and multilateral, rather than bilateral, cooperation. Structure and responsibilities are statutory, rather than negotiated, often based on federal and state laws. They take a variety of forms. The most common form in the U.S. are regional councils of governments (COGs) and metropolitan planning organizations (MPOs), designed to manage federal transportation issues in metropolitan areas by allocating federal funds.

Multilateral interlocal agreements are entered into voluntarily by local units. Some obligations may be negotiable but they generally require participants to accept common terms of agreement and obligations for action. Mutual aid agreements for emergency management are a prominent example.

Contract networks link individual units through joint ventures and service contracts that require the consent of those involved. This set of governance tools preserves local autonomy while providing a formalized mechanism for resolving externalities and other issues of concern to the parties. Contract networks link local governments in legally binding agreements, but because agreements often overlap they may also be supported by norms of reciprocity (Thurmaier and Wood 2002). Andrew (2009) argues that contractual ties developed locally produce general patterns of regional integration as bilateral ventures, agreements, and contracts create a unique formation of contractual ties at the macro level.

Partnerships are multilateral associations of diverse actors often including both public and private organizations. For example, regional economic development partnerships have become an increasingly popular approach to organizing regional economic development efforts (Feiock et al. 2009). A development partnership is an "alliance formed by local governments, often with the help of private sector firms and nonprofit organizations, which has a mission of enhancing the economy of a multijurisdictional area" (Olberding 2002, 253). Watershed partnerships are another example of regional partnership institutions that collectively address water-related issues at the watershed level relying on collaborative participation by governmental and nongovernmental actors (Lubell et al. 2002).

Informal groups or councils are voluntary associations of elected or appointed public officials that meet on an informal basis to share information and coordinate service activities. Informal group decisions can take the form of collectively reinforced shared understandings and expectations that, although only socially enforced, are binding. For example, in the Milwaukee metro region local development officials informally agreed to inform one another when a firm currently operating in one jurisdiction approached another regarding location incentives to move (Steinacker and Feiock 2003). Working-group coordination can also take the form of routine interactions through professional associations or community conferences (LeRoux 2007). In the Tampa Bay, Florida, area, the coastal communities meet monthly over lunch to share ideas, information, and informally coordinate actions through mutual consent absent any formal authority or enforcement mechanism.

Policy networks provide the greatest local autonomy in cooperative governance of local services. Network interactions can foster norms of trust that help participants identify partners where defection is less likely. Repeated face-to-face interaction is especially important in order for norms of reciprocity to develop and cooperative agreements to form (Axelrod 1984). Unlike formal authority structures that are defined in statute, policy network structures emerge unplanned from interactions among local actors. Informal networks coordinate complex decisions within the formal structure. They preserve full local autonomy and require no formal authority, although higher-level government can influence their development (Schneider et al. 2003).

It can be seen therefore that the institutional collective action problems engendered in "irrationalist" forms of government can be mitigated or solved in a multiplicity of ways evolving to solve specific problems faced by local governments of all forms. How efficient these methods are is difficult to empirically examine, but they are often preferred by local actors both to preserve local autonomy and power but also to ensure local variation.

5. Conclusions

Arguments for consolidated or fragmented government will not go away. And these ideas do not only apply at the urban level. Hooghe and Marks (2003) have argued that these competing ideas are replicated in the urban literature, writing on the European Union, within international relations and with public administration and public policy fields. As we argued, empirically examining the efficiency, effectiveness, and equity of different institutional forms is difficult and problematic; hence the issues will continue to be debated. We have examined arguments for competition both theoretically and reviewed some of the empirical evidence. It is clear that as pure conditions for competition cannot be maintained in the urban sphere—the complex nature of the goods and services provided, the high search and exit, and noisy signals for public authorities from such market movements—competition alone will not bring efficiency. For that reason in complex governance settings, many forms of institutional collective action need to develop. In our final section we reviewed these multiple forms. It is too soon to give definitive views on the efficiency of these processes, but there is no doubt that in the "irrationalist" forms of complex service delivery both citizen and public sector organizations respond to inefficiencies by attempting to coordinate activities. This does demonstrate that Hayekian evolutionary ideas do help to form local government structures where there is a lack of central "rationalized" organization. However, it is far from clear how efficient any equilibrium institutions that emerge will prove to be.

Competition might bring gains, but given the public good quality, externalities and spillover effects of many urban services, and the demand of equity and equality in public provision, cooperation is more important. In theory cooperation reduces the efficiency of competitive processes, but no pure competition exists anyway because of transactions and information costs. The past twenty years have seen growing irrationalism at the local level, not only in its heartland of the U.S. but also in the state-centered systems of Europe. Given this growing trend the types of cooperative systems that we have reviewed are likely to continue and will need to be strengthened.

REFERENCES

ACIR. 1987. *The Organization of Local Public Economies, A-109*. Washington, DC: U.S. Government Printing Office.

Agranoff, Robert, and Michael McGuire. 2003. *Collaborative Public Management: New Strategies for Local Governments*. Washington, DC: Georgetown University Press.

Anderson, R. E. 1973. "Consumer Dissatisfaction: The Effects of Disconfirmed Expectancy on Perceived Product Performance." *Journal of Marketing Research* 10:38–44.

Andrew, Simon A. 2010. "Adaptive versus Restrictive Contracts: Can They Resolve Different Risk Problems?" In *Self-Organizing Federalism: Collaborative Mechanisms to Mitigate Institutional Collective Action Dilemmas*, ed. Richard C. Feiock and John T. Scholz. Cambridge: Cambridge University Press.

Appleby, J., and A. Alvarez-Rosete. 2003. "The National Health Service: Keeping Up with Public Expectations." In *British Social Attitudes: The Twentieth Report: Continuity and Change over Two Decades*, ed. A. Park, J. Curtice, K. Thomson, L. Jarvis, and C. Bromley. London: Sage.

Atkinson, Antony B., and Joseph E. Stiglitz. 1980. *Lectures on Public Economics*. London: McGraw-Hill.

Axelrod, Robert. 1984. *The Evolution of Cooperation*. New York: Basic Books.

Bardach, Eugene. 1998. *Getting Agencies to Work Together: The Practice and Theory of Managerial Statecraft*. Washington, DC: Brookings Institute.

Bickers, Kenneth N., and Robert M. Stein. 1998. "The Microfoundations of the Tiebout Model." *Urban Affairs Review* 34 (1):76–93.

Bish, Robert L. 1971. *The Political Economy of Metropolitan Areas*. Chicago: Markham.

Bish, Roger L., and Vincent Ostrom. 1973. *Understanding Urban Government*. Washington, DC: American Enterprise Institute.

Blackorby, C., and C. Brett. 2000. "Fiscal Federalism Revisited." *Journal of Economic Theory* 92 (2):300–17.

Boyne, George. 1997. "Comparing the Performance of Local Authorities: An Evaluation of the Audit Commission Indicators." *Local Government Studies* 23 (4):17–43.

———. 2002. "Concepts and Indicators of Local Authority Performance: An Evaluation of the Statutory Frameworks in England and Wales." *Public Money and Management* 22 (2):17–24.

Boyne, George, P. Day, and R. Walker. 2002. "The Evaluation of Public Service Inspection: A Theoretical Framework." *Urban Studies* 39 (1197–212).

Brennan, Geoffrey, and James M. Buchanan. 1980. *The Power to Tax: Analytical Foundations of a Fiscal Constitution*. Cambridge: Cambridge University Press.

Breton, Albert. 1996. *Competitive Governments: An Economic Theory of Politics and Public Finance*. Cambridge: Cambridge University Press.

Brierly, Allen. 2004. "Issues of Scale and Transaction Costs in City-County Consolidation." In *City-County Consolidation and Its Alternatives: Reshaping the Local Government Landscape*, ed. J. G. Carr and R. C. Feoick. Armonk, NY: M. E. Sharpe.

Brown, K., and C. Coulter. 1983. "Subject and Objective Measures of Public Service Delivery." *Public Administration Review* 43: 50–58.

Buchanan, James M. 1965. "An Economic Theory of Clubs." *Economica* 32 (125):1–14.

Campbell, R. J. 2004. "Leviathan and Fiscal Illusion in Local Government Overlapping Jurisdictions." *Public Choice* 120:301–29.

Carr, Jered B., and Richard C. Feoick, eds. 2004. *City-County Consolidation and its Alternatives*. Armonk, NY: M. E. Sharpe.

Chicoine, D. L., and L. Walzer. 1985. *Government Structure and Local Public Finance*. Boston: Oelgeschlanger, Funn and Hain.

Coase, Ronald. 1960. "The Problem of Social Cost." *Journal of Law and Economics* 3:1–44.

———. 1988. *The Firm, the Market, and the Law*. Chicago: University of Chicago Press.

Craw, Michael. 2008. "Taming the Local Leviathan: Institutional and Economic Constraints of Municipal Budgets." *Urban Affairs Review* 43 (5):663–90.

Cullis, John, and Philip Jones. 1992. *Public Finance and Public Choice: Analytical Perspectives*. London: McGraw-Hill.

DeHoog, Ruth Hoogland, David Lowery, and W. E. Lyons. 1990. "Citizen Satisfaction with Local Governance: A Test of Individual, Jurisdictional and City-Specific Explanations." *Journal of Politics* 2:807–37.

Deno, K. T., and S. L. Mehay. 1987. "Municipal Management Structure and Fiscal Performance: Do City Managers Make a Difference?" *Southern Economic Journal* 53 (3): 627–42.

DiLorenzo, T. J. 1983. "Economic Competition and Political Competition: An Empirical Note." *Public Choice* 40:203–9.

Dolan, D. A. 1990. "Local Government Fragmentation; Does it Drive Up the Cost of Government?" *Urban Affairs Quarterly* 26 (1):28–45.

Dowding, Keith. 2008. "A Pandemonium of Confusions: Kay and Marsh on Tiebout." *New Political Economy* 13 (3):335–348.

Dowding, Keith, and Peter John. 2008. "The Three Exit, Three Voice and Loyalty Framework: A Test with Survey Data on Local Services." *Political Studies* 56 (2):288–311.

———. 2009. "The Value of Choice in Public Policy." *Public Administration* 87 (2):219–33.

Dowding, Keith, Peter John, and Stephen Biggs. 1994. "Tiebout: A Survey of the Empirical Literature." *Urban Studies* 31 (4–5):767–97.

Dowding, Keith, Peter John, Thanos Mergoupis, and Mark Van Vugt. 2000. "Exit, Voice and Loyalty: Analytic and Empirical Developments." *European Journal of Political Research* 37 (4):469–95.

Dowding, Keith, and Peter John. 2012. "Exits, Voices and Social Investment: Citizens' Responses to Public Services." Cambridge: Cambridge University Press.

Dowding, Keith, and Thanos Mergoupis. 2003. "Fragmentation, Fiscal Mobility and Efficiency." *Journal of Politics* 65 (4):1190–207.

Eberts, R. W., and T. J. Gronberg. 1990. "Structure, Conduct, and Performance in the Local Public Sector." *National Tax Journal* 43 (2):165–73.

Farnham, P. G. 1987. "Form of Government and the Median Voter." *Social Science Quarterly* 68 (3):569–82.

———. 1990. "The Impact of Citizen Influence on Local Government Expenditure." *Public Choice* 64 (3):201–12.

Feiock, Richard C. 2004. "Politics, Governance, and the Complexity of Local Land Use Regulation." *Urban Studies* 41 (2):363–77.

———. 2009. "Metropolitan Governance and Collective Action." *Urban Affairs Review* 44:356–77.

Feiock, Richard C., and John Scholz, eds. 2010. *Self-Organizing Federalism: Collaborative Mechanisms to Mitigate Institutional Collective Action Dilemmas*. Cambridge: Cambridge University Press.

Feiock, Richard C., Annette Steinacker, and Hyung Park. 2009. "Institutional Collective Action and Joint Ventures for Economic Development." *Public Administration Review* 69:256–70.

Forbes, Kevin F., and Ernest M. Zampelli. 1989. "Is Leviathan a Mythical Beast?" *American Economic Review* 79 (3):568–77.

Foster, Kathryn A. 1997. *The Political Economy of Special-Purpose Government*. Washington, DC: Georgetown University Press.

Frey, Bruno S., and Reiner Eichenberger. 1996a. "To Harmonize or Compete?. That is Not the Question." *Journal of Public Economics* 60:335–49.

———. 1996b. "FOCJ: Competitive Governments for Europe." *International Review of Law and Economics* 16:315–27.

———. 1999. *The New Democratic Federalism for Europe: Functional, Overlapping and Competing Jurisdictions*. Cheltenham: Edward Elgar.

Gerber, Elizabeth R., and Clark C. Gibson. 2006. "Cooperative Municipal Service Provision: A Political Economy Framework." In *Resource Sharing in Urban Areas*, ed. J. G. Carr. Armonk, NY: M. E. Sharpe.

Goodsell, C. 1990. *The Case for Bureaucracy: A Public Administration Polemic*. Chatham, NJ: Chatham House.

Graddy, Elizabeth A., and Bin Chen. 2006. "Influences on the Size and Scope of Setworks for Social Service Delivery." *Journal of Public Administration Research and Theory* 16 (4): 533–52.

Gramlich, E. M. 1977. "A Review of the Theory of Intergovernmental Grants." In *The Political Economy of Fiscal Federalism*, ed. W. E. Oates. Lexington, MA: Lexington Books.

Gramlich, E. M., and H. Galper. 1973. *State and Local Fiscal Behavior and Federal Grant Policy*: Brookings Papers on Economic Activity 1. Washington, DC: Brookings Institution.

Hayek, Friedrich. 1982. *Law, Legislation and Liberty: A New Statement of the Liberal Principles of Justice and Political Economy*. London: Routledge and Kegan Paul.

Hayes, K., and S. Chang. 1990. "The Relative Efficiency of City Manager and Mayor-Council Government: Implications for Policy Instrument Choices." *Public Administration Review* 63:616–25.

Heil, J. B. 1991. "The Search for Leviathan Revisited." *Public Finance Quarterly* 19:334–46.

Hendrick, Rebecca, Yonghong Wu, and Jacob Benoy. 2007. "Tax Competition Among Municipal Governments: Exit Versus Voice." *Urban Affairs Review* 43 (2): 221–55.

Hirschman, Albert O. 1970. *Exit, Voice and Loyalty: Responses to Decline in Firms, Organizations and States*. Cambridge, MA: Harvard University Press.

Hooghe, Liesbet, and Garry Marks. 2003. "Unraveling the Central State, but How? Types of Multi-Level Governance." *American Political Science Review* 97 (2):233–43.

James, Oliver. 2009. "Evaluating the Expectations Disconfirmation and Expectation Anchoring Approaches to Citizen Satisfaction with Local Public Services." *Journal of Public Administration Research and Theory* 19:107–23.

John, Peter, Keith Dowding, and Stephen Biggs. 1995. "Residential Mobility in London: A Micro-level Test of the Behavioural Assumptions of the Tiebout Model." *British Journal of Political Science* 25:379–97.

Jung, C. 2006. "Forms of Government and Spending on Common Municipal Functions: A Longitudinal Approach." *International Review of Administrative Sciences* 72 (3):363–76.

Kahneman, Daniel. 1999. "Objective Happiness." In *Well-Being: The Foundations of Hedonic Psychology*, ed. D. Kahneman, E. Diner, and N. Schwarz. New York: Russell Sage Foundation.

Kahneman, Daniel, and J. Snell. 1990. "Predicting Utility." In *Insights Into Decision Making*, ed. R. Hogarth. Chicago: University of Chicago Press.

Kahneman, Daniel, and Amos Tversky. 2000. "Choices, Values and Frames." In *Choices, Values and Frames*, ed. D. Kahneman and A. Tversky. Cambridge: Cambridge University Press.

King, D. 1984. *Fiscal Tiers: The Economics of Multi-Level Government*. London: George Allen and Unwin.

Le Grand, Julian. 2007. *The Other Invisible Hand: Delivering Public Services Through Choice and Competition*. Princeton, NJ: Princeton University Press.

LeRoux, Kelly. 2007. *Councils of Government and Nonprofit Community Conferences*. Working Paper: Wayne State University.

Link, M. W., and R. W. Oldendick. 2000. "The Role of Survey Research in the Benchmarking Process." *Journal of Public Budgeting, Accounting and Financial Management* 12 (1):138–64.

Lubell, Mark, Mark Schneider, John Scholz, and Mihriye Mete. 2002. "Watershed Partnerships and the Emergence of Collective Action Institutions." *American Journal of Political Science* 46 (1):148–63.

Lyons, W. 1978. "Reform and Response in American Cities: Structure and Policy Reconsidered." *Social Science Quarterly* 59 (1):118–32.

Lyons, W. E., David Lowery, and Ruth Hoogland DeHoog. 1992. *The Politics of Dissatisfaction: Citizens, Services and Urban Institutions*. Armonk, NY: M. E. Sharpe.

Mandell, Myrna P., ed. 2001. *Getting Results through Collaboration: Networks and Network Structures for Public Policy and Management*. Westport, CT: Quorum Books.

Martin, R. M., and R. Wagner. 1978. "The Institutional Framework for Municipal Incorporation: An Economic Analysis of Local Agency Formation Commissions in California." *Journal of Law and Economics* 21:409–25.

McGinnis, Michael D., ed. 1999. *Polycentricity and Local Public Economies: Readings from the Workshop in Political Theory and Policy Analysis.* Ann Arbor: University of Michigan Press.

McLean, Iain, Dirk Haubrich, and Roxanna Guitierrez-Romero. 2007. "The Perils and Pitfalls of Performance Measurement: The CPA Regime for Local Authorities." *Public Management and Money* 27 (2):111–17.

Mehay, Stephen L. 1984. "The Effect of Governmental Structure on Special District Expenditures." *Public Choice* 44:339–48.

Meier, Kenneth J., and J. O'Toole. 2001. "Managerial Strategies and Behavior in Networks: A Model with Evidence from U.S. Public Education." *Journal of Public Administration Research and Theory* 11:271–95.

Millward, H. B., and K. G. Provan. 2000. "How Networks are Governed." In *Governance and Performance: New Perspectives*, ed. C. J. Heinrich and L. E. Lynn. Washington, DC: Georgetown University Press.

Moesen, W., and P. van Cauwenberge. 2000. "The Status of the Budget Constraint, Federalism and the Relative Size of Government: A Bureaucracy Approach." *Public Choice* 104 (3–4):207–24.

Monkkonen, Eric H. 1988. *America Becomes Urban: The Development of U.S. Cities and Towns 1780–1980.* Berkeley: University of California Press.

Morgan, D. R., and J. P. Pelissero. 1980. "Urban Policy: Does Political Structure Matter?" *American Political Science Review* 74 (4):999–1006.

Mullin, Megan. 2010. "Special District Expansion versus Interlocal Contracts: Complements or Substitutes?" In *Self-Organizing Federalism: Collaborative Mechanisms to Mitigate Institutional Collective Action Dilemmas*, ed. Richard C. Feiock and John T. Scholz. Cambridge: Cambridge University Press.

Nelson, Michael A. 1987. "Searching for Leviathan: Comment and Extension." *American Economic Review* 77 (1):198–204.

Niskanen, William A. 1971. *Bureaucracy and Representative Government.* Chicago: Aldine Press.

Oates, Wallace E. 1972. *Fiscal Federalism.* New York: Harcourt Brace.

———. 1979. "Lump-sum Grants Have Price Effects." In *Fiscal Federalism and Grants-in-Aid*, ed. P. Mieszkowski and W. H. Oakland. Washington, DC: Urban Institute.

———. 1985. "Searching for Leviathan: An Empirical Study." *American Economic Review* 75 (4):748–57.

———. 1988. "On the Nature and Measurement of Fiscal Illusion." In *Taxation and Fiscal Federalism: Essays in Honour of Russell Mathews*, ed. G. Brennan, B. S. Grewal, and P. Groevewegen. Canberra: Australian National University Press.

———. 1999. "The Problem of Fiscal Federalism." *Journal of Democracy* 10 (2):83–86.

Oakerson, Ronald J. 1999. *Governing Local Public Economies: Creating the Civic Metropolis.* Oakland, CA: ICS Press.

Oates, Wallace E., and Robert M. Schwab. 1991. "The Allocative and Distributive Implications of Local Fiscal Competition." In *Competition Among States and Local Governments: Efficiency and Equity in American Federalism*, ed. D. Kenyon and J. Kincaid. Washington, DC: Urban Institute Press.

Olberding, Julia C. 2002. "Dividing into the 'Third Waves' of Regional Governance Strategies: A Study of Regional Partnerships for Economic Development in U.S. Metropolitan Areas." *Economic Development Quarterly* 16:251–72.

Olson, Mancur. 1969. "The Principle of Fiscal Equivalence." *American Economic Review* 59 (2):470–87.

Ostrom, Vincent. 1987. *The Political Theory of a Compound Republic: Designing the American Experiment.* 2nd ed. Lincoln: University of Nebraska Press.

Ostrom, Vincent, Robert Bish, and Elinor Ostrom. 1988. *Local Government in the United States.* San Francisco, CA: ICS Press.

Palumbo, G. 1983. "City Government Expenditures and City Government Reality: A Comment on Sjoquist." *National Tax Journal* 236 (2):249–51.

Parks, Roger B. 1983. "Linking Objective and Subjective Measures of Performance." *Public Administration Review* 44:118–27.

Percy, Stephen L., and Brett W. Hawkins. 1992. "Further Tests of Individual-level Propositions from the Tiebout Model." *Journal of Politics* 54:1149–57.

Prest, John. 1990. *Liberty and Locality: Parliament, Permissive Legislation, and Ratepayers' Democracies in the Mid-Nineteenth Century.* Oxford: Clarendon Press.

Provan, Keith G., and Patrick Kenis. 2008. "Modes of Network Governance, Structure, Management and Effectiveness." *Journal of Public Administration Research and Theory* 18 (2):229–52.

Reifschneider, Alexandra Petermann. 2006. *Competition in the Provision of Local Public Goods.* Cheltenham: Edward Elgar.

Roch, Christine H., and Theodore Poister. 2006. "Citizens, Accountability, and Service Satisfaction." *Urban Affairs Review* 41 (3):292–308.

Romer, Thomas, and Howard Rosenthal. 1980. "An Institutional Theory of the Effect of Intergovernmental Grants." *National Tax Journal* 33:451–58.

Ruhil, Anirudch V. S. 2003. "Structural Change and Fiscal Flows: A Framework for Analysing the Effects of Urban Events." *Urban Affairs Review* 38 (3):396–416.

Samuelson, Paul A. 1954. "The Pure Theory of Public Expenditure." *Review of Economics and Statistics* 36:387–89.

———. 1955. "Diagrammatic Exposition of a Theory of Public Goods." *Review of Economics and Statistics* 38:350–56.

———. 1958. "Aspects of Public Expenditure Theories." *Review of Economics and Statistics* 40:332–38.

Savas, E. S. 1987. *Privatization: The Key to Better Government.* Chatham, NJ: Chatham House.

Schneider, Mark. 1989. *The Competitive City: The Political Economy of Suburbia.* Pittsburgh, PA: University of Pittsburgh Press.

Schneider, Mark, Mark Lubell, John Scholz, Denisa Mindruta, and Matthew Edwardsen. 2003. "Building Consensual Institutions: Networks and the National Estuary Program." *American Journal of Political Science* 47 (1):143–58.

Schwartz, Barry. 2004. *The Paradox of Choice: Why More Is Less.* New York: HarperCollins.

Shapiro, T. J., and J. Sonstelie. 1982. "Did Proposition 13 Slay Leviathan?" *American Economic Review* 72 (2):184–90.

Sjoquist, D. L. 1982. "The Effect of the Number of Local Governments on Central City Expenditures." *National Tax Journal* 35 (1):79–97.

Spreng, R. A., S. B. MacKenzie, and R. W. Olshavsky. 1996. "A Re-Examination of the Determinants of Consumer Satisfaction." *Journal of Marketing* 60 (3):15–32.

Stein, R. M. 1987. "Tiebout's Sorting Hypothesis." *Urban Affairs Quarterly* 23:140–66.

Stein, Robert M. 1993. "Arranging City Services." *Journal of Public Administration Research and Theory* 3 (1):66–92.

Steinacker, Annette, and Richard C. Feiock. 2003. "A Bargaining Framework for Local Development and Policy Choices." Presented to Meetings of the American Political Science Association, Philadelphia.

Stipak, B. 1979. "Citizen Satisfaction with Urban Services: Potential Misuse as Performance Indicator." *Public Administration Review* 39:46–52.

———. 1980. "Local Government's Use of Citizen Surveys." *Public Administration Review* 40:521–25.

Stumm, T. J., and M. T. Corrigon. 1998. "City Managers: Do They Promote Fiscal Efficiency?" *Journal of Urban Affairs* 20 (3):343–51.

Teske, Paul, Mark Schneider, Mark Mintrom, and Samuel Best. 1993. "Establishing Micro Foundations of a Macro Theory: Information, Movers, and the Competitive Local Market for Public Goods." *American Political Science Review* 87 (3):702–13.

Thurmaier, Kurt, and Curtis Wood. 2002. "Interlocal Agreements as Social Networks: Picket Fence Regionalism in Metropolitan Kansas City." *Public Administration Review* 62:585–98.

Tiebout, Charles M. 1956. "A Pure Theory of Local Expenditures." *Journal of Political Economy* 64:416–24.

———. 1957. "Location Theory, Empirical Evidence and Economic Evolution." *Regional Science Association, Papers and Proceedings* 3:74–86.

Turnbull, G. K., and S. S. Djoundourian. 1993. "Overlapping Jurisdictions: Substitutes or Complements?" *Public Choice* 75 (3):231–45.

Van Ryzin, G. G. 2004. "Expectations, Performance and Citizen Satisfaction with Urban Services." *Journal of Policy Analysis and Management* 23:443–48.

———. 2006. "Testing the Expectation Disconfirmation Model of Citizen Satisfaction with Local Government." *Journal of Public Administration Research and Theory* 16:599–611.

Van Ryzin, G. G., D. Muzzio, S. Immerwahr, L. Gulick, and E. Martinez. 2004. "Drivers and Consequences of Citizen Satisfaction: An Application of the American Customer Satisfaction Index Model to New York City." *Public Administration Review* 64:321–41.

Westbrook, R. A., and M. D. Reilly. 1983. "Value-Percept Disparity: Alternatives to the Disconfirmation of Expectations Theory of Consumer Satisfaction." *Advances in Consumer Research* 10:256–61.

Zax, Jeffrey S. 1988. "The Effects of Jurisdiction Types and Numbers on Local Public Finance." In *Fiscal Federalism: Quantitative Studies*, ed. H. S. Rosen. Chicago: University of Chicago Press.

———. 1989. "Is There a Leviathan in Your Neighbourhood?" *American Economic Review* 95 (3):560–67.

CHAPTER 4

URBAN POLITICS AND THE NEW INSTITUTIONALISM

JONATHAN S. DAVIES AND
JESSICA TROUNSTINE

1. Introduction

When political science first emerged as a social scientific discipline in the early 1900s scholars tended to study the political world by carefully describing the legal and formal structures that defined the state. At midcentury, a revolution occurred as they began to argue that the narrow focus on institutions failed to explain important political outcomes like the rise of Nazism or the domination of elite preferences in policymaking. The field as a whole came to embrace the tools of social psychology, focusing on the behavior of individuals to understand political phenomena. But, over time, these explanations also came to be viewed as incomplete as Marxist and other structural explanations came to the fore. The rise of new institutionalism from the mid-1980s represented yet another field-wide turning point. Scholars turned toward analyzing the ways in which formal and informal institutions create and constrain individual behavior and the ways in which individuals affect the establishment and transformation of the structures themselves. Since this time the study of institutions has played a prominent role in political science research.

This chapter explores the development and applications of neoinstitutionalist thought in urban politics, evaluating the strengths and weaknesses of different approaches and identifying gaps in the field for further research. It demonstrates how institutional theories have, in various guises, come to dominate urban political research. The chapter suggests that institutionalism has a bright future in urban politics, although there are potent criticisms and lacunae, which the next generation of studies will need to address. The chapter proceeds by first outlining the distinction between "old" and "new" institutionalisms and then exploring the dominant neoinstitutional approaches in the urban field: rational choice, sociological and historical institutionalisms. It subsequently looks at ways in which new institutionalist theory has been applied in practice, then discusses controversies and limitations and suggests directions for future research. In conclusion, we argue that there is tremendous opportunity for growth in the field of urban institutionalism.

In order to help organize our discussion, we begin by explaining what we mean by "institution." Lowndes (1996: 182) provides a helpful three-part umbrella definition of the term. She argues that institutionalism is a meso-level concept, meaning that institutions are both "created by, and constraining of, political actors" and are situated within macro social structures (Lowndes 2001: 1963). Additionally, institutions may have formal or informal aspects and finally, they have some legitimacy and persist over time. Institutions also allocate authority and divide labor among participants such that different actors are assigned particular rights and obligations. Institutions are the embedded legacies of past human action and thus prefigure the actions of the people who constitute them, making decisions seem routine and unproblematic. Thus, an overarching definition of "institution" might be "rules, structures and norms that create and enforce cooperative behavior among individuals and groups." Although institutions are not immutable, they are difficult to change and they embody power; so understanding an institution requires understanding its origin and how (and whether) it has been altered over time.

2. Institutionalisms Old and New in Urban Politics

At the turn of the twentieth century, as cities rapidly expanded with the force of industrialization and immigration, many students of municipal affairs became deeply worried about the possibility of successfully managing the modern American city (Murphy 2002). Political machines dominated local politics through party organizations, created corrupt and inefficient government, and maintained office by supposedly bribing immigrant masses into loyalty (Bryce 1888). Formal institutions in this environment were a facade; the locus of power was the party hierarchy headed by the infamous boss. The solution for many was the reinvention of city government through municipal reform. The clearest expression of reform ideals was offered by the National Municipal League, founded in 1894. Throughout the early 1900s the League produced a series of model city charters intended to produce incorruptible city government run by experts and supported by a knowledgeable, decisive electorate (National Municipal League 1916). It was thought that these were the necessary preconditions to allow elected officials the freedom to pursue growth and development, and to undermine the control of bosses (Murphy 2002). Reformers firmly believed that their goals could be achieved through the revision of city charters and state constitutions. Thus, we might say that the first informal institutionalists in urban politics were those scholars who conducted detailed studies of political machines, while the first formal institutionalists were scholars and practitioners committed to the promotion of municipal reform.

The reform agenda supported a range of institutional changes intended to increase the efficiency and efficacy of government by limiting the effects of political forces like parties, voters, and elected officials on city government. Reformers argued that the "right to good government" should take precedence over the "right to self-government," which required a focus on hiring professional administrators to run municipal affairs and eliminating "politics" from city government. The result was a push for council-manager systems, decreased pay for elected officials, and civil service systems for hiring city workers; in other words changes to institutions thought to be beneficial to political machines.

Additionally, reform organizations supported the enactment of nonpartisan local elections, arguing that parties should be irrelevant to urban administration. Because reformers argued that they had identified the most appropriate approach to good government, political institutions that made governance conflictual, like parties, served to stymie progress. Nonpartisan elections on the other hand promised "to take the city government out of politics" ("Tired of Bossism" 1888: 1). Along these lines, reformers also promoted citywide (at-large) elections to prevent narrow interests from influencing local government. Finally, reformers proposed, lobbied for, and supported the passage of suffrage restrictions at the state and local level including literacy tests, abolition of alien suffrage, registration requirements, poll taxes, obscure polling places, and measures that decreased the visibility or comprehensibility of politics, like nonconcurrent, off-year elections. In essence, municipal reformers sought to limit the size of the electorate and to reduce participation by their opponents in order to establish dominance (Bridges and Kronick 1999, Trounstine 2008). Because reform opposition tended to be comprised of the working class and people of color, these tactics and goals were often imbued with racism, producing political, economic, and social inequality where they were successful (Bridges 1997).

Although the commitment to efficiency was being challenged within the world of public administration by the middle of the 20th century, it took urban scholars another decade to begin to critically analyze the effects of the institutional changes reformers had promoted and come to see that the elimination of politics was neither possible nor desirable. This delay was due in part to the commitment of political scientists like Frank Goodnow, Charles Merriam, Woodrow Wilson, and Richard Childs to the reform view that city governance ought to be apolitical and in part to the early institutionalist stance that government could be understood by describing and prescribing particular formal institutions.

As was true in political science more broadly, new research emerged in the 1950s that strove empirically to explain politics and government in cities. Much of this work was either behaviorally focused or concentrated on forces external to municipal government. A large portion of this work was concerned with who *really* has the power to influence municipal policy, regardless of their legal authority to do so; in other words regardless of the formal institutional setting. This "community power debate" dominated the urban politics literature for the next thirty years (see Harding 2009 for a critical review). Represented by Floyd Hunter's 1953 study of Atlanta, elite theorists argued that local decision-making was dominated by entrenched socio-economic elites. Community policy in Hunter's view was determined by a handful of men in the larger, private corporate world who persuaded public officials to act on their behalf when necessary. In response, the pluralist school of thought, exemplified by Dahl and his students, argued that power is fragmented and decentralized and that policy outcomes are the result of bargaining among competing pressures and preferences in the local political arena (Judge 1998).

To the extent that formal and informal institutions distribute power, one could imagine a place for institutions in either elite theory or pluralism. But early elite theorists and pluralists paid scant attention to differences in power distributions via institutions. The primary emphasis in both theories was on the preferences of political actors in their pursuit of municipal policy. For elite theorists these actors are elites outside of the formal governmental structure; for pluralists they are interested members of the community. The assumption in much of the work was that strong preferences will make their way into the political system, irrespective of the institutional setting (although Dahl did indicate that fragmented institutions generated multiple access points for diverse pressures to influence policy).

In the 1980s the focus swung back toward institutions as scholars began to argue that the preferences and power of political actors both generated and was influenced by formal governmental structures and informal patterns of interaction. These "new" institutionalists tend to claim that the "old" institutionalists (e.g. Goodnow 1900) were overly concerned with formal rules and organizations, particularly the structures of representative democracy and the formal organizational structures of city government, effectively reducing the study of urban politics to the study of urban government (Lowndes 2001: 1954). Neoinstitutionalism typically allows for a broader set of influences in decision-making than the old. For example, in *A City in the Republic* (1984), Bridges offered an institutional explanation for the appearance of political machines as the most common form of city politics in the nineteenth- and early twentieth-century United States. Although the dominant explanations of the appearance of machines attributed their origin to the political culture of Irish immigrants (Moynihan 1964) or working-class "self-regardingness" (Banfield and Wilson 1963), Bridges argued that the appearance of machines was best understood as the consequence of conflicts associated with early industrialization in the context of widespread suffrage. In addition to bringing nongovernmental actors into the picture, neoinstitutionalism also depicts the state itself as internally differentiated, a "distinct ensemble of institutions and organizations," as Jessop (2008: 9) put it.

Kjaer (2004: 2) argues that since the late 1980s neoinstitutionalism has become central to political science and that it grounds studies of governance across the subdisciplines. New-institutionalist thinking also spans other social science disciplines, including economics (North 1990), organization theory (DiMaggio and Powell 1991), and sociology (Granovetter 1973). In political science, March and Olsen led the way (1989). They distinguished rational choice from normative (or sociological) approaches, the former explaining behavior in terms of the "logic of consequentiality," the latter in terms of the "logic of appropriateness" (March and Olsen 1989: 160–62). The distinction was essentially between the rational actor's calculation of her options and their likely outcomes and the norm-governed actor's instinctive or conscious evaluation of whether a course of action conforms to given values. The "sociological" interpretation of political institutions as rule-governed decision-making environments composed of "rule-following individuals" dominates institutional approaches in urban politics, although rational choice variants which depict institutions as constraints on the choices of otherwise rational actors, do retain some influence (Ostrom 1991: 238) as does historical institutionalism (e.g., Davies 2004). We explore the rational choice, sociological, and historical variants of neoinstitutionalism in greater depth below.

Milestone publications followed March and Olson, including Hall and Taylor's (1996) article, categorizing the rational choice, sociological, and historical forms of institutional theorizing; Peters's (1999) book, which identified six varieties; and Lowndes's (2001) article in *Urban Studies*, which mounted a robust case for institutional analysis in urban politics (see also Lowndes 2009). Thus, as Kjaer maintains, new institutionalist thinking of various kinds quickly became established in political science and the urban politics subfield.

In Britain, real-world changes in the structure of local governance lent support to new institutionalist thinking, with the wave of "new public management" reforms fragmenting local government and endowing undemocratic agencies, business, and voluntary sector providers with new roles in public service delivery (Lowndes 2001: 1955). In the United States too, the rise of public-private partnerships and an emphasis on nongovernmental service providers underscored the need to adopt an expansive definition of institutions (see Ammons 2003). In this fragmented environment, urbanists began examining the informal ways in which the rules of the game, or "logics of appropriateness" are established, maintained, and embedded in the common sense of diverse political actors, thus giving shape and continuity to political action (e.g., Lowndes and Wilson 2003: 279).

Over the past twenty-five years, or so, this understanding of the local political arena as involving both public and private actors has led urban institutionalists to focus primarily on informal institutions with stability seen as a defining feature of the political landscape (Kooiman 2000: 158). This preoccupation has been, to some extent, at the expense of analyses of formal institutions. For instance an enduring debate over who has power has led urban scholars away from analyzing the legal structure of city governments, toward a focus on the informal but stable relationships between elected officials and economic elites (e.g., Stone 1989). It is often argued that insufficient attention has been paid to the formal and informal context in which these relationships develop and change (see Clarke 1995, or Goodwin and Painter 1997 for a longer explanation of this criticism), although Torfing (2001), Hay (1999), and Crouch (2005), among others, have developed analyses that are sensitive to the dynamics of change. We reflect below in greater depth on institutional continuity and change, in the context of historical institutionalism.

3. New Institutionalist Approaches

While there are strong links among different approaches, the neoinstitutionalist tradition is internally differentiated. Scholars invoke varied definitions of the term "institution" and so have divergent foci and reach different conclusions. Above, we define institutions as the "rules, structures, and norms that create and enforce cooperative behavior among individuals and groups." Some scholars focus on rules and structures while others focus on norms. Similarly, some scholars focus on the ways in which institutions constrain behavior and outcomes, while others are most concerned with the factors that generate the institutions in the first place. It is thus important to examine alternative institutional approaches and this section explores three that are salient to the study of urban politics: they are the rational choice, sociological, and historical institutionalisms.

3.1. Rational Choice Institutionalism

Rational choice institutionalism takes a deductive approach, frequently invoking the tools and language of game theory to depict institutions as limitations on the choices of rational actors. By analyzing the incentive structures institutions create, rational choice theorists seek to make testable predictions regarding individual behavior and aggregate political outcomes. Some rational choice theorists take institutions as predetermined constraints that shape preferences, behavior, action, and ultimately outcomes. Other scholars study institutions as creations of the actors themselves; as collectively agreed upon ways of acting (Shepsle 2006). This means that a rational choice perspective can be brought to bear on either formal or informal institutions; however, a focus on formal institutions has tended to dominate research in this tradition.

An important issue for rational choice theorists is the difficulty in achieving collective action given the attractiveness of free-riding on others' efforts (Olson 1965). Thus, the rational choice perspective often views institutions as having arisen as solutions to particular collective action problems and as generating and maintaining equilibrium outcomes. Some work in local politics, primarily in the field of urban economics, takes this approach. For example, Tiebout (1956) starts from the position that residents select the location of their home based on the package of public goods and taxes offered by the municipal government; the more municipalities from which residents can choose, the closer residents will come to having their preferences realized. This leads to the conclusion that in equilibrium, competition among localities results in homogenous preferences among residents where no individual can be made better off by moving. Peterson (1981) builds on Tiebout's theory to argue that the competition among localities for population and business will lead cities to offer a package of public goods and taxes that emphasizes redevelopment and de-emphasizes redistribution.

Despite his enormous intellectual impact on urban politics scholarship few scholars followed Peterson's lead in consciously invoking a rational choice theoretical framework for studying institutions.[1] This is, perhaps, unsurprising given the predilections of the urban subfield (see Imbroscio 2010). There is a large literature that analyzes the effects of formal governing arrangements and electoral rules on representation and policy, but little work within political science has explained why institutions work by focusing on individual rationality. Furthermore, there are virtually no urban political science scholars who have used formal (e.g., game) theory in their work. This tendency has contributed to the marginalization of urban scholarship from the larger political science discipline, although the causes of the estrangement are hotly disputed.

However, the last two decades have seen a growing body of scholarship influenced by rational choice institutional approaches to local level politics. For instance, Trounstine (2008) argues that machine and reform political coalitions took advantage of formal institutions to increase their probability of reelection. The insulation from political threat altered elected officials' behavior in predictable ways; the benefits of municipal policy were directed toward a core group of supporters at the expense of the broader public. Berry and Gersen (2007) draw on principal-agent theory in an analysis of the relationship between the number of elected officials per capita and the representation of constituent preferences. They show that increasing the density of officials increases specialization in fiscal policy but also increases the costs of monitoring for voters, leading to a U-shaped relationship between density and efficiency. Mullin (2008) also takes a rational choice approach to argue that special districts isolate policymaking and encourage the development of expertise among officials. She finds that districts can therefore lead to policy outcomes that differ from those produced by general purpose governments, but only when the issue lacks salience. It is under these conditions that general purpose officials will be disinclined to pay attention to and devote resources toward the issue. In the UK, Keith Dowding and Patrick Dunleavy both developed rational choice accounts of urban politics based on adaptations of urban regime theory (e.g. Dowding, Dunleavy, and King 2000). However, rational choice institutionalism has otherwise had little influence on analysis of UK urban politics.

1. Many scholars in the economics, planning, and policy fields do invoke an overtly rational institutional approach but the tradition has been uncommon among political scientists.

3.2. Sociological Institutionalism

Sociological institutionalism, which has been influential in British urban studies, is often called normative institutionalism (e.g., March and Olsen 1989) because shared norms are the source of institutional stability. Institutionalists in this tradition draw inspiration from Granovetter (1973) and are skeptical of claims that groups of actors like states and ruling classes can dominate, or that seemingly weaker groups are entirely subordinate. According to Granovetter strong ties are the basis of group integrity, for example families, formal organizations, and cliques, while strong-weak ties link members of different social groups, and groups to other groups. Granovetter sees building weak ties as a good way to create a positive relationship between diverse groups, because they facilitate information flows. Weak ties are made strong by "bridges," for example two groups organized around distinct goals finding that they have a purpose in common and realizing that they need to cooperate to achieve it. Strong-weak ties of this kind are just as effective constraints on action as command or coercion. As Lowndes (2001: 1962) put it, the notion of weak ties does not imply ineffectiveness; it "refers to the manner rather than the impact of constraint." The bridges making weak ties strong include trust, empathy, and common or congruent purposes, which generate logics, or senses, of appropriate action.

In the urban field, sociological institutionalists often treat power as dispersed and governing capacity as contingent on mobilizing governing coalitions to marshal fragmented resources. According to Pierre and Stoker:

> Today, the role of the *government* in the process of *governance* is much more contingent. Local, regional, and national political elites alike seek to forge coalitions with private businesses, voluntary associations and other societal actors to mobilize resources across the public-private border in order to enhance their chances of guiding society towards politically defined goals. (2002: 29)

Peters and Pierre (2001: 131) argue, in a similar vein, that political power and institutional capacity now derive more from the ability of governments to wield and coordinate resources from across the public and private sectors than from formal or coercive powers. Thus, urban politics is about "blending and coordinating public and private interests" (Pierre 1999: 374). Different institutional models of urban governance describe the variety of systems, values, norms, beliefs, and practices that make collaborative governance possible (Pierre 1999: 375).

This conception of governance has become very influential, providing a clear perspective on the changing role of the state and offering scholars a framework for explaining the variety of collaborative institutions that have been built by central and local governments. Many scholars now agree that in modern cities, the social, political, and economic context is favorable to the development of collaborative governing institutions. While hierarchies and markets remain an important part of the institutional mix, "the new ingredient is networks" (Lowndes 2001: 1962). In addition to providing a framework for scholars, nurturing strong-weak ties among diverse actors who bring different resources to the ever-more complex governing arena has also become an urgent priority for political and managerial leaders (Valler and Betteley 2001: 2397).

One contribution of sociological institutionalist thinking is that it invites scholars to consider how individuals and groups create these strong-weak ties enabling stable, effective collaborative governance, features it also has in common with network and regime analysis (see Pierre and Stoker, this volume). Starting from a heterarchical perspective on the fragmentation of power, this strand of neoinstitutionalism draws attention to the contingency and fragility of successful governing arrangements. Its primary concern, like urban regime theory, is how cooperatively to generate the "power to" act rather than the struggle to achieve "power over," or domination of some actors by others (see Stone 1989).[2] It demands that attention be paid to resource mobilization, coalition building, and leadership, key themes in contemporary governing agendas. It tends to focus on how cooperative efforts can be mobilized toward a putative common, or public interest.

3.3. Historical Institutionalism

Historical institutionalism views institutions as the "legacy of concrete historical processes," and tends to be more concerned with temporal processes than other institutional approaches (Steinmo et al. 1992). The urban variant of historical institutionalism frequently focuses on how patterns of socioeconomic and political development are established and maintained and places considerable emphasis on the persistence of social structures and power asymmetries. For historical institutionalists, today's power struggles are regulated by institutional rules and conventions that are the legacy of previous struggles (e.g. Torfing 2001: 294). The origins of historical institutionalism are to be found near the beginning of the twentieth century when Veblen asked the question, posed by many before and since, of how capitalism sustains itself despite its manifest injustices. He argued that through a variety of psychological, ideological, economic, and political investments in the system actors are led to replicate it in their actions day-by-day; a positive feedback loop rendering it an unquestioned, almost unnoticed, part of daily life. This notion of the impact of sunk investment on social action underpins the concept of "path dependency," central to historical institutionalism. According to Pierson, the cost of exit from a course of action once it is embarked on tends to rise with every step along that path (2000: 252). The cost of exit rises because of the increasing levels of investment in a given course of action over time, even if the path is not necessarily

2. Stone explains the difference between these two concepts as follows: "If distrust and wariness prevail, relationships tend toward conflict—and certainly toward noncooperation. If trust and mutuality develop there is basis for cooperation. When players come together to take on a task that neither could accomplish singly, they constitute a form of power to achieve a purpose. To distinguish this form of power from 'power over' (the capacity to prevail in a contest of wills), we can label it 'power to'" (Stone 2003: 131).

the optimal one.[3] Put another way, past actions impose constraints on some future actions, while enabling others. Historical institutionalists are particularly sensitive to the ways in which institutions produce constraints and opportunity structures that favor the powerful.

If sociological institutionalism emphasizes informality and rational choice concentrates on formal structures, historical institutionalism straddles both sides of the debate. Like informal networks, the formal structures, organizations, and practices of government also arise from path-dependent action (Immergut 1998). Path dependency arises from the internalization of shared rules, purposes, and norms, from the imposition and routine acceptance of command structures, as in the military, or from infrastructural constraints associated with material and physical structures, for example the size and shape of a building or the financial implications of embarking on a new course, or not continuing with a current one.

One criticism of institutional theory, particularly its historical variant, has been that it is unable to explain institutional change, the theory of path dependency emphasizing stability (Alexander 2001: 254). One way out of this conundrum, as Alexander notes, is to attribute change to shocks exogenous to the institutions in question (also Torfing 2001: 284). Hypothetically, the collapse of the banking system could be seen as an external shock to the policy system, creating in its wake a breakdown in trust between city governments and defaulting city developers, thus potentially shattering long-standing urban regimes. In circumstances such as this, where conventions are directly contradicted by experience, or following an existing path suddenly appears potentially ruinous, there is likely to be conflict and uncertainty among institutional actors, opening up the possibility of change, a "path shaping" moment (Torfing 2001) or institutional collapse.

What might be called "dialectical institutionalism" (a term used by Hay and Wincott 1998: 956, in a footnote) is an alternative to exogenous theories of change within the historical institutionalist tradition, situating institutional change in a more dynamic account of social development. According to Torfing (2001: 288), any institution has a degree of elasticity. It can account for and cope with unexpected events by mobilizing resources, stretching the interpretation of rules, and modifying rule-governed practices. But there are limits to how far it can stretch and radical change can occur when the limits of elasticity are breached. Torfing calls this a "window of opportunity," in which old and new forces can potentially restructure the policy path. However, this account of institutional elasticity needs to be supplemented with one that explains the dynamics of continuity and change.

Hay (1999) offers a more substantive conception of dialectical institutionalism, exploring the relationship between path dependency and path shaping and characterizing the moment of institutional change as "punctuated evolution." This idea draws on the evolutionary concept of punctuated equilibrium, used by Krasner

3. See Crouch 2005, for an alternative account of path-dependent action and institutional innovation.

(1984) in the field of international relations to denote a social world characterized by stasis and sudden change. The concept of punctuated evolution seeks to explain both the success of a particular path of development and its dislocation (Hay 1999: 327). In Hay's model, the gradual accumulation of contradictions in times of "normal" policy (evolution) is the precondition for crises (punctuation). As Alexander (2001) argues, however embedded they may be, institutions are always vulnerable to low-intensity conflicts, even where they lower the risk of noncompliance by ensuring that "losers" maintain a stake in the system. This conception points to a theory of co-determination in which agents create, sustain, and undermine structures in societies inherently prone to crises. These crisis tendencies must then achieve "narration," or political and ideological articulation. If and when accumulated contradictions are so great that they cannot be overlooked (it would be hard, for example, to overlook the sovereign debt crisis), they enter the realm of public debate and a moment of crisis is upon us. Alternative systems can then compete for domination and a new institutional settlement is reached when one path-shaping strategy wins out in a battle of ideas and strategy, proves successful, and structures future choices through the cycle of increased returns described above.

Davies (2004) applies this account of dialectical institutionalism in his study of urban politics in the UK. He argues that the emergence of collaborative urban governance followed the crisis of bureaucratic statism in the late 1970s and the divisive Thatcher governments of the 1980s. During the 1990s, successive Conservative and Labour governments began to experiment with institutional mechanisms, predominantly at the urban scale, designed to reconcile and mobilize civil society in a partnership with state and market actors. Urban partnerships, network-like institutions bringing together state, business, and citizen actors, presented the possibility of a new institutional settlement and are now ubiquitous in local politics. However, Davies argues that dominant ideologies favoring partnership and the slew of policy initiatives to promote collaboration have, as yet, failed to generate strong path-dependent institutions with value conflicts persisting. Thus, Britain is still in a "punctuated" phase in the development of urban governing structures and a variety of outcomes is possible.

4. The Extended Family of Institutionalist Theories

Neoinstitutionalist thinking is present in a variety of theories of urban politics. Perhaps the most influential and far-reaching bodies of literature in this vein are urban regime theory in the United States (Stone 1989) and network governance theory in the UK (Rhodes 1997). These approaches use different vocabularies and draw on distinct theoretical traditions, while addressing similar intellectual and political challenges; determining how governmental and nongovernmental actors mobilize and blend resources to achieve effective governance, or how diverse governmental and nongovernmental actors build stable governing arrangements to deliver on the congruent elements of their political agendas. In studying these subjects, they focus on the problem of institutionalization and the modes of constraint that hold institutions together.

The mode of constraint varies depending on the version of institutionalism in play. For example, historical institutionalists emphasize the effect of sunk investment in generating path dependencies (e.g., Pierson 2000), whereas sociological institutionalists focus on shared norms and trust and the development of weak ties between different groups and actors (Granovetter 1973). In essence, they ask "how are formal rules and informal "rules in use" (Lowndes et al. 2006) established and maintained in a manner that binds governing coalitions together and generates stability in the governing system"? While the same language is not used, the "mode of constraint" is also of vital concern for both regime and network theorists. For regime theorists, it is the congruence of economic and political interests around development, or "resource dependency" that binds actors together in institutions. For Rhodesian network theorists, "trust" is the bind, although earlier iterations of Rhodes's work with Marsh (Rhodes and Marsh 1992) saw resource dependency as the key. There is consequently a significant familial relationship between several influential theories of urban politics discussed in this volume (e.g. Pierre and Stoker) even though scholars of each use a distinctive grammar and appeal to different intellectual traditions.

While some scholars stay in one or other camp, the similarities between these approaches mean that others can move easily between them. The British scholar Gerry Stoker is a good example of a leading urbanist who has, over time, been influenced by a wide range of political approaches including regulation theory, regime theory, network theory, and neoinstitutionalism (see Orr 2005). Using a toolbox of concepts, Stoker's principal message is that local politics matters; be it in the form of different regime-types (Stoker and Mossberger 1994), the influence of local institutions on leadership styles (Greasley and Stoker 2009), or the impact of local "rules in use" on patterns of political participation in cities (Lowndes et al. 2006).

5. Formal Institutionalisms

As explained above, the largest body of urban institutional research is about informal institutions. However, some new institutionalist scholars focus on the centrality of formal structures (Sharp 2002, 1991, Pelissero and Krebs 1997, Sass 2000). This body of scholarship tends to be concerned with the impact of government institutions on the quality of democratic life and public spending. Unlike the study of informal institutions, there is little work that might be considered an overarching theory of formal institutions; and few scholars invoke any of the institutionalist traditions overtly other than to begin from the stance that institutions ought to matter for political outcomes.

Given the historical importance of the reform movement in the American context, much of the scholarship analyzing formal institutions evaluates the effects of reformed structures on participation, representation (particularly descriptive), responsiveness (particularly to group concerns), and spending patterns. A large body of work analyzes the effects of manager versus mayoral executive structures, at-large versus district selection methods for city council, partisan versus nonpartisan elections, the size of city councils, concurrent versus nonconcurrent elections, direct democracy, civil service and unionization, and the structure and degree of privatization in service delivery.[4] Many scholars conclude that reform institutions meant to increase the efficiency of the political system "both in theory and in practice meant heeding some citizens and not others... [and] the cost of greater efficiency [is] less democracy" (Eakins 1976: 3). As a result lower-class and minority interests suffered under reform structures (see for instance Welch and Bledsoe 1988 or Lineberry and Folwer 1967). However, the research in this tradition is heterogeneous, with many contradictory findings (e.g. Morgan and Pelissero 1980 find no institutional effects, Trounstine 2008 finds conditional effects, and Ruhil 2008 finds short-term effects of reformed institutions). In the UK too, the evidence about institutional effects on political outcomes is mixed. Greasley and Stoker (2009: 127) note that while organizational culture may indeed influence individual behavior, "further research is required to examine just how important this influence is relative to the influences of structural features and individual interests." This conclusion is particularly apt in relation to the small number of elected mayors in English cities (Greasley and Stoker 2009: 131), whose capabilities as would-be "institutional entrepreneurs" (Crouch 2005) have yet to become clear. Furthermore, scholars have paid insufficient attention to testing the mechanisms by which these formal structures induce particular outcomes and analyzing when the institutions ought to matter. Going forward, scholars might use game theoretic tools or historical institutional approaches to explain the development of formal institutions and make predictions about their effects.

Another type of formal institutional approach focuses on the relationships among governments both horizontally and vertically. For instance, scholars investigate the effect of intergovernmental funding on municipal policy (Brooks et al. 2008) with some (Stein 2003) arguing that local politics do not significantly affect local outcomes as a result of the mandates and constraints imposed by state and federal governments. Other scholars analyze the causes and effects of decentralized governance and the preponderance of governments at the local level. Some argue that fragmentation increases negative outcomes such as racial and income segregation (Morgan and Mareschal 1999, Danielson 1976) and undersupplied public goods

4. The number of works is too long to list here. See Welch and Bledsoe 1988, Ruhil 2008, Pelissero 2003 for reviews of much of the literature.

(Orfield 2002), while others offer evidence that municipal officials effectively cooperate to serve resident needs (Feiock 2004), and argue that small communities allow residents to better articulate their preferences (Tiebout 1956).

6. Critique and Future Directions in Institutionalist Research

This account of institutional theory and its applications in urban politics demonstrates the richness of the field, but perhaps also exposes its vulnerability to claims that institutionalism is too broad to be a distinct body of theory. Marxists and rational choice theorists may agree that "institutions matter in political explanation," but hold incompatible views about how and why they matter. Thus, it might be more accurate to argue that while institutions are central to many theories, the idea of a unified institutionalist theory, based on common theoretical precepts, is a mirage.

In a similar vein, Przeworski (2004: 527) argues that institutional theorizing often makes it difficult to distinguish between institutional and noninstitutional effects. He draws attention to the problem of "how to distinguish effects of institutions from those of the conditions that give rise to them." If institutions simply replicate the causal conditions that give rise to them, for example the structural power inequalities embedded in collaborative urban governance, then they play no autonomous role and merely articulate the relations in question (Przeworski 2004: 527). Davies' (2007) argument that urban partnerships replicate the iniquitous social and economic power relations in which they are situated is an instance of this kind of claim. He presents partnership conflicts as instances of broader social conflicts, explained in terms of the structural contradictions of neoliberalism. In Davies' work urban institutions are not a strong causal force. Lowndes et al. (2006), by way of contrast, meet Przeworski's demand for counterfactual studies to demonstrate institutional effects. They find that even in local settings with similar socioeconomic characteristics, political participation varied according to distinct "rules in use" and that while path-dependent effects were visible, local actors were able to "shape and bend institutional forces in new directions" (2006: 559). Thus, for them, local institutions clearly matter.

Secondly, despite the body of work dedicated to the task, neoinstitutionalist theory has not entirely laid to rest the perception that it is weak in explaining institutional change. A valuable insight in the dialectical account of institutional change is that the potential for instability is embedded in the very rules and norms that enable institutions to function. Institutions bear the imprint of societal contradictions. "Exogenous" factors may explain some change, but endogenous tensions or contradictions are often crucial to understanding why institutions, once enacted, appear dysfunctional or even self-destructing (Lindner and Rittberger 2003: 468). Furthermore, Cammack argues that these supposed external shocks can be seen as endogenous if they are situated within a "whole systems" theory of social development, such as Marxism (1990: 161). The outstanding challenge, then, is to invoke a *theory* of change, which specifies the locus of the contradictions within institutions and by what means these contradictions build up and eventually render them unsustainable.

The critique of collaborative governance offered by Davies (2004), thirdly, highlights the limits of the sociological institutionalist account of urban politics. Emphasizing the role of norms in generating productive cross-sectoral governing coalitions, it tends to overstate the extent to which "trust" is the glue in urban governance and understate the degree to which "hierarchy matters" in holding together cross-sectoral institutions based on distrust, the "suppression of mutual loathing in pursuit of government money" (Parker and Gallagher 2007: 15). At the same time, it understates the extent to which collaborative institutions have developed into, or been forced by government to become, formal bureaucracies. While formality does not preclude networking and trust, sociological institutionalism further understates the apparent tendency for some collaborative governing institutions to become more hierarchical and less amenable to nongovernmental influences over time. This trend may mean that governance relies less on trust among interest groups and more on the power accorded to particular institutions by the state. If the momentum in the system of urban governance is toward closed, elite networks then sociological institutionalism lacks a convincing norm- or rule-based account for it. More attention could be paid to the formalization of collaborative arrangements and the constraining effects of these and other formal institutions. In general, urban institutionalism would benefit from more sophisticated accounts of the mechanisms by which institutions rise, fall and shape political processes.

These studies pose questions to institutionalists that can only be resolved in the context of meta-debates about the relationship between structure and action and empirical studies capable of evaluating competing explanations. For example, are social structures and by extension urban institutions, reducible to the immediate actions of the agents who create them and the relationships between those agents? Alternatively, are they reducible to the socioeconomic structures that give rise to them? Or, can we arrive at a defensible conception of structure and action, where structure generates and modifies the conditions in which action occurs? Whatever position is taken on structure, it is also necessary to stipulate the nature and conditions of human agency, the causal power of individuals and groups of actors exercised voluntarily, which is often asserted and rather less often conceptualized (but see Emirbayer and Mische 1998). Urban variants and institutional studies more broadly need greater clarity about their position in these debates; goals which are most likely to be served if urban scholars develop precise and detailed theories in the context of comparative study.

7. Conclusion

This chapter highlights the two-decade domination of urban politics by neoinstitutionalist theory. In this time, new institutionalists have developed a variety of highly insightful accounts of the ways that urban politics works, particularly the manner in which political actors with diverse interests find sufficient common ground to develop and sustain workable governing agendas. At the same time, institutional theory remains controversial and in many ways theoretically underdeveloped. We suggest that there is a clear forward research agenda for urban institutionalists and call for special attention to the dynamics of institutional formality and informality. The recent prominence of regime theory and sociological institutionalism has tended to occlude hierarchy and processes of bureaucratization, which in some accounts (e.g. Davies 2007) are growing rather than diminishing. In addition, we urge urban institutionalists to focus on the testable implications of their arguments and to test hypotheses with rigorous empirical evidence. This will undoubtedly require new data collections and perhaps new methodologies. For instance, game theoretic analysis might be a useful addition to urban institutionalists' toolboxes. In addition, ethnographic approaches are fairly rare in urban politics and these too have the potential to cast new light inductively on the micro-dynamics of institutional formation, maintenance, and change. Finally, we echo previous calls for further work on the dynamics of continuity and change and the presence of institutional effects in urban politics. As authors we struggled to define "exogenous" and "endogenous" drivers of change, suggesting that further research on boundary questions could help determine where urban institutions begin and end. Studies tackling these questions will add as much to our knowledge of urban politics as previous generations of institutionalist research.

References

Alexander, G. 2001. "Institutions, Path Dependence and Democratic Consolidation." *Journal of Theoretical Politics* 13(3): 249–70.

Ammons, David. 2003. "Urban Services." In *Cities, Politics, and Policy*, ed John Pelissero. Washington, DC: DC Press.

Banfield, Edward and James Q. Wilson. 1963. *City Politics*. Cambridge, MA: Harvard University Press and MIT Press.

Berry, Christopher and Jacob Gersen. 2007. "The Fiscal Consequences of Electoral Institutions." Available at http://papers.ssrn.com/sol3/papers.cfm?abstract_id=996445. Accessed August 14, 2011.

Bridges, Amy. 1997. *Morning Glories: Municipal Reform in the Southwest*. Princeton: Princeton University Press.

Bridges, Amy and Richard Kronick. 1999. "Writing the Rules to Win the Game: The Middle Class Regimes of Municipal Reformers." *Urban Affairs Review* 34(5): 691–706.

Brooks, Leah, Justin Phillips, and Tom Ogorzalek. 2008. "Can Municipal Governments Be Trusted with Policy Implementation?: A Re-Evaluation of Federal Block Grants." Typescript.

Bryce, James. 1888. "Rings and Bosses." *American Commonwealth.* Vol. 2. London: Macmillan.

Cammack, P. 1990. "Statism, New Institutionalism and Marxism." In *Socialist register 1990*, ed. R. Miliband and L. Panitch. London: Merlin Press.

Clarke, S. E. 1995. "Institutional Logics and Local Economic Development: A Comparative Analysis of Eight American Cities." *International Urban and Regional Research* 18:513–33.

Crouch, C. 2005. *Capitalist Diversity and Change: Recombinant Governance and Institutional Entrepreneurs.* Oxford: Oxford University Press.

Danielson, Michael N. 1976. *The Politics of Exclusion.* New York: Columbia University Press.

Davies, J. S. 2004. "Conjuncture or Disjuncture? An Institutionalist Analysis of Local Regeneration Partnerships in the UK." *International Journal of Urban and Regional Research* 28(3): 570–85.

Davies, J. S. 2007. "The Limits of Partnership: An Exit-Action Strategy for Local Democratic Inclusion." *Political Studies* 55(4): 779–800.

DiMaggio, P. and W. Powell. 1991. *The New Institutionalism in Organizational Analysis.* Chicago: University of Chicago Press.

Dowding, K., P. Dunleavy, and D. King. 2000. "Understanding Urban Governance: The Contribution of Rational Choice." In *The New Politics of British Local Governance*, ed. Gerry Stoker. Basingstoke: Palgrave Macmillan.

Eakins, David, ed. 1976. *Businessmen and Municipal Reform: A Study of Ideals and Practice in San Jose and Santa Cruz.* San Jose: Sourisseau Academy for California State and Local History, San Jose State University.

Emirbayer, M. and A. Mische. 1998. "What is Agency?" *American Journal of Sociology* 103(4): 962–1023.

Feiock, Richard, ed. 2004. *Metropolitan Governance: Conflict, Competition, and Cooperation.* Washington, DC: Georgetown University Press.

Goodnow, Frank. 1900. *Politics and Administration.* New York: Macmillan

Goodwin, M. and J. Painter. 1997. "Concrete Research, Urban Regimes and Regulation Theory." In *Reconstructing Regime Theory: Regulating Urban Politics in a Global Economy*, ed. Mickey Lauria. London: Sage.

Granovetter, M. 1973. "The Strength of Weak Ties." *American Journal of Sociology* 78:1360–80.

Greasley, S. and G. Stoker. 2009. "Urban political leadership." In *Theories of Urban Politics*, ed. Jonathan S. Davies and David Imbroscio. London: Sage. 2nd ed.

Hall, P. and R. Taylor. 1996. "Political Science and the Three Institutionalisms." *Political Studies* 44(5): 936–57.

Harding, A. 2009. "The History of Community Power." In *Theories of Urban Politics*, ed. Jonathan S. Davies and David L Imbroscio. London: Sage. 2nd ed.

Hay, C. 1999. "Crisis and the Structural Transformation of the State: Interrogating the Process of Change." *British Journal of Politics and International Relations* 1(3): 317–44.

Hay, C. and D. Wincott. 1998. "Structure, Agency and Historical Institutionalism." *Political Studies* 46(5): 951–57.

Imbroscio, D. L. 2010. "Keeping It Critical: Resisting the Lure of the Mainstream." In *Critical urban studies: new directions*, ed. Jonathan S. Davies and David Imbroscio. New York: SUNY Press.

Immergut, E. 1998. "The Theoretical Core of the New Institutionalism." *Politics and Society* 26(1): 5–34.

Jessop, B. 2008. *State Power*. Cambridge: Polity Press.

Judge, David. 1998. "Pluralism." In *Theories of Urban Politics*, ed. David Judge, Gerry Stoker, and Harold Wolman. Thousand Oaks, CA: Sage.

Kjaer, A. M. 2004. *Governance*. Cambridge: Polity Press.

Kooiman, J. 2000. "Societal Governance: Levels, Models and Orders of Social-Political Interaction." In *Debating Governance*, ed. J. Pierre. Oxford: Oxford University Press.

Krasner, S. D. 1984. "Approaches to the State: Alternative Conceptions and Historical Dynamics." *Comparative Politics* 16(2): 223–46.

Lindner, J. and B. Rittberger. 2003. "The Creation, Interpretation and Contestation of Institutions—Revisiting Historical Institutionalism." *Journal of Common Market Studies* 41(3): 445–73.

Lineberry, R. L. and E. P. Fowler. 1967. "Reformism and Public Policies in American Cities." *American Political Science Review* 61:701–16.

Lowndes, V. 1996. "Varieties of New Institutionalism: A Critical Appraisal." *Public Administration* 74(2): 181–97.

Lowndes, V. 2001. "Rescuing Aunt Sally: Taking Institutional Theory Seriously in Urban Politics." *Urban Studies* 38(11): 1953–71.

Lowndes, V. 2009. "The New Institutionalism." In *Theories of Urban Politics*, ed. Jonathan S. Davies and David Imbroscio. London: Sage. 2nd ed.

Lowndes, V., L. Pratchett, and G. Stoker. 2006. "Local Political Participation: The Impact of Rules-in-Use." *Public Administration* 84(3): 539–61.

Lowndes, V. and D. Wilson. 2003. "Balancing Revisability and Robustness? A New Institutionalist Perspective on Local Government Modernisation." *Public Administration* 81(2): 275–98.

March, J. G. and J. P. Olsen. 1989. *Rediscovering Institutions: The Organizational Basis of Politics*. New York: Free Press.

Morgan, David R. and Patrice Mareschal. 1999. "Central-City/Suburban Inequality and Metropolitan Fragmentation." *Urban Affairs Review* 34:578–95.

Morgan, David R. and John Pelissero. 1980. "Urban Policy: Does POLITICAL Structure Matter?" *American Political Science Review* 74(4): 999–1006.

Moynihan, Daniel Patrick. 1964. "The Irish." In *Beyond the Moo65lting Pot*, by Nathan Glazer and Daniel Patrick Moynihan. Cambridge, MA: MIT Press.

Mullin, Megan. 2008. "The Conditional Effect of Specialized Governance on Public Policy." *American Journal of Political Science* 52 (1): 125–41.

Murphy, Russell. 2002. "Politics, Political Science, and Urban Governance: A Literature and a Legacy." *Annual Review of Political Science* 5:63–85.

National Municipal League. 1916. "A Model City Charter and Municipal Home Rule." As prepared by the Committee on Municipal Program of the National Municipal League, March 15, 1916. Available at http://openlibrary.org/books/OL23379393M/A_model_city_charter_and_municipal_home_rule_as_prepared_by_the_Committee_on_municipal_program_of_the_National_municipal_league.

North, D. 1990. *Institutions, Institutional Change and Economic Performance*. Cambridge: Cambridge University Press.

Olson, Mancur. 1965. *The Logic of Collective Action: Public Goods and the Theory of Groups*. Cambridge, MA: Harvard University Press.

Orfield, Myron. 2002. *American Metro Politics: The New Suburban Reality*. Washington, DC: Brookings Institution Press.

Orr, K. 2005. "Three Versions of Stoker." *Public Administration* 83(2): 297–321.
Ostrom, E. 1991. "Rational Choice Theory and Institutional Analysis: Towards Complementarity." *American Political Science Review* 85(1): 237–50.
Parker, S. and N. Gallagher. 2007. "Introduction." In *The Collaborative State, ed.* Simon Parker and Niamh Gallagher. London: Demos. http://eprints.utas.edu.au/2631/1/Collaborative_State_-_web.pdf. Accessed December 15, 2008.
Pelissero, J. P., ed. 2003. *Cities, Politics, and Policy*. Washington, DC: Congressional Quarterly Press.
Pelissero, John P. and Timothy B. Krebs. 1997. "City Council Legislative Committees and Policy-Making in Large United States Cities." *American Journal of Political Science* 41(2): 499–518.
Peters, B. G. 1999. *Institutional Theory in Political Science: The New Institutionalism.* London: Pinter.
Peters, B. G. and J. Pierre. 2001. "Developments in Intergovernmental Relations: Towards Multi-level Governance." *Policy and Politics* 29(2): 131–35.
Peterson, Paul. 1981. City Limits. Chicago: University of Chicago Press.
Pierre, J. 1999. "Models of Urban Governance: The Institutional Dimension of Urban Politics." *Urban Affairs Review* 34(3): 372–96.
Pierre, J. and G. Stoker. 2002. "Toward Multi-level Governance." In *Developments in British Politics 6*, ed. P. Dunleavy, A. Gamble, R. Heffernan, I. Holliday, and G. Peele. Basingstoke: Palgrave.
Pierson. P. 2000. "Increasing Returns, Path Dependency and the Study of Politics." *American Political Science Review* 94(2): 251–67.
Przeworski, A. 2004. "Institutions Matter?" *Governance and Opposition* 39(4): 527–40.
Rhodes, R. A. W. 1997. *Understanding Governance: Policy Networks, Governance, Reflexivity and Accountability*. Buckingham: Open University Press.
Rhodes, R. A. W. and D. Marsh. 1992. "New Directions in the Study of Policy Networks." *European Journal of Political Research* 21:181–205.
Ruhil, Anirudh. 2008. "Structural Change and Fiscal Flows: A Framework for Analyzing the Effects of Urban Events." *Urban Affairs Review* 38(3): 396–416.
Sass, Tim R. 2000. "The Determinants of Hispanic Representation in Municipal Government." Southern Economics Journal 66:609–30.
Sharp, Elaine. 1991. "Institutional Manifestations of Accessibility and Urban Economic Development Policy." *Western Political Quarterly* 44(1): 129–47.
Sharp, Elaine. 2002. "Culture, Institutions, and Urban Official's Responses to Morality Issues." *Political Research Quarterly* 55(4): 861–83.
Shepsle, Kenneth. 2006. "Rational Choice Institutionalism." In *Oxford Handbook of Political Institutions*, ed. Sarah. Binder, R. A. Rhodes, and Bert Rockman. New York: Oxford University Press.
Stein, Robert. 2003. "The Politics of Revenue and Spending Policies." In *Cities, Politics, and Policy*, ed. J. P. Pelissero. Washington, DC: Congressional Quarterly Press.
Steinmo, S., K. Thelen, and F. Longstreth. 1992. *Structuring Politics: Historical Institutionalism in Comparative Analysis*. Cambridge: Cambridge University Press.
Stoker, G. and K. Mossberger. 1994. "Urban Regime Theory in Comparative Perspective." *Environment and Planning C: Government and Policy* 12(2): 195–212.
Stone, C. N. 1989. *Regime Politics: Governing Atlanta 1946–1988*. Lawrence: University of Kansas Press.
Stone, C. N. 2003. "Power and Governance in American Cities." In *Cities, Politics, and Policy*, ed. J. P. Pelissero. Washington, DC: Congressional Quarterly Press.

Tiebout, Charles. 1956. "A Pure Theory of Local Expenditures." *Journal of Political Economy* 64:416–24.

"Tired of Bossism." *Los Angeles Times*, June 30, 1888.

Torfing, J. 2001. "Path Dependent Danish Welfare Reforms: The Contribution of the New Institutionalisms to Understanding Evolutionary Change." *Scandinavian Political Studies* 24(4): 277–309.

Trounstine, Jessica. 2008. *Political Monopolies in American Cities: The Rise and Fall of Bosses and Reformers*. Chicago: University of Chicago Press.

Valler, D. and D. Betteley. 2001. "The Politics of 'Integrated' Local Policy in England." *Urban Studies* 38(13): 2393–413.

Welch, Susan and Timothy Bledsoe. 1988. *Urban Reform and Its Consequences*. Chicago: University of Chicago Press.

CHAPTER 5

URBAN GOVERNANCE

JON PIERRE AND B. GUY PETERS

This chapter provides an overview of urban governance as a theory and research field in urban politics. Like all overviews, it does not claim to cover the entire range of the field but rather seeks to exemplify the research that is typical to the field and its core underlying perspectives and assumptions. The chapter first briefly discusses various constraints on local government before it proceeds to outline the urban governance field. The following section is devoted to a discussion about different challenges to urban governance. We then look more closely at the role of institutions and different types of objectives in urban governance before we assess the urban governance perspective. A concluding section closes the chapter.

Urban governance, simply defined, is about the formulation and pursuit of collective goals at the local level of the political system. Unlike traditional accounts of urban politics, governance theory makes no prejudgment about which social actors are most central to the pursuit of collective goals. Stoker (1998, 17) argues: "Governance refers to the development of governance styles in which boundaries between and within public and private sectors have become blurred. The essence of governance is its focus on governing mechanisms which do not rest on the recourse to the authority and sanctions of government."[1] As is the case in all forms of democratic governance, however, we expect political institutions and elective office to play a leading if not dominant role in urban governance. Those institutions, along

Pierre's research for this chapter has been supported by a grant from the Swedish Science Council and a sabbatical grant from the Wenner-Gren Foundations. We appreciate the helpful comments on an earlier draft of the chapter from the *Handbook* editors.

1. This is not the place to rehearse the entire range of different definitions of governance, from Rhodes (1997) society-centred definition of governance as self-organizing networks to Bell and Hindmoor's (2009) more state-centric argument that different modes of governance are different strategies of the state to govern society.

with processes of popular input and democratic accountability, were put in place to define collective goals and to ensure the provision of financial resources and organizational control to pursue those goals. But one of the lessons coming out the governance research during the past twenty years is that the role of institutions and politicians has changed considerably. This is true for the role of national institutions in their governance context but it is an even more accurate description of local political institutions and actors (see Pierre and Peters 2005; Stoker 2000).

What makes urban governance distinct from governance at the national level is that the role of formal political institutions and their leaders at the urban level has probably never been as predominant as it is often said to be at the level of the state. Cities, to a much higher degree than national government, are deeply embedded in a web of institutional, economic, and political constraints which creates a set of complex contingencies in the process of governing. Since, as we argue in this chapter, much of the leverage of local political institutions is derived from different forms of concerted action with key societal players, managing these contingencies in a strategic way is the main governance challenge to the local political leadership.

The constraints on institutional capacity and political leadership are considerable. One important set of constraints is related to different aspects of the economy. Cities face more complex contingencies to their business sector compared to the macroeconomic interdependencies that the nation-state is embedded in. Cities, particularly smaller cities, often have fairly homogenous business sectors, which makes them vulnerable to structural changes in the economy. Secondly, taxes and service fees, which make up the bulk of the city's income, are delicate variables in the urban economy; voters will not accept dramatic tax increases but will see such measures as incentives to relocate to more moderately taxed jurisdictions. These economic constraints on urban politics tend to reinforce each other into either upward spirals with economic growth and low social costs, or downward spirals with low growth, increasing unemployment, and rising welfare expenditures.

A second type of constraint is related to institutional variables. Cities are subordinate to constitutional arrangements defining their autonomy and to mandates defined by national government. Central-local relationships vary considerably across different national contexts (Norton 1994). In the United States and the UK, local autonomy has historically speaking been very limited; local governments in America are in the classical "Dillon's Rule" seen as "creatures of the state"[2] and similarly in Britain the *ultra vires* principle states that local governments may only undertake those activities which Parliament has authorized them to do (see Gurr and King 1987).[3] At the other end of the spectrum we find the Swedish local government arrangement which accords local authorities considerable autonomy

2. That said, states do delegate substantial authority to sub-national governments, e.g. through home rule charters for cities.

3. Please note that recent legislation in the UK has accorded local government somewhat more autonomy.

(Westerståhl 1987). Seen in the context of urban governance these constitutional arrangements define to a significant degree the range of policy choice available to a city. They also define ex officio channels of communications among local, regional, and national institutions.

A third set of constraints are political or related to public policy. Again, there are important variations among jurisdiction with regard to the significance of these constraints. Local governments are embedded in national, sometimes also transnational institutional and policy frameworks which prescribe or prohibit specific forms of political and administrative behavior among the local governments. In addition, countries such as Japan and the UK have from time to time witnessed ideologically based conflicts between central and local government (Gurr and King 1987; Harding 1998; Muramatsu 1997; Steiner, Krauss, and Flanagan 1980). The basic issue here is that central and local governments sometimes disagree about what is the best policy to address a particular societal problem. Although local governments are expected to implement the policies of central government, the reality is often more complex. In addition, most countries have probably experienced some disagreements between central and local government concerning the degree to which central mandates are funded. Thus, central-local relationships are more complex and contested than the constitutional blueprint suggests.

The above political constraints are linked to the nature of policies themselves, and the difficulties in addressing many public problems within the confines of individual urban areas. For example, transportation is only effective when it links cities to suburbs and the hinterlands. Likewise, crime does not respect the political boundaries within an area, so effective policing must be considered in a regional manner. Economic development issues also extend to regions, often even transnational regions (Morgan 2007).

Together, these economic, institutional, and political constraints on cities define a rather limited scope of local policy choice. At the same time, the urban policy agenda is a challenging political project, accommodating global pressures such as migration and a concentration of urban space (Hambleton and Gross 2007). This is the backdrop against which theories of urban regimes and urban governance have evolved (Stone 1989; 2008a). In his seminal study of urban politics in Atlanta, Clarence Stone (1989) describes the gap between the challenges facing a city and the capabilities of that city as "overwhelming." Essential to the present discussion, Stone also argues that it is precisely in order to increase their "capacity to act" that the urban political leadership forges alliances with resourceful societal actors, primarily the corporate sector.

Stone's urban regime theory defined much of the urban politics research agenda in the United States for two decades, if not more as it still maintains a predominant position in U.S. urban politics (Orr and Johnson 2008). In some important aspects, urban regime theory could be seen as a precursor to the evolving analytical models of urban governance, or what Stone himself refers to an "alternative lens" (Stone 2008b) in the study of urban politics. Both theories look at local political institutions, political leadership, and policy choice in a contextualized perspective and both theories highlight the political strategy of mobilizing a variety of strategic and resourceful actors in the urban territory toward collective objectives. Both theories also define a capacity for choice as related to (i.e. both facilitated and confined by) the political entrepreneurialism of building coalitions with social partners to attain political goals and both theories argue that cities seek to enhance their capabilities through social partnerships; the rationale for city hall to engage those social partners is that it facilitates a blending of public and private resources.

We can now somewhat elaborate our definition of urban governance. Unlike many previous studies that look at the formal powers of local political and administrative institutions, the urban governance perspective is focused on the role of those institutions in steering and coordinating the local community. Political power in the governance perspective is highly contextualized. It is conceptualized almost identically to Clarence Stone's "social production" model of power in his 1989 book on urban regimes: "power to, not power over." The formal power bases of local institutions are to some degree used as bargaining chips with which cities gain access to resources controlled by private business or other social partners.

Thus, urbanists' attention has shifted from local government to urban governance. The core research issues in urban governance relate to the role of local institutions in the process of urban governance. The pursuit of collective objectives is conducted through a process involving a wide variety of actors among which public actors are but one category. Services are produced and delivered in cooperation with the market or civil society (see Clarke 2001). The role of the city in this process is to set up goals and coordinate the actions of public institutions, market actors, and voluntary associations. Urban governance thus sees the steering and coordination of the local society as a process wherein the role of the local government is not fixed as a constitutional mandate but rather a variable both in terms of its strength and its functions.

Some forms of exchange between the local government and its external environment have always taken place; indeed, it is impossible to think of any system of government that does not, in some way or other, utilize societal resources for its purposes or conducts dialogue with significant societal players. This means that we should be careful to think of governance as a new phenomenon that evolved in the 1980s. Governance—the process of societal steering and coordination—is as old as government. What has changed, rather, is the role of government in governance (Bell and Hindmoor 2009; Pierre and Peters 2000). This applies to all levels of government but arguably most strongly to local government. We are therefore uncomfortable with the common statement that there has been a "shift from government to governance" (see, for instance, Rhodes 1997). Government is still there, just as governance is an old feature of society. Its role has changed in important aspects; society's complexity has increased; and globalization urges us to rethink much of what we previously knew about domestic institutional capacity. But all of that being said, government remains, for the time being, the key player in governance albeit in a slightly different than before.

The new forms of urban governance that emerged during the 1980s and 1990s in the UK referred not so much to what local governments do but rather to how they do it, and what role they play in governing (Stoker 1998). Comparative analyses of urban governance argue that local governments "differ more in what they govern than in how they govern" (Teune 1995, 16). A slightly different way of describing these changes would be to say that the "governance turn" is primarily related to changes in governance style and to a lesser extent as a matter of changes in the substantive issues at the core of local government service delivery. From both perspectives, however, there has not been a distinct "shift" from government to governance but the role of government in governance has certainly changed.

In addition, there are also normative and ideological aspects of the concept of governance that need to be separated from governance as an object of academic study. The urban governance perspective accords nonelected actors a significant role in the process of collective goal definition, implementation, and service delivery. This involvement of societal actors in the process of governing is at the heart of the (urban) governance discourse. That having been said, however, cities must maintain a delicate balance between a broad societal mobilization of external resources on the one hand, and maintaining a leading role in the governance process on the other. In many contexts, this notion of political and democratic control over the urban space might well be wishful thinking as there are powerful corporate actors involved in urban governance which have the capacity to make a powerful imprint on the city if they so choose.

The normative claim that elected and accountable officials ought to have the final word on collective matters in urban governance is just that—a normative claim which may or may not be reflective of the ways things actually work. Jill Simone Gross and Robin Hambleton suggest that to some, governance "is less a creative process for solving societal problems than a mechanism for allowing the state to abdicate its responsibilities for providing social care and support" and that "governance in the absence of strong government can lead to urban breakdown" (Hambleton and Gross 2007, 9). Again, there has been less of a "shift from government to governance" than a change in the role of government in governance. These transformations of the role of political institutions and elected officials in the process of governing have, as Hambleton and Gross argue, both direct normative implications and also raise questions about the quality of governance.

The blending of public and private resources which is the sustaining logic of both urban regime theory and urban governance theory raises important questions about accountability and democratic control. Public-private partnerships represent in many ways the epitome of this problem. Today there is a wide range of such partnerships at all levels of government created for a number of different purposes (see Osborne 2000; Pierre 1998). The partnerships that emerged at the local government level during the 1980s and 1990s were primarily set in place to help boost economic development. They were also meant to signal, in the spirit of Thatcherism, the idea that the role of politics was not to regulate and control business but instead to promote economic development.

1. Challenges to Urban Governance

We discussed previously the economic, institutional, and political constraints on local government and urban governance. The significance of these constraints comes into play as the city addresses different types of challenges to its governance. Cities are for the most part dynamic creatures that adapt to changes in their external environment at the same time as they seek to reshape and develop their urban space and economic base. The historical record suggests that some cities have adapted successfully to changes in their environment; consider for example cities that were quick to embark on the transition toward a postindustrial economy. However, history also provides ample evidence that not all cities possess this capacity to adapt to changes in the external environment.

Some time ago now John Mollenkopf (1983, 40) devised a simple typology of American cities based on their economic history and transformative capacity. He differentiated between the old industrial cities, which were not able to regenerate the local economy as structural change hit the industry; the formerly industrial cities which have successfully redefined their economic base into a service-sector economy; and the "new" cities, for example cities in the American Southwest which could enjoy an economic boom without having to carry a financial and social legacy of declining industries. The typology suggests that transformative capacity is not a "given" but rather, we suggest, a quality related to urban governance. While economic restructuring urges the city leadership to play a reactive rather than a proactive role, that role can be executed in many different ways. Most importantly, perhaps, forging or maintaining close relationships with the corporate sector is an important strategy for city leaders to address issues related to the impact of economic restructuring and thus mitigate its effects on the city. Some cities simply appear to be better at changing than others, whether that change is in response to external shocks or initiated by the city leadership. By nourishing close contacts with all strategic players in the city, its leaders increase their capability to act and maintain some degree of policy choice. Whether that capacity to accommodate change depends on political leadership or the corporate sector's commitment to place or the involvement of civil society in the governance process is an issue beyond this chapter.

1.1. Globalization

It is difficult to avoid globalization as a key impetus for change at the local level. The literature on the impact of globalization on cities and regions argues with some consistency that global and transnational flows of financial resources, goods, information, and people have exposed urban and regional economies which previously were protected by the state to a new set of powerful pressures, but also that the institutions of the state mitigate those pressures (see for instance Beauregard 1995). Domestic institutions, through regulation and financial and institutional support, cushion the impact of global competition on businesses that had previously been secluded from overseas competition. This arrangement presupposes a rather proactive, regulatory state and intergovernmental relationships which facilitate this set of roles.

Reality has offered a more dismal account; cities and regions that have found themselves in dire economic circumstances as a result of overseas competition have for the most part been offered precious little support from central government. Such support was much more common during the structural crises of the 1960s or 1970s than in the globalization era. And, where support indeed has been offered it has typically been short-term remedies to accommodate labor or to help facilitate retraining. This pattern seems to hold true for a wide variety of countries, for example, Japan, the Scandinavian countries, the UK, and the United States (for an overview, see Hall 1987; see also Boyer and Drache 1996; Hirst and Thompson 1999). Thus, cities and regions frequently find themselves more alone in the accommodation of global economic pressures than much of the literature on global-local connections seems to suggest (cf. Clarke 2003).

The increasing speed of economic restructuring which is a trademark of the global economy thus places a major challenge on the urban political agenda. The task is not so much related to accommodating laid-off labor; that would be a task above and beyond what most cities are capable of. Instead, the governance challenge is to mobilize the political and economic spheres of the community toward a strategy of economic modernization which makes the city less vulnerable to rapid changes in the global economy. For the vast majorities of cities, this has meant promoting a long-term increased diversification of the local economy with an emphasis on service-sector businesses and management services.

Again, since these strategies include all major players in the city, the urban governance perspective seems better geared to conceptualize and account for these strategies compared to an analytical focus solely on the city's political and administrative institutions. In some cases (Melbourne being one example) it is the business community, not the city's elected leadership, which initiates a proactive strategy to accommodate global economic pressures. Private-sector-led economic development puts some pressure on city government to deliver on its part of the project.

1.2. Migration

Robin Hambleton and Jill Simone Gross (2007) argue that urbanization and migration are the two main manifestations of globalization at the urban level. If urbanization is more typical of those countries that industrialized during the global era, like China, migration has risen on the urban policy agenda in both developing and developed countries. Today, a major city like Toronto has a population where 45 percent are immigrants to the city (Simone Gross 2007, 86). It goes without saying that accommodating and integrating these large groups of immigrants poses a major challenge to the city.

Migration as a policy and administrative problem plays out slightly differently in different national and political contexts. The Scandinavian and European welfare states were built on the tacit assumption that the political economy would be a fairly closed system with only marginal movement in and out of the system. With increasing migration, large groups of immigrants have become eligible for welfare-state services compelling central and local government to increase their financial input into welfare-state programs. Local government, which provides the basic safety net in the welfare system in most European countries, has had to prioritize these social expenditures as part of the accommodation of migration.

Migration covers a wide range of cross-border movements (see Cornelius et al. 1994; Geddes 2003). The demographics of many European and Asian countries with a growing population in postretirement ages have meant that these countries face labor shortages and therefore actively seek to recruit labor from the outside world. Moreover, a large part of contemporary migration is caused by armed conflict or climate change. National and local governments have a major challenge in trying to link migration to labor demand. At the local level, such local labor market programs probably benefit from networks between the city administration and the business community.

1.3. Balancing Market Forces against Collective Objectives

The city's relationship to private capital, or urban political economy, was a major field in urban politics alongside urban regime analysis.[4] Ironically, urban political economy lost momentum at about the same time as globalization entered the urbanists' agenda. For the present context we will not go into the urban political economy terrain, other than to point out that as is the case with urban regime theory, urban political economy has a governance dimension which is essential to an understanding of the potential for coordinated action.

More broadly, cities must nourish a delicate balance in their relationship with private business. Market actors generate the growth in the local economy, provide jobs, and (in many countries) pay tax to the city. This tends to give private business what Charles Lindblom (1977) once referred to as a "privileged position" in urban governance; even if there is a pattern of interdependence between city and business it is an asymmetrical interdependence where business is more important to the city than *vice versa*.

The challenge to urban governance that comes out of this asymmetrical interdependence could be defined as one of integrating the business community into

4. See chapters by Chapter 23, Kantor and Turok, and Chapter 24, Garcia and Judd in this Handbook.

collectively defined projects without imposing so much political control that business decides to relocate to more probusiness locales. As a key societal player in most cities, the business sector has the capacity, through action or inaction, to determine much of the outcome of the city's policies. In his classic study of the political struggle in Gary, Indiana, to reduce air pollution from the local steel mills, Matthew Crenson notes that "though U.S. Steel never really threw its weight against the antipollution forces, its weight was felt all the same... In spite of its political passivity, U.S. Steel seems to have had the ability to enforce inaction on the dirty air issue" (Crenson 1971, 78). Cities do not bite the hand that feeds them and tend to avoid enforcing tough regulation on local business. At the same time, cities have a responsibility not just toward the business sector but the local community as a whole.

A somewhat different aspect of this problem is related to the privatization of public space in many cities, not least in the United States. As Margaret Kohn shows, privatizing public space in cities has major ramifications on public debate and discourse as the right to free speech can only be claimed in public spaces, not in privately owned facilities such as shopping malls (Kohn 2004). Since urban politics from Tocqueville onward has been described as the unsurpassed setting for democratic training and political socialization, removing free speech from that space represents a serious encroachment on (urban) democratic governance. Again, however, the city has to balance the interests of its business community against collective values and objectives.

1.4. Playing the Multilevel Governance Game

As we pointed out earlier in this chapter, cities are embedded in national, sometimes also transnational institutional and constitutional arrangements. These arrangements define to a large extent the formal and actual autonomy of local governments. In addition, however, they also provide opportunity structures for cities to extract financial and other resources from higher echelons of government. With the growing importance of transnational institutions—the European Union (EU) being the prime example—or transnational or even global agreements, "agendas" or "protocols" that identify local government as a key policy agent, the vertical relations between the city and institutions and actors become increasingly important as well. These complex webs of vertical exchanges between institutions and actors from the global to the local levels are referred to as multilevel governance (see for instance Bache and Flinders 2004; Berger 2003; Betsill and Bulkeley 2004; Hooghe and Marks 2003; Peters and Pierre 2001).

Multilevel governance differs in several important aspects from traditional models of intergovernmental relationships (Torfing et al. 2012). One such important difference is that unlike traditional intergovernmental relationships, multilevel governance is essentially nonhierarchical; for instance, cities can engage transnational institutions, or *vice versa*, without having to consult the nation-state government level. This is the typical modus operandi of the EU structural funds or agricultural support programs. Second, these contextually defined institutional relations are negotiated, more than they are a matter of control and subordination. Third, participation, too, is defined by context and agency zeal rather than by legal requirements or regulation. Funds are created for specific purposes; conferences involving potential stakeholders are organized at short notice and circulated selectively; or a task-specific network to address an issue which includes several institutional levels is formed in an informal way and those actors and interests that are "in the know" may get access to these forums. This is part of the reason why so many European cities and regions spend large amounts of financial resources on lobbyists in Brussels or on maintaining permanent offices in the EU capital.

Taken together, all of this suggests that for a city to become involved in multilevel governance it is essential to have an open organization and to be involved in networks of various types. For the urban political leadership there is a distinct challenge in maintaining productive horizontal networks with strategic players in the local community while at the same time participating in the wide variety of regional and transnational forums, networks, and institutions which constitute the city's vertical environment. The vertical linkages are in many ways as important, if not more so, than the horizontal networks within the community, particularly in order to mobilize resources or be present when decisions that concern the city are made.

2. Urban Governance: Institutions and Objectives

Although urban governance should be perceived as a process, institutions play important roles in that process. However, one of the major topics of debate among governance scholars revolves around the role of institutions. In the more general governance debate, the standpoints cover the entire range from "state-centric" models of governance in which institutions are seen as leading actors, to "society-centric" governance which accords little or no role for government (see Kjaer 2004; Kooiman 1993; 2003; Pierre and Peters 2005; Rhodes 1997). The short answer to the question of who is more right is probably "it depends"; different levels of government, different national context, different policy sectors, and different specific issues show different roles for political institutions and actors and societal actors. In the urban setting, institutions are more constrained and contingent on external resources, as we pointed out earlier. We therefore expect urban governance, all else being equal, to have a stronger component of society-centrism than, say, governance at the nation-state level.

One of the problems in the literature on urban governance is that it, perhaps for obvious reasons, has been almost exclusively concerned with various aspects of collaborative strategies at the urban level. Thus, a great deal of effort has gone into studying the roles of networks and other governance structures and into understanding what facilitates or complicates collaborative governance. We argue, however, that in order to understand the composition of any governance structure and its key players you need to understand the objectives of governance. Who you decide to team up with depends to a very large extent on what it is that you seek to accomplish. If economic growth is the chief governance objective, political officials in the city will typically approach the corporate elite to see how closer cooperation can promote economic development (Pierre 2011). The consequence of that strategy, as Clarence Stone (1989) demonstrates, is that other urban policy objectives such as neighborhood development or distributive programs are given less political attention.

Another way of describing this relationship between the composition and the objectives of urban governance is to say that gaining access to the governance structure is imperative to societal players who wish to have a say in the process of defining the urban policy agenda. This means that the formation of a governance network or any other governance structure is far more contentious and controversial process than is often assumed. Governance networks are typically said to be composed by a constellation of actors sharing the same basic interests and objectives (see Sörensen and Torfing 2007). Thus, composition and objectives are defined in one and the same process. Where there is a stronger component of political institutions and actors in the governance structure, however, deciding on the governance forms, procedures, and participants (what is referred to as meta-governance) becomes critical to the objectives of governance.

The reader might summarize what we have said thus far by thinking that urban governance is an urban political strategy to define and pursue, in concert with other major players in the urban context, collective objectives. These objectives could be either "defensive," that is, aimed at accommodating or resolving policy problems in the face of significant restrictions on the city's capacity to act, or "offensive," that is, defining the ideal scenario for the city and a strategy on how to attain those goals. Just as globalization offers both challenges and opportunities to a city, so do policy contexts like climate change, migration, and sustainable development. Urban governance, in this perspective, becomes a process where an eclectic mix of actors, each with their own interest, is mobilized toward a collective goal. Political institutions and actors may or may not play a leading role in this governance. The outcomes are only marginally contingent on the success of the local agency, as national or transnational forces frequently redefine the preconditions for the urban governance. Another way of describing this could be to say, quite simply, that urban governance is messy, as Leach and Percy-Smith (2001) portray urban governance in the UK.

Admittedly, this is a bleak image of urban governance. While it is not very difficult to think of empirical cases that fit this pessimistic account of urban governance, it is also easy to think of a large number of cases where urban governance has been much more successful. A large number of cities (Baltimore, San Francisco, Manchester, Melbourne) have conducted a redevelopment of their downtown or waterfront areas, creating new spaces for housing, leisure, and consumption. Other cities (New York City) have been able to curb staggering crime rates. Yet other cities have been able to redefine their economic base from traditional industry to a postindustrial economy based in service sectors like health care, financial management, trade, fashion, design, entertainment, or the arts (Pittsburgh, Milan, Cleveland, Osaka, Gothenburg, Glasgow). These major projects would not have been possible without a broad mobilization of actors in the local territory combined with the influx of external resources. Needless to say, the role of the political leadership in these cases varies but it is extremely difficult to think of successful cases that did not see that leadership playing a mobilizing and coordinating role.

Such political leadership is perhaps not only critical to the success of large urban regeneration projects; it is also to a large extent a precondition for democratic accountability. The vast majority of such projects were enabled by a cocktail of financial resources from the local government, the business community, national government, and, in the European context, transnational funds from the EU. The role of private actors cannot be generalized, nor can we say something about the institutional arrangements within which different monies were pooled. What does seem clear, however, is that holding political officials to account in these complex processes is a rather daunting task. Accountability is preconditioned on control but we have no chance of ascertaining that elected politicians were, in fact, in control. This problem is not just typical to mega-projects redefining the economy of a city; it is present also in local public-private partnerships in small municipalities.

The broad mobilization of societal actors which is a defining feature of urban governance also holds one of the key problems associated with that governance; the problematic accountability and the limited role of popular input into the urban political agenda. True, such governance significantly enhances the city's "capacity to act" (Stone 1989), but that capacity comes at the price of a distinct political leadership which can be assessed against democratic criteria. It could be that output-based accountability makes up for the loss in traditional, input-based accountability; "if it works it's good, if it doesn't it isn't." There is growing empirical evidence that such output-based legitimacy is becoming as important as legitimacy from the input side of the political system, if not more so (see Gilley 2009; Peters 2011). Result-based accountability is not without significant conceptual problems—how do we know with some degree of certainty who is responsible for specific outcomes?—but its role is clearly growing.

3. Assessing the Governance Approach in Urban Politics

A perennial problem in governance research is that it sometimes conflates the normative, empirical, and analytical meanings of the concept of governance (see Pierre and Peters 2005). Today, governance refers to a particular interactive form of governing, to a normative model of how cities and states should be governed, and to a political science theory of governing. Governance became a buzzword among both political scientists and practitioners during the 1990s and early 2000s. It represented a fresh perspective on the preconditions for governing increasingly complex societies. Instead of trying to break through social complexity, government should "steer, not row" (Osborne and Gaebler 1992; but see Peters 1997). In the normative model of urban governance, local government is seen as a political and organizational "hub" in the local community, defining objectives and making priorities but delivering services and promoting economic development in concert with societal players.

Urban governance as an analytical model emerged alongside this normative redefinition of the role of local government. There is, to be sure, not yet a theory of urban governance. Instead, urban governance has, as mentioned earlier, been seen as an "alternative lens" through which urban politics can be understood (Stone 2008b) or as a framework identifying phenomena "worthy of study" (Stoker 1998, 18). As such, this approach will ask many of the same questions that more conventional models would ask, but also adds other dimensions. In particular, the governance approach emphasizes the extent to which government is not alone in the processes of steering and can employ a range of other actors.

Perhaps the biggest strength of the urban governance approach to urban politics is that it helps conceptualize what appears to be the practice of urban politics and leadership—to seek coalitions and cooperation with other resourceful players in the local community. Thus, theory corresponds nicely with real-world behavior in the processes of steering economy and society. At the same time, the theory asks pertinent and important questions about the extent to which this model of governance delivers on baseline democracy requirements like transparency, accountability, and popular input.

Also, urban governance is more apt to describe the relationships between the complexities of the contemporary local government organization, particularly in bigger cities, and their equally complex local environment. Approaches that look solely at formal institutional arrangements fail to note the significance of agency and political entrepreneurialism. That said, there may be additional institutional structures created that link government, society, and market actors. These institutions may be more complex than conventional public sector organizations, and more difficult to manage, but they are crucial for steering in the complex environment within which contemporary urban governance occurs.

4. Concluding Comments

Urban governance as an analytical framework or proto-theory has helped scholars understand the incentives, but also challenges, related to collaborative forms of governing. Collaborative forms of urban governance could be seen as a strategy of purchasing organizational capabilities at the expense of some of the traditional values associated with democracy such as popular input, transparency, and accountability. This is not to suggest that those values are completely lost, but it is to say that the manifestation of those values will have a different appearance compared to more traditional forms of governing. Accountability becomes tied more to performance and less to representation; goal definitions reflect the increasingly complex and fragmented society and less the collective objectives of the polity; transparency prevails but will uncover processes that are less and less the real loci of political power; and equal treatment becomes neither possible nor desirable in the context of diversifying public service and the empowerment of the customers of those services.

At some stage or other, assessing governance arrangements becomes almost impossible without some normative benchmarks. Some standards of good governance apply regardless of the level being considered. We have already demonstrated that effectiveness is important for urban governance, whether that involves collaborative means or not. Likewise, any properly devised governance arrangements must emphasize accountability, and we would hope that governance would also be participative and democratic. These normative standards are not, however, unambiguous and they must be considered in light of the particular urban settings and the goals of the actors involved.

REFERENCES

Bache, I. and M. Flinders, eds. 2004. *Multi-level Governance.* Oxford: Oxford Univ. Press.

Beauregard, R. A. 1995. "Theorizing the Global-Local Connection." In P. L. Knox and P. J. Taylor, eds. *World Cities in a World-System.* Cambridge: Cambridge Univ. Press.

Berger, G. 2003. "Reflections on Governance: Power Relations and Policy Making in Regional Sustainable Development." *Journal of Environmental Policy and Planning* 5:219–34.

Bell, S. and A. Hindmoor. 2009. *Rethinking Governance: The Centrality of the State in Modern Society.* Cambridge: Cambridge Univ. Press.

Betsill, M. M. and H. Bulkeley. 2004. "Transnational Networks and Global Environmental Governance: The Cities for Climate Program." *International Studies Quarterly* 48:471–93.

Boyer, R. and D. Drache, eds. 1996. *States Against Markets: The Limits of Globalization.* New York: Routledge.

Clarke, S. E. 2001. "The Prospects for Local Governance: The Roles of Nonprofit Organizations." *Policy Studies Review* 18:129–45.

Clarke, S. E. 2003. "Globalism and Cities: A North American Perspective." In R. Hambleton, H. V. Savitch, and M. Stewart, eds. *Globalism and Local Democracy: Challenge and Change in Europe and North America.* Basingstoke: Palgrave.

Cornelius, W. A., P. L. Martin and J. F. Hollifield, eds. 1994. *Controlling Immigration: A Global Perspective.* Stanford: Stanford Univ. Press.

Crenson, M. A. 1971. *The Un-Politics of Air Pollution.* Baltimore: Johns Hopkins Univ. Press.

Geddes, A. 2003. *The Politics of Migration and Immigration in Europe.* London: Sage.

Gilley, B. 2009. *The Right to Rule: How States Win and Lose Legitimacy.* New York: Columbia Univ. Press.
Gurr, T. R. and D. S. King. 1987. *The State and the City.* Chicago: University of Chicago Press.
Hall, P. A. 1987. "The Anatomy of Job Creation: Nations, Regions and Cities in the 1960s and 1970s." *Regional Studies* 21:95–106.
Hambleton, R. and J. Simone Gross, eds. 2007. *Governing Cities in a Global Era.* Basingstoke: Palgrave.
Harding, A. 1998. "Public-Private Partnerships in the UK." In J. Pierre, ed. *Partnerships in Urban Governance: European and American Experience.* Basingstoke: Macmillan.
Hirst, P. and G. Thompson 1999. *Globalization in Question: The International Economy and the Possibilities of Governance.* Oxford: Polity Press.
Hooghe, L. and G. Marks. 2003. "Unravelling the Central State, but How? Types of Multi-level Governance." *American Political Science Review* 97:233–43.
Kjaer, A. M. 2004. *Governance.* Cambridge: Polity Press.
Kohn, M. 2004. *Brave New Neighborhoods.* New York: Routledge.
Kooiman, J., ed. 1993. *Modern Governance: New Government-Society Interactions.* London: Sage.
Kooiman, J. 2003. *Governing as Governance.* London: Sage.
Leach, R. and J. Percy-Smith. 2001. *Local Governance in Britain.* Basingstoke: Palgrave.
Lindblom, C. E. 1977. *Politics and Markets.* New York: Basic Books.
Mollenkopf, J. H. 1983. *The Contested City.* Princeton: Princeton Univ. Press.
Morgan, K. 2007. "The Learning Region: Institutions, Innovations and Regional Renewal." *Regional Studies* 41:147–59.
Muramatsu, M. 1997. *Local Power in the Japanese State.* Berkeley: Univ. of California Press.
Norton, A. 1994. *International Handbook of Local and Regional Government: A Comparative Analysis of Advanced Democracies.* Cheltenham: Edward Elgar.
Orr, M. and V. C. Johnson, eds. 2008. *Power in the City: Clarence Stone and the Politics of Inequality.* Lawrence: Univ. Press of Kansas.
Osborne, D. and E. Gaebler. 1992. *Reinventing Government.* Reading, MA: Addison-Wesley.
Osborne, S. P., ed. 2000. *Public-Private Partnerships: Theory and Practice in International Perspective.* London: Routledge.
Peters, B. G. 1997. "Shouldn't Row, Can't Steer: What's A Government to Do?" *Public Policy and Administration* 12:51–61.
Peters, B. G. 2011. "Bureaucracy and Democracy: Towards Output-based Legitimacy?" In J-M. Eymeri-Douzans and J. Pierre, eds. *Administrative Reforms and Democratic Governance.* London: Routledge.
Peters, B. G. and J. Pierre. 2001. "Developments in Intergovernmental Relationships: Towards Multi-level Governance." *Policy and Politics* 29:131–35.
Pierre, J. ed. 1998. *Partnerships in Urban Governance: European and American Experience.* Basingstoke: Macmillan.
Pierre, J. 2011. *The Politics of Urban Governance.* Basingstoke: Palgrave.
Pierre, J. and B. G. Peters. 2000. *Governance, Politics and the State.* Basingstoke: Palgrave.
Pierre, J. and B. G. Peters. 2005. *Governing Complex Societies.* Basingstoke: Palgrave.
Rhodes, R. A. W. 1997. *Understanding Governance: Policy Networks, Governance, Reflexivity, and Accountability.* Buckingham: Open Univ. Press.
Simone Gross, J. 2007. "Diversity and the Democratic Challenge: Governing World Cities." In R. Hambleton and J. Simone Gross, eds. *Governing Cities in a Global Era.* Basingstoke: Palgrave.

Simone Gross, J. and R. Hambleton. 2007. "Global Trends, Diversity and Local Democracy." In R. Hambleton and J. Simone Gross, eds. *Governing Cities in a Global Era.* Basingstoke: Palgrave.

Sörensen, E. and J. Torfing, eds. 2007. *Theories of Democratic Network Governance.* Basingstoke: Palgrave.

Steiner, K., E. S. Krauss, and S. C. Flanagan, eds. 1980. *Political Opposition and Local Politics in Japan.* Princeton: Princeton Univ. Press.

Stoker, G. 1998. "Governance as Theory: Five Propositions." *International Social Science Journal* 155:17–28.

Stoker, G. 2000. "Urban Political Science and the Challenge of Urban Governance." In J. Pierre, ed. *Debating Governance: Authority, Steering, and Democracy.* Oxford: Oxford Univ. Press.

Stone, C. N. 1989. *Regime Politics: Governing Atlanta, 1946–1988.* Lawrence: Univ. of Kansas Press.

Stone, C. N. 2008a. "Urban Regimes and the Capacity to Govern: A Political Economy Approach." *Journal of Urban Affairs* 15:1–28.

Stone, C. N. 2008b. "Urban Politics Then and Now." In M. Orr and V. C. Johnson. eds. *Power in the City: Clarence Stone and the Politics of Inequality.* Lawrence: Univ. Press of Kansas.

Teune, H. 1995. "Local Government and Democratic Political Development." *Annals of the American Academy of Political and Social Science* 540:11–23.

Torfing, J., Peters, B. G., J. Pierre and E. Sörensen. 2012. *Interactive Governance.* Oxford: Oxford University Press.

Westerståhl, J. 1987. *Staten, kommunerna och den kommunala självstyrelsen* [The State, Municipalities and Local Autonomy]. Stockholm: Civildepartementet.

CHAPTER 6

ELECTIONS AND POLICY RESPONSIVENESS

ALISTAIR CLARK AND TIMOTHY B. KREBS

1. Introduction

The ability to elect representatives to govern is a cornerstone of representative democracy. Elections ensure an element of accountability and responsibility upon governments. Consequently, they are central to political science. Given the proximity of local and urban political institutions to their citizens, electoral politics ought to be particularly important in such settings. The electoral dimension is ultimately a key aspect of urban politics which differentiates local government from local administration, and can determine the control of local councils and local public policy. Moreover, urban electoral politics offers the political scientist considerable research potential; the nature of local politics means that analysts theoretically have greater numbers of observations both within and across jurisdictions upon which to base their research, thereby potentially leading to more robust findings and increasing knowledge about political behavior more generally.

Despite this, elections and their outcomes have largely been overlooked in the study of urban politics in recent years. What this chapter therefore aims to do is to bring elections and electoral behavior back toward the foreground of urban politics in order to provide insights from political behavior and examine how, if at all, these insights have been applied to the field of urban politics. The chapter proceeds in five parts. The first section highlights the importance of local elections and sets out key aspects and questions that form the background to any analysis of urban elections. The second part provides an assessment of the range of methods utilized in the study of urban elections and asks about their potential strengths and weaknesses. The third section discusses urban voters' vote choice and its consequences for accountability, electoral competition, responsiveness, and representation. The fourth part broadens this discussion to reflect upon the comparative dimension, and how this has contributed to understanding urban electoral behavior. Pulling these strands together, the concluding section sets out an agenda for future theory and research in urban and local electoral politics.

2. Urban Elections: Important or Irrelevant?

Although electoral studies are a central aspect of political science, people could easily be forgiven for thinking elections largely irrelevant to the study of urban politics. Electoral politics merit barely a passing mention in two key introductory collections on urban politics (Judge et al. 1995; Davies and Imbroscio 2009). In a study of the relationship between the disciplines of political science and urban politics, Sapotichne et al. (2007, 96–97) found that works on voting behavior and electoral mobilization are considerably underrepresented in citations in big urban politics journals. Indeed, they suggest that urban politics has diverged from the broader discipline to the extent that it has become a "black hole" where broader political science insights are rarely felt. Even if one does not wish to accept the strength of that criticism—urban elections scholars may publish their work elsewhere for instance—it is clear that national elections in the U.S., the UK, and elsewhere receive much more academic attention than elections to local councils and mayoralties.

It is therefore worth setting out clearly both why elections are important to the study of urban politics, while also reflecting on some of the issues which may contribute to them not having the profile that they enjoy in the broader discipline. Regular democratic elections have a number of key functions. On the input side, they allow citizens a degree of control over their elected representatives. When they are contested, elections provide voters with a choice of competing candidates, platforms, and parties. They therefore provide a key mechanism for holding representatives to account for their performance in office. In theory, elections provide representation for different social groups and also act as a key means of educating and integrating citizens into political life. On the output side, elections determine the control of governments. This is important, because control and leadership of an administration can lead to very different public policies being pursued. Moreover, decisive electoral results and high levels of participation both confer a mandate to govern, and provide legitimacy to the broader political system (Dahl 1956).

The functions of elections are as important at the local level as at the national (Vetter 2007). Indeed, a key assumption about voting behavior is that the more a voter thinks their vote is likely to make a difference, the more likely they are to turn out to vote. Given that urban elections take place at the level closest to the voter, such elections ought to be at the forefront of local political considerations. Consequently, at least two British reports into local government have highlighted the role of elections as "the essence of local democracy" (Miller 1988, ch. 1), and as the central way in which councils are held to account (Lyons Inquiry 2006, 33 and 66).

Equally important for the conduct of democratic politics, urban voters choosing to vote differently can have important consequences beyond the initial urban setting. Sonenshein and Drayse (2006), for instance, have traced the development of immigrant urban electoral coalitions, something which also feeds into national developments. Secondly, since winning representation in local elections is often more accessible than at the national level, it is often at local elections that small and radical parties and candidates make a breakthrough; high profile cases include the Belgian Vlaams Blok/Belang, the British National Party, and the election of a post-Fascist mayor of Rome (Di Franco 2009; Rhodes 2009; Swyngedouw 2000). In major U.S. cities, minority candidates have achieved great electoral success in large part due to their ability to translate local demographic advantages into political victories (Browning, Marshall, and Tabb 2003). Finally, urban elections can also lead to new coalition lineups between parties which have not worked together at national level such as the German CDU and Greens in Hamburg (Jou 2009). Urban elections can therefore become almost a "testing ground" for, and a harbinger of, broader social and political developments.

2.1. The Rules of the Game: Urban Electoral Institutions

Local institutional arrangements are regularly pointed to as an important determinant of participation in urban elections (Kelleher and Lowery 2004; Wood 2002). Most importantly for this chapter, considerable diversity is found in the variety of electoral arrangements used for urban elections. The first issue is the timing of elections. In England, metropolitan boroughs elect three councillors to each multimember district within the council and hold "partial" elections where a third of the councillors are reelected each year. By contrast, London boroughs hold all-out elections where the whole council is elected every four years, as do some other authorities elsewhere in the UK (Rallings and Thrasher 1997, ch. 3). These local elections are often combined with elections to a higher level of office. Concurrent multilevel elections have become a regular feature of the political landscape in, for instance, the UK, Sweden, Italy, and Germany (van der Kolk 2007). In the U.S., 83 percent of cities employ staggered terms for city councillors, meaning that roughly one-half of the council is up for election during each election cycle. Only 9 percent limit the terms of their elected officials (MacManus and Bullock 2003). Approximately 64 percent of cities use at-large elections, that is, multimember districts, in which voters citywide select councillors, while approximately 14 percent employ district elections, in which voters within a particular district or ward select the councillor for that seat. Furthermore, about 21 percent of cities use mixed systems, or ones that combine district and at-large representation schemes. At-large systems have grown slightly more popular over time, while mixed systems have become somewhat less popular (MacManus and Bullock 2003, 16). Most cities also elect their officials in off years, or at times when state and national elections are not being held.

A second issue relates to the type of electoral system used. This often varies within countries. In the UK most urban elections are held under first-past-the-post rules, although those in Scotland and Northern Ireland are held under the Single Transferable Vote (STV), those for the London Assembly are held under Mixed-Member Proportional (MMP) and the London mayor, and all other directly elected mayors, are elected by Supplementary Vote. Similar diversity exists across Europe. Van der Kolk (2007) highlights differences between municipalities in a number of countries. Thus, closed list systems are used in larger Spanish municipalities, while open lists are used in smaller municipalities. Similar municipal variation is also found in Germany, Luxembourg, and France. In the U.S., the typical system is for council and mayoral candidates to compete first in a nonpartisan primary election. If no one passes a certain vote percentage threshold—usually 50 percent—then a runoff election is held between the top two vote getters. In cities with partisan ballots, the winners of each party's primary election will face each other in a general election contest. Nonpartisan election systems are by far the norm in the U.S., with approximately 77 percent of cities employing this type of ballot structure (MacManus and Bullock 2003, 15).

A third institutional aspect is the autonomy and power of local administrations to both deliver public policy and raise or lower local taxation. The argument is that the more powers councils have, the more likely citizens will be motivated to participate in local elections. Conversely, the less powers local councils have, the less citizens will be interested in participating. In the UK, the perceived lack of autonomy of local authorities, combined with the increase of unelected local governance networks, is regularly associated with a lack of interest among local citizens, at the same time as these elections have become more important to the political parties (Rallings et al. 2005; Wilks-Heeg and Blick 2009; Wilks-Heeg and Clayton 2006). In the U.S. the powers of local government are constrained by the legal doctrine known as Dillon's Rule, the legal principle that cities are "creatures of the state" and thus subject to all manner of state restrictions. Although 48 of 50 states grant some form of home rule to cities, the vast majority of states impose restrictions on cities' taxation, borrowing, and spending policies (Ross and Levine 2006, 133–38). The more pertinent issue for elections and policy responsiveness is the extent to which the power of local elected officials varies across cities within states. In council manager cities, unelected, appointed managers have more power, whereas in mayor council cities, elected officials are expected to lead on policy issues. Underlining this idea, Hajnal and Lewis (2003, 658–59) found that citizens were more inclined to participate where cities were directly responsible for delivering their own services, whereas those with less responsibility had lower participation, although others have challenged this conclusion (van der Kolk 2009).

2.2. Voter Turnout in Urban Elections

Electoral turnout is in decline in many advanced democracies. Low turnout is often most obvious in local elections where turnout can be much less than in national parliamentary contests. Vetter (2009, 5), for instance, demonstrates that while average national turnout in Germany has been relatively steady at around 77–79 percent from the late 1980s, local turnout has fallen to a mean of 50.9 percent between 2004 and 2008. Germany is not unique. In his study of local turnout in 24 European countries van der Kolk (2009, 29) found that all had lower levels of local turnout than national turnout. In six of these countries, the gap was greater than 20 percentage points, in ten the gap was 10–20 percent, while in the remainder the gap was less than 10 percent. Those countries with lower national-local turnout gaps tended to have either compulsory voting or concurrent local and national elections. The country with the biggest local-national gap, at 26.5 percentage points, is the UK.

Figure 6.1 underlines the disparity between national and urban elections in the UK from 1997 onward. While national turnout fell to around 60 percent in the 2001 and 2005 general elections, turnout in both metropolitan and London boroughs is considerably lower. Metropolitan turnout peaked at 41.3 percent in 2004 due to the elections being held concurrently with those to the European Parliament, but otherwise varies between around 25–35 percent, while London turnout varies between around 32 and 38 percent. For much of this period, turnout in more rural areas, represented by shire districts, has also been higher than in urban areas, despite a degree of convergence due to being held concurrently with European elections in 2004. Turnout in many urban areas would therefore seem to be consistently lower than that in different contexts, thereby suggesting that there is something about the urban polity that encourages people to stay at home.

There is no central database that allows scholars to gauge urban voter turnout in the U.S. Knowledge of urban voter turnout comes from the efforts of individuals or teams of scholars collecting data on samples of cities. According to Caren's (2007) study of large U.S. cities (peak population of 500,000), average turnout between 1978 and 2003 was 27 percent of eligible voters. Moreover, average turnout had declined 20 percent during this time frame. It is apparent then that broader trends in voting seen in American politics apply locally as well (but see McDonald and

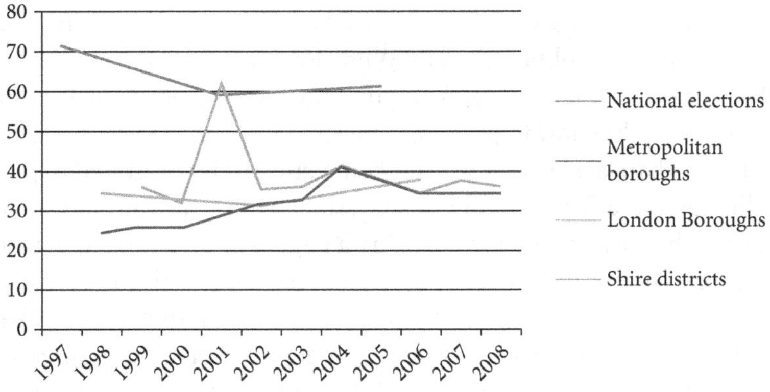

Figure 6.1. Turnout in National & Local Elections in England

Source: Adapted from LGC Elections Centre, http://plymouth.ac.uk/elections (March 10, 2010).

Popkin 2001), despite the fact that local elections take place in relatively smaller jurisdictions, where the value of each vote cast is, theoretically, higher.

How might local turnout be explained? As nationally, those who vote in local elections are different than those who do not—they tend to be better educated and higher income—potentially biasing the local electoral and policy process. Other factors may interact with the upward socioeconomic bias. For example, there is a good deal of evidence that institutional arrangements such as council manager government, nonpartisan ballots, and the timing of local elections influence local voter turnout (Caren 2007; Hajnal and Lewis 2003; Karnig and Walter 1983; Schaffner, Streb, and Wright 2001; Wood 2002). Reformed cities and cities that hold their elections in years in which state and national partisan elections are not being held usually experience lower turnout compared to cities that are unreformed and that hold their elections concurrently. Cities that are economically diverse may stimulate greater interest in local political issues, thus increasing turnout (Oliver 1999). Turnout is greater in areas where there is less neighborhood poverty and more social connectedness (Alex-Assensoh 1997); it is also higher in smaller cities (Oliver 2000; but see Kelleher and Lowery 2004).

Others point to campaign effects. Turnout is greater in places where there is aggressive door-to-door canvassing, whether by party organisations or candidates (Bledsoe and Welch 1987; Bochel and Denver 1971; Green et al. 2003; Erie 1988; Pelissero et al. 2000; Wolfinger 1963) or where there is strong electoral competition (Trounstine 2008). Minority voter turnout is higher when a candidate of the same race or ethnicity is on the ballot (Barreto et al. 2005; Kleppner 1985). In U.S. cities, the need for greater turnout may be most pressing for minority groups. Hajnal and Trounstine's (2005) research on simulated election turnout and mayoral election outcomes in ten large U.S. cities indicates that had whites and minorities voted at the same rate, election outcomes would have been different in three of the ten cases they examined, and the candidate favored by Latinos would have won. They also found, based on a sample of nearly 1,700 cities, that higher actual turnout was linked to significantly greater levels of city council representation of Latinos and Asian Americans.

In addition to affecting who wins and who loses, turnout is widely held to indicate the legitimacy of a political system. While low turnouts are nothing new in the UK, Wilks-Heeg and Blick (2009, 9) argue that local turnouts of the magnitude described above are "too low to provide sufficient democratic legitimacy." They suggest that at the urban level people are not being effectively integrated to political life in a way that democratic theory might suggest. Such low turnouts also make it difficult to argue that urban elections provide a degree of control and accountability over local representatives. Low turnouts also make it difficult to suggest that clear preferences are being communicated to local councillors. In countries like the UK with strong party systems, local elections are regularly seen as little more than large scale "opinion polls" on how the national government is performing. Both points suggest that local political elites are the key locus of local power, running the administration under little scrutiny from their electorate. When combined with a lack of interest and knowledge about local politics, these issues have clear implications. As Miller (1988, 3–4) puts the problem:

> [I]f the majority of electors ignore local elections altogether and refuse to vote, while most of those that do vote use the local election to pass judgment on national government, we can argue that local elections are meaningless and irrelevant...the message that local elections then send to local government is almost completely irrelevant because few voters are evaluating local government's performance when they vote.

Moreover, low turnouts also raise key questions about the equality of participation in urban elections; turnout often tends to be dominated by the unrepresentative groups with lower-class and minority groups often less inclined to participate (Hajnal and Lewis 2003, 655). Research suggests that skewed voter turnout may affect the policy priorities of local government. Hajnal (2010, ch. 5) finds that low voter turnout in U.S. cities produces less redistributive spending, and more spending on economic development and basic services. It also leads to less taxes and debt, thus smaller government overall thereby suggesting "that when disadvantaged groups fail to vote, local officials are more likely to be unresponsive to their concerns. Moreover, the effects are substantial. Expanded turnout could increase the amount of money going to redistributive programs by a third" (Hajnal 2010, 139). Moreover, dominant regimes in cities work to restrict electoral competition, which not only reduces turnout but biases election outcomes in favor of coalition-backed incumbents. With electoral control in hand, dominant regimes have few incentives to provide policy benefits to a broad audience, favoring instead a narrow set of policy benefits to core coalition supporters, usually to the detriment of lower income, nonwhite residents (Erie 1988; Trounstine 2008).

3. Methodological Approaches to the Study of Urban Elections

To what extent have different methodological approaches contributed to research findings on urban election and policy responsiveness? In short, it is difficult to suggest that different approaches have done so to equal degrees. Research into urban elections and policy responsiveness has predominantly been carried out using quantitative techniques. To some degree this is unsurprising; elections produce considerable amounts of quantitative data, while measures of policy output such as spending per head of population are also easily quantifiable. This is not to say that qualitative research has not contributed to the study of urban elections and policy responsiveness. Through a range of interviews, Gregory (1969), for instance, highlights the reasons, which are unlikely to have changed much over the years, why councillors may or may not be responsive to their voters in one English city. Similarly, Rhodes (2009) presents a qualitative study of the rise of the far right British National Party (BNP) through local elections in another English city. These studies highlight the fact that case study methods have also contributed a considerable degree of insight, although often as part of a broader study of the conduct of local politics than elections by themselves (Di Franco 2009; Newton 1976; Wilks-Heeg and Clayton 2006). Likewise, U.S. urban scholars have generated a mix of qualitative case studies that explore political incorporation and regime analysis, and more quantitative studies that try not only to explain election outcomes, but also what happens after elections in terms of policy and, especially, allocational outputs. The case studies also have tended to deal with broader issues of systemwide significance, while quantitative work has been more narrowly focused (but see Trounstine 2008). This notwithstanding, the predominant approach to studying local elections is through quantitative methods.

One of the key benefits of studying urban elections and politics more generally is that they potentially allow the deployment of the comparative method to subnational political settings. This allows comparisons both within countries, and between different countries. One key point is that there are many more urban administrations than there are national governments. As John (2009, 22) indicates, this is potentially a "massive advantage" for the researcher in urban elections (and urban politics more generally) because the large number of cities allows statistical inferences to be drawn about relationships between variables on a basis of much higher confidence than comparative politics findings based on a small number of countries. Wood (2002), for instance, carried out a random sample of 57 cities in his study of voter turnout. Pierre (2005) points to the importance of such comparative research in uncovering causal mechanisms and the drivers of urban political change. Denters and Mossberger (2006, 557–58) demonstrate how such a comparative approach can contribute to building a theory of local election turnout.

Most studies of urban elections and policy responsiveness utilize aggregate data in relation to either election results or policy outputs, whether at the level of the city or districts within the city. Aggregate data has considerable potential to help examine urban political dynamics. Ranney (1962) highlights the fact that such aggregate data tend to be quite reliable for this purpose because they are not reliant on the individual perceptions and misperceptions of survey data and consequently are more comparable over time. Nevertheless, a reliance on aggregate-level data leaves researchers prone to accusations of ecological fallacy, of making inferences about individual behavior from aggregate-level data which may not exist when individuals are considered. Indeed, studies using individual-level data relating to local elections are rare (but see Heath et al. 1999; Miller 1988) and this does present a considerable lacuna in knowledge. Nevertheless Rallings and Thrasher (1997, 8–9) note that both aggregate and individual data tend to support the analysis, discussed below, that some voters do indeed vote on the basis of local policy-related factors. This notwithstanding, there is an important need for more individual-level analyses of local voting behavior both to counter suspicions of ecological fallacy, and to provide more detailed insights into individuals' local policy preferences and voting behavior (James and John 2007, 578).

Despite its potential, there are nevertheless considerable difficulties which have to be faced in studying urban elections and policy responsiveness comparatively. The first is the fundamental difficulty of collecting data across many different local authorities. Not all data is necessarily openly available and local authorities may decline to provide the relevant data, or may record it in a way which is not comparable across local governments (Hajnal and Lewis 2003, 650–51; Kelleher and Lowery 2004, 735; Wood 2002, 221). The second difficulty is to ensure that the measures used, whether as independent or dependent variables, are actually comparable. In studies of participation, different measures of turnout are used. Wood (2002) measures turnout in both city council and mayoral elections as the average percentage of registered voters who participated in the city's previous two elections. By contrast, Kelleher and Lowery (2004) measure turnout as a percentage of voting age population, but only consider voting in city council elections. Hajnal and Lewis (2003) employ both voting age population and registered voters in constructing their measure of voter turnout, while Oliver (2000) relies upon survey respondents' self-reports of voting in local elections in the previous five years. Hansen (1994, 13) uses the proportion of eligible voters who voted. Even at the most basic level, this issue of equivalency is a problem. This whole book is about urban politics. Even in apparently similar research, different terms are used; for instance, in American studies, Wood (2002) discusses city elections, Kelleher and Lowery consider metropolitan contexts, and Hajnal and Lewis (2003) discuss municipal institutions. In cross-country comparisons, this difficulty is also present. The British tendency is to discuss local elections generically even when it is the urban setting that is the focus (Rallings and Thrasher 1997), a confusion of terms which is also evident elsewhere (Hansen 1994). While to some degree these terms may reflect a difference in urban political structures in different countries, this basic point also highlights the difficulties of achieving proper equivalency in comparative studies.

A related difficulty is the need for models to be clearly specified. Thus, Boyne (1985, 490) points to the wide range of dependent variables in output studies——a variety of financial and nonfinancial policy outputs——and highlights how they tap quite different aspects of policy output, yet are still grouped under the heading of output studies. Berry et al. (1993) also highlight difficulties in actually measuring policy responsiveness, particularly in measuring the demand that local authorities are meant to be responding to. Similar issues are faced when specifying political and environmental independent variables. Not only are there differences between urban political structures, between, for instance, political and bureaucratic council leadership, Boyne (1985, 489) also highlights a tendency across local output studies for too many independent variables to be used somewhat atheoretically in "fishing expeditions" to try to explain outputs.

The final point to consider in this section is the extent to which there are different research approaches to urban elections and policy responsiveness across countries. This can be answered in two ways. At one level, Boyne (1985) notes considerable difference between how these topics are approached between British and American scholars. American scholars he argues are more innovative and broad in their selection of political variables by contrast with British scholars who have tended to concentrate on what he called "parties and elections" type variables. This situation is fortunately changing, as the work of James and John (2007) and Boyne et al. (2009) on local government performance indicate, although American scholars such as Berry and Howell (2007) and Webber (2010) are innovating further by looking at single-function elections and performance, in these cases relating to schools. At the more general level however, the key point is simply that most studies, from whichever country, tend to adopt quantitative methods using aggregate data to make inferences about political behavior.

4. The Impact of Vote Choice in Urban Elections

Why do urban elections matter? Despite the fact that the urban administration is likely to be the closest level of government to voters, discussion so far suggests that, regardless of how they are studied, urban elections are "second order" contests largely irrelevant to the majority of voters. Second order elections are those to a level of government other than the national government, where less is perceived to be at stake (Reif and Schmitt 1980). In such elections, participation is expected to be much lower than in those to the national parliament. Under these circumstances, city leaders would appear to have little or no reason to be responsive to their local electorate. In Gregory's (1969) version of this argument, electors would be perceived to have short memories, be confused or ignorant about the responsibilities of local authorities and incapable of distinguishing between local and national levels.

4.1. Accountability——How Voters Choose

It is first necessary, however, to understand why urban voters might vote the way they do. Do they hold local governments accountable—at least at times? The key question is to what extent have political scientists been able to link broader knowledge about voting behavior to specific concerns about local political issues. Intuitively there would seem to be a case for doing so; split-ticket voting between UK national and local elections when both are held concurrently suggests that some voters do choose to vote on specifically local factors (Heath et al. 1999; Rallings and Thrasher 2003).

There is a considerable literature on vote choice, developed primarily at the national level. Where strong party systems extend to the urban level, such as the UK, party identification may play a role, as might the effects of social structure. A variety of closely-related approaches can be grouped under the general heading of "rational choice" voting. Firstly, voters can vote on the basis of their proximity to the issues offered by parties and candidates (Butler and Stokes 1969, ch. 8). Secondly, they can choose how to vote on "valence" issues that there is broad agreement upon. Electors choose between candidates and parties on the basis of their performance and competence in handling these key issues (Butler and Stokes 1969; Clarke et al. 2009). Thirdly, there is the question of whether voters choose on the basis of retrospective judgments, attributing either blame or credit for performance in office (Fiorina 1981). Fourth, egocentric "economic voting" is where voters choose through a consideration of how economic policies are likely to affect them. A version of this idea is derived specifically from urban politics. Fischel's (2001, 4) "homevoter hypothesis" states that homeowners "balance the benefits of local policies against the costs when the policies affect the value of their home, and they will tend to choose those policies that preserve or increase the value of their homes."

Evidence for most of these explanations of vote choice can be found at the local level. In the U.S., because of nonpartisan ballots, elections held in off years, and fundamentally different local policy agendas, the results of local elections shed very little light on the future political prospects of national parties. In a study of local elections in England, however, Miller (1988) found, in common with other studies (Heath et al. 1999; Rallings and Thrasher 2003) that party vote choice at the national level was the most important determinant of local vote choice; around four-fifths of voters chose to vote the same way at both levels. Despite this, around two-thirds of Miller's sample suggested that local factors did form part of their calculation when choosing how to vote. Of the fifth of voters whose choice led them to diverge from their national choice, Miller (1988, 165) therefore speculated that local issues, personalities, and campaigns were key to determining how they voted. Rallings and Thrasher (2003) suggest that local political context is crucial in explaining deviation in local voting from the national norm, particularly where voters have experience of local incumbents and active campaigns from parties, in this case the British Liberal Democrats, other than those holding power at the national level. Heath et al. (1999, 402) make a similar point, but indicate that issues related to local autonomy helped explain differential voting at the local level and suggest that voters did vote instrumentally on the basis of local issues.

Studies based on aggregate data also suggest that urban electorates are sensitive to policy changes in the way that egocentric economic voting approaches might suggest. Hansen's (1994, 23–28) study of turnout in Norwegian municipalities found that higher turnout was associated with increased level of local service provision, thereby leading him to conclude that local voters were acting in a rational manner and therefore making it "likely that a consumer's approach to the study of the pattern of voting is of more relevance at the local than the national level."

In a series of studies, Gibson (1988; 1994; Gibson and Stewart 1992) investigated this question in a different way asking whether or not voters were responsive to rises in local taxation by assessing the swing away from the incumbent party in elections in both London and Birmingham. In each of these studies local tax increases were statistically significant determinants of swing against incumbent parties, although James and John (2007, 576) find local taxation less important in a more recent study. Gibson's studies also highlighted the impact of changes of service levels, measured as expenditure per head of population over the total period between elections, in explaining vote swings in urban elections.

Gibson's studies implicitly suggest a retrospective orientation toward vote choice among urban voters, with some attribution of blame for levels of performance. Recent innovations have assessed these questions in more detail. Berry and Howell (2007) examine retrospective voting in U.S. school board elections, arguing that as local single-function elections, they allow a more direct attribution of accountability than can be established by looking at elections to multipurpose local councils. While they find some evidence of retrospective voting behavior, this is only limited. They highlight the key role of media attention in providing information sources to allow voters to make judgments about incumbent performance. They suggest that when this wanes, so does voters' ability to judge performance retrospectively, a finding they argue raises questions about the true scope of retrospective voting.

Boyne et al. (2009) closely examine the idea of "valence" or performance voting in English local governments by using data from the publicly available Comprehensive Performance Assessment (CPA) of local council's performance. This provides a five point overall ordinal assessment of council performance, ranging from zero to four stars, with the highest reflecting the best performance. Performance on this scale is assessed in relation to the proportion of the total vote for the incumbent administration. As they rightly observe (Boyne et al. 2009, 1274), "if performance voting is still found in this [local] context, it is a phenomenon potentially of broad relevance." In an earlier analysis, James and John (2007) had found no evidence of local economic voting, whereas Boyne et al. (2009) did find a relationship between measured performance and vote choice. The key finding in both studies using CPA data was that a "negativity bias" exists where parties are punished for poor performance, but don't necessarily receive a boost for good performance. This means that, contrary to Webber's (2010) suggestion that increased levels of participation improves performance in a school-based single-function election, the same incentive may not exist when a multipurpose council is considered. In other words, a key premise of representative democracy—that participation and electoral incentives promote responsible government beyond a certain level of performance—may be crucially flawed at the local level, if not beyond.

This all feeds into the debate about whether or not urban elections are irrelevant, second order contests. Research findings crucially depend on the starting point of the researcher. From a national perspective, urban elections may indeed appear irrelevant to some because they experience low turnout and appear to be low interest contests where national issues dominate. From an urban perspective however, it is evident from the above discussion that they are not irrelevant for all voters. Indeed, it is clear that local political issues and their assessment by voters when deciding how to vote contributes a crucial additional element to understanding local voting behavior. Oliver and Ha (2007) find that, while suburban voters may be unrepresentative, they also tend to exhibit high levels of involvement, knowledge, and interest in local affairs. In other words, they come close to the normative democratic ideal of active, knowledgeable citizens, choosing representatives on the basis of information available to them. This is an important finding which, replicated elsewhere, would underline the importance of a broader understanding of urban electorates and elections and highlight the fact that they are far from irrelevant or second order to a large and active section of the population.

4.2. Electoral Competition and Accountability

Whether or not voters are interested in and knowledgeable about local issues may nevertheless be beside the point in ensuring policy accountability. If elected officials think that they care, and if political opposition is capable of being mobilized, then their behavior in office is more likely to be responsive (Gregory 1969). The key ingredient might therefore be electoral competition and not turnout per se, although the two are clearly related. Unfortunately, despite Oliver and Ha's (2007) finding that incumbent councillors enjoy less of a personal advantage in suburban elections, they still tend to be reelected, especially in larger cities (Howell and Oiler 1981; Krebs 1998). Although systematic data are hard to come by, the local council incumbent advantage appears to have increased over time, from around 72 percent in 1962 to around 85 percent in 2001 (DeSantis and Renner 1994, 40; Karnig and Walter 1977, 66). Weaker incumbency effects can still be traced in party-dominated urban elections such as England, although incumbency is unlikely to save a councillor in the face of a sizeable swing against their party (Rallings and Thrasher 1997, 79–84).

Incumbents are strong because they have greater name recognition, have developed a strong personal vote through policy advocacy and constituent service, and because they are able to raise more campaign money than challengers (Krebs 1998). In large cities at least challengers need money to translate their experience and qualifications into votes, and to undermine support for the incumbent. This, however, is hard to come by given the strategic behavior of donors who hedge their bets and protect their interests by giving disproportionately to incumbents and candidates for open seats (Adams 2007; Arrington and Ingalls 1984; Fleischmann and Stein 1998; Krebs 2001). More data are needed to determine if campaign money is important across cities or only in larger municipalities. For candidates running either as challengers or for open seats, name recognition, familiarity, and legitimacy among voters are key electoral resources (Lieske 1989). Newspaper endorsements and endorsements from party organizations and/or influential community groups also have been shown to be important predictors of election outcomes (Fraga 1998; Krebs 1998; Stein and Fleischmann 1987). In multiracial contexts, a candidate's race may play a pivotal role in election outcomes (Hajnal 2007; Lieske 1989).

4.3. Responsiveness and Representation

To what extent are urban authorities responsive to their electorates? This is central to the idea of elections providing accountability and providing an electoral mandate. It also goes the core of Laswell's (1936) famous definition of politics being about "who gets what, when and how." Gregory (1969) highlights a number of reasons why local councillors feel they have to be responsive to their electorates in what he calls the "rule of anticipated reactions." However, as suggested above, these reactions are not necessarily only anticipated; some voters do seem to attribute blame and penalize poor performance. Gregory's reasons include: the worry that many voters will correctly attribute blame for local issues with the local council; regular elections must be taken seriously so as not to lose control in the future; and the idea that a councillor's own local performance may serve to counter national swings away from their party.

The degree to which authorities in U.S. cities are responsive to their electorates is clouded by a number of factors. In strong party systems, like those found in Europe, voters can evaluate incumbents on the basis of their party affiliation, whether their party is in control, and whether they approve of what the party in power is doing. This is considerably less clear in the U.S. context because parties generally are not active locally, candidates in most cities do not officially represent political parties (a result in part of nonpartisan ballots), and opinion data on the performance of local governments and the policy preferences of local elected officials is limited (but see MacManus 1998). There also is something of a norm of volunteerism in local political service that potentially threatens the reelection incentive crucial to policy responsiveness (MacManus 1998; Prewitt 1970). If people are serving their communities as volunteers with little regard for reelection, there may be little incentive to strive to adequately represent constituent concerns.

U.S. urban elections, especially contests for mayor, are often decided on the basis of racial considerations (Bullock 1984; Hajnal 2007; Hill, Moreno, and Cue 2001; Kaufmann 2004; Kleppner 1985; Liu and Vanderleeuw 2007; Sonenshein 1993). If voters choose candidates on the basis of race, it would seem that the ability of local elected officials to be responsive to a broad constituency is compromised. On the other hand, candidates elected in racially charged campaigns may work harder to the address the policy needs of those who did not vote for them in an effort to broaden their base of support, and possibly short-circuit potential challengers, such as with Harold Washington in Chicago following his 1983 victory over Bernard Epton in a racially charged contest (Pinderhughes 2003).

If race is not a factor, things like party and ideology matter more to local voters' choices (Kaufmann 2004). If voters are able to determine candidates' party and ideology and if they act on it, the prospect of broader policy responsiveness is enhanced (Gregory 1969). There is also evidence that race recedes in importance as a cue in voting when minority candidates run as incumbents. In this case, performance becomes a more important criterion (Hajnal 2007; Stein, Post, and Ulbig 2006). When performance is the key criterion in candidate selection, voters are in a better position to hold elected officials accountable (Lay 2009). Likewise, elected officials are in a position to alter their behavior to respond to the perceived policy needs of city residents, and/or their own policy weaknesses. In general, policy performance matters in evaluations of mayors, but given the diversity of larger cities, the issue of race and how it affects individuals' evaluations is a complicating factor (Howell and McLean 2001).

The issue of policy representation has been a mainstay in U.S. urban politics for decades. Indeed, electoral reforms such as nonpartisan ballots and at-large election systems were sold on the basis of making local government more democratic and responsive to the needs of all residents. The target of these reforms was the urban machines that dominated U.S. city politics in the late 19th and early 20th centuries. Reformers, though, had their own agenda, namely to ensure that lower income, typically nonwhite interests were kept out of office where they might use their power to harm the interests of urban business elites (Bridges 1997).

Although at-large elections never became popular in older industrial cities of the Northeast and Midwest, they were widely adopted elsewhere. As the U.S. diversified, the constitutionality of at-large elections came into question, however. Consequently, urban scholars have spent considerable time evaluating the electoral consequences of at-large systems for the descriptive representation of minorities and women in city politics. In general, at-large elections harm the chances of minorities to be adequately represented on city councils (Engstrom and McDonald 1981; 1982; Trounstine and Valdini 2008; Welch 1990; Zax 1990). Due to lower levels of residential concentration, though, at-large systems harm Latinos less than they harm African Americans (Sass 2000). And it would appear that the deleterious effect of at-large systems on African American representation has diminished overt time (Sass and Mehay 1995). By contrast, women generally do better under at-large arrangements (Alozie and Manganaro 1993; MacManus and Bullock 1993; Trounstine and Valdini 2008). District elections also appear to benefit gay and lesbian candidates (Button, Wald, and Rienzo 1999).

The debate over descriptive representation and election method is not merely academic. A major topic in the U.S. urban politics literature is how descriptive representation leads to or produces substantive policy gains for minority groups. Perhaps the most extensive and sustained examination of the responsiveness of city governments to the concerns of the minority community is Browning, Marshall, and Tabb's *Racial Politics in American Cities*. This presents a series of qualitative case studies on the linkage between minority incorporation, defined as the extent to which group interests are effectively represented in policymaking and policy benefits. Results of these case studies indicate that government responsiveness in the form of city government hiring, minority political appointments, and police-community relations improves in response to minority political incorporation, but that group economic advancement does not. Time series analyses on the revenue and spending policies in cities with minority mayors, however, shows few effects (Pelissero, Holian, and Tomaka 2000). Garbaye (2005) demonstrates similar dynamics in the UK and France, with a "virtuous circle" existing between prominority policies, geographical concentration, open local opportunity structures, and the election of minority groups to urban administrations.

In the U.S., the composition of local elected bodies is a key factor in local policy responsiveness, as there is a direct link between minorities and women officeholders and the diversity of local bureaucracies. A large literature focuses on the link between racial/ethnic and gender composition of elected bodies, and employment diversity in city bureaucracies (Eisinger 1982; Joyce 1997; Kerr and Mladenka 1994; Kerr, Miller, and Reid 1998; Mladenka 1991; McClain and Karnig 1990; Mladenka 1989; Stein 1986; Saltzstein 1986; Welch, Karnig, and Eribes 1983). Early work was largely cross-sectional in nature, examining workforce diversity in cities over a certain size. More recent work has employed pooled cross-sectional analysis in an effort to explore cross-sectional and temporal variation in minority and female employment in cities (Kerr and Mladenka 1994; Kerr, Miller, and Reid 1998; Kerr et al. 2008). Although the latter approach provides more in the way of analytical leverage, both cross-sectional and longitudinal studies indicate a strong connection between who is elected and the diversity of the city workforce.

More diverse local bureaucracies, in turn, lead to more favorable policy outputs for historically underserved populations. Although a great deal of evidence suggests that city services are delivered in a neutral fashion according to apolitical decision rules (Jones et al. 1978; Levy, Meltsner, and Wildavsky 1974; Lineberry 1977; Mladenka 1980; Mladenka and Hill 1977), other work indicates more of a role for electoral politics (Koehler and Wrightson 1987; Miranda and Tunyavong 1994). That politics matters in urban service delivery also has been shown in a series of studies linking black and Latino elected representation on urban school boards to improvements in education outcomes for minority students (Fraga, Meier, and England 1986; Meier, Stewart, and England 1991; Leal, Martinez-Ebers, and Meier 2004). Similarly, the election of gay officials is positively related to progay policies at the city level (Haider-Markel, Joslyn, and Kniss 2000; Wald, Button, and Rienzo 1996). Black city residents also report greater satisfaction with their neighborhoods, public schools and police services, when represented by African Americans in city government and school boards (Marschall and Ruhil 2007).

Urban electoral arrangements influence the nature of policy dynamics. Councils elected by districts experience more ward-based conflict, and those elected by partisan ballots tend to be more partisan in their deliberations than those elected by nonpartisan ballots (Welch and Bledsoe 1988). District representatives are more likely to favor government programs targeted to particular groups or constituencies than at-large councillors, in part because of their desire to serve constituents with tangible benefits (Clingermayer and Feiock 1995). District councillors, especially those with diverse campaign networks, are also more likely to receive requests for service than at-large councillors and those with less diverse campaign networks (Clingermayer and Feiock 1994). Urban structural arrangements appear to influence the outlooks, priorities, and responsiveness of those charged with making city policy.

Some evidence also suggests that mayoral turnover influences both the policy decisions and priorities of local government, especially in mayor council cities. The policy effects of electoral shifts are greatest when a challenger defeats an incumbent, followed by change that results from an open seat election, suggesting that newly elected officials seek to make good on their mandate for change (Wolman, Strate, and Melchior 1996). The electoral cycle itself may cause officials to redirect policy in ways to appeal to voter concerns, for example by hiring more police officers to capture the "law and order" vote, or by lowering taxes (Bhattacharyya and Wassmer 1995; Levitt 1997; Strate, Wolman, and Melchior 1993).

In sum, research on U.S. cities indicates that electoral politics matters for urban policy responsiveness. Often the linkage between elections and policy responsiveness is indirect through the bureaucracy, a key agent of political responsiveness in U.S. city politics. What makes assessing accountability in local government in the U.S. difficult is the near total absence of responsible parties at the local level. In the non-U.S. context, parties matter because they stand for something distinct. Voters choose candidates on the basis of party labels and if the party fails to deliver on its policy goals it runs the risk of having its officials defeated at the next election. Although party and ideology are important in local elections, especially at the city-wide level, a number of factors are also critical in predicting voters' choices—race, incumbency, performance—being chief among them. Another issue is the degree to which voters know what they are voting for in choosing among candidates. Although Oliver and Ha (2007) suggest that suburban voters are knowledgeable and thus are able to link their policy preferences to the candidates on the ballot, because one's knowledge of and interest in local politics declines with city size (Oliver 2000), this may not hold in the context of large city elections. Complicating matters we have little information on the campaigns run by local candidates—apart from studies of deracialization (Austin-Wright and Middleton 2004), and even here measures of the campaigns are often weak—thus assessing what is discussed in campaigns and what happens in policy is very difficult.

Elections then play a role in local policy responsiveness, if only because local councillors feel that they may be held accountable and punished for their decisions. For example, Newton (1976, ch. 9) highlights how housing became a key election issue in local campaigns, leading local councillors and administrations of all parties in one English city to keep rents down for fear of retribution at the ballot box. Moreover, Gibson (1988) indicates that service levels are important, finding a positive relationship between higher service levels and a swing toward the incumbent administration. As James and John (2007, 576) point out, even if the national level may be important, good performance at local level still matters.

A number of points are important nevertheless. Firstly, elections tend to be important in ensuring policy responsiveness not on their own, but in combination with other political activity. Newton's (1976, ch. 9) finding regarding local housing policy also highlighted the fact that elections were effective because local interest groups were also highly active on the issue, creating an awareness about it in local policymakers' minds which they then reacted to. Others have also highlighted the importance of local pressure groups (Berry et al. 1993, ch. 6; Schumaker and Getter 1977). Secondly, local administrations do not necessarily respond equally to all their constituents. In a study of 51 communities, Schumaker and Getter (1977) found that there was a bias in responsiveness toward the more affluent citizens, with only a few cities showing responsiveness toward the disadvantaged. If Oliver and Ha (2007) are correct about the nature of the suburban voter exhibiting high levels of involvement, knowledge, and interest in local affairs, then these would seem to be the voters that are having their preferences responded to, not those who may lack voice in the system. Most of the attention from urbanists is on larger places that tend to have less informed and less engaged voters, and less electoral competition (Lascher 2005). Thirdly, Berry et al. (1993 ch. 6) however clearly highlight the fact that the cities with greater levels of local participation are more responsive to the majority of their populations. If this speaks to the importance of an open local opportunity structure to allow access for local groups, it also speaks to the importance of increasing levels of urban turnout since the more people who do so, the more responsive local representatives are likely to be.

One aspect of local elections that might narrow the scope of policy responsiveness is campaign contributing. Although the research is in this area of the urban literature is very thin, what we do know, not surprisingly, is that business interests are dominant actors (Adams 2007; Fleischmann and Stein 1998; Krebs 2005; Krebs and Pelissero 2001). Perhaps more importantly for understanding the potential for policy responsiveness in cities is research indicating that candidates draw funds from the same types of corporate interests (Adams 2007). Even if candidates start out with a set of donor interests that is more inclusive of noncorporate, progressive interests, when they seek reelection, especially if they are mayors, their fund-raising coalition will expand to include more corporate contributors (Krebs and Pelissero 2001). This is so because the most active donors behave strategically to protect their access to sitting incumbents, who are heavily favored to win reelection. In sum, the initial advantage that corporate concerns enjoy is reinforced by strategic behavior on the part of donors (Stein and Fleischmann 1998).

5. Comparative Perspectives

While there may be similarities in the methodological approach to this subject, to what extent are differences between countries evident in understanding local elections and policy responsiveness? There is one very important difference between the UK and Europe on the one hand and the U.S. on the other. This is that parties are central to the study of urban elections in the UK and Europe, in a way that they are not, or at least have not been for some time, in the U.S. Rallings and Thrasher (1997) note how historically political parties were quick to see the opportunities to extend their influence in urban government in the UK. This continues to the present day, with patterns of party competition in metropolitan boroughs extending beyond the main two parties to often include the third party in the British system, the Liberal Democrats. Some cities, such as Liverpool and London, are highly party politicized (Rallings and Thrasher 1997, ch. 6). Indeed, the proportion of seats contested by the two main parties in London is consistently above 90 percent (Rallings et al. 2005, 395–96). As electorates become more volatile, this party politicization has been complemented in recent years by growing numbers of small parties and nonpartisan organizations and candidates contesting urban elections (Copus et al. 2008).

By contrast, the U.S. has predominantly nonpartisan urban elections. Indeed, as noted above about three-quarters of all U.S. cities employ nonpartisan ballots. The effects are far reaching; nonpartisan ballots tend to negatively affect voter turnout, and have reduced significantly the role of local political parties. Together, these effects bias the local political process in favor of upper status interests. A lasting effect of the reform era, nonpartisan ballots undermined political parties, in particular machine organizations, but at a cost of greater economic and political diversity in the local political process (Welch and Bledsoe 1988).

As a consequence, these differences mean that findings from different contexts are often not directly transferable. Nevertheless, issues such as incumbency apply across different jurisdictions regardless of whether the incumbent is a party politician or an independent. The principle of incumbency conferring an advantage on candidates due to their being more visible throughout the electoral cycle and thereby cultivating a personal vote is well established at the national level. Incumbency effects are also in evidence at the local level in the UK, although not to the same degree as at the national level. Indeed, Rallings and Thrasher (1997, 79–84) observe that incumbency is unlikely to protect a councillor from a large-scale swing of public opinion away from their party. Incumbency advantage is also clear in the U.S., but its effect is delinked to national parties and platforms. The key issue, and a clearly understudied one, is the nature of the local incumbent advantage (i.e., what is at the root of it) and what characteristics of challengers and electoral context might lessen it.

6. Conclusions: New Directions for Theory and Research

Policy responsiveness is an essential component of life in democracies. Electoral politics plays a key role in this as the central mechanism by which the public has its say in the policy agenda of government. A difficulty present in efforts to understand the linkage between elections and policy responsiveness is the content of what is being communicated between voters and elected officials. In partisan political systems, like those present in European cities, elections revolve far more around party platforms and issues. It is more straightforward then to surmise that the public wants a change in government policy upon the election of a new party, especially if policy differences between the outgoing party and the incoming party are clear. In the U.S. candidates for local offices are to a much greater degree, free agents with an ability to craft whatever policy message and personal image they deem fit for their objectives.

In addition to what is being communicated is the question of responsiveness to whom or to what interests? Is politics and governing set up to be broadly representative at all times? Research suggests a somewhat mixed response to this question. The election of more minority and female candidates in U.S. cities has no doubt brought substantive gains for minority groups and women, not only in terms of policy but in the critical areas of city hiring and service provision. In this respect we see that elections have the potential to broaden policy responsiveness to groups and concerns historically marginalized. At the same time, however, the fact that voter turnout is declining both in European and in U.S. cities suggests that broad policy representation is not possible, let alone probable. Clearly low voter turnout is a problem, especially with the severe upper status bias typical of most electorates, and research indicates greater responsiveness in cities with greater turnout especially among minority groups. Another challenge for policy responsiveness, in both European and U.S. contexts is what to make of the fact that in some cities at certain times particular coalitions gain power and then use it to promote the narrow interests of dominant coalition actors over time. Regime theory of course suggests as much but scholars have tended to be preoccupied with the nature of the regime, its actors, and electoral coalition and less with the notion of the narrowing of policy responsiveness inherent in the theory. This issue has been far more explicit in the work of those investigating the role of machine and reform monopolies in U.S. cities (Erie 1988; Bridges 1997; Trounstine 2008).

Given the centrality of elections generally and electoral competition specifically to broader and more effective policy responsiveness, it is important for urban scholars to focus more attention on electoral politics. As noted at the outset, this topic within urban politics is badly understudied. To more fully understand elections and policy responsiveness, urban scholars should strive to understand what campaigns are about, how voters consume and act on campaign messages, and then how these are translated in governing bodies. In other words, what is the connection between issues, electoral success, and policy change in cities? Candidates and parties standing for public office spend a great deal of time discussing their issue positions, yet there is little attention given to either the issues they run on or if and how they act on them (but see Atkeson and Krebs 1998).

In addition to the role of voters, urban scholars would do well to pay more attention to the interests that fund the campaigns, and therefore make it possible for candidates to communicate with voters why they should be elected and what they stand for. Urbanists have forever it seems discussed the issue of community power—whether it be from a pluralist, elitist, or regime theory perspective, but rarely have scholars delved into the foundations of group power, namely the ability to participate in elections. We of course have some sense that urban policy agendas are dominated by financial concerns, whether they are in real estate, banking, and finance, but we have little understanding of the role these groups play in urban campaigns. This is so despite the tremendous attention this topic has received at the national level, especially in the U.S. For too long urban politics scholars have ignored elections, preferring instead to see urban politics and policy as largely reactive to the mobility of people and firms, or the relatively weak place of cities in the economic and intergovernmental systems (Peterson 1981). Even when elections have been central to theorizing about urban politics (as in regime theory), they have either been glossed over or insufficiently grounded empirically. It is to this research agenda we hope urban politics scholars turn in the future.

REFERENCES

Adams, B. E. 2007. Fundraising coalitions in open seat mayoral elections. *Journal of Urban Affairs* 29:481–99.

Alex-Assensoh, Y. 1997. Race, concentrated poverty, social isolation, and political behavior. *Urban Affairs Review* 33:209–27.

Alozie, N. O., and L. L. Manganaro. 1993. Black and Hispanic council representation: Does council size matter? *Urban Affairs Quarterly* 29:276–98.

Arrington, T. S., and G. L. Ingalls. 1984. Effects of campaign spending on local elections: The Charlotte case. *American Politics Quarterly* 12:117–27.

Atkeson, Lonna Rae, and Timothy B. Krebs. 2008. "Press coverage of mayoral candidates: The role of gender in news reporting and campaign issue speech." *Political Research Quarterly* 61:239–252.

Austin Wright, S. D., and R. T. Middleton IV, 2004. The limitations of the deracialization concept in the 2001 Los Angeles mayoral election. *Political Research Quarterly* 57:283–93.

Barreto, M. A., M. Villarreal, and N. D. Woods. 2005. Metropolitan Latino political behavior: Voter turnout and candidate preference in Los Angeles. *Journal of Urban Affairs* 27:71–91.

Berry, C. R., and W. G. Howell. 2007. Accountability and local elections: Rethinking retrospective voting. *Journal of Politics* 69:844–58.

Berry, J. M., K. E. Portney, and K. Thomson. 1993. *The rebirth of urban democracy.* Washington, DC: Brookings Institution.

Bhattacharyya, D. K., and R. W. Wassmer. 1995. Fiscal dynamics of local elected officials. *Public Choice* 83:221–49.

Bledsoe, T., and S. Welch. 1987. Patterns of political party activity among U.S. cities. *Urban Affairs Quarterly* 23:249–69.

Bochel, J. M., and D. T. Denver. 1971. Canvassing, turnout and party support: An experiment. *British Journal of Political Science* 1:257–69.

Boyne, G. A. 1985. Theory, methodology and results in political science—the case of output studies. *British Journal of Political Science* 15:473–515.

Boyne, G. A., O. James, P. John, and N. Petrovsky. 2009. Democracy and government performance: Holding incumbents accountable in English local governments. *Journal of Politics* 71:1273–84.

Bridges, A. 1997. Textbook municipal reform. *Urban Affairs Review* 33:97–119.

Browning, R. P., D. R. Marshall, and D. H. Tabb, eds. 2003. *Racial politics in American cities.* 3rd edition. New York: Longman.

Bullock, III, C. S. 1984. Racial crossover voting and the election of black officials. *Journal of Politics* 46:238–51.

Butler, D. and D. Stokes. 1969. *Political change in Britain.* London: MacMillan.

Button, J. W., K. D. Wald, and B. A. Rienzo. 1999. The election of openly gay public officials in American communities. *Urban Affairs Review* 35:188–209.

Caren, N. 2007. Big city, big turnout? Electoral participation in American cities. *Journal of Urban Affairs* 29:31–46.

Clarke, H. D., D. Sanders, M. C. Stewart, and P. F. Whiteley. 2009. *Performance politics and the British voter.* Cambridge: Cambridge University Press.
Clingermayer, J. C. and R. C. Feiock. 1994. Campaigns, careerism, and constituencies: Contacting council members about economic development policy. *American Politics Quarterly* 4:453–68.
———. 1995. Council views toward targeting of development policy benefits. *Journal of Politics* 57:508–20.
Copus, C., A. Clark, and K. Bottom. 2008. Multi-party politics in England? Small parties, independents and political associations in English local politics, in M. Reiser and E. Holtmann (eds.) *Farewell to the party model? Independent local lists in Eastern and Western European countries.* Wiesbaden: VS Verlag: 253–76.
Dahl, R. A. 1956. *A preface to democratic theory.* Chicago: University of Chicago Press.
Davies, J. S., and D. L. Imbroscio, eds. 2009. *Theories of urban politics.* 2nd edition. London: Sage.
Denters, B. and K. Mossberger. 2006. Building blocks for a methodology for comparative urban research. *Urban Affairs Review* 41:550–71.
DeSantis, V., and T. Renner. 1994. Term limits and turnover among local officials. In *Municipal year book, 1994.* Washington, DC: International City Management Association.
Di Franco, G. 2009. Alemanno's surprising victory in Rome. *Italian Politics* 24:99–116.
Eisinger, P. K. 1982. Black employment in municipal jobs: The impact of black political power. *American Political Science Review* 76:380–98.
Engstrom, R. and M. McDonald, 1981. The election of blacks to city councils: Clarifying the impact of electoral arrangements of the seats/population relationship. *American Political Science Review* 75:344–54.
———. 1982. The underrepresentation of blacks on city councils: Comparing the structural and socioeconomic explanations for south/non-south differences. *Journal of Politics* 44:1088–99.
Erie, S. P. 1988. *Rainbows end: Irish-Americans and the dilemmas of urban machine politics, 1840–1985.* Berkeley: University of California Press.
Fiorina, M. 1981. *Retrospective voting in American national elections.* New Haven: Yale University Press.
Fischel, W. A. 2001. *The homevoter hypothesis: How home values influence local government taxation, school finance and land-use policies.* London: Harvard University Press.
Fleishmann, A. and L. Stein. 1998. Campaign contributions in local elections. *Political Research Quarterly* 51:673–89.
Fraga, L. R. 1988. Domination through democratic means: Nonpartisan slating groups in city electoral politics. *Urban Affairs Quarterly* 23:528–55.
Fraga, L. R., K. J. Meier, and R. E. England. 1986. Hispanic Americans and educational policy: Limits to equal access. *Journal of Politics* 48:850–76.
Garbaye, R. 2005. *Getting into local power: The politics of ethnic minorities in British and French cities,* London: Blackwell.
Gibson, J. G. 1988. Rate increases and local elections: A different approach and a different conclusion. *Policy and Politics* 16:197–208.
———. 1994. Voter reaction to tax change: The case of the poll tax. *Applied Economics* 26:877–84.
Gibson, J. G., and J. D. Stewart. 1992. Poll tax, rates and local elections. *Political Studies* 40:516–31.
Green, D. P., A. S. Gerber, and D. W. Nickerson. 2003. Getting out the vote in local elections: results from six door-to-door canvassing experiments. *Journal of Politics* 65:1083–1096.

Gregory, R. 1969. Local elections and the rule of anticipated reactions. *Political Studies* 17:31–47.

Haider-Markel, D. P., M. R. Joslyn, and C. J. Kniss. 2000. Minority group interests and political representation: Gay elected officials in the policy process. *Journal of Politics* 62:568–77.

Hajnal, Z. L. 2007. *Changing white attitudes toward black political leadership.* Cambridge: Cambridge University Press.

———. 2010. *America's uneven democracy: Race, turnout, and representation in city politics.* Cambridge: Cambridge University Press.

Hajnal, Z. L., and P. G. Lewis. 2003. Municipal institutions and voter turnout in local elections. *Urban Affairs Review* 38:645–68.

Hajnal, Z., and J. Troustine. 2005. Where turnout matters: the consequences of uneven turnout in city politics. *Journal of Politics* 67: 515–35.

Hansen, T. 1994. Local elections and local government performance. *Scandinavian Political Studies* 17:1–30.

Heath, A., I. McLean, B. Taylor, and J. Curtice. 1999. Between first and second order: A comparison of voting behaviour in European and local elections in Britain. *European Journal of Political Research* 35:389–414.

Hill, K. A., D. V. Moreno, and L. Cue. 2001. Racial and partisan voting in a tri-ethnic city: The 1996 Dade county mayoral election. *Journal of Urban Affairs* 23:291–307.

Howell, S. E., and W. P. McLean. 2001. Performance and race in evaluating minority mayors. *Public Opinion Quarterly* 61:321–44.

Howell, S. E., and W. Oiler. 1981. Campaign activities and local election outcomes. *Social Science Quarterly* 62:152–60.

James, O., and P. John. 2007. Public management at the ballot box: Performance information and electoral support for incumbent English local governments. *Journal of Public Administration Research and Theory* 17:567–80.

John, P. 2009. Why study urban politics? In J. S. Davies and D. L. Imbroscio (eds.) *Theories of urban politics.* 2nd edition. London: Sage: 17–23.

Jones, B. D., S. R. Greenberg, C. Kaufman, and J. Drew. 1978. Service delivery rules and the distribution of local government services: Three Detroit bureaucracies. *Journal of Politics* 40:334–68.

Jou, W. 2009. The 2008 Hamburg *Bürgerschaftswahl*: Birth of a new coalition formula. *German Politics* 18:96–102.

Joyce, P. D. 1997. A reversal of fortunes: Black empowerment, political machines, and city jobs in New York City and Chicago. *Urban Affairs Review* 32:291–318.

Judge, D., G. Stoker, and H. Wolman, eds. 1995. *Theories of urban politics.* London: Sage.

Karnig, A. K. and O. Walter. 1977. Municipal elections: registration, incumbent success, and voter participation. In *Municipal Yearbook, 1977.* Washington, DC: International City Management Association.

———. 1983. Decline in municipal voter turnout. *American Politics Quarterly* 11:491–506.

Kaufmann, K. 2004. *The urban voter: group conflict and mayoral voting behavior in American cities.* Ann Arbor: University of Michigan Press.

Kelleher, C., and D. Lowery. 2004. Political participation and metropolitan institutional contexts. *Urban Affairs Review* 39:720–57.

Kerr, B., and K. Mladenka 1994. Does politics matter? A time series analysis of minority employment patterns. *American Journal of Political Science* 38:918–43.

Kerr, B., W. Miller, and M. Reid. 1998. Determinants of female employment patterns in U. S. cities. *Urban Affairs Review* 33:559–78.

Kleppner, P. 1985. *Chicago divided: The making of a black mayor.* DeKalb: Northern Illinois University Press.

Koehler, D., and M. Wrightson. 1987. Inequality in the delivery of urban services: A reconsideration of the Chicago parks. *Journal of Politics* 49:80–99.

Krebs, T. B. 1998. The determinants of candidates vote share and the advantages of incumbency in city council elections. *American Journal of Political Science* 42:921–35.

———. Political experience and fundraising in city council elections. *Social Science Quarterly* 82:537–51.

———. 2005. Urban interests and campaign contributions: Evidence from Los Angeles. *Journal of Urban Affairs* 27:165–75.

Krebs, T. B., and J. P. Pelissero. 2001. Fund-raising coalitions in mayoral campaigns. *Urban Affairs Review* 37:67–84.

Lascher, E. M. 2005. Constituency size and incumbent safety: A reexamination. *Political Research Quarterly* 58:269–78.

Laswell, H. 1936. *Politics: Who gets what, when and how.* Chicago: Chicago University Press.

Lay, J. C. 2009. Race, retrospective voting, and disasters: The re-election of C. Ray Nagin after Hurricane Katrina. *Urban Affairs Review* 44:645–62.

Leal, D. L., V. Martinez-Ebers, and K. J. Meier. 2004. The politics of Latino elections: The biases of at-large elections. *Journal of Politics* 66:1224–44.

Levitt, S. D. 1997. Using electoral cycles in police hiring to estimate the effect of police on crime. *American Economic Review* 87:270–90.

Levy, F. S., A. J. Meltsner, and A. Wildavsky. 1974. *Urban outcomes.* Berkeley: University of California Press.

Lieske, J. 1989. The political dynamics of urban voting behavior. *American Journal of Political Science* 33:150–74.

Lineberry, R. L. 1977. *Equality and urban policy.* Beverly Hills, CA: Sage.

Liu, B., and J. Vanderleeuw. 2007. *Race rules: Electoral politics in New Orleans, 1965–2006.* Lanham, MD: Lexington Books.

Lyons Inquiry. 2006. *National prosperity, local choice and civic engagement: A new partnership between central and local government for the 21st century.* London: HMSO.

MacManus, S. A. 1998. Seniors in city hall: Causes and consequences of the graying of city councils. *Social Science Quarterly* 79:620–33.

MacManus, S. A. and C. S. Bullock III. 1993. Women and racial/ethnic minorities in mayoral and council positions. *The municipal year book 1993.* Washington, DC: International City/County Management Association. Pp. 70–84.

———. 2003. The form, structure, and composition of America's municipalities in the new millennium. In *The municipal year book 2003.* Washington, DC: International City/County Management Association. Pp. 3–18.

Marschall, M. J., and A. V. S. Ruhil. 2007. Substantive symbols: The attitudinal dimension of black political incorporation in local government. *American Journal of Political Science* 51:17–33

McClain, P., and A. Karnig. 1990. Black and Hispanic socioeconomic and political competition. *American Political Science Review* 84:535–45.

McDonald, M. P. and S. L. Popkin. 2001. The myth of the vanishing voter. *American Political Science Review* 95:963–74.

Meier, K. J., J. Stewart, and R. E. England. 1991. The politics of bureaucratic discretion: Education access as an urban service. *American Journal of Political Science* 35:155–77.

Miller, W. L. 1988. *Irrelevant elections: The quality of local democracy in Britain.* Oxford: Clarendon Press.

Miranda, R. A. and I. Tunyavong. 1994. Patterned inequality? Reexamining the role of distributive politics in urban service delivery. *Urban Affairs Quarterly* 29:509–34.
Mladenka, K. R. 1980. The urban bureaucracy and the Chicago political machine: Who gets what and the limits of political control. *American Political Science Review* 74:991–98.
———. 1989. Blacks and Hispanics in urban politics. *American Political Science Review* 83:165–91.
———. 1991. Public employee unions, reformism, and black employment in 1200 American cities. *Urban Affairs Quarterly* 26:532–48.
Mladenka, K., and K. Q. Hill. 1977. The distribution of benefits in an urban environment: Parks and libraries in Houston. *Urban Affairs Quarterly* 13:73–94.
Newton, K. 1976. *Second city politics: Democratic processes and decision-making in Birmingham.* Oxford: Clarendon Press.
Oliver, J. E. 1999. The effects of metropolitan economic segregation on local civic participation. *American Journal of Political Science* 43:186–212.
———. 2000. City size and civic involvement in metropolitan America. *American Political Science Review* 94:361–73.
Oliver, J. E., and S. E. Ha. 2007. Vote choice in suburban elections. *American Political Science Review* 101:393–408.
Pelissero, J. P., D. B. Holian, and L. Tomaka. 2000. Does political incorporation matter? The impact of minority mayors over time. *Urban Affairs Review* 36:84–92.
Pelissero, J. P., T. B. Krebs, and S. Jenkins. 2000. Asian Americans, political organizations, and participation in Chicago electoral precincts. *Urban Affairs Review* 35:750–69.
Peterson, P. E. 1981. *City limits.* Chicago: University of Chicago Press.
Pierre, J. 2005. Comparative urban governance: uncovering complex causalities. *Urban Affairs Review* 40:446–62.
Pinderhughes, D. M. 2003 *Chicago politics: Political incorporation and restoration.* In *Racial Politics in American Cities.* 3rd edition, eds. R. P. Browning, D. R. Marshall, and D. H. Tabb. New York: Longman. Pp. 143–63.
Prewitt, K. 1970. *The recruitment of political leaders: A study of citizen-politicians.* New York: Bobbs-Merrill Company.
Rallings, C., and M. Thrasher. 1997. *Local elections in Britain.* London: Routledge.
———. 2003. Explaining split-ticket voting and the 1979 and 1997 general and local elections in Britain. *Political Studies* 51:558–72.
Rallings, C., M. Thrasher, and D. Denver, D. 2005. Trends in local elections in Britain, 1975–2003. *Local Government Studies* 31:393–413.
Ranney, A. 1962. The utility and limitations of aggregate data in the study of electoral behaviour. In A. Ranney (ed.) *Essays on the Behavioural Study of Politics.* Urbana: University of Illinois Press. Pp. 91–102.
Reif, K-H., and Schmitt, H. 1980. Nine second-order national elections—a conceptual framework for the analysis of European elections results. *European Journal of Political Research* 8:3–44.
Rhodes, J. 2009. The political breakthrough of the BNP: The case of Burnley. *British Politics* 4:22–46.
Ross, B. H. and M. A. Levine. 2006. *Urban politics: Power in metropolitan America.* Belmont, CA: Thomson Wadsworth.
Saltzstein, G. H. 1986. Female mayors and women in municipal jobs. *American Journal of Political Science* 30:140–64.
Sapotichne, J., B. D. Jones, and M. Wolfe. 2007. Is urban politics a black hole? Analysing the boundary between political science and urban politics, *Urban Affairs Review* 43:76–106.

Sass, T. R. 2000. The determinants of Hispanic representation in municipal government. *Southern Economic Journal* 66:609–30.
Sass, T. R., and S. L. Mehay. 1995. The Voting Rights Act, district elections, and the success of black candidates in municipal elections. *Journal of Law and Economics* 38:367–92.
Schaffner, B. F., M. Streb, and G. Wright. 2001. Teams without uniforms: The nonpartisan ballot in state and local elections. *Political Research Quarterly* 54:7–30.
Schumaker, P. D., and R. W. Getter. 1977. Responsiveness bias in 51 American communities. *American Journal of Political Science* 21:247–81.
Sonenshein, R. 1993. *Politics in black and white: Race and power in Los Angeles.* Princeton, NJ: Princeton University Press.
Sonenshein, R., and M. Drayse. 2006. Urban electoral coalitions in an age of immigration: Time and place in the 2001 and 2005 Los Angeles mayoral primaries. *Political Geography* 25:570–95.
Stein, L. 1986. Representative local government: Minorities in the municipal workforce. *Journal of Politics* 48:694–713.
Stein, L. and A. Fleischmann. 1987. Newspaper and business endorsements in municipal elections: A test of conventional wisdom. *Journal of Urban Affairs* 9:325–36.
Stein, R. M., S. Post, and S. Ulbig. 2006. Voting for minority candidates in multi-racial/ethnic communities. *Urban Affairs Review* 41:157–81.
Strate, J., H. Wolman, and A. Melchior. 1993. Are there election-driven tax and expenditure cycles for urban governments? *Urban Affairs Quarterly* 28:462–79.
Swyngedouw, M. 2000. Belgium: Explaining the relationship between Vlaams Blok and the city of Antwerp. In P. Hainsworth (ed.) *The Politics of the Extreme Right.* Pinter: London. Pp. 121–43.
Trounstine, J. 2008. *Political monopolies in American cities: The rise and fall of bosses and reformers.* Chicago: University of Chicago Press.
Trounstine, J. and M. E. Valdini. 2008. The context matters: The effects of single-member versus at-large districts on city council diversity. *American Journal of Political Science* 52:554–69.
van der Kolk. H. 2007. Local electoral systems in Western Europe. *Local Government Studies* 33:159–80.
———. 2009. Local electoral participation in Europe: Is it really declining? Paper Presented to ECPR General Conference, University of Potsdam, September 10–12.
Vetter, A. 2007. *Local politics: A resource for democracy in Western Europe?* Plymouth: Lexington Books.
———. 2009. Do preference vote systems affect turnout: Evidence from German local elections, 1978–2008. Paper Presented to ECPR General Conference, University of Potsdam, September 10–12.
Wald, K. D., J. W. Button, and B. A. Rienzo. 1996. The politics of gay rights in American communities: Explaining antidiscrimination ordinances and policies. *American Journal of Political Science* 40:1152–78.
Webber, D. J. 2010. School district democracy: School board voting and school performance. *Politics and Policy* 38:81–95.
Welch, S. 1990. The impact of at-large elections on the representation of blacks and Hispanics. *Journal of Politics* 52:1050–76.
Welch, S., and T. Bledsoe. 1988. *Urban reform and its consequences.* Chicago: University of Chicago Press.
Welch, S., A. Karnig, and R. A. Eribes. 1983. Changes in Hispanic local public employment in the southwest. *Western Political Quarterly* 36:660–73.

Wilks-Heeg, S., and A. Blick. 2009. *What are local elections for? Three questions, ten problems and a democratic solution*. Liverpool: Democratic Audit.

Wilks-Heeg, S., and S. Clayton. 2006. *Whose town is it anyway? The state of local democracy in two northern towns.* York: Joseph Rowntree Charitable Trust.

Wolfinger, R. 1963. The influence of precinct work on voting behavior. *Public Opinion Quarterly* 27:387–98.

Wolman, H., J. Strate, and A. Melchior. 1996. Does changing mayors matters? *Journal of Politics* 58:201–23.

Wolfinger, R. 1963. The influence of precinct work on voting behavior. *Public Opinion Quarterly* 27:387–98.

Wood, C. 2002. Voter turnout in city elections. *Urban Affairs Review* 38:209–31.

Zax, J. S. 1990. Election methods and black and Hispanic city council membership. *Social Science Quarterly* 71:338–55.

CHAPTER 7

URBAN POLITICS AS MULTILEVEL ANALYSIS

DANIEL KÜBLER AND
MICHAEL A. PAGANO

1. Introduction

At the beginning of the twenty-first century, several tendencies accentuate the entwining of cities with dynamics that occur at other territorial levels. City governance cannot be understood within the confines of the political institutions of a municipal government and the interplay of interest group pressures and political party posturing within city boundaries. Besides the complex arrangements between municipal and state/provincial governments within federal systems, many unitary states have also decentralized and intergovernmental relations have become more complex as a result. Additionally, nongovernmental actors and private sector associations have become increasingly important in guiding and shaping power relations and policy within cities and within broader metropolitan regions. There is thus a need to develop concepts and theories that are able to systematically account for the increasingly multileveled aspect of urban politics and policy.

This article unwraps the multileveled aspect of urban politics and policy by focusing on three main topics. First, we focus on the issues related to the nesting of cities within specific nation-state contexts. Going beyond purely institutional settings and intergovernmental relations, the "vertical" nesting of cities in national contexts also encompasses aspects such as the structuring of the party system, interest group representation, as well as welfare state characteristics. Gaining an understanding of this aspect of multilevel politics is especially important for internationally comparative analyses of urban politics and policy as we are challenged to carefully account for contextual elements that vary across countries (see Denters and Mossberger 2006). Second, we focus on the issues related to the more "horizontal" nesting of cities within wider metropolitan areas. As metropolitanization has proceeded and urban regions have become the predominant form of human settlement in the twenty-first century (Hoffmann-Martinot and Sellers 2005), individual cities have increasingly become entwined in functional interdependencies that contribute to the shaping of politics and governance within them. Finally, the chapter moves beyond the vertical and horizontal nesting of cities in order to examine issues related to the role of cities in the realm of international relations. Indeed, cities across the world have become increasingly involved in international relations (Lefèvre and D'Albergo 2007), not only as a consequence of global competition, but also due to new incentives provided to them through the strengthening of international intergovernmental organizations such as the European Union, the WTO, or some thematic branches of the UN. In the conclusion, we offer a few themes for further research.

2. Cities within Nation-States

Except for the rare contemporary city-states such as Singapore, the Principality of Monaco, or the Vatican, cities are normally local governments from a constitutional point of view. Throughout the world, cities are under the influence of upper level governments, notably national governments and, in most cases, other subnational government levels such as regions, states, or provinces. Urban politics and policy dwell within this constitutional framework where higher-level institutions structure constraints and opportunities. While the general picture of cities as constitutionally subordinate is certainly correct for most countries today, it is important to note the divergence of the historical trajectories that have produced the current setting. A distinction can notably be made between an Old World and a New World context that can also be seen to be a source of the fundamental difference between European and American cities (Bagnasco and Le Galès 1997).

For the Old World it is important to note that cities were not always "just" local governments. Many European cities have known long periods of glory as autonomous city-states, when they were global centers of political power, economic wealth, as well as social and cultural innovation. The city republics of northern Italy come to mind (e.g. Florence, Genoa, Venice), but also the cities of the Hanseatic league to the North (e.g. Bremen, Hamburg, or Lübeck). The medieval European city, studied as a driver of the modernization process by Max Weber in his classic work (1978), remains associated with civility and urbanity. It has left a heritage whose accumulated legacy is still tangible in terms of arts and architecture. As Patrick Le Galès (2002, 40ff.) has shown, the process of state formation in Europe involved the conquest and domination over medieval cities, most of which had succumbed by the end of the sixteenth century. With the creation of modern nation-states, cities were squeezed to the very bottom of the new constitutional architectures—where they remain until the present day.

In a New World context, such as in the Americas or in Australia, cities had a different role in the process of constructing the constitutional order. They were the outposts of European settlement and therefore always at the core of any constitutional project. The construction of higher-level governments was typically made with the understanding that local governments were critical constitutional entities with, in many cases, important autonomous rights. In a New World context, relations between cities and higher-level governments were originally more likely to follow a rationale of collaboration rather than one of competition. This notwithstanding, the modern constitutional orders in the New World countries also foresee a clearly subordinate status for cities, albeit in the context of states/provinces rather than that of the nation.

2.1. City Autonomy and Intergovernmental Relations in a Comparative Perspective

What does this subordinate constitutional status of cities mean for the analysis of urban politics and policy? It means to acknowledge that city governments are constrained entities, as their autonomy is limited by authority at higher levels. Hence a very prominent approach to conceptualize the vertical nesting of urban politics and policy has consisted in accounting for the nature and the extent of the limits imposed on cities by higher-level governments. There is an abundant literature on the ways in which to systematize and measure city autonomy, and to compare differences in nature and degree across countries (see Goldsmith's chapter in this volume). This work conveys an analytical perspective where city autonomy is thought of as a form of agency that is structured both by legal rules (constitutional and financial decentralization) and political practice (the access of local elites to higher-level arenas) that shape urban politics and policy, not only by posing limits, but also by providing opportunities. Both dimensions vary independently from each other across countries and thereby coin nationally distinct local government traditions.

However, this perspective on city autonomy provides an overtly static picture in the sense that local government traditions are assumed to be stable over time—a fact that should be questioned. As Goldsmith shows in his contribution to this volume, local government systems throughout the industrialized democracies have substantially changed from the 1980s onward. This is mainly—but not only—a consequence of reforms in intergovernmental relations, especially in former unitary states such as France, Spain, and even Britain. Local governments' discretion has been increased in the wake of decentralization reforms, and a new intermediate tier has been established at the regional level. With the regional tier being increasingly important for determining local autonomy, all these former unitary states "are beginning to share something in common with the federal countries" (Goldsmith 2002, 99).

In federal countries, cities have an important, if sometimes ambiguous, role in the constitutional order. In the US, for example, creating, terminating, and consolidating local governments can only be realized with the express approval of the state. The classic description of local governments' lives was presented by Judge John Dillon from the state of Iowa in 1868: "Municipal corporations owe their origin to, and derive their powers and rights wholly from, the legislature. It breathes into them the breath of life, without which they cannot exist. As it creates, so it may destroy." States create local governments through powers of incorporation and states can abolish local governments, regulate their behavior, limit their taxing authority, and in all ways make them comply with their demands within constitutional limits. Those who believed that "localism" or local autonomy best reflected the wishes and interests of the citizenry have clamored ever since to loosen the strictures of Dillon's Rule by supporting greater local autonomy (or what's referred to as "Home Rule"), which would favor expansive local powers to tax, legislate, provide services, and otherwise meet the needs of local citizens. Thirty-six states have granted some form of Home Rule to local governments (typically municipalities) and eight states have provided Home Rule statutorily (Richardson et al. 2003). Canadian federalism follows a similar framework to that of the US, namely, the key relationship with cities is legally prescribed by provinces. Nevertheless, an extensive network of contacts between cities and the federal government as well as with the provinces challenges a clear rendering of the situation. Under Liberal governments, the federal government engages in more projects with cities, while the Conservative governments maintain political distance from cities. Yet, the strength and well-being of increasingly autonomous municipalities rests on their capacity to access adequate fiscal resources, which is not considered to be strong (Horak 2009). The growing scholarship on multilevel governance in Canada explores the interactions between the provinces and municipalities on the one hand and the episodic intervention of the federal government on the other. The ebb and flow of federal and state support and withdrawal creates an uncertain environment for cities and their capacity to plan for long-term growth (Young and McCarthy 2009). The fiscal and political crises of the past decade have pushed municipal issues to the front line of Canadian politics, raising calls for more autonomy and greater access to financial resources while creating different patterns of governance across the provincial landscape.

Today, as local governments in Europe and North America have become more "autonomous" in the exercise of certain powers, power is shifting away from the center and toward more decentralized and dispersed centers of power. Peters and Pierre discuss this as a "logical extension of these [decentralization] developments" (2001, 131). Central governments throughout the world seem to have reduced their control on local authorities and consequently placed more responsibility on the intermediate tiers. But in many countries, such disengagement has been paralleled by a change in policy instruments, emphasizing collaboration and incentives rather than coercion and directives, creating an environment in which relations between local government and higher-level authorities are increasingly based on willing cooperation. Consequently, the networks, governmental layers, contracts, and connections between and among municipalities and a host of other entities, governmental and nongovernmental at various territorial levels, have created a spiderweb of interactions, a complex, multilevel arrangement of layers and nodes of contact that certainly appear to have order, but only if one examines the intricacies closely. And that is precisely the problem. Few citizens, or even academics, of these local democratic polities take the time or have the interest to understand the complex web of relations.

2.2. The Multilayered Nature of Urban Politics and the Need for Decentered Analysis

Given the changing nature of intergovernmental relations, as well as the "flattening" of constitutional orders in the wake of decentralization and regionalist reforms, it might no longer be adequate to view the vertical nesting of cities simply in terms of (constrained) local autonomy. At least since the 1950s political scientists around the world have attempted to understand power and the distribution of authority and influence in cities and urban regions. That a power elite might control (Mills 1956), that community elites govern (Hunter 1953), or that a pluralist model prevails (Dahl 1961) divided the academic research on the distribution of power and authority. Stone's (1989) influential work on Atlanta extended Dahl's pluralist model of government institutions by recognizing that nongovernmental actors have a seat at the governance table, and that coalitions of interest groups, if they worked through the political process—informing and influencing decisions of the elected officials—could exert change on the allocation of resources and authority.

Fifty years of research have built on those models and findings to present a more robust and explanatory framework for the distribution and exercise of power and authority. Today, the analytic lenses of scholars on the distribution of power are much better, stronger, and illuminating. Political power, and the power to change and influence the distribution of public resources, is more dispersed, networked, and shared than political scientists had described a half century ago. In the US, scholars began to notice some changes when nongovernmental organizations (NGOs) began taking on greater responsibilities in service delivery. Contracting between local governments and nonprofit service providers was recognized as a legitimate (and quite pervasive) governing arrangement; this became particularly important in the 1980s as "sorting out" questions dominated the national discussion and (local) social service systems were pressured by federal aid reductions. Scholars began to think of NGOs as partners in the distribution of public services. Social service agencies are, in many cases, NGOs that contract service provision with municipalities, counties, and the state.

As the analytic lens of urban governance broadened to include others in governing and in service delivery, another element was reintroduced in understanding the exercise and authority of political power at the local level, and that was the rediscovery of federalism. The nearly worldwide calls for regional control in transitioning nations (e.g. South Africa), as well as in established orders (e.g. Italy), were clearly for some sort of "shared governance" system in which not only provinces or states were strengthened, but also regional or municipal governments. What this has meant for research on power and authority in cities and urban regions is the refocusing of the analytic lens on the controlling influence of states over the behavior of municipalities. It has also encouraged an examination of how municipal services are delivered, especially intergovernmental cooperative agreements between municipalities and other local governments.

Following Sellers (2002) we can therefore argue that the nested character of urban politics and governance goes far beyond the familiar tenet of the institutional context. Of course, intergovernmental relations and systems of interest aggregation continue to play a role. But in parallel to the rising importance of business and nongovernmental actors, the nature of capitalist institutions (prevailing systems of corporate governance, industrial relations, educational systems, etc.) becomes an increasingly important contextual factor that contributes to shaping urban politics and policy, as it confronts "the protagonists of urban governance with different patterns of economic organization as well as different economic policies" (Sellers 2002, 620). In addition, the types of the welfare state play a role, as they tend to produce characteristic patterns of policies and constituencies that can be relevant at the city level, such as housing or welfare programs. For instance, the social democratic welfare state in the Nordic countries has been found to parallel, as a prerequisite, local governments with strong fiscal and politico-administrative capacities needed to implement the wide range of public policies that are on the agenda (Sellers and Lidstrom 2007).

There are thus not only multiple dimensions to the nested character of city governments with respect to their specific national context. But the multidimensionality of this subnational nesting produces specific mixes that shape urban politics and governance in specific ways. This leads Sellers (2005) to argue that the role of the national context should be reconceptualized: rather than in terms of a top-down account of constrained local autonomy, the national should be analyzed as an *infrastructure* for the agents of urban politics and governance: "Like the physical infrastructure in its relation to economic and social life, this infrastructure consists of taken-for-granted conditions for political processes within and among localities" (Sellers 2005, 425). Governmental and political institutions, economic structures, even social and cultural practices and values provide a national infrastructure for local agency and thereby shape urban politics and governance. According to Sellers, analysts should therefore abandon the nation as the unit of analysis, as it implies explaining variations in urban politics and governance as a result of varying national patterns of constraints and opportunities imposed on local actors. Rather, students of urban politics and governance should adopt "de-centered comparative analysis" (Sellers 2005, 435), where the focus lies on the city or an urban region as a unit of analysis, and variations of outcomes are analyzed as a result of both local strategies and nationally specific infrastructures of urban governance that shape local agency. Such an approach usually implies a comparison of cities located in one country combined with a comparison of cities located in at least one other country. As an illustration for such an approach, we can quote Savitch and Kantor's (2002) important study of the ways in which cities have responded to the challenge of globalization. More particularly, Savitch and Kantor selected ten cities located in five countries in North America and Western Europe, and provide an account of how these cities have grappled with the forces of global restructuring over the last thirty years. They show how local strategies combine with economic fortune, but also with national urban policies and intergovernmental resources that expand and contract the scope for individual cities' choice.

3. From Metropolitan Governance to Multilevel Governance

Urban growth and urban sprawl have continued throughout the twentieth century and into the twenty-first century. As the world's urban areas became increasingly dense in response to declining agricultural opportunities, the urban centers spread from their core, creating multiple centers within urban areas and sprawling from those centers in networks of residential and low-density commercial and industrial zones. It is increasingly inaccurate to speak of cities; rather, we must speak of metropolitan areas. However, the territorial institutional framework has not always followed the spatial expansion of the functional urban territory. As a result, high degrees of governmental fragmentation are found in most metropolitan areas across the OECD (Hoffmann-Martinot and Sellers 2005).

3.1. The Classic Debate

Some observers of metropolitan areas that are characterized by fragmented and overlapping governments contend that fragmentation is bad and institutional consolidation is the way out. Besides consolidation or amalgamation, this school of thought has also called for the metropolitan government model, thereby explicitly acknowledging the multilevel dimension to metropolitan government (see Lowery 1999; Kelleher and Lowery 2004). Forces toward consolidation contend that both negative externalities and destructive competition among local governments for economic development opportunities can be addressed under a more centralized/integrated governing system. Economies of scale can enhance productivity and performance and positive externalities can be encouraged. Drawing on these arguments, institutional reforms have been initiated in metropolitan areas throughout the world (Lefèvre 1998). During the 1960s and the 1970s, two-tier metropolitan governments were created in France (the *Commnunautés urbaines*), England (the *Metropolitan Counties*—abolished in 1986), but also in Canada (e.g. *Metro Toronto*, *Communauté urbaine de Montréal*) and the United States (e.g. *Portland Metro, Twin*

Cities). Yet, political factors (e.g., loss of local control) and place identity often conspired to maintain fragmented institutional patterns.

As arguments for consolidation for efficiency and equity reasons were gaining a foothold, a new perspective on metropolitan governance emerged in the late 1950s. It draws heavily on Tiebout's (1956) article in which he formulated a coherent public choice critique of the earlier arguments of the metropolitan reform tradition. Although Tiebout's theoretical interests were in explaining an optimal sized municipality, the framework he elucidated introduced tax burden and service delivery as key variables in firm and people migration. He argues that, while it is true that cities are monopolistic providers of services to their residents, city governments must be responsive to taxpayer-voters' preferences (demand) for a bundle of city services and provide these services at an acceptable or competitive tax-price. Should a city fail to deliver on either count, people and firms will migrate to other cities that come closer to providing an appropriate bundle of services at an acceptable tax-price. In other words, people and firms can express their assessment of a city's performance by "voting with their feet."

That citizens and firms can register their satisfaction or dissatisfaction with city tax policies and the performance of city service delivery allows analysts to examine competition among municipalities for jobs, resources, and people. This approach also provides a supporting platform for fragmentation and decentralization. The classic public choice perspective in defense of fragmentation, or at least a critique of local government consolidation, was presented by Ostrom, Tiebout, and Warren (1961). Their assessment suggests that municipal competition advanced greater service delivery efficiency and ensured that municipalities' monopolistic tendencies could be curbed, knowing that people and firms could migrate to neighboring locations if their municipality were not competitive. To the extent that decentralization and fragmentation in political organization are beneficial from the perspective of flexibility, efficiency and innovation, these decentralized political institutions are challenged in their ineffectiveness at addressing spillovers, small size, coordination, and redistributing income. This was the conclusion of Frey and Eichenberger (2001) who offer a framework of fragmented governance, by proposing a decentralized political structure based on an explicit recognition of the beneficial characteristic of functional, overlapping, and competing jurisdictions (FOCJ).

As a result of the public choice challenge the "intellectual foundation of progressive reform institutions [was] in tatters" (Lowery 1999, 30). In the 1980s, consolidationist reform initiatives came to a halt, and the abolishment of metropolitan governments in some places did not spark particularly strong protest—as was the case with the metropolitan counties and the Greater London Council in England, dissolved by the Thatcher government in an attempt to regain control over Labour dominated councils (Goldsmith 2005). Nevertheless, metro reforms were back on the agenda in the 1990s, with metropolitan governments re-created in England (the *Greater London Authority*) but also in Germany (*Stuttgart* , *Hannover*) and other places (Heinelt and Kübler 2005).

The push toward both fragmentation *cum* competition and consolidation *cum* cooperation has enormous implications for the future of metropolitan governance in the twenty-first century (Pagano 2007). Under the fragmentation scenario, local governments will be locked in competition for resources by bundling just the right type and quality of services at just the right tax-price, an activity that characterizes much of the local government landscape today. More likely, however, is that the competition among municipalities can only refer to the actions not only of "municipal governments" but also the attendant relationships they have developed with civic and philanthropic organizations, private entities, and other local governments with whom the incorporated municipalities must negotiate, contract, and compete, and which they must include.

3.2. Multilevel Metropolitan Governance

Consolidation or fragmentation? Disappointed by the dispute between the two classic schools of thought, researchers have started to focus on the role of policy networks in metropolitan governance and discovered a "new regionalism" (see Savitch and Vogel 2009). This third approach is based on the argument that coordinated behavior cannot only be produced via hierarchic decision-making (metro reform tradition) or competition (public choice tradition), but also via negotiation. It thereby echoes the work on multilevel governance in Europe (e.g. Hooghe and Marks 2003) emphasizing the importance of voluntary cooperation and joint-decision systems as a means to coordinate policymaking across territorial state levels in a context of increasing interdependencies.

New regionalist thinking allows for and recognizes the fact that the authority to govern over a spatially contiguous area is no longer the purview of the standard players, namely, the various (overlapping) local governments, subnational government, and central government. Metropolitan governance must now recognize and include the diversity of nonprofit service providers (especially the rapidly growing influence of faith-based organizations), the intrusion and involvement of the academic, real estate, banking, chambers of commerce, and the broader corporate communities (especially with regard to their engagement in economic development, transportation, land-use, and housing policies), and the service delivery responsibilities and rule-making authority of residential community associations. Moreover, the rapid rise in nongovernmental, nonprofit service providers which rely on local governmental contracts as crucial revenue sources has led some observers to refer to the "hollow state" (Milward and Provan 2000). In turn, third party government has become an important part of the lexicon of governance as well, which is a formal recognition of the importance of nongovernmental stakeholders in both shaping and implementing public policy.

The scale of complexity in managing program delivery that requires input or communication with a variety of organizations and governmental players has spawned increasing interest in how the intergovernmental system can be managed. More precisely, how can service delivery by one level of government (or a contractor of one level of government) be coordinated effectively with other governments and stakeholders? The intertwining of the relevant governmental actors requires collaboration at some basic level to ensure that the intergovernmental system meets citizen demands (Agranoff and McGuire 2003; Feiock 2004). Local governments may have the power to create public authorities—not uncommon in the US—often for infrastructure revenue-raising purposes (e.g. debt issuance) or incorporate under enabling legislation of a state to form new local governments, such as special districts, for the express purpose of providing a specific service. Creation of such institutions as public authorities, tax increment districts, business improvement districts, special taxing districts, and the like, are often in response to constraints imposed by states on local governments. Cities transfer services to newly created public authorities and special districts that operate separately from the municipal government. The public authority, as usually defined, is governed by a city-appointed board and lacks taxing authority, yet it still often possesses the power of eminent domain, which allows governments to take private property for public purposes with fair compensation to the owner. The special district, on the other hand, often has an elected governing board and possesses taxing and rate-setting authority. In both cases, the jurisdictions exist separately from general purpose municipal governments and may issue revenue debt, which pledges a portion of the income stream that is generated by users (payers) of the services. The major purposes of public authorities and special districts are "to provide a vehicle for using nonguaranteed debt and to finance activities out of fees and charges or special benefits taxes." (Aronson and Schwartz 1975, 166). These single-purpose local governments are nested within a complex web of interrelationships with overlapping or contiguous general-purpose governments, requiring increased organizational engagement and resulting in possibly higher transaction costs to manage such a complex network.

Recent research has begun examining interlocal cooperation among a multiplicity of networked local governments as adapting behaviors on the part of fragmented and proximate governments (Feiock 2009). This neoinstitutional analysis examines the complexity in organizational design that inheres in a multiplicity of local governments cooperating in the production of services with other local governments as well as with the nonprofit sector. If early public choice scholars were focusing on the costs of service delivery, the quality of services, the tax burden on individuals and firms, and migration as indicators of the efficacy of the market-like behavior of municipalities, other municipal behaviors were being overlooked, such as cooperation. Proponents of consolidation have argued that a key benefit of eliminating duplicative governments is that economies of scale reduce costs and, as a consequence, tax burdens. Public choice scholars were not persuaded, but they overlooked until recently the flexible, informal consolidation that results from cooperating in service provision. Municipalities find that to the extent they can keep transaction costs low (costs of negotiating between local governments for service delivery) and legal options open (the authority to negotiate with other potential providers of the same service), cooperative agreements hold down service delivery costs and simultaneously allow municipalities to seek even more cost-effective arrangements (Andrew 2009).

The web of interconnectedness among local governments within a region is not only a horizontal relationship, but also a linkage to states/provinces and the federal government. Collaborative public management, as Agranoff and McGuire (2003) describe it, is a necessary outgrowth of multilevel relationships among and between local governments as well as among and between higher-order governments.

4. Cities as Actors beyond the Nation-State

So far, we have shown that a multilayered analysis of urban politics and governance implies to take into account the effects of cities being nested both (vertically) within a national context, as well as (horizontally) within the dynamics of the larger urban region they belong to. In both these realms, recent trends and developments point toward a growing complexity of the set of actors relevant for urban politics and governance. Besides political institutions and state agencies at various territorial levels, nongovernmental organizations stemming from business and the civil society are of increasing importance in the complex web of multilevel governance. At the beginning of the twenty-first century, the world of urban politics and governance is characterized by a strong interdependence of actors whose coordination increasingly depends on negotiated agreements rather than unilateral action or hierarchical direction (on this distinction see Scharpf 1997). In the wake of this process, intergovernmental hierarchies become flattened and cities are rising, ever more, toward acting at eye level with upper level authorities who, from a formal legal point of view, are hierarchically superior. Hypothetically at least, this process of hierarchical reordering may well lead to a situation where "in the most extreme form, local actors become the principals, and hierarchical superiors within the state become the potential agents" (Sellers 2005, 433).

A case in point is the new role that cities seek to play in the realm of international relations (Lefèvre and D'Albergo 2007). Historians have shown that international relations have been a playground for city politics throughout the twentieth century. The Urban Internationale movement (Saunier 2001) is an early example, while town twinning and international networking initiatives have been pursued throughout the twentieth century (Ewen and Hebbert 2007). Historically, there is thus nothing new to the presence of cities in the international arena. However, changes that have occurred in the international arena in the late twentieth century make cities' presence in the international arena appear in a wholly new light.

4.1. European Cities and the European Union

Without any doubt, European integration has boosted cities' transnational activities since the 1980s, when cities came under the wing of various European policy programs (Ewen and Hebbert 2007). These programs have provided a new set of constraints and opportunities for urban politics and policy in cities located within the EU, thereby starting the Europeanization of European cities: a process of mutual institutional adaptation and adjustment in which cities not only have developed new strategies and policies but in which they have also gained increased weight at the supranational level (Kübler and Piliutyte 2007).

Focusing on the effects of EU Structural Funds in British cities, Marshall (2005) aptly distinguishes between "download" and "upload" Europeanization. Download Europeanization entails the changes in policies, practices, and preferences within cities as a consequence of the adaptation to incentives and constraints linked to the participation in EU programs. Among those changes, there is the increased participation of European cities in international city networks at the European level, such as Eurocities, for instance. These networks help cities to stay informed about European legislation and policies and therefore reduce information costs. They also foster policy transfer and learning, and therefore allow cities to keep up with an European or international "state of the art," requested for eligibility in eventual EU funding programs. The activation of cities in the international realm thus appears as a consequence of European integration. The motivation to "download" the EU and its programs provides strong incentives for cities to get involved in international networking and clarify their position with respect to an increasingly integrated supranational arena for European cities. This is especially the case for less wealthy and problem-ridden cities, or cities in accession countries, as they can expect to meet the criteria for EU funding.

Upload Europeanization, on the other hand, relates to cities' getting involved in international lobbying of the EU. As they have become stakeholders in EU policies, cities seek to influence the legislative process at the EU level. Heinelt and Niederhafner (2008) have shown that cities have used various channels to access decision-making at the EU level. Cities and their organization play a crucial role in providing the information and expertise needed by the European Commission for the formulation and the implementation of EU policies. In addition, members of the European Parliament are also receptive of expertise and knowledge produced by cities, and can be activated for the articulation of territorial interests that may be at stake in their local constituencies. Cities have the possibilities to "upload" their points of view at the level of the EU and have increasingly engaged in collective supranational action in order to be successful. Although some national local government associations or individual cities have opted for the establishment of an office in Brussels to lobby their interests individually, transnational city networks have clearly become the main thrust for cities' interest representation at the European level during the 1990s.

The growing importance of transnational city networks in the EU also intensifies the relationships between cities across national borders. They exchange experiences and cooperate to formulate policy solutions to similar problems. Europeanization thus provides new opportunities for transnational city-to-city relationships. This aspect of "horizontal Europeanization" as Kern and Bulkeley (2009) call it has become an increasingly common feature in Europe: "cities learn from one another when they jointly develop solutions for shared problems; they compete with each other when they engage in benchmarking exercises or vie awards for their local activities" (2009, 328).

The EU multilevel system of governance has thus become increasingly relevant for urban politics and policy in Europe, especially for smaller and midsize cities (Le Galès 2002).

4.2. Cities and the Wider Field of International Relations

But also beyond Europe, cities increasingly play the wider international game. More than two decades ago, Fry (1990) noted that more than 1,000 US cities had been engaged "in long-term international activities" in large part due to the rapidly increasing global economy. Promoting local industry for export purposes or for investment topped the reasons for city government involvement in international relations. Especially important has been cities' involvement in GATT (later WTO) and the Canada-US Free Trade Agreement (replaced by NAFTA). More recently Lefèvre (2009, 92ff.) found that cities and local governments play an increasingly important role in the realm of the United Nations and its agencies. A case in point is the creation, in 2004, of the United Cities and Local Governments (UCLG) association, whose mission is to engage in lobby and advocacy to promote the role and status of local government in the international arena and to influence international policymaking. The UCLG enjoys significant influence in the development and the implementation of UN programs, such as the United Nations Advisory Committee of Local Authorities (UNACLA), the Habitat Agenda, the Millennium Development Goals, and many others. This increasing engagement in the field of international relations makes clear that cities emerge at the global level not only as territorial nodes of economic exchange, but they also surface as political players intending to influence development and politics at the global scale.

These international activities also have domestic effects (van der Heiden 2010). Since the Westphalian treaty, international relations have been the prerogative of nation-states. National foreign policy and cities' transnational activities are often complementary to each other, as was shown for cities in EU accession countries (Kübler and Piliutyte 2007). Sometimes, however, city governments engage in issues of world politics in order to deliberately oppose national foreign policy goals, such as in London and Rome, whose mayors have openly opposed their national governments' decision to participate in the US invasion of Iraq. But besides tensions added to vertical intergovernmental relations, cities' international activities might also affect power relations at the city and the metropolitan level. Lefèvre (2009, 99–104) notes that core-cities of metropolitan areas are much more likely to engage in international activities than suburban municipalities. Core city mayors seek to use international activities to increase their resources and strengthen their position with respect to other powerful actors and other municipalities in the wider metropolitan areas. The development of international activities therefore also appears as a strategy to construct political leadership at the metropolitan level.

5. Conclusion

The "who rules?" question that has undergirded urban politics for generations can no longer be viewed in a formalistic or institutional manner, nor as elite control or multiple and overlapping elite groups, nor focus on the embedded or nested nature of municipal authorities within intergovernmental systems. Rather, it must embrace a catholic understanding of the broader interests in the exercise of political power and include civic associations, philanthropies, nonprofits, private providers, as well as the business and labor sectors. And these broader interests are actuated within the overarching legal, financial, and political architecture. More accurate and complex assessment of city governance must reach beyond the traditional foci of urban politics and embrace the many layers and levels of influence and political power.

There are, of course, many topics for future scholarship on issues of networked, multilevel urban politics and governance. In order to better understand the vertical nesting of cities in various settings, more research needs to be done in the perspective that Sellers (2005) has termed decentered analysis. Most notably, it would be useful to implement large-N comparative research designs on issues of urban politics and governance in various countries, in order to assess the generalizability of the findings generated by the comparative case studies approach that has characterized this field of research up to today. With respect to issues of metropolitan governance, and overcoming the old debate of consolidation versus fragmentation, the challenge ahead is to investigate the innumerable and undocumented intergovernmental cooperative arrangements and their effect on city autonomy and politics. Metropolitan areas are increasingly recognized as growth engines of the national economies by upper-level governments, and collaborative relations are strengthened but also rearranged in this process. The third field of multilevel urban politics and governance, cities as actors beyond the nation-state, is arguably the one that has been the least analyzed. While transnational city networks have started to be investigated recently—especially with respect to the various features of Europeanization—much less is known about cities engaging in politics at the global level, whether or not related to the UN or other international organizations. There is, to date, a flagrant lack of systematic evidence on the role of cities in world politics, the impact they can have at that level, but also on the domestic effects related to such international engagements.

References

Agranoff, Robert and Michael McGuire. 2003. *Collaborative Public Management: New Strategies for Local Governments.* Washington, DC: Georgetown University Press.

Andrew, Simon. 2009. Regional Integration through Contracting Networks: An Empirical Analysis of Institutional Collective Action Framework. *Urban Affairs Review* 44(3): 378–402.

Aronson, J. Richard and Eli Schwartz, eds. 1975. *Management Policies in Local Government Finance*. Washington, DC: International City Management Association.

Bagnasco, Arnaldo and Patrick Le Galès, eds. 1997. *Villes en Europe*. Paris: La Découverte.

Dahl, Robert A. 1961. *Who Governs?* New Haven: Yale University Press.

Denters, Bas and Karen Mossberger. 2006. Building Blocks for a Methodology for Comparative Urban Political Research. *Urban Affairs Review* 41(4): 550–71.

Ewen, Shane and Michael Hebbert. 2007. European Cities in a networked World during the Long 20th Century. *Environment and Planning C: Government and Policy* 25(3): 327–40.

Feiock, Richard C., ed. 2004. *Metropolitan Governance: Conflict, Competition, and Cooperation*. Washington, DC: Georgetown University Press.

Feiock, Richard C. 2009. Metropolitan Governance and Institutional Collective Action. *Urban Affairs Review* 44(3): 356–77.

Frey, Bruno S. and Reiner Eichenberger. 2001. Metropolitan Governance for the Future: Functional Overlapping Competing Jurisdictions (FOCJ). *Swiss Political Science Review* 7(3): 124–30.

Fry, Earl. 1990. State and Local Governments in the International Arena. *Annals of the American Academy of Political and Social Science* 509 (May): 118–27.

Goldsmith, Michael. 2002. Central Control over Local Government—a Western European Comparison. *Local Government Studies* 28(3): 91–112.

Goldsmith, Michael. 2005. The Experience of Metropolitan Government in England. In: Hubert Heinelt and Daniel Kübler, eds. *Metropolitan Governance: Capacity, Democracy and the Dynamics of Place*. London: Routledge.

Heinelt, Hubert and Daniel Kübler, eds. 2005. *Metropolitan Governance: Capacity, Democracy and the Dynamics of Place*. London: Routledge.

Heinelt, Hubert and Stefan Niederhafner. 2008. Cities and Organized Interest Intermediation in the EU Multi-level System. *European Urban and Regional Studies* 15(2): 173–87.

Hoffmann-Martinot, Vincent and Jeffrey Sellers, eds. 2005. *Metropolitanization and Political Change*. Opladen: Verlag für Sozialwissenschaften.

Hooghe, Liesbet and Gary Marks. 2003. Unraveling the Central State, but How? Types of Multi-Level Governance. *American Political Science Review* 97(2): 233–43.

Horak, Martin. 2009. Governance Reform from Below: Multilevel Politics and the "New Deal" Campaign in Toronto, Canada. Nairobi, Kenya: UN-Habitat. On-line at: http://www.ppm-ppm.ca/pdf/Horak%20New%20Deal%20paper.pdf.

Hunter, Floyd. 1953. *Community Power Structure: A Study of Decision Makers*. Chapel Hill: University of North Carolina Press.

Kelleher, Christine and David Lowery. 2004. Political Participation and Metropolitan Institutional Contexts. *Urban Affairs Review* 39(6): 720–57.

Kern, Kristine and Harriet Bulkeley. 2009. Cities, Europeanization and Multi-level Governance: Governing Climate Change through Transnational Municipal Networks. *Journal of Common Market Studies* 47(2): 309–32.

Kübler, Daniel and Jolita Piliutyte. 2007. Intergovernmental Relations and International Urban Strategies: Constraints and Opportunities in Multilevel Polities. *Environment and Planning C: Government and Policy* 25(3): 357–73.

Le Galès, Patrick. 2002. *European Cities: Social Conflicts and Governance*. Oxford: Oxford University Press.

Lefèvre, Christian. 1998. Metropolitan Government and Governance in Western Countries: A Critical Review. *International Journal of Urban and Regional Research* 22(1): 9–25.

Lefèvre, Christian 2009. *Gouverner les métropoles*. Paris: LGDJ—lextenso éditions.
Lefèvre, Christian and Ernesto D'Albergo. 2007. Theme Issue: International Strategies of Cities: Explaining Divergence and Convergence. *Environment and Planning C: Government and Policy* 25(3): 317–409.
Lowery, David. 1999. Answering the Public Choice Challenge: A Neoprogressive Research Agenda. *Governance* 12(1): 29–55.
Marshall, Adam. 2005. Europeanization at the Urban Level: Local Actors, Institutions and the Dynamics of Multi-level Interaction. *Journal of European Public Policy* 12(4): 668–86.
Mills, C. Wright. 1956. *The Power Elite*. New York: Oxford University Press.
Milward, H. Brinton and Keith G. Provan. 2000. Governing the Hollow State. *Journal of Public Administration Research and Theory* 10(2): 359–79.
Ostrom, Vincent, Charles M. Tiebout and Robert Warren. 1961. The Organization of Government in Metropolitan Areas: A Theoretical Inquiry. *American Political Science Review* 55:831–42.
Pagano, Michael A. 2007. In the Eye of the Beholder: The Dynamics of Federalism. In: Michael A. Pagano and Robert Leonardi, eds. *The Dynamics of Federalism in National and Supranational Political Systems*. Basingstoke: Palgrave.
Peters, B. Guy and Jon Pierre. 2001. Developments in Intergovernmental Relations: Towards Multi-Level Governance. *Policy & Politics* 29(2): 131–35.
Richardson, Jesse J., Jr., Meghan Zimmerman Gough, and Robert Puentes. 2003. *Is Home Rule the Answer? Clarifying the Influence of Dillon's Rule on Growth Management*. Brookings Institution Center on Urban and Metropolitan Policy. http://www.brookings.edu/es/urban/publications/dillonsrule.pdf (viewed September 21, 2009).
Saunier, Pierre-Yves. 2001. Sketches from the Urban Internationale, 1910–50: Voluntary Associations, International Institutions and US Philanthropic Foundations. *International Journal of Urban and Regional Research* 25(2): 380–403.
Savitch, Hank V. and Paul Kantor. 2002. *Cities in the International Marketplace: The Political Economy of Urban Development in North America and Western Europe*. Princeton: Princeton University Press.
Savitch, Hank and Ronald K. Vogel. 2009. Regionalism and Urban Politics. In: Jonathan S. Davies and David L. Imbroscio, eds. *Theories of Urban Politics*. London: Sage.
Scharpf, Fritz. 1997. *Games Real Actors Play. Actor-Centered Institutionalism and Policy Research*. Boulder, CO: Westview.
Sellers, Jeffery M. 2002. The Nation-State and Urban Governance: Toward Multilevel Analysis. *Urban Affairs Review* 37(5): 611–41.
Sellers, Jeffrey. 2005. Re-placing the Nation: An Agenda for Comparative Urban Politics. *Urban Affairs Review* 40(4): 419–45.
Sellers, Jefferey. M. and Anders Lidstrom. 2007. Decentralization, Local Government, and the Welfare State. *Governance* 20(4): 609–32.
Stone, Clarence. 1989. *Regime Politics: Governing Atlanta, 1946–1988*. Lawrence: University Press of Kansas.
Tiebout, Charles M. 1956. A Pure Theory of Local Expenditures. *Journal of Political Economy* 44:416–24.
van der Heiden, Nico. 2010. *Urban Foreign Policy and Domestic Dilemmas: Insights from Swiss and EU City-Regions*. Essex: ECPR Press.
Weber, Max. 1978. Economy and Society. Berkeley: University of California Press.
Young, Robert and Kelly McCarthy. 2009. Why Do Municipal Issues Rise on the Federal Policy Agenda in Canada. *Canadian Public Administration* 52(3): 347–70.s

PART II

INSTITUTIONS AND DEMOCRATIC PRACTICE

CHAPTER 8

CITIES IN INTERGOVERNMENTAL SYSTEMS

MIKE GOLDSMITH

1. Introduction

This essay reviews the relationship between cities and higher levels of government. It first considers theoretical perspectives on intergovernmental relations, then examines the relationship between cities and higher levels of government in Europe and North America, before reviewing briefly the situation in developing countries. It concludes by offering some suggestions for further research.

The position of cities in intergovernmental systems has changed considerably over the last twenty years. Major cities today are involved in a competitive struggle to maintain or improve their position in a global market for investment and employment. Whether they compete by trying to attract new economic activities, such as finance or high tech, or because they contain large pools of cheap skilled labor (as is the case with many Chinese, Indian, or some East European cities), or because they seek to make themselves attractive to tourists through the development of cultural, sporting, or other facilities, major cities across the world seek to improve their world status. And in doing so, their relationship with cities elsewhere, and with higher levels of government within and without their own country, has changed. Cities now exist in a far-reaching network of multilevel governance, markedly different from the kind of relationships which existed even only twenty or thirty years ago.

Yet it would be wrong to assume that this pattern of relationships is entirely new. As urban historians have shown, cities have always existed within a network of intergovernmental relationships in which cities have been subordinate to national or state/provincial/regional governments over time (Goldsmith and Garrard 2000; Morris 2000; Trainor 2000). The research issue is how this network has changed and for what reasons, and how do we explain the position of cities within it. As a subject for comparative research, intergovernmental relations still remain somewhat under-researched, partly for methodological reasons, partly for theoretical ones (Wolman 2008). Most studies (e.g. Rhodes 1981; 1986; Wright 1988) are focused on a single country. The few comparative studies (Page and Goldsmith 1987; Hesse 1991) are edited collections depending on a number of single-country studies to provide general insights or a basis for the classification of local government in different countries. Even here the emphasis may be less on intergovernmental relations than on some other question, generally the amount of discretion or autonomy which regions/states/provinces and local governments have within a particular political system. When we examine the current comparative situation of cities (Goldsmith and Page 2010), what we find is a diversity of relationships, in which individual cities can find themselves working with other cities in the same country; with cities in neighboring or far away countries, with an intermediate tier, with other government agencies or quangos, with national government(s) and even with supranational bodies such as the EU and UN agencies. Cities therefore have a host of vertical and horizontal relationships with a large range of other governmental, private, and voluntary sector bodies—a world now known in political science as one of multi-level governance (Hooghe and Marks 2001).

For some authors (e.g. Le Galès 2002), this world creates more opportunities and space for cities to act more independently than was the case twenty or thirty years ago. In the European context, Le Galès highlights the increasing importance of major cities as actors on the urban stage. Decentralization has meant that higher levels of government have developed policy instruments designed to encourage collaboration, offering cities incentives to cooperate with others and across sectors. However, other authors (e.g. Goldsmith 2005; Goldsmith and Page 2010) point to increasing governmental regulation, often taking new forms involving standardization of services, auditing, and benchmarking as well as the use of specific conditional grants, which further complicates the rules of the now multilevel intergovernmental game and places greater constraints on what cities can do.

2. Intergovernmental Relations and Theory

How do we begin to understand these multidimensional relationships? Three perspectives, one drawn from economics and two from political science, are particularly of relevance.

The economics literature is that associated with fiscal federalism and is classically represented in the work of Wallace Oates (1972). The fiscal federalism approach sees local government as a subordinate tier in a multilevel system and outlines principles for defining the functions and duties of different levels of government. Thus in federal systems such as the US and Canada, local governments are subordinate to state or provincial governments, According to Oates, the level which determines the level of provision of services (public goods) should include precisely those who consume the services. A related aspect is Oates's decentralization theorem under which "each public service should be provided by the jurisdiction having the minimum geographic area that would internalize benefits and costs of such provision" (Oates 1972, 55). The rationale for this argument lies in the classic justifications for local government—namely that local governments understand what citizens want and are accountable to them. Such an approach supposedly encourages fiscal responsibility and efficiency, especially if financing the services is decentralized. But there are links between this approach and that of public choice theorists such as Tiebout (1956), since this model is seen as encouraging competition and innovation among local governments while avoiding unnecessary levels of government. However, as with the public choice literature, such an approach is likely to lead to a multitude of jurisdictions and agencies at the local level. The fiscal federalism approach is important, however, because it has been influential with agencies like the World Bank and the IMF in their approach to tackling institutional structural problems in developing countries.

From a political science perspective, we have the work of R. A. W. Rhodes on the UK and Deil S. Wright on the United States. Comparatively we also have the work of Page and Goldsmith on unitary systems in Europe, and that of Marks and Hooghe on multilevel governance.[1]

Rhodes (1981) sets out what is generally known as his power-dependency model of intergovernmental relations. Drawing on interorganizational analysis, he saw intergovernmental relations as a process through which different levels of government achieve their goals by exchanging resources through a bargaining process, with each level being constrained by its dependence on other levels to achieve policy goals. The discretion of different levels reflected "the product of the goals and the relative power potential of interacting organisations" (Rhodes 1981, 99). Thus a city might increase its "power" by the skillful deployment of its resources and by exchanging resources with other levels of government and other organizations, but was dependent on them to implement its goals. Central governments needed local governments and vice versa. And the resources employed covered a wide range, from constitutional-legal to hierarchical, financial, informational, and political. The bargaining between these different parts was conducted in what were well-understood "rules of the game."

While this framework attracted some criticism (for example in its initial format it seemed to imply a degree of symmetry in the nature of the relationships between center and locality), it was widely employed as a research framework for the analysis

1. In an excellent comparative study Bolleyer (2009) concentrates her attention on the relations between central and intermediate tiers of government. Unfortunately no mention is made in the text of cities, local government, or special purpose bodies in the text.

of intergovernmental relations in the UK during the 1980s. Drawing together a large body of research, Rhodes (1986) modified his initial position. Though retaining the essentials of the power-dependency model, he recognized that at least as far as the UK was concerned intergovernmental relations were asymmetrical, and he introduced the idea of policy communities into his model. For Rhodes, policy communities are networks who share similar functional interests, have extensive membership, are vertically interdependent, are relatively insulated from each other, and stable over time. Intergovernmental relations were largely conducted through these policy communities and networks, and, one might add, largely outside or in parallel to the formal processes of everyday politics.

Wright's (1978) classic study of intergovernmental relations in the US provides a different perspective from that of Rhodes, though it shares some common features. Wright also stresses the need to move from a simple legal understanding of intergovernmental relations, and also notes the importance of nonhierarchical relations and the importance especially of financial resources. But Wright's model is first and foremost applied to a federal rather than a unitary system. In this respect Wright provides three models of national, state, and local relationships. The first is the *coordinate authority* model in which distinct boundaries separate out the different levels and in which national and state governments are independent and autonomous from each other. In practice, by the time Wright was writing, this model was largely seen as obsolete and based on outdated interpretations of US constitutional practice. His second model—the *inclusive-authority* model—is one which implies centralization, hierarchy, and dependency. Wright suggests that two strategies exist under which effectively national government reduces the authority of states and local governments. The first simply reduces the power of states or local governments or both, while increasing that of the national government. The second, commonly called "enlarging the pie" (Wright 1988, 43), involves extending the power of the national government without reducing that of either the states or local governments.

Wright suggests that while there is some evidence supporting this model through Supreme Court decisions, statutes, and administrative regulations, the idea of a federal government controlling or governing everything cannot be sustained. His third model—the *overlapping authority* model—is his preferred way of analyzing intergovernmental relations in the United States. Here substantial areas of governmental activities involve all three levels simultaneously; the space for autonomous action and the power of any one level is "significantly limited" (Wright 1988, 49). At this model's heart is the idea of the different levels being involved in a bargaining process and exchange—a view not too dissimilar to that employed by Rhodes in his model.

Both of these models were designed to provide a framework for understanding intergovernmental relations in the context of a single state, although there is a case for their employment more widely. In practice researchers have not generally followed that line. Two examples drawn from that literature draw on different models. The first, employed by Page and Goldsmith (1987) in their comparative study of seven European unitary states, uses a simple model as a framework for their analysis, which sought to identify the position of local governments in different political systems.

They suggest that central-local relations could be understood in terms of how functions were distributed between center and locality; the discretion that different levels had in performing their functions, and the degree of influence, or access, which localities had with the center. Put simply, the more functions local governments perform, the more discretion they have over the way in which these functions are performed, and the more they are able to influence central government policy decisions and programs, the stronger the position of local government in the political system as a whole. But in practice a comparative analysis is difficult to perform. On paper a comparison of functions across local governments in different countries should be relatively easy to make—but the more one explores the details of separate functions, the more difficult comparison becomes. Municipalities everywhere appear to have responsibility for such functions as housing, education, welfare, environmental matters, and so on, but the details of these vary enormously between and across countries. Page and Goldsmith's solution to this problem was to measure the importance of local government in functional terms by examining the municipalities' share of public expenditure, as well as their share of public employment. The more public expenditure is accounted for by municipalities and the greater their share of public employment, the greater their responsibility for governmental functions.

Discretion is also difficult to measure and can take various forms. First, there is legal or constitutional discretion—do municipalities have general competence powers or are they subject to laws passed at national or state/provincial/region levels? In Clark's (1984) terms, a general competence power allows cities to act independently from higher levels of government—they are free to act. Second, there is administrative discretion—to what extent do higher levels of government constrain what cities can do in policy terms by regulating their behavior administratively? Again in Clark's terms, how far are cities free from control from above? A simple distinction is between those functions which are mandatory—which cities *have* to provide—and those which are permissive—cities *may* decide to undertake these functions. Third, there is financial discretion: are cities free to raise their own income through local taxes or are these limited in some way? Does central government provide financial assistance through an unhypothecated general grant which cities can then spend as they see fit, or do they use specific grants, often with conditions attached as to how the monies must be spent? And while one dimension of discretion may lead us to consider cities as relatively autonomous in terms of intergovernmental relations, when examined from another dimension, cities appear to be constrained. Thus, for example, a city may decide *not* to engage in some form of cultural activity only to find the incentives offered under some specific grant scheme push it toward providing such activities. But in turn these might be constrained by the conditions which are attached to the specific grants... So clearly discretion is a dimension difficult to measure and one relying quite heavily on qualitative judgments as much as quantitative ones.

Access was used by Page and Goldsmith to examine the ways in which cities could bring influence to bear on higher levels of government. The idea draws on Tarrow's (1977) comparative analysis of France and Italy, in which he drew attention to the way in which multiple office-holding in France or the party networks in Italy gave local politicians wide-ranging access to the center, often allowing them to deliver specific benefits to their community. Even today French mayors may hold office at a number of levels—local, national, regional, European—though the number they may hold and which ones they can hold is now limited. But in other countries Page and Goldsmith found that localities had very limited access to the center, being represented by national organizations whose ability to influence policy and programs at the center could well vary, as the Scandinavian and British cases demonstrated in the 1987 study. Overall it was one factor which led Page and Goldsmith to draw a distinction between local governments in northern European countries, who had wide functional responsibility and considerable discretion in how they performed these functions, but individually had limited access to the center, and those in southern Europe, where local governments were small, with limited functional responsibility, limited discretion (being subject to considerable central oversight and regulation), but which had some means of influencing the center through the direct access they possessed.

Twenty years further on, such a distinction in Europe is no longer valid (Goldsmith and Page 2010). The functions, discretion, access model is still useful for analyzing intergovernmental relations in specific countries, including federal systems where in most cases it is the relationship between municipalities and the intermediate tier which is of greatest importance. But Europe has changed since the 1987 study was undertaken. There has not only been the collapse of communism and the creation of new democracies in central and eastern Europe, but the EU itself has become a major actor on the world stage and has increased in size, with twenty-seven members today. What has been called the "Europeanisation of local government" (Goldsmith 1993) now means that cities deal not only with intermediate and national levels of government, but also with various European bodies, whether it be in grantsmanship games as they seek funding for various activities under EU programs, or whether it be as a result of processes of EU regulation (Majone 1996; 2005) which apply across the EU as a whole. Furthermore, given that two of the basic rules of the EU in its programs are the principles of subsidiarity (things should be done at the lowest possible level) and partnership (to win funds cities have to work with a wide range of partners, including higher levels of government, other localities, and the private and voluntary sectors), the nature of intergovernmental relationships in Europe has become more extensive and complicated. Thus cities not only have to work vertically with different levels of government, but also horizontally with other partners, often including partners from outside their own country. The term *multilevel governance* more aptly describes intergovernmental relations in Europe today.

Multilevel governance is perhaps most associated with the work of Hooghe and Marks (Hooghe and Marks 2001; Marks and Hooghe 2003; 2004). Most of their work is written in the context of the European Union, but (2003) analytically they distinguish between two types of multilevel governance, which they simply call Types 1 and 2. Type 1 is the most common and largely derives from federalism. It involves a limited number (usually three) of general purpose jurisdictions with noninteracting membership, whose architecture is system wide. Thus Type 1 multilevel governance would be reflected in the usual federal pattern of national, state/regional/provincial and local levels of government, but it is also to be found in the structure of the European Union (Marks and Hooghe 2003, 236–37; 2004). But it is Type 2 multilevel governance which clearly attracts Hooghe and Marks. Type 2 can have an unlimited number of task-specific jurisdictions with intersecting membership and is characterized by its flexibility (Marks and Hooghe 2003, 237–39). The classic example of Type 2 multilevel governance is the fragmented system of governance found in most metropolitan areas in the United States where special districts, overwhelmingly single function bodies, can be found. Hooghe and Marks note that such districts have increased by over 300 percent between 1952 and 2002 (Marks and Hooghe 2003, 237). Switzerland also makes use of such bodies: Frey and Eichenberger (2001) identify six types of functional, overlapping, competitive jurisdictions (FOCJ) which operate alongside general purpose municipalities. But such special purpose bodies are to be found in many countries, contributing to the fragmentation of local government found in countries such as the United Kingdom, France, and Italy in Europe, as well as in federal systems such as Canada and Australia.

Characteristic of Type 2 multilevel governance is the fact that the institutions involved often have overlapping or at least intersecting membership. Schmitter (1996) uses the term *condominio* to describe such bodies. For him, they are "dispersed overlapping domains" with "incongruent membership" that "act autonomously to solve common problems and produce different public goods." The result is that Type 2 governance is widespread at the local level, with several fragmented institutions characteristic of most large cities. This fragmentation poses coordination problems for intergovernmental relations, but also offers considerable flexibility, allowing both for experimentation in institutional design and for the subsequent abolition of institutions which either do not work or which have satisfactorily dealt with the issues for which they were established. Single purpose bodies are all too easy to establish, as those who argue for an integrationist approach to city government willingly note.

Type 2 governance depends on the existence of Type 1 governance, for it is Type 1 institutions who characteristically establish such bodies. Considering the EU and its different policy sectors, for example, the EU competence to act in different sectors varies, and even within the same sector there may well be varying rules and regulations (Balme and Chabanet 2002). The EU's preference for policy programs targeted at specific problems gives rise to institutional arrangements and networks which characterize Type 2 governance by example—crossing borders, bringing in different partners, requiring different kinds of commitments by the players involved. The establishment of each and every program is itself a lesson in multilevel governance, involving different levels—the Commission, member states, intermediate and local tiers—as well as different partners—private and voluntary sector bodies, for example.

While the EU is the best international example of multilevel governance, Hooghe and Marks argue that Type 2 governance is especially to be found at the national/international level. International governmental organizations have increased in number considerably in recent years, though, as Marks and Hooghe (2003) note, they have a high mortality rate. Bodies such as NATO and SEATO, the World Trade Organization, and the World Bank are mostly concerned with coordinating governments rather than private sector bodies. Furthermore, Type 2 governance crosses national borders—again within the EU, with its long-established program of cross-border cooperation, but also within the North America Free Trade area—Canada/US and Mexico/US cooperation, for example. Most bodies established under cross-border arrangements tend to be functionally specific, or else constructed on a bottom-up basis within a flexible wider program, as with the EU's INTERREG program. In this context cities begin to take on an international dimension to their governmental relations: space does not allow a full discussion of this theme, but its growing importance should not be underestimated (Pallard 1999; Aldecoa and Keating 1999).

One consequence of these developments is the need to reflect on the nature of the political spaces in which cities operate. Here the work of Keating (1998), Carter (2008), Pasquier (2004), Smith (2008), Carter and Pasquier (2010) and others is relevant. These authors suggest that the formal institutional position of cities is only one definition of the political space in which cities operate and criticize some of the multilevel governance literature for its emphasis on vertical institutional relationships rather than the wider cross-sectoral nature of multilevel governance. This perspective is best thought of as a new form of territorial politics in which cities are but one actor among many, a theme echoed by Piattoni (2010).

Notwithstanding these perspectives, the formal nature of institutional intergovernmental relationships remains important. The constitutional position of subnational bodies, including cities and local governments; their functions; the way in which they are financed; as well as the formal intergovernmental arrangements within which they operate set the context within which multilevel governance operates, as well as determining the autonomy or discretion cities have to decide for themselves how best to provide for their citizens.

3. Decentralization: Strengthening Cities in Intergovernmental Relations?

According to a United Cities and Local Governments 2008 report, there has been a trend toward decentralization in most countries of the world recently (UCLG 2008). In effect this development has meant a strengthening of the subnational level at the expense of national governments, with the emphasis in many cases being on an intermediate tier between the center and locality. However, the extent of this decentralization process varies greatly, with some countries doing little to decentralize powers and authority to subnational levels. Great differences remain between those countries in the developed North and those in the developing South. In particular, limitations on resources, especially in terms of finance and trained personnel, in the South mean that where decentralization has occurred, it is limited in practice. In part this difference can be demonstrated by the percentage of public expenditure accounted for by local governments: a World Bank report of 2004 shows local government in countries like Botswana, Belarus, Costa Rica, and Nicaragua accounting for less that 10% of public spending, whereas in Denmark the figure is closer to 55% (UCLG 2008, 296).

The result of these differences is that there is great *diversity* in the patterns of intergovernmental relations around the world. This diversity is most marked in federal systems, where constitutional responsibility for local governments is generally to be found at the intermediate level—region, state, or province. If local governments are the responsibility of this intermediate tier, then in effect each such unit creates its own local government system and the main rules of intergovernmental relations. Thus, in the case of the United States, there are fifty different local government systems. But even in a well-known and centralized state such as the United Kingdom, one can also find a number of different systems, with Scotland, Wales, Northern Ireland, and England each having their own system of local government and different patterns of intergovernmental relations.

This diversity makes comparison difficult. One thing is relatively clear, however, and that is the position of capital cities. Nearly all are major metropolitan areas with some form of area-wide governance in place. Many have elected mayors who may well enjoy a special relationship with national government officials: no national government would wish to see its capital city as a backwater! In developed countries this situation is the case with such capitals as Canberra, Ottawa, Washington, London, and Paris for example. Furthermore, in the developed world there has been a tendency recently to establish some form of area-wide metropolitan governance arrangements. Though in some cases, for example Toronto, these take the form of an area-wide government, in most cases the arrangements come about as a result of some voluntary agreement among municipalities within the metropolitan area to cooperate, such cooperation being encouraged by central government through legislation containing various sticks and carrots designed to encourage cooperation: France's Chevenement Act of 2000 provides a good example. Following this act, over 100 voluntary areas were created within three years, together with five or six new urban communities also being established. Similar developments can be found in parts of North America, where states or provinces have encouraged some form of cooperation over a metropolitan region (Savitch and Vogel 1996). But the United States in particular is an example where special single purpose agencies proliferate: bodies generally designed to deal with a specific problem or service. This kind of agency, often found in most metropolitan areas, further complicates intergovernmental relations, and we still lack a sufficiently developed framework for analysis of it (Marks and Hooghe 2003).

4. Intergovermental Relations—European Developments

Turning more generally to intergovernmental relations, a review of recent European developments serves to highlight their diverse nature. Three factors have brought about considerable change: globalization and Europeanization; the continuing rise of the intermediate tier, and new forms of regulation.

4.1. Globalization and Europeanization

In practice globalization and Europeanization is in some ways both the most and least important. It is the most important because globalization has increased the interdependence of the world economy, undermining the ability of nation-states to determine their own economic future. Cities compete to maintain or improve their position in the world hierarchy of economic centers. But globalization/Europeanization is also the least important, largely because national governments still set the political agenda and mediate the effects of both globalization and Europeanization. The development of the EU has been important for intergovernmental relations in a number of ways (Bache 2008). First, through regional and other programs it has provided opportunities for cities to engage in grantsmanship games whereby they seek funding to support local objectives within an EU determined framework. But even here national governments play an important role as intermediaries between the locality and Brussels. The EU's rules of the game determine who is eligible to participate in its programs as well as the basis for participation: localities can determine for themselves whether or not they wish to play. To do so they are likely to have to join with others in a partnership, though the EU emphasis on the subsidiarity principle gives localities a stronger role to play in this game than might otherwise be the case. Partnerships not only involve national and intermediate tiers, but along with partners from other neighboring localities, private sector organizations as well as the third sector, and may also involve partners who come from other countries.

The EU has had an impact on intergovernmental relations in Europe in other ways. It has been a major source of regulation in many areas, from the working hours' directive through consumer affairs via environmental matters and financial contracts, all often impacting directly on how cities and localities conduct their business. It is difficult to judge how important this regulation has been for intergovernmental relations, partly because it is mediated by national governments (who largely determine who enforces EU regulations), partly because such regulation is only part of the battery of forms of regulation under which many European cities now operate. Overall, given the importance of national governments within the EU generally, the impact of Brussels directly on cities must be considered marginal. But it is also marginal for two other reasons. First, not all cities may be eligible to play the European game, not being identified as a place suitable for or even needing EU support. Second, not all cities or localities choose to play the European game, even if they are eligible (Goldsmith and Klausen 1997).

4.2. The Growing Importance of the "Meso"

The second factor—the continuing rise of the intermediate tier—is well brought out in a range of recent studies and literature (Sharpe 1993; Loughlin 2001). Marks, Hooghe, and Schakel (2008) clearly show the importance of the meso in their study, findings further supported by a recent survey of intergovernmental relations in thirteen European countries (Goldsmith and Page 2010). Clearly, as one would expect, the intermediate tier is important in federal systems such as Germany,

Belgium, and Switzerland. But its importance has also increased in the UK, where devolution has given considerable power to the governments of Scotland, Wales, and Northern Ireland; Italy (where regions are clearly more important than twenty years ago); Spain; and in central European countries such as the Czech Republic and Hungary (albeit regions remain weak here). In France, where decentralization created regional governments in the early 1980s, regions have not increased greatly in importance over time, remaining one among a number of subnational units. But even in countries like Denmark, Norway, and Sweden, which remain strongly unitary in practice, there are the beginnings of some form of regional tier, albeit of a limited nature. Nevertheless, even where this intermediate tier is of limited importance, its presence further complicates the nature of intergovernmental relations.

4.3. The Impact of New Forms of Regulation

New forms of regulation may well have had the greatest impact on intergovernmental relations in Europe in recent years. Initially following from the pressures to adopt ideas associated with New Public Management, such as privatization of services, contracting out, and so on, more recently many national governments have introduced new measures such as specifying service standards and benchmarking, together with rewards and punishments for those localities who excel or fail. The UK provides an extreme example of this kind of development (Sullivan 2010; Chandler 2007), but echoes of it can be found in Scandinavia (Fimreite and Tranvik 2010; Back and Johansson 2010). Another new feature is the growing use of contractual relationships between the center and locality, as found in countries like Holland and France (Pinson 2010; Denters and Rose 2005). Last, but not least, on the financial front, though general block grants are widely used in most European countries, the use of specific conditional grants remains widespread, and may well be increasing in some countries. These latter especially constrain how cities and local governments undertake their functions, but changes in forms of regulation in other areas also affect their behavior.

The general pattern of decentralization noted earlier has also taken place in Europe, with intermediate and local governments being expected to undertake more and more functions. Taken with the changes in regulation and the increase in status of the intermediate tier in most countries, this increase in functional responsibilities means that cities do more, but generally have less discretion over the way in which they perform these functions. Both cities also have less direct access to the center than was previously the case, their interests being represented by one or more national association. There has also been a decrease in multiple office-holding (for example in France) (Pinson 2010) while party ties may well be weaker than before (for example in Italy) (Bobbio and Piperno 2010). As a result cities have generally been less able to secure specific benefits for themselves, a trend only partly mitigated by the increasing use of directly elected mayors in many countries (again Italy and Germany provide examples).

Yet, as LeGalès (2002) argues, cities have become more important actors on the European stage. This importance reflects the importance given within the European Union to the subsidiarity principle, which in turn underpins much of European policy aimed at promoting cohesion (Hooghe 1996) and dealing with urban disparities.

In both cases cities have been places best able to benefit from such policies. But large cities have been the ones to develop a strong lobbying capacity in Brussels, as evidenced by the number which have or share an office there or who belong to networks and organizations such as Eurocities. Even where the EU's regional policy shifted direction away from some of the declining areas of western Europe (such as the North West of England), these networks were sufficiently persuasive in Brussels that the switch in policy was moderated or possible alternative funding was made available through other programs, such as URBAN. Not all cities who benefited from the former regional policy continued to do so after the late 1990s, and some may well have chosen not to continue playing the kind of grantsmanship games which European funding demands—for example, the building of extensive vertical, horizontal, and cross-national partnerships, together with the provision of matched funding. But cities are at the heart of most national government attempts to restructure municipal institutions in urban areas, as seen by the extensive voluntary cooperation found in major metropolitan areas in France, reorganization in Denmark, or the failure to achieve metropolitan reform in Italy. And, as major centers of population, their voice is likely to be heard on all policy matters affecting their interests. For all these reasons cities are important actors in intergovernmental systems in western Europe.

5. Intergovernmental Relations: North America

How far does this assessment apply in other parts of the world? In countries like the United States, Canada, and Australia—all federal systems—cities are subordinate to state or provincial governments; the federal government, constitutionally and practically, has a smaller direct role in matters affecting cities and municipalities. Each state or province is free to decide how local government, including that of major cities, is organized and run, resulting in a wide variety of different systems in each country. They are also likely to guard their constitutional position strongly, as demonstrated by the way in which the federal governments of Australia and Canada diminished their role in urban matters in the 1970s. For example, an attempt to include a mention of local government in the federal constitution in an Australian 1988 referendum was defeated. Similarly it was part of Ronald Reagan's policy to withdraw the federal government from involvement with cities in the 1980s in an attempt to redefine the allocation of functions between different levels of government (Salomon and Lund 1984; Chubb and Peterson 1985; Wright 1990). The result is a great diversity in local political systems, together with a considerable use of special purpose bodies.

Nevertheless, there is evidence of continuing decentralization and further reform of these systems (Bolleyer 2009). Writers such as O'Toole (1997; 2004) have stressed how, in the United States, "intergovernmental programs have become more the rule than the exception": national programs are implemented with "the active involvement of states and localities," thus providing "a heavy tilt toward collaborative intergovernmental arrangements" (O'Toole and Meier 2004, 469) in which networks of officials, agencies, and private and voluntary sectors come together. This focus has led commentators such as Wright (1990) to stress the importance of intergovernmental management as a further dimension to the analysis of intergovernmental relations. And in this context Wright also stresses the growing importance of new forms of regulation in intergovernmental relations (Wright 1990, 175).

6. Intergovernmental Relations in Developing Countries

As table 1 reveals, there are very large and heavily populated cities and metropolitan areas around the world. Of the top twenty cities listed here, fourteen are capital cities and only two are from Western countries. But most of the urban political science

Table 1. World's Largest Cities

City	Population (millions)	Population density/lm	Governmental Structure
Shanghai	13.8	7,174	Core district plus suburbs
Mumbai	13.8	22,937	Municipal corporation
Karachi	12.9	3,783	City district
Delhi*	12.6	29,149	Municipal corporation
Istanbul	11.4	6,211	Metropolitan municipality
São Paulo	11.0	7,247	Municipality
Moscow*	10.5	9,722	City proper
Beijing*	10.1	7,400	Core plus inner suburbs
Mexico City*	8.8	5,954	Federal district
Tokyo*	8.8	14,254	23 special wards
Jakarta*	8.5	12,738	Special capital district
New York City	8.4	10,452	City proper
Lagos*	7.9	7,938	Statistical area
Tehran*	7.9	10,359	City proper
Kinshasa*	7.8	787	City province
Lima*	7.6	2,848	Province
London*	7.6	4,863	GLC + boroughs
Bogota*	7.3	4,566	Capital district

* Capital city.

Source: Esa.un.org: *World Urbanization Prospects: The 2007 Revision—Population Database*, http://data.un.org/Data.aspx?d=POP&f=tableCode%3a240, accessed October 8, 2010.

literature on intergovernmental relations is based on experience in Western cities, mainly North American or European. Explanations or understandings of such cities may well be less relevant when considering cities and metropolitan areas in less developed parts of the world.

Many Third World cities are characterized by weak governmental arrangements, are poorly financed and staffed, and with inadequate infrastructure and services, and with socially segregated populations. Such segregation is also a feature of cities in more advanced countries, whose infrastructure and services are generally much better, as is the finance and staffing of their governments. But metropolitan areas are still characterized by fragmented governmental systems, often relying on voluntary cooperation between municipalities to tackle problems, and with a wide range of special purpose bodies designed to manage specific policy areas. This fragmentation in the face of often rapid urban growth (especially in the less developed countries) means that metropolitan areas lack control and even guidance on how to tackle problems. A multiplicity of units also means insufficient qualified staff to deal with issues on an area-wide basis. In many cases, especially in the less developed countries, there may be a lack of political will either to create new metropolitan-wide structures or to bring about the intermunicipal cooperation necessary to tackle issues such as increasng social segregation. Problems may be aggravated by the increasing competition between cities as a result of economic globalization, a process which is also leading to extended metropolitan regions, a development often referred to in the literature as "the new regionalism" (Savitch and Vogel 1996; Sellers 2008).

While metropolitan areas and cities in both developed and developing countries share some features in common, clearly many problems are much greater in the South. In both cases, however, it is the possibilities for both horizontal and vertical governance arrangements that dominate their intergovernmental linkages. In the language of multilevel governance, metropolitan areas are characterized by both Type 1 and Type 2 governance arrangements (Marks and Hooghe 2003). Cities need to cooperate with each other; special purpose bodies abound and have to be brought into governance networks, and vertical relationships with higher government levels may be crucial if problems of institutional fragmentation and lack of resources are to be overcome.

One exception to some of the features outlined above is the position of capital cities. In many cases the central government has chosen to create some special institutional structure to cover the capital city and its hinterland. In some cases an area-wide body has been established as for example with Tokyo in Japan; Greater London in the UK; Metro Manila in the Philippines, and Seoul in South Korea. However, even in these cases, the area covered by the institutional structure is less than that covering the economic and social metropolitan area as a whole, a feature much more aggravated in metropolitan areas generally, and especially in the South. For example, spatial expansion outside the formal institutional boundaries means that the metropolitan area only covers 45% of the metropolitan population in Seoul, 38% in Johannesburg, and 50% in Mexico City (Sellers 2008).

Space prohibits a wide-ranging account of intergovernmental relations in the developing countries of the world. In most cases systems remain highly centralized with the local level, even in cities, somewhat underdeveloped (UCLG 2008; Shah 2006). To take Latin America as an example, with its mix of federal and unitary systems, this region is highly urbanized (average % is 77.8%), on average, yet subnational government accounts for less than 20% of total governmental expenditures. Some countries, such as Brazil, have undertaken processes of decentralization (Asensio 2006). In this case subnational government accounts for over 40% of governmental expenditure (UCLG 2008, 174). Cities are characterized by fragmentation, yet more than half the population of Latin America lives in cities with more than a million inhabitants. Buenos Aires covers the autonomous city plus a further thirty-two municipalities; São Paulo covers thirty-nine prefectures, and Mexico City encompasses more than forty-one municipalities. As the UCLG (2008, 181) report notes, "Territorial administration and management of the big cities poses a major problem.... few have a metropolitan government that allows them to manage the urban territory in an integrated manner." Exceptions include Lima, Caracas, and Bogotá. In other cases some form of intermunicipal cooperation has been introduced, as in the case of Argentina and Ecuador. UCLG conclude their Latin American survey by suggesting that the continent remains one with "a high degree of political, territorial and economic centralization, exacerbated by concentration in the metropolises and immense social and territorial disparities" (UCLG 2008, 203).

Subnational government in the Asia-Pacific region is also highly variable. The region contains over half of the forty largest metropolitan areas in the world, characterized by fragmented governmental systems and a multiplicity of special purposes agencies. Some countries (e.g. India, Malaysia, Australia, and Pakistan) are federal systems in which subnational governments have a greater or lesser degree of autonomy. Other countries (e.g. China, Japan, New Zealand, and Vietnam) have unitary systems, and here central government is dominant. There are few examples of single metropolitan governments (Brisbane is an exception), though a reasonable degree of voluntary cooperation between municipalities within metropolitan areas occurs in some cases—Bangkok and Tokyo being two examples. One needs to distinguish between those countries with well-established democratic local government systems (e.g. Japan, Australia, and New Zealand and perhaps India) from those where subnational government is still developing (e.g. China, Indonesia, Korea, and the Philippines). In the former, central and state governments have recently undertaken reform processes to tackle problems of metropolitan fragmentation: in the latter, reform is more difficult, mainly for finance and personnel reasons. In India for example, there are separate forms of government for urban and rural areas. In the former in 2001 there were over 400 municipalities with a population of over 100,000, covering in total over 172 million. Within this figure there were thirty-five municipalities with populations in excess of a million—and with a total population of almost 108 million (Mathur 2006, 172). Mumbai alone has a population of around 14 million, as does Delhi. Both are dwarfed by the Tokyo-Yokohama metropolitan area with a population estimated at around 33 million. Both Mumbai and Tokyo have some form of area-wide metropolitan governance—the essential difference is that Tokyo has gone further in developing its structures than Mumbai and has far greater resources to tackle the problems it faces.

These two examples of cities and intergovernmental relations in developing countries indicates the generally weak position of cities, mainly due to a lack of finance, underqualified staff, and lack of political will to reform the system, especially in the less advanced countries. Such a picture would be repeated in gloomier terms in countries in Africa, Eurasia, and the Middle East: rapidly expanding urban populations, rapid development in some cases, little in others, and political and administrative systems which lag behind these processes of economic and social change.

7. Concluding Remarks and Further Research

This chapter has sought to highlight the diverse nature of intergovernmental relations across a wide range of countries. Diversity is found almost everywhere. As such, cities find themselves in a wide range of relationships with different levels of government, from neighboring local authorities through special purpose bodies, up to higher levels of government—state/provincial/regional—and even to the international level, especially in the case of Europe with the development of the European Union. In the European case we highlighted the importance of *Europeanization/globalization*, together with *continuing decentralization* to intermediate or local tiers of government, and *new forms of regulation* as important factors affecting intergovernmental relations. There is some evidence to suggest that globalization, regionalization, and regulation are also important factors affecting intergovernmental relations and the position of cities in other countries such as the United States, Canada, and Australia, as well as in developing countries. In all cases ideas about the nature of multilevel governance and its workings, as well as an understanding of the kinds of networks in which cities are involved and how they operate, are important for our understanding of intergovernmental relations.

However, while there is considerable research evidence on the workings of multilevel governance in terms of vertical relations between different levels of government particularly in the European context (what Marks and Hooghe [2003] call Type 1 governance), there is much less evidence about how horizontal and cross-sectoral Type 2 governance operates, and how especially cities are able to work within such a framework to secure their policy goals across different policy sectors. In an era of fiscal austerity, in which national governments frequently set broad policy goals, but expect lower tiers of government to develop and implement such policy programs, often within a strong centrally or regionally determined regulatory framework, cities have to use all their skills and resources to secure their policy aims. In this context, an increased understanding of Type 2 governance becomes an important research objective. As part of this research, we need to consider cities in their international dimension—the international relations of cities are important at a time of increasing globalization.

A second gap in our understanding of cities and their intergovernmental relations concerns cities in developing countries. These countries contain by far the world's largest cities—yet our understanding of how they operate is still limited. Some comparative studies of such cities and their intergovernmental relations would both provide us with a broader understanding of intergovernmental relations more generally, but would also provide a stimulus to new theoretical thinking.

Lastly, while the number of comparative studies is on the increase and our theoretical capacity improving, we still need more comparative work and theoretical development in this field. With notable exceptions, far too many studies are still single country or are based on snapshots taken of different countries at a particular point in time, or fail to capture all possible levels of intergovernmental relationships (Bolleyer 2009).

REFERENCES

Aldecoa, F. and Keating, M., eds. 1999. "Paradiplomacy in Action: The Foreign Relations of Sub-national Governments." Special issue of *Regional and Federal Studies* 9: 1.

Asensio, M. A. 2006. "Local Government Organisation and Finance: Argentina." In Shah, A., ed. *Local Governance in Developing Countries.* Washington, DC: World Bank, 347–80.

Bache, I. 2008. *Europeanization and Multilevel Governance.* Lanham, MD: Rowan and Littlefield.

Back, H. and Johansson, V. 2010. "Sweden." In Goldsmith, M. and Page, E., eds. *Changing Intergovernmental Relations in Europe.* London: Routledge, 198–209.

Balme, R. and Chabanet, D. 2002. *Collection Action in Europe.* Paris: Presses de Science-Po.

Bobbio, L. and Piperno, S. 2010. "Italy." In Goldsmith, M. and Page, E. C., eds. *Changing Government Relations in Europe.* London: Routledge, 127–44.

Bolleyer, N. 2009. *Intergovernmental Cooperation.* Oxford: Oxford University Press.

Carter, C. 2008. "Globalization, Scottish Fisheries and 'Political Work': EU-Local Dialectics." In Julien, B. and Smith, A., eds. *Industries and Globalization: The Political Causality of Divergent Responses.* London: Palgrave, 149–81.

Carter, C. and Pasquier, R., eds. 2010. "The Europeanization of Regions as Spaces for Politics." Special issue of *Regional and Federal Studies* 20(3): 281–295.

Chandler, J. 2007. *Explaining Local Government.* Manchester: Manchester University Press.

Chubb, E. and Peterson, P., eds. 1985. *The New Directions in American Politics.* Washington, DC: Urban Institute Press.

Clark, G. 1984. "A Theory of Local Autonomy." *Annals of the Association of American Geographers* 74: 195–200.

Denters, B. and Rose, L. eds. 2005. *Comparing Local Governance.* Basingstoke, Palgrave.

Fimreite, A-L. and Tranvik, T. 2010. "Norway." In Goldsmith, M. and Page, E., eds. *Changing Intergovernmental Relations in Europe.* London: Routledge, 163–78.
Frey, B. S. and Eichenberger, R. 2001. "Metropolitan Governance for the Future: Functional Overlapping Competing Jurisdictions (FOCJ)." *Swiss Political Science Review* 7(3): 124–30.
Goldsmith, M. 1993. "The Europeanization of Local Government." *Urban Studies* 30(4–5): 83–70.
———. 2005. "A New Intergovernmentalism." In Denters, S. A. H. and Rose, L., eds. *Comparing Local Governance.* Basingstoke: Palgrave, 228–45.
Goldsmith, M. and Garrard, J. 2000. "Urban Governance: Some Reflections." In Morris, R. J. and Trainor, R. H., eds. *Urban Governance: Britain and Beyond Since 1750.* Aldershot: Ashgate, 15–27.
Goldsmith, M. and Klausen, K. K., eds. 1997. *European Integration and Local Government.* Cheltenham: Edward Elgar.
Goldsmith, M. and Page, E., eds. 2010. *Changing Intergovernmental Relations in Europe.* London: Routledge.
Hesse, J. J., ed. 1991. *Local Government and Urban Affairs in International Perspective.* Baden-Baden: Nomos Verlagsgesellschaft.
Hooghe, L., ed. 1996. *Cohesion Policy and European Integration.* Oxford: Oxford University Press.
Hooghe, L. and Marks, G. 2001. *Multi-Level Governance and European Integration.* Lanham, MD: Rowan and Littlefield.
Keating, M. 1998. *The New Regionalism in Western Europe: Territorial Restructuring and Political Change.* Cheltenham: Edward Elgar.
Le Galès, P. 2002. *European Cities.* Oxford: Oxford University Press.
Loughlin, J., ed. 2001. *Subnational Democracy in the European Union.* Oxford: Oxford University Press.
Majone, G. 1996. *Regulating Europe.* London: Routledge.
———. 2005. *Dilemmas of European Integration.* Oxford: Oxford University Press.
Marks, G. and Hooghe, L. 2003. "Unravelling the Central State. But How? Types of Multi-level Governance." *American Political Science Review* 97(2): 233–43.
———. 2004. "Contesting Visions of Multi-Level Governance." In Bach, I. and Flinders, M., eds. *Multi-level Governance.* Oxford: Oxford University Press, 15–30.
Marks, G., Hooghe, L. and Schakel, A. H. 2008. "Regional Authority in 42 Countries, 1950–2006: A Measure and Five Hypotheses." Special issue of *Regional and Federal Studies* 18(2–3): 111–302.
Mathur, O. P. 2006. "Local Government Organization and Finance: Urban India." In Shah, A., ed. *Local Governance in Developing Countries.* Washington, DC: World Bank, 169–204.
Morris, R. 2000. "Governance: Two Centuries of Urban Growth." In Morris, R. J. and Trainor, R. H., eds. *Urban Governance: Britain and Beyond since 1750.* Aldershot: Ashgate, 1–14.
Oates, W. E. 1972. *Fiscal Federalism.* New York: Harcourt Brace Jovanovich.
O'Toole, L. 1997. "Treating Networks Seriously: Practical and Research-Based Agendas in Public Administration." *Public Administration Review* 57(1): 45–52.
O'Toole, L and Meier, K. 2004. "Public Management in Intergovernmental Networks: Matching Structural Networks and Managerial Networking." *Journal of Public Administration Research and Theory* 14(4): 469–94.
Page, E. C. and Goldsmith, M., eds. 1987. *Central and Local Government Relations.* London: Sage.

Pallard, J., ed. 1999: "Les Relations Internationales des Regions En Europe." Special issue of *Etudes Internationales* 30(4).
Pasquier, R. 2004. *La Capacite politque des Regions: Une comparison—France: Espagne.* Rennes: Presses Universitaires de Rennes.
Pinson, G. 2010. "France." In Goldsmith, M. and Page, E., eds. *Changing Government Relations in Europe.* London: Routledge, 68–87.
Rhodes, R. A. W. 1981. *Control and Power in Central-Local Government Relations.* Farnborough: Gower.
———. 1986. *The National World of Local Government.* London: Allen and Unwin.
Salomon, L. and Lund, M. S., eds. 1984. *The Reagan Presidency and the Governing of Urban America.* Washington, DC: Urban Institute Press.
Savitch, H. and Vogel, R., eds. 1996: *Regional Politics: America in a Post City Age.* Newbury Park: Sage.
Schmitter, P. 1996. "Imagining the Future of the Euro-Polity with the Help of New Concepts." In Marks, G., Scharpf, F. W., Schmitter, P. C., and Streeck, W. *Governance in the European Union.* London: Sage, 121–51.
Sellers, J. 2008. "North America." In UCLG: *Decentralization and Local Democracy in the World.* Barcelona: UCLG, 234–55.
Shah, A., ed. 2006. *Local Governance in Developing Countries.* Washington, DC: World Bank.
Smith, A. 2008. "Territory and the Regulation of Industry: Examples from Scotland and Aquitaine." *Regional and Federal Studies* 18(1): 37–53.
Sharpe, L. J., ed. 1993. *The Rise of Meso Government in Europe.* London: Sage.
Sullivan, H. 2010. "The United Kingdom." In Goldsmith, M. and Page, E. C., eds., *Changing Government Relations in Europe.* London: Routledge, 228–46.
Tarrow, S. 1977. *Between Center and Periphery: Grassroots Politicians in Italy and France.* New Haven: Yale University Press.
Tiebout, C. 1956. "A Pure Theory of Local Expenditures." *Journal of Political Economy* 64(5): 416–24.
Trainor, R. H. 2000. "The 'Decline' of British Urban Governance since 1850." In Morris, R. J. and Trainor, R. H., eds. *Urban Governance: Britain and Beyond since 1750.* Aldershot: Ashgate, 28–46.
UCLG. 2008. *Decentralization and Local Democracy in the World.* Barcelona: UCLG.
Wolman, H. 2008. "Comparing Local Government Systems across Countries: Conceptual and Methodological Challenges to Building a Field of Comparative Local Government Studies." *Environment and Planning C: Government and Policy* 26(1): 87–103.
Wright, D. S. 1976. *Understanding Intergovernmental Relations: Public Policy and Participants' Perspectives in Local, State, and National Governments.* North Scituate, MA: Duxbury Press.
———. 1988. *Understanding Intergovernmental Relations.* 3rd ed. Pacific Grove, CA: Brooks/Cole.
———. 1990. "Federalism, Intergovernmental Relations and Intergovernmental Management: Historical Reflections and Conceptual Comparisons." *Public Administration Review* 50(2): 168–78.

CHAPTER 9

BUREAUCRACY AND DEMOCRACY IN LOCAL GOVERNMENT

NIELS EJERSBO AND JAMES H. SVARA

1. Introduction

Bureaucracy constitutes the core organizational capacity of local governments to carry out the government's work of enforcing laws, implementing policies, and delivering services. In the past century, bureaucracies emerged as the dominant model for organizing the salaried staff of the government. Bureaucracy does not exist in isolation, because it is linked to the political leadership of the local government and to the residents of the city or county. Beyond enforcement, implementation, and service delivery, it also supports the development of mission and goals by elected officials in those areas in which local governments have autonomy. The nature of the relationships to elected officials and citizens may be determined by one (or both) of two perspectives: the characteristics of bureaucracy, on the one hand, or the instruments of formal or political control, on the other.

According to the first perspective, bureaucracy dominates the relationships. It is common to think of the bureaucracy as a monolith that operates according to its own rules, resists change, ignores outsiders, and stymies those who try to control it or hold it accountable. The administrative structure has characteristics that reflect the internal logic, inner workings, and accumulated resources of autonomous large-scale organizations. Stated differently, the organization created to serve the city may be relatively impervious to control. Altering the characteristics and consequences of urban bureaucracies requires moving beyond the bureaucratic state to a new organizational paradigm.

An alternate perspective is to recognize that the administrative structure and process is an essential feature of local government that can be organized and linked to politicians and citizens in various ways that may change over time. The administrative structure may be subject to external design and control, and it may interact constructively with the elected officials and the citizens that it serves. Thus, the nature of relationships is a key issue to explore. Administrative arrangements and characteristics of bureaucracy also vary with the formal constitutional structure in which they operate.

Defining bureaucracy narrowly in terms of specific features might lead to the conclusion that bureaucracy as an organizational form was found in local government during an extended period from the late nineteenth century to the 1980s when it started to be replaced by a new organizational form. This interpretation, however, would run up against the common view that the permanent administrative structure of government has been and continues to be a "bureaucracy." We acknowledge this view and decline to accept the argument that societies are or should be entering a new era without bureaucracy, nor do we accept the view the "bureaucracy" remained static until the changes of the last three decades. "Bureaucracy" can take different shapes and relate to other key actors in differing ways. It is useful to acknowledge a period of the "classic bureaucracy" while recognizing the classic bureaucracy itself absorbed substantial changes and that different and less obviously "bureaucratic" formal organizations are emerging as the characteristics of classic bureaucracies decline. Urban areas in Western countries, and many outside the West, have bureaucracies as central actors in their process of governance. The bureaucracies differ across countries with differing state traditions of governance and differing degrees of local autonomy, but they all share certain common features.

In this discussion, bureaucracy is considered to be the institution in urban governance characterized by continuity in personnel, methods, structure, and values that plays a special role (along with elected officials and citizens) in formulating public policy and a central role in implementing public policy and delivering public services whatever its exact features and methods. The initial topics to be examined are the nature of bureaucracy and how it is manifested in local government. These topics provide a baseline set of characteristics associated with the increasingly complex classical bureaucracy as it has evolved in the twentieth century. Changes since 1980 are examined to determine whether bureaucracy is being replaced by new models of organization, on the one hand, or being transformed to add new elements and perspectives that coexist with traditional features. The aim of this chapter is not to rule one of the approaches as winner or emphasize a particular perspective to the study of local government organization. Rather, this chapter will use insights from various perspectives and approaches to discuss developments in local government bureaucracy and how these changes have altered the way local government bureaucracies function today. We argue that despite major changes, bureaucratic structures and hierarchies with traditional and modern elements are continuously a part of the local government organization. Stated simply, cities cannot survive without a bureaucracy, but the bureaucracy must evolve and has evolved continuously to meet new needs and conditions.

2. Nature of Bureaucracy

Organizational models reflect the social, economic, and technological conditions in the period when they are created. Thompson (2003) has argued that "transformations in organizational arrangements must be largely driven by changes in information costs." Classic bureaucracies had a technological advantage over less well-managed organizations, both private and public. Examples of prebureaucratic options included the monarch, the political party organization, and voluntary actions by common citizens. Thompson credits the Prussians with perfecting the bureaucratic model during the nineteenth century and recognizes it as a technological breakthrough that incorporated superior methods of handling information. Centralized, functional, hierarchical structures relying on "ex-ante control" and government provision and control had advantages relative to decentralized, process-oriented, self-organizing, part-dominated, and private structures in the late nineteenth and early twentieth centuries (Reschenthaler and Thompson 1996). By balancing the features of coordination and specialization of tasks in an era of high information costs, bureaucracies won out over other forms of organizations, and larger organizations won out over smaller ones.

The characteristics of bureaucracy as an ideal type have been defined by Weber (1946) and further elaborated by other scholars (e.g., Chandler and Plano 1988; Olsen 2005). A bureaucracy operates on the basis of the following characteristics:

- rules by which tasks are organized
- division of labor which produces specialization
- hierarchy to provide control and coordination
- decisions by technical and legal standards
- administration based on filing systems and institutional memory
- institutionalized civil service
- administration as a vocation
- neutral competence; separation of politics and administration
- consistency, fairness, and equity

In time, these characteristics came to be challenged. For example, rules were countered with calls for deregulation and use of incentives. Still, the traditional characteristics supported the emergence of an organizational form that moved beyond the disadvantages of the prebureaucratic institutions that had preceded it.

There are certain conditions that must be met for an organization to operate according to these characteristics. The organization must be relatively self-contained and sufficiently independent to preserve these characteristics in the face of pressures to deviate from the standards. In government, it is particularly important that the organization be insulated from political values, for example, using resources to win friends and punish opponents, and practices, for example, patronage, that would conflict with bureaucratic standards. The insulation of administrative practice from political manipulation was an early step toward creating the administrative state (Rutgers 1997). Beyond these ideal type characteristics, bureaucracies are commonly assumed to have certain negative attributes, such as being rigid, authoritarian, and self-directed with entrenched staff motivated by pay, benefits, and security (Lowi 1967; Denhardt and Denhardt 2003).

These negative characterizations are often at odds with or fail to recognize the variation in bureaucracies in practice and ignore adaptations made by bureaucracies over time preceding the fundamental challenges starting in the 1980s and then accelerated by changes since then. Bureaucracies have rules but also guide behavior with goals and objectives. The division of labor permits management of complexity (Meier and Hill 2005) and advances in communication permit more decentralized coordination. The traditional hierarchy was designed to provide simultaneously for control and coordination of specialized parts of the organization. Technical and legal standards broadened over time loosening supervisory controls, and the reliance on paper filing systems and routing of information through fixed channels and strict controls over filing of records relaxed as information costs declined. Civil service systems have opened up with lateral entry, flexible pay-systems, and a wider range of incentives. Administrative professionals have long been guided by public service values. Consistency and fairness remain central concerns and the scope of equity considerations has broadened to address inequalities between social and racial/ethnic groups. The separation of politics and administration (as opposed to the insulation of administration from political interference) has been a myth from the beginning—a topic considered more fully in the discussion of the relationship between bureaucracy and elected officials. The values and methods of administrators can advance the public interest (Meier 1997) and enhance the credibility of elected officials (Miller 2000).

The bureaucracy is not static even though its essential logic is preserved. It is continuously challenged and changes on an ongoing basis (Meier and Hill 2005; Kouzes and Posner 2002; Collins 2001). However, its essential position in governance is preserved. Fundamental changes in organizational arrangements are driven by changes in values, political resources, and information costs. Bureaucracy had been challenged by and partially absorbed three movements by the 1970s that altered the character of bureaucracy and some of its assumptions. Scientific management had put more emphasis on efficiency and established performance as an important factor along with rules in shaping work. Rather than simply carrying out prescribed duties, staff members focused on the task to be accomplished. Knowledge was increasingly important along with authority, and Frederick Taylor's commitment to research-based methods challenged hierarchy and established methods (Schachter 1989). The human relations movement in organization theory elevated the importance of leadership, intrinsic rewards, and informal factors in organizations.

Although it was critical of classical bureaucracy, many of its assumptions and methods have been incorporated into bureaucratic practice. Finally, there was increased attention to the normative ends of administration (Waldo 1948), linkages with citizens (Arnstein 1969), and social equity (Marini 1971).

Originally, the classic bureaucracy came to be seen as the superior structure of public organizations because it addressed the issues of the prebureaucratic models—lack of fairness and accountability, incompetence and partisan favoritism, and limited capacity and continuity—and it provided a mechanism for linking the administrative structure to the political process that regularized political control while reducing political interference. Critics of bureaucracy have characterized it as undemocratic, impersonal, slow, rigid, and inefficient, and today the classic bureaucracy is mostly associated with negative connotations (Osborne and Gaebler 1992). These criticisms may indicate the frustration with large organizations that fail (or are slow) to incorporate new philosophies and technologies that permit more public serving modes of operation.

Others who have made the case for bureaucracy have argued that public bureaucracy is far better than its reputation (Goodsell 1983). Furthermore, there is more variation in the relationship of classic bureaucracy and the democratic process than critics acknowledge. To be sure, the connection between bureaucracy and democracy is problematic. Bureaucrats carry out decisions made by elected officials, but they also help to shape the decisions. Bureaucratic power and bureaucratic politics may interfere with the translation of political goals into administrative action (Vigoda-Gadot and Miller-Mor 2008). The examination of bureaucracy must consider to what extent political and professional values are balanced and how the two sets of officials interact.

3. Bureaucracy in Local Government

The desirability of using bureaucracy has always been debated heavily whether it is replacing other organizational approaches or defending itself against attacks. In cities, some stable organizational structure is needed to handle the collective needs of large numbers of people (often quite diverse) living in close proximity to each other, but this structure has varied widely and has evolved over time.

Local government bureaucrats as a group do not fit the bureaucratic model in several important respects. The unique formal structure, the close proximity of elected officials and administrators, the high interaction of both with residents of the city, and the programmatic and fiscal controls exerted by higher levels of government reduce the isolation and autonomy that bureaucracies might have in the abstract or at the national level. Thus, in addition to the deviations from the classic bureaucratic model already noted, bureaucracy in local government is likely to have unique characteristics with respect to the roles of the top administrator and links to elected officials, the relationship between politics and administration, and the characteristics of employment within the municipal organization. Each is briefly examined.

3.1. Role of Top Administrator and Links to Elected Officials

It is common to think of the bureaucracy as a pyramid with a top administrator at the pinnacle who interacts with external, nonprofessional authorities. Most cities have an appointed chief administrative officer (CAO) who oversees the administrative structure and reports to elected officials.[1] How these officials are formally organized, however, varies considerably between cities and affects both the interface between elected officials and administrators as well as the roles and influence of the top administrator (Mouritzen and Svara 2002).[2] Although the political governing structure is different from country to country in specifics, there are common features that can be clustered in four "forms" of government—the formal provisions that structure how governmental authority and political power are obtained, maintained, and exercised in municipal government.

The form of government in a particular country may be described by its proximity to or distance from one of four ideal types (Mouritzen and Svara 2002, ch. 3):

- *The strong mayor form*: The elected mayor overshadows the city council and is in full charge of all executive functions. The CAO serves at the mayor's will, and political considerations can affect the behavior of professional civil servants. France, Spain, Italy, Portugal, Germany, and U.S. cities with the mayor-council form approximate this model.[3]
- *The committee-leader form*: One person is clearly "the political leader" of the municipality—with or without the title of mayor—but executive powers are shared with the elected heads of standing committees composed of elected politicians as well with the CAO. Illustrative countries are Denmark, Sweden, and the United Kingdom before reforms starting in 2000 (Asquith 2008).
- *Cabinet/collective form*: The decision center is one collegiate body consisting of a mayor and "minister" for each department. The executive committee is responsible for all executive functions and delegates authority to the CAO. Illustrative countries are the Netherlands and Belgium. The cabinet form is one of the new models available in the U.K., an experiment being introduced in Oslo, and an experiment being phased out in the three largest Danish cities.

1. Not all the countries have an appointed CAO in all municipal governments. The office is missing in over half of the mayor-council cities in the United States over 10,000 in population and in small towns in France and Italy.

2. This section draws extensively from Mouritzen and Svara (2002), chapters 3 and 10.

3. The U.S. cities vary in the power of the mayor, the extent of the mayor's support in the council, and, if there is a CAO, the method of selecting this official.

- *The council-manager form:* All executive functions are in the hands of a professional administrator—the city manager—who is appointed by the city council which has general authority over policy but is restricted from involvement in administrative matters. Illustrative countries are Ireland, Norway, Finland, and the United States council-manager cities. It was formerly found in *Stadtdirektor* form in Nordrhein-Westfalen and Niedersachsen.

Analysis of role performance by the CAO across countries uncovers important similarities as well as differences related to form of government. The highest level of involvement is found in activities related to policy innovation and the least involvement is in traditional management functions. The extent of involvement as a political and legal adviser to politicians shows the greatest variation.

The four forms of government are associated with some systematic differences in the roles, interactions, and influence of elected officials and administrators. Three types of CAOs based on their perception of their own political influence relative to politicians are dependent (less influence), interdependent (approximately the same influence), and independent (more influence) (Mouritzen and Svara 2002, ch. 9). In mayor-council cities, the formal powers of the mayor are highest compared to cities with other forms, and this official is clearly the leading politician. The CAOs in these cities are actively involved in policy innovation but they are also the most highly involved in classical administrative tasks and the least active in providing political advice to their mayor. The influence level of the CAOs is moderately high but lower than in cities with other forms of government. There are more CAOs who perceive their influence to be substantially lower than the top politician, that is, dependent administrators, than in other forms (47%), although interdependent CAOs are slightly more common (48%).

The committee-leader cities have the greatest dispersion of authority among the mayor, executive committee, standing committees, CAO, and department heads. The CAOs tend to view themselves as independently competent but political servants who are accountable to politicians rather than to the public. They are very active as policy innovators and have the highest scores for giving advice to politicians among all CAOs. They are least involved in filling classical administrative functions. They have high influence levels but work with politicians who are themselves also very influential. Consequently, there is a high proportion of interdependent CAOs in the committee-leader cities (68%).

The collective cities give extensive authority to the executive committee. The CAOs are likely to see themselves as agents of the executive committee, responsive to their views and reliant on the top politicians rather than other actors for their ability to function effectively as CAO. These CAOs report the lowest activity level in policy innovation, advice to politicians, and classical administration. In these cities, the CAOs tend to have moderate influence. A slight majority are interdependent CAOs (51%).

The council-manager cities place substantial authority in the office of the CAO and give no executive authority to elected officials. Council-manager CAOs are very active in policy innovation and somewhat active in administration. They seek to shape the decision-making process and coordination of work with elected officials but steer clear from offering political advice. These CAOs have the highest influence among all the forms of government, and their relative influence is also the highest. As a consequence, council-manager cities have the fewest dependent CAOs (5%) and the most independent types (39%), although interdependent types are the majority (56%).

The differences in linkages based on form might suggest that only council-manager cities have the clear separation between politicians and administrators that is presumed in the classic bureaucratic model. Mayors can control the bureaucracy in strong mayor cities and there are multiple points of interaction between politicians and administrators in the committee-leader and executive committee forms. In actuality, as we see in the next section, the relationship is more complex and nuanced in cities of all kinds. The legal framework for city government does not capture all the important differences between countries shaped by factors such as the political culture of the population (Hofstede 1997), the scope of governmental functions, and the degree of local autonomy. The preferred form may reflect societal attitudes about power, social relationships, and uncertainty (Mouritzen and Svara 2002, ch. 3). Administrators operating under the same form of government will differ somewhat in, for example, U.S. council-manager cities with a narrow range of functions and a tradition of local autonomy and Norwegian council-manager cities with broad functions of central government control. Comparatively, the attitudes and behavior of administrators are affected by country and structural differences even though the nature of bureaucracy produces strong similarities across time and space.

3.2. Relationship between Bureaucracy and Elected Officials

The preconditions for a legitimate and workable bureaucracy in local government are to provide for external control and accountability, on the one hand, and prevent political interference in the working of the organization that would undermine the professional competence and fairness of administrators, on the other. Furthermore, the purpose and policies of the public organization must reflect the preferences of elected officials but also incorporate the values and expertise of administrators if the policies are to be democratic, effective, and feasible. Balancing these potentially conflicting characteristics is an enduring challenge, and administrators with their extensive resources can easily undermine the control of elected officials.

There are four major models for understanding political-administrative relations: political responsiveness, separation, autonomy, and interaction or overlapping roles (Aberbach, Putnam, and Rockman 1981; Svara 2006; Lee and Raadschelders 2008).[4] These models do not focus on explanation of the behavior of individuals

4. The literature of models of political-administrative relations draws on empirical research as well as conceptual and normative work noted in the discussion. Empirical studies have been conducted in national governments (e.g., Aberbach, Putnam, and Rockman 1981; Aberbach and Rockman 2000) and in city government (e.g., Mouritzen and Svara 2002). Portions of this section appeared in Svara (2006).

and organizations as public choice or normative institutionalist models (Peters 1999) do, although the assumptions of these general models are incorporated in efforts to explain how administrators relate to politicians and elected officials. To proponents of bureaucracy, the first model violates the norms of the classic bureaucracy. Under the responsive administrator model, there is close political alignment of politicians and administrators reflected in the efforts of administrators to please their political masters. Administrators act as the political agent of the elected executive or party majority. This model is based on the presumption that politicians are looking for politically "responsive competence" as opposed to "neutral competence" from administrators and that administrators find it to be in their interests to provide it (Moe 1985). Politicians may want administrators who not only do what they are told, but believe in the political aims of elected officials—a quality not found among professional bureaucrats. The strong mayor form provides formal resources for the mayor to command responsiveness, but most CAOs in these cities do not report political interference (Mouritzen and Svara 2002).

The separate roles model is the simple and standard way of conceptualizing the political-administrative relationship. In the U.S., the separate roles model has been associated with the dichotomy concept, although it used to some extent in Europe as well (Overeem 2008). Defined in the strictest terms, the bureaucracy accepts policy directions from elected officials with no involvement in the formation of the policy and is fully responsible for the independent implementation of the policy.[5] In contrast, less stringent separation is envisioned by Kettl (2000) who simply calls for distinguishing the political and administrative spheres and clear political control of administration. Viewed in this way, the separate roles model is populated by elected officials who view themselves as detached governors, on the one hand, and by Putnam's (1975, 89–91) "classical bureaucrats," on the other, who contribute to policy decisions and exert modest influence. The separate roles model also serves as a check to particularistic politics, that is, a protective shield against political interference in the actions of administrators. Montjoy and Watson (1995) propose a "reinterpreted dichotomy" that permits a policymaking role for the manager, but still helps managers resist the forces of particularism.[6] This model presumes that administrators limit the scope of their policy involvement to technical advice and minimize efforts to be directly responsive to citizens while asserting that elected

5. In Sayre's (1958, 103) view of dichotomy, "politics and policy were separate from administration, which was concerned exclusively with the execution of assignments handed down from the realm of politics," and his definition was very influential in shaping the definition of the dichotomy in the United States and its association with the early scholars in public administration according to Svara (1999a). As the concept was described prior to Sayre's article, it was permissible for administrators to propose policy but the dichotomy idea was deemed useful as it helped to focus public attention on elected officials and to shield administrators from interference.

6. In contrast, Frederickson (1997, 227–29) uses a "sanitized" version of the dichotomy to remind administrators to focus on administrative matters and avoid policymaking.

officials should keep their hands off administration.[7] Although spheres are separate, clear remote control of bureaucracy by politicians is presumed (Hood 2002). Administrators are neutral vis-à-vis their political masters while at the same time being committed to upholding professional competence.[8]

If there is separation of politicians and administrators but the accountability of administrators to politicians is weak, the conditions of the autonomous administrator model are present. This administrator is self-directing to the extent that political control is questionable. Weber (Gerth and Mills 1946) recognized that the bureaucracy can be resistant to control and change. There is a fundamental asymmetry in experience and specialized knowledge that undermines the formal principal-agent relationship between the elected principal and the administrative agent (Banks and Weingast 1992). Public choice theorists argue that administrators act in terms of their own interests or their own perception of the public interest rather than the public interest as translated by elected officials (Tullock 1965; Niskanen 1971; Dunleavy 1991). Bureaucracies are the "new machines" in local government that operate beyond political control or central coordination (Lowi 1967, 86; Jones 1995). Often it is suspected that administrative agencies are "bureaucratic fiefdoms . . . that cannot be held accountable through the normal mechanisms of representative democracy" (Stein 1991, 1), a view shared by others (Gruber 1987; Golden 2000). The widespread popular perception of administrators is that bureaucracies are lumbering, unresponsive, self-interested, and out of control (Wood and Waterman 1994, 141).

Despite the popularity of the separate roles and autonomous administrator models, there are a variety of approaches that share the characteristic of seeing administrators and elected officials as having roles that overlap each other and recognize the shared influence of politicians and administrators (Farazmand 1997, xi). Elected officials and bureaucrats accommodate each other's perspectives and preferences. There is extensive interaction, overlapping functions, and reciprocal influence (Self 1972). The thinking of the originators of the council-manager form illustrates acceptance of overlapping roles (Woodruff 1919). They envisioned a government with cooperative relationships between officials who reflected distinct values and perspectives. A study of chief executives who head the bureaucracy in British local government by Norton (1991) finds the same conditions as those advocated by

7. This view approximates image 2 of Aberbach et al. (1981, 6–9) in which politicians bring values and administrators facts to the policy process. Image 1 is essentially the dichotomy model, i.e., a divided world in which the "politicians make decisions; bureaucrats merely implement them."

8. In this model and others, the definition of "neutral competence" is an active one. "Neutral" means neither value-free (and certainly not value-less) nor passive. Asmeron and Reis (1996, 8–9) come to the same conclusion in their review of studies in a number of countries. As Rohr (2005, 10) described this quality among British administrators, "senior civil servants stand ready to serve loyally the governments chosen by the British people." Viewed in this way, neutral competence can be compatible with any of the approaches with the possible exception of the "responsive administrator" model.

the early American political reformers. Despite new challenges in both countries (Svara 2007; Boyne et al. 2010), administrators use their strategic position and the organizational resources to initiate change, but they are in turn dependent on the shared responsibility with or support from the political leadership for their success (SOLACE 2005). For the local government to be effective, mutual understanding and a joint working relationship between political and administrative leaders is essential. There are a number of observers who support a model of overlapping roles (Putnam 1975, 90; Nalbandian 1994; Svara 1989; 1999b; Doig and Hargrove 1990; Schneider and Teske 1992). Administrators are a source of change or energy as well as stability (Nardulli and Stonecash 1981; Stein 1991, 61–62).

The widespread incidence of the overlapping roles model, however, does not mean that some aspects of the other models are not commonly found as well. Each of the models has a central feature that is important for understanding the role and contributions of administrators (Svara 2006). The responsive administrator model asserts the importance of administrative responsiveness that is expected of the bureaucracy as an instrumental organization and need not undermine independence nor professionalism. The separate roles model supports differentiation and professionalism that continue to be important despite extensive sharing and interaction. The autonomous administrator stresses the importance of administrative independence that need not be accompanied by aloofness. Finally, the overlapping roles model captures the widespread sharing and interaction in the governmental process. The importance of differentiation even when there are overlapping roles is illustrated by Dunn's conclusion that administrators in Australia are invited to the policy table because they are viewed as neutral (Dunn 1997, 162). In this example, one finds overlapping roles and separation of spheres at the same time. Thus, rather than viewing the models of competitors, a different approach is to accept the possibility of these characteristics can be combined and coexist. The concept of complementarity in political-administrative relations (Svara 2006; 2007) presumes that a coherent bureaucracy is functioning along with elected officials. Politicians and administrators have reciprocal influence and interdependency along with distinct roles and values.

Thus, just as the classic bureaucracy has incorporated changes and new perspectives on management, so too has the relationship of the bureaucracy to elected officials evolved and become more complex and nuanced. Certainly, bureaucracies can come to be dominated by politicians, defy political control, or operate in a separate sphere with limited exchanges. Most commonly, however, they interact in complex ways with elected officials shaped by the formal structure in which they operate, and this has more or less been the situation throughout the twentieth century (Lynn 2001; Svara 2001).

The implications of this revised view of classic bureaucracy are that the formal administrative structure in local government is more open, more interactive, and more subject to external control than has commonly been presumed. Although the manpower, informational, and organization resources make the bureaucracy in a city a powerful force, the power is not exercised in a vacuum. Although the bureaucracy can block some changes it opposes or withhold support for innovations (Lowi 1967; Yates 1977), acceptance of change is common as well and the goals of political principals and administrative agents are often consistent (Waterman and Meier 1998).

3.3. Characteristics of Employment in Urban Bureaucracies

The expectation of lifelong employment within the same organization with leaders who have worked their up through the ranks is not necessarily found in urban bureaucracies. A study of local government CEOs show how the bureaucratic career, defined as controlled from central government or an internal bottom-up career is only one of several career patterns (Magnier 2002). Even though the bureaucratic model would suggest that the mobility of local government CEOs is limited (except in countries with centrally controlled career systems) leaving the job as CEO due to career advancement seems more common than expected (Ejersbo and Dahler-Larsen 2002). Local government CEOs "are 'local' mainly in the sense that their work histories tie them to the world of local government, but they have few roots in the local community" (Magnier 2002, 56).

Changes at the political level also seem to influence the turnover of senior management in local government and emphasize that bureaucratic careers are influenced by changes at the political level. A study of English local authorities concludes that "senior managers are not insulated from political change, and that appointing new top officials is one way in which new ruling parties seek to pursue their policy preference" (Boyne et al. 2010). U.S. studies document the "push" of administrators out of top positions by political forces as well as the new opportunities that "pull" them to other cities (DeHoog and Whitaker 1990). The U.Di.T.E. study shows how different systems of local government have different career patterns for CEOs and different levels of influence exerted by the local authority in matters of hiring and firing. In the group of southern European countries entry to the position as CEO and the following career is often controlled by statute giving the local authority little influence. In the northern European and Anglo group local governments have more freedom to choose candidates for the position as CEO (Pless and De Leemans 2002). This movement across organizations is uniquely possible in local government and reinforces the characteristics of responsiveness and strategic orientation in local bureaucracies. In the United Kingdom, despite legal protections for the chief executive, there is likelihood of removal with a change in party majority and a prior record of low administrative performance (Boyne et al. 2010). Thus, turnover in leaders introduces new ideas into the supposedly stable bureaucracy, and the boundary between the political and administrative spheres is "negotiated" between top politicians and administrators at the apex of local government. The general change in management and control systems seen in local government also influences the linkage between managers and the local government organization. In a number of countries top managers are frequently hired on contracts with a set number of years. In addition, we see the use of individual performance contracts for top managers.

The contracts do not necessarily follow the election cycle and should not be seen as a way to introduce appointment of top managers according to their political beliefs. However, it becomes easier for the political level to make changes at the top management level—sometimes with reference to poor performance. The civil service system is in flux and lifelong appointments are not necessarily the standard anymore. However, the flexible system coexists with a traditional system of nonpolitical appointments.

Thus, the simple model of the bureaucracy as an ideal type is more complex in actuality given the way it evolved during the twentieth century. The bureaucracy in local government evidences substantial variation and interacts extensively with politicians. These conditions should be recognized as the baseline from which to assess the substantial change that has occurred in the past three decades.

4. Change in Local Bureaucracies

The conditions of cities and the characteristics of the administrative structure continue to change. There is a debate over how to understand today's local government organizations and consequently how these organizations should be studied. It is possible to detect three major approaches to studying local government bureaucracy—the classic bureaucracy and its two alternatives (see also Kjaer 2009, 139). The first approach that has been examined up to this point focuses on the formal structure in a bureaucratic setup and studies actors and their relationships based upon their position within a formal structure and a hierarchical organization (e.g. Mouritzen and Svara 2002; Mouritzen 1995). The second relates to New Public Management and portrays local governments as transforming organizations that emphasize the use of private sector management methods, contractual relationships, and changing organizational structures (Øgård 2000; Greve and Ejersbo 2005; Stoker 1999; Osborne and Gaebler 1992). A third position is represented by a governance perspective emphasizing partnerships, networks, participation, and the interaction between the local bureaucracy and external partners as key elements in understanding of local government (John 2000; Kjaer 2009; Bogason 2000) or a perspective that emphasizes public service over hierarchy or private sector values (Denhardt and Denhardt 2003).

These approaches may be interpreted as bureaucracy and its successors or, reflecting an eclectic view of bureaucracy, as "three theoretical models of bureaucracy" (Kjaer 2009, 139), even though only the first reflects the traditional or classic bureaucratic model. As pointed out by Meier and Hill (2005), bureaucracy faces various challenges but is still important to the governmental process generally and in local government. Olsen (2005, 2) also points to the importance of bureaucracy as an administrative form, an analytical concept, and a set of ideas and observations about public administration and formally organized institutions.

4.1. Forces of Change

The bureaucracy challenged by Thatcher and Reagan in the 1980s with the stereotypical charges of being rigid, authoritarian, and detached organizations had in fact already adapted considerably to new values, new social and political conditions, and new technologies, as we have seen. It was not uniform across countries and differing constitutional frameworks and political cultures as Pless and De Leemans (2002) demonstrate. Neither was bureaucracy strictly separated from the elected officials as a purely instrumental organization. The accelerated changes of the past three decades reflect new political currents that have challenged the "assured" position of administrators (Svara 2007) and also new ways of thinking about organizations in an era of social and technological change.

The comparative advantage of the classic bureaucracy has been altered by the revolution in information technology as well as increased activism by elected officials and citizens alike. These outside actors benefited from easier access to information, but they had already been mobilized by the social and political changes from the 1960s onward to demand a larger role in the governmental process. The expansion in nongovernmental philanthropic organizations supplemented and challenged the monopoly of government in addressing social needs, and businesses expanded the range of services that they could provide under contract with local governments. Thompson (2003, 332) argues that "the organizational arrangements invented at the dawn of the industrial era have become increasingly anachronistic." Improvements in education and expansion of automation and information technology have curtailed the relative advantage of bureaucratic personnel systems and centralized, large-scale organizations. With lower costs of communication, logistics, and information-processing, smaller and diversified organizations can outperform those based on large-scale and vertical integration. Consequently, Thompson (2003, 333) observes, "even large companies are mimicking their smaller competitors by shrinking head offices, removing layers of bureaucracy, and concentration on core businesses." Governmental bureaucracies that led the way in reorganization in the early twentieth century have lagged behind the changes that are occurring in business.

Although it was perhaps natural that urban bureaucracies would resist changes that were viewed initially as efforts to dismantle government (Eggers and O'Leary 1995), it appears that local governments are incorporating new approaches into the way they think about organizing their work and delivering services. Change although still halting at times is coming under the banners of New Public Management and New Governance. It is appears that these movements change the essential logic and form of bureaucracy in important ways but do not necessarily replace it.

4.2. New Public Management and Governance

New public management (NPM) has been a key concept in the discussion of local government organization during the past couple of decades (Peters 2001). Despite—or perhaps because of its popularity, there is no common understanding of the concept.

Instead of clarity, NPM often turns into slogans and contradictory reform programs (John 2000, 97). Sometimes, it seems like NPM is used as a convenient way to conceptualize and group rather diverse developments instead of going through the difficulty of treating each of the developments separately. It has been debated whether NPM results in convergence or divergence (Lynn 1996). While this seems to continue to be an open question (Kettl 2000, 66), along with questions about intended and unintended consequences of different NPM tools, it is beyond question that NPM has had an impact on the way local governments are organized and operate.

Hood (1991) has summarized NPM in the following categories: hands-on professional management, explicit standards and measures of performance, output control, disaggregation of units in the public sector, competition, private sector styles of management practices, and discipline and parsimony in resource use. Many of these features have found their way into local government. Marketization and competition is perhaps the feature most often associated with NPM. It has had a big impact on local government in many countries. In Britain local governments have experienced several centrally initiated reforms such as Compulsory Competitive Tendering (CCT) and Best Value both aimed at increased public-private competition and efficiency gains in local government (Higgins, James, and Rober 2004). In some countries like New Zealand and Australia similar types of reforms have been implemented while other countries have followed a different and less radical path in order to increase competition in local government.

Following the U.S. model of NPM (Meier and Hill 2005), American cities have reexamined what services they should provide, that is, offer under governmental auspices, as well who should deliver the service. Public provision is declining. From a standard list of services, government were responsible for 66% in 1992 and 51% in 2007 (Warner and Hefetz, 2004; 2009; Hefetz and Warner 2004). After a shift toward delivery services by contracting in the 1990s, U.S. local governments are mixing contracting out with contracting back in. They are increasingly using mixed modes of delivery with public and private contributions (e.g., privately provided services in a public facility), dividing tasks in process (e.g., public screening and private training in workforce training), and managed competition when government

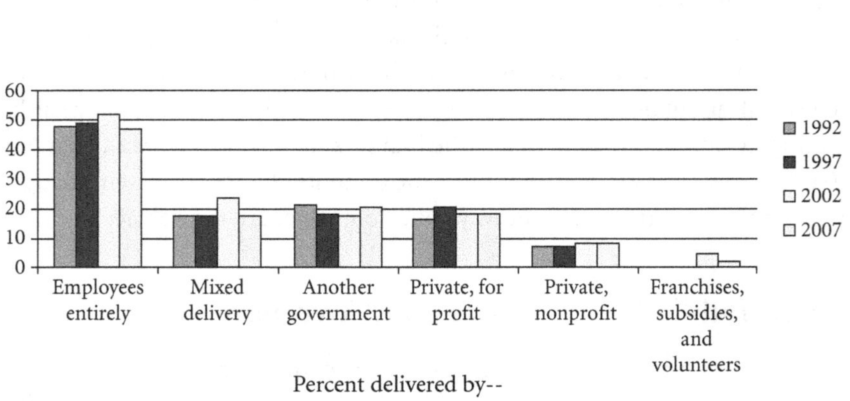

Figure 9.1. Who Delivers Services in U.S. Local Government, 1992–2007.

departments and private contracts submit bids to deliver a service (Morgan, England, and Pelissero 2007). Setting aside the reduction in the number of services provided, Warner and Hefetz find that the mix of service delivery in U.S. cities in 2007 once again is very similar to 1992, as indicated in figure 1.

Use of contracting out and managed competition may have changed the name of the service provider, but it also has had an impact on the internal organization of local government. In order to open up for bids from departments inside the local government and at the same time secure a fair competition between private companies and internal bids, local government organization has been organized according to a purchaser-provider split (Higgins, James, and Rober 2004). Contracting out of services to a private provider is one example of challenges to the hierarchy within local government. Although decisions on level of service are determined within the local government hierarchy, and funding for the service is a matter for local government, major decisions are detached from the traditional hierarchy within local government. As services are contracted out, it may be difficult to know who to hold accountable—especially with complex subcontractor relationships (Romzek and Johnston 2002). The recent increase in "contracting back in" does not represent a rejection of NPM but a more selective use of its techniques.

Performance management (usually accompanied by internal contracting or specification of standards or targets) is another element of the NPM toolkit that has found its way into the local government organization. It can be shown that performance management has been used in local government for several decades, but has over the past years grown in importance. Use of performance management serves the purpose of political control over the local bureaucracy and transparency to citizens in order to underpin user choice and voting (Askim 2007, 8). On the one hand, it can be argued that performance management challenges the rule-driven bureaucracy and puts more emphasis on fulfillment of contract obligations and performance indicators. On the other, hand performance management results in new forms of bureaucratization and increasing transaction costs (Kuhlmann 2008).

There is more emphasis on values and objectives than rules. Strategic management entails more purposeful direction of organizational performance toward preferred ends rather than the maintaining stable levels of performance in disparate programs managed separately (Ingraham 2007; Svara 2007; Klausen 2004). Cities are increasingly using statistical analysis of problems and concentrating resources to produce remedies starting with the Citistat analysis of crime in New York City and replicated in cities such as Baltimore (Behn 2007). Innovation has become a salient goal (Borins 2000), and more attention is being given to the factors that promote adoption of innovations in local government (Kearney 2005).

Division of labor is still characteristic of local government administration. The administration is often divided into departments or sections based on area of service, professional expertise, or function. This arrangement is challenged by more holistic views on local government services. This view argues that the organizing principle should be the citizen and the need of the citizen, as opposed to functional or professional considerations. Inspired by service concepts from the private sector, local governments introduced "one-stop shops" in which citizens could get the help needed without running from the one department to the next (Gaster and Rutqvist 2000). Motivated by the same holistic approach, local government has reformed its department structures amalgamating functions, for example social services and education, in order to provide a more holistic approach.

Taken together, NPM has had an impact on bureaucracy in local government. Some of the elements of NPM have a direct effect and changed the functioning of the bureaucracy while others have had a more indirect impact on the organization of local government. Regardless of the level of impact, it is important to note that NPM has not replaced the bureaucratic organization in local government. It has changed and modified the traditional bureaucratic characteristics, but it is not a replacement or a shift from A to B. As discussed above, NPM may not always have had the intended consequences or the level of impact projected by its proponents.

4.3. New Governance and Relations with Residents

Governance has like New Public Management been associated with many different definitions, perspectives, and understandings (Kjær 2009; Klijn 2008; Sørensen 2002; Rhodes 1997). Studies of reform trends in local government argue that a significant trend is a shift from public management to governance (Denter and Rose 2005; Proeller 2006). In the study of local government, governance has most often been associated with networks and the interaction between local government and third parties. By extension, the approach encompasses expanded interactions with citizens and residents.

Whereas the classic bureaucracy had an ideal relationship with elected officials that called for limited overlap and an actual relationship characterized by extensive interaction, the relationship with citizens was more limited in theory and in practice. The preconditions for classical bureaucracy were to avoid direct ties with citizens except in the delivery of services to prescribed recipients. Limited contact helps to preserve central hierarchical control and maintain consistency in service delivery. The reform movement viewed neighborhood concerns as parochial and short-sighted. In many U.S. cities, ward representation and constituency service was removed from the city council by making council elections at-large in the city as a whole and nonpartisan (Banfield and Wilson 1963). Professional standards took precedence over citizen input in the development of policy proposals and the design and delivery of services. Administrators did have contact with community groups. In 1948, International City/County Management Association president C. A. Harrell (1948, 290–94) identified the city manager as a "community leader" who is a "positive, vital force in the community" and "visualizes broad objectives, distant goals, far-sighted projects." Still, it is likely that top administrators focused their community contacts on the leadership stratum, particularly in business and civic affairs.

Even though bureaucracy traditionally is portrayed as closed and avoiding direct contact with citizens, it has a high volume of interaction with residents through citizen-initiated contacts. It is suggested that this type of contract is the most frequent form of contact and higher than other types of political participation (Thomas and Melkers 1999).

In recent decades, the connections have broadened and deepened. Top administrators have become committed to advancing citizen participation and strengthening community attachment (Nalbandian 1999). Handling complaints from citizens has become a important concern of administrators, and measuring citizen satisfaction is a common performance indicator (Hatry et al. 2006). Thomas (1986) observes that it was consistent with early views of neighborhoods for two city managers to veto funds for expanded community planning teams. Now community engagement activities are common in Cincinnati and other cities.

Lowndes, Pratchett, and Stoker (2006) show how the structures and conventions of public management influence public participation. If institutional arrangements in local government are informed by "public value management," citizen participation is more likely. With this approach, citizens and the public are looked upon as overseers of government, the funders of government, and the users of services instead of "clients" or "consumers."

In many Western countries new ways of citizen involvement at the local level have been introduced. John (2001) comments on a number of new mechanisms of participation and show how these have spread across west European countries. Common practices in Scandinavia include community councils; neighborhood bodies (especially Sweden); user boards for service institutions such as schools, homes for the elderly, and day-care centers for children (especially Denmark); consultation programs; and citizens juries. Experiences with mechanisms of citizen involvement are also covered in Amnå and Montin (2000) including country reports from Spain, Poland, and Japan among others. The forms of "deliberative democracy" and their utilization are expanding in the United States (Lukensmeyer and Torres 2006; Roberts 2004).

The different types of mechanisms for citizen involvement affect the functions of the local government bureaucracy. In some cities community councils and neighborhood bodies have their own administrative body. This may complicate the general bureaucratic organization of a local government and change hierarchical structures and work relations. Introducing user boards in service institutions forces the public officials into a more open and consultative role. In general, the new forms of citizen participation may short-circuit the hierarchy and chain of command and give citizens alternative channels of communication within the local government organization. They may also alter the roles of the bureaucrats and professionals. They force bureaucrats to interact and respond in new ways with citizens and the broader community.

5. Future Research

Changes in local government highlight the need for a new research agenda aimed both at important questions at the local level and also at addressing important issues in public administration generally. Research on urban bureaucracy has informed broader discussions. For example, the tensions between bureaucratic expertise and democratic accountability and control have been clarified by combining limited cases at the national level with the extensive number of local governments. Insights about the changing roles of top administrators in a new political era can be derived from examining how chief administrators in local government are adapting to new conditions, involving, for example, research conducted at the local level. Governments in the United States and other countries are bracing for a large-scale generational turnover in their personnel (Benest 2003)—as great as the infusion of new staff in the early 1970s—at the same time as the revolution in information technology is cresting and—in part as a consequence of this change—citizen expectations about their involvement in public affairs is being transformed. Changes in governance and the increased importance of partnerships and networking will alter how services are delivered (Sørensen and Torfing 2003). The introduction of new welfare service technologies and a more systematic use of Internet-based authority decisions will change not only the interaction with citizens but also the internal organization of the local government organization.

The structure of the bureaucracy and roles of administrators will be impacted at all levels of government. Local governments will be the testing ground for the organizations of the future.

6. Conclusion

Local governments depend on administrative organizations for effective governance. They may be organized in terms of different models—bureaucracy, NPM, or networks—but more likely, they blend these models. There is a tendency to view development of new ideas and approaches in public administration as disjointed and lacking continuity (Svara 2001). The bureaucratic model described in stereotypical ways persisted with little change until the NPM model that was in turn challenged and replaced by a public service or network governance model (Denhardt and Denhardt 2003). State-centered models of bureaucracy are being replaced with society-centered models (Bogason 2000). Viewing changes in the field as developmental puts them in a different light. The recognition that the classical bureaucracy was adaptable and incorporated new approaches, for example, replacing authoritarian control with participative management, helps to explain why "old" bureaucrats could accept more fundamental recent changes. The awareness that bureaucrats have had an interdependent relationship with elected officials and exert considerable influence on policy formation helps to explain why new approaches to governance could be incorporated into the practices of administrators. When the British Society of Local Association Chief Executives calls the CAO the chief strategic officer (SOLACE 2005), this is not such a big change as would be the case if top administrators actually operated under a separate roles model or had never networked.

There is both continuity and the gradual incorporation of new models to develop a new blended model of bureaucracy. A number of developments challenge the hierarchical structure in local government administration. Local governments form networks in order to increase capacity or to enjoy possible economics of scale. Collaboration and creation of networks between local governments are sometimes accentuated by structural reforms as these are seen as alternatives to amalgamation of local governments (Dollery et al. 2006). Some networks are formed among local governments while others include private or voluntary organizations. In any case, these types of arrangement often run counter to the traditional lines of authority in local government. Still, Bell and Hindmoor (2008, 2) stress continuity as well as change:

> We agree that governments have, in recent decades, adopted a broader range of governance strategies. But we disagree that this constitutes a "fundamental transformation." This is partly because alternative governance strategies have a far longer pedigree than many of those writing about governance recognize, and also because states generally retain effective control over such arrangements. States are constantly choosing new policy goals and learning to pursue them in different ways. But while much has changed, the state remains a central actor in governance arrangements.

Bureaucracies continue to do most of the work of the state and continue to be the "pivotal player" even in situations "when governments *choose* to govern in alternative ways" (Bell and Hindmoor 2008, 3, emphasis in original).

The wide spread of contracting out, networks, and intermunicipal corporation and types of fragmentation could give the impression that bureaucratic characteristics have lost their importance for understanding local government. However, other forces may have the opposite effect. A large proportion of local governments in Western democracies have been through amalgamation reform reducing the number of municipalities and increasing its size (Pless and De Leemans 2002; Dollery et al. 2006; Sancton 2000). Larger local governments may have an increased capacity and have to rely less on cooperation and networks in order to deliver public services. Likewise, larger organizations may depend more on formal hierarchy than smaller organizations.

The bureaucracy as a modern form of organization emerged in the late nineteenth century. It was a significant change in itself and evolved substantially over the next 100 years. New models have challenged and in theory might replace the adapted classic bureaucracy. The evidence offered suggests, however, that the bureaucracy continues to fill core functions in governance while becoming more open, more accepting of new incentives and methods of organizations, and more extensively linked to other organizations in network arrangements.

Early in this discussion, the classic characteristics of bureaucracy were presented. If the bureaucratic form persists, what are the characteristics of modern, blended, adapted bureaucracy? Some traditional elements remain but they have been altered by changes inside and outside government, and some new elements are present. Rather than offering a new paradigm to replace the bureaucratic paradigm, the original paradigm itself has continued to evolve. We suggest the bureaucracies can now be understood to operate on the basis of the following characteristics:

- Complex organization with specialized and generalized units that operate in integrated strategic way;
- Concentration (but not monopoly) of knowledge, expertise, and experience combined with transparency;
- Open system with links to public, nongovernmental organizations, and participation in networks (some initiated by government) with internal integration and control by enhanced information technology;
- Principles (e.g., equal treatment, public over self-interest), standards (e.g., performance), and rules by which tasks are organized;
- Multiple divisions and combinations of labor including matrix/task force/ temporary organizations;
- Identifiable authority combined with decentralized decision-making;[9] flattened organization with reduced middle-level managers;
- Decisions by consideration of multiple sources of technical/professional knowledge and values, political responsiveness, legal standards, and dialogue with persons and groups outside the organization;
- Administration based on shared knowledge and accessible records;
- Open civil service;
- Separation of service provision and delivery with some use of outsourcing and co-production with residents; mixture of state-centered and society-centered approaches;
- Administration as a profession;
- Professional value commitments, consistent service to changing political masters and accountability to public;
- Complementarity of politics and administration;
- Consistency, fairness, and social equity.

These characteristics are not unique to local bureaucracies, but they are more evident at this level and developed there first. The smaller scale of local governments, the closer proximity to persons served, and the extensive interaction of administrators and elected officials in policymaking and policy implementation / service delivery all tend to challenge hierarchical control internally, the separation of administrators and politicians, and the aloofness of bureaucrats from citizens. It is not new for local administrators to network with other governments and nongovernmental organizations or to make provision for direct participation by citizens. The finding that local governments in the United States are back at the level of contracting out service delivery that they were at in 1992 indicates both that the

9. As Meier and Hill (2005, 65) observe, "to the extent that policy makers seek to create governance systems that can be held accountable, we are likely to see hierarchy as a basic principle."

outsourcing bloom has faded but also that there was already a high level of shared service delivery at the onset of "reinventing government."

The new bureaucracy represents an amalgam of continuity and change, and it will continue to evolve in the future. The modified bureaucracy will persist, however, as the adviser of elected officials, link with residents, provider of a wide range of services at the local level, and delivery agent for many of those services.

Stated simply, as we asserted in the introduction, cities cannot survive without a bureaucracy. That statement can be expanded to incorporate the themes developed in this discussion: Democratic governance in cities cannot survive without a competent, independent, open, responsible, and evolving bureaucracy.

REFERENCES

Aberbach, Joel B., Robert D. Putnam, and Bert A. Rockman. 1981. *Bureaucrats and Politicians in Western Democracies.* Cambridge: Harvard University Press.

Aberbach, Joel D., and Bert A. Rockman. 2000. *In the Web of Politics: Three Decades of the U.S. Federal Executive.* Washington, DC: Brookings Institution Press.

Amnå, E., and S. Montin, eds. 2000. *Towards a New Concept of Local Self-Government.* Oslo: Fagbokforlaget.

Arnstein, Sherry R. 1969. A Ladder of Citizen Participation. *Journal of the American Institute of Planners* 35:216–24.

Askim, J. 2007. Local Government by Numbers: Who Makes Use of Performance Information, When, and for What Purposes? Series of dissertations submitted to the Faculty of Social Sciences, University of Oslo, No. 91.

Asmeron, Haile K., and Eliza P. Reis, eds. 1996. *Democratization and Political Neutrality.* London: Macmillan.

Asquith, Andy 2008. A Bullock, a Monkey and Robocop: An Assessment of the Directly Elected Mayor in English Local Government. *Policy & Politics* 36:39–53.

Banfield, Edward C., and James Q. Wilson. 1963. *City Politics.* New York: Vintage Books.

Banks, Jeffrey S., and Barry R. Weingast. 1992. The Political Control of Bureaucracies under Asymmetric Information. *American Journal of Political Science* 36:509–24.

Behn, Robert D. 2007. What All Mayors Would Like to Know about Baltimore's CitiStat Performance Strategy. IBM Center for the Business of Government.

Bell, Stephen, and Andrew Hindmoor. 2008. *Rethinking Governance: The Centrality of the State in Modern Society.* Cambridge: Cambridge University Press.

Benest, F. 2003. *Preparing the Next Generation.* Washington, DC: International City/County Management Association.

Bogason, P. 2000. *Public Policy and Local Governance.* Cheltenham: Edward Elgar.

Borins, Sandford. 2000. Loose Cannons and Rule Breakers, or Enterprising Leaders? Some Evidence about Innovative Public Managers. *Public Administration Review* 60:498–507.

Boyne, G., O. James, P. John, and N. Petrovsky. 2010. Does Political Change Affect Senior Management Turnover? An Empirical Analysis of Top-Tier Local Authorities in England. *Public Administration* 88:136–53.

Chandler, R. C., and J. C. Plano. 1988. *The Public Administration Dictionary.* New York: Wiley.

Collins, Jim. 2001. *Good to Great.* New York: HarperCollins.

DeHoog, Ruth, and Gordon Whitaker. 1990. Political Conflict or Professional Advancement: Alternative Explanations of City Manager Turnover. *Journal of Urban Affairs* 12:367–77.

Denhardt, Janet V., and Robert B. Denhardt. 2003. *The New Public Service: Serving, Not Steering*. Armonk, NY: M. E. Sharpe.

Denters, B., and L. Rose, eds. 2005. *Comparing Local Governance: Trends and Developments.* London: Palgrave.

Doig, J. W., and E. C. Hargrove, eds. 1990. *Leadership and Innovation: Entrepreneurs in Government.* Baltimore: Johns Hopkins University Press.

Dollery, Brian, Lin Crase, and Andrew Johnson. 2006. *Australian Local Government Economics.* Sydney: UNSW Press.

Dunleavy, Patrick. 1991. *Democracy, Bureaucracy, and Public Choice: Economic Explanations in Political Science.* London: Harvester Wheatsheaf.

Dunn, Delmer. 1997. *Politics and Administration at the Top: Lessons from Down Under.* Pittsburgh: University of Pittsburgh Press.

Eggers, William D., and John O'Leary. 1995. *Revolution at the Roots.* New York: Free Press.

Ejersbo, N., and P. Dahler-Larsen. 2002. Leaving the Job as CEO. In P. Dahler-Larsen, ed., *Social Bonds to City Hall.* Odense: Odense University Press.

Farazmand, Ali. 1997. Introduction. In Ali Farazmand, ed., *Modern Systems of Government Exploring the Role of Bureaucrats and Politicians.* Thousand Oaks, CA: Sage Publications.

Frederickson, H. George. 1997. *The Spirit of Public Administration.* Tuscaloosa: University of Alabama Press.

Gaster, L., and H. Rutqvist. 2000. Changing the "Front Line" to Meet Citizens Needs. *Local Government Studies* 26(2): 53–70.

Gerth, H. H., and C. Wright Mills, trans. 1946. *From Max Weber: Essays in Sociology.* New York: Oxford University Press.

Golden, Marissa Martino. 2000. *What Motivates Bureaucrats? Politics and Administration during the Reagan Years.* New York: Columbia University Press.

Goodsell, C. 1983. *The Case for Bureaucracy*, Chatham, NJ: Chatham House.

Greve, C., and N. Ejersbo. 2005. Contracts as Reinvented Institutions in the Public Sector: A Gross-Cultural Comparison. New York: Praeger.

Gruber, Judith E. 1987. *Controlling Bureaucracies.* Berkeley: University of California Press.

Harrell, C. A. 1948. The City Manager as a Community Leader. *Public Management* 30:290–94.

Hatry, Harry, et al. 2006. *How Effective Are Your Community Services?* 3rd ed. Washington, DC: ICMA.

Hefetz, Amir, and Mildred Warner. 2004. Privatization and Its Reverse: Explaining the Dynamics of the Government Contracting Process. *Journal of Public Administration Research and Theory* 14:171–90.

Higgins, P., P. James, and I. Rober. 2004. Compulsory or Not Compulsory? The Use of Competition in British Local Government. *Asia Pacific Journal of Public Administration* 26(2): 95–114.

Hofstede, G. 1997. *Cultures and Organizations: Software of the Mind.* New York: McGraw-Hill.

Hood, Christopher. 1991. A Public Management for All Seasons? *Public Administration* 69(1): 3–19.

Hood, Christopher. 2002. Control, Bargains, and Cheating: The Politics of Public-Service Reform. *Journal of Public Administration Research and Theory* 12(3): 309–22.

Ingraham, Patricia. 2007. *In Pursuit of Performance: Management Systems in State and Local Governments.* Baltimore: Johns Hopkins University Press.

John, P. 2000. *Local Governance in Western Europe.* London: Sage.

Jones, Bryan D. 1995. Bureaucrats and Urban Politics: Who Controls? Who Benefits? In David Judge, Gerry Stoker, and Harold Wolman, eds. *Theories of Urban Politics.* Thousand Oaks, CA: Sage Publications.

Kearney, R. C. 2005. Reinventing Government and Battling Budget Crisis: Manager and Municipal Government Actions in 2003. *Municipal Yearbook 2005,* 27–32.

Lukensmeyer, C. J., and L. H. Torres. 2006. Public Deliberation: A Manager's Guide to Citizen Engagement. IBM Center for the Business of Government.

Kettl, Donald F. 2000. Public Administration at the Millennium: The State of the Field. *Journal of Public Administration Research and Theory* 10:7–34.

Kjaer, A. M. 2009. Governance and the Urban Bureaucracy. In J. S. Davies and D. L. Imbroscio, eds., *Theories of Urban Politics.* London: Sage.

Klausen, K. K. 2004. *Strategisk ledelse. De mange arenaer.* Odense: Syddansk Universitetsforlag.

Klijn. E. H. 2008. Governance and Governance Networks in Europe. *Public Management Review* 10(4): 505–25.

Kouzes, James H., and Barry Z. Posner. 2002. *The Leadership Challenge.* San Francisco: Jossey-Bass.

Kuhlmann, S. 2008. Reforming Local Public Services: Trends and Effects in Germany and France. *Public Management Review* 10(5): 573–96.

Lee, K-H., and J. C. N. Raadschelders. 2008. Political-Administrative Relations: Impact of and Puzzles in Aberbach, Putnam, and Rockman, 1981. *Governance* 21(3): 419–38.

Lowi, Theodore. 1967. Machine Politics—Old and New. *The Public Interest* 9:83–92.

Lowndes, V., L. Pratchett, and G. Stoker. 2006. Local Political Participation: The Impact of Rules-in-Use. *Public Administration* 84(3): 539–61.

Lynn, Laurence E., Jr. 1996. The New Public Management as an International Phenomenon: A Skeptical View. *International Public Management Journal* 1:573–91.

Lynn, Laurence E., Jr. 2001. The Myth of the Bureaucratic Paradigm: What Traditional Public Administration Really Stood For. *Public Administration Review* 61:144–60.

Magnier, A. 2002. Beyond the City Hall: Municipal Administrative Leadership and Local Community. In P. Dahler-Larsen, ed., *Social Bonds to City Hall.* Odense: Odense University Press.

Marini, Frank. 1971. *Toward a New Public Administration: The Minnowbrook Perspective.* San Francisco: Chandler.

Meier, Kenneth J. 1997. Bureaucracy and Democracy: The Case for More Bureaucracy and Less Democracy. *Public Administration Review* 57:193–99.

Meier, K. J., and G. C. Hill. 2005. Bureaucracy in the Twenty-First Century. In E. Ferlie, L. E. Lynn Jr., and C. Pollitt, eds. *The Oxford Handbook of Public Management Administration.* Oxford: Oxford University Press.

Miller, G. 2000. Above Politics: Credible Commitment and Efficiency in the Design of Public Agencies. *Journal of Public Administration Research and Theory* 10(2): 289–328.

Moe, Terry M. 1985. The Politicized Presidency. In John E. Chubb and Paul E. Peterson, eds., *The New Direction in American Politics.* Washington, DC: Brookings Institution.

Montjoy, Robert S., and Douglas J. Watson. 1995. A Case for Reinterpreted Dichotomy of Politics and Administration as a Professional Standard in Council-Manager Government. *Public Administration Review* 55:231–39.

Morgan, David R., Robert E. England, and John P. Pelissero. 2007. *Managing Urban America.* 6th ed. Washington, DC: CQ Press.

Mouritzen, Poul Erik. 1995. A Comparative Research Project on Chief Executives in Local Government. The U.D.I.T.E. Leadership Study. Local Government Studies No. 5/1995. Odense University.

Mouritzen, Poul Erik, and James H. Svara. 2002. *Leadership at the Apex: Politicians and Administrators in Western Local Governments.* Pittsburgh: University of Pittsburgh Press.

Nalbandian, John. 1994. Reflections of a "Pracademic" on the Logic of Politics and Administration. *Public Administration Review* 54:531–36.

Nalbandian, John. 1999. Facilitating Community, Enabling Democracy: New Roles for Local Government Managers. *Public Administration Review* 59:187–97.

Nardulli, Robert F., and Jeffrey M. Stonecash. 1981. *Politics, Professionalism, and Urban Services.* Cambridge: Oelgeschlager, Gunn, and Hain, Publishers.

Niskanen, William. 1971. *Bureaucracy and Representative Government.* Chicago: Aldine.

Norton, Alan. 1991. *The Role of Chief Executive in British Local Government.* Birmington: University of Birmington, Institute of Local Government Studies.

Øgård, M. 2000. New Public Management. Markedet som redningsplanke? In H. Baldersheim and L. Rose, eds., *Det kommunale laboratorium.* Bergen: Fagbokforlaget.

Olsen, J. P. 2005. Maybe It Is Time to Rediscover Bureaucracy. *Journal of Public Administration Research and Theory* 16:1–24.

Osborne, D., and T. Gaebler. 1992. *Reinventing Government.* New York: Addison-Wesley.

Overeem, Patrick. 2008. Beyond Heterodoxy: Dwight Waldo and the Politics–Administration Dichotomy. *Public Administration Review* 68:36–45.

Peters, B. Guy. 1999. *Institutional Theory in Political Science: The "New Institutionalism."* London: Pinter.

Peters, B. Guy. 2001. *The Future of Governing.* 2nd ed. Lawrence: University Press of of Kansas.

Pless, Y., and K. De Leemans. 2002. The Glass Cage: The Institutional Structure Around the Position of Municipal CEO. In P. Dahler-Larsen, ed., *Social Bonds to City Hall.* Odense: Odense University Press.

Proeller, Isabella. 2006. Trends in Local Government in Europe. *Public Management Review* 8(1): 7–29.

Putnam, Robert D. 1975. The Political Attitudes of Senior Civil Servants in Britain, Germany, and Italy. In Mattei Dogan, ed. *The Mandarins of Western Europe: The Political Role of Top Civil Servants.* New York: John Wiley & Sons.

Reschenthaler, G. B., and F. Thompson. 1996. The Information Revolution and the New Public Management. *Journal of Public Administration Research and Theory* 6(1): 125–43.

Rhodes, R. A. W. 1997. *Understanding Governance.* Buckingham: Open University Press.

Roberts, N. 2004. Public Deliberation in an Age of Direct Citizen Participation. *American Review of Public Administration* 34:315–53.

Rohr, John A. 2005. Comparative Observations Concerning Administrative Ethics in Europe and the United States: A Constitutional Perspective. Keynote address prepared for the International Conference on Ethics and Integrity of Governance: A Transatlantic Dialogue. Public Management Institute of the Katholieke Universitat, Leuven, Belgium. June.

Romzek, B., and J. Johnston. 2002. Effective Contract Implementation and Management: A Preliminary Model. *Journal of Public Administration Research and Theory* 12(3): 423–53.

Rutgers, Mark R. 1997. Beyond Woodrow Wilson: The Identity of the Study of Public Administration in Historical Perspective. *Administra tion & Society* 29(3): 276–300.

Sancton, Andrew. 2000. *Merger Mania.* Montreal: McGill-Queens University Press.

Sayre. Wallace. 1958. Premises of Public Administration: Past and Emerging. *Public Administration Review* 18:102–5.
Schachter, Hindy Lauer. 1989. *Frederick Taylor and the Public Administration Community: A Reevaluation*. Albany: State University of New York Press.
Schneider, Mark, and Paul Teske. 1992. Toward a Theory of the Political Entrepreneur: Evidence from Local Government. *American Political Science Review* 86:737–47.
Self, Peter. 1972. *Administrative Theories and Politics: An Inquiry into the Structure and Processes of Modern Government*. London: George Allen & Unwin Ltd.
SOLACE. 2005. *Leadership United: Executive Summary*. London: Society of Local Authority Chief Executives and Senior Managers.
Sørensen, E. 2002. Democratic Theory and Network Governance. *Administrative Theory and Praxis* 24(4): 693–720.
Sørensen, E., and J. Torfing. 2003. Network Politics, Political Capital, and Democracy. *International Journal of Public Administration* 26(6): 609–34.
Stein, Lana. 1991. *Holding Bureaucrats Accountable: Politicians and Professionals in St. Louis*. Tuscaloosa: University of Alabama Press.
Stoker, G., ed. 1999. *The New Public Management of British Local Governance*. Basingstoke: Macmillan.
Svara, James H. 1989. Policy and Administration: City Managers as Comprehensive Professional Leaders. In H. George Frederickson, ed., *Ideal and Practice in City Management*. Washington, DC: International City Management Association.
Svara, James H. 1999a. Complementarity of Politics and Administration as a Legitimate Alternative to the Dichotomy Model. *Administration & Society* 30:676–705.
Svara, James H. 1999b. The Shifting Boundary between Elected Officials and City Managers in Large Council-Manager Cities. *Public Administration Review* 59:44–53.
Svara, James H. 2001. The Myth of the Dichotomy: Complementarity of Politics and Administration in the Past and Future of Public Administration. *Public Administration Review* 61:176–83.
Svara, James H. 2006. Politicians and Administrators in the Political Process: A Review of Themes and Issues in the Literature. *International Journal of Public Administration* 29(12): 953–76.
Svara, James H. 2007. Leadership by Top Administrators in a Changing World: New Challenges in Political-Administrative Relations. In Ricardo S. Morse and Terry F. Buss, eds., *Transforming Public Leadership for the 21st Century*. Armonk, NY: M. E. Sharpe.
Thomas, J., Melkers. J. 1999. Explaining Citizen-Initiated Contacts with Municipal Bureaucrats: Lessons from the Atlanta Experience. *Urban Affairs Review* 34(5): 667–90.
Thomas, John Clayton. 1986. *Between Citizen And City: Neighborhood Organizations and Urban Politics in Cincinnati*. Lawrence: University Press of Kansas.
Thompson. Fred. 2003. Why a New Public Management? Why Now? *Review of Public Personnel Administration* 23:329–36.
Tullock, Gordon. 1965. *The Politics of Bureaucracy*. Washington, DC: Public Affairs Press.
Vigoda-Gadot, Mizrahi, and Tevet Miller-Mor. 2008. The Bureaucracy-Democracy Tango: A Dual-Source Empirical Revalidation by Structural Equation Modeling in the Israeli Public Sector. *Policy and Politics* 36(3): 431–48.
Waldo, Dwight. 1948. *The Administrative State: A Study of the Political Theory of American Public Administration*. New York: Ronald Press Co.
Warner, M. E., and Amir Hefetz. 2004. Pragmatism over Politics: Alternative Service Delivery in Local Government, 1992–2002. In *The Municipal Year Book 2004*. Washington, DC: International City County Management Association.

Warner, M. E., and Amir Hefetz 2009. Cooperative Cooperation: Alternate Service Delivery 2002–2007. In *The Municipal Year Book 2009*. Washington, DC: International City County Management Association.
Waterman, Richard W., and Kenneth J. Meier. 1998. Principle-Agent Models: An Expansion? *Journal of Public Administration Research and Theory* 8:173–202.
Wood, Dan B., and Richard W. Waterman. 1994. *Bureaucratic Dynamics: The Role of Bureaucracy in a Democracy*. Boulder, CO: Westview Press.
Woodruff, Clinton Rogers. 1919. *A New Municipal Program*. New York: D. Appleton and Company.
Yates, Douglas. 1977. *The Ungovernable City*. Cambridge: MIT Press.

CHAPTER 10

REFORMING LOCAL GOVERNMENT INSTITUTIONS AND THE NEW PUBLIC MANAGEMENT

HELLMUT WOLLMANN AND
KURT THURMAIER

1. Introduction

This chapter discusses institutional local government reforms, particularly those inspired by the New Public Management, in an internationally comparative perspective. Since the late 1970s the reform of municipal administration has been formulated and encouraged by a conceptual current that developed into the internationally known and influential New Public Management (Hood 1991). Emerging out of New Zealand and Australia into the UK, and rapidly expanding particularly into Anglo-Saxon countries, the New Public Management (NPM) reform program focused on three points (Pollitt and Bouckaert 2003, 2011). First, NPM was imbued with the neoliberal policy directed at rolling back the welfare state, including its local government dimension, to a lean state format by reducing functions and by privatizing as many tasks as could be taken over by the market. Second, it postulated that the production and delivery of the remaining public functions should be outsourced and contracted to NGOs or private providers by way of competitive tendering.

Third, in its managerialist component, NPM aimed at undoing the hierarchical Weberian public administration model and its alleged shortcomings (rigidity, fixation on legal correctness, and neglect of economic efficiency) by importing private sector managerialist concepts and tools into public administration. Reminiscent of the policy/administration dichotomy advocated in U.S. public administration doctrine, policymakers were to be restricted to setting general policy goals while the managers were to be given flexibility and autonomy to attain these goals. Most famously, political leaders should "steer" while the managers should "row" (Osborne and Gaebler 1992). Internally, hierarchical control should be replaced by performance-based monitoring and evaluation.

The NPM reforms have evolved differently in U.S. and European local governments. First, local governments on each side of the Atlantic are rooted historically in different institutional contexts. Second, they have different political and managerial starting points from which the reforms could be adopted and adapted. Our chapter analyzes the effect of NPM reforms on local governments in the U.S. and European contexts, and concludes with an intercontinental comparison and suggestions for future research.

The geographical bases of the comparative analysis are the U.S. (296 million inhabitants) and Europe (491 million inhabitants). We define Europe as the European Union's 27 member countries. Germany, France, and the UK, the three largest countries demographically, account for 16.7 percent, 12.6 percent, and 12.2 percent of the population, respectively. (Norway and Switzerland are outside the EU.) This regional scope invites three comparative dimensions: an intra-European, an intra-U.S., and an intercontinental ("transatlantic" Europe-U.S.).

We take essentially an institutionalist approach to comparatively address institutional change in local government administrative and operational structures. Our analytical and explanatory frame draws on *historical institutionalism* (Peters 1995; Thoenig 2003), emphasizing the historically grown institutional and cultural traditions, or path-dependencies (Pierson and Skocpol 2002) that may impinge on the institutional trajectory (such as *civil culture* versus *rule of law* traditions), on *discursive institutionalism* (Schmidt 2008) which hypothesizes the influences of discourses (such as New Public Management), and on *actors-centered institutionalism* which highlights the possible impact of actors and their policy decisions (such as individual policymakers or the European Commission). Directing our developmental analysis at the period since 1980, we choose the concept of *starting conditions* or *starting point* (Pollitt and Bouckaert 2011) to capture the specific institutional setting and problem constellation which propelled or retarded the development at this point.

We begin (section 2) by discussing the functional and territorial structure of local governments. This provides essential background information for the analysis in section 3 of how local governments have evolved in response to NPM reforms and other pressures. We focus on three dimensions of institutional change: leadership, internal reorganization, and external reorganization. Section 4 analyzes how local governments have altered their external operations to respond to a market orientation, most noticeably in increased efforts at contracting for services. The concluding section provides a comparative assessment and theoretical interpretation of local government reforms under *government* versus *governance* auspices.

2. Functional and Territorial Profile of Local Government Level

We begin with a sketch of the functional and territorial profiles at the local government level. Setting a pattern for the chapter, we begin with Europe and then present the U.S. comparison.

2.1. Functional and Territorial Profile of European Local Governments

Dating back to medieval times, European towns took on important tasks, such as providing marketplaces, basic local infrastructure and safety, as well as local charities looking after the urban poor. The expansion of the functions of modern local government was, in the course of the 19th century, prompted by and geared to industrialization and urbanization with Britain as Europe's frontrunner and other countries, particularly Germany, following suit. As the central government levels typically left it largely to the local government level to deal with the social ills and infrastructural problems caused by rampant industrialization and urbanization, a multifunctional profile of local government took shape which was scorned by contemporary market-liberal and conservative critics as municipal socialism. Absorbing traditionally existing single-purpose boards and organizations, local governments arrived most pronouncedly at first in England's Victorian local government model, at a *multifunctional* profile that has become the path-dependent hallmark of European local government (Wollmann 2004a).

With the advent of the (national) welfare state in the early 20th century, which expanded after 1945 and climaxed during the 1960s and early 1970s, the multifunctional role of the local government levels was ever more accentuated, particularly in the UK, Germany, and Sweden, in which the national governments put the local authorities in charge of implementing the lion's share of the advanced welfare state and proceeded to buttress their territorial basis and capacity by (large-scale) territorial consolidation (see also below section 3). Exemplary of this development has been Sweden in making the local government levels the operational basis and pillar (Pierre 1994) of the Swedish Welfare State Model.

Varying in functional composition and importance between the countries (see Marcou and Wollmann 2008), the local government responsibilities in most European countries typically cover urbanism and urban planning (often including issuance of building permits), social services (including social benefits in Sweden and Germany), leisure and culture, public utilities (particularly in Germany in the traditional form of multifunctional city works (*Stadtwerke*), and infrastructural facilities.[1] The local authorities are commonly responsible for the construction and upkeep of primary and secondary school buildings and technical personnel, while in half of the EU countries they are also financially responsible for staff (teacher) remuneration (e.g., in Sweden since 1990). The involvement of local government in health care varies according to the country-specific health care system, be it public or insurance-based. In Sweden the operational and financial responsibility for the public health system has been entirely placed on the *landsting kommuner* (the upper local government level). In the UK since 1948, it has been completely turned over to the National Health Service, a self-standing public agency.

Sweden has the largest municipal sector (87 percent in 2005; see table 1), and they enjoy a remarkably high degree of local autonomy, financed predominantly from locally levied taxes. In the UK, local government staff account for more than half of the total public employment (Wilson and Game 2006), although since the Thatcherist centralist shift, it has experienced increasing central government control. With some 30 percent of local level personnel, Germany and France are in the middle, with the labor-intensive school function lying with the Länder and central government, respectively. The data on Spain evidence the dramatic shift of functions which the country has experienced in being transformed since 1978 and the end of the Franco regime. It has become a quasi-federal state with the public functions transferred from the central state level largely to regions and to a distinctly lesser degree to the municipalities. Finally it should be highlighted that, notwithstanding decentralization in France since 1982 and in Italy since the late 1990s, the local percentage of total personnel still stands at 51 and 54, respectively, which reveals the continued dualism of central and local administrative units and personnel in the subnational space, with the legacy of the centralist Napoleonic state still shining through.

From its origins in the 19th century, the development of modern local government in European countries has been shaped by the organizational principle of multifunctional territoriality, according to which special functions, single-purpose actors, and institutions should be absorbed and integrated within a territorially defined local space to be operated and coordinated by the multifunctionally responsible elected local authority. Two groups of countries are distinguished in the further development of the European local government systems. Group 1 is exemplified by the UK, Sweden, and some of the German Länder and hence is classified as the *North European* pattern (see Norton 1994, 40). The territorial consolidation of the municipal level was promoted by the national governments particularly during the 1960s and 1970s by merging existing small-size municipalities.

In line with the then prevalent reformist *zeitgeist*, the underlying concept and driving political will was to prepare the territorial and institutional ground for further expanding the functional role of the local governments in the implementation

1. For detailed and substantiated overviews see Dexia 2008, 63ff.; Marcou and Wollmann 2008, 115; for an earlier "classic" treatment see Norton 1994.

Table 1. **Structural Data on Municipalities and Intermunicipal Bodies (in 2005)**

	Number	Average population	Average area (km^2)	% less than 5,000 pop.	Intermunicipal bodies
Germany	12,340	6,690	29	77	1,708[a]
France	36,683	1,720	15	95	15,440[b]
Italy	8,401	7,270	37	71	634[c]
Sweden	290	31,310	1,552	4	0
England	389	139,480	562	0	0
Spain	8,111	5,430	62	85	1,080[d]
Hungary	3,175	3,170	29	91	2,590
EU (27)	**92,506**	**5,410**	**47**	**82**	

[a] *Verwaltungsgemeinschaften, Ämter* etc.
[b] 12,840 *syndicats* plus 2,601 *communautés* (*à propre fiscalité*).
[c] 356 *comunità montane* plus 278 *unioni di comuni* (plus numerous *consorzi*).
[d] 81 *comarcas* + some 1,000 *mancomunidades.*

of the national welfare state, as epitomized in the Swedish notion of the local welfare state (Pierre 2004). Hence the basic idea was to further accentuate the organizational principle of *territoriality* geared to *multifunctionality.* The North European type territorial reforms characteristically hinged on the assumption (and political will) that, while the affected municipalities should be given the opportunity to be heard, it was seen to fall to the power of the national government level to carry through such reforms, and in the last resort, coercively by way of binding legislation. Among the North European type reforms, the one carried out in the UK in 1974 stood out by its unparalleled scale in arriving at bottom level local government units (districts/boroughs) averaging 140,000 inhabitants (see Stewart 2000 for criticizing the "sizeism" of the British reform variant); it was followed by Sweden with municipalities averaging 34,000 people (for further comparative data see Norton 1994, 40; Dexia 2008).

By contrast, the *South European* pattern appears in most other European countries; the often extremely small-size municipalities have been left more or less unchanged, while a new layer and type of intermunicipal body has been put in place, meant to operationally support their member municipalities in the delivery of public services.[2] France has become exemplary of generating a complex multitude of intermunicipal bodies (*intercommunalité*) with the *syndicats* and *communautés* adding some 15,400 units). Other countries of the South European territorial format have similar, but less numerous, intermunicipal patterns (see Norton 1994,

2. Insofar as in these countries central governments took the policy initiative to bring about territorial consolidation, such policy moves were typically premised on *voluntariness* (in French *volontariat*), that is, making amalgamation contingent on the consent of the local councils or local populations. Such voluntary consolidation attempts almost completely failed in France and Italy during the early 1970s (Norton 1994, 40ff.).

40; Dexia 2008, 67 with overview on all European countries concerned). Generally speaking, in these countries the organizational principle of multifunctional territoriality embodied in the municipalities has remained relatively weak while the intermunicipal bodies come close to a single deterritorialized organizational logic.

In recent years a new round of local level territorial consolidation has been under way in a growing number of countries (Wollmann 2010). It has been conceptually and politically driven by mounting criticism of the function of small-size municipalities and intermunicipal bodies, and by the intention to improve the administrative performance (e.g., coordination capacity) of local government by having territorially enlarged and viable municipalities. Local government consolidation has occurred in a radical way in Denmark in 2007 (arriving at municipalities averaging 55,000 inhabitants), but more moderately in East German Länder. France has recently (2008–10) embarked on a legislative reform process which, according to the recommendations of the high-caliber reform commission (see Comité Balladur 2009), might pave the ground for having territorially consolidated multifunctional new municipalities (*communes nouvelles*). So the territoriality-based multifunctional organizational logic of local government aiming at providing for its operational and administrative capacity appears to be in line with the classical European local government model (Wollmann 2010).

2.2. Territorial and Functional Profile of U.S. Local Governments

U.S. local governments developed structure and function from the bottom up, as creatures of the 50 states; the U.S. Constitution is silent about local governments. Consequently, NPM and any other reform is unlikely to be adopted in the same fashion and degree across all U.S. local governments. Second, the neoliberal argument (Tiebout 1956) for structuring local governments to maximize economic efficiency (i.e., to match as closely as possible local preferences for goods and services), has precedent in the peculiar feature of primary and secondary education in the U.S. being a function of independent school districts that do not conform to the boundaries of multifunctional general local governments such as counties and municipalities. More recently, the territorial profile of local governments in the U.S. has been shaped by a trend of layering new single-purpose special districts across the jurisdictional boundaries of traditional multifunctional local governments.

States in the U.S. typically use a two-tier system of multifunctional local governments, with counties as the upper level and municipalities as the lower level. The default powers of U.S. local governments are established on a principle known as Dillon's Rule (Dillon 1911), that local governments are "creatures of the legislature" and have only those corporate powers that are specifically delegated to them by their state government (Goodnow 1895, 1). The alternative regulatory framework is *home rule*, in which local governments are allowed broad powers to act as they wish—unless the legislature specifically prohibits an activity (Krane et al. 2001; Wood 2006).

School districts are single-purpose districts that usually cross two or more general-purpose local government jurisdictions, *and* have independent property tax authority. The U.S. Constitution is also silent on education, reserving this power to the states, which, in turn, largely have left education policy to local school districts.[3] Yet school districts account for over half of all state aid to local governments.[4] They account for about half of all local government employment in the U.S., and 31 percent of all U.S. civilian employees. School district consolidations have reduced the number of districts 14 percent over 30 years (table 2), but the number of employees has not declined concomitantly.

Aside from education, cities and counties are multifunctional. Public safety accounts for 20 percent of general fund municipal expenditures, housing and environment 20 percent, and social services 9 percent. Distinct county responsibilities include revenue collection and administration, local corrections, and they are delegated by the states for welfare and income maintenance administration.

Many public policy problems span traditional local government jurisdictional boundaries. Table 2 highlights the explosion of special local government districts, increasing 44 percent in the last 30 years. For example, independent watershed districts are created to govern a watershed area. These are independent, single-purpose local government units, usually spanning two or more municipal or county jurisdictions. Many special districts were created to bypass the property tax limitations on counties and municipalities, implemented with the property tax revolts in the 1970s and 1980s. Each special district can have a specific revenue source (a property tax, sales tax, or fees). Many of these special district governing bodies are directed by boards populated with members chosen by separate direct elections. In others, the governing boards are populated by representatives of specific member governments, such as on a metropolitan planning council.

An alternative solution to transjurisdictional service delivery problems, used more frequently in recent years, is to create interlocal service delivery agreements (ILAs), whereby multiple units of general local governments (counties and municipalities) agree to share sovereignty to provide a service or regulate a problem that affects each of them and is better addressed jointly.[5] ILAs allow local governments

3. Curriculum and personnel policies are decided almost exclusively at the school district level (sometimes within some broad state guidelines).There is a growing movement by governors and state school superintendents to adopt "a uniform set of academic standards" at the national level to replace "the patchwork of standards" across the states (Dillon 2010).

4. This is a consequence of states being forced by state courts to equalize educational opportunities across school districts to conform to state constitutional requirements. In some southern states (e.g., Virginia), the budget and taxing authority of school districts is shared with county governments.

5. Interlocal agreements (ILAs) can take many forms, ranging from an informal handshake agreement to elaborate contracts structured according to statutory requirements and filed with a state agency and county recorder.

Table 2. Numbers of U.S. Local Governments, and Change 1977–2007

	Counties	School districts	Special districts	Municipal	Town or township
1977	3,042	15,174	25,962	18,862	16,822
1987	3,042	14,721	29,532	19,200	16,691
1997	3,043	13,726	34,683	19,372	16,629
2007	3,033	13,051	37,381	19,492	16,519
Change 1977–2007	**Insignificant**	**-14%**	**+44%**	**+3%**	**-2%**

Source: U.S. Census of Governments.

to respond to a specific service market through collaboration instead of creating a special district (although some ILAs in fact create special districts, e.g., for rural fire service). Research on ILAs suggests that a majority of cities and counties are involved in at least one ILA (Henderson 1984; U.S. ACIR 1985; Agranoff 1989). Unfortunately, since most states do not collect systematic data on interlocal agreements, there is no reportable total number of agreements.

Some states have permitted directly elected metropolitan governing bodies as a new local government level, including Portland, Oregon, and Minneapolis–St. Paul, Minnesota (Sellers 2008, 236). However, city-county consolidation (i.e., amalgamation) is a rare event in the U.S. The most famous consolidated governments (New York City, New Orleans, St. Louis, and Indianapolis) were created by legislative fiat. Consolidated city-county governments only make up slightly more than 1 percent of the 3,043 county governments in the U.S. and about 1.5 percent of the 19,371 city governments (Durning 2003; Leland and Thurmaier 2004; 2006). Most consolidations are created by referendum, and since 1974 there have only been 40 successful referenda to politically consolidate the principal city with its county. The difficulty in consolidating general local governments predates the NPM reform movement, suggesting that NPM arguments against consolidated governments resonated with citizens well before NPM advocates reiterated them.

3. Institutional Reforms of Local Government

This section addresses the leadership, management, and other institutional changes which have occurred in local level administrative and operational structures since the 1980s, with attention to the influences of New Public Management reforms. Local government leadership reforms are essentially aimed at strengthening the operational capacity of local government. Although also inaugurated during the 1980s, they did not conceptually hail from NPM but emerged from a widely shared perception of a performance deficit (as well as democracy deficit) of local government. Internal management reforms have focused on overcoming the rigidity and hierarchical inefficiencies of Weberian organizations with flattened hierarchies and performance-based evaluation and compensation. External reorganization includes two forms of privatization. One form is the transfer of local government functions to organizations outside local government, but still remaining in municipal ownership (e.g., with municipal corporations). Alternatively, it may refer to selling local government assets into private sector ownership.

3.1. European Institutional Reforms

In European countries, local administration using local level organization and professionalized staff was first built up in Britain and in Germany in order to cope with the rising local government tasks in the course of the 19th century (Schröter and Röber 2000). By contrast, in Sweden, local level tasks were carried out primarily by laymen, being a latecomer to industrialization and a largely rural country well into the 20th century (Strömberg and Engen 1996, 267; Wollmann 2008a, 293ff.; 2008b: 226ff.). With the advent of the advanced national welfare state after 1945 and its climax in the 1960s and 1970s, local government and its administration reached an unprecedented scope of welfare state-driven activities going hand in hand with the claim that this repertoire of welfare services was best performed in house, by local public personnel. The UK and Sweden went furthest in claiming and practicing this monopolist public service production. Germany developed quite differently under the *subsidiarity principle*; social services were delivered largely by nongovernmental organizations (NGOs) (Bönker et al. 2010). In France public tasks were discharged almost exclusively by central government personnel essentially until the decentralization of 1982, so that the buildup of local level administration came correspondingly late. Among other historically Napoleonic centralist states, municipal administration was built up in Spain after 1978, and in Italy after decentralization in the late 1990s (albeit still in limited scale).

3.2. Leadership Reforms in European Countries

Two major reform currents can be distinguished among European countries (see Borraz and John 2004; Berg and Rao 2005; Reynaert et al. 2009; Wollmann 2009). A minority of European countries historically are based on the *government by committee* local government system (UK, Scandinavian countries). Most other Continental European countries are premised on the *council/mayor* local government form.[6] In the *government by committee* system, executive decision-making and

6. For overviews see Borraz and John 2004; Wollmann 2008c, 2009. A conspicuous recent spree of publications on local leadership reforms evidences the salience of that issue. See the special issues in *International Journal of Urban and Regional Research* 28(1) (2004); and *Local Government Studies* 34(2) (2008); Berg and Rao 2008; and Reynaert et al. 2009.

control over local administration is exercised by sectorally responsible, collectively deciding standing committees of local administration. It has been increasingly criticized on two scores. First, the sectoralizing of committee responsibility has been conducive to the sectoralization and departmentalization in the conduct of local government functions. Second, collective decision-making has impeded identifiable political accountability. Hence, the reforms of the *government by committee* system were essentially directed at concentrating the executive (decision-making as well as administrative) functions upon one (executive) committee and at decollectivizing decision-making by individualizing responsibilities and accountability.

In England, the reform introduced by parliamentary legislation in 2000 laid down various options (Wilson and Game 2006, 93ff.; Rao 2005). In the *cabinet with leader* variant, a council-elected executive committee with a council-elected leader is installed; this is somewhat tailored on the national level cabinet government, with the leader resembling a local prime minister. About 300 of the 311 local councils have adopted this form. The second option (*directly elected mayor with cabinet*) is a conspicuous novelty in the British local government tradition, largely inspired by the U.S. example of directly elected mayors; a directly elected mayor and a cabinet are put in place whose members the mayor may, from among councilors, appoint and dismiss at pleasure. This option may be understood as a presidential form of local government; the introduction requires approval by local referendum and only 7 of the 311 local councils have adopted this form (Copus 2009, 48). The third legislative option (*directly elected mayor with council-appointed city manager*) is also an institutional novelty, drawing on the prevalent council/city manager local government form in the U.S.; it was installed in 2002 by local referendum in only one local authority and it was abolished in 2008, again by local referendum.

The operational performance of Sweden's traditional *government by committee* system also has been criticized for functional fragmentation and blurred accountability since the 1980s. Different from the UK's top-down legislative intervention, Sweden's municipalities have been reforming their local government from bottom up and individually, within their organizational autonomy. While leaving the traditional system of sectorally responsible standing committees still in place, the chairpersons of these committees as well as the chairperson and most members of the most influential executive committee (*kommunstyrelse*) are now elected by the council majority party (see Montin 2005); the chairperson of the executive committee comes close to the position of local prime minister. Thus, Sweden's municipalities have, in a bottom-up development, also moved toward a local parliamentary form.

The *council and council-elected mayor* form which is prevalent throughout Continental European countries historically dates back to France's municipal legislation adopted in 1790 immediately after the Great Revolution. The revolutionary institutional novelty was that local government was conceived as a quasi-parliamentary system in which the legislative decision-making function was given to the elected council while the council-elected mayor was assigned the executive function. This was construed as a dualistic scheme in which the mayor executed the decisions passed by the council as well as public functions delegated to him/her by the central government. The quasi-parliamentary institutional arrangement of having a council-elected executive mayor, acting in a dualistic task model, has become the institutional blueprint throughout the Continental European countries, including central and eastern Europe. With some slight variations between countries, the *elected council plus council-elected executive mayor* form was in place in Continental European countries well into the 1980s—with the sole exception of two South German Länder (Baden-Württemberg and Bavaria) where, drawing on the U.S. example in the 1950s, they introduced the direct election of the executive mayor (Wollmann 2004b).

Since 1990, the directly elected executive mayor reform has been introduced in a growing number of Continental European countries to address the perceived performance deficit and democracy deficit. The German Länder, in a form of institutional isomorphism, were the first European countries to sequentially (DiMaggio and Powell 1983) enact this reform, followed by Italy in 1993 (Bobbio 2005, 41ff.). As a noticeable peculiarity, some Länder have included a referendum procedure to recall as sitting mayor, drawing on a U.S. model to counterbalance the powerful position of the mayor. Cities in Italy, in 1997, inaugurated the position of a city manager (*direttore generale*—appointed by the mayor, not by the council), adopting NPM ideas and also leaning on U.S. examples (Lippi 2003, 152). An increasing number of central east European countries have also turned to installing directly elected executive mayors (Wollmann 2009).

The quasi-parliamentarian *council-elected executive mayor* concept originated in 1790 in France and has remained in place to this day. It should be added though that in France's local council election system, the local council election process comes very close to the direct election of the executive mayor. In fact, for a number of country-specific peculiarities (especially the practice of multiple memberships of mayors. sitting also in upper level elected bodies, including the Assembée Nationale, dubbed *cumul de mandats*), French mayors have become arguably the strongest among European mayors, rising to a powerful position likened to a local president—if not a local "monarch" (Mabileau 1997, 353; Hoffmann and Martinot 2003, 166ff.).

3.3. Internal Management Reforms in European Countries

The range, focus, and timing of NPM-driven local administrative modernization have shown noticeable differences between European countries, particularly along the legal and cultural divide between the Anglo-Saxon common-law based *civil culture* tradition and the Continental European Roman law-rooted *rule of law* (*Rechtsstaat*) tradition (Wollmann 2000a; Pollitt and Bouckaert 2011). The acceptance and implementation of NPM concepts in Anglo-Saxon countries, with the UK taking the lead, was essentially facilitated by the common-law tradition in which a distinction is not made between public law and private law, nor between public and private sector, so that transferring managerialist principles and tools from the business sector to local administration did not have to struggle with legal and cultural barriers.

By contrast, the Roman law-rooted rule of law tradition in major Continental European countries made them legally and culturally much less accessible for and receptive to the NPM message. In Germany, for instance, the NPM discourse (manifest in the New Steering Model) made its entry only in the early 1990s, while in France it has, at least in explicit terminology, hardly been taken on. In Sweden which stands somewhat between the rule of law and the Civil Culture traditions, and where managerialist concepts (e.g., management by objectives) had already been accepted and implemented in the planning reform movement during the 1970s, NPM entered the administrative reform agenda during the 1990s (see Wollmann 2000b).

As to the initiation of NPM-inspired local level modernization drive, the UK stands out as an all but exceptional case, in that the modernization of local administration was largely imposed on the local authorities by central government, be it by making competitive tendering (CCT) obligatory by national legislation, or by introducing centrally designed and controlled indicator-based performance management for the local authorities (e.g., the Best Value regime). Similarly in Italy (in 1993), national top-down legislation had a strong NPM-related tendency for the municipalities, particularly by obliging them to adopt performance reviews (Bobbio 2005, 42; Lippi 2003, 144).

In most other European countries, NPM-inspired reforms were initiated bottom-up by the local authorities themselves, often also involving local government associations. Germany and Sweden are cases in point. The focus and accentuation of conceptual NPM components have varied according to country-specific starting points. In the UK, the NPM modernization drive was directed at dismantling the local government production monopoly by introducing market-type principles and procedures into local government operations. By contrast, in Continental Europe the rule of law tradition went hand in hand with a Weberian bureaucratic administrative model, with municipal administration being externally regulated by detailed legal provisions while being internal hierarchically directed and controlled. The NPM-inspired reform discourse largely singled out the managerialist component directed at the Weberian bureaucratic model.

As comprehensive national comparative evaluation studies on NPM-inspired local level modernization are still largely lacking, only scant and fragmentary empirical findings are available on results and impacts of NPM modernization in local government. Drawing on a recent evaluation study on NPM- / New Steering Model–inspired modernization of German local authorities (probably the most comprehensive pertinent evaluation study yet internationally available), it could be argued that, after NPM-inspired municipal sector modernization aiming at overcoming Weberian administration gathered rhetorical and practical dynamics in an early takeoff phase, it has in the meantime noticeably faded and even given way to some re-Weberization. However, there are reliable hints at a distinct shift in the administrative culture, complementing, if not replacing, the previous fixation on legal correctness with an economic efficiency orientation (Bogumil et al. 2007; Kuhlmann 2008; Kuhlmann et al. 2008).

3.4. External Reorganizing Reforms in European Countries

In European countries the external reorganization of local governments has been driven by the market-oriented components of NPM, by the market-liberalization policy ever more actively pursued by the European Commission, as well as by budgetary pressures besetting most of the countries. While the general current has been pointing at the outsourcing of local government activities and responsibilities, the focus, timing, and rate of the pertinent changes have varied depending on country-specific starting conditions and path-dependent legal and cultural givens. The following is only a selective and exemplified picture of a much more diversified development.

In the UK, social services were entirely delivered in house by local government staffs into the late 1970s; under central government pressure since then, the local authorities have gone furthest in outsourcing social services to outside (mainly commercial) providers by way of competitive tendering (Wilson and Game 2006, 353ff.; Bönker et al. 2010; Hill et al. 2010). Another far-reaching change in the conduct of public functions has occurred since the 1980s, when central government has proceeded to create self-standing, local level, single-purpose institutions known as *quangos* (quasi-nongovernmental organizations) for the implementation of administrative tasks. These are meant to carry out public functions largely under central government direction and intentionally outside local government (Skelcher 1998); the quangoization of the local level is a unique feature of England's subnational local space. By now there are some 5,000 quangos (Wilson and Game 2006, 145).

In Sweden, where social services were also delivered almost entirely in house by local government personnel, the NPM has had only limited repercussions, with 80 percent of local level activities and services still being rendered by in-house local government personnel. This probably reflects and is caused by the still broad public support of the municipal sector-based service regime (Montin 1993; Wollmann 2008a, 329ff.). German social services were traditionally delivered by NGO welfare organizations. In 1994 new federal legislation on the care of old and frail people stipulated that the care market which had come to be increasingly oligopolized by the NGOs was open to all providers, including private commercial ones (Bönker and Wollmann 2000; Bönker et al. 2010).

Cross-country commonalities as well as divergence characterize the field of public utilities (e.g., water, sewage, energy, and public transport). In the UK significant segments of public utilities (e.g., water, energy) were transferred to national agencies in the 1940s and have been materially privatized since the 1980s. In France, as early as the 19th century, many municipalities (due to their small size and lack of operational resources) proceeded to outsource the provision of public utilities by way of *gestion déléguée* to external public and private enterprises, which has been identified as the early French variant of public private partnerships (Lorrain 1995;

Marcou 2002, 21). In Germany and Sweden (and to a lesser extent Italy), the provision of a broad scope of public utilities has traditionally been a key function of local government. The services were produced either by municipal administration or in organizationally self-standing (typically multiutility) municipal corporations, with the German *Stadtwerke* as an exemplar.

The production of public services and public utilities has in recent years seen far-reaching changes. First, shifts were pushed by the market-liberalization drive of the European Commission which criticizes the existing local production as "protected local markets, if not local monopolies" and appears determined to make market competition prevail. Second, the municipalities have been increasingly beset by budgetary woes. Thus, they sought to improve their operational economy and competitiveness by *outsourcing* to outside "corporatized" (but still municipal) units. Second, international and national providers of services and public utilities have increasingly sought to have access to local markets; the municipalities have been ready to cash in and partially or wholly sell their municipal assets, particularly public utilities, to profit seeking firms.

The local actor levels throughout Europe have shown an organizational fraying of territorially defined, multifunctional, elected local government as the dominant actor in the local arena. There has been a corresponding increase in pluralization of actors, be they municipal, semipublic, NGO, or for-profit organizations. The UK represents an extreme case of the quangoization of the local level, with a multitude of single-purpose local level actors directly financed and controlled by central government.

As traditional multifunctional local government is increasingly surrounded and "satellitized" (see Huron and Spindler 1998, 74) by a multitude of single-purpose actors, it is increasingly challenged to live up to its political, democratically legitimated mandate to advocate and ensure the common interest of the community in coordinating multiple policies and functions.[7] However, there are empirical signs of a remunicipalization of services in reaction to the negative fallouts of some material privatization, such as the loss of political accountability of service production and uncontrollable rise in tariffs (Wollmann et al. 2010; Wollmann and Marcou 2010b).

4. U.S. Reforms

The primary NPM manifestation in the U.S., the Reinventing Government Movement promoted by Osborne and Gaebler (1992) and Vice President Gore, arguably had three effects on local governments. First, more services were devolved

7. For a discussion of the juxtaposition of the multifunctional and single-function organizational logic see Wollmann 2004.

from the federal to state and especially local governments, but without funds to support provision. Second, personnel systems came under pressure to be more flexible and more responsive to environmental changes (political and economic). Third, the increased demands from devolution combined with the lack of concomitant funds to increase pressure on local governments to contract with private sector firms and NGOs to provide services. Yet the increased pressure to contract for service delivery does not represent a radical departure from previous local government management practices.

4.1. U.S. Leadership Reforms

Within the limitations of state constitutions and statutes, residents of communities in the U.S. can choose their form of local government, including the arrangement for political leadership. Counties use a commission form similar to the government by committee group in Europe, or a chief executive-council form. County elected executives and commissioners normally are elected in partisan elections. The two main models at the municipal level are the *directly elected mayor-council* form and the *council-manager* form. The *town meeting* form of local government is found mostly in a few New England states; in this form, the directly elected town president conducts the meetings of town residents in a direct democracy model.

The mayor-council form uses a directly elected mayor with a two- to four-year term, and a city council that is usually elected by districts, although there can be variants with at-large or mixed (at-large and district) representatives. The directly elected mayor-council form is the oldest, and continues to be very popular, especially in large cities; about 43 percent of all U.S. cities over 2,500 population used the mayor-council form in 2007. It has the highest use in cities under 5,000 population and over 500,000 population (Svara and Nelson 2008). Especially in the large cities, the mayoral and councilor elections are based on partisan campaigns. The directly elected mayor is also an executive mayor, that is, exercising the chief executive function.

The council-manager form of government was first adopted in 1908 and in 2008 was the form used by more than 3,500 cities with populations over 2,500 and more than 370 counties (Svara and Nelson 2008). The council-manager plan suggests electing council members at-large and choosing a mayor from among the elected councilors, usually rotating the mayor each year among council members. Elections for the mayor and councilors are almost always nonpartisan. In addition, it calls for appointing a generalist administrator (i.e., city manager) to be the chief administrative officer (CAO) for the municipality. The council-manager form was a response to the 19th century mayoral and council electoral spoils system that was often viewed as corrupt (especially by those who were not in power). It has strong managerialist roots to bring business-like practices—where appropriate—to management of municipal services, and predates NPM reform efforts. Efficiency is a core value of council-manager governments, but not to the exclusion of equity and service effectiveness, as made clear by the ICMA Code of Ethics (ICMA 2010).

The current controversy in local government political leadership is the argument by Frederickson et al. (2004, 7) that municipalities have been increasingly fusing the two basic forms of government into a "dominant modern form of American local government, the 'adapted city,'" whereby the mayors are directly elected, the councils adopt a hybrid representation (at-large and district seats), and they retain a professional city manager as the CAO. Frederickson and others identify similar pressures for change as found in European governments: citizens desiring stronger, more focused leadership of the community, responsive to dominant constituencies, and able to develop and execute an economic development vision for the community.

Svara and Nelson (2008, 10) strongly disagree, arguing that the council-manager form has always operated with various combinations of electoral features and differing degrees of shared executive authority with the mayor. In their view, the key feature of the council-manager form is that the professional top administrator is assigned the executive responsibilities, and is accountable to the entire council, regardless of whether or not the mayor is directly elected, either in partisan or non-partisan elections. They also note (table 3) that the use of a chief administrative position is slowly expanding in local governments that use elected executive forms of government although the United States lags behind European countries. In 2008, they report that almost half of mayor-council governments and over half of town meeting governments also have a chief administrative officer (CAO) or city administrator (2008, 8). Increasingly, counties are hiring professional county managers with the same basic educational training that city managers have (a Master of Public Administration), whether they operate in the commission or the executive-council form.

The hybrid system of a directly elected *non*-executive mayor and an executive municipal (or county) manager (CAO), working with an elected council, highlights the strategic leadership potential of an elected mayor without sacrificing the professional executive management of routine tasks of public service delivery. It comports with the NPM prescription for elected officials to steer and managers to mange. If Svara and Nelson are correct, however, the credit for this reform does not belong to NPM.

4.2. Internal Management Reforms of U.S. Local Governments

Apart from restructuring local governments into a hybrid council-manager form of government, there have been few noticeable enduring reforms to restructure the internal operations of U.S. local governments. Historically local governments have operated with their own-source personnel, including independent personnel systems. States traditionally do not dictate civil service structures for their local governments, even for municipalities without home rule powers. The rise in federal social welfare activities in the 1960s and 1970s resulted in increased numbers of local

Table 3. Major Forms of U.S. Local Government (cities over 2,500 population), 1990–2007

Form of government	1990	2007	Change in form of government		
	% (number)	% (number)	% (number)	Cities smaller than 10,000	Cities larger than 10,000
Mayor-council	54.5%	43.5%	−14.1%	−515	1
	(3,645)	(3,131)	(−514)		
Council-manager	36.2%	48.9%	45.5%	574	526
	(2,420)	(3,520)	(1,100)		
Other	9.2%	7.5%	−12.0%	−47	−27
	(617)	(543)	(−74)		
Total	100.0%	100.0%	7.7%		
	(6,682)	(7,194)	(512)		

Source: *The Municipal Year Book* 1991 and 2008. The number of cities under 10,000 was 3,914 in 1990 and 3,926 in 2007. The number of cities over 10,000 was 2,768 in 1990 and 3,268 in 2007. Adapted from Svara and Nelson (2008).

personnel being funded wholly or partly with federal funds, especially for urban development, labor training, and welfare programs. However, the number of federally funded personnel has declined after the 1978 peak in federal grants to states and local governments. On the other hand, counties increasingly have state funded program personnel, especially regarding elderly healthcare, income maintenance programs, and services for troubled youth. School districts receive some federal funds for remedial education activities, but these are usually small shares of total school budgets; most school district positions are considered own-source FTE even when a majority of the district's budget may be funded by a state subsidy.

The NPM reform prescriptions are but a variation on a consistent theme of U.S. local administration that emphasizes efficiency in service delivery. Local government management has not been immune to the influences of various reform waves at the national level, for example, performance management in the 1950s, 1970s, and the 1990s. And the influence of the equity emphasis from the New Public Administration of the 1970s (Frederickson and others) is evident in local affirmative action policies and preferential contracting policies for women- and minority-owned firms. Yet the enduring value in local administration has been delivery of basic public services in an efficient (i.e., low cost) manner. The indictment by Osborne and Gaebler (and other NPM advocates) of local government administration seemed out of place to many local government managers, at least those operating under the council-manager form.

Recent reforms in personnel practice in U.S. local governments represent a somewhat paradoxical shift to market-oriented practices in the face of increased professionalization in the council-manager form of government. To what extent the shift to market-oriented practice is a consequence of the NPM arguments is debatable, although inflexible civil service systems were a principal target of the Reinvention Movement (Osborne and Gaebler). Market reforms take several forms, and the consequences of these changes include less job security for employees and less predictable wages for those who retain positions.

Conforming to the NPM critique against hierarchical organizations, many municipalities are moving away from narrow pay step systems and pay grades, to broader pay bands for greater flexibility in hiring and moving people around, for example, from 25 pay grades to 5 (Gerhart and Rynes 2003). There also is some movement toward team based management and group incentives for gain-sharing; group gains result in group profit shares (Graham-Moore and Ross 1990; and Perry, Mesch, and Paarlberg 2006). Third, there is movement toward skill based pay for job enrichment and horizontal job enlargement; this involves doing more with less, multitasking, and using a smaller workforce to accomplish more (Hackman and Oldham 1980). Finally, local governments are increasingly integrating HR functions with strategic planning and budgeting; hiring decisions are made more carefully today in terms of how they dovetail with the central priorities of the organization and how well the organization can afford these.

Taken alone, these changes would indicate a slide back to the spoils days of Tammany Hall. Yet the ability to respond to market environments is possible, in part, because local governments have become increasingly more professionalized in executive management, as noted by Svara and Nelson (2008). As city/county managers are increasingly rewarded (or not) based on performance metrics applied by their city councils, they have increasingly been inclined to use the same structure throughout their organizations, and especially with department heads.

The International City/County Management Association (ICMA) has recently (2006) formally and explicitly supported research and recognition of local government management innovations with a renewed partnership with the Alliance for Innovation (www.transformgov.org) which seeks to join the research capacities of universities with public administration scholars with the local government managers who are management innovators. Research on local government innovations is rather scarce (Nelson, et al. 2011), especially compared with the vast supply of innovation literature related to private sector management practices. While there are some general works on government innovation (e.g., Borins 2000; 2008; Light 1998; Abramson and Littman 2002; Bekkers, van Duivenboden, and Thaens 2006; and Veenswijk 2005), there is only a smattering of innovation studies specific to local governments in the U.S. For example, Ihrke et al. (2003) study city council member perspectives on innovation, while Johnson and Walzer's volume (2000) focuses on innovations in contracting for services. Other research focuses on e-government or specific services. It is difficult to discern any major reform trends from this literature, although internal operations innovations surely are implemented across a wide range of U.S. local governments.

4.3. External Market Orientations of U.S. Local Governments

One consequence of NPM reforms at the central government level has been the devolution of more functional responsibilities to local (and state) governments. Given the constraints on local own-source revenues, local governments have responded to these mandates by increasingly contracting with NGOs, private firms, and other local governments to deliver services.

Some services have been particularly identified for contracting to the private sector. Municipalities and counties are increasingly contracting with NGOs for social service delivery, funded by local and state funds. Municipalities and counties have long contracted with private firms for the repair and replacement of roads and highways; only minor repairs (such as filling potholes) is provided by in-house employees. A clear trend in the last 20 years has been for municipalities to contract with private firms for solid waste collection, supported by fees in pass-through contracts instead of funding municipal workers through property tax bills. In some cases residents pay for services directly to the private firms, while in many municipalities, residents pay for water, sewer, and solid waste services directly to the city, and the fees are passed through to the private firm. Privatization of solid waste collection services has allowed municipalities to reallocate those property tax dollars to other services (and sometimes to reduce taxes).

Increasingly, ILAs are used as an alternative service delivery mechanism to increase service effectiveness (e.g., solid waste collection and collective use of landfills) and to reduce costs (e.g., pooling resources to support a single crime lab in a metropolitan area instead of each entity maintaining its own lab). Shared sovereignty over collective (joint) service delivery via ILAs must be agreed to by the elected officials (councils and mayors), and it must be implemented by personnel in the collaborating local governments. Understanding the impetus for agreements, the effects on local governments, and the management *of* networks and management *within* networks is an active area of research for many public administration scholars in the U.S. (e.g., Agranoff 2007; Agranoff and McGuire 2001; Carr, LeRoux, and Shres 2009; Chen and Thurmaier 2009; Wood 2006; and others).

Increasing use of contracts with NGOs and private firms to deliver services is affecting the internal accountability structures and personnel requirements of U.S. local governments. There is increasing demand for contract management skills, and employees find themselves operating in networks of local governments with multiple and blurred accountability lines. Brown, Potoski, and Van Slyke (2006) note that local governments often lack contracting capacity, and they must carefully evaluate whether contracting is a viable option for each service.

The privatization agenda of NPM (a large component in the models exported from New Zealand and Australia) has been relatively unimportant in the U.S. Few parastatals have existed in the U.S. to privatize (e.g., no airlines, and Amtrak is small). With the exception of certain states (e.g., Iowa, Kansas, and Ohio), most power utilities in the U.S. are investor-owned corporations, while the water and sewer services are almost always municipally owned utilities. There was a brief period when some municipalities experimented with privatization of water supply, but the efforts evaporated quickly and without widespread adoption. The municipal water and sewer utilities are operated as quasi-independent enterprises, dependent on fees for services as the business revenues model. County governments are seldom involved in water and sewer services (except in consolidated city-county governments), and rural water and sewer services are most often the responsibility of individual property owners (who usually drill their own wells and install their own septic (sewer) systems), subject to state (and sometimes county) regulations. Similar to the trend observable in European countries, a reversal of privatization in the water supply sector and other services appears to be under way (Hefetz and Warner 2007).

5. Intercontinental ("Transatlantic") Analysis

We conclude this chapter with a summary intercontinental ("transatlantic") comparative analysis and with a brief discussion of its conceptual government versus governance implications.

5.1. Comparative Intercontinental Analysis

An intercontinental comparison and interpretation of our accounts identifies some crucial features and differences between the European and the U.S. local government systems. While in both systems the subnational local space generally has a two layer structure, it exhibits important differences in the territorial organization, size, and functional profile. In Europe, the municipalities as the lower local government layer have been traditionally designed and put in place as elected local authorities with comprehensive territorial as well as functional coverage, beyond which special-purpose authorities do not exist. From the arrival of the national welfare state, the local authorities have been charged with a range of welfare state responsibilities. On average the local government levels of the EU countries (see Dexia 2006) employ about 30 percent of the entire public sector personnel (though in Sweden it is 87 percent). Territorial consolidations (during the 1960s, 1970s, and more recently in the 2000s) have aimed at strengthening the operational potential of local administration by achieving economies of scale through consolidations (amalgamations). The current average population of municipalities in the 27 EU countries is 5,000, ranging between 140,000 in the UK (as result of aggressive consolidations) and 1,560 in France (in the absence of consolidations).

In the U.S., the territorial and functional setting of the local government level is distinctly different. Local governments in the U.S. employ about 64 percent of the public sector workforce, twice as large as in EU countries. Special-purpose districts, most importantly school districts, have historically coexisted with the general-purpose counties and municipalities. Thus, local government institutions are not only territorially, but also functionally fragmented. Territorial consolidation has been negligible. The significant differences in the territorial, functional, and personnel profiles of the two local government systems have a bearing on the rate and direction of institutional reforms. Different institutional and cultural traditions also weigh on their institutional developments.

European countries have recently shown a remarkable reform dynamic with regard to local political and executive leadership, both in the government by committee group (UK and Sweden) and in the mayoral group (Continental European countries). The driving forces are generally perceived as performance and democracy deficits. In both reform strategies (executive committee with leader and directly elected executive mayor) the political and executive leadership has been institutionally merged without singling out a city director as a self-standing executive position, meant to avoid the politically and operationally costly role conflicts between the two position-holders. (Italy has so far been an exception, institutionally separating the political role of the directly elected mayor and the administrative executive function of a city director [in line with NPM].)

In the U.S., in contrast, there has been considerable continuity in the institutional setting of local leadership in that the directly elected mayor has been introduced and retained since the end of the 19th century. For much of the 20th century there were two stark models of municipal administration: a directly elected mayor as political and administrative executive, versus a council-manager form with an appointed executive and collective political leadership. In the last decades, there has been a gradual institutional hybridization of these forms, with more and more municipalities adding the position of an executive city manager to an elected mayor, and council-manager cities choosing to elect a mayor at-large for political leadership. The hybrid model has the virtue of blending traditional public administration as well as NPM concepts, emphasizing the separation between the political and the administrative functions, and an efficient operations approach to city management.

With regard to internal administrative reorganization, European local government systems shared the starting condition of a local administrative fabric which was tailored to the in-house implementation of multifunctional welfare state tasks. In Continental European countries, the rule of law context accentuated a legalist and hierarchical Weberian administrative model. The NPM-inspired modernization strategies were fueled in some European countries (such as the UK) by neoliberal policy tenets directed at overcoming the hierarchical model by introducing private sector managerialist concepts. Although the NPM modernization drive energy has faded, still there have been noticeable managerialist changes in local administration throughout European countries. In the U.S., local governments have experimented with more flexible and flatter organizational hierarchies, reducing the number of pay grades and moving performance evaluations and remuneration from individuals to work teams responsible for collaborative results within the organization.

Regarding external reorganization, the starting condition in most European countries was again marked by a traditional multifunction model which, in the heydays of the welfare state, included the provision of social services as well as public utilities. Under the impact of the marketization imperatives of NPM and the European Commission's market liberalization policy, local governments in most European countries turned to hiving off, outsourcing, and privatization to external actors and providers. The impact has, by and large, been significant through the pluralization and extension of governance-type actor networks.

U.S. local governments have increased their willingness to contract with private sector firms, NGOs, or local governments to deliver services. The NPM focus on contracting for services instead of providing them in-house is widely adapted by U.S. cities and counties. Solid waste disposal, for example, largely has been shifted to a fee for service basis using private waste haulers for collection services. Airports and major recreation venues (such as sports stadiums) are operated as quangos using a business financial model even if wholly owned by the local government. But the privatization drive from NPM fell flat in the U.S. because there were few entities to privatize, especially at the local government level. Alternatively, special districts cover a range of functions and usually span two or more municipal or county jurisdictions. While in some regards they are similar to intercommunal bodies in European countries (particularly to the syndicates and *communautés* in France), they are in principle self-standing local government units, independent of the traditional multifunctional local governments. That said, it is not clear that one can attribute the development of U.S. local governments to NPM ideology alone, as the historical starting point for special districts and lean governments was set in the U.S. long before NPM was born.

5.2. From Local Government to Local Governance?

Local *government* is understood as the traditional, territorially defined, multipurpose elected local authority, while local *governance* is conceived as networks of typically single-purpose actors and organizations operating outside the realm of the local government organization to provide public services (Rhodes 1997; Berry et al. 2004; Thurmaier and Wood 2002). Under our definitional and conceptual auspices the development of the local institutional setting and actor constellation presents a somewhat conflicting and contradictory pattern.

On the one hand, the preceding comparative analysis points to traditional local government having been strengthened in two crucial dimensions. First, in most European countries the political and operational leadership capacity of local government has been enhanced through a type of local parliamentarism in England and Sweden, and through a form of local presidentialism in most of the continental European countries. Second, internal administrative reorganization has improved its operational capacity particularly through the NPM-induced introduction of cost-accounting, performance monitoring, and economic thinking in municipal administration. Thus, the political and operational stances of the traditional local government have been consolidated and reinforced. This also pertains to its political mandate and legitimacy to represent, advocate, and ensure the common interest of the local community in the local level political process.

On the other hand, the position and the role of the traditional local government have been influenced and challenged by the emergence and expansion of actors and institutions resulting from hiving off, outsourcing, and privatizing local government functions to external actors and organizations; these constitute local governance networks essentially operating outside and beyond the immediate organizational fabric and reach of local governments. The previously tightly defined and public-sector-centered institutional fabric of local government has tended to fray out. These governance actors and organizations are premised on their special-purpose logic of operational flexibility and single function efficiency, as well as an ability to mobilize additional nonpublic (voluntary or private sector) financial and human resources in local level activities. They are likely to challenge, and run counter to, the logic of general-purpose local government and its common interest commitment and mandate (Wollmann 2004a).

In order to cope with these challenges local governments have embarked upon various strategies. In conspicuously deviating from the organizational scheme of traditional local government, some municipalities have exhibited institutional isomorphism and radically changed their organizational fabric by borrowing a variant of organizational structure from private sector companies. For example, a cohort of neoliberal policy-committed French mayors during the 1980s set on devising their municipality as *ville entrepreneuriale* or *ville stratège* (Maury 1997; Wollmann 2008a, 230ff.; Kuhlmann 2009). Likewise, in Hungary, in the early post-1990 transformation period, NPM-inspired "entrepreneurial local government" was attempted as an organizational blueprint (Soos 2003, 248f.). In Germany, a significant number of municipalities adopted an organizational scheme dubbed *Konzern Stadt* (city holding), tailored on the organizational principle of private sector holding companies (Bogumil and Holtkamp 2006, 96). However, the *Konzern Stadt* design has apparently lost attraction and momentum also among German local authorities in recent years. Overall, these entrepreneurial overtures have been short-lived.

Another strategy explicitly anchored in the traditional local government structure creates intra-administrative special operational units and/or special council committees that are meant to keep in check the single-purpose dynamics and centrifugal drift inherent in the governance network that includes entirely or partially corporatized (hived off) municipally owned companies "satellitizing" local government (Huron and Spindler 1998, 74).[8]

Local government's potential to influence and coordinate local level activities and services in a governance framework has been bolstered through the recent strengthening of its government structures, particularly of its political and executive leadership. The evidence presented in this chapter suggests that these developments of leadership, external contracting, and interorganizational governance forms have occurred, in U.S. local governments, more independently from the NPM reforms than this was, by and large, the case in European countries. In the U.S., the contracting for services (to private, public, and nongovernmental organizations) takes advantage of market efficiency, but simply continues the historical push for increased efficiency as a high value of U.S. local governments. The increased use of special districts to address complex service problems can be mistaken as an outcome of NPM's market orientation, but they are better understood as consequences, perhaps unintended, of restrictive local tax policies, as well as the transjurisdictional solutions to transjurisdictional problems (Chen and Thurmaier 2009; Thurmaier 2006).

In general terms, vis-à-vis the multitude of governance-type single-purpose organizations each pursuing its specific goals and particular interests, traditional local government has the crucial task to mediate between and coordinate the multifarious functions of interests of a plurality of local level actors—ideally with the aim to arrive at the elusive common good and public interest. Among the modalities to bring about multiactor coordination, the distinction has been made between hierarchy, negotiation, and market (Kaufmann et al. 1986; Wollmann 2002). Coordinating functions and activities of actors in governance networks requires

8. For intralocal government arrangements to steer corporatized companies and operational units, *Beteiligungssteuerung*, in the case of German municipalities, see Bogumil and Holtkamp 2006, 95ff.

interaction, persuasion, and bargaining. Depending on the public service and the competencies of the governance actors, the local government may act as a network hub, a network node, or a peripheral network actor (Friend 1976; Berry et al. 2004; Thurmaier and Wood 2002).

Since the traditional general-purpose elected local government is politically mandated to pursue the common interest of the local community vis-à-vis a plurality of single-purpose and particular-interest actors, while the governance-type actors strive for optimal flexibility and efficiency in the fulfillment of their specific functions and interests, the structures and logics of local government and local governance can be viewed as mutually complementary and supportive rather than contradictory and mutually exclusive (see Wollmann and Bouckaert 2006, 34f.).

6. Perspectives and Needs of Internationally Comparative Research

Finally we turn to discuss the need for, and potential of, internationally comparative research on local government reforms. The desirability of further comparative work includes the study of local government systems at large. This holds true for cross-European countries research (for available overviews—with varying country coverage—see John 2001; Bobbio 2002; Kersting and Vetter 2003; Denters and Rose 2005; Dexia 2008; Marcou and Wollmann 2008; Wollmann 2007, 2008a, 2008b; Kersting et al. 2009; Kuhlmann 2009; and, still indispensable, Norton 1994). The UK/England is somewhat overrepresented in existing comparative literature, probably still reflecting, besides an Anglophone dominance (Baldersheim and Wollmann 2006), the pace-setting role which British local government has historically played in the development of European local government. The inclusion of south European and central east European countries has been neglected, arguably also for language reasons. Finally, the scarcity of internationally comparative work shows a conspicuous gap in the intercontinental (Europe/U.S.) comparative dimension, with the noteworthy exceptions of Norton (1994), Sellers (2002), and Bobbio (2002). The emerging paradigm shift from government to governance offers a fresh opportunity for intercontinental research; the ways in which governance can evolve on each continent is conditioned by the historical nature and role of its local governments, and careful comparative research could provide insights and lessons for practice to benefit practitioners and scholars on both sides of the Atlantic.

When it comes to the NPM-induced local government reforms, the need for comparative research is even more manifest. Some internally comparative research has been conducted on NPM-guided public sector modernization on the central government level. For example, Pollitt and Bouckaert (2011) include the comparative analysis and international overviews by international organizations, such as

OEDC. More typically they are focused on the central government level, and broadly comparative work and publications on local level administrative modernization are still missing, except for treatments on selected countries (Wollmann 2008a; Kuhlmann and Fedele 2010).

Further research is needed regarding comparative analyses on local level, NPM-inspired modernization that singles out and focuses on policy and service fields to analytically track the reforms. Such policy-related research may be particularly penetrating and revealing. For an attempt at combining cross-country country and cross-policy comparisons see Wollmann and Marcou (2010a; 2010b). While available studies on NPM-inspired local level reforms have largely focused on the concepts and the implementation of such reforms, the evaluative analysis of the results and outcomes has so far been largely neglected.[9] This seems understandable in view of the formidable methodological and empirical problems of analyzing public sector reforms (Pollitt and Bouckaert 2003), but needs to be tackled and overcome.

REFERENCES

Abramson, Mark A. and Ian D. Littman, eds. 2002. *Innovation*. Lanham, MD: Rowman & Littlefield.

Agranoff, Robert. 1989. "Managing Intergovernmental Processes." In *Handbook of Public Administration*, edited by James L. Perry, 131–47. San Francisco, CA: Jossey-Bass.

Agranoff, Robert. 2007. *Managing within Networks: Adding Value to Public Organizations*. Washington, DC: Georgetown University Press.

Agranoff, Robert and Michael McGuire. 2001. "Big Questions in Public Network Management Research." *Journal of Public Administration Research and Theory* 11(3): 295–326.

Baldersheim, Harald and Hellmut Wollmann. 2006. "An Assessment of the Field of Comparative Local Government." In Harald Baldersheim and Hellmut Wollmann, eds., *The Comparative Study of Local Government and Politics: Overview and Synthesis.* Opladen: Barbara Budrich Publishers.

Barry, Gerhart and Sara Rynes. 2003. *Compensation*. Thousand Oaks, CA: Sage.

Bekkers, Victor, Hein van Duivenboden, and Marcel Thaens, eds. 2006. *Information and Communication Technology and Public Innovation: Assessing the ICT-Driven Modernization of Public Administration. Amsterdam: IOS Press.*

Berg, Rikke and Nirmila Rao, eds. 2005. *Transforming Local Political Leadership*. Houndmills: Palgrave.

Berry, Frances S., Ralph S. Brower, Sang O. Choi, Wendy X. Goa, HeeSoun Jang, Myungjung Kwon, and Jessica Word, eds. 2004. "Three Traditions of Network Research: What the Public Management Research Agenda Can Learn from Other Research Communities." *Public Administration Review* 64(5): 539–52.

Bobbio, Luigi. 2002. *I governi locali nelle democrazie contemporanee.* Rome: Editori Laterza.

9. On internationally comparative evaluation of central level public sector reforms see Furubo et al. 2002; Pollitt and Bouckaert 2004; Wollmann 2003a, 2003b.

Bobbio, Luigi. 2005. Italy: "After the Storm" In Bas Denters and Lawrence E. Rose, eds., *Comparing Local Governance: Trends and Developments*. Houdmills: Palgrave.
Bogumil, Jörg, Stephan Grohs, Sabine Kuhlmann, and Anna K. Ohm. 2007. *Zehn Jahre Neues Steuerungsmodell*. Berlin: Sigma.
Bogumil, Jörg and Lars Holtkamp. 2006. *Kommunalpolitik und Kommunalverwaltung*. Wiesbaden: VS Verlag.
Bönker, Frank, Anna Marzanati, and Michael Hill. 2010. "The Changing Role of Local Government in Long-Term Care in England, France, Germany and Italy." In Hellmut Wollmann and Gérard Marcou, eds., *The Provision of Public Services in Europe: Between State, Local Government and Market*. Cheltenham: Edward Elgar.
Bönker, Frank and Hellmut Wollmann. 2000. "The Rise and Fall of a Social Service Regime." In Hellmut Wollmann and Eckhard Schröter, eds., *Comparing Public Sector Reform in Britain and Germany*. Aldershot: Ashgate.
Borins, Sandford. 2000. "Loose Cannons and Rule Breakers, or Enterprising Leaders? Some Evidence about Innovative Public Managers." *Public Administration Review* 60(6): 498–507.
Borins, Sandford, ed. 2008. *Innovations in Government: Research, Recognition, and Replication*. Washington, DC: Brookings Institution Press.
Borraz, Olivier and John, Peter. 2004. "The Transformation of Urban Political Leadership in Western Europe." *International Journal of Urban and Regional Research* 29(1): 107–21.
Brown, Trevor L., Matthew Potoski, and David M. Van Slyke. 2006. "Managing Public Service Contracts: Aligning Values, Institutions, and Markets," *Public Administration Review* 66(3): 323–331.
Carr, Jered B., Kelly LeRoux, and Manoj Shres. 2009. "Institutional Ties, Transaction Costs, and External Service Production." *Urban Affairs Review* 44(3): 403–27.
Chen, Yu-Che and Kurt Thurmaier. 2009. "Interlocal Agreements as Collaborations: An Empirical Investigation of Impetuses, Norms, and Success." *American Review of Public Administration* 39(5): 536–52.
Comité Balladur. 2009. "Comité pour la réforme des collectivités locales." http://www.reformedescollectiviteslocales.fr/home/index.php.
Copus, Collin. 2009. "English Elected Mayors: Developing a New Form of Local Political Leadership in England, or Moving On the Same Old Style?" In Herwig Reynaert, Kristof Steyrers, Pascal Delwit, and Jean-Benoit Pilet, eds., *Local Political Leadership in Europe*. Brugge: Vanden Broele.
Denters, Bas and Lawrence E. Rose, eds. 2005. *Comparing Local Governance: Trends and Developments*. Houndmills: Palgrave.
Dexia. 2006. *Les fonctions publiques locales*. Paris: Dexia.
Dexia. 2008. *Sub-national Governments in the European Union: Organisation. Responsibilities and Finance*. Paris: Dexia.
Dillon, John F. 1911. *Commentaries on the Law of Municipal Corporations*. 5th ed. Boston: Little, Brown.
Dillon, Sam. 2010. "Panel Proposes Single Standard for All Schools." *New York Times*, March 10. http://www.nytimes.com/2010/03/11/education/11educ.html (accessed March 24, 2010).
DiMaggio, Paul J. and WalterW. Powell. 1983. "The Iron Cage Revisited: Institutional Isomorphism and Collective Rationality in Organizational Fields." *American Sociological Review* 38(2): 147–60.
Durning, Daniel. 2003. "Consolidated Governments." In Jack Rabin, ed., *Encyclopedia of Public Administration and Public Policy*. Vol. 1. New York: Marcel Dekker.

Frederickson, H. George, Gary A. Johnson, and Curtis H. Wood. 2004. *The Adapted City: Institutional Dynamics and Structural Change.* Armonk, NY: M. E. Sharpe.

Friend, John. 1977. "Community and Policy: Coordination from Above or Below." *Linkage* 2:4–10.

Gains, F. 2004. "The Local Bureaucrat. A Block to Reform or a Key to Unlocking Change?" In Gerry Stoker and David Wilson, eds., *British Government into the 21rst Century*. Basingstoke: Palgrave Macmillan.

Goodnow, Frank J. 1895. "Municipal Home Rule." *Political Science Quarterly* 10(1): 1–21.

Graham-Moore, Brian and Timothy Ross. 1990. *Gainsharing: Plans for Improving Performance*. Washington. DC: Bureau of National Affairs.

Hackman, Richard and Greg Oldham. 1980. *Job Redesign*. Reading, MA: Addison-Wesley.

Hefetz, Amir and Mildred Warner. 2007. "Beyond the Market versus Planning Dichotomy: Understanding Privatisation and Its Reverse in US Cities." *Local Government Studies* 33(4): 555–72.

Henderson, Lori M. 1984. "Intergovernmental Service Arrangements and the Transfer of Functions." *Municipal Year Book*. Washington DC: International City and County Management Association.

Hill, Michael, Martine Long, Anna Marzanati, and Frank Bönker. 2010. "The Local Government Role in Pre-school Child Care in France, Germany, Italy and the UK." In Hellmut Wollmann and Gérard Marcou, eds., *The Provision of Public Services in Europe: Between State, Local Government and Market.* Cheltenham: Edward Elgar.

Hoffmann-Martinot, Vincent. 2003. "The French Republic: One Yet Divisible." In Norbert Kersting and Angelika Vetter, eds., *Reforming Local Government in Europe.* Opladen: Leske + Budrich.

Hood, Christopher. 1991. "A Public Management for All Seasons." *Public Administration* 69(1): 3–19.

Huron, D. and J. Spindler. 1998. *The Management Public Local.* Paris: LGDJ.

Ihrke, Douglas, Rick Proctor, and Jerry Gabris. 2003. "Understanding Innovation in Municipal Government: City Council Member Perspectives." *Journal of Urban Affairs* 25(1): 71–90.

International City/County Management Association (ICMA). 2010. Code of Ethics. http://www.icma.org/main/bc.asp?bcid=40&hsid=1&ssid1=2530&ssid2=2531, (accessed on February 10, 2010).

John, Peter. 2001. *Local Governance in Western Europe.* London: Sage.

Johnson, Robin A. and Norman Walzer, eds. 2000. *Local Government Innovation: Issues and Trends in Privatization and Managed Competition.* Westport, CT: Quorum Books.

Kaufmann, Franz-Xaver, Giandomenico Majone, and Vincent Ostrom, eds. 1987. *Guidance, Control and Evaluation in the Public Sector.* Berlin: deGruyter.

Kersting, Norbert, Janice Nickson Caulfield, Dele Andrew/Olowu, and Hellmut Wollmann. 2009. *Local Governance Reforms in Global Perspective. URI book series.* Wiesbaden: VS Verlag.

König, Klaus. 1997. "Entrepreneurial Management or Executive Administration: The Perspective of Classical Administration." In Walter Kickert, ed., *Public Management and Administrative Reform in Western Europe.* Cheltenham: Edward Elgar.

Krane Dale, Rigos Platon, and Melville Hill, Jr., eds. 2001. *Home Rule in America: A 50-State Handbook.* Washington, DC: Congressional Quarterly Books.

Kuhlmann, Sabine. 2008. "'Tires les leçon de l'économisation' de la politique de l'administration locale en Allemagne. Le 'Neues Steuerungsmodell' a-t-il échoué?" *Pouvoirs Locaux* 79:115–20.

Kuhlmann, Sabine. 2009. *Politik- und Verwaltungsreform in Kontinentaleuropa. Subnationaler Institutionenwandel im deutsch-französischen Vergleich*. Baden-Baden: Nomos.

Kuhlmann, Sabine, Jörg Bogumil, and Stefan Grohs. 2008. "Evaluating Administrative Modernisation in German Local Government: Success or Failure of the 'New Steering Model'?" *Public Administration Review* 68(5): 851–63.

Kuhlmann, Sabine and Paolo Fedele. 2010. "Local Government Modernization in Germany and Italy." In Hellmut Wollmann and Gérard Marcou, eds., *The Provision of Public Services in Europe: Between State, Local Government and Market*. Cheltenham: Edward Elgar.

Leland, Suzanne and Kurt Thurmaier, eds. 2004. *Case Studies of City-County Consolidation*. Armonk, NY: M. E. Sharpe.

Leland, Suzanne and Kurt Thurmaier. 2006. "When Efficiency Is Unbelievable: Normative Lessons from 30 Years of City-County Consolidations." *Public Administration Review* 65(4): 475–89.

Light, Paul. 1998. *Sustaining Innovation: Creating Nonprofit and Government Organizations That Innovate Naturally*. San Francisco: Jossey-Bass.

Lippi, Andrea. 2003. "'As a Voluntary Choice or a Legal Obligation': Assessing New Public Management Policy in Italy." In Hellmut Wollmann, ed., *Evaluation in Public-Sector Reform*. Cheltenham: Edward Elgar.

Lorrain, Dominique. 1995. "Le changement silencieux." In Dominique Lorrain and Gerry Stoker, eds., *La privatisation des services urbains en Europe*. Paris: Editions La Découverte.

Mabileau, Albert. 1997. "Les génies invisibles du local." *Revue Française de Science Politique* 47:340–75.

Marcou, Gérard. 2000. "L'application de la loi du 12 juillet 1999. Stratégies et problèmes de mise en oeuvre." In *Annuaire 2000 des Collectivités Locales*. Paris: CNRS.

Marcou, Gérard. 2002. "Le partenariat public-privé: retrait ou renouveau d'intervention publique?" In Caisse des Dépôts, ed., *Partenariat public-privé et collectivités territoriales*. Paris: La Documentation Française.

Marcou, Gérard and Hellmut Wollmann. 2008. "Europe." In UCLG, *GOLD Report*. www.cities-localgovernments.org/gold/gold_report.asp(accessed August 10, 2011).

Maury, Yann. 1997. "Les contradictions du néo-liberalisme gestionnaire." *Revue Politiques et Management Public* 15(4): 145–69.

Montin, Stig. 1993. *Swedish Local Government in Transition*. Örebro: University of Örebro.

Montin, Stig. 2005. "The Swedish Model: Many Actors and a Few Strong Leaders." In Rikke Berg and Nirmila Rao, eds., *Transforming Local Political Leadership*, Houndmills: Palgrave.

Nelson, K. L., C. H. Wood, and G. T. Gabris. 2011. "Innovation management in local government: An empirical analysis of suburban municipalities." *International Journal of Organization Theory and Behavior*, 14(3): 301–328.

Norton, Allan. 1994. *International Handbook of Local and Regional Government*. Aldershot: Edward Elgar.

Olson, Johan P. 1988. "Administrative Reforms and Theories of Organisation." In Colin Campbell and Guy B. Peters, eds., *Organising Governance—Governing Organisations*. Pittsburgh: University of Pittsburgh Press.

Osborne, David and Ted Gaebler. 1992. *Reinventing Government: How the Entrepreneurial Spirit Is Transforming the Public Sector*. Reading, MA; Addison-Wesley.

Perry, James, D. Mesch, and L. Paarlberg. 2006. "Motivating Employees in a New Governance Era: The Performance Paradigm Revisited." *Public Administration Review* 66 (4): 89–122.

Peters, Guy B. 1995. "Political Institutions: Old and New." In Robert Goodin and Hans-Dieter Klingemann, eds., A *New Handbook of Political Science*. Oxford: Oxford University Press.

Pierre, Jon. 1994. *Den lokala staten*. Stockholm: Almquist & Wiksell.

Pierson, Paul and Theda Skocpol. 2002. "Historical Institutionalism in Contemporary Political Science." Unpublished paper, Harvard University, http://arilson.favareto.googlepages.com/Pierson_Skocpol.pdf (accessed August 10, 2011).

Pollitt, Christopher and Geert Bouckaert. 2003. "Evaluating Public Sector Management Reforms: An International Perspective." In Hellmut Wollmann, ed., *Evaluation in Public-Sector Reform*. Cheltenham: Edward Elgar.

Pollitt, Christopher and Geert Bouckaert. 2011. *Public Management Reforms*. 3nd ed. Oxford: Oxford University Press.

Rao, Nirmala. 2005. "From Committees to Leaders and Cabinets: The British Experience." In Rikke Berg and Nirmala Rao, eds., *Transforming Local Political Leadership*. Houndmills: Palgrave Macmillan.

Reynaert, Herwig, Kristof Steyrers, Pascal Delwit, and Jean-Benoit Pilet, eds. 2009. *Local Political Leadership in Europe*. Baden-Baden: Nomos Vanden Broele.

Rhodes, Rod. 1997. *Understanding Governance*. London: Macmillan.

Rogers, Everett M. 2003. *Diffusion of Innovation*. 5th ed. New York: Free Press.

Schmidt, Vivien. 2008. "Discursive Institutionalism: The Explanatory Power of Ideas and Discourses." *Annual Review of Political Science* 11:8–25.

Schröter, Eckhard and Manfred Röber. 2000. "Local Government Services in the United Kingdom and Germany." In Hellmut Wollmann and Eckhard Schröter, eds., *Comparing Public Sector Reform in Britain and Germany*. Aldershot: Ashgate.

Sellers, Jeffery. 2002. "Governing from Below." *Urban Regions and the Global Economy*. Cambridge: Cambridge University Press.

Sellers, Jeffery. 2008. "North America." In UCLG, *GOLD Report*. www.cities-localgovernments.org/gold/gold_report.asp (accessed August 10, 2011).

Skelcher, Chris. 1998. *The Appointed State*. Buckingham: Open University Press.

Stewart, John. 2000. *The Nature of British Local Government*. Houndmills: Macmillan.

Soos, Gabor. 2003. "Local Government Reforms and the Capacity for Local Governance in Hungary." In Norbert Kersting, and Angelika Vetter, eds., *Reforming Local Government in Europe*. Opladen: Leske + Budrich.

Strömberg, Lars and Tone Engen. 1996. "Sweden." In Erik Albaek, Lawrence Rose, Lars Strömberg, and Krister Stahlberg, eds., *Nordic Local Government*. Helsinki: Association of Finnish Local Authorities.

Svara, James H. and Kimberly L. Nelson. 2008. "Taking Stock of the Council-Manager Form at 100." *PM* 90(7): 6–15.

Thoenig, Jean Claude. 2003. "Institutional Theories and Public Institution: Traditions and Appropriateness." In B. Guy Peters and Jon Pierre, eds., *Handbook of Public Administration* London: Sage.

Thurmaier, Kurt. 2006. "High Intensity Interlocal Collaboration in Three Cities." *Public Administration Review* 66 (Supplement 1): 144–46.

Thurmaier, Kurt and Curtis H. Wood. 2002. "Interlocal Agreements as Overlapping Social Networks: Picket-Fence Regionalism in Metropolitan Kansas City." *Public Administration Review* 62(5): 585–98.

Tiebout, Charles M. 1956. "A Pure Theory of Local Expenditures." *Journal of Political Economy* 64(5): 416–24.

United States Advisory Commission on Intergovernmental Relations (U.S. ACIR). 1985. *Intergovernmental Service Arrangements for Delivering Local Public Services: Update 1983*. Washington, DC: United States Government Printing Office.

Veenswijk, Marcel, ed. 2005. *Organizing Innovation: New Approaches to Cultural Change and Intervention in Public Sector Organizations*. Amsterdam: IOS Press.

Wilson, David and Chris Game. 2006. *Local Government in the United Kingdom*. 4th ed. Houndmills: Palgrave.

Wollmann, Hellmut. 2000a. "Comparing Institutional Development in Britain and Germany." In Hellmut Wollmann and Eckhard Schröter, eds., *Comparing Public Sector Reform in Britain and Germany*. Aldershot: Ashgate.

Wollmann, Hellmut. 2000b. "Local Government Modernisation in Germany between Incrementalism and Reform Waves." *Public Administration* 78(4): 915–36.

Wollmann, Hellmut. 2003. "Evaluation of Public Sector Reforms: Trend, Potentials and Limits in International Perspective." In Hellmut Wollmann, ed., *Evaluation in Public-Sector Reform*. Cheltenham: Edward Elgar.

Wollmann, Hellmut. 2004a. "Local Government Reforms in Great Britain, Sweden, France and Germany, between Multi-Function and Single-Purpose Organisation." *Local Government Studies* 30(4): 639–65.

Wollmann, Hellmut. 2004b. "Urban Leadership in German Local Politics: The Rise, Role and Performance of the Directly Elected (Chief Executive) Mayor." *International Journal of Urban and Regional Research* 28(1): 150–65.

Wollmann, Hellmut. 2007. "Changes, Ruptures and Continuities in European Local Government Systems." In Fred Lazin, Matt Evans, Vincent Hoffmann-Martinot, and Hellmut Wollmann, eds., *Local Government Reforms in Countries in Transition*. Lanham, MD: Rowman & Littlefield.

Wollmann, Hellmut. 2008a. "Comparing Local Government Reforms in England, Sweden, France and Germany." *Wüstenrot Stiftung*. www.wuestenrot-stiftung.de/download/local-government (accessed 2010).

Wollmann, Hellmut. 2008b. *Reformen in Kommunalpolitik und –verwaltung. England, Schweden, Frankreich und Deutschland im Vergleich*. Wiesbaden: VS Verlag.

Wollmann, Hellmut. 2008c. "Reforming Local Leadership and Local Democracy: The Cases of England, Sweden Germany and France in Comparative Perspective." *Local Government Studies* 34(2): 279–95.

Wollmann, Hellmut. 2009. "The Ascent of the Directly Elected Mayor in European Local Government in West and East." In Herwig Reynaert, Kristof Steyrers, Pascal Delwit, and Jean-Benoit Pilet, eds., *Local Political Leadership in Europe*. Brugge: Vanden Broele.

Wollmann, Hellmut. 2010. "Comparing Two Logics of Interlocal Cooperation: The Cases of France and Germany." *Urban Affairs Review* 46(2): 263–92.

Wollmann, Hellmut, Harald Baldersheim, Gérard Marcou, Giulio Citroni, and John McEldowney. 2010. "From Public Service to Commodity: The Demunicipalizsation (or Remunicipalization?) of Energy Provision in Germany, Italy, France, the U.K. and Norway." In Hellmut Wollmann and Gérard Marcou, eds., *The Provision of Public Services in Europe: Between State, Local Government and Market*. Cheltenham: Edward Elgar.

Wollmann, Hellmut and Gérard Marcou, eds. 2010a. *The Provision of Public Services in Europe: Between State, Local Government and Market*. Cheltenham: Edward Elgar.

Wollmann, Hellmut and Gérard Marcou. 2010b. "From Public Sector Based to 'Privatised' Service Provision: Is the Pendulum Swinging Back Again?" In Hellmut Wollmann and Gérard Marcou, eds., *The Provision of Public Services in Europe: Between State, Local Government and Market*. Cheltenham: Edward Elgar.

Wood, Curtis H. 2006. "Scope and Patterns of Metropolitan Governance in Urban America." *American Review of Public Administration* 36(3): 337–53.

CHAPTER 11

A PLACE TO PARTY?: PARTIES AND NONPARTISANSHIP IN LOCAL GOVERNMENT

COLIN COPUS, MELVIN WINGFIELD, KRISTOF STEYVERS, AND HERWIG REYNAERT

1. Introduction

Two notions of local government have been in constant competition. The first is of a nonpartisan, politically neutral local government, dedicated to the common good and seeking rational and technical solutions to public service issues from which political partisanship simply distracts (see Fallend, Ignits, and Swianiewicz 2006). The second notion is of local government as a place where wider national party battles are fought and refought and where ideological concerns and party interest dominate decision-making (see Hennock 1973, Owen 1982). Schattschneider (1942) maintained that "modern democracy is unthinkable save in terms of political parties"; Lapalombara and Anderson (1992: 393) argue "It is not simply that parties are central to elections and to policy making, or that they make or break governments.... Under their aegis, mass publics are mobilised...political systems of every conceivable variety seem unable to function without one or more political party."

Sections of this chapter result from recent research funded by grant F/094/AP "Small parties: Influence and effect on democratic engagement and local politics" from the Leverhulme Trust. The authors gratefully acknowledge this support and assistance.

More recently, Montero and Gunther (2002: 2f.) added that "parties have always been... absolutely essential for the proper functioning of representative democracy." That logic does not stop at national government and has found reflection in debates about local government throughout the 19th and 20th centuries resulting in national parties coming to control the localities, bringing with them highly partisan modes of governing, particularly in Europe (Jones 1969, Newton 1976, Green 1981).

In this chapter we explore which of the two visions—nonpartisan, neutral, and technocratic, or partisan, partial, and ideological—provides the model for most local government.

Nonpartisan local government has been prevalent in the U.S. for the past century since the era of Progressive reform, although both partisan and nonpartisan governments can be found there. Indeed, Ferreira and Gyourko (2009: 421) conclude that national and state elections differ from local elections, in part, due to the absence of strong partisanship which itself was facilitated by homogenous social groupings. Historically, we find a different story in large cities. When it comes to the partisan nature of local politics, the U.S., for some time, followed and often led party politicization when compared to Europe. Indeed, machine politics had an easier time developing at the municipal level in the U.S. than nationally and was subject to detailed excoriation as early as the turn of the 19th century by Ostrogorski (1902). His praise of the Independent Republican and reform minded "Mugwumps" and Independent municipal reformers (1902: 481) for improving the state of U.S. local government did not mean the end of machine politics, which lasted well into the 20th century (see for an example, Royko 1971). The Democratic Party's Tammany Hall machine, which had a stranglehold on the politics of New York for almost 80 years, became a watchword for party-based political corruption and cronyism (Allen 1993, Finegold 1995, Burrows and Wallace 1999). The Progressives—municipal reformers—aimed to remove national party politics from American local elections and over time U.S. local politics has seen a radical shift with nonpartisanship becoming widespread, if not the norm (see Hofstadter 1955, DeSantis and Renner 1991). Contemporary U.S. local politics distinguishes itself from those European countries where national political parties dominate local government, and the details of these differences in the U.S. are discussed further by Clark and Krebs in their contribution to this volume.

But, partisanship is changing at the local level in Europe as well, with the emergence of local parties and nonpartisanship in some cases. But, do nonpartisan elections and politics simply mean a disguising of national party allegiances (much as in Europe during the 19th and early 20th centuries) and an adoption by nonpartisan groups of a shape and form to their politics that is barely distinguishable from the national parties they eschew? Indeed, we question, given the strength and depth of national party penetration into the localities, whether nonpartisan local government can survive in an urban setting in Europe. To elaborate our arguments and provide illuminating examples of the dynamics and effects of partisan and nonpartisan politics in the localities, we take two contrasting but representative cases in contemporary Europe from which we generalize (see Wollmann 2006): England, where rapid industrialization and urbanization resulted in large, professionalized, service-oriented, welfare-based local government, circumscribed by national government and the *ultra vires* principle; and, Belgium, where local government was late to nationalization (and only partially so) and where it has been characterized by fragmented territorial organization, laymen rule, and the principle of local self-government, with few functions and discretion compensated for by direct access to central power, via party networks and dual mandate holding. The contrasting local electoral systems with a first-past-the-post majoritarian, multimember ward system closely associated with two (and a half) parties in England, and in Belgium semiopen lists for at-large elections producing a segmented multiparty system (Van der Kolk 2007), provide a further distinction from which to explore the party politicization of urban politics.

Local government across much of contemporary Europe and the U.S. has long been a place where national parties seek power (see Hjellum 1967). National parties have had a long and complex relationship with local government and have been, in one guise or another, a permanent feature of the local political landscape. Indeed, the political practices of national parties have long set the tone for the conduct of local politics showing the extent to which it can be seen as having been nationalized (Gyford 1985. The nationalization of local politics is however a process which Hansen and Rose (2007) rightly separate from a solely electoral dynamic and note that the relative strength of parties in different council areas has an impact on the longer-term character of local democracy. The impact of party politics in an urban setting is seen less on the level of electoral participation and more in how it influences the conduct of local politics, the engagement of the public in a wide range of nonelectoral political activities, and how councils' service-providing role speeds the nationalization process by responding to calls for national standards of local public services (Hansen and Rose 2007).

Despite the strength of national parties in local government, they face competition from small and local parties and independent candidates (Holtmann 2008, Rieser and Holtmann 2008). Parties must coexist in a messy local political dynamic where they are one player among many, with some not sharing the party rules of the game and displaying varying levels of organizational coherence or shape. A complex dynamic exists between local politics structured, organized, and conducted by national parties in the contest for control of local government and an array of smaller parties and independent local politicians, challenging major party dominance. There is a nonpartisan and smaller party dimension to European local politics that provides an alternative vehicle for political engagement and which can signal discontent to the local political elite, recruited through the national parties.

There are compelling and interesting reasons for using the English and Belgium cases to elaborate our discussion: a differing constitutional model for local government, contrasting electoral systems, the gradual prospect that the UK will move to a Belgium solution to its internal national tensions, particularly when the English get fed up with an unbalanced political system. Despite these differences, national parties play a powerful role in local politics, meaning considerable benefits arise from studying these distinctive nations to understand why that may be the case as they throw light on the partisan nature of much of urban politics and help identify where the pockets of nonpartisan resistance may exist. Also, much of the research on local party and nonpartisan politics is context specific and located within a nation's local political system. Therefore, by examining in some detail our two exempla nations we can illuminate the experiences and practices of party politics in more general terms.

Section 2 of this chapter sets the party political context within which local politics operates and surveys the ground where nonpartisan alternatives or smaller parties must exist. Section 3.1 examines the way parties organize to conduct council business and the politics of the locality. Section 3.2 looks at the range of political alternatives to the main parties and examines their contribution to and the implications for local politics. It does this by considering only those that take part in electoral politics and provide a representative alternative to the main parties in local government. The conclusion draws out the lessons from party controlled local government and what challengers to the main parties can offer the localities.

2. Local Government and the Emergence of Party

National political parties have had to cope with different historical, constitutional, social, economic, and political forces and trends in their rise to prominence in their respective local governments. That process was, as a result of different national settings, an uneven one which in some countries like England and Norway has resulted in a comprehensive control of local politics by the national parties (see Aars and Offerdal 1998, Denters and Rose 2005); yet, in others the process has resulted in less comprehensive control by parties, but with parties still holding a dominance across the system (Dewachter 1994). Even though parties dominate local government, local conditions have a role to play in how each party will fare within any given locality (Midtbo and Stromsnes, 1996, Hansen and Rose 2007). While we have compelling evidence from across Europe that local factors matter, it appears that it now really only matters to the fortunes of the main parties in competition with each other and less about whether some other players will provide effective competition to the main parties, which they can do in limited circumstances (see, Kjear and Jorgen 2010).

The first municipal elections in England of December 1835 (after 1835 Municipal Corporations Act) and even the campaigns for incorporation under the Act were local party political battles (Fraser 1979). The emergence of local democratic institutions reflected a series of debates and concerns which made the newly formed 19th century councils ready-made battlegrounds for national party disputes (see Chandler 2007). Indeed, early Victorian fears of a majority turning political institutions against the property owners drove concerns about wholesale involvement in local government as it did for the Founding Fathers of American national democracy (see Beloff 1948). A system of local representation was needed to reconcile popular democracy with the protection of property rights. The system also needed to guarantee that elected local elites would be drawn from property owners and be supporters of the then two main national parties: the Conservatives or Liberals; a trick which national representative democracy and government had been able to pull (see Beloff 1948, Crick 1982, Held 1993, Tocqueville 1994). Local government was to be ratepayer rather than representative in nature and would ensure property could not be threatened by municipalization and local redistributionary policies (Soldon 1974, Gyford 1986, Young 1989, Davis 1989, Gillespie 1989). Moreover, the 19th century development of the local government franchise ensured that voters and candidates fulfilled property qualifications (see Keith-Lucas 1952 and Hennock 1973).

Gyford (1985) identified five stages of party politicization (in English local government): *diversity* (1835–65), *crystallization* (1865–1905), *realignment* (1905–45), *nationalization* (1945–74), and *reappraisal* (1974–). Through these stages national parties took increasing interest in local government and a stable two-party system emerged in English local government, which reflected the national party contest (Gyford 1976: 125–32). Nationalization was a party process and meant a reciprocal acknowledgment by key political actors of the benefits of assimilating local with national party concerns. *Reappraisal* from 1974 involved a further escalation in the spread of party politics and the development, at different times by the three main parties, of codified and uncodified means of ensuring councillors conducted their business fully cognizant of their role in a national party. While policy autonomy suggests a *stratarchic* party relationship, behavioral and organizational requirements show parties, in English local government, as monolithic. Rokkan (1966) also referred to the politicization of local government as a process where national parties enter local elections and disturb and distort the existing local political dynamic, transforming it into a system which reflects national rather than local political rule. Thus, gradual politicization of local government finds echoes across Europe and in countries such as Portugal, Germany, and Spain (see De Almeida 2008, Sweeting 2009, and Vetter 2009) where despite different contextual factors, party presence in local government and the conduct of local politics is remarkably similar. What we find across Europe is parties not just nationalizing their own local government but organizing and behaving in ways that cut across national boundaries. A councillor in England would find little to surprise him if he should wake to find himself a councillor in Spain and—language to one side—could quite happily get on with the job of pursuing party interest in the local setting.

National party domination of local government and the increase in central party control over local parties and councillors means we can conclude that *reappraisal* is at an end; English local government has now fully entered a period of *partisanship*, After the May 2010 English local elections the three main political parties held 16,825, or just over 92 percent of all English council seats; they regularly take over 90 percent of all council seats in England (Rallings and Thrasher 2007) and this striking penetration into English council chambers means that councillors take with them attitudes, approaches, and party interactions that have resulted in the importation of Westminster style politics into local government. Party control of seats and councils and councillor attitudes toward their role as a national party member and they conduct of council business, are good measures of the *partisan* nature of local government. It is a pattern replicated across Europe where we see national parties dominating candidacy, vote share, and seats won (Goldsmith and Page 2010, *passim*). Moreover, in places like France and Italy we see party control of local government being institutionalized by the award of a "winners" seat supplement to strengthen the position of the mayor (Fabbrini 2000, Hoffmann-Martinot 2003).

In Belgium the 19th century introduction of local representative democracy reflected the success of political parties at the national level but driven by the development of the local electoral system and its wider effect on parties in the century following Belgian independence (i.e. 1830–1920). Two fundamental shifts occurred: first, from property qualifications for the franchise to universal suffrage; and, second, the introduction of proportional voting as an alternative to the majoritarian system (Witte 1994). Local government was used as a laboratory for political experiments (with localities serving as safe havens for progressive reforms of which potentially "damaging effects" on the national order would be limited to the local) as well as a mechanism for balance—to countervail reforms at the national level considered quite progressive to ensure conservatives had a firm local power base. Such tendencies interacted with the contrasts between urban localities (where liberalism and later socialism dominated) and their rural counterparts (dominated by conservative, catholic forces). Hence, shifts in the local electoral system reflected national party power struggles played out, over time, in the localities (see, D'Hoore 1994, Vanschoenbeek 1994, Pasture 1994).

In Belgium the regional local party systems should be distinguished (Wayenberg et al. 2011). Paralleling the evolution from a unitary to a federal state, traditional national parties have split since the 1970s into Flemish and Walloon chapters and newcomers (such as the Greens) have followed this pattern. The nationalization of the local party system can be discerned in the second half of the 20th century, albeit later and less comprehensive than in the English case (see table 1). When England commenced the phase of partisan reappraisal in the 1970s, nationalization of the Belgium local party system had just started. The municipal landscape was highly fragmented in terms of territory and inhabitants. As an example of the so-called Franco group of countries (Hesse and Sharpe 1991), until the 1970s Belgium had a multitude of small municipalities (more than 2,500) with few inhabitants (averaging a bit more than 4,000). Second, and conjointly, these municipalities had relatively few functions (Sellers and Lidström 2007). Whereas a collectivist consensus comparable to the English case did emerge in the Belgium of that era, the main welfare state functions were carried out by central government or the third sector (due to societal pillarization).

In these small, relatively homogenous local polities with limited functions national parties were either not viable and/or of little political meaning. Consequently, until 1970 Belgian municipalities were characterized by uncontested elections (Dewachter 1994). Similarly, in some of the smaller German municipalities, national parties abdicate political space to independent voter lists (see, Gohlert et al. 2008). The Belgium local elections of 1976, after the number of municipalities was reduced to 589 national parties, became more prevalent in local government (De Ceuninck et al. 2010). Suddenly, national parties found fertile local ground and although structural reform was not followed by extensive decentralization the political stakes were much higher.

Kjear and Jorgen (2010) have argued that increased municipal size is one of the determinants of the nationalization of local politics as parties see a point to controlling large, political powerful municipalities. In the Flemish region, the Christian-Democrats have traditionally been the most successful national party at the local level with the socialists coming second and liberals, third. In Wallonia, socialists and Christian-Democrats swap places locally but the liberals still remain in third place locally. Such averages of course mask variation over time and divergence between municipalities (Wille and Deschouwer 2007). But, there is now a much stronger national feel to local politics in Belgium than has previously been the case (Steyvers and Reynaert 2010).

There are parallels in our discussion so far with the U.S. experience of party politics in local government. Indeed, the Founding Fathers, at various times, grappled with two worrying concerns: how big the democratic element of the American republic should be and the damaging effects of factions (parties) on the body politic (Beloff 1948). These latter fears proved well founded as machine-based politics gripped the urban municipal landscape, with party machines exchanging favors for the continual electoral support of individuals and blocs of voters (Guterbock 1980, Brown and Halaby 1987, Finegold 1995). Brown and Halaby (1987) identify machine politics declining during the 1970s and 1980s, at just the time, in England, when local party politics was developing in intensity and ideological passion.

3. Partisan Local Government

3.1. The Effects of National Party Politics on Local Government and Representation

The debate continues as to whether the presence of national parties in local government has a damaging effect on local democracy, public engagement, and open debate, or whether national party involvement strengthens political leadership and accountability. The debate is conducted in the knowledge that the electorate has an ambivalent attitude toward party involvement in local government (Young and Rao 1995). In addition, distaste of party political intrusion into council affairs has been blamed for deterring well qualified potential candidates from seeking local office and for subjugating the needs of the community to the needs of the party (Clements

1969, Committee on the Management of Local Government 1967). But, parties represent their supporters' interests and merge the national and local political battle fought between the parties, but do so, across Europe, at a cost of marginalizing nonpartisan groups (see Jones 1969, Kerrouche 2005).

Case studies show that national parties in England are a long-standing feature of local government and they conduct local politics by adopting the adversarial nature of national party interaction (Bealey et al. 1965, Jones 1969, Saunders 1979, Dearlove 1973 Glassberg 1981, Green 1981). They also show that rurality is no guarantee against the worst excesses of party political behavior and over time, parties can change the nature of the rural political landscape (Birch 1959, Stacey 1960, Lee 1963). Parties as a principal feature of liberal democracy permeate the local level to become the primary bodies through which local views, preferences, and needs are articulated and promoted, to such an extent that the key political relationship is not between the councillor and the community but between the party group and the council leader (Meny 1992, Leach and Wilson 2000).

Partisan and adversarial local politics is ensured when parties act as unified and disciplined blocs of councillors—speaking and voting as one on issues decided before formal council meetings. To add to this partisanship, national parties often produce rules setting out the way councillors should behave and the disciplinary procedures and sanctions available to the party to ensure councillors follow the line. But councillors are loyal to their parties not just because the rules say so, but also because they agree with them and where they do not, their long-standing membership and unwillingness to provide opposition groups with evidence of a party split outweigh their discontent. It is the rigidity of the boundaries that party groups place between themselves that is the key factor in understanding the nature of partisanship in local government.

It is the party rather than the citizen that is the focus of councillors' attention and it is the party that the councillor represents. Parties develop a partisan based assessment of the local common good, which is linked to a broad ideological frame and which is secured by pursuing party advancement. In our two exemplar countries and across Europe we find different reasons for the same outcome in local government: party discipline is tight and parties are the ultimate frame of reference and loyalty for the councillor (Sweeting 2009, for the Spanish example). What exists at the local level is less a democracy and more a *partyocracy* (Dewinter and Dumont 2006). The local partyocracy can manifest itself through access, by councillors to the center. In the southern local government tradition such access is frequent and direct, often by means of dual mandate holding (Ackaert, De Ceuninck, et al. 2007). In the Belgian Parliament around four-fifths of MPs are also councillors and about a third hold local executive office. Such a *cumul des mandats* has a twofold effect. First, it is a mechanism for patronage and interest mediation: local officeholders with a direct link to the center serve as a broker for their municipality through a series of informal networks. Second, local officeholders with national links have more resources to assist citizens with problems. Such a clientelist approach is not without advantages in terms of personal votes. Also, parties recruit candidates for parliamentary elections that are embedded locally and so strengthen the parties electoral standing (Ackaert 1994).Yet, what parties at the local level consider as important during local elections largely corresponds to their national identity and profile. In Belgium, for example, Christian-Democrats attach much importance to the third sector and associational life; Socialists emphasize social affairs; and, Liberals favor trade, economy, and tax politics; although some pragmatism in the localities still remains, local politics is largely nationalized (Buelens et al. 2008).

Despite the control of local government that national parties have developed, a common trend across Europe is for parties to experience a declining resource base as well as facing competition from single-issue groups (see Lapalombara and Anderson 1992, Schmitt and Holmberg 1995 Game and Leach 1996, Deschouwer and Rihoux 2008). Indeed, since the 1990s, there has been a recognition of the disconnection between parties and local citizens linked to the notion that parties are organizations in decline (see Montero and Gunther 2002, Blyth and Katz 2005: 40, Seyd and Whiteley 2004: 358, Ackaert, De Ceuninck, et al. 2007). Measures have been proposed across Europe to close this gap by giving citizens a more direct say in local matters through the direct election of the mayor, a more proportional voting system, the introduction of mechanisms for public participation, and prohibition of forms of accumulating mandates. Despite the weakening of their position, parties still dominate local government and continue to conduct its business as though their legitimacy remained unchallenged. Through the domination of council seats, and a conflation of local and national political processes and interests, parties have squeezed out of the local political arena diversity of practice and form. National parties have a homogenizing effect on local politics. Thus, it is outside the walls of those parties that we must look if we wish to observe expressions of the rich, deep, and diverse local political environment that still survives.

3.2. The Alternative to Mainstream Party Politics

Small party and independent politics in local government had been largely ignored since Grant (1971: 204 and see 1973) identified the importance of local conditions to political mobilization. Such local conditions can transcend voters' national political affiliation as they are not catered for by the left-right division of the national political parties and so require different organizational outlets locally. There has recently been a growing interest in the study of independents, nonpartisan groupings, and small parties in local government, which reflects the fertile ground local politics provides for alternatives to the main political parties (Reiser and Holtmann 2008).

There has been a flourishing of local bodies confronting the major parties in local contests; many of these bodies display their local roots by including the name of the locality in their titles, such as the Better Bedford Party, Doncaster First Party, Boston By-Pass Party, the Camberwell Party, Canvey Island Independent Party, or the Devizes Guardians. These were formed with the aim of contesting elections within a council area only, but can still be defined as a *political group identified by an official label that presents at elections and is capable of placing through elections (free or not free) candidates for public office* and which formulates comprehensive policies (see Sartori 1976: 52–59; see also Mair 1989, Katz and Mair 1995, Blyth and Katz 2005). Moreover such local parties are formed with the specific intention of engaging in electoral politics and this is a defining characteristic of the local party.

Other nonparty organizations, such as residents or tenants associations, local community groups, or single-issue groups, stimulated by local conditions or issues also present themselves for local election (see Boogers 2008). These *political associations* can be distinguished from local parties because they were originally formed for a purpose other than to enter the local electoral fray. But, local political circumstances, prominent local issues, and the failure of the main parties to adequately deal with, or respond to, these concerns leaves them with no alternative but to contest local elections (Copus, Clark, and Bottom 2008: 262–64). Such bodies are a coming together of a group of people who combine to produce a jointly declared and loose aggregation of shared ideas, notions, and intentions, with a confederal relationship between the architecture and objectives of the organization and its members: they are indeed, associations but ones which adopt a local political purpose: *political associations*.

Of the 1,380 councillors in England that, after the May 2010 elections were not from the three parties, 84 were from eight small political parties. In addition, there were some 110 Greens, but as the Greens now have their first MP they have distinguished themselves from other small parties in England. The British National Party (BNP) has the second largest haul of small party seats, but those were reduced from 57 to 28 after the 2010 elections (not all English councils have elections each year and some councils elect only a third of councillors at an election). Copus et al. (2008) argue that small national parties conduct council business in broadly similar ways to the main parties, that is cohering in disciplined blocs—no matter what their size—and rarely, if ever speaking or voting with councillors from other parties. Indeed, they readily accept the role of a representative as one who has a considerable degree of freedom from the voter, is not bound by instructions from constituents, and pursues the policies of the party. Smaller parties accept the logic and language of partisanship and are prepared to act accordingly.

In seeking an alternative approach to local politics we are left with those councillors that eschew party and stand as independents or as candidates of *political associations* and it is here that we find a greater variation in the conduct of local politics from the national parties. Independents present themselves as antidotes to national parties and deliberately eschew, in some cases, any form of organization—linking organizational coherence to the way political parties act in local government. Independent councillors fall into four broad categories (Copus et al. 2008): the *fully independent*, that is, the candidate/councillor that has no organization behind him or her, save a group of friends, family, and well-wishers who do nothing more than conduct electioneering and expect, nor demand, any say over the campaign. Once elected, the supporters expect no influence over what the councillor does. The *fully independent* councillor decides each issue without formally consulting other councillors (although informal discussions and interactions will no doubt occur).

In addition to Grant's (1971) *concealed* Conservative, we have the *revealed party-independent*: the candidate who places "independent" before the label of a national political party. The emergence of such candidates often comes from an internal local party dispute or reselection battle. If deselected as party candidate they stand against their former party, but display their political sympathies by referring to it in their candidacy. Next we find the *situational* independent, whose political predilections are to operate, as far as possible as an independent, but, when circumstances dictate, are prepared to work alongside other councillors—including those from political parties—but that cooperation is driven by issues and circumstances rather than a broad need to join with other councillors. Finally, we have the *conjoined independent*. Here, an local independent political organization exists and acts as a loose coordinating body, with the resources to secure the return of independent candidates. Once elected, the *conjoined independents* form a group, which meets to discuss policy, and may or may not make decisions about how to act in council meetings; they may indeed employ some loose disciplinary mechanisms to ensure councillors go along with the policies and decisions of the independent group. *Conjoined independents* can be further subdivided into weakly and strongly conjoined, depending on the nature and level of interaction they have with other independent councillors (see Bottom and Copus 2011).

There is a range of political behavior displayed by independents which shows they are able to operate in ways that vary from the rigid organization of the main parties. But, independents can also display similar organizational characteristics to the parties they eschew. *Political associations* also adopt a range of approaches to council business. Single-issue groups and groups such as residents associations have displayed both a coherent approach to council business and also more fissiparous tendencies which have seen groups experience divisions and councillors leaving to form new council blocs—such as with the Boston By-Pass Party.

We see among independents and *political association* councillors a greater willingness than their party counterparts to put the needs of their wards above the council as a whole and a greater willingness to demur from the decisions of a group and act accordingly. Indeed, nonpartisan councillors consistently display stronger localist tendencies than their party counterparts (see Reiser 2008, Boogers and Voerman 2010a, Boogers and Carter 2010b). Interest aggregation for the party councillor is ideologically or party political and relies on meeting the perceived needs of a broadly perceived constituency. Interest aggregation for the nonpartisan councillor is driven by the needs of a locality and the need to pursue and promote an issue-based politics not a broad ideological position.

It is clear that independents and *political associations* can provide a different approach to local politics than the national parties, alternative sources of local political leadership, a different recruitment route, and act as a conduit between the voters and the council. Indeed, independents strive to develop an apolitical agenda which allows them to distance themselves from national parties (Aars and Rinkjob

2005). By being free from any national political perspective and objective such councillors can and indeed are local representatives of a type rarely found in political parties—even among Liberal Democrats who pride themselves on community politics (see Copus 2007). Given this conclusion, it is all the more surprising, that across English local government, such alternatives to the mainstream parties are largely rejected at the polls (Copus et al. 2008).

Since the municipal reformers in the U.S. managed to see off the worse excesses of the machine politics typified by the Tammany Hall regime, a new period of nonpartisan local politics has emerged. Much of the drive for that nonpartisanship was to bring business-like approaches to local government and to raise the caliber of councillors—a debate not unfamiliar to the European discourse. The way to achieve these things was through a weakening, or even removal, of party politics from the local arena. Indeed, the expression: "there being no Republican way to pave a street and no Democratic way to lay a sewer" (Adrian 1952: 766, Northup 1987: 1679) has a direct parallel in the English expression: "there is no Socialist or Conservative way to dig a ditch." But, of course, there is a Republican and Democratic, Socialist and Conservative view about how many of these things there are, who builds them, who maintains them, where they are and who pays for them. Nonpartisan politicians still have to solve contentious local political issues and make overtly political decisions—if not for party political reasons. Nonpartisan elections may weaken parties—except, of course, that candidates may disguise their party allegiances—but, it appears that nonpartisanship strengthens the position of the incumbent local politician, not because of good stewardship of the local office, but because of a recognition by voters of name alone (Schaffner et al. 2001).

But very broadly we find similar tendencies among nonpartisans in the U.S. as we do in Europe: a desire to bring a new form of politics to bear on the government of the localities; a policy profile that does not match a firm ideological frame of reference; a belief in harmonic/factual politics; a localist perspective about where political power and decision-making should rest; and, a more fissiparous tendency when it comes to council meetings and speaking and voting—if you present yourself as the antidote to party politics, bloc voting and speaking with one voice must be the first causality of your approach to politics.

Electoral systems matter for the nonpartisan candidate, and countries employing the list system for local elections have seen alternatives to the main parties fragmenting the local political arena. But, the list system implies a gathering of political candidates for local elections; hence, single independent candidates are exceptional. Candidates adhere to an organization that resembles a political party, albeit often only as an electoral machine. Second, the proportional electoral formula and municipal-wide election lower the threshold for electoral success and trigger the emergence of alternatives to the main parties in a way that the first-past-the-post system cannot (Steyvers and Reynaert 2010).

Two main categories of nontraditional parties may be discerned at the local level where the list system operates. The first comprises of alternative national parties. If we look at Belgium as an example we see that a group of regionalist parties have emerged—which have been particularly strong in Flanders and weak at the local level in Wallonia. In Flanders, the regionalist VU was present in approximately 60 percent of all municipalities, winning an average 15 percent of the vote. From the 1990s onward, the party's presence in municipal elections almost halved and lists were presented only where electoral success seemed guaranteed. The formation of electoral cartels with other parties or using a local name (see below) was often seen as an alternative (Sebberechts 1994). As the VU disintegrated, the N-VA as one of its successors followed a similar path. Regionalist parties can become a victim of their own success at the national level either determining or at least influencing a political agenda and program of reform implicating them in a governing agenda. But, such parties can lose their monopoly as the sole alternative to national parties and themselves fall victim to more localist alternatives.

Two other such newcomers started to penetrate the Belgium party system in the late 1980s: the Greens and the far right (Walgrave 1994) (see table 1). In Flanders, the Vlaams Blok (later Vlaams Belang) is not far behind Agelev (later on Groen!) in terms of electoral strength. Whereas the Greens have never reached double digits where they presented municipal lists, the far right has become an established force at the local level. This is not the case in Wallonia, where the Greens, since 2000, score consistently and above the 10 percent threshold and the far right faces more difficulties embedding itself locally (Ackaert, Reynaert, et al. 2007).

These newcomers bring different policies and politics to the local level, but often do so in accordance with their national profile. The Greens favor environmentalism, participatory democracy, and developmental aid. The far right emphasize safety and immigration (Buelens et al. 2008). Hence, the emergence of these alternatives to the main parties is in fact an extension of the nationalization of the local party system.

Even when looking at what may at first sight appear to be a local list care is needed as such lists can be used to disguise national affiliations (Deschouwer 1996). There are lists however that do not bear a national party name and/or number and appear in the shape of genuine local parties, single-issue movements, or constituencies of independents (Steyvers et al. 2008, Gohlert et al. 2008). For example, in three out of four Belgium municipalities local lists are presented in the preelectoral configuration. Moreover and depending on the region considered, one out of every four (Walloon) or five (Flemish) voters seems to entrust genuinely local lists with their vote. Indeed, when present electorally, they are often successful and when successful their chances increase for being included in ruling coalitions or with an overall majority (Steyvers et al. 2009).

Organizationally, genuine local lists are more loosely structured, less ideologically driven, and oriented toward (often against) issues of municipal development; they are less affected by the dominant transformations in the patterns of descriptive representation at the local level (feminization, professionalization, and rejuvenation) probably referring to a more static power structure in which they are successful. Local lists, independents and councillors from political associations have a specific profile suggesting that they indeed lead to a different and distinct type of

Table 1. Penetration and Share of Parties/Lists in Belgian Local Elections 1976–2006

Flanders	Electoral year											
	1976		1982		1988		1994		2000		2006	
Party/list	%M	%V	%M	%V	%M	%V	%M	%V	%M	%V	%M	%V
Christian Democrat	91.9	42.8	92.5	37.6	92.5	37	83.4	36.4	85.1	30.6	88.0	33.7
Socialist	84.4	21.3	86.7	21.6	85.7	21.1	73.4	19.6	71.4	18.5	56.5	21.2
Liberal	54.9	16.3	65.9	16.1	71.1	17.6	77.9	20.3	81.2	24.3	74.4	19.4
Regionalist	57.8	14.7	60.7	14.6	56.5	11.7	35.4	9.1	41.6	8.8	13.3	7.5
Green	–	–	25.3	6.2	48.7	6.9	52.2	8.2	62.0	8.4	36.0	7.0
Extreme right	–	–	7.8	2.5	16.6	6.1	42.5	10.3	58.8	13.4	72.1	17.1
Local	72.1	20.5	71.1	18.6	68.8	17.4	77.6	21.0	63.9	17.3	87.0	19.1

Wallonia	Electoral year											
	1976		1982		1988		1994		2000		2006	
Party/list	%M	%V	%M	%V	%M	%V	%M	%V	%M	%V	%M	%V
Christian Democrat	66.8	28.3	60.7	27.8	59.9	27.8	73.7	27.3	71.4	22.5	48.1	26.3
Socialist	74.8	41.8	76.3	41.3	76.7	43.3	77.9	37.8	75.2	38.5	53.1	35.7
Liberal	40.8	16.8	46.2	22.2	45.8	21.9	62.2	21.1	66.4	23.7	48.1	22.8
Green	0.8	2.1	28.6	7.2	32.4	8.5	50.8	8.5	71.0	12.1	51.5	10.6
Extreme right	–	–	1.1	1.4	3.1	1.9	17.2	7.9	8.4	4.1	9.2	8.1
Local	82.4	28.2	–	–	84.0	28.5	82.1	21.7	69.8	24.7	76.3	22.9

%M = percentage of municipalities where the list considered contested local elections under (national) name/number%V = percentage of votes the list considered collected in municipalities where it contested local elections.

local politics and policies that are not based on the ideological certainties of national parties, nor on the need to pursue national party interests. Some of the characteristics of nonpartisan local politicians link with the classic notion of local government as nonpartisan, politically neutral, and dedicated to a nonideological local common good mentioned in the introduction.

4. Conclusions

When candidates of national political parties are elected to councils they bring with them a set of preconceptions about the nature of political exchanges and decision-making. They also share—despite party label—a set of interpretations of key political concepts such as democracy, accountability, representation, about the role of parties in local government and the nature of nonpartisan politics. National parties set the tone, context, and working practices of councils and local politics and generate a set of behavioral expectations of councillor activity. National parties in local government focus far more on governing the locality and representing the party than offering channels for citizen opinion into council decision-making process. Indeed, party domination of local government has strengthened over time and has occurred despite very real differences between systems of local government, its constitutional status, electoral systems used and despite the differing avenues and opportunities for nonpartisans to be elected locally.

Parties conduct local politics and council business in very similar ways, wherever they are based. While it may be that large, urban councils are more attractive to national parties—because of the resources and power that such councils have—smaller and more rural areas are not completely isolated from party politics and the practices and approaches they bring with them. Parties have the effect of nationalizing local government not only because they bring national concerns to the local setting, but also because they also organize and behave in ways that cut across national boundaries, making party practices, organizational form, party interactions, and councillor loyalty familiar territory for the councillor wherever he is located.

The defining characteristic of party presence in local government is the loyalty that councillors—across the spectrum—willingly grant to their party—over and above that which they give to their voters and the cohesive and disciplined approach to local politics that comes in its wake. Party loyalty is generated by different factors such as: party rules, ideological beliefs, a predisposition to support the party; the comfort gleaned from the mutual support enjoyed by colleagues bound together by membership of a national party; and a degree of fear at the political and social consequences of publicly dissenting from the party. Parties are strong in local government because of the loyalty councillors grant to them. Parties are not however, strong, robust organizations when it comes to civil society where they are seen as little more than electoral machines, which many citizens do not wish to join (see Aars and Ringkjøb 2005, Whiteley 2008).

The lack of deep roots national parties have within the communities they represent and govern locally means they are vulnerable to challenges from smaller parties and from nonpartisan contenders for local council office. It is clear that the electoral system—list or first-past-the-post—has an impact on not only the success rate of the nonpartisan alternative to the main national parties in local government, but also on the way they organize. But, even without the centripetal force of the list system, nonpartisans may cohere to varying degrees in council, partly because the only model of politics in town is that presented by the parties and partly because organization and coherence enhance the likelihood of success in votes if not debate. Yet, nonpartisan alternatives to national parties offer an opportunity for a different style and approach to local politics and provide the chance for councillors to respond to purely local political stimulus, unhindered by a national political or ideological frame of reference.

We asked in the introduction if nonpartisan politics could survive, particularly in an urban setting: we find that it can, but it is under constant pressure from national parties and the practices they bring with them into local government. Moreover, nonpartisans exist in a local government largely dominated by national parties who have shaped the form and processes of local politics. Yet, not only are nonpartisans a constant and growing element of the local political landscape they also offer an alternative to the national parties in local government by enhancing the quality of local representation; influencing the policy agenda; and motivating citizens to engage with, and participate in, the political process. Nonpartisans and indeed, smaller parties, open up local democracy; provide a range of alternative voices for local citizens; enhance democratic accountability; provide space for public political discourse; present challenges to the major parties; refocus local politics on local issues; and can provide a challenge to notions of party loyalty superseding loyalty to the electorate. The continual struggle faced by the nonpartisan is to convince the voter that this is an alternative worth supporting.

REFERENCES

Aars, J., and A. Offerdal. 1998. "Local Political Recruitment in Crisis? A Comparison of Finland and Norway." *Scandinavian Political Studies* 21(3): 207–30.

Aars, J. and H.-E. Ringkjøb. 2005. "Party Politicisation Reversed? Non-partisan Alternatives in Norwegian Local Politics." *Scandinavian Political Studies* 28(2): 161–81.

Ackaert, J. 1994. "De nationalisatie van de gemeentepolitiek. Een onderzoek naar de verwevenheid tussen nationale politiek en gemeentepolitiek op het niveau van politieke mandatarissen." In Gemeentekrediet, ed., *De gemeenteraadsverkiezingen en hun impact of de Belgische politiek (1890–1970).* Brussels: Gemeentekrediet.

Ackaert, J., K. De Ceuninck, H. Reynaert, K. Steyvers, and T.Valcke. 2007. "Doen (wijzigende) instituties ertoe? De invloed van het gemeente(kies)decreet op de gemeenteraadsverkiezingen van 2006." *Res Publica* 49(1): 15–33.

Ackaert, J., H. Reynaert, K. De Ceuninck, K. Steyvers, and T. Valcke. 2007. "De gemeenteraadsverkiezingen van 28 Oktober 2006. Evolutie sinds 1975." *Res Publica* 49(2–3): 413–42.

Adrian, C. 1952. "Some General Characteristics of Nonpartisan Elections." *American Political Science Review* 46(3): 766–76.

Allen, O. 1993. *The Tiger: The Rise and Fall of Tammany Hall.* Reading, MA: Addison-Wesley.

Bealey, F., J. Blondel, and W. P. McCann. 1965. *Constituency Politics: A Study of Newcastle-under-Lyme.* London: Faber and Faber.

Beloff, M., ed. 1948. *The Federalist Papers or the New Constitution.* Oxford: Basil Blackwell.

Birch, A. H. 1959. *Small Town Politics: A Study of Political Life in Glossop.* London: Oxford University Press.

Blyth, M., and R. Katz. 2005. "From Catch-all Politics to Cartelisation: The Political Economy of the Cartel Party." West European Politics 28(1): 33–60.

Bottom, K., and C. Copus. 2011. "Independent Politics: Why Seek to Serve and Survive as an Independent Councillor?" *Public Policy and Administration*, 26(3): 279–305.

Boogers, M. 2008. "Local Political Parties in the Netherlands: Anomaly or Prototype?" In M.Reiser and E. Holtmann, eds., *Farewell to the Party Model? Independent Local Lists in Eastern and Western European Countries.* Wiesbaden: VS Verlag.

Boogers, M., and G. Voerman. 2010a. "Independent Local Political Parties in the Netherlands." *Local Government Studies* 36(1): 75–90.

Boogers, M., and G. Carter. 2010b. "The Specific Nature of Local Groups." *Res Publica* 52(2): 263–65.

Brown, M., and N. Halaby. 1987. "Machine Politics in America, 1870–1945." *Journal of Interdisciplinary History* 17(3): 587–612.

Buelens, J., P. Dumont, B. Rihoux, and B. Heyndels. 2008. "Het standpunt van de partij: wat is belangrijk voor de lokale afdelingen?" In J. Buelens, B. Rihoux, and K. Deschouwer, eds., *Tussen kiezer en hoofdkwartier. De lokale partijafdelingen en de gemeenteraadsverkiezingen van 2006.* Brussels: VUB Press.

Burrows, E., and M. Wallace. 1999. *Gotham: A History of New York City to 1898.* New York: Oxford University Press.

Chandler, J. A. 2007. *Explaining Local Government: Local Government in Britain Since 1800.* Manchester: Manchester University Press.

Clements, R. V. 1969. *Local Notables and the City Council.* London: Macmillan.

Committee of Inquiry into the Conduct of Local Authority Business. 1986. Research vol. 2, *The Local Government Councillor.* London: HMSO.

Committee on the Management of Local Government. 1967. *Report of the Committee.* Vol. 1. London: HMSO.

Copus, C. 2007. "Liberal Democrat Councillors: Community Politics, Local Campaigning and the role of the Political Party." *Political Quarterly* 78(1): 128–38.

Copus, C., A. Clark, and, K. Bottom. 2008. "Multi-Party Politics in England? Small Parties, Independents and Political Associations in English Local Politics." In M. Reiser and E. Holtmann, eds., *Farewell to the Party Model? Independent Local Lists in Eastern and Western European Countries.* Wiesbaden: VS Verlag.

Crick, B. 1982. *In Defence of Politics.* Harmondsworth: Penguin.

Davis, J. 1989. "The Progressive Council, 1889–1907." In A. Saint, ed., *Politics and the People of London: The London County Council 1889–1965.* London: Hambledon Press.

Dearlove, J. 1973. *The Politics of Policy in Local Government: The Making and Maintenance of Public Policy in the Royal Borough of Kensington and Chelsea.* London: Cambridge University Press.

De Almeida, M. 2008. "Party Politics in Portugal." *European Societies* 10(3): 357–78.
DeSantis, V., and T. Renner. 1991. "Contemporary Patterns and Trends in Municipal Government Structure." In *The Municipal Year Book*. Washington, DC: International City/County Management Association.
Denters, Bas, and Lawrence E. Rose. 2005. "Towards Local Governance?" In B. Denters and L. E. Rose, eds., *Comparing Local Governance: Trends and Developments*. Basingstoke: Palgrave Macmillan.
Deschouwer, K. 1996. "Nationale partijen en gemeenteraadsverkiezingen." In J. Buelens and K. Deschouwer, eds., *De Dorpsstraat is de Wetstraat niet. Een onderzoek naar de opvattingen van plaatselijke woordvoerders van nationale partijen*. Brussels: VUB Press.
Deschouwer, K., and B. Rihoux. 2008. "De lokale partijafdelingen: van hiërarchie naar stratarchie." In J. Buelens, B. Rihoux, and K. Deschouwer, eds., *Tussen kiezer en hoofdkwartier. De lokale partijafdelingen en de gemeenteraadsverkiezingen van 2006*. Brussels: VUB Press.
Dewachter, W. 1994. "Gestalten van gemeenteraadsverkiezingen en de samenvoeging der gemeenten." In Gemeentekrediet, ed., *De gemeenteraadsverkiezingen en hun impact of de Belgische politiek (1890–1970)*. Brussels: Gemeentekrediet.
Dewinter, L., and P. Dumont. 2006. "Do Belgian Parties Undermine the Democratic Chain of Delegation?" *West European Politics* 29(5): 957–76.
D'Hoore, M. 1994. "Les libéraux et les elections communales (1895–1940): Un état des questions." In Gemeentekrediet, ed., *De gemeenteraadsverkiezingen en hun impact of de Belgische politiek (1890–1970)*. Brussels: Gemeentekrediet.
Fabbrini, S. 2000. "Presidentialization of Italian Local Government? The Nature and the Effects of Semiparliamentarism." Paper presented at the workshop on "The Presidentialization of Parliamentary Democracies." ECPR Joint Sessions of Workshops, Copenhagen, Denmark, April 14–19.
Fallend, F., G. Ignits, and P. Swianiewiczs. 2006. "Divided Loyalties: Mayors between Party Representation and Local Community Interests." In H. Bäck, H. Heinelt, and A. Magnier, eds. *The European Mayor: Political Leaders in the Changing Context of Local Democracy*. Wiesbaden: VS Verlag.
Ferreira, F., and J. Gyourko. 2009. "Do Political Parties Matter? Evidence from U.S. Cities." *Quarterly Journal of Economics* 124(1): 399–422.
Finegold, K. 1995. *Experts and Politicians: Reform Challenges to Machine Politics in New York, Cleveland, and Chicago*. Princeton, NJ: Princeton University Press.
Fraser, D. 1979. *Power and Authority in the Victorian City*. New York: St Martin's Press.
Game, C., and S. Leach. 1996. "Political Parties and Local Democracy." In L. Pratchett and D. Wilson, eds., *Local Democracy and Local Government*. London: Macmillan.
Gillespie, J. 1989. "Municipalism, Monopoly and Management: The Demise of Socialism in one County 1918–1933." In A. Saint, ed., *Politics and People of London: The London County Council 1889–1965*. London: Hambledon Press.
Glassberg, A. 1981. *Representation and Urban Community*. London: Macmillan.
Gohlert, S., E, Holtmann, A. Krappidel, and M. Reiser. 2008. "A Bridging Case? Independent local Lists in East and West Germany." In M. Reiser and E. Holtmann, eds., *Farewell to the Party Model? Independent Local Lists in Eastern and Western European Countries, Urban and Regional Research International*. Wiesbaden: VS Verlag, 127–48.
Goldsmith, M., and E. Page. 2010. *Changing Government Relations in Europe: From Localism to Intergovernmentalism*. London: Routledge.

Grant, W. P. 1971. "Local Parties in British Local Politics: A Framework for Empirical Analysis." *Political Studies* 19(2): 201–12.
Grant, W. P. 1973. "Non-partisanship in British Local Politics." *Policy and Politics* 1(3): 241–54.
Green, D. 1981. *Power and Party in an English City: An Account of Single-Party Rule*. London: Allen and Unwin.
Guterbock, T. 1980. *Machine Politics in Transition: Party and Community in Chicago*. Chicago: University of Chicago Press.
Gyford, J. 1976. *Local Politics in Britain*. London: Croom Helm.
Gyford, J. 1985. "The Politicisation of Local Government." In M. Loughlin, M. Gelfand, and K. Young, ed., *Half a Century of Municipal Decline*. London: Allen and Unwin.
Gyford, J. 1986. "Diversity, Sectionalism and Local Democracy." In Committee of Inquiry into the Conduct of Local Authority Business, Research vol. 4, *Aspects of Local Democracy*. London: HMSO.
Committee of Inquiry into the Conduct of Local Authority Business. 1986. Research vol. 2, *The Local Government Councillor*. London: HMSO.
Hansen, T., and L. E. Rose. 2007. "Assessing the Vitality of Local Democracy: What Considerations Apply?" Paper prepared for the 4th ECPR General Conference, Pisa, Italy, September 6–8.
Held, D. 1993. *Models of Democracy*. Oxford: Polity Press.
Hennock, E. P. 1973. *Fit and Proper Persons: Ideal and Reality in Nineteenth-Century Urban Government*. London: Edward Arnold.
Hesse, J., and L. Sharpe. 1991. "Local Government in an International Perspective: Some Comparative Observations." In J. Hesse, ed., *Local Government and Urban Affairs in International Perspective: Analyses of Twenty Western Industrialized Countries*. Baden-Baden: Nomos-Verlagsgesellschaft.
Hjellum, T. 1967. "The Politicization of Local Government: Rates of Change, Conditioning Factors, Effects on Political Culture." *Scandinavian Political Studies* 2:69–93.
Hoffmann-Martinot, V. 2003. "The French Republic, One Yet Divisible?" In N. Kersting and A. Vetter, eds., *Local Government Reform in Europe—Closing the Gap between Democracy and Efficiency*. Opladen: Leske + Budrich.
Hofstadter, R. 1955. *The Age of Reform: From Bryan to FDR*. New York: Knopf.
Holtmann, E. 2008. "Lists in Europe." In M. Reiser and E. Holtmann, eds., *Farewell to the Party Model? Independent Local Lists in Eastern and Western European Countries*. Wiesbaden: VS Verlag.
Jones, G. W. 1969. *Borough Politics: A Study of Wolverhampton Borough Council 1888–1964*. London: Macmillan.
Katz, R., and P. Mair. 1995. "Changing Models of Party Organisation and Party Democracy: The Emergence of the Cartel Party." *Party Politics* 10:5–28.
Keith-Lucas, B. 1952. *The English Local Government Franchise*. Oxford: Basil Blackwell.
Kerrouche, E. 2005. "The Powerful French Mayor: Myth and Reality." In R. Berg and N. Rao, eds., *Transforming Local Political Leadership*. Houndsmills: Palgrave.
Kjaer, U., and E. Jorgen. 2010. "Local Party System Nationalisation: Does Municipal Size Matter?" *Local Government Studies* 36(3): 425–44.
Lapalombara, J., and J. Anderson. 1992. "Political Parties." In M. Hawkesworth and M. Kogan, eds., *Encyclopaedia of Government and Politics*. Vol. 1. London: Routledge.
Leach, S. 2006. *The Changing Role of Local Politics in Britain*. Bristol: Policy Press.
Leach, S., and D. Wilson. 2000. *Local Political Leadership*. Bristol: Policy Press.
Lee, J. M. 1963. *Social Leaders and Public Persons: A Study of County Government in Cheshire since 1888*. Oxford: Clarendon Press.

Mair, P. 1989. "The Problem of Party System Change." *Journal of Theoretical Politics* 1(3): 251–76.
Meny, Y. 1992. "La Re´publique des fiefs." *Pouvoir* 60:55–71.
Midtbo T., and K. Stromsnes. 1996. "Voter Turnout in Norway: Time, Space and Causality." *Scandinavian Political Studies* 19:379–400.
Montero, J. R., and R. Gunther. 2002. "Introduction: Reviewing and Reassesing Parties." In R. Gunther, J. R. Montero, and J. J. Lintz, eds., *Political Parties: Old Concepts and New Challenges.* Oxford: Oxford University Press.
Newton, K. 1976. *Second City Politics: Democratic Processes and Decision-Making in Birmingham.* Oxford, Clarendon Press.
Northup, N. 1987. "Local Nonpartisan Elections, Political Parties and the First Amendment." *Columbia Law Review* 87(8): 1677–701.
Ostrogorski, M. 1902. *Democracy and the Organisation of Political Parties.* 2. vols. New York: Macmillan.
Owen, D. 1982. *The Government of Victorian London. 1855–1889: The Metropolitan Board of Works, the Vestries, and the City Corporation.* Cambridge: Harvard University Press.
Pasture, P. 1994. "De katholieke partij en de doorbraak van de standenvertegenwoordiging in de gemeenteraden 1895–1921." In Gemeentekrediet, ed., *De gemeenteraadsverkiezingen en hun impact of de Belgische politiek (1890–1970).* Brussels: Gemeentekrediet.
Reiser, M., and E. Holtmann, eds. 2008. *Farewell to the Party Model: Independent Local Lists in East and West European Countries.* Wiesbaden. VS Verlag.
Reiser, M. 2008. "Independent Local Lists in Eastern and Western European Countries." In M. Reiser and E. Holtmann, eds., *Farewell to the Party Model? Independent Local Lists in Eastern and Western European Countries.* Wiesbaden: VS Verlag.
Rokkan, S. 1966. "Electoral Mobilization, Party Competition, and National Integration." In J. LaPalombara and M. Wiener, eds., *Political Parties and Political Development.* Princeton, NJ: Princeton University Press.
Royko, M. 1971. *Boss: Richard. J. Daley of Chicago.* New York: Signet.
Sartori, G. 1976. *Parties and Party Systems.* Cambridge: Cambridge University Press.
Saunders, P. 1979. *Urban Politics: A Sociological Interpretation.* London: Hutchinson.
Schaffner, B., M. Streb, and G. Wright. 2001. "Teams without Uniforms: The Nonpartisan Ballot in State and Local Elections." *Political Research Quarterly* 54(70): 6–30.
Schmitt, H., and S. Holmberg. 1995. "Political Parties in Decline?" In H.-D. Klingemann and D. Fuchs, eds., *Citizens and the State.* Oxford: Oxford University Press.
Sebberechts, F. 1994. "De Vlaams-nationale partijen in de gemeenteraadsverkiezingen na de Tweede Wereldoorlog." In Gemeentekrediet, ed., *De gemeenteraadsverkiezingen en hun impact of de Belgische politiek (1890–1970).* Brussels: Gemeentekrediet.
Sellers, J., and A. Lidström. 2007. "Decentralization, Local Government, and the Welfare State." *Governance* 20(4): 609–32.
Seyd, P., and P. Whiteley. 2004. "British Party Members: An Overview." *Party Politics* 10(4): 355–66.
Schattschneider, E. E. 1942. *Party Government.* New York: Holt, Rinehart and Winston.
Soldon, N. 1974. "*Laissez-faire* as Dogma: The Liberty and Property Defence League 1882–1914." In K. Brown, ed., *Essays in Anti-Labour History: Responses to the Rise of Labour in Britain.* London: Macmillan.
Stacey, M. 1960. *Tradition and Change: A Study of Banbury.* New York: Oxford University Press.
Steyvers, K., and H. Reynaert. 2010. "De gemeenteraadsverkiezingen als brandpunt van de lokale representatieve democratie." In H. Reynaert, ed., *De kerktorenpolitiek voorbij. Lokale politiek in Vlaanderen.* Brugge: Vanden Broele.

Steyvers, K., H. Reynaert, K. De Ceuninck, and T. Valcke. 2008. "All Politics is Local, Partisan or National? Local Lists in Belgium." In M. Reiser and E. Holtmann, eds., *Farewell to the Party Model? Independent Local Lists in East and West European Countries.* Wiesbaden: VS Verlag.

Steyvers, K., H. Reynaert, K. De Ceuninck, T. Valcke, and T. Verhelst. 2009. "Bird of Paradise or Ugly Duckling? On the Meaning of Local Lists for Municipal Politics in Belgium." Paper presented at the conference "Minor Parties and Independents in Local Politics. Do They Make a Difference?" University of Halle-Wittenberg. Germany, November 27–28.

Sweeting, D. 2009. "The Institutions of "Strong' Local Political Leadership in Spain." *Environment and Planning C: Government and Policy* 27(4): 698–712.

Tocqueville, Alexis de. 1994. *Democracy in America.* Ed. J. P. Mayer. London: Fontana Press.

Van Der Kolk, H. 2007. "Local Electoral Systems in Europe." *Local Government Studies* 33(2): 159–80.

Vanschoenbeek, G. 1994. "De doorbraak van de social-democratische aanwezigheid in de Vlaamse gemeentepolitiek." In Gemeentekrediet, ed., *De gemeenteraadsverkiezingen en hun impact of de Belgische politiek (1890–1970).* Brussels: Gemeentekrediet.

Vetter, A. 2009. "Citizens versus Parties: Explaining Institutional Change in German Local Government, 1989–2008." *Local Government Studies* 35(1): 125–42.

Walgrave, S. 1994. "Agalev en de gemeenteraadsverkiezingen van 1982 en 1988." In Gemeentekrediet, ed., *De gemeenteraadsverkiezingen en hun impact of de Belgische politiek (1890–1970).* Brussels: Gemeentekrediet.

Wayenberg, E., F. De Rynck, K. Steyvers, and Pilet Jean-Benoit. 2011. "Belgium: A Tale of Regional Divergence?" In J. Loughlin, F. Hendriks, and A. Lidström, eds., *The Oxford Handbook of Local and Regional Democracy in Europe.* Oxford: Oxford University Press.

Whiteley, P. 2008. "Where Have All the Members Gone? The Dynamics of Party Membership in Britain." *Parliamentary Affairs 2008.* Oxford: Oxford University Press / The Hansard Society.

Wille, F., K. and Deschouwer. 2007. "Het beschermde dorp. Nationale tendensen bij gemeenteraadsverkiezingen." *Res Publica* 49(1): 67–88.

Witte, E. 1994. "Tussen experiment en correctief. De Belgische gemeentelijke kieswetgeving in relatie tot het nationale kiesstelsel." In Gemeentekrediet, ed., *De gemeenteraadsverkiezingen en hun impact of de Belgische politiek (1890–1970).* Brussels: Gemeentekrediet.

Wollmann, H. 2006. "The Fall and the Rise of the Local Community: A Comparative and Historical Perspective." *Urban Studies* 43(8): 1419–38.

Young, K. 1975. *Local Politics and the Rise of Party: The London Municipal Society and the Conservative Intervention in Local Elections, 1894–1963.* Leicester: Leicester University Press.

Young, K. 1989. "Bright Hopes and Dark Fears: The Origins and Expectations of the County Councils." In K. Young, ed., *New Directions For County Government,* London: Association of County Councils.

Young K., and N. Rao. 1995. "Faith in Local Democracy." In J. Curtice, R. Jowell, L. Brook, and A. Park, eds., *British Social Attitudes: The Twelfth Report.* Aldershot: Dartmouth.

CHAPTER 12

LOCAL DEMOCRACY AND CITIZENSHIP

HUBERT HEINELT

1. Introduction

Personal relationships in local communities (where everybody knows everybody) offer specific conditions for political self-determination as the core notion of democracy. At the local level is seems possible that those affected by a decision are also able to take part in this decision. In addition, a local community seems to be a political unit in which members are easily able to mutually recognize each other as equals in taking decisions affecting this community. This mutual recognition as equals forms the basis understanding of citizenship and it can be argued that it was effective before citizenship rights were established and ensured by the (nation) state.[1]

Dahl (1971) and Dahl and Tufte (1973) are prominent examples of a much broader debate in which the formation of spatially grounded political communities and identities as well as associated ideas about forms of democratic self-governing is linked to the city (or *polis*) as an *ideal type* of community. However, it was also Dahl who recognized a problem that for most citizens, participation in very large units becomes minimal and in very small units it becomes trivial. At the extremes, citizens may participate in a vast range of complex and crucial decisions by the single act of casting a ballot; or else they have almost unlimited opportunities to participate in decisions over matters of no importance. At the one extreme, then,

1. This chapter is partly based on an article on "Debating the Democratic Legitimacy of the European Union" (Heinelt 2007) and pieces of a book on *Governing Modern Societies: Towards Participatory Governance* (Heinelt 2010).

the people vote but they do not rule; at the other, they rule—but they have nothing to rule over (Dahl 1971: 97).

In his book on "size and democracy" written with Tufte (Dahl and Tufte 1973) the question was raised: "Can we say, then, that there is any optimal size for a political system?" It was unequivocally answered: "In our view, the answer is clearly no. Different problems require political units of different size" (Dahl and Tufte 1973: 135).

This statement will be used as a starting point for this chapter. However, in the following not only structures of a multilevel system will be considered in which local democracy is constrained by *territorial* political units placed above the local level, that means, upper-level government. Instead (and going beyond the reflections of Dahl and Tufte), also functionally determined *sectoral* political units will be taken into account which complement vertically layered territorial political units. In section 2 structures of such multilevel systems are considered. This is done with the aim to outline impacts of such systems on the meaning of democracy. In a next step (in section 3), these reflections are related to the debate about a "shift from government to governance" and challenges of democracy related to the observation that the sphere of governance extends far beyond a government centered vision of policymaking. The relevance of participation as well as criteria of the democratic quality of governance arrangements are reflected in section 4, and to demonstrate how differently political participation of individual actors can be, three governing orders will be distinguished and "three worlds of democratic action" outlined (in section 5). Within such a web of various forms of participation the concept of citizenship needs to be reconceptualized (which will be done in section 6).

2. The Local Level in Multilevel Governance

The statement (quoted above) that "different problems require political units of different size" (Dahl and Tufte 1973: 135) was related by Dahl and Tufte (1973: 20–25) to two aspects characterizing a political system as one of democratic self-government, namely *citizen effectiveness* and *system capacity*—or *citizen participation* and *system effectiveness* (as these two aspects were phrased by Dahl in his later works [1989; 1994; 1998]). Dahl and Tufte argued that, on the one hand, participation is necessary to underpin the idea that those allowed to take decisions and those affected by them are effectively determining policymaking. On the other hand, the capacity of the political system is crucial to solve complex problems in accordance with expressed demands—in an efficient way.

Although Dahl and Tufte did not provide a clear answer to the question of how big a political system ideally should be to allow democratic self-government, they offer instructive starting points for further analysis.

First of all their statement that "different problems require political units of different size" points to the conclusion that one should think about a sort of *flexible political geometry* which implies a structure of coupled political units in which problems are addressed according to their specific challenges and opportunities to solve them on the part of different political units each covering a differing space. In the words of Dahl and Tufte:

> Rather than conceiving of democracy as located in a particular kind of inclusive, sovereign unit, we must learn to conceive of democracy spreading through a set of interrelated political systems, sometimes though not always arranged like Chinese boxes, the smaller nesting in the larger. (Dahl and Tufte 1973: 135)

This does not necessarily mean (although Dahl and Tufte point in this direction) that we have to think about a multilevel system of vertically layered territorial units. Instead, a multilevel system clearly structured in a vertical sense by layered territorial units each responsible for particular tasks and equipped with distinct competences can be complemented horizontally by functionally determined (sectoral) political entities.

With such a flexible political geometry particular problems can be addressed effectively which means that *system capacity* can be built or secured. In addition, this structure also offers a broad spectrum of potential forms of participation which goes beyond affecting the membership of representative bodies periodically through elections. These forms of participation are linked not only to the different territorial layers of a multilevel system but also to the flanking functionally determined (sectoral) political units. Such a broad spectrum of participation can contribute to *citizen effectiveness*.[2]

Following Dahl and Tufte, what is crucial is not only the problem-solving capacity (i.e. "system capacity") of a flexible political geometry of this kind. Likewise, it is vital that those taking decisions and are at the same time affected by those decisions are convinced that they can effectively influence policymaking. This is central because the ability of a political unit to actually solve problems, that is, to be effective, is measured in relation to the demands (the intended effects) of those collectively trying to influence their living in a particular way and direction.

3. The Democratic Challenges of Governance

Reflections on functionally determined sectoral political entities complementing horizontally or overlapping single territorial levels of government lead inevitably to the debate on a "shift from government to governance." This debate is linked to the

2. These reflections can be linked to the distinction between two (ideal) types of jurisdictions and related multilevel system made by Hooghe and Marks (2003).

diagnosis that in modern societies the sphere of governance extends far beyond a government centered vision of policymaking. In this sense policy-making is extended to society at large (for an overview see Pierre 2000; Pierre and Peters 2000). This observation concerns all territorial levels—including the local one—and questions the traditional distinction between state and society. Additionally, participation in governing activities can no longer be perceived only as a matter of being indirectly involved in governmental affairs by voting and through representation but can be seen also through extended engagement in different forms of policymaking.

The creation of forms of governance beyond the governing activities of the state as well as of local government is considered to be closely related to actual transformations of the economic, social, cultural, and physical ways in which various aspects of collective life can be organized. This diagnosis is mainly based on two observations.

On the one hand, it is argued that "system effectiveness" (Dahl 1994) can only be achieved through bargaining systems in which a number of interdependent but autonomous public and private actors are involved. This refers to global issues as well as to domestic or local ones. This questions not only the sovereignty of the state—or the states—but also traditional forms of democratic citizen participation, meaning the image of self-governing through equal voting rights and accountable representation.

On the other hand, it is argued that societal interactions have become politicized in the sense that nearly everything impacts on one's life and has the potential of turning into a societally binding decision. Regarding technological change this is highlighted by Philip Frankenfeld's dictum: "To innovate is to legislate" (Frankenfeld 1992: 460). What he highlights for technology also applies to other aspects of societal interactions and social change:

> Technology increases impacts of humans upon their world and upon other humans.... It creates power. It creates political communities or realms of common impact, often ex nihilo. Technology thus compels us to increase the reach and binding power of the politics and ethics through which we order human independence. (Frankenfeld 1992: 460–61)

What are the implications of such a diagnosis where (i) the sovereignty of the state and the abilities of people to influence their lives democratically through societally binding decisions of representative bodies are limited and (ii) at the same time societal interactions are subordinated to the realms of binding decisions taken in unknown arenas? To perceive these realms where societally binding decisions are taken to coordinate interactions as spheres of governance is important because this means politicizing them. This means that societally binding decisions are seen as a political issue. However, from a democratic point of view, this is only a first step. The next step should be to transform governance into participatory governance by enhancing the realm of democracy, that is by "bringing citizens back in."

4. Advantages and Standards of the Democratic Quality of Participatory Governance

Participation is traditionally not only seen as a value in itself but as a means to legitimize decision-making. This is argued on several grounds (see for example Mills 1977: chapter 8, and for an overview Schmalz-Bruns 2002). First, one basic *normative* assumption of democratic theory, starting from the idea of the natural rights of man, is that those who are affected by a decision also have to be given a right to participate in the decision. Thus, even if the final decision is not based on their ideas, they have had a say and a chance to make their argument heard. Second, participation by a broad range of interests, if undertaken in an open and free way, makes everybody give good reasons for their position. This can help to eliminate both egoistic and logically wrong positions. Third, Charles Lindblom (1965) developed an argument called the "intelligence of democracy": those who are given the right to participate might have the relevant knowledge necessary to produce better results or to achieve the politically defined objectives (see also Cohen and Sabel 1997: 320).

In referring to the second and third grounds (which can be classified as *functional*) one can summarize that participatory governance arrangements

> would contribute in three distinctive ways to improving the quality of decision-making: (1) they enhance the opportunities for mutual accommodation through exchanges of reasoned arguments; (2) they serve to generate higher levels of trust among those who participate and this, in turn, (3) allows them to introduce a longer time-horizon into their calculations since sacrifices and losses in the present can be more reliably recuperated in future decisions. (Gbikpi and Grote 2002: 21, referring to Schmitter 2002: 53–54)

If it is the task to transform governance into participatory governance by enhancing the realm of democracy, the democratic quality of participatory governance has to be reflected. "Traditional" attempts to define democracy seem to be insufficient, as they are either explicitly or implicitly oriented at state-centered decision-making and the model of representative or "liberal" democracy. Instead, criteria should be employed that go beyond state-centered decision-making by representative bodies and are broad enough to capture "a degree of participation so great and so fairly spread about that no one feels neglected and everyone feels, with justice, that his viewpoint has been pretty fairly attended to" (Dahl 1971: 112). The following criteria—suggested by Papadopoulos and Warin (2007)—form a starting point to assess the democratic quality of governance arrangements:

- their *openness and accessibility*,
- the *quality of deliberation* taking place within them,
- their *effectiveness* and
- their *links to the public sphere.*

More specifically, the *quality of deliberation* should be linked to "reasoning together among equals" (Cohen 2007: 220) where "the reasoning must in some recognizable way be the reasoning of the equal persons who are subject to the decisions" (Cohen 2007: 220),[3] and *effectiveness* should be considered in relation to the ability to achieve the objectives determined by collective decisions, that is, effective collective self-determination.

Additionally (and going beyond the views of Papadopoulos and Warin 2007),

- those who are potentially affected by policy outputs flowing out of governance arrangements should directly or indirectly (through representative bodies) participate in the *making and enforcement of rules* for these governance arrangements.[4]

The last point emphasizes not only the links to and coupling with forms of direct and representative democracy based on voting, and in this respect with opportunities of citizens to influence forms of participatory governance. It also highlights that especially the openness and accessibility of (participatory) governance arrangements as well as their links to the public sphere should be regulated in a binding form through forms of direct and representative democracy. This implies that such governance arrangements have to be established in a reliable form and for a certain period of time. In such arrangements foreseeable interactions can occur which is especially important against the background of possible conflicts. Furthermore, both the reliability and a certain durability of governance arrangements are crucial insofar as it cannot always be expected that governance arrangements develop in reliable and durable form endogenously from societal interactions.

If participatory governance is about enhancing the realm of democracy by "bringing citizens back in" then participation is *not* necessarily related to collective or even "corporate actors." Without any doubt do those collective actors and corporate actors[5] play an unneglectable role

> whose resources and cooperation are perceived as useful to compensate or overcome state—or market—failure in the provision of common goods or at least avoidance of common bads by cooperative action in governance arrangements. (Greven 2007: 236)

3. This can be related to the relevance of "arguing" as a governance mode (as discussed in section 3).

4. On this see Schmitter's (2002: 58ff.) considerations on "design principles for governance arrangements."

5. For a distinction between collective and corporate actors on the one hand and individual actors on the other see Scharpf 1997. *Corporate actors* are characterized by "a high degree of autonomy" in the definition and pursuit of their objectives in relation to their members or "the ultimate beneficiaries of their activities" (Scharpf 1997: 54). By way of contrast, *collective actors* are composite actors "that are dependent on and guided by the preferences of their members" (Scharpf 1997: 54).

However, to demonstrate that reflections on participatory governance neither entail a factual nor a "normative de-individualization of political participation" (Greven 2007: 237), different governing orders will be distinguished and "three worlds of democratic action" outlined (see section 5). Against the background of these governing orders and the "three worlds of democratic action," the political and legal equality of every human being and the right to participate among equals in political decisions are linked to different themes—namely either (i) to agreements on general or just on policy-specific cognitive or normative points of reference relevant for framing (inter-)actions, (ii) to the political design of institutional settings and policies (programs), or (iii) to their implementation. Furthermore, the forms of participation and the way to influence political decisions differ between these governing orders. This affects the opportunities to exercise influence individually or collectively in a particular way.

5. Different Dimensions of Governance—and the "Three Worlds of Democratic Action"

Jan Kooiman (2000: 143ff.; 2002: 86–87; 2003: 133ff.) distinguishes different governing orders: namely first order, second order, and meta governing).[6] *Meta governing* can be linked to the formation of general or policy-specific images (or paradigms, *Leitbilder*).[7] A specific context-related (local) understand of sustainability can be such an image. It is underpinned by communicative rationality based on deliberation. Meta governing and the development of images implies a linguistic coding of problem definitions and patterns of action which are binding through "ethical standards"—as Kooiman (2002: 92) phrased it. But one can argue (see Heinelt 2010: 22) that it is not just ethical standards in the sense of normative images or ideas of appropriateness[8] that are a matter of concern when

6. For a similar approach to the "three worlds of action"—with a "constitutional choice," "collective choice," and "operational choice" level—see Kiser and Ostrom 1982 as well as Ostrom 1990: 50–55.

7. Jessop (2002) uses the expression "meta-governance." For him meta-governance "involves re-articulating and 'collibrating'" (Jessop 2002: 49) of different governance modes—namely *hierarchy* or hierarchical interventions in society relying on and being legitimized in a democratic political order by majoritarian decisions, the *market*, and nonhierarchical *networks* of autonomous but interdependent public and private actors. In other words: "[Meta-governance] is the organisation of the conditions for governance and involves the judicious mixing of market, hierarchy, and networks" (Jessop 2002: 49).

8. I refer here to the distinction between the "logic of appropriateness" and the "logic of consequentiality" made by March and Olsen (1989).

it has to be considered how and why a certain linguistic coding of problem definitions and patterns of action becomes binding for interactions. Crucial are also shared or commonly accepted and therefore dominant assumptions about causality and "factual matters" (how the world works). In these kinds of interaction in which normative images of appropriateness and assumptions about causality are developed, participants can use their *voice* to influence debate through "good reasons." For the development of this kind of participation it is important to consider the distribution of "voice-options" and the conditions under which it is possible to be influential by (public) reasoning.

Such conditions can be laid down by law (as is the case for instance with the legislation on environmental impact assessment, see Heinelt et al. 2001). But against the background of the multitude of specific local circumstances, the use of legally fixed formal "voice-options" depends heavily on local adaptation or local institutional design taking specific spatial conditions into account (Haus and Heinelt 2005: 34).

First order governing is oriented toward operational actions with more or less narrow institutionally defined *choice* options. This is the world of implementation and concerns mainly the local level where local government and its administration meet those who are affected by a specific policy or where policy addressees (such as enterprises but also—like in the case of "area-based initiatives"—neighborhoods) implement a program autonomously but not unrelated to the influences from and on other actors. Participation in this context means that those who could be affected by a policy have to be involved in its implementation. *Voice* again can be an important element of such an engagement. But the importance of participation (by *voice*) in the context of first order governing is less related to ethics or images of appropriateness than to effectiveness. This means that through participation the implementation of a program can be secured in line with policy objectives by taking the motives and concerns of the policy addressees into account. Furthermore, the willingness of policy addressees to comply can be secured by their participation. And finally, the knowledge necessary for achieving a given policy objective can be developed through participation. This underlines not only the importance of creating "voice" options but also of reflecting on the circumstances and conditions under which specific actors can be influential. However, there is another kind of participation based on communication in the context of first order governing, namely bargaining. *Bargaining* rests on a specific kind of power which derives from exit options, the option of noncompliance or holding back relevant knowledge. This has to be contrasted with *arguing*, which can be of influence only if "good reasons" referring to assumptions about causality can be put forward or if normatively binding images are employed, developed at the meta governing level.[9]

9. "To argue is to engage in communication for the purpose of persuading an opponent, i.e. to make the other change beliefs about factual or normative matters.... To bargain is to engage in communication for the purpose of forcing or inducing the opponent to accept one's claim" (Elster 1991: 3).

How do circumstances and conditions develop under which specific actors can be influential by *voice*—or, more precisely, by arguing and/or bargaining? They can develop endogenously in society or autonomously from politics—like in local "agenda 21" / LA 21 initiatives (see Lafferty 1999) where beyond legally fixed formal "voice-options" opportunities to be influential by (public) reasoning can develop from local discourses. However, usually such "voice-options" develop or are established by political design and are related to certain statuses or features of citizenship (which is addressed in section 6). The political design of conditions under which specific actors can be influential by *voice* is a task of second order governing, as Kooiman called it.

Second order governing is geared toward institution building and the creation of policy instruments or programs. Effectiveness can be seen as a standard of second order governing, just as in first order governing. By achieving effectiveness, second order governing can acquire a specific kind of legitimacy, that is, output legitimacy.[10] However, this kind of legitimacy is not only poor in a normative sense, but it is also insufficient in relation to sustaining and changes in institutions, or, to put it in general terms, the political order. This requires input legitimation by participation, and it is questionable if forms of participation relying on *voice* (arguing as well as bargaining) are sufficient in this respect because (depending on the specific regulation in question) broader aspects of the political order can be affected. Depending on the (perceived) extent of being affected, input legitimation by participation through voting (*vote*) can become indispensable, that is, a legitimation based on the equal right of all citizens to participate in systems of majoritarian decision-making. In summary, the traditional forms of participation through the election of representative bodies or through directly expressed agreement or disagreement by referendums are crucial for second order governing. This underlines the crucial role of traditional forms of participation through representation and parliamentary structures for second order governing. Furthermore, it is important that representative bodies and "parliamentary politics" associated with them have a "holistic character" (Lord 2007: 147) in so far as they offer a place for political decisions

> in which all problems can be comprehended in relation to all others. This . . . is important if representatives are to influence trade-offs of value across the range of public policy, and control the externalities and cumulative unintended consequences associated with individual actions. (Lord 2007: 147)

However, a strict and isolated coupling of second order governing with majoritarian decision-making is already broken by the embeddedness of second order governing in processes of meta governing through which second order governing is

10. For the distinction between legitimacy and legitimation as well as the different dimensions of input, output, and throughput, see Haus and Heinelt 2005: 14–16 (by referring to Scharpf's distinction between an input and an output dimension of the legitimacy of the political system; see Scharpf 1970: 21–28).

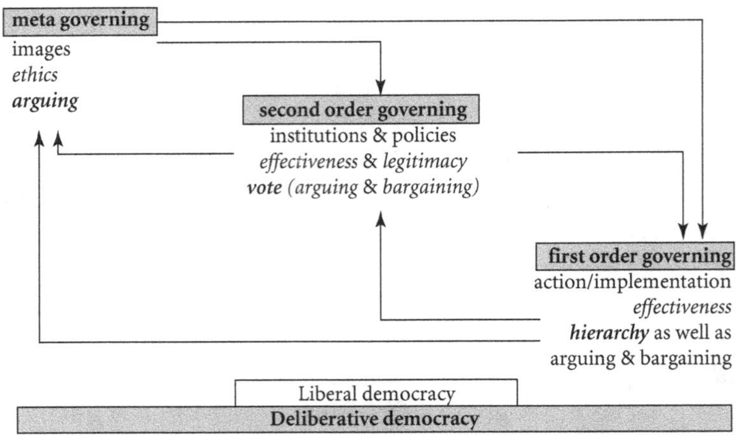

Figure 12.1. The Three Worlds of Democratic Action

(Based on Kooiman 2002.)

influenced *indirectly* by communicative rationality and by the forms of participation based on (public) arguing. Furthermore, at the level of second order governing itself, a lot of opportunities of *direct* influence by communicative interactions (i.e. by *voice*) do exist—using either the mode of arguing or that of bargaining (for instance by lobbying).

Against the background of the distinction between the three governing orders, it is possible to reflect on the interrelation between participation and the aspects of the democratic quality of governance arrangement outlined above (in section 4). These reflections can be focused on relations between different forms (or common perceptions) of democracy whose key features are captured by the models of liberal and of deliberative democracy.[11]

- "Liberal democracy" stresses the individual's right to participate in general elections and, by this, the aggregation of individual preferences to form guidelines for those in representative bodies or in government and the option to make the latter accountable to the individual citizen, can be related to second order governing.
- "Deliberative democracy" giving emphasis to free, open, and public reasoning is important for meta governing as well as for first order governing. However, it has limited direct importance for second order governing.

These reflections can be transformed into a model of "the three worlds of democratic action" (to modify the expression of the "the three worlds of action" from Kiser and Ostrom 1982): the world of meta-governance, the world of second order governing, and the world of first order governing (see figure 1). In such a model the specific features of individual levels as well as linkages between them can be addressed conceptually.

11. See Habermas 1996: 289–302; Bohman and Regh 1997; Pierre and Peters 2000: 137–41; or Cohen 2007; and for early debates Pateman 1970.

"One person—one vote" is applicable in only one of these worlds (the world of second order governing), and the same applies for arguing in another world (the world of meta-governance).

Because meta governing is about the clarification of what problems are about and how to solve them in a way perceived as appropriate, it is related to cognitive and normative questions. Answers to cognitive questions (how the world is functioning or from which assumptions of causality one starts thinking) as well as answers to normative questions (how the world should function or look like) are based on communicative rationality, that is, on communication characterized by the exchange of reason as well as the necessity to justify the validity claim resulting out of an articulated reason (Habermas 1984). In other words (and to use the terms introduced above): "ethical standards" and images can only be generated by arguing or "good reasons." As shared norms or understandings they cannot be negotiated by bargaining, but rather their relevance in a certain situation can be agreed through this mode of communicative interaction. The same applies to majoritarian decisions, especially those made by representative bodies. What has been agreed upon as appropriate can be recognized through majoritarian decisions (by law) either in a particular situation or for a certain time.

Meta governing impacts on second as well as on first order governing through "framing" (see for "framing" Goffman 1974; Campbell 1998; Hay 2002: 194–215), and by this meta governing influences answers to the questions of who should participate in governance arrangements. But it should be emphasized (as aforementioned) that second order governing is crucial for creating conditions for being involved (and how) in first order and in meta governing by setting up entitlements to participate. By this conditions for arguing and bargaining are established through majoritarian decisions.

It has to be emphasized that the levels distinguished above do *not* represent territorial levels. Instead it has to be highlighted that meta governing, for instance, concerns local discourses about images of city or regional development, such as where a particular understanding of sustainability is developed. However, these local discourses (for instance of local "agenda 21" / LA 21 initiatives; see Lafferty) are embedded in arguments at "upper," even global, levels about a linguistic coding of problem definitions and the appropriateness of particular strategies and actions.

The same applies to second order governing. Decisions on policies as well as on institutional settings are not only taken by upper-level authorities. Depending on the competencies and financial resources of local government within national political systems (see for a distinction the typology developed by Hesse and Sharpe 1991 and its further elaboration by Heinelt and Hlepas 2006) the local level can play an important role in this respect.

Furthermore, decisions of upper-level authorities (governments) regarding policies as well as the political design of institutional settings (e.g. municipal codes) and procedural rules (e.g. in planning) do of course play a crucial role in second order governing. However, in relation to the application of particular policies and procedural rules as well as institutional settings decisions of upper-level authorities simply represent instructions or guidelines *for* "subordinate" (especially local) actors. But these instructions or guidelines form a "channel of policy choices" and define feasible options (a more or less broad "feasible set"). Within such a "channel of policy choices" decisions have to be taken *by* "subordinate" actors—from the politically defined feasible options. This opens up opportunities for the design of particular forms of problem solving, the involvement of specific actors to govern in a way that is adapted to the particular (local) context (see, for instance, the contributions in Boddy and Parkinson 2004).

6. From Citizens to Holders—and Back

Participation based on citizenship is related to legal entitlement underpinned by the state as the authority traditionally seen as ultimately responsible and—because of the monopoly of power—capable of taking binding decisions. This is not only the case for the right to participate in elections. The same also applies to shareholders or owners whose legally secured property rights are the basis for their involvement, when specific collective decisions affect the private world of ownership. There can also be a legal entitlement for individuals to come together collectively and attain the legal (or licensed) status of a corporate actor involved in institutionalized forms of interest intermediation.

What do the assumptions about governance mean for the concept of citizenship? To put it precisely, because governing and the sphere of governance extend far beyond a state-centered vision of policymaking, citizenship based answers to the question "Who should participate?" seem to be insufficient.

Against this background, Schmitter's reflections on "holders" are interesting, that is, on "persons/organizations who could potentially be invited or allowed to participate [because] they possess some quality or resource that entitles them to participate" (Schmitter 2002: 62). Based on the specific "quality or resource that entitles them to participate" he distinguishes specific holder categories (Schmitter 2002: 62–63). Only one of them refers to

> [r]ights that are attached to membership in a national political community and that presumably entitle all those having them to participate equally in all decisions made by that community[.] In this case, the holders are usually called citizens. (Schmitter 2002: 62).

Beside these "rights holders" Schmitter distinguishes between the following other "holders" according to the quality or resource they possess:

- *spatial holders*, that is, residents;
- *share holders*, that is to say, owners;

- *stake holders*, or those who "regardless of where they live, what their nationality is or what their level of information/skills may be...could be materially or even spiritually affected by a given measure" (Schmitter 2002: 63);
- *interest holders*, specifically someone who "demonstrates sufficient awareness about the issue being decided and makes known the desire to participate in the name of some constituency" (Schmitter 2002: 63), for example "(voluntary) spokespersons" or the interested public;
- *knowledge holders* who are experts of different kinds holding specific knowledge (or skills) which are "presumably needed if the policies taken are going to be technically effective" (Schmitter 2002: 62); and finally
- *status holders*, i.e. actors (according to Schmitter, usually organizations) "that have been recognized by the authorities ultimately responsible for decision and formally accorded the right to represent a designated social, economic or political category" (Schmitter 2002: 63) or; more precisely: "(corporate) representatives."

However, because Schmitter concentrates on "the apposite criterion according to the substance of the problem that has to be solved or the conflict that has to be resolved" (Schmitter 2002: 63) his answer to the question: "Who should participate?" has a bias toward effectiveness. In short, only those possessing some quality or resource to solve a particular problem or to resolve a specific conflict are entitled to participate. Based on Kooiman's reflections on the three governing orders—and the related concept of the "three world of democratic action" outlined above (in section 5)—this seems to be plausible for first order governing. However, second order governing and meta governing are also guided by standards other than effectiveness—namely in the case of second order governing by legitimacy and in the case of meta governing by shared assumptions about causality and normative images of appropriateness. Additionally, as is shown at the end of this section, legitimacy and concepts of appropriateness play a role in first order governing as well. Legitimacy, assumptions about causality, and normative standards of appropriateness are important because the design of forms of participation and of entitlement is a political task in the purest sense, that is, a task based on an intentional and binding coordination of societal interactions.

To recognize the design of forms of participation and of entitlement as a political task and to relate it to standards of legitimacy and appropriateness is important, if it can be assumed that it is participatory governance that brings democracy in the sense outlined above into the wider sphere of policymaking opened up by the shift from government to governance. This emphasizes the importance of the question: How should the concept of citizenship be reframed in a way that the question "Who should participate?" can be answered in a society in which governing extends far beyond a state-centered vision of policymaking?

To answer this question it is necessary to perceive citizenship not within a static concept but within a historical and dynamic one (see, for instance, Marshall 1964). This means that—depending on changing societal conditions—one can and should imagine new forms of citizenship beyond the familiar civil, political, and social forms of citizenship. Consequently, the development of citizenship has to be seen as a reflexive mechanism dealing with the negative consequences of societal change. Against this background it can be argued that due "to its dynamic character 'full citizenship' will never be reached but will remain always a goal" (Roth 2002: 79).

How new forms of citizenship develop can be observed for instance in the cases of "ecological" (Roth 2002) and "technological citizenship" (Saretzki 2002), as well as in relation to ethnic groups or gender issues (see for example Rossili 2000). What one can draw out of the relevant political and academic debate is that new statuses develop incrementally and "locally," that is, from the "world of action," and not a priori from an authority ultimately responsible and capable of taking binding decisions and that one should not construct new citizenships "apart from and unrelated to existing political 'polities'" (Saretzki 2002: 103).

Whatever citizenship can mean, one aspect remains fundamental: Citizenship is based on the design of a certain "status"[12] secured by the authority ultimately responsible for the political coordination of societal interaction, that is, the state.

This fundamental feature of citizenship can be related to Schmitter's holder concept in respect to the category of *status holders*. Particular holders have a status by being "recognised by the authorities ultimately responsible for decision and formally accorded the right to represent a designated social, economic or political category" (Schmitter 2002: 63). It can be argued (and demonstrated empirically; see for instance Heinelt 2002: 20–22) that these particular holders have been "recognized" and formally accorded a specific right of representation because otherwise a particular policy runs the risk of losing or never acquiring legitimacy, or political and societal acceptance. In this respect, the "granting" of a status addresses the effectiveness of a policy, but not in a mere economic or technical sense, rather in an essentially political way, that is, by addressing the issue of legitimacy. Usually, such a status is introduced in parallel to politically defined and legally required procedures and contents of a specific policy, where such procedures and contents are crucial, because the policy and the likelihood and/or credibility of its implementation are—in the shadow of (potential) political conflicts—politically and socially accepted only when the procedures and contents have been securely underpinned.

Furthermore, assumptions about causality and normative standards of appropriateness or ethics can play a role. They are underpinned by communicative rationality about what is "good" or "bad" or even "appropriate" or "inadequate"—for a society as a whole or for a specific sector of society or within a particular (local) context. Provided such assumptions and images have acquired the status of a shared "meaning system" (Scott 1994: 70ff.), they can have an influence on the answer to the "question of political design" for participatory governance in a similar way to statuses "granted" to actors by political authorities. This is because such

12. See the debate about "status" and "contract" in Marshall 1964.

assumptions about causality and images of normative appropriateness influence the choice of the "apposite criterion" for identifying those who should participate based on the nature of the problem to be solved.

Returning to Schmitter's category of "status holder" which is (as mentioned above) related by him to corporate actors, especially to the "social partners" in neo-corporatist arrangements, it can be reinterpreted and broadened in two respects.

On the one hand, the right "to represent a designated social, economic or political category" (Schmitter 2002: 63) can also be given to groups which are not organized as corporate actors (like classical neocorporatist associations such as trade unions or employer organizations) but as collective ones. This applies especially to civil society organizations which for instance articulate and represent concerns like the protection of the environment, or advocate consumer or human rights. As collective actors they are "composite actors" (Scharpf 1997: 54) but they neither show a high ability to commit their members or supporters nor do they have a monopoly to represent particular concerns or interests. Instead, they articulate concerns or interests in a pluralistic way.

On the other hand, the right "to represent a designated social... category" can also be granted to social groups without an organizational structure. This can be illustrated by the case of gender rules which grant especially women a particular status which can be claimed by individuals for themselves and on behalf of others for the whole group. The same applies to disabled people as well as increasingly to elderly people, and, in particular, in societies characterized by ethnic and religious cleavages, rules do exist which grant not only such groups a specific status but also their individual members.

It is crucial that with the recognition as a "status holder" actors gain an authorized "quality" and resource which allows them to participate in a particular range of decisions. But this authorized "quality" and resource is not from the outset bound by law and secured by the state (or any governmental agency). Instead, it can endogenously develop from and become embedded in societal interactions.

To sum up, participation may be determined mainly by effectiveness. Nevertheless, legitimacy plays a crucial role. To guarantee political and societal acceptance of political interventions, some actors are assigned a specific political status which permits them to participate. Such a status implies bargaining power which can limit the discretion of other actors. Furthermore, particular assumptions or beliefs about factual and normative matters are needed to agree on the "apposite criterion" for identifying those who should participate. Politically determined statuses and commonly developed understandings of causality and images of appropriateness have to be understood as elements for defining a new kind of citizenship, not just for defining holders. As mentioned above, such new statuses develop incrementally and "locally" and are not usually built up from nothing by an authority ultimately responsible and capable of taking such binding decisions (or by second order governing). Instead, what is crucial is the recognition of such a status in societal interactions embedded in a specific (usually spatially defined) "action arena."

To identify conditions for the creation of (new) statuses or normatively and legally determined entitlements to participate, the so-called "Institutional Analysis and Development (IAD) framework" developed by Ostrom et al. (1994) is helpful. According to the IAD framework actors who have to interact in a particular action situation to produce a policy outcome are placed in an action arena. In this arena actors are not interacting freely. They have to refer to (i) given "attributes of the physical world," (ii) "attributes of the community/communities" surrounding them, and (iii) "rules-in-use" because these three components structure their interactions (Ostrom et al. 1994: 37; Ostrom 2011: 9–10).

In the following, only reflections of Ostrom et al. on "rules-in-use" are considered because they offer options for systematic thinking about opportunities for participation. The "rules in use" are characterized as "rules in the head" (Ostrom 1999: 53) which puts emphasis on their conceptualization beyond formal rules. Ostrom et al. (1994) distinguish seven types of rules (see also Ostrom 1990):

- *Position rules* establish positions and assign them to participants. They essentially determine who is responsible for what, who has what kind of formal powers etc. Therefore they are forming the starting-point for other types of rules.
- *Boundary rules* regulate the entry and exit of actors.
- *Authority rules* assign the set of actions related to a particular position, allocate rights and obligations to positions, settle the means available for the positions to carry out their tasks, and specify alternatives to act at a certain position.
- *Aggregation rules* determine how decisions in the arena have to be taken or outcomes have to be reached through contributions of the different position holders.
- *Scope rules* stipulate possible outcomes and spell out how the outcomes are related to other arenas.
- *Information rules* regulate which information should be available for which position holder.
- *Payoff rules* allocate benefits and costs of the interactions in the arena as well as of achieved outcomes.

These rules can be related to the question of how "holders" can have an impact on governing activities through their participation and what the creation of (new) statuses may imply. Furthermore, specific problems resulting from particular combinations of these rules can occur.

Take the case of the "rights holder," the traditional role of the citizen as voter. "Boundary rules" identify who in a particular territorially defined spatial unit is allowed to vote; "position rules" determine the role as a voter; "authority rules" define how to vote; "aggregation rules" fix the forms of the majority rule as the decision mode; and "information rules" provide opportunities to inform and to be informed. Problems arising from arrangements in which "rights holders" act in

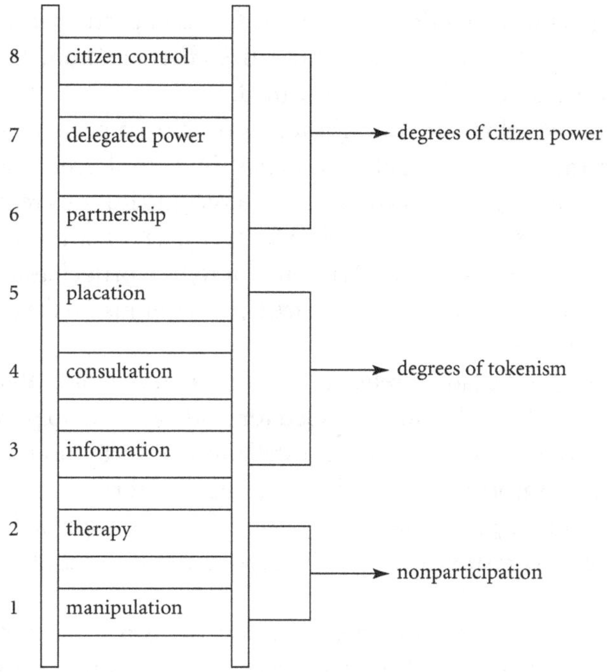

Figure 12.2. Ladder of citizen participation

Source: Arnstein 1969: 217.

accordance with certain rules can also be highlighted by considering the other "rules in use" in those same arrangements. Against the background of the very evidence of spatial interdependencies of decisions (for instance in metropolitan regions; see for an overview Heinelt and Kübler 2005) taken by voters and representative bodies, problems can be highlighted when looking at the "scope rules" and "payoff rules" because it cannot be taken for granted that what "rights holders" have tried to achieve can actually be achieved and have an impact just on them but not also on others.

In thinking broadly about the design of particular "status holders," it is important to consider (i) how "boundary rules" determine conditions for entering the "action arena" and therefore the participation of particular actors; (ii) how "position rules" fix their role within the "action arena"; (iii) whether or not "authority rules," for instance, either allow them just to articulate their concerns or "good reasons" or grant them a kind of veto power; (iv) whether or not "aggregation rules" specifying how decisions are taken offer them an opportunity to participate effectively; (v) how "scope rules" ensure the relevance of decisions in which they have been involved (not least in relation to a particular scope respecting the autonomy of others or other "action arenas"); and (vi) how "payoff rules" regulate the distribution of costs and burdens as well as the benefits and advantages of decisions in which they have been involved.

By referring to the distinction between the forms of participation articulated by Arnstein (1969) in her model of a "ladder of citizen participation," the reflections on the aforementioned seven rules can be clarified.

For Arnstein only three out of eight forms of "citizen participation" were relevant insofar as they facilitate that "'nobodies' in several arenas are [becoming] 'somebodies' with enough power to make the target institutions responsive to their views, aspirations, and needs" (Arnstein 1969: 217). The other five forms of participation (see figure 2) were shown by Arnstein not to be worth characterizing as such because they either do not really lead to participation or just make pretence of leading to participation.

The third rung of the ladder refers to the provision of *information* to citizens by decision-makers "with no channel provided for feedback and no power for negotiation" (Arnstein 1969: 219). In such a constellation "information rules" may have broadened access to information for a larger group of actors but "position," "boundary," "authority," and "aggregation rules" do not allow the informed actors "to make the target institutions responsive to their views, aspirations, and needs" (Arnstein 1969: 219).

Consultation is, according to Arnstein, also tokenism "since it offers no assurance that citizen concerns and ideas will be taken into account" (Arnstein 1969: 219). In the case of *consultation* "information rules" may have broadened access to information for actors and "boundary rules" allow them to enter a related action arena. Furthermore, "position rules" assign particular actors an active role ("position") in this arena so they can articulate concerns, ideas, and suggestions. But "authority" and "aggregation rules" do not allow them to ensure that the articulated concerns, ideas, and suggestions are taken into account in decisions (the "choice of action"). Different kinds of advisory groups are examples of this form of participation. In addition, a legal right to be actively involved in hearings (for instance within environmental impact assessment) opens up an opportunity for this form of participation. But advisory groups can—according to the rules enhancing participation—also be subsumed under partnership as a form of participation.

In the case of *partnership* "power is in fact redistributed" and in particular rules are made

> to share planning and decision-making responsibilities through such structures as joint policy boards, planning committees and mechanisms for resolving impasses. After the ground rules have been established..., they are not subject to unilateral change. (Arnstein 1969: 221)

In contrast to the aforementioned forms of participation, rules are different in the case of partnership insofar as articulated concerns, ideas, and suggestions cannot just be ignored because the "authority rules" grant all those involved in the action arena bargaining power and the "aggregation rules" lay down decision-making procedures which reflect shared decision-making (or planning) competences.

"*Delegated power*" refers to cases where responsibilities for specific tasks are transferred. In such cases the 'information," "position," "boundary," "authority," and "aggregation rules" allow the involved actors to take decisions quite autonomously. But through "scope rules" the range and the compulsory nature of decisions are limited to those who have taken them or to a particular group of affected people. Furthermore, "payoff rules" can play a crucial role in two ways. First, they can put a limit on costs which have to be covered by those beyond the actors directly involved or those who should be intentionally affected (for instance by limiting the funding of activities). Second, they can influence intended gains and their distribution, for instance, by defining funding objectives or tasks to be undertaken. An example of "delegated power" is the transfer of the implementation of a program—including the spending of funds—to (nongovernmental) independent bodies according to fixed general objectives. Such independent bodies could be responsible for developing and implementing of area-based initiatives in a city, like those in England in charge of a specific area-based "action plan" within the context of the EU structural funds (DETR 1997a; 1997b).

With respect to "*citizen control*," Arnstein emphasized that "no one in the nation has absolute control" (Arnstein 1969: 223)—"including the President of the United States" (Arnstein 1969: 216). By "citizen control" she meant those forms of participation which refer to self-administration (for instance of schools) or the self-government of city districts or neighborhoods with respect to single policies or programs. In contrast to the forms of "delegation" the "payoff rules" are designed in the case of "citizen control" in such a way that available financial resources can be used according to decisions of the involved actors (citizens) and the effects these actors are trying to achieve.

7. Conclusion

This chapter concentrates on local democracy beyond the governmental structures. It starts from a summary of issues and commentaries (in section 2.1) which emphasizes that governing modern societies inevitably implies governance beyond governmental structures. Against this background it was argued that it is a political task to turn the inevitability of governance into a participatory form. This required some reflection about participatory governance and the notion of democracy and how they relate to each other. In a further step, different governing orders were outlined. Each of these governing orders offers particular forms of participation which relate to certain models of democracy. This leads to a model of different "worlds of democratic action." This model shows that democratic political systems have to be considered as a complex and broad web of various forms of interest articulation and intermediation as well as decision-making. Within such a web the concept of citizenship needs to be reconceptualized. It was argued that the incremental and reflexive processes of identifying and recognizing the actors who should be participating are crucial. It was argued that the way actors acquire an opportunity—and under certain conditions a right—to participate relies on particular "rules in use" in specificaction arenas.

In respect to such "rules in use," the question can be raised (see, for instance, Klok and Denters 2005: 43): who should and could interpret the rules in a binding way and secure compliance? The authoritative interpretation of the rules does not necessarily flow from a particular formal position within an action arena because some action arenas are characterized by nonhierarchical relations between actors and by the availability of exit options. Therefore, compliance strongly depends on perceptions of appropriateness, and deviant behavior can lead to a new reading of the rules. Against this background it is important to be aware that rules can be defined and changed at different levels, namely, through deliberative design at "superior" levels (meta or second order governing) or through processes of adaptation at the "operational" level (first order governing).

REFERENCES

Arnstein, Sherry R. 1969: A Ladder of Citizen Participation, in: Journal of the American Institute of Planners, Vol. 35, No. 4, 216–24.

Boddy, Martin/Parkinson, Michael (eds.) 2004: City Matters. Competitiveness, Cohesion and Urban Governance, Bristol: Policy Press.

Bohman, James/Regh, William (ed.) 1997: Deliberative Democracy. Essays on Reason and Politics, Cambridge (Mass.): MIT Press.

Campbell, John L. 1998: Institutional Analysis and the Role of Ideas in Political Economy, in: Theory and Society, Vol. 27, No. 3, 377–409.

Cohen, Joshua 2007: Deliberative Democracy, in: Rosenberg, Shawn R. (ed.): Deliberation, Participation and Democracy. Can the People Govern? New York: Palgrave Macmillan, 219–36.

Cohen, Joshua/Sabel, Charles F. 1997: Directly-deliberative Polyarchy, in: European Law Journal, Vol. 3, No. 4, 313–42.

Dahl, Robert A. 1971: The City in the Future of Democracy, in: Cook, Morgan (ed.): Participatory Democracy, San Francisco: Canfield Press, 85–114 (first published 1967 in American Political Science Review, Vol. 61, No. 4, 953–69).

Dahl, Robert A. 1989: Democracy and Its Critics, New Haven (Conn.): Yale University Press.

Dahl, Robert A. 1994: A Democratic Dilemma. System Effectiveness versus Citizen Participation, in: Political Science Quarterly, Vol. 10, No. 1, 23–34.

Dahl, Robert A. 1998: On Democracy, New Haven: Yale University Press.

Dahl, Robert A./Tufte, Edward R. 1973: Size and Democracy, Stanford: Stanford University Press.

DETR (Department of Environment, Transport and the Regions) 1997a: EC Structural Fund Programmes in England. Action Plans for European Regional Development Fund and European Social Fund. Guidance Note No. 1, London.

DETR (Department of Environment, Transport and the Regions) 1997b: EC Structural Fund Programmes in England. Action Plans for European Regional Development Fund and European Social Fund. Guidance Note No. 2, London.

Elster, Jon 1991: Arguing and Bargaining in Two Constituent Assemblies, The Storrs Lectures, Yale Law School, unpublished manuscript.

Frankenfeld, Philip J. 1992: Technological Citizenship: A Normative Framework for Risk Studies, in: Science, Technology & Human Values, Vol. 17, No. 4, 459–84.

Gbikpi, Bernard/Grote, Jürgen R. 2002: From Democratic Government to Participatory Governance, in: Grote, Jürgen R./Gbikpi, Bernard (eds.): Participatory Governance. Political and Societal Implications, Opladen: Leske & Budrich, 17–34.

Goffman, Erving 1974: Frame Analysis, Cambridge: Harvard University Press.

Greven, Michael Th. 2007: Some Considerations on Participation in Participatory Governance, in: Kohler-Koch, Beate/Rittberger, Berthold (eds.): Debating the Democratic Legitimacy of the European Union, Lanham, MD: Rowman & Littlefield, 233–48.

Habermas, Jürgen 1984: The Theory of Communicative Action, Vol. 1: Reason and the Rationalization of Society, Boston: Beacon Press.

Habermas, Jürgen 1996: Between Facts and Norms. Contributions to a Discourse Theory of Law and Democracy, Cambridge: Blackwell Publishers.

Haus, Michael/Heinelt, Hubert 2005: How to Achieve Governability at the Local Level? Theoretical and Conceptual Considerations on a Complementarity of Urban Leadership and Community Involvement, in: Haus, Michael/Hei-nelt, Hubert/Stewart, Murray (eds.): Urban Governance and Democracy: Leadership and Community Involvement, London: Routledge, 12–39.

Hay, Colin 2002: Political Analysis. A Critical Introduction, Basingstoke/New York: Palgrave.

Heinelt, Hubert 2002: Civic Perspectives on a Democratic Transformation of the EU, in: Grote, Jürgen R./Gbikpi, Bernard (eds.): Participatory Governance. Political and Societal Implications, Opladen: Leske & Budrich, 97–120.

Heinelt, Hubert 2007b: Participatory Governance and European Democracy. Bringing Empirical Evidence to a Theoretical Debate, in: Kohler-Koch, Beate/Rittberger, Berthold (eds.): Debating the Democratic Legitimacy of the European Union, Lanham MD: Rowman & Littlefield, 217–32.

Heinelt, Hubert 2010: Governing Modern Societies: Towards Participatory Governance, London: Routledge.

Heinelt, Hubert/Hlepas, Nikolaos-K. 2006: Typologies of Local Government Systems, in: Bäck, Henry/Heinelt, Hubert/Magnier, Annick (eds.): The European Mayor. Political Leaders in the Changing Context of Local Democracy, Wiesbaden: VS Verlag, 21–42.

Heinelt, Hubert/Kübler, Daniel (eds.) 2005: Metropolitan Governance. Capacity, Democracy and the Dynamics of Place, London: Routledge.

Heinelt, Hubert/Malek, Tanja/Staeck, Nicola/Töller, Annette E. 2001: Environmental Policy. The European Union and a Paradigm Shift, in: Heinelt, Hubert/Malek, Tanja/Smith, Randall/Töller, Annette E. (eds.): European Union Environment Policy and New Forms of Governance, Aldershot: Ashgate: 1–32.

Hesse, Joachim J./Sharpe, Laurence J. 1991: Local Government in International Perspective: Some Comparative Observations, in: Hesse, Joachim J./Sharpe, Laurence J. (eds.): Local Government and Urban Affairs in International Perspective. Analyses of Twenty Western Industrialised Countries, Baden-Baden: Nomos, 603–21.

Hooghe, Liesbet/Marks, Gary 2003: Unraveling the Central State, but How? Types of Multi-level Governance, in: American Political Science Review, Vol. 97, No. 2, 233–43.

Jessop, Bob 2002: Governance and Metagovernance. On Reflexivity, Requisite Variety, and Requisite Irony, in: Heinelt, Hubert/Getimis, Panagiotis/Kafkalas, Grigoris/Smith,

Randall/Swynge-douw, Eric (eds.): Participatory Governance in Multi-Level Context. Concepts and Experience, Opladen: Leske & Budrich, 33–58.

Kiser, Larry/Ostrom, Elinor 1982: The Three Worlds of Action, in: Ostrom, Elinor (ed.): Strategies of Political Inquiry, Beverly Hills: Sage, 179–222.

Klok, Pieter-Jan/Denters, Bas 2005: Urban Leadership and Community Involvement. An Institutional Analysis, in: Haus, Michael/Heinelt, Hubert/Stewart, Murray (eds.): Urban Governance and Democracy. Leadership and Community Involvement, London: Routledge, 40–64.

Kooiman, Jan 2000: Societal Governance, in: Pierre, Jon (ed.): Debating Governance. Authority, Steering, and Democracy. Oxford: Oxford University Press, 138–64.

Kooiman, Jan 2002: Governance. A Social-Political Perspective, in: Grote, Jürgen R./Gbikpi, Bernard (eds.) 2002: Participatory Governance. Political and Societal Implications, Opladen: Leske & Budrich, 71–96.

Kooiman, Jan 2003: Governing as Governance, London: Sage.

Lafferty, William M. 1999: Implementing LA 21 in Europe. New Initiatives for Sustainable Communities, Oslo: Pro Sus.

Lindblom, Charles 1965. The Intelligence of Democracy. Decision Making through Mutual Adjustment. New York: Free Press.

Lord, Christopher 2007: Parliamentary Representation in a Decentered Polity, in: Kohler-Koch, Beate/Rittberger, Berthold (eds.): Debating the Democratic Legitimacy of the European Union, Lanham, MD: Rowman & Littlefield, 139–56.

March, James G./Olsen, Johan P. 1989: Rediscovering Institutions. The Organizational Basis of Politics, New York: Free Press.

Marshall, Thomas H. 1964. Class, Citizenship and Social Development, New York: Doubleday.

Mill, John Stuart 1977: The Collected Works of John Stuart Mill, Vol. 19, Part 2, Toronto: University of Toronto Press.

Ostrom, Elinor 1990: Governing the Commons. The Evolution of Institutions for Collective Action, Cambridge: Cambridge University Press.

Ostrom, Elinor 1999: Institutional Rational Choice. An Assessment of the Institutional Analysis and Development Framework, in: Sabatier, Paul A. (ed.): Theories of the Policy Process, Boulder, CO: Westview, 35–71.

Ostrom, Elinor 2011: Background on the Institutional Analysis and Development Framework, in: Policy Studies Journal, Vol. 39, No. 1, 7–27.

Ostrom, Elinor/Gardner, Roy/Walker, James 1994: Rules, Games and Common-Pool Resources, Ann Arbor: University of Michigan Press.

Papadopoulos, Yannis/Warin, Philippe 2007: Are Innovative, Participatory and Deliberative Procedures in Policy Making Democratic and Effective? in: European Journal of Political Research, Vol. 46, No. 4, 445–73.

Pateman, Carole 1970: Participation and Democratic Theory, Cambridge: Cambridge University Press.

Pierre, Jon (ed.) 2000: Debating Governance. Authority, Steering, and Democracy, Oxford: Oxford University Press.

Pierre, Jon/Peters, B. Guy 2000: Governance, Politics and the State, London: Macmillan.

Rossili, Mariagrazia (ed.) 2000: Gender Policies in the European Union, New York: Peter Lang.

Roth, Roland 2002: Participatory Governance and Urban Citizenship, in: Heinelt, Hubert/Getimis, Panagiotis/Kafkalas, Grigoris/Smith, Randall/Swynge-douw, Eric (eds.) 2002: Participatory Governance in Multi-level Context. Concepts and Experience, Opladen: Leske & Budrich, 75–82.

Saretzki, Thomas 2002: Technological Governance—Technological Citizenship? in: Heinelt, Hubert/Getimis, Panagiotis/Kafkalas, Grigoris/Smith, Randall/Swyngedouw, Eric (eds.) 2002: Participatory Governance in Multi-level Context. Concepts and Experience, Opladen: Leske & Budrich, 83–106.
Scharpf, Fritz W. 1970: Demokratie zwischen Utopie und Anpassung, Konstanz: Cornelsen Verlag Scriptor.
Scharpf, Fritz W. 1997: Games Real Actors Play. Actor-Centered Institutionalism in Policy Research, Boulder, CO: Westview.
Schmalz-Bruns, Rainer 2002: The Normative Desirability of Participatory Democracy, in: Heinelt, Hubert/Getimis, Panagiotis/Kafkalas, Grigoris/Smith, Randall/Swyngedouw, Eric (eds.): Participatory Governance in Multi-level Context. Concepts and Experience, Opladen: Leske & Budrich, 59–74.
Schmitter, Philippe C. 2002: Participation in Governance Arrangements: Is There Any Reason to Expect It Will Achieve "Sustainable and Innovative Policies in a Multi-level Context"? in: Grote, Jürgen/Gbikpi, Bernard (eds): Participatory Governance. Political and Societal Implications, Opladen: Leske & Budrich, 51–69.
Scott, W. Richard 1994: Institutions and Organizations. Towards a Theoretical Synthesis, in: Scott; W. Richard/Meyer, John W. (eds.): Institutional Environment and Organizations. Structural Complexity and Individualism, London: Sage, 55–80.

CHAPTER 13

NEIGHBORHOODS AND CIVIC PRACTICE

MARTIN HORAK AND TALJA BLOKLAND

1. The Political Significance of Neighborhoods

Neighborhoods are long-standing concerns in urban politics. Democratic theorists from Tocqueville (2000) to Dahl (1970) have argued that small units of political participation foster a citizen's sense of political efficacy and identification with the polity. Urban political elites and residents alike often see the neighborhood as the smallest unit of political participation; as such, neighborhoods are potentially crucial sites for enacting citizenship rights and making political claims. Across the industrialized world, city governments, nongovernmental organizations, political parties, and other agents frequently use neighborhoods as units for mobilizing participation, organizing political processes, and addressing policy problems.

Yet the definition of "neighborhood" is contested. Government officials often presume that political-administrative units are also social units through which residents can be reached or mobilized. Meanwhile, residents have various understandings of what a neighborhood is, defining it either spatially or on the basis of social interactions (Guest and Lee 1984; Kuschenbach 2003), so the term has an "inherent ambiguity" (Guest and Lee 1984, 35; Wellman and Leighton 1979).

Scholars in Europe and the United States—the regions in our focus—identify many ways in which neighborhoods matter in urban politics. We divide these into three categories. First, there is research on how the social and economic characteristics of neighborhoods can affect residents' access to citizenship rights and opportunities for political participation. This literature has two main related analytical foci. One involves understanding the forces that shape the social and economic characteristics of neighborhoods over time. The other involves understanding how such neighborhood-level variables in turn affect people's likelihood to be active participants in neighborhood politics. In short, this literature focuses on the *neighborhood as a context of opportunities,* including social, economic, civic, and political opportunities.

A second strand of research examines neighborhoods as sites for policy intervention. Some interventions involve explicit efforts by outside actors to mobilize or empower residents at the neighborhood level, either in a general sense (for example, by instituting neighborhood councils) or around particular issues (such as environmental justice or integration of immigrants). Other interventions involve spatially targeted initiatives whose primary goal is to address neighborhood problems (such as high crime rates or joblessness), rather than to mobilize residents. In practice, many interventions pursue both aims, since getting residents involved is often seen as a means of addressing neighborhood problems. The academic literature on interventions has a number of analytical objectives, including explaining the outcomes of mobilization efforts, evaluating policy processes and outcomes, and describing changes in neighborhood-level governance. Here, the *neighborhood* is seen as *an object of policy.*

Finally, there is a body of research that looks at collective agency within neighborhoods. The focus here is on how residents come together to defend or advance their collective interests at the neighborhood level. While such collective action often addresses broader political structures directly through electoral mobilization or political lobbying, it also includes self-help initiatives such as neighborhood watch programs or neighborhood improvement committees. These are all means though which neighborhood agents collectively seek to define, defend, or advance their place in the stratification of places (Logan and Molotch 1987). A central theoretical question concerns the effectiveness of neighborhood mobilization—the extent to which neighborhood mobilization actually has a significant impact on urban politics in general. This, then, is a central concern of the literature on *neighborhood as collective agent,* and it provides one lens through which researchers can integrate a neighborhood focus with wider questions of urban structure and inequalities.

Despite their different analytical foci, all of these perspectives share a concern with civic skills, and with the neighborhood as a site to develop or mobilize these. Civic skills are the capabilities of individuals and groups to pursue goals that are broader than their personal needs. As Pateman (1970) argues, political participation serves to develop a "democratic community... in which each person develops his or her talents to be part of the public cause" (Blokland 2005, 275). Put differently, civic skills are what Robert Dahl called "the arts and habits of democratic life" (quoted in Blokland 2005, 276). Yet such civic skills are unequally distributed and deployed across neighborhoods. We can only develop civic skills if we are given the opportunity to develop these, and we can only use these skills effectively if we have opportunities to access the broader political power structure (Blokland 2006). The promise of the neighborhood as a foundation for democratic practice thus depends on the available opportunities to develop and exercise civic skills at that level.

The rest of this chapter explores the three perspectives on neighborhood politics identified above through a comparative historical analysis of empirical developments and academic work in the United States and Europe. Neighborhood politics and its academic study in the United States are cohesive enough to allow for a broad survey. Empirical developments and academic work in Europe are too heterogeneous to permit more than a selective account. Our approach focuses primarily on literature and examples drawn from the Netherlands and Germany. These do not represent Europe as a whole, since civic traditions and urban political systems vary so widely, but they do illustrate patterns typical of the welfare states of continental northern Europe, and provide illuminating contrasts with the dynamics of American neighborhood politics.

2. The Unequal Landscape of Opportunity in American and European Neighborhoods

Many urban researchers see neighborhoods as wellsprings for political engagement—sites in which civic skills can be developed and put into practice through the making of political claims. This conception of the neighborhood is particularly prominent in the United States, where the Jeffersonian ideal of grassroots democracy holds a deep and abiding place. It is far less important in Europe, where there is neither a dual party system nor direct territorial representation (see below).

Yet, in both Europe and the United States, urban neighborhoods are stratified along economic and ethno-racial lines. This produces a highly unequal distribution of social and economic opportunities, impacting political practice. As we will see, there is ample evidence that in the United States, socio-spatial inequality translates into unequal opportunities to develop and deploy civic skills. In European cities, the political consequences of socio-spatial inequality are different—due in part to differences in the structure of urban governance—but also significant. Political claims are made not only through party politics, but also through various other channels, and differences in social and economic resources between neighborhoods affect how well neighborhood residents can mobilize to influence citywide political agendas. Our understanding of the potential of neighborhoods to function as wellsprings for political engagement thus requires us to first understand how socio-spatial inequality evolves at the neighborhood level.

2.1. The Evolution of Neighborhood Inequality in the United States and Europe

In both the United States and Europe, the spatial distribution of wealth and ethnoracial segregation across neighborhoods has changed markedly since the early 20th century. The landscape of most large European cities developed in the late 19th century due to migration from rural areas to industrializing towns; American cities were shaped by the arrival of immigrants from Europe in the late 19th and early 20th centuries. Most immigrants to the United States went to the northeastern industrializing cities, where they often settled in neighborhoods with concentrations of particular ethnic groups. In Europe, too, migrants from specific regions clustered in particular neighborhoods, creating social divisions visible only on a very small scale (Burgers and Kalb 1995).

In the United States, a second major wave of migration between the 1940s and 1960s brought some five million rural African-Americans from southern states into the industrial cities of the northeast (Judd and Swanstrom 2008, 213). By the early 1970s, a sharp divide had emerged in many urban areas between poor, predominantly African-American central cities and affluent white suburban municipalities. Many older central cities saw population decreases, and were increasingly marked by distressed neighborhoods plagued by joblessness and violence. Conversely, many suburbs became wealthy enclaves that pursued social, political, and physical separation from the central city (see Hero and Orr, in this volume). Northern European cities saw mass migration from Mediterranean countries after World War II, which reached its high point in the 1960s when "guest workers" from Turkey and Morocco were brought in, while postcolonial migration further diversified the ethnic makeup of many cities. Yet segregation remained less pronounced than in America, for reasons that we will explore below.

Most scholars agree that racialized socio-spatial segregation in the United States has now decreased, due to factors such as the rise of an African-American middle class and an increase in Hispanic and Asian immigration (Glaeser and Vigdor 2001). Yet aggregate nationwide income inequality between neighborhoods has continued to intensify (Wheeler and La Jeunesse 2008), and poor African-American residents remain heavily segregated in many cities (Rogers 2006). In European cities, segregation seems to be on the increase. Segregation index research demonstrates that Dutch and German cities have become increasingly divided along ethno-racial lines (Van Kempen and Bolt 1997; Musterd 2005), and gentrification is widespread in cities like Berlin and Amsterdam, creating new patterns of class-cum-race segregation (Wiest and Hill 2004; Van Weesep 1994; Lees 2009).

2.2. Understanding Neighborhood Inequality and Change

Efforts to explain neighborhood change and persistent socio-spatial inequality have given rise to a vast and varied literature. Early American work on neighborhood change is associated with the ecological perspective developed by Chicago School sociologists (Park, Burgess, and McKenzie 1925; Hoover and Vernon 1959), a perspective that also had influence in European urban studies (Bahrdt 1961; Haussermann and Siebert 2004). Widely accepted in its time, much of the ecological work has since been discredited for viewing both ethnic segregation and neighborhood change as "natural" processes (Aldrich 1975).

The spread of deeply distressed African-American neighborhoods in the 1970s spurred some American scholars to turn to macro-level economic explanations. Wilson (1987; 1996), for example, argues that the migration of poor African-Americans into industrial cities was followed by deindustrialization, which resulted in persistently high rates of unemployment for these low-skilled workers. The result, according to Wilson, has been the emergence of a spatially and racially segregated "underclass." There has been extensive discussion as to whether this model also applies to Europe. In an influential comparative analysis of French and American distressed neighborhoods, Wacquant (1999) argues that differences in the character of the welfare state and in neighborhood policy intervention create very different intersections of class and race in the Parisian *banlieues* than in the ghettoes of Chicago. That said, immigrants in European areas of disadvantage do face structural unemployment, poverty, and segregation—but due to higher minimum wages, better public transportation, and smaller cities, of a different quality (Andersson and Musterd 2005; Farwick 2001; Friedrichs and Blasius 2000; Kronauer 2002).

For all their merits, economically oriented arguments cannot fully explain the correlation of race and social disadvantage, nor can they explain why social disadvantage is so spatially concentrated in particular neighborhoods (Kraus 2004, 101). These issues have been tackled by scholars who emphasize political variables. One body of American work emphasizes the United States' history of officially sanctioned or tolerated segregation, targeted primarily at African-Americans. Until 1968 residential racial segregation was not prohibited by federal law, and was actively pursued in many cities. Racially discriminatory practices by the housing industry, such as "redlining" (the refusal to lend money to home buyers in certain, usually African-American neighborhoods) were widely used until they were banned in 1977 (Judd and Swanstrom 144–47). A number of studies document the deep cumulative impact of segregationist practices on the neighborhoods of American cities (Davis 1990; Kraus 2004; Satter 2009). European cities, of course, developed in a different context. Since the destruction of Jewish enclaves during World War II, explicitly segregationist urban policies have not existed in north European cities. However, the contemporary concentration of immigrants in parts of European cities cannot be fully explained by a "natural" selection process or by the preferences of specific migrant groups (Van der Laan Bouma Doff 2007; Musterd and de Winter 1998). Aalbers (2005) has suggested that in Amsterdam and Rotterdam, too, redlining is one of the practices applied with institutional racist consequences.

A second body of politically oriented work in the United States, urban political economy, explores how the structure of local government helps to reproduce socio-spatial inequalities. For a variety of reasons, including dependence on property taxes and the consequent need to compete with other municipalities for investment, American local governments are particularly responsive to the interests of business actors and of middle-class homeowners. This "system bias" (Stone 1976) produces a local politics that privileges growth in property values over social redistribution (see also Peterson 1980; Logan and Molotch 1987; Stone 1989). In this context, distressed neighborhoods are usually either ignored by local politicians, or they are "redeveloped"/gentrified, and their residents displaced to other high-poverty neighborhoods (Stone 1976; Hackworth 2002). Both phenomena tend to reproduce socio-spatial inequalities. At the same time, the fragmentation of most U.S. metropolitan areas into multiple local government units exacerbates inequalities across municipalities (Rusk 1995; Blair and Carroll 2007).

The causal connection between local government structure and neighborhood inequality is clearly illustrated when we contrast the American context with the European one. Europe's national tax systems, national redistribution of resources, and lower dependency on property taxes produces less severe socio-spatial inequalities than those in the United States. That said, the privatization of various public services in European countries is starting to accentuate inequalities. For example, in Germany Haussermann et al. have found a correlation between the role of the state in housing and the homogeneity of new neighborhoods, with market-driven housing provision resulting in increasingly segregated cities (Haussermann, Läpple, and Siebel 2008, 90).

The perspectives we have discussed so far view neighborhood inequality and change as largely driven by external forces. A different body of work examines how the *internal* social characteristics of neighborhoods shape inequality and change. One strand of this work is the sociological literature on "neighborhood effects," which posits that concentrated social and economic disadvantage in distressed neighborhoods produces behaviors, such as crime and drug use, that perpetuate disadvantage. While researchers have identified strong correlations among these variables, causal mechanisms remain hard to demonstrate (Sampson et al. 2002).

There is also a more optimistic strand of work on social organization in neighborhoods, which focuses on the concept of social capital. The social capital thesis suggests that networks of trust among local residents, developed and maintained through social and voluntary associations, can serve as a micro-level foundation for collective political action. This argument, articulated most notably by Putnam (1993; 2000), has received significant attention in recent years in Europe and the United States alike. Yet empirical support for these claims in the United States is rather weak. Hays and Kogl, for example, find that neighborhood residents who are more involved in social associations are not more involved in local political activity (2007, 183). That said, in the European context Dekker (2007) does find that neighborhood social capital affects participation, but only in combination with resident attachment to place and local ties with neighbors (2007, 355).

In a trenchant critique of the political arguments in the social capital literature, De Filippis (2001) holds that a vigorous associational life is necessary but not sufficient to empower neighborhood residents as collective actors. What also matters, De Filippis argues, is the ability of neighborhood residents to identify access points to the broader system of political and economic power (2001, 790). Similarly, Lelieveldt (2004) argues on the basis of Dutch data that social capital may facilitate people's capacity to participate in urban governance and lobby for change, but that governmental action remains central for a range of local problems (see also Dekker and Van Kempen 2006). In other words, consideration of broader power structures needs to be systematically integrated into social capital analysis. One way of doing this, De Filippis argues, would be to borrow from Bourdieu (1985), who sees social capital as the product of social relationships *plus* access political and economic power (De Filippis 2001).

These analyses point us toward a more general problem in the writing on neighborhood inequality and change: The writing on social organization in neighborhoods and the writing on macro-level economic and political forces are often disconnected. Neighborhoods tend to be seen either as victims of forces beyond their control, or as communities that can take charge of their own destiny through appropriate social organization. Relatively few analysts have bridged these perspectives. As we will see, the gap between the two dominant academic understandings of neighborhood inequality and change is reflected in divided views regarding neighborhood-level policy intervention and the promise of neighborhood political action.

3. Policy Intervention and Collective Action: Politics at the Neighborhood Scale

Research on neighborhood politics in both the United States and Europe has focused on two main phenomena: Patterns of policy intervention targeted at neighborhoods, and patterns of political mobilization by neighborhood actors themselves. The stories of neighborhood policy intervention and political mobilization are closely intertwined, as is the academic interpretation of these stories, so the two will be discussed in tandem here, first in the American context, and then in the very different context of the Netherlands. While politics in middle-class and wealthy neighborhoods has been treated in the literature, especially with respect to American suburbs (see Hero and Orr, in this volume), the pervasive and politically pernicious problem of socio-spatial inequality has made poor neighborhoods the primary focus of both policy intervention and academic interest. Consequently, our review focuses primarily on these neighborhoods.

3.1. Neighborhood Intervention and Collective Action in the United States

One of the most striking characteristics of policy aimed at poor neighborhoods in the United States is the prominence of federal intervention. With local governments largely focused on the development and servicing of property, the federal government has repeatedly addressed urban socio-spatial inequality through spatially targeted policies. In the 1950s federal officials sponsored a large-scale program of urban renewal, which was enthusiastically embraced by local political and business elites in many cities (Stone 1976; O'Connor 1995). Housing stock in poor urban neighborhoods was destroyed and replaced either with new commercial real estate, or with large-scale, high-rise public housing projects. It soon became apparent, however, that this program did not reduce socio-spatial segregation (Rae 2003); instead, it tended to further concentrate the poor (Anderson 1964; Fainstein 1986).

At the local level, urban renewal often spurred the emergence of vigorous neighborhood-level protest groups. At the federal level, the failure of urban renewal as social policy led Lyndon Johnson's administration to shift in the 1960s to a strategy of helping neighborhood-level actors to organize themselves. Under the auspices of the War on Poverty, Congress authorized the creation of neighborhood-level Community Action Agencies (CAAs) and Model Cities Agencies (MCAs). These received federal funding directly, which effectively cut municipal politicians out of the neighborhood development equation (Rae 2003). Introduced in the context of the civil rights movement, these policies helped to give birth to a new politics in poor neighborhoods, focused on grassroots mobilization around economic and social development goals. In addition, when combined with the increased electoral strength of African-Americans in many central cities, federal initiatives helped to spur the incorporation of African-Americans into municipal politics (Browning, Marshall, and Tabb 1984). By the mid-1970s several large central cities had African-American mayors whose support was grounded in neighborhood mobilization.

In the 1970s, the Nixon and Ford administrations moved away from direct funding for poor neighborhoods. The new Community Development Block Grant (CDBG) program funneled federal assistance through municipal officials, who disbursed a significant proportion of it to middle-class neighborhoods. In a number of cities, coalitions of middle-class neighborhood associations in turn steered local governing agendas toward neighborhood and quality-of-life concerns, and pressed local political elites to decentralize control over service delivery and policymaking to neighborhood-level decision-making bodies (Boyte 1980; Diers 2004).

The 1980s saw a dramatic scaling back of federal community development funding under the Reagan administration. Remaining funds were reallocated in the service of a new focus: Using public funding to leverage private investment, and focusing on neighborhood-level job creation and small business development. This basic approach was maintained through the 1990s and into the new century. For example, the Clinton administration introduced the Empowerment Zones program, which provides tax credits for local business development and local hiring in poor neighborhoods. The focus on economic development and private investment has in turn changed the landscape of neighborhood mobilization. Service delivery and economic development in poor neighborhoods are now often dominated by professionalized Community Development Corporations (CDCs)—nongovernmental, nonprofit entities that manage contracts with federal, state, and/or local governments, and that leverage private and foundation investment. Protest-based and advocacy-oriented neighborhood associations continue to thrive in many middle-class neighborhoods, but the 1960s and 70s momentum toward a broader decentralization of local power has dissipated.

Policy intervention and political mobilization in American neighborhoods since the 1960s have been subject to a great deal of academic inquiry. We can identify a consistent clustering of scholarly work into two dominant streams. The first stream, which we will call "decentralist," shares many foundational assumptions with the work on neighborhood social organization discussed earlier. Neighborhoods are seen as spatial loci for the development of community, and as basic building blocks of democratic participation in America. Founded mainly on micro-level case studies, decentralist work champions neighborhood political mobilization as a means to pursuing broader policy change, and tends to treat socio-spatial inequality as a second-order problem.

Early decentralist work on neighborhood politics was often heavily prescriptive. For example, Kotler (1969) advocates the radical decentralization of municipal power toward the neighborhood level, while Boyte (1980) celebrates the rise of middle-class neighborhood activism. Over the last 20 years, more explicitly analytical work has emerged. Berry, Portney, and Thomson (1993) draw on evidence from five case cities to argue that decentralization of municipal power to the neighborhood level produces increased citizen participation and more effective local governance, an argument echoed by Fung and Wright (2003). Other decentralist work assesses positively the activity of CDCs. Grogan and Proscio (2000) and Von Hoffman (2003) both argue that an "urban renaissance" is occurring in inner cities, and they credit market-based strategies, often enacted by CDCs, for bringing jobs and investment into poor areas.

Such conclusions lead these authors to support further decentralization of powers and governmental resources to the neighborhood level as a means of increasing political participation and empowering neighborhood actors. However, decentralist work is subject to some significant analytical limitations. Much of it focuses on "best cases" of decentralized governance, a strategy that limits insights into the conditions under which decentralization might emerge in the first place. In addition, the same selection bias limits the generalizability of the literature's findings regarding the positive impact of decentralized governance and policy on inner-city poverty.

A second body of American work draws on the theoretical frame provided by urban political economy. Its key research concern is accounting for the persistence of deep inequalities across neighborhoods *despite* 50 years of intervention and mobilization. As noted earlier, while neighborhood racial segregation has declined modestly from its peak in the United States, there has been no aggregate decrease in income inequality across neighborhoods in recent decades. Indeed, scholars suggest that patterns of intervention and mobilization have in some ways worked to reinforce socio-spatial inequality. Community organizing remains strongest in middle-class and wealthy neighborhoods (Goetz and Sidney 1994; Harwood 2007), and neighborhood mobilization is most effective in addressing property development issues, rather than social welfare and redistribution (Ferman 1996; Fagotto and Fung 2006). Why is this so?

Scholars of urban political economy argue that it is because broader political structures contain and/or subvert the redistributive aspirations of neighborhood intervention and mobilization. As we have seen, municipalities are pivotal players in neighborhood governance in the United States, and aside from a brief period in the 1960s, federal aid has flowed through municipal officials. As noted earlier, the structure of local government in the United States privileges propertied interests, and this in turn leads local politicians in most cities to marginalize neighborhood associations with redistributive aims and co-opt them into a local politics focused on property development (Stone 1976). In a sweeping historical analysis, Katznelson (1981) argues that the organization of American municipal politics around the confluence of neighborhood and race/ethnicity prevents the emergence of a citywide politics of class. As other scholars point out, community activists with redistributive aspirations then face a difficult choice between remaining marginal outsiders and becoming co-opted insiders (Marston and Towers 1993). Meanwhile, federal government emphasis on market-based intervention since the 1980s has further encouraged CDCs to privilege property and business development, even if these do not address the needs of poor residents (Halpern 1995; Stoecker 1997; DeFilippis 2004). Current research on neighborhood regeneration initiatives in several American cities further suggests that such initiatives lack citywide cohesion, and are often shaped by the investment potential of individual neighborhoods (Shiau, Musso, and Sellers 2010; Stoker, Stone, and Worgs 2009).

Given such arguments, it is unsurprising that many political economy scholars have been skeptical of the utility of decentralization. Crenson (1983) argues that decentralization of decision-making and resources to neighborhood associations only accentuates socio-spatial inequality. Katznelson (1981) suggests that the neighborhood mobilization and municipal political incorporation of African-Americans in the late 1960s neutralized the radical class demands of the civil rights movement at the national level and contained them within socially regressive local political structures. Instead of advocating decentralization, some scholars thus suggest ways in which the structure of the local political economy could be altered to empower residents of disadvantaged neighborhoods. Williamson et al. (2002), Imbroscio (1997), and DeFilippis (2004), for example, all advocate strategies to bring capital under local community control. New regionalist scholars (Rusk 1995; Levine 2000) advocate city-regional structures that can share suburban wealth with distressed central cities. Yet such ideas appear politically infeasible in most American cities.

Are the goals of fostering grassroots political agency and decreasing socio-spatial inequality thus fundamentally incompatible? Our review suggests that, the arguments of decentralist authors notwithstanding, there are, at the very least, fundamental tensions between these goals in the American context. Is this condition unique to the United States, or does it obtain in other contexts as well? We can shed light on this question by turning our attention to the Netherlands and Germany. As we will see, research in these contexts offers a different version of the same conclusion, suggesting that these goals stand in tension not only in the American context, but possibly in any Western democracy.

3.2. Neighborhood Intervention and Collective Action in the Netherlands and Germany

In the late 19th century and early 20th century the first surveys of living conditions of the poor were developed in the Netherlands and Germany and, since these data clustered by neighborhoods, deprivation became defined as a neighborhood issue, and community development took place through both religious and social institutions at the local level. Community development initiatives led by local social-democratic and communist political party organizations had broad social components, ranging from newspaper displays where left-wing papers could be read to the active organization of protests and demonstrations. In the 1930s, for example, such demonstrations in Rotterdam and Amsterdam took the form of local rent-strikes, with specific neighborhoods developing a radical reputation (Hendrikx 1977). After World War I, political parties began organizing more on a national level, but their broad membership base within local communities continued to form the backbone of community development efforts. This rather decentralized and often radical form of grassroots political agency did not return after World War II.

The years immediately after World War II in western Europe were characterized by housing shortages, and a consequent focus on producing new dwellings. But by the 1960s, city regeneration through functionalist planning and the large-scale removal of old housing emerged as an important policy focus. In this context, citizens mobilized against the demolition of their neighborhoods in a manner that paralleled developments in the United States (Ostendorf 2004). In the Netherlands, they did so rather successfully. In response, the national social democratic government designed a form of urban regeneration in which piecemeal renovation or rebuilding at the block level became the norm. Political protests, often in the same neighborhoods that had developed a radical reputation in the 1930s, resulted in a right to return for residents. Such urban renewal increased the public housing stock, as redeveloped properties remained state-owned. By the 1980s, however it became clear that this form of urban renewal had shortcomings. First, the focus on improving the physical housing conditions came at the expense of attention to the economic and social position of neighborhood residents. Second, the right to return minimized resident displacement, but in combination with rent-control, it made entire inner-city neighborhoods inaccessible to residents with higher incomes, creating socioeconomically homogeneous areas dominated by a variety of immigrant groups (De Kleijn 1985; Van der Pennen and Wuertz 1986).

In the 1960s and 1970s the German and Dutch welfare states expanded in all spheres of life, including the social infrastructure of neighborhoods. Social service agencies of all kinds mushroomed, and developed professionalized staff (De Swaan 1989; Derksen and Verplanke 1987; Schuyt 1995). State-funded community workers sought to organize, mobilize, and emancipate the residents and activate their political participation at the neighborhood level (Peper 1973). Yet the position of immigrants in such participatory efforts was weak, due both to the common presumption that many immigrants were only temporary residents, and to a widespread belief in the necessity and potential of ethnic minorities to self-mobilize (Cain et al. 1985).

Furthermore, while professionals organized citizens to participate in planning processes in their neighborhoods, this participation receded quickly once renewal was over (Blokland 2003). It became apparent that the multiple problems of disadvantaged residents were not being dealt with adequately, and that newly renovated areas decayed quickly again, since residents seemed to have little sense of collective responsibility for their livability. In an attempt to address the deficiencies of the physical approach of early urban renewal, Dutch authorities organized residents to take responsibility for the cleanliness and safety of public spaces in their neighborhoods through street cleanups, neighborhood watch initiatives, and the like (De Kleijn 1985). In Germany, a similar program, dubbed "Social City," instituted neighborhood management offices to organize residents to get involved in improving the quality of life in their area.

Interestingly, neighborhood collective organization is hardly present in nondeprived areas, so the conclusion of American scholars that neighborhood organizing is most effective in middle-class neighborhoods does not apply in this context. Given the overall good quality of public facilities and infrastructure, and the fact that most political-economic decision making and planning does not take place at the local level, there appears to be little motivation for middle-class neighborhood organizing. Indeed, professionals in the field strongly associate community development and community organizing with emancipating the poor (and, increasingly, immigrants), while housing associations view it as a means to facilitate neighborhood change. In both the Netherlands and Germany, however, this rather simple contrast to the United States is complicated by the recent emergence of private charities and nonprofit foundations as neighborhood development actors, as well as by intensified competition for international investment, which often marginalizes neighborhood interests. In addition, the retreat of the welfare state and the emergence of self-help ideologies have spurred new private-sector initiatives that embrace goals reminiscent of the civic concerns of the charities in the 19th century.

Attempts to decrease socio-spatial inequality are now common in Dutch, German, and other European cities, where state-led gentrification is becoming the norm and mixing neighborhoods by race, ethnicity, and class is a policy goal. Bringing middle-class residents into deprived areas by changing the housing stock (again) is seen as an effective strategy to combat segregation, as well as to strengthen neighborhoods, since middle classes are seen as more likely to participate politically (Kleinhans 2004; Berube 2005; Bailey et al. 2006; Kearns and Mason, 2008; Galster 2007). In the Netherlands, selling good quality public housing to tenants is one of the tactics used, based on the belief that home-ownership will increase local participation (Elsinga 2005). In Germany, the large-scale privatization of housing has diminished state control over neighborhood change. While inner-city neighborhoods gentrify, large estates on the edges of cities are increasingly socially segregated.

Whether or not policies of mixing benefit low-income and marginal residents remains unclear, however, given the inconclusive findings of the "neighborhood effects" research (see above). Moreover, European scholars have argued neither social capital strategies nor demographic strategies create new avenues to access resources for those in disadvantaged positions (Van Eijk 2010; Blokland and Van Eijk 2010). Social capital strategies do not address broader structural inequities (Taylor 2000, 1019; Noordhoff 2008). If and when deindustrialization is the cause of unemployment creating ties among the unemployed will not get them jobs, although it may create companionship and solidarity (Hofmann 2009). Mixing strategies may introduce more neighborhood-level social heterogeneity, but this does not automatically create social ties, let alone social capital (May 1991; Butler and Robson 2003).

4. Understanding Neighborhoods in Urban Politics: Avenues of Further Inquiry

Neighborhoods are paradoxical entities in urban politics. Often seen as seedbeds of civic practice and democracy, they are also geographical instantiations of broader inequalities in contemporary societies. Despite decades of policy intervention and research in both the United States and in Europe, it is not clear whether and how the tensions between the democratic potential of neighborhoods and the realities of socio-spatial inequality can be reconciled. Understanding of the interplay between policy, agency, and inequality at the neighborhood level remains a key task for researchers. We thus conclude with some thoughts on how this task might be approached.

It is clear that the study of neighborhood politics would benefit from more variation-finding work, both within individual countries, and cross-nationally. Some recent American analyses, such as Ferman's (1996) study of neighborhood politics in Pittsburgh and Chicago, suggest that relationships between neighborhood agents and municipal officials vary tremendously across cities. Our own review in this chapter demonstrates the potential of cross-national comparison to illuminate the factors that account for varied mobilizational, political, and social outcomes at the neighborhood level. Yet cross-national comparative work on neighborhood politics is almost entirely absent. Both domestic and cross-national comparative work can provide a basis for theorizing the conditions under which effective collective agency in neighborhoods may be realized. Existing work provides some possible conceptual frames. Concepts such as political opportunity and resource mobilization, drawn from social movement theory, provide one frame. Bourdieu's (1985) conception of social capital as social relationships plus access to power provides another. Although they do not draw explicitly on Bourdieu, Stone et al. (2001) articulate a closely related concept, "civic capacity," which refers to an institutionalized set of inclusive elite-grassroots relationships (see also Foster-Fishman et al. 2006).

Second, the study of neighborhood politics would benefit from more multilevel analysis. The prospects for neighborhood agency are fundamentally affected by forces operating at multiple spatial scales, a fact that has long been recognized by researchers (Durose and Lowndes 2010). Yet, with few exceptions (Orr 2007) there has been little work that focuses on how neighborhood agents themselves might themselves develop political strategies that identify points of leverage beyond the local scale. Existing work suggests that developing multilevel strategies is a difficult undertaking for neighborhood agents, but given the very limited research on the subject, we do not really know what possibilities and practices exist in this regard. As we have seen above, it appears that historically, the multiparty political systems of northern Europe provided more opportunities to "scale up" neighborhood concerns than they do today. Yet new opportunities may also be opening up. For example, thanks to the emergence of new media, anti-globalization movements such as the Right to the City Movement (http://www.righttothecity.org/) can link with neighborhood-level organizations in ways that were not possible in the past.

Third, work on the role of race in American neighborhood politics has long been dominated by a concern with African-Americans, yet the ethno-racial landscape of neighborhood politics is now a diverse one, both in the United States and in Europe. In what ways do prospects for and barriers to neighborhood mobilization differ by race and ethnicity in this new reality? Does an increasingly complex landscape of ethno-racial neighborhood politics open up new possibilities for neighborhood agency, or, conversely, do rapid demographic change and neighborhood instability introduce new constraints and challenges? And how do recent immigrants who are not (yet) citizens get involved in collective agency at the neighborhood level? A small but growing body of work addresses these promising avenues of inquiry (Marston and Towers 1993; Rogers 2006; Clarke et al. 2006). Furthermore, in both the United States and Europe, the tremendous ethnic diversity of immigrant neighborhoods raises questions as to whether neighborhoods are capable of providing residents a frame for identification that has more weight than their ethnic or racial identities.

Finally, research on neighborhood politics and policy in the United States and Europe alike might benefit from a more historical turn. Some of the best work in the field (Stone 1976; Katznelson 1981; Halpern 1995) covers significant spans of time, but the field is dominated by case studies that often lack deeper historical context. Setting such studies in the context of a longer historical trajectory may help to distinguish short-term barriers and opportunities from the longer-term systemic variables that shape the possibilities for neighborhood agency in urban politics.

REFERENCES

Aalbers, M. B. 2005. Who's afraid of red, yellow and green? Redlining in Rotterdam. *Geo-forum* 36: 562–80.

Aldrich, H. 1975. Ecological succession in racially changing neighborhoods: A review of the literature. *Urban Affairs Quarterly* 10: 327–48.

Anderson, M. 1964. *The federal bulldozer: A critical analysis of urban renewal, 1949–1962.* Cambridge, MA: MIT Press.

Andersson, R. and S. Musterd. 2005. Housing mix, social mix, and social opportunities. *Urban Affairs Review* 6: 761–90.

Bahrdt, H. P. 1961. *Die moderne Großstadt. Soziologische Überlegungen zum Städtebau.* Hamburg: Rowholt.

Bailey, N., A. Haworth, T. Manzi, P. Paranagamage and M. Roberts. 2006. *Creating and sustaining mixed income communities. A good practice guide.* Coventry/York: The Chartered Institute of Housing/Joseph Rowntree Foundation.

Berube, A. 2005. *Mixed communities in England. A US perspective on evidence and policy prospects.* York: Joseph Rowntree Foundation.

Berry, J., K. Portney, and K. Thomson. 1993. *The rebirth of urban democracy.* Washington, DC: Brookings Institution.

Blair, J. and M. Carroll. 2007. Inner-city neighborhoods and metropolitan development. *Economic Development Quarterly* 21: 263–77.

Blokland, H. 2005. *Pluralisme, Democratie & Politieke Kennis: Ontwikkelingen in de Moderne Tijd*, Assen: Van Gorcum.

Blokland, H. 2006. *Modernization and its political consequences.* New Haven: Yale University Press.

Blokland, T. 2003. *Urban bonds.* Cambridge: Polity.

Blokland, T. 2006. Civic participation and social capital: Mixing networks in diverse neighbourhoods. In A. Heimgartner, ed. *Face of research on European social development: Community work, civil society and professionalization of social work*: 19–29. Vienna: LitVerlag.

Blokland, T. and G. Van Eijk 2010. Do people who like diversity practice diversity in neighborhood life? Journal of Ethnic and Migration Studies 36(2): 313–32.

Bourdieu, P. 1985. The forms of capital. In J. G. Richardson, ed. *Handbook of theory and research for the sociology of education*: 241–58. New York: Greenwood.

Boyte, H. C. 1980. *The backyard revolution.* Philadelphia, PA: Temple University Press.

Browning, R., D. R. Marshall, and D. H. Tabb. 1984. *Protest is not enough: The struggle of blacks and Hispanics for equality in Urban Politics.* Berkeley: University of California Press.

Burgers, J. and D. Kalb. 1995. Economic restructuring and local consequences: The case of Drents Dorp, Eindhoven. *Journal of Housing and the Built Environment* 10(2): 127–39.

Butler, T and G. Robson. 2003. Living in the bubble: gentrification and its "others" in North London. *Urban Studies* 40(9): 1791–809.

Cain, G. G. et al., eds. 1985. *Etnische minderheden: wetenschap en beleid.* Meppel: Boom.

Clarke, S. N., R. Hero, M. Sidney, L. Fraga and B. Erlichson. 2006. *Multiethnic moments: the politics of urban education reform.* Philadelphia: Temple University Press.

Crenson, M. A. 1983. *Neighborhood politics.* Cambridge, MA: Harvard University Press.

Dahl, R. 1970. *After the revolution? Authority in a good society.* New Haven, CT: Yale University Press.

Davis, M. 1990. *City of quartz: excavating the future in Los Angeles.* London: Verso.

DeFilippis, J. 2001. The myth of social capital in community development. *Housing Policy Debate* 12: 781–806.

DeFilippis, J. 2004. *Unmaking Goliath: community control in the face of global capital.* New York: Routledge.

De Kleijn, G. 1985. *De staat van de stadsvernieuwing.* Utrecht: Vakgroep Stadsstudies RUU.

Dekker, K. 2007. Social capital, neighbourhood attachment and participation in distressed urban areas: a case study in the Hague and Utrecht, the Netherlands. *Housing Studies* 22(3): 355–79.

Dekker, K. and R. Van Kempen. 2006. Large housing estates in Europe: a contemporary overview. In R. van Kempen, K. Dekker, S. Hall, and I. Tosics, eds. *Restructuring large Housing Estates in Europe*: 19–46. Bristol: Policy Press.

Derksen, A. and L. Verplanke. 1987. *Geschiedenis van de onmaatschappelijkheidsbestrijding in Nederland 1914–1970*. Meppel: Boom.

De Swaan, A. 1989. *De mens is de mens een zorg. Opstellen 1971–1981*. Amsterdam: Meulenhoff.

Diers, J. 2004. *Neighbor power: building community the Seattle way.* Seattle: University of Washington Press.

Durose, C. and V. Lowndes. 2010. Neighbourhood governance: contested rationales within a multi-level setting—a study of Manchester. *Local Government Studies* 36(3): 341–59.

Elsinga, M. 2005. Affordable and low risk home ownership. In P. J. Boelhouwer, J. Doling, and M. Elsinga, eds. *Home Ownership: getting in, getting from, getting out*: 75–94. Delft: DUP Science.

Fagotto, E. and A. Fung. 2006. Empowered participation in urban governance: the Minneapolis Neighborhood Revitalization Program. *International Journal of Urban and Regional Research* 30(3): 638–55.

Fainstein, S. 1986. *Restructuring the city: the political economy of urban redevelopment.* New York: Longman.

Farwick A. 2001. *Segregierte Armut in der Stadt: Ursachen und soziale Folgen der räumlichen Konzentration von Sozialhilfeempfängern*. Opladen: Leske & Budrich.

Ferman, B. 1996. *Challenging the growth machine: neighborhood politics in Chicago and Pittsburgh*. Lawrence: University Press of Kansas.

Foster-Fishman, P., K. Fitzgerald, C. Brandell, B. Nowell, D. Chavis, and L. Van Egeren. 2006. Mobilizing residents for action: the role of small wins and strategic supports. American Journal of Community Psychology 38: 143–52.

Friedrichs, J. and J. Blasius 2000. *Leben in benachteiligten Wohngebieten*. Opalen: Leske & Budrich.

Fung, A. and E. Wright. 2003. *Deepening democracy: institutional innovations in empowered participatory governance*. London: Verso.

Galster, G. 2007. Should policy makers strive for neighborhood social mix? An analysis of the western European evidence base. *Housing Studies* 22(4): 523–45.

Glaeser, E. and J. Vigdor. 2001. Racial segregation in the 2000 census: promising news. *Survey Series*. Washington, DC: Brookings Institution.

Goetz, E. and M. Sidney. 1994. Revenge of the property owners: community development and the politics of property. *Journal of Urban Affairs* 16(4): 319–34.

Grogan, P. and T. Proscio. 2000. *Comeback cities: a blueprint for urban neighborhood revival.* Boulder: Westview Press.

Guest, A. and B. Lee. 1984. How urbanites define their neighborhoods. *Population and Environment* 7: 32–56.

Hackworth, J. 2002. Post-recession gentrification in New York City. *Urban Affairs Review* 37: 815–43.

Halpern, R. 1995. *Rebuilding the inner city: a history of neighborhood initiatives to address poverty in the United States*. New York: Columbia University Press.

Harwood, S. 2007. Geographies of opportunity for whom? Neighborhood improvement programs as regulators of neighborhood activism. *Journal of Planning Education and Research* 26(3): 261–71.

Häussermann, H., D. Läpple, and W. Siebel 2008. *Stadtpolitik*. Frankfurt am Main: Suhrkamp.

Hays, R. and A. Kogl. 2007. Neighborhood attachment, social capital building, and political participation: a case study of low- and moderate-income residents of Waterloo, Iowa. *Journal of Urban Affairs* 29: 181–205.

Hendrikx, H. G. M. 1977. Rellen en huurstakingen in Rotterdam tijdens de jaren dertig [Riots and rent strikes in Rotterdam during the 1930s], Ph.D. thesis, Erasmus Universiteit, Rotterdam.

Hofmann, Barbara. 2009. Do more placement officers lead to lower unemployment? Evidence from Germany. IAB Discussion Paper 13/2009.

Hoover, E. and R. Vernon. 1959. *Anatomy of a metropolis*. Cambridge, MA: Harvard University Press.

Imbroscio, D. 1997. *Reconstructing city politics: alternative economic development and urban regimes*. Thousand Oaks, CA: Sage.

Judd, D. and T. Swanstrom. 2008. *City politics: the political economy of urban America*. New York: Pearson.

Katznelson, I. 1981. *City trenches: urban politics and the patterning of class in the United States*. New York: Pantheon.

Kleinhans, R. 2004. Social implications of housing diversification in urban renewal: a review of recent literature. *Journal of Housing and the Built Environment* 19(4): 367–90.

Kearns, A. and P. Mason. 2008. Mixed tenure communities and neighbourhood quality. *Housing Studies* 22: 661–91.

Kotler, M. 1969. *Neighborhood government: the local foundations of political life*. Indianapolis: Bobbs-Merrill.

Kraus, N. 2004. The significance of race in urban politics: the limitations of regime theory. *Race and Society* 7: 95–111.

Kronauer, M. 2002. *Exklusion. Die Gefährdung des Sozialen im hoch entwickelten Kapitalismus*. Frankfurt am Main: Campus Verlag.

Kuschenbach, M. 2003. Street phenomenology. *Ethnography* 4(3): 455–85.

Lees, L. 2009. Urban renaissance in an urban recession: the end of gentrification? *Environment and Planning A* 41(7): 1529–33.

Lelieveldt, H. 2004. Helping citizens help themselves: neighborhood improvement programs and the impact of social networks, trust and norms on neighborhood-oriented forms of participation. *Urban Affairs Review* 39(5): 531–51.

Levine, M. V. 2000. A third-world city in the first world: Social exclusion, racial inequality, and sustainable development in Baltimore. In M. Polese and R. Stren, eds. *The social sustainability of cities*: 123–56. Toronto: University of Toronto Press.

Logan, J. and H. Molotch. 1987. *Urban fortunes: the political economy of place*. Berkeley: University of California Press.

Ludwig-Mayerhofer, Wolfgang, Olaf Behrend, and Ariadne Sondermann· 2009. *Auf der Suche nach der verlorenen Arbeit· Arbeitslose und Arbeitsvermittler im neuen Arbeitsmarktregime*. Konstanz: UVK.

Marston, S. and G. Towers. 1993. Private spaces and the politics of places: spatioeconomic restructuring and community organizing in Tucson and El Paso. In R. Fisher and J. Kling, eds. *Mobilizing the community: Local politics in the era of the global city*: 75–102. Newbury Park, CA: Sage.

Musterd, S. 2005. Social and Ethnic Segregation in Europe: Levels, Causes, and Effects. *Journal of Urban Affairs* 27:331–48.

Musterd, S. and M. de Winter. 1998. Conditions for spatial segregation: some Europe an perspectives. *International Journal of Urban and Regional Research* 22: 665–73.

Noordhoff, F. 2008. *Persistent poverty in the Netherlands.* Amsterdam: Amsterdam University Press.

O'Connor, T. H. 1995. *Building a new Boston: politics and urban renewal, 1950–1970.* Boston: Northeastern University Press.

Orr, M. 2007. ed. *Transforming the city: community organizing and the challenge of political change.* Lawrence: University Press of Kansas.

Ostendorf, W. 2004. The neighbourhood as a context of responsibility. *Dela* 21:319–28.

Park, R., E. Burgess and R. McKenzie. 1925. *The city: suggestions for the study of human nature in the urban environment.* Chicago: University of Chicago Press.

Pateman, C. 1970. *Participation and democratic theory.* Cambridge: Cambridge University Press.

Peper, B. 1973. *Vorming van welzijnsbeleid, evolutie en evaluatie van het opbouwwerk.* Boom: Meppel.

Peterson, P. 1980. *City limits.* Chicago: University of Chicago Press.

Putnam, R. 1993. *Making democracy work: civic traditions in modern Italy.* Princeton: Princeton University Press.

Putnam, Robert. 2000. *Bowling alone: collapse and revival of American community.* New York: Simon & Schuster.

Rae, D. W. 2003. *City: Urbanism and its end.* New Haven, CT: Yale University Press.

Rogers, R. 2006. *Afro-Caribbean immigrants and the politics of incorporation.* Cambridge: Cambridge University Press.

Rusk, D. 1995. *Cities without suburbs*, 2nd ed. Washington, DC: Woodrow Wilson Center Press.

Sampson, R. J., J. D. Morenoff, and T. Gannon-Rowley. 2002. Assessing "neighborhood effects": social processes and new directions in research. *Annual Review of Sociology* 28: 443–78.

Satter, B. 2009. *Family properties: race, real estate, and the exploitation of black urban America.* New York: Metropolitan Books.

Schuyt, K. 1995. *De verdeelde samenleving: een inleiding in de ontwikkeling van de Nederlandse verzorgingstaat.* Leiden: Stenfert Kroese.

Shiau, E., J. Musso and J. Sellers. 2010. Institutions and civil society: the political dynamics of neighborhood regeneration in Los Angeles. Paper presented at Midwest Political Science Association Conference, Chicago.

Stoecker, R. 1997. The CDC model of urban redevelopment: a critique and an alternative. *Journal of Urban Affairs* 19(1): 1–22.

Stoker, R., C. Stone and D. Worgs. 2009. Policy subsystems and the politics of neighborhood policy in Baltimore. Paper presented at American Political Science Association annual meeting, Toronto.

Stone, C. N. 1976. *Economic growth and neighborhood discontent: system bias in the urban renewal program of Atlanta.* Chapel Hill: University of North Carolina Press.

Stone, C. N. 1989. *Regime politics: Governing Atlanta.* Lawrence: University Press of Kansas.

Stone, C. N., J. R. Henig, B. D. Jones and C. Pierannunzi. 2001. *Building civic capacity: the politics of reforming urban schools.* Lawrence: University Press of Kansas.

Taylor, Marilyn. 2000. Communities in the Lead: Power, Organisational Capacity and Social Capital. *Urban Studies* 37(5–6): 1019–35.

Tocqueville, A. 2000. *Democracy in America*, trans. G. Lawrence. New York: Perennial Classics, 2000.

Van der Laan Bouma Doff, W. 2007. Involuntary isolation: ethnic preferences and residential segregation. *Journal of Urban Affairs* 29(3): 289–309.

Van der Pennen, T. , and K. Wuertz. 1985. *Bouwen voor de kleurrijke buurt.* The Hague: VUGA.

Van Eijk, G. 2010. *Unequal networks: spatial segregation, relationships and inequality in the city.* Delft: IOS Press.

Van Kempen, R. and G. Bolt. 1997. Turks in the Netherlands: urban segregation and neighborhood choice. *American Behavioral Scientist* 41(3): 374–95.

Van Weesep, J. 1994. Gentrification as a research frontier. *Progress in Human Geography* 18: 74–83.

Von Hoffman, A. 2003. *House by house, block by block: the rebirth of America's urban neighborhoods.* New York: Oxford University Press.

Wacquant, L. 1999. Red Belt, Black Belt: Racial Division, Class Inequality, and the State in the French Urban Periphery and the American Ghetto. In Enzo Mingione, ed. *Urban poverty and the "underclass": a reader*: 234–74. Oxford: Basil Blackwell.

Wellman, B. and B. Leighton. 1979. Networks, neighborhoods and communities: approaches to the study of the community question. *Urban Affairs Quarterly* 14(3): 363–90.

Wheeler, C. H. and E. La Jeunesse. 2008. Trends in neighborhood income inequality in the U.S.: 1980–2000. *Journal of Regional Science* 48(5): 879–91.

Wiest, K. and A. Hill. 2004. Sanfte Gentrifizierung, Studentifizierung und Inseln ethnischer Konzentration in ostdeutschen Cityrandgebieten. Das Beispiel Leipzig. *Raumforschung und Raumordnung* 4: 361–74.

Williamson, T., D. Imbroscio and G. Alperovitz· 2002. *Making a place for community: local democracy in a global era.* New York: Routledge.

Wilson, W. J. 1987. *The truly disadvantaged: the inner city, the underclass, and public policy.* Chicago: University of Chicago Press.

Wilson, W. J. 1996. *When work disappears: the world of the new urban poor.* New York: Random House.

CHAPTER 14

SOCIAL MOVEMENTS IN URBAN POLITICS: TRENDS IN RESEARCH AND PRACTICE

MARGIT MAYER AND
JULIE-ANNE BOUDREAU

1. Introduction

Mobilization around urban conflicts and their efforts to influence urban politics have a long history. As urbanization advanced, cities became increasingly viewed as sites where social struggles and emancipatory politics were concentrated. In the 19th and early 20th centuries, First World cities were sites of politically mobilized working classes and harbored vibrant proletarian public spheres. Since the post-World War II period, they have become sites of struggles around collective consumption, particularly in the 1960s when contestations over public infrastructures and public space were perceived by ruling classes across the advanced Western countries as unrest threatening broader catalytic effects. While cities in the global North seem to have lost this potential of radiating transformative change into society at large, social movements of various kinds still mobilize and intervene in local politics, and cities in the global South have become sites of new forms of resistance which, however, in many ways defy the explanatory frameworks provided by prevalent movement theories. Globalization and global urbanization have deeply affected the transnational division of labor, and thus the class composition of cities worldwide, spawning significant reconfigurations within both practice and theories of social movements in urban settings.

This chapter traces first, the genealogy of urban movements and second, of the theories and methodologies developed to explain their dynamics primarily in European and North American settings, where different legacies have generated different "schools" of analysis. Their respective strengths and weaknesses are then evaluated against the emergence and increasingly salient role of "glocal" movements influenced by transnational antiglobalization activism, as well as against the novel forms of urban micro- and infra-politics[1] (which may be read as manifesting an impact of urbanity on forms of political action) with the potential of reaching a global scale because of the scope and interdependencies of the current historical period. Finally, and on the basis of our reading of the deficits and lacunae of current urban research and action, we suggest some lines for a future research agenda.

2. Tracing the Genealogy of "Urban Social Movements"

Even though urban social movements have a long history, they have not explicitly been identified in social science literatures until the 1960s. The term "urban social movement" was first introduced in studies by Manuel Castells and other French researchers in order to challenge a view then prevalent in urban sociology, which saw social problems and spatial structures primarily from the perspective of social integration. In contrast to this sociological view, and inspired by the widespread struggles over housing policies, urban renewal, and squatting, which these researchers were observing at the time, they developed a concept of urban conflicts as structured by struggles over (political) power. They saw urban movements as not only articulating the structural contradictions of late-capitalist societies, but also as capable of bringing about, together with labor unions and political parties, fundamental change in politics and society (Castells 1977, 432). This definition, though later abandoned by Castells (1983), has spread not only across Western metropoles, but also across Latin America and the newly industrializing countries of Asia, and has become influential in guiding the research of the "new urban sociology" (cf. Lebas 1982; Pickvance 1976).

This early concept of urban social movements was more interested in the (potential) function and effects of the movements than in their concrete origins, their specific forms of organizing and mobilizing, and the various ways in which they pursued their interests. Analysis focused on the structural contradictions articulated by the movements, less on their frames and ideologies, action repertoires, and organizational patterns. As a consequence, what was studied were primarily

1. The term was coined by Scott (1990) to designate a "hidden transcript of power," actions taken in uncoordinated manner in everyday settings and difficult to detect from the perspective of those in power.

those movements that seemed or promised to bring about social and political change—less promising, localist, or small-scale mobilizations that did not reflect the large structural contradictions of class society remained outside the radar screen of these scholars.

By the mid-1980s, as urban conflicts intensified and cities experienced more and more varied forms of protest and political mobilization, this narrow definition of social movements was displaced by less normative views of urban activism. Castells as well, in his central study of the topic (1983), redefines urban movements in a less charged way as "urban-oriented mobilizations that influence structural social change and transform the urban meanings" (305). These movements combine activism around collective consumption with struggles for community culture as well as for political self-management; "transforming urban meanings" thus implies the undermining of the social hierarchies that structure urban life and producing, instead, a city organized on the basis of use values, autonomous local cultures, and decentralized participatory democracy (319–20).

Another neo-Marxist, yet less structuralist strand of analysis of urban movements developed on the basis of Lefebvre's writings on the critique of everyday life and on cities. Lefebvre's concept of the Everyday Life connotes, as that of the Situationists, both a space of resistance against alienation and the permanent colonization of the lifeworld through the commodity form. While commodification of all realms of life is accelerated by the global process of "urbanization" of society, it is also urban space which becomes a new productive force. Lefebvre wrote *La révolution urbaine* (1970) under the impression of the 1968 events in Paris, viewing "revolution" both as technocratic, neoliberal conquest of the world, as well as urban praxis as utopian critique, thus laying the basis for a more ambiguous yet emancipatory concept for interpreting movements for the right to the city.

David Harvey, concerned with the diversity and fragmentation of place-based resistance movements which he viewed as incoherent and fraught with internal contradictions (Harvey 1996; 2000), suggested identifying the underlying class content in the broad range of issues of "militant particularism," thereby providing the foundation for a more universal socialist resistance politics. Borrowing the notion from Raymond Williams (1989), Harvey argued that militant particularisms are often profoundly conservative, resting upon the perpetuation of patterns of social relations and community solidarities. Left to themselves, he sees such place-based movements easily dominated by the power of capital, unable to transcend the narrow solidarities and particular affinities shaped in particular places. He concludes that movements need to develop a politics of solidarity reaching across space, without abandoning their militant particularist base(s) (1996, 400).

Distinct from such (neo-)Marxist perspectives on the reality and possibilities of the city, which shaped urban movement research particularly across the European countries (cf. Mayer et al. 1978), North America saw primarily another, more pragmatic, perspective take hold. Most scholars here initially focused on empirical studies of protest movements of urban minorities in the context of local political structures (e.g. Fainstein and Fainstein 1974) and on the long established tradition of community organizing (cf. Fisher 1994), which saw a massive renaissance in the context of struggles against renewal and displacement, but also on homeowner movements (cf. Fainstein and Hirst 1995, 190).

Latin American authors had also started to devote themselves to empirical investigations of local political actions exploding onto the scenes of newly democratized countries (cf. Escobar and Alvarez 1992; Wignaraja 1993). Both in North and South America, where structuralist traditions have been less influential than in Europe, questions of mobilization, organization, and empowerment of discriminated and marginalized urban groups gained attention and were moved into the foreground of research far sooner than in Europe. This led to a more open and broader definition of urban social movements, including a wide variety of forms of mobilization taking place within and oriented toward the city.

Identity-based movements have also made their mark in urban politics and have been studied from within a variety of perspectives. In Western cities, struggles for recognition of marginalized identities were particularly intense in the 1980s and 1990s, accompanied by academic debates on the relationship between identity and redistributional politics. Iris Young's chapter on city life in her 1990 book nicely summarizes the tensions in the North American context. While movements based on ethnic and racial identities were soon dealt with in the context of urban politics literatures, as well as increasingly in studies of urban social movements, the role of gay and lesbian movements in urban life was viewed in more ambiguous terms. Castells (1983) devoted a chapter to analyzing the gay community in San Francisco, highlighting its success in transforming the local political system and in upgrading property values and built environment (similarly Lauria and Knopp 1985), but bemoaning its failure to align with the women's movement and thus to build a new hegemonic culture. Bailey's (1999) study of gay and lesbian activism in four U.S. cities combined political-economic with identity-related approaches, thus allowing for a fuller understanding of gay residential concentration and electoral prowess. While North American authors have emphasized how sexual minorities have claimed territory in the city from which to build inclusion and representation, in the European debates, gay and lesbian space has been considered more in terms of resistance and transgression. In eastern European cities, gay and lesbian activism still mainly revolves around the contestation of the criminalization and marginalization of homosexuality, whereas in the West since the 1990s, gay pride marches, CSD demonstrations, and gay scenes more generally have increasingly become commercialized, which has reoriented research into exploring the normalizing effects of a "lesbian and gay equality" rhetoric (Richardson 2005) and the impetus of sexual politics commodified as "cosmopolitan and incorporated spatiality" (Binnie and Skeggs 2004), but also its new radical potential when the capitalization of cultural difference is tactically harnessed (e.g. Bassi 2006).

Generally, the international debate now speaks of *social* movements to the extent that collective actors intervene, through mobilization, in processes of social and/or political change, and of *urban* movements to the extent that their goals and activities concern the city and its decision-making structures and processes. However, new research currently goes beyond this definition of "urban movement" by exploring how urbanity affects wider types of political acts as well (see section 4 below).

Urban movements have not only appeared in different shapes and sizes, but they have also undergone significant changes. To this day, urban movements in the so-called transformation societies follow different patterns from those challenging the urbanism of Western democracies. And within the former, the different eastern European countries' movements, though sharing characteristics and concerns, particularly over housing and environmental degradations, exhibit significant differences depending on the strength of their respective civil societies (cf. Pickvance 2000). Unlike their postsocialist counterparts, the urban movements that emerged in (post-military dictatorship) Latin American countries were part of broad popular struggles not only around issues of consumption and workforce reproduction, but also civil liberties, democratization of daily life, and the organization of cooperatives. Though the World Bank and IMF thrust most Latin American countries into severe economic crisis, and homegrown repressive regimes forced social movements onto the defensive, these precarious decades were survived thanks to self-organizing *barrios*, where neighborhood women played important roles nourishing the need for warm food and basic services as well as for dignity. Country after country has seen new (workers) parties or indigenous movements gain strength and oust repressive regimes, creating space for more participatory democracy and empowering the local movements against neoliberalism and imperialism. Also, struggles were won by the gay and lesbian movements in cities such as Mexico City, where gay marriage was recently recognized in the wake of numerous other progressive policies implemented by the leftist government since the 1990s, with the impressive result of having challenged the authoritarian regime of the PRI nationwide.

Our knowledge of urban movements in the new growth regions of Asia appears to be more scattered if we look exclusively under the familiar labels, that is, look for literatures applying the social movement theories elaborated within Western contexts (e.g. Ho Kwok-laung 2000). But if we cast the net more widely, we find that, as with Latin American urbanism, there is sustained research on the marginalities of the South Asian city, but also work on the possibilities of urban citizenship. South Asian scholarship is shaped by traditions of postcolonial theory and studies of the South Asian city are concerned with the hegemonic production of urban subjects, specifically with how subaltern subjects consent to and participate in projects of urban redevelopment and inequality (Roy 2003a). This as well as scholarship on urban movements in South Asia, Africa, or the Middle East open windows to forms of agency that go beyond the hegemonic theoretical frameworks, and future research will be well served to incorporate it more systematically if we want to understand the trajectory of urban social movements.

The prevailing theoretical approaches, even though they have been developed mostly on the basis of urban conflict in Western democracies, fall short in accounting for the significant changes First World urban activism has undergone since globalization and neoliberalism have fundamentally reconfigured cityscapes here—as well as, of course, in the Second and Third Worlds. As First World cities have transformed into something like "global suburbs," having outsourced much of their manufacturing to platforms in the global South, they now constitute privileged spaces for more and less gentrified "creative classes," and breeding grounds for a mix of alternative, critical, and "bohemian" milieus.

This generates a new antagonism (and hence new types of conflict) between top-end users of the city versus growing advanced marginality, creating fundamentally restructured movement terrains and new relationships between municipalities and civil society actors. Privatization, security measures, the proliferation of zones of segregation, and the retrenchment of municipal services and infrastructures are all contributing to the disappearance of spaces for collectivization, and to the disintegration of the role public space might play in the formation and politicization of (class) subjects and for building alliances. Yet, at the same time, as (low) waged work has expanded to include more women and more immigrants, First World cities increasingly become important sites of anticolonial struggles as well as struggles against racism and sexism, and the trends to pit "creative urban lifestyles" against suburban dwellers are also being contested, as for example by the Creative Class Struggle group in Toronto.[2]

3. Social Movement Theories and Urbanity

This genealogy of the concept of urban social movements demonstrates that it developed as a fairly autonomous self-standing body of literature, separated from social movement theories. Social movement theories, whether of the "American" or the "European" traditions,[3] have some trouble with the urban specificity of movements

2. When Richard Florida moved to Toronto in 2007 (with public subsidies to pay for his salary and support his research at the University of Toronto), local residents began to mobilize against the dominance of creative class policies. According to the group, "'Creative class' policies are designed to build money-making cities rather than secure livelihoods for real people. These policies celebrate a society based on inequality, in which a select group of glorified professionals is supported by an invisible army of low-wage service workers. Seduced by the promise of prosperity and growth, governments around the world are reorienting their economies along these 'creative' class lines without consulting immigrants, women, people of colour, low-wage workers, and others directly affected by their decisions. Divisive 'creative class' policies, implemented in the midst of the worst financial crisis since the Great Depression, serve only to increase the vulnerability of the vulnerable and further empower the powerful" (http://creativeclassstruggle.wordpress.com/mission/, retrieved August 4, 2010).

3. By now, the division between "American" and "European" social movement theories (cf. Mayer 1991, 1995) has been broken down by many contributions (see for instance della Porta and Diani 1999). Yet its legacies are still palpable—as illustrated even

as it runs counter to the categorization logic of environmental, women's, LGBT, peace, antinuclear, or other new social movements. The "American" perspective, led among others by Tarrow, Zald, McAdams, and Tilly, is primarily preoccupied with understanding the conditions enabling political mobilization, with the concept of political opportunity structure at the center of their analytical framework (see Tarrow, 1998; McAdam, McCarthy, and Zald, 1996; McAdam, Tarrow, and Tilly, 2001). In addition to identifying the conditions for mobilization, this approach seeks to unveil the mechanisms through which various forms of political contention (from social movements to revolution) unfold in relation to the state. Resources, organizational form, framing processes, repertoires of action serve as foci of analysis for understanding the mechanics of political contention. This literature does not consider urbanity as a factor worthy of analysis. More recent work suggests instead (as we will show in the last section) that urbanity, understood as a historically-situated and unevenly distributed condition, also has an impact on the logic of political contention. The idea that contention works in cycles (the concept of a cycle of protest), with the 1960s and 1970s as the epitome of such cycles in the "American" theoretical perspective, does not consider the urban quality of such cycles as a relevant explanatory factor.

The "European" perspective, known as new social movement theory, has been more sensitive to the role of urbanity, but without explicitly reflecting on its influence on mobilization. The interrogation here centers on uncovering the structural socioeconomic and cultural transformations that led to the emergence of newly politicized issues (such as sexual orientation, environmentalism, ecology, etc.) outside of the labor-capital nexus (see for instance Melucci 1989; Touraine 1992; Mayer and Roth 1995). These movements, to quote Ruggiero, are "not preoccupied with struggles over the production and distribution of material goods, but rais[e] cultural challenges to the dominant language and to official codes" (Ruggiero, 2001, 43–44). More influenced by Marxism than rational choice theory (as are the American scholars), this "European" approach is concerned with defining what counts as "social movement" (rather narrowly as opposed to the concept of political contention generally used by American scholars). Inspired by Marx's idea of labor as the motor of history, they define a social movement as a force that has social transformative power. This, of course, eliminates many urban struggles, where the connection between their practice and a potentially society-wide transformative effect is less clear. Yet, the fact that new social movement theory is interested in newly politicized issues that are particularly visible in cities might have initiated a reflection on the impact of urbanity on social mobilization. Lefebvre (1968; 1970),

by recent publications such as an 'urban social movements' entry published in the U.S. (Rabrenovic 2009). It describes urban social movement theory exclusively in terms of American approaches "including most prominently resource mobilization theory, political opportunity structure theory and framing theory" (241), mentioning neither the influence of Lefebvre or Harvey, nor the European new social movement perspective.

though not a social movement theorist per se but widely perceived as writing within this context, is the only author who explicitly raised this question. For this, he was criticized by Castells (1972) and Harvey (1973). In *The Urban Question* (1972, 1977), Castells emphasized that there is nothing specifically urban about the way history progresses. According to this young Castells, the prevailing motor of action was still class struggle. He rejected the idea that an urban mode of production was displacing the industrial capital-labor nexus. His analysis interpreted political claims arising in cities as the contemporary manifestation of the capital-labor conflict, shifted from the workplace to the collective consumption spaces of the city. In *Social Justice and the City* (1973), Harvey made a similar argument, suggesting that the urban was still heavily dependent on industrial capital and thus cannot be analyzed as a new mode of production. His evidence was that industrial capital was still far stronger than land capital.

As the global political economic context drastically changed in the following decades, both Castells and Harvey later nuanced these arguments from the 1970s and offered important reflections on the urbanity of social movements. While Castells (1996–98) turns more toward the networked organizational form of social and political claims, Harvey (1989; 2008) revisits Lefebvre's early claims to the right to the city and highlights the shifts in the political economic context that have enabled the rise of urban movements around the globe. As urbanization globalizes through the integration of financial markets and through the dictates of international organizations pushing for urbanizing policies in the South in order to foster economic development, more and more movements rally under the banner of the "Right to the City" (Mayer 2009).

Especially as the fallout of the financial and economic crisis has been making itself felt, and as growing numbers of urban residents see long-accustomed rights erode, the slogan "Right to the City" has come to merge and concentrate a set of highly charged issues: it has the potential to bring together deprived and excluded groups with culturally alienated, discontented groups, and also to forge connections between struggles in First World metropoles and those in cities of the global South, where the fight against privatization, speculation, eviction, and displacement is even far more existential.

But the claim is being invoked in rather different, not always reconcilable ways. On the one side, movements are building on the Lefebvrian conception, where urbanization stands for a transformation of society and everyday life through capital. Against this transformation Lefebvre sought to *create* rights through social and political action: the street, and claims to it, are establishing these rights. In this sense, the right to the city is not a juridical right, but rather an oppositional demand. It is a right to redistribution, not for all people, but for those deprived of it and in need of it. And it is a right that exists only as people appropriate it (and the city). In this sense, many local struggles in European and American cities have recently invoked the claim and used it to form alliances across town and across issues, between housing activists and artists, leftist groups and cultural workers, small business owners and the new precarious groups—as all of them feel threatened by contemporary forms of development entailing gentrification, mega projects, and displacement. In the U.S. it is even used as an organizational principle as with the Right to the City Alliance (cf. Leavitt et al. 2009).

At the same time the slogan has also gained traction in another context, where international NGOs and advocacy organizations have adopted it with somewhat different connotations. Beginning in the mid-1990s, a variety of inter- and transnational policy networks and international NGOs have developed "Urban Agendas" and in 2001, now in the framework of the World Social Forum (WSF), a process was opened to formulate a *World Charter on the Right to the City*. A couple events in particular stood out in the revision, negotiation, and dissemination process: at the Social Forum of the Americas in Quito, Ecuador, in 2004 the Habitat International Coalition together with other transnational organizations promoted instruments through which to broaden and activate social mobilization around this new right; during the World Social Forum in Porto Alegre in 2005 a "World Charter of the Right to the City" was adopted. The UN-Habitat decision to organize the fifth World Urban Forum in 2010 around the theme of the right to the city further contributed to propel the topic to the worldwide arena. Parallel to these initiatives, some governments, at various levels, have been generating charters in order to legislate human rights in the urban context.

The objective of such charters is to establish effective legal monitoring mechanisms and instruments to ensure the enforcement of recognized human, social, and citizenship rights. In their effort to put "our most vulnerable urban residents" rather than investors and developers at the center of public policy, these charters enumerate specific rights which a progressive urban politics should particularly protect. All of these listed rights (such as: to housing, social security, work, leisure, information, organization, free association, food and water, freedom from dispossession, etc.) are supposed to hold for all "urban inhabitants," but some groups are highlighted as deserving particular protection (poor, ill, handicapped, and migrants get mentioned). (These and further details to be found on the website UNESCO.ORG; cf. also Sugranyes and Mathivet 2010; on how the Right to the City has become materialized in legal terms in Brazil, see Fernandes 2007.)

Fully realized, such rights might spell improvements for disadvantaged groups. However, such institutionalized sets of rights invariably boil down to claims for inclusion in the contemporary city as it exists; they do not aim at transforming the existing system—and in that process ourselves. They target particular aspects of neoliberal policy, but not the underlying structures which systematically produce exploitation, poverty, and marginalization. Perhaps one promising movement potentially able to merge the city-based transformative struggles with transnational urban agendas might develop out of claims by urban indigenous peoples. Tapping into transnational postcolonial theories and practices, urban indigenous people in North America are increasingly claiming the right to the city, with transformative potential.

Both "European" and "American" theoretical perspectives on social movements, and particularly the depoliticized version of "the right to the city," which echoes many assumptions of the latter, lack attention to urbanity as a condition that transforms the practice of political contestation. In many ways, this can be explained by disciplinary divisions, with political scientists and sociologists on one side, and geographers and urbanists on the other. The latter have been at the forefront of discussions on the emancipatory city, linking urban movements with the broader political economic context, while political scientists and sociologists have been more concerned with conflicts between social movements and state institutions. While political scientists and sociologists have had their respective contingent of scholars working on urban politics and urban sociology, these subfields have largely been narrowly defined around municipal politics and apolitical social interactions.

Hence it seems to us an urgent task of the contemporary period, as we argue below, to bring these various disciplinary, theoretical, and methodological strands together. In a study of how the urban poor movements of Mexico have contributed to major institutional and political-economic changes in this country, Haber (2006) develops an interesting methodological framework combining tools from "American" social movement theories (political opportunity structure, cycles of protest, as well as influences from Piven and Cloward 1979) with a phenomenological approach to understand the construction of activist subjectivity, something closer to the heart of the "European" approach to social movements. He focuses on relationships between activists because understanding what difference it makes "to a middle-aged, low income woman living in a shantytown [for instance] if she refers to her neighbour as *señora* or *compañera*" "deepens our appreciation for the experience of movements; it also contributes to our analytical understanding of how this resource is generated and its power implications" (Haber 2006, 19). Along with this, he offers an interesting reflection on changing intergovernmental relations and the rise of cities as political actors in the global neoliberal context of the 1980s and 1990s.

4. Global Urbanity and Political Mobilization

At the height and yet beginning crisis of neoliberalism (with the dot.com crash of 2001), urban movements entered a new phase, where urbanization has gone global through the integration of financial markets that have used their flexibility to debt-finance urban development around the world (Harvey 2008, 30). Economic growth rates began to stagnate in the "old" industrial nations, and sharper social divides became expressed in intensifying socio-spatial polarization, while reforms of social security systems replaced welfare with workfare that seeks to "activate" the urban underclass into downgraded and informal labor markets. But still, the benefits of the growth of the last 30 years have overwhelmingly gone to those living in the West/North under immeasurably higher living standards than the greater part of the world, even higher than for most but the very rich in the dynamic economies which have been keeping the world economy going. The emerging economies in formerly "underdeveloped" regions have seen unprecedented growth rates in industrialization and urbanization driven by neoliberal market rule. Whether in Africa, Latin America, South or East Asia, this intense development usually privileges upper- and middle-class propertied interests, while shack-dweller communities, pavement dwellers, and slum and favela regions have sprawled at the outskirts or within exploding mega cities, marginalizing and discriminating their inhabitants in multiple ways. However, their daily struggles for survival, usually at the grassroots level and most often hidden from view, have been challenging and reframing the association of civilization and urbanization characteristic of the neoliberal notion of development. For them, development "has become synonymous with a combination of crises (food, environmental, energy, financial, and climate)" (McMichael and Morarji 2010, 238). The emergence of such new collective actors—out of the lower, indigenous, feminist, and other (post)colonial cultures—is gradually being acknowledged, but still constitutes a significant break both within the world of social movements and that of academic research.

One of the reasons for the invisibility of these struggles in research and in the world of social movements arguably lies in the definition of the "political" underlying activist and research circles. The idea of social movement implies that the state-citizen relationship is inherently "political" in the sense that it is based on competitive and often confrontational claim-making. Yet, politicization is only one way to interact with the state; negotiation is another (for instance, bribing a corrupted official). Hiding from the state is yet another way (e.g. squatting). In an interesting text on informal settlements, Roy and AlSayyad (2004) show how the dominance of studies on Latin American urban informality has led to the general assumption that squatters and people active in the informal economy tend to mobilize collectively against the state. However, studies on urban informality in the Middle East show that many individuals prefer to hide, or keep a low profile, rather than confronting authorities. Bayat (2004, 81 and 94) suggests that political subjectivity comes more in the form of a "quiet encroachment of the ordinary," which he defines as "noncollective, but prolonged, direct action by individuals and families to acquire the basic necessities of life (land for shelter, urban collective consumption, informal work, business opportunities, and public space) in a quiet and unassuming, yet illegal fashion... The struggle of the actors against the authorities is not about winning a gain, but primarily about defending and furthering what has already been won." In other words, it is not necessarily socially and politically transformative or revolutionary. In many ways, as Bayat writes speaking of street vendors and squatters, "*theirs* is not a politics of protest, but of redress, the struggle for an immediate outcome through individual direct action" (Bayat 2004, 93, emphasis original). This is not to say that collective action is absent. But, as with the mobilization of migrant domestic workers in Los Angeles in the marches against the right-wing proposals to reform immigration in the U.S. in 2006, it is mostly through continuities between everyday life and protest action that one can understand political mobilization (Boudreau et al. 2009).

Within the Euro-American core, neoliberal globalization and the rise of global urbanity can be said to have narrowed the space for social contestation in many ways, but nevertheless collective mobilization does continue, especially around three urban fault lines: challenges to corporate urban development, claims for social and environmental justice, and antiglobalization (see Mayer 2007). Also, urban riots have reemerged on the scene, a type of militancy that seems to refuse to be linked to articulated political demands. French suburbs have become sites of what many described as "prepolitical" protest by young people, mostly of migrant background. Similarly, Athens and other European cities have erupted in protests against police violence and have seen disturbances triggered by the financial meltdown of 2008. If many continue to see urban riots as prepolitical, others insist that for some groups riots can be the only way to enter the political space and find a way to negotiate (Rea 2006; Balibar 2007).

Reflecting these novel developments, various theoretical debates have emerged around the world, not all of which we can possibly reflect on here. Our limitation to only parts of English, French and German speaking academia will hopefully not be read as reproduction of Eurocentric forms of colonialism, but as merely a first step toward understanding the diversity of practices and theories of today's global-local movements.

With the rise of antiglobalization movements at the end of the 1990s, the relation between urban movements and resistance to neoliberal globalization inspired much research on the dialectic between global and local as new sites of resistance (e.g. Hamel, Lustiger-Thaler, and Mayer 2000; Merrifield 2002; INURA 2003; Köhler and Wissen 2003; Conway 2004). A special issue of *Space and Polity* was dedicated to uncover the urban orientation of justice movements (Nicholls and Beaumont 2004). The *International Journal of Urban Regional Research* published a special issue exploring the changes urban social movements have undergone since the 1970s (Pickvance 2003), and a recent issue of *CITY* is dedicated to questions these recent changes have thrown up for critical urban theory (Brenner, Marcuse, and Mayer 2009).

As transnational antiglobalization movements, after coming together in the World Social Forum and other global gatherings, began to discover "the local," their city, as places where globalization "touches down" and materializes, where global issues become localized, they sparked off not only new alliances and new action repertoires within urban movement scenes, but also new research exploring the role of scale and global-local connections for and within urban contestation. Organizations such as the Social Fora or Attac have expanded their demands to include not only the democratization of international institutions, but have taken the message of "global justice" to the city (Portaliou 2007). Here they defend public services and institutions, campaign against welfare cuts, and for rights for migrants as well as workfare workers. In the course of their countersummits or Social Forum meetings, they have discovered that issues such as privatization and infringement of social rights are connecting them with movements across the globe. Conversely, preexisting urban movements that have long been struggling for a better city are now articulating the "global" in contestations that take place "locally," and are importing action repertoires gleaned from antiglobalization protests. Together with the antiglobalization movements, they now seek to build alliances with local unions, social service organizations, churches, and newly emerging labor/community centers.

Ongoing research seeks to detect patterns and causal relationships in this multiscalar jumble (cf. Ashman 2004; Glassman 2001; Routledge 2003; Sites 2007; Tarrow and McAdam 2005; Wissen et al. 2008). The interplay of these different clusters of "glocal" movements seems to create a novel multi-scalar architecture of urban protest, in which impetus from supranational scales may boost and strengthen local grassroots movements, or specific urban initiatives may turn into beacons of the global social justice movement. While there is, to our knowledge, little research as yet exploring the tensions and conflicts that have emerged between mobile transnational activism and the locally based groups, it is increasingly clear that the new dialectic between global and local sites of resistance emerges as an important focus of theorizing the significance of today's urban movements. Also, work done in Latin American, African, and Asian cities on the respective urban movements, squatters' and shack- or pavement-dwellers' struggles, and their respective forms of self-organization and resistance to the everyday violence needs to be brought into the debates going on in social movement circles far more than has been the case so far, if we are to understand the possibilities and trajectories of an emancipatory urban politics (for instance, Roy and AlSayyad 2004).

Beyond the urban social movement literature but also inspired by Lefebvre's work on the right to the city (1968), the dynamic literature on urban citizenship stresses the importance of recognizing the legitimacy of political action for people without legal citizenship (Holston 1995; Holston and Appadurai 1996; Sassen 1996; Dikeç and Gilbert 2002; Mitchell 2003). The right to be politically active brings to the fore the issue of the possibility to act. These studies locate political mobilization in everyday life, because people *inhabit* a world on which they wish to act. However, by focusing on the legitimacy to act without legal citizenship, this literature does not explain why people decide to act. In the "American" social movement approach discussed above, these two questions (the possibility to act and the motive for taking action) could not be separated. Indeed, the concept of a political opportunity structure (Tarrow 1998) posits that action can be initiated only if a window of opportunity enables people to seize it and take action. The opportunity provides the motive. On the other hand, this framework neglects a fundamental aspect of urban daily life: politics in daily rhythms, which is invisible if we only focus on more or less organized mass mobilization.

These small acts of reappropriation of urban space are at the core of another body of literature, which is also claiming much influence from Lefebvre, but also from Hardt and Negri's notion of the multitude (see for instance a special issue of the French journal *Multitudes* on the *agir urbain*, urban acts [Petrescu et al. 2008]). The "multitude" for Hardt and Negri (2004) is the mass of self-organizing people whose cumulative actions lead to a revolutionary contestation of contemporary imperialism. In their conversation with Negri, the authors of this special issue on urban actions explore what acting in the city looks like. They emphasize the researcher's duty to look for political acts in unexpected liminal places, such as the street corner, the artist collective, or the vacant space between buildings. They never define why they call this type of politics "urban." Nevertheless, one can infer that the small gestures investigated can be found mostly in dense city settings and because the type of political subjectivity they see is largely a function of intense interactions among diverse people in close contact. Indeed, a recent exhibition at the Canadian Center for Architecture was dedicated to numerous examples of such urban acts of resistance, mostly conceived by architects, artists, and radical urban planners (Borasi and Zardini 2009). Such forms of urban resistance range from guerrilla gardening to skateboarding, from the occupation of public parks to the creation of sandboxes and soccer fields on freeways. These micro- and infra-practices, according to Negri (2008), cumulate into "irreversible thresholds" which gradually constitute collective revolutionary actors.

While indeed, political action in the city is deeply entrenched into everyday life, which means that it is defined by interdependencies, unpredictability, and nonstrategic actions, this challenges some of the underlying assumptions of classical social movement theories. Studies of social movements have mostly been constructed on an antagonistic ontology aiming to uncover the workings of domination in order to foster resistance. There is an identified enemy and the focus of the studies is on analyzing strategies of resistance. Yet, if resistance can also be conceived as unorganized, diffuse, and nonstrategic, and if we emphasize the construction of individual political subjectivity more than the organization of collective movements, what would be a future critical research agenda?

5. An Agenda for Future Research

One of the characteristics of contemporary urban movements, whether those influenced by the open space concept typical of the Social Forum process or those involved in micro-actions in the city, is that they do not have a consensual and defined idea of the ideal society for which they are struggling. When the organizers of the Montreal Citizen Summit, for instance, call for the *City We Want*, they know very well that the various claims and activities that will stem out of the event (just like in any other social forum) will not necessarily converge. At the core of this logic of action is the idea that conflicts are beneficial for keeping democracy alive (a clear position against the consensual bent of neoliberalism; see Mertes 2004) and that the results of conflicts are always unpredictable. Unpredictability is integrated into political strategies. Unpredictability, as well as intensified interdependencies and mobilities, accelerating paces of change and intensified affects, are also central characteristics of urbanity. We define urbanity as a historically-situated and geographically unevenly distributed condition that affects the way we act politically. One important question for future research could be: What is it in urbanity that would energize political action? Is there a specifically urban way of acting politically (Boudreau 2010)? What is the emancipatory potential of the city today?

As First World cities have transformed into privileged "global suburbs" inhabited by, on the one hand, upscale top-end users and "creative classes," on the other by low-wage and precarious groups of excluded and marginalized "urban outcasts" (Wacquant 2007), they become sites of different types of urban movements: they are sites of anticolonial and antiracist struggles, which are only occasionally visible; more visibly, they are sites of antigentrification and other defensive struggles, in which heterogeneous actors seek to save a piece of urbanity or protect their alternative lifestyles. For some of these, the risk of co-optation and (partial) integration into an urban model in the image of corporate and financial interests is immense. Especially among former squatters and the newly engaged cultural activists, many have become more interested in projecting a city where their own—self-determined, autonomous, and politically-correct—liberated space is guaranteed (and less concerned with the exclusion and repression of less fortunate ones). Such activists increasingly succeed today in securing their own survival by buying into the new, entrepreneurial "creative city" policies that exploit their vibrant cultural scenes for branding, as a locational asset in the intensifying interurban competition.

Under such conditions, where dissent is often limited to defending "alternative biotopes" and/or easily incorporated into creative city policies, we need to ask whether First World cities, whose class composition has been structurally transformed as global production chains asserted themselves, are still capable of bringing forth the social forces with an interest in transforming them into more equitable and attractive living environments for all. In whose interest would it be to form alliances that would challenge the structures of *global* inequality? Do the comparatively privileged urban activists in the global North have the motivation for *global* justice?

Given the increasingly tight global interconnections that define urban social movements, comparative urban politics would seem to be another crucial area for future research. Precisely because of these interdependencies, comparative methodologies ought not to be conceived as the comparison of fixed and mutually-exclusive units (e.g., two or several cities in different regions of the world), but rather the comparison of processes and the use of interconnections for blurring the limit between the compared elements. The objective of comparing should not be simply to highlight contrasts and similarities, but rather to use a different lens to shed light on a local process. For instance, in comparing homeless activism in the U.S. to slum dwelling in India, Roy does not hesitate to "use one site to pose questions of another" because she sees transnationalism as an "interrogative technique" (Roy 2003b, 466).

Thus, looking ahead it seems that more interpenetration between various research traditions (sociology, political science, urban studies, geography, etc.) and worlds of political action (North, South, East, and West) is urgently needed. We need to beware of zero-sum games between local action and transnational struggles, "creative" inner city politics and outcasts of global suburbs. The very definition of the political, long understood in social movement worlds as a strategically-organized confrontation between the dominant and the dominated, may need to be enlarged if we are to recognize forms of action increasingly important in our urban world. From spontaneous riots to the "quiet encroachment" and negotiated practices of informality, these struggles are part of the politics of our cities, yet still analytically unconnected to the (urban) social movement literature.

REFERENCES

Ashman, S. 2004. "Resistance to Neoliberal Globalisation: A Case of 'Militant Particularism'?" Politics 24(2): 143–53.

Bailey, R. W. 1999. Gay Politics, Urban Politics: Identity and Economics in the Urban Setting. New York: Columbia University Press.

Balibar, E. 2007. "Uprisings in the Banlieues." Constellations 14(1): 47–71.

Bassi, C. 2006. "Riding the Dialectical Waves of Gay Political Economy: A Story from Birmingham's Commercial Gay Scene." Antipode 38(2): 213–35.

Bayat, A. 2004. "Globalization and the Politics of the Informals in the Global South." In A. Roy and N. AlSayyad, eds. Urban Informality: Transnational Perspectives from the Middle East, Latin America, and South Asia. Lanham, MD: Lexington Books.

Binnie, J. and B. Skeggs. 2004. "Cosmopolitan Knowledge and the Production and Consumption of Sexualised Space: Manchester's Gay Village." Sociological Review 52(1): 39–61.

Borasi, G. and M. Zardini, eds. 2009. Actions: Comment s'approprier la ville. Montreal: Canadian Center for Architecture. (Also available in English.)

Boudreau, J. A. 2010. "Reflections on Urbanity as an Object of Study and a Critical Epistemology." In J. S. Davies and D. L. Imbroscio, eds. Critical Urban Studies: New Directions. New York: SUNY Press.

Boudreau, J. A., with the collaboration of N. Boucher and M. Liguori. 2009. "Taking the Bus Daily and Demonstrating on Sunday: Reflections on the Formation of Political Subjectivity in an Urban World." City 13(2–3): 336–46.

Brenner, N., P. Marcuse and M. Mayer 2009. "Introduction" to "Cities for People, Not for Profit." Special issue of CITY 13(2–3): 176–84.

Castells, M. 1972. La question urbaine. Paris: F. Maspero.

Castells, M. 1977. The Urban Question: A Marxist Approach. London: Edward Arnold.

Castells, M. 1983. The City and the Grass-roots: A Cross-cultural Theory of Urban Social Movements. London: Edward Arnold.

Castells, M. 1996–98. The Information Age: Economy, Society and Culture. 3 vols. Cambridge, MA: Blackwell.

Conway, J. 2004. Identity, Place, Knowledge: Social Movements Contesting Globalization. Toronto: Fernwood Publishing.

Della Porta, D. and M. Diani. 1999. Social Movements: An Introduction. London: Blackwell.

Dikeç, M. and L. Gilbert. 2002. "Right to the City: Homage or a New Societal Ethics?" Capitalism, Nature, Socialism 11(2): 58–74.

Escobar, A., and S. E. Alvarez, eds. 1992. The Making of Social Movements in Latin America: Identity, Strategy and Democracy. Boulder: Westview Press.
Fainstein, N. I. and S. Fainstein. 1974. Urban Political Movements. The Search for Power by Minority Groups in American Cities. Englewood Cliffs, N.J.: Prentice-Hall.
Fainstein, S. and C. Hirst, 1995. "Urban Social Movements." In D. Judge, G. Stoker, and H. Wolman, eds. Theories of Urban Politics. London: Sage.
Fernandes, E. 2007. "Constructing the 'Right to the City' in Brazil." Social and Legal Studies 16/2 : 201–19.
Fisher, R. 1994. Let the People Decide: Neighborhood Organizing in America. New York: Twayne.
Glassman, J. 2001. "From Seattle (and Ubon) to Bangkok: The Scales of Resistance to Corporate Globalization." Environment and Planning D: Society and Space 19: 513–33.
Haber, P. L. 2006. Power from Experience: Urban Popular Movements in Late Twentieth-Century Mexico. University Park: Pennsylvania State University Press.
Hamel, P., H. Lustiger-Thaler and M. Mayer, eds. 2000. Urban Movements in a Globalising World. London: Routledge.
Hardt, M. and T. Negri. 2004. Multitude: War and Democracy in the Age of Empire. New York: Penguin.
Harvey, D. 1973. Social Justice and the City. London: E. Arnold.
Harvey, D. 1989. The Urban Experience. Baltimore: Johns Hopkins University Press.
Harvey, D. 1996. Justice, Nature and the Geography of Difference. Oxford: Blackwell.
Harvey, D. 2000. Spaces of Hope. Edinburgh: Edinburgh University Press.
Harvey, D. 2008. "The Right to the City." New Left Review 53: 23–40.
Ho Kwok-leung, D. 2000. Polite Politics: A Sociological Analysis of an Urban Protest in Hong Kong. Ashgate: Aldershot.
Holston, J. 1995. "Spaces of Insurgent Citizenship." Planning Theory 13: 35–51.
Holston, J. and A. Appadurai. 1996. "Cities and Citizenship." Public Culture 8: 187–204.
International Network for Urban Research and Action, ed. 2003. The Contested Metropolis: Six Cities at the Beginning of the 21st Century. Basel: Birkhäuser-Verlag.
Köhler, B. and M. Wissen. 2003. "Glocalizing Protest: Urban Conflicts and Global Social Movements." International Journal of Urban and Regional Research 27(4): 942–51.
Lauria, M. and L. Knopp. 1995. "Towards an Analysis of the Role of Gay Communities in the Urban Renaissance." Urban Geography 6: 152–69.
Leavitt, J., T. S. Samara and M. Brady. 2009. "The Right to the City Alliance: Time to Democratize Urban Governance." Progressive Planning 181 (Fall): 4–10.
Lebas, E., ed. 1982. "Urban and Regional Sociology in Advanced Industrial Societies: A Decade of Marxist and Critical Perspectives." Special issue of Current Sociology/La Sociologie Contemporaine: The Journal of the International Sociological Association 30(10).
Lefebvre, H. 1968. Le droit à la ville. Paris: Anthropos.
Lefebvre, H. 1970. La révolution urbaine. Paris: Gallimard.
Mayer, M. 1991. "Social Movement Research and Social Movement Practice: The U.S. Pattern." In D. Rucht, ed. Research on Social Movements: The State of the Art in Western Europe and the USA. Frankfurt am Main: Campus/Boulder, CO: Westview.
Mayer, M. 1995. "Social Movement Research in the United States: A European Perspective." In Stanford M. Lyman, ed. Social Movements: Critiques, Concepts, Case Studies. London: Macmillan.
Mayer, M. 2007. "Contesting the Neoliberalization of Urban Governance." In Helga Leitner, Jamie Peck, and Eric Sheppard, eds. Contesting Neoliberalism: The Urban Frontier. New York: Guilford Press.

Mayer, M. 2009. "The 'Right to the City' in the Context of Shifting Mottos of Urban Social Movements." City 13(2–3): 362–74.
Mayer, M. and R. Roth. 1995. "New Social Movements and the Transformation to Post-Fordist Society." In Marcy Darnovsky, Barbara Epstein, and Richard Flacks, eds. Cultural Politics and Social Movements. Philadelphia: Temple University Press.
Mayer, M., R. Roth and V. Brandes, eds. 1978. Stadtkrise und soziale Bewegungen: Texte zur internationalen Entwicklung. Frankfurt am Main: Europäische Verlagsanstalt.
McAdam, D., J. D. McCarthy and M. N. Zald, eds. 1996. Comparative Perspectives on Social Movements: Political Opportunities, Mobilizing Structures, and Cultural Framings. Cambridge: Cambridge University Press.
McAdam, D., S. Tarrow and C. Tilly. 2001. Dynamics of Contention. Cambridge: Cambridge University Press.
McMichael, P., ed. 2010. Contesting Development: Critical Struggles for Social Change. New York: Routledge.
McMichael, P. and K. Morarji, 2010. "Development and Its Discontents." In Philip McMichael, ed. Contesting Development. New York: Routledge.
Melucci, A. 1989. Nomads of the Present. London: Hutchison Radius.
Merrifield, A. 2002. "Seattle, Quebec, Genoa: Après le déluge... Henri Lefebvre?" Environment and Planning D: Society and Space 20(2): 127–34.
Mertes, T., ed. 2004. A Movement of Movements: Is Another World Really Possible? London: Verso.
Mitchell, D. 2003. The Right to the City: Social Justice and the Fight for Public Space. New York: Guilford Press.
Negri, T. 2008. "Qu'est-ce qu'un événement ou un lieu biopolitique dans la métropole?" Multitudes 31: 17–30.
Nicholls, W. J. and J. Beaumont 2004. "Introduction to the Special Issue: The Urbanization of Justice Movements?" Space and Polity 8(2): 107–17.
Petrescu, D., A. Querrien and C. Petcou. 2008. "Agir urbain" Multitudes 31: 11–15.
Pickvance, C., ed. 1976. Urban Sociology: Critical Essays. London: Tavistock.
Pickvance, C. 2003. "From Urban Social Movements to Urban Movements: A Review and Introduction to a Symposium on Urban Movements." International Journal of Urban and Regional Research 27(1): 102–9.
Pickvance, K. 2000. "The Diversity of Eastern European Social Movements: Urban Movements, New Social Movements and Nationalist Movements." In P. Hamel, H. Lustiger-Thaler, and M. Mayer, eds. 2000. Urban Movements in a Globalising World. London: Routledge.
Piven, F. F. and R. A. Cloward. 1979. Poor People's Movements: Why They Succeed, How They Fail. New York: Vintage Books.
Portaliou, E. 2007 "Anti-global Movements Reclaim the City." City 11(2): 165–75.
Rabrenovic, G. 2009. "Urban Social Movements." In Jonathan S. Davies and David L. Imbrosio, eds. Theories of Urban Politics. Los Angeles: Sage.
Rea, A. 2006. "Les émeutes urbaines: Causes institutionnelles et absence de reconnaissance" Déviance et Société 30(4): 463–75.
Richardson, D. 2005. "Desiring Sameness? The Rise of a Neoliberal Politics of Normalisation." Antipode 37(3): 515–35.
Routledge, P. 2003. "Convergence Space: Process Geographies of Grassroots Globalization Networks." Transactions of the Institute of British Geographers 28: 333–49.
Roy, A. 2003a. City Requiem, Calcutta: Gender and the Politics of Poverty. Minneapolis: University of Minnesota Press.

Roy, A. 2003b. "Paradigms of Propertied Citizenship: Transnational Techniques of Analysis." Urban Affairs Review 38(4): 463–91.
Roy, A. and N. AlSayyad, eds. 2004. Urban Informality: Transnational Perspectives from the Middle East, Latin America, and South Asia. Lanham, MD: Lexington Books.
Ruggiero, V. 2001. Movements in the City: Conflict in the European Metropolis. Essex: Prentice Hall.
Sassen, S. 1996. "Whose City Is It? Globalization and the Formation of New Claims." Public Culture 8: 205–23.
Scott, J. C. 1990. Domination and the Art of Resistance: Hidden Transcripts. New Haven: Yale University Press.
Sites, W. 2007. "Contesting the Neoliberal City? Theories of Neoliberalism and Urban Strategies of Contention." In Helga Leitner, Jamie Peck, and Eric Sheppard, eds. Contesting Neoliberalism: The Urban Frontier. New York: Guilford.
Sugranyes, A. and Ch. Mathievet, eds. 2010. "Cities for All: Proposals and Experiences towards the Right to the City." Habitat International Coalition (http://www.hic-net.org/content/Cities%20fol%20All-ENG.pdf).
Tarrow, S. 1998. Power in Movement: Social Movements and Contentious Politics. Cambridge: Cambridge University Press.
Tarrow, S. and D. McAdam 2005. "Scale Shift in Transnational Contention." In Donatella della Porta and Sidney Tarrow, eds. Transnational Protest and Global Activism. Lanham, MD: Rowman and Littlefield.
Touraine, A. 1992. "Beyond Social Movements?" Theory, Culture and Society 9: 125–45.
Wacquant, L. 2007. Urban Outcasts: A Comparative Sociology of Advanced Marginality. Oxford: Polity.
Wignaraja, P. ed. 1993. New Social Movements in the South: Empowering the People. London: Zed Books.
Williams, R. 1989. Resources of Hope. London: Verso.
Wissen, M., B. Röttger and S. Heeg, eds. 2008. Politics of Scale: Räume der Globalisierung und Perspektiven emanzipatorischer Politik. Münster: Westfälisches Dampfboot.
Young, I. M. 1990. Justice and the Politics of Difference. Princeton: Princeton University Press.

PART III

POLITICS AND THE CHANGING SOCIAL ORGANIZATION OF CITIES

CHAPTER 15

SOCIAL CAPITAL

RODNEY E. HERO AND MARION ORR

The quality and durability of democracy at the nation-state and subnational levels of Western countries are, according to "social capital" theorists, often attributable in significant part to the richness and density of civic association, the nature of "civil society," particularly sense of "community," and to levels of social trust, that is, to social capital. In the United States, and in U.S. political science, such arguments are often traced to Tocqueville's (1835) observations about the extensive and notable civic engagement in American politics and society. Those views have been echoed and advocated by other prominent scholars over recent decades to the point that the social capital thesis has become a major influence, a prominent school of thought, in the study of American and comparative politics, advanced by a number of scholars (Putnam 1993; 1995; 2000; Skocpol 2000; Skocpol et al. 2000; cf. Rice and Sumberg 1997; Elazar 1966; 1984; Knack 2002). Social capital (and related concepts, such as "political culture" and "civic culture") are said, and have ostensibly demonstrated, to be essential correlates of procedural and substantive democracy as well as civic and economic equality in America (and other countries)—historically and into the present.

Theory and research on social capital has been linked to more general theoretical concerns and broad issues of politics, such as democracy, to some degree to certain dimensions of equality, as well as to social outcomes and governmental "performance." On the other hand, social capital's relation to other common political theoretical concerns, such as "power" and "space" and "institutions" have been less explicit and clear (cf. Hero 2007). Nor, do we think, has the social capital literature been adequately juxtaposed with other urban politics theoretical frameworks.

This chapter explores the concept of social capital and its consequences and the relevance for the practice and study of urban politics, particularly as discussed in the political science literature, by addressing several topics. First, we consider the question of what social capital is; that is, we briefly define and look at social capital as a "dependent" variable. We then summarize research on the ostensible impacts or consequences of social capital; that is, treating it as a core independent variable. We suggest how findings on this have varied somewhat by context and, at the same time, the unit of analysis studied.

As will be apparent, relatively few studies of social capital and politics have been directly focused on urban politics. This in turn, leads us to consider institutional as well as social contexts of social capital; we touch upon the relevance of federal/unitary structures; states, cities; welfare state; political economy and prevalence/dominance of certain types of groups. We will briefly sketch how that might be done with regard to one or two such frameworks.

1. Understanding Social Capital

The social capital thesis as developed by Robert Putnam (2000) concerning the role of civil society, particularly claims about social capital's significance for the general well-being of American society, received extraordinary scholarly attention among political scientists and other social scientists, as well as in public intellectual circles. That thesis initially emerged in a widely heralded and highly influential study of Italy, *Making Democracy Work: Civic Traditions in Modern Italy* (1993). The argument was later further developed and applied to the United States, first in brief, article form (1995) and then in a full-length book, *Bowling Alone: The Collapse and Revival of American Community* (Putnam 2000; hereafter referred to as "*BA*"). The first book (1993) delineated the correlates of democracy in Italian regions, particularly the importance of civil society as operationally defined in the concept of social capital. The second book represents the most elaborate statement of social capital's purportedly profound and beneficial impacts in American society, by providing extensive empirical evidence and evaluation. For the sake of simplicity if nothing else, we take the analysis in *BA* as a benchmark source of the social capital thesis and politics in the U.S., and more generally.

There have been somewhat disparate definitions of social capital, as the discussion above has already implied (also see Sullivan 2009, 221–23). One way to understand the essence of social capital is to describe how it has been studied—more specifically, how it has been "operationally defined"—in the literature.

In his effort to systematically assess the social capital thesis, Putnam developed a "social capital index" (for 1990), which served as his major explanatory variable regarding the importance of civic republicanism and community for various aspects of American society and politics (Putnam 2000, chs. 16–22). Putnam's social capital index has five components and 14 specific variables; the components include measures of community organizational life, engagement in public affairs, community volunteerism, informal sociability, and social trust (Putnam 2000, 291). These components and variables are combined into the social capital index and serve as markers of social behaviors and of attitudes which are then examined relative to an array of social and political outcomes.

Putnam's analysis of social capital also made an important distinction between "bonding" social capital, that is, exclusive and inwardly focused associations and groups, from "bridging" ones, that is, inclusive, open groups that reach out to others and ostensibly focus on a larger, broader public good. Putnam's own examination (2000) did not identify nor separate groups on this basis in the construction of its social capital index, however. In a study designed to test social capital and particularly this bridging/bonding distinction, Hill and Metsubayashi (2005), guided by suggestions offered by Putnam in *BA*, categorized "fraternal organizations, labor unions, fraternities, sororities, farm organizations, study clubs and professional societies as bonding groups" and "service clubs, veterans organizations, political organizations, sports associations, school service organizations, and hobby organizations as bridging groups" (2005, 218). This suggests a further definition and another illustration of the conceptualization of social capital.

Knack's (2002) understanding of the concept is indicated in his study which used several indicators of the concept of social capital—volunteering, percent of those in a state who respond to census questionnaires, social trust, informal socializing, club meetings, and membership in "good government" groups. Rice and Sumberg (1997, 105), in analyzing "civic culture," a concept closely related to social capital, used four components and 11 specific indicators of the idea. One component, *engagement*, is measured by newspaper circulation per capita, library books per capita in public libraries, community improvement and philanthropy/voluntarism groups per capita, and the gender distribution of public school teachers. Another component, *equality*, includes percent of state legislators who are women, civil rights groups per capita of nonwhites, and income inequality. A third, called *solidarity, trust, and tolerance*, includes crime rate, lawyers per capita, and default rate on Perkins student loans. A final component of this civic culture indicator, *social structures of cooperation*, is "a per capita composite index of twenty-six different types of nonprofit organizations." These were then examined regarding their impact on policy outcomes. (Note that some of what are used in this study as indicators of civic culture and/or social capital, as independent variables, such as equality and crime rates, are used in other studies [such as Putnam 2000] as dependent variables. This hints at a common criticism of the social capital thesis; viz., it is rather ambiguous as to whether social capital is cause or effect. Social capital is often said to "go together" with various social phenomena, but which leads to which is often unclear.)

An examination of the impact of civic participation on policy in eight cities in two European countries (Germany and France) and three cities in the U.S. (Sellers 2002, 338–70) used indicators suggesting the similarities, and differences, in the elements and forms and ways of measuring social capital across countries. In Germany (four cities studied), and France (four cities studied), measures of the electoral success of Green Party and Ecologist parties, respectively, along with newspaper readership and association memberships were taken to be indicative of social capital-like factors. On the other hand, in the U.S. cities studied (Madison, WI; Durham, NC; and New Haven, CT) data on Green Party and/or Ecologist-type parties' successes seemed not relevant and not available. The indicators of social capital / civic participation used, then, in these cities included membership in the Sierra Club, National Audubon Society, League of Women Voters, and Boys and Girls Clubs, along with "annual blood donation" and newspaper subscription rates.

The several studies, two focusing on cities (in Europe and the U.S.—Hill and Metsubayahi, and Sellers), and several on the American states (Putnam, Knack, Rice and Sumberg) proffer both considerable commonalities but also some differences in their understanding of social capital.

2. Consequences of Social Capital

Beyond discerning the essence and elements of social capital, a great deal of attention to its *consequences* as social capital is distributed within and across polities has been an important question in the political science research. In assessments of the *implications* of social capital for social and political outcomes, much of the research has focused most heavily on the states of the U.S. (see, e.g., Putnam 2000 especially chs. 16–20, also chs. 21–22; Knack 2002; Rice and Sumberg 1997; Hero 2007). A central claim by Putnam is that as there has been more or less social capital across the states (and communities) of the U.S., that is, where there is and has been more aggregate social capital, there is greater sense of community and, perhaps most significantly, markedly *better social outcomes* (chs. 16–22; cf. Fishman 2004). Furthermore, Putnam asserts a strong link between social capital and *equality*, especially "civic" and "economic" equality. In short, Putnam makes a series of forceful assertions about social capital's impact on substantive policies, procedural democracy, and social equality.

Data for the variables to be explained (dependent variables, which are generally from the 1990s; see, Putnam 2000, especially chs. 16–20, also chs. 21–22) provide evidence for numerous analyses of social capital's impact on social outcomes and send a very clear and powerful message: higher social capital is strongly related to a vast array of beneficial outcomes. Social capital is consistently shown to provide the leading explanation of outcomes (even after accounting for factors such as states' overall racial composition, poverty levels, and others). Thus, for various indicators of "child welfare" and "educational performance" (ch. 17), "safe and productive neighborhoods" (ch. 18), "economic prosperity" (ch. 19), and "health and happiness" (ch. 20) higher levels of social capital are strongly related to "better" outcomes.

Along with assertions that higher social capital is strongly associated with better substantive outcomes (Putnam 2000, chs. 16–20), a strong link between social capital and civic and economic dimensions of equality is found (Putnam 2000,

358–63, and ch. 22 more generally). An examination in the states of relationships between social capital and measures of economic and civic equality—measured with gini coefficients, and a civic equality index, respectively—finds that these strongly "go together" with social capital (Putnam 2000, 360–61). With specific reference to "economic" and "civic" equality, Putnam declares: "[b]oth across space, and across time, equality and fraternity [community] are strongly positively correlated" (359). Indeed, it is emphatically argued that equality and community are connected (Putnam 2000, 358; also see Elazar 1984; Rice and Sumberg 1997).

Other studies have very strong similarities with the social capital thesis, and have drawn comparable conclusions about social and political outcomes. These studies commonly produce evidence that supports the social capital thesis and/or similar arguments, although some of the findings do depart from social capital's claims to some degree.

Social capital has been found to have important effects on aspects of politics well beyond the numerous dimensions identified in *BA*. Knack (2002) analyzed several indicators of states' social capital (see above) to asses their impact on the "quality" and "performance" of state governments. Quality essentially equates to government "accountability" and "efficiency" and was measured based on the adoption and implementation a number of administrative practices such as financial management, capital management, human resources, managing for results, information technology, and an overall indicator of quality. Knack reasons that the quality of state administrative practice both reflects and furthers openness and trust in government that one would or should expect to be associated with social capital. He finds that indicators of states' level of social capital are indeed related to some of the indicators of government quality that are examined separately. In general, then, this study clearly supports the social capital thesis, albeit with qualifications. Knack argues that aspects of social capital identified with "generalized reciprocity" (such as social trust, volunteering, and willingness to respond to census takers) are in fact associated with better governmental performance. On the other hand, aspects of social capital identified with "social connectedness" (including activity in associations and informal socializing) are generally *not* related to governmental performance, although membership in "good government" groups is a notable exception. An empirical analysis of 305 Flemish municipalities in 2000 supported the view that social capital leads to better government performance at the local level (Coffé and Geys 2005), rather like what was found in Knack's (2002) study of the state-level in the U.S. (see above).

Hill and Metsubayashi analyzed *the responsiveness of elected officials to the mass public* in 64 American communities relative to levels of (bridging and bonding) social capital, using data from the early 1970s. With this focus, Hill and Metsubayashi may go beyond issues considered by most social capital analysis, which tend not to address actions of formal governmental institutions and officials, per se, but it seems consistent with the spirit of social capital arguments. Hill and Metsubayashi found that "membership in bridging social capital associations is *unrelated*" to public officials' responsiveness; this is not consistent with Putnam's claims. They also found that "bonding social capital membership is *negatively associated* with" governmental responsiveness. In short, this study offered little support for the claims about beneficial effects of social capital but strong evidence indicating negative effects of bonding group membership on representation (cf. Brehm and Rahn 1997).

In general, the connotations of the concept and its link to democracy and accountability are summarized in several comments. Social capital contributes to democracy in two different ways, according to Putnam (2000, 338). "Externally, voluntary associations ... allow individuals to express their interests and demands on government and to protect themselves from abuses of power from political leaders. Political information flows through social networks, and in these networks public life is discussed" (cf. Knack 2002). At the same time, "Internally, associations and less formal networks of civic engagement instill in their members habits of cooperation and public-spiritedness, as well as the practical skills necessary to partake in public life" (cf. Verba, Schlozman, and Brady 1995). In a related vein, Knack (2002) argues that "social capital can broaden government accountability, so that government must be responsive to citizens at large rather than to narrow interests" (Knack 2002, 773; see Hero 2007, ch. 2).

Rice and Sumberg use three indicators of "government performance" (which differ somewhat from those used by Knack). "Policy liberalism" refers to "the extent to which societies have adopted the types of policies generally associated with modern liberalism, such as extensive welfare systems, progressive tax structures, and consumer protections standards." They use "a ranking of states that combines eight policy measures"; those measures "reflect the usual ideological divisions between liberals and conservatives." A second aspect of government performance is "innovation," which they analyze with data "from a comprehensive index of state policy creativity based on more than sixty types of policies." The third indicator, administrative effectiveness, is based on an average of two indices, one on the "quality of state administration" and the other on "the capacity of state government legislatures to make effective and efficient decisions."

Examining their central questions thusly, Rice and Sumberg conclude that a "link between [civic] culture and [government] performance is indisputable," and, further, "... the strength of the relationship between civic culture and government performance in the states is pronounced" (Rice and Sumberg 1997, 109–10). These findings hold even when a number of other variables are considered, including a measure of state "diversity," which is found to have no impact itself. It is perhaps telling that the diversity measure used in this civic culture (social capital) study was from 1973 and was based on "percent foreign born" in a state, which is (was) surely a questionable measure then and now because, among other reasons, "minority groups"—the vast majority of blacks / African Americans, most Hispanics/Latinos who trace their ancestry to the American southwest, and Native Americans—would not be counted in this measure of diversity. Rice and Sumberg's findings affirming social capital claims are another in a tradition of similar analyses associated with political and civic culture in America (cf. however, Hero 2003).

3. Social Capital Controversies and Questions

There have also been a number of questions, issues, and controversies surrounding much of the empirical work on social capital. As the discussion above suggests, social capital does not have a widely understood definition. The definition associated mostly with Putnam is not the same as some other social capital scholars. For Putnam, social capital is mostly defined in terms of the nature and extent of one's involvement in various informal networks and formal civic organizations. Other political scientists writing about social capital have followed Putnam, treating social capital as a multidimensional concept with a wide number of variables and measure about peoples involvement in civic associations and religious organizations. Social capital is sometimes discussed in terms of resources (such as information, ideas, support) that one can gain by virtue of being connected into a network of relationships with other people (see Portes 1998; Loury 1987). When social capital is conceptualized in this fashion, researchers often conclude that the flow of resources varies with the composition of the network. "Those who occupy key strategic positions in the network, especially those whose ties span important groups, can be said to have more social capital than their peers" (Grootaert et al. 2004, 5). There is no combination of variables that researchers have consistently used across time and space to measure social capital. The use of multiple definitions raises questions about measurement and potential measurement error.

As mentioned, there have long been issues among political scientists over whether social capital is an independent or a dependent variable. Putnam, for example, implies that social capital is an independent variable, asserting that good stocks of social capital lead to positive societal outcomes and more effective government. However, a number of scholars have noted that government institutions may be a source of social capital. Levi contends that state institutions can lay the groundwork for social capital and can work to undermine social capital. Brehm and Rahn (1997, 1014–15) argue that "poor performance by government can initiate downward spirals in social capital by first undermining trust, and then feeding into the reciprocal cycle." Sidney Tarrow followed this line of critique noting that the lack of state focus in Putnam's model "is one of the major flaws of [Putnam's] explanatory models." In short, Putnam misconstrued the causal chain between associational involvement and effective governance. He assumes that good government and positive social outcomes are the result of social capital.

There is some empirical evidence from cities that bolsters the claim of some of the Putnam's critics that the causal arrow could just as easily run from governmental institutions to social capital. For example, Fung (2004) and Fagotto and Fung (2006) have shown how citizen engagement and robust relationships among neighborhood organizations can be accomplished by local government institutionalizing public involvement in decision-making. Their research in Chicago and Minneapolis suggests that properly designed and implemented governmental institutions that incorporate broad democratic participatory principles can spark social capital and improve government effectiveness. In Minneapolis, for example, a coalition of city council members developed the Neighborhood Revitalization Program (NPR) that allocated millions of dollars to neighborhood groups to spend on local improvement projects. "Prior to NPR, community organizations were present in most neighborhoods, but only some were well staffed and effective. The resources, support, and authority provided by NPR, however, contributed to the formation of associations in neighborhoods where there were none and strengthened existing associations throughout the city (Fagotto and Fung 2006, 651). In Chicago, a similar process involving public schools and police-community relations has occurred (Fung 2004). Programs like those in Minneapolis and Chicago reversed "the causal arrow that runs from social capital to the performance of democratic institutions" (Fung 2004, 122). This is consistent with earlier work on government-sponsored neighborhood associations in five large American cities. Finally, a group of European scholars examined social capital in Birmingham, UK, and found that the city council development of an "innovative democratic framework" for engagement that played a central role in "the creation and evolution of a number of self-organized ethnic and faith-based" community organizations. From their case study of Birmingham, Maloney, Smith, and Stoker (2001, 96) concluded that research on social capital should focus on "the effect of governmental-associational relationships on social capital."

There is also considerable ambiguity about what is the proper "unit of analysis" to study social capital. Brehm and Rahn show that social capital "manifests itself in individuals." Specifically, Brehm and Rahn show that "the greater trust that citizens hold for others, the more likely they are to participate" in community association, civic groups, PTAs, and civic organizations. Brehm and Rahn posit a reciprocal relationship between civic engagement and interpersonal trust. As they explain: "It is not, after all, a 'community' that participates or builds trust, but the people who comprise that community who belong to civic organizations and acquire positive feelings" (1997, 1001). Brehm and Rahn make the strong case that social capital researchers would do well to focus the unit of analysis on the individual antecedents of social capital. However, Putnam and others postulate social capital as a property of people living in a common location; as a property of communities.

For most social capital studies, a common approach has been to use states as the common location to study its impact (Putnam, Hero, Knack, Rice and Sumberg). The consistent focus on states has broader implications because we do not expect politics in general to "play out" the same way at different levels of politics. This argument has been especially emphasized regarding the American political system. Many decades ago, V. O. Key, Jr. (1949) illustrated how wide variations in political practices tend to exist at different levels of government despite similar regional tendencies. For example, in some southern states, Key found that racial politics and party politics at the county level could be dramatically different than at the state level. Moreover, there are clear theoretical reasons to think that politics is different in different domains of the political system as the arenas of interactions are larger or smaller which, in turn, has implications for the types of politics and public policy (Schattschneider 1960). For example, community organizers have long shown that the most effective way to get people involved is by engaging them in struggles related directly to their everyday experiences in their neighborhood (Alinsky 1962; Smock 2004; Orr 2007). Policy questions are more likely to be viewed as more abstract and philosophical or ideological in larger political arenas such as at the national level, where broader issues concerning procedural and substantive equality are central. On the other hand, in narrower political arenas, proximate, material, interest-based issues are more likely to predominate. Morris (1984) has shown that many of the leaders of the civil rights movement understood this and practiced it. Chong (1991) went a step further showing how reputational concern—what those in your immediate neighborhood and community might think about you—can be sufficient to encourage civic engagement. This would presumably be important for the impact/ consequences of social capital and might influence its formation as well:

Robert Dahl (1967) once described the city as the "optimal" site for analysis of democracy, and given the diversity of their populations and the fact that the number of cities makes for potentially hundreds of observations, cities would seem appropriate to explore social capital. However, there are theoretical tensions between social capital and the reigning urban theoretical models that emphasize political economy. Social capital as a theoretical framework, however, is largely inattentive to political economy concerns. Social capital stresses the socialization of individuals that occurs through associational life. Social capital emphasizes the noneconomic aspects of civil society. The urban political economy framework emphasizes that policy is made and power exercised through the interaction of the public sector with private economic factors (Stone 1989). Social capital as a framework is concerned with shared norms and the development of trust that develops primarily through the basis of face-to-face interactions. Implicit in the social capital framework are strong notions of consensus generated through "norms of generalized reciprocity" (Putnam 2000, 21). The urban political economy framework, on the other hand, often emphasizes the unequal distribution of resources, the complexity of political and economic relationships, and the competitive politics typically found in urban settings. These broad theoretical tensions have rendered social capital influence in urban politics research to be somewhat limited (cf., however, Sellers 2002, 335–73). The social capital concept would need some modification to make room for an urban political economy perspective (see Orr 1999, 5–16).

If diversity or heterogeneity is seen as a central feature of urban, especially big city politics, this suggests that social capital may be limited in its analytical reach. According to Putnam's measures, U.S. states with high levels of social capital are also among the least urban and/or do not have any very large cities relative to the rest of the U.S. For example, the states with the highest aggregate levels of social capital in Putnam's (2000) analysis are among the very smallest of the American states in overall population and with scarcely a major city or metropolitan area within or between them. Indeed, in more recent research, Putnam (2007) presents the case that social capital does not exist in most urban centers. He shows that ethnic diversity is negatively correlated with social capital. In large ethnically diverse metropolitan areas such as Chicago, Los Angeles, Houston, and Boston, Putnam (2007) very low levels of social capital compared to more homogeneous areas. Curiously, cities like Chicago, Los Angeles, Houston, and Boston have national reputations for having vibrant community organizations (see von Hoffman 2003). This should give analysts immediate pause about what social capital is and what it means (or meant) in the twenty-first century. Surprisingly, however, early social capital arguments scarcely took note of such basic information. And despite subsequent attention to the impact of racial diversity on the formation of social capital, there has been less attention to the consequences of diversity for the impacts of social capital, particularly on "relative" versus "absolute" social outcomes (see Hero 2007).

On the whole, various social capital, political culture, and civic culture arguments, which share strong similarities and come to broadly similar conclusions, appear to have a blind spot in that their civic republican orientations understate the role of race, and ascriptive hierarchy in America (Smith 1993). This highlights the need for more direct consideration of racial diversity factors that are suggestive of the legacies of the philosophical tradition of inegalitarianism, particularly *racial* inegalitarianism and two-tiered pluralism (Hero 1992).

Stone et al. offer an explanation of why social capital may be similarly ambiguous, one which is not unlike Knack's distinction between "generalized reciprocity" and "social connectedness dimensions" of social capital and argument that the former but not the latter had impacts on government performance (see above). Despite its apparent focus on social dimensions, "Social capital concerns behavior that is largely interpersonal and private" and not necessarily "activities that are squarely in the public arena and involve governance institutions and major group representatives." When talking about a large public arena [in contrast to such inclinations as skills, social trust and reciprocity, associated with social capital] "habits of cooperation that develop in small and close meetings do not necessarily come into play" (Stone et al. 2001, 5–6).

One suspects social capital's impacts may be relevant to the civic arena but much less so to the political realm (cf. Stone et al. 2001; Theiss-Morse and Hibbing 2005). Social capital analyses have not usually considered *policy outputs*—as distinct from *social outcomes*. But there are good reasons to consider *policies* based on the assumption that we might, and perhaps should, expect some congruence between formal governmental actions and such purportedly significant forces in society as social capital and race.

The social capital thesis scarcely recognizes much less seeks to account for the role or impact of *formal governmental institutions and practices*, including *public policies* or *outputs* (e.g., Lowndes and Wilson 2001). There appears something of a grudging acceptance of the role of formal institutions, that is, government, in the leading social capital studies. For example, Putnam (2000, 147) states that: "For better or worse, we rely increasingly—*we are forced to rely increasingly—on formal institutions*, and above all on the law, *to accomplish what we used to accomplish through informal networks reinforced by generalized reciprocity—that is, through social capital*" (emphases added). Except to suggest that increases in public policies hasten the decline of social capital through "displacement," social capital analyses seldom take up the question of what relationship there is or might be between the two (Putnam 2000). Some studies have assessed the relation of social capital to government "performance" (Rice and Sumberg 1997) and government "accountability" (Knack 2002). However, the dependent variables examined in those studies are different, and the measurement of social capital varies from what we take to be the authoritative study of social capital, that is, Putnam's (2000); there are also various other differences in those studies, including the set of independent variables considered and how some of those are measured.

The most prominent social capital arguments suggest that there are troubling implications associated with the increased reliance on formal versus more informal methods of pursuing social goals (Putnam 2000). But this raises a question: when formal public policies regarding aspects of basic fairness and general well-being *are* adopted, do they follow a pattern that corresponds to, is affected by the levels of social capital? Do different levels of social capital in a society influence or transmit to ostensibly parallel *formal* public policies?

Social capital studies have generally provided little specific guidance on what to expect regarding a relationship between levels of social capital and the public policy inclinations of cities (cf. Rice and Sumberg 1997). Some years prior to the publication of the authoritative book on social capital in America, *Bowling Alone* (Putnam 2000), Robert Putnam had suggested that "social capital is not a substitute for effective public policy"; and social capital is both a "prerequisite" for effective public policy and, "in part, a consequence of it." Furthermore, "wise policy can encourage social capital formation, and social capital itself enhances the effectiveness of government action" (Putnam 1993, as quoted in Putzel 1997, 948). It is not clear whether this is meant to suggest that the implementation and/or the very formulation of public policy were aided by social capital, but it may be so. And what is meant by "effective" policy is not manifestly obvious nor is the substantive content of policies that would be seen to accord with social capital arguments self-evident. Furthermore, the primary causal direction apparent—policy to social capital, or vice versa—is ambiguous. However, higher social capital would seem to be associated with more "positive" public policies.

4. Future Social Capital Research

In considering future research, we think it useful for researchers to consider social capital with other forms or avenues for civic engagement. A useful issue for future research would be to consider how social capital, along with another approach to the study of politics that focus on urban masses or "the people"—social

Comparing Social Capital and Social Movements Analytical Approaches

Dimension	*Social CAPITAL*	*Social MOVEMENTS*
Social arena focus	civic (apolitical); 'society-centered'	politics/government
'Policy' focus	varied, diffuse Outcomes	justice/equality/ Environmental Govtl. decisions/outputs
Concern for equality	ambiguous, limited	central
Style	cooperative; 'service,' 'assistive' (civil)	more contentious
Attainment of democracy defined in terms of…	participatory; 'good government'	substantive policy outputs; grass-roots inclusion
View of status quo	implicit affirmation	need for change, (fundamental) reform
Type of change called for	relatively specific (*not* socio-economic 'structural')	broader, social structural; emphatically substantive
Impacts on politics	Indirect (spillover of civic into political)	Direct
Social class Orientation	Middle (upper) class (not disadvantaged)	Working/lowerclass (the 'marginalized' or often 'excluded')
Racial/ethnic conditions and recognition	homogeneity; similarity	heterogeneity; difference
Civic participation	End in itself	Means and End
Link to American Political tradition (implicit)	Civic republican (consensus)	Liberal (competitive); brings attention to *In*egalitarian tradition

movements—informs our understanding of urban politics. That is, beyond the impact of regimes (which do include, "electoral coalitions"), what might social capital and social movements separately and together tell us about urban politics? Here, we briefly sketch out some ideas on this, recognizing that not all (maybe not very many) of the specific claims and distinctions we make would be readily agreed upon by scholars. Nonetheless, we hope this will generate some discussion (see figure 1).

Social movements provide a way for connecting individuals and groups across cities, neighborhoods, and regions to forge collective solution to social problems (Gamson 1990; Pastor, Benner, and Matsuoka 2009). They offer a forum for working together to develop community power, and collaborate with others in making fundamental shifts in the political and social arrangements that have caused inequities, exclusions, and subordination. In a social movement, the actors engaged in the collective action are linked by dense informal networks of organizations and individuals (McAdam 1982; Morris 1984). They share a collective identity or sense of shared mission. People feel connected by a common purpose, and share commitment to a cause; they feel linked or at least compatible with a broader collective mobilization (Chong 1991).

There are some dimensions that social capital and social movements have in common. Diani (2001), for example, shows how social movements and social capital have a kind of symbiotic relationships, arguing that social movements can generate new forms of social capital. In addition, both are relatively loose organizational entities (especially compared to "interest groups" or political parties). Social capital and social movements display fluidity in the level and longevity of participants' association (Diani 2001). Social capital networks are often transformed. Similarly, social movements start and eventually end with most of the participants moving on. Terms like "associations" and "movements" generally connote loose organization. The structure of social capital and social movements is characterized by flowing relationships. Individuals can move from one social capital network into another. These relationships are nevertheless significant. Social capital, as Putnam (2000, 19) described it, is about how "lives are made more productive by social ties." Moreover, trust is a significant variable in social movements and social capital. The relationships that are central to social movements and social capital are cemented in part by high levels of interpersonal and organizational trust (Putnam 2000, 136–39; Hetherington 1998). Finally, Diani (2001) has shown how social movements have the capacity to generate new social capital and networks.

Nevertheless, there are dimensions of social capital and social movements that diverge. Perhaps one of the central areas of divergence centers on issues related to social justice and equality. The policy focus of social movements is on ideals of justice and equality (Tilly 1978; Tarrow 1998). Social capital policy focus is much more varied and diffused depending on the composition of the social network. Social capital's limited concern for equality is not at all unexpected given that social capital networks tend to be narrow and homogeneous. Social capital has an implicit affirmation of the status quo. Its social-class orientation tends to be more linked to the upper class and middle class with very limited incorporation of the poor and working class (Levi 1996). The participants' commitment to the social capital network is more instrumental or affective and seldom normative. As Smock (2004, 67), "People who participate in networks for normative reasons are committed to a common abstract mission or ideology."

Social movements are more directly concerned with shaping and altering governmental decisions that perpetuate inequality, especially inequality premised on social-class status (Morris 1984; McAdam 1989). Participants join in to see that governmental institutions and decisions are consistent with these ideals justice and equality (Payne 1995). While social capital's implicit linkage to America's political tradition are anchored in civic republicanism and consensus, social movements' connection is through the country's liberal traditions of social and political competitiveness. Social movements are more likely to bring attention to America's inegalitarian tradition (Smith 1997). Critics argued that Putnam's embrace of social capital as something nearly always positive missed the kind of "unsocial capital" like the many neighborhood improvement associations that operated to prevent African Americans and other minorities from purchasing homes (Levi 1996). Social capital's concern for equality is typically ambiguous and limited. When change is on the social capital agenda—it tends to be relatively specific (e.g. more playgrounds, improved street lighting, new choir uniforms, etc.)—not the kind of change that is socioeconomic and structural (Smock 2004). A need for change and fundamental reform are central to social movements. Social movements call for broader and socio-structural changes (Pastor, Benner, and Matsuoka 2009).

Given their divergence in the areas of social justice and equality, it is not surprising that social capital and social movement arenas of social action are also different. Social capitalists tend to focus on the civic arena (see Ferman 1996). Putnam's original formulation of social capital was decidedly civic in orientation—birdwatching clubs; bowling leagues, PTA. Social capital is more society related and it is not necessarily politicized. If it is politicized, social capital networks are likely to work to mobilize the government's formal institutions to address specific problems, much like the "civic fauna" Rae (2003) described in New Haven. The social capital is deployed as mechanism for co-production. Social capital is not just for participants of the network, but also for governance.

Social movements work within the political arena, challenging government and private institutions that are obstacles to social justice (Gamson 1990). Because of this, social movements' political style is often more contentious while social capital is much more cooperative, often working alongside and assisting government all the while remaining anchored in the civic arena. Indeed, social capital views the attainment of democracy as defined by a capacity to see government put to use best practices and achieve "good" government. Meanwhile, substantive policy outputs with robust grassroots inclusion is what social movements strive for (Anyon 2005). Social movements are interested in directly impacting politics and social capital is satisfied with a more indirect impact. With social capital, there is a hope that the civic will somehow spillover into the political arena. From the social capital perspective, civic participation is an end of itself. From the social movement perspective, civic participation is both a means and end.

5. Conclusion

Unless it is modified, social capital does not fit with much of the reigning approach to urban political science—the urban political economy approach. This approach focuses on the interplay between polity and the economy at the local level and its consequences for public policy. The political arena is an important component of the urban political economy perspective. Social capital, on the other hand, is centered more in the civic arena. In addition, it is not clear how issues of race and ethnicity—central variables in urban politics—are addressed through social capital. Issues of racial justice are typically central to social movements. Although they also occur in rural areas, social movements have historically had their roots in the experience of urban residents (Tarrow 1994).

As a developing political science concept, social capital has many strengths and weaknesses. We have attempted to outline and discuss some of the significant theoretical and methodological issues surrounding the concept. Since the publication of *Bowling Alone*, social capital has garnered a lot of attention among political scientists and other social scientists. As we described earlier, one of the consequences of the growth in attention has been the development of divergent measures used to operationalize the concept. This has led to a number of questions and controversies surrounding the utility of social capital. The definitional looseness will allow other researchers to venture an effort to create a robust conceptualization of the concept.

REFERENCES

Alinsky, Saul. 1962. *Rules for Radicals*. New York: Vintage.

Anyon, Jean 2005. *Radical Possibilities: Public Policy, Urban Education and a New Social Movement*. New York: Routledge.

Brehm, John and Wendy Rahn. 1997. "Individual-Level Evidence for the Causes and Consequences of Social Capital." *American Journal of Political Science* 41(4): 999–1023.

Chong, Dennis. 1991. *Collective Action and the Civil Rights Movement*. Chicago: University 006Ff Chicago Press.

Coffé, Hilde and Benny Geys. 2005. "Performance and Social Capital: An Application to the Local Government Level." *Journal of Urban Affairs* 27(5): 485–501.

Dahl, Robert. 1967. "The City in the future of Democracy." *American Political Science Review* 61: 953–70.

Diani, Mario. 2001. "Social Capital as Social Movement Outcome." In *Beyond Tocqueville*, edited by Bob Edwards, Michael W. Foley, and Mario Diani. Hanover, NH: Tufts University Press. Pp. 202–18.

Elazar, Daniel J. 1966. *American Federalism: A View from the States.* New York: Crowell.

Elazar, Daniel J. 1984. *American Federalism: A View from the States.* 3rd ed. New York: Harper and Row.

Fagotto, Elena and Archon Fung. 2006. "Empowered Participation in Minneapolis: The Neighborhood Revitalization Program." *International Journal of Urban and Regional Research* 30(3): 638–55.

Ferman, Barbara. 1996. *Challenging the Growth Machine.* Lawrence: University Press of Kansas.

Fishman, Robert M. 2004. *Democracy's Voices: Social Ties and the Quality of Public Life in Spain.* Ithaca: Cornell University Press.

Fung, Archon. 2004. *Empowered Participation: Reinventing Urban Democracy.* Princeton: Princeton University Press.

Gamson, William. 1990. *The Strategy of Social Protest.* Belmont, CA: Wadsworth.

Grootaert, Christiaan, Deepa Narrayan, and Veronica Jones. 2004. *Measuring Social Capital: An Integrated Questionnaire.* New York: World Bank.

Hero, Rodney E. 1992 *Latinos and the U.S. Political System: Two-Tiered Pluralism.* Philadelphia: Temple University Press.

Hero, Rodney E. 2003. "Multiple Traditions in American Politics and Racial Policy Inequality." *Political Research Quarterly* 56(4): 401–8.

Hero, Rodney E. 2007. *Racial Diversity and Social Capital: Equality and Community in America.* New York: Cambridge University Press.

Hetherington, Marc J. 1998. "The Political Relevance of Political Trust." *American Political Science Review* 92(4): 791–808.

Hill, Kim Q. and Tetsuya Metsubayashi. 2005. "Civic Engagement and Mass-Elite Policy Agenda Agreement in American Communities." *American Political Science Review* 99(2): 215–24.

Key, V. O., Jr. 1949. *Southern Politics.* New York: Knopf.

Knack, Stephen. 2002. "Social Capital and the Quality of Government: Evidence from the States." *American Journal of Political Science* 46(4): 772–85.

Levi, Margaret. 1996. "Social and Unsocial Capital: A Review Essay of Robert Putnam's Making Democracy Work. *Politics and Society* 24: 45–55.

Lowndes, Vivien and David Wilson. 2001. "Social Capital and Local Governance: Exploring the Institutional Design Variable." *Political Studies* 49(4): 629–45.

Loury, Glenn. 1987. "Why Should We Care About Group Inequality." *Social Philosophy and Policy* 5: 249–71.

Maloney, William, Graham Smith, and Gerry Stoker. 2001. "Social Capital and the City." In *Beyond Tocqueville: Civil Society and the Social Capital Debate in Comparative Perspective*, edited by Bob Edwards, Michael W. Foley, and Mario Diani. Hanover, NH: Tufts University Press. Pp. 83–96.

McAdam, Doug. 1982. *Political Process and the Development of Black Insurgency.* Chicago: University of Chicago Press.

Morris, Aldon. 1984. *The Origins of the Civil Rights Movement.* New York: Free Press.

Orr, Marion. 1999. *Black Social Capital: The Politics of School Reform in Baltimore, 1986–1998.* Lawrence: University Press of Kansas.

Orr, Marion, ed. 2007. *Transforming the City: Community Organizing and the Challenge of Political Change.* Lawrence: University Press of Kansas.

Pastor, Manuel, Jr., Chris Benner, and Martha Matsuoka. 2009. *This Could Be the Start of Something Big: How Social Movements for Regional Equity Are Reshaping Metropolitan America.* Ithaca, NY: Cornell University Press.

Payne, Charles. 1995. *I've Got the Light of Freedom: The Organizing Tradition and the Mississippi Freedom Struggle*. Berkeley: University of California Press.
Portes, Alejandro. 1998. "Social Capital: Its Origins and Applications in Contemporary Sociology." *Annual Review of Sociology* 24: 1–24.
Putnam, Robert D. 1993. *Making Democracy Work: Civic Traditions in Modern Italy*. Princeton: Princeton University Press.
Putnam, Robert D. 1995. "Bowling Alone: America's Declining Social Capital." *Journal of Democracy* 6(1): 65–78.
Putnam, Robert D. 2000. *Bowling Alone: The Collapse and Revival of American Community*. New York: Simon and Schuster.
Putnam, Robert D. 2007. "E Pluribus Unum: Diversity and Community in the Twenty-first Century." The 2006 Johan Skytte Prize Lecture. *Scandinavian Political Studies* 30(2): 137–74.
Putzel, James. 1997. "Accounting for the 'Dark Side' of Social Capital: Reading Robert Putnam on Democracy." *Journal of International Development* 9(7): 939–49.
Rae, Douglas W. 2003. *City: Urbanism and Its End*: New Haven: Yale University Press.
Rice, Tom W. and Alexander Sumberg. 1997. "Civic Culture and Government Performance in the American States." *Publius* 27(1): 99–114.
Schattschneider, E. E. 1960. *The Semi-sovereign People*. Hinsdale, IL: Dryden Press.
Sellers, Jeffrey. 2002. *Governing from Below: Urban Regions and the Global Economy*. New York: Cambridge University Press.
Skocpol, Theda. 2003. *Diminished Democracy: From Membership to Management in American Civic Life*. Norman: University of Oklahoma Press.
Skocpol, Theda, Marshall Ganz, and Ziad Munson. 2000. "A Nation of Organizers: The Institutional Origins of Civic Voluntarism in the United States." *American Political Science Review* 94(3): 527–46.
Smith, Rogers M. 1993. "Beyond Tocqueville, Myrdal, and Hartz: The Multiple Traditions in America." *American Political Science Review* 87(3): 549–66.
Smith, Rogers. 1997. *Civic Ideals: Conflicting Visions of Citizenship in U.S. History*. New Haven: Yale University Press.
Smock, Kristina. 2004. *Democracy in Action: Community Organizing and Urban Change*. New York: Columbia University Press.
Stone, Clarence N. 1989. *Regime Politics: Governing Atlanta, 1946–1988*. Lawrence: University Press of Kansas.
Stone, Clarence N., Jeffrey R. Henig, Bryan D. Jones, and Carol Pierannunzi. 2001. *Building Civic Capacity: The Politics of Reforming Urban Schools*. Lawrence: University Press of Kansas.
Sullivan, Helen. 2009. "Social Capital." In *Theories of Urban Politics*, edited by Jonathan S. Davies and David Imbroscio. 2nd ed. Los Angeles: Sage. Pp. 221–38.
Tarrow, Sidney, 1994. *Power in Movement: Collective Action, Social Movements and Politics*. Cambridge: Cambridge University Press.
Theiss-Morse, Elizabeth and John R. Hibbing. 2005. "Citizenships and Civic Engagement." *Annual Review of Political Science* 8: 227–49.
Tilly, Charles. 1978. *From Mobilization to Revolution*. Reading, MA: Addison-Wesley.
Tocqueville, Alexis de. 1958 [1835]. *Democracy in America*. Richard D. Heffner, editor. New York: New American Library.
Verba, Sidney, Kay L. Schlozman and Henry E. Brady. 1995. *Voice and Equality: Civic Voluntarism in American Politics*. Cambridge, MA: Harvard University Press.
von Hoffman, Alexander. 2003. House by House, Block by Block: The Rebirth of America's Urban Neighborhoods. New York: Oxford University Press.

CHAPTER 16

THE CENTRALITY OF RACIAL AND ETHNIC POLITICS IN AMERICAN CITIES AND TOWNS

PARU SHAH AND MELISSA MARSCHALL

For more than 40 years, scholars have turned to cities to examine the intersection of race/ethnicity and politics. In particular, they have considered how race/ethnicity shapes racial and political attitudes, policy preferences, voting behavior, and political processes and outcomes. The dramatic racial and ethnic transformation of the U.S. population taking place over the last several decades means that scholars must be ever more mindful of the changing landscape in their conceptualizations, theories, and empirical analyses of local politics and governance. How has the rapid increase of Latino and Asian populations across the U.S. affected the likelihood of minority representation and what are the future prospects for minority groups? Will we see more intergroup cooperation in the future or are heightened competition and conflict the more likely outcomes? What are the implications of multiracial and multiethnic cities for how race influences the attitudes and behaviors of local residents? How do these trends shape the nature, process, and outcomes of local politics and public policy?

In this chapter, we begin by first reviewing the significant developments in the racial and ethnic composition of local places in the U.S.[1] in order to set the stage for our analysis of why racial and ethnic politics plays such a central role in

1. All cities in our analysis are defined by the census as a "place," or a locality established to provide governmental functions for a concentration of people. Thus, we include cities, towns, villages, and boroughs.

American local politics and perhaps more importantly, what the future holds as the U.S. continues the transformation to a multiracial and multicultural nation. As others have acknowledged, similar demographic changes are underway in Europe (OECD 2007; Bloemraad et al. 2008), and although our chapter focuses exclusively on the U.S., these parallel developments suggest that race and ethnicity are becoming increasingly central to local politics in Europe as well. From here we examine three areas of inquiry that scholars studying racial and ethnic dimensions of local politics have and will likely continue to focus on. We begin with minority representation and the role of race and ethnicity in shaping the electoral and officeholding fortunes of minority candidates. Second, we consider the implications of minority representation, both symbolically as a precursor to psychological shifts in political efficacy and trust, and substantively, moving policy toward co-racial/ethnic preferences. Lastly, we turn our attention to the literature on the relationship between racial/ethnic context and individual-level attitudes and political behaviors.

To be sure, the literature on the racial/ethnic dimensions of cities and local politics is vast and we cannot begin to capture the incredible diversity of questions, approaches, and theories included in this literature. Thus, our strategy is to focus on some of the persistent puzzles in the literature while at the same time outlining a set of new questions posed by the changing racial/ethnic paradigm in the U.S. We conclude by outlining several specific ways in which future scholarship can proceed in addressing these lines of inquiry.

1. The Changing Racial and Ethnic Landscape of America, 1980–2000

There was a time in U.S. history when the term "racial minority" was synonymous with African American. Since other racial and ethnic minorities constituted a very small portion of the population, they were assumed to be insignificant as a political force. However, demographic changes over the past several decades have introduced complications to this conceptualization and more generally, to the study of race/ethnicity in America. For example, between 1980 and 2000, the Asian and Latino populations increased 204% and 142% respectively. Today, the U.S. population is roughly three-fourths non-Hispanic white, but Latinos, blacks, and Asians are expected to comprise the majority by the year 2042 (Brookings 2010). These changes have a number of important consequences for local politics. First, there have been important shifts in the distribution and diffusion of racial minorities across regions and cities of different sizes. And second, the growth of Latino and Asian populations has led to profound changes within cities, both in terms of composition and concentration of populations.

1.1. The Growth and Shift in Biracial/Ethnic Places

As the U.S. population becomes increasingly multiracial/ethnic, to what extent are cities, towns, and suburbs reflecting this change? Historically, minority populations have exhibited strong regional concentrations: blacks in the South, Asians in the West, and Latinos in the Southwest. By 2000, however, each group had made considerable inroads in every region of the U.S. To what extent are these groups concentrated in cities within these regions and has this shifted over time? The answer to this question has important implications for descriptive representation across place and time and also provides the backdrop for understanding one critical facet of racial/ethnic politics in American cities and towns: majority voting strength (i.e., politics in local jurisdictions where one racial or ethnic group comprises at least 50% of the population).

While the greater part of cities in the U.S. have been and continue to be comprised of predominantly white residents, the past three decades have witnessed an overall increase in both the depth and breadth of predominantly black and Latino cities. The total number of majority black cities increased from 714 to 1,026 between 1980 and 2000. While majority black cities are concentrated in the South (85% or 636 of 714 in 1980 and 881 of 1,026 in 2000), regions outside the South have witnessed the largest gains over the past three decades. The Midwest in particular saw strong growth, increasing over 100% between 1980 and 2000 (from 49 to 108 majority black places).

Yet this growth seems modest in comparison to that of Latino-dominant cities, which increased from 289 in 1980 to 416 in 1990 to 825 in 2000. Before 2000, the majority of Latino-dominant cities were located in the West (56% or 123 of 289 in 1980 and 55% or 229 of 416 in 1990); by 2000, however, the South housed the majority of cities with Latino populations greater than 50% (52% or 430 of 825). In 1980, there were no majority Asian cities in the continental U.S., but by 2000 Asians were the majority in seven cities—six in California, and one in Pennsylvania.[2]

In addition to regional variation in the overall growth of biracial cities, there are also interesting distinctions in population distributions by city size. First, although blacks and Latinos are found in greatest numbers in big cities (populations greater than 250,000), they have made the largest inroads in small cities (less than 25,000 people): in 2000, 93% of majority black places (955 of 1,026) and 89% of majority Latino places (736 of 825) were small cities. Second, over time, the steepest increases occurred in medium-sized cities (between 25,000 and 250,000 people): a two-fold increased in majority black places (from 29 in 1980 to 62 in 2000), and a four-fold increase in majority Latinos places (22 in 1980 to 84 in 2000).

2. In California: Walnut City, Milpitas City, Monterey Park City, Rowland Heights, Cerritos City, and Daly City; in Pennsylvania: Millbourne Borough.

1.2. The Rise of Multiracial Cities

Given the historical differences in settlement patterns for blacks, Latinos, and Asians, it is perhaps not surprising that the majority of places with sizeable minority populations have been biracial. The influx of Latinos, particularly in southern states with large black populations, has changed this pattern, and has resulted in the rise of truly multiracial cities. Conceptions of multiracial cities vary, but from a political perspective, we believe cities where multiple groups reside but where none constitutes a majority is a particularly apt definition since it implies that no racial or ethnic group is large enough to rely solely on its own population to sway electoral politics.

Using this definition, tables 1 and 2 display the growth of multiracial places over time by average population size and region, and highlight a number of salient features of these cities. First, the total number of multiracial cities has increased almost fourfold in the span of 20 years, from 167 in 1980 to 601 in 2000. The composition of these cities has also been in flux, with white and black population shares decreasing between 1980 and 2000 and average Latino and Asian population shares increasing. Second, each region of the U.S. witnessed an increase in the number of multiracial places, with the most dramatic growth in the South and West. Within these regions however, multiracial cities are generally confined to a few states, including Texas, California, Florida, Georgia, New York, and New Jersey. Lastly, while these places include some of the largest U.S. cities—New York, Chicago, Houston—the vast majority (69%) are small cities (populations less than 25,000), such as Crescent City, FL; Omega, GA; and Ossining, NY.

1.3. Changes in Segregation Patterns

Equally central to the study of cities is the concentration and dispersion of racial and ethnic groups within cities. The extent and nature of racial/ethnic segregation within local jurisdictions have critical implications for a whole range of phenomena,

Table 1. Average Percent of Population, by Race, for Multiracial Cities, 1980–2000

	1980	1990	2000
Percent white	44.7	43.5	41.5
Percent black	30.1	24.3	24.3
Percent Latino	19.4	22.9	25.2
Percent Asian	3.7	7.2	5.8
Number of cities	167	280	601

Source: US Census Summary 3 File, 1980, 1990, 2000.

Table 2. Regional Distribution of Multiracial Cities, 1980–2000

	1980	1990	2000
North	15	34	68
Midwest	9	11	29
South	94	132	332
West	49	103	172
Number of cities	167	280	601

Source: US Census Summary 3 File, 1980, 1990, 2000.

including minority candidate emergence in local elections, the formation or alteration of racial attitudes, stereotypes, and political orientations, and the distribution and quality of local public goods and services.

Analyses of the 1980–2000 censuses generally suggest that whereas residential segregation has declined for blacks (who nevertheless remain the most segregated group), it has been on the rise for both Asians and Latinos (Fischer et al. 2004; Iceland et al. 2002; Logan et al. 2004). Studies find that the decline in black-white segregation is usually found in multiracial cities or in cities with smaller proportions of blacks, and that the movement of Asians and Latinos into predominantly black-white places does little to change black-white segregation patterns (Logan et al. 2004). Segregation for Latinos and Asians is greatest in places where they comprise a large proportion of the population (Frey and Farley 1996; Logan et al. 2004; Johnston et al. 2006). Research on these groups also finds that the foreign-born are more segregated than their native-born counterparts (Iceland and Scopilliti 2008).

Although studies have done a relatively good job describing segregation patterns of particular groups (primarily vis-à-vis whites), far less is known about how shifts in city or neighborhood racial/ethnic composition affect segregation patterns among all groups (but see Logan & Zhang 2010; Pais et al. 2009). Thus, additional work on segregation patterns in multiracial cities is needed, as is research investigating how increases in Latino and Asian populations affect their residential segregation both within and across cities. Finally, we know almost nothing about patterns of segregation in smaller places.

To sum, a number of forces have transformed the racial and ethnic landscape of the U.S. since the 1980s. Latinos and Asians have made significant gains in the overall population, multiracial/ethnic places are on the rise, and segregation patterns within and across cities are in flux. Shifts in the size and geographic concentration of minority populations have important implications and consequences for the study of race and politics. In the following sections, we examine three primary areas of inquiry, focusing on how these new racial and ethnic paradigms challenge extant theories and models.

2. Minority Candidates and Elected Officials in Local Politics

At the heart of research investigating minority representation in local elections and politics is the question of what factors contribute to success. Researchers have tended to examine this question in the context of either local legislatures (city councils or school boards) or executives (mayors). Consequently this work has developed along somewhat different trajectories. In the case of councils and school boards, studies typically involve cross-sectional analyses that rely on relatively large samples. These studies have focused on descriptive representation and have paid particular attention to the ways in which electoral arrangements facilitate or inhibit the proportional representation of minorities in local legislatures. While much of this research concludes that single member districts (SMD) are most efficacious in translating minority votes into minority seats (Engstrom and McDonald 1981; Karnig and Welch 1982; Marschall, Ruhil, and Shah 2010; Robinson and Dye 1978; Taebel 1978; Bullock and MacManus 1987; Zax 1990; Welch 1990), studies have also shown that blacks in particular have made considerable progress in multimember or at-large (AL) systems (Sass and Mehay 1995; Sass and Pittman 2000; but see Marschall et al. 2010).

On the other hand, research on minority mayors most typically involves case studies of big-city mayoral elections or the political experiences and governing styles of big-city mayors (Ardrey and Nelson 1990; Colburn and Adler 2001; Hahn and Almy 1971; Kaufmann 1998; Munoz and Henry 1986; Perry 1990; Preston 1987; Sheffield and Hadley 1984; Sonenshein 1986; Summers and Klinkner 1990; but see Marschall and Ruhil 2006). This area of inquiry focuses explicitly on elections (rather than officeholding or representation) and employs a relatively expansive analytic lens. Examining campaign and candidate attributes as well as the broader historical, political, and economic context in which mayoral elections take place, this body of work seeks to explain who votes for, and more specifically, which groups are pivotal in the electoral success of minority candidates.

Although research on legislative versus executive representation relies on different data and methods, and approaches its subject from alternative theoretical lenses, it shares a number of commonalities as well. First, the vast majority of research on mayoral candidates and legislative officeholding has focused on large U.S. cities. A second common feature is the tendency of scholarly work to examine the electoral and representational experiences of a single group, in most cases African Americans, rather than comparing experiences across groups. Third, only occasionally, and typically in only a limited fashion, has research on minority mayors or local legislatures attempted to explain changes in electoral fortunes or minority officeholding over time. Finally, whether it is the mayor's office, city council, or school board seats, studies have consistently found the relative size of the minority population and racial bloc voting to be the most powerful explanations for minority electoral success (Bullock and Campbell 1984; Murray and Vedlitz 1978; Engstrom and McDonald 1981; 1982; Karnig and Welch 1982; Robinson and Dye 1978; Taebel 1978; Bullock and MacManus 1987; Zax 1990; Welch 1990; Sass and Mehay 1995; Sass and Pittman 2000).

Though this body of work has contributed significantly to our understanding of minority officeholding in local politics, a number of questions have nevertheless been largely overlooked. And, whereas this oversight was somewhat unavoidable in the past given data limitations and the predominantly biracial (black-white) context of the cities where minorities historically lived, this is no longer the case. Indeed, as the demographic trends outlined in the previous section make clear, it is imperative that future research attends more vigorously to the places where minorities (blacks, Latinos, and Asians) live and are concentrated today. This means shifting attention from large urban centers to suburbs and smaller towns, and developing better tools to measure within-city racial/ethnic characteristics. In addition, future studies need to develop new theoretical and empirical approaches to study multiracial places and multigroup outcomes. For example, rather than looking exclusively at the number of legislative seats held by one group in isolation, studies should also analyze the racial/ethnic composition of the legislature as a whole (see e.g., Grimmer and Nall 2009). Finally, scholars need to focus more energy and attention on understanding and explaining changes in minority electoral fortunes and representation over time.

2.1. Patterns of Black versus Latino Council Representation

In tables 3 and 4 we report data from the International City/County Management Association (ICMA) showing black and Latino representation on city councils by city size for the first and most recent year this organization conducted surveys of municipal governments in the U.S. (1981 and 2006).[3] As these data illustrate, when looking at the total number of black and Latino councilors, the vast majority are found in the smallest U.S. cities. On the other hand, small cities are also most likely to have no Latinos or blacks serving on their councils. This seemingly contradictory pattern is explained by the large number of cities with populations under 25,000 in the ICMA sample (and U.S. more generally). Yet, these patterns highlight two important questions that remain largely unexamined by urban politics scholars. First, what explains minority representation in these smaller U.S. cities and do models developed and tested for the largest U.S. cities explain Latino and black officeholding in these more typical localities? Second, to what extent is the absence

3. Asian American representation is not included here due the very small number of councilors reported in the ICMA data (45 in 1981 and 95 in 2006). Even across all municipalities, their numbers remain small: 332 in 2000 according to the Gender and Multicultural Leadership Project (www.gmcl.org).

Table 3. African Americans Serving on City Councils by City Size, 1981 and 2006

City size	1981			2006		
	Total	Pct of all blacks	Pct with no blacks	Total	Pct of all blacks	Pct with no blacks
<25,000	543	54.4	89.0	830	64.7	84.9
25–69,999	203	20.3	80.1	241	18.8	75.9
70–199,999	134	13.4	67.7	127	9.9	65.6
>200,000	118	11.8	22.8	85	6.6	20.5
Total	998	100		1,283	100	

Source: ICMA 1981, 2006.

Table 4. Latinos Serving on City Councils by City Size, 1981 and 2006

city size	1981			2006		
	Total	Pct of all Latinos	Pct with no Latinos	Total	Pct of all Latinos	Pct with no Latinos
<25,000	259	67.8	96.8	454	66.3	92.6
25–69,999	59	15.4	94.0	109	15.9	87.7
70–199,999	39	10.2	87.3	85	12.4	74.4
>200,000	25	6.5	75.4	37	5.4	51.3
Total	382	100		685	100	

Source: International City/County Manager Association (ICMA), *Form of Government Surveys*, 1981, 2006.

of Latino and black council representation a function of supply: that is, minority candidates not running for local office in these jurisdictions?

The data in tables 3 and 4 also highlight some important differences across groups and underscore the value of more focused cross-group analyses. In particular, changes in black and Latino council representation over time exhibit quite different patterns, with the strongest black gains occurring in the smallest localities (an increase of over 50%) and decreases occurring in medium and large cities, and Latinos witnessing gains across cities of all sizes with roughly the same percent changes. A second noteworthy difference across groups relates to the percentage of cities with no minority elected councilors. For blacks, the likelihood of observing no councilors decreases steadily as the size of the city increases. Indeed, in the largest U.S. cities, only about a fifth of cities have no blacks on their councils. Further, the pattern is nearly identical for both 1981 and 2006. For Latinos, the likelihood of observing no council representation is much greater across all city sizes and remains high even in the largest cities (75% in 1981). By 2006, observing Latino elected councilors was still a rare event; however, the percentage of cities with no Latino councilors had decreased considerably—a trend not observed for blacks. A third question then, is what accounts for the formidable hurdle in minority officeholding on local councils and why is this hurdle substantially greater for Latinos? Finally, have the inroads Latinos made in big cities come at the expense of black representation?

2.2. Accounting for Gains in Minority Representation

Despite the substantial gains blacks and Latinos have made in local officeholding since passage of the Voting Rights Act in 1965, very little research has systematically examined the factors contributing to these gains or even where these gains have been strongest (Marschall et al. 2010; Sass and Mehay 1995; Sass and Pittman 2000; Trounstine and Valdini 2008). Moreover, the most reliable variable linked to representation, minority population size, cannot account for these increases. For example, between 1984 and 2000, black and Latino representation in municipal offices increased at almost identical rates (49.3% versus 48.7%). The number of blacks holding municipal offices increased from 2,735 (including 255 mayors) to 4,083 (451 mayors) and the number of Latinos grew from 987 (including 142 mayors) to 1,468 (including 213 mayors) (NALEO and Joint Center, various years). Yet between 1980 and 2000, the black population increased just 30% (from 26.1 million to 33.9 million), whereas the Latino population grew 142% (from 14.6 million to 35.3 million) (U.S. Census Bureau 2008).

Beyond simply the size of the minority population (and preferably, the eligible, voting age population) we need to know how the population is *concentrated*. And, since electoral arrangements play a critical role in determining whether and how minority voting strength is concentrated, these must be considered too. While a handful of studies have attempted to investigate the efficacy of district (SMD) versus at-large (AL) electoral systems on legislative officeholding over time, it is not clear what to make of their findings given limitations of the data and methods employed. In particular, most studies have untenably used the ICMA's *Form of Government Survey* as panel data to make inferences about changes in this relationship overtime (see e.g., Sass and Pittman 2000; Trounstine and Valdini 2008). And, even studies employing a constant sample of cities (Marschall et al. 2010) continue to measure minority voting strength exclusively at the city-level regardless of whether councilors are elected citywide or by district. This inability to accurately or reliably measure how and where minority voting strength is concentrated means that to date, our understanding of how electoral structures influence minority electoral success and representation is not only incomplete, but potentially biased. Thus, future research must address this fundamental problem and employ proximate (i.e., district-level) indicators that measure the distribution and concentration of minority residents within the city.

2.3. Election, Voting, and Representation in Multiracial Contexts

Lastly, urban scholarship has centered on the question of who votes for, and more specifically, which groups are pivotal in the electoral success of minority candidates. This body of work is based almost entirely on black mayors, although a smaller body of literature has focused on Latino mayors (Baretto 2007; Baretto, Villarreal, and Woods 2005; Hero and Beatty 1989; Hill et al. 2001). For both blacks and Latinos, the earliest mayors emerged in predominantly minority cities. Browning et al. (1984) argued for the possibility of "rainbow coalitions" or the courting of "crossover" voters (including other minority groups and liberal whites) in places where the minority population constituted less than a majority, but to date empirical tests of this thesis have been mixed (e.g., Rocha 2007; Marschall and Ruhil 2006). In the context of legislative representation, Marschall et al. (2010) and Shah (2010) find blacks and Latinos are more likely to work together to get a single minority elected, but are far less likely to cooperate once that seat has been filled.

The rise of multiracial places, coupled with success of black mayors in these places (Marschall and Ruhil 2006) (see figure 1), underscores the need for further examination of "crossover" voting and the building of theories that move beyond racialized voting. For one, the ways in which past experience with minority representation shapes future representation have not been sufficiently addressed. In part, an overreliance on cross-sectional data means we know little of how the election of a black mayor at one point in time impacts the likelihood of electing either another black mayor or a Latino mayor at a future date.

Second, while the election (and in most cases, reelection) of a single minority mayor in cities where blacks or Latinos do not comprise an electoral majority appears to be the rule (e.g., David Dinkins in New York, Harold Washington in Chicago, Lee Brown in Houston, Ron Kirk in Dallas, Tom Bradley in Los Angeles,

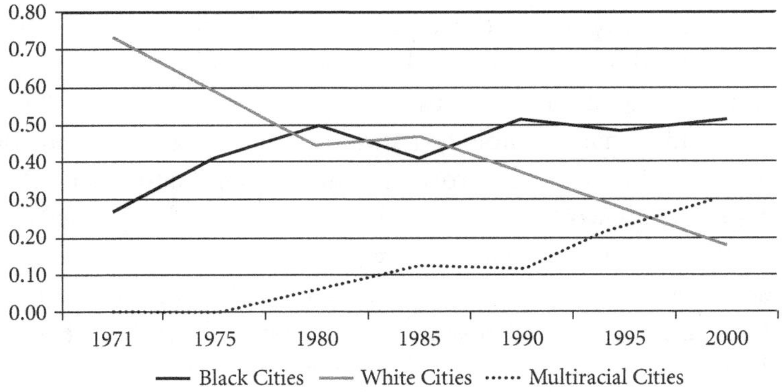

Figure 16.1. Proportion of All Black Mayors by City Type, 1975–2000

Based on a sample of 309 cities, see Marschall and Ruhil (2006) for more details.

Sharon Sayles Belton in Minneapolis, Rice Norman in Seattle, Willie Brown in San Francisco), some cities have elected multiple black or Latino mayors (Wilson Goode and John Street in Philadelphia, James McGee and Richard Dixon in Dayton, OH), or in rare cases, one of each (Wellington Webb and Federico Pena in Denver, Tom Bradley and Antonio Villaraigosa in Los Angeles). What explains this? Is it greater acceptance and support among white voters as Hajnal's (2007) information theory might suggest? Is the incidence of multiple minority mayors a function of more liberal electorates or an institutionalized bi- or multiracial electoral coalition?

Finally, we are ill equipped to answer questions about the supply side of minority candidates in local elections. At the most basic level, the question of whether minorities are underrepresented because they are not running or not winning remains completely unaddressed. And, as the U.S. becomes increasingly multiracial, understanding what happens when multiple racial/ethnic candidates run against one another is ever more pressing. These and other questions can be fruitfully explored at the local level now, providing both critical insights about how race and ethnic politics shape local elections and officeholding, and a foundation for studying state and federal elections in the future.

3. Implications of Minority Officeholding in Local Politics

Beyond the question of whether and how minorities are represented in local politics and government is the more substantive matter of whether it makes a difference. In other words, do blacks, Latinos, and Asians need black, Latino, or Asian elected officials to represent their interests or are nonminority representatives just as effective in serving these constituencies? To date, political scientists have examined the implications of minority descriptive representation by documenting the value of symbolic representation or recording the substantive benefits emanating from a particular office. Research on symbolic representation builds on theoretical insights from political and social psychology (Abramson 1983; Gilliam 1996; Bobo and Gilliam 1990), including work on procedural justice (Lind and Tyler 1988; Thibaut and Walker 1975). This work focuses on the individual and examines the psychic and behavioral effects of representation, irrespective of whether representatives are actually responsive to the constituents they serve (Eulau and Karp 1977). On the other hand, research examining substantive representation builds more directly on work in urban politics and public administration, particularly service delivery, and tends to take a more macro-level approach.

While a number of studies find empirical evidence consistent with the symbolic representation model for African Americans (Abney and Hutcheson 1981; Bobo and Gilliam 1990; Howell and Fagan 1988) and Latinos (Shah 2009), important questions remain. In the first place, most analyses have focused on within-group effects, and have neglected causal relationships among and between groups. Consequently, we know much less about how black elected officials impact levels of trust and political efficacy among nonblack constituents and vice versa. Such questions are increasingly salient given the rise of multiracial places, and are particularly important in the context of new immigrant destinations in the South—places that have witnessed dramatic growth in their foreign-born populations (see e.g. Singer 2004)—where the likelihood of Latinos confronting black leadership is high. A second set of questions entails the relationship between symbolic and substantive representation. To what extent are these separate phenomena? Can these effects be isolated from one another, and if so, how can we design empirical tests to best assess this? Several recent studies suggest that symbolic effects of minority representation may be fleeting (Spence, McClerking, and Brown 2009) or present only in when improvements in local services are conspicuous (Marschall and Ruhil 2007; Marschall and Shah 2007).

Beyond symbolic effects, studies have tended to find substantive outcomes originating from minority representation. Focusing on minority mayors, research finds positive effects on the racial/ethnic composition of the municipal workforce (Eisinger 1982; Mladenka 1989; Stein 1986; Stein and Condrey 1987), the distribution of government expenditures and public services (Karnig and Welch 1980; but see also Pelissero et al. 2000), and the share of city contracts granted to minority business owners (Jones 1978; Nelson 1987; MacManus 1990). Other research has attempted to document the substantive effects of minority representation in specific policy arenas where minority policy preferences or a minority policy agenda are most discernible. Two policy areas that have featured most prominently in this research include public schooling (Fraga et al. 1986; Meier and England 1984; Polinard et al. 1990; Polinard et al. 1995), and policing and public safety (Browning, Marshall, and Tabb 1984; Saltzstein 1989).

A particular challenge in all research on substantive representation is identifying a set of policy preferences that is unique or at least more strongly held by the specific group in question (as compared to other racial/ethnic groups). In other words, can policy preferences really be defined along racial/ethnic lines (independent of socioeconomic status, neighborhood location, or partisanship) and if so, for which policies are these preferences most starkly differentiated? Even when this can be done, the case must be made that such preferences are stable and consistently held by minority communities across cities that may differ in a number of important respects.

For example, expectations about and realities of public services in small cities versus large cities or racially homogeneous versus heterogeneous cities might be quite disparate. Consequently, we may need different methodological approaches and conceptions of substantive representation depending on the type of local jurisdiction in question. And, since services are delivered in a very localized manner, it is incumbent that future studies begin to look at disaggregated indicators of service provision and/or quality. Doing this will require multilevel and ideally, geocoded data, as well as analytic methods appropriate for these relatively complex data and relationships. Finally, it will also require attention to the capacity of local elected officials to act in ways consistent with the policy preferences and expectations of their constituents. As other studies have shown (Saltzstein 1989; Spence et al. 2009), constraints on minority mayors (or other elected officials) may prevent them from acting upon the policy preferences of their core constituents, and lead them to define their representational roles in more complex terms.

4. Race and Place: The Influence of Context on Racial Attitudes and Behaviors

Perhaps the most fundamental way in which the racial and ethnic features of local jurisdictions shape local politics is via their effects on individual attitudes and behaviors. Indeed, the racial and ethnic context of neighborhoods and cities plays an important role in shaping the way individuals understand both their own racial/ethnic identities and those of others (see e.g. Key 1949). Because these understandings have important implications for how local residents engage in political and civic life, political scientists have devoted considerable attention to understanding how racial and other contextual features of local places operate on the development of individual-level attitudes and behaviors.

As with research on minority representation in local elections and politics, most of the work examining how race/ethnicity and place intersect has focused on black-white relationships, looking only occasionally at how Latinos and Asians fit into existing theories and models. Furthermore, much of this work, particularly with regard to attitudes, focuses on unidimensional changes in the racial/ethnic context. In other words, how do increases in the size of one racial group (e.g., blacks) affect the attitudes of individuals from a different racial group (e.g., whites)?[4] What these studies tend to find is that whereas whites living in contexts with more blacks exhibit increasing racial hostility and prejudice toward blacks (Fosset and Kiecolt 1989; Giles 1977; Giles and Hertz 1994; Glaser 1994; Key 1949; Stein et al. 2000; Taylor 1998; Wright 1997), blacks living in contexts with larger concentrations of whites tend to develop lower levels of group solidarity and stronger attachments to whites and other groups in society (Pettigrew 1998; Bledsoe et al. 1995).[5]

4. There is also a considerable body of work examining the behavioral effects of racial context (see e.g., Leighley 2001; Oliver 2010; Uslaner and Brown 2005; Cho et al. 2006). Given space constraints and the fact that much of this literature focuses on electoral and political participation in presidential and other nonlocal contests, we largely omit it from this chapter.

5. More recent analyses suggest that other factors play a key role in conditioning the effects of racial context, namely the socioeconomic status of neighborhood or city

In examining the dynamic racial and ethnic changes taking place within and across U.S. cities, towns, and suburbs, a number of unanswered questions emerge. First, how do existing theories regarding the relationship between racial/ethnic context and individual attitudes and behaviors apply to Asians and Latinos? Latinos and Asians present a unique challenge because of within-group heterogeneity on a number of characteristics relating to racial attitudes (Kaufmann 2003; Frey 2001; Lai 2003). The racial heterogeneity of Latinos in particular, means that in- and out-group orientations will vary significantly depending on racial identity and to a lesser extent, country of origin.[6] Based on the 2000 census, there are nearly one million black Hispanics in the U.S., and data suggest that black Hispanics have a socioeconomic profile much more similar to non-Hispanic blacks than to other Hispanic groups. For example, black Hispanics tend to live in neighborhoods with roughly the same number of black and Hispanic residents, and black Hispanic children tend to have a non-Hispanic black mother or father (Logan 2003). In addition to racial differences, ongoing immigration means there are important generational and linguistic differences within Asian and Latino groups, and these differences have important implications for how individuals within groups identify in- and out-groups (Oliver 2010; Ramakrishnan 2005).

The second unaddressed question focuses more specifically on the ways in which immigration shapes the effects of racial/ethnic context, particularly in light of the myriad and distinctive differences between traditional and new immigrant destinations. Again, this area of inquiry is particularly salient to Latino and Asian populations, which differ significantly in the extent, nature, and recency of their immigration. While scholars have begun to examine the implications of rapid growth in immigrant populations for both local politics and racial and political attitudes (Barreto et al. 2010; Fennelly 2008; Jones-Correa 2005; 2008; Kochar, Suro, and Tafoya 2005; McClain 1993; McClain et al. 2006; Oliver and Wong 2003; Rocha 2007) this work has only scratched the surface. How does the influx of a young, mainly Spanish speaking, population challenge the traditional black-white racial dynamics of many new destination places? Do behavioral and attitudinal effects of racial/ethnic context operate on local residents in communities that have undergone rapid racial/ethnic transformations in the same ways as in communities with long histories of foreign immigration or racial minorities?

Finally, a third set of questions deal more with methodological and conceptual issues than any one substantive area in particular. In the first place, empirical explorations of the racial threat and intergroup contact theories have primarily been conducted using survey data not necessarily collected with this purpose in mind. In particular, surveys typically have only a few respondents from any given city (let

residents (Marschall and Stolle 2004; Oliver and Mendelberg 2000) and the extent of intergroup contact (Jackman and Crane 1986; Stein et al. 2000).

6. More Dominicans (12.7%) than any other group identified themselves as black in the 2000 census, followed by Puerto Ricans (8.2%) and Cubans (4.7%). Only 1.1% of Mexicans identified as black (Logan 2003).

alone neighborhood), thereby making it impossible to examine how residents within *the same city* (or neighborhood) are similarly or differentially affected by their racial/ethnic context.[7] Since the number of Latinos and Asians included in these samples tends to be relatively small, this data problem has especially important implications for studying how contextual effects operate on the attitudes and behaviors of Latinos and Asians.

Another vexing problem is how to best measure the concentration and dispersion of racial groups. What is the appropriate unit of analysis (e.g., city, census tract)? And, at what level does segregation impact attitudes and behaviors? How do we best capture the dynamics of multigroup segregation? Lastly, the "levels of analysis" problem goes beyond segregation and measurement issues. Majority black cities may be conceptually different from majority black neighborhoods, or majority black suburbs. Put differently, how do size and other salient aspects of local jurisdictions (e.g., level and nature of service provision) intersect with racial/ethnic context? Again, given the dispersion of racial and ethnic minorities in small- and medium-sized places, the omission of these jurisdictions suggests our current understanding of the relationship between race and place is incomplete.

5. Conclusion and Future Directions

The increasing racial/ethnic heterogeneity of the U.S. population is perhaps nowhere more evident than at the local level, which means that American cities, towns, and neighborhoods continue to be the best arena for testing theories about the role of race/ethnicity in politics. In this chapter we surveyed but a few of these theories as we examined three prominent areas of inquiry in the fields of urban and racial politics—elections and officeholding, the implications of minority representation, and the role of racial/ethnic context on attitudes and behaviors. As we noted earlier, this is a large and diverse literature and we could hardly do justice to it in this essay. In addition, we highlighted how transformations in America's racial/ethnic landscape challenge current theories, conceptualizations, and findings, and identified a set of questions that we believe deserve greater attention. In this final section, we synthesize these ideas in order to outline an agenda for future research.

First, as we noted consistently in this chapter, current understandings of the interaction and implications of race and politics are too narrowly developed within the context of biracial settings (most often black-white) and large central cities. Given dramatic increases in foreign immigration over the past several decades and the fact that the majority of Americans now live in suburbs, future research needs to expand and modify existing theories and concepts in order to accommodate

7. Exceptions include the Multi-city Study of Inequality, the Detroit Area Study, and to a lesser extent, the Social Capital Benchmark Survey.

these realities. The rise of multiracial/ethnic cities also suggests the need for more nuanced comparisons within and across different contexts. Beyond this, additional work that places the racial/ethnic transformations in American localities within a global context that seeks to compare these processes across countries is clearly needed. As many other chapters in the volume argue, a cross-national comparative framework is necessary as the processes of immigration and migration transform understandings of national identity and racial/ethnic consciousness across the globe.

Second, our ability to access, measure, and compile appropriate data has fallen behind theoretical and conceptual developments, limiting in many ways our ability to assess some of the most vital and pertinent questions about race/ethnicity and politics. The glaring omissions include data on Latinos and Asians and studies of small and middle-sized places. However, we are also in need of reliable and accurate information about the supply of minority candidates in elections, more proximate measures of the distribution and concentration of minority residents within cities, valid indicators of minority preferences for local services and policies, and comparable policy outputs/outcomes across multiple cities (and the neighborhoods within them). Conceptually and theoretically, we must continue to struggle with identifying the most relevant levels of analysis in examining the concepts of "context" and "place," entertaining the ways in which multiple contexts impose their effects independently and simultaneously. These types of inquiry will hopefully also lead to innovations in analytic methods (e.g., compositional data analysis, multilevel modeling, systematic content analysis, matching), and provide more leverage and enhanced validity to empirical tests of complex theories of racial and urban politics.

Lastly, is the question of change. To date, urban scholars have paid scant attention to the questions of transformations over time, most often because of data limitations. Yet the shifting racial/ethnic realities in U.S. cities and towns require models that both describe and explain change (i.e. increases in the number of minority representatives over time), and conceptualize change as an important variable in understanding current and future patterns (i.e. the effects of prior minority representation on likelihood of future representation). Thus, while the racial and ethnic changes taking place in American cities, towns, and suburbs over the last 30 years provide new challenges to scholarship, we have an opportunity to look back and examine these transformations through both historical and contemporary lenses, establishing a critical looking glass into the future of electoral processes and representative democracy in the U.S.

REFERENCES

Abney, F. Glenn and John D. Hutcheson. 1981. "Race, Representation, and Trust: Changes in Attitudes after the Election of a Black Mayor." *Public Opinion Quarterly* 45: 91–101.

Abramson, Paul R. 1983. *Political Attitudes in America*. San Francisco: W. H. Freeman.

Ardrey, Saundra and William E. Nelson. 1990. "The Maturation of Black Political Power: The Case of Cleveland." *PS: Political Science and Politics* 23: 148–51.

Barreto, M. A., B. F. Gonzalez, and G. R. Sanchez. 2010. "Rainbow Coalition in the Golden State? Exposing Myths, Uncovering New Realities in Latino Attitudes towards Blacks." In Laura Pulido and Josh Kun, eds., *Black and Brown Los Angeles: A Contemporary Reader*. Berkeley: University of California Press.

Bledsoe, Timothy, Susan Welch, Lee Sigelman, and Michael Combs. 1995. "Residential Context and Racial Solidarity among African Americans." *American Journal of Political Science* 39(2): 434–58.

Bloemraad, Irene, Anna Korteweg, and Gokce Yurdakul. 2008. "Citizenship and Immigration: Multiculturalism, Assimilation and Challenges to the Nation State." *Annual Review of Sociology* 34: 153–79.

Bobo, L. and F. Gilliam. 1990. "Race, Sociopolitical Participation, and Black Empowerment." *American Political Science Review* 84(2): 377–93.

Brookings Institution Metropolitan Policy Program. 2010. *State of Metropolitan America: On the Front Lines of Demographic Transformation*. Washington, DC: Author.

Browning, Rufus P., Dale R. Marshall, and David H. Tabb. 1984. *Protest is Not Enough*. Berkeley: University of California Press.

Bullock, Charles S., II Iand Bruce A. Campbell. 1984. "Racist or Racial Voting in the 1981 Atlanta Municipal Elections." *Urban Affairs Quarterly* 20: 149–64.

Bullock, Charles S. and Susan A. MacManus. 1987. "Staggered Terms and Black Representation." *Journal of Politics* 49: 543–52.

Colburn, David R., and Jeffrey S. Adler. 2001. *African-American Mayors: Race, Politics, and the America City*. Urbana: University of Illinois Press.

Eisinger, Peter K. 1982 "Black Employment in Municipal Jobs: The Impact of Black Political Power." *American Political Science Review* 76: 380–92.

Engstrom, Richard, and Michael McDonald. 1981. "The Election of Blacks to City Councils: Clarifying the Impact of Electoral Arrangements on the Seats/Population Relationship." *American Political Science Review* 75(2): 344–54.

———. 1982. "The Underrepresentation of Blacks on City Councils." *Journal of Politics* 44: 1088–105.

Eulau, Heinz and Paul D. Karps. 1977. "The Puzzle of Representation: Specifying Components of Responsiveness." *Legislative Studies Quarterly* 2: 233–54.

Fennelly, Katherine. 2008. "Prejudice Toward Immigrants in the Midwest." In D. S. Massey, ed., *New Faces in New Places: The Changing Geography of American Immigration*. New York: Russell Sage Foundation.

Fischer, Claude, Gretchen Stockmayer, Jon Stiles, and Michael Hout. 2004. "Distinguishing the Geographic Levels and Social Dimensions of US Metropolitan Segregation, 1960–2000." *Demography* 41(1): 37–59.

Fosset, Mark and K. Jill Kiecolt. 1989. "The Relative Size of Minority Populations and White Racial Attitudes." *Social Science Quarterly* 70: 820–35.

Fraga, L. R., K. J. Meier, and R. E. England. 1986. "Hispanic Americans and Educational Policy: Limits to Equal Access." *Journal of Politics* 48: 850–76.

Frey, William. 2001. *Melting Pot Suburbs: A Census 2000 Study of Suburban Diversity.* Washington, DC: Brookings Institution.

Frey, W. H. and R. Farley. 1996. "Latino, Asian and Black Segregation in the US Metropolitan Areas: Are Multiethnic Metros Different?" *Demography* 33: 35–50.

Giles, Michael W. 1977. "Recent Black and Racial Hostility: An Old Assumption Revisited." *Social Science Quarterly* 58: 412–17.

Giles, Michael W. and K. Hertz. 1994. "Racial Threat and Partisan Identification." *American Political Science Review* 88: 317–26.

Gilliam, Frank D., Jr. 1996. "Exploring Minority Empowerment: Symbolic Politics, Governing Coalitions and Traces of Political Style in Los Angeles." *American Journal of Political Science* 40(1): 56–81.

Glaser, J. 1994. "Back to the Black Belt: Racial Environment and White Racial Attitudes in the South." *Journal of Politics* 56(1): 21–41.

Grimmer, Justin and Clayton Nall. 2009. "The Turnout-Representation Disconnect in Local Elections." Retrieved March 18, 2009 from http://www.people.fas.harvard .edu/~jgrimmer/PARevised2.pdf.

Hahn, Harlan and Timothy Almy. 1971. "Ethnic Politics and Racial Issues: Voting in Los Angeles." *Western Political Quarterly* 24: 719–30.

Hajnal, Zoltan L. 2007. *Changing White Attitudes toward Black Political Leadership*. New York: Cambridge University Press.

Hero, Rodney E. and Kathleen M. Beatty. 1989. "The Elections of Federico Pena as Mayor of Denver: Analysis and Implications." *Social Science Quarterly* 70(2): 300–310.

Hill, Kevin A., Dario V. Moreno, and Lourdes Cue. 2001. "Racial and Partisan Voting in a Tri-Ethnic City: The 1996 Dade County Mayoral Election." *Journal of Urban Affairs* 23: 291–307.

Howell, Susan E. and Deborah Fagan. 1988. "Race and Trust in Government: Testing the Political Reality Model." *Public Opinion Quarterly* 52(3): 343–50.

Iceland, J., D. H. Weinberg, and E. Steinmetz. 2002. *Racial and Ethnic Segregation in the United States: 1980–2000*. U.S. Census Bureau, Series CENSR-3. Washington. DC: US GPO.

Iceland, John and Melissa Scopilliti. 2008. "Immigrant Residential Segregation in US Metropolitan Areas, 1990–2000." *Demography* 45(1): 79–94.

International City/County Manager Association (ICMA). 1981, 2006 *Form of Government Surveys*. Washington DC: Author.

Johnston, Ron, Michael Poulsen, and James Forrest. 2006. "Blacks and Hispanics in Urban America: Similar Patterns of Residential Segregation?" *Population, Space and Place* 12: 389–406.

Joint Center for Political and Economic Research. 1970–2002. *Annual Roster of Black Elected Officials*. Washington, DC: Joint Center for Political and Economic Research.

Jones, Mack H. 1978. "Black Political Empowerment in Atlanta: Myth and Reality." *Annals of the American Academy of Political and Social Science* 439 (September): 90–117.

Jones-Correa, Michael. 2008. "Race to the Top? The Politics of Immigrant Education in Suburbia," In D. S. Massey, ed., *New Faces in New Places: The Changing Geography of American Immigration*. New York: Russell Sage Foundation.

———. 2005. "Bringing Outsiders In: Questions of Immigration Incorporation." In R. Hero and C. Wolbrecht, eds., *The Politics of Democratic Inclusion*. Philadelphia: Temple University Press.

Karnig, Albert K. and Susan Welch. 1980. *Black Representation in Urban Policy*. Chicago: University of Chicago Press.

Karnig, Albert K., and Susan Welch. 1982. "Electoral Structure and Black Representation on City Councils." *Social Science Quarterly* 63: 99–114.

Kaufmann, Karen. 1998. "Racial Conflict and Political Choice: A Study of Mayoral Voting Behavior in Los Angeles and New York." *Urban Affairs Review* 33: 655–85.

———. 2003. "Black and Latino Voters in Denver: Responses to Each Other's Political Leadership." *Political Science Quarterly* 118: 107–26.

Key, V. O. 1949. *Southern Politics in State and Nation*. New York: Knopf.

Kochar, Rakesh, Roberto Suro, and Sonya Tafoya. 2005. *The New Latino South: The Context and Consequences of Rapid Population Growth*. Washington, DC: Pew Hispanic Center.

Lai, James. 2003. "Asian Pacific Americans and the Pan-Ethnic Question." In Don T. Nakanishi and James Lai, eds., *Asian American Politics: Law, Participation, and Policy*. Lanham, MD: Rowman and Littlefield.

Lind, E. Allan and Tom R. Tyler. 1988. *The Social Psychology of Procedural Justice*. New York: Plenum.

Logan, John R. 2003. "How Race Counts for Hispanic Americans." Lewis Mumford Center University at Albany. Available at: http://mumford.albany.edu/census/BlackLatinoReport/BlackLatinoReport.pdf.

Logan, John R., Brian Stults, and Reynolds Farley. 2004. "Segregation of Minorities in the Metropolis: Two Decades of Change." *Demography* 41(1): 1–22.

Logan, John R. and Charles Zhang. 2010. "Global Neighborhoods: New Pathways to Diversity and Separation." *American Journal of Sociology* 115(4): 1069–109.

MacManus, Susan A. 1990. "Minority Business Contracting with Local Government." *Urban Affairs Quarterly* 25: 455–73.

Marschall, Melissa and Anirudh Ruhil. 2007. "Substantive Symbols: The Attitudinal Dimension of Black Political Incorporation in Local Government." *American Journal of Political Science* 51(1): 17–33.

———. 2006. "The Pomp of Power: Black Mayoralties in Urban America." *Social Science Quarterly* 87(4): 828–50.

Marschall, Melissa and Paru Shah. 2007. "The Attitudinal Effects of Minority Incorporation: Examining the Racial Dimensions of Trust in Urban America." *Urban Affairs Review* 42: 629–58.

Marschall, Melissa, Anirudh Ruhil, and Paru Shah. 2010. "The New Racial Calculus: Electoral Institutions and Black Representation in Local Legislatures." *American Journal of Political Science* 54(1): 107–24.

McClain, Paula A. 1993. "The Changing Dynamics of Urban Politics: Black and Hispanic Municipal Employment—Is There Competition?" *Journal of Politics* 55(2): 399–414.

McClain, Paula D., et al. 2006. "Racial Distancing in a Southern City: Latino Immigrants' Views of Black Americans." *America Journal of Political Science* 68(3): 571–84.

Meier, Kenneth J. and Robert E. England. 1984. "Black Representation and Educational Policy: Are they Related?" *American Political Science Review* 78(2): 392–403.

Mladenka, Kenneth R. 1989. "Blacks and Hispanics in Urban America." *American Political Science Review* 83(1): 165–91.

Munoz, Carlos Jr. and Charles Henry. 1986. "Rainbow Coalitions in Four Big Cities: San Antonio, Denver, Chicago and Philadelphia." *PS: Political Science and Politics* 19(3): 598–609.

Murray, Richard and Arnold Vedlitz. 1978. "Racial Voting Patterns in the South: An Analysis of Major Elections from 1960–1977 in Five Cities." *American Academy of Political and Social Science Annals* 439: 29–39.

NALEO. 1984–2009. *National Roster of Hispanic Elected Officials*. Los Angeles: NALEO.

Nelson, William E. Jr. 1987. "Cleveland: The Evolution of Black Political Power." In Michael Preston, Lenneal J. Henderson Jr., and Paul L. Puryear, eds., *The New Black Politics: The Search For Political Power*. New York: Longman.

OECD. 2007. International Migration Outlook: SOPEMI 2007 Education. Paris: OECD.

Oliver, J. Eric. 2010. *The Paradoxes of Integration: Race, Neighborhood, and Civic Life in Multiethnic America*. Chicago: University of Chicago Press.

Oliver, J. Eric and Janelle Wong. 2003. "Intergroup Prejudice in Multiethnic Settings." *American Journal of Political Science* 47(4): 567–82.

Pais, Jeremy, Scott South, and Kyle Crowder. 2009. "White Flight Revisited: A Multiethnic Perspective on Neighborhood Out-Migration." *Population Research and Policy Review* 28(3): 321–46.

Pelissero, John P., David B. Holian, and Laura A. Tomaka. 2000. "Does Political Incorporation Matter? The Impact of Minority Mayors over Time." *Urban Affairs Review* 36:84–92.

Perry, Huey L. 1990. "The Reelection of Sidney Barthelemy as Mayor of New Orleans." *PS: Political Science and Politics* 23: 156–57.

Pettigrew, Thomas F. 1998. "Intergroup Contact Theory." *Annual Review of Psychology* 49: 65–85.

Polinard, Jerry L., Robert D. Wrinkle, and Tomas Longoria. 1990. "Education and Governance: Representational Links to Second Generation Discrimination." *Western Political Quarterly* 43: 631–46.

Polinard, Jerry L., Robert D. Wrinkle, and Kenneth J. Meier. 1995. "The Influence of Educational and Political Resources on Minority Students' Success." *Journal of Negro Education* 64: 463–74.

Preston, Michael B. 1987. "The Election of Harold Washington: An Examination of the SES Model in the 1983 Chicago Mayoral Election." In Michael B. Preston, Lenneal J. Henderson, Jr., and Paul L. Puryear, eds., *The New Black Politics: The Search for Political Power*. New York: Longman.

Ramakrishnan, Subramanian Karthick. 2005. *Democracy in Immigrant America: Changing Demographics and Political Participation*. Stanford, CA: Stanford University Press.

Robinson, Theodore and Thomas R. Dye. 1978. "Reformism and Black Representation on City Councils." *Social Science Quarterly* 59: 133–41.

Rocha, Rene. 2007. "Black-Brown Coalitions in Local School Board Elections." *Political Research Quarterly* 60(2): 315–27.

Saltzstein, Grace Hall. 1989. "Black Mayors and Police Policies." *Journal of Politics* 51(3): 525–44.

Sass, Tim R. and Stephen L. Mehay. 1995. "The Voting Rights Act, District Elections, and the Success of Black Candidates in Municipal Elections." *Journal of Law and Economics* 38(2): 367–92.

Sass, Tim R. and Bobby J. Pittman, Jr. 2000. "The Changing Impact of Electoral Structure on Black Representation in the South, 1970–1996." *Public Choice* 104: 369–88.

Shah, Paru R. 2010. "Racing toward Representation A Hurdle Model of Latino Incorporation." *American Politics Research* 38(1): 84–109.

———. 2009. "Motivating Participation: Estimating the Impact of Symbolic Representation on Latino Parent Involvement." *Social Science Quarterly* 90(1): 212–30.

Sheffield, James F., Jr. and Charles D. Hadley. 1984. "Racial Voting in a Biracial City: A Reexamination of Some Hypotheses." *American Politics Quarterly* 12: 449–64.

Singer, Audrey. 2004. "The Rise of New Immigrant Gateways." Washington, DC: Brookings Institution.

Sonenshein, Raphael J. 1986. "'Biracial Coalition Politics in Los Angeles.'" *PS: Political Science and Politics* 19: 582–90.

Spence, Lester K., Harwood K. McClerking, and Robert Brown. 2009. "Revisiting Black Incorporation and Local Political Participation." *Urban Affairs Review* 45(2): 274–85.

Stein, Lana. 1986. "Representative Local Government: Minorities in the Municipal Work Force." *Journal of Politics* 48: 694–713.

Stein, Lana and Stephen E. Condrey. 1987. "Integrating Municipal Workforces: A Comparative Study of Six Southern Cities." *Publius* 17: 93–104.

Stein, Robert, Stephanie Post, and Allison L. Rinden. 2000. "Reconciling Context and Contact Effects on Racial Attitudes." *Political Research Quarterly* 53: 285–303.

Summers, Mary and Philip Klinkner. 1990. "The Election of John Daniels as Mayor of New Haven." *PS: Political Science and Politics* 23: 142–45.

Taebel, Delbert. 1978. "Minority Representation on City Councils: The Impact of Structure on Blacks and Hispanics." *Social Science Quarterly* 59: 142–52.

Taylor, Marylee C. 1998. "How White Attitudes Vary with the Racial Composition of Local Populations: Numbers Count." *American Sociological Review* 63(4): 512–35.

Thibaut, John W. and Laurens Walker. 1975. *Procedural Justice: A Psychological Analysis.* New York: L. Erlbaum Associates.

Trounstine, Jessica L. and Melody E. Valdini. 2008. "The Context Matters: The Effects of Single-Member versus At-Large Districts on City Council Diversity." *American Journal of Political Science* 52(3): 554–69.

U.S. Census Bureau. 2008. 1970, 1980, 1990, and 2000 Decennial Censuses; Population Projections, July 1, 2010 to July 1, 2050. Available at: http://www.census.gov/population/www/socdemo/hispanic/files/Internet_Hispanic_in_US_2006.pdf.

———. 1980, 1990, 2000. Decennial Census, Summary File 3. Washington, DC: U.S. Census Bureau.

———. N.d. 1970, 1980, 1990, and 2000 Decennial Censuses. Available at: http://www.census.gov/population/www/socdemo/race/black.html.

Welch, Susan. 1990. "The Impact of At-Large Elections on the Representation of Blacks and Hispanics." *Journal of Politics* 52(4): 1050–76.

Wright, Gerald C. 1977. "Contextual Models of Electoral Behavior: The Southern Wallace Vote." *American Political Science Review* 71: 497–508.

Zax, Jeffrey S. 1990. "Election Methods and Black and Hispanic City Council Membership." *Social Science Quarterly* 71: 339–55.

CHAPTER 17

POVERTY AND SOCIAL EXCLUSION

ROB ATKINSON AND TODD SWANSTROM

In this chapter we compare the scholarly research and policy approaches to poverty in the United States and western Europe. The United States has always had a culture of poverty approach, largely missing in Europe, that places more emphasis on individual striving and the voluntary institutions of civil society, instead of government, to address poverty. By contrast, the European discourse on poverty has always stressed the structural causes of poverty and the importance of the national welfare state. Since the 1970s, however, an interesting convergence has occurred as the discourse about poverty on both sides of the Atlantic has shifted from a focus on incomes to a focus on relationships, or what is termed social exclusion. Although the shift to social exclusion has expanded the research on poverty in fruitful directions, we argue that the impact on policy has been less profound, partly because it is so difficult to measure. Moreover, the contested nature of the concept of social exclusion has often obscured the hard political choices that need to be made to reduce poverty.

1. Why Concepts and Research Matter for Poverty Policy

A concern with and debates over poverty are by no means new; in Europe one can trace a concern with poverty back at least to the UK's Elizabethan Poor Laws[1] and while the emergence of social/inclusion exclusion is more recent, arguably originat-

1. Although one should note that a concern with addressing poverty through forms of charitable action has existed for much longer in the major world religions—e.g.,

ing in France in the 1960s, one can trace the *problematique*[2] within which these concepts are located back to nineteenth century social theorists such as Durkheim. How the causes are understood plays a major role in determining how the issue is addressed. If the problem is located in individual deficiencies or moral shortcomings, then the solutions developed will be very different from an approach that locates the causes within local communities or the structures of the capitalist economy. These debates are not abstract esoteric ones but have a profound impact on how we, as societies, choose to address poverty and social exclusion. In the "real world" different conceptual approaches have become embedded within institutional systems that strongly condition how we address questions of poverty and social exclusion/inclusion.

Moving down a level, but linked to these "higher" level issues, there are also important debates about who or what in society should take primary responsibility for addressing these issues. For instance, should this lie with the state or civil society organizations (e.g. charitable organizations, the churches, philanthropy by the wealthy, etc.) or the individual? Broadly speaking Europe has opted for a leading role for the state,[3] funded through taxation, while the United States has tended to looked more toward civil society and individuals with the state playing a more subordinate role.

More concretely, there have been extensive debates over the most appropriate policy approach to adopt—should poverty and exclusion/inclusion be addressed through universal social policies, such as child allowances and retirement systems, or by more targeted approaches that focus on particular groups and/or areas in which concentrations of affected groups may be found. These are not arcane issues because, as critics of the more focused approach point out, it misses those experiencing problems that do not live in the targeted areas (and these are often the majority of the poor/excluded) and it assumes that the causes lie within the areas targeted thereby ignoring wider structural causes. Over time the emphasis on the main-

Christianity, Islam, and Judaism—for whom action on the part of religious organizations and individuals to address poverty was often seen as part of doing "God's work" and necessary for individual salvation.

2. The term has its origins in French thought and denotes the constellation of concepts and questions that constitute a way of thinking about and understanding the world. It is broadly similar to the English term "paradigm."

3. In Europe, as part of the European social model, there has been a general acceptance that the central state has the primary responsibility; however, this does not mean that subnational levels have been excluded. In many European countries (e.g., Denmark) the local state is a key element in the provision, delivery, and financing of policies to tackle poverty and social exclusion. In other countries with a federal structure (e.g., in Germany where the *Länder* have significant powers) the regional state plays a similar role. In countries with a unitary structure (e.g., France and the United Kingdom) the major onus resides with the central state, although even here local government plays an important role in service delivery. While this emphasizes the diversity of responses to the "who or what" issue, overall responsibility has largely been assigned to the state.

stream versus targeted approach has tended to swing back and forth with the current conventional wisdom in Europe tending to argue that welfare state approaches should take the lead role with targeted initiatives functioning as part of a wider integrated approach. In the United States, broad social entitlements are mostly confined to the elderly (Social Security and Medicare). Means-tested social programs for the poor were never as generous as the universal programs in Europe and the have been cut significantly in recent decades. Compared to Europe, in the United States the debate has been much more about how best to change the behavior, or culture, of "aberrant" individuals and/or groups in order to move them out of poverty.

The different ways in which the issues outlined above are resolved has tended to become embodied in political settlements (e.g., what is often referred to as the post–World War II social democratic consensus in western Europe or the New Deal welfare state in the U.S.) that in turn become embedded within societal and state institutions. These settlements will partly structure how societies deal with problems of poverty and exclusion for relatively long periods of time, but they are not immutable and are subject to revision or radical change particularly during periods of "crisis" (e.g. as occurred in the 1930s and 1970s).

The broad pattern we see on both sides of the Atlantic since the 1970s is a shift in the discourse from an incomes approach to poverty to a relational approach or one that focuses on the participation of marginalized groups in society. Up to the 1950s and 1960s the tendency under the incomes approach was to define poverty as the lack of sufficient resources to live a "decent" life, however that was defined. Under an incomes approach, the obvious solution to poverty is to redistribute income to the poor in order to pull them out of poverty. The social exclusion approach suggests that the problem is not just a lack of income but exclusion from full participation in the economic, social, and political relations of society. Solving social exclusion may require a much broader array of targeted policies that address the needs of places as well as targeted groups. We conclude that the political and policy implications of the social exclusion approach are highly ambiguous and politically contested.

2. Poverty and Social Exclusion: The United States Debate

When Michael Harrington published *The Other America* in 1962, the United States had no official poverty count. According to conventional wisdom, the poor were gradually being lifted out of poverty by the rising tide of postwar prosperity. After Harrington mailed the manuscript to the publisher, he went off to Paris for a few months, expecting the book to fall into obscurity—just like its subject matter. When he got back a few months later, he found that he was a minor celebrity. The new young president, John Kennedy, had reportedly read the book and it was almost required reading for liberals. Harrington became the man who "discovered" poverty in America.

Politicians pay attention to things that can be measured and there was still the problem of how to count the poor. At about the same time that Harrington published his book, an obscure economist in the Social Security Administration was laboring to come up with a way of measuring poverty. Mollie Orshanky's method was simple: she first determined the minimum basic diet needing to survive; she then determined how much that would cost; and finally, she multiplied that by three—based on survey research showing that the average American family spent about one-third of its income on groceries. Orshansky called her measure of poverty a "relatively absolute" standard (Orshansky 1965). It was absolute because it was based on the science of nutrition—the minimum nutrition needed to survive. It was relative because the poverty cut off was higher in a wealthy nation like the United States where only about a third of income was spent on food. In poor societies, families spend 50 percent or more of their incomes on food.

The assassination of President Kennedy in 1963 put Lyndon Johnson in the presidency. Johnson wanted a signature political issue that would cement his place in history. He chose poverty and called his program the War on Poverty or the Great Society. Johnson wanted a method for measuring poverty that would decline as the economy grew. Orshansky's measure fitted the bill. The government took the original calculations and then simply updated them using the Consumer Price Index (CPI). This has been the official poverty measure of the United States ever since.

Over time the official U.S. poverty standard has lost its relative quality and become much more of an absolute consumption standard; this is because the CPI has not increased as much as incomes and therefore those who fall below the poverty line have fallen further and further behind the average American. When the poverty standard was originally calculated it fell at about 50 percent of median income; it now stands at about 29 percent (Swanstrom, Stigers, and Ryan 2008). With Americans today spending less than one-seventh of their incomes on food, the official poverty cut-off, if recalculated following Orshansky's method, would be much higher and thus many more families would be considered poor.

Scholars have frequently criticized the official poverty standard and in 1995 the National Academy of Sciences, a prestigious government-supported research organization, recommended an alternative for calculating the poverty line (Citro and Michaels 1995). Their recommendations have been consistently rejected by Congress and the executive branch. Recalculating poverty would, of course, result in more people being deemed poor—something no government wants. Moreover, the official poverty standard is used to qualify people for many government benefits and a new definition would boost the number of beneficiaries, unless adjustments were made.[4]

4. In 2011 the Obama Administration's Census Bureau implemented a Supplemental Poverty Measure along the lines recommended by the National Academy of Sciences. It does not replace the official poverty measure, which is still being used for program eligibility (Tavernise and Gebeloff 2011).

As flawed as it is, the official poverty standard undoubtedly played a significant role in putting poverty on the national policy agenda. Johnson's War on Poverty stimulated a great deal of research on poverty, much of it by sociologists, which rooted poverty in structural factors like racial discrimination, human capital shortages, and family structure. This work helped to form the intellectual basis for specific policies that were enacted as part of the War on Poverty, including affirmative action, job training, and early childhood education (Head Start). With the Vietnam War draining the federal treasury, Johnson's War on Poverty was never adequately funded.

2.1. Conservative Backlash: The Culture of Poverty Approach

In the midst of the War on Poverty federal antipoverty policies came under attack by conservative scholars who succeeded in reframing the dominant discourse on poverty. Edward Banfield's *The Unheavenly City* (1968) is the fount of the conservative critique of structural theories of poverty and defenses of the welfare state. Banfield argued that class is not defined by income but by cultural orientations passed on during childhood. More specifically, he defined the lower class, or the poor, as those who are radically present-oriented and uninterested in saving for the future. Thus, giving a man a job will not bring him out of poverty because he will still have the same cultural orientation for immediate experiences and short-term gratification, especially sex, undermining work discipline and savings. Although Banfield's cultural explanation of poverty was never rigorously tested, it served to justify a policy of "benign neglect" by the federal government as welfare policies were rolled back.

The book that rivaled Harrington's *The Other America* in its influence on national poverty policy is Charles Murray's *Losing Ground: American Social Policy 1950–1980* (1984). Murray argued that not only were welfare policies ineffective, they actually were the *cause* of poverty. By funding single mothers, welfare policies made it possible (and rational) for women to eschew work and marriage. Once these behaviors became dominant in a community, they created a "culture of poverty" where dropping out of school, not working, and having children out of wedlock was the norm. A libertarian, Murray believed that any intervention to help people in trouble constituted a moral hazard that would only encourage more problematic behavior. Despite the apparent plausibility of this argument, evidence for the strong incentive effects of welfare has always been weak (Wilson 1987).

At a time when women were entering the workforce in droves, however, the view that society should support women to stay home with their children was rapidly losing political support. A view that had been far outside the mainstream in the 1960s and 1970s became mainstream in the 1980s under President Ronald Reagan. The culture of poverty critique of the welfare state aided the triumph of welfare reform in 1995 that ended the federal entitlement to welfare and enacted widespread work requirements for receipt of welfare. Since then welfare rolls in the United States have fallen by more than two-thirds.

2.2. Contextualizing Poverty: The Concentrated Poverty Approach

About the same time as the conservatives scholars were developing the culture of poverty perspective, liberal scholars began to focus on another dimension of poverty—its concentration—that has had a significant influence on public policy. In many ways this work parallels the European research on social exclusion/inclusion. William Julius Wilson's *The Truly Disadvantaged* (1987) can be viewed as the seminal work in the study of concentrated poverty. Wilson argued that there was indeed a kind urban underclass, but it was rooted in the loss of industrial jobs in inner city ghettos, not in welfare payments. Unemployed men could not support a family and the prevalence of female-headed households led to problematic behaviors. Wilson implied that the underclass, rooted in the disconnection from opportunity, could be changed by reconnecting the ghetto poor to opportunities.

A vigorous debate followed the publication of *The Truly Disadvantaged* over the role of race in ghetto formation. Wilson acknowledged that past discrimination played a role in ghetto formation but he downplayed the role of present-day racism. In fact, he argued that the triumphs of the civil rights movement played a negative role by enabling successful blacks to flee to the suburbs, leaving behind pockets of concentrated poverty. Other scholars argued that (racial) discrimination in labor and especially housing markets was a major cause of ghetto poverty (Massey and Denton 1993). The negative effects of deindustrialization and the location of new jobs in the suburbs were concentrated on blacks because housing discrimination prevented them from following jobs out to the suburbs.

Wilson's research set off a new wave of poverty research on the effects of living in areas of concentrated poverty independent of individual characteristics. By the late 1990s 100 scholarly articles a year were being published on "neighborhood effects," mostly the neighborhood effects of concentrated poverty (Sampson, Morenoff, and Gannon-Rowley 2002). Scholars disagree about the magnitude of the effects of concentrated poverty and its causal pathways, but preponderance of the evidence favors significant neighborhood effects.[5] If concentrated poverty is a public policy problem, there are two basic ways to attack it: either lift up areas of concentrated poverty through community development or help poor people to disperse to mixed-income areas. Both strategies have been tried and each has been subject to criticism.

The community development approach has deep roots in American traditions of localism and self-help. The modern community development movement in the United States can be traced back to a tour that Robert Kennedy took of the

5. For syntheses of the research literature on the negative effects of concentrated poverty, see Ellen and Turner 2003 and Dreier, Mollenkopf, and Swanstrom 2004, ch. 3.

Bedford-Stuyvesant section of Brooklyn in 1966. Appalled by the poverty and hopelessness, Kennedy helped to pass legislation that provided federal support for locally controlled nonprofit institutions, called community development corporations (CDCs). Supported by federal funding, the number of CDCs has increased from a few hundred in the 1970s to over 4,000 today. Scholars have extensively studied the successes and failures of CDCs. There seems little doubt that well-supported community development initiatives can succeed, as a study of the Dudley Street Initiative in Boston documented (Medoff and Sklar 1994).

Most CDCs are quite small, however, and critics argue that local development efforts have severe limits (Rusk 1999). New regionalism represents a school of thought in urban scholarship arguing that poverty must be approached from a broader regional perspective, linking community development to the broader region and helping the poor to disperse to mixed-income suburbs (Orfield 1997; Rusk 1999; Dreier, Mollenkopf, and Swanstrom 2004). The dispersal strategy has influenced federal antipoverty policy. The federal government enacted a Moving to Opportunity (MTO) program in 1993 that included a controlled experiment to test for the effects of moving poor families from areas of concentrated poverty to mixed-income areas. So far the results of the experiment are mixed and somewhat disappointing for advocates of dispersion (Goering 2003; Goering and Feins 2003). Poor families feel safer and have some positive outcomes, but they often feel estranged from their neighbors.

More recently, scholars have begun to attack the regionalism and dispersal strategy for poverty reduction.[6] New regionalism is viewed as undermining democracy and taking power away from minorities who now represent an electoral majority in many American cities. The dispersal strategy is criticized for undermining local communities and facilitating the takeover of valuable central city real estate by developers.

The shift in the discourse in the U.S. from an incomes approach to a concentrated poverty or social exclusion approach has opened up researchers to a wide range of new factors influencing poverty, especially spatial relations. The policy implications of the concentrated poverty approach, however, are highly ambiguous and it can be spun in many different directions politically. Is poverty basically a question that local communities can address or do we need a regional strategy? Does focusing attention on the contextual causes of poverty distract attention from the broader dynamics of inequality in a global capitalist system? Both the degree of poverty and the degree of inequality have risen in the United States since the 1970s. Furthermore, the United States lacks the non-place-based entitlement programs that pull many people out of poverty in European social democracies (Rainwater and Smeeding 2005). Critics have argued that the targeted approach implied by

6. See Goetz 2003 and Imbroscio's attack on new regionalism (2006) and on the dispersal strategy (2008), along with rebuttals by Swanstrom, Briggs, Goering, and Feins in the same issues.

research on concentrated poverty distracts attention from the need for the broad entitlement programs necessary to cushion families, no matter where they live, from the risks inherent in a global capitalist economy.

3. Poverty and Social Inclusion/Exclusion: The European Debate

Since the late 1970s the notion of poverty has experienced something of a decline in significance within European academic and political debates and to a certain extent has been replaced by a focus on social inclusion/exclusion. In part this has occurred because since the early 1980s governments in the European Union were reluctant to acknowledge the continued existence of poverty (measured in relative terms). Nevertheless, for much of the 1980s they could not deny the continued existence of high levels of unemployment, and by association poverty, that affected many people across Europe. Given this reality concepts were required that explained the persistently high levels of long-term and permanent unemployment, poverty, and the associated decline in social cohesion and solidarity. These developments were seen as threatening the European Social Model.[7] In this context notions such as social inclusion/exclusion seemed to offer an alternative to poverty. Consequently social exclusion meant "different things to different people" and this ambiguity allowed "a continuing dialogue about matters that some would equate with, or at least include within, the concept of poverty" (Walker 1995, 102).

In addition, the years since the early 1980s have witnessed a new and intensified phase in the process of globalization that has led many to argue that it is no longer possible to continue with traditional social democratic policies focusing on social egalitarianism. Furthermore, the recognition that societies were becoming increasingly diverse (in terms of ethnicity, gender, sexuality) reduced the emphasis on class based differences and the focus moved toward that of social cohesion and by extension social inclusion.

What should be clearly stated is that there are no generally agreed definitions of social inclusion/exclusion—they are contested concepts. We will therefore focus on two broad attempts to construct concepts of social exclusion which may be seen as illustrative of the wider debate. The first concept derives from the

7. The European Social Model of society: "seeks to combine a system of economic organisation based on market forces, freedom of opportunity and enterprise with a commitment to the values of internal solidarity and mutual support which ensures open access for all members of society to services of general benefit and protection" (Commission of the European Communities 1996, 13).

"French tradition" while the second has its origins in debates concerning citizenship.

3.1. The French Tradition

The notion of social exclusion is deeply embedded in French social and political discourse; however, it should be acknowledged that a single unified concept of exclusion does not exist in France (see Silver 1994; Béland 2007). Despite this proviso, two factors unite French accounts. For French researchers the concept of poverty has been embedded within an Anglo-Saxon liberal individualist *problematique* that understands society as fragmented with groups in open competition with one another. Furthermore, poverty is viewed as a static concept—an outcome rather than a dynamic process—mainly concerned with income distribution and defining what constitutes an adequate level of income (e.g. Townsend 1979 and 1993).

This French approach is aware of the importance of income distribution, but emphasizes the need to create social solidarity and to ensure that all individuals are integrated into and participate in a national social and moral order. Here exclusion is essentially concerned with relational issues and the dynamic processes that produce a breakdown in social integration and the associated marginalization of groups in relation to the nation. Social exclusion is thus conceived as the outcome of processes of social and economic restructuring within contemporary capitalism. These processes produce mass long-term unemployment and isolated spaces that are socially and spatially segregated from the wider society, thus the importance of social inclusion.

Within the French approach perhaps the most interesting notion of social exclusion is found in the work of Serge Paugam (1995 and 1996). For Paugam (1996) those categorized as poor are not defined by their own internal relationships but by the collective attitude that society adopts towards them—what he terms the "social orientation to poverty." He constructs three ideal types of the social orientation to poverty: 1) integrated poverty, 2) marginal poverty; 3) disabling poverty. Integrated poverty exists in societies where poverty is the norm for significant numbers of people; such societies are often described as semi-industrial or traditional (e.g. Mediterranean societies such as Portugal, Greece, or southern Italy). Here poverty is not stigmatized and the poor are not socially excluded. Marginal poverty exists in advanced industrial societies where the poor are a heavily stigmatized minority—a residuum—that has failed to adapt to modern life. In these societies the poor are outside traditional working-class institutions (e.g. trade unions) but pose no threat to social order and are disciplined by the welfare state (Germany is cited as an example). In the third ideal type, disabling poverty, social exclusion is the central focus rather than poverty. In such societies there are rapidly increasing numbers of people who exist outside the labor market, but also experience inadequate housing, poor health, and high levels of welfare dependency, that is, cumulative disadvantage. The excluded are widely perceived as posing a threat to social cohesion and social order as they become increasingly isolated from the rest of society. Such situations are most commonly found in societies experiencing high unemployment and unstable labor markets (e.g. the UK and France).

Paugam retains the concept of poverty but locates it in the wider context of exclusion; poverty is a necessary, but not a sufficient, condition for the creation of exclusion. He makes the crucial point that the poor do not constitute a homogeneous category and that poverty is also a multidimensional phenomenon—a dynamic process. For him the problem with the traditional definition of poverty is that it aggregates different groups thereby obscuring the multiple processes that, over time, create social exclusion. Thus, it is vital to identify "indicators of economic and social precariousness (precarious employment, marital instability, economic poverty, inadequate social and family life, inadequate support networks and low levels of participation in social activities)" (Paugam 1995, 50).

3.2. Citizenship and Social Exclusion

A second approach has sought to reconcile the French and Anglo-Saxon traditions through the use of the concept of citizenship rights. Robbins (1994) explicitly used T. H. Marshall's (1965) theory of citizenship as a means to identify social exclusion. As Room (1995) argues this approach:

> sought to investigate social exclusion in both relational and distributional terms. To evaluate, on the one hand, the extent to which some groups of the population are denied access to the principal social and occupation milieux and to the welfare institutions that embody modern notions of social citizenship; to examine on the other hand, the patterns of multidimensional disadvantage to which these groups are vulnerable, especially insofar as these persist over time. (Room 1995, 7)

Exclusion is conceived "in terms of the denial—or non-realisation—of citizenship rights" (Berghman 1995, 19).

Berghman focused attention not simply on citizenship rights but on the societal institutions in which those rights are embedded and materialized, namely:

1. the democratic and legal system, which promotes civic integration;
2. the labour market which promotes economic integration
3. the welfare system promoting what may be called social integration;
4. the family and community system which promotes interpersonal integration. (Commins 1993 quoted in Berghman 1995, 10)

Thus social exclusion occurs when one or more of the systems break down, allowing us to identify and focus on a comprehensive, multidimensional, and dynamic process. However, he still wished to retain poverty, but to restrict it to a lack of disposable income:

> Poverty then is part of, a specific form of, social exclusion. The latter is broader and should not necessarily always encompass an element of poverty. In between poverty and social exclusion is the concept of relative deprivation. (Berghman 1995, 10)

The central issue is the extent to which individuals and groups are "embedded" within these institutional systems.

Despite the considerable work carried out to elaborate and specify the concept of social exclusion and develop it in policy terms there is still no widely accepted definition of the concept and there is an almost complete lack of reliable data to empirically identify and investigate it. Governments and researchers continued using well-established indicators such as those associated with income (e.g. poverty and inequality in the distribution of income), unemployment (particularly extent and length), health (e.g. mortality rates), housing (e.g. indicators of substandard accommodation), and spatial concentration of these factors. Various combinations and methods were available to operationalize these indicators and construct composite indicators of "multiple deprivation." However, none of these approaches is without its problems and it is questionable whether they actually *measure social exclusion*, or at least the cultural and relational dimensions of exclusion, and there are no generally reliable empirical measures of social inclusion.

4. Where Are We Today?

This situation described above represents the position in the late 1990s; since then European researchers have still not been able to develop a widely accepted concept of social exclusion/inclusion and associated indicators/measures that go beyond the material dimension. This is not to deny that there have been impressive attempts to develop sophisticated ways of measuring material deprivation and its various dimensions at the European level and to support comparative European research (cf. Stewart 2003; Berthoud 2004; Ogg 2005). However, we still lack the means to measure the nonmaterial dimensions of exclusion and inclusion within countries let alone comparatively across Europe. This partly relates to the contested nature of the concepts, but also because the nonmaterial dimension is notoriously difficult to capture through large-scale data collection methods at the national, let alone the European level, and any such effort would be extremely expensive. While creative use has often been made of household surveys the problem is that such surveys are usually not designed to investigate exclusion/inclusion per se making it somewhat difficult to confidently use their results.

Moreover, while it is recognized that poverty and social exclusion are not the exclusive preserve of urban areas in Europe the emphasis has undoubtedly been on the incidence of poverty and social exclusion in run-down urban neighborhoods. We can see clear evidence of this in the fact that over the last 20–30 years a number of European countries (e.g. Denmark, France, Germany, the Netherlands, and the United Kingdom) have had ongoing area-based regeneration programs directed at urban neighborhoods. Since the mid-1990s other countries (e.g. Italy, Spain, and Portugal) have also developed similar initiatives. Moreover, at the European level, under the auspices of the European Union, a range of area-based programs targeted on urban neighborhoods (most notably URBAN) have been supported since the late 1990s.

Despite the developments outlined above it is interesting to note in two recently published overviews (Béland 2007; O'Brien and Penna 2008) how little the debates have changed. It is arguable that most progress has been achieved by comparative research utilizing a case study approach to investigate various dimensions of exclusion in depth and then to draw (tentative) conclusions from this research. It is to an example of one of these that we will now briefly turn.

A number of research projects have been funded by the European Framework Programmes (operated by the European Commission) that have supported sustained research into neighborhoods experiencing social exclusion. URBEX is perhaps one of the most significant and best known of these (see Murie and Musterd 2004; the chapters in Kazepov 2005 also draw in part from this project). This research focuses on the "role of place or neighbourhood in social exclusion" (Murie and Musterd 2004, 1442) and in particular "the different opportunity structures provided by different neighbourhoods" (1443). In part the research was concerned with how the excluded experienced social exclusion and what they could do to mitigate its effects both individually and collectively (i.e. as a neighborhood). This work draws upon arguments developed by Mingione (1991, 1994, 1995, and 2005) concerning the interaction of market exchange and redistribution and reciprocity within the context of European societies and their associated welfare regimes. One of the significant findings of this research is that the resources generated (or not generated) within neighborhoods can contribute either to the opportunities available to residents that ameliorate the effects of social exclusion or to forms of entrapment that intensify social exclusion. However, the research also suggests that not all neighborhoods have this impact (positively or negatively); indeed Murie and Musterd argue:

> The research suggests that in some cities there is a lack of impact of neighbourhood and the key factors affecting the experience of social exclusion [are] related to the economy...or to the welfare state. (Murie and Musterd 2004, 1456)

What the URBEX works add, among other things, to our understanding of social exclusion is a clear focus on reciprocal relations and how the neighborhood can operate as a source of amelioration or intensification of social exclusion and how it is experienced. But it is does not detract from the argument that the primary causes of social exclusion are to be found outside the neighborhood in wider factors such as the economy and the labor market and the nature of the welfare system and how it operates. Clearly the labor market still occupies a crucial role as an integrating mechanism to combat social exclusion and facilitate social inclusion (Clasen et al. 1997) but it is not the only mechanism and on its own may well fail to address wider issues related to the marginal position of some individuals and groups who are unlikely to gain access to the core labor market, experience intermittent employment, and be engaged in permanent low-paid forms of employment. In order to address these groups it is necessary to have a wider range of policies than simply getting people back into paid work.

What should be clear from the above is that the concepts of social exclusion and social inclusion are intimately related; indeed they constitute two sides of the same coin and cannot be understood in isolation from one another (i.e. they are relational). Moreover, in terms of both the European academic and policy debates they are closely tied to a number of other concepts such as citizenship, social solidarity and social cohesion. It remains difficult to clearly draw a line between the "included" and the "excluded," particularly those who are close to either side of the "dividing line." Nor should one assume that the "included" constitute a homogenous category in which everyone has the same access to services in terms of their relationships to and embeddness in the societal institutions Berghman (1995) identifies. Much the same applies to the "excluded"; they too do not constitute an undifferentiated category. It is this that makes it so difficult to adopt single-track policies that see the solution to exclusion and the route to inclusion as simply getting people into work, particularly as the nature of work has become much more "flexible" and impermanent for many people today.

5. Conclusion: The Shifting Discourse on Poverty in Europe and the United States

Most commentators on poverty research have emphasized the differences between western Europe and the United States. Those differences are certainly great. Lacking a social democratic tradition, the United States does not have the wide range of universal entitlement programs present in Europe that cushion those at the bottom from the worst deprivations. Europe largely lacks the "culture of poverty" perspective that is so powerful in the United States and that has assigned responsibility for addressing poverty to individuals or to voluntary institutions in civil society. Even the shift to social exclusion has taken different forms on the two sides of the Atlantic. In the U.S. the research has been mostly about the contextual effects of concentrated poverty using the federal poverty measure, which over the years has become more and more an absolute standard based on consumption and still dominates policy discussions (Swanstrom, Stigers, and Ryan 2008). If EU nations use a quantitative cutoff for poverty, it generally is a relative standard (50 or 60 percent of median income). More importantly, European research on poverty has shifted dramatically to a social exclusion/inclusion approach that has received substantial public research funds and this work is reflected in official policy statements, although often less so in actual policies.

In many ways, however, the similarities of the U.S. and western Europe are more striking than the differences. On both sides of the Atlantic the incomes approach to poverty has shifted to a broader relational approach. Even if American researchers less commonly use the term "social exclusion," American research on concentrated poverty raises similar issues of full participation in society as the social exclusion approach does in Europe. The shift to social exclusion has broadened research by directing the attention of researchers away from purely economic factors to examine all types of social relations. As Nobel Prize–winning economist Amartya Sen argues, we need to understand poverty in terms of concrete "capabilities and functionings" instead of focusing simply on the purchasing power of households (Sen 1983). The comprehensiveness of the social exclusion/inclusion approach, however, means that the policy implications of research are not clear and that social exclusion has become a politically contested concept that can be used to support very different policies.

First, while progress has been made in measuring social exclusion it cannot be quantified and tracked nearly as easily as income. Devising an agreed measure of social exclusion would require agreement on what social relations are most important and how to combine them, an almost impossible task. A second problem with the social exclusion approach is deciding the scale at which social relations should be monitored. Should we focus on the community, region, nation-state, or global level? The scale at which social exclusion operates determines the level at which policies should aim. In the United States, the social exclusion approach has been used to legitimate local community development policies, but critics argue that exclusion is largely generated by regional dynamics and policies therefore need to be directed there. Others would go further and argue that only national, or even global, policies will truly address social exclusion. In Europe the focus has tended to swing between the neighborhood and national level, with a growing recognition that at the European level regional differences need to be addressed, particularly with regard to what are described as "peripheral regions." In parallel there has been a growing acknowledgment that action needs to be coordinated between all levels if social exclusion is to be addressed and social inclusion achieved at a societal level and across Europe. This latter point is closely related to the idea of territorial and social cohesion of the European territory that lies at the heart of the European Union project.

Although the social exclusion/inclusion discourse has enriched our understanding of poverty and, arguably, improved public policies, it has also encouraged a depoliticized approach to poverty that obscures the underlying conflicts inherent in poverty policies. A common perspective is that economic competitiveness depends on social cohesion, or inclusion.[8] Attacking social exclusion is necessary for postindustrial economic prosperity. When the interests of the rich and poor are not contradictory but complementary, the conventional trade-offs between effi-

8. Buck et al. (2005) refer to the presumed tight connections between economic competitiveness and cohesion (and responsive governance) as the "new conventional wisdom."

ciency and equality, between growth and redistribution, fade away. While poverty and social exclusion can serve as a drag on the economy, this perspective obscures fundamental issues of power and entrenched interests. The economic, social, and political systems are connected, but they are not so tightly connected that social exclusion cannot coexist with rapid economic growth. There are still tough choices that need to be made and poverty is still a political and moral question with few easy answers.

REFERENCES

Banfield, William. 1968. *The Unheavenly City: The Nature and Future of Our Urban Crisis.* Boston: Little, Brown.

Béland, D. 2007. "The Social Exclusion Discourse: Ideas and Policy Change." *Politics and Policy* 35(1): 123–39.

Berghman, J. 1995. "Social Exclusion in Europe: Policy Context and Analytical Framework." In G. Room, ed., *Beyond the Threshold.* Bristol: Policy Press.

Berthoud, R. 2004. *Patterns of Poverty across Europe.* Bristol: Policy Press.

Buck, Nick, Ian Gordon, Alan Harding, and Ivan Turok. 2005. *Changing Cities: Rethinking Urban Competitiveness, Cohesion and Governance.* New York: Palgrave Macmillan.

Citro, Constance F. and Robert T. Michael, eds. 1995. *Measuring Poverty: A New Approach.* Washington, DC: National Academy Press.

Clasen, J., A. Gould, and J. Vincent. 1997. *Long-Term Unemployment and the Threat of Social Exclusion.* Bristol: Policy Press.

Commins, P., ed. 1993. *Combating Exclusion in Ireland.* Brussels: European Commission.

Commission of the European Communities. 1996. *First Report on Economic and Social Cohesion.* Brussels: European Commission.

Dreier, Peter, John Mollenkopf, and Todd Swanstrom. 2004. *Place Matters: Metropolitics for the Twenty-first Century.* 2nd ed. Lawrence: University Press of Kansas.

Ellen, Ingrid Gould and Margery Austin Turner. 2003. "Do Neighborhoods Matter and Why?" In John Goering and Judith D. Feins, eds., *Choosing a Better Life? Evaluating the Moving to Opportunity Social Experiment.* Washington, DC: Urban Institute Press.

Goering, John. 2003. "Political Origins and Opposition." In John Goering and Judith D. Feins, eds., *Choosing a Better Life? Evaluating the Moving to Opportunity Social Experiment.* Washington, DC: Urban Institute Press.

Goering, John and Judith C. Feins, eds. 2003. *Choosing a Better Life? Evaluating the Moving to Opportunity Social Experiment.* Washington, DC: Urban Institute Press.

Goetz, Edward G. 2003. *Clearing the Way: Deconcentrating the Poor in Urban America.* Washington, DC: Urban Institute Press.

Harrington, Michael. 1962. *The Other America: Poverty in the United States.* New York: Macmillan.

Imbroscio, David. 2006. "United and Actuated by Some Common Impulse of Passion: Challenging the Dispersal Consensus in American Housing Policy Research." *Journal of Urban Affairs* 30(2): 111–30.

Imbroscio, David. 2008. "Shaming the Inside Game: A Critique of the Liberal Expansionist Approach to Addressing Urban Problems." *Urban Affairs Review* 42(2): 224–48.

Kazepov, Y., ed. 2005. *Cities of Europe: Changing Context, Local Arrangements and the Challenge to Urban Cohesion*. Oxford: Blackwell.

Marshall, T. H. 1965. *Class, Citizenship and Social Development*. New York: Anchor.

Massey, Douglas S. and Nancy A. Denton. 1993. *American Apartheid: Segregation and the Making of the Underclass*. Cambridge, MA: Harvard University Press.

Medoff, Peter and Holly Sklar. 1994. *Streets of Hope: The Fall and Rise of an Urban Neighborhood*. Boston: South End Press.

Mingione, E. 1991. *Fragmented Societies. A Sociology of Economic Life beyond the Market Paradigm*. Oxford: Blackwell.

Mingione, E. 1994. "Life Strategies and Social Economies in the Postfordist Age." *International Journal of Urban and Regional Research* 18: 24–45.

Mingione, E. 1995. "New Aspects of Marginality in Europe." In C. Hadjimichalis and D. Sadler, eds., *Europe at the Margins: New Mosaics of Inequality*. Chichester: John Wiley & Sons.

Mingione, E. 2005. "Urban Social Change: A Socio-historical Framework of Analysis." In Y. Kazepov, ed., *Cities of Europe: Changing Context, Local Arrangements and the Challenge to Urban Cohesion*. Oxford: Blackwell.

Murie, A. and S. Musterd. 2004. "Social Exclusion and Opportunity Structures in European Cities and Neighbourhoods." *Urban Studies* 41(8): 1441–59.

Murray, Charles. 1984. *Losing Ground: American Social Policy 1950–1980*. New York: Basic Books.

O'Brien, M. and S. Penna. 2008. "Social Exclusion in Europe: Some Conceptual Issues." *International Journal of Social Welfare* 17: 84–92.

Ogg, J. 2005. "Social Exclusion and Insecurity among Older Europeans: The Influence of Welfare Regimes." *Aging and Society* 25: 69–90.

Orfield, Myron. 1997. *Metropolitics: A Regional Agenda for Community and Stability*. Washington, DC: Brookings Institution Press.

Orshansky, Mollie. 1965. "Counting the Poor: Another Look at the Poverty Profile. *Social Security Bulletin* 28: 3–29.

Paugam, S. 1995. "The Spiral of Precariousness: A Multidimensional Approach to the Process of Social Disqualification in France." In G. Room, ed., *Beyond the Threshold*. Bristol: Policy Press.

Paugam, S. 1996. "Elements of a Comparative Research Perspective on Poverty in European Societies." Paper presented at European Science Foundation Conference on "Social Exclusion and Social Integration in Europe." Blarney, March.

Rainwater, Lee and Timothy M. Smeeding. 2005. *Poor Kids in a Rich Country: America's Children in Comparative Perspective*. New York: Russell Sage Foundation.

Robbins, D. 1994. *Observatory on National Policies to Combat Social Exclusion: Third Annual Report*. Lille: A & R.

Room, G. 1995. "Poverty and Social Exclusion: The New European Agenda for Policy and Research." In G. Room, ed., *Beyond the Threshold*. Bristol: Policy Press.

Rusk, David. 1999. *Inside Game/Outside Game*. Washington, DC: Brookings Institution Press.

Sampson, Robert J., Jeffrey D. Morenoff, and Thomas Gannon-Rowley. 2002. "Assessing 'Neighborhood Effects': Social Processes and New Directions in Research." *American Review of Sociology* 28: 443–78.

Sen, Amartya. 1983. "Poor, Relatively Speaking." *Oxford Economic Papers* 35(2): 153–69.

Silver, H. 1994. "Social Exclusion and Social Solidarity: Three Paradigms." *International Labour Review* 133: 531–77.

Stewart, K. 2003. "Monitoring Social Inclusion in Europe's Regions." *Journal of European Social Policy* 13(4): 335–56.

Swanstrom, Todd, Katy Stigers, and Rob Ryan. 2008. "Measuring Concentrated Poverty: The Federal Standard vs. a Relative Standard." *Housing Policy Debate* 19(2): 295–321.

Tavernise, Sabrina and Robert Gebeloff. 2011. "New Way to Tally Poor Recasts View of Poverty." New York Times (November 7).

Townsend P. 1979. *Poverty in the United Kingdom*. London: Penguin.

Townsend P. 1993. *The International Analysis of Poverty*. London: Harvester/Wheatsheaf.

Walker R. 1995. "The Dynamics of Poverty and Social Exclusion." In G. Room, ed., *Beyond the Threshold*. Bristol: Policy Press.

Wilson, William Julius. 1987. *The Truly Disadvantaged: The Inner City, the Underclass, and Public Policy*. Chicago: University of Chicago Press.

CHAPTER 18

POLARIZATION AND ENCLAVES IN CITIES

EVAN McKENZIE

Tendencies toward social segregation, polarization, and the formation of enclaves have been observed in cities ancient, modern, and postmodern, and concerns about the consequences of these processes have been among the most enduring themes in urban literature. There are many reasons why particular places become identified with certain groups of people. The situation can arise from the need to reside near places of employment, as with factory workers who need to walk or take public transportation to work. It can result from bonds of solidarity that draw people of a certain ethnic background, religion, or age to choose like-minded neighbors. In certain cases, most notably African-Americans in the US, residential segregation has been imposed by actions of government and the real estate industry, establishing patterns of residential isolation that have persisted for decades. Many urban scholars believe that the processes associated with globalization as well as recent trends in the housing industry have accelerated the partitioning of cities into distinct sectors, and that similarities can be seen in cities around the world. This chapter outlines the main concepts associated with urban segmentation and enclave formation, and then considers the way enclaves, segregation, and polarization have been, and continue to be, major concerns in current policy debates in the US and other nations.

1. Enclaves

An enclave, as understood in urban studies, is a place that has become identified as having a high concentration of residents with some particular characteristic, so that the location attracts other people who share that characteristic. Enclaves can be urban neighborhoods, suburban subdivisions, or for that matter even rural compounds. What is essential, as Mark Abrahamson notes, is that the residents share a sense of identity that they associate with a certain place, and that place has attributes that facilitate the expression of their sense of identity. "An enclave involves a special relationship between a distinctive group of people and a particular place" (Abrahamson 2006, 3). Once an enclave is established it becomes a magnet for other members of the subculture and it may serve this purpose with as little as 25% of its population belonging to the group with which the enclave is identified (Abrahamson 2006, 4). Often an enclave begins to form because of proximity to employment, goods and services, or amenities that are important to a particular group or subculture. In some cases it may simply be that housing is available to the group in one particular area, and nowhere else, and that factor alone begins the enclave formation process.

Generally enclaves do not have hard boundaries but are socially defined. Moreover, typically enclaves do not correspond to census tracts or other official districts and therefore can be hard to study using the sort of data that are collected routinely by government agencies. Examples of enclaves include the Castro Street neighborhood in San Francisco, which is a mecca for gay residents; concentrations of artists and bohemians in various cities; Hasidic Jewish neighborhoods in New York City; elite residential areas and gated communities such as Beacon Hill in Boston and Bel Air in Los Angeles; Liberdade, a Japanese neighborhood in São Paolo, Brazil; and neighborhoods in several European nations where large numbers of immigrants from predominantly Muslim nations cluster and in some cases live according to the laws of their religious faith. Enclaves may be neighborhoods, but not all neighborhoods share the sense of group identity that is associated with an enclave.

Peter Marcuse draws distinctions between ghettos, enclaves, and "citadels." Ghettos, he asserts, are spatial concentrations of people who have been involuntarily identified as inferior, separated, and limited in their residential and other opportunities by the dominant interests in the society. An enclave, by contrast, is a place where a self-defined group locates itself in order to enhance its social, economic, political, or cultural development. There are immigrant enclaves, cultural enclaves, and exclusionary enclaves that are formed in part to isolate the residents, who are of intermediate status and thus somewhat insecure, from those below them. A citadel is a place where an elite group that is defined by its position of superiority over others isolates itself, and often fortifies itself, in order to protect their superior position (Marcuse 1997).

2. Segregation

The term "segregation" could be used simply to describe demographic separation, but in the US the term is nearly always understood in the context of the various private and public tactics and policies used by white elites in government and the real estate industry to keep African-Americans concentrated in densely populated and impoverished urban neighborhoods, such as Harlem in New York City, Watts in south-central Los Angeles, and the south side of Chicago.

Integration and segregation, used in a demographic sense, describe the way the group members are distributed within a city or some other area. Demographers use various statistical measures to characterize levels of integration or segregation in diverse communities, the most commonly used being the *dissimilarity index*, which compares the actual distribution of group members with what would be expected by chance. An entirely random distribution of individuals of different groups would be expected to yield a dissimilarity index of zero, or perfect demographic integration, and a perfectly segregated community, where members of each group live in complete isolation from all members of other groups, would have a dissimilarity index of 1.0.

The demographic usages of diversity and integration are neutral social scientific terms used to facilitate accurate description and mathematical analysis. But when we move beyond these neat demographic definitions and consider the way the words are used in political discourse, matters become more complicated and contentious, because the words encompass understandings of the power relationships in our society and the identity, status, and even the existence of racial groups.

Segregation is often used to mean the systematic exclusion of black people from all-white communities, schools, occupations, and other venues. It is a set of practices used to maintain white supremacy by denying black people access to resources. Massey and Denton argue that "Not only is the depth of black segregation unprecedented and utterly unique compared with that of other groups, but it shows little sign of change with the passage of time or improvements in socioeconomic status" (Massey and Denton 1993, 2). Many all-black neighborhoods have come to be associated with crime and other social disorders, and the role of segregation in producing those conditions is a subject of concern to scholars. William Julius Wilson asserted that the out-migration of the black middle class was the primary factor in the creation of the black urban underclass (Wilson 1996). Massey and Denton argue instead that the cause was racial segregation itself: "Segregation created the structural condition for the emergence of an oppositional culture that devalues work, schooling, and marriage and that stresses attitudes and behaviors that are antithetical and often hostile to success in the larger economy" (Massey and Denton 1993, 8).

The distinction is often made between *de jure* and *de facto* segregation. *De jure* segregation is mandated by law, as was the case under the "separate but equal" doctrine of *Plessy v. Ferguson*, 163 US 737 (1896). Such practices are akin to the *apartheid* system that prevailed in South Africa. In the US, government practices that intentionally separate people on the basis of race violate the Equal Protection Clause of the United States Constitution, as decided in *Brown v. Board of Education*, 347 US 483 (1954). *De facto* segregation is that which occurs as the result of other social conditions, usually because private racial discrimination is involved, as, for example, when schools are segregated as a consequence of complex patterns of discrimination and institutional racism in the housing market which create distinct white and black neighborhoods. Many private real estate industry practices that discriminate on the basis of race are violations of federal laws, such as Title VIII of the Civil Rights Act of 1968, known as the Fair Housing Act.

3. Segregation, Ethnic Enclaves, and Urban Theory

Many ethnic enclaves in Europe came into existence because of massive, multiple waves of immigration resulting directly or indirectly from decolonization, the collapse of Communism in eastern Europe, and the demands of the labor market. Although many of these immigrants were in a sense recruited to solve temporary labor shortages, "the foreign workers, migrant workers, or guest workers of the 1950s and 1960s have become permanent or at least quasi-permanent settlers" (Heisler 1986, 77).

There are many unresolved issues regarding how these immigrant enclaves should be regarded in the public policy framework of their respective nations. Ethnicity, it is said, has positive and negative aspects. Living among an "in group" of people with a shared ethnicity creates feelings of belonging and provides important social support. However, in some cases a group's isolation from the larger national culture can be problematic and even lead to discrimination and political conflict. Questions about national identity are being raised, such as to what degree European nations should define themselves as "multicultural" or "plural" societies (Guibernau and Rex 1997). However, "there is no necessary connection between ethnicity and conflict," and a great deal depends on whether social cleavages reinforce each other (Hutchinson and Smith 1994, 3). For example, ethnic residential separation may or may not reinforce economic inequalities. Because there are many different immigrant cultures and multiple European nations involved, it is difficult to generalize except to say that the host countries are now confronted with a set of thorny issues.

Urbanists have studied American racial segregation for many decades and it is instructive to trace the evolution of theories they developed to explain it. The models of race relations and patterns of residency that emerged from the Chicago School of urban studies in the 1920s suggested that racial segregation and the exclusionary practices that created it were natural conditions that resulted from the operation of neutral social laws.

This view was articulated by Robert Park and Ernest W. Burgess who founded the "human ecology" school of urban theory. "Chicago School" theorists viewed the city as analogous to a natural habitat in which various racial and ethnic groups struggled for niches to survive and perpetuate themselves. Much of the work of the

Chicago School revolved around understanding how groups of European immigrants and black migrants from the south were to be assimilated into American cities, particularly Chicago, where they would have to adapt to a new cultural environment. The theory of human ecology was set forth in the classic sociology text entitled *The City* (Park and Burgess 1925).

Burgess followed the book with an article that applied human ecology theory in an effort to explain "Residential Segregation in American Cities" (Burgess 1928). Burgess concluded that the residential isolation of African-Americans was simply the result of the same factors that determined the location and movement of all other immigrant groups.

Based on his observations of Chicago and other cities, Burgess observed that a city could be divided into neighborhoods. Each neighborhood, he observed, tended to be predominantly inhabited by some one racial, ethnic, or economic group. He conceived of the city as consisting of five concentric circles or zones. From the center outward, they were "the loop," or central business district, the "zone in transition," the "zone of workingmen's homes," the "residential zone," and "the commuter's zone." Burgess then argued that there were two forces operating to move people outward from one zone to another. One was the "push" of business interests that sought to expand from the center, intruding into residential neighborhoods as they did so. The other was the "pull" toward the outside exerted by new and more attractive residential areas.

These two forces, along with a desire of every group to stay together that he called "local community," set in motion a natural migration from the center to the periphery. Any new social group entering the city would typically find it easiest to settle in the zone of transition, because it would be near sources of employment and offer the least resistance to intrusion by a new group. He then identified a "principle of radial extension" at work that caused each ethnic or racial group—Poles, Scandinavians, Irish, African-Americans, and others—to extend outward from the center along distinct corridors, as the "push" and "pull" forces caused them to move toward the periphery. As these groups entered new territory, they encountered the existing inhabitants. Thus began the process of "succession," which had four stages: invasion, reaction of the existing inhabitants in the form of resistance, followed by abandonment of the area, and climax, or the achievement of a new equilibrium as the "invading" group became identified with the area.

Seen in the light of urban ecology, Burgess argued, the segregation of black people was not unusual, nor was the resistance they encountered that included violence. All this was consistent with the overall theory of urban ecology. Perhaps the most significant thing about Burgess's model is what it does not include. The model does not allow for the existence of integrated communities. The new equilibrium is not a balanced, integrated community, but means simply that the old group has abandoned the neighborhood and the new one has fully occupied it. A neighborhood which houses two groups at the same time is, by definition, in transition from the old, higher status group to the new, lower status one. Stable, racially integrated neighborhoods are an oxymoron from this perspective.

Burgess was one of the most influential social scientists in America, and the explanation for residential segregation set forth in this article that he offered, bolstered by Park's work on the race relations cycle, was considered quite credible for many years. Here were some of the most prominent social scientists in the nation saying in essence that racial segregation was the result of immutable laws of social behavior. Higher and lower status social groups, including racial groups, were incompatible, and the higher status groups would seek separation from the lower status groups.

Eventually as statistical and data analysis techniques developed, empirical confirmation for this general perspective came in the form of major national studies based on census tract level data (Duncan and Duncan 1955; Taueber and Taueber 1965). These studies tended to confirm the notion that racially integrated neighborhoods were unstable and would soon transition to black neighborhoods. The most refined theoretical formulation of this perspective was Schelling's "tipping point" model. It came to be believed in social science that the preferences of whites and blacks might be structured so that once a relatively small number of blacks moved into a neighborhood it was only a matter of time before all the whites moved out (Schelling 1978).

Although this perspective was influential in its time, and informed public policy decisions, more recent research provides evidence that there are, indeed, stable integrated neighborhoods across the nation. Numerous metropolitan areas have multiracial and multiethnic neighborhoods, and there is an emerging body of literature on what makes them stay that way. One notable work is the recent large-scale study by Ingrid Gould Ellen, that finds substantial evidence of stable racial integration (Ellen 2000). Using data from the 1990 census and other sources, Ellen finds that over 15% of non-Hispanic whites and over one-third of blacks lived in integrated census tracts in 1990, and that over three-fourths of the tracts that were integrated in 1980 remained integrated in 1990.

Ellen's study finds no support for the theory that racial transition is caused by the departure of existing white residents. It is caused, Ellen finds, by the unwillingness of whites to move into a neighborhood that they think is undergoing rapid racial transition, which, they believe, will bring declining quality in local institutions, property values, and public safety. She calls this phenomenon "neighborhood racial stereotyping."

Race based neighborhood stereotyping, Ellen explains, is the belief that a neighborhood which is undergoing rapid racial transition will experience structural decline in the form of worsening public schools, an increase in crime, and a decrease in property values. This form of stereotyping, she argues, is different than simple racial prejudice. It is not an unwillingness to have black neighbors per se, based on stereotypes about individuals. It is a belief about how the world works—specifically, a belief that rapid racial transition brings with it certain consequences. Ellen argues that her own study, as well as many studies done by others and using different methodologies, support the neighborhood stereotyping explanation.

Ellen also criticizes the "tipping point" explanation for racial transition. Tipping assumes that white and black people have fixed preferences regarding neighborhood composition, and when the black population reaches a relatively low level that some whites consider too high, those whites leave. That increases the black percentage in the neighborhood to the level that still more whites find unacceptable, so they leave, and so on, until the neighborhood is all black. But Ellen demonstrates that the initial percentage of black population in a neighborhood does not explain whether or not it subsequently resegregates. Instead, the more significant variable is the rate at which the black population had increased in the previous decade. In other words, the black proportion of a neighborhood's population in 1980 does not explain whether it will remain integrated during the decade of the 1980s. Instead, the amount of change in the black population during the 1970s is significant in explaining resegregation or stable integration during the 1980s. If a neighborhood changed a great deal during a ten-year period, it will be perceived as unstable. If it changed only gradually, it is not. Ellen argues, then, that racial groups do not have fixed preferences for a neighborhood with a certain racial composition. Rather, they have a set of beliefs about what happens in neighborhoods undergoing rapid racial transition.

The neighborhood stereotyping hypothesis has practical implications for any community wishing to remain diverse. Ellen's research suggests that racial transition is caused by failure of white demand—that is, by the unwillingness of whites to move in—rather than the decision of whites to move out. Existing residents, Ellen says, have information about the community and are already invested in it, and moving has costs, so they have incentives to stay and observe what happens rather than flee. But outsiders shopping for a new home have already decided to pay the costs of moving from their current location, are not invested in any particular place but are choosing among several, and are prone to rely on neighborhood stereotyping because they lack the knowledge insiders have.

Ellen's census-based findings on the viability of integrated neighborhoods are supported by survey research showing some softening of racial attitudes toward integration, even in such hotbeds of racial tension as the Detroit area (Welch et al. 2001), and by recent studies of other urban neighborhoods (Maly 2005).

4. Public Policies and Segregation

For many years, the real estate industry and the Federal Housing Administration shared the same perspective as leading social scientists such as Park and Burgess. They believed that racial segregation was a natural phenomenon, and their private and public policies in essence put succession theory into practice. If whites would not live in neighborhoods with black residents, it was believed, then those who sold real estate should keep the races separate, because racial integration was bad for property values. The National Association of Real Estate Boards promoted until 1950 a Code of Ethics that contained a provision, enforceable by penalty of expulsion from the organization, that prohibited realtors from introducing into a neighborhood a member of any race or nationality whose presence would be "detrimental to property values." Charles Abrams's book, *Forbidden Neighbors*, analyzes in detail the way real estate texts and policies advanced the belief that maintenance of racial segregation was good for property values and lucrative for realtors. This approach was institutionalized as early as the 1920s and continued well into the 1950s. Abrams's 1955 study found that there was not a single real estate textbook that disputed what he called this "racist gospel" (Abrams 1955).

The Federal Housing Administration's underwriting manuals, used to determine whether to offer federal mortgage insurance on a particular property, explicitly advocated the maintenance of racial segregation. The agency also recommended the use of race restrictive covenants banning sale to blacks. As historian Kenneth Jackson observed, the FHA "helped to turn the building industry against the minority and inner-city housing market, and its policies supported the income and racial segregation of suburbia. For perhaps the first time, the federal government embraced the discriminatory attitudes of the marketplace... FHA exhorted segregation and enshrined it as public policy" (Jackson 1987, 213).

The civil rights movement and federal, state, and local Fair Housing Acts have made illegal the many industry practices—such as racial steering and using various deceptive techniques to induce panic selling—that helped to produce racial segregation. However, the ghettos and enclaves that formed during the years when segregation was actively pursued as a goal have persisted in many cities across the US.

Public policies, especially at the local level, can also be used to limit or prevent segregation. During the 1960s, the civil rights movement produced groups with a focus on particular housing issues, such as fair housing groups and tenants' rights organizations. One of these branches, the neighborhood stabilization movement, developed to address a particular problem. Once a community was opened up to minority entry through fair housing efforts, some whites would leave and others would be reluctant to move in, and the result of all these fair housing policies, it seemed, was creation of yet another all-minority community. Neighborhood stabilization advocates asked how this segregation-integration-resegregation process could be prevented, so that the community could remain integrated. In short, they believed that residential integration was a good thing, but they believed that fair housing laws were only half of the picture because they opened up a community to black residents, but did nothing to keep the white population from leaving. The goal of the policies was labeled "neighborhood stabilization," "managed integration," "integration maintenance," and more recently has come to be called "diversity assurance" (Saltman 1990).

This movement focused on the beliefs and actions of white people as the key variables in the resegregation process. One challenge was preventing the departure of a community's existing white population, and the other was ensuring that the community would remain attractive to potential new white residents, which went under the label of "affirmative marketing. Resegregation, these advocates believed, was not a natural process but instead the result of people's actions, and ultimately a self-fulfilling prophecy that did not need to come true. Integration advocates attributed this pattern to calculated, predatory, and highly profitable practices by realtors and bankers who exploited the fears of white sellers and the vulnerability of black buyers.

A number of communities and neighborhoods adopted such policies in the 1970s, and some continue to enforce them. These include Oak Park, Illinois, which is generally considered to have been a successful undertaking in the sense that it remains an attractive location for a diverse population and has strong housing values (Goodwin 1979). However, the effectiveness and motives of the efforts in Chicago's South Shore neighborhood have been questioned (Molotch 1972). The notion that it is legitimate for a community to attempt to limit the percentage of black residents, while deliberately enticing white residents, is so offensive to many people that these programs are hard to put in place and generate enormous controversy, along with potential litigation.

The public choice, or rational choice, approach to urban studies makes the argument that public policies should encourage governmental fragmentation and residential sorting into small neighborhoods. Charles Tiebout (1956) contends that inefficiencies associated with the large-scale provision of public goods can be overcome if a quasi-market can be set up in a metropolitan area, so that small units of government compete with each other for residents by offering different packages of goods and services from which current and prospective residents can choose. The theory assumes that residents will relocate in order to obtain the optimal package, given their preferences. However, questions have been raised about the validity of the assumptions of Tiebout's model. Creating new governments is much more difficult than founding new business corporations. Business collusion is normally seen as damaging to consumers, but government agreements not to compete with each other may be beneficial to citizens, such as agreements not to offer tax reduction incentives to businesses. And not all consumers of local public goods are equally mobile, so that if governments are responsive to relocations, their policies might evolve to favor more mobile constituencies (Donohue 1997).

The empirical claims of Tiebout's theory have been challenged as well. There is little evidence to confirm that a greater number of local governments leads to increased competition among them. The evidence that more governments leads to greater citizen satisfaction is marginal, and increasing the number of alternatives does not in and of itself empower citizens (Dowding and John 1994; 2009). The institutional structure of Great Britain more closely approach the assumptions of Tiebout's model than the conditions that prevail in the US, and research in Britain shows that the three largest metropolitan areas would benefit from reducing, not increasing, the amount of government fragmentation (Dowding and Mergoupis 2003).

5. Polarization, Globalization, and the Mass Production of Enclaves

Polarization refers to a type of separation or segregation in which the differences between groups become extreme, and there are scholars within the field of critical urban studies who argue that processes associated with globalization, including architectural and real estate industry practices, are increasing and intensifying social and economic polarization within cities and metropolitan areas across the globe.

Judd and Fainstein argue that many cities have responded to global competition, tax resistance, and deindustrialization by adopt a deliberate fiscal and economic strategy of catering to tourists. This strategy seeks to tax outsiders instead of their own residents. In order to do this, they remake the city at great public expense, creating clusters of museums, stadiums, restaurants, theaters, shopping areas, casinos, and other attractions in or near downtown areas that are made safe as "tourist bubbles." There, tourists can play, consume a carefully constructed version of the city, and spend their money (Judd and Fainstein 1999).

Critical urban theory reflects postmodern analyses of urbanization, some of which are often associated with the "L.A. School" of urban studies. In this literature, Los Angeles is viewed as a place where emerging trends can be identified, and one of the most significant of those trends is the creation of private enclaves for the affluent. The L.A. School focuses on the politics of space. Enclosure, separation, segregation, and the idea of the "gated community" are central to these analyses. It has been argued that in addition to the physical separation of private enclaves, there is an institutional separation that is facilitated by the creation of private local governments in these enclaves, representing a potential deterioration of the public realm and portending an intensified polarization of society (McKenzie 1994; Dear and Dishman 2003). Private governance is seen as an institutional vehicle that the wealthy and powerful can use to retreat from the public realm and place their lives and their assets beyond control by public governments that are subject to the vicissitudes of the democratic process. Perhaps the most scathing depiction of this process is Mike Davis's *City of Quartz* (1990), which describes a Los Angeles that, in his view, has been divided into fortified enclaves for the affluent and militarized public spaces where a hostile police force terrorizes the poor.

Fragmentation of society and the body politic figure prominently in studies of the national political culture as well as in urban studies. In 1992, Arthur M. Schlesinger, Jr. published *The Disuniting of America: Reflections on a Multicultural Society*, advancing the idea that the nation is coming apart under the strain of multiculturalism. Civil society, he and others argue, is fragmenting as any sense of common national identity becomes unsustainable. In a related vein, political scientist Benjamin Barber (1996) argues that the nation-state is being pulled apart from above and below by globalism and tribalism. From above, the forces of "McWorld" are those of global corporations that tend to homogenize people into a common world of mass consumption. But from the bottom comes what Barber calls "Jihad," or intense local social movements based on religion, language, or ethnicity (1996). These identity-based local movements can be the basis for enclave formation, and pose challenges to the existence of the nation-state.

It appears that the proliferation and niche marketing of private communities are promoting the creation of enclaves. Gun lovers, boat aficionados, golfers, senior citizens, young singles, young marrieds—each can have its own homogeneous community, targeted to a very specific income range and marketed carefully to exactly the right groups. These cultural and lifestyle enclaves dovetail with a long-term trend toward fragmentation of general-purpose governments into various kinds of special-purpose districts—transportation management authorities, port authorities, business improvement districts, special improvement districts, special assessment districts, tax increment financing districts, and so on. Business improvement districts, for example, came into existence in 1975 and have spread rapidly, so that there are now more than a thousand such districts in the nation. Like private communities, business improvement districts do not observe the standards of liberal democratic governance despite being a hybrid of public and private (Briffault 1999).

Some theorists contend that this segmentation of urban space and governance into various forms of special districts is largely political in nature. They contend that processes are driven by business interests that are creating special-purpose urban governments that allow affluent citizens to "acquire services, to keep their taxes low, to wall out the poor, and to indulge their taste for racial exclusion" (Burns 1994, 5). These independent microgovernments, they say, permit economic and social elites to put resources beyond the reach of democratic processes and do things by contract, such as setting property qualifications for voting, that would otherwise be impossible in a public setting where constitutional rights and liberties apply. Nancy Burns, in her study of special districts, notes that "in recent years, citizens have been forming cities that provide few services" (1994, 9). It can be argued that private communities fit into this picture as yet another kind of special district providing municipal services and as such could be seen as an integral part of urban governmental fragmentation. Such processes have been described as the creation of a sort of "parallel state" of private institutions performing what were formerly public functions (Mallett 1993).

6. Privately Governed Housing Developments and Gated Communities

Fortified residences and cities are found among the oldest known human habitations, but in the US until recently only wealthy people were found living behind walls and gates by choice. However, in the mid-1990s developers had begun to create such preserves for the middle class. By now, much has been written about the social, economic, and political ramifications of the spread of "gating" (Blakely and Snyder 1997; Atkinson and Blandy 2006). Scholars have tried to understand why this is happening, and whether it is evidence that the affluent are retreating into fortified enclaves and accelerating the social division between society's haves and have-nots. Blakely and Snyder's *Fortress America* (1997) classified gated communities into three categories. "Lifestyle communities" are intended to provide a secure environment for enjoying golf courses and other amenities and are often set up for retirees. "Elite communities" use isolation to create prestige and offer seclusion to the rich or famous. "Security zones" offer those who are fearful of crime a refuge to protect life and property.

Blakely and Snyder contend that gating as a social phenomenon is driven by the conditions and conflicts of urban living. The middle and upper classes use gated communities to separate themselves from urban problems, such as immigration and a growing underclass. From their perspective, gated communities exemplified and amplified the overall patterns of segregation by race and class in American society.

Anthropologist Setha Low argues that those who live in gated communities are driven to such enclaves by what she calls a "culture of fear." Those who choose this lifestyle, she observes, are often driven by nostalgia and seeking a mythical past of intimate, predictable, village life that is rich with a sense of community and free from the stresses of contemporary existence. Preventing strangers from entering is an important factor for them, in part because of a generalized fear of outsiders, and in order to alleviate concerns about child molestation and abduction (Low 2003). Low conducted ethnographic studies of gated communities in New York City and San Antonio, and on the basis of those studies writes of the "discourse of urban fear" that leads people to live in gated communities, where the physical environment produces "loss of a sense of place... increasing class separation... [and] a landscape that encodes class relations and residential (race/class/ethnic/gender) segregation more permanently in the built environment" (Low 2001, 45). She views the secure private community as a reflection of demand among the affluent for a safe haven that they control: "Gated communities respond to middle-class and upper middle-class individuals' desire for community and intimacy and facilitate avoidance, separation, and surveillance" (Low 2001, 48). Other scholars have emphasized the centrality of fear in the formation of private gated enclaves and speak of a new "architecture of fear" (Ellin 1997).

There is a certain level of demand for the private community lifestyle that can lead to the creation and marketing of corporate employee enclaves, some of them gated. Middle- and upper-class home buyers, concerned about crime and disenchanted with government, are in many cases searching for a privatized utopia offering a sense of neighborhood control, enhanced security, a homogenous population, and small-scale managerial private government that enforces high standards of property maintenance. Lang and Danielson (1997) suggest that the private community lifestyle appeals to corporate managerial employees who are very mobile and live in neighborhoods where there is a high degree of transience. Such neighborhoods, they observe, lack relationship-based informal social controls to manage conflicts over routine neighborhood issues. In such "corporate migrant communities," the formal social controls emanating from a homeowners' association are seen as a positive feature (Lang and Danielson 1997, 883).

On balance it seems that the attraction of gated communities is related to the desire for neighborhood homogeneity and control over one's neighborhood space, especially given the fact of an increasingly diverse nation where there may be multiple sets of expectations and norms regarding social behavior, as well as news and entertainment media that foreground crime and violence. However, the observations about US gated communities and those in affluent parts of European nations may not apply universally. Gated communities have become prevalent in many nations and are now the subject of a substantial international literature (Caldeira 2001; Glasze et al. 2006). There are places where the fear of crime is very real and police protections widely considered inadequate. In such situations private security measures can become the norm.

Apart from cultural yearnings for security and isolation, there are supply-side economic considerations that drive the spread of private communities. Developers seeking to mass-produce housing for the middle class have found that they can build higher-density developments in private communities with their own private governments. If they can create commonly owned parks, swimming pools, and other amenities, they can put more people on less land and also provide these amenities to buyers to compensate for small lots. For these reasons, private communities enable developers to maintain profits and keep prices relatively affordable despite rising land prices. Moreover, municipalities have discovered that private communities offer a tax windfall for cities. Their residents pay a full share of property tax, but receive fewer municipal services and amenities, and must pay a second time to provide these services through their private governments. For this reason, many municipalities view private communities as "cash cows" and are now requiring that all new construction be in common interest housing developments (Siegel 2006).

These dynamics operating on developers and local governments produce a mutuality of interests that leads to a joint decision by government and the private sector to build common interest housing, often to the exclusion of anything else. A study of California shows that the fiscal incentives affecting developers and local governments explain about two-thirds of the variance in private community construction (McKenzie 1998). This suggests that developers and local governments are primarily responsible for the rapid spread of private communities, rather than a sudden surge of demand for private communities among the buying public.

The cohousing movement should be considered as a variant or hybrid of the developer-created private community, and is seen by some as being more consistent with communal values and shared property ownership (McCamant and Durrett 1993). Residents take turn cooking meals for each other in a common dining hall, make their own rules to live by, and in fact start the entire development through common effort. These are obvious and significant differences between a cohousing project and the typical developer-created version. However, there are significant obstacles to owners undertaking such efforts. Mark Fenster's comparison of a cohousing community and a conventional private community suggested that the use by cohousing advocates of existing common interest housing forms, as required by lending institutions, prevents them from overcoming many of the problems associated with private communities (1999).

There are also private communities dedicated to environmental goals that can take on some of the characteristics of an enclave in that they attract residents with a strong interest in preserving the natural environment. Prairie Crossing, a planned community in Lake County, Illinois, is designed in both its physical and legal structure to advance the preservation of the prairie environment that prevailed in the area before it was substantially inhabited. Residents are taught how to burn their lawns instead of mowing them, there is a charter school and a communal vegetable garden, and two commuter train stations make it easy to commute without using a private vehicle.

Although gated communities and other forms of common interest housing first became prevalent in the US and therefore most early research on the subject was US-based, this type of housing is now found in substantial quantities in nations all over the world. There are private gated communities in eastern and western Europe, the Middle East, sub-Saharan Africa, Asia, Central and South America, Australia, and New Zealand. Scholars from many of these nations have set up an international collaborative research effort that is producing a substantial body of literature. Among the questions being examined is whether a US model has been exported elsewhere, or whether instead certain conditions associated with globalization and postmodernity are producing the same sorts of housing and enclaves in many different nations (Glasze, Webster, and Frantz 2006; Atkinson and Blandy 2006; Blandy, Dupuis, and Dixon 2010). It is possible that these conditions may include a rapidly escalating demand for housing in particular cities, coupled with low capabilities on the part of local government to provide necessary services to new residents. In such conditions, private developers and contractors may step into the gap and create new communities with private infrastructure, managed by private local governments.

REFERENCES

Abrams, Charles *Forbidden Neighbors.* New York: Harper and Bros., 1955; reprint, Port Washington, NY: Kennikat, 1971.

Abrahamson, Mark. 2006. *Urban Enclaves: Identity and Place in the World.* 2nd ed. New York: Worth Publishers.

Atkinson, Rowland, and Sarah Blandy. 2006. *Gated Communities.* New York: Routledge.

Barber, Benjamin. 1996. *Jihad vs. McWorld: How Globalism and Tribalism Are Reshaping the World.* New York: Ballantine.

Blakely, Edward J., and Mary Gail Snyder. 1997. *Fortress America: Gated Communities in the United States.* Washington, DC: Brookings Institution.

Blandy, Sarah, Ann Dupuis, and Jennifer Dixon, eds. 2010. *Multi-Owned Housing: Law, Power, and Practice.* Abingdon: Ashgate.

Briffault, Richard. 1999. "A Government for Our Time? Business Improvement District and Urban Governance." *Columbia Law Review* 99(2):365–477.

Burgess, Ernest W. 1928. "Residential Segregation in American Cities." *Annals of the American Academy of Political and Social Science* 140:105–15.

Burns, Nancy. 1994. *The Formation of American Local Governments: Private Values in Public Institutions.* Oxford: Oxford University Press.

Davis, Mike. 1990. *City of Quartz: Excavating the Future in Los Angeles.* London: Verso.

Dear, Michael J., and J. Dallas Dishman. 2002. *From Chicago to L.A.: Making Sense of Urban Theory.* Thousand Oaks, CA: Sage Publications.

Donohue, John D. 1997. "Tiebout? Or Not Tiebout? The Market Metaphor and America's Decolution Debate." *Journal of Economic Perspectives* 11(4):73–81.

Dowding, Keith, and Peter John. 1994. "Tiebout: A Survey of the Empirical Literature." *Urban Studies* 31(4–5):767–97.

Dowding, Keith, and Peter John. 2009. "The Value of Choice in Public Policy." *Public Administration* 87(2):219–33.

Dowding, Keith, and Thanos Mergoupis. 2003. "Fragmentation, Fiscal Mobility, and Efficiency." *Journal of Politics* 65(4):1190–207.

Duncan, Otis, and Beverly Duncan. 1955. *The Negro Population of Chicago: A Study of Residential Succession.* Chicago: University of Chicago Press.

Ellen, I. 2000. *Sharing America's Neighborhoods: The Prospects for Stable Racial Integration.* Cambridge: Harvard University Press.

Ellin, Nan, ed. 1997. *Architecture of Fear.* New York: Princeton Architectural Press.

Fenster, Mark. 1999. "Community by Covenant, Process, and Design: Cohousing and the Contemporary Common Interest Community." *Journal of Land Use and Environmental Law* 15(3):3–54.

Glasze, Georg, Chris Webster, and Klaus Frantz. 2006. *Private Cities: Global and Local Perspectives.* New York: Routledge.

Goodwin, Carole 1979. *The Oak Park Strategy: Community Control of Racial Change.* Chicago: University of Chicago Press.

Guibernau, Montserrat, and John Rex. 1997. *The Ethnicity Reader: Nationalism, Multiculturalism and Migration.* Cambridge: Polity Press.

Heisler, Barbara S. 1986. "Immigrant Settlement and the Structure of Emergent Immigrant Communities in Western Europe." *Annals of the American Academy of Political and Social Science* 486:76–86.

Hutchinson, John, and Anthony D. Smith, eds. 1994. *Ethnicity.* Oxford: Oxford University Press.

Jackson, Kenneth. 1987. *Crabgrass Frontier: The Suburbanization of the United States.* Oxford: Oxford University Press.

Judd, Dennis R., and Susan S. Fainstein, eds. 1999. *The Tourist City.* New Haven: Yale University Press.

Lang, Robert E., and Karen A. Danielson. 1997. "Gated Communities in America: Walling Out the World?" *Housing Policy Debate* 8(4):867–99.

Low, Setha M. 2001. "The Edge and the Center: Gated Communities and the Discourse of Urban Fear." *American Anthropologist* 103(1):45–58.

Low, Setha M. 2003. *Behind the Gates: Life, Security and the Pursuit of Happiness in Fortress America.* London: Routledge.

Mallett, William J. 1993. "Private Government Formation in the D.C. Metropolitan Area." *Growth and Change* 24(3):385–415.

Maly, Michael. 2005. *Beyond Segregation: Multiracial and Multiethnic Neighborhoods in the United States*. Philadelphia: Temple University Press.

Marcuse, Peter. 1997. "The Ghetto of Exclusion and the Fortified Enclave: New Patterns in the United States." *American Behavioral Scientist* special issue, "The New Spatial Order of Cities" 41(3):311–26.

Massey, Douglas, and Nancy A. Denton. 1993. *American Apartheid: Segregation and the Making of the Underclass*. Cambridge: Harvard University Press.

McCamant, Kathryn, and Charles Durrett. 1993. *Cohousing: A Contemporary Approach to Housing Ourselves*. Berkeley, CA: Ten Speed.

McKenzie, Evan. 1994. *Privatopia: Homeowner Associations and the Rise of Residential Private Government*. New Haven: Yale University Press.

McKenzie, Evan. 1998. "Homeowner Associations and California Politics: An Exploratory Analysis." *Urban Affairs Review* 34(1):52–74.

Molotch, Harvey L. 1972. *Managed Integration: Dilemmas of Doing Good in the City*. Berkeley: University of California Press.

Park, Robert E., and Ernest W. Burgess. 1925. *The City*. Chicago: University of Chicago Press.

Saltman, Juliet. 1990. *A Fragile Movement: The Struggle for Neighborhood Stabilization*. New York: Greenwood Press.

Schelling, T. 1978. *Micromotives and Macrobehavior*. New York: Norton.

Schlesinger, Arthur M. Jr. 1992. *The Disuniting of America: Reflections on a Multicultural Society*. New York: Norton.

Siegel, Stephen. 2006. "The Public Role in Establishing Private Residential Communities: Towards a New Formulation of Local Government Land Use Policies That Eliminate the Legal Requirements to Privatize New Communities in the United States." *Urban Lawyer* 38(4):859–948.

Taueber, K., and A. Taueber. 1965. *Negroes in Cities: Residential Segregation and Neighborhood Change*. Chicago: Aldine.

Tiebout, Charles M. 1956. "A Pure Theory of Local Expenditures." *Journal of Political Economy* 64(3):416–24.

Welch, Susan, Lee Sigelman, Timothy Bledsoe, and Michael Combs. 2001. *Race and Place: Race Relations in an American City*. Cambridge: Cambridge University Press.

Wilson, William Julius. 1996. *When Work Disappears: The World of the New Urban Poor*. New York: Random House.

CHAPTER 19

IMMIGRANT INCORPORATION INTO URBAN POLITICS

ROMAIN GARBAYE AND JOHN MOLLENKOPF

Over the last four decades, immigrants and their children have become an increasing presence in the large cities of west Europe and North America.[1] Their arrival has introduced many new challenges into the various domains of urban politics. On one side is the question of reception—what rights of citizenship and denizenship do local and national political systems grant to new immigrant ethnic groups, how do established actors and constituencies respond to the growth of these groups, and where, if at all, do they fit into the prevailing patterns of political competition and empowerment? How do public services respond to the challenges of serving these new clients? On the other side is the question of mobilization—how do new immigrant ethnic groups *want* to fit in, how do they define their interests within their new political destinations and express their needs or desires, what strategies do they employ to get positive responses from government, what allies seek to help or thwart them, when and how do immigrant-origin candidates succeed, and under what circumstances do immigrant constituencies and their representatives come to wield genuine political influence?

A great many factors shape the answers to these questions. The political opportunity structure is defined by national citizenship laws, naturalization practices, election rules, systems of party representation, and formal and informal modes of electoral

1. The authors are grateful for insightful and helpful comments on this chapter from Els de Graauw, Jennifer Hochschild, Laure Michon, Laura Morales, and Karen Schönwälder. All remaining errors are our own.

mobilization and competition. Patterns of immigrant political mobilization reflect experiences in the previous country of origin, leadership and organizational development in the country of residence, and political creativity and innovation in response to the opportunities presented. The outcomes range hugely depending on specific circumstances. In some cases, cohesively organized new immigrant groups have entered the urban political arena easily and have achieved substantial influence, as in the case of Cubans in Miami or the more recent success of Dominicans in Providence, Rhode Island. In most other situations, however, immigrant political mobilization faces various obstacles to entry and success within urban political settings that has yielded partial, ambiguous, or tentative results in terms of the empowerment of newly emerging immigrant constituencies. And some groups in some places, particularly unauthorized immigrants arriving in new destinations that lack experience with immigrants, experience nonrecognition and exclusion.

At the individual level, foreign-born residents and their children face many barriers to electoral participation, such as lack of citizenship, relative youthfulness, low rates of enrollment in voter lists, difficulty with reading or understanding the national language, and low rates for such correlates of political participation as education, labor force participation, income, home ownership, and organizational membership. Of course, even denizens who lack official standing in the national polity can still participate—through community, ethnic, religious, or civic organizations or through the consultative bodies that many local governments have established to communicate with new immigrant groups. Still, such consultative bodies rarely have much influence over policymaking and there is no substitute for a group's being able to vote cohesively and especially to provide the margin of victory to an electoral majority.

Immigrant-origin dwellers in urban areas also face a wide range of institutional and systemic barriers to them as groups. Nations vary widely in how they recognize, categorize, and count groups. Terms that are as common as apple pie in the U.S., such as "race," are anathema to French and other European ways of distinguishing populations. Everyone born in the U.S. is automatically a U.S. citizen, including the children of illegal immigrants or those just passing through temporarily, but no European nation grants such unfettered birthright citizenship, even in countries with a strong *jus soli* traditions, such as Great Britain and Ireland. To the contrary, some European nations classify members of the second or even third generation as foreign nationals lacking political rights, despite their cultural and social integration. (For the European cases, see Bauböck 2006, Bauböck 2010, Goodman 2010.) Moreover, even though the U.S. Constitution and the European Commission's Common Agenda for Integration espouse equality on the basis of national origin, the advanced democracies continue to display racial and ethnic hierarchies and demonstrate many types of informal prejudice and discrimination. Finally, conservative populist politicians have successfully mobilized anti-immigrant sentiment in many recent national elections in west Europe and the United States, leading to more restrictive national and local enforcement practices.

Two tropes commonly applied to the relationship between population trends and electoral influence are "demography is [political] destiny," a saying attributed to August Comte, and "all politics is local," commonly attributed to Thomas P. O'Neill, the long-serving congressman from North Cambridge, Massachusetts, who became Speaker of the House. These thoughts rest on a profoundly true basis: local office-holders represent specific electoral constituencies in competitive democratic systems and they better be closely attuned to changes in these constituencies or they will be challenged by someone representing the new groups. At the same time, as Jennifer Hochschild (2010) has trenchantly pointed out, things never work out in such a simple and direct way. The structure and dynamics of national and local political systems filter and regulate the ways in which underlying demographic changes come to have meaning for political representation. The relationship is always contingent on the passage of time and the actions and reactions of players in the game of politics.

As a result, the changing makeup of city council members and local legislators and the coalition that elects mayors and other higher level executives always lags that of the population at large. New York City is home to the largest number of first and second-generation immigrants of any city in the U.S. and fewer than one in five residents is a native born white person with native born parents, but such people hold the mayoralty, another citywide elected position, and half the seats on the city council. One-fifth of the population of Paris has a foreign nationality and many more are French nationals from immigrant backgrounds, yet only nine members of the 163 person council are from immigrant backgrounds. Similarly, Turkish-origin residents make up more than 10% of Berlin's population but hold only seven seats in its 149 member legislature.

1. What Immigrants Arrived in Which Cities?

The west European and North American stocks of immigrants constitute a bit less than half of the UN's estimate of the world's total migrant population (99 out of 214 million) (UN 2009). The U.S. alone accounts for 37 million and Canada another 6 million. The major west European recipients of migrants are Germany (7.2 million), the UK (6.6 million), Spain (6.5 million), and France (5 million). Within west Europe, however, more than a third of this migration comes from nearby rich countries and Canada and the U.S. both send large numbers of migrants to each other. These white Christian or Jewish migrants from or to west European or North American sources are not generally considered to be problematic in their urban destinations.

The "non-Western" migrants who form the new urban minority groups, by contrast, are often considered to be problematic by the native born (white) populations in the rich democracies. Making up the majority of the migrants since 1960, they have followed a number of distinct paths from their homelands into the large cities of west Europe and North America. In west Europe, major flows included guest workers recruited from Turkey, southern Europe, and North Africa during the late 1950s and 1960s, residents of former English, French, or Dutch colonies such as the West Indies, Surinam, French-speaking sub-Saharan Africa, and the Maghreb arriving after independence in the 1960s, refugees from Balkan conflicts in the 1990s, and recent labor migrants from the new EU accession countries, such as Poland, after 2000. In addition, former countries of mass emigration like Italy, Spain, Portugal, and Ireland, have now become major recipients of immigration. While numbers from individual sending countries, such as Turkey, may be relatively small compared to the total number of foreign born, they tend to be highly concentrated in the older working-class neighborhoods of the largest cities, where they form a significant fraction of the population.

As table 1 shows, the largest countries have received the largest numbers of immigrants, but the smallest countries often have higher shares of foreign-born residents. The U.S. and Canada have both large numbers and high shares; they have received labor migrants from diverse sources, including Latin America, the Caribbean, Africa, Central Europe, China, and the Philippines, although the U.S. has also accepted many refugees from Cuba, Vietnam, Nicaragua, El Salvador, and perhaps will get them from Iraq and Afghanistan in the future. Mexican migrants are by far the largest group in the U.S., while migrants from Turkey, North Africa, and the former Yugoslavia constitute the largest non-EU groups in west Europe.

These migration flows often follow long-established kinship networks and transnational commercial relationships that link specific sending places to specific urban destinations. Each national flow usually has ethnic and religious diversity: Turkish migrants include a substantial number of Kurds, while Algerians include Berbers and Indians include Muslims. Indeed, subordinated minorities within a sending country may be more likely to emigrate than members of the majority. Upon arrival, most international migrants move to economically vibrant big cities, often port cities or major transportation centers, which already sustain their countrymen or even their townspeople. In Europe, guest workers were recruited to the old industrial cities; this is much less common in the U.S. (For Europe, see Eurostat 2010, Chapter 2, Map 2.4, p. 44.) In the U.S., low wage migrant workers that originally concentrated in traditional gateways like New York and Los Angeles have now diffused toward some deindustrialized places where the flight of native born workers from low wage labor has opened some opportunities (as in Fall River, Massachusetts) and to the booming areas of the mid-2000s (such as Las Vegas or Phoenix or Atlanta) (Singer, Hardwick, and Brettell 2008).

Prominent immigrant destinations include the major cities of Germany, France, Spain, the UK, the Netherlands, and Belgium (Rogers and Tillie 2001: 4). Non-EU nationals make up about 7% of their total population; when naturalized immi-

Table 1. Total Population, Foreign-Born Population, and Largest Non-EU Immigrant Groups in West Europe and North America (millions of people in 2008)

Country (2008)	Total	FB	EU/NA	Largest non-EU/NA	Second largest	Third largest
Austria	8.387	1.277	0.290	Former Yugo 0.322	Turkey 0.158	Albania 0.060
Belgium (2007)	10.667	1.380	0.659	Moroccan 0.211	Turkey 0.080	Algeria 0.064
Denmark	5.476	0.402	0.093	Former Yugo 0.770	Turkey 0.042	Somalia 0.016
Finland	5.300	0.219	0.047	Former USSR 0.046	Turkey 0.012	Somalia 0.010
France	64.004	5.040	1.283	Algeria 2.123	Morocco 0.761	Vietnam 0.624
Germany (2007)	81.221	7.225	2.516	Turkey 1.830	Russia 0.188	Ukraine 0.127
Ireland (2006)	4.562	0.602	0.392	Filipino 0.093	Chinese 0.018	Lebanese 0.011
Italy (2001)	59.821	1.445	0.934	Albania 0.402	Morocco 0.366	Chinese 0.128
Luxembourg (2001)	0.441	0.206	0.177	Former Yugo 0.013	N. African 0.006	Cape Verde 0.003
Netherlands	16.573	1.794	0.688	Turkey 0.196	Surinam 0.187	Morocco 0.169
Norway	4.840	0.485	0.138	Former Yugo 0.034	India 0.035	Iraq 0.021
Portugal	10.643	0.651	0.115	Brazil 0.070	Cape Verde 0.065	Angola 0.083
Spain	44.729	6.481	2.112	Morocco 0.732	Ecuador 0.471	Colombia 0.355
Sweden	9.275	1.282	0.241	Former Yugo 0.135	Iraq 0.109	Turkey 0.039
Switzerland (2009)	7.555	1.714	1.078	Former Yugo 0.181	Albania 0.096	Turkey 0.076
United Kingdom	51.579	6.647	1.614	India 0.601	Pakistan 0.401	Jamaica 0.142
Canada (2006)	33.890	6.187	NA	China 0.469	India 0.444	Philippines 0.303
U.S.	299.1	37.264	NA	Mexico 11.845	Philippines 1.813	India 1.632

Sources: Total Populations for Europe (2008): Eurostat Database, http://epp.eurostat.ec.europa.eu/; foreign-born totals and source countries for Europe and Canada: Organisation for Economic Co-operation and Development International Migration Database at *http://stats.oecd.org*; U.S.: March 2008 Current Population Survey; supplemental data from national statistical databases. EU/NA = European Union or North America (excluding Mexico).

grants and their children are taken into account, that share probably more than doubles. West European cities where non-EU nationals make up more than 10% of the total include Frankfurt (15%), Munich (15%), Stuttgart (15%), Mainz (13%), Dortmund (12%), Hamburg (11%), Düsseldorf (11%), and Berlin (10%) in Germany; Paris (11%) but not Marseille or the other major cities of France; Madrid (12%) and Barcelona (10%) in Spain; Milan (10%) but not the other major Italian cities; none of the big four cities in the Netherlands; Brussels (11%) but not Antwerp in Belgium; and Vienna (14%) in Austria (Eurostat Urban Audit 2011).

The foreign-born shares of cities in the UK are generally substantially higher, although the current sources are not broken out in detail by the UK Office of National Statistics. About a third of London's population is foreign born, as well as one-fifth of Birmingham, and a quarter of Manchester. The 2001 UK Census indicated that the percentage of non-UK citizens born outside the EU (7% in England) was particularly high in Manchester (11%), Blackburn (10%), Bradford (10%), Leicester (21%), Birmingham (13%), Luton (15%), Cambridge (13%), and almost all of inner and outer London (22% overall). With relatively liberal naturalization of the first generation and nearly universal citizenship for the second, the immigrant-origin population shares are far higher in each of these places.

The same is true in the United States, with the cities of New York (36%) and Los Angeles (40%) containing the largest overall numbers of immigrants, while Miami (50%) has the largest immigrant population share. Boston (25%), Providence (30%), Chicago (21%), San Francisco (24%), and San Diego (22%) also have large immigrant-origin populations as do emerging destinations like Charlotte, NC (14%). Well more than half of their central cities are immigrants or their children and the same is true in the larger metropolitan regions. In Canada, metropolitan Toronto 2.3 million of the 5 million residents are foreign born, almost half of whom are from Asia. Similarly, 740,000 of greater Montreal's 3.6 million people are foreign born, as are 831,000 of greater Vancouver's 2 million (Murdie 2008). Taken together, immigrant-origin populations already account for significant shares of the actual and potential electorate in these North American cities and their influence is destined to grow steadily in the coming decades.

Migrant flows from outside of west Europe and North America have thus settled among the native born residents of large metropolitan areas to produce many different mixes of racial and ethnic groups. Although these cities of immigration share certain broad characteristics—immigrants live disproportionately in older housing in disadvantaged neighborhoods, work in low skilled jobs, tend to be relatively poor and reliant on social provision, and have children who attend poorly performing schools with few native born white pupils—each place has distinct mix of immigrant and native born groups. Their relations and interactions vary from friendly neighboring to what the native born may regard as "parallel societies." As yet, we have little systematic evidence in many countries of patterns of segregation and interaction (or lack of it) on a small, neighborhood scale.

As will be detailed below, these specifics matter a great deal for how immigrants are mobilized into urban politics (or not). The comparative study of this important new phenomenon is just beginning, but a number of comparative research projects have been mounted, edited volumes published, and research networks and websites established. Recent edited volumes leading the field of study of immigrant political mobilization and incorporation in urban areas include Ramakrishnan and Bloemraad (2008) and Lee, Ramakrishnan, and Ramírez (2006) for the U.S., Bird, Saalfeld, and Wüst (2011), Penninx et al. (2004) and Peró and Solomos (2010) for Europe, and Hochschild and Mollenkopf (2009) for comparing the two settings.

2. The Warmth of Welcome

The mixing of immigrants and natives in the large cities of west Europe and North America has triggered many debates over the prevalence of racial discrimination, the ways in which the majority should recognize ethnic, cultural, and religious differences, and the motivation of new immigrant groups to become full members of their host cities. The arrival of new immigrant groups from non-Western racial and religious backgrounds has triggered anti-immigrant responses from natives, sometimes with racist overtones. For example, in the 1950s and 1960s, strident anti-immigrant campaigns against West Indian immigrants in Birmingham prompted the Conservative governments of that era to pass the first large restrictions on immigration of the postwar era in the UK (Hill and Issacharoff 1971: 50). Likewise French far-right leader Jean-Marie Le Pen's first electoral successes came in the city of Dreux, after a campaign that played on the fear of ethnic minorities of immigrant background. Pim Fortuyn of the Netherlands founded his anti-immigrant List Pim Fortuyn in Rotterdam, where members of the declining white working class found themselves side by side with new immigrant neighbors. The citizens of Arizona adopted state legislation to require law enforcement officers to demand papers from anyone who might plausibly be unauthorized. In a number of cases, most notably Austria, France, the Netherlands, and Switzerland, these parties have achieved considerable political influence, and indeed the current government of the Netherlands depends on votes from the LPF to stay in power.

In Europe, Minkenberg (2009) argues that traditional far-right populist political entrepreneurs seized on the perceived threat posed by immigrants to a native working class facing deindustrialization to enhance their political influence. This in turn has led conservative parties within the normal spectrum of political parties to provide openings to them, reflected both in the composition of national governments (for example Austria as well as the Netherlands) and the adopting of anti-immigrant measures. Ivarsflaten (2005) argues that the presence of highly visible anti-immigrant elites and an underlying mass anxiety over the immigrant threat to national cultural unity both serve as important factors driving anti-immigrant political responses. Indeed, the strength of anti-immigrant parties can even push parties on the left to adopt tougher positions on immigrants (Alonso and da Fonseca 2009). Howard (2010) has also noted the ways in which anti-immigrant party influence hampers the liberalization of citizenship laws.

Christopher Bail (2008) has used the European Social Survey to distinguish three distinct patterns of native responses to immigrants in Europe: a relatively tolerant one in the Scandinavian counties (Norway, Denmark, Sweden, but also Switzerland), all small countries with strong welfare states and high shares of immigrants, but also characterized by a lack of clear religious or racial boundaries; a set of larger peripheral countries that have all recently become immigrant destinations (Spain, Portugal, Italy, Ireland, Greece) where the discourse is relatively new and unsophisticated and marked by stronger racial and religious boundaries, and the core countries of west Europe (Britain, France, Germany, Austria, Netherlands, Belgium) which have longer histories of migration, substantial guest worker and former colonial migration, and highly developed discourses over immigrant integration, but not without natives articulating their anxieties over whether they can maintain the integrity of their national cultures. Other cross-national attempts to measure receptiveness to immigrants include the Multicultural Index created by Banting, Johnston, Kymlicka, and Soroka (2006) based on the International Social Survey Programme and the MIPEX index of the Migration Policy Group (2011).

Canadian social scientists have also been exploring how immigrants and their children are actually faring in a nation formally committed to multiculturalism. In comparative perspective, Canada may be the most explicitly pro-immigrant nation of the group. Like the U.S., it was built up on the basis of immigration, but unlike the U.S. it strongly emphasizes labor market qualifications in admitting immigrants and has an array of federal and provincial programs to enhance their integration. Sociologist Irene Bloemraad (2006) has underscored the importance of this difference in advancing citizenship acquisition in Canada as compared to the U.S. Canadian politics has not been marked by right-wing anti-immigrant political campaigns, although language politics in Quebec set a quite different framework for the interaction between immigrants and natives in Montreal as compared to Toronto or Vancouver. Still, political scientist Martin Papillon (2002: 1) concluded that, despite Canada's pro-immigrant stance, "visible minorities, which now constitute the majority of immigrants to urban Canada, face greater systemic barriers to social inclusion than earlier groups of immigrants."

Given that its population is almost four times greater than that of the largest west European country—and that it contains highly diverse combinations of native and immigrant racial and ethnic groups—the U.S. inevitably shows distinctively different regional patterns of immigrant reception. The large cities with continuous immigrant inflows, such as New York, Chicago, and Los Angeles, tend to react in more positive way than those which lack such a heritage, such as Phoenix or Charlotte. But the suburban periphery may be far less friendly even in metropolitan areas with long histories of immigration. Moreover, as Foner and Alba (2010, see also Alba and Foner 2009) and Hochschild and Mollenkopf (2010) have noted, we must always put migration-drive ethnic diversity in the U.S. in the context of its shameful legacy of slavery and persisting black-white differences.

In the U.S. political scientists are exploring why some cities are more likely than others to adopt a hostile stance toward immigrants (Hopkins 2010, Ramakrishnan and Wong 2010). They have underscored the importance not only of the formation of individual negative attitudes (a dynamic with a long history in America), but how local political opportunity structures and other contextual factors shape those individual responses. A rapid influx of recent immigrants, especially those lacking authorization, certainly makes American cities and suburbs more prone to anti-immigrant responses (O'Neil 2010). As in the European scholarship, however, these scholars find that anti-immigrant mobilization occurs mainly where local (and national) political actors think they will benefit from mobilizing resentment and outrage against these groups. Conversely, long experience with large immigrant populations, a prevalence of Democratic local officeholders, and greater urban density all tend to insulate against such responses. Hopkins's analysis of larger data suggests, however, that local outcomes are also highly sensitive to the tenor of national debate about immigration.

On the other hand, even in areas where immigrants are a new phenomenon, local public service systems—education, welfare, health, law enforcement—must interact with them and find some sort of *modus vivendi*. Particularly when immigration has not been negatively politicized at a city or regional level, public agencies can often fly "under the radar" and deal with immigrants, even the undocumented, in ways that local public opinion might not accept were these practices to become more visible (Jones-Correa 2008, Cattacin 2009, Marrow 2009). The extent and shape of local immigrant-serving organizations in the central city also provides a reference point for suburban jurisdictions reacting to the spread of immigrant populations (deGraauw, Gleeson, and Bloemraad 2010).

In this respect, interaction between immigrants and their children and public service agencies is also concentrated in the big cities where they have settled. This creates a host of specific issues for local elected officials even where immigrants are at best marginal political actors: discrimination on the basis of national origin, the official recognition by local governments of cultural and religious diversity, police treatment of immigrants as victims, perpetrators or witnesses, the regulation of hate crimes against members of immigrant communities, the construction of custom-built places of worship (mosques, Sikh or Hindu temples), reaction to seemingly illiberal cultural practices (wearing the veil, ritual slaughtering of animals), school responses to speakers of nonnational languages, and regulation of open-air labor markets. Even in the absence of formal political participation, immigrant associations and community groups often play a crucial role in bringing these issues to the fore.

Local political authorities have reacted in a variety of ways to such issues. In the 1960s and 1970s, local governments frequently set up "consultative councils" for first-generation immigrants with foreigner status—and therefore no voting rights. These structures reflected a widespread perception that immigrants first needed to be trained in political participation before becoming naturalized voters who could access "real" politics. In most cases, these experiments failed to advance migrant claims significantly. Local political establishments only began to take immigrant-related issues seriously when more immigrants and their children obtained the vote, started using it, and first elected candidates from immigrant backgrounds.

3. Gaining Citizenship and Exercising the Right to Vote

National-level politics of immigration and nationality set strong institutional parameters for immigrant participation in local politics. Until recently, the trend in Europe was toward a convergence on liberal, American-style nationality and citizenship regimes, with easy access to citizenship through naturalization for first-generation migrants, and citizenship automatically or by choice for their children born in their host country (Joppke 2007, 2010, Vink and de Groot 2010). In recent years, however, the politicization of immigrant "otherness," particularly for Muslim groups, has been accompanied by widespread debate over whether such immigrants can become fully "German" or "French" as well as by the adoption of more restrictive policies. Moreover, in some countries, particularly Switzerland, local administration of national regulations may deter eligible groups from attaining citizenship.

The effects of the sometimes stark contrasts among national policies in the postwar decades are still evident. Even in the case of Germany, which liberalized its citizenship rules in 1999, naturalization has remained limited because it refuses to recognize dual nationality and imposes other requirements. Naturalization of the major immigrant group, Turks, peaked when the law went into effect in 2000 and declined subsequently. In Britain, the extremely liberal citizenship regime in place in the 1950s and 1960s automatically gave colonial or postcolonial immigrants voting rights in all British elections upon arrival in the UK. As a result, political participation by these groups developed more rapidly in the UK than elsewhere in Europe, with political parties noting the importance of minority voters as early as the general elections of 1974 (Saggar 1998: 25, LGIU 1996). At the local level, "visible minorities" began winning local council and parliamentary seats starting in London in the early 1980s and spreading to other areas of concentration thereafter (Adolino 1998, Geddes 1993, Saggar 1991).

In some instances, European governments have granted local voting rights to noncitizens who have legal permanent residence. Scandinavian countries, which host growing migrant populations, took the lead in granting such rights, with Sweden enacting them in 1976, Denmark in 1981, Norway in 1982, and the Netherlands in 1986 and Belgium in 2004. (LeCour Grandmaison and Wihtol de Wenden [1993] provide a comprehensive study of local voting rights for foreigners in Europe in this period.) In most cases, this led to the gradual growth of immigrant political constituencies and greater attention from political parties. In the Netherlands, participation in local elections surged after the granting of local voting rights in 1985 and minority representation in large Dutch cities increased steadily (Hartman 2007, Van Heelsum 2002, 2004). In Belgium, local voting rights granted in 2004 produced substantial participation in the 2006 local elections, and, as in the Netherlands, a corresponding rise in representation on local councils with large immigrant minority populations. In France and Germany, however, proposals to grant local voting rights never garnered much attention from national decision-makers and participation by first generation immigrants remains more limited. Only a few U.S. municipalities have granted local voting rights to noncitizens, most notably Takoma Park, Maryland (although the practice was common at the end of the 19th century) and voters recently defeated efforts to extend this right in Portland, Maine, and San Francisco, California.

France has a liberal citizenship regime, with easy naturalization for first-generation migrants and citizenship (at age 18) for the second generation. In the past several decades, however, the naturalization rate has remained comparatively low because the procedure is complex and little advertised (Weil 2002: 251). On the other hand, the coming of age of the second generation, combined with first-generation migrants who have naturalized, have made immigrant communities a potential electoral force in some localities. However, established political parties have not paid much attention to them and immigrant-origin representation on local councils has remained low in most cities. Only in the 2008 local elections, 30 years after the process began in Britain, did a significant number of ethnic minority candidates win election to the councils of such large French cities as Marseille or Lyon.

In Britain, Conservatives and the Labour Party reached a bipartisan consensus in the 1960s on a dual policy of restricting immigration and promoting harmonious "race relations." As a result, public discourse shifted from immigration to racial discrimination and the recognition of diversity. The race relations framework put in place in the 1960s encouraged local authorities to manage racial tensions on their territory. This approach was facilitated by the relatively high separation of national and local politics in Britain (sometimes referred to as "high" and "low" politics). All of this constituted a favorable context to the rise of locally focused antiracist campaigns, the creation of antidiscrimination policies by local councils, and the emergence of a "black" and "Asian" personnel in local Labour Party organizations, who then went on to win election on local councils.

Given the high levels of citizenship attained by immigrants in Canada and their concentration in the three biggest cities, especially Toronto, one would expect that they would emerge as important voting constituencies in city politics. Yet the rapidity with which they emerged, combined with the preponderance of the relatively conservative native born white population, a low level of partisanship, and the absorption of the city of Toronto into a metropolitan government led to comparatively low levels of immigrant electoral mobilization in a context of a conservative political establishment (Siemiatycki et al. 2001; Andrew et al. 2008, Hicks 2006). Despite these constraints, however, the 44-member council includes four members from East Asian backgrounds, one born in Portugal, and one born in Ecuador. (It also has one black member.)

No comprehensive documentation of local elected officials from immigrant backgrounds is currently available for the U.S., but the November 2008 Current Population Survey election supplement details the scope of the potential electorate with immigrant origins (table 2). As of November 2008, just under a quarter of the total U.S. population was foreign born or had at least one foreign-born parent. Since all of the children born in the U.S. are citizens, they make up a larger share of the immigrant-origin citizens, while the foreign-born share of the citizen population is smaller because only 42.6% of them had naturalized. Since the native stock population is older relative to the total and the children of immigrants are still relatively young, the native stock population makes up a larger share of the potential electorate. Still, one out of every six potential voters in the November 2008 presidential election was an immigrant or the child of an immigrant. For reasons that are similar to those operating in Canada and west Europe, however, members of the immigrant first and second generation who are voting age citizens are less likely than natives to have registered or actually cast ballots. Still, 14.6% of the voters in 2008 were immigrants or their children, a share that exceeds that of African Americans (11.5% of total voters) and far outweighs native born Hispanics (3.3%).

Table 2 also demonstrates that immigrant-origin voters are an even more consequential part of the active electorate in the large cities which have received the most immigrants in recent decades. Taken together, the immigrant-origin electorate exceeds one-third of the total in these cities. The two largest local jurisdictions in the U.S., the five counties of New York City (8.1 million people) and Los Angeles County (9.8 million people), have populations comparable to smaller European nations like Austria, Sweden, or Switzerland. In the November 2008 presidential election, foreign-born voters made up a quarter of their voters and their native born children made up 17% more, while native stock whites was barely a quarter of the electorate in New York and a third in Los Angeles. These two cities may be considered, therefore, forerunners or harbingers of electoral conditions that may gradually emerge in many other major urban areas in North America and west Europe. Given their demographic similarities, their considerable political differences—a highly partisan New York compared to a nonpartisan Los Angeles—make them a particularly interesting comparison regarding how local political structures or dynamics shape immigrant political mobilization and incorporation (Mollenkopf 2008, Sonenshein and Drayse 2006).

Immigrant first- and second-generation political candidates have been making steady headway in winning legislative offices in New York City. The first Dominican and West Indian candidates were elected to the 51-member City Council after its enlargement and redistricting in 1991, along with an increased number of African Americans and Puerto Ricans. In the subsequent two decades, the immigrant-origin council delegation has grown to four Dominicans (one first generation and three second generation), three West Indians (one first generation and two second), and two Chinese (both foreign born), or one-fifth of the total. The Council also has six

Table 2. **Total Population, Citizen and Voting Age Population, Registration and Voting by Immigrant Status, United States (November 2008 presidential election, totals in 000s)**

Status	Total	Citizens	Citizens 18+	Registered voters	2008 voters	Immigrant city voters
Native stock	76.6%	82.6%	83.8%	85.2%	85.4%	63.8%
One FB parent	4.5%	4.9%	4.4%	4.5%	4.5%	6.0%
Two FB parents	6.3%	6.8%	4.4%	3.9%	3.8%	9.6%
Foreign born	12.5%	5.8%	7.5%	6.4%	6.3%	20.6%
Total	299,700	278,144	205,739	146,252	131,091	10,388

Source: Authors' calculation from the November 2008 Current Population Survey. Immigrant cities are New York, Los Angeles, Chicago, Houston, San Francisco–Oakland, San Jose, Miami, and Boston.

Puerto Rican and 11 African American members, giving minority members a slim majority of the votes. While the regular Democratic Party organizations in the Bronx, Queens, and Brooklyn managed this process of racial and ethnic succession by choosing immigrant-origin candidates who typically beat more community-based competitors, the city's highly partisan political system has clearly allowed the diversity of the city's demographic changes to be reflected in the nature of its representatives.

Minority and immigrant-origin candidates in New York did not have much success in running for citywide offices until 2009, when John Liu, who migrated with his family from Taiwan at age five, was elected comptroller, the city's second highest office. (His father renamed him John and his brothers Robert and Edward after the Kennedy family.) In 2001, with support from native born as well as immigrant blacks and Latinos, Fernando Ferrer, a Puerto Rican from the Bronx, sought but failed to get the Democratic mayoral nomination. Republican Michael Bloomberg ultimately won office in that year, while William C. Thompson, an African American Democrat with a West Indian grandparent, became comptroller. Ferrer ran for mayor again in 2005. Narrowly winning the Democratic nomination against Congressman Anthony Weiner, he then resoundingly lost the general election to the incumbent Mayor Bloomberg, who assiduously courted and won votes in various immigrant communities, including West Indian neighborhoods.

In 2009, after suspending term limits in conjunction with the City Council, Mayor Bloomberg narrowly won a final reelection campaign against Comptroller Thompson, who drew well in African American and West Indian neighborhoods, but lost support in Puerto Rican and Dominican neighborhoods compared to Ferrer's shares in 2005. Meanwhile, Bloomberg focused his campaign on the more conservative immigrant neighborhoods, drawing strongly in Russian and Chinese areas and even doing comparatively well in Latino immigrant areas. In the same election, however, Liu won the comptroller's race, becoming the first recent citywide elected official from an Asian or immigrant background. His victory not only reflected the Democratic Party's ability to consolidate the vote behind a minority candidate for this citywide office, but was an artful electoral coalition building effort that successfully crossed racial and ethnic lines.

In Los Angeles, four immigrant-origin members currently serve on the 15-seat City Council, one born in Mexico and three with Mexican ancestry, for just over one-quarter of the seats. Achieving these seats was a long, hard struggle, for the first Mexican American Council member, Edward Roybal, was gerrymandered out of his seat in 1959 and the next, Richard Alatorre, was not elected until 1985. Along with three African American members, minority officeholders wield slightly less than half the Council votes. This balance reflects the predominance of Mexican Americans within the immigrant-origin population of Los Angeles, as distinct from the great diversity characterizing the immigrant communities of New York City, but additional representation of Latino communities may come at the expense either of African American or Jewish officeholders there.

The great breakthrough of immigrant representation in Los Angeles occurred, however, with the election of Antonio Villaraigosa, a former union organizer and Democratic speaker of the state Assembly, in 2005 (Sonenshein 2005). Having grown up in a poor, single parent family on the East Side of LA, a predominantly Mexican American neighborhood, he attended UCLA, worked as an organizer for the Teacher's Union, and served in the State Assembly before losing a mayoral campaign in 2001 (to James Hahn, a liberal white whose father had become a political icon representing the black neighborhoods of LA in the County Board of Supervisors) and winning a city council seat in 2003. After Hahn lost black support by forcing out the African American chief of police (who then became a member of the City Council), Villaraigosa was able to forge a coalition of Hispanic, black, and white liberal voters to win the 2005 election and to be reelected against weak challengers in 2009. While his inability to radically transform Los Angeles politics and policies has disappointed some and his divorce and use of free tickets to high profile events has dented his reputation, the Villaraigosa administration successfully championed school reform, building a new subway line from downtown to Santa Monica, and efforts to reduce crime and gang activity.

New York and Los Angeles thus provide contrasting routes by which immigrant constituencies have gained access to decision-making power in urban politics. Politicians from the largest immigrant groups in New York—Dominicans, West Indians, and Chinese—have won a steadily increasing number of city and state legislative offices and one—Comptroller John Liu—has attained a position of considerable power, since the comptroller approves all substantial contracts issued by the city, has the power to audit all city departments, and manages the huge city pension funds. Yet immigrant, native minority, and white liberal constituencies have not been able to coalesce behind a mayoral candidate who can win a majority of votes in the general election and overcome the racial polarization that has characterized mayoral elections for 30 years. Nor does the Democratic Party appear to be a vehicle by which that can easily be accomplished in approaching mayoral elections. Still, the importance of the immigrant vote in city elections has yielded not only pervasive influence on the margins of power, but a strongly pro-immigrant stance by successive mayors of New York, even when their victories have not been attained with substantial minority support.

Los Angeles provides an inverse picture: only the largest immigrant ethnic group, Mexican Americans, has achieved significant political representation, and many others that make up significant shares of the electorate (Filipinos, Iranians, Indians, Koreans) have not. This reflects a variety of factors, including the low spatial concentrations of these groups, the large areas covered by each council district, and the absence of party organizations recruiting candidates from these backgrounds. Yet despite the long road Mexican American political leaders have had to follow, they succeeded in winning substantial numbers of legislative districts and the foremost among them, Antonio Villaraigosa, forged a progressive coalition that reached across racial and ethnic boundaries.

4. The Influence of Local Representation Systems

The urban settings described previously demonstrate widely varying levels of immigrant political incorporation, in the form of mobilizing for elections, winning office, and being part of local government. Some cities demonstrate virtually no capacity or willingness to represent immigrant ethnic communities as groups—in these cities, immigrant-origin candidates have succeeded only because parties have chosen them, not their not communities. In other cities, especially the relatively open, winner-take-all, single member districts of the UK, Canada, and the U.S., immigrant-origin political entrepreneurs have successfully organized an immigrant ethnic voting base to win legislative, and upon occasion executive, positions. Indeed, they have sometimes been able to exert real political influence on behalf of the interests of their constituencies.

Apart from the ways in national and local citizenship practices filter broad demographic patterns to create bodies of potentially eligible voters, what accounts for this variation? A gradually developing body of comparative research highlights a number of political and institutional factors that may account for these variations, although some studies have placed more emphasis on the national than the local context (Keating 1991, Ireland 1994, Blommaert and Martiniello 1996, Favell 1998, Oriol 1998, Vertovec 1998, Guiraudon 2000, Hansen 2000, Bousetta 1997 and 2001, Geisser and Oriol 2002, Garbaye 2002, Le Galès 2003, Joppke and Morawska 2003, Garbaye 2005, Koopmans et al. 2005, Alba and Foner 2009, Hochschild and Mollenkopf 2009, Bird, Saalfeld, and Wüst 2010, Michon 2010, de Graauw and Andrews 2011). These works highlight the interplay between political opportunities and group strategies for political advancement and conclude that, in addition to national immigration selection policies, nationality laws, and governmental approaches to "integrating" immigrants, local patterns of party politics and community organization play a particularly important role in immigrant political incorporation.

The process of urban political incorporation—mobilizing immigrant-origin electoral constituencies, electing immigrant-origin candidates to local office, and their taking part in local governing coalitions—is advancing slowly but steadily across the large cities of west Europe and North America, though it has gone further in the U.S. than Europe (Mollenkopf and Hochschild 2010). Within this general trend, the degree and forms of incorporation vary strikingly both within and across countries. Some cities show levels of minority representation on city councils that begin to approach those of New York or Los Angeles. As Hochschild and Mollenkopf (2009: 11) note, "the forty-five member city council of Amsterdam has approximately seven members from immigrant backgrounds" (see also Dekker and Fattah 2007). And Brussels has by far the most representation of people descended from non-Europeans—twenty (22.5 percent) out of eighty-nine total seats in the

Brussels Parliament (Jacobs, Phalet, and Swyngedouw 2004). In Britain, most of the large cities with minority concentrations have also achieved roughly proportionate levels of representation on city councils since the early 1990s (Le Lohé 1998: 89).

In other countries, however, immigrant incorporation has been much more limited, or began only recently, even though migrants, their children, and even grandchildren have been established in large numbers for decades. In French cities, for example, significant levels of representation began to appear only belatedly, in the 2008 municipal elections. One reason is that French system of representation works against immigrant political representation. The *cumul des mandats* system permits members of the French National Assembly, including those forming the government, simultaneously to hold mayorships of large cities or other local mandates. As a result, ambitious politicians view political control over large cities as a fast track to national prominence and they often retain their local mandates throughout their national careers. The *cumul des mandats* is and indicator of the high local salience of national politics, which has taken on a markedly illiberal tone on immigration and integration issues. In this context, it has been particularly difficult for immigrant leaders or their liberal allies to raise issues of discrimination or recognition of diversity.

In Germany, Karen Schönwälder and Christiane Kofri (2010) have carried out the most comprehensive analysis of immigrants in urban politics, focusing on the city councils in North Rhine–Westphalia. They found the number of immigrant council members, although still far from parity, has slowly risen, so that they now hold about 4% of the seats in the larger cities, with the thicker networks of organizations in Turkish communities helping them make particularly good progress. They did not find that the Social Democratic Party had been a important engine of representation, in contrast to the role of left parties in other European urban settings.

Da Fonseca (2011) has similarly analyzed the degree to which German political parties advanced immigrant candidates in the five federal elections before and after the citizenship reform of 1999 and the surge of naturalizations that peaked around that date. She distinguishes former ethnic Germans from other immigrants in her analysis. The Germany party system involves a mixture of lists (proportional representation) and single member districts. She finds that although the number of such candidates remains quite small, it has also increased slowly for the Christian Democrats and the Social Democrats and more rapidly for the smaller left parties, the Greens and the Left Party. Despite these increases in nominations, however, the number of foreign-born officeholders remains extremely small, with only 11 deputies in the Bundestag, five of whom are Turkish (see also Miera 2009).

This result may be interpreted in terms of the larger catchall parties not wishing to undermine their appeal to native German constituencies by going very far in the direction of small immigrant constituencies, combined with a generally negative approach toward multiculturalism (Miera 2009). Meanwhile, the smaller parties on the left have put such candidates forward in their efforts to create comparative advantage, especially in urban jurisdictions where immigrant-origin voters are more numerous. Still, despite high proportions of Turkish and other immigrant-origin dwellers in cities like Berlin, they are a far smaller proportion of the electorate and hold only a few positions in either the Berlin Parliament or the district councils.

The national modes of organizing local politics are also important. The structure of local councils and their executives, as well as local electoral and districting systems, combine to create more or less favorable opportunities for immigrant incorporation. In Belgian municipal elections, ethnic minority candidates have benefited from the possibility afforded to voters to give an additional vote to a individuals of their choice on party lists. In Brussels communes with large populations of voters with migrant backgrounds, voters have used this additional vote to favor candidates of similar origins with considerable success, as was evident in the 2000 local elections (Jacobs, Martiniello, and Réa 2001). (This produced complaints from majority candidates placed higher on the list of "ethnic" voting.) A similar system of preferential voting in Dutch local elections has also facilitated the election of candidates of immigrant background (Van Heelsum 2002: 189, 2004).

The British local system favors minority incorporation in a different way. Because a simple plurality vote can win and the local election districts or wards are small, covering a neighborhood of around 20,000 people, a concentrated minority population can elect the candidate of its choice in the inner-city wards of large British cities. As in the U.S., they often form ethnic voting blocs at the ward level that have facilitated the election of ethnic minority candidates from the early 1980s onward.

In France, by contrast, municipal elections are held on a citywide basis, which means that ethnic minority voting blocs are "diluted" by a much larger group of white, middle-class voters. The French use of a list (proportional representation) system for municipal elections has not alleviated the problem because party leaders routinely place ethnic minority candidates low on the list, even though this may sometimes help minority candidates if they manage to obtain places on the dominant party's slate. In addition, immigrant-origin voters do not have an additional vote to give to specific candidates, as is the case in Belgium. In practice, the leading list (from parties that are less likely to nominate immigrant-origin candidates) grabs at least half of the council seats.

Finally, specific local political traditions contribute to the sometimes spectacular differences in styles and levels of immigrant incorporation from one city to another. Such local factors as the weight of political personalities (for example in the French system where the mayor dominates the local council), specifically local configurations of party competition (where the party favors established native constituencies over immigrant interests), and traditional relations between political authorities and civil society can all mitigate national election practices or systems designed to increase immigrant political participation.

5. Patterns of Party Competition

The levels and forms of party competition are central to determining the styles and levels of immigrant participation. In the absence of competition, local parties have little incentive to empower new or emerging voter constituencies like new immigrant ethnic groups. The crucial point is whether local party nominations are open to challenge and frequently changing or on the contrary are repeatedly dominated by the same groups or factions. Michael Jones-Correa (Jones-Correa 1998) has described how the regular Democratic county party organization in Queens has maintained a monopoly of access to elected office in the borough thanks to a long-standing system of rewards for supporters. Jones-Correa shows how this set of political arrangements worked over a considerable period of time to contain electoral challenges from the borough's massive new immigrant population and to dampen their electoral mobilization. When demographic change became too great to be ignored, the county party organization backed its own candidates from immigrant backgrounds. In his first Council race in 2001, for example, John Liu received their support and continued to have it in his subsequent races, although he was also endorsed for comptroller by a wide range of organizations, many of which had a reform orientation. Nevertheless, "party machines," whether located in the U.S. or France, can act as a barrier, unlike the turn-of-the-last-century urban machines of the U.S., which are considered to have been vehicles for immigrant inclusion.

Some European cities definitely produced an equivalent of the Queens County machine. Many large French cities are dominated, sometimes for decades, by powerful figures who have successfully played on the at-large electoral system and the *cumul des mandats* system to build tight networks of loyal supporters across local party structures and municipal bureaucracies. In these cities, as in Queens, they have become sufficiently entrenched to win easy reelection against competing parties. As a result, they have little incentive to respond to newcomers or such marginal groups as recent immigrants. They may treat such groups with benign neglect, give token recognition, or fund them to carry out innocuous, depoliticized activities (Bousetta 1997: 227–28, Garbaye 2005: ch. 5). When new immigrant groups have attempted to challenge the municipal machines head-on by putting up their own municipal slates, the municipal leadership typically has little difficulty fending them off by promising jobs to their leaders or funding to their associations.

French municipal politics have produced generations of immigrant groups and activists whose dependence on public jobs and funds ensures their obedience to the local powers that be, earning them the derogatory nickname of "Beur-geois." (This is a contraction of the word *beur*, slang for young, second-generation North Africans, and *bourgeois*.) Césari (1993) describes several urban examples of this phenomenon while Wihtol de Wenden and Leveau (2001) provide an overall analysis of North African associations in France since the 1970s. Such dynamics can also be found in some British cities, where traditional Labour Party networks, supported by trade unions, retained a sufficiently large base of activists to obviate the need for appealing for support from ethnic minorities (for example the case of Wolverhampton, outside Birmingham, as described by Joly and Candappa 1994).

In cities with more vigorous party competition and more open primary systems, immigrant ethnic minorities have more opportunity to enter the fray and are more likely to be viewed as valuable allies by party leadership. This can be seen in some French cities, where the minority vote has not been confined just to left-of-center parties, as is usual, but where right-wing lists have also sought to co-opt minorities. This has also been the case in British cities in the 2000s. Labour's declining popularity allowed the smaller Liberal Democrats to challenge it in some of its strongholds. Some disenchanted minority Labour councilors were among the first to defect to the Liberal Democrats.

The organization of local party organizations and the degree of competition between them thus fundamentally affects the prospects for immigrant minority political incorporation. When no group or leader has a clear grip on a party that dominates the city, competing factions will be more likely to seek support from such groups in order to build a citywide majority. They may assiduously court these constituencies and back candidates for lesser office that come from these backgrounds. Just such a dynamic sparked the spectacular rise of minority representation in Birmingham in the 1980s and 1990s, where a new, "intellectual," environmentalist, and pro-minority "Left" of the Labour Party waged a long and hard fight against the prevailing traditional "Right" of the party, leading both sides seeking to co-opt minority voters. Facing mounting challenges from the Left, embattled, aging "right-wing" Labour politicians handpicked black and Asian community leaders to be the city councilors from their backgrounds in the early and mid-1980s to renew their base of support in the poor, ethnic minority wards of the inner city. Eventually the "Left" claimed leadership both of the party and the city council in the mid-1990s with ethnic support from such varied minority activists as black churches, Muslim networks, student organizations, and trade unions (Solomos and Back 1995).

Situations of durable exclusion of minorities at the hands of an entrenched machine may, however, persist where local parties have a tradition of paternalism associated with a city's industrial history. Yet minority activists can try to carve out a place for themselves in municipal politics even in some of these situations. In the northern French textile town of Roubaix, the Catholic business leadership and the local Socialists co-managed the municipality for decades, but this produced a fragmented electoral scene and a lively community organization along ethnic lines, an inheritance from a rich earlier history of migration. The electoral fragmentation allowed leaders and activists from new immigrant organizations to bargain for positions on party lists.

At this point, lessons drawn from these urban situations are suggestive rather than systemic. Although research projects and networks devoted to comparing the forms and extent of immigrant political incorporation across urban settings have begun to emerge over the last decade, the field still lacks comprehensive information on immigrant electoral outcomes and political antecedents across a large number of settings. To date, scholarship on west European and North American cities has rested mainly on case studies of one city or a few strategically chosen cities. No systematic inventory exists of first- or second-generation immigrant candidates and elected officials across cities in either continent. In part this reflects the great multiplicity of different ways in which groups are defined, census statistics gathered, urban electorates and party systems organized, and so on. Some important ground-clearing is under way, such as the EU-funded LOCALMULTIDEM (http://www.um.es/localmultidem) and EMILIE (http://emilie.eliamep.gr) projects, which focus on immigrant political participation in urban settings (Morales and Giugni 2011, EMILIE 2009) and the forthcoming volume on models of immigrant political incorporation being developed by Jennifer Hochschild, Claudine Gay, Michael Jones-Correa, and Jacqueline Chattopadhyay. The challenge of doing systematic, rigorous comparison across a large number of urban settings in West Europe and North America has yet to be addressed, however.

6. The Future of Immigrant Political Empowerment

In looking forward, factors working both against and for immigrant political mobilization and incorporation can clearly be identified. Working against them are the fragmentation of and large cultural and socioeconomic differences among the immigrant groups that have flowed into the largest and most important cities of the rich democracies, the unwillingness of the dominant political parties to recruit new constituencies, the difficulties that immigrant-origin political candidates have in shifting from mobilizing a concentrated ethnic constituency in a relatively small legislative district or municipality to building the cross-cutting coalitions of groups necessary for success at higher levels, and finding solutions to the fundamental and persisting question of whether an official represents the interest of specific groups or represents the solution to a policy challenge facing the whole of society.

Even in the open and competitive of political environments that are most conducive to the entry of new immigrant minority groups, these groups are doubly heterogeneous. That is to say, not only do immigrant groups have quite varied cultural, social, and economic origins, but each group is typically divided by religion, class, subregion, and political leanings. Mexican immigrants to Los Angeles or New York may differ depending on the region of Mexico from which they come or whether they are purely indigenous people or lighter-skinned mestizos. Immigrants from South China literally do not speak the same language as those from the North, although they use exactly the same characters. Many new immigrants do not know where to place themselves in America's black-white racial dichotomy, nor do they want to do so. (Similar comments can be made about European immigrants.) While Asian and

Latino immigrants often live among each other or nearby, many other groups as well contribute to the emergence of "global" neighborhoods. While all of the new immigrant groups may share certain interests—for example in translation services, fair treatment by the police, good schooling for their children, or access to jobs—their differences are even more salient. The task of mobilizing immigrant communities for political engagement is thus an inherently difficult task that will require the passage of time—and most likely their "ethnicization" (Morawksa 2005).

The large cities in North America and west Europe that have experienced the greatest volume of immigrant arrivals in recent decades—New York, Los Angeles, Chicago, Toronto, London, Manchester, Birmingham, Paris, Marseille, Brussels, Rotterdam, Amsterdam, Berlin, Hamburg, Frankfurt, Munich, Vienna, Zurich, Geneva, Milan, Rome, Barcelona, and Madrid—all have rich and complicated political traditions involving powerful competing and sometimes clashing interests. Immigrants introduce a new element into the choreography of this political competition. Under many prevailing circumstances, none of the established forces may have an interest in enlisting their support. Indeed, it is clear that some groups think they will benefit by mobilizing native sentiment against their inclusion.

Yet these cities are democracies and sooner or later immigrant communities will become active citizens, not just passive denizens. This process will start on a neighborhood and community scale, with groups forming to advance or protect local interests. The agents who form these groups—the emerging immigrant-origin political class—will begin their work within relatively narrow or closed social networks, but to succeed they will have to spread steadily outward, both to get the resources necessary for political organizing and to widen their base of support. Even one of the most successful immigrant-origin politicians in any urban setting, John Liu, could not win his first election for city council on the basis of Chinese voters alone, because they made up only a sliver of his electorate. So the speed of immigrant political incorporation will be hindered by the difficulty of staring in once place but growing into quite a different one—and how fast immigrant-origin politicians develop the skill at doing this.

Finally, as successful candidates are fond of saying, they cannot be the city councilor or the mayor of the (blank) people, they are the (blank) councilor or mayor for all the people, where the (blank) can be African American, West Indian, Chinese, Algerian, Moroccan, or Turkish. At the material level, urban politics will probably always have a significant element of ethnic patronage and policy decisions will always be evaluated in part on the basis on the good or bad they do for different ethnic groups. But to succeed, urban political leaders and their governing coalitions must be about a lot more—identifying and solving the basic problems facing the city. Rising immigrant-origin political leaders will also have to translate the concerns of their community into terms that touch on universal principles and questions. Learning this, too, will take time.

Balancing these factors that are sure to slow the progress of immigrant political incorporation are others that will hasten it. Most profoundly, the rich democracies simply cannot abide a situation in which they are committed to the principle that all members of the community should have equal rights but in practice systematically exclude or subordinate some of those members. Immigrant communities organizing to make urban political systems pay better attention to their needs will always have a moral wind blowing at their back. (Granted, rights come with duties, so it is fair for native born citizens to expect immigrants to meet certain tests, such as learning the national language, being patriotic, and following the rules.)

Although demography is emphatically not destiny in this matter, demographic trends will also favor immigrant political incorporation over the long run. The native white populations of west Europe and North America are aging and bearing fewer children. These nations have a structural need for immigrants both to sustain their labor forces and populations and to pay into the social security systems that will sustain the white natives in their old age (Myers 2007). They will have to provide paths of upward mobility for new immigrant groups simply to sustain themselves (Alba 2009). As a result, even where first generation immigrants remain locked in the lower part of the social order, their children are quite likely to rise, if not always as quickly as we or they would like. Their successes will provide society with the chance to redefine immigrants from being "problems" to being "solutions." Certainly, in a globalizing world, the transnational ties and transcultural abilities of immigrants and their children can be an important asset and cultural diversity a strength, not a weakness.

The final impact of demographic change is that it will eat away the social base of political parties and force them to look for new supporters (at least in democratic systems). Students of party realignment and succession often point to this dynamic as fundamental in creating the conditions for change. Immigration is having a sufficiently pervasive impact on many big cities to lead to this sort of change. Just as a Mexican American, Antonio Villaraigosa, became mayor of Los Angeles in 2005, John Liu comptroller of New York in 2009, and the Dutch Labor Party appointed Ahmed Aboutaleb mayor of Rotterdam at the end of 2008, the dominant parties (or dominant electoral coalitions in nonpartisan cities) in many other cities can be expected to reach out to promote rising immigrant candidates. For their part, as immigrant communities develop succeeding generations with more political skills and resources, they too will push hard toward this end.

REFERENCES

Adolino, Jessica, 1998. *Ethnic minorities, electoral politics and political integration in Britain.* London: Pinter.

Alba, Richard. 2009. *Blurring the color line: The new chance for a more integrated America.* Cambridge: Harvard University Press.

Alba, Richard, and Nancy Foner. 2009. "'Entering the precincts of power: Do national differences matter for immigrant-minority political representation." In Jennifer Hochschild and John Mollenkopf, eds., *Bringing outsiders in: Transatlantic perspectives on immigrant political incorporation.* Ithaca, NY: Cornell University Press.

Alonso, Sonia and Sara Claro da Fonseca. 2009. "Immigration, left and right." Madrid: Instituto Juan March, Working Paper 2009.247.

Andrew, Caroline, John Biles, Myer Siemiatycki, and Erin Tolley, eds. 2008. *Electing a diverse Canada: The representation of immigrants, minorities, and women*. Vancouver: University of British Colombia Press.

Bail, Christopher. 2008. "The configuration of symbolic boundaries against immigrants in Europe." *American Sociological Review* 73:37–59.

Banting, Keith, Richard Johnston, Will Kymlicka, and Stuart Soroka. 2006. "Do multiculturalism policies erode the welfare state?" In Keith Banting and Will Kymlicka, eds., *Multiculturalism and the welfare state: Recognition and redistribution in contemporary democracies*. Oxford: Oxford University Press.

Bauböck, Rainer. 2006. "The acquisition and loss of nationality in fifteen EU states. Results of the comparative project NATAC." Vienna: IMISCOE Policy Brief.

Bauböck, Rainer. 2010. "Studying citizenship constellations." *Journal of Ethnic and Migration Studies* 36(5): 847–959.

Bird, Karen, Thomas Saalfeld, Andreas M. Wüst, eds. 2011. *The political representation of immigrants and minorities: Voters, parties and parliaments in liberal democracies*. New York: Routledge/ECPR Studies in European Political Science.

Bloemraad, Irene. 2006. *Becoming a citizen: Incorporating immigrants and refugees in the United States and Canada*. Berkeley: University of California Press.

Blommaert, Jan, and Marco Martiniello. 1996. "Ethnic mobilization, multiculturalism and the political process in two Belgian cities, Antwerp and Liège." *European Journal of Social Sciences* 9(1): 51–73.

Bousetta, Hassan. 1997. "Citizenship and political participation in France and the Netherlands: Reflections on two local cases." *New Community* 23(3): 215–31.

Bousetta, Hassan. 2001. *Immigration, post-immigration politics and the political mobilization of ethnic minorities: A comparative case study of Moroccans in four European cities*. Doctoral dissertation, Catholic University, Brussels.

Cattacin, Sandro. 2009. "Differences in the city: Parallel worlds, migration, and the problem of inclusion of differences in urban space." In Jennifer Hochschild and John Mollenkopf, eds., *Bringing outsiders in: Transatlantic perspectives on immigrant political incorporation*. Ithaca, NY: Cornell University Press.

Césari, Jocelyne. 1993. "Les leaders associatifs issus de l'immigration Maghrébine: Intermédiaires ou clientèles?" *Horizons Maghrébins* 20–21: 80–95, special issue, "Le droit à la mémoire, élites Maghrébines de France."

———, ed. 1998. *Musulmans et républicains, les jeunes, l'Islam et la France*. Paris: Complexe.

Da Fonseca, Sara Claro. 2011. "New citizens, new candidates? Candidate selection and the mobilization of immigrant voters in German elections." In Karen Bird, Thomas Saalfeld, and Andreas M. Wüst, eds., *The political representation of immigrants and minorities: Voters, parties and parliaments in liberal democracies*. New York: Routledge.

De Graauw, Els, Shannon Gleeson, and Irene Bloemraad. 2010. "Immigrant suburbs and central cities: Understanding differences in municipal support for immigrant organizations and suburban free-riding." Unpublished paper, April 29.

De Graauw, Els, and Caroline Andrew. 2011. "Immigrant political incorporation in American and Canadian cities." In Carlos Teixeira, Wei Li, and Audrey Kobayashi, eds., *Immigrant geographies of North American cities*. Don Mills, Ontario: Oxford University Press.

Dekker, Lisette, and Brahim Fattah. 2007. "Meer diversiteit in de gemeenteraden." Research note, Amsterdam.
Eurostat. 2010. *Eurostat regional yearbook 2010*. Luxembourg: Publications Office of the European Union.
EMILIE. 2009. *EMILIE project final report*. Athens: Hellenic Foundation for European and Foreign Policy.
Favell, Adrian. 1998. *Philosophies of integration, immigration and the idea of citizenship in France and Britain*. London: Macmillan.
Foner, Nancy and Richard Alba. 2010. "Immigration and the legacies of the past: The impact of slavery and the Holocaust on contemporary immigrants in the United States and Western Europe." *Comparative Studies in Society and History* 52(4): 798–819.
Garbaye, Romain. 2002. "Ethnic minority participation in a British and French city: A historical-institutionalist perspective." *International Journal of Urban and Regional Research* 26(3): 555–70.
Garbaye, Romain. 2005. *Getting into local power: The politics of ethnic minorities in British and French cities*. Oxford: Blackwell.
Geddes, Andrew. 1993. "Asian and African-Caribbean Representation in Elected Local Government in England and Wales." *New Community* 20(1): 43–57.
Geisser, Vincent and Paul Oriol. 2002 "Les Français d'origine etrangère aux elections municipales de 2001." *Migration et Société* 13(77): 41–53.
Goodman, Sara Wallace. 2010. "Naturalisation policies in Europe: Exploring patterns of inclusion and exclusion." Florence: European Democracy Observatory, European University Institute.
Guiraudon, Virginie. 2000. *Les politiques d'immigration en Europe, Allemagne, France, Pays-Bas*. Paris: L'Harmattan.
Hansen, Randall. 2000. *Citizenship and immigration in post-war Britain*. Oxford: Oxford University Press.
Hartman, Ivo. 2007. "Overall report: European exchange of good practices in the field of participation and citizenship of underrepresented groups." Amsterdam: Center for Political Participation, Instituut voor Publiek en Politiek.
Hicks, Bruce M. 2006. "Are marginalized communities disenfranchised? Voter turnout and representation in post-merger Toronto." Montreal: Institute for Research on Public Policy, Working Paper No. 2006–03.
Hill, Ruth, and Michael Issacharoff. 1971. *Community and race relations: A study of community relations committees in Britain*. Oxford: Oxford University Press.
Hochschild, Jennifer. 2010. "International migration at a crossroads: Will demography change politics before politics impedes demographic change?" Paper presented to the conference on "Citizenship in a Globalized World: Perspectives from the Immigrant Democracies." University of New South Wales, Australia, July 13–15.
Hochschild, Jennifer and John Mollenkopf. 2009. "Understanding immigrant political incorporation in comparative perspective." In Jennifer Hochschild and John Mollenkopf, eds. *Bringing outsiders in: Transatlantic perspectives on immigrant political incorporation*. Ithaca, NY: Cornell University Press.
———. 2010. "Immigrant political incorporation: Comparing success in the United States and Western Europe." *Ethnic and Racial Studies* 33(1): 19–38.
Hopkins, Daniel J. 2010. "Politicized places: Explaining where and when immigrants provoke local opposition." *American Political Science Review* 104:1: 21–39.
Howard, Marc Morjé. 2010. "The impact of the far right on citizenship policy in Europe: Explaining continuity and change." *Journal of Ethnic and Migration Studies* 36(5): 735–51.

Ireland, Patrick. 1994. *The policy challenge of ethnic diversity*. Cambridge: Harvard University Press.

Ivarsflaten, Elisabeth. 2005."Threatened by diversity: Why restrictive asylum and immigration policies appeal to voters in Western Europe." *Journal of Elections, Public Opinion and Parties* 15(1): 21–45.

Jacobs, Dirk, Marco Martiniello and Andrea Rea. 2001. "Changing patterns of political participation of immigrants in the Brussels capital region, the October 2000 elections." Presentation to Metropolis Conference, November 27.

Jacobs, Dirk, Karen Phalet, and Marc Swyngedouw. 2004. "Associational membership and political involvement among ethnic minority groups in Brussels." *Journal of Ethnic and Migration Studies* 30(3): 543–59.

Joly, Danièle, and Mano Candappa. 1994. *Local authorities, ethnic minorities and pluralist integration: A study in five local authorities*. Coventry: Center for Research in Ethnic Relations, University of Warwick.

Jones-Correa, Michael. 1998. *Between two nations: The political predicament of Latinos in New York City*. Ithaca, NY: Cornell University Press.

Jones-Correa, Michael. 2008. "Race to the top? The politics of immigrant education in suburbia." In *New faces in new places: The changing geography of American immigration*, ed. Douglas Massey. New York: Russell Sage.

Joppke, Christian. 2007. "'Beyond national models: Civic integration policies for immigrants in Western Europe." *West European Politics* 30(1): 1–22.

Joppke, Christian. 2010. *Citizenship and immigration*. Cambridge: Polity Press.

Joppke, Christian, and Ewa Morawska, eds. 2003. *Toward assimilation and citizenship: Immigrants in liberal nation-states*. London: Palgrave.

Keating, Michael. 1991. *Comparative urban politics: Power and the city in the United States, Canada, Britain, and France*. Aldershot: Elgar.

Koopmans, Ruud, Paul Statham, M. Giugni, and F. Passy. 2005. *Contested citizenship: Immigration and cultural diversity in Europe*. Minneapolis: University of Minnesota Press.

Le Cour de Grandmaison, Olivier, and Catherine Wihtol de Wenden. 1993. *Les etrangers dans la cité*. Paris: Expériences Européennes, La Découverte.

Le Galès, Patrick. 2002. *Le retour des villes européennes. Sociétés urbaines, mondialisation, gouvernement et gouvernance*. Paris: Presses de Sciences Po.

Le Lohé, Michel. 1998. "Ethnic minority participation and representation in the British electoral system." In Shamit Saggar, ed., *Race and British electoral politics*. London: University College Press.

LGIU. 1996. Report on the first all party convention of Black, Asian, and ethnic minority councilors. London.

Lee, Taeku, S. Karthick Ramakrishnan, and Ricardo Ramírez, eds. 2006. *Transforming politics, transforming America: The political and civic incorporation of immigrants in the United States*. Charlottesville: University of Virginia Press.

Marrow, Helen B. 2009. "Immigrant bureaucratic incorporation: The dual roles of professional missions and government policies." *American Sociological Review* 74(5): 756–76.

Martiniello, Marco. 1998. "Les élus d'origine étrangère à Bruxelles: Une nouvelle etape de la participation politique des populations d'origine immigrée." *Revue Européenne des Migrations Internationales* 14(2): 123–49.

Michon, Laure. 2010. "Political careers of ethnic minority municipal councilors in Amsterdam and the region of Paris, 1990–2007." Doctoral dissertation, Political Science, University of Amsterdam.

Miera, Frauke. 2009. "Political participation of migrants in Germany." Frankfurt am Oder: European University Viadrina, EMILIE Policy Brief.

Migration Policy Group. 2011. *Migration Policy Index III.* Brussels: Migration Policy Group (www.integrationindex.eu).

Minkenberg, Michael 2009. "Anti-immigrant politics in Europe: The radical right, xenophobic tendencies and their political environment." In Jennifer Hochschild and John Mollenkopf, eds., *Bringing outsiders in: Transatlantic perspectives on immigrant political incorporation.* Ithaca, NY: Cornell University Press.

Mollenkopf, John 2008. "Immigrant political empowerment in New York and Los Angeles." In Gary Orfield and Andrew Grant Thomas, eds., *Color lines: Exploring the frontiers of America's multiracial present and future.* Philadelphia: Temple University Press.

Morales, Laura and Marco Giugni, eds. 2011. *Social capital, political participation and migration in Europe: Making multicultural democracy work?* London: Palgrave.

Morawska, Eva. 2005. "Immigrants, transnationalism, and ethnicization: A comparison of this great wave and the last." In Gary Gerstle and John Mollenkopf, eds., *E pluribus unum? Contemporary and historical perspectives on immigrant political incorporation.* New York: Russell Sage Foundation.

Murdie, Robert A. 2008. "Diversity and concentration in Canadian immigration: Trends in Toronto, Montreal, and Vancouver, 1971–2006." *Research Bulletin* 42, Centre for Urban and Community Studies, University of Toronto.

Myers, Dowell. 2007. *Immigrants and boomers: Forging a new social contract.* New York: Russell Sage Foundation.

O'Neil, Kevin. 2010. "Challenging Change: Immigrant population growth and local anti-immigration ordinances." Paper presented to the conference "Migration: A World in Motion," Center for International Policy Exchanges, University of Maryland, Maastricht, Netherlands, February 18–20.

Oriol, Paul. 1998. "Les immigrés et les elections municipales de 1995." *Migrations et Sociétés* 10(56): 5–17.

Papillon, Maurice. 2002. "Immigration, diversity, and social inclusion in Canada's cities." Ottawa: Canadian Policy Research Networks.

Penninx, Rinus, Karen Kraal, Marco Martiniello and Steven Vertovec, eds. 2004. *Citizenship in European cities: Immigrants, local politics, and integration policies.* Aldershot: Ashgate.

Peró, Davide and John Solomos. 2010. "Introduction: Special issue on migrant politics and mobilization." *Ethnic and Racial Studies* 33(1): 1–18.

Ramakrishnan, S. Karthick, and Irene Bloemraad, eds. 2008. *Civic hopes and political realities: Immigrants, community organizations, and political engagement.* New York: Russell Sage Foundation.

Ramakrishnan, Karthick and Tom Wong. 2010. "Partisanship, not Spanish: Explaining municipal ordinances affecting undocumented immigrants." In *Taking local control: Immigration policy activism in U.S. cities and states*, ed. Monica Varsanyi. Stanford, CA: Stanford University Press.

Rogers, A and Jean Tillie, eds. 2001. *Multicultural policies and modes of citizenship in European cities.* Aldershot: Ashgate.

Saggar, Shamit. 1991. *Race and public policy.* Aldershot: Avebury.

Saggar, Shamit, ed. 1998. "Analysing race and elections in British politics: Some conceptual and theoretical concerns." In Saggar, Shamit, ed., *Race and British electoral politics.* London: University College Press.

Schönwälder, Karen and Christiane Kofri. 2010. "Diversity in Germany's political life? Immigrants in city councils." MMG Working Paper 10–17. Max Planck Institute for the Study of Religious and Ethnic Diversity Göttingen.

Siemiatycki, Myer, Tim Rees, Roxana Ng, and Khan Rahi, 2001. "Integrating community diversity in Toronto: On whose terms?" Toronto: CERIS—The Ontario Metropolis Centre, Working Paper 14.

Singer, Audrey, Susan W. Hardwick and Caroline B. Brettell, eds. 2008. *Twenty-first-century gateways: Immigrant incorporation in suburban America*. Washington, DC: Brookings Institution.

Solomos, John, and Les Back. 1995. *Race, politics and social change*. London: Routledge.

Sonenshein. Raphael. 2005. "Latino incorporation reaches the urban summit: How Antonio Villaraigosa won the 2005 Los Angeles mayor's race." *PS: Political Science & Politics* 38: 713–21.

Sonenshein, Raphael and Mark Drayse. 2006. "Urban electoral coalitions in an age of immigration: Time and place in the 2001 and 2005 Los Angeles mayoral primaries." *Political Geography* 25(5): 570–95.

United Nations. 2009. "International migration 2009." Population Division, Department of Economic and Social Affairs, at http://www.un.org/esa/population/publications/2009Migration_Chart/.

Van Heelsum, Anja. 2002. "The relationship between political participation and civic community of migrants in the Netherlands." *Journal of International Migration and Integration* 3(2): 179–200.

Van Heelsum, Anja. 2005. "Political participation and civic community of ethnic minorities in four cities in the Netherlands." *Politics* 25(1): 19–30.

Vertovec, Steve. 1998. "Politiques multiculturelles et citoyenneté dans les villes européennes." *Revue Internationale des Sciences Sociales* 156: 211–24.

Vink, Maarten P. and Gerard-René de Groot. 2010. "Citizenship attribution in Western Europe: International framework and domestic trends." *Journal of Ethnic and Migration Studies* 36(5): 713–34.

Weil, Patrick. 2002. *Qu'est ce qu'un français? Histoire de la nationalité française depuis la Révolution*. Paris: Grasset.

Wihtol de Wenden, Catherine, and Rémy Leveau. 2001. *Le Beurgoisie: Trois générations d'associations maghrébines*. Paris: Presses du CNRS.

CHAPTER 20

CULTURAL CONFLICTS, RELIGION, AND URBAN POLITICS

ELAINE B. SHARP AND MICHAEL BROWN

1. Introduction

As urban historians and philosophers would remind us (Erie 1990; Arkes 1981), there have always been cultural and moral dimensions to American city politics. Yet they have not always been the focus of urban politics scholarship. By the early 1990's, the idea that the U.S. was embroiled in a series of "culture wars" was well-established by writers such as James Davison Hunter (1991; 1994) and "morality politics" had become a compelling category for scholars of public policy at the national and state levels (Meier 1994). A decade of high-profile conflict over abortion, the political mobilization of the religious right, and political battles over the death penalty, drug control, pornography, and other morality-based topics had drawn the attention of a number of scholars with interests in the distinctive ways in which this category of politics and policymaking plays out at the federal level and in state capitals.

Urban political science was somewhat slower to enter this domain, perhaps because of the dominance of theorizing geared toward economic development matters in the urban field, perhaps because political parties and partisanship, which are so key to understanding morality politics at the state and national levels, are not as important in explaining urban phenomena, or perhaps because the theoretical framework of "diffusion of innovations" which provided such an important framework for state politics scholars to tackle the issue has not been used much in urban scholarship. But by the second half of the 1990's, case studies and a smaller number of larger-n studies of local government involvement in the culture wars began to emerge.

For urban and political geography, the turn toward culture involved even more profound changes. Not only were there shifts toward topics and issues that had hardly been probed but seemed timely and urgent at the end of the 20th century; in addition, this "cultural turn" also meant profound methodological and epistemological shifts—away from positivist or realist epistemologies that privileged explanatory scholarship and quantitative analyses and toward postmodern frameworks that stressed interpretation, theory-development, and qualitative approaches such as ethnography and discourse analysis (Wheeler 2002; Marston 2004). Following Castells (1983), the field also sought a break from the economism and reductionism of both rational-choice and structural Marxist urban theory that seemed increasingly unhelpful (Marston and Pratt 2003).

The progeny of this approach seek not to *explain* urban politics through culture but to *understand*, interpret, and theorize the role of cultural conflict in producing politics in the city. Scholars in this genre drew upon a wide array of interdisciplinary sources to conceptualize culture. These included the critical theory of the Frankfurt School (Held, 1980), the cultural anthropology of Geertz (1973), the cultural Marxism of Raymond Williams (1989), the cultural studies of the Birmingham School in the UK and postmodern and poststructural approaches that encouraged studies of discourse and texts (Rosneau 1992). The result is an emphasis on culture as a *process* of meaning-making (Mitchell, 1995) that, while sometimes spectacular, is also always "ordinary" (Williams 1989, 3). Culture is viewed as an ontological dimension of all other social variables, forming webs of signification and power/knowledge. These networks allow for "maps of meaning" that could be read and deconstructed in ways that drew in richer, social dimensions of city life (Jackson 1989).

This chapter describes developments in the literatures from both the urban field of political science and urban political geography as scholars in these fields began to focus more heavily on cultural conflict, religion and urban politics, and morality issues. We consider the American culture wars at the urban scale as well as other forms of cultural conflict in advanced capitalist cities around the world.

2. Urban Scholarship Turns to the Culture Wars

Some of the early work in political science on culture wars in American cities appeared in an edited volume by Sharp (1999), which attempted to systematize the outcome variable of interest by laying out a series of roles that city governments play in culture war controversies. The continuum of roles ranged from actions explicitly favorable to activists challenging the moral standards of the community (responsiveness, or even hyperactive responsiveness) through evasion of the issue to the opposite extreme of repression of those challenging the status quo standards of the community. In the absence of strong theory geared specifically to explain variation in local governments' actions in the morality politics arena however, studies in the Sharp (1999) volume and elsewhere have drawn upon a wide variety of different explanatory approaches.

2.1. Social Movements and Civil Society

Studies of abortion protest and government response in Columbia and Greenville, South Carolina (Woliver 1999) and Denver (Clarke 1999), for example, relied heavily upon social movement theory. To a large extent, Button, Wald, and Rienzo's (1997) pioneering work on the adoption of gay rights legislation in U.S. communities also relies upon social movement theory. The key difference between the studies is that Woliver's and Clark's works are case studies which draw upon concepts from social movement theory, such as strategic adaptation, networks of activism, and the routinization of collective action for case interpretation. By contrast, Button, Wald, and Rienzo's (1997) quantitative analysis of 126 cities or counties with gay rights ordinances as compared with 125 communities chosen at random develops empirical indicators to test the explanatory power of concepts drawn from the resource-mobilization arm of social movement theory, such as resource mobilization of lesbians and gay men, the political opportunity structure, and the "communal protest" level of local religious institutions. All three were found to be important.

Consistent with this emphasis on the state-civil society nexus and the role of social movements, historical studies in both the U.S. and UK have shown the role of the local state in oppressing and marginalizing "homosexuals" on the basis of moral and cultural pathos (e.g. Atkins 2002; Houlbrook 2005). These policies have run the gamut across local state institutions from the police to public health to welfare and social service agencies. Since the post-Stonewall era, the resistance to these cultural exclusions has taken the form of pressures from gay and lesbian liberation to rights-based claims pressed through urban social movements and directed at local and higher tier state apparatuses in the city. There are a small handful of case studies of early gay rights battles in American cities (e.g. Gay Writer's Group 1983; Atkins 2002). Other scholars have explored the ways that class and sexuality intersect either harmoniously or conflictually in areas such as gentrification by gays, or local gay rights legislation (e.g. Shilts 1988; Bailey 1998; Knopp 1990; Brown, Knopp, and Morrill 2005).

Research on the regulation of sex work in cities also carries the theme of the local state's occasionally repressive role, though not necessarily social movement pressures for change. Hubbard (2004) investigates the efficacy of so-called "zero-tolerance" policies in London around prostitution, finding that the impetus is often the local state's role in facilitating capital accumulation via gentrification. In Toronto, Larsen (1999) found that police crackdowns on prostitution had little efficacy, despite high rates of conviction. The ways that police action and local government policies can complicate sex workers' attempts to make their work safer have been detailed by Sanders (2004) in her Birmingham, UK study. In terms of policymaking, Kerkin's (2004) research in Melbourne, Australia demonstrates how discourse analysis can be used in the local planning office to spatially "reorder" street prostitution into safer forms.

In the same vein, there is scholarly attention to the fact that urban cultural politics is increasingly taking the form of so-called "quality-of-life" policies in which city government attempts to regulate allegedly antisocial behavior. These range from antipanhandling and vagrancy ordinances to public drug use, the exclusion of convicted drug users from various parts of the city (Kubler and Walti 2001; Belina and Helms 2003; England 2008), and enforcements of "respectability" that cleave working-class British masculinities (McDowell 2007). Prior (2008) has highlighted the role that city planning offices play in governing and regulating sexuality. In Sydney, commercial-sex establishments such as gay bathhouses are interpreted in contradictory ways in policy documents. Debates over alcohol consumption in public space are an especially salient instance of cultural conflict in urban Britain (Jayne, Valentine, and Holloway 2008).

But urban politics is not simply focused on the state, a point that is often shown to be true in studies of cultural issues. Some literature shows that gays and lesbians can play progressive roles when they are part of the local state. Cooper's (2006) work in Britain, Andrucki and Elder's (2007) work in Vermont, and Brown's (1997) work in Vancouver, Canada each cautions us against sharp categorical distinctions between local government and social movements, because often members of the latter are employed in key positions in the former, and because of the tightening links between the state and the nonprofit sector.

Furthermore, in his ethnography of the local response to AIDS in Vancouver in the 1990s, Brown (1997) demonstrates how a narrow focus on state-centered urban politics occludes extremely important politics across the realms of civil society, the home, and family. Indeed, the public space of civil society has been a battleground of city politics for gays and lesbians engaging in what Fraser (1995) deems "the politics of recognition' (though see Nash 2006). Because a fundamental dimension of heteronormativity is "the closet" (Brown 2000), access to and occupation of urban public space has been both a strategy and goal of queers in a wide variety of cities. Thus a great deal has been written about gay pride parades and festivals in this literature. Oswin's (2005) study of Capetown, South Africa demonstrates the limits of pride festivals as their growth and success in combating homophobia leads to corporatism that also has racist and neoliberal effects. Browne's (2007) comparative study in Brighton, UK and Dublin, Ireland similarly questions the political limits of a commodified festival most respondents saw as mere "fun." There have been several studies of gay pride parades that demonstrate the importance of sexual minorities to claim public space visibly and loudly in order to combat shaming and closeting by homophobia and heteronormativity in city life (Johnston 2007 and 2008; Brickell 2000). Simultaneous claims to urban public space with parades by sexual minorities and racial or ethnic groups have produced a territorial politics with quite different effects, which have been explored in New Orleans (O'Reiley and Crucher 2006) and New York City (Marston 2002).

2.2. Regime Theory

Other studies of morality issue developments at the local level have drawn interpretive inspiration from the version of political economy that is most distinctive to the study of urban politics—regime theory. DeLeon (1999), for example, interprets the striking 1990's developments in gay rights legislation in San Francisco as resulting from the combination of the character of the durable governing coalition in San Francisco (i.e., its regime), in which gays were strongly incorporated, and San Francisco's economic importance in a global economy, which allowed it to play a moral vanguard role. Similarly, Rosenthal's (1999) comparative case study of policy responsiveness to gays and lesbians in four cities in New York state emphasizes differences in the cities' governing regimes, not differences in the political mobilization of gays, as accounting for the policy differences.

The significance of various constituencies or organized interests tends to be merged with economic considerations in urban regime theory, which identifies distinctive regimes based upon key participants to a governing coalition defined largely in terms of their economic stakes. This makes regime theory somewhat problematic for the study of local morality politics and culture wars for two reasons. First, the extent to which economic considerations are relevant at all when culture war issues are at stake (and how important they are compared with morality activism) is an open and interesting question, given that culture war issues by definition are ones where religious convictions or other basic value principles are involved (Mooney 2001, 4; Brown 2006). In his study of the local politics of AIDS in Christchurch, New Zealand Brown (1999) noted the theoretically narrow economistic definition of the public-private couplet through which regime theorists frame city politics, suggesting there are multiple publics and privates beyond "state and market" in other forms of urban politics. Chong and Marshall (1999) depict a complex interplay of economic considerations and morality preferences in their case study of controversy in a conservative Texas county over proposed tax breaks to attract Apple Computer Company despite its provision of health benefits to unmarried partners of employees. Similarly, debates over the so-called "pink dollar" often emerge in the local politics of tourism promotion and development more generally (Waitt and Markwell 2006; Oswin 2005). Other research suggests that while economics trumps morality in some issue areas (regulation of sexually explicit businesses, casino gambling development), economic considerations do not appear to influence decision-making on other morality issues such as support for needle exchange programs and abortion-related policymaking at the local level (Sharp 2005a).

Second, while land development and downtown business interests anchor the seemingly most prevalent type of governing coalition depicted in urban regime theory, research on morality politics at the state level suggests that other organized interests, none of which are featured in the other regime types, may be involved in morality policy development. Norrander and Wilcox (2001), for example, find that the relative strength of pro-life versus pro-choice interests in each state constitutes a very powerful predictor of the direction of state policy on abortion and Roh and Haider-Markel (2003) find that interest group activity is an important predictor of voting patterns on state and local ballot initiatives and referenda on abortion policy. Meanwhile, some local-level case study evidence suggests the importance of organized religious interests in local conflicts over casino development (Penning and Storteboom 2007) and gay rights (Djupe, Neiheisel, and Sokhey 2007). Regime theory, which focuses on durable governing coalitions, incorporates into its definition of regime types the kinds of organized interests that are relatively continuously involved in community decision-making. By contrast, culture war controversies tend to be explosive but episodic and the organized interests involved therein may not necessarily be continuously involved in other areas of local governance. Hence, the importance of the very different organized interests that are involved in culture war controversies may be overlooked by regime theory.

2.3. Morality Issues, Cultural Explanation, and Interpretation

Cultural (or more properly subcultural) cleavage might seem to be an obvious candidate for explaining variation and change in local governments' handling of the kinds of issues that fit under the culture war banner. But at least among political scientists in the United States, doing so has been complicated by matters of definition and conceptualization. At one extreme, the concept of culture can be defined so broadly as to include virtually any and all human phenomena. If everything about politics (interests, values, styles of participation, rules and institutions, and more) and everything about society (living arrangements, modes of work, kinship definitions, artistic traditions, class divisions, ethnic divisions, and much, much more) is part of what we mean by "culture," then culture becomes a dysfunctionally bloated concept, scholars talk past each other, and cultural attributions can become relatively meaningless explanations for variation in what happens.

The key to avoiding these problems is more specific conceptualization of the dimension of culture that is theoretically relevant as well as the development of cultural explanations and understandings based either on distinctions in types of subcultures along that dimension or on specific variables reflecting that dimension. Among urban politics scholars in the U.S., research using cultural explanations has evolved into two different conceptualizations of culture based on identification of two different dimensions of culture. One focuses more specifically on *political* (or civic) culture—that is, those attitudes, practices, and meaning systems that define the prevailing character of governing systems and of citizens' relationship with government. The second focuses on *social* culture—that is, the beliefs, values, and ways of living that distinguish one civil society from another.

With respect to work in the *political (or civic)* culture vein, Elazar's classic studies of the political subcultures of the United States (1966; 1984)were once the touchstone for urban as well as state politics scholars. While empirically developed from information on ethnic and religious group settlement patterns in historical context, Elazar depicts three basic subcultures (moralistic, individualistic, and traditionalistic) that are said to differ from each other in terms of the shared understandings that citizens and elites still have about matters such as the role of government in society, the need for political participation, and the significance of partisan and ideological interests. Elazar's mapping of the U.S. into the three subcultural categories and their hybrids and Lieske's (1993) updating of Elazar into a larger set of subcultural categories based largely on religious affiliation and racial and ethnic composition of the population have provided the grounds for scholars to test for the explanatory importance of this version of political culture in matters ranging from the adoption of progressive collective bargaining practices (McCurdy 1998) to differences in urban environmental policy (Budd et al. 2008) to female representation in state legislatures (Camobreco and Barnello 2003). However, with rare exceptions (Fischer and Pratt 2006), research on morality policy at both the state and local levels has largely eschewed Elazar's typology. State politics scholars turned instead to more contemporary and more direct cultural measures for the assessment of morality policy adoption—most notably, level of religious adherence and prevalence of evangelical Protestants in the states (Gibson 2004). Urban politics scholars turned to the conceptualization of *social* culture that is outlined in the next section.

Meanwhile, a new conceptualization of civic culture has been developed by Reese and Rosenfeld (2002) specifically for the study of local economic development. Their conceptualization of civic culture includes "local government structures and governing (regime) systems, community visions and goals, responses to the external environment as well as local economic exigencies, community power systems, decision-making processes, and ultimately local policies" (2002, 14). Additional key elements include the "structure of the economic development enterprise, locus of power and input arrangements, and decisionmaking styles" (Reese and Rosenfeld 2002, 45). While this very comprehensive listing of elements means that their conceptualization might in principle be usable for analysis of government action in any policy domain, the conceptualization is clearly geared toward analysis of communities' economic development activities and may or may not be as relevant for explaining culture war issues.

By contrast, urban scholarship on culture war issues turned to a developing conceptualization of *social* culture that seemed particularly relevant given its roots in acknowledgment of the postindustrial social transformations that writers on culture wars point to as the source of the cleavages that pit cultural progressives against the culturally orthodox or traditional. Drawing upon not only Hunter's (1991) work but also earlier writings on postindustrial society (Bell 1973), a variety of scholars began to converge on a conceptualization of social culture that highlights the contrast between (a) a new or unconventional subculture that has emerged, albeit unevenly, in postindustrial societies and (b) the conventional or traditional subculture that it replaces. In this line of work (Sharp 2002; 2003; 2005a; 2005b; Sharp and Joslyn 2008; DeLeon and Naff 2004; Florida 2002; Clark and Inglehart 1998; Rempel and Clark 1997; Rosdil 1991 and 1998) the new or unconventional subculture is characterized by change in women's social roles, greater prevalence of postsecondary education, increases in nontraditional household arrangements, the growing importance of high-tech and "creative-class" occupations and the decline in traditional religious attachments. Places that have been in the vanguard of these trends have subcultures that are characterized by greater tolerance of social diversity based on race, ethnicity, sexual orientation, country of origin, and the like (Florida 2002; Sharp and Joslyn 2008) and a predilection for progressive policies (Rosdil 1991), at least on social issues if not always on fiscal issues (Clark and Inglehart 1998). Conversely, cities that, by contrast, have smaller numbers of highly educated and creative class individuals, fewer gays, more married couple-with-kids household arrangements, and a higher level of religiosity would manifest cultural orthodoxy. Focusing on change in nation-states over time, Clark and Inglehart (1998) also characterize the new political culture as exhibiting heightened political participation in social movements, the decreasing relevance of political parties and class-based politics, and heightened support for civil right, civil liberties, and individual freedom of choice (Clark 1996).

This conceptualization of an important cleavage in contemporary society between new or unconventional subculture and traditional or orthodox subculture has been used to understand phenomena other than morality issues, such as citizen preferences for local growth controls (Baldassare 1998) and social welfare program support (Clark and Inglehart 1998); DeLeon and Naff (2004) find that cities that score higher on a New Political Culture index have much more liberal populaces, slightly higher levels of electoral participation, and much higher levels of political protest activity than more conventional cities.

However, this conceptualization of new or unconventional versus traditional or orthodox subculture has been especially important in analyses of the morality issue controversies and identity politics that are central to the "culture wars." The volume *Morality Politics in American Cities* (Sharp 2005a) investigates whether it is these differences in subcultural type, or economic health of the community, or differences in political institutions that accounts for differences in ten cities' handling of abortion access and protest, gambling policy, stance toward the sex industry, policies toward gays, and drug policies. Consistent with earlier work on the topic, the study finds little evidence that institutional arrangements (reformed versus unreformed matter). However, depending upon the specific issue, cultural explanation can be highly important. For morality issues that also involve substantial material stakes (sex industry, casino gambling), the pattern of cities' responses is better explained by cities' economic circumstances than by differences in cities' subcultures; by contrast, the pattern of cities' responses to "pure morality issues" (abortion, drug courts, and needle exchanges) is well explained by subcultural differences, and the economic health of the community appears to be irrelevant. Gay rights is a hybrid morality issue that does not fit comfortably into either of the above categories;

and both cultural and economic explanations were found to be important in accounting for city governments' actions in this issue area.

Similarly, DeLeon and Naff (2004) find that the distinction between cities with new or unconventional subcultures and cities with traditional or orthodox subcultures has explanatory importance for identity politics. Focusing on the nearly 40 communities where random sample surveys were conducted as part of the Social Capital Benchmark Survey (SCBS), they find that in a number of ways, a community's political culture conditions the character of identity politics within it. For example, the association between religiosity and mobilization for electoral politics is highest in cities with conventional political cultures but diminishes in cities with increasingly higher scores on the new political culture.

2.4. Religion and Urban Politics

Cultural explanations in urban politics in one sense give a featured place to religion—for example, religion is part of the conceptualization of the subcultural types discussed above. But despite its inclusion in these conceptualizations, religiosity is sometimes neglected when empirical work on unconventional versus traditional culture is pursued (Rosdil 1991; 1998; Clark and Inglehart 1998) or difficulty is encountered in finding evidence that an aggregate data-based measure of religiosity hangs together with the other elements of unconventional culture (Sharp 2005b).

But this does not mean that the role of religion in various aspects of local politics has been completely neglected. Rather, it means that the role of religion and religiosity in local politics is not always explicitly investigated within the framework of the broader, culturalist explanations outlined above.

In fact, two quite distinct lines of scholarship on religion and urban politics have emerged, largely independent of those broader, culturalist explanations. The first focuses on the role of churches and religiosity in the development and handling of controversies over the very "morality issues" that have already been discussed in this chapter. The emphasis here is typically on churches as important institutional players (and clergy as important activists) in opposing gambling (Penning and Storteboom 2007), gay rights (Djupe, Neiheisel, and Sokhey 2007; Musser 1999), the sex industry, and the like. While it is not necessarily based upon broader theorizing about a cultural divide between orthodox and progressive forces, the findings of this predominantly case study line of work are quite consistent with that theoretical approach. These case studies portray activists from fundamentalist churches as moral crusaders against gay rights (Musser 1999) and reveal that while clergy from all religious denominations in Columbus were to some extent caught up in Ohio's political campaign over same-sex marriage, clergy from evangelical Protestant churches were the most involved and were the most frequent targets of conservative interest groups mobilizing against same-sex marriage (Djupe, Neiheisel, and Sokhey 2007). Still other case studies reveal that clergy, and especially fundamentalist clergy, played an instrumental role in opposing the Wayland casino development in western Michigan (Penning and Storteboom 2007) and that the presence of conservative churches and churchgoing publics were important factors in the trajectory of abortion clinic protest and its management by local government in Greenville and Columbia, South Carolina (Woliver 1999).

The second line of scholarship on religion and local politics focuses on the role of churches and faith-based organizations more broadly in community development or local social justice issues. For example, Reese and Shields (2000) outline the important role of clergy in community development activities in Detroit, Alex-Assensoh (2004) depicts the role of the Black Baptist Pastors' Conference in furthering community development issues (such as inner-city revitalization, affordable housing, redress of lending discrimination, and job development for the disadvantaged) in Columbus, Ohio, and Hula, Jackson, and Orr (1997) present a comparative case study showing the progressive agenda potency of BUILD—a Baltimore-based organization of about 50 churches, most of which are predominantly African-American, and three labor groups—compared to two nonprofits in Detroit and Los Angeles that are not religiously based. In the same vein, Crawford (2007) offers a case study of the important role that both conservative Protestant and Catholic clergy played in developing successful community coalitions for health care for the poor in Omaha, and Olson (2007) shows how a faith-based organization mobilized to provide services for the homeless in Racine, Wisconsin.

A key concept that ties together much of this literature is congregation-based community organizing. It is a concept that subsumes the more frequently used concept of faith-based organizing. According to Hart (2001, 28), congregation-based community organizing may be "the largest coherent contemporary movement for economic justice—either secular or religious—that engages grassroots Americans locally in face-to-face political activity." Congregation-based community organizing is diverse on denominational, ethnic, and racial grounds, and draws its strength from its development of a "systematic religio-political language combining themes from the tradition of community organizing developed by Saul Alinsky with religious social action traditions" (Hart 2001, 27). According to Hart, its willingness to merge practical politics with the passionate language of values and religion give this form of organizing the kind of power in pursuing a progressive agenda in cities that we have seen in conservative religious activism on morality issues (Hart 2001, 28).

In the same vein, Swarts (2008) draws upon comparative case study analysis of two congregation-based community organizing alliances (PACT in San Jose and Metropolitan Congregations United for St. Louis) and ACORN activities in those same two communities to highlight a distinctive "cultural strategy" for mobilization that faith-based organizations have successfully used. But the concept of a "cultural strategy" here is quite distinct from any notion of culture war divisions. In contrast with the literature on the role of conservative churches in morality policy conflicts, she notes that divisive issues such as abortion and gay rights are usually not on the agenda of these congregation-based community organizing coalitions. Rather, they focus on a broad array of progressive politics issues. Her case study of PACT, for example, reveals an organization successfully pressuring city and county officials to adopt PACT's affordable housing plans, to commit to new programs dealing with youth, drugs, crime, and neighborhood needs, and to fund a plan to insure all children in the county.

The predominantly case study literature on the role of religion in development and social justice issues in communities is in many ways inspiring. However, it tends to be one-sided. That is, it typically extols the special advantages that either churches or congregation-based community organizing have for mobilizing resources for community development and advancement of a progressive agenda; and it typically describes one or two cases of successful faith-based involvement in progressive community development issues without providing adequate information about how rare or common such success might be, what the obstacles to church involvement are, and how important faith-based activism is relative to other, competing explanations of what local officials do. One important exception to this critique is Musso, Kitsusea, and Cooper's (2002) study of faltering efforts to get faith-based organizations involved in the development of neighborhood councils in Los Angeles—a study that outlines not only the "civic promise of faith organizations" but also the obstacles to their involvement in local political issues. Reese and Shields (2000) also lay out a set of variables that should affect the involvement of clergy or congregation members in issues such as housing development, job training, business development support, and the like, but their study of a limited number of churches in a single city is not able to adequately test hypotheses drawn from that set.

Internationally, questions of religion and urban politics do not often fit the American theoretical template. Both religion and the form and structure of subnational politics vary across countries in ways that make overgeneralization dangerous. For example, McNeill (2003) documents the powerful role that the Vatican plays in Roman city politics, critiquing planning efforts for a gay pride march during that city's Jubilee 2000 festival. Another example is the intense, often micro-level segregation between Protestants and Catholics in Belfast, Northern Ireland that for years has impacted all manner of urban life there (Boal 2002; Gallaher and Shirlow 2006). More recently, Shirlow (2006) has found that despite its reputation as a post-conflict city, Belfast remains culturally segregated and conflicts still appear along sectarian lines in urban governance. Religious conflicts also play themselves out in local politics as they reflect different immigration and demographic mixes. Hemka (2002) interprets the clash in Rotterdam over a Muslim cleric's homophobic comments about Dutch gays that drew in the minister of urban affairs as one instance of pre- and postmodern dimensions of national culture.

The differential geographies of urban religious conflict can be made more broadly with respect to cultural conflict overall. The culture wars of the (urban) United States are not necessarily paralleled in other cities around the world, even in the global North. Instead, conflicts over traits like religion and language raise the importance of appreciating nationalism as a framework for understanding social and electoral cleavages in many world cities. There are cultural conflicts around postcolonial and linguistic cleavages in Canadian cities (Wood 2006). Linguistic forms of cultural conflict affect places as diverse as Montreal (Sancton 1983), local government districts in Northern Ireland (Chriost 2001), and the northeast of

Scotland (Knox 2001). Jones and Desforges (2003) demonstrate the role that localities play in the reproduction of Welsh nationalism in that part of the United Kingdom. Dietz (2004) shows the role that nongovernmental organizations can play in fostering nationalist clashes between Spanish nationalists and Islamic immigrations in Anadalucia, Spain. Nagel's (2002) work on Beirut has traced the issues of nationalism in the urban politics of redevelopment of the ruins in that war-torn city.

A fascinating new strand of literature details a variety of global city politics whose conflict (often quite state-centric) pivots on the construction and planning of memorials in urban public space, showing the importance of national and local memory as a cultural dimension of city politics. For example Till (2005) offers a fascinating urban political geography of a reunifying Berlin in the 1990s where the city politics of neighborhood coalitions, redevelopment permitting, gentrification, and public service delivery were worked through questions of how that city memorialized its role in the Holocaust during the era of National Socialism and its role during the cold war as a divided city that challenged notions of a single, authentic German nationalism. Similar locational conflicts around city memorials have been detailed by Burk (2003) in Vancouver, Canada, Power and Sidaway (2005) in Lisbon, Fenster (2004) in Israel, Bosco in Argentina (2004), and Dwyer (2002) in southern American cities. The subculture of "gypsy-travelers" in British localities is another example of a particularly intense national phenomenon that differentiates the geography of the local culture wars (e.g. Bancroft 2000).

3. Future Directions for Theory and Research

In this concluding section, we outline some possible future issues that urban political scholarship might take in its continued interest in cultural conflict. But here we run up against the authors' differing epistemological standpoints and visions. Rather than letting one intellectual tradition dominate or negotiating toward some middle point of consensus, we pose two sets of suggestions—first a more conventionally social-scientific approach reflecting Sharp's orientation and second a more postmodern approach indicative of Brown's standpoint in political and cultural geography. Our voices are in many ways dissonant. We juxtapose them here because that is the truth of where studies of urban cultural-conflict are these days, and in the spirit of mutual respect and interdisciplinarity.

3.1. Sharp's Suggestions

Some of the early work conceptualizing a new or unconventional culture (as distinct from traditional culture) characterizes the former as being significant in part because it crosscuts class and familiar left-right ideological lines (Rempel and Clark

1997). Yet both DeLeon and Naff (2004) on the one hand and Sharp (2005b) on the other find different indices measuring new or unconventional culture to be *very* highly linked to the usual left-right ideological divide, and Florida's (2002) work on the "creative class" is part of both the conceptualization and the measurement of unconventional culture for writers in this field. This may be one reason that Reese and Rosenfeld (2008) characterize this whole dimension of culture as "ideological." Further theoretical development is needed to lay out the implications of a heavy left-right component to the new or unconventional culture:

Further conceptual work is also required because of the urban field's long tradition of attention to matters of race. It is not clear whether racial diversity, racial tolerance and other aspects of the politics of race should be part of the conceptualization of what the new, unconventional culture means; or whether these are two separate phenomena. (Sharp 2005b)

Measurement issues also need attention. For example, state politics scholars have largely eschewed any effort to use a complex, multi-item measure of new or unconventional culture in their analyses, instead using only one or two individual indicators of characteristics (most notably percent of the population that is evangelical) that are hypothesized to be culturally relevant. By contrast, urban scholarship so far emphasizes multi-item indices. One possible disadvantage of using a multi-item index of a complex conceptualization of cultural types rather than individual, culturally relevant indicators is the possibility that the greater explanatory importance of one or more of the index items is being obscured. Urban scholars might find it useful to have an explicit conversation about which analytical approach is preferable.

Finally, the disjunction between case studies and large-N quantitative analyses poses a challenge. In this topical area, studies from the two methodological traditions sometimes nicely complement each other. For example, quantitative studies have provided evidence that places with larger evangelical Protestant populations are less likely to adopt gay rights ordinances, while case studies show the sometimes subtle mechanisms through which clergy and congregations exert that influence. However, this complementarity or synergy between quantitative hypothesis testing and qualitative theory building and interpretation is more the exception than the rule. Rather than developing without much reference to each other, it would be highly desirable if there could be a greater mesh between two forms of scholarship.

3.2. Brown's Suggestions

There is a need for more frequent and meaningful conversation between different approaches to the study of urban politics and culture. Such conversations are immensely difficult because the interlocutors are separated not simply by methods or types of data. Differences are often epistemological—as in the case of positivist or realist approaches typical of American urban political science versus poststructuralism of critical human geography. These different standpoints in relation to the nature of truth and knowledge itself, leading to interlocutors talking past one another about what and how we research (for an excellent example see Dixon and Jones 1998).

Secondly, I would like to see critical cultural and political theory used to open up new lines of inquiry—in both theoretical and empirical directions. Questions of how to theorize "culture," problems of reification, essentialism, and reductionism could be dealt with through engagement with the decades of intellectual work on culture. New ways of thinking about the cultural elements of the state, and power itself, for instance, might be gained from Foucault's (1980) poststructuralism, Duggan's (1995) queer theory, or Taussig's (1997) experimental anthropology. These move us away from limiting notions of urban politics as essentially "access, rent, and property" (Pahl 1975, 296), collective consumption (Dunleavy 1980), or the confluence of state and market (Elkin 1987). Cultural theory might also broaden our empirical search for urban politics. For instance, the relative absence of urban politics research on public health seems odd when it is theorized as a question of biopower and governmentality (Brown 2009).

Finally, I think we could be more methodologically plural and creative in our study of urban cultural conflicts. The possibility for mixed methods seems terrific, even when they produce different findings in the same study (e.g. Brown, Knopp, and Morrill 2005). There is a greater role for theory building, inductive empirical work in order to build more interested and durable theories to test. Longitudinal designs might help us appreciate cultural change in place over time, just as comparative analysis has allowed us to distinguish common from particular trends. A greater use of modes of analysis such as ethnography, projective techniques, as well as critical discourse or textual analysis, for example, could provide refreshing insights that would help us build better theory to understand—and yes, explain—cultural conflict (and consensus) in cities.

REFERENCES

Alex-Assensoh, Yvette M. 2004. "Taking the Sanctuary to the Streets: Religion, Race, and Community Development in Columbus, Ohio." *Annals of the American Academy of Political and Social Science* 594 (July): 79–91.

Andrucki, Max, and Glen Elder. 2007. "Locating the State in Queer Space: GLBT Non-profit Organizations in Vermont, USA." *Social and Cultural Geography* 8:89–104.

Atkins, Gary. 2002. *Gay Seattle*. Seattle: University of Washington Press.

Arkes, Hadley. 1981. *The Philosopher and the City: The Moral Dimensions of Urban Politics*. Princeton: Princeton University Press.

Bailey, Robert. 1998. *Gay Politics/Urban Politics*. New York: Columbia University Press.

Baldassare, Mark. 1998. "Citizen Preferences for Local Growth Controls: Trends in U.S. Suburban Support for a New Political Culture Movement." In *The New Political Culture*, edited by Terry N. Clark and Vincent Hoffman-Martinot, 261–78. Boulder: Westview Press.

Bancroft, Agnes. 2000. "No Interest in the Land: Legal and Spatial Enclosure of Gypsy-Travellers in Britain." *Space and Polity* 4:41–56.

Belina, Bernd, and Gesa Helms. 2003. "Zero Tolerance for the Industrial Past and Other Threats." *Urban Studies* 40:1845–67.
Bell, Daniel. 1973. *The Coming of Post-industrial Society*. New York: Basic Books.
Bell, David, and Jon Binnie. 2004. "Authenticating Queer Space: Citizenship, Urbanism, and Governance." *Urban Studies* 41:1807–20.
Boal, F. W. 2002. "Belfast: Walls Within." *Political Geography* 21:687–94.
Bosco, Fernando. 2004. "Human Rights Politics and Scaled Performances of Memory: Conflicts among the Madres de Plaza de Mayo in Argentina." *Social and Cultural Geography* 5:381–402.
Brickell, Chris. 2000. "Heroes and Invaders: Gay and Lesbian Pride Parades and the Public/private Distinction in New Zealand Media Accounts." *Gender, Place and Culture* 7:163–78.
Brown, Michael. 1997. *RePlacing Citizenship: AIDS Activism and Radical Democracy.* New York: Guilford Press.
———. 1999. "Reconceptualizing Public and Private in Urban Regime Theory." *International Journal of Urban and Regional Research* 23:45–69.
———. 2000. *Closet Space: Geographies of Metaphor from the Body to the Globe*. London: Routledge.
———. 2006. "Sexual Citizenship, Political Obligation, and Disease-Ecology in Gay Seattle. *Political Geography* 25:874–98.
———. 2009. "Public Health as Urban Politics, Urban Geography: Venereal Biopower in Post-war Seattle." *Urban Geography* 30:1–29.
Brown, Michael, Larry Knopp, and Richard Morrill. 2005. "The Culture Wars and Urban Electoral Politics: Sexuality, Race, and Class in Tacoma, Washington." *Political Geography* 24:267–91.
Browne, Kath. 2007. "A Party without Politics?" *Social and Cultural Geography* 8:63–87.
Budd, William, Nicholas Lovrich, Jr., John C. Pierce, and Barbara Chamberlain. 2008. "Cultural Sources of Variations in U.S. Urban Sustainability Attributes." *Cities* 25:257–67.
Burk, A. L. 2003. "Private Griefs, Public Places." *Political Geography* 22:317–33.
Button, James W., Kenneth D. Wald, and Barbara A. Rienzo. 1997. *Private Lives, Public Conflicts: Battles over Gay Rights in American Communities*. Washington, DC: CQ Press.
———. 1999. In *Culture Wars & Local Politics*, edited by Elaine B. Sharp, 81–99. Lawrence: University Press of Kansas.
Camobreco, John F., and Michelle A. Barnello. 2003. "Postmaterialism and Post-Industrialism: Cultural Influences on Female Representation in State Legislatures." *State Politics and Policy Quarterly* 3: 117–38.
Castells, Manuel. 1983. *The City and the Grassroots*. Berkeley: University of California Press.
Chong, Dennis, and Anna-Maria Marshall. 1999. "When Morality and Economics Collide (or Not) in a Texas Community." *Political Behavior* 21:91–121.
Chriost, Diarmait. 2001. "Implementing Political Agreement in Northern Ireland: Planning Issues for Irish Language Policy." *Social and Cultural Geography* 2:297–313.
Clark, Terry N. 1996. "Structural Realignments in American City Politics." *Urba Affairs Review* 31(3): 367–403.
Clark, Terry Nichols, and Ronald Inglehart. 1998. "The New Political Culture: Changing Dynamics of Support for the Welfare State and Other Policies in Postindustrial Societies." In *The New Political Culture*, edited by Terry Nichols Clark and Vincent Hoffmann-Martinot, 9–72. Boulder, CO: Westview Press.

Clarke, Susan E. 1999. "Ideas, Interests, and Institutions Shaping Abortion Politics in Denver." In *Culture Wars and Local Politics*, edited by Elaine Sharp, 43–62. Lawrence: University Press of Kansas.
Cooper, Davina. 2006. "Active Citizenship and the Governmentality of Local Lesbian and Gay Politics." *Political Geography* 25:921–43.
Crawford, Sue E. S. 2007. "Religious Interests in Community Collaboration: The Quiet Fight for Health Care in South Omaha." In *Religious Interests in Community Conflict: Beyond the Culture Wars*, edited by Paul A. Djupe and Laura R. Olson, 103–22. Waco, TX: Baylor University Press.
DeLeon, Richard E. 1999. "San Francisco and Domestic Partners: New Fields of Battle in the Culture War." In *Culture Wars & Local Politics*, edited by Elaine B. Sharp, 117–36. Lawrence: University Press of Kansas.
DeLeon, Richard E., and Katharine C. Naff. 2004. "Identity Politics and Local Political Culture." *Urban Affairs Review* 39:689–719.
Dietz, Gunther. 2004. "Frontier Hybridization or Culture Clash? Transnational Migrant Communities and Sub-national Identity Politics in Andalusia, Spain." *Journal of Ethnic and Migration Studies* 30:1087–112.
Dixon, Deborah, and J. P. Jones. 1998. "My Dinner with Derrida: Or Spatial Analysis and Poststructuralism Do Lunch." *Environment and Planning* 30:247–60.
Djupe, Paul A., Jacob R. Neiheisel, and Anand Edward Sokhey. 2007. "Clergy and Controversy: A Study of Clergy and Gay Rights in Columbus, Ohio." In *Religious Interests in Community Conflict*, edited by Paul A. Djupe and Laura R. Olson, 73–102. Waco, TX: Baylor University Press.
Duggan, Lisa. 1995. "Queering the State." In *Sex Wars: Sexual Dissent and Political Culture*, edited by L. Duggan and N. Hunter, 179–93. London: Routledge.
Dunleavy, Patrick. 1980. *Urban Political Analysis*. London: Macmillan.
Dwyer, Owen. 2002. "Location, Politics and the Production of Civil Rights Memorial Landscapes." *Urban Geography* 23:31–56.
Elazar, Daniel. 1966. *American Federalism: A View from the States.* New York: Thomas Y. Crowell.
———. 1984. *American Federalism*. 3rd ed. New York: Harper & Row.
Elkin, Stephen. 1987. *City and Regime in the American Republic.* Chicago: University of Chicago Press.
England, Marcia. 2008. Stay Out of Drug Areas: Drugs, Othering and Regulation of Public Space in Seattle, Washington." *Space and Polity* 12:197–213.
Erie, Steven. 1990. *Rainbow's End*. Berkeley: University of California Press.
Fenster, Tovi. 2004 "Belonging, Memory and the Politics of Planning in Israel." *Social and Cultural Geography* 5:403–17.
Fraser, Nancy. 1995. "Recognition or Redistribution." *Journal of Political Philosophy* 3:166–80.
Fisher, Patrick, and Travis Pratt. 2006. "Political Culture and the Death Penalty." *Criminal Justice Policy Review* 17:48–60.
Florida, Richard. 2002. *The Rise of the Creative Class*. New York: Basic Books.
Foucault, Michel. 1980. *The History of Sexuality*, vol. 1. New York: Vintage.
Gallaher, Carol, and Peter Shirlow. 2006. "The Geography of Loyalist Paramilitary Feuding in Belfast." *Space and Polity* 10:149–69.
Gay Writer's Group. 1983. *It Could Happen to You*. Boston: Alyson Press.
Geertz, Clifford. 1973. *The Interpretation of Cultures*. New York: Basic Books.
Gibson, M. Troy. 2004. "Culture Wars in State Education Policy: A Look at the Relative Treatment of Evolutionary Theory in State Science Standards." *Social Science Quarterly* 85:1129–49.

Hart, Stephen. 2001. *Cultural Dilemmas of Progressive Politics*. Chicago: University of Chicago Press.

Held, David. 1980. *Introduction to Critical Theory*. Berkeley: University of California Press.

Hemka, Gert. 2006. "Imams and Homosexuality: A Post-gay Debate in The Netherlands." *Sexualities* 5:237–48.

Houlbrook, Matt. 2005 *Queer London*. Chicago: University of Chicago Press.

Hubbard, Phil. 2004. "Cleansing the Metropolis: Sex Work and the Politics of Zero Tolerance." *Urban Studies* 41:1687–702.

Hula, Richard C., Cynthia Y. Jackson, and Marion Orr. 1997. "Urban Politics, Governing Nonprofits, and Community Revitalization." *Urban Affairs Review* 32:459–90.

Hunter, James Davison. 1991. *Culture Wars*. New York: Basic Books.

———. 1994. *Before the Shooting Begins: Searching for Democracy in America's Culture War*. New York: Free Press.

Jackson, Peter. 1989. *Maps of Meaning*. Boston: Unwin Hyman.

Jayne, Mark, Gill Valentine, and Sarah Holloway. 2008. "Fluid Boundaries—British Binge Drinking and European Civility: Alcohol and the Production and Consumption of Public Space." *Space and Polity* 12:81–100.

Johnston, Lynda. 2007. "Mobilising Pride/Shame: Lesbians, Tourism, and Parades." *Social and Cultural Geography* 8:29–45.

———. 2008. "Queen('s) Street or Ponsonby Poofters?" *New Zealand Geographer* 53:29–33.

Jones, Rhys, and Luke Desforges. 2003. "Localities and the Reproduction of Welsh Nationalism." *Political Geography* 22:271–92.

Kerkin, Kate. 2004. "Discourse, Representation, and Urban Planning." *Australian Geographer* 35:185–92.

Knopp, Lawrence. 1990. "Some Theoretical Implications of Gay Involvement in an Urban Land market." *Political Geography Quarterly* 9:337–52.

Knox, Dan. 2001. "Doing the Doric: The Institutionalization of Regional Language and Culture in the North-east of Scotland." *Social and Cultural Geography* 2:315–31.

Kubler, Daniel, and Sonja Walti. 2001. "Drug Policy-Making in Metropolitan Areas: Urban Conflicts and Governance." *International Journal of Urban and Regional Research* 25:35–54.

Larsen, Nick. 1999. "Urban Politics and Prostitution Control." *Canadian Journal of Urban Research* 8:28–38.

Lieske, Joel. 1993. "Regional Subcultures of the United States." *Journal of Politics* 55:888–913.

Marston, Sallie. 2002. "Making Difference: Conflict over Irish Identity in the New York City St. Patrick's Day Parade." *Political Geography* 21:373–92.

———. 2004. "Space, Culture and the State: Uneven Developments in Political Geography." *Political Geography* 23:1–16.

Marston, Sallie, and Geraldine Pratt. 2003. "Coming of Age: Urban Geography in the 80's." *Urban Geography* 24:340–51.

McCurdy, Arthur H. 1998. "Political Culture, Local Government and Progressive Personnel Practices." *Review of Public Personnel Administration* 18:23–38.

McDowell, Linda. 2007. "Respect, Deference, Respectability, and Place." *Geoforum* 38:276–86.

McNeill, D. 2003. "Rome, Global Cty? Church, State and the Jubilee 2000." *Political Geography* 22:535–56.

Meier, Kenneth J. 1994. *The Politics of Sin: Drugs, Alcohol, and Public Policy*. Armonk, NY: M. E. Sharpe.

Mitchell, Don 1995. "There's No Such Thing as Culture: Towards a Reconceptualisation of the Idea of Culture in Geography." *Transactions of the Institute of British Geographers*, n.s. 20: 102–16.

Mooney, Christopher Z. 2001. "The Public Clash of Private Values." In *The Public Clash of Private Values*, edited by Christopher Mooney, 3–20. New York: Chatham House.

Musser, Rick. 1999. "Fred Phelps versus Topeka." In *Culture Wars & Local Politics*, edited by Elaine B. Sharp, 158–77. Lawrence: University Press of Kansas.

Musso, Juliet Ann, Alicia Kitsuse, and Terry L. Cooper. 2002. "Faith Organizations and Neighborhood Councils in Los Angeles." *Public Administration and Development* 22:83–94.

Nagel, Caroline. 2002. "Reconstructing Space, Re-creating Memory: Sectarian Politics and Urban Development in Post-war Beruit." *Political Geography* 21:717–25.

Nash, Catherine Jean. 2006. "Toronto's Gay Village (1969–1982): Plotting the Politics of Gay Identity." *Canadian Geographer* 50:1–16.

Norrander, Barbara, and Clyde Wilcox. 2001. "Public Opinion and Policymaking in the States: The Case of Post-Roe Abortion Policy." In *The Public Clash of Private Values*, edited by Christopher Mooney, 143–59. New York: Chatham House.

Olson, Laura R. 2007. "Homelessness, Ecumenism, and Politics in Racine, Wisconsin." In *Religious Interests in Community Conflict: Beyond the Culture Wars*, edited by Paul A. Djupe and Laura R. Olson, 123–44. Waco: Baylor University Press.

O'Reilly, Kathleen, and Michael Crutcher. 2006. "Parallel Politics: The Spatial Power of New Orleans' Labor Day Parades." *Social and Cultural Geography* 7:245–65.

Oswin, Natalie. 2005. "Researching 'Gay Cape Town', Finding Value-added Queerness." *Social and Cultural Geography* 6:567–86.

Pahl, Ray. 1975. *Whose City?* Harmondsworth: Penguin.

Penning, James M., and Andrew Storteboom. 2007. "God and Gaming: Community Conflict over a Proposed Indian Casino in West Michigan." In *Religious Interests in Community Conflict*, edited by Paul A. Djupe and Laura R. Olson, 17–50. Waco, TX: Baylor University Press.

Power, Marcus, and James Sidaway. 2005. "Deconstructing Twinned Towers: Lisbon's Expo'98 and the Occluded Geographies of Discovery." *Social and Cultural Geography* 6:865–83.

Prior, Jason. 2008. "Planning for Sex in the City: Urban Governance, Planning, and the Placement of Sex-industry Premises in the City." *Australian Geographer* 39:339–52.

Reese, Laura A. and Raymond A. Rosenfeld. 2002. *The Civic Culture of Local Economic Development*. Thousand Oaks, CA: Sage Publications.

———. 2008. "Introduction: Comparative Civic Culture." *Journal of Urban Affairs* 30:355–74.

Reese, Laura A., and Gary Shields. 2000. "Faith-Based Economic Development." *Review of Policy Research* 17:84–103.

Rempel, Michael, and Terry Nichols Clark. 1997. "Post-Industrial Politics: A Framework For Interpreting Citizen Politics since the 1960s." In *Citizen Politics in Post-Industrial Societies*, edited by Terry Nichols Clark and Michael Rempel, 9–54. Boulder: Westview Press.

Roh, Jongho, and Donald P. Haider-Markel. 2003. "All Politics Is Not Local: National Forces in State Abortion Initiatives." *Social Science Quarterly* 84:15–31.

Rosdil, Donald. 1991. "The Context of Radical Populism in U.S. Cities: A Comparative Analysis." *Journal of Urban Affairs* 13:77–96.

———. 1998. "Rethinking Local Policy Analysis: The Challenge of Culture to Political Economy." Paper presented at the annual meeting of the Midwest Political Science Association, Chicago, Illinois, April 23–25.

Rosenthal, Donald B. 1999. "Regime Change and Gay and Lesbian Politics in Four New York Cities." In *Culture Wars & Local Politics*, edited by Elaine B. Sharp, 63–80. Lawrence: University Press of Kansas.

Rosneau, Pauline. 1992. *Postmodernism and the Social Sciences: Insights, Inroads, and Intrusions*. Princeton, NJ: Princeton University Press.

Sancton, Andrew. 1983. "Montreal." In *City Politics in Canada*, edited by W. Magnusson and A. Sancton, 66–89. Toronto: University of Toronto Press.

Sanders, Teela. 2004. "The Risks of Street Prostitution: Punters, Police, and Protesters." *Urban Studies*. 41:1703–17.

Sharp, Elaine B. 1999. "Introduction." In *Culture Wars & Local Politics*, edited by Elaine B. Sharp, 1–20. Lawrence: University Press of Kansas.

———. 2002. "Culture, Institutions, and Urban Officials' Responses to Morality Issues." *Political Research Quarterly* 55:861–93.

———. 2003. "Local Government and the Politics of Decency." *Social Science Quarterly* 84:262–77.

Sharp, Elaine B. 2005a. With Y. Alex-Assensoh, S. Clarke, R. DeLeon, J. Flammang, M. Rich, and M. Sarbaugh-Thompson. *Morality Issues and City Politics*. Lawrence: University Press of Kansas.

———. 2005b. "Cities and Sub-Cultures: Exploring Validity and Predicting Connections." *Urban Affairs Review* 41:131–56.

Sharp, Elaine B., and Mark Joslyn. 2008. "Culture, Segregation, and Tolerance in Urban America." *Social Science Quarterly* 89:573–91.

Shilts, Randy. 1988. *The Mayor of Castro Street*. New York: St. Martin's Press.

Shirlow, Peter. 2006. "Belfast: The Post-Conflict City." *Space and Polity* 10: 99–107.

Swarts, Heidi J. 2008. *Organizing Urban America: Secular and Faith-based Progressive Movements*. Minneapolis: University of Minnesota Press.

Taussig, Michael. 1997. *The Magic of the State*. London: Routledge.

Till, Karen. 2005. *The New Berlin*. Minneapolis: University of Minnesota Press.

Waitt, Gordon, and Kevin Markwell. 2006. *Gay Tourism*. New York: Haworth Press.

Wheeler, James. 2002. "From Urban Economic to Social/Cultural Urban Geography: 1980–2001." *Urban Geography* 23:97–102.

Williams, Raymond. 1989. *Resources of Hope*. London: Verso.

Woliver, Laura R. 1999. "Abortion Conflicts and City Governments: Negotiating Coexistence in South Carolina." In *Culture Wars and Local Politics*, edited by Elaine Sharp, 21–42. Lawrence: University Press of Kansas.

Wood, Patricia. 2006. "The 'Sarcee War': Fragmented Citizenship and the City." *Space and Polity* 10:229–42.

PART IV

URBAN POLICY: CHALLENGES FOR THE TWENTY-FIRST CENTURY

CHAPTER 21

WHAT CITIES DO: HOW MUCH DOES URBAN POLICY MATTER?

HAROLD WOLMAN ASSISTED BY
ROBERT McMANMON

1. Introduction

How much does urban policy matter? This at first glance deceptively simple question requires a good deal of preliminary explanation. What do we mean by urban and, for that matter, by "urban policy." And "matter" in what ways, to whom, and for what?

For the purposes of this chapter we take "urban" to mean, unless noted otherwise, general purpose local government. Where possible we will focus on local government in metropolitan areas or conurbations and particularly core city urban governments; however much of the political science literature does not distinguish between these large city governments and municipal government more generically. Urban policy is policy generated and implemented by these units of urban (local) governments through local government political processes (i.e., not national policy toward urban areas).

By "matter" we mean has an impact, whether intended or unintended, on the welfare (well-being) of residents of the area or on characteristics of the area that in turn affect the welfare of local residents, such as the functioning of the local economy. By welfare, we follow Wolman and Goldsmith (1990, 4) who define welfare as "the satisfaction individuals derive from the life circumstances they experience."

They note that operationally welfare is frequently measured by income, but that, in addition, "people also derive satisfaction from circumstances that have nothing directly to do with their level of income," including the physical, recreational, and social amenities of their living environment, the social networks of which they are a part (e.g., family, church, community), their relationship to institutions with which they identify, participation in civic and community affairs, their physical and mental health, personal safety and security, and so forth. By welfare we thus include important outcomes such as the level and distribution of income, employment status, poverty and social exclusion, security (public safety), and enjoyment of amenities. Thus, this chapter—and the question of whether urban policy "matters"—is concerned with the impact of urban policies on *outcomes*.

We proceed as follows. In the next section we set forth what city governments *do* and how that differs across Western nations. We then consider why policies produced by urban governments *might* matter in terms of outcomes. This is followed by a review of literature on the effect of various urban policies on outcome levels and on outcome distribution. Finally we review the literature on the effect of institutional choice on outcomes.

2. Urban Policy in Comparative Perspective

In a cross-national or comparative context the answer to "does urban policy matter?" will depend upon differences across countries in the importance of local government within the overall public sector and in the assignment of functional responsibilities to local government (what functions are local governments responsible for).

As table 1 indicates, there is a substantial variation among developed countries in the importance of the local sector.[1] The table shows the percentages of local government spending as a share of all general government spending for nondefense purposes and also local government spending as a percentage of total spending for each of nine specific services. These percentages can be thought of as rough indicators of the importance or responsibility of local governments.[2] Focusing on the percentage of local government spending as a share of all public sector nondefense spending, the importance of local government in the major developed Western nations ranges from substantial (66.5% in Denmark and 44.7% in Sweden) to extremely modest (7% in Australia and 10.5% in New Zealand). Local governments in the United States account for 30.1% of all nondefense spending, which is above both the median (22.1%) and the mean (25.4%). In general, local governments play

1. "Local government" in these tables and the ensuing discussion refers to all local governments (including local special districts and, in the U.S., local school districts) rather than only general purpose local governments.

2. In some cases final local spending reflects the use of local government as a delivery mechanism for national government programs, particularly in the social welfare functional area.

a less important role in service provision in federal countries than in unitary ones, but this is largely due to the existence of a strong intermediate subnational level of government (state, province, lander) in the federal countries that does not exist in the unitary ones. In federal countries, the median perecentage of all nondefense spending accounted for by local governments was 16.2% compared to 26.3% in the unitary countries.

Using local government spending for a specific function above 25.0% of general government spending for that function as an indicator that local government has an important role as a provider for a specific service area (see bolded figures in table 1), differences in local government functional responsibility are easily spotted. In most countries local governments provide the majority of funding for categories such as environmental protection; housing and community amenities; and recreation culture and religion. There is mixed experience among countries in the importance of local governments in some other areas, such as health, education, and public services with local government systems in some countries responsible for substantial spending and others relatively little. And, in most countries, local governments tend not to finance a substantial share of programs such as social protection; and public order and safety.[3]

Providing public order and safety and education are widely regarded as two of the most important local government functions in the U.S. and UK. But the table clearly shows that is not the case across the developed world. Local governments in the United States and the United Kingdom account for over 52% of total public spending on public order and safety, while local governments in Denmark, the Czech Republic, Hungary, Iceland, Australia, and New Zealand all account for less than 10%; the median is 13.6%. While 12 of the 23 local government systems in the table account for 50% or more of overall education spending (51.5% in the U.S.), local governments in Spain, New Zealand, and Australia all spend less than 10% of all education public sector spending. In the social protection area, local governments account for more than 25% of all social protection spending, led by Denmark (78.8%), followed by Sweden (28.3%), and Iceland (25.0). In 14 of the 24 countries local governments spend less than 10% of overall public sector spending on social protection (8.2% in the U.S.). Although there is substantial variation within both the federal and the unitary group of countries—and in some cases local government plays a more important role in the federal countries than in the unitary ones—nonetheless, in each of the service categories the median local government percentage of total public sector expenditure is lower in federal countries than in unitary ones.

Substantial local government responsibility for a function does not necessarily mean the function accounts for a large share of local government expenditure. Table 2 displays the allocation of local government spending among the various functions for which local government has some responsibility. In many of the

3. For detailed descriptions of the spending programs that fall under these categories see the International Monetary Fund government statistics manual, starting on page 86: http://www.imf.org/external/pubs/ft/gfs/manual/pdf/all.pdf.

Table 1. Local Expenditures on Key Public Services as a Percentage of All General Governments Spending on that Service, 2006

	All nondefense spending	Administrative services	Public order and safety	Economic affairs	Environment protection	Housing and community amenities	Health	Recreation, culture, and religion	Education	Social protection
Federal										
Australia	7.0%	14.8%	3.5%	14.7%	**45.5%**	**33.2%**	0.4%	**40.8%**	0.2%	1.4%
Austria	16.1%	18.7%	11.5%	22.9%	**57.5%**	**38.7%**	18.4%	**57.7%**	23.2%	8.1%
Belgium*	14.2%	18.4%	**47.9%**	13.7%	**57.0%**	**43.3%**	2.4%	**50.5%**	22.7%	6.4%
Canada	19.4%	12.3%	**34.6%**	**28.4%**	**67.7%**	**69.3%**	1.5%	**51.1%**	**50.6%**	3.5%
Germany	16.2%	23.3%	20.6%	**25.0%**	**83.6%**	**48.7%**	2.2%	**70.5%**	**28.7%**	11.2%
Switzerland	26.3%	**34.5%**	20.3%	20.1%	**85.4%**	**54.3%**	**46.5%**	**59.7%**	**35.7%**	11.3%
United States***	30.1%	20.9%	**52.6%**	**21.6%**	n/a	23.7%	10.2%	**69.4%**	**51.5%**	8.2%
Mean	18.5%	20.4%	**27.3%**	20.9%	**66.1%**	**44.5%**	11.7%	**57.1%**	**30.4%**	7.2%
Median	16.2%	18.7%	20.6%	21.6%	**62.6%**	**43.3%**	2.4%	**57.7%**	**28.7%**	8.1%
Unitary										
Czech Republic	26.2%	**32.1%**	8.7%	**31.8%**	**67.9%**	**62.8%**	4.0%	**70.2%**	**74.1%**	7.8%
Denmark	66.5%	**30.9%**	9.1%	**45.1%**	**57.5%**	**26.8%**	**98.5%**	**58.2%**	**55.5%**	**78.8%**
Finland*	40.8%	**41.2%**	**27.0%**	**26.2%**	**42.4%**	**35.7%**	**82.4%**	**75.9%**	**67.2%**	21.8%
France*	21.1%	**29.1%**	22.2%	**49.4%**	**92.6%**	**91.1%**	0.9%	**74.9%**	**28.7%**	7.7%
Hungary*	26.5%	**26.1%**	7.5%	13.0%	**80.9%**	**98.7%**	**35.8%**	**38.5%**	**66.1%**	9.8%
Iceland	32.4%	**28.5%**	8.4%	**26.7%**	**49.7%**	**94.7%**	1.3%	**65.0%**	**60.3%**	**25.0%**
Ireland*	19.0%	20.8%	14.1%	**35.8%**	**100.0%**	**100.0%**	0.0%	**53.4%**	**32.2%**	3.8%
Italy*	33.3%	**25.6%**	11.8%	**59.9%**	**91.5%**	**94.8%**	**98.4%**	**56.4%**	**27.0%**	3.9%
Luxembourg	13.3%	18.6%	8.5%	17.5%	**58.4%**	**47.3%**	0.4%	**35.7%**	**25.2%**	0.8%
New Zealand	10.5%	20.3%	0.0%	**37.6%**	**100.0%**	**30.5%**	0.0%	24.6%	0.0%	1.7%
Norway	32.4%	30.7%	13.6%	23.0%	**82.2%**	**84.6%**	**27.8%**	**61.8%**	**65.9%**	20.8%

Poland	32.2%	22.2%	12.8%	**47.6%**	**90.6%**	**77.3%**	**46.3%**	**76.1%**	**71.3%**	11.0%
Slovak Republic	17.9%	19.2%	3.7%	21.4%	**61.9%**	**81.8%**	0.4%	**46.3%**	**64.9%**	4.2%
Spain*	16.1%	**43.0%**	**25.2%**	17.9%	**67.0%**	**66.1%**	1.3%	**45.3%**	6.0%	3.7%
Sweden**	44.7%	**35.6%**	17.0%	**27.3%**	**60.0%**	**82.3%**	**96.8%**	**76.1%**	**73.1%**	**28.3%**
United Kingdom****	22.1%	21.6%	**52.1%**	**29.0%**	n/a	**41.1%**	n/a	**65.0%**	**67.1%**	20.3%
Mean	**28.4%**	**27.8%**	15.1%	**31.8%**	**73.5%**	**69.7%**	**33.0%**	**57.7%**	**49.0%**	15.6%
Median	**26.3%**	**27.3%**	12.3%	**28.2%**	**67.9%**	**79.6%**	4.0%	**60.0%**	**62.6%**	8.8%
Overall mean	25.4%	25.6%	18.8%	**28.5%**	**71.4%**	**62.0%**	**26.2%**	**57.5%**	**43.4%**	13.0%
Overall median	22.1%	23.3%	13.6%	**26.2%**	**67.7%**	**62.8%**	3.2%	**58.2%**	**50.6%**	8.1%

Source: IMF Government Statistics Yearbook (2007).

Local expenditures in excess of 25% bolded, signifying local government important for that sector.

*2005 accounts.

**2004 accounts.

***2001 accounts was last available data, ratio of federal, state, and local to local.

****1998 accounts, ratio of central and local to local; some outlay categories were changed after 2001.

Table 2. Allocation of Local Spending by Function, 2006

	Administrative services	Public order and safety	Economic affairs	Environment protection	Housing and community amenities	Health	Recreation, culture, and religion	Education	Social protection
Federal									
Australia	24.4%	2.6%	26.7%	9.5%	13.7%	1.2%	15.7%	0.4%	5.8%
Austria	16.9%	2.1%	14.2%	2.6%	2.8%	16.3%	7.1%	17.7%	21.3%
Belgium*	24.0%	11.3%	9.6%	4.9%	2.2%	2.5%	9.3%	19.9%	16.4%
Canada	8.7%	9.2%	13.2%	5.9%	7.8%	1.5%	6.9%	41.2%	5.5%
Germany	14.6%	4.5%	11.4%	5.7%	6.4%	1.9%	6.0%	16.2%	33.3%
Switzerland	14.4%	4.8%	8.8%	5.3%	2.5%	20.6%	5.6%	21.9%	16.3%
United States***	16.2%	10.4%	7.4%	n/a	2.1%	8.4%	3.4%	44.8%	7.3%
Mean	17.0%	6.4%	13.0%	5.7%	5.4%	7.5%	7.7%	23.1%	15.1%
Median	16.2%	4.8%	11.4%	5.5%	2.8%	2.5%	6.9%	19.9%	16.3%
Unitary									
Czech Republic	15.0%	1.8%	22.2%	7.6%	9.4%	2.3%	7.8%	28.6%	9.1%
Denmark	6.1%	0.3%	4.7%	0.9%	0.4%	20.4%	2.7%	12.9%	51.5%
Finland*	14.0%	2.1%	6.1%	0.7%	0.4%	28.4%	4.6%	20.5%	23.3%
France*	19.2%	2.8%	13.1%	6.9%	15.2%	0.6%	10.2%	16.1%	15.8%
Hungary*	19.3%	1.2%	5.7%	3.9%	6.9%	15.4%	4.8%	29.9%	12.8%
Iceland	10.2%	0.9%	11.7%	2.4%	4.5%	0.8%	17.3%	37.2%	15.0%
Ireland*	11.9%	3.4%	25.0%	9.1%	23.8%	0.0%	4.3%	21.7%	5.6%
Italy*	14.3%	1.5%	14.6%	4.5%	4.6%	43.3%	3.0%	8.2%	4.5%
Luxembourg	20.9%	1.7%	15.9%	12.1%	7.6%	0.3%	13.1%	24.6%	3.9%
New Zealand	18.4%	0.0%	35.2%	21.4%	7.3%	0.0%	12.2%	0.0%	5.6%
Norway	10.7%	1.0%	6.5%	3.6%	4.2%	15.2%	4.8%	28.5%	25.6%

Poland	9.4%	1.8%	14.8%	4.0%	5.6%	15.3%	5.2%	29.6%	14.3%
Slovak Republic	18.5%	1.1%	16.7%	6.5%	10.4%	0.4%	7.5%	37.3%	7.0%
Spain*	32.7%	7.6%	14.2%	9.8%	9.4%	1.2%	10.7%	4.4%	8.0%
Sweden**	11.2%	1.0%	5.5%	0.9%	2.9%	28.1%	3.2%	22.5%	28.6%
United Kingdom****	4.0%	12.3%	6.0%	n/a	5.4%	n/a	3.1%	28.7%	32.5%
Mean	14.7%	2.5%	13.6%	6.3%	7.4%	11.4%	7.2%	21.9%	16.4%
Median	14.2%	1.6%	13.6%	4.5%	6.3%	2.3%	5.0%	23.5%	13.6%
Overall Mean	15.4%	3.7%	13.4%	6.1%	6.8%	10.2%	7.3%	22.3%	16.0%
Overall Median	14.6%	2.1%	13.1%	5.3%	5.6%	2.4%	6.0%	21.9%	14.3%

Source: IMF Government Statistics Yearbook (2007).

*2005 accounts.

**2004 accounts.

***2001 accounts.

****1998 accounts; some outlay categories were changed after 2001.

Note: percentages do not always total 100% because of other accounts, including local defense spending.

Table 3. Cluster Analysis: Local Expenditures on Key Public Services as a Share of All General Governments Spending on That Service, 2006

	All nondefense spending	Administrative services	Public order and safety	Economic affairs	Environment protection	Housing and community amenities	Health	Recreation, culture, and religion	Education	Social protection
Group A: 11 nations										
Mean	17.4%	22.4%	**25.2%**	22.6%	**69.1%**	**45.1%**	8.3%	**51.8%**	**28.3%**	7.0%
Median	16.1%	20.3%	20.6%	21.6%	**67.0%**	**43.3%**	1.9%	**51.1%**	**25.2%**	6.4%
Group B: 8 nations										
Mean	**26.0%**	**26.1%**	11.4%	**31.1%**	**78.2%**	**86.4%**	14.6%	**60.8%**	**57.9%**	11.2%
Median	**26.3%**	**27.3%**	10.7%	**29.2%**	**81.5%**	**87.9%**	2.6%	**63.4%**	**65.4%**	8.8%
Group C: 2 nations										
Mean	**42.7%**	**36.1%**	18.1%	**35.7%**	**49.9%**	**31.3%**	**90.5%**	**67.0%**	**61.3%**	**50.3%**
Median	**42.7%**	**38.4%**	22.0%	**26.8%**	**51.2%**	**59.0%**	**89.6%**	**76.0%**	**70.1%**	**25.1%**
Group D: 1 nation										
Italy	33.3%	**25.6%**	11.8%	**59.9%**	**91.5%**	**94.8%**	**98.4%**	**56.4%**	**27.0%**	3.9%
Group E: 1 nation										
Denmark	66.5%	**30.9%**	9.1%	**45.1%**	**57.5%**	**26.8%**	**98.5%**	**58.2%**	**55.5%**	**78.8%**

Group A	*Group B*	*Group C*	*Group D*	*Group E*
Australia	Czech Republic	Finland	Italy	Denmark
Austria	France	Sweden		
Belgium	Hungary			
Canada	Iceland			
Germany	Norway			
Luxembourg	Poland			
New Zealand	Slovak Republic			
Spain				
Switzerland				
United Kingdom				
United States				

countries (8) education is the largest local government expenditure category, but social protection is the top expenditure in several other countries (5), and in other countries public administration services (3), health (2), economic affairs (1), and housing and community development (1) constitute the greatest proportion of local government spending. As the table indicates in two countries (the U.S. and Canada) over 40% of all local government spending is for education; health accounts for 43.3% of local government spending in Italy; social protection for 51.5% in Denmark, 33.3% in Germany, and 32.5% in the UK; and economic affairs for 35.2% of local government spending in New Zealand. In all of these cases the percentage listed also represents the service for which local government spending is the highest.

Finally, we use formal cluster analysis to group the various countries into those that are most like one another and most unlike other groups in terms, first, of the importance of total public sector spending accounted for by local governments in each of the various service functions and, next, in terms of the percentage allocation of local government spending across expenditure categories. The resulting empirically derived groupings provide a much different picture than previous a priori groupings of country local government systems.

Cluster analysis is a means of creating typologies. It begins with every unit of analysis (country, in our case) as a separate group and then creates fewer clusters by merging like cases with one another. There is no objective "correct" number of clusters; we begin with eight clusters among which our 23 nations are grouped and continue down to three clusters.

In the importance of local government cluster analysis the United States and United Kingdom are grouped together as one among eight groups, but by the fifth cluster stage they are merged with nine other countries (New Zealand, Australia, Austria, Belgium, Canada, Germany, Switzerland, Luxembourg, and Spain) as a single group of 11 countries (see table 3). All of the 11 countries in this group (Group A), with the exception of the UK, Luxembourg, New Zealand, and Spain, are federal countries and all federal countries in the sample are part of this group. Another eight countries (group B) are also grouped together at the fifth cluster stage—the Czech Republic, France, Hungary, Iceland, Ireland, Norway, Poland, and the Slovak Republic. All of these are unitary countries. The other three groups are Finland and Sweden (group C, two Scandinavian countries), Denmark (which remains in its own group down through the third cluster), and Italy (which is its own separate group until the fourth cluster at which point it joins Finland and Sweden as a group of three).

Comparing the two groups with the most members (groups A and B), compared to those in group B, group A consists of countries whose local governments play a much less important role in public sector spending in all nondefense spending and in every functional category *with the exception of public order and safety*. In that category group A country local governments account for an average of 25.2% of total public sector expenditures compared to 11.4% for group B countries.

A cluster analysis of the allocation of local government spending by function across the 23 countries yielded three major groups at the first stage plus two groups

Table 4. Cluster Analysis: Allocation of Local Spending by Function, 2006

	Administrative services	Public order and safety	Economic affairs	Environment protection	Housing and community amenities	Health	Recreation, culture, and religion	Education	Social protection
Group A: 9 nations									
Mean	12.7%	3.4%	8.8%	3.3%	4.1%	17.7%	4.9%	23.9%	23.1%
Median	14.0%	2.1%	6.5%	3.8%	4.2%	15.8%	4.8%	22.5%	23.3%
Group B: 7 nations									
Mean	14.5%	4.0%	16.0%	7.3%	9.4%	1.9%	8.6%	33.6%	7.6%
Median	15.0%	1.8%	15.9%	7.0%	7.8%	0.8%	7.5%	37.2%	7.0%
Group C: 5 nations									
Mean	23.7%	4.9%	19.7%	10.5%	9.6%	1.1%	11.6%	8.2%	10.3%
Median	24.0%	2.8%	14.2%	9.5%	9.4%	1.2%	10.7%	4.4%	8.0%
Group D: 1 nation									
Italy.	14.3%	1.5%	14.6%	4.5%	4.6%	43.3%	3.0%	8.2%	4.5%
Group E: 1 nation									
Denmark	6.1%	0.3%	4.7%	0.9%	0.4%	20.4%	2.7%	12.9%	51.5%
Group A		*Group B*		*Group C*		*Group D*		*Group E*	
Austria		Canada		Austria		Italy		Denmark	
Finland		Czech Republic		Belgium					
Germany		Iceland		France					
Hungary		Ireland		New Zealand					
Norway		Luxembourg		Spain					
Poland		Slovak Republic							
Sweden		United States							
Switzerland									
United Kingdom									

of one member each (see table 4). Group A consisted of nine countries (Austria, Switzerland, Finland, Hungary, Norway, Poland, Sweden, Germany, and the UK) that spent more than 40% of their budget on health and social welfare expenditures, more than twice the percentage spent on these functions by either of the other two main groups. Group B, which consisted of seven countries (Ireland, Canada, the Czech Republic, Iceland, Luxembourg, the Slovak Republic, and the United States), allocated a very high percentage of their budget (compared to the other two groups) to education expenditures and a low percentage to health and social welfare. The five countries in group C (Australia, New Zealand, Belgium, France, and Spain) had a higher proportion of their local expenditure on recreation, environmental protection, and general government administration relative to the other two groups.

3. How Might Urban Policies Matter?

What kinds of policies do urban governments produce that *might* matter, that is, that might affect important outcomes? Wolman and Goldsmith (1990) observe that while individual welfare is profoundly affected both by the operations of the private market and by the activities of national (and intermediate level) governments, there is nonetheless scope for local government effect. While unlike national government, local government cannot affect the local economy through use of monetary or fiscal policy, urban governments often engage in efforts to affect the number and quality of local jobs, local wages, and the local unemployment rate, all of which can have an effect on individual income and employment status.

Local governments can potentially affect the local economy by efforts to attract jobs to the area through specific economic development policies and subsidies or through more general efforts to improve the city's competitive advantage as a location for economic activity. The latter may be pursued through local *infrastructure policies* that improve the area's transportation and communications networks, *human capital policies* (formal education and job training) that improve the quality and productivity of the labor force, *community amenity policies* that make the area an attractive place to live for highly-educated, high-skilled labor, thereby increasing the quality of an area's labor supply, and *local taxation and expenditure policies* that affect the cost of businesses locating within the city and the value of the public services they receive.

However, unless the city government is region-wide or nearly region-wide in scope, there are quite strong limitations on what an individual local government, acting on its own, can accomplish. An individual local government may pursue a particular policy or strategy, but that does not imply that other local governments in the region or the region as a whole will do so. Yet, the local economy is regional in scope and, if our concern is the welfare of residents of a city, their economic welfare will be affected by the functioning of the *regional* economy and labor market rather than simply activity occurring in the city in which they reside. In a fragmented local government system such as exists in metropolitan areas in the United States, the actions of a single local government, while they may have spillover effects on the region, are unlikely to have a major impact on the region's competitive advantage.

Moreover, actions taken by a single local government may provide only a limited benefit to its own residents because of leakages to the broader regional economy. Improving a city's infrastructure or providing tax and expenditure policies attractive to businesses may serve to attract additional economic activity into the city's boundaries, but the additional jobs and income created do not necessarily all accrue to residents of the city, since the resulting jobs are open to anyone from the entire regional labor market. On the other hand, human capital policies, if successful, will improve the employment and income potential of city residents competing in the regional labor market and thus are clearly welfare enhancing for city residents. Amenity policies adopted by a major city may similarly benefit not only the city's residents, but make the entire region more attractive as a location for economic activity and expand employment and income opportunities for residents of the entire region (including city residents).

The problem in the United States is that fiscal incentives for city government are not aligned with incentives for them to undertake activities that would improve the welfare of their residents (as well as other residents in the region). Since most city governments are overwhelmingly dependent on the local property tax, a city gains fiscal benefit from additional regional economic activity only if that activity locates within its boundaries. Thus, the incentives facing a local government are to undertake policies (particularly favorable local tax and expenditure policies and infrastructure policies) to attract business within its boundaries. At the same time there are disincentives to engage in activity that may accrue to the benefit of the region as a whole (such as human capital policies) since the benefits generate positive externalities for the region as a whole while the costs are completely borne by the local government.

In addition to the kinds of activity described above, local governments in some countries might also affect personal income through income redistribution, either via income transfer payments (if determined or paid for by local government rather than simply administered through local government), through local taxes that are redistributive in nature, or through the provision of public sector employment to preferred classes of recipients. However, as Peterson (1981) observes, redistributive local government policy in a metropolitan area with many local governments risks wealthy households and businesses simply moving to other local governments within the area.

Local governments can also affect important outcomes (and the welfare of their residents) through providing local services that the community desires efficiently. Providing services not desired by the local community but funded through local taxes reduces community welfare, while providing services inefficiently raises the cost of services and thus effectively reduces community income. Local governments might also attempt to affect important outcomes through regulatory behavior that protects public health and welfare, through activity that enhances public safety and security, through policies that improve community amenities, and through regulatory and other efforts to shape the urban form. All of these, if effective, would contribute to the welfare of community residents.

4. Research on Urban Policy Outcomes

What does the research literature tell us about the actual effects of policies of urban governments on outcomes? The answer is surprisingly disappointing. There are two obvious problems that confront analysis of the effect of urban government policies on outcomes. The first is the counterfactual problem: how do we know what would have occurred in the absence of policy? Urban policy occurs among a tangle of factors that potentially affect outcomes related to well-being, including the market and private and nonprofit sector activity, activities of higher levels of government, local social institutions, family relationships, and the social and demographic characteristics of the population. Unless urban policy efforts occur under conditions of random assignment social experiments or fortuitously occurring natural experiments any effort to sort out the effect of policy will require models that control for these other factors and will be fraught with difficulty. The second problem is the extremely difficult question of how to measure local policy or urban governments in order to estimate its value added effect.

Political scientists have not made much of an effort at this task. We began by examining several standard American political science textbooks on urban politics and urban policy (Morgan et al. 2007; Ross and Levine 2006; Denters and Rose 2005; Dreier et al. 2004; Saltzstein 2003; John 2001; Harrigan and Vogel 2000) to assess the extent to which they cover in a systematic way the *effects* of policy, or, more broadly, of institutions, which are a form of policy choice. Many texts contain chapters on the institutional structures of local governments and sections discussing the process of local policymaking, the nature and causes of urban problems, and descriptions of policies (frequently at the federal level) and policy design that address them. Only rarely, however, do they address outcomes. When they do occur, discussions of outcomes are most frequently related to bureaucratic service delivery and the distributive equity and efficiency of local services, local fiscal and zoning policies and processes that result in segregation, Tiebout type policy consequences and sorting resulting from the system of fragmented governments in metropolitan areas, winners and losers from growth and development policies, and the effects of government structure (reform vs. nonreform) on public policy outcomes. The political science research literature in these areas is relatively rich, and we refer to it below.

The economics literature is more likely to focus on welfare-related outcomes as a dependent variable, but it rarely employs policy or institutional characteristics as independent variables to explain outcomes. There are some exceptions, particularly in the area of local fiscal policy, in the use of the degree of fragmentation in metropolitan area governments as an explanator of Tiebout generated outcomes, and, to a lesser extent and more recently, in the effects of local government institutional structure (strong mayor vs. council-manager, etc.) on fiscal outcomes. (For a review, see Helsley 2004.)

4.1. Fiscal Policy Outcomes

There has been a substantial economics literature on the effects of local government taxes and spending policies on local economies. The findings of this literature can be summarized, at one level, quite succinctly. If the level of spending and quality of public services are held constant, *increases in taxes* negatively affect employment and economic activity. If the level of taxes is held constant, *increases in public services* positively affect employment and economic activity. Put another way, for any given level of taxes, an area that can provide services more efficiently and/or more appropriately for the needs of business will have a competitive advantage over other areas. For any given level and mix of services, a community that can provide these at a lower tax burden to business will have a competitive advantage over other areas. Both of these effects have a much larger effect on the competitive advantage of municipalities relative to one another within a metropolitan area than they do on the competitive advantage of a metropolitan area relative to other metropolitan areas.

Within a metropolitan area changes in tax policy will have a much more pronounced impact on economic growth for the individual jurisdiction increasing (or reducing) local taxes. For example, summarizing research on how differences in property tax rates across local governments within a metropolitan area affect economic growth and development, Bartik concludes that a 10% reduction in a community's local business property tax will increase business activity in the community by around 20%—*assuming all other communities leave their property tax rates unchanged and there is not an offsetting decrease in local spending* (Bartik 1994, 853, italics added). Again, the caveat that all things must remain equal to realize these results is not a realistic assumption when local governments within a metropolitan area are likely to engage in interjurisdictional competition.

These findings are consistent with subsequent research by Mark, McGuire, and Papke (1998). Looking at population and employment growth across local governments within the Washington, DC metropolitan areas, they find that employment growth rates are highly sensitive to the levels of personal property tax and sales tax. In each case, a 10% reduction in the tax would be expected to increase employment by approximately 20% over the long term. Their empirical results suggest that local real property taxes are not important influences in either residential or business location decisions. Similarly, they conclude that taxes on individuals (personal income, sales, and residential property taxes) are not important influences on residential choice (Mark et al. 2000, 121).

On the service side, government services can be considered either a cost reduction to a firm located in the area (e.g., the higher the quality of the education system, the lower the firm's cost for on-the-job training) or an amenity to it or its employees. However, not all public expenditures are of equal value to a firm. Fisher (1997, 54), in his review of the literature concludes, "In many studies, government spending, public capital, or public services are estimated to exert a positive and statistically significant effect on economic development...But the results vary greatly. Perhaps the most that can be concluded is that some public services clearly have a positive effect on some measures of economic development in some cases." Of the public services reviewed, Fisher finds that only for transportation are there consistent findings of a positive relationship, while the other services—public safety, education, and public capital—have different effects across different studies.

Many local governments also provide specific economic development incentives. The literature is virtually unanimous in agreeing that such incentives are likely to have a much greater effect at the intrametropolitan level than at the intermetropolitan level. A mobile firm approaches its location decision first by making a choice among regions and then, having made a regional choice, by deciding in which local jurisdiction within the region they wish to locate. At the interregional level other considerations, particularly labor supply and transport, are likely to overwhelm specific economic development incentives in importance. Once the regional decision is made—and labor and transport considerations are relatively equal throughout the region—economic development incentives offered by local governments within the region may make a difference.

Anderson and Wassmer (2000) review the literature on economic development incentives and find that such incentives are prevalent at the local level across the U.S. and take on a number of different forms. They conclude that "there are both theoretical and empirical reasons to believe that local taxes, business-related expenditures, and economic development incentives can influence the intrametropolitan location of business firms" (2000, 59).

Economists argue that the value of specific features of a house and its environment—including taxes and public services provided—is "capitalized"[4] into the price of housing. Thus, if a public service is particularly valued or if taxes are deemed too high, then the price of a house in that jurisdiction ought to, respectively, be higher or lower, than it otherwise would be or than it would be in another community in which those characteristics did not apply but all else were equal. Fischel (2001, 45) cites research literature to argue that capitalization is widespread with respect to a very wide range of environmental and governmental characteristics. One way of assessing the effect of public policy on outcomes—if we define outcomes as changes in well-being—is thus to model the effect of specific public

4. Fischel (2001, 7) explains capitalization thus: "the expected future flow of benefits or costs that accrue to something you own...is systematically reflected in the present value of your asset."

policies on housing values via the capitalization process. Fischel (ch. 3) presents evidence that high property taxes (relative to those of other communities in a region) are capitalized into lower housing prices and that high quality schools are capitalized into higher home values (p. 154).

4.1.1. *Urban Policy and Tiebout Outcomes*

An important theoretical development—one that has been the subject of a substantial amount of research—also suggests that the *level and composition* of local government taxes and services *relative to those of other communities in the region* will have an important effect on outcomes. Within a metropolitan area with several local governments, and providing the local governments vary in the types and levels of public services they provide and the tax price they charge for them, Tiebout (1956) posited that households in the area would make residential location decisions based on the extent to which these various tax/service packages matched their own preferences. Given a large number of such local governments, the result would be local governments comprised of residents with relatively homogenous preferences receiving services that corresponded to their tastes, given their budget constraints. The resulting outcomes would maximize resident welfare and reflect allocative efficiency.

Although Tiebout's original article did not provide local governments with a policy role in bringing about these outcomes, later additions added explicit local government policy roles either through utilizing the median voter model as a means for citizens to exercise voice as well as exit or through allowing local policymakers to alter tax/service packages in order to induce desired fiscal ends (for reviews of the development of the Tiebout model, see Fischel 2006; Oates 2006; Oates 2009). In addition, Hamilton (1975) noted that in order for the Tiebout hypothesis to work, local government would have to engage in land use regulation and zoning policy designed to prevent lower-income households from moving into areas with high fiscal capacity per capita and thus having their tax price subsidized by other residents of these areas. Oates (1969) noted that local government tax/service packages were capitalized into the value of property located within the government's boundaries, thus affecting the wealth of local property owners. Thus, if a community provided good educational services using tax revenues efficiently to do so, the result would be higher property values for homeowners. On the other hand, if it provided poor educational services for the same tax price—or if it raised taxes beyond the value of the services citizens desired or provided those services inefficiently or ineffectively, the result would be capitalized into lower property values.

A substantial amount of research has been devoted to testing the implicit predictions of the Tiebout model and its additions. Oates (2009, 13) provides a review of the literature and concludes that people do, in fact, vote with their feet in a local context. He observes that "the preponderance of the evidence is consistent with the basic insight that fiscal decentralization can provide important welfare gains by allowing a diversity of local policies that accord more closely with local preferences, especially in a setting where individual households can vote with their feet." Fischel (2001, 47ff.) also reviews the literature on capitalization of tax/service differentials into house prices and argues that the literature overwhelmingly supports the proposition that capitalization occurs, and, while acknowledging that there is substantial debate, argues that the capitalization is complete. Reviews by Yinger et al. (1988) and Dowding and John (1994) also conclude that capitalization occurs, but that the evidence suggests it may be, depending upon conditions, considerably less than 100%.

Other research and literature reviews of the research support the Tiebout model (Bickers et al. 2006; Dowding and John 1994). However, there is a body of literature that argues mobility decisions are more responsive to neighborhood composition, particularly with respect to race and class, than to public policy as embodied in tax/service packages and that these concerns are often hidden because they are cloaked within the language of public policy (see Neiman 1976; Lowery and Lyons 1989; and Weiher 1991). Weiher (1991) and Lewis and Neiman (2009) both emphasize that municipal jurisdiction, existing demographics, and, to some extent, reputations, serve as proxy signals to potential movers that result in sorting by race and class as opposed to by classic Tiebout effects.

Land use policy and zoning regulation by urban governments play an important role in the sorting required by the Tiebout model. Assuming local governments manipulate their land use policy, as is frequently alleged, to create a fiscal surplus, the result will be relatively homogenous communities economically (and, given the high correlation between income and race) and racially (for a review of this literature, see Altshuler et al. 1999). In addition, some research suggests many decisions, particularly relating to local government incorporation, are explicit reflections of racial discrimination without regard to fiscal considerations (see Burns 1994).

Residential location patterns in many middle and higher-income communities in U.S. metropolitan areas are consistent with the logic of the Tiebout model. On the other hand, there is very little political science research that focuses directly on land use policymaking and that illuminates the actual behavior and motivations that underlie the resulting location patterns (although see Lewis and Neiman 2009, whose findings rely on surveys of California city planning directors, city economic development directors, and city managers). The application of the Tiebout model, which has been enormously influential in the United States, is less obvious in other countries whose local government systems do not share the requisite features of the model, that is, a large number of relatively homogenous local governments within a metropolitan area that differ with respect to the tax/service packages that they offer.

While the resulting small and relatively homogenous local governments may be "efficient" in an economic sense, they have obvious social and political implications that are not so benign. The system creates substantial fiscal disparities among local governments (i.e., tax base per capita varies substantially, with local governments with low-income and high-need populations usually having lower tax base per capita and thus less ability to provide locally financed services than local governments comprised of wealthier taxpayers). In addition, since tax/service preferences frequently vary by income and race (often reinforced by discriminatory preferences), it also creates economic and racial segregation (Pendall 2000). The consequences for outcomes may be substantial. Research suggests that racial segregation is associated with a variety of adverse welfare-related outcomes for blacks including lower earnings, lower high school graduation rates, and greater black-white income differentials (see Altshuler et al. 1999, 56–59).

4.2. Nonfiscal Urban Policy and Outcomes

The measures used by economists in most of the above studies take fiscal outputs (money spent) as the measure of urban public policy. As such they capture only one dimension of urban policy. In a recent study of urban performance in the UK, Greasley, Wolman, and John (2011) attempt to move beyond simply fiscal outputs. They assess the effect of local government service competence and professional capacity on area employment growth between 1995 and 2005. To do so they utilize several indicators from the Audit Commission's Comprehensive Performance Assessment which include measures assessing the quality of various services, the corporate capacity of local government, and the speed with which planning applications are processed. While all of these measures are positively related to area employment growth, only the service performance score attains statistical significance (at the .10 level).

Other studies of the effect of nonfiscal output urban policies on outcomes include research, conducted in a variety of fields, on the effects of specific policies.[5] To what extent, for example, have city police strategies—community policing, broken windows, increases in police force numbers—actually had an impact on city crime (particularly violent crime) and on resident fear of crime. Surely this is an important outcome affecting resident well-being. Levitt (2004, 184) reviews a wide variety of studies and estimates that, controlling for other factors, increases in the number of local police accounted for an approximately 5.5% decline in homicide and violent crime between 1991 and 2001. However, Eck and Maguire (2000) review 27 empirical studies on the effect of the number of police on violent crime and conclude (217) conclude that, while some studies found that increasing police resulted in a decrease in violent crime, others did not and that, "Overall the evidence suggests that hiring more police officers did not play an independent or consistent role in reducing violent crime in the United States." They also review evidence on a myriad of other local police strategies such as community policing, broken windows (zero tolerance), and so on, and, although they find individual studies that indicate one or more of these is effective in reducing violent crime, they

5. We are excluding research on the effect of local education policies and practices on educational outcomes—of which there is a very substantial amount—because, at least in the United States, education policy is not a responsibility of general purpose local government but, instead, of independent single-purpose school districts.

conclude that, with one exception, "there is little evidence that generic changes in policing are responsible for reducing violent crime." The one exception is a strong focus of police efforts on concentrations of repeated crime, what they term the three repeats: "repeat offenders, repeat places, and repeat victims."

Similarly, does service privatization, a strategy pursued by some cities, improve residents' well-being by providing services of the same quality at lower tax cost? In a review of the existing literature, both U.S. and international, Ammons (2003, 262) concludes that, "The evidence from surveys of local government officials and empirical studies is mixed, but most of it appears to confirm in general the cost advantages of contracting."

5. Urban Policy and Distributive Outcomes

Much of the political science literature on the effect of urban policy on outcomes focuses on distributive questions of who the winners and losers are or are perceived to be. Paul Peterson (1981) follows the logic of the Tiebout model when he argues that local governments are unable to engage effectively in redistributive policy. Local governments that try to do so will find that businesses and wealthier residents upon whom the burdens of these redistributive policies are imposed will simply respond by moving out of the local government boundaries to another local government in the same region that does not have such policies (taking the exit alternative; see Hirschman 1970). However, Kantor and Savitch (1993) argue that in some cases local redistributive policies can be financed through imposing burdens on business. They note that some businesses are essentially immobile or would incur a very high cost from moving. They also observe that market conditions in some cities may make location there so desirable that businesses will be willing to pay higher taxes in order to take advantage of the high demand.

Research on the existence of "progressive policy regimes," local governments engaging in redistributive policies particularly with respect to housing and local economic development, suggests that such regimes are often characterized by high market demand for land (see Goetz 1994 and Elkins 1995 for reviews of research on this topic as well as empirical research).

Service distribution output studies (Levy et al. 1974; Lineberry 1977; Jones 1980; Cingranelli 1981; Mladenka 1989; for a review, see DeHoog 1997) have attempted to trace the actual rather than the perceived distribution of local services among different groups or neighborhoods. Services examined have included streets, libraries, schools, parks, and neighborhood and community development. The earlier studies (Levy et al. 1974; Lineberry 1977) found "unpatterned inequalities"—inequality in the delivery of most services, but with some services favoring low-income people or neighborhoods, while others favored middle or wealthy households/neighborhoods. As DeHoog reports, later studies have found more systematic bias in service distribution against low-income households and neighborhoods.

In addition to studies on service distribution, researchers have examined how the awards of office—political appointments, patronage, procurement contracts—are distributed among groups. Most of this research has focused on how mayoral change, particularly the election of nonwhite mayors and/or council members, affects public employment and receipt of government contracts. Not surprisingly, elected politicians are found to reward their base constituencies (Behr 2000, 244). Both Behr (2000) and Stein (1997) review existing literature and cite an early generation of studies that found minority municipal employment was related to a city having a mayor of the same minority status (see particularly Eisinger 1982). However, later studies have been more nuanced. Kerr and Mladenka (1994) used a pooled time-series design (unlike earlier cross-sectional work) and found that presence of a Black or Hispanic mayor had little impact on Black or Hispanic municipal employment. However they did find that minority municipal employment was related to the extent of minority representation on city council. Browning et al. (2003 and prior editions) conducted a series of case studies and concluded that the degree of political incorporation of minorities—the extent to which minority council members were part of the dominant political condition—had strong effects on minority employment as well as other minority political objectives.

6. Institutions as Urban Policy Choices and Outcomes

In some countries local governments have a choice, though usually a somewhat restricted one, about the nature and structure of local government institutions (see Mouritzen and Svara 2002, ch. 3). In the United States, for example, local government institutions can be considered as the most fundamental of urban policy choices, since these are the equivalent of constitutional choices as embodied in municipal charters. To what extent do these institutional choices affect the well-being of local government residents?

The major institutional structure variations in U.S. local government have to do with form of government. In mayor-council local governments, councils and mayors are separately elected and the mayor serves as chief executive. In council-manager systems the elected council appoints a professional city manager who is responsible to the council but who effectively performs chief executive functions. The mayor is usually selected from among council members (although in some council-manager cities the mayor is separately elected) and has little formal power (though the mayor may play important informal roles. See Svara 1990 and Frederickson et al. 2004).

A substantial amount of research, both in political science and in economics, has been devoted to the first part of that question. Early political science research (Lineberry and Fowler 1967) indicated that council-manager systems produced lower levels of taxing and spending and were less responsive to citizen input than did mayor-council systems. Later research using time-series techniques (Morgan and Pelissero 1980) found that differences in government structure had very little effect on taxing and spending decisions. Haughwout and Inman (2002), on the other hand, find that "weak city governance"—city governance characterized by council-manager systems and where a majority of council members are elected by wards—is associated with higher spending (because of logrolling among district-representing council members) and lower growth in home values and income. Clearly these findings do relate to resident well-being. Stumm and Corrigan, on the other hand, find that council-manager cities have lower taxes and expenditures (1998). Nunn (1996) examines differences in the allocation of spending between council-manager and mayor-council cities and finds that council-manager cities allocate more to water, sewer, and road infrastructure spending, a reflection of the professional training and longer time horizons of appointed (rather than elected) managers. However, Rauch (1995) found that council-manager cities spent less on infrastructure than did mayor-council cities. As the above suggests, the literature, which is characterized by a wide divergence in methods employed, does not provide consistent findings (see Frederickson et al. 2004, who call the research results "ambiguous," 50).

7. Conclusion

In this chapter we have asked "how much does urban policy matter?" By "matter" we mean what do we know about its effects on outcomes related to the well-being of residents of the local government that generates the policy.

We find, perhaps somewhat surprisingly, that this is an underresearched area and that the brutally honest answer to the question we pose is "we don't really know" or, perhaps a bit more accurately, "we know very little." To summarize, we do know that the fiscal activities of local government matter, that is, local taxes and spending have effects on local economic activity that relate to resident welfare. Thus, in a ceteris paribus condition, high local taxes relative to those of other communities in the region will reduce local economic activity and high-quality public services will increase it. Both of these also directly affect resident well-being as evidenced by capitalization studies that show high taxes reduce home values in an area, while high-quality public services (particularly education) increase home values. Research on more specific policy areas provide quite mixed results.

Much of the research related to outcomes of local government policy is situated within the context of Tiebout effects on mobility. These effects are posited to occur within a system of multiple general purpose local governments in a region competing with one another for residents and tax base. This is a system that is descriptive of the U.S., but much less so of other local government systems in many of the developed Western nations. The literature does support the existence of positive Tiebout effects on local government efficiency (which is welfare enhancing), but another set of literature finds that the logical consequences of the Tiebout process are local municipalities segregated by race and class and that such segregation has negative effects on social welfare.

One of the interesting features of the research literature on the effects of policy on outcomes and on well-being is the predominance of research by economists and the relative paucity of research by political scientists on these questions. Perhaps this simply reflects the nature of the question we have asked—social well-being is a concept within the standard economic paradigm and economists have a long history of trying to measure it, however imperfectly. Perhaps it reflects the fact that the tool-kit and methodologies of economics are more appropriate for the task. In the absence of experiments with random assignment or fortuitous natural experiments, researchers face the task of estimating effect through observational studies. Econometric analysis is a standard tool for modeling the effect of government policy, controlling for other and frequently quite powerful potentially confounding factors, on outcomes, and, as the term "econometric" implies, it is a tool that economists are quite comfortable with. While political scientists within the general discipline now routinely use econometric models and multivariate analysis, the intensive qualitative case study has been utilized more intensively by political scientists in urban policy research than it has in many other parts of the discipline. Case study research has produced a body of deep and nuanced studies of urban policymaking processes, of how policy is produced, and of power, influence, and control structures at the urban level. However, it is not well-suited for generalization across local governments on the effects of urban policies.

The relative lack of political science studies on outcomes and the divergent approaches of the two disciplines to urban policy is not necessarily a bad thing—it may simply represent an efficient division of labor between the disciplines with respect to public policy, with political scientists focusing on the process through which policy is made and economists concentrating on the effects or outcomes of urban policy.

In any case, the methodological problems associated with conducting research on the effects of urban policy on resident well-being are daunting regardless of discipline, and they are particularly so in more fragmented systems of local government such as characterizes the United States. Policies of a local government have spillover effects and leakages that result in benefits accruing to nonresidents. Counterfactuals are difficult to establish. Local policies are only one of many factors affecting resident well-being and controlling for these other factors—many of which are quite powerful—is extremely difficult, even with highly sophisticated econometric models.

Finally, policy as a variable is difficult to measure. How, for example, can and should local economic development policy be operationalized? Assuming data are available for analysis across a large number of local governments, local economic development activity could be measured as the amount expended (in total or per capita) for that function by each local government. This has the merit of nicely capturing variation in policy related behavior across local governments. The disadvantages of this approach clearly outweigh this merit, since the approach assumes that it doesn't matter what the actual activities that local governments engage in are (and they are likely to vary substantially across local governments), so long as the activity can be classified as economic development. But it is quite plausible, if not likely, that some local economic development activities are likely to have a greater impact on resident well-being than are others, even if the same amount of money is spent for each.

Another approach has been to count the number of different kinds of economic development activities utilized by a local government as a measure of local economic development policy, but clearly the same objection applies here (see Wolman and Spitzley 1999 for a discussion and critique of measurement issues in local economic development policy). The right way of approaching this question is to turn the various different kinds of local economic development activities and their design characteristics into variables, but collecting this data across a large number of local governments would be a major task. Paradoxically, it may be that the only way to capture local government policy and its effects is through case studies—but quantitative rather than qualitative—that examine the effect of local policies with specific design characteristics in one or a small number of different local governments.

REFERENCES

Altshuler, Alan; Morrill, William; Wolman, Harold; and Mitchell, Faith (eds.) 1999. *Governance and Opportunity in Metropolitan Areas.* Washington, DC. National Academy Press.

Ammons, David. 2003. "Urban Services." In John Pelissero (ed.). *Cities, Politics, and Policies: A Comparative Analysis.* Washington, DC. CQ Press.

Anderson, John and Wassmer, Robert. 2000. *Bidding for Business: The Efficacy of Local Economic Development Incentives in a Metropolitan Area.* Kalamazoo, MI. The W. E. Upjohn Institute for Employment Research.

Bartik, Timothy. 1994. "Jobs, Productivity, and Local Economic Development: What Implications Does Economic Research Have for the Role of Government?" *National Tax Journal* 47 (4) 847–61.

Behr, Joshua. 2000. "Black and Female Municipal Employment: A Substantive Benefit of Minority Political Incorporation." *Journal of Urban Affairs* 22 (3) 243–64.

Bickers, Kenneth; Salucci, Lapo; and Stein, Robert. 2006. "Assessing the Micro-Foundations of the Tiebout Model." *Urban Affairs Review* 42 (1) 57–80.

Browning, Rufus; Marshall, Dale Rogers; and Tabb, David (eds.). 2003. *Racial Politics in America's Cities.* New York. Longman Publishers (3rd ed.).

Burns, Nancy. 1994. *The Formation of American Local Governments: Private Values in Public Institutions.* New York. Oxford University Press.
Cingranelli, David. 1981. "Race, Politics, and Elites: Testing Alternative Models of Municipal Service Distribution." *American Journal of Political Science* 25: 664–92.
DeHoog, Ruth. 1997. "Urban Service Delivery." In Ronald Vogel (ed.). *Handbook of Research on Urban Politics and Policy in the United States.* Westport, CT. Greenwood Press.
Denters, Bas and Rose, Lawrence (eds.). 2005. *Comparing Local Governance.* New York. Palgrave Macmillan.
Dowding, Keith and John, Peter. 1994. "Tiebout: A Survey of the Empirical Literature." *Urban Studies* 31 (4–5): 767–97.
Eck, John and Maguire, Edward. 2000. "Have Changes in Policing Reduced Violent Crime? An Assessment of the Evidence." In Alfred Blumstein and Joel Wallman (eds.). *The Crime Drop in America.* Cambridge. Cambridge University Press.
Eisinger, Peter. 1982. "Black Employment in Municipal Jobs: The Impact of Black Political Power." *American Political Science Review* 76 (2) 380–92.
Elkins, David. 1995. "Testing Competing Explanations for the Adoption of Type II Policies." *Urban Affairs Review* 30 (6) 809–39.
Fischel, William. 2001. *The Homevoter Hypothesis.* Cambridge, MA. Harvard University Press.
Fischel, William. 2006. "Footloose at Fifty: An Introduction to the Tiebout Anniversary Essays." In William Fischel (ed.). *The Tiebout Model at Fifty.* Cambridge, MA. Lincoln Institute of Land Policy.
Fisher, Ronald. 1997. "Tax and Spending Incentives and Enterprise Zones." *New England Economic Review* March/April. 109–30.
Frederickson, H. George; Johnson, Gary; and Wood, Curtis. 2004. *The Adapted City: Institutional Dynamics and Structural Change.* Armonk, NY. M. E. Sharpe.
Goetz, Edward. 1994. "Expanding Possibilities in Local Development Policy: An Examination of U.S. Cities." *Political Research Quarterly* 47: 85–109.
Greasely, Stephen; Wolman, Harold; and John, Peter. 2011. "Does Government Performance Matter: The Effects of Local Government on Urban Outcomes in England." *Urban Studies* 48: 1835–51.
Hamilton, Bruce. 1975. "Zoning and Property Taxation in a System of Local Governments." *Urban Studies* 12: 205–11.
Harrigan, John and Vogel, Ron. 2000. *Political Change in the Metropolis.* New York. Addison Wesley, Longman.
Haughwout, Andrew and Inman, Robert. 2002. "Should Suburbs Help Their Central Cities?" In William Gale and Janet Rothenberg Pack (eds.). *Brookings-Wharton Papers on Urban Affairs, 2002.* Washington. DC. Brookings Institution Press.
Helsley, Robert. 2004. "Urban Political Economics." In J. V. Henderson and J. F. Thisse (eds.). *Handbook of Regional and Urban Economics.* Vol. 4. Amsterdam. Elsevier.
Hirschman, Albert. 1970. *Exit, Voice and Loyalty.* Cambridge, MA. Harvard University Press.
John, Peter. 2001. *Local Governance in Western Europe.* London. Sage Publications.
Jones, Bryan. 1980. *Service Delivery in the City: Citizen Demand and Bureaucratic Response.* New York: Longmans.
Kantor, Paul and Savitch, H. V. 1993. "Can Politicians Bargain with Business?" *Urban Affairs Quarterly* December. 230–55.
Kerr, Brinck and Mladenka, Kenneth. 1994. "Does Politics Matter? A Time-Series Analysis of Minority Employment Patterns." *American Journal of Political Science* 38 (4) 918–43.
Levitt, Steven. 2004. "Understanding Why Crime Fell in the 1990s." *Journal of Economic Perspectives* 18 (1) 163–90.

Levy, Frank; Meltsner, Arnold; and Wildavsky, Aaron. 1974. *Urban Outcomes.* Berkeley. University of California Press.

Lewis, Paul and Neiman, Max. 2009. *Custodians of Place: Governing the Growth and Development of Cities.* Washington, DC. Georgetown University Press.

Lineberry, Robert. 1977. *Equality and Urban Policy: The Distribution of Urban Public Services.* Beverley Hills, CA. Sage Publications.

Lineberry, Robert and Fowler, Edmund. 1967. "Reformism and Public Policies in American Cities." *American Political Science Review* 61: 701–16.

Lowery, David and Lyons, William. 1989. "The Impact of Jurisdictional Boundaries: An Individual Level Test of the Tiebout Model." *Journal of Politics* 51: 73–97.

Mark, S. T.; McGuire, T. J.; and Papke, L. E. 1998. *Taxing Simply, Taxing Fairly: Report to the Mayor and the District of Columbia Tax Revision Commission.* Available at: http://ntanet.org/dctax/Chap.%20BTaxes%20&%20Econ%20Dev.pdf.

Mark, S. T.; McGuire, T. J.; and Papke, L. E. 2000. "The Influence of Taxes and Employment on Population Growth: Evidence from the Washington, DC Metropolitan Area." *National Tax Journal* 53: 105–24.

Mladenka, Kenneth. 1989. " The Distribution of an Urban Public Service." *Urban Affairs Review.* 24: 556–583.

Morgan, David; England, Robert; and Pelissero, John. 2007. *Managing Urban America.* Washington, DC. Congressional Quarterly Press (6th ed.).

Morgan, David, and Pelissero, John. 1980. "Urban Policy: Does Political Structure Matter?" *American Political Science Review* 74: 999–1006.

Mouritzen, Poul Eric and Svara, James. 2002. *Leadership at the Apex: Politicians and Administrators in Western Local Governments.* Pittsburgh. University of Pittsburgh Press.

Neiman, Max. 1976. "Social Stratification and Government Inequality." *American Political Science Review* 54 (4): 149–80.

Nunn, Samuel. 1996. "Urban Infrastructure Strategies and Capital Spending in City Manager and Strong Mayor Cities." *American Review of Public Administration* 26 (1) 93–112.

Oates, Wallace. 1969. "The Effects of Property Taxes and Local Public Spending on Property Values." *Journal of Political Economy* 77: 957–71.

Oates, Wallace. 2006. "The Many Faces of the Tiebout Model." In William Fischel (ed.). *The Tiebout Model at Fifty.* Cambridge, MA. Lincoln Institute of Land Policy.

Oates, Wallace. 2009. "Local Government: An Economic Perspective." Paper presented at Lincoln Institute of Land Policy and George Washington Institute of Public Policy Property Tax Roundtable, Washington, DC, February 13.

Pendall, Rolf. 2000. "Local Land Use Regulation and the Chain of Exclusion." *Journal of the American Planning Association* 66 (2) 125–42.

Peterson, Paul. 1981. *City Limits.* Chicago. University of Chicago Press.

Rauch, J. E. 1995. "Bureaucracy, Infrastructure, and Economic Growth: Evidence from US Cities During the Progressive Era." *American Economic Review* 85: 968–79.

Ross, Bernard and Levine, Myron. 2006. *Urban Politics: Power in Metropolitan Areas.* Belmont, CA. Thompson Wadsworth. (7th ed.).

Saltzstein, Alan. 2003. *Governing America's Urban Areas.* Belmont, CA. Thompson Wadsworth.

Stein, Lana. 1997. "Equal Opportunity in the City." In Ronald Vogel (ed.). *Handbook of Research on Urban Politics and Policy in the United States.* Westport, CT. Greenwood Press.

Stumm, Theodore and Corrigan, Matthew. 1998. "City Managers: Do They Promote Fiscal Efficiency?" *Journal of Urban Affairs* 20 (3) 343–51.

Svara, James. 1990. *Official Leadership in the City.* New York. Oxford University Press.

Tiebout, Charles 1956. "A Pure Theory of Local Expenditures." *Journal of Political Economy* 64 (5). Reprinted in William Fischel (ed.). *The Tiebout Model at Fifty*. Cambridge, MA. Lincoln Institute of Land Policy.

Weiher, Gregory. 1991. *The Fractured Metropolis: Political Fragmentation and Metropolitan Segregation*. Albany. State University of New York Press.

Wolman, Harold and Goldsmith, Michael. 1990. "Local Autonomy as a Meaningful Analytical Concept." *Urban Affairs Review* 26 (1) 3–27.

Wolman, Harold with Spitzley, D. 1999. "The Politics of Local Economic Development." *Economic Development Quarterly* 10 (2) (1996) 115–50. Reprinted in John Blair and Laura Reese (eds.). *Approaches to Economic Development*. Beverly Hills, CA. Sage.

Yinger, John; Bloom, Howard; Borsch-Supan, Axel; and Ladd, Helen. 1988. *Property Taxes and Housing Values: The Theory and Estimation of Intrajurisdictional Property Tax Capitalization.* Boston. Academic Press.

CHAPTER 22

SETTING CITY AGENDAS: POWER AND POLICY CHANGE

JOSHUA SAPOTICHNE AND BRYAN D. JONES

1. Introduction

On February 16, 2005, the United Nations Kyoto Protocol, the agreement to address climate change through collective stabilization of greenhouse gas emissions, took effect in 141 nations. Absent from the list of ratifiers was the U.S. government. Despite the role of Clinton and Bush administration officials in shaping the international climate change agenda, then-President George W. Bush chose not to submit the treaty for Senate ratification. On that very same day, former Seattle mayor Greg Nickels launched a new initiative called the U.S. Conference of Mayors (USCM) Climate Protection Agreement. The chief objective of the Agreement was simple: participating mayors would pledge to advance the goals of the Kyoto Protocol at the city level by reducing carbon dioxide emissions in their cities by 7 percent below 1990 levels by the year 2012.

At the time the event appeared to be little more than political stagecraft. Yet support for an aggressive city-level climate change strategy slowly, then more rapidly, began to mount (Rabe 2007; Schreurs 2008). Indeed, as we go to press, 1,054 mayors representing about 40 percent of the U.S. population have adopted the Agreement for their cities.[1] Moreover, this groundswell of support advanced, as well

1. According to findings from a 2007 USCM survey, nearly 90 percent of mayors require or anticipate requiring in the next year that new city government buildings be constructed following green building standards; 72 percent have employed alternative

as was aided by, a USCM-led lobbying campaign to petition the U.S. Congress for resources to help city governments devise, enact, and implement energy efficiency strategies. The culmination of this effort came in 2007 in the form of Energy Efficiency and Conservation Block Grants (EECBG), a program for which $3.2 billion was appropriated in the 2009 American Recovery and Reinvestment Act.

What makes EECBG so attractive to urban policymakers is that it is more than a simple climate program, but one component of an increasingly popular strategy opaquely characterized as the federal commitment to a "green collar economy" (Jones 2008). This is not your father's energy policy, but a fresh approach that attempts to tackle core aspects of both poverty reduction and climate change though a mix of loosely related policy tools ranging from the subsidization of sustainable building practices, to antisprawl land-use policies, to tax incentives for building retrofits and new energy efficiency constructions, to increased public investment in transportation infrastructure.

Not surprisingly, the growing popularity of what Thomas Friedman (2008) termed a "win, win, win, win, win" strategy currently has subnational interests clamoring to accent the relative "greenness" of existing and prospective policy initiatives (see Kennedy 2009; Marcus 2009; Apollo Alliance et al. 2008). Numerous state and local governments have adopted U.S. Green Building Council, LEED, and Energy Star standards to signal a commitment to energy efficiency (Koski 2010). Policies adopted to reconfigure industrial infrastructure from Pittsburgh, Pennsylvania to Des Moines, Iowa are touted for their creation of "green jobs." Transit programs in cities as diverse as Chicago, Illinois and Grand Rapids, Michigan are pitched as strategies for improving city and suburban ambient air quality. In all, the U.S. urban policy agenda, or at least the strategic rhetoric employed by urban policymakers to describe various policy initiatives, has undergone a substantial "greening".

For political scientists studying urban politics in the U.S., abroad, or from a comparative bent, the case of climate change policy raises fundamental questions about how urban policy agendas are built, how urban agendas change, and the ways in which these processes are affected by intergovernmental dynamics. U.S. urban scholars might predict that the structure and biases of federalism would drive urban growth interests to eschew environmental policy aims. Yet, by strategically linking city policy innovations with broader federal energy objectives, urban interests helped expand the scope and tenor of discussion to legitimize the notion that clean energy investment can serve as a catalyst for employment and growth. Indeed the climate change "benefits coalitions," in the words of Thomas Anton (1989), has

fuels for city fleets or have fully accepted hybrid-electric technology; two-thirds have institutionalized climate protection activities in the city government through the appointment of personnel devoted to climate change concerns; and just under three-quarters have changed or are in the process of changing residential and commercial building codes and ordinances to encourage construction of new energy efficient and environmentally sustainable building (USCM 2007).

reinforced the need for the formulation and administration of policies that balance the stimulation of growth, with, for instance, distributive efforts to promote fairness in hiring practices as well as federal regulation of carbon emissions.

In the case of U.S. climate policy, city-level innovation sparked federal intervention, which then facilitated and codified urban policy change—a bottom-up-top-down process, if you will.[2] As the issue of climate change gained in status, policy attention and activity cascaded across the U.S. federal system, resulting both in substantial federal change as well as nontrivial transformations in city-level institutions. How frequently does this "type" of policy change occur? Moreover, how do institutional and systemic difference across cities, states, regions, or nations structure urban agenda-setting opportunities? These questions are difficult to address in light of the paucity of research on agenda setting in U.S. and comparative urban politics. For a variety of reasons that we address in the following pages, models of policy agenda setting—that is, the process by which issues come up for consideration within and across different public and institutional venues—are mostly built and applied to national policymaking, both in the U.S. and abroad,[3] rather than in the domain of city government. In this chapter, we offer an explanation for this phenomenon and show why the divergence in scholarship is detrimental to theorizing on city politics and policy, as well as to a more comprehensive understanding of agenda dynamics and policy change more generally. Our problem is not with a particular theory or framework, but with the more common pursuit of representing urban policymaking in ways that tend to exclude choice and innovation. We endeavor to make a simple point: that the complex dance between institutional change and policy change so prevalent in national-level research on the policy process does not end at the city limits. We conclude with a discussion of a research strategy that can both refocus our understanding of urban politics in the U.S. and abroad and contribute profitably to theories of policy agenda setting.

2. Urban Policymaking and the Imminence of Agenda Dynamics

From the early works of David Easton (1965), Peter Bacharach and Morton Baratz (1962), and Edward Banfield and James Q. Wilson (1963), scholars studying all manner of political conflict have acknowledged that structural biases inherent in the

2. Federalism theorists might forecast that the federal government would preempt the "patchwork quilt" of subnational policies through coordinated regulation (see Zimmerman 2008), but this is certainly not the case here.

3. We mainly focus on western European nations since a relatively recent outpouring of research on the EU multilevel system has addressed aspects of these key questions.

U.S. federal system influence when, how, and why some controversies reach the attention of policymakers, and, conversely, when, how, and why some controversies are denied consideration. In the field of urban politics and policy, institutional biases are of particular interest to scholars given the relative weakness of city governments in the U.S. system, as well as the enduring division of labor between state and market (Stone 1987, 5). Due in large measure to these commanding forces, urban policy agendas are studied by scholars operating from within public choice and political economy paradigms as veritable manifestations of what Stephen Elkin (1987) called the "commercial public interest".

Research on the management of political conflict also has a home in the body of research on policy agendas. Most agendas research addresses a specific query: the manner by which the public comes to understand, and the receptiveness of policymaking institutions to, a particular policy problem. The expansion and containment of political conflict is a central aspect of the agenda building process (Cobb and Elder 1983, 36–62). Much like the work in urban politics, dozens of empirical studies on policy agendas have illustrated that new issues or ideas meet considerable resistance from prevailing political arrangements.[4] But sometimes the disadvantaged succeed in expanding political conflict or circumnavigating unreceptive policy venues as a means of breaking through institutionalized barriers, a process that nearly always results in dramatic policy change. Indeed, research in this vein tends to treat institutional structure more as a variable in a complex model of policy change, and less as a governing principle that may only be altered through formal rule changes. To the agenda-setting scholar, stasis, incremental adjustments, and policy punctuations are all part of the same evolutionary process that links institutional change and policy change.

A few years back, we became interested in what we consider the inbuilt theoretical connection between urban politics and agenda-setting processes—that is, shared foci on the interplay of the structure of political conflict and policy agendas. So we (along with coauthor, Michelle Wolfe) collected and analyzed citation data to systematically analyze the extent to which ideas developed outside the field have penetrated urban scholarship over time, and the extent to which scholars from outside the field have embraced urban politics theorizing. To our dismay, we found that urbanists publishing within the subfield's top journals tend to pay scant attention to policy agendas research (Sapotichne, Jones, and Wolfe 2007, 89–91; also see Sapotichne, Jones, and Wolfe 2008).[5]

But why? Some time ago, Thomas Anton (1989) famously argued that structure-induced, status quo biases may constrain intergovernmental actors, yet the

4. A number of works in recent years have shifted focus back to the potency of institutional and structural biases to policy change and the countermobilization strategies of actors with an interest in preserving the status quo (see Pralle 2006; Givel 2006; Wood 2006; Miller 2008).

5. As pointed out in a recent analysis of the field of Canadian urban politics (Eidelman and Taylor 2010), this isolation is not strictly American.

federalized system of overlapping jurisdictions and "counterpart bureaucracies" also facilitates change by providing direct channels of access (also see Yin 1980). Familiar examples abound. U.S. federal and state officials frequently intervene to restructure metropolitan institutions and shape urban policy (Burns 2002, 2003; Judd and Smith 2007). Issues, such as smoking regulation, creep onto the European Union's (EU) agenda as a result of strategic machinations of substate actors from within member nations (Princen and Rhinard 2006). City-level officials in the U.S. seek to engage state and special-purpose governments to sidestep local opposition (Berman 2003; Sapotichne and Smith forthcoming). Both in the U.S. and abroad, reform-oriented entrepreneurs at the subnational level challenge and limit downtown growth through the initiative process by catalyzing electoral mobilization, and through new collective governing arrangements (DeLeon 1992; Schneider and Teske 1993; Sellers 2002). Structure matters. Global, national, and subnational equilibrating forces mostly prevail. Policy output is mostly stable. But it is striking that city-level strategies of conflict management and agenda setting bear a strong resemblance to comparable federal policy processes in both U.S. and non-U.S. contexts.

In this section, we offer an explanation for why this resemblance is not made more manifest in the literature. To this end, we explain that scholarship on the urban policy process has essentially bifurcated into two organizing frameworks: *domain theory*—the view that the nature of the political process is driven by the particular policy area at hand; and *regime theory*—the study of building public-/private-sector governance coalitions in the face of structural limitations of city governments. While scholars in both traditions seek to explain the antecedents to the urban policy process, we contend that the frameworks' overwhelming focus on the structural limitations of city policy agendas places too great an emphasis on seemingly static public-private relationships while ignoring the prospects for change.

2.1. Domain Theory

Primarily set forth in urban politics in Paul Peterson's *City Limits* (1981) and, more generally, through the works of Theodore Lowi (1964, 1972) and Ripley and Franklin (1990), the basic tenet of domain theory is that "policy begets politics", or that the content of policy influences its politics. The notion here is that distinct policymaking environments will form to surround different issues (see May, Sapotichne, and Workman 2006) and will vary based upon a number of factors including constituency mobilization, issue politicization, levels of conflict, and agenda status.[6] For instance, Peterson's influential model of urban policymaking suggests that elite interests in a relatively closed policymaking system will dominate issues regarding the stimulation of economic growth. Debates concerning allotment and delivery of city services, on the other hand, will tend to be more

6. See Elaine Sharp's chapter in the *Handbook of Research on Urban Politics and Policy in the United States* (1997b) for a thorough rendering of what she terms the "policy spheres paradigm" in the study of urban politics and policy.

open and pluralistic. Redistributive issues should be more open as well, but these issues tend to occupy more marginal positions on most cities' policy agendas. As such, questions of formulation and resource allocation are fundamentally contingent upon the particular policy under consideration (Sharp 1997b, 275). In this view, urban fiscal angst and other exogenous forces may prohibit city governments from providing certain goods to needy populations (Peterson, Rabe, and Wong 1986); yet proposals aimed at growing the urban physical space are considered nondiscretionary and immune from these forces (Kantor and David 1988; Peterson 1995). Agenda status is fundamentally predetermined by city governments' "unitary interest" in local economic vitality.

Peterson's work on urban policymaking has left an ineradicable mark on the urban field by suggesting an unambiguous way in which the nature of urban politics is influenced by the type of issue at hand. However, substantial shortcomings plague core descriptive and predictive elements of the domain approach. For one, programs and policies are multidimensional and frequently crosscut policy types (Baumgartner and Jones 1993, 40–55). Given ample time for examination, "issue transformation is perhaps more the rule than the exception" when it comes to policy politics (Rochefort and Cobb 1994, 56). As a result, it is difficult to determine how some, if not most, policies should be classified over time. Ed Goetz (1990), in an analysis of housing and development policy in 281 localities, emphasizes that a great many projects contain "mandated benefits" which range from affordable housing subsidies, to mandates for the hiring of local residents, to set-asides for minority businesses. More generally, "social" policies aimed at improving elementary and secondary education, health services, and urban environmental ecology all intersect with growth objectives, and indeed may be employed as instruments of economic stimulus (Wolman and Spitzley 1996; Altshuler and Gomez-Ibanez 1993). Given the recurrence of similar policy tools for promoting the distribution of direct economic and social goods to otherwise disadvantaged groups (Fleischmann, Green, and Kwong 1991; Imbroscio 1997; Sellers 2002) and the use of seemingly discrepant policies for raising city revenue (Altshuler and Gomez-Ibanez 1993), analytical categorization quickly becomes murky.

Moreover, predicting a policy's politics is increasingly difficult as the composition of issues evolves over time. What frequently determines the political feasibility of a certain set of policy proposals, and indeed the process by which proposals reach the formal agenda, is both elite and public *perception* (see May 1986). Issues evolve—once conflictual issues may now be widely accepted; just as those once considered consensual may now be highly conflictual. From AIDS to air pollution, scholars have shown that an issue's collective definition is subject to a high degree of manipulation (Hilgartner and Bosk 1988, 56). Peterson suggests that urban policymaking predicts that a city's interest in growth drives preference convergence among urban populations, representative institutions, and export industries, resulting in an agenda centered almost entirely on economic development. There is considerable evidence, however, that in U.S. and non-U.S. cities alike, a great deal more conflict occurs over growth policy than the model predicts (see, for instance, Sanders and Stone 1987;

Purcell 2000; Sellers 2002; Altshuler and Luberoff 2003). In cities all over the globe urban development exists in relation to a bevy of other issues with each embedded in complex systems of strategic problem definition. New attributes of growth with less favorable connotation—such as energy usage, congestion, and pollution—can rise to gain more attention. The more general point is this: To establish how any issue reaches the urban agenda, one must consider how it transforms into a political problem and how that problem comes to be publicly and privately defined.[7]

2.2. Regime Theory

Urban domain theorists contend that city policy is driven almost entirely by a competitive need for growth. Regime theorists, on the other hand, focus on the web of local political relationships and the cooperation necessary between governmental and nongovernmental actors to both formulate a policy agenda, as well as construct a supportive set of governance arrangements to guide the agenda through the political process.[8] For regime theorists, the key factor in regime formation and maintenance is the "social production" of governance capacity. Successful coalitions are formed when key actors exhibit the political and institutional capability to align resources around the cooperative task of governing (Stone 2005).[9]

Regime analysts argue that the structure of particular governance arrangements is strongly associated with policy objectives. Some regimes, for instance, may establish economic development departments or special purpose districts to institutionalize a preferred development agenda and foster cooperation across relevant interests. But development policy can take many forms, such as incentives to attract industry, downtown commercial development, and targeted residential enhancement, each approach involving a different causal connection between problem, policy, and impact. How development regime players chose to *emphasize* a certain conception of development and its connection with preferred policy solution, defines the regime. To fully grasp regime formation and evolution, asserts Stone (2001), "it is important to think about ideational matters at two levels—the level of broad purpose, but also the broad level of program construction. The two levels give the regime its identifying agenda" (21).

7. The example at this chapter's outset on the reconstitution and reframing of urban environmental and energy initiatives provides an apt case of entrepreneurial activism in response to changing political conditions.

8. In the last decade or so, a number of comprehensive summaries have been written on the concept of urban regimes. Regarding U.S. regime formations, see, for instance. Mossberger (2008); Stone (2005); Mossberger and Stoker (2001); and Stoker (1995). From a comparative perspective, see Harding (1994); Stoker and Mossberger (1994); John and Cole (1998); Davies (2003); and Sellers (2002).

9. The "iron law of regimes" according to Gerry Stoker (1995) holds that regime viability is dependent upon the mobilization of interests commensurate with its main policy agenda (61).

One shortcoming of most regime analysis is that it generally fails to specify the process of regime *change*.[10] As maintenance rather than responsiveness begins to dominate a regime's purpose, preferred solutions have been shown to fall out of favor, leading to inadaptability to changing internal or external conditions (see Jones and Bachelor 1993, 15–19). Not surprisingly, scholars who have chosen to examine regimes in a dynamic perspective have found evidence of change in response to a rapid rise in fresh policy proposals and symbolic representations that cascade through the system to break down existing arrangements (Jones and Bachelor 1993; Bachelor 1994). Others point to slower periods of regime transition in which repeated questioning of existing arrangements chips away at regime legitimacy, gradually leading to institutionalization of a new policy agenda (Orr and Stoker 1994). As Gerry Stoker intimated some 15 years ago (1995, 68), to understand the process of regime change, what is needed is a greater "recognition of the impact of shifts in exogenous conditions as well as developments in the internal dynamics of coalition building".

A second deficiency of regime analysis results from the shortage of regime scholarship that examines issues of coalitional formation, maintenance, and evolution in the context of intergovernmental complexity.[11] Regime analyses invariably note the significance of decision-making processes at higher levels of government. Yet when push comes to shove, the crucial variable for achieving governing capacity to carry out a policy agenda is "the internal politics of coalition building" (Stone 1989, 178). Jonathan Davies (2003) argues that this is particularly problematic in the UK, where the expansion of bureaucratically controlled urban regeneration partnerships has been driven in large measure by a series of central government initiatives and direct interventions. Similarly, in a comparative study of two British and two French cities, Peter John and Alastair Cole (2000) illustrate that the structure and capacity of intergovernmental education policy networks are more a function of intrastate variations in the centrality of federal and local bureaucratic officials than of city-level political motivations.[12]

10. A few possible causes of this phenomenon include lack of conceptual clarity regarding regime type, or, for that matter, the actual presence of a cohesive governing coalition (Mossberger and Stoker 2001); a shortage of attention to higher levels of government and the implications of state and federal policy on regime formation and continuity (Altshuler and Luberoff 2003); and an overriding focus on economic development policy at the expense of examining the full range of issues on which city governments focus and in which business interest play a less dominant role (Sapotichne, Jones, and Wolfe 2007).

11. Altshuler and Luberoff (2003, 72) argue that, in light of the venerated position of the Atlanta regime in the concept's theoretical and methodological tradition, this omission may have done a great deal to impel the field toward overly localist conceptions of urban governance.

12. However, in the domain of economic development, the authors observe greater cross-national similarities in network structure.

Not surprisingly, scholars who do consider the intergovernmental politics of urban governance arrangements, both in the U.S. and abroad, find that regime *context* matters a great deal. Thomas Anton's (1989, 30) seminal work on the role of city politics in the intergovernmental system suggests a more dynamic process of coalition formation by which evolving patterns of interests at all levels of government may "mobilize to develop, support, and implement government benefit programs". Jeffrey Sellers (2002), in an expansive comparative analysis of 11 cities in three nations, illustrates that cross-national variations in the structure of multilevel institutions clearly shapes the capacity of urban governments to maintain federal policy aims as well as provides certain opportunities for establishing and maintaining urban policy agendas. Richard DeLeon's (1992) study of San Francisco politics demonstrates that shifting patterns of federal funding facilitated the breakup of the Bay Area's progressive/slow-growth coalition by mobilizing opposing downtown business interests. Altshuler and Luberoff's (2003) influential work on the evolution of urban public investment outlines a more general pattern of urban policy transformation in response to federal policy change. The authors show that shifts in federal spending after the 1970s drove widespread city-level resistance to new taxes and mega-project financing, leading growth entrepreneurs to eschew traditional clearance-based urban renewal in favor of creatively funded and implemented "infrastructure of play" projects (also see Judd 2003 Fainstein and Judd 1999; Eisinger 1998).

2.3. Regimes, Domains, and Agendas

The bifurcation of the study of city policymaking has driven a mostly static depiction of the process by which urban governments the world over choose to do what they do. Domain theory's primary contribution to the field of urban politics is its concern with the policy environment—for example, intensity and commensurability of preferences, differential mobilization of interests and institutions—when considering processes of policy formulation, enactment, and implementation. The somewhat static and deterministic depiction of urban policymaking that results from its application, however, ignores changing perceptions of policy issues over time (Orr and Stoker 1994), the degree of conflict surrounding contemporary development issues (Altshuler and Luberoff 2003), and the interdependence of the panoply of concerns that occupy the attention of urban policymakers. In short, domain theory ignores policy dynamics.

Regime theorists, at least to a certain degree, address the conflictual nature of city policymaking by offering convincing explanations for why urban governance coalitions form and why particular problem definitions are codified over others. As we have pointed out in an earlier article (Sapotichne, Jones, and Wolfe 2007), Stone's initial conception of systemic power provided a fresh lens through which to view urban policymakers' "power to" form governing coalitions around a particular policy agenda—growth-oriented or otherwise. Indeed much of Stone and his associates' recent work addresses fundamental aspects of urban conflict management, including the prospects of city-level policy entrepreneurs for fostering long-standing reform coalitions (Stone, Orr, and Worgs 2006) and the role of extraurban actors in affecting substantive urban policy change through intergovernmental agenda building strategies (Stone 2001).

We are not suggesting that regime theory per se is the problem, any more than we are placing blame on the shoulders of those applying domain theory to urban policymaking. Our issue is with the more common pursuit of representing urban policymaking in ways that tend to exclude choice, innovation, and change. Regime analysts tend to overlook questions regarding the ways in which national-, regional-, or state-level dynamics lead to the emergence of new policy ideas or when fresh conceptions of old issues achieve public interest. Do multilevel systems of governance, such as in the EU, hinder or facilitate such information cascades? More generally, when a regime's agenda shows signs of failing, do solutions more aligned with dynamics at the national or supranational level (or indeed those offered by nonregime players) gain support and generate positive feedback? As with the case of climate change policy from this chapter's introduction, it seems plausible that in the U.S. these dynamics can flow through the federal system to create policy change at all levels of government. Indeed, a large body of literature on processes of policy transfer (Radaelli 2000), policy diffusion (Busch and Jorgens 2005), and resultant cross-national policy convergence (Knill 2005) in western Europe highlights dynamic policy feedback across institutional settings. In what follows, we highlight research that addresses similar questions of policy dynamics.

3. Agenda Dynamism in Urban Politics

As we mentioned above, some scholars have successfully studied urban politics and policy through the policy agendas lens. We contend that agenda-setting theory has influenced the study of urban politics in two specific respects: first, in considering the role of policy entrepreneurs in managing political conflicts, and second, in contemplating the role of information processing and policy feedback in policy change.

3.1. Policy Entrepreneurship and Political Conflict

As has been pointed out with great vigor, development issues occupy a privileged position on the urban agenda. But the reality of urban policymaking is that city agendas are comprised of many issues—from education, to pollution, to plant closings, to morality policy—that at different points in time occupy the attention of urban officials. The predominance of regime and domain theorizing in urban scholarship has another consequence: an unhealthy preoccupation with economic development policy. Given the struggles that face actors operating from outside the development domain to gain public status (see, for instance, Crenson 1971, 159–76; Sharp 1997a), it comes as no great surprise that more consideration is given to agenda-setting processes in nondevelopment policy arenas.[13]

In light of the recent concern over the performance of urban public schools and the explosion of city takeovers in Chicago, Cleveland, Boston, and New York, a number of studies have applied agenda-setting theorizing to the examination of urban education. The most comprehensive effort, the "Civic Capacity and Urban Education project," consists of an 11-city cross-sectional analysis that addresses the cities' capacity to mobilize around broad educational goals. In the resultant work most pertinent to this chapter, Stone et al. (2001) examine why many of the cities under investigation were able to craft a sustained development agenda, yet have achieved varying levels of success with respect to education reform? A number of impediments, ranging from a high amount of jurisdictional competition, to incommensurate interests of relevant actors, to a basic ambiguity about the "problem" of urban education, have conspired to create an environment in which policymaking equilibrium is easily upset. Within what the authors refer to as "high reverberation subsystems," the key for achieving and sustaining a reform agenda is the capacity of local entrepreneurs to translate the particularistic desires of public and private actors into a well-articulated "purpose" (also see Stone 2001; Stone, Orr, and Worgs 2006). Indeed, in a spin-off article on how mayoral leadership impacts the politics of education reform, Melissa Marschall and Paru Shah (2005) show that the involvement of diverse interests with incongruent incentives for cooperation places a premium on the capacity of city mayors in particular to exploit institutional power and catalyze a shared reform identity (also see Jones and Hill 1998).

Scholarship on local policy entrepreneurs focuses on the strategies utilized by change-oriented actors to mobilize latent publics, manipulate policy images, and navigate the labyrinthine system of government institutions to propel gainful issues onto the policy agenda.[14] Perhaps most notably, Mark Schneider, Paul Teske, and Michael Mintrom (1995) engaged in a comprehensive research project to offer a theory of policy entrepreneurship and test its propositions in the suburban laboratory. In applying their theory of entrepreneurial emergence and strategy, the authors illustrate how the recent success of antigrowth movements in local debates over urban and suburban growth has hinged on the interplay of entrepreneurial rhetoric

13. Two classic studies from the early 1970s fit the bill: Matthew A. Crenson's (1971) comparative case study of the (un)politics of urban air pollution, and Peter Bacharach and Morton Baratz's (1971) study of poverty decision-making processes in Baltimore, Maryland.

14. In an analysis of the city of Miami's dissolution referendum, Annette Steinacker (2001, 100) argues that the processes of changing the structure of metropolitan governance arrangements "need to be understood as the outcomes of an agenda-setting process". She shows that that the issue advocacy of a prominent sponsor of neighborhood incorporation, coupled with support by entrepreneurial politicians in response to scandal and fiscal crisis, combined to explain how disincorporation gained a hearing, but ultimately failed.

and the mobilization of diffuse populist interests around the dimension of neighborhood preservation (also see Schneider and Teske 1993). More recently, Elaine Sharp (1996, 1997, 2007) applies the theory of public entrepreneurship to explain the distinctive function played by "culture war" entrepreneurs in gaining agenda access and promoting a favorable issue definition in local morality policy debates. A central factor in Sharp's narrative is the capacity of these actors to navigate the intense controversies and substantial community costs to action that characterize cultural politics.

Scholars of EU policy processes have shed some light on the relationship between group capacity and the successful strategic negotiation of multilevel governance systems (see Zahariadis 2008). Eising (2007), in a recent article drawing on survey data from 800 German, French, UK, and EU business associations, argues that, to varying degrees, interest group access to EU institutions is contingent upon a bevy of factors, including group-level resources and the division of labor among EU and national associations. In a similar vein, Beyers (2004) illustrates how institutional conditions and interest group resources mediate the relative effectiveness of public (outside access) and inside lobbying strategies by European interest associations (also see Constantelos 2007). Richardson (2000) has argued that the "Europeanization" of national and subnational policy sectors has legitimized the use of strategic rhetoric that highlights EU policy goals, even in certain cases in which these goals conflict with national strategies. As such, insider groups and actors have access to potential frames that outsider groups and change-oriented entrepreneurs do not.

In a related example in the U.S., Sapotichne (2011a), in a study of the debate in the mid-1990s over the public financing of two new sports stadiums in Seattle, blends work on agenda-setting with rhetorical strategy to offer a framework for explaining how groups generate, evaluate, and adjust "frames" in mega-project financing debates. Progrowth interests utilize slack resources, public relations expertise, and editorial page support to set the terms of debate by highlighting the issue dimension most likely to garner maximum support. Antistadium interests that tend to be more heterogeneous mostly employ "insurgency" strategies: Rather than attempting to reframe the debate by highlighting a more favorable issue dimension, these actors tend to *engage* existing dimensions by challenging their validity—for example, disputing spurious claims of substantial economic impact.

A second core dimension of conflict management and entrepreneurism is the notion of "venue shopping", or the strategy of seeking out alternative and ostensibly more favorable policy arenas (see Pralle 2003, 2006; Baumgartner and Jones 1993, 35–37). Whereas some issues are firmly within the jurisdiction of a single institution or level of government, "federalized" policy issues are more likely to display competitive environments in which jurisdictional boundaries either overlap or are less well established (see Miller 2008). As such, decision-making authority is not institutionally static and, based on a number of interrelated forces, may move up and down the governmental hierarchy.

In light of what has been termed EU "multilevelness"—that is, the interconnectivity as well as dispersion of policy politics across governmental levels (Beyers et al. 2008, 1294)—scholars have paid attention to how interest group opportunities are structured within and across western European governments. For instance, Bryan Wendon's (1998) work illustrates how actors within EU governing institutions in their quest for developing a comprehensive European social policy have worked to create new institutional arrangements that decrease the influence of member governments and create points of access for advocacy groups. In a thoughtful piece on the structure of agenda-setting opportunities within the EU, Princen (2007) contends that despite difficulties in public mobilization at the supranational level, a number of western European policy issues ranging from immigration (see Guiraudon 2000), to member-nation sanctions (see Van de Steeg 2006), to human and civil rights (Mahoney and Baumgartner 2008), have expanded to the European level (see also Kerber and Eckardt 2007; Knill 2005).

More pertinent to this chapter is the work on vertical venue-shopping: The processes by which actors from within subnational governments, or interest organizations operating at the local level, will turn to higher-level governments—for example, state, national, or supranational institutions (such as the European Council or other EU governing bodies)—to bypass unreceptive political environments "at home"; or a more top-down process by which entrepreneurial actors will seek out ostensibly more favorable decision venues at the subnational and urban levels.[15] Regarding the latter, Durose and Lowndes (2010) illustrate that rationales for urban revitalization that focused on place-based notions of civic pride were more effective in mobilizing neighborhood advocates and interest organizations, whereas economic rationales worked better within city government institutions. Lisa Miller (2007, 2008), in a set of studies of crime control policy, shows that citizen groups that challenge status quo crime policies frequently found local and city governments to be more accessible and hospitable to their interests than larger constituencies of state and national governments. Similarly, Shipan and Volden's (2006) recent work on U.S. smoking policy illustrates how antismoking advocates sought out large metropolitan governments when state legislatures were indifferent to smoking regulation.

Interesting work has also been conducted on the process of "bottom-up" venue shopping. In a recent piece on the process of "territorial state-bypassing" by subnational interest groups in the EU, Tatham (2010) illustrates that "domestically strong" regional and local interests frequently engage in coordinative EU lobbying strategies with member nations, though they may bypass these nations when governed by competing political parties (see also Keating and Hooghe 2006; Jeffery 2000). In a comparative study of mega-project debates in Seattle and Chicago, Sapotichne and Smith (forthcoming) show that as the local consensus for economic growth has deteriorated and growth politics have become more conflict-laden, city-level actors

15. A great deal of scholarship has highlighted the influence of outside institutions in city growth policy—including state governments (Eisinger 1998; Sbragia 1996; Burns and Gamm 1997) and quasi-governmental authorities (Judd 2003; Judd and Smith 2007).

have chosen to relocate political conflict to more receptive state-run institutions, a strategy that permits greater control over the scope and tenor of debate. In a similar vein, Stone's (2001) recent reexamination of the Atlanta growth regime demonstrates how contemporary regionalization of urban development policy has influenced the coalitional strategies of Atlanta business elites (2001). According to Stone, business lobbying efforts have shifted to the Georgia state government as Atlanta's governmental institutions prove more and more incapable of crafting a coherent agenda around the city's physical reconstruction (26–27). These arguments advance agenda-setting theory as well: it seems that under certain endogenous and exogenous conditions, venue shopping may be employed to *suppress* political conflict rather than expand it (also see Pralle 2006, 13–31; Princen 2007, 31–32).

3.2. Information Processing and Policy Feedback

One burgeoning line of research in the policy processes field focuses on the ways in which governments process information and prioritize problems. Of primary interest is how the cognitive limits of individual decision-makers and the collective limitations of groups of actors influences the assemblage, interpretation, and prioritization of policy signals (see Jones and Baumgartner 2005, 7–17). Recently, a model of disproportionate information processing was introduced to explain how boundedly rational processes of decision-making lead to patterns of extreme policy stability punctuated by periods of rapid change. Across a number of subfields and institutional venues, scholars applying this framework have illustrated time and again that policy agendas, though often proceeding smoothly with marginal or incremental accommodations, are regularly torn by lurches and considerable departures from the incremental past.[16] Indeed, scholars of policy formation in the EU have uncovered similar, boundedly rational processes of policy search (see Cairney 2009; Zahariadis 2008; Princen 2007).

Though structurally dependent (see Kantor and David 1988), city government agendas are far from fixed. The instability of urban agendas is particularly apparent in analyses of decision-making process of urban leaders and in studies of the punctuated politics of city budgeting. With respect to the former, analyses of economic development in Detroit by Bryan Jones and Lynn Bachelor (1993) show that reliance on previous growth solutions and attendant policy approaches, termed "solution sets," hampers the responsiveness of governance coalitions to environmental dynamics (also see Bachelor 1994). The authors illustrate that throughout the 1980s, Detroit public officials, particularly Mayor Coleman Young, obstinately and unsuccessfully adopted outdated commercial development tactics to address fundamentally different issues of industrial decay, a strategy characterized by the motto "there is nothing wrong with Detroit that three or four factories can't solve" (Jones and Bachelor 1993, 249). The development strategy, which was readily available and

16. For a review of this literature, see Baumgartner, Green-Pedersen, and Jones (2006).

codified within existing city agencies, exemplified the boundedly rational political strategy of connecting an old solution to an emerging problem.

As Bachelor (1994, 1998) illustrates in follow-up analyses, Detroit officials were seemingly unfazed as similar strategies were adopted in future debates over the siting and financing of a Chrysler plant, as well as casino and stadium development over a decade later. The upshot: While urban political elites may command sufficient leverage in shaping development agendas, cognitive and institutional constraints characterize urban decision-making processes leading to insufficient search and policy imitation that frequently results in evolving rather than fixed patterns of coalitional politics and policy outcomes.

An additional line of research builds on theories of disproportionate information processing and error accumulation to explain processes of urban budgeting. Agenda-setting theorizing has recently been extended to produce an agenda-based model of U.S. federal budgeting (Jones, Baumgartner, and True 1998; True 2000). Federal institutions have been shown to magnify, rather than offset, the general human tendency toward "punctuated equilibrium"—that is, stasis, interspersed with rapid change (Jones, Sulkin, and Larsen 2003). As attention shifts to new attributes, so too do outcomes. And the process is often equally as volatile. Breunig and Koski (2006) find punctuated budget change for U.S. state budgets; Jones and Baumgartner (2005) find similar patterns for U.S. national outlays since the early 19th century.

But what of the process of urban budgeting? Meagan Jordan (2003) extends punctuated equilibrium theory to urban budgeting in the 38 largest cites in the U.S. to show that city expenditures, much like those at the state and federal levels, exhibit high kurtosis scores. Yet variation exists across functional categories: nonallocational budget functions, such as public buildings, parks and recreation, and highways, are more prone to rapid increases or decreases and thus hold less stable positions on local policy agendas. Allocational functions, such as basic day-to-day deliveries of policy, fire, and sanitation services, are considerably less punctuation-prone and occupy more stable positions on local policy agendas. These findings reinforce the imperative of service delivery, particular during times of fiscal stress when decision-makers seem more likely to sacrifice economic growth policies. With respect to the agenda status of urban problems, however, Jordan's analysis calls into question the centrality of urban development.

3.3. Patterns in City Agendas Research

What role do agenda-setting processes play in urban policymaking? At first blush, the research on this subject may seem a bit schizophrenic—an obvious upshot of scholarly heterogeneity. Indeed, this schizophrenia is particularly acute when considering how the work on U.S. urban agendas relates to findings from Canada, Europe, and beyond. For the purposes of this chapter, we contend that a set of findings emerge from our survey that, on the whole, point to a more dynamic portrait of city-level conflict management and agenda building as well as a more levelheaded view of the composition and bias of city policy agendas.

Attention, as it is in all systems of government, is in short supply in urban policymaking institutions. As such, a number of elements of policy entrepreneurship, including problem definition (Portz 1994; Stone et al. 2001), coalition building and management (DeLeon 1992; Marschall and Shah 2005), and social and political perspicacity (Stone, Orr, and Worgs 2006), have been highlighted as important factors in driving urban policy change, as well as in sustaining reform coalitions. Some have pointed out the circumstances under which city or state level officials may attempt to manage political conflict through strategic rhetoric. To be sure, local media play a role in these processes. As is the case of federal and state models of policy agenda building and policy change, television and newspaper coverage facilitates the transmission of issue salience and the mobilization of attentive publics in cities (Crow 2010). Yet the specific role of urban and local media in the setting of urban agendas is far from settled as limited capacity (Nicodemus 2004) and structural imperatives (Molotch 1976) have been shown to influence the coverage of urban politics.

Some of the most intriguing research in our survey attempts to draw out the interplay between urban autonomy, institutional structure, and the intergovernmental system. In the U.S. context, a number of scholars have recently pointed out that decision-making over the scope and nature of city policymaking is happening in more, and in different, venues (Judd and Simpson 2003). State officials frequently intervene to command control over the design and implementation of city development initiatives (Burns 2002). Other instruments such as quasi-governmental and special-purpose authorities—replete with comparatively high levels of fiscal capacity and taxing and spending authority—have been crucial to urban policymaking decisions regarding transportation, environmental degradation, waste, housing, and development (Mitchell 1990; see also Judd and Smith 2007). These institutions frequently codify the policy strategies of dominant regime interests (Judd 2003).

However, some recent work in the U.S. has shown that state agencies and legislative institutions, as well as special-purpose governments, may also operate as alternative venues for city-level interests whose agendas are meeting resistance within other governmental levels (Sapotichne and Smith forthcoming; Sonenshein and Hogan-Esch 2006). Effective venue shopping in the intergovernmental context is contingent upon a number of forces, including partisanship, network interconnectivity, and group- and individual-level resources. Moreover, whereas multilevel characteristics offer agenda-setting opportunities, these actors are similarly faced with what Princen and Kerremans (2008) have labeled "political opportunity structures" at each level that determine the relative receptiveness of decision venues.

Nascent research on comparative policy venues has, to a certain degree, helped to tease out the significance of these contingencies. Constantelos (2010), in a piece comparing lobbying strategies by U.S. and Canadian interest groups in response to the economic crisis, illustrates that subnational governments at the provincial, state, and county levels provide attractive alternative decision venues when they are controlled by "sympathetic" political parties. In other words, partisanship is a key factor in determining the favorability of venue opportunity structures. In one of the more thorough treatments of venue shopping and conflict management to date, Sarah Pralle (2006) also goes to pains to remind us that venue shopping is highly contextually dependent. She shows that a hodgepodge of subnational forestry advocates in the U.S. and Canada were able to overcome powerful timber interests and governmental institutional constraints by "internationalizing" the issue of Clayoquot Sound. Globalizing the conflict, she contends, led to domestic policy change through a policymaking "boomerang effect"—international actors who were far way from the original locus of conflict pressured domestic decision-makers to take action to address environmental degradation.

In all, this mixture of empirical findings raises more questions than it answers. Similarities in U.S. and Canadian federal systems, for instance, provide institutional controls for comparative analysis, but also limit the findings' generalizability. Yet, a few factors are particularly salient. To be sure, the role of extraurban actors and institutions in the U.S. urban policy process has changed the "ecology" of urban decision-making. In the EU and Canada, research on the opportunity structure of decision venues within the multilevel system draws out how partisan politics, institutional structure, and the nationalization and supra-nationalization of European advocacy groups affect the highly contextualized nature of issue mobilization and venue openness. As policy process and interest group literatures continue to cross-pollinate (Mahoney and Baumgartner 2008), we anticipate that scholars in the coming years will provide us with a much stronger sense of how institutional arrangements influence, and are influenced by, agenda-setting strategies.

In general, urban political scientists, both in the U.S. and abroad, are inattentive to the portfolio of issues and programs that comprise city policy agendas. However, a smattering of research does provide a few important insights. In a recent paper, Daniel Hopkins (2008) offers preliminary insights into the determinants of urban policy agendas through an analysis of data set of 97 State of the City Addresses. Though coefficient estimates are far from conclusive, his descriptive findings are perhaps most impactful as he shows that mayors, on average, spend as much time on issues of the environment, education, crime, and transportation, as they do on economic and community development.[17] Jordan's (2003) work on urban budgeting, which we survey above, also calls into question the fixed centrality of the urban "growth imperative." Her analyses suggest that whereas rapid enhancements in expenditures on development are more common, so too are drastic decreases, illustrative of a more multifarious and contingent process of urban policy politics.

In all, we contend that our survey draws out a consistent storyline. This storyline is not meant to be derisory. However, it is meant to complicate existing explanations of urban policymaking. As scholars of urban politics have illustrated,

17. Gerber and Hopkins (2009) examine the impact of mayoral partisanship on city budgetary spending to show that public safety spending, an area with a high degree of mayoral discretion, is most affected by partisanship (Democrats spend more; especially in close elections). Other urban issue areas, such as taxation and social concerns, are undetermined by partisan shifts.

structure matters in urban politics. Consequently, issues of land use, taxation, and community vitalization occupy a great deal of urban policymakers' limited attention. Or at least we think this is the case. Moreover, enough evidence exists to show that, when a particular "solution set" is disrupted by either external or internal perturbations, considerable positive feedback can be generated to effect substantive policy change. We do not know much about the context of these changes from a cross-sectional standpoint. Nor do we have a systematic understanding of the temporal connection between agenda building, policy continuity, and policy change. Indeed, we know even less about how national political climate and the structure of political institutions interact to manipulate agenda-setting opportunities for strategic actors. But we do have a sense of the processes, albeit in one or another city, one country or another, or at one or another point in time, by which change occurs. Not surprisingly, our survey indicates that city-level strategies of agenda setting, conflict expansion, and policy change bear a strong resemblance to comparable processes at the federal level.

4. Conclusion: The Promise of Urban Policy Agendas Research

This chapter began with a vignette about the dynamic intergovernmental politics of climate change policy. The example illustrates what we believe is an interesting phenomenon: The cascading of a particular policy issue across different levels of the U.S. system to drive spikes in attention, multilevel policy adoptions, and institutional restructuring. Yet, current theories of urban politics and policymaking are inattentive to such dynamics. Models that focus on the structural determinants of coalition formation, or that employ social choice models of policymaking, are inadequate for explaining urban agenda dynamics, particularly in the context of intergovernmental politics in the U.S. and abroad. A smattering of works focuses on these issues; though we are hard-pressed to mold these findings into even the roughest of frameworks concerning the determinants of urban policy agenda construction or the context for policy change. This is particularly dispiriting in light of the prevalence of city-level strategies of agenda setting.

We end this chapter, however, not on a discouraged note, but on a note of sanguinity. While many of the works we have surveyed (and others that we did not include) have offered more robust explanations for urban policy processes by incorporating elements of policy agenda dynamics, the enterprise has a long way to go. As Cobb, Ross, and Ross (1976) pointed out some time ago, the issue of agenda setting is principally appropriate for comparative analysis.

So, why not a comparative analysis of urban agendas? This prospective research program encompasses two core elements. The first addresses the issue of within-nation comparison. This is particularly relevant in the U.S. given the relative policymaking autonomy of subnational governments. Indeed, as we go to press, Xinsheng Liu and his associates (2010) have published a recent piece in *Policy Studies Journal* that relies upon 271 in-depth interviews with stakeholders from three U.S. Gulf Coast localities to illustrates how governmental actors and key interest groups influence local policy agendas. This study is certainly a step in the right direction. One must overcome a number of hurdles, including the lack of centralized data and the uniqueness of particular metropolitan structures, to conduct a large-scale comparative study of cities and localities. Yet, the leverage gained from examining the interplay of city-level policy inputs (e.g., newspaper, televised media, public agenda, elections) and outputs (e.g., budgetary outlays, spending, mayoral executive orders, statutes), contingent upon variations in formal structures (e.g., weak-mayor, strong-mayor, council-manager), regime or machine type (e.g., progressive, developmental, environmental), regional effects (e.g., Northeast, Midwest, Southeast), and other relevant factors, is exceedingly large.

How do urban agenda-setting processes vary across national boundaries? In the past, this question amounted to little more than a thought experiment. Yet globalizing political economic forces, along with the sustained development of multilevel governance in Europe, has guided a semiconvergence of "Western" policy processes across North America and Europe. It goes without mentioning that this convergence is far from absolute. Our simple point is that greater similarities in many facets of the policy process, ranging from the complexity of multilevel governing in the face of jurisdictional messiness, to intergovernmental approaches to issue advocacy, allow for more useful comparisons of how urban agendas are constructed and maintained in systems in which national parties play a much larger role in local decision-making or where federal systems are much more centralized.

To borrow from Sellers's (2002) delineation of national structures of local policymaking, one could address these questions through a comparison of city agendas in southern European cities, whose governments operate within a centralized federal system but also enjoy a relatively high agenda status in supralocal governing institutions, to policy agendas in urban governments operating within the highly decentralized U.S. federal system.[18] As has been a central theme in this chapter, evidence from the mishmash of studies on various dimensions of Western policy processes, if nothing else, illustrates one vital point: to understand how policy agendas are set, one must not simply consider the strategies of agenda-setting operatives, but how political environments structure agenda-setting opportunities and constraints. For urbanists, in both the U.S. and abroad, the chief promise of an urban agenda-setting research program is a more thorough understanding of the extent to which findings from the agenda-setting tradition can be generalized to city governments and, as a result, a more thorough understanding of urban policy politics.

18. To be sure, there are limitations to cross-national agenda studies. For instance, one might find less utility in comparing urban agendas across more centralized, "corporatist"-style federal systems (such as those found in the Germanic and Scandinavian nations) where central governments formally standardize most of what local officials can do and local policy agendas are driven by political parties and highly organized economic interests.

A second, and perhaps less obvious, payoff should also result from a study of urban policy agendas. Throughout this chapter, we have suggested that agenda-setting frameworks developed at the national level have much to offer scholars with an interest in explaining the origins and composition of urban policy agendas. We are also confident that research on urban policy agendas will enrich our more general understanding of policy agendas and policy change. The literature on policy agendas has been largely developed inside the U.S. context; consequently, scholars tend to focus on single policymaking systems over a substantial period of time. The field has a much weaker sense, for instance, of why certain problems gain agenda status at particular points in time or of the level of influence assigned to various factors that are important to theories of policy change. In most analyses, significant determinants of major policy change—such as exogenous shocks, interest group mobilizations, entrepreneurial machinations, and internal system dynamics—are shown to occur at roughly the same time. The ability of policy scholars to discern among these forces is associated with the number of comparable cases in which the scholar is interested, with more cases obviously permitting additional "degrees of freedom."

It was not until recently that scholars have begun to apply theories of agenda setting to comparative politics of policymaking (Baumgartner, Green-Pedersen, and Jones 2006). A current research program extends the U.S. Policy Agendas Project to a number of European nations as a means of determining the transportability of punctuated equilibrium theory for explaining budgetary changes (Jones et al. 2009) and policy outputs more generally (Baumgartner et al. 2009). What these scholars are finding is that they can offer more authoritative explanations of evolving policy dynamics based on systematic variations across nations in institutional "friction", party politics, and the relative strength of different branches of government. Not surprisingly, as comparative policy scholars devote more attention to agenda dynamics, the import and consequence of institutions in the agenda-setting process becomes increasingly clear (see Mahoney and Baumgartner 2008). In a recent analysis of the relationship between urban governance arrangements and budget volatility, Sapotichne (2011b) applies the "comparative friction" logic to illustrate that the consolidation of policymaking authority in either branch of city government seems to reduce volatility in spending patterns. Changes to the institutional cost structure through the incorporation of empowered bodies or transactive processes, however, lead to stepwise increases in volatility. Though far from definitive, this early finding underscores the importance of comparative urban agendas work for isolating the sources of incremental and punctuated policy processes.

In all, comparative studies of policy agendas have opened the door for less overdetermined theories of the policy process as they provide insights that both reaffirm the dynamic processes of policy change, while also contextualizing and clarifying the significance of particular forces. For us, this encapsulates the promise of comparative urban agendas research—a systematic analysis of city-level public and formal policy agendas over a significant amount of time that will assuredly provide important lessons that transcend political and jurisdictional boundaries.

REFERENCES

Altshuler, A. A. and J. A. Gomez-Ibanez. 1993. Regulation for revenue: The political economy of land-use exactions. Washington, DC: Brookings.

Altshuler, A. A. and D. Luberoff. 2003. Mega-projects: The changing politics of urban public investments. Washington, DC: Brookings.

Anton, T. 1989. American federalism and public policy. Philadelphia: Temple University Press.

Apollo Alliance, Green for All, Center for American Progress, and Center on Wisconsin Strategy. 2008. Green-collar jobs in America's cities. Accessed online August 25, 2009, from http://www.americanprogress.org/issues/2008/03/pdf/green_collar_jobs.pdf.

Bacharach, P. and M. S. Baratz. 1962. The two faces of power. *American Political Science Review* 56: 947–52.

———. 1970. Power and poverty. New York: Oxford University Press.

Bachelor, L. W. 1998. Stadiums as solution sets. *Review of Policy Research* 15: 89–102.

———. 1994. Regime maintenance, solution sets, and urban economic development. *Urban Affairs Review* 29: 596–616.

Banfield, E. C. and J. Q. Wilson. 1963. City politics. Cambridge, MA: Harvard University Press.

Baumgartner, F. R. et al. 2009. Punctuated equilibrium in comparative perspective. *American Journal of Political Science* 533: 603–20.

Baumgartner, F. R., C. Green-Pedersen, and B. D. Jones. 2006. Comparative studies of policy agendas. *Journal of European Public Policy* 13: 959–74.

Baumgartner, F. R. and B. D. Jones. 1993. Agendas and instability in American politics. Chicago: University of Chicago Press.

Berman, D. R. 2003. Local government and the states: Autonomy, politics, and policy. Armonk, NY: M. E. Sharpe.

Beyers, J. 2004. Voice and access: Political practices of European interest associations. *European Union Politics* 5: 211–40.

Beyers, J., R. Eising, and W. Maloney. 2008. Embedding interest group research. *West European Politics* 31: 1292–302.

Breunig, C. and C. Koski. 2006. Punctuated equilibria and budgets in the American states. *Policy Studies Journal* 34: 363–79.

Burns, N. and G. Gamm. 1997. Creatures of the state: State politics and local government, 1871–1921. *Urban Affairs Review* 33: 59–96.

Burns, P. 2003. Regime theory, state government, and a takeover of urban education. *Journal of Urban Affairs* 25: 285–303.

———. 2002. The intergovernmental regime and public policy in Hartford, Connecticut. *Journal of Urban Affairs* 24: 55–73.

Busch, P. O. and H. Jorgens. 2005. The international sources of policy convergence: Explaining the spread of environmental policy innovations. *Journal of European Public Policy* 12: 860–84.

Cairney, P. 2009. The role of ideas in policy transfer. *Journal of European Public Policy* 16: 471–88.

Cobb, R. W. and C. E. Elder. 1983. Participation in American politics. Baltimore: Johns Hopkins University Press.

Cobb, R., J.-K. Ross, and M. H. Ross. 1976. Agenda building as a comparative political process. *American Political Science Review* 70: 126–38.

Constantelos, J. 2010. Playing the field. *Publius* 40: 460–83.
———. 2007. Interest group strategies in multi-level Europe. *Journal of Public Affairs* 7: 39–53.
Crenson, M. A. 1971. The un-politics of air pollution. Baltimore: John Hopkins University Press.
Crow, D. A. 2010. Local media and experts: Sources of environmental policy initiation? *Policy Studies Journal* 38: 143–64.
Davies, J. S. 2003. Partnerships versus regimes. *Journal of Urban Affairs* 25: 253–69.
DeLeon, R. 1992. Left coast city: Progressive politics in San Francisco, 1975–1991. Lawrence: University Press of Kansas.
Durose, C. and V. Lowndes. 2010. Neighbourhood governance: Contested rationales within multi-level setting study of Manchester. *Local Government Studies* 36: 341–59.
Easton, D. 1965. A systems analysis of political life. New York: Wiley.
Eidelman, G. and Z. Taylor. 2010. Canadian urban politics: Another "black hole"? *Journal of Urban Affairs* 32: 305–20.
Eising, R. 2007. Institutional context, organizational resources and strategic choices. *European Union Politics* 8: 329–62.
Eisinger, P. K. 1998. Partners for growth: State and local relations in economic development, In Hanson, R. L., ed., Governing partners. Boulder, CO: Westview Press.
———. 2000. The politics of bread and circuses. *Urban Affairs Review* 35: 316–33.
Elkin, S. L. 1987. City and regime politics in the American republic. Chicago: University of Chicago Press.
Fainstein, S. S. and D. R. Judd. 1999. Cities as places to play. In Judd, D. R. and S. S. Fainstein, eds., The tourist city. New Haven, CT: Yale University Press.
Fleischmann, A., G. P. Green, and T. M. Kwong. 1991. What's a city to do? Explaining differences in local economic development policies. *Western Political Quarterly* 45: 677–99.
Friedman, T. L. 2008. Win, win, win, win, win... *New York Times*, December 28: WK8.
Gerber, E. R. and D. J. Hopkins. 2011. When mayors matter: Estimating the impact of mayoral partisanship on city policy. *American Journal of Political Science* 55: 326–39.
Givel, M. 2006. Punctuated equilibrium in limbo: The tobacco lobby and U.S. state policy making from 1990–2003. *Policy Studies Journal* 34: 405–418.
Goetz, E. G. 1990. Type II policy and mandated benefits in economic development. *Urban Affairs Review* 26: 170–90.
Guiraudon, V. 2000. European integration and migration policy: Vertical policy-making as venue shopping. *Journal of Common Market Studies* 38: 251–71.
Harding, A. 1994. Urban regimes and growth machines: Towards a cross-national research agenda. *Urban Affairs Quarterly* 29: 356–82.
Hilgartner, S. and C. L. Bosk. 1988. The rise and fall of social problems. *American Journal of Sociology* 94: 53–78.
Hopkins, D. J. 2008. The origins of the urban political agenda. Paper presented at the Annual Meeting of the American Political Science Association, Boston, August 30.
Imbroscio, D. L. 1997. Reconstructing city politics. Thousand Oaks, CA: Sage.
Jeffery, C. 2000. Sub-national mobilization and European integration. *Journal of Common Market Studies* 38: 1–23.
John, P. and A. Cole. 1998. Urban regimes and local governance in Britain and France: Policy adoption and coordination in Leeds and Lille. *Urban Affairs Review* 33: 382–404.
———. 2000. When do institutions, policy sectors, and cities matter? *Comparative Political Studies* 33: 248–68.

Jones, B. D. et. al. 2009. A general empirical law of public budgets. *American Journal of Political Science* 534: 855–973.

Jones, B. D. and L. W. Bachelor. 1993. 2nd ed. The sustaining hand: Community leadership and corporate power. Lawrence: University Press of Kansas.

Jones, B. D. and F. R. Baumgartner. 2005. The politics of attention. Chicago: University of Chicago Press.

Jones, B. D., F. R. Baumgartner, and J. L. True. 1998. Policy punctuations: U.S. budget authority, 1947–1995. *Journal of Politics* 60: 1–33.

Jones, B. D., T. Sulkin, and H. Larsen. 2003. Policy punctuations in American political institutions. *American Political Science Review* 97: 151–70.

Jones, C. L. and C. Hill. 1998. Strategy and tactics in subsystem protection: The politics of education reform in Montgomery County, Maryland. In Stone, C. N., ed., Changing urban education. Lawerence: University Press of Kansas.

Jones, V. 2008. The green collar economy: How one solution can fix our two biggest problems. New York: Harper One.

Jordan, M. M. 2003. Punctuations and agendas: A new look at local government budget expenditures. *Journal of Policy Analysis and Management* 22: 345–60.

Judd, D. R. 2003. Building the tourist city, editor's introduction. In Judd, D. R., ed., The infrastructure of play: Building the tourist city. Armonk, NY: M. E. Sharpe.

Judd, D. R. and D. Simpson. 2003. Reconstructing the local state: The role of external constituencies in building urban tourism. *American Behavioral Scientist* 46: 1056–69.

Judd, D. R. and J. M. Smith. 2007. The New ecology of urban governance: Special purpose authorities and urban development. In Hambleton, R. and J. S. Gross., eds., Governing cities in a global era: Urban innovation, competition and democratic reform. Hampshire, UK: Macmillan.

Kantor, P. M. and S. M. David. 1988. The dependent city: The changing political economy of urban America, New York: Scott Foresman.

Keating, M. and L. Hooghe. 2006. Bypassing the nation-state? Regions and the EU policy process. In Richardson, J., ed., European Union: Power and policy-making. New York: Routledge.

Kennedy, D. 2009. Urban renewal: An approach to building and sustaining a green-collar economy. *EDA America: Quarterly Insights and Best Practices in Economic Development*, Spring: 1–3.

Kerber, W. and M. Eckardt. 2007. Policy learning in Europe: The open method of co-ordination and laboratory federalism. *Journal of European Public Policy* 14: 227–47.

Knill, C. 2005. Introduction: Cross-national policy convergence: Concepts, approaches and explanatory factors. *Journal of European Public Policy* 12: 764–74.

Koski, C. 2010. Greening America's skylines: The diffusion of low-salience policies. *Policy Studies Journal* 38: 93–117.

Liu, X., E. Lindquist, A. Vedlitz, and K. Vincent. 2010. Understanding local policymaking: Policy elites' perceptions of local agenda setting and alternative policy selection. *Policy Studies Journal* 38: 69–91.

Lowi, T. J. 1964. Review: American business, public policy, case-studies, and political theory. *World Politics* 16: 677–715.

———. 1972. Four systems of policy, politics and choice. *Public Administration Review* 32: 298–310.

Mahoney, C. and F. R. Baumgartner. 2008. Converging perspectives on interest group research in Europe and America. *West European Politics* 31: 1292–302.

Marcus, C. 2009. Greening a brick city: A look at Newark's collaborative process to building a green economy. *EDA America: Quarterly Insights and Best Practices in Economic Development*, Spring: 6–7.
Marschall, M. and P. Shah. 2005. Keeping policy churn off the agenda: Urban education and civic capacity. *Policy Studies Journal* 33: 161–80.
May, P. J. 1986. Politics and policy analysis. *Political Science Quarterly* 101: 109–25.
May, P. J., J. Sapotichne, and S. Workman. 2006. Policy coherence and policy domains. *Policy Studies Journal* 34: 381–403.
Miller, L. L. 2008. The perils of federalism. New York: Oxford University Press.
———. 2007. The representational biases of federalism. *Perspectives on Politics* 5: 305–21.
Mitchell, J. 1990. The policy activities of public authorities. *Policy Studies Journal* 18: 928–42.
Molotch, H. 1976. The city as a growth machine: Toward a political economy of place. *American Journal of Sociology* 82: 309–32.
Mossberger, K. 2008. Urban regime analysis. In Davies, J. S. and D. L. Imbroscio, eds., Theories of urban politics, 2nd ed. Los Angeles: Sage.
Mossberger, K. and Stoker, G. 2001. The evolution of urban regime theory: The challenge of conceptualization. *Urban Affairs Review* 36: 810–35.
Nicodemus, D. M. 2004. Mobilizing information: Local news and the formation of viable political communities. *Political Communication* 21: 161–76.
Orr, M. and G. Stoker. 1994. Urban regimes and leadership in Detroit. *Urban Affairs Quarterly* 30: 48–73.
Peterson, P. E. 1981. City limits. Chicago: University of Chicago Press.
———. 1995. *The Price of Federalism*. Washington, DC: Brookings.
Peterson, P. E., B. G. Rabe, and K. Wong. 1986. When federalism works. Washington, DC: Brookings.
Portz, J. 1994. Plant closings, community definitions and local response. In Rochefort, D. A. and R. W. Cobb, eds., The politics of problem definition. Lawrence: University Press of Kansas.
Pralle, S. B. 2003. Venue shopping, political strategy, and policy change. *Journal of Public Policy* 23: 233–60.
———. 2006. Branching out, digging in: Environmental advocacy and agenda setting. Washington, DC: Georgetown University Press.
Princen, S. 2007. Agenda setting in the European union. *Journal of European Public Policy* 14: 21–38.
Princen, S. and B. Kerremans. 2008. Opportunity structures in the EU multilevel system. *West European Politics* 31: 1129–46.
Princen, S. and M. Rhinard. 2006. Crashing and creeping: Agenda-setting dynamics in the European Union. *Journal of European Public Policy* 13: 1119–32.
Purcell, M. 2000. The decline of the political consensus for urban growth: Evidence from Los Angeles. *Journal of Urban Affairs* 22: 85–100.
Rabe, B. G. 2007. Beyond Kyoto: Climate change policy in multilevel governance systems. *Governance* 20: 423–44.
Radaelli, C. 2000. Policy transfer in the European Union: Institutional isomorphism as a source of legitimacy. *Governance* 13: 25–43.
Richardson, J. 2000. Government, interest groups and policy change. *Political Studies* 48: 1006–25.
Ripley, R. B. and G. A. Franklin. 1990. Congress, the bureaucracy, and public policy. Chicago: Dorsey Press.

Rochefort, D. A. and R. W. Cobb, eds. 1994. The politics of problem definition. Lawrence: University Press of Kansas.

Sanders, H. T. and C. N. Stone. 1987. Development policy reconsidered. *Urban Affairs Review* 224: 521–39.

Sapotichne, J. 2011a. Regime capacity and strategic rhetoric: how to frame the debate over publicly financed sports stadiums. Working paper, Michigan State University.

———. 2011b. Why some institutions produce more punctuated outputs than others: institutional costs and urban policy agendas. Paper presented at the Comparative Agendas Conference, University of Catania, Catania, Italy, June 23–25.

Sapotichne, J., B. D. Jones, and M. Wolfe. 2007. Is urban politics a black hole? Analyzing the boundary between political science and urban politics. *Urban Affairs Review* 43: 76–106.

———. 2008. Response to the black hole debate. *Urban News* 22: 16–19.

Sapotichne, J. and J. M. Smith. Forthcoming. Venue shopping and the politics of urban development: Lessons from Chicago and Seattle. *Urban Affairs Review*.

Sbragia, A. M. 1996. Debt wish: Entrepreneurial cities, U.S. federalism and economic development. Pittsburgh: University of Pittsburgh Press.

Schneider, M. and P. Teske. 1993. The antigrowth entrepreneur: Challenging the equilibrium of the growth machine. *Journal of Politics* 553: 720–36.

Schneider, M., P. Teske, and M. Mintrom. 1995. Public entrepreneurs. Princeton, NJ: Princeton University Press.

Schreurs, M. A. 2008. From the bottom up: Local and subnational climate change politics. *Journal of Environment and Development* 17: 343–55.

Sellers, J. M. 2002. Governing from below: Urban regions and the global economy. Cambridge: Cambridge University Press.

Sharp, E. B. 1996. Culture wars and city politics: Local government's role in social conflict. *Urban Affairs Review* 31: 738–58.

———. 1997a. A comparative anatomy of urban social conflict. *Political Research Quarterly* 50: 261–80.

———. 1997b. Policy process. In Vogel, R. K., ed., Handbook of research on urban politics and policy in the United States. Westport, CT: Greenwood.

———. 2007. Revitalizing urban research: Can cultural explanations bring us back from the periphery? *Urban Affairs Review* 43: 55–75.

Shipan, C. R. and C. Volden. 2006. Bottom-up policy federalism. *American Journal of Political Science* 50: 825–43.

Sonenshein, R. J. and T. Hogan-Esch. 2006. Bringing the state (government) back in: Home rule and the politics of secession in Los Angeles and New York City. *Urban Affairs Review* 41: 467–91.

Steinacker, A. 2001. Prospects for regional governance: Lessons from the Miami abolition vote. *Urban Affairs Review* 37: 100–18.

Stoker, G. 1995. Regime theory and urban politics. In Judge, D., G. Stoker, and H. Wolman, eds., Theories of urban politics. London: Sage.

Stoker, G. and K. Mossberger. 1994. Urban regime theory in comparative perspective. *Environment and Planning C: Government and Policy* 12: 195–212.

Stone, C. N. 1987. The study of the politics of urban development. In Stone, C. and H. Sanders, eds., The politics of urban development. Lawrence: University Press of Kansas.

———. 1989. Regime politics. Lawrence: University Press of Kansas.

———. 2001. The Atlanta experience re-examined. *International Journal of Urban and Regional Research* 25: 20–34.

———. 2005. Looking back to look forward: Reflections on urban regime analysis. *Urban Affairs Review* 40: 309–41.

Stone, C. N., J. Henig, B. D. Jones, and C. Pierannunzi. 2001. Building civic capacity: The new politics of urban school reform. Lawrence: University Press of Kansas.

Stone, C. N., M. Orr, and D. Worgs. 2006. The flight of the bumblebee. *Perspectives on Politics* 4: 529–46.

Tatham, M. 2010. With or without you? Revisiting territorial state-bypassing in EU interest representation. *Journal of European Public Policy* 17: 76–99.

True, J. L. 2000. Avalanches and incrementalism: Making policy and budgets in the United States. *American Review of Public Administration* 30: 3–18.

United States Conference of Mayors 2007. Survey on mayoral leadership on climate protection. http://www.usmayors.org/climateprotection/climatesurvey07.pdf. Accessed February 1, 2009.

Van de Steeg, M. 2006. Does a public sphere exist in the EU? An analysis of the content of the debate on the Haider case. *European Journal of Political Research* 45: 609–34.

Wendon, B. 1998. The commission as image-venue entrepreneur in EU social policy. *Journal of European Public Policy* 5: 339–53.

Wolman, H. and D. Spitzley. 1996. The politics of local economic development. *Economic Development Quarterly* 10: 115–50.

Wood, R. S. 2006. Tobacco's tipping point: The master settlement agreement as a focusing event. *Policy Studies Journal* 34: 419–36.

Yin, R. K. 1980. Creeping federalism: The federal impact on the structure and function of local government. In Glickman, N. J., ed., Urban impacts of federal policies. Baltimore: Johns Hopkins University Press.

Zahariadis, N. 2008. Ambiguity and choice in European public policy. *Journal of European Public Policy* 15: 514–30.

Zimmerman, J. F. 2008. Contemporary American federalism. Albany: SUNY Press.

CHAPTER 23

THE POLITICS OF URBAN GROWTH AND DECLINE

PAUL KANTOR AND IVAN TUROK

THE politics of urban growth and decline involves governments at all levels in addressing the complexity of socioeconomic change in specific places. These are more than purely *local* matters concerning the location of new development, the design of the urban fabric, or the quality of community services. Broader tiers of government are increasingly engaged in the fortunes of particular places on the grounds that they matter greatly to the achievement of wider regional and national goals. Metropolitan areas, in particular, have come to be seen as drivers of national economic development and sources of resilience in a context of intensified global competition (Castells 2000; Scott 2001; Hall and Pain 2006; Sassen 2006; 1998). Recognition of the heightened significance of cities and metropolitan regions has been accompanied in many countries by greater decentralization of policy responsibilities from national government to regional and local institutions, although the extent to which this has occurred and the explanations for it are contested (Brenner 2004; Rodriguez-Pose and Gill 2005; Pike and Tomaney 2009).

Urban growth and decline is also a key field of study in urban politics. Political scientists and sociologists regard the engagement of urban political systems with the economy and demographic change as central to understanding local policy and politics. Indeed, some critics caution that focus on urban development politics is excessive, and call for shifting the attention of theory to other dimensions of local political life that are sometimes marginalized in contemporary investigation (Sapotichne, Jones, and Wolfe 2007).

Over the last two decades urban policy itself has been transformed in many countries from an agenda dominated by concerns about employment decline, social distress, and physical decay, to one that is also associated with economic dynamism, social vitality, and physical renaissance (Buck et al. 2005; Cochrane 2007). Cities are increasingly perceived to be places that can help nations and regions to gain competitive advantage through innovation and productivity growth, and by attracting mobile talent and investment (OECD 2006; European Commission 2006; World Bank 2009). The long tradition of piecemeal urban initiatives and remedial social projects is also being replaced in some places by a more integrated, multilevel approach to urban policy—essentially taking cities more seriously. In the process, many cities are becoming more discriminating about the nature or "quality" of growth pursued, with a preference for high value, socially inclusive, and durable development rather than maximizing the sheer quantity of investment and activity (Buck et al. 2005; Turok 2009).

The purpose of this chapter is to explore the literature and arguments that have emerged over the last two decades about the politics of urban policy in Europe and North America. We consider the debates about the emergence of a stronger economic dimension to urban policy and what this means for social cohesion and democracy. We also discuss the significance of policy decentralization and the consequences for different kinds of places and people. We argue that local political processes matter to the social and economic trajectories of cities and that decentralization can be a positive force for prosperity and participation, although it can also be subverted for narrower political purposes and exacerbate inequalities.

The structure of the chapter is as follows: The next section considers the economic sources and impacts of recent urban growth. The second section discusses the political processes that contribute to urban success. The third section contrasts different political theories of urban policy. Section 4 compares different perspectives on developments in Europe and North America. The fifth section examines who benefits from urban policy. The conclusion draws the threads together and outlines some directions for future research.

1. Economic Dimensions of Urban Growth

Growing policy interest in metropolitan areas partly reflects a popular argument that urban communities make a disproportionate contribution to national prosperity, particularly in advanced economies where knowledge, ideas, and intellectual resources are increasingly the basis of competitive success (Taylor 2004; Hall and Pain 2006; HM Treasury 2008; World Bank 2009). The argument certainly has some foundation, although it has tended to run well ahead of the evidence to the point where it has become uncritically accepted as a universal truth among many national and international organizations (Buck et al. 2005; Turok and Mykhnenko 2008). Cities are believed to be engines of wealth creation through the spatial concentration of productive activity, entrepreneurs, workers, and consumers. Proximity facilitates sharing infrastructure and information, matching the distinctive requirements of firms for specialized labor and suppliers, and learning about new techniques, products, and processes through face-to-face contact. This is thought to lower business costs, increase flexibility, reduce risks, stimulate creative thinking, and improve product quality—a potent mixture.

The forces for agglomeration are also said to be reinforced by globalization and the accelerated pace of contemporary economic change. The spread of information and communications technology (ICT) and the decline in transport costs privilege access to international markets for well-connected places, or "hubs" in the wider system of information, trade, and financial flows (Castells 2000; Sassen 2006). In a more competitive environment, specialization among firms and among cities helps them to gain differential advantage, and is reinforced by knowledge spillovers, localized learning, and cooperation among firms, their suppliers, and service providers (Porter 1998; Storper 1997). The faster pace of change also makes it more important for cities to be alert and responsive to external developments, including opportunities to attract new forms of investment and threats arising from environmental and regulatory changes. The increasing openness of national borders means that the fortunes of cities are linked more closely to international events and therefore vulnerable to forces beyond their control, such as the recent global financial crisis.

Contemporary demographic trends have arguably strengthened the position of cities as well. Within many parts of Europe and North America the average household size has been falling and personal mobility has been rising. Single adult households, couples with no children, and families with two or more people in work have been increasing (Turok and Mykhnenko 2007). Their demand for proximity to central city jobs, amenities, and lifestyles is stronger than for the archetypal suburban family of two parents and several children but only one breadwinner. Cities also contain the social infrastructure, universities, and career choices to help regions and nations in the competition to attract students, young professionals, and other talented workers required to generate and exploit knowledge (Glaeser and Gottlieb 2006; Florida 2004). Falling barriers to international migration within the enlarged European Union and, to a lesser extent, the North American Free Trade Association have made it easier for people to move between countries. Migrant workers have usually settled in major cities, where the choice of jobs, housing, and community services is better than elsewhere. Illegal immigration has also grown in response to global inequalities in labor markets, and new migrants are becoming a major presence in selected cities and suburbs. The political consequences of the changing social composition of these urban areas have not been widely studied, although it appears from media reports that xenophobia is increasing in many places.

This process of concentrated growth or "urban resurgence" has been offset by other forces promoting the dispersal or deconcentration of activity and population, including congestion, rising property prices, and high labor costs. This has occurred at different scales—within metropolitan areas from central cities to suburbs; within regions from large to smaller cities and towns; and within nations from primate cities to secondary cities—making it all the more important to work with a clear and consistent definition of the "city." The net effect or overall outcome has varied among countries depending on factors such as the size and economic structure of cities and the role of public policy in seeking to contain or support urbanization (Turok 2004; Turok and Mykhnenko 2008). Cities with a large manufacturing sector, for example, have tended to suffer both from employment decentralization and deindustrialization, often with devastating effects on the well-being of local communities and tarnishing the city's image as a business location. Apart from this, the pattern of strong and weak performing cities in Europe and North America has not been adequately explained by researchers.

A parallel argument has been that changes associated with globalization have made location less significant and cities less important. Pronouncements about the "death of distance," "end of geography," and, most recently, the "world is flat" (Friedman 2005 claims that developments in ICT (such as the Internet, standardized software, and videoconferencing), deregulated markets (allowing outsourcing and offshoring), and the integration of regional and national economies are eliminating the "friction of distance" and flattening the world economy. Firms, workers, and urban areas everywhere are said to have access to a whole new platform that enables them to connect, compete, and collaborate in a more interconnected global economy. These provocative ideas run counter to the conventional understanding that access to this new facility is uneven, and that other wealth-creating factors (such as investment capital, innovation capacity, and skilled labor) are still very unequally distributed (Christopherson, Garretsen, and Martin 2008). The prevailing view is that some places (particularly major cities with high levels of connectivity and amenity) are better positioned than others to prosper from the enlarged international markets and access to resources afforded by globalization.

In sum, most scholars believe that globalization and economic integration heighten rather than diminish the importance of place-specific social and political institutions in the process of economic development and wealth creation (Barnes and Ledebur 1998; Storper 1997; Porter 1998). Indeed some see closer integration of private and public sectors in various "local production systems" (Crouch et al. 2001), suggesting that political and economic dimensions cannot be separated very easily.

2. Political Dimensions

Lively debates about prevailing economic tendencies indicate that the underlying forces are not immutable and particular outcomes are not inevitable. It is also clear that governments are potentially important in influencing the course of urbanization. To take a simple example from the above, they can help or hinder access to the new information and communications platform by their stance toward regulating and investing in electronic and physical connectivity. In addition, in a more market-oriented and volatile economy with greater mobility of capital and labor, there is little doubt that civic leaders feel under increasing pressure to compete in order to attract and retain investment, jobs, skills, knowledge, and other resources. Government conditions the competition through its structures, procedures, rules, and signals, both deliberately and unintentionally. Broadly speaking, North American governments have traditionally been more supportive of territorial competition than those in Europe, although some of the latter have shifted their position over time in recognition that it can serve useful political purposes at a time when macroeconomic policies are constrained by globalization (Turok 2004). During the early 1990s, for example, the UK government deliberately introduced competitive bidding into the allocation of selected public funds in order to alter the mind-set and culture of local authorities toward emphasizing enterprise and opportunity rather than need and entitlement. Government is also forced to deal with many of the social and environmental consequences of growth and decline at the local level, and to manage the macroeconomic effects, which may include higher unemployment and welfare spending (in the case of decline) and inflated house prices and wage costs (in the case of rapid or imbalanced growth).

Different levels of government act in different ways and with different tools and techniques. At the local level, efficient basic infrastructure and an effective supply of serviced land are among the preconditions for urban economic development (Bartik 2009). A high quality education and training system is another essential function of the public sector to ensure adequate human capital and to retain the benefits of growth within the locality (Donegan et al. 2008). Experience suggests that practical advice, financial support, and venture capital for small business formation and growth can also be worthwhile tasks for local authorities. Former industrial cities may need special public investment in urban amenities and cultural facilities to shift popular perceptions and broaden their appeal to mobile workers, visitors, and investors, although this is controversial because of the uncertain economic impacts and potentially narrow beneficiaries (Florida 2004; Bartik 2009; Donegan et al. 2008). An underlying dilemma is whether the strategic emphasis is on promoting cities as centers of production (including advanced producer services, creative industries, and modern manufacturing) or consumption (including entertainment, culture, universities, and tourism) (Glaeser and Gottlieb 2006; Turok 2009).

Governments influence urban economies indirectly too. Differences in organizational structures, responsibilities, and financial arrangements among local, regional, and national authorities can shape the course of city development. For example, the United States federal system of fiscal decentralization makes local and state governments more reliant on self-generated revenues than in many countries. This has made urban prosperity and the welfare of residents more dependent on private investment and created powerful incentives to compete (Sbragia 1999). This, in turn, has contributed to uneven development as businesses and residents quit established locations with higher social costs in favor of lower tax jurisdictions. Since the 1980s, fiscal decentralization and federal cuts in urban aid programs have grown, linked to the conservative political tide in national politics. This has increased the disparities between rich and poorer localities, and encouraged business and household relocation to areas with lower taxes and weaker regulations. These forms of decentralization often have exacerbated inner city poverty, although it has also been suggested that they have expanded the choices of selected citizens and made government more efficient (Kantor 1995; Fainstein and Fainstein 1989; Dreier, Mollenkopf, and Swanstrom 2004).

In contrast, western European governments tend toward stronger national welfare policies and fiscal equalization schemes to limit the disparities between local authorities and to stabilize those experiencing economic decline. Principles underpinning the allocation of public resources include territorial equity (or "fairness"), and common social citizenship (or "solidarity"), reflected in the pooling of risks and sharing of resources across communities so that differential needs can be met more effectively. These policies are reinforced by European Union "territorial cohesion" programs serving similar purposes, although with much more modest funding. In recent years the situation has begun to change with European governments embarking on a (selective) process of scaling back equity-based spatial policies and decentralizing responsibilities to regions and localities. This has often been justified in the interests of efficiency (or "competitiveness") in the sense of reducing state constraints on business and enabling places to realize their potential. It should improve the flexibility and responsiveness of economic policy to diverse circumstances on the ground and encourage greater policy variety and innovation. Nevertheless, their fiscal systems remain more centralized than in the US and Canada and many universal welfare programs are unaffected. Some scholars have been critical of the direction of these changes on grounds that they expose vulnerable urban communities to the vicissitudes of the market and weaken national redistributive and democratic arrangements (Lovering 1999; Peck 2002; Brenner 2004).

3. Political Theory and Urban Development

Urban growth and decline are part of the same process of urban economic development. Put rather crudely, "winner" and "loser" communities share a common landscape or operating environment, but experience different fortunes. Most of the theoretical literature on the politics of urban development does not distinguish these outcomes as separate phenomena. Rather, they are perceived to reflect different degrees of success in the same basic system of institutional rules, procedures, and incentives. From an economic perspective, a potential criticism is that there appears to be an implicit assumption of a zero-sum process, namely that the benefits for one city come at the expense of another, with no net contribution to economic output or jobs across the economy. Some economic development policies may well conform to this assumption because they are essentially diversionary, such as competitive bidding for mobile investment or to host prominent sporting or cultural events. The activity is relatively discrete, it has to go somewhere, and its growth prospects are limited. However, other policies may have more productive outcomes, such as providing technical assistance to firms to enhance their processes, encourage product innovation, and sell their output into wider markets. Policies that result in more effective utilization of unemployed resources, such as labor and land, may also be considered productive from a national economic perspective (Bartik 2009).

The traditional urban development focus is on growth politics, on the assumption that local communities generally seek growth and avoid decay. This view is most evident in Peterson's landmark study *City Limits* (1981). Peterson argued that cities must avoid redistributive services, provide basic services at an adequate level, and devote most attention to policies that stimulate economic growth. He suggested that the social health of a city depends above all on its economic prosperity. When the economy is growing, tax revenues increase, city services can be improved, donations to charities become more generous, and the social and cultural life of the city is enhanced. He also suggested that civic leaders cannot leave economic growth to chance, especially since they lack the broad economic powers available to national government. If the local business environment is not conducive, investors and firms will go elsewhere. Recognition of this reality encourages cities to compete with each other to minimize taxes, avoid costly red tape, and offer business subsidies. There is an economic imperative at work, whatever the complexion of local politics.

Although other theoretical perspectives also portrayed growth politics as central to what cities do (Logan and Molotch 1987), Peterson's theory ignited years of controversy among political scientists. Many took Peterson to task for his assertion that growth benefits everyone. Others argued that he ignored the significance and complexities of urban politics. Some cautioned that there are different ways of promoting growth, which require political choices to be made by decision makers. Furthermore, whatever growth paths are chosen, they cannot be realized unless governing elites mobilize sufficient political support for them (Kantor and Judd 2008; Stone and Saunders 1987).

This alternative view was favored by the literature on "urban regimes." This focused on understanding the ways in which the tensions between the economy and local democracy are managed in promoting urban development. Proponents of regime theory argued that government officials lack the resources to do much on their own and need the cooperation of the business community in order to maintain the city as a place for investment and political stability. Regime participants—the dominant public and private players in local politics—learn to work together to accomplish mutual goals. All are empowered in the sense that they can accomplish things that none of them working alone could achieve. Business leaders are thought to remain particularly important on major development issues, even biasing critical public policies in their favor (Stone 1989).

Although this perspective was embraced by many urban scholars, particularly in the US, critics argue that the regime concept lacks explanatory power and theoretical rigor. Many of these criticisms are described elsewhere in this volume. In respect to urban development, however, critics generally fault regime theory for describing local governing coalitions without having much to say about powerful forces framing and influencing their decisions, such as global economic dislocations. (Sapotichine, Jones, and Wolfe 2007; Stoker 1995; Savitch and Kantor 2002; Mossberger 2009). Most important, regime theory has been difficult to apply outside North America, although it has oriented some Anglo-American comparative research (DiGaetano and Klemanski 1999). In western Europe, more centralized governmental conditions, the power of the public sector, and different civic traditions diminish the role of private elites in local development. This is one of the reasons why European and American scholarship has often differed. European scholarship focuses more on public sector dynamics than do many North American investigators. European researchers have also been more informed by social theories derived from Marxist and other radical traditions. In these perspectives, urban politics is usually regarded as an aspect of managing the social and political tensions of an inherently conflict-ridden and crisis-prone system of capitalism (Katznelson 1993). The local state has struggled to balance the contradictory requirements to support social reproduction and enable profitable private production.

Many western European scholars identify the shift from a "Fordist" (traditional mass production) to a "post-Fordist" (modern service-dominated) economy as central to understanding the processes of urban economic development and political change. Although usually neo-Marxist approaches assign a minor place to local politics in managing this transition, some afford it greater importance or "relative autonomy" from core accumulation and production processes (Jessop 1999a; 1999b). For instance, Castells (1977) regards urban social movements and the local provision of "collective consumption" activities (social services and welfare safety nets) as integral to the development of capitalism. Neo-Marxist theories and concepts are less influential than they once were in contemporary political analysis of urban growth and decline. Many critics find the ideas too abstract, functionalist (deterministic), and difficult to apply or evaluate empirically. Some of the underlying assumptions about the structure of society and the trajectory of capitalist development appear dated and out of step with the contemporary world. They cannot easily account for the variety of political and economic systems that coexist.

More recent works in the radical tradition has sought to overcome some of these criticisms. "Regulation" and related theorists argue that economic changes depend upon and partially reflect local developments in politics, culture, and social life (Painter 1995; Geddes 2009), indicating complex two-way relationships at work. In another direction, a body of work on the "varieties of capitalism" (Hall and Soskice 2001) also offers an alternative macro-view of public-private sector relations, although this has had limited application to the politics of cities and regions as yet (Crouch et al. 2001). Most recent European studies of the politics of urban development are quite eclectic. They rely on theoretical insights from organization theory, urban geography, and communications, as well as applied scholarship in planning and public administration (Le Galès 2002; Salet, Thornley, and Kreukels 2003; Jouve and Lefevre 2002; Terhorst and van de Ven 1997).

In sum, contemporary studies of the politics of urban economic development in Europe and North America are marked by fragmentation and the failure of any overarching theory to steer the agenda. This does not necessarily signify a lack of progress since the rich history of theoretical debate has enlivened this field of study. It could be argued that the lack of a dominant theoretical paradigm is a positive feature. It opens the subfield to sharing with and drawing upon competing ideas from the disciplinary mainstreams in political science, sociology, economics, and public policy (Sapotichne, Jones, and Wolfe 2007).

4. Global Influences and Comparative Urban Research

Awareness of global influences on local politics has been responsible for much greater stress on comparative urban research in recent years. As noted earlier, the emergence of interconnected cities playing specialized roles in the world economy has gained particular attention. In the past, most comparative research on urban development politics was often limited to Anglo-American comparisons or case studies of western European cities. More recent work has been broader in reach and more rigorous in comparative methodology. In addition, increasing attention is paid to understanding the political processes associated with urban decline as well as growth.

One line of comparative scholarship focuses on the "rescaling" of government (that is changes in the functions or decision-making of the state at different levels) in the process of urban development. This subject is described in detail elsewhere in this volume, highlighting how the functional area of cities has been expanding and how cities, suburbs, and the surrounding countryside are becoming more interdependent. Consequently, some have begun to explore the political implications of this "city-region" reality (Kantor 2006; Kantor et al. 2012; Basolo 2003; Macleod 2001). Sellers (2002) argues that nation-states rely increasingly upon constituting, but not dominating, local initiatives in their attempts to address economic stresses and environmental challenges. Governing from below appears to be replacing more prescriptive, top-down approaches. The UK government, for example, has stressed repeatedly in recent years that "city-regions will increasingly be critical to driving national and regional growth" (HM Treasury 2008, 52), and encouraged local authorities to work together on transport infrastructure, skills, and other policies for growth promotion.

Brenner (2004) also suggests that cities and regions have been undergoing major state restructuring in Europe and North America in response to globalizing capitalism. In his view, government action has been precipitated at the regional scale in order to accommodate new economic pressures. He argues that changing geographical arrangements of state institutions are connected to shifts in economic and social policy, and that policies once aimed at narrowing regional disparities are being replaced by neoliberal approaches that focus on boosting economic competitiveness. This chimes with the arguments of other authors that the "new regionalism" is primarily concerned with raising indigenous productivity and enabling each city or region to reach its own potential, rather than reducing spatial inequalities (Keating 1998; Scott 2001; Pike, Rodriguez-Pose, and Tomaney 2006).

Other comparative studies see less convergence among governments around neoliberal policies or state restructuring. They emphasize variation among national, regional, and local governments in responding to the changing international economy (Salet and Faludi 2000; Harding 2007; Newman and Thornley 2005; Kantor 2007; Kantor et al. 2012). Savitch and Kantor (2002) describe how cities draw upon particular bargaining positions as they compete for investment, concluding that local politics really matters to local economic outcomes. They observe that cities can potentially draw upon three different kinds of resources—their economic position, access to government support, and local democratic forces. First, cities with favorable economic circumstances are less vulnerable to the threat of private disinvestment and can therefore be more demanding about the social and environmental conditions they set in regulating new development. Cities with weak or shrinking economies are more dependent on the whims of investors. Second, cities in vertically integrated political systems usually enjoy access to national government resources and support in business regulation. Cities left largely to fend for themselves, as in federal systems, are under greater pressure to chase tax revenues and jobs. Finally, localities can bargain most effectively when their citizens demand public benefits from development and accountability from public officials. Thus, cities having well-developed popular control institutions and a quality-of-life demanding citizenry motivate more effective bargaining with the private sector than poorly governed cities dominated by citizens sharing low economic expectations.

In their survey of ten North American and western European cities, Kantor and Savitch describe how cities with greater cumulative bargaining resources tend to secure more public benefits from economic development than less resourceful cities. They also find that prosperous cities are not invariably capable of achieving better social outcomes than cities with weak economies. Less competitive cities can sometimes compensate for their lack of private investment with fiscal or regulatory support from central government. Although the mere possession of bargaining resources is not sufficient to ensure influence in the development process, these resources count if they are effectively mobilized by governing coalitions determined to extract concessions from investors and other business interests.

This bargaining perspective also suggests different ways in which local governments can manage decline. Few cities have no bargaining resources at all. Some kinds of resources, such as well-organized responsive political systems, can be created over time by committed citizens and local leaders. Whether these resources are used to address urban economic decay depends upon the presence of particular kinds of governing regimes with the strategic capacity and foresight to do so.

One response to decline is attempting to offset it, using strategies to leverage special public sector resources, such as urban renewal programs or one-off cultural events or sporting fixtures, instead of targeting private investment. The introduction of competitive bidding by some national governments to allocate this kind of discretionary spending may have encouraged this approach (Turok 2004). This strategy is most effective if it operates within a framework of longer-term objectives for the city so there is a degree of consistency and cumulative development over time—a kind of "structured opportunism." This was utilized with some success during the 1980s and 1990s by cities such as Marseilles in France, Manchester in England, and Glasgow in Scotland. The closest contemporary equivalent may be cities in central and eastern Europe that are currently facing significant population decline but also benefiting from European structural funds for infrastructure upgrading, business support, and skills training.

Alternatively, local governments may organize a "vendor" strategy, which involves governing elites accommodating private sector requirements with few demands made for additional public benefits beyond the immediate self-interest of the investors. It may mean granting businesses special privileges and simplified rules and procedures in the hope of attracting their money and jobs. The city seeks to build a reputation for being business-friendly through its speedy decision-making and undemanding requirements on issues such as the environment, social responsibility, and contributions to infrastructure costs. Detroit has been following this logic for decades in an effort to compensate for its abandonment by the auto industry and the state government, but with limited success (Savitch and Kantor 2002; Jones and Bachelor 1993).

Other approaches to managing decline mean ignoring investor demands in favor of purely local political goals. This is exemplified by the city of Naples, Italy, where public officials play down practical policies that might help revive the local economy in preference for running a political machine dominated by sustaining those in power. This kind of clientele politics is absorbed with exploiting business and government programs for short-term payoffs to individuals and their supporters, leaving the city's economic fortunes to chance. Although this may appear self-destructive, it can prove highly resilient because of its deep political entrenchment and local access to public funds in order to fuel the system.

Finally, there are uncommon cases when local government leaders pursue blatant confrontation with centers of economic and political power, sometimes abandoning pragmatic programs aimed at economic revitalization. This occurred in a range of British cities during the 1980s in response to a highly ideological Conservative Government under Margaret Thatcher which was intent on cutting local authority budgets and constraining their powers. It was most apparent and lasted longest in Liverpool, where a radical faction took over the local Labor Party and directly confronted the government (Savitch and Kantor 2002). This strategy of ideological challenge is invariably unstable and transitory because the targets of local challenge are so powerful and socially embedded, from central governments to the private marketplace with its system of corporate power. Central governments can mandate or abolish nonconformist local authorities, while private decision-makers can relocate their capital (Portz 1990).

5. Who Benefits From Urban Growth and Development?

There is considerable debate among policy researchers about whether the increasing range and sophistication of government programs has been effective at boosting urban economic performance. This is partly attributable to major methodological difficulties involved in disentangling policy impacts from other changes in the economic environment, and taking displacement and multiplier effects into account. It is also clearly difficult to generalize about policy effects in different places and indeed the available evidence seems to be quite mixed. Studies of incentives offered by local governments in the US and Canada find that the costs can escalate and the impact on business location decisions may be limited (Anderson and Wassmer 2000; Fisher and Peters 1998). In Europe, subsidies to support business relocation have fallen out of favor for similar reasons and are now regulated by the European Commission to avoid excessive incentives distorting competition unfairly. Efforts by cities in both continents to induce growth by promoting professional sporting activities, building exhibition centers, cultural amenities, and tourist attractions have often been criticized as wasteful and unproductive. Urban development trajectories reflect the interaction of complex economic and social systems, frequently beyond the reach of special local government programs, at least in the short term (Blair and Reese 1999).

There is also much debate about who the main beneficiaries are from public policies to promote urban development and growth. Vacant land may be redeveloped, businesses may become more productive and profitable, and local economic output may increase, while sections of the population remain impoverished. Many researchers have questioned whether urban policies are adequately targeted to benefit poor and vulnerable residents rather than landowners, speculative investors, business proprietors, and highly educated citizens (Blair and Reese 1999; Fainstein 2001; Sites 2003; see Frieden and Sagalyn 1989 for a contrasting view). For instance, policies aimed at revitalizing run-down business districts do not automatically benefit poor residential communities. In a context of excess labor supply, any jobs created from business support measures will probably not filter through to workless groups with low skills. Further, growth strategies aimed at entertainment, tourism, and other consumer service industries may produce mostly low paid, part-time, and temporary jobs that are not worthwhile for household heads on welfare benefits to pursue (Judd and Fainstein 1999; Foglesong 2001).

There is always a risk that urban development projects divide communities rather than draw them together. Older industrial cities sometimes seek ways of elevating their image and reinventing themselves as something more up-market and exclusive, which may alienate existing communities who feel cast aside. Efforts to attract new consumers and investors often produce gated communities and other segregated environments with poor and minority groups separated off from other citizens. American downtowns such as Atlanta, Los Angeles, and Boston have been remodeled with skywalks, park-like atriums in corporate buildings, new commercial centers, and protected tourist enclaves that are supposed to function like public spaces and parks. Yet they are often designed to deter ordinary city residents in the hope of making them more attractive to visitors and business people (Davis 2002; Judd 2002). Private shopping malls in the suburbs commonly discourage nonshoppers and may even be built to exclude pedestrians. Observers fear that historic squares, parks, and other public open spaces are being replaced by privately controlled spaces (Zukin 1995; Kohn 2004). The political struggle over "whose city?" has many faces.

In European cities, there is generally a stronger commitment to the public realm, although similar commercial pressures exist to privatize such spaces or to exclude the less well-off through strategic urban design measures and surveillance schemes. The outcomes vary greatly depending on the stance of civic leaders and the vigilance of voluntary bodies and community groups. A rather different source of tension has arisen in many European cities around immigration and the pressure on jobs, housing, schools, and other public services in poor inner city neighborhoods. New settlers put additional strains on already stretched facilities, which create resentment from existing communities, especially if special urban program resources are skewed to incoming groups. Many city leaders have shown courage and imagination in promoting social inclusion and cohesion by providing social housing, special instruction in schools, distinctive places of worship, and sponsoring religious and cultural festivals to raise awareness, celebrate diversity, and boost civic pride. Some have also supported minority group representation in different social sectors and helped to establish intercultural forums to promote dialogue and interaction between different religious and ethnic communities.

6. Conclusion

There has been increasing scholarly attention to the politics of growth and decline in Europe and North America over the last two decades. This is partly related to the rising interest among governments in the economic possibilities of cities and awareness of the importance of politics in shaping the economic well-being of urban places. Although the study of urban development politics and policy lacks a dominant theoretical perspective, most research supports the conclusion that political forces at multiple governmental levels are critical influences in the changing fortunes of cities, suburbs, and even whole metropolitan regions.

The idea of a broad economic imperative driving urban growth and decline hardly captures the complex reality that many social forces are at play in the course of urban change and that political choices always matter. For example, some observers (Brenner 2003, 2004) have interpreted the trend toward political decentralization as reflecting governmental adaptation to the imperative of making cities more competitive in an increasingly globalized economy. In this view globalization demands more sensitive, fine-grained policy responses tailored to localities, instead of broad-brush macroeconomic measures. The implications are that local and regional authorities are obliged to promote narrow economic objectives above wider social and environmental goals, and have limited discretion in relation to whose interests are served by their strategies. This outcome is generally understood to mean greater territorial inequality—both between and within regions. Thus, the transfer of powers and responsibilities downward is seen essentially as detrimental to the values of social cohesion, equity, and democracy.

Other observers (Savitch and Kantor 2002; Newman and Thornley 2005; Sellers 2002) have questioned these interpretations of policy developments. Decentralization does not necessarily mean that economic goals are predetermined or narrow, or that they outweigh social and environmental objectives. Civic leaders have scope to follow different strategies depending on local circumstances and bargaining resources. And policy decentralization does not invariably mean central government reneging on its responsibilities to reduce territorial inequalities—policies at different levels can be complementary, rather than one replacing the other. In short, there are many forms of growth politics. Local political processes still can be a positive force for economic and social prosperity. Decentralized governance arrangements may be subverted for narrow political purposes and may widen spatial disparities, but they may also be used for opposite objectives. The multilayered governmental nature of urban development policy, and the opportunities for alternative political responses to problems of growth and decline ensure that political choices always matter.

What of the implications for future research? One priority is to develop richer and more nuanced comparative analyses of the diverse institutional arrangements for economic development and their concrete effects on economic performance and social conditions. The politics of decentralization in urban development especially merits attention since this trend in government is accelerating throughout the Western industrial world. These accounts need to recognize that the transfer or sharing of powers and responsibilities is often variable and inconsistent across government departments and between regions, reflecting different considerations, political interests, and levels of resistance. The role of local and regional politics is also important in shaping the nature and scope of decentralization. Policy devolution does not reflect crude economic imperatives, nor does it occur in isolation of economic considerations. Future research requires a more balanced and detailed account, reflecting real-world complexities.

Another research priority is to explore the social, political, and economic consequences of urban economic growth and decline more fully. The benefits and costs of economic change may be distributed in different ways among those who live in urban places. Landowners, speculative investors, business proprietors, and people with different levels of human capital are likely to view the value of economic upheaval in their communities differently. There may be even more variable responses to population growth and in-migration involving different social groups. Yet the actual costs and benefits of change may be quite different to those perceived and they beg to be discovered. Similarly, better public policies to ameliorate problems associated with economic modernization and demographic change are always dependent upon better knowledge of the actual consequences for the citizens who live in communities undergoing transformation.

More work on comparative methods is also important. Greater clarity is needed to ensure that the language and variables used to describe phenomena in different countries are equivalent, even terms such as urban growth, decline, and decentralization. Are we sure that ideas and concepts mean the same thing? Methods of selecting appropriate cases and units for comparison also warrant further attention. And finding ways of taking account of the specificity and unique historical context of different national systems and cultures will remain a major challenge.

Finally, there is an intangible dimension of urban growth and decline that warrants greater political analysis. Urban economic performance also includes the image and perception of cities. Perceived performance may often bear little relation to objective conditions. How and why perceptions and reality differ or converge constitutes a matter of compelling research interest that has far-ranging consequences for policy. The politics of urban change constitutes a vast field of inquiry, rich in issues of theory and practice, and touching on some of the most compelling social questions of our time.

REFERENCES

Anderson, J. E. and R. W. Wassmer. 2000. *Bidding for Business*. Kalamazoo, MI: W. E. Upjohn Institute.

Barnes, R. A. and L. C. Ledebur. 1998. *The New Regional Economics*. Thousand Oaks, CA: Sage.

Bartik, T. J. 2009. "The Revitalisation of Older Industrial Cities: A Review Essay of Retooling for Growth." *Growth and Change* 40:1–29.

Basolo, V. 2003. "US Regionalism and Rationality." *Urban Studies* 40:447–62.

Blair, J. P. and L. A. Reese. 1999. *Approaches to Economic Development*. Thousand Oaks, CA: Sage.

Brenner, N. 2003. "Metropolitan Institutional Reform and the Rescaling of State Space in Contemporary Western Europe." *European Urban and Regional Studies* 10:297–324.

———. 2004. *New State Spaces*. New York: Oxford University Press.

Buck, I., I. Gordon, A. Harding, and I. Turok, eds. 2005. *Changing Cities: Rethinking Urban Competitiveness, Cohesion and Governance*. London: Palgrave.

Castells, M. 1977. *The Urban Question*. Cambridge, MA: MIT Press.
———. 2000. *The Information Age: Economy, Society and Culture*. Volume 1: *The Rise of the Network Society*. 2nd ed. Oxford: Blackwell.
Christopherson, S., H. Garretsen, and R. Martin. 2008. "The World Is Not Flat: Putting Globalization in its Place." *Cambridge Journal of Regions, Economy and Society* 1: 343–49.
Cochrane, A. 2007. *Understanding Urban Policy: A Critical Approach*. Oxford: Blackwell.
Crouch, C., P. Le Galès, C. Trigilia, and H. Voelzkow, eds. 2001. *Local Production Systems in Europe: Rise or Demise?* Oxford: Oxford University Press.
Davis, M. 2002. "Fortress Los Angeles, The Militarization of Public Space."
DiGaetano, A. and J. S. Klemanski. 1999. *Power and City Governance*. Minneapolis: University of Minnesota Press.
Donegan, M., J. Drucker, H. Goldstein, N. Lowe, and E. Malizia. 2008. "Which Indicators Explain Metropolitan Economic Performance Best?" *Journal of the American Planning Association* 74:180–95.
Dreier, P., J. Mollenkopf, and T. Swanstrom. 2004. *Place Matters*. 2nd ed. Lawrence: University Press of Kansas.
European Commission. Directorate-General for Regional Policy. 2006. *Cohesion Policy and Cities: The Urban Contribution to Growth and Jobs in the Regions*. Luxembourg: Office for Official Publications of the European Communities. July.
Fainstein, S. 2001. *The City Builders*. Lawrence: University Press of Kansas.
Fainstein, S. and N. Fainstein. 1989. "The Ambivalent State: Economic Development Policy in the U.S. Federal System under the Reagan Administration." *Urban Affairs Quarterly* 25:41–62.
Fisher, P. S. and A. H. Peters. 1998. *Industrial Incentives*. Kalamazoo, MI: Upjohn Institute.
Florida, R. 2004. *The Rise of the Creative Class*. New York: Basic Books.
Foglesong, R. E. 2001. *Married to the Mouse*. New Haven: Yale University Press.
Frieden, B. J. and L. B. Sagalyn. 1989. *Downtown Inc.* Cambridge: MIT Press.
Friedman, T. L. 2005. *The World is Flat. New York: Farrar, Straus and Giroux.*
Geddes, M. 2009. "Marxism in Urban Politics." David, J. S. and D. L. Imbrioscio, eds., *Theories of Urban Politics*, 2nd ed. Los Angeles: Sage Publications.
Glaeser, E. and J. Gottlieb. 2006. "Urban Resurgence and the Consumer City." *Urban Studies* 43:1275–99.
Hall, P. and K. Pain. 2006. *The Polycentric Metropolis*. London: Earthscan.
Hall, P. A. and D. Soskice, eds. 2001. *Varieties of Capitalism: The Institutional Foundations of Comparative Advantage*. Oxford: Oxford University Press.
Harding, A. 2007. "Taking City Regions Seriously? Response to Debate on 'City Regions': New Geographies of Governance, Democracy and Social Reproduction." *International Journal of Urban and Regional Research* 31:443–58.
HM Treasury. 2008. *The UK Economy: Addressing Long-Term Strategic Challenges*. London: HM Treasury.
Jessop, B. 1999a. "Narrating the Future of the National Economy and the National State: Remarks on Remapping Regulation and Reinventing Governance." Steinmetz, G., ed., *State/Culture*. Ithaca, NY: Cornell University Press.
———. 1999b. "Globalization and the National State: Reflections on a Theme of Poulantzas." Aaronowitz, S. and P. Bratisis, eds., *Rethinking the State*. Minneapolis: University of Minnesota Press.
Jones, B. D. and L. W. Bachelor. 1993. *The Sustaining Hand*. 2nd ed. Lawrence: University Press of Kansas.

Jouve, B. and C. Lefévre. 2002. *Local Power, Territory and Institutions in European Metropolitan Areas*. London: Frank Cass.

Judd, D. 2002. "Enclosure, Community and Public Life." Judd, D. and P. Kantor, eds., *The Politics of Urban America*, 3rd ed. New York: Longman.

Judd, D. and S. Fainstein. 1999. *The Tourist City*. New Haven: Yale University Press.

Kantor, P. 1995. *The Dependent City Revisited: The Political Economy of Urban Development and Social Policy*. Boulder: Westview.

———. 2006. "Regionalism and Reform: A Comparative Perspective on Dutch Urban Politics." *Urban Affairs Review* 41:800–29.

———. 2007. "Globalization and the American Model of Development: Making the Market." *Métropoles* 1:31–68. http://metropoles.revues.org.

Kantor, P. and D. R. Judd, eds. 2008. *American Urban Politics in a Global Age*. New York: Longman.

Kantor, P., C. Lefevre, A. Saito, H. V. Savitch, and A. Thornley. 2012. *Struggling Giants: City Region Governance in London, New York, Paris, and Tokyo*. Minneapolis: University of Minnesota Press.

Katznelson, I. 1993. *Marxism and the City*. Oxford: Clarendon Press.

Keating, M. 1998. *The New Regionalism in Western Europe: Territorial Restructuring and Political Change*. Cheltenham: Edward Elgar.

Kohn, M. 2004. *Brave New Neighborhoods*. New York: Routledge.

Le Galès, P. 2002. *European Cities*. Oxford: Oxford University Press.

Logan, J. and H. Molotch. 1987. *Urban Fortunes*. Berkeley: University of California Press.

Lovering, J. 1999. "Theory Led by Policy: The Inadequacies of 'The New Regionalism'." *International Journal of Urban and Regional Research* 23:379–95.

MacLeod, G. 2001. "New Regionalism Reconsidered: Globalization and the Remaking of Political Space." *International Journal of Urban and Regional Research* 25:804–29.

Mossberger, K. 2009. "Urban Regime Analysis." David, J. S. and D. L. Imbrioscio, eds., *Theories of Urban Politics*, 2nd ed. Los Angeles: Sage Publications.

Newman, P. and A. Thornley. 2005. *Planning World Cities*. New York: Palgrave Macmillan.

OECD. 2006. *Competitive Cities in the Global Economy*. Paris: OECD.

Painter, J. 1995. "Regulation Theory, Post-Fordism and Urban Politics." Judge, D., G. Stoker, and H. Wolman, eds., *Theories of Urban Politics*. London: Sage.

Peterson, P. E. 1981. *City Limits*. Chicago : University of Chicago Press.

Peck, J. 2002. "Political Economies of Scale: Fast Policy, Interscalar Relations and Neoliberal Workfare." *Economic Geography* 78:332–60.

Pike, A., A. Rodriguez-Pose, and J. Tomaney. 2006. *Local and Regional Development*. London: Routledge.

Pike, A. and J. Tomaney. 2009. "The State and Uneven Development: The Governance of Economic Development in England in the Post-Devolution UK." *Cambridge Journal of Regions, Economy and Society* 1:1–22.

Porter, M. E. 1998. "Clusters and the New Economics of Competitiveness." *Harvard Business Review*, December, 77–90.

Portz, J. 1990. *The Politics of Plant Closings*. Lawrence: University Press of Kansas.

Rodriguez-Pose, A. and N. Gill. 2005. "On the Economic Dividend of Devolution." *Regional Studies* 39:405–20.

Salet, W. and A. Faludi, eds. 2000. *The Revival of Strategic Spatial Planning*. Amsterdam: KNAW Edita.

Salet, W., A. Thornley, and A. Kreukels. 2003. *Metropolitan Governance and Spatial Planning*. London: Spon Press.

Sapotichne, J., B. Jones and M. Wolfe. 2007. "Is Urban Politics a Black Hole? Analyzing the Boundary between Political Science and Urban politics." *Urban Affairs Review* 43:76–106.
Sassen, S. 1998. *Globalization and Its Discontents*. New York: New Press.
———. 2006. *Territory, Authority, Rights*. Princeton: Princeton University Press.
Savitch, H. V. and P. Kantor. 2002. *Cities in the International Marketplace*. Princeton, NJ: Princeton University Press.
Sbragia, A. 1999. *Debt Wish*. Pittsburgh: University of Pittsburgh Press.
Scott, A. J., ed. 2001. *Global City-Regions: Trends, Theory, Policy*. Oxford: Oxford University Press.
Sellers, J. M. 2002. *Governing from Below*. Cambridge: Cambridge University Press.
Sites, W. 2003. *Remaking New York*. Minneapolis: University of Minnesota Press.
Stoker, G. 1995. "Regime Theory and Urban Politics." Judge, D., G. Stoker, and H. Wolman, eds., *Theories of Urban Politics*. London: Sage.
Stone, C. N. 1989. *Regime Politics: Governing Atlanta, 1946–1988*. Lawrence: University Press of Kansas.
Stone, C. N. and H. Saunders., eds. 1987. *The Politics of Urban Development*. Lawrence: University Press of Kansas.
Storper, M. 1997. *The Regional World: Territorial Development in a Global Economy*. New York: Guildford Press.
Taylor, P. 2004. *World City Network: A Global Urban Analysis*. London: Routledge.
Terhorst, P. and J. C. L. van de Ven. 1997. *Fragmented Brussels and Consolidated Amsterdam*. Amsterdam: Netherlands Geographical Society.
Turok, I. 2004. "Cities, Regions and Competitiveness." *Regional Studies* 38:1069–83.
———. 2009. "The Distinctive City: Pitfalls in the Pursuit of Differential Advantage." *Environment and Planning A* 41:13–30.
Turok, I. and V. Mykhnenko. 2007. "The Trajectories of European Cities, 1960–2005." *Cities* 24:165–82.
———. 2008. "Resurgent European Cities?" *Urban Research & Practice* 1:54–77.
World Bank. 2009. *World Development Report 2009: Shaping Economic Geography*. Washington: World Bank.
Zukin, S. 1995. *The Cultures of Cities*. Oxford: Blackwell.

CHAPTER 24

COMPETITIVE CITIES

MARISOL GARCIA AND DENNIS R. JUDD

OUTSIDE the United States, the idea that cities compete for investment, capital, and people was almost absent in the scholarly literature until quite recently. These lacunae arose from no defect in non-U.S. urban scholarship; instead, the situation reflected divergent paths of urban development. As historians have long noted, cities in the U.S. grew through schemes of local promotion of town development, and virtually all politics revolved around the singular imperative of growth. By contrast, in most of the world, cities have been the centers of political and administrative power and cultural expression, a role that became elaborated and institutionalized with the rise of the nation-state. The history of the city was thus interpreted through the lens of the state and its priorities, as a reading of Lewis Mumford's *The City in History* confirms.

In the 1980s and 1990s the concept of the competitive city became relevant to comparative urban scholarship because of the impact of deindustrialization and globalization. These interlocking forces have torn the urban hierarchy of the industrial era apart. As a result, in the U.S. the competition among cities has become as intense as it was before a stable system of cities emerged in the late nineteenth century. Elsewhere, where urban systems were maintained in part by national economic policies and state expenditures, the protections offered by national policy were quickly eroded. For cities, the results have been historic and profound; suddenly, cities were plunged into a fight for survival in an expanding global arena. This explains why scholars all over the world have become preoccupied with issues related to the competitive city.

1. The Conditions for Interurban Competition

The historic pattern of urban expansion in the United States has been unique. The great cities of Europe, Asia, and elsewhere evolved not only as places of commerce and trade, but also as centers of religious, military, cultural, and political power. The city-state preceded the nation-state, and it collected within it the institutions that held societies together. Later, cities like Rome and London defined and dominated emerging national cultures and presided over vast bureaucracies that managed imperial ambitions. Their historical dominance survives to the present day.

Urban development in the United States traces a different arc. Lacking a long cultural, social, and political history, cities came into being and prospered mainly for economic reasons. The urban historian Sam Bass Warner could only have been referring to the U.S. context when he coined the term "privatism" to refer to the politics and local culture its cities. Since its purpose was economic, the city could survive only if it succeeded on those terms. As a result, historians who have written the literature on urban development in the U.S. have focused upon the pursuit of individual opportunity and the way this impulse was given collective expression by the policies of the local state.

There are two periods of particularly intense interurban competition in the U.S.: one associated with the rise of the industrial city, the other with its decline. What makes both periods similar is that the national and international urban system was in a period of rapid change. As the nation spread into the frontier, cities tried to place themselves at critical points within emerging patterns of trade and economic development. By now a familiar narrative describes their attempts to secure rail connections by investing heavily in railroad stock. This story has a central place in nineteenth-century American history because public subsidies helped the railroads become the first large corporations, and the fight for public subsidies lead to economic crises and political corruption. This period came to a close when the industrial hierarchy became well defined, and cities found secure niches within it.

A century later, deindustrialization and the economic restructuring associated with globalization reignited an intense interurban rivalry in the U.S. But deindustrialization hit all of the economies of the developed nations at the same time, and with similar effects. The deindustrialization of the 1970s exerted its effects most deeply in the cities and regions that relied upon extractive and manufacturing activities. For example, unemployment in some places reached levels as high as 20 percent in Pittsburgh (steel), Sheffield (coals and steel), Liverpool and Glasgow (shipbuilding; shipping), and cities throughout continental Europe were similarly affected. By the late 1980s almost every economic sector was involved in the global movement of capital and goods. It soon became clear that countries, regions, and cities would have to compete in the emerging global economy. Despite profound differences in political traditions, strategies of urban revitalization converged in the sense that all of them emphasized the goal of making cities competitive.

In the United States, the combination of economic restructuring and changes in urban policy seemed to be merely the last phase in a long-term process of decentralization from the urban core, which had been taking place for decades, comprising also the post–World War II urban crisis of suburbanization and racial conflict. Older industrial cities and metropolitan regions were plunged into a deep economic malaise for which there seemed to be no obvious remedy. Rather than responding to help the cities recover, in the early 1980s the administration of President Ronald Reagan declared that national economic growth was more important than the economic health of particular cities and regions. Cities were left on their own to devise strategies to regenerate their local economies.

Regeneration policies were composed of two major elements: a close collaboration between government and business, and the invention of policy from the bottom up. Cities were put in the position of saving themselves, and the strategies for doing so became increasingly creative and complex over time. What began as direct public subsidies by cities in the form of tax abatements, land subsidies, and infrastructure development mushroomed into an incredibly complex institutional web made up of municipalities, special-purpose authorities, and special districts. These arrangements evolved more rapidly in the U.S. than elsewhere because higher-level governments were relatively absent in local economic development.

Economic restructuring and changes in urban policy unfolded in the UK and in continental Europe at about the same time, and with similar, often disastrous social and economic effects. Old port and industrial cities across Europe, places like Glasgow, Sheffield, Liverpool, Hamburg, and Marseilles, slid into sudden decline. But the policy responses differed in important respects. What distinguished Europe from the U.S. was a general assumption that central governments should be closely involved in making the industrial policies that affect regions and cities. However, within this broad consensus there were significant national differences.

2. Political Culture and Strategies of Competition

The policy response in Britain resembled the U.S. more closely than anywhere else. After the Conservatives took power in 1979, Margaret Thatcher led a movement to change the ideological climate in Britain by replacing state action with market forces. At least rhetorically, markets replaced governmental expenditures as the primary response to urban decline; the values of entrepreneurialism replaced public intervention; wealth creation replaced the distribution of public welfare. To push forward these principles, the Thatcher government took steps to centralize public power and weaken local autonomy. A variety of initiatives sprang up: city action teams, task forces, enterprise zones, free ports, urban development grants, urban regeneration grants, urban development corporations. Cities were expected to use such policies aggressively if they wanted national government assistance. Unlike the U.S., however, the local coalitions preserved a strong policy and planning role by the local state. Business and other private actors played important roles, but within the context of state-led priorities.

There were many national variations on the theme of interurban competition, but in general the countries of continental Europe continued to involve the central state closely in the task of urban revitalization. For example, in the 1970s the French government initiated a program to nationalize and provide state support for key industries. The nationalization of basic industries increased public-sector employment, but they also made French industry uncompetitive in the emerging global economic order. Beginning in 1983, national policies underwent a dramatic shift to encourage French industry to become more competitive. These policies bore superficial similarities to those identified with Reaganism and Thatcherism: privatization, deregulation, and tax incentives to attract private investment. Nevertheless, the tradition of a centralized state with strong ties to local affairs led to the organization of powerful and complex coalitions of elite leadership at the local level. The central state identified "growth poles" as a way of establishing national priorities for urban development, but the coalitions formed at the city level were capable of mobilizing significant resources on their own.

Likewise, in Germany, the government initially responded to deindustrialization by attempting to shore up declining industries, but by the 1980s these policies gave way to strategies to protect regions; for example, the ability of firms to close shop and move elsewhere was strictly regulated. West German cities possessed very significant powers of their own. Thus, urban policy was much more decentralized than in the French case, with local political elites possessing the power and resources to define and implement economic regeneration strategies with little oversight. However, the pressure to compete led to similarities in the local strategies, with the cities providing bureaucratic personnel and substantial public subsidies for schemes to make them more attractive to affluent residents and investors.

3. Competitive Cities under Globalization

Cities have adjusted in various ways and with varying levels of success to the global economy. Though it is still in flux, a new urban hierarchy has emerged that reflects these differences. At the top of the pyramid are the big global cities such as New York, Tokyo, Paris, Miami, and Chicago. Among this group of cities there are important distinctions, but all of them have attracted layer upon layer of highly educated white-collar professionals—for example, corporate managers, management consultants, legal experts, accountants, computer specialists, financial analysts, media and public relations specialists. Cities further down the hierarchy have also converted to economies based upon a combination of services, and many are heavily dependent upon tourism. Some cities have never fully recovered, and continue to struggle to find a niche. Despite signs of renewal, they continue to be haunted by the specter of urban decline. The worst cases, such as Detroit, Michigan, tend to be located in the U.S., where national policies for regional development and economic restructuring have been absent. The pressures to find a niche in the global urban hierarchy ensure that individual cities will compete, some of them desperately.

For some time there was a question about whether the cities most affected by economic restructuring could successfully compete for mobile capital. For the most part, this question has been answered. The cities at the top of the urban hierarchy have, by definition, thoroughly restructured their economies. Secondary cities have mostly recovered as well, though to varying degrees. The cities that relied most heavily upon manufacturing had the longest path to travel. In Britain, cities such as Newcastle, Liverpool, and Glasgow have turned around to a remarkable degree, and the recovery can be traced to a combination of enormous amounts of central and local public funds and private investment. In some cities in the U.S., such as Cleveland, Philadelphia, and St. Louis, recovery has been accomplished, but it remains somewhat fragile and uneven. These types of cities have the fewest resources to devote to the task of recovery, but they are forced to compete with whatever they are able to bring to the task.

A systematic pattern has emerged that distinguishes how and with what success cities have been able to compete. Hank Savitch and Paul Kantor (2002) have made a distinction between social-centered and market-centered policies. Social-centered policies rely heavily upon formal planning and impose requirements and restrictions on investors, such as the provision of public amenities. These approaches incorporate labor and social-welfare policies meant to spread the social benefits of urban regeneration. Market-centered strategies attempt to induce investment through low taxes, public subsidies in the form of land, relaxed regulation, and infrastructure financed by public funds. Generally, unionized labor and generous social programs are seen as hindrances to investment.

In effect, these categories reflect the political cultures that distinguish the U.S. from Europe. Virtually all European cities studied by Savitch and Kantor relied upon social-centered policies, while most of the U.S. cities employed market-based approaches. But within these two groups, important differences exist. Cities in both contexts that are the most desperate for capital are in the worst position to bargain. Even when they face big problems, cities that operate within a political culture that supports strong public intervention have some room to maneuver in deciding among alternative strategies. By contrast, cities that operate without a strong central or local state have few choices but to bend to the demands of investors. These pressures are modified as regeneration takes hold, but cultural differences remain fundamentally important.

In Europe the European Union plays an important part, with two roles in the development of cities. One approach of the EU encourages urban competition, especially with the territorial agenda linked to the implementation of the Lisbon agenda (2000–2010) fostering not just urban regeneration and international image but also promoting the investment in knowledge and innovation and the identification of innovative clusters, where the business communities are encouraged to work together with administrators. Competition is encouraged also by the distribution of funds through Europe-wide bidding. The other EU approach focuses on social cohesion policies emphasizing employment opportunities or community programs (such as the URBAN program implemented from 1994 until 2006) related to national, regional, or metropolitan policies (Commission of European Communities 2008). The ambiguity of the EU can be seen in a recent Green paper on territorial cohesion stressing the need for sustainable territorial development, strengthening economic competitiveness and capacity for growth while ensuring social cohesion (COM 2008, 6).

4. Theoretical Approaches to Urban Competition

Different theoretical approaches have emerged to explain the strategies employed by cities to gain comparative advantages in the international marketplace. One line of explanation, following regulation theory, focuses on the ways in which industrial decline and post-Keynesian policies have forced cities and regions to assume new responsibilities. The new "regimes of accumulation" are based upon a recognition that national states have largely abandoned central planning controls. Public leaders have, as a result, been forced to become entrepreneurial (Jessop 2004; Le Galès 1998, 2002). Scholars focusing on urban regions have emphasized the interlocking relationships between cities and regions in devising competitive strategies (Keating 1998). In analyzing the competitive strategies employed by European cities, theorists have stressed the transition to a post-Fordist model that has incorporated neoliberalism as a guiding principle (Jessop 2003; Scott 2008) and/or the restructuring of the state power in political scales (Brenner 2004). All have argued that cities and regions must restructure their institutional frameworks and policy choices in order to adapt to the challenges and constraints of globalization.

Urban tourism plays an independent and mediating role in the emergence of post-Fordist urban economies (Fainstein et al. 2003, 241–42). Cities of all sizes seek to enhance their competitive position in the global economy through an explicit focus on culture and identity, reflected as much in the physical transformation of the city as in the development of a distinctive cultural life in the city (Degen 2008). The strategy of cultural urban tourism has been followed by urban leaders around the world with variable success. Some cities—for example, New York, Paris, Berlin, Rome, Barcelona, Chicago—have been extremely successful in using their symbolic capital to gain competitive advantages in the international marketplace. The risks are considerable and often the subsidies, infrastructure, and other incentives are sizable, but virtually all major cities must compete for culture, leisure, and tourism because these are some of the most rapidly growing sectors of the world economy (Judd and Fainstein 1999).

A complementary approach focuses on the increasing role played by transnational corporations (Scott 2008) and the rediscovery of cities as sites of the specialized labor and service support of the knowledge economy (Amin and Graham 1997). In the European context neo-Schumpeterians[1] and new institutionalists have stressed the role of institutions in underpinning market entrepreneurship (Harding 1997; Jessop 2002). Attention has been focused upon nationally based institutional regulations and governance processes as key elements determining how cities position themselves in the global economic order. A study published in 2007 argued that a combination of institutional structure and cultural path-dependency explains the competitive strategies. This approach constitutes a critical appraisal of neoliberal policies and emphasizes bottom-up strategies for innovation which can improve competitive advantage (Moulaert et al. 2007).

Economic and economic geography analysis, on the other hand, has focused on the particular factors that confer competitive advantage. What makes some cities more competitive than others? For cities the interplay of location and strengths of firms and other economic agents is crucial (Begg 2002). These factors interact with governance and policy influence. More specific characteristics have also been identified, such as the assertion that a high income elasticity of demand helps to promote full employment, and that job creation should aim at high-skill, high income jobs (Kresl 1995 in Begg 1999, 800). As a factor of urban competitiveness, human capital has gained considerable attention with the seminal work of Richard Florida on the creative class. But others factors also deserve attention, such as the "competitive ethos," which has, according to its advocates, encouraged city leaders to invest in marketing the cities they manage and identifying and reinforcing their assets (Gordon and Cheshire 1998 in Begg 1999, 805).

Some attempts have been made to bring these strands together into one framework. In the U.S., "resurgent" cities are associated with a well-educated professional population (a "creative class"), loyalty to the city by the middle classes, and the attraction of foreign migrants, all elements that secure a complex social and racial mix (Beauregard 2004).

Storper and Manville (2006, 1265) have argued that accessibility to jobs instead of the acquisition of cultural capital in flashy cities filled with shopping centers

1. The relevance of Schumpeter is manifested in the broad role given to the entrepreneur as a creative actor and initiator of innovative activities, who develops efficient new ways of doing things to generate above average profits. Some authors like Jessop go further in their analysis, pointing at the emerging Schumpeterian competition state that aims at securing economic growth within its borders. This type of state is highly concerned with technological change, innovation, and enterprise as well as with new governance techniques to pursuit these aims (Jessop 2002, 133–34).

constitutes a more convincing explanation for urban regeneration. Mobile workers and immigrants move into or stay in cities that offer job opportunities and an urban environment that fulfills the promise of life chances. However, "the making of a place is a joint project of architects, developers, engineers, regulators and others . . . , the coordination is highly imperfect and a tremendous amount of information is still lost as to what is required to make a city grow or to be transformed." It is been pointed out that urban renaissance is not the same as urban competitiveness; "success in terms of physical regeneration, cultural development and international profile is not the same necessarily as competitive success and one does not automatically lead to the other" (Boddy and Parkinson 2004, 424).

Economic and social efficiency is associated with successful governance (Stone 2005). In the UK the virtuous duo of competitiveness and governance has developed into a triangle by adding social cohesion as the third pillar (Buck et al. 2005). Perhaps the most debated of all concepts born from the political economy perspective has been the urban regime. The strengths and weaknesses of the concept have provoked a long-standing debate. In the U.S., urban regime analysis has treated economic policies, social policies, and governance as interconnected phenomena. Decisions about local policies on these matters are accomplished through a stable coalition that allows public and private leaders to cooperate in achieving mutual aims and setting the local agenda. Where it exists, the urban regime, in other words, is regarded as the main instrument of political agency in a city (Stone 2005).

5. A Critical Assessment of Key Theoretical Controversies

Regime analysis has been critically assessed in Europe on several grounds. There is by now a long-standing debate pursued by authors who see urban regime analysis as an abstraction based upon arrangements exclusive to cities in the United States, making the concept of limited use when applied to cities elsewhere (Pierre 2005, Di Gaetano and Lawless 1999, Harding 1997). Kantor and Savitch have argued that urban regime analysis, as a conceptual tool for comparative analysis between North American and European cities, is inadequate because "of the differences in the composition and power business interests in European cities" (2005, 136). The major difference is that cities in Europe have a stronger public-sector presence in urban landownership, bureaucratic authority, and planning regulations. For these reasons European academics consider different notions of urban governance to be more useful not only for their own context, but also for comparative analysis. These studies focus on several features of governance:

(a) The importance of national and regional institutional contexts in defining urban regimes. Harding, for example, initially admits the explanatory capacity of the urban regime concept as compared to growth machines for explaining strategies led by business interests to mobilize resources for local economic restructuring (Harding, 1997). However, in a closer look at several specific cases—Amsterdam, Copenhagen, Edinburgh, Hamburg, and Manchester—he draws the conclusion that competitive strategies in these cities have worked hand in hand with national responses to globalization, and that the differences between the way urban coalitions work is best understood by incorporating their respective national frameworks and ways of regulating than by extrapolating them from those contexts. Unitary state structures (Denmark, the Netherlands, and the UK) are associated with the subordination of local policies to the priorities of state agencies (1997, 308). In federal countries like Germany, city leaders have more autonomy and yet are no less bound (if not constrained) by national regulations. In highly decentralized states (Spain, Italy), the strong role played by regional institutions creates a highly complex framework of governance mechanisms for the planning and implementation of urban regeneration projects (Salet and Gualini 2007). In the United States, by contrast, regional involvement in city planning is infrequent and tenuous (Kantor and Savitch 2005).

(b) The central role of political legitimacy in urban governance. In U.S. cities, entrepreneurial coalitions claim the legitimacy of the state, but the winners are sharply divided from the losers, and state autonomy is ambiguous. Harding and others point out that economic growth as an engine for urban intervention in European cities is strongly related to increasing revenues, protecting the national welfare state, and overcoming fragmentation and social exclusion. Particularly interesting is the marriage created in European normative literature between competitiveness and social cohesion. Moreover, economic development partnership is often led by local public administration actors who combine central government resources with local tax revenues and who engage private actors. This is done not without critical distance from sectors of the city councils, which are more concerned with social cohesion than with urban competitiveness.

(c) The variability and stability of a particular regime. Comparative analyses have shown a variety of outcomes in public-private partnerships which do not necessarily correspond to a coherent and stable urban regime (Mossberger and Stoker 2001, 820).[2] In the late 1980s a cross-national literature began to emerge in which a variety of responses to economic change were apparent (Judd and Parkinson 1990 in Mossberger and Stoker 2001, 819). This variability is another reason why European scholars have increasingly adopted a perspective focusing on broader conceptions of governance that consider the way that government, defined as a vertical and

2. Mossberger and Stoker (2001, 829) include a series of core properties of "urban regimes" such as: (a) partners draw from government and nongovernmental sources, requiring but not limited to business participation; (b) collaboration is based on social production—the need to bring together fragmented resources for the power to accomplish tasks; (c) identifiable policy agendas are related to the composition of the participants in the coalition and (d) a long-standing pattern of cooperation rather than a temporary coalition is necessary.

institutional structure for exercising power and implementing policy, incorporates "a diversification and proliferation of politically relevant coalitions" composed of state and nonstate actors. Pierre(2005, 452) goes further, claiming that a governance perspective goes beyond local institutions to "search for processes and mechanisms through which significant and resource-full actors coordinate their actions and resources in the pursuit of collective defined objectives." He has characterized four modes of urban governance: "managerialist," "corporatist," "pro-growth," and "welfare-oriented." Only the pro-growth model resembles the U.S. model, but even in that case, governing coalitions do not need to be stable, but can work temporarily and with shifting networks that deal with specific issues. In addition, a city can follow several governance strategies at the same time, depending upon whether the emphasis is on economic competitiveness or on social cohesion.

(d) The other European reality that challenges the concept of urban regimes is the multiscale institutional framework in which European cities are embedded. EU funding thorough Structural Funds has been a major stimulus to all types of partnerships (public-public and public-private) to improve the competitive capacity of cities. Thus, in the European arena, local actors involved in coalitions and networks do not only shift according to specific issues, but are encouraged by European institutions to do so with financial support. Although the "Europe of cities" has not materialized into a strong power bloc, the large proportion of European regulations and financial programs pouring down to cities from European institutions is not to be neglected analytically (Kazepov 2005). Multilevel governance clearly stresses the strong ties that connect state institutions and regulations to urban regulations and policies. Of course the European arena is far from uniform, and contains significant differences. What is common to cities in the European context is the close relations between several tiers of government, which creates a complicated institutional and policy picture that challenges the view that policy is a local choice.

6. Comparative Research

The field of urban affairs has turned strongly in the direction of cross-national analysis and systematic comparative research to overcome the limitations of local case studies (Pierre 2005, 4; Beaumont and Nichols 2008). Part of the problem of comparative work is that it is difficult to untangle the deep structural differences that make countries, regions, and cities differ. The problem has been challenging enough even when it was confined mainly to research involving cities in North America and Europe. But the scope of the field is widening rapidly. In recent years there has been an outpouring of research on the interurban competition among the global cities and the newly industrialized and transitional economies of Asia. This competition has intensified since the 1990s. In that decade, the Chinese government collaborated with an aggressive leadership in Shanghai to transform that city into a global power. In reaction, Tokyo, Singapore, and Hong Kong have offered subsidies, tax breaks, streamlined business regulations, and other incentives in an attempt to lure investment capital (Chen 2009). The emerging economies have gone past the stage of export platforms to encourage the development of a variety of high-tech and service centers. In the future, scholarship in other parts of the world, especially including Latin America, is bound to come into the literature in a significant way. Trying to draw comparisons among very diverse cases in such widely varying contexts will make the task of urban theory more challenging than ever before.

The problems of comparison have been daunting even within the relatively restricted contexts covered in previous research. For example, in America local chambers of commerce are separated from government and historically rooted as interest groups, whereas in Europe the relationship between city councils and local chambers of commerce is such that city mayors have a considerable capacity to preempt them (2005, 135–51). Comparability problems emerge also from the generalization of public-private partnerships as an element of both urban regime analyses (U.S.) and governance structures that rely on complex institutional mechanisms to promote economic development (Europe). Since regime analysis assumes a strong role for private sector interests and business in local decision making, research carried out in Europe has looked for similar behavior, and has found that private-public partnerships are indeed practiced in urban redevelopment projects, especially the ones that involved large-scale projects (Moulaert et al. 2003). However, as we have discussed, the literature reveals widely divergent cultural norms, political practices, and institutional structures.

A fundamental issue is that it is often difficult to tell even whether the language used transfers from one context to the next. This problem becomes apparent when considering what is meant by strategic planning. In the U.S. it generally refers to exercises involving large numbers of participants who agree on abstract goals, while in European cities it is often led by city administrations, and has a direct connection to action (Salet and Gualini 2007). Some terms, however, do seem to pass the comparativity test. In all contexts, coalitions in some form are present. Nowhere is government so strong that it can operate alone, which in any case could not occur in a democratic context. Savitch and Kantor have shown a useful way forward, with their focus on the relationship between the nature of coalitions and the bargaining position of cities. They define bargaining as the city's ability to "garner resources in order to maximize its choices and realize its objectives in the capital investment process" (2002, 43).

One of the methodological contributions of Savitch and Kantor's work is a definition of the variables *driving forces* (market conditions and intergovernmental support) and *steering forces* (popular control, local culture), which helps them to explain how the conditions faced by cities circumscribe choice, and also how context shapes the coalitions that make decisions. This systematic comparative work concludes that the availability of political choice is crucial, but that choices also reflect the political forces at work. Policy choices and outcomes result mainly from the way leaders make use of their bargaining positions. In a more recent methodological article they have analyzed the difficulties researchers face in measuring support by higher levels of government for cities' efforts to define their competitive strategies. (By "support" they understand greater intergovernmental fiscal and planning integration.) Institutional support is relevant because it can counteract unfavorable market conditions, which is the case of some European cities included in their work (Glasgow, Liverpool, Marseilles, and Naples). In order to get support, local leaders have to be actively involved in bargaining. Thus the concept of *bargaining* has an explanatory value for relating political choice with economic competition among cities (Kantor and Savitch 2005, 148).

Given the high variability of institutional contexts in Europe some may argue that comparability may be more fruitful when conducting research within a given institutional frame. This is what has been done in the UK,[3] where a large-scale comparative study showed that the variables of most importance in local regeneration efforts are diversified industrial structures (with a concentration of knowledge-based industries); land property and planning systems availability; market size and diversity; amenities and infrastructure; capacity to attract and retain a skilled and highly qualified labor force; quality of life, and local environment and educational provision (Boddy and Parkinson 2004, 407–32). The outcomes of this comparative study may appear to contradict that of Savitch and Kantor (2002) to the extent that in the British case no strong correlation was found between competitiveness and local governance. Instead, the researchers stress the overriding importance of long-term structural factors. However, and somewhat contradictorily, the authors of the British study propose a policy recommendation to promote permanent institutional arrangements to strengthen personal contacts between key players as well as to encourage partnerships in innovative centers (Boddy and Parkinson 2004, 413). This recommendation is derived from their finding that strategic alliances between interested partners holding strategic visions concerning resources and territories constitute the way forward to a consistent capacity for urban competitiveness. In the end, then, the study conforms quite well to Kantor and Savitch's research.

7. Research Directions

Recent theoretical and empirical contributions have indicated the importance of human capital and more specifically the emergence of a "creative class" as a key factor for economic development. Although related to labor market analysis, the role of talent becomes central and in interaction with other factors, such as the openness and

3. A major research program "*Cities: Competitiveness and Cohesion Research Programme*" was set up in 1997 by the Economic and Social Research Council in the UK, which included 23 different projects, 30 universities, and almost 100 researchers. For a summary of the main arguments and findings of the different project see Boddy and Parkinson (2004).

tolerance of the urban environment and social diversity (Florida 2002). The argument stresses that the geographical concentration of talent is correlated with low entry barriers for human capital. Moreover, the creative class is located preferably where there is a high concentration of sectors based on advanced technology. The innovative contribution of this approach is that it gives priority to the pooling of highly qualified human capital in the attraction for firms and industrial clusters (Florida 2002, 754). This analysis also recommends the pursuit of strategies that favor the diversity of people and services as a way of enlarging the concentration of the creative class.

These conclusions have generated fierce debate at the same time that they have stimulated research in European cities.[4] Critics have argued that there is nothing new in the perception that talent is crucial for cities to prosper (as shown in historic Athens, Florence, and Vienna, for example). In addition, critics have pointed out that the constitution and concentration of a creative cluster tends to follow a path-dependent route, which partially determines the strategies that make sense for particular places. Nevertheless, it must be granted that some key factors are necessary to become the nesting territory for the concentration of creativity and innovation, and it is important to identify these. Some research questions have been put forward, and are now the subject of research. These include, among others: "What are the conditions for creating or stimulating 'creative knowledge regions'?" and "What is the role of so-called 'soft' factors such as quality of life in creating and stimulating 'creative knowledge regions'?" (Musterd et al. 2007).

These studies, however, seem to take for granted the premise that city and regional competitiveness must be market driven, and that the tendency toward greater social inequality is happening everywhere. Would it be possible to envisage creativity and innovation with a larger participation of sectors of society than the "creative core?" (Fainstein 2001, 887). Is the European welfare state tradition receding and letting the dream of a just city drift further away? Questions such as these indicate that the concept of the Just City is likely to become as important as the Competitive City in future research.

The current economic crisis has put issues of social justice back on the political agenda. Investment in urban property markets has slowed, contributing to an increase in unemployment and problems in the housing sector. Loan foreclosures have increased the risk of homelessness and put pressure on local and national governments to engage in coordinated Keynesian and monetary policies in order to combat a decline in middle-class living standards as well as rising levels of poverty. These problems are as likely to stimulate as to reduce interurban competition. Research questions, such as how city leaders are able to redirect their priorities toward issues of social and environmental sustainability and to influence their respective national governments priorities, are likely to follow.

4. See for example Accommodating Creative Knowledge—Competitiveness of European Metropolitan Regions within the Enlarged Union (ACRE) coordinated by Sako Musterd. Starting date 2006.

Several issues have been raised in this entry. Although cities have competed historically, with economic globalization a systematic pattern has emerged showing the variability of strategies for competition and the degrees of success. The literature shows that in the post-Fordist model of accumulation, cities have not only incorporated competitive principles but have also engaged in restructuring their institutional frameworks and governance mechanism to accommodate cooperation with other levels of government as well as noninstitutional actors. Governance cultures have followed a path-dependency but are also dynamic and innovative. One of the factors that most vigorously drives innovation is surely the need for cities to compete, in whatever context they operate within.

REFERENCES

Amin, A. (1999) "An Institutionalist Perspective on Regional Economic Development." *International Journal of Urban and Regional Research* 23(2): 365–78.

Amin, A. and S. Graham (1997) "The Ordinary City." *Transactions of the Institute of British Geographers* 22: 411–29.

Begg, I. (1999) "Cities and Competitiveness." *Urban Studies* 36(5–6): 795–809.

Begg, I. (ed.) (2002) *Urban Competitiveness: Policies for Dynamic Cities*. Bristol: Policy Press.

Beaumont, J. and W. Nichols (2008) "Plural Governance, Participation and Democracy in Cities (Symposium)." *International Journal of Urban and Regional Research* 32(1): 87–94.

Beauregard, R. A. (2004) "Are Cities Resurgent? A Conference Report." *City* 8(3): 421–27.

Boddy, M. and M. Parkinson (eds.) (2004) *City Matters*. Bristol: Policy Press.

Brenner, N. (2004) "Urban Governance and the Production of New State Spaces in Western Europe 1960–2000." *Review of International Political Economy* 11(3): 447–88.

Buck, N., I. Gordon, A. Harding, and I. Turok (eds.) (2005) *Changing Cities: Rethinking Urban Competitiveness, Cohesion and Governance*. Basingstoke: Palgrave Macmillan.

Chen, Xiangming (ed.) (2009) *Shanghai Rising: State Power and Local Transformations in a Global Megacity*. Minneapolis: University of Minnesota Press.

COM (2008) Green Paper on Territorial Cohesion: Turning Territorial Diversity into Strength—2008: Communication from the Commission to the Council, the European Parliament, the Committee of the Regions and the European Economic and Social Committee.

Commission of European Communities (2008) http://ec.europa.eu/regional_policy/sources/docoffic/2007/working/urban_dimension_en.pdf, visited September 2009.

Degen, M. (2008) *Sensing Cities: Regenerating Public Life in Barcelona and Manchester*. London: Routledge.

Di Gaetano, A. and P. Lawless (1999) "Urban Governance and Urban Decline: Governing Structures and Policy Agenda in Birmingham and Shefield, England and Detroit, Michigan, 1980–1997," *Urban Affairs Review* 34(4): 546–77.

Fainstein, S. (2001) "Competitiveness, Cohesion and Governance: Their Implications for Social Justice." *International Journal of Urban and Regional Research* 25: 884–88.

Fainstein, S., L. Hoffman, and D. Judd (2003) "Making Theoretical Sense of Tourism." In Hoffman, L., S. Fainstein, and D. Judd (eds.) *Cities and Visitors*. Oxford: Blackwell.

Florida, R. (2002) "The Economic Geography of Talent." *Annals of the Association of American Geographers* 92(4): 743–45.

Geddes, M. (2000) "Tackling Social Exclusion in the European Union? The Limits to the New Orthodoxy in Local Partnership." *International Journal of Urban and Regional Research* 24(4): 782–800.

Harding, A. (1997) "Urban Regimes in a Europe of the Cities?" *European Urban and Regional Studies* 4(4): 291–314.

Jessop, B. (2002) *The Future of the Capitalist State*. Cambridge: Polity.

Jessop, B. (2003) "Good Governance and the Urban Question: On Managing the Contradictions of Neo-Liberalism." Department of Sociology, Lancaster University. http://www.comp.lancs.ac.uk/sociology/soco75rj.html.

Jessop, B. (2004) Governance, Multi-Level Governance and Metagovernance. In Bache, I. (ed.) *Multi-level Governance*. Oxford: Blackwell.

Judd, D. R. and S. Fainstein (eds.) (1999) *The Tourist City*. New Haven: Yale University Press.

Kantor, P. and H. V. Savitch (2005) "How to Study Comparative Urban Development Politics: A Research Note." *International Journal of Urban and Regional Research* 29(1): 135–51.

Kazepov, Y. (2005) *Cities of Europe: Changing Contexts, Local Arrangements and the Challenge to Urban Cohesion*. Oxford: Blackwell.

Keating, M. (1998) *The New Regionalism in Western Europe*. Cheltenham: Edward Elgar.

Le Galès, P. (1998) "Regulations and Governance in European Cities." *International Journal of Urban and Regional Research* 22(3): 482–506.

Le Galès, P. (2002) *European Cities, Social Conflicts and Governance*. Oxford: Blackwell.

Mossberger, K. and G. Stoker (2001) "The Evolution of Urban Regime Theory: The Challenge of Conceptualisation." *Urban Affairs Review* 36: 810–35.

Moulaert, F, F. Martinelli, and S. Gonzalez (2007) "Social Innovation and Governance in European Cities: Urban Developments between Path Dependency and Radical Innovation." *European Urban and Regional Studies* 14(3): 195–209.

Moulaert, F., F. Martinelli, and A. Rodriguez (2003) *The Globalized City: Economic Restructuring and Social Polarization in European Cities*. Oxford: Oxford University Press.

Musterd, S, M. Bonje, C. Chapain, Z. Kovácks, and A. Murie (2007) *Accommodating Creative Knowledge: A Literature Review from a European perspective*. ACRE Report 1. http://www2.fmg.uva.nl/acre/index.html.

Pierre, J. (2005) "Comparative Urban Governance: Uncovering Complex Causalities." *Urban Affairs Review* 40(4): 446–62.

Salet, W. and E. Gualini (2007) *Framing Strategic Urban Projects: Learning from Current Experiences in European Urban Regions*. London: Routledge.

Savitch, H. V. and P. Kantor (2002) *Cities in the International Marketplace: The Political Economy of Urban Development in North America and Western Europe*. Princeton, NJ: Princeton University Press.

Scott, A. J. (2008) "Resurgent Metropolis: Economy, Society and Urbanization in Interconnected World." *International Journal of Urban and Regional Research* 32(3): 548–64.

Stone, C. (2005) "Looking Back to Look Forward. Reflections on Urban Regime Analysis." *Urban Affairs Review* 40(3): 309–41.

Storper, M. and M. Manville (2006) "Behaviour, Preferences and Cities: Urban Theory and Urban Resurgence." *Urban Studies* 43(8): 1247–74.

CHAPTER 25

URBAN VIOLENCE IN THE UNITED STATES AND FRANCE: COMPARING LOS ANGELES (1992) AND PARIS (2005)

SOPHIE BODY-GENDROT AND
H. V. SAVITCH

1. America and Europe in Perspective

Collective violence is hardly new to cities and has a long history in America and Europe. We examine this subject by closely comparing mass rioting in Los Angeles in 1992 and Paris in 2005. Our approach uses an interactive framework that incorporates key variables. These variables identify how riots begin, how they mature, and how they end. Highlighting these processes enables us to understand how the conjunction of critical events can set off a social conflagration as well as shape interrelationships between key actors. An interactive approach also reveals a good deal about the dynamics of collective violence in different societies.

Collective violence does seem to occur in waves characterized by periods of upheaval and followed by periods of quiescence. In the United States the most memorable time occurred during the 1960s when cities were aflame with burning buildings and demonstrators took to the streets. The civil strife began with four major upheavals in 1965; 21 in 1966; 83 in 1967, and more than a hundred in 1968

(U.S. Riot Commission 1968). During these years collective violence brought about the deaths of 250 people, it left 12,000 injured, and approximately 83,000 people were arrested. Europe also had its memorable incidents of collective violence. In France and Germany, radicals staged demonstrations which sometimes turned violent. Although officially, no deaths occurred among the students confronting the police on the streets of Paris and other large cities in France, clashes between police and young workers on strike in 1968 caused at least three deaths and over one hundred demonstrators were badly injured. Approximately 400 people were arrested. In Germany, the clashes were also violent.

In the United States the violence of the 1960s was often explained as the result of socioeconomic conditions in black neighborhoods. The scholarly literature either assumed or claimed that poverty and segregation were responsible for collective violence. Besides this, the urban context plays a role in channeling collective violence. The relatively dense spaces of cities allow crowds to gather and facilitate mass mobilization. Urban densities also permit news and rumors to circulate more easily and are likely to serve as a source of mobilization. When combined with poverty and social exclusion this can be a lethal combination and precipitate collective violence.

It was against this backdrop that civil rights leaders called for increased federal aid to the poor and their neighborhoods, lest the hardships produce still more calamitous violence (Piven and Cloward 1971; Hobsbawm 2005; Olzak, Shanahan, and McEneaney 1996). A presidential commission, named after its chair and former governor of Illinois Otto Kerner, reported on the course of events. In what has become a familiar quote, the Commission bluntly wrote, "Our society is moving toward two societies, one black, and one white—separate and unequal" (U.S. Riot Commission 1968). The Kerner Commission blamed white racism for conditions that led to mass rioting, adding that the nation was deeply implicated in having created black ghettos (U.S. Riot Commission 1968). The violence in Europe was explicitly more political. Nevertheless, some form of deprivation lay at the root of French and German protestors who were motivated by an urge to remake the social order.

Much of the 1970s and 1980s saw a relative lessening of collective violence, both in the United States and western Europe. Those incidents that did occur were singular and isolated. A radicalization of young political activists emerged with direct action groups resorting to extreme violence to make their political cause visible. Action Directe in France, the Red Brigades in Italy, and the Baader band in Germany attacked lethally, not just political leaders but economic members of the elite as well. But in France starting in 1981, clashes repeatedly opposed bands of youths, frequently of immigrant origin, to the police after incidents in neighborhoods in crisis.

By the early 1990s and into the millennium, two major episodes of civil strife burst upon the scene. Collective violence erupted in Los Angeles during 1992 and large scale disorder reared its head again in the greater Paris area during 2005. Both of these major incidents were marked by waves of violence and had immense impact in their respective societies. Again the urban context helped mobilize the demonstrators. In the United States, other cities experienced mass, violent attacks at the turn of the 1990s. Different triggering incidents set off collective violence in New York (1991 and 1992), Detroit (1992), and Miami (1989). These episodes had a clear racial or ethnic content.

Much the same scenario occurred on the other side of the Atlantic during the 1980s. In the United Kingdom riots occurred in major inner-city areas containing relatively compact and highly segregated African-Caribbean populations such as Bristol (1980), Manchester, Liverpool, Birmingham, Leeds, and Brixton. In the 1990s, they involved white youth from working-class high-rise projects and police after some incidents such as car thefts or ram-raiding (Waddington, Jobard, and King 2009). At the beginning of the 2000s, riots occurred between white and immigrant youth in the northern textile towns of Oldham, Burnley, and Bradford. Some of these incidents revealed the racial content of events, too often hidden by the generic term "riot."

In France, the riots of 2005 were directly connected to rioting that erupted in 210 cities as well as limited copycat attacks in Germany, Belgium, Denmark, Spain, Greece, and Italy (Body-Gendrot 2008). The incidents had a racial/ethnic overtone with a majority of participants from Arab, African, and Muslim background clashing with the police in core cities (Roy 2005; Silverstein and Tetreault 2006). Four out of five neighborhoods hit by disorders benefited from territorial affirmative action. "We are not aware of any riots having occurred (with) actors...from middle-class or affluent neighborhoods" (Lagrange 2009: 109).

We now have an opportunity to learn from the perspective of this urban violence. Using Los Angeles and Paris as centerpieces, we ask: What was the basis of these disorders? Can they best be explained as the major product of economic disadvantage and social prejudice—or as some theorists call it, "deprivation theory"? Does deprivation theory alone provide the best explanation or are there political/bureaucratic conditions that can shed light on these episodes? How might we identify these political/bureaucratic conditions? Further, if a complexity of conditions brought on the urban violence, what policy steps can be taken to ensure public safety?

2. Reconsidering Theory

As applied to the urban context, deprivation theory stresses mounting and cumulative burdens on the poor and minority groups. In the United States, research points to the withdrawal of federal assistance from inner cities, shrinking welfare assistance, and inequality (Castells 1983; Harris and Wilkins 1988; Feagin and Hahn 1973). Similar explanations are offered for collective violence experienced by immigrant neighborhoods in France, sometimes with an emphasis on abuse stemming from France's colonial past (Stora 2002).

While there is something to be said for deprivation theory, it does not provide a sufficient explanation for the events which transpired in Los Angeles. If deprivation alone explained the Los Angeles riot, one would expect that Los Angeles would compare unfavorably to other cities in its level of economic hardship. Both our analysis and others suggest otherwise. Indeed Los Angeles did and continues to do comparatively well on most indices of economic hardship (Nathan and Adams 1976, 1989; Ledebur and Barnes 1992; Savitch et al. 1993). Levels of poverty, unemployment, and other distress factors show that Detroit, Cleveland, Newark, St. Louis, and a host of other cities fared far worse than Los Angeles.

Moreover, nationwide disturbances would have occurred in the wake of scant federal assistance to inner cities and would have subsided as federal aid increased. However, the historical record shows the opposite. The era of the mid to late 1960s showed the highest levels of urban collective violence, and this was a high point for the War on Poverty. By comparison the period between 1982 and 1988 was one of dramatic federal withdrawal and cities remained relatively quiescent. Also, well after the Los Angeles disorders George W. Bush's White House severely cut federal aid and urban strife was at an all-time low.[1]

Last, deprivation theory depended upon violence being caused by a vertical hierarchical relationship between the establishment (in the form of social class or a controlling government) and an underclass minority. In fact the Los Angeles case (and many others) involved the major conflict as lateral, between ethnic/racial minorities occupying the same city space. Collective violence in Los Angeles entailed serious multisided communal conflict between blacks, Latinos, and Korean Americans. Two-thirds of the Latino migration clustered within four formerly black communities and Koreans succeeded Jewish shopkeepers in those neighborhoods. Many African Americans feel Latinos have taken jobs from them, and believe themselves to be treated rudely by Korean shopkeepers. About one-third of blacks surveyed felt that Mexican Americans "didn't try hard enough to speak English," while 39% of Latinos felt blacks were more violent than other Americans; nearly half of Asian Americans believe that blacks lack motivation (Oliver and Johnson 1984; Bobo et al. 1992). These considerations suggest that a skein of factors, including but not limited to deprivation, caused the April 1992 riot in Los Angeles.

Much the same could be said for France. Collective violence occurred in French neighborhoods benefiting from specific public subsidies within what is called *politique de la ville* (a prototype for diversified forms of preferential treatment in selected

1. The U.S. Conference of Mayors estimates that federal aid to state and local governments fell by $34 billion in adjusted dollars in the 1980s (O'Cleireacain, 1991: 276). Betgween 1980-1990, federal aid as a percentage of city budgets was reduced by nearly 64%, falling from an average of 17.7% in 1980 to just 6.4% in 1990 (Simmons, 1991). In Los Angeles, federal aid plummeted from nearly 15% of the city budget in 1968 to 9% in 1988 (U.S. Bureau of the Census, 1968, 1988). George W. Bush (2000-2008) continued to cut aid to the cities. From 2000 to 2006 Community Development funding was reduced by $1.25 billion (NMI, 2006).

problem neighborhoods). This mode of territorial affirmative action was launched at the beginning of the 1980s after the return of the Left to power. It targeted 184 experimental zones in 1984. But, four years later, under pressures from concerned mayors, this policy was extended to 500 neighborhoods in a context of economic changes and massive unemployment and marked by outbursts of collective violence (Body-Gendrot 2000). Currently, after reaching 1,300 in 1999, the number of subsidized neighborhoods (referred to as sensitive urban zones—ZUS—by the French administration) is 751. The majority of them are located in the Greater Paris. They are characterized by a large component of unemployed and large, immigrant families living in massive public housing.

These data could give substance to the relative deprivation theory. But the correlation is affected by a complexity of factors. First of all, the data give a static picture of neighborhoods. They do not reveal the high turnover of residents which is more important in these zones than elsewhere. As families experiencing economic and social upward mobility move out, the statistics of a place get worse. The maximum priority given by authorities to sites where the 2005 riots occurred was not due to their level of deprivation, but to their risks of violence. Numerous riots occurred in free enterprise zones (Lagrange 2009: 111). Usually located in the most deprived zones, they had generated a high level of unmet expectations that led to anger, especially among the youth.

Also undermining the deprivation theory in the Paris case, interviews reveal a wide diversity of attitudes and perceptions among the residents. Research on recent urban renewal programs in metropolitan Paris reveals that only 20% to 25% of the residents wanted to leave their neighborhood (Lelévrier 2008). A majority of residents preferred to stay, hoping to benefit from larger or better apartments. The voice of the marginalized and angry youth or of disenfranchised and older "whites," usually echoed in the media, do not convey a wholly accurate picture.

3. An Interactive Framework

Our interactive approach emphasizes the operation of multiple forces which, in the course of events, come together to produce a particular outcome (Skocpol 1979; Goldstone 1991; Savitch and Useem 1992). These forces may be independent of each other initially, but interpenetrate as events unfold. Thus, the decline of employment opportunities for inner-city residents may be independent of discord within city government, yet in combination with other circumstances which debilitate the community (increased schooı dropout rates which put youth on the street, interethnic tensions which augment police-community tensions), these factors can combine to create a highly combustible compound.

The murky problem of why riots occur can also be illuminated by thinking about the obverse: why do riots not occur more often in situations where we might

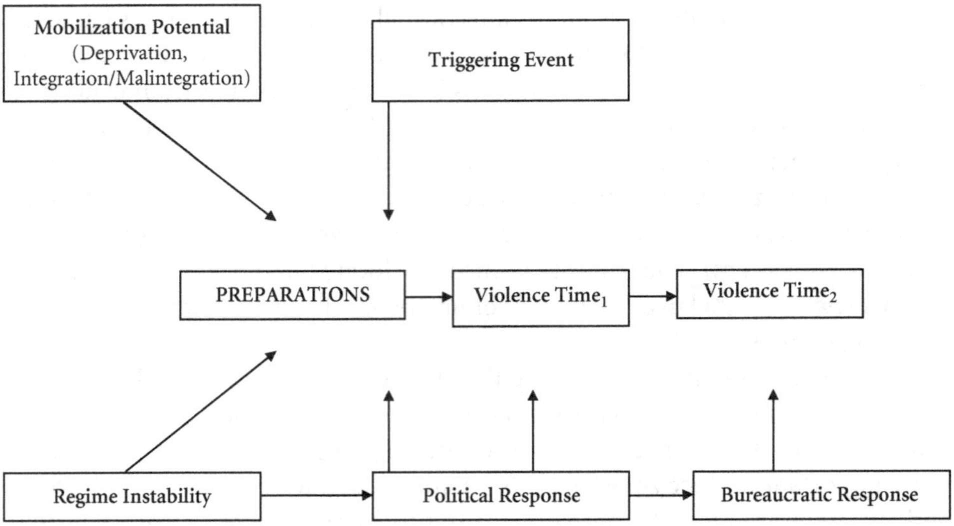

Figure 25.1 An Interactive Framework for Understanding Urban Rioting

expect them? The answer can best be obtained initially, by acknowledging that civil strife is relatively rare, and next, by suggesting that when collective violence does occur, it is catalyzed through a labyrinth of relatively discreet, highly dispositional events which, at a defining moment, fold into one another. It is this combination of chance, context, and causation which guides our study.

Using an interactive framework, we suggest that collective violence can be understood in terms of figure 1. The figure displays the components of urban rioting as mobilization potential, triggering events, preparations, regime stability, and political/bureaucratic response.[2]

By *mobilization potential* we mean the relationships and attitudes that facilitate or inhibit collective violence (Goldstone 1991). We identify this potential as having two constituent parts: (a) deprivation and (b) integration/disintegration. As we see it (a) deprivation occurs within logical and causative contexts. The collective violence in Los Angeles did not emanate from Beverly Hills but from impoverished neighborhoods in south central Los Angeles. In Paris the demonstrators were not drawn from the Champs Elysées, but from depressed housing projects in the northern suburbs (*banlieues*) of Paris. By deprivation we mean economic hardship, the diminution of real and/or perceived chances for social mobility, and widening inequalities between the status of one ethnic group relative to others. By (b) integration/malintegration we mean the kinds of organization that potential demonstrators join or associate with. Is there integration into traditional family or civic structures in an atmosphere of peace? Or, is there malintegration on the streets or into gangs of youth amid a mood of anger?

2. The figure and framework are modified and the original drawn from H.V. Savitch and Bert Useem (1992).

A *triggering event* is viewed here as a publicized episode that brings to a head or catalyzes cumulative grievances. Triggering events are usually filled with drama or tragedy of one kind of another. *Preparations* refer to a process in which potential rioters become mentally ready to engage in collective action/violence. Since this may occur in phases we have designated its ramification in terms of $Time_1$, $Time_2$, and so on. *Regime stability* is defined as the formal and informal arrangements through which conflict and social change can be managed (Stone 1989; Elkin 1987). When regimes are stable they will be unified and act in clear, decisive terms. This includes (a) political response and (b) bureaucratic response. By political response we mean effective policy decisions made by publicly elected officials. By bureaucratic response we mean the ability to swiftly implement those policies. Naturally, both responses depend upon effective leadership. In examining the stages of collective violence we are interested in the direction taken by the demonstrators as well as whether the participants changed.

We now conduct a "running comparison" between Los Angeles (1992) and Paris (2005) by employing the framework posed above (Savitch and Kantor 2005). We begin with a summary of the facts.

4. Los Angeles and Paris under Pressure

4.1. Facts in Los Angeles and Paris

Los Angeles: At 3:10 P.M. on April 29, 1992, a jury announced the acquittal (on all but one count) of four Los Angeles police officers charged with beating Rodney King. Almost immediately, crowds began to collect on street corners around the city and there were several minor disturbances. About 6:30 P.M. a hostile crowd began to form at an intersection (Florence and Normandie) in south central Los Angeles, the heart of the city's African American population. The crowd grew to an estimated 600 participants and began to assault passing motorists (including the infamous beating of trucker driving through the area). About 100 officers collected at an emergency field post, but they did not deploy. By about 7:00 P.M., the violence began to spread to other parts of the city and continued for the next five days. Property damage was estimated at $1 billion and the episode caused 60 deaths.

Paris: The 2005 outbursts occurred on October 27, in Clichy-sous-Bois, a deprived urban zone in Seine-Saint-Denis north of Paris. Three youth (one of Turkish descent, the other two of African heritage) trying to escape a police patrol, came upon an electric power substation. They ignored the "Danger/High Voltage" signs and went into the area. Two of the three youth misstepped and were instantly electrocuted. A rumor immediately spread that the police had provoked the incident. Within hours about 100 young men descended onto the streets, chanting

"Dead for nothing!" They threw rocks at city buses and the police, then set 23 cars ablaze (Waddington, Jobard, and King 2009: 4). Two additional nights of intermittent rioting followed. The fire station was stoned, windows were broken, bus shelters vandalized. and the postal center set ablaze. The next day, 400 antiriot police were sent into the neighborhood of Chêne Pointu. The violence subsided and a silent march ensued, gathering 500 protesters. Three nights later, a tear gas canister fell into the entrance of a store-front mosque, causing panic. The youth accused the police of having perpetrated this, while the police denied any wrongdoing. Thereafter seven localities north of Paris experienced large scale violence before reaching provincial cities. After six days of unrest, 200 cars had been torched, violent clashes and heavy damages had occurred, but the outbursts remained contained to the North of Greater Paris (Body-Gendrot 2008). On the whole, after 20 days of massive violence, the total cost was estimated between 200 and 250 million Euros (Body-Gendrot 2008).

4.2. Mass Mobilization Potential

Deprivation in Los Angeles: During the decades prior to 1992, Los Angeles or parts of it had become poorer. The proportion of families below the poverty line rose from 9% in 1970 to over 13% in 1990, and in years prior to 1992 joblessness has risen substantially from 4.9 to 7.8%. Still, Los Angeles was by no means at or near the bottom of the deprivation ladder. As of the 1990s the city's "hardship" relative to 55 major cities in the nation was roughly in the middle, and its income disparity with surrounding suburbs compared favorably with most other cities (Ledebur and Barnes 1992; Savitch et al. 1992).[3]

Low income and joblessness were compounded by endemic hopelessness, especially for youth. For the whole of Los Angeles, roughly 60% of high school students graduate and 40% drop out. In south central Los Angeles the figure was reversed and in some schools roughly three-quarters of the school age population dropped out (Johnson, Cloyzelle, et al. 1992).

Integration/Malintegration in Los Angeles: We find evidence in the African American community that gangs played a significant role in initiating mass violence. Gangs have strong horizontal integration and weak vertical integration. While estimates of gang membership should be viewed skeptically, police data suggest that half of all black males 21 to 29 years old belong to gangs. The figures for Latinos (8%) and Asian Americans (6%) are substantially lower (Dentler 1992). It appears that collective action within the Latino community came from recent immigrant groups, located in south and central Los Angeles. These groups appear to perceive

3. Calculations of hardship of 55 cities between 1970 and 1980 show that Los Angeles actually reduced its level of deprivation and is in third quintile (Nathan & Adams, 1989). Calculations on city-suburban income disparities show Los Angeles as holding 67.7% of the per capita earnings of its suburbs. This puts Los Angeles as the 41st least disparate metropolis among 56 others (Ledebur & Barnes, 1992).

themselves as having little stake in the existing political and social order. In contrast, the long established Mexican American community in East Los Angeles did not experience serious disorders. This may be due to greater political integration in East Los Angeles as reflected by and stemming from recent electoral victories. The progressive political integration of Mexican American immigrants has reached a new stage by the election of a mayor from that group.

Deprivation in Paris: The department (county) experiencing most of the violence, Seine-Saint-Denis, has the highest unemployment rate in France. The percentage of unemployed households was 13.9% at the end of the summer of 2005 (versus 9.8% in France). The number of those receiving public assistance went from 38,000 to 48,000 between 2002 and 2005 (Kokoreff 2008: 156).

Clichy-sous-Bois (referred to by its shortened nomenclature as Clichy) is the poorest locality in the Department of Seine-Saint-Denis. Its rate of unemployment reached 23.5% in 2004 (16% in 1993) and 31% for those under 25. Dependent families make up 67.4% of the population and 46.6% are under the poverty threshold; 33% of the residents are nonnational immigrants and among them, 60% are jobless. In the neighborhood of Chêne Pointu immigrants comprise 45% of the population (Kokoreff 2008: 166).

Integration/Malintegration in Paris. The topic of integration is all the more difficult to handle here as there is no ethnic/racial categorization in France. Only the distinction French/nonnational applies, ignoring the importance of French second or third generations of foreign origin in these *banlieues*. H. Lagrange offers some clues. In the second week of unrest, a number of localities with large families of African origin were the scene of riots and as he observed among these families, "there is clearly a marked tendency toward delinquency and school under-achievement." "The concentration of large families correlates very significantly with the geography of the riots... and their level of segregation" (Lagrange 2009: 113).

The segregation of a place translates into poor schooling, stigmatization, delinquency, and economic disinvestment. The feeling of being segregated adds to that of unfairness. "The rate of unemployment among the 15–25 year old does not appear empirically as a factor fuelling riots" (Lagrange 2009: 120). The localities where the sub-Saharan families settled were not riot zones in the 1980s and the 1990s. These young rioters have no stake in the existing political and social order and due to their isolation, they have no spokesmen. There is no transmission of a culture of protest from the older ones to the youngest. Community organizations deliver services; they are not advocates for the have-nots. The political representation of these residents is nonexistent.

Over two-thirds of the delinquent gangs in France are located in the Greater Paris and they involve several thousands of young people. There are not structured gangs as in Los Angeles and youngsters are not divided by race and ethnicity, but there are groups of idle youngsters between 13 and 25 making a living out of various activities who live in what might be called a counterculture. They are responsible for numerous street crimes; they guard their own turfs and attack those who do not belong to their neighborhoods. More and more firemen are attacked along with postmen, teachers, social workers, bus drivers, not to mention doctors, delivery people, and storekeepers. This has led to the abandonment of whole areas, where the police hesitate to enter (Body-Gendrot 2000: 189–93).

4.3. Triggering Event

Los Angeles: The Rodney King beating reinforced a widely held perception among African Americans, that some police not only acted as racially motivated brutes, but can do so without fear of sanction. Further, the acquittals became the focus of a sharp public debate. The verdict created a sense of unity within the African American community. Charges of racism and police brutality, long made by some activists within the African American community, were instantly grasped by a great majority and achieved mass expression.

Paris: The mishandling of the Clichy incident by the minister of interior (Nicolas Sarkozy) occurred in a highly charged political atmosphere. Sarkozy had referred to the demonstrators as *racaille* (rabble or riffraff). In a context of pain and grief, this and other remarks struck some as offensive. One local teen-ager explained that,

> things accumulated. It had been in the air for a long time, it needed to explode and it will explode again…The two youngsters who died in Clichy, many of us knew them. Had we engaged in peaceful demonstrations, it would have achieved nothing. The only means for us to be heard was to torch cars while on TV. I would say it worked. (Kokoreff 2008: 149–50)

4.4. Preparations

Los Angeles: Following the announcement of acquittals (3:10 P.M.), residents milled in the streets and engaged in acts which tested authority (rock throwing, halting traffic). For the most part, these acts were carried out with impunity. That is, they demonstrated that citizens could take to the streets and defy authority without much cost, restraint, or penalty. Around dusk, the nature of the activity changed in two important ways. First, those engaging in acts of defiance did not flee after committing a crime; instead, they remained in the area and exercised control over it. Second, the attacks widened and became more lethal.

Paris: Several sets of actors were involved among the rioters. First, a fraction of 15- to 20-year-old young men from Clichy frequently of immigrant origin (because immigrants are the major component of the working classes in France) started the disorders, acting out, displaying their emotion and anger after the two deaths.

Second, more violent and older individuals brought the chaos to a head. Their diverse motivations had to do with revenge (some of them had been fired from firms or institutions) or a will to destroy the status quo or mental disorder or other causes. In between, a lot of passive watchers hesitated to join in, while others tried in vain to stop the violence.

4.5. Times

Los Angeles effectively experienced two stages of collective violence. The first stage occurred at Florence and Normandie and involved brutal attacks upon persons. These acts were done by young African Americans who gathered on the streets. The second stage evolved as stores were progressively looted and buildings were set on fire. During this later stage young Latinos joined African Americans and participated in assaults against property. As for those who did not engage in civil strife, Asian Americans refrained from manifest acts of lawlessness. In fact Korean Americans stood armed guard over their endangered property and tried to preserve public order.

In France no locality experienced more than four nights of riots (Cinchelli et al. 2006: 3). What was unusual in 2005 was the contagion over a number of weeks that spread from the north of Paris to three hundred neighborhoods in various localities in France and the length of time the unrest went on—roughly 21 days.

There are several explanations for the increasing contagion over time. As mentioned, the local mayors' calls at first were not heard by the headquarters in Paris, choosing to protect a game at the national stadium in Saint-Denis rather than stop the rioters four nights after the beginning of the mobilization. They did not anticipate the media coverage either.

The drama of massive arson also attracted international television. As soon as the numbers of cars ablaze were seen on prime time news, it was interpreted as a further stimulus. At the start, the media began counting the number of burned cars, the number of cities, and affected neighborhoods. This did not help. The result was a Top Ten of the "hottest" cities, which stimulated youth of nearby cities to engage in still more violence and damage (Cincelli et al. 2006: 35). After ten days, the number of torched cars and acts of vandalism exceeded 1,400 in 274 localities. On November 7, after the prime minister delivered a solemn speech on TV, about 1,200 cars were burned in 300 localities. That night marked the apex of the contagion; 40% of problem areas in three regions, the most industrialized and the most socially polarized, were hit by disorders. As the weather turned cold the violence subsided.

In the French case, the media acted as a magnifying glass for isolated incidents, rewarding negative heroes, making sense out of their acts but after a while, denouncing them for their excess. The media were the translators of the events, using the same images to weave isolated events into a single narration (Balibar 2006: 95). Most adults in the affected localities did not support the offenders, but a lot of them said that they "understood" these violent reactions.

4.6. Regime Stability

Los Angeles: Beginning in the 1970s, the regime gained strength through a coalition of business and a liberal Anglo-Jewish-black alliance, whose crowning achievement was to elect a black mayor (Tom Bradley) by an overwhelmingly white electorate.

Bradley's soft, low key style enabled city leaders to push an agenda of economic development, racial progress, and some civilian control over the police (Saltzstein and Sonenshein 1991).

Over the last decade much of that has changed. The once quiet Bradley coalition has been superseded by a heightened competitive politics where ethnic groups vie for control, rewards, and recognition. Neighborhood and ethnic interests have grown reactive over a shortage of low income housing, declining school performance, and strained municipal services. As a new regime struggled to achieve stability, it came into conflict with the police department. Well before the violence of 1992, relations between the mayor and police were strained. Members of the City Council quarreled with the Police Chief Daryl Gates over the introduction of a community policing program. The police commission also fought with Gates over issues of departmental organization and management ("Gates Sharply Scolded," January 12, 1992; "Police Commissioners," January 14, 1992). Just before the outbreak of violence, the feud with Gates came to a head. Politicians denounced his actions as "bizarre and crazy" and accused him of violating the city charter. Gates returned the insults by charging that politicians had enfeebled the police, torn down morale, and "scared officers to death" about using any kind of force. Usually sedate downtown interests found themselves in the imbroglio and took up collections to revise the city charter, so that Gates might be controlled (Gates 1992; "Corporate Cash," March 24, 1992).

From both theoretical and empirical perspectives, the feud was even deeper and a symptom of an unstable regime in transition. The regime was caught in factional warfare between established liberal-downtown interests (critical of police performance and anxious about racial conflict), African American residents (angry at the police and deeply aggrieved), rising Latino and Asian American groups (uncomfortable with the police and anxious to win representation), and a humiliated police force (defensive about their conduct and confronted by everyday dangers). Finally, the regime was plainly divided with some favoring tough police action to stop crime and others accusing the police of racism and bigotry. When it came to the issue of police brutality, potential demonstrators could easily perceive that important elements of the regime were on their side against the police.

Paris: By the end of the 1980s most national efforts to combat poverty and social exclusion were diluted. Antipoverty and antiexclusion policies like America's Model Cities were targeted at improving public spaces, reducing poverty, and promoting educational opportunities. Increasing crime brought, however, about a popular backlash among white citizens and numerous left-wing mayors lost their positions during the elections in 1987. Stricter law enforcement was then invoked and 1997 marked the return of the National Police as a major actor. Antipoverty and antiexclusion policies found themselves in disfavor.

Riots covered by the media had occurred every year in the 1980s and the 1990s. Repetitive riots since the beginning of the 1990s seemed to have produced nothing but political shifts within the French public sphere (evoking fear of crime, fear of immigration, hate crimes, extreme voting patterns, etc.), which finally nurtured and legitimated law-and-order policies as the main strategic option (Waddington, Jobard, and King 2009: 235). Meanwhile, the situation in the most deprived neighborhoods deteriorated. The instability and destabilization of work, one of the bases of social integration, turned a swath of the population into a marginal population (Castel 2000: 528).

In 2001, fear of crime became the first concern of the French. During the first round of presidential elections, the choice of the extreme-right leader by a large number of voters caused alarm among some voters and apathy among others (28.4% of the French did not vote). When the disorders of 2005 spread across the country, the country turned further rightward, bringing about further schisms.

4.7. Political and Bureaucratic Response

Los Angeles: While the Rodney King episode was a powerful catalyst, the conflagration was far from inevitable. We suggest that failures at the conjunction of a precipitating event and the response of politicians and bureaucrats transformed verbal protest into an incendiary chain of violence. To begin with political elites, as the signs of civil strife emerged, a leadership forum was held at the First A.M.E. Church. This was a highly organized attempt to bring community leaders and constituents together. While this meeting included the upper stratum of black leadership (politicians, civil right proponents, clergy), it is not clear whether this black elite affected grassroots behavior. Much of the leadership seemed complacent about the possibility of mass violence. Not only was there an absence of constraint from black leadership, but some had put political pressures on the police to refrain from taking action. A member of the City Council warned ranking police officers that "a display of force would precipitate rather than defuse the situation" (Useem 1997: 370). All this only led to increased confusion about both the coherence and the intent of the regime.

On the bureaucratic (police) side, the fumble at Florence and Normandie was only one element of a generally disorganized and poorly executed response to the violence. Two-thirds of the police department's area captains were attending a conference at a seaside retreat and were not notified of the disorder until hours after its occurrence. While some expected that violence might break out as a result of the acquittals, police were mistakenly not put on alert. As a result hundreds of officers were off-duty as the verdicts were being read (Useem 1997).

Other elements include: near breakdown in the operation of the Emergency Operation Center (the department's command post); poor deployment of resources, particularly in the decision to use the Metro Unit (the department's elite unit); and failure to draw on other law enforcement agencies, such as the Los Angeles County Sheriff's Department. Most would agree that quick, decisive intervention was required to meet the impending volatility, and this was not only missing but clumsily managed. Indeed, some police actually fled from volatile areas because they were outnumbered and lacked adequate preparations. As the violence erupted, helicopters flew over the city streets, broadcasting coverage of numerous crimes while the police were absent (Useem 1997).

In sum, a combination of political divisions and bureaucratic ineptitude allowed the violence to advance without impediment. Political/bureaucratic confusion was as much responsible for the devastation of south central Los Angeles as any other factor.

Paris: At the local level, numerous mayors in the greater Paris mobilized their city police forces, made use of private safety agents, and mobilized antiviolence committees. Mediators, volunteers, religious leaders, parents undertook surveillance of the riskiest sites and sought to pacify the youths.

At the national level, the national police and the gendarmerie concentrated on particular zones and arrested the rioters. Yet these forces could not be backed up everywhere; 11,500 civil servants, including 4,500 police officers and gendarmes (60 units per night) were mobilized; 271 of them were injured during the outbursts. All told, 4,770 persons were arrested (Rivayrand 2006: 56–57).

A state of emergency was pronounced by decree on November 9, based on a law from 1955. It allowed curfews and home searches night and day all over the territory, the ban of youth assembly, and the closure of cafés and entertainment places in 25 territorial departments. Prefects were required to deport undocumented foreigners implicated in the violence. However, only 5% of the concerned localities resorted to curfews, demonstrating that mayors who knew their own communities exercised their own judgment in dealing with the situation.

In sum, the riots of 2005 shook the nation but only briefly. Many voters turned toward the right and some to the extreme right. Others remained indifferent or as a symbol of protest abstained from the political process. The reaction deepened already existing social schisms.

5. Collective Violence, Public Policy, and Policing Strategies

Perforce, any attempt to deal with collective urban violence needs to confront the issue of deprivation. In the United States this brought on the "War on Poverty" in the 1960s and "Empowerment Zones" in the 1990s. In France rioting prompted the initiation of "sensitive urban zones" and "*politique de la ville*" during the last two decades. Whether or not collective violence actually leads to public policy benefits is debatable. To be sure, findings in the United States indicate that under certain conditions welfare programs were expanded as a result of collective violence (Piven and Cloward 1971; Fording 1997, 2001). Similarly, findings in the United Kingdom on the effects of mass rioting on budgets also lend credence to this proposition (John 2006). On the other hand, our own assessment of rioting in France showed a public backlash after 2002 against increasing public assistance for marginalized communities. That the issue was not even a theme during the presidential campaign in France in 2006–2007 shows the indifference of mainstream France toward granting policy benefits.

These differences may very well be explained by differing contexts in which the rioting occurred, so the French experience may not be at odds with American and British studies. Nevertheless, the public policy benefits gained from rioting may very well be temporary. Certainly, in the United States the reduction of welfare benefits and contraction of welfare roles during the 1990s reversed any policy benefits that might have accrued as a result of earlier rioting. In the United Kingdom, the Thatcher government's response was not very different. Apart from the normative implications, it is difficult to argue that rioting brings long-term gains to the affected populations.

The only viable public policy course is via conventional routes of programmatic change. We know full well the difficulties and strings of failure associated with redistributive programs Nevertheless, without some reduction in levels of disparity, violence of one kind or another (collectivized rioting, individualized crime) is likely to persist. The avenues to success are familiar—reinforced education, jobs, decent housing, improved municipal services, and the like. The task here heavily falls on government, but government should also enlist nonprofit and private sectors into viable programs.

We should also recognize that any gains with regard to ameliorating deprivation will be incremental rather than sudden and it will experience periods of frustration. The uncomfortable reality is that liberal democratic states often do not have the political capacity to eliminate deep-seated poverty and broken families, much less do away with malintegration. Still and all, we can chip away at the problem and the sheer effort serves as a symbol of public commitment.

At the same time the amelioration of collective violence hardly ends with the issue of deprivation. Another course of action relates to police performance and stems from the train of events outlined above. Given the choices, police strategy could focus at any number of points. Traditional strategies are basically reactive, concentrating on the occurrence of criminal acts. Police respond to complaints or see a violation in progress and they take action. Other strategies have come to be known as community policing. Police departments take a holistic view of a neighborhood, set up ministations, engage the residents in deterring and identifying crime, and integrate activities around neighborhood needs. The latter often requires police to work more closely with community residents, who request that officers become more deeply involved in problem-solving and restoring order to an urban environment (Skogan 2004; Elmsley 2007).

Any strategy can be understood as tied to a particular organization structure. Police forces modify chains of command, allocate functional responsibilities, divide work into territorial units, and incorporate appropriate managerial techniques to fulfill a particular strategy. Simply put, for most police departments strategy shapes organizational structure. Traditional strategies for combating collective violence are usually supported by professional hierarchy models of organization. Management is carried out through centralized chains of command, departments are treated as efficient machines, personnel are deployed as needed, and specialized units are trained to handle particular problems (Brodeur 1995).

Proactive strategies which employ area sweeps may use matrix organizations where specialized officers are drawn from a variety of units to form teams. These teams may serve as supplements to existing forces or be assigned on a long-term basis. As one type of proactive strategy, community policing requires a decentralized geographically-based organization. If police are to enlist local help and interact with residents and civilian agencies, departments need to be more responsive, quicker, and flexible, requiring flat rather than tall hierarchies. A good example of this approach is offered by the "reassuring police patrols" launched by Police Commissioner Ian Blair which gained the approval of numerous residents in London. But concern with proximity between police and population is meaningful within a conception in which the police are not only serving the state but are accountable to the public and this requires that citizens should be partners or referents of policemen. In France where order maintenance is the police major mission, proximity with the population appears as a handicap (Zauberman and Levy 2003).

Finally, the effectiveness of a police strategy may depend upon the communities toward which they are directed. One can readily understand that if community policing is to be effective, it requires the existence of a community, that is, a neighborhood which shares common bonds, possesses social, religious, and civic institutions, and holds confidence in its ability to prosper. Without linkages to such a community, police organization is bound to collapse. Even with the same degree of community integration and organization, neighborhoods may vary in their attitudes toward police and openness toward mutual identification and cooperation. If these attitudes can be readily changed by immediate experience, then a program of community policing can engender the attitudes needed to support it. Attitudes toward police, however, may resist change, perhaps because they are embedded in a longer historical experience couched in animosity. If police are perceived with suspicion, community policing will be difficult to achieve.

In France, citizen input is not welcome in matters of law-and-order. Taking the law into one's hands to ensure safety is seen as an insurgent form of privatization. Self-defense, different from legitimate defense, is not considered as an appropriate response to problems of delinquency and it is condemned by courts. Moreover, because a lot of high risk places are immigrant neighborhoods, there is a tendency to denounce forms of civil organization involving older young men as communitarism which substitutes unwelcome allegiances for citizenship. It is feared that if ethnicized groupings were encouraged to involve residents into problem-solving, they would turn into "tribes" fighting one another. Sarajevo and Los Angeles are quickly evoked in such assumptions.

However, such fears, also fueled by the media, are not grounded in reality. In fact, serious offenses, gangs, weapons possession, and riots are not frequent, either in Los Angeles, in London, or in Paris. Three sets of actors, the media, the experts, and the political elites amplify urban risks, from youth antisocial behaviors to threats of Islamic terrorism, making the formalization of insecurity a unified and unifying category. In our noisy and competitive democracies, they cultivate the appearance of effectiveness with symbols such as the principle of precaution and opportunistic uses of urban concerns. However public opinion is not so gullible. It engages and disengages according to specific events or to the place given to risk in their culture. Changes relative to security are not just constructed at the top; they result from complex interactions with a variety of social, economic, and political factors differentiating one country, one city from another.

REFERENCES

Balibar. Etienne (2006). "Uprisings in the Banlieues." *Lignes*, November, 50–101.

Body-Gendrot, Sophie (2000). *The Social Control of Cities? A Comparative Perspective.* Oxford: Blackwell.

Body-Gendrot, Sophie (2007). "Police, Justice and Youth Violence in France." In Tyler T. (ed.) *Legitimacy and the Criminal System: International Perspectives.* New York: Russell Sage.

Body-Gendrot, Sophie (2008). "Urban Violence in France: Anything New ?" In L. Cachet (ed.) *Governance of Security in the Netherlands and Belgium.* Den Haag, Netherlands: Boom Legal Publishers, pp. 263–80.

Brodeur, Jean-Paul, ed. (1995). *Comparisons in Policing: An International Perspective.* Aldershot: Avery.

Castel, Robert (2000). "The Roads to Disaffiliation: Insecure Work and Vulnerable Relationships." *International Journal of Urban and Regional Research* 24(3): 519–35.

Castells, Manuel (1983). *The City and the Grassroots.* Berkeley: University of California Press.

Cinchelli, Vincent, Olivier Galland, Jacques de Maillard, and Serge Misset (2006). " Enquête sur les violences urbaines. Comprendre les émeutes de novembre 2005. L'exemple d'Aulnay-sous- bois." Centre d'analyse stratégique, November.

Dentler, Robert (1992). "The Los Angeles Riots of Spring 1992: Events, Causes, and Future Policy." *Sociological Practice Review* 3: 222–44.

Elkin, Stephen (1987). "State and Market in City Politics: Or, the 'Real' Dallas." In Clarence A. Stone and Heywood T. Sanders (eds.) *The Politics of Urban Development.* Lawrence: University Press of Kansas.

Elmsley, Clive (2007). "Community Policing/Policing Communities: Some Historical Perspectives." *Policing* 1(2): 235–43.

Feagin, Joe E., and Harlan Hahn (1973). *Ghetto Revolts.* New York: Macmillan.

Fording, Richard (1997). "The Conditional Effect of Violence as a Political Tactic: Mass Insurgency, Welfare Generosity and Electoral Context in the American States." *American Journal of Political Science* 41(1): 1–29.

Fording, Richard (2001). "The Political Response to Black Insurgency: A Critical Test of Competing Theories of the State." *American Political Science Review* 95(1): 115–30.

"Gates Sharply Scolded by Commission" (1992). *Los Angeles Times*, January 12.

Goldstone, Jack A. (1991). *Revolution and Rebellion in the Early Modern World.* Berkeley: University of California Press.

Gurr, Ted (1968). "A Causal Model of Civil Strife: A Comparative Analysis Using New Indices." *American Political Science Review* 62: 1104–24.

Harris, Fred R., and Roger W. Wilkins (1988). *Quiet Riots: Race and Poverty in the United States: The Kerner Report Twenty Years Later.* New York: Pantheon.

Hobsbawm, E. (2005). "Cities and Insurrection." *Global Urban Development* 1(1): 1–8.

John, Peter (2006). "Explaining Policy Change: The Impact of Media, Public Opinion and Violence on Urban Budgets in England." *Journal of European Public Policy* 13(7): 1053–68.

Johnson, James H., Jr., Cloyzelle K. Jones, Walter C. Farrell Jr. and Melvin L. Oliver (1992). "The Los Angeles Rebellion: A Retrospective View." *Economic Development Quarterly* 6: 356–72.

Johnson, James H., Jr., Melvin L. Oliver, Lawrence Bobo, and Walter C. FarrellJr. (1992). "Evaluating Public and Private Sector Responses of the Los Angeles Civil Unrest of 1992." Center for the Study of Urban Poverty, UCLA, September 16.

Kokoreff, Michel (2008). *Sociologie des émeutes.* Paris: Payot.

Lagrange, Hugues (2005). "Des banlieues prises au feu." *Libération*, November 4.

Lagrange, Hugues (2009). "The French Riots and Urban Segregation." In David Waddington, Fabien Jobard, and Mike King (eds.) *Rioting in the UK and France: A Comparative Analysis.* Cullompton, UK: Willan, 107–23.

Ledebur, Larry C., and William R. Barnes (1992). *Metropolitan Disparities and Economic Growth.* Washington, DC: National League of Cities.

Lelévrier C. (2008). "Les mobilités et la politique de la ville. Mobilités, un enjeu d'égalité." Saint-Denis, *Cahiers de Profession banlieue*, April, 11–40.

Nathan, Richard A., and Charles Adams (1976). "Understanding Central City Hardship." *Political Science Quarterly* 91: 47–62.

Nathan, Richard A., and Charles Adams (1989). "Four Perspectives on Urban Hardship." *Political Science Quarterly* 104: 488–608.

O'Cleireacain, Carol (1991). "Cats of New Federalism." *Dissent*, Spring, 276–78.

Oliver, Melvin L., and James H. Johnson (1984). "Interethnic Conflict in an Urban Ghetto: The Case of Blacks and Latinos in Los Angeles." *Research in Social Movements, Conflict, and Change* 6: 67–94.

Olzak, Susan, Suzanne Shanahan, and Elizabeth H. McEneaney (1996). "Poverty, Segregation, and Race Riots, 1960–1993." *American Sociological Review* 61: 590–613.

Piven, Frances Fox, and Richard A. Cloward (1971). *Regulating the Poor: The Functions of Public Welfare.* New York: Pantheon.

"Police Commissioners Urged to Block Gates" (1992). *Los Angeles Times*, January 14.

Rivayrand, Serge (2006). "L'action de la police nationale dans la lutte contre les violences urbaines." *Regards sur l'actualité* 319 (March): 56–57.

Roy, Oliver (2005). "The Nature of the French Riots." In the *Riots in France*, November 18, http://riotsfrance.ssrc.org/Roy/ (arguing that the rioting is not new, but the "extension of space and time" is the news of these riots).

Rubenstein, Richard E. (1992). "The Los Angeles Riots: Causes and Cures." *National Civic Review* 81: 819–26.

Saltzstein, Alan L., and Raphael J. Sonenshein (1991). "Los Angeles: Transformation of a Governing Coalition." In H. V. Savitch and John C. Thomas (eds.) *Big City Politics in Transition.* Newbury Park, CA: Sage.

Savitch, H. V., David Collins, Daniel Sanders, and John P. Markham (1993). "Ties That Bind: Central Cities, Suburbs, and the New Metropolitan Region." *Economic Development Quarterly* 7(4): 341–57.

Savitch, H. V., and Paul Kantor (2005). "How to Study Comparative Urban Development Politics: A Research Framework." *International Journal of Urban and Regional Research* 29(1): 135–51.

Savitch, H. V., and Bert Useem (1992). "Explaining Urban Disorders with Special Reference to Los Angeles (1992)." Proposal to the National Science Foundation. Unpublished manuscript.

Silverstein, Paul A. and Chantal Tetreault (2006). "Post Colonial Urban Apartheid." In *Riots in France*, June 11, http://riotsfrance.ssrc.org/Silverstein_Tetreault/ (explaining that similar, but more localized riots occurred in 1981, 1990, 1991, and 1995).

Skocpol, Theda (1979). *States and Social Revolution: A Comparative Analysis of France, Russia and China*. Cambridge: Cambridge University Press.

Skogan, Wes, ed. (2004). *Community Policing: Can It Work?* Belmont, CA: Wadsworth/Thomson.

Stone, Clarence A. (1989). *Regime Politics: Governing Atlanta, 1946–1988*. Lawrence: University Press of Kansas.

Stora, Benjamin (2002). *Histoire de la guerre d'Algérie*. Paris: La Découverte.

U.S. Riot Commission (1968). *Report of the National Advisory Commission on Civil Disorders*. Washington, DC: U.S. Government Printing Office.

Useem, Bert (1997). "The State and Collective Disorder: The Lost Angeles Riot/Protest of April, 1992." *Social Forces* 76(2): 357–77.

Waddington, David, Fabien Jobard, and Mike King, eds. (2009). "Introduction and Overview: The British and French Riots." In David Waddington, Fabien Jobard, and Mike King (eds.) *Rioting in the UK and France: A Comparative Analysis*. Cullompton, UK: Willan.

Zauberman, Renée, and Levy René (2003). "Police, Minorities and the French Republican Ideal." *Criminology* 41(4): 1065–100.

CHAPTER 26

CITIES AND THE POLITICS OF SUSTAINABILITY

ROGER KEIL AND MARK WHITEHEAD

1. On the Waterfront—Introducing the Duplicitous Nature of the Sustainable City

If you had taken a stroll along the gentrified public spaces of Toronto's Waterfront during the summer of 2007 you would have encountered an arresting piece of urban redevelopment. A sustainable "minihome" had been temporarily erected on the shore of Lake Ontario to provide a bespoke showcase for the area's sustainable urban development plan. A sign attached to the sidewall of the home proclaimed the goals of this new paradigm of urban development:

> WATERFRONToronto is committed to making the city's waterfront a national and global model for sustainability... We understand that sustainable development is imperative for the city, the province and the country as a whole. WATERFRONToronto wants to be defined and judged by our ability to deliver on our sustainable development principles: energy efficient buildings; green roofs; district energy for heating and cooling; brown field clean-up; 300 hectares of parks of public spaces; public transit within a five minute walk of all residences; cycling and pedestrian connections across the water front.

There is a geo-historical significance to Toronto's plans for sustainable urban waterfront development.[1] Nestled in among the marinas, condos, and affluent play-spaces

1. These plans have since come under review and contestation by a new municipal government under Rob Ford, who was elected mayor in November 2010. These newer developments are not taken into account in the current analysis.

of gardens and musical amphitheater, this exhibition of sustainable urban *imagineering* sits in a landscape that encapsulates the culmination of the late twentieth-century drive toward gentrification. In fact, the reclaiming of once derelict waterfront land has been interpreted as a chief example of "new built gentrification" (Bunce 2004 and a formidable case study of mega-project development (Lehrer and Laidley 2008). The City of Toronto, in cooperation with private and public corporations, has set out to make wasteland into choice real estate built on an ideology of social and ecological reform. The area has been an ongoing battleground of old and new, industrial and natural, water and land for decades. At each stage, new societal relationships with nature were developed, tested, rejected and existing political ecologies retreaded (Desfor and Keil 2004). The land where the city meets the lake has been produced through complex processes of urban ecological politics.[2] During the past generation, the area became the subject of a Royal Commission and a Regeneration Trust under the leadership of former Toronto mayor David Crombie, and it provided the screen onto which Toronto's Olympic Dreams were projected in both unsuccessful bids for 1996 and 2008. Crombie's waterfront plans introduced the notion of sustainable urban development into the local discourse at an expansive scale—covering hundreds of kilometers of shoreline and dozens of water courses that run down from the glacial moraine north of the city into Lake Ontario. The Royal Commission's battle cry was to produce—true to the mantra of ecological modernization—a "clean, green waterfront" to the benefit of the economic development of a city which had fallen into a deep slump in the early 1990s.[3]

2. The histories of the port and the portlands in Toronto have conjugated various fashionable waves of urban society, and nature, regional economies, and ecologies were to be entwined. A multiscale, historically complex story of socio-natures has been imprinted on the terrains and waters that have defined the city from its beginning (Desfor and Vesalon 2008). Once a bustling place of precontact aboriginal activity at the mouths of canoeable rivers teeming with fish, the waterfront has been a piece in the puzzle of the British Empire at least since the City of York, today's Toronto, was founded there in 1791. Later, it became the site of Toronto's nascent industrialization in the nineteenth century, and the scene for much of its unwanted heavy industrial and metabolic abuses in the twentieth.

3. Meanwhile, at a more local scale, an extensive artificial peninsula—the Leslie Street Spit—extends from the shore east of the city center and envelopes the Toronto Islands that sit like turtles a small ferry ride south of the downtown. A giant cyborgian landscape, the Spit was made by truckload after truckload of rubble excavated from the building of this emergent global city's downtown since the early 1960s. Yet, this was no regular waste disposal site but also a field of dreams that attracted the passions of various political communities and user groups from recreational sailors to bird watchers, from coyotes to cyclists (Hartmann 1999). The Islands, themselves, have become both refuge to a small population of residents who hold out in their bucolic cottages on the mercies of a 99-year lease and one of Toronto mass recreational destinations, particularly in the summer. But the Islands have also been the site of an iconic struggle over the new social ecology of Toronto's waterfront. Toronto's former "green" Mayor David Miller was first

There are two important insights that emerge from WATERFRONToronto's account of sustainable urban development. First, it reveals the all-encompassing nature of urban sustainability thinking: the sustainable city is defined in terms of its energy use/efficiency, the nature of its architecture, its framing of public space, its dominant modes of transportation, and the spatial patterning of its land-uses. It has been widely recognized that conceptualizing the city in integrated social, economic, and ecological terms is a defining characteristic of the sustainable city movement (see Girardet 2006). Second, it also emphasizes the ways in which sustainable urban development challenges urban policy to think beyond the narrow bounds of the city-limits, to consider the broader ecological and ethical footprints of a metropolis. The sustainable city is a call to understand the complex internal and external socio-environmental relations that enable a city to function. Thus while enmeshed in an urban space that has, to all intents and purposes, been pacified by a cappuccino-culture of conspicuous consumption and elite living, the sustainable urban development exhibition suggests a less avaricious vision of the urban future: a paradigm of urban development that recognizes the ecological costs of urban wealth creation, and the need for a more socially inclusive and energy restrained metropolitan future.

What interests us most about this expression of urban sustainability is not what it brings to light about the nature of sustainable urban place-making, but what it tells us about its associated politics. While it is clear that sustainable urban development (hereafter SUD) offers a potentially radical position from which to challenge conventional patterns of urban development, what is occurring on the shores of Lake Ontario is typical of the reformist depoliticization of urban policy that has became synonymous with the sustainable city vision. WATERFRONToronto (formerly known as the Toronto Waterfront Revitalization Corporation) is a public-private partnership of local government and corporate interests overseen by an appointed board of directors. In addition to a small number of elected officials, this body has typically been composed of executives of financial and industrial corporations. This elite group of urban executives are utilizing the values associated with SUD, as a way of continuing to legitimate their power over urban space, inventing all kinds of new features of a less regulated planning processes on the way (Bunce 2004). Where once business power over urban space was secured through the promise of growth and greater efficiency, it now appears to be assured by the visions of ecological modernization, green innovation, and creative environmental thinking promoted by the private sector. Whether it is being used to challenge the socio-environmental injustices associated with certain patterns of urban development, or to support the elite control

elected, in 2003, on a ticket that explicitly included the termination of flight activity from the City Centre Airport on the westernmost isle in the archipelago (Boudreau et al. 2009). That Miller's desire to stop planes from flying in and out of the city center may have more to do with the protection of the rising property values along the shining row of condominiums that have sprung up adjacent to the flight path than with urban ecologies in the physiological sense gets us back to the notion of "new built gentrification."

of urban space, SUD is an inherently political process. While the politics of sustainable city formation is routinely overlooked, it cannot be ignored.

We claim that the relationship between the sustainable city agenda and urban political studies has been crucial to the development of new perspectives on both the spatial politics of sustainable urbanism, and the socio-ecological dynamics of metropolitan governance. New ecological considerations now appear to be central to the formation of various modes of urban political mobilization. At the same time urban political studies has enabled the analyses of SUD to move from anodyne accounts of the technological implementation of sustainable city plans, to consider the power dynamics that are shaping what types of sustainable cities are being built, and for whom such urban places are being created. This line of analysis ultimately enables us to reveal how the sustainable city vision simultaneously embodies a radical perspective on the political and ecological functioning of cities, and at other times a powerful consensual device for claiming and shaping space around a relatively narrow set of reformist agendas.

2. The Genealogies of Urban Sustainability: From Vancouver to Istanbul

In order to view the formative moments of sustainable city ideal it is necessary to move from the shoreline of Toronto in 2007, to another Canadian city some thirty-one years previously. In May and June of 1976 the first United Nations Conference on Human Settlements was held in Vancouver. This conference led to the creation of the United Nations Centre for Human Settlements (hereafter UNCHS), which was charged with devising and implementing programs of human settlement that would supported key UN agreements on environmental protection, civil liberties, and economic advancement. Although the Vancouver Declaration, which followed the 1976 conference, did not discuss sustainable urbanism explicitly, it did map out the key principles upon which future policies and programs for sustainable cities would be based. The Vancouver Declaration envisaged cities as key sites in and through which international agreements could take material effect, and change the lives of target populations (see UNCHS 1976: 1). In many ways, this was the first time that the city had been put forward as a vehicle for international policy delivery. The Declaration did not, however, simply construct cities as neutral arbiters of social-environmental policy. It recognized that the rapid and sprawling development associated with *uncontrolled urbanism* was actively contributing to the forms of socioeconomic, political, and ecological injustice that the UNCHS was trying to address. The Vancouver Declaration thus envisaged a strategically planned, *orderly process of urbanization*, which would provide the basis for the forms of sustainable urbanism we are so familiar with today (UNCHS 1976).

The vision of future urban development established by in 1976 reveals something of the bewildering complexity of urban sustainable development policy. Equitable economic growth, improved food, health, and water supply systems, energy conservation, investment in safe shelter and accommodation, and antidiscriminatory policies, were just some of the goals of the Vancouver Declaration. The UNCHS's vision also contained a radical, progressive element, which asserted that in attempting to improve the quality of urban life for all "priority should be given to the needs of the most disadvantaged people" (UNCHS 1976: 4). The role of the Vancouver Declaration in shaping urban sustainable developing thinking can be discerned in two key ways. First, under the rubric of *life supporting resources*, it drew crucial lines of connection between social, economic and environmental justice (UNCHS 1976: 2). Second, through a strong emphasis on planned urban development and "the right and duty to participate," it established that sustainable urbanism was as much a political process as a planning goal (UNCHS 1976: 5). The connection between urban development and associated systems of open-governance, effective participation, and the *freedom to choose* are crucial, if often overlooked, dimensions of the sustainable city ideal.

The radical ideas of the Vancouver Declaration and UNCHS would be further codified by the World Commission on Environmental and Development and within the Local Agenda 21 process that followed the United Conference on Environment and Development in 1992 in Rio de Janeiro. In fact, some of the members of the Brundtland Commission, like Frankfurt's mayor Volker Hauff, carried the message of sustainable development directly into urban agendas. Peter Brand has noted that "[t]he Rio Summit of 1992 laid down a practical challenge and put the emphasis on action (now, before it's too late!), so that urban environmental management took on a technical and performative guise. Progress towards urban sustainability became a question of the adoption of good practice, to be promoted through international programmes and city networks, and measured through indicators, supported by a now huge literature on sustainable urban development" (Brand 2007: 619). Indeed, whereas many national governments at the end of the Cold War were slow in jumping on the sustainable development bandwagon, municipal authorities grasped onto the process with enthusiasm and practical success. Cities as diverse as Curitiba and Porto Alegre in Brazil, Freiburg and Münster in Germany, or Toronto and Vancouver in Canada became global showcases for sustainable development and workshops for practical applications of climate change policy, waste diversion experiments, pilot studies in innovative public transportation, green roof ordinances, bicycle networks, and the like.

While the World Commission on Environmental and Development and the LA21 process would align the diverse views on urban development associated with the UNCHS with the emerging principles of sustainable urbanism, it is clear that the sustainable city agenda emerged out of existing ways of thinking about the city, as opposed to embodying a confluence of urban policy with the orthodoxies of sustainable development. Confusion did, however, continue during the 1990s concerning precisely what the principles of sustainable urban development were.

In order to rectify this confusion the second Conference of the UNCHS (also known as Habitat II, or the "City Summit"), which was held in Istanbul in 1996, sought a more detailed articulation of what sustainable urban development involved. The *Habitat Agenda*, which emerged from this summit, contained over 100 commitments and 600 recommendations on urban development (see United Nations 2009). While now couched in the language of sustainability, the Habitat Agenda largely reaffirms the principles articulated in the Vancouver Declaration. According to Girard et al. (2003) there is an overt politics to the Habitat Agenda to the extent that it "[e]ffectively acknowledges that the neoliberalist 'laissez-faire' approach, based on the reduction in control, on deregulation, and so on, is not adequate enough to ensure the sustainable governance of the city...the Habitat Agenda sees the city as an 'engine of development' but also as an 'engine of social change'" (11–12).

While we recognize that the all-encompassing nature of sustainable urbanism has meant that it has been subjected to a range of more or less radical interpretations, we take as our starting point in this chapter the assumption that the sustainable city ideal represents a challenge to the political structures, economic imperatives, and environmental relations associated with neoliberal urbanization. Sustainable urbanization, at least in its formative articulations, proposes a city marked by five key processes: 1) a degree of control over the urbanization process; 2) new systems of procedural justice to ensure a broader cross-section of urban denizens have the opportunity to influence the nature of urban development; 3) deliberative attempts to secure more socioeconomic justice through active redistribution; 4) more integrated and holistic systems of urban planning; and 5) increased levels of local government intervention within urban systems in order to secure the objectives outlined above. While we acknowledge that not all, or indeed any, of these characteristics can necessarily be found within contemporary policies or initiatives that carry the label sustainable urbanism, we adopt these urban policy goals as contexts through which to explore the relationships between SUD and the study of urban politics.

2. Sustainabilities within the Machine: Urban Political Theory Meets SUD

2.1. The Sustainable City as Urban Countercoalition and Spatial Fix

It is tempting to interpret the arrival of the sustainable city agenda as a disruptive moment within the history of urban political study: a moment when the existing canons of urban political analysis were disturbed by new ways of viewing the city and of intervening within urban space. However, not only have preexisting theories of urban politics been vital in analyzing the varied processes associated with SUD, but a premonition of the sustainable city can itself be discerned within the urban political oeuvre. In 1976, the year of the first UNCHS conference in Vancouver, Harvey Molotch published his now classic intervention into the debate on community power, "The City as Growth Machine" (Molotch 1976). The growth machine thesis played a crucial role in shaping how urban theorists interpreted the nature of metropolitan development and the motivational dynamics of city politics (see also Logan and Molotch 1987). The essence of modern urban place-making was presented here as the conversion of an ever-expanding dowry of land into a marketable commodity (through lease and sale). It is thus the physical expansion of the city (in relation to both population and surface area), which, according to Molotch, facilitates the commercialization of complex systems of private land and enables growth to become the prime *operative motivation* for urban political elites (Molotch 1976: 1).

At one level, the growth machine thesis exposed the operational logics of the uncontrolled and unsustainable city systems that the UNCHS was trying to rein-in at Vancouver. The imperative of urban growth exposed by Molotch revealed that low-density, high energy consuming, car-based cities of suburban sprawl and exurbia—which had been the heart and soul of American spatial development, emulated increasingly in some form or another around the world—were not the accidental outcome of an aggregate of lifestyle choices, but were part of the political and economic logic of capitalist urbanization. But in his account of the decline and death of growth machines, Molotch also reveals the grassroots context within which the local political will for more sustainable patterns of urban development started. Consequently, at the same time as we see the first internationally sanctioned efforts to control the unregulated growth of cities, Molotch charted the rise of antigrowth movements in university towns like Santa Barbara, and larger cities such San Diego (1976). While we do not wish to claim that the urban countercoalitions identified by Molotch were direct equivalents to the sustainable city movement, it is clear that in their concerns with the impacts of uncontrolled urban growth on the urban living environment (particularly in relationship to air pollution and amenity) that the emerging politics of antigrowth urbanism was the local harbinger of SUD.

The urban growth machine thesis has provided a valuable framework within which to position and analyze SUD, and it has enabled accounts of sustainable city building to move beyond fairly apolitical accounts, which position SUD as largely a technical problem of planning and design, to recognize the fundamental challenge of this urban vision to capitalist urbanization (cf. Haughton and Hunter 1994; Harvey 1996: chs. 13 and 14). But if the environmental imperatives of SUD appear to challenge the growth logics of modern urbanism, more recent work has shown that the developmental goals of sustainable urbanism are compatible with the *ecological masking* of growth machines (see While et al. 2004). The growth machine politics of both Frankfurt and Toronto since the 1990s have, for example, relied on significant rhetorical and procedural articulations of growth with environmentalism rather than pitting one against the other (Keil and Graham 1998; Keil and Ronneberger 1994). Indeed, we now note that the sustainability and urban form debate has reached the pages of the conservative Manhattan Institute. Edward Glaeser (2009) wrote for the neoliberal think tank's *City Journal* recently: "So California environmentalists have things exactly backward. If climate change is the major environmental challenge that we face, the state should actively encourage new construction, rather than push it toward other areas. True, increasing development in California might increase per-household carbon emissions within the state if the new development, following the current model, took place on the extreme edges of urban areas. A better path would be to ease restrictions in the urban cores of San Francisco, San Jose, Los Angeles, and San Diego. More building there would reduce average commute lengths and improve per-capita emissions. Higher densities could also justify more investment in new, low-emissions energy plants."[4] Yet such applications of SUD need to be viewed cautiously and critically. In their work on SUD in Manchester and Leeds, for example, While et al. (2004) describe the emergence of sustainable development policies that have been forged at the interface of new regimes of economic neoliberalism and deregulation, and a rising sense of ecological responsibility within the urban polity. Exploring the links between the entrepreneurial and environmental city agendas, While et al. (2004) reveal the inherent tension between a model of urban development which prioritizes greater market freedoms (allied to looser restrictions on air and water pollution; intensified patterns of consumption; and greenfield sprawl); and an urban commitment to ecological care. According to While et al. (2004), it is the discourses and practices of SUD that provide uneasy *spatial fixes* to these apparently contradictory urban tendencies (551). But *sustainable urban fixes*[5] tend to focus on policy areas where it is possible to reconcile social, economic, and environmental priorities, while allowing *urban growth as usual* to continue where the costs of environmental and social policy bear down too heavily on the economic competitiveness of a place (While et al. 2004: 554).[6]

4. There is no page reference for this quote, but it is taken from the online version of the paper available at http://www.city-journal.org/2009/issue_19_1.html (accessed September 29, 2009).

5. The notion of a sustainable urban fix is deployed by While et al. as a way of capturing the spatial compromises that characterize the sustainable city. Deriving from the popular Marxian notion of spatial fix (which denotes the spatial orchestration of particular systems of infrastructure, housing, production systems, and social amenities that enable the socioeconomic contradictions of capitalism to be temporarily managed), the sustainable urban fix reflects how certain cities attempt to instigate patterns of spatial development that address the demands of sustainable urbanism and the political pressures which emanate from the socio-ecological costs of urbanization.

6. Research by While, Jonas, and Gibbs (2004) consequently reveals that while the city of Leeds has been able to make steady progress in its sustainable city agenda, the *high-octane* urbanism of Manchester has exposed serious contradictions between the economic and environmental goals of city leaders (this was expressed most prominently in the political debates and tensions that surrounded the expansion of Manchester airport).

Theories of Urban Growth Machines have exposed SUD studies to the role of elite politics within the shaping of urban futures. At one level, this perspective has laid bare the ways in which urban sustainability is compromised in its consensual alignment with urban orthodoxies of growth. At another level, related work has excavated the political geographies associated with the sustainable city project. Just as the nature of the urban elites who govern and control cities varies from metropolis to metropolis, so do the opportunities for different versions of SUD to develop, flourish, and flounder. But the political geography of SUD is more than just a question of the spatial variability of political institutions and culture: the political geography of urban sustainability is also a product of the geographical structure of a place (compact or low density; an expanding and developable airport or an airport site with little potential for expansion; a well-integrated set of land-uses or a series of single-use urban zones) and the political process that flow from these geographies. It is important to note that in recent years theories of the urban growth machine have been supplemented and extended by the application of Urban Regime Theory (Stone 1989). While also stressing the importance of urban coalition formation in the crystallization of urban power, Urban Regime Theory adopts a more pluralist take on metropolitan politics: suggesting that the power to initiate urban mobilizations is not the preserve of a patrician class, and that coalition formation can be based upon more than the orthodoxy of growth. At one level, Urban Regime Theory has offered a creative context for exploring the possible role of sustainable development in the formation of more open and ecologically-oriented urban political coalitions. It appears, however, that although "*green regimes*" may embrace aspects of environmental sustainability, they are still undergirded by the normalcy of growth and interurban competition (see Tretter 2009).

2.2. Sustainable Coherences and the Urban Class Politics of SUD

The growth machine theory has provided a powerful framework for the interpretation of SUD within the entrepreneurial spaces of urban postindustrial redevelopment. Although its premises are shaped by the particularities of the highly liberalized and localized American process of spatial growth, it has had a surprisingly strong resonance in Europe and elsewhere where scholars have distilled the principles of growth driven politics from the work of Logan, Molotch, and others, and have applied those analytical principles to their local and regional circumstances. It has, however, offered far less analytical purchase within urban spaces that have been subject to long-term economic decline. Studies of the application of SUD principles within old industrial spaces of structural economic decline have uncovered a very different set of political processes cutting across the sustainable city agenda (see here Whitehead 2003; 2007; Dunion and Scandrett 2003; Bernt 2009). Focusing on the *in-between* spaces of the city—spaces that have neither been able to remake themselves as the recreational play-spaces of the wealthy (as with the downtown) nor the manicured securities of WASP (White Anglo-Saxon Protestant) enclaves (as with the suburbs)—such studies have revealed the ways in which the persistent contours of class challenge and transform SUD. Related research has drawn on a diverse body of Marxist scholarship on the city, mainly anchored upon the transformative work of David Harvey (1973; 1989; 1996). Laying bare the connections between the spatial logics of capitalism and the urbanization process, Harvey develops two key concepts, which have particular significance for the political framing of SUD: *structured coherence* and the *regional class alliance.* According to Harvey, urban space under capitalism is marked by the gradual (and always contradictory) emergence of various spatial compatibilities between the use of cities as sites of economic production and of social reproduction (Harvey 2001: 328). These *territorial coherencies, inter alia,* relate to the location of industrial resources, the presence of key labor skills, the availability plentiful and affordable housing, and the presence of a publicly subsidized infrastructure of transport networks, power supply, and waste treatment. At a very simple level, Harvey suggests that the structured coherence of a city is determined by attempts to minimize the necessary movement of goods and services required for economic production, and the needs of daily labor substitution (i.e. commuting ranges). In many ways the regional class alliance is a political constellation that derives directly from the structured coherence of a place. Comprised of landowners, state and local government officials, as well as certain sections of the working-class community, the regional class alliance is essentially a coalition of interests who each benefit from the functioning of the urban space economy (see Harvey 2001: 333–34).

Although there are clear parallels between the analytical focus on Harvey's and Molotch's work, the exploration of structured coherences exposes dimensions of the politics of SUD that the growth machine fails to reveal. At one level an appreciation of the structured coherences of a city exposes the varied economic barriers that exist to SUD, and which often range beyond the expanded commercialization of land emphasized within the growth machine thesis. As Whitehead's work on sustainable urban health initiatives in Stoke-on-Trent illustrates, for example, reform on the factory floor is often conditioned by the broader economic fortunes of a given city's dominant economic sectors (Whitehead 2003). In the case of Stoke, with its dependence on the older industrial trades associated with the pottery and ceramics industries, we find a structured coherence unable and unwilling to make concessions to the demands of socio-environmental sustainability.[7] Consequently, while the commercial gains associated with the ecological modernization of production processes may be technically available to all, some cities are better positioned to embrace these opportunities than others. Theories of urban structured coherence always draw attention to the varied and ever shifting terrains of class alliance and conflict that SUD must navigate. Additionally, the attention that theories of structured coherence bring to the role of publicly-funded infrastructure in the

7. This resistance stems both from the large costs associated with restructuring the production process and the high level of international competition now being experienced in this sector.

operation of a city reveals how certain cities are politically locked into unsustainable patterns of development (Young and Keil 2009).

Consequently, while the nature of urban development in the Brazilian city of Curitiba may make the development of sustainable public transport systems economically viable for the local authority, cities characterized by low settlement densities, vast swathes of exurban sprawl, greenfield factories, and unifunctional zoning, may find the public costs associated with the restructuring of a metropolis's infrastructural DNA economically prohibitive and governmentally impossible (cf. Girardet 2006; Hall 2003; Martinez-Alier 2003; Rogers 1997). This is not the Manichean politics of class or community resistance to SUD that is commonly described in academic discussions, and is based upon a divided and irreconcilable beliefs concerning the balancing of urban economic need with environmental care. It is the unyielding politics that derives from urban inertia.

3. Sustainability and the Reconfiguration of Urban Justice: Toward a Planetary Structured Coherence

The central impacts of SUD to the urban political arena can be discerned through a consideration of changing approaches to questions of urban justice. SUD has not only led to a new interest in the connections between social and environmental justice, but also with the fundamental reframing of what counts as legitimate objects of contestation within the political struggles that surround urban justice.

Several sets of issues arise here. One is the issue of *spatial justice*. This speaks at one level to the fact that urban authorities are increasingly constructing their policies in relation to processes and events that extend well beyond their jurisdictional boundaries. At another level it also relates to the inability of institutions set up in a state-centered system of nested governmental hierarchies to address concerns of sustainability and social justice in a world that rapidly becomes more complex and more diverse. In this context, it is argued that cities may be more important now as instruments and locales of state strategies because they are constituted in a multiscale process of state rescaling (Jonas, Gibbs, and While 2009: 6). Furthermore this implies that despite the decidedly territorial connotations of the "sustainability fix" it must not distract from the fact that environmental governance is currently expanded at and across all existing scales, and that municipal sustainability efforts are constituted by and suspended astride networks that span the globe and that include state and nonstate actors (Bulkeley 2005; Toly 2008). The notion of a "fix" also must not be used to suggest that (local) states, despite their rhetoric and best attempts, are actually in the position "to save societies from the various threats associated with environmental fluctuations" (Whitehead 2008: 415). In fact, the sustainability fix at the local or regional scale suffers from an "institutional void" between the necessary policies and the shifting polities of a post-Westphalian world (Hajer 2003).

Second, SUD presents challenges of *temporal justice* to urban political communities. It has been a common characteristic of environmentalism to demand longer-term, transgenerational visions of political action. Building sustainable societal relationships with nature in the city, it is believed, means moving beyond the short-termism of the rent-seeking-growth-machine-ethic and the electoral cycles and parochial logics of local political activity. In addition to stretching the temporal framework within which urban politics operates, contemporary forms of SUD are also beginning to politicize urban time in new ways. Consequently, in the context of the likely socio-environmental threats associated with climate change, the politics of SUD is increasingly emphasizing the need for more rapid policy responses to climate change abatement and mitigation. This new temporal politics is perhaps demonstrated most clearly in the 100-Months (to Save Our Climate) partnership and its call for urgent transformations in current ways of life.[8]

The third set of issues that SUD brings into the center ground of urban politics is the question of *environmental justice*. The idea that specific urban areas are more polluted or subject to greater environmental harm than others has led to the notion of environmental racism. First used in the United States, but also since in South Africa, Canada, and other parts of the world, environmental racism denotes the coincidence of racialized (or otherwise excluded or stigmatized) populations and environmental "bads." Related grievances have been taken up by a movement for environmental justice which seeks the protection of affected populations and areas from future damage and, if appropriate, compensation for injustices that have been experienced by a community or by individuals. The environmental justice paradigm has been a powerful tool for activists, enabling oppressed communities to intervene in debates on urban sustainability debates (Agyeman, Bullard, and Evans 2003). Exemplary for a large and rapidly growing body of work on the subject has been the research of Robert Bullard (2007) who has made a direct connection between the unsustainability of sprawl in American cities and the question of environmental racism. While the political and analytical dynamics of environmental justice has come under much recent critical scrutiny, it is clear that the emphasis that it places on the complex interconnections that exist between social and environmental systems connect it directly to the broader goals of SUD (Debbané and Keil 2004).

The final set of issues that SUD presents to the urban political realm concern *transspecies justice*. As Jennifer Wolch (1996) has pointed out in her pioneering work on human-animal relations, in order to truly speak of justice and sustainability, cities need to be attentive to the challenges of the nonhuman to the ways in which we construct urban political communities and systems of metropolitan representation and participation. There are two aspects to the transspecies problematique in the context of urban sustainability. On one hand, there is an ethical component about

8. See http://www.onehundredmonths.org/.

human-animal differentiation and relationality (widely discussed in the wake of Singer 1975). In this context it is asserted that any discussion of sustainability and justice in the city must incorporate animal welfare. Whether cities can survive in the long term on a system of meat production which includes unethical production, slaughter and consumption of animals, or, more radically put, whether just and sustainable cities can be sustained on the basis of subjecting animals to (ab)use at all, is now a core ethical, but also pragmatic issue in the new environmental politics of the city (Wolch 1996; Wolch and Emel 1998). While important, this argument is not of predominant importance in our current context. On the other hand, then, each form of human-animal relations has metabolic, (infra)structural, and physical consequences that are central to the process, structure, and form of the city and its sustainability. In addition, the notion of the posthuman city has entered the debate from the experience of recent pandemic threats such as SARS, Avian Flu (H5N1), Influenza A (H1N1). In all such cases, problematic relationships of humans and animals in accelerated urbanization processes have been seen at the base of newly emerging infectious diseases that threaten life in cities. The globalization of infection has now also become a lens through which urban human-animal relations are being discussed in the context of sustainable urban living (Ali and Keil 2007; 2008). From this problematique, critical urban theorists have developed notions of posthuman urbanism, evoking the powerful insight that there can be no intellectual or practical separation of human from nonhuman life in the sustainable city (Braun 2008).

Despite its critical deconstruction in the sense presented above, the municipal and regional institutional level of policymaking and politics is an important *real-political* arena of action when it comes to the relationship of justice and sustainability. The chief challenge of this aspect of urban sustainability politics will be how to create *planetary structured coherences* out of the myriad local struggles over socio-environmental justice in the urban world. But if nothing else, it is clear that SUD has expanded both the complexity and extent of what is considered to be political in the urban context.

4. From the Sustainable to the Resilient City: Urban Political Ecologies, Climate Change, and Catastrophe

4.1. On New Analytical Trajectories

The varied convergences between SUD and urban political study have had transformative impacts on how we understand both the elusive goal of the sustainable metropolis and the nature of early twenty-first-century city politics. In this section we move our concern with the interdisciplinary gains associated with studying SUD from a resolutely political perspective so as to explore how changes in the epistemologies of urban political science, and the realities of urban environmental existence, are combining to render the sustainable city an increasingly anachronistic goal.

At a conceptual level, recent developments within studies of SUD and the nature of urban environmental politics have problematized the normative and analytical value of studying urban socio-environmental justice from a sustainable development perspective. In a normative context Krueger and Agyeman (2005) have cast serious doubt on the methodological imperative of those studying sustainable urban development to focus their attention on cities that explicitly declare their sustainable desires. Drawing on extensive empirical studies of cities with and without named SUD initiatives (see Lake 2000; Portney 2003), Krueger and Agyeman argue that the relative success of a city in achieving sustainability gains is not necessarily correlated to the presence of approved SUD schemes (2005: 414) and assert the value of studying *actually existing urban sustainabilities* (2005: 414). We like to think of the actually existing forms of SUD as *ambient urban sustainabilities*. These ambient sustainabilities include the tougher enforcement of environmental pollution legislation, the improvement of public parks, the provision of more regular public transport, the removal of asbestos from urban buildings, and collective campaigns to preserve labor rights. While these processes may not exhibit the integrative logics, or democratic aspirations of SUD, they may just be where the real business of SUD is being realized in our cities.

The emergence of urban political ecology has presented more wholesale challenges to the interpretative logics of SUD studies. Urban political ecology (hereafter UPE) has been an emergent theme in political and urban studies over the past decade (Keil 2003; 2005; Heynen et al. 2006; Swyngedouw and Heynen 2003). While the holistic sense of urban environmental study that is suggested by the ecological focus of UPE is reminiscent of the integrative intent of SUD studies, the political sensibilities of UPE set it apart (see here Heynen et al. 2006). The radical political intent of UPE is thus not only to foreground the politicization of nature within the city, but to fundamentally challenge the nature of what counts as "urban" politics. It is in this context that proponents of UPE have argued that in order to understand the nature of the political forces that shape urban ecologies it is necessary to move beyond narrowly defined accounts of the urban political field. As part of this emergent debate, attention has been drawn to the impacts of regional formations, state projects and the globalized, neoliberalized world economy on urban political ecologies (Brenner 2004; Swyngedouw 2004): the result has been an increasing realization that it is not just the ecologies of cities that are integrated into varied scales of bio-ecology and planetary systems of climate, but also that urban politics is a multiscalar phenomenon.

In addition to drawing attention to the role of regional political formations within the co-option of SUD agendas by groups who are beyond the traditional systems of metropolitan political accountability,[9] UPE has also stressed the importance of positioning the sustainable city firmly within the frame of the national state politics (see Whitehead 2008; Whitehead, Jones, and Jones, 2006; Swyngedouw 2009). While the rise of SUD has at one level been equated with a broader shift away from the powers of the nation-state, and depicted either as one of a series of neoliberal localisms (Tretter 2009) or transnational municipalisms (Toly 2008), work within UPE has been keen to connect the politics of SUD with the imperatives of national state ideology and strategy. Clearly, the role of the state (at all geographical scales and institutional levels) remains crucial in shaping the politics of urban sustainability.[10] At one level, it is thus possible to see SUD as one of a series of strategies that are remaking governmental territories into a series of urban state spaces, which are better able to adapt and respond to global economic and ecological challenges/opportunities than cumbersome national territories (see Brenner 2004). At another level, it is also clear that what is possible and desirable to achieve in terms of SUD is not only determined by urban fiat, but also by the broader landscapes of resource needs and economic investment opportunities determined by national agro-economic and industrial-military systems (see Swyngedouw 2004).

If UPE has questioned the scalar constitution of "urban" sustainability politics, more recent work has started to question the normative impacts of SUD on personal conduct and freedom. Urban sustainability has increasingly been recognized as a constitutive part of changing governmentalities under the neoliberal reign

9. It has been noted, for example, that the rise of new regionalisms of various kinds, and the construction of new city-regions (to govern metropolitan society and foster economic development), are connected to a politics of sustainable development. At one level there appears good reason for reconstituting SUD at a regional scale. Thinking about SUD in regional terms has the practical advantage that it mimics in territorial terms the metabolic relationships sustaining the city: incorporating the water, land, materials for construction, chemicals, energy, food, etc. as well as their reverse recycling and disposal as wastes that stretch well beyond the boundaries of the metropolis (Gibbs and Jonas 2001: 275; Keil and Boudreau 2006; Swyngedouw 2006; Toly 2008: 343). As Gibbs and Jonas insist, "[t]he environment needs to be a key component of the economic development strategy for a region, rather than marginal to it" (2001: 281). The regionalization of SUD, has, however, also been interpreted as more political than pragmatic, as new, unelected regional power blocs and alliances utilize the discursive promises of sustainable development and ecological modernization in order to gain strategic power over urban policy and key metropolitan resources (Gibbs 2006; Gibbs and Jonas 2000; Jonas, Gibbs, and While 2004a; 2004b; While, Jonas, and Gibbs, 2004; Tretter 2009). This "regional fixing" of SUD coincides with an opening and deterritorialization of urban policy which continues to stretch the capacities of local and regional decision-makers to deal with the challenges in front of them (Bulkeley 2005; Hodson and Marvin 2009; North 2009).

10. Jonas, Gibbs, and While call this development "ecostate restructuring wherein the liberal ecologically-modernizing state takes a more active and directed role in regulating the environmental inputs and outputs of mainstream economic and social activities including resource extraction, production, consumption, and to some extent also urban development" (2009: 5).

during which "the environment has become transformed into a sphere of social discipline and personal obligation. The liberating aspirations of much early environmental thought have all but disappeared, leaving in their wake an uninspiring field of limits, restrictions and risk...bringing environmental constraints into everyday spatial practices" (Brand 2007: 617). Urban sustainability agendas have at least three advantages in the promotion of these forms of diffuse power, as they allow them "[to create] sensations of wellbeing/welfare in and through the environment...[to reconstruct] of a sense of social unity and collective purpose, and to operate as a legitimation strategy in uncertain, neoliberalized times" (Brand 2007: 620). Urban sustainability lends itself to be consumed in this way as an ideological master-discourse and as a blueprint for urban governmentalities that easily bridge institutional, practical, and conceptual rifts between multiple discourses: technical, political, experiential, pedagogical, and so on. The retooling of an urban waste regime and the minds of eager grade-schoolers on recycling detail, global corporations mining the waste stream, and the organization of individual households are all "in the game" and are connected through the pragmatic politics of the "sustainability fix."

4.2. On New Urban Challenges

Various publications on the analytical prioritization of cities labeled sustainable, the emergence of UPE, and the development of theories of green governmentality have cast critical light on the theoretical and normative constitution of SUD studies. Recent events have, however, challenged SUD in more overtly material ways. The rising incidence of urban environmental catastrophes (relating to flooding, firestorms, tidal surges, and seismic disturbances), threats over urban water and food security, and the looming threats of peak oil production and climate change, have all contributed to a critical reevaluation of the SUD agenda. Each of these varied events has raised concern about the empirical assumptions that undergird sustainable development: namely that the environment provides enough predictable stability to enable sustainable socioeconomic systems to prevail, and that stable and virtuous relations can be established between ecological and socioeconomic systems. In this situation, a new proposition is being made that would, if accepted widely, historicize the urban politics of sustainability as a period rather than a process of more long-term reach. This proposition is to replace the universal discourse of urban sustainability with a more precise and programmatic set of global policy collaborations among cities and citizens. There are two main thrusts. First, there is the notion that "the reduction of reliance on fossil fuels—or what we term *carbon control*—could be emerging alongside, or even replacing altogether, sustainable development as the principle discourse and rationality underpinning new ecostatist modes of regulation" (Jonas et al. 2009: 5). This makes the local state a pivot in international climate regulation (Jonas et al. 2009: 8).

Second, there is an increased sense of crisis that has now begun to characterize urban ecological politics. Rather than being concerned predominantly with the positive virtues of urban sustainability, some have now topped the sustainability dynamic with a program of vulnerability and resilience. In view of recent disasters (from urban terrorism and warfare, to Hurricane Katrina and pandemic threats), cities have been the focus of increased concern about systemic breakdown linked to environmental and other factors (Clarke and Chenoweth 2006). A "passion of the catastrophe" has gripped cities and their politics (Citton 2008). Whether it is talk of a "planet of slums" (Davis 2005), or whether there is a "monster at our door" (Davis 2006), it is clear that politics of nature in the city is not just about redirecting material streams into more sustainable channels. It is ostensibly about survival itself. Talking in terms of resilience instead of sustainability prioritizes the possibility that urban society may actually be confronted by a series of severe step changes in their social economies and environmental relations, which are not easy to predict, or to prevent. Whereas sustainability highlights the importance of creating harmonious feedback between social, environmental, and economic systems, a politics of resilience openly recognizes that even if this goal were possible, the time for its potential achievement has long since passed most cities by. Resilience thus prioritizes *diversity* (in relation to urban transport systems, energy generation, food production), *modularity* (in terms of energy delivery systems etc.), and *tightness of feedbacks* (or the ways in which transformations in one part of an urban system are recognized and responded to by others) (see Hopkins 2008: 54–57; Keil 2009). The politics of resilience accepts, to a degree, that a new paradigm of "ecological security" (Hodson and Marvin 2009) has begun to emerge as a central preoccupation of cities and their polities. This impression is shared by those who have noted the heightened necessity of cities to add global pandemic preparedness to their sense of sustainability and security (Keil and Ali 2007). But a politics is not one of blind fatalism: quite the contrary, it suggests that new forms of community cohesion, working together, local empowerment, and ecological intimacy can not only prepare cities for the worst the twenty-first-century environment and economy can throw at them, but also make being-in-cities a more hopeful and rewarding experience. In this line of thought, a more foundational political discourse has started to seep up through the bureaucratic, institutionalized practice of urban politics. This, to use a phrase Isabelle Stengers has attached to Donna Haraway's politics, entails "fabricating hope at the rim of the abyss" (Stengers 2009b: 24). Or to use Stengers's own mode of thinking beyond the rim: "nothing will 'save' us if not our capacity to mend together the dispositifs of trial and error" (Citton 2009 based on Stengers 2009a).

5. Conclusion

In this chapter we have examined the urban politics of sustainability. We started from some concrete dilemmas present in today's urban development where growth (or decline) and environment/nature are repositioned toward each other in novel ways. The discourse and practice of "urban sustainability" has given these processes a new frame. We discussed how sustainability can mask cynical gentrifying strategies at one end of the spectrum, while it may be the matrix on which the tactics of an environmental justice politics grow at the other end. We have outlined some of the major historical developments through which the notion of sustainability has been linked to cities; and we have discussed major conceptual debates that relate to "urban sustainability." We can conclude that a new urban "politics of nature" (Latour 2004) must, by necessity, address ecological relationships in the context of human sociality.

We have shown that to some sustainability has been a "bureaucratic-ecological program for the stabilization of the economy" (Riesel and Semprun 2008: 57), which originated in such elite initiatives as the Club of Rome in the 1970s and which during its genealogy morphed into the sustainable development discourse of the 1980s and the ecological modernization of the 1990s (Keil 2007). Others are more hopeful and positive and highlight the potential of socio-ecological transformation for which the concept offers a rallying cry. Be that as it may, the sustainability agenda has introduced urban and regional politics to a political horizon way beyond the usual four-year electoral rhythm of municipal government and the one-year half-life of municipal budgets. Urban politicians are now expected to speak knowledgably and plausibly about events way in excess of their own terms in office.

The arrival of sustainability in the city has reopened debate on how to view cities: as scale (which simply means "local" really) or as level (in the Lefebvrian sense, which is the medium level between the universal and the individual) (Kipfer 2009). The urban as *level* points to the problematique of urban lifestyles, of the negotiating of societal differences, of modes of housing and transportation, of politics, and of what Jonas, Gibbs, and While call "the politics of the living space" (2009: 17). The urban as *scale* points to the necessity of negotiating sustainability politics locally and it assumes—in most cases—that the local is a place of natural democracy and basic forms, that is, more genuine or authentic forms of democracy, although such authenticity, like the entire idea of local, needs to be reevaluated in a world of unbounded electronic communication and high mobility, globalized rescaling, and topological networks that establish place in a web of far-flung relationships. Whether SUD represents the collective paradigm for our collective urban futures, or merely a passing trace in an evolving history of urban politics, it is clear that the meeting of sustainability and the city has had transformative impacts upon how we understand each category.

REFERENCES

Agyeman, J., Bullard, R.D., and Evans, B. 2003. *Just Sustainabilities: Development in an Unequal World*. London: Earthscan.

Ali, S. Harris and Keil, R. 2007. Contagious cities. *Geography Compass* 1, 1207–26.

Ali, S. Harris and Keil R. eds. 2008. *Networked Disease: Emerging Infections in the Global City*. Oxford: Wiley Blackwell.

Bernt, M. 2009. Partnerships for demolition: The governance of urban renewal in East German shrinking cities. *The International Journal of Urban and Regional Research* 29, 740–70.

Brand, P. 2007. Green subjection: The politics of neoliberal urban environmental management. *International Journal of Urban and Regional Research* 31, 616–32.

Brenner, N. 2004. *New State Spaces: Urban Governance and the Rescaling of Statehood.* Oxford: Oxford University Press.

Braun, B. 2008. Thinking the city through SARS: Bodies, topologies, politics. In S. Harris Ali and R. Keil, eds. *Networked Disease: Emerging Infections in the Global City.* Oxford: Wiley Blackwell.

Bulkeley, H. 2005. Reconfiguring environmental governance: Towards a politics of scales and networks. *Political Geography* 24, 875–902.

Bullard, R. ed. 2007. *Growing Smarter: Achieving Livable Communities, Environmental Justice, and Regional Equity.* Cambridge, MA: MIT Press.

Bunce, S. 2004. The emergence of "smart growth" intensification in Toronto: Environment and economy in the new official plan. *Local Environment* 9, 177–91.

Citton, Y. 2008. La passion des catastrophes. *La revue internationale des livres & des idées*, November–December, 7–11.

Citton, Y. 2009. La pharmacie d'Isabelle Stengers: Politiques de l'experimentation collective. *La revue internationale des livres & des idées*, March–April, 19–23.

Clarke, S. and Chenoweth, E. 2006. The politics of vulnerability: Constructing local performance regimes for homeland security. *Review of Policy Research* 23, 95–114.

Davis, M. 2005. *Planet of Slums.* London: Verso.

Davis, M. 2006. *The Monster at Our Door.* New York: New Press.

Debbané, A-M. and Keil, R. 2004. Multiple disconnections: Environmental justice, urban sustainability and water. *Space and Polity* 8, 209–25.

Desfor, G. and Keil, R. 2004. *Nature and the City: Making Environmental Policy in Toronto and Los Angeles.* Tucson: University of Arizona Press.

Desfor, G. and Vesalon, L. 2008. Urban expansion and industrial nature: A political ecology of Toronto's port industrial district. *International Journal of Urban and Regional Research* 32, 586–603.

Dunion, K. and Scandrett, E. 2003. The campaign for environmental justice in Scotland as a response to poverty in a northern nation. In J. Agyeman, R. D. Bullard, and B. Evans, eds. *Just Sustainabilities: Development in an Unequal World.* London: Earthscan.

Gibbs, D. 2006. Prospects for an environmental economic geography: Linking ecological modernization and regulationist approaches. *Economic Geography* 82 (2), 193–215.

Gibbs, D., and Jonas, A. 2000. Governance and regulation in local environmental policy: The utility of a regime approach. *Geoforum* 31(3), 299–313.

Gibbs, D. and Jonas, A. E. G. 2001. Rescaling and regional governance: The English Regional Development Agencies and the environment. *Environment and Planning C: Government and Policy* 19, 269–88.

Girard, L. F, Forte, B., Cerreta, M., De Toro, P., and Forte, F., eds. 2003. *The Human Sustainable City: Challenges and Perspectives from the Habitat Agenda.* Aldershot: Ashgate 89–106.

Girardet, H. 2006. *Creating Sustainable* Cities. Dartington: Green Books.

Glaeser, E. 2009. Green cities, brown suburbs. *City Journal* 19. http://www.city-journal.org/2009/19_1_green-cities.html (accessed March 21, 2009).

Hajer, M. 2003. Policy without polity? Policy analysis and the institutional void. *Policy Sciences* 36, 175–95.

Hall, P. 2003. The sustainable city in an age of globalization. In L. F. Girard, B. Forte, M. Cerreta, P. De Toro, and F. Forte, eds. *The Human Sustainable City: Challenges and Perspectives from the Habitat Agenda*. Aldershot: Ashgate.

Hartmann, F. 1999. Nature in the City: Urban Ecological Politics in Toronto. PhD dissertation, Department of Political Science. York University, Toronto.

Harvey, D. 1973. *Social Justice and the City*. London: Edward Arnold.

Harvey, D. 1989. *The Urban Experience*. Oxford: Blackwell.

Harvey, D. 1996. *Justice, Nature and the Geography of Difference*. Oxford: Blackwell.

Harvey, D. 2001. *Spaces of Capital: Towards a Critical Geography*. Edinburgh: Edinburgh University Press.

Haughton, G. and Hunter, C. 1994. *Sustainable Cities*. London: Jessica Kingsley Publishers/Regional Studies Association.

Heynen, N., Kaika, M., and Swyngedouw, E., eds. 2006. *In the Nature of Cities: Urban Political Ecology and the Politics of Urban Metabolism*. London: Routledge.

Hodson, M. and Marvin, S. 2009. Urban ecological security: A new urban paradigm? *International Journal of Urban and Regional Research* 33, 193–215.

Hopkins, R. 2008. *The Transition Handbook: From Oil Dependency to Local Resilience*. Totnes, Devon: Green Books.

Jonas, A. E. G., Gibbs, D. C., and While, A. H. 2009. The new urban politics as a politics of carbon control. Presentation at the Association of American Geographers Conference, Las Vegas, March 23.

Jonas, A. Gibbs, D. and While, A. 2004a. State modernization and local strategic selectivity after Local Agenda 21: Evidence from three northern English localities. *Policy and Politics* 32(2): 151–68.

Jonas, A. Gibbs, D. and While, A. 2004b. Uneven development, sustainability, and city-regionalism contested: English city regions in the European context. In H. Halkier and I. Sagan, eds. *Regionalism Contested: Institution, Society and Territorial Governance*. London: Ashgate.

Keil, R. 2003. Progress report 1: Urban political ecology. *Urban Geography* 24, 723–38.

Keil, R. 2005. Progress report 2: Urban political ecology. *Urban Geography* 26, 640–51.

Keil, R. 2007. Sustaining modernity, modernizing nature: The environmental crisis and the survival of capitalism. In R. Krueger and D. Gibbs, eds. *The Sustainable Development Paradox: Urban Political Economy in the US and Europe*. New York: Guilford Press.

Keil, R. 2009. Global cities: Connectivity, vulnerability and resilience. In B. Hahn and M. Zwingenberger, eds. *Global Cities*. Heidelberg: Universitätsverlag Winter.

Keil, R. and Ali, S. H. 2007. Governing the sick city: Urban governance in the age of emerging infectious disease. *Antipode* 39, 846–73.

Keil, R. and Boudreau, J.-A. 2006 Metropolitics and metabolics: Rolling out environmentalism in Toronto. In N. Heynen, M. Kaika, and E. Swyngedouw, eds. *In the Nature of Cities: Urban Political Ecology*. London: Routledge.

Keil, R. and Graham, J. 1998. Reasserting nature: Constructing urban environments after Fordism. In B. Braun and N. Castree, eds. *Remaking Reality: Nature at the Millennium*. London: Routledge.

Keil, R. and Ronneberger, K. 1994. Going up the country: Internationalization and urbanization on Frankfurt's northern fringe. *Environment and Planning D: Society and Space* 12, 137–66.

Kipfer, S. 2009. Why the urban question still matters: Reflections on rescaling and the promise of the urban. In R. Keil and R. Mahon, eds. *Leviathan Undone? Towards a Political Economy of Scale*. Vancouver: University of British Columbia Press.

Krueger, R and Agyeman, J. 2005. Sustainability schizophrenia or "actually existing sustainabilities"? Toward a broader understanding of the politics and promise of local sustainability in the US. *Geoforum* 36, 410–17.

Lake, R. 2000. Contradictions in the local state: Local implementation of the U.S. sustainability agenda in the USA. In N. Low, B. Gleeson, I. Elander, and R. Lidskog, eds. *Consuming Cities: The Urban Environment in the Global Economy after the Rio Declaration*. London: Routledge.

Latour, B. 2004. *Politics of Nature*. Cambridge: Harvard University Press.

Lehrer, U. and Laidley, J. 2008. Old mega-projects newly packaged? Waterfront redevelopment in Toronto. *International Journal of Urban and Regional Research* 32, 786–803.

Logan, J. and Molotch, H. 1987. *Urban Fortunes: The Political Economy of Place*. Berkeley: University of California Press.

Martinez-Alier, J. 2003. Urban "unsustainability" and environmental conflict. In L. F. Girard, B. Forte, M. Cerreta, P. De Toro, and F. Forte, eds. *The Human Sustainable City: Challenges and Perspectives from the Habitat Agenda*. Aldershot: Ashgate.

Molotch, H. 1976. The city as a growth machine: Toward a political economy of place. *American Journal of Sociology* 82, 309–32.

North, P. 2009. Beyond entrepreneurial cities: Towards a progressive urban politics of climate change and resource constraint. Presentation at the Association of American Geographers Conference, Las Vegas, March 23.

Portney, K. 2003. *Taking Sustainable Cities Seriously*. Cambridge, MA: MIT Press.

Riesel, R. and Semprun, J. 2008. *Catastrophisme, administration du désastre et soumission durable*. Paris: Editions de l'encyclopédie des nuisances.

Rogers, R. (with Gumuchdjian, P.) 1997. *Cities for a Small Planet*. London: Faber.

Singer, P. 1975. *Animal Liberation: A New Ethics for Our Treatment of Animals*. New York: New York Review/Random House.

Stengers, I. 2009a. *Au temps des catastrophes. Résister a la barbarie qui vient*. Paris: La Découverté.

Stengers, I. 2009b. Fabriquer de l'espoir au bord du gouffre. *La revue internationale des livres & des idées*, March–April, 24–29.

Stone, C. 1989. *Regime Politics: Governing Atlanta, 1946–1988*. Lawrence: University Press of Kansas.

Swyngedouw, E. 2004. *Social Power and the Urbanization of Water: Flows of Power*. Oxford: Oxford University Press.

Swyngedouw, E. 2006. Metabolic urbanization: The making of cyborg cities. In N. Heynen, M. Kaika, and E. Swyngedouw eds. *In the Nature of Cities: Urban Political Ecology and the Politics of Urban Metabolism*. Abingdon, Oxon: Routledge.

Swyngedouw, E. 2009. The antinomies of the post-political city. *International Journal of Urban and Regional Research* 33, 601–20.

Swyngedouw, E. and Heynen, N. 2003. Urban political ecology and the politics of scale. *Antipode* 35, 898–918.

Toly, N. J. 2008. Transnational municipal networks in climate politics: From global governance to global politics. *Globalizations* 5, 341–56.

Tretter, E. 2009. Sustainability and neoliberal urban development: An Austin case study. Presentation at the Association of American Geographer Conference, Las Vegas, March 23.

UNCHS. 1976. *The Vancouver Declaration on Human Settlements*. Habitat: United Nations Conference on Human Settlements.

United Nations. 2009. *Istanbul Declaration on Human Settlements*. General Assembly resolution 51/177 of December 1996 and 53/242 of July 28, 1999.

While, A. H., Jonas, A. E. G., and Gibbs, D. C. 2004. The environment and the entrepreneurial city: Searching for the urban "sustainability fix" in Manchester and Leeds. *International Journal of Urban and Regional Research* 28, 549–69.
Whitehead, M. 2003. (Re)analysing the sustainable city: Nature, urbanization and the regulation of socio-environmental relations in the UK. *Urban Studies* 40, 1183–206.
Whitehead, M. 2007. *Spaces of Sustainability: Geographical Perspectives on the Sustainable Society*. London: Routledge.
Whitehead, M. 2008. Cold monsters and ecological Leviathan: On the relationships between states and the environment. *Geography Compass* 2, 414–32.
Whitehead, M., Jones, R., and Jones, M. 2006. *The Nature of the State: Excavating the Political Ecologies of the Modern State*. Oxford: Oxford University Press.
Wolch, J. 1996. Zoopolis, *Capitalism, Nature, Socialism* 7, 21–48.
Wolch, J. and Emel, J. 1998. *Animal Geographies: Place, Politics and Identity in the Nature-Culture Borderlands*. New York: Verso.
Young, D. and Keil, R. 2009. Seeking the urban in-between: Tracking the urban politics of infrastructure in Toronto. Presentation at the Association of American Geographers Conference, Las Vegas, March 25.

PART V

EMERGING RESEARCH AGENDAS

CHAPTER 27

JUSTICE, URBAN POLITICS, AND POLICY

HEATHER CAMPBELL AND
SUSAN S. FAINSTEIN

1. Introduction

The growth in income inequality characteristic of the developed world that began in the 1970s has prompted renewed calls for redistribution within the urban political arena (H. Campbell 2006; S. Fainstein 2000). At the grass roots, activists have framed redistributive demands within the World Social Forum and the Right to the City Alliance.[1] Among scholars, distress over rising inequality in urban regions has stimulated an outpouring of conferences, articles, and books dealing with the question of spatial justice.[2] Concern with the meaning of justice in the urban arena has nudged urban theorists to examine the works of philosophers, especially those of John Rawls and his supporters and critics, and to seek to make them applicable within the practice of urban politics and policymaking (Meagher 2008; Merrifield 2002). It has also stimulated a renewed interest in the writings of Henri Lefebvre,

1. See their web page at http://www.righttothecity.org/RTTC_Funder_Guide_Web.pdf (accessed December 31, 2008) for a description of their aims and list of their member organizations.

2. See, *inter alia*, Marcuse et al. (2009) and the new journal *Justice Spatiale/Spatial Justice*. Recent conferences include the Spatial Justice Symposium (University of Paris, Nanterre, March 2008); the Conference on the Right to the City (Technical University of Berlin, November 2008); and the Conference on Justice and the American Metropolis (Washington University in St. Louis, May 2008).

whose call for a "right to the city" has been associated with the concept of justice (Mitchell 2003).

Concern with the just city does not assume that the urban level is the most important locus for policies affecting social relations. Cities are nested within larger jurisdictions, and, as Paul Peterson (1981) notes, city governments are limited in their ability to effect redistribution. At the same time they constitute relatively autonomous bodies with a range of discretion that allows them to make life better or worse for their citizens.[3] The variation among cities in terms of the extent to which they provide social services, public housing, access to amenities, high-quality education, protection against displacement, public transit; criminalize deviant behavior; and discriminate against minorities reflects the extent to which local actions can be more or less just. Even where the amount of resources available to local governments depends on national governmental policy, how these resources are expended does not ensue automatically as a result of national fiat. Groups based at the local level contest the allocative and developmental policies of urban regimes, making urban politics frequently contentious. Furthermore, cities are the arenas in which many of the issues that become salient at the national level are framed. Thus, for example, the American civil rights movement developed out of a series of local rebellions.

The focus on outcomes associated with discussions of the just city marks a move away from the emphasis on process characterizing progressive theorists and grassroots organizations until recently. Ever since the urban protest movements of the 1960s, demands for participation have topped the agenda of urban activists in Western liberal democracies,[4] and calls for justice have been framed in terms of power to the people. These demands have, to some extent, resulted in the establishment of more participatory institutions. Participation has been valued in itself and also been considered as the vehicle through which a fair distribution of benefits would be achieved (Purcell 2008; Young 2000). During this same time period, however, proponents of neoliberalism have succeeded in framing urban policy in terms of competitiveness, and in most cities the triumph of neoliberal ideology has been accompanied by increasing inequality. Seemingly, increased democracy alone is insufficient to force redistribution of resources. Although arguably even greater openness or stronger popular mobilizations might have produced different, more equitable results, so far the hope that citizen activism would pressure governments into promoting a more egalitarian society has not borne fruit. Moreover, some of the more successful grassroots movements have used participatory mechanisms to push policy toward regressive outcomes, as they have pressed for tax reductions and restrictions on immigrants.

3. Elster (1992, 27) indicates that for "core cases of local justice... the relevant good is allocated... by a relatively autonomous institution." Elster is not referring to local governments but rather to bodies like admissions offices and hospital boards, but the principle applies as well to municipal authorities.

4. Bronner (1999, 18) asserts: "Democracy has become the answer to every question and the solution to every problem. Its critical edge has been lost."

This chapter summarizes discussions of the definition of justice and of the relation between process and outcome incorporated within it, identifies key debates over the role of the state in ensuring justice, examines the way in which the issue is framed in the US and UK, discusses the importance of the national context for urban politics, and finally indicates an agenda for future scholarship. Our purpose is both to analyze the implications of different theoretical approaches and to evaluate urban politics and policy in relation to justice.

2. Rawls, His Antecedents, His Critics, and the Applicability of Theories of Justice to the Urban Milieu

Within the Anglo-American liberal tradition, utilitarian thought was long the principal basis for the prevailing conception of justice. The origin of utilitarianism lies in the British social reform movement of the nineteenth century, although it is now often perceived as closely tied to mainstream economics and inherently conservative in nature. Bentham's (1789) original formulation is concerned with the moral consequences of action in terms of the balance of pleasure over pain. This balance is assessed through the summation of individual self-interests, with appropriate actions determined on the basis of the achievement of the good or in the classic utilitarian phrase, "the greatest happiness of the greatest number." In the context of those times, a notion valuing the interests of all members of society has a strongly reformist orientation. However, as utilitarianism becomes reduced to the notion of a hedonic calculation, its reformist sense diminishes. The representation of individual preferences in monetary terms within the discipline of economics is in itself problematic, but more profoundly, in a diverse world, linking the notion of the good to a majoritarian view of happiness is questionable.

John Rawls's work represents a challenge to utilitarian conceptions of justice. Rawls, one of the major political thinkers of the twentieth century, returns Anglo-American philosophy to its roots in Aristotelian concerns with universal values and Enlightenment concepts of liberty and equality. For much of the twentieth century Anglo-American philosophy dwelled on linguistic issues and eschewed the concern with justice characteristic of the Marxist-influenced Frankfurt School of critical theory. While renewing a focus on justice, Rawls does not turn to Marxism but remains deeply rooted within liberal concepts of social democracy and the welfare state. His approach is to establish an analytic framework for examining distributional questions that fits with contemporary models of rationality, especially within rational choice theory. He thus surmounts the rigidity of previously dominant philosophical logical positivism and its strict separation of fact and value (H. Putnam

2002), overcoming the premise within economics that there can be no interpersonal comparisons of welfare, yet still not resorting to subjectivism.

Rawls's (1971) argument for the priority to be granted equality of primary goods depends on a simple thought experiment. Famously, he argues that individuals, in the "original position" where they cannot know their eventual social position ("behind a veil of ignorance"), will opt for an egalitarian society out of fear that they may find themselves at the bottom of the economic hierarchy. The choice therefore does not arise out of either natural law—the justification for equality used by the Enlightenment theorists—or a soft humanitarianism but rather out of a rational calculation of self-interest. As applied to cities, Rawls's "difference principle" (i.e. equality of primary goods) means that urban policy should most benefit those people who have least. Thus, even if, as Paul Peterson (1981) contends, redistribution cannot succeed at the urban level because of competition among cities for investment, the failure of urban regimes to adopt redistributional measures must be regarded as a matter of incapacity not of principle. According to the logic of Rawls, justice always requires the attainment of material equality as a goal.

Rawls's formulation has been challenged by philosophers of culture and gender who consider injustice to be based primarily in the failure to recognize "the other." Iris Marion Young's (1990, 2000) work is particularly significant in this respect, especially as regards the notion of justice in the context of the city. She begins by taking the concepts of oppression and domination as her starting point. Then, instead of focusing on individuals she examines institutionalized forms of oppression and the impacts these have for decision-making procedures, the social division of labor, and culture. She considers that Rawls overlooks matters concerning "the just organization of government institutions, and just methods of political decision-making" (1990, 22). She also insists that concepts of justice must take context into account and be sensitive to group differences. She calls for a concept of "differentiated solidarity" and for consideration of justice at the scale of the city region, thereby precluding reliance solely on face-to-face discussion, as is required under concepts of deliberative democracy.

Building on recent discussions of diversity, Nancy Fraser (Fraser and Honneth 2003) does not reject Young's emphasis on group difference but rather argues that recognition and redistribution are analytically separable, and both are fundamental to justice.[5] Fraser intends that the politics of equality and economic perspectives should not be displaced by concerns with identity and culture. Distribution and recognition are seen as mutually irreducible aspects of justice, and "only a framework that integrates the two... can grasp the imbrication of class inequality and status hierarchy in contemporary society" (Fraser and Honneth 2003, 3).

Sen's (1999) and Nussbaum's (2000) capabilities approach offers a further avenue for establishing values appropriate to the just city. Like Rawls they intend their strictures to be generally applicable. They criticize him, however, for his restriction of justice to equality of primary goods. They argue both for a broader set of entitlements and for

5. The term recognition is used by philosophers to mean that a cultural grouping is acknowledged respectfully and granted legitimacy (see Fraser and Honneth 2003).

favoring those who require advantages, not simply equality (e.g., the mentally or physically handicapped), if they are to thrive. Instead of material goods, they emphasize a number of dimensions for calibrating justice, using the term "capabilities" to describe the opportunities to which individuals are entitled in a just society. By capabilities they are referring to what people have the potential to do. One does not need to exercise one's capabilities if one chooses not to (e.g. one can choose asceticism), but the opportunity has to be available, including a consciousness of the value of these capabilities. According to this reasoning, each person should be treated as an end, and there is a threshold level of each capability beneath which human functioning is not possible. Applying this approach to cities means establishing a threshold level of resources below which no one is allowed to sink. The level is determined not only by economic status but by a variety of indicators including health, self-respect, access to education, and political rights.

For all the abovementioned theorists, the concept of justice transcends simple economic equality, although Rawls has sometimes been interpreted as meaning only that. Except for Young they do not, however, take into account the question of spatial justice.[6] The writings of the French philosopher Henri Lefebvre, by introducing the concept of the right to the city, incorporate spatial relations within an egalitarian argument. Lefebvre alerts us to the way in which space and society are mutually constituted: "Space and the politics of space 'express' social relationships but [also] react against them" (Lefebvre 2003, 15). In delineating a right to the city, Lefebvre (1996, 147) is referring both to an individual right in relation to equal access to space and also to a joint aim: a city providing for human needs that are satisfied through social relationships developed in lived space. He thus goes beyond the liberal individualism of Rawls and his successors, pointing to qualities immanent in the collectivity.

The question of what constitutes a just urban policy, and whether inclusive processes necessarily produce just outcomes, underlies many of the debates over service delivery and regeneration within metropolitan areas. A discussion of this question must confront the tensions among the various objectives that constitute justice, as the aims of democracy, equality, sustainability, and development may, and indeed often do, lead to differing policies (S. Campbell 1996). In the next section we examine some of the key issues that arise when we seek to increase justice within urban contexts.

3. Issues

Once we start to envisage the everyday context of actual places and people, the questions asked of a conception of justice become more immediate and also often less appealing. Difficult choices may have to be made, involving the loss

6. A more extensive analysis of the issue of spatial justice than is incorporated in this chapter would examine urban/rural and global South/global North questions. Here we restrict ourselves to urban areas within Western liberal democracies.

of opportunities and freedoms for some in the quest to realize the greater good of others.

To give some context to the subsequent discussion of the issues which are raised, let us start by considering the (not so) hypothetical characteristics of a contemporary Western city, through the eyes of those acting and living in such environments:

> A local official looks down at the colorful shadings of a series of maps of the city region. They indicate: the disparity between average household income in the wealthiest districts of the city compared to the poorest districts increased by 26 percent between 2001 and 2005; a significant correlation between the poorest localities and higher than average proportions of ethnic minority and single parent (overwhelmingly female headed) households, and lower average life expectancy and adult literacy; home ownership across the city increased from 48 percent in 1979 to 68 percent in 2009, while housing conditions in the poorer areas deteriorated.
>
> An elected councilor heads to a full Council meeting, where a vote is to be taken on whether to sell off publicly owned playing fields. A large developer will build 25 "affordable" housing units on a former industrial site in exchange for permission to develop a gated community of executive homes on the playing fields site. Feedback from the "Citizen Assemblies" is ambivalent, with the exception of the property owners adjoining the playing fields, who claim part of the site to have several species of wild orchids. In private, concern centers on the loss of views and decline in property values. For the City Council, very tight education and social services budgets make maximizing revenue an important priority.
>
> The official sees out of a window a man going into the Citizens' Advice Bureau (CAB) (a not-for-profit organization). He wants help with sorting out his mounting debts. Six months ago his wife and two children had to find a new house to rent as their previous home was to be demolished as part of a mixed-income regeneration scheme. Their new location forced his wife to give up her part-time job as there is no public transport. The children's new school is short staffed, they've been burgled, and his wife's health is suffering. He gets occasional work as a laborer, and while a rent supplement lowers the cost of their new dwelling, as they already had debts, his wages do not cover the bills.
>
> His new neighbors are a third generation Pakistani family and next door to them the housing department placed a Somali family. The latter receive lots of visits from government officials. He met someone in the bar who was giving out leaflets with the slogan: "Local jobs for local hard working families." Maybe he'll vote for the first time at the next elections?

So what does "justice" in an urban context look like? What should be done, about what and by whom? The above highlights the complexity, and often contradictory nature, of the issues involved. Targeting aid to disadvantaged communities may lead to stigmatization; attempts at community redevelopment can produce spatial displacement, gentrification, and residualization; and the costs of environmental protection may fall disproportionately on the poorest. Given this, should the "heavy hand" of the state be supplemented or replaced by the market (and its management practices) or nongovernmental organizations and civil society bodies? Does greater democracy lead to more economic and social equality, or does it exacerbate divisions arising out of different social positions and reinforce prejudice? Identifying injustice is part of the task of rectifying it, but deciding who has a responsibility to take which sorts of actions on behalf of whom, raises an equally searching range of issues. Arguably if the concept of justice is to have real purchase on the lives of everyday people, it has to do so in an existing urban context where circumstances are uncertain and dynamic, choices problematic, and actions likely to be accompanied by unintended outcomes.

The remainder of this section seeks to identify the key issues raised when a concern for justice turns from the abstract to the level of the city. It starts with consideration of general issues that have long been the subject of debate but need to be reviewed afresh in the context of the city and then moves on to more specific aspects of urban justice.

3.1. General Issues

3.1.1. *Conception of Interests and their Representation*

Underlying assumptions about interests constitute an important starting point for discussions of justice. Who knows best what our interests are (or should be)? Liberal approaches place priority on individuals and their perceptions of their needs or wants, while communitarian writers argue that individuals develop an understanding of their interests through association with others. When it comes to policymaking, the "who knows best" question becomes a key political issue.

Traditional forms of representative democracy assume that elected and appointed government officials possess sufficient objectivity to act on behalf of their constituents (Mansbridge 2009). Usually they justify their decisions not as comprising the sum of individual interests, but as embodying a wider and somewhat different conception: the "public interest" (Flathman 1966; Marquand 2004). Skepticism concerning the probity and representativeness of public officials, however, has produced calls for restricting the authority of officeholders. One view is that more inclusive, often community-based, forms of deliberative democracy would better serve the public (Dryzek 2000; Gutmann and Thompson 1996). A different analysis concludes that interests are only truly expressed through choices made by individuals in markets, and hence deregulation and privatization should be pursued (Pennington 2002; Osborne and Gaebler 1992).

3.1.2. *Conceptions of Rights*

Understandings of justice also embody assumptions about freedoms and rights: how much freedom (and hence which rights) should be traded for how much equality and in what areas (Sen 1999)? For example, a concern about equality of opportunity will likely clash with property rights, and a focus on the interests of the majority will have implications for minority rights to self-expression and recognition. Moreover, the realization of one's rights (whether negative or positive) depends on both the ability to exercise them and also the acceptance by others that such rights should be upheld. More specifically, in relation to goods and services, the prioritization, protection, and delivery of such rights must entail some form of collective action (O'Neill 2000).

3.1.3. *Remedies for Injustice*

Analyses of the nature of injustice lead on to questions of how best they can be remedied. On the left, long-standing concern with economic processes focuses attention on the operation of capital (and its collusion with the state) as the crucible of class-based inequalities and injustice (Harvey 1973, 1996). In contrast, while also maintaining a focus on the economic realm, neoliberal economists argue that it is overregulation of markets, leading to inefficiency, which creates destabilizing inequalities (Pennington 2002). At the same time group-defined difference has been identified by philosophers such as Axel Honneth as the basis of disadvantage (Fraser and Honneth 2003). Paradoxically while the ideological underpinnings of the economic and cultural critiques are hugely different, the state and its urban policies have become a commonly perceived source of injustice (Storper 2001), although in light of recent economic events, there are signs of renewed appreciation of the interventionist state as an enabler rather than merely as a constraint or, more sinisterly, oppressor. Furthermore, experiments in participatory democracy have demonstrated the exclusionary capacities of local communities and the injustices that can arise out of expressions of self-determination (Campbell et al. 2005; Cooke and Kothari 2001).

3.1.4. *Emphasis of Focus on Justice*

The preceding arguments fuse together into a focus on fair processes or on just outcomes. On the "just process" side, be that in relation to democratic, market-based, or bureaucratic processes, lie arguments which suggest that, given the variety of ways to live a good life, justice should not concern itself with end states. But, as Mulhall and Swift (1997) ask (in a slightly different context), is the ability to choose more important than the choice? Those who consider that the choice does matter question whether just processes produce just outcomes and note that ostensibly neutral processes are actually biased toward particular outcomes (Connor 1993; Nussbaum 2000). They therefore argue that justice must concern itself with matters of substance, outcomes and the meaning of greater equality in goods, services, and opportunities.

3.2. Specific (Urban Policy) Issues

3.2.1. *Which Substantive Aspects of Interests Matter?*

When we move to determining actions that create greater justice in actual cities, substantive content becomes central to debate. In circumstances of limited resources, policy options have to be prioritized. Differences among political opponents revolve around economic impacts; in discussions of how to reduce poverty, opposing arguments support regulation of the private sector and redistribution, on the one hand,

Table 1. Conceiving of Justice in (urban) Public Policy—General Issues

Generalized models	Conception of interests	How interests are discovered	Emphasis of just urban policy
Welfare state: paternalistic city	Public interest—based on an undifferentiated public.	Representative democracy plus technical professional expertise	Redistribution
Neo-liberal state: entrepreneurial city	Individualistic wants (private utility)—based on interests of capital and consumers.	Consumption through markets or quasi-markets	Competition/pluralism
Politics of difference: multicultural city	Communal interests based on shared identity	Deliberative democracy and inclusive participation	Recognition leading to redistribution
Equitable distribution: just city	Collective needs—individual as an end but within a context based on interdependency	Representative democracy, supported by deliberation, and practical judgment, and equity-oriented expertise	Redistribution and recognition

and facilitating capital accumulation on the premise that the benefits will trickle down on the other. Issues of social and cultural diversity (based on gender, ethnicity, sexuality, disability, etc.) have further defined the substantive focus, as indicated by the use of terms like social exclusion or more positively diversity and social inclusion. In addition, concern with climate change and environmental hazards raises questions of which economic and cultural groups will bear the opportunity costs of regulation and siting of unwanted land uses (HM Treasury 2007).

3.2.2. *Spatial or Place-Based Concern*

A spatial component to justice has normative implications in terms of whether resources should target people or places, and more profoundly whether emphasis centers on individuals (and their families) or on collectivities. Issues of spatial justice also link to questions of whether our concern for justice includes strangers and transcends geographic boundaries (Fraser 2008; O'Neill 2000; Young 2000). The issue of scale has significant substantive implications (Brenner 1999). What may seem just to local communities (for example, no wind farm in our backyard or the imposition of strict pollution controls causing Western corporations to locate noxious processing plants in countries of the global South) may take on a different quality at the scale of the city, the region, the nation, or globally.

3.2.3. *Emphasis of "Just" Urban Policy*

These concerns lead to approaches that give varying prominence to redistribution, recognition, or competition as ways of addressing injustice. In terms of policy perspectives, these might be crudely summarized as: the paternalistic city, the multicultural city, and the entrepreneurial city, as represented in table 1. The fourth category in table 1—the just city—indicates the approach involved in a substantive conception of justice involving both redistribution and recognition. In addition to providing a partial summary of the preceding discussion, this figure suggests how links can be made between these issues, intellectual debates, and urban policy discourses. Some simplification is inevitable, but the table highlights how groups of ideas have reinforced one another to produce distinct approaches to justice in the context of urban policy. Each model involves a critique and a guide to action.

The next section examines the extent to which these models have exerted leverage in urban policy in the US and UK and to what effect.

4. Local Strategies

Within the United States and western Europe scholars and policymakers have used different vocabularies and emphasized different kinds of policies in their efforts to improve the situation of the disadvantaged (as defined by race, ethnicity, class, or gender). In the US considerable emphasis has been placed on segregation and concentrated poverty in cities and their contribution to the perceived accumulation of dysfunctional characteristics among the poor (Logan et al. 2004). European approaches have stressed the impacts of social exclusion, in particular the effects of detachment from the labor market (see Levitas 1998; Murie and Musterd 2004). At the same time, on both continents policymakers have stressed the necessity of competitiveness in a globalized world, and there is considerable similarity in policies aiming at stimulating economic growth. In this section we examine the debates and policy impacts in the United States and the United Kingdom.[7]

4.1. The United States

Since World War II the American national government has only intermittently paid much attention to specifically urban issues. The 1949 Housing Act launched the public housing and urban renewal programs, which worked on the assumption that physical changes would transform cities, reversing the patterns of disinvestment and growing poverty that had accelerated during the postwar years. Disillusionment with these programs led to their abrogation in 1974 and the substitution of block grant programs that resulted in a substantially lessened federal presence. Community resistance had forced a reassessment of urban renewal based on large-scale demolition, while the physical deterioration of public housing, along with its minority demographic occupation, caused it to be perceived by the general public as counterproductive. After the mid-1970s domination by conservative national regimes and the growth of a suburban electoral majority caused the emphasis in urban policy to shift away from concern with poor neighborhoods and toward stimulating economic competitiveness.[8] The War on Poverty, commenced by President Lyndon Johnson in 1964, faded away, and urban fiscal crises led city governments to make economic development their first priority. To the extent that poverty remained on the agenda, its remedy was increasingly seen to be spatial dispersal rather than assistance to low-income residents. Although an array of programs continued to exist for affordable housing, neighborhood economic development, and employment training and placement, they were poorly funded and without strong political support. In the absence of a strong federal urban policy, there has been considerable variation from city to city in the extent to which public programs address disadvantage.

7. Due to lack of space, we do not present examples from continental Europe. Our purpose in presenting these examples is not to provide a comprehensive overview of approaches to urban justice but rather simply to illustrate the kinds of issues that arise at the urban level.

8. The Democratic administrations of Jimmy Carter, Bill Clinton, and Barack Obama, while somewhat more responsive than Republican regimes to poor inner-city constituencies, did not mark significant changes in the trajectory.

Ever since the publication of William Julius Wilson's books *The Declining Significance of Race* (1978) and *The Truly Disadvantaged* (1987), debate has raged concerning the extent to which spatial factors produced an isolated underclass prevented by geography from grasping opportunities for upward mobility. Wilson's arguments concerning the negative effects of the spatial concentration of poverty have become embodied in governmental policies aimed at dispersing the poor, allegedly for their own good. This stress on spatial isolation has led, within the urban politics literature, to a neglect of the structural factors producing inequality (N. Fainstein 1993) even while discussions of the national political economy have increasingly highlighted growing disparities of income. Yet, obviously, if low wages, unemployment, and underemployment afflict growing numbers of people, and these people must live somewhere, then relative poverty will persist, regardless of where they are located.

In relation to the issue of neighborhood poverty, the question of how to promote a more just city is fought out in the urban political arena over two related lines of conflict: deconcentration of the poor and gentrification. Supporters of deconcentration have succeeded in having their views embodied in several federal programs: HOPE VI, which demolishes troubled public housing developments and replaces them with mixed-income projects that house only a fraction of the previous residents (Schwartz 2006, 117–24); Moving to Opportunity, an experimental program that promotes out-migration from inner-city areas (Briggs et al. 2009); and rental housing vouchers[9] that are allocated according to need, but which only go to a fraction of those eligible due to limited funding. These programs are based on the assumption that moving the poor to more heterogeneous neighborhoods will improve their life chances through providing better role models, access to jobs, and better services.

The pressure for moving poor people out of central locations has been especially significant in cities undergoing gentrification. In such places gentrification is frequently justified as benefiting not just the in-movers but also the remaining low-income residents (Bennett et al. 2006), who gain an upgrading of services and neighborhood amenities through living in mixed-income neighborhoods (Freeman and Branconi 2004; Freeman 2006). Opponents of gentrification and of city governments' efforts to attract the "creative class" through encouraging historic preservation, appealing urban design and mixed use regard the whole effort at urban transformation as depriving ordinary people of the right to the city (N. Smith 1996). Although rationalized in terms of diversity (Fainstein 2005), the effect of gentrification, even if it does not directly displace households, leads to the symbolic, and eventually material, takeover of desirable neighborhoods by the well-to-do.

Advocates for low-income groups contend that dispersal programs destroy existing communities, undermine whatever political influence the poor might have,

9. Called Section 8 certificates after their authorization under the Housing and Community Development Act of 1974, they are now labeled "housing choice vouchers," although the term Section 8 is still commonly used.

and fail to offer recognition to differing cultures (Goetz 2003). Iris Marion Young (2000) argues that integration of culturally disparate groups would not prevent the harm of racial and class discrimination. She gives four reasons why "this ideal tends wrongly to focus on patterns of group clustering while ignoring more central issues of privilege and disadvantage" (p. 216): (1) it favors the dominant group; (2) it rejects people's desire to associate with affinity groups; (3) it usually meets resistance and the subordinate group typically is blamed; (4) it does not eliminate the material disadvantage underlying segregating processes (pp. 216–18). In other words, externally imposed dispersal programs provide neither redistribution of primary goods nor recognition. That they are rationalized in terms of promoting diversity—an ostensibly progressive value—is ironic, if not cynical.

The other prominent debate in relationship to urban justice within American cities revolves around programs aimed at achieving economic development through spatial restructuring and subsidies to developers and corporations. The retreat of the federal government from aiding redevelopment programs that began in the 1970s gave rise to a variety of state and local programs using regulatory relief, direct capital expenditures, and tax subsidies to promote construction and attract business investment. Relying on public-private partnerships, these efforts funneled public money into the hands of the already prosperous (G. Squires 1989). Their justification has always been trickle-down—everyone would benefit from new investment that would produce employment and tax revenues. Cities that failed to offer enticements would lose out to other places that did.

The politics surrounding redevelopment programs brings into sharp focus the contradictions between growth and equity, democracy and just outcomes. Unlike the projects characteristic of urban renewal in the decades following World War II, contemporary large redevelopment projects do not usually involve massive displacement of residents as they typically take place in disused waterfronts and industrial sites (Diaz Orueta and Fainstein 2008). Consequently relatively few people suffer immediate injury, and substantial popular support exists for them. The equity question involves the choice of investment object, as the developments usually consist of luxury housing, upscale retailing, tourist spaces, and sports facilities. The latter represent a particularly egregious form of assisting the rich, since a great body of research shows little economic effect, while team owners and players receive enormous income flows (Long 2005). Although the new mega-projects often include a public benefit in the form of recreational spaces, beautification, and some affordable housing, the bulk of public money flows into the hands of the already well-off. This is money that is not spent on education, health services, or social housing. It is doubtful, however, whether substantially more public participation would change these investment choices, as economic growth remains a broadly popular goal.

4.2. The United Kingdom

Policy debates about urban justice in the UK exhibit parallels with experience in the US. The creation of "balanced," "mixed," and "sustainable communities," in combination with the facilitation of "urban renaissance,"[10] particularly through market-led physical investment in historic city centers, have all featured in British urban policy. The resulting policy developments have been accompanied by concerns about gentrification and displacement, and more recently diversity and multiculturalism. However, the European tradition of a strong state, in Britain characterized by the dominance of central government, means that the tone, rhetoric, and parameters of debate are constructed differently.

During the postwar period British urban policy shifted away from a focus on material redistribution to the cultivation of individual choice and opportunity for all. The current social exclusion agenda is about ensuring individuals acquire the appropriate skills (and even morals, in the case of criminal young men and lone parents, especially young women) to gain paid employment and contribute to economic productivity, while not disrupting or being a burden on society (Levitas 1998). In this view individual deficiencies rather than the operation of structural forces become the source of disadvantage (J. Squires 2007; Phillips 2006). Poverty is defined less in purely economic terms—the absence of money—and more as a social and cultural phenomenon, with significant implications for policy priorities. Recent urban policy despite a profusion of area-based initiatives is in practice ambivalent about place: its real concern is with individual social mobility, either directly or if necessary through replacement of the disadvantaged by the more affluent.

This individualistic bias is in stark contrast to the prevailing ideology of the immediate postwar years. Urban policy then appears remarkable to the contemporary eye for its unabashed redistributive confidence. Massive programs of slum clearance and reconstruction combined with policies of urban containment. The goal was to achieve environmental improvements for those living in the poorest parts of cities, including access to utilities and the newly available services of the welfare state. Perhaps even more striking were attempts at intra- and interregional spatial redistribution. "London overspill housing" for disadvantaged inner-city residents was built in the leafy suburban home counties, a series of new towns were constructed, and a system of permits encouraged employers (and developers) to locate away from the South-East to the less prosperous cities of the North. This was spatial redistribution without subtlety and centralized control was enormous. It was not the "gas and water socialism" of earlier eras based on local civic activism. Utilities and services (like hospitals) were taken out of local control and nationalized. The clumsiness and demeaning paternalism of some of the policies have lived

10. Reference to "mixed" and "balanced" communities in the UK has endured from the social reform debates following the rapid urbanization of the nineteenth century, exemplified in Victorian philanthropic urban experiments, then moving into Ebenezer Howard's "garden city" of the early twentieth century and postwar reconstruction and development initiatives. The New Labour rhetoric of "sustainable communities" and "urban renaissance" has a more specific policy focus (see respectively, Office of the Deputy Prime Minister 2003 and Urban Task Force 1999).

long in critical thinking and popular imagination. What is remembered are the slum clearances which broke up long established communities and incarcerated families in anonymous tower blocks or the urban motorways which sliced through the heart of many cities, not the improvements in basic living conditions and opportunities.

Policies adopted after the mid-1970s under both Conservative and Labour governments reflected the negative reactions to the postwar programs. Critics of massive redevelopment projects argued that physical change alone could not create enriching living environments.[11] They (and policymakers sympathetic to their arguments) called for greater public involvement to challenge technocratic expertise, especially by low-income communities.[12] Further by 1979 Peter Townsend's seminal work, *Poverty in the United Kingdom*, underlined the multidimensional nature of poverty. It demonstrated that material deprivation was only one facet of poverty; at least as important to the experience of disadvantage was wider exclusion from customary ways of living. Recent reference to "social exclusion" and "social inclusion" rather than poverty, reflects this thinking and the influence of continental European policy agendas. New Labour has also consciously used the social exclusion discourse to indicate a move away from the clumsy redistribution of the "nanny state," toward the cultivation of opportunity for all.[13] As Tony Blair put it in his conference speech of 1999, "Not equal incomes. Not uniform lifestyles or taste or culture. But true equality: equal worth, an equal chance of fulfilment, equal access to knowledge and opportunity. Equal rights. Equal responsibilities. The class war is over" (quoted in Levitas 2000, 364).

In the interim between Townsend's mention of "exclusion" and the arrival of New Labour, the intellectual and political underpinnings of urban policy changed. Despite very different intellectual origins and aims, ideas of social diversity intermingled with neoliberal sentiments of opportunity and aspiration to emphasize the rights of the individual and to critique the "oppressive" practices of the state and its accompanying bureaucracy. More specifically, following Thatcher's extension of private property rights through the "Right to Buy" program for the privatization of public housing,[14] housing aspirations became central to urban policy. Owner occupation was turned into the tenure of choice and the remaining council housing and

11. For critical studies of British postwar redevelopment schemes, see, for example, Dennis (1970). Critical studies of the outcomes of American urban redevelopment initiatives also influenced UK debates (see Gans 1962; Jacobs 1961).

12. American critics were influential. See Davidoff's (1965) work on "advocacy" and Arnstein's (1969) much celebrated critical review of public participation practices. The Seebohm (Committee on Local Authority 1968) and Skeffington (Committee on Public Participation in Planning 1969) committee reports led to the requirement for public involvement in planning in Britain.

13. See the creation of the Social Exclusion Unit (SEU) in December 1997, despite no mention in Labour's manifesto. It aimed to provide "joined up solutions to joined up problems" (see for example SEU 1998).

14. Between 1979 and 1997 1.25 million council houses were sold to their tenants.

occupants stigmatized and disparaged. Tellingly, the crude statistics on the share of national income indicate inequality was rising.[15] Delivery mechanisms were increasingly privatized. Public services were turned into quasi-markets, partnerships encouraged with the private sector and third sector organizations, capital projects delivered through public/private partnerships (PPPs), and compliance secured through contracts and performance targets. In a few areas the free market agenda was sidelined. The number and location of new regional shopping developments were restricted so as to maintain the vitality of existing city centers, and property tax on business was collected nationally then redistributed by formula, eliminating the cutthroat competition for "ratables" characteristic of the United States.

Labour's election in 1997 saw its modest aspiration toward redistribution set against an acceptance of the imperative of economic growth, a wish to appeal to "Middle England's" perceived expectation of social mobility and owner occupation, and the existence of a highly fragmented governance landscape. In contrast to the postwar years there was little emphasis on interregional redistribution. However, the deterioration of the big industrial cities, especially the cumulative deprivation and lack of productivity (in employment terms) of certain communities, was a concern. Against this background Labour embarked on the largest program of area-based redevelopment since the 1960s. It involved a complex tapestry of initiatives, action zones, and partnerships, including 39 New Deal for Communities (NDC) areas and nine Housing Market Renewal (HMR) Pathfinders. These initiatives espoused a (joined-up) multidimensional perspective of deprivation. Community participation and multicultural recognition were central to their operation, if in the case of the latter, there was little clarity over the implications.

This phase of urban policy was shaped by assumptions concerning economic and cultural imperatives. The sense was that, given a service-based economy and contemporary housing aspirations, mass social housing estates for the working class were no longer appropriate. The rhetoric of HMR, as in the US HOPE VI program, proclaims the aim of creating "greater housing choice." In practice only the more affluent truly enjoy greater choice (Cameron 2003, 2006), while the disadvantaged find themselves with fewer options. Despite protests by local activists, the sentiments of most residents are not necessarily opposed to these measures (Cameron 2003; Goodchild and Cole 2001). Moreover, the displacement of those with reputations for "antisocial behavior" is generally welcomed. "Who knows best?" remains an enduring question for urban policymakers and one which is complicated by time and geographical scale.

Genuine commitment to participation has resulted in far greater and more wide-ranging community engagement than previously, despite the fragmented and transient nature of the communities (Lawless 2004, 387–88). However, links between participation and results are complex. The NDC evaluation shows that while there are

15. The share of the national income among the poorest 10 percent halved, while the proportion held by the top 10 percent increased from 21 percent in 1979 to 27 percent in 1991 (Department for Work and Pensions 2003).

signs of positive changes in attitudes, such as lessened fear of crime, "only modest evidence [exists] as yet of positive change in relation to ultimate outcomes: more jobs, less unemployment, fewer crimes, higher education rates, etc." (Lawless 2006, 1996). Under the Labour government of the first decade of this century, British urban policy showed greater sensitivity to issues of recognition and equality of opportunity, as measured by outcomes calibrated in terms of improved standards of living; the measurable effects, however, have been limited. Since the financial crisis that began in 2007 and the budget cutting of the Conservative government that took office in 2010, commitment to programs targeted toward the disadvantaged has lapsed.

5. The Significance of Context

The influence of urban justice debates are evident in policy development and its analysis in the US and UK. Despite contextual differences the underlying substantive dilemmas display parallels: *what* and *who* matters, *how* best to improve the lot of disadvantaged individuals and communities, and *which* delivery agents are most effective. Urban policy is not a function merely of the actions of city authorities. Its form represents the expression of multiple layers of policy activity from residents' associations, through national and transnational governmental institutions to global financial bodies. However, these sometimes remote decisions have their effects in the places where people live.

In contrast to the greater income inequality and diversity of the US and UK, the continental northern European welfare states have been distinguished by their success in ensuring that all citizens achieve a threshold level (Fainstein 2001; OECD 2008). National and EU policies mean city governments in these contexts rely less on their own resources in order to promote social justice and are therefore more insulated from the pressure of developers and high-income taxpayers than in the US. However, over the last decade, growing ethnic diversity has increasingly challenged the claims to spatial justice of northern Europe (Novy and Mayer 2009). Generally European immigration law is more restrictive than in the US and Canada, and immigrant neighborhoods tend to be perceived as dangerous and disorderly (Body-Gendrot and Martiniello 2000). In relation to the question of justice, the issue of recognition—whether ethnic groups should be acknowledged or pressed to assimilate—remains a political issue in both Europe and the United States, especially in the American West where Mexicans dominate the transnational flow. On the other hand, the debate over whether immigrant neighborhoods should be broken up or maintained is much more contentious in Europe than in America. In contrast to their generally negative view of African-American neighborhoods, American urban regimes have celebrated immigrant entrepreneurs and residents as agents of revitalization in depleted neighborhoods and have advertised ethnic enclaves as tourist attractions (Rath 2007).

In both Europe and the United States toleration of gendered space has grown remarkably in recent times. Because gays have clustered in cities, some urban neighborhoods have become identified with gay culture. In some places, for example San Francisco, gays have been leaders in movements for historic preservation and succeeded in transforming declining neighborhoods into the most desirable parts of the city. To the extent that they became the shock troops of gentrification, however, their effects indicate the tension between economic equality and recognition.

6. The Politics of Justice in the City: Future Research Agenda

Three questions require continued attention from scholars concerned with the political economy of the just city. First is the development of a set of normative criteria by which urban policy at various scales can be evaluated (see Fainstein 2009, 2010). Such a formulation requires the nesting of urban theory within geographical and philosophical approaches to questions of justice. In particular, it calls for introducing spatial considerations into philosophy and moving between abstract deductive logic and practical questions of the possible at any specific historical moment. For example, in relation to the problems presented by unassimilated groups, arguments for and against geographic dispersion have greater or lesser purchase at different times. If dispersal requirements had been in effect during the years of massive suburbanization in America, the template that froze suburban exclusion and inner-city ghettoization into place would not have been set. Undoing what has been done, however, raises different questions of justice than was initially the case.

A second question concerns how normative concerns can be incorporated into social scientific analysis (Bridge 2005, ch. 7). This is especially important in relation to the framing of research questions. There are important differences between asking which policies can mitigate poverty and which can alleviate inequality. Likewise, investigation of factors creating competitiveness or cohesion leads to different kinds of metrics from the examination of the production of equity or cosmopolitanism. Political scientists and planning theorists have concerned themselves rather single-mindedly until recently with levels and forms of participation. This focus need not be discarded, but it ought not to be at the neglect of addressing the hoary questions of who gets what and who should get what.

Third, we need to examine the effects of two factors currently leading to important new policy directions: the global economic crisis that began in 2007 and the threat of climate change. The set of pressures on land development caused by the real estate bubble of past decades disappeared with the rise of foreclosures, inability of developers to gain financing for their projects, and declining value of both residential and commercial property. President Obama's former chief of staff Rahm Emanuel has been quoted as saying "You never want a serious crisis to go to waste"

(*Wall Street Journal*, November 21, 2008). The financial crisis and its aftermath seem to both legitimate greater government intervention and delegitimate private capital, especially property capital. The outcome could be an opening for more redistributive actions by government, particularly in relation to housing provision. So far, however, debt reduction has greatly exceeded improvements in social welfare as a governmental aim.

Less precipitously, greater awareness of the implications of climate change has already caused much greater emphasis on sustainability than previously. Whether implementation of measures to produce "green cities" results in greater or less justice depends on the strategies adopted. More compact development in the interest of energy conservation could simply raise property values at the expense of low-income groups, or, if combined with housing and transit subsidies, improve their access to housing and jobs. The important point is that a connection is made, rather than viewing environmental policies in isolation from their social and economic implications.

Thus, the stories told here of policies reinforcing maldistribution of resources might yield to a more just urban politics. The situation with reference to cultural difference is indeterminate: on the one hand, openness to diversity and multiculturalism appears to be increasing; on the other, opposition to immigration has become more vocal in both the United States and western Europe. The effect of economic hardship on attitudes toward minority groups competing for scarce jobs may be to exacerbate hostility, but it may also serve to reduce the flow of new immigrants, thereby facilitating absorption. Crucially, just urban policy will need to pay attention to the socioeconomic forces shaping cities and the current discourse of opportunity will need to confront serious substantive questions.

REFERENCES

Arnstein, Sherry. 1969. The ladder of citizen participation. *Journal of the American Institute of Planners* 35(4), 216–24.

Atkinson, Rowland, and Keith Kintrea. 2001. Disentangling area effects: Evidence from deprived and non-deprived neighbourhoods. *Urban Studies* 38(12), 2277–98.

Bennett, Larry, Janet L. Smith, and Patricia A. Wright (eds.). 2006. *Where Are Poor People to Live?* Armonk, NY: M. E. Sharpe.

Bentham, Jeremy. 1789 [1948]. *An Introduction to the Principles of Morals and Legislation.* Oxford: Basil Blackwell.

Body-Gendrot, Sophie, and Marco Martiniello (eds.). 2000. *Minorities in European Cities.* New York: St. Martin's Press.

Brenner, N. 1999. Globalization as reterritorialisation: The re-scalingof urban governance in the European Union. *Urban Studies* 36, 431–52.

Bridge, Gary. 2005. *Reason in the City of Difference.* London: Routledge.

Briggs, Xavier de Souza, Susan J. Popkin, and John Goering. 2009. *Moving to Opportunity.* Oxford: Oxford University Press.

Brenner, N. 1999. Globalisation as reterritorialisation: The re-scaling of urban governance in the European Union. *Urban Studies* 36, 431–52.

Bronner, Stephen Eric. 1999. *Ideas in Action*. Lanham, MD: Rowman and Littlefield.

Cameron, Stuart. 2003. Gentrification, housing redifferentiation and urban regeneration: "Going for Growth" in Newcastle upon Tyne. *Urban Studie*, 40(12), 2367–82.

———. 2006. From low demand to rising aspirations: Housing market renewal within regional and neighbourhood regeneration policy. *Housing Studies* 21(1), 3–16.

Campbell, Heather. 2006. Just planning: The art of situated ethical judgment. *Journal of Planning Education and Research* 26. 92–106.

———. (ed). 2005. Interface: The darker side of local communities: is this the *real world* of planning? *Planning Theory and Practice* 6(4), 517–41.

Campbell, Scott. 1996. Green cities, growing cities, just cities? Urban planning and the contradictions of sustainable development. *Journal of the American Planning Association* 62(3), 296–312.

Committee on Local Authority and Allied Personal Social Services. 1968. *Report of the Committee on Local Authority and Allied Personal Social Services*. Cmnd 3703. London: HMSO.

Committee on Public Participation in Planning. 1969. *People and Planning: Report of the Committee on Public Participation in Planning*. London: HMSO.

Connor, Steven. 1993. The necessity of value. In Judith Squires, ed., *Principled Positions: Postmodernism and the Rediscovery of Value*. London: Lawrence and Wishart.

Cooke, Bill, and Uma Kothari. 2001. *Participation: the New Tyranny?* London: Zed Books.

Davidoff, Paul. (1965) Advocacy and pluralism in planning. *Journal of the American Institute of Planners* 31, 331–38.

Dennis, N. 1970. *People and Planning: The Sociology of Housing in Sunderland*, London: Faber.

Department for Work and Pensions. 2003. *Households Below Average Income 2000/1*. London: The Stationery Office.

Diaz Orueta, Fernando, and Susan S. Fainstein (eds.). 2008. Symposium on the new mega-projects: genesis and impacts. *International Journal of Urban and Regional Research* 32(4), 759–840.

Dryzek, John. 2000. *Deliberative Democracy and Beyond*. Oxford: Oxford University Press.

Elster, Jon. 1992. *Local Justice*. New York: Russell Sage Foundation.

Fainstein, Norman. 1993. Race, class and segregation: Discourses about African Americans. *International Journal of Urban and Regional Research* 17(3), 384–403.

Fainstein, Susan S. 2000. New directions in planning theory. *Urban Affairs Review* 35(4), 451–78.

———. 2001. Inequality in global city-regions. In Allen J. Scott, ed., *Global City-Regions*. New York: Oxford University Press.

———. 2005. Cities and Diversity: Should we want it? Can we plan for it? *Urban Affairs Review* 41(1), 3–19.

———. 2009. Planning and the just city. In Peter Marcuse, James Connolly, Ingrid Olivo Magana, Johannes Novy, Cuz Potter, and Justin Steil, eds., *Searching for the Just City*. New York: Routledge.

———. 2010. *The Just City*. Ithaca, NY: Cornell University Press.

Flathman, Richard. 1966. *The Public Interest: An Essay Concerning the Normative Discourse of Politics*. New York: Wiley.

Fraser, Nancy. 2008. *Scales of Justice: Reimagining Political Space in a Globalizing World*. Cambridge: Polity.

Fraser, Nancy, and Axel Honneth. 2003. *Redistribution or Recognition?* (Trans. Joel Golb, James Ingram, and Chritiane Wilke). London: Verso.

Freeman, Lance. 2006. *There Goes the 'Hood.* Philadelphia: Temple University Press.
Freeman, Lance, and Frank Branconi. 2004. Gentrification and displacement: New York City in the 1990s. *Journal of the American Planning Association* 70(1), 39–52.
Gans, Herbert. 1962. *The Urban Villagers: Group and Class in the Life of Italian-Americans.* New York: Free Press.
Goetz, Edward G. 2003. *Clearing the Way.* Washington, DC: Urban Institute Press.
Goodchild, Barry, and Ian Cole. 2001. Social balance and mixed neighbourhoods in Britain since 1979: A review of discourse and practice in social housing. *Environment and Planning D* 19(1), 103–21.
Gutmann, Amy, and Dennis Thompson. 1996. *Democracy and Disagreement.* London: Belknap Press.
Harvey, David. 1973. *Social Justice and the City.* London: Edward Arnold.
———. 1996. *Justice, Nature and the Geography of Difference.* Oxford: Blackwell.
HM Treasury. 2007. *The Economics of Climate Change: The Stern Review.* Cambridge: Cambridge University Press.
Jacobs, Jane. 1961. *The Death and Life of Great American Cities.* New York: Vintage.
Lawless, Paul. 2004. Locating and explaining area-based urban initiatives: New Deal for Communities in England. *Environment and Planning C* 22, 383–99.
———. 2006. Area-based urban interventions: rationale and outcomes: The New Deal for Communities programme in England. *Urban Studies* 43(11), 1991–2011.
Lefebvre, Henri. 1996. The right to the city. In Eleonore Kofman and Elizabeth Lebas, eds. and trans., *Writings on Cities.* Oxford: Blackwell.
———. 2003. *The Urban Revolution.* Minneapolis: University of Minnesota Press.
Levitas, Ruth. 1998. *The Inclusive Society? Social Exclusion and New Labour.* Basingstoke: Macmillan.
———. 2000. What is social exclusion? In David Gordon and Peter Townsend, eds., *Breadline Europe: The Measurement of Poverty.* Bristol: Policy Press.
Logan, John R., Brian J. Stults, and Reynolds Farley. 2004. Segregation of minorities in the metropolis: Two decades of change. *Demography* 41(1), 1–22.
Long, Judith Grant. 2005. Full count: The real cost of public funding for major league sports facilities. *Journal of Sports Economics* 6(2), 119–43.
Mansbridge, Jane. 2009. A "selection model" of political representation. *Journal of Political Philosophy* 17(4), 369–99.
Marcuse, Peter, James Connolly, Ingrid Olivo Magana, Johannes Novy, Cuz Potter, and Justin Steil (eds.). 2009. *Searching for the Just City.* New York: Routledge.
Marquand, David. 2004. *Decline of the Public.* Cambridge: Polity Press.
Meagher, Sharon M. (ed.). 2008. *Philosophy and the City.* Albany: SUNY Press.
Merrifield, Andy. 2002. *Dialectical Urbanism.* New York: Monthly Review Press.
Mitchell, Don. 2003. *The Right to the City: Social Justice and the Fight for Public Space.* New York: Guilford Press.
Mulhall, Simon, and Andrew Swift. 1997. *Liberals and Communitarians.* 2nd ed. Oxford: Blackwell.
Murie, Alan, and Sako Musterd. 2004. Social exclusion and opportunity structures in European cities and neighbourhoods. *Urban Studies* 41(8), 1441–45.
Novy, Johannes and Margit Mayer. 2009. As "just" as it gets? The European city in the "just City" discourse. In Peter Marcuse, James Connolly, Ingrid Olivo Magana, Johannes Novy, Cuz Potter, and Justin Steil, eds., *Searching for the Just City.* New York: Routledge.
Nussbaum, Martha C. 2000. *Women and Human Development.* Cambridge: Cambridge University Press.

OECD. 2008. *Growing Unequal? Income Distribution and Poverty in OECD Countries*. Paris: OECD.
Office of the Deputy Prime Minister (ODPM). 2003. *Sustainable Communities: Building for the Future*. London: ODPM.
O'Neill, Onora. 2000. *Bounds of Justice*. Cambridge: Cambridge University Press.
Osborne, David, and Ted Gaebler. 1992. *Reinventing Government*. New York: Plume.
Pennington, Mark. 2002. *Liberating the Land: The Case for Private Land Use Planning*, London: Institute of Economic Affairs.
Peterson, Paul. 1981. *City Limits*. Chicago: University of Chicago Press.
Phillips, Anne. 2006. "Really" equal: Opportunities and autonomy. *Journal of Political Philosophy* 14(1), 18–32.
Purcell, Mark. 2008. *Recapturing Democracy*. New York: Routledge.
Putnam, Hilary. 2002. *The Collapse of the Fact/Value Dichotomy*. Cambridge: Harvard University Press.
Rath, Jan (ed.). 2007. *Tourism, Ethnic Diversity and the City*. New York: Routledge.
Rawls, John. 1971. *A Theory of Justice*. Cambridge, MA: Harvard University Press.
Schwartz, Alex F. 2006. *Housing Policy in the United States*. New York: Routledge.
Sen, Amartya K. 1999. *Development as Freedom*. New York: Oxford University Press.
Smith, Neil. 1996. *The New Urban Frontier: Gentrification and the Revanchist City*. New York: Routledge.
Social Exclusion Unit. 1998. Bringing Britain Together: A national strategy for neighbourhood renewal. Cmnd 4045. London: The Stationery Office.
Squires, Gregory D. 1989. *Unequal Partnerships*. New Brunswick, NJ: Rutgers University Press.
Squires, Judith. 2007. Negotiating equality and diversity in Britain: Towards a differentiated citizenship? *Critical Review of International Social and Political Philosophy* 10(4), 531–59.
Storper, Michael. 2001. The poverty of radical theory today: From the false promises of Marxism to the mirage of the cultural turn. *International Journal of Urban and Regional Research* 25, 155–79.
Townsend, Peter. 1979. *Poverty in the United Kingdom*. Harmondsworth: Penguin.
Urban Task Force. 1999. *Towards an Urban Renaissance*. London: E&FN Spon.
Wilson, William Julius. 1987. *The Truly Disadvantaged*. Chicago: University of Chicago Press.
———. 1978. *The Declining Significance of Race*. Chicago: University of Chicago Press.
Young, Iris Marion. 1990. *Justice and the Politics of Difference*. Princeton, NJ.: Princeton University Press.
———. 2000. *Inclusion and Democracy*. Oxford: Oxford University Press.

CHAPTER 28

CITIES AND POLITICS IN THE DEVELOPING WORLD: WHY DECENTRALIZATION MATTERS

RICHARD STREN

1. The Context: Urbanization across the World

The potential parameters for this chapter could be enormous. How to tell the essential story, and to analyze the major political trends in urban areas in what we conventionally call the "developing world" of Asia, Africa, and Latin America, when we are dealing with thousands of cities and with at least 165 countries?[1] The story is complex, and it varies considerably among major world regions. But there are three major parts to this narrative: the growth and increasing importance of cities in the developing world; the trend to decentralize; and the related movements of democratization and burgeoning of civil society. To set the stage for this larger discussion, we first need to delineate three major parameters of the urban universe. In this introductory section, we explain the spread of urbanization in developing countries, the increasing size of cities in the developing world, and the increasing economic importance of the largest cities.

1. The number of countries is based on the list provided in the most recent demographic survey produced by the United Nations, *World Urbanization Prospects: The 2009 Revision* (United Nations 2010).

1.1. Creeping Urbanization

Over the next twenty years, most of the world's population growth will take place in the cities and towns of poor countries. Some of this growth will be in very large cities, but intermediate size cities (between 1 and 5 million)—are growing even more rapidly (National Research Council 2003). The general point here is that the "urban revolution"—an idea developed by Henri Lefebvre in 1970 to reflect on social movements in France in the late 1960s (2003)—has now become a worldwide phenomenon (see Brugmann 2009). Although some regions, such as Africa and Asia have lower absolute rates of urbanization (40.0 percent and 42.2 percent respectively of their total populations live in cities) than do, say, Latin America (at 79.6 percent), the overall proportion of population living in cities was estimated to have reached 50.1 percent in 2010 (United Nations 2010, 5). Thus, as of the end of the first decade of the current millennium, the world became officially urban rather than rural! While some may wish to celebrate this statistical fact (the World Bank, for example, has declared the post-2009 decade "The Decade of the City" [World Bank 2009, 1]), we must observe that, in spite of precise numbers often cited, the aggregate results represent trends rather than an exact condition. The main reason for this is that the aggregate figures compiled by the United Nations Population Division are drawn from figures supplied by all the countries in the world, in which definitions of what is "urban" are anything but consistent. And aside from definitions of what is "urban," some countries use a variety of designations for their cities, from the central city in a large metropolitan area, to the whole metropolitan area itself (National Research Council 2003, 139). In spite of these inconsistencies, the general trends we report in this chapter represent the situation in many different countries with a reasonable degree of accuracy and validity.

1.2. Size

Cities in the so-called "less developed" regions of Asia, Africa, and Latin America (including the Caribbean) were not always as large and important as many of them have now become. In 1950, when 29.1 percent of the world lived in cities and towns, almost all of the largest cities in the world were in the so-called "developed" regions of Europe and North America. In that year, only one city—New York—had a population of more than 10 million. By 2007, 19 cities had populations greater than 10 million; and of these only three (Tokyo, New York, and Los Angeles) were in the "more developed" areas. Out of the top 10 cities in population size in 2007, eight were in Latin America and Asia. As Mattei Dogan and John Kasarda put it two decades ago, "[t]he world is becoming more and more a world of giant cities, and these cities are increasingly located in less-developed countries" (Dogan and Kasarda 1988, 12).

1.3. Economic Influence

Cities all over the world, but particularly large cities, and particularly large cities in developing countries, are increasing in economic influence. This is most evidently the case for extended city regions—or metropolitan areas—in Asia, Africa, and Latin America. And as they become more important economically, "the urban space [that they represent] has become subject to new or sharpened contestation" (Sassen 2004, 379). That is, they are becoming more of a focus for the political, whether it plays itself out on the local level (as in local politics) or at a more national or international level.

Definitions of what is "metropolitan" as opposed to merely "urban" abound, but the Canadian definition of a "census metropolitan area" can stand as a useful starting point. These areas are defined as "cities with a very large urbanized core, together with adjacent urban and rural areas which have a high degree of economic and social integration with that core" (United Nations 2001, 131). In the United States, a detailed study has shown that the 361 metropolitan area economies are responsible for 86 percent of the total GDP of the whole country. If it were a country, the metropolitan region of New York would have the tenth largest economy in the world (US Conference of Mayors 2007, 12). Using different figures based on similar calculations, we can compare the GDP of selected major world cities with the GDP of the countries in which they are located. The results are shown in table 1. The figures show clearly that the proportion of the country's GDP generated by these major cities is well in excess of the proportion of the country's population that they represent. Comparing columns (3) with (6) we see that, while New York City is 6.2 percent of the population of the United States, its economy represents 9 percent of the country's GDP. This represents a positive, or disproportionate economic contribution of 45 percent, giving a "location quotient" (Isserman 1977) of 1.45. Similarly, for Mexico City, São Paulo, Shanghai, and Mumbai the corresponding location quotients are 2.27, 2.86, 5.45, and 9.41, respectively. In proportion to their populations—which are already very large—these metropolitan areas make a very important contribution to the economies of their respective countries.

Table 1. Comparisons of Major World Cities' GDP with Country GDP, 2005

City	(1) City population (millions)	(2) Country population (millions)	(3) City/ cntry (%)	(4) City GDP ($billions)	(5) Country GDP ($billions)	(6) City GDP/ country GDP (%)
New York	18.7	298	6.2	1133	12,417	9
Mexico City	19.4	107	18.1	315	768	41
São Paulo	18.3	186	9.8	225	796	28
Shanghai	14.5	1,323	1.1	139	2,234	6
Mumbai	18.2	1,103	1.7	126	805	16

Sources: United Nations 2006; World Bank 2006; "City Mayors" website, http://www.citymayors.com/statistics/richest-cities-2005.html; at http://siteresources.worldbank.org/DATASTATISTICS/Resources/GDP.pdf.

As large city regions come into their own, we have seen more studies of metropolitan governance and politics in the developing world (Cameron 1999; Collin and Robertson 2007; Laquian 2005; McCarney and Stren 2003; Myers and Dietz 2002; Rao 2007; Rojas, Cuadrado-Roura, and Guell 2008; Segbers 2007; Slack and Chattopadhyay 2009). Four of the major themes of this very provocative literature are the fragmentation of the urban system as cities expand geographically and grow in terms of population; the difficulty of finding an acceptable formula for dealing with other (higher) levels of government; the consistent pressures to respond adequately to the infrastructure and service needs of a large—and often very poor and marginalized—population; and the appropriate planning and local governance institutions required for these new city forms (UN-HABITAT 2008, chapter 4.5).

1.4. Competitive Cities

These large cities, and many more like them, are part of a world system of cities. Whether they are classified as "global cities" (functioning as "strategic sites for the managing and specialized servicing of global economic operations" [Sassen 2004, 373]) or "world cities" (whose internal politics and external policies are directly related to their place and status in the larger world economy) (Friedmann 1995) or even just "ordinary cities" (all the rest [Robinson 2006]) they aspire to improvement. But if they wish to maintain their place in the global system they must also compete. At least this is what they (and we) are told in much of the urban planning literature. In an introduction to a book entitled *Competitive Cities: Succeeding in the Global Economy* (Duffy 1995), the former mayor of Seattle says, "[s]uccessful cities of the future, both large and small, and regardless of where they are on the world map, must use all their resources if they hope to compete and prosper in a new world economy" (Royer 1995, x).

In this system, cities and city regions compete intensely with each other for investment, for the location of headquarters of transnational corporations, for hosting international agencies, for tourist streams, for large conventions, for major events such as the Olympics or the World Cup, or for major political meetings. A recently completed, and very well publicized study of the competitiveness of Latin American cities illustrates some important elements of this competitive international culture. The study, which was produced by a Colombian university and a Chilean consulting firm, lists 48 Latin American cities in terms of their attractiveness for external investment. The five leading cities are, in order, São Paulo, Mexico City, Santiago, Rio de Janeiro, and Buenos Aires. The key elements composing the overall index of "attractiveness to investment" are the size and wealth of the city, the number of global firms with offices in the city, the depth and specialization of the financial market, and what is called "urban comfort." The latter term includes both quality of life and security ("*Ranking de Ciudades...*" 2010). Aside from the criteria used to measure "attractiveness" it is worth noting that the most desirable cities are among the very largest in the region.

1.5. A Competitive "Tool": The City Development Strategy

For more than a decade, cities have been told by development agencies and international urban specialists that they need to develop better "strategic plans" or "visions" if they wish to be among the world's winners rather than losers. For cities in developing countries, the most widely used "tool" (a term used in planning to connote some practical approach or organizational model) proposed to achieve such an objective is the City Development Strategy, or CDS approach. Although the CDS is defined only in very general terms by its major proponent, the Cities Alliance (a development agency supported by the major bilateral donors, some large developing countries such as Brazil, South Africa, and India, the World Bank, and UN-HABITAT) it can be understood as a collaborative effort—involving all major stakeholders including businesses, governments, and civil society groups—to create a common vision for a city, and to develop a plan of action based on this vision (Cities Alliance 2006). While there have been literally hundreds of attempts at CDS projects in the cities of Africa, Asia, and Latin America (personal communication to the author), many (if not most) have foundered one way or another on the shoals of local or national politics. On the one hand, local arrangements, even when they are genuinely collaborative, need the support of higher levels of government and the political system if (previously) weak/poor cities are going to pull themselves out of their torpor; on the other hand, there is a major tendency in all assistance projects (which in most cases operate at the initiative of governments—usually national governments) for top-down rather than more balanced programs, thus bypassing many genuinely important but politically weak voices at the community level.

A number of studies of Johannesburg, South Africa show the various ways in which the city's very early approach to a collaborative development project eventually lost steam. As South Africa moved from apartheid to the current plural democratic phase of its political development, significant reformulation of local government institutions took place (Cameron 1999). At first, Johannesburg, the largest city in the country with a population of about 3 million in the late 1990s, was in dire financial straits. To improve municipal finances, and to move to another level of municipal organization, an impressive and ambitious urban reform process (called iGoli 2002 and then iGoli 2010) was put in place by a new city manager at the end of the 1990s (Parnell and Robinson 2006). The promotion of this scheme—which was to involve the municipal unions, the major leaders of the ANC, and civil society groups—began just as the larger metropolitan area was being consolidated into a single "unicity" by a national agency, and as new local elections were being organized. In the midst of resistance from the unions, who feared their positions would be threatened by reform of urban service delivery, delay on the part of an external consultancy team, and stalling on the political side as new leaders took over, this phase of the visioning process came "to a sticky halt" (Robinson 2006, 136). Later in the decade, citywide redistributive agendas remained, to be potentially accomplished through some undefined participatory visioning exercise, but there were too many difficulties and internal contradictions for this to result in a successful CDS-type plan, as had previously been proposed. Rather, formal participatory mechanisms through the machinery of local government seemed to be the best option for the future (Lipietz 2008).

Critics of this approach to urban policymaking in developing countries often point out that, by attempting to compete internationally, cities may be shortchanging their most important constituent groups—at least numerically—the poor and marginal. A study of Cape Town by David McDonald begins with the assertion that "politicians and policymakers in Cape Town, as well as business leaders and the media, have become fixated with the idea of being a 'world city'. From Cape Town's claim to offering world-class amenities, to its promotion of itself as a lucrative investment center, one can barely read a policy statement or promotional brochure that does not make some kind of reference to Cape Town's world city ambitions" (McDonald 2008, 1). Starting with this premise, McDonald then deploys an analysis of a broad range of local policy issues in Cape Town—including the pricing of services; pressures for the privatization of public transport, electricity supply, solid waste disposal and water; and the skewing of investments in the built environment toward middle- and upper-income residential areas and business clusters—to support his argument that the neoliberal approach of the world-city model almost intrinsically diverts the attention of urban planners and politicians away from the more pressing challenges of dealing with persistent poverty. Of course, the use of "mega-events" such as Olympic bids (whether they succeed or fail) by planners to promote certain kinds of infrastructure rather than others is well known (Hiller 2000), as is the "branding" and "placemaking" approach to promoting cities internationally in order to attract investment and major events (Zhang and Zhao 2009). But as even successful Olympic cities have learned, the "developmental" image they wish to project internationally may be at cross-purposes with the "redistributive" issues that many (including both local and international civil society groups) wish them to respond to in their local constituencies (Gold and Gold 2007). And overall, as Eleanora Pasotti has argued, more and more cities internationally are adopting "political branding" strategies to distinguish their internal and external policies from other cities. These branding strategies go along with the weakening of political party and clientelistic ties at the local level, the strengthening of the "image" of the mayor through direct elections, and appeals for votes through a mass communication strategy which offers collective, rather than individual benefits to the mayor's local constituency (Pasotti 2010).

2. The Last Three Decades: Attempts at Decentralization

The increasing importance of cities—especially large cities—in the international system is not a random tendency. True, cities are generating more wealth than they were in previous decades; and because of the globalization of culture, society and the economy they are more connected to major forces in the international political economy. But they would not be able to exert much influence, or be well connected, if they did not have more power and authority in their own local sphere. Enter decentralization—widespread and major redistribution of power that has taken place, roughly since the mid- to late 1980s, in most important regions of the developing world. While we do not have precise figures, by the mid-1990s, all but 12 of the world's 75 developing or transitional countries with a population of 5 million or more claimed to be engaged in some kind of program of transfer of political power to local units of government (Dillinger 1994, 8). Much more recently, but again without precise figures, we are told by the worldwide agency United Cities and Local Governments (UCLG) that "in the last 20 years decentralization has established itself as a political and institutional phenomenon in most countries around the world." As a result, in more than 130 countries "[t]he notions of '*autonomía local*', 'local self-government', '*Selbsverwaltung*' and '*libre administration*' have gradually become the norm in territorial administration in every region" (United Cities and Local Governments 2009, 20).

Before we proceed further, we must discuss briefly the *meaning* of decentralization. Essentially, by decentralization we mean the transfer of significant powers and functions, along with fiscal responsibility to carry out these powers and functions, from the national to the local level of government. For this transfer to be meaningful, Philip Mawhood argues, the decentralized local body should have its own budget, a separate legal existence, and the authority to allocate substantial resources on a range of different functions, the decisions being made by representatives of the local people (Mawhood 1983, 9–10). In federal states, decentralization may involve both the transfer of powers and functions from the national to the state or provincial level, as well as the transfer of powers and functions from the state or provincial level to the local. In both unitary and federal systems, the essential point is that local authorities (however they are defined) are strengthened. And when we speak of decentralization, it is common to distinguish among political, fiscal, and administrative decentralization; progress in one area (for example administrative decentralization) may not necessarily lead to political, let alone fiscal decentralization in all countries.

2.1. Three "Moments" of Decentralization

In spite of the current support for decentralization in many (if not all) developing countries, it has had a checkered history. In Africa and Asia, there have been three important historical "moments" (or phases) of decentralization. We can almost call them "the three decentralizations." Each of the first two historical phases has left its institutional footprint on the subsequent phase. It is important to understand each of these phases in order because, as Douglas North explained, an institutional or technological innovation, once accepted, creates limitations for the future based on fixed costs, learning effects, coordination effects (by which there are advantages to cooperation with other agents taking similar action), and adaptive expectations (whereby the more an approach is used, the more there is as belief in its further prevalence) (North 1990, 94). This idea is the basis of the "path dependency" approach to economic change.

A second important idea is the notion that, across nations, institutional reforms often occur in regional clusters. The regionalization of innovations (or policy reforms) is explained by Kurt Weyland using the example of the diffusion of pension reform legislation across Latin America. The immediate background to this wave of changes is that from the 1970s onward, most Latin American countries were in serious financial difficulties with their social security systems. A bold attempt to respond to this problem was made by Chile in 1981, through a radical privatization scheme under the Pinochet regime. Eventually, many other Latin American countries reformed their pension systems, almost all of them referring (either positively or negatively) to the Chilean example. (Brazil reformed its pension system, but did not take a privatization approach [Pinheiro 2004]). But the fact that other countries and their technical experts knew about the Chilean case, the fact that some of them bordered on Chile or were close to the country geographically, and that their populations learned about the Chilean example, played a large role in the spread of the reform throughout the continent. Weyland explains:

> As people are disproportionately influenced by events they witness directly, so drastic policy change enacted next door has particular immediacy, salience, and thus, availability. Decision makers cannot fail to pay attention to a bold reform adopted by a neighboring country. Such a nearby innovation is on their mind, whereas a change occurring halfway around the globe usually escapes their attention.... As decision makers do not scan the environment systematically and comprehensively for the relevant information but more passively let themselves be influenced disproportionately by experiences that happen to grab their attention, the unique availability of a reform enacted [nearby] often puts that innovation on the policy-making agenda in a whole region. (Weyland 2005, 285–86)

As we discuss the advance of decentralization through its three "moments" it is quite clear that regional clustering has played an important role in both the pace and the spread of this process. While we pay some attention to Asia, many of our examples will be taken from decentralization experiences in Latin America and Africa, where decentralization has—at least formally—spread very widely since the 1980s.

2.2. The First Moment of Decentralization

The *first moment* consolidated itself just before and at the point of independence (from the late 1940s through the early 1960s) in Africa and Asia, when local (and state) authorities were being established by mutual agreement between the nationalists and the departing colonial authorities. These local authorities were attempts to formalize existing understandings about the democratic delivery of local services, in the form of institutions that closely resembled local governments and communes in the metropole. To the British, local government was a "school for democracy," while for the French the *commune* was the arena for the exercise of rational civic rights on the part of both urban and rural citizens. In the waning years of colonialism (up to the 1960s), the colonizing powers attempted to develop both the spirit and effective administrative capacity of these local bodies, in both rural and urban areas, as multipurpose governments with responsibility for a variety of local functions. Many important nationalist leaders—who later became powerful politicians as ministers or presidents—had experience in these local bodies (Stren and Eyoh 2007).

After independence, the various pressures of the one-party state, military regimes, and the ideology of central planning began to deprive local governments (except residually in South Asia) of many of their powers and much of their original autonomy. In some countries, strengthening local authorities was viewed by national political leaders as tantamount to reinforcing regional sentiments, when these differences might produce opposition to the central government. But as a result of increasing restrictions on local government, failures throughout the system were more and more attributed to the center alone. Here we move into a period of about two to three decades, during which—at least in sub-Saharan Africa—"the removal of decentralized government" (Kasfir 1983) was the norm. Central government came to be the focus of almost all political and administrative initiative, and the ideology of development stressed central planning and national integration. Eventually, there was a reaction.

2.3. The Second Moment of Decentralization

The reaction came in the late 1970s and early 1980s. We may call this a *second moment* of decentralization, when in a response to overcentralization and problems with local project implementation, central governments throughout the developing world looked for administrative means of relocating development committees, technical ministries, and even large projects, at the district level, "closer to the people." But this trend at decentralization in Africa during the 1970s and 1980s was more like deconcentration than true, political decentralization. Perhaps typical of the reasoning behind this second attempt to "rescue" local institutions was the argument by President Julius Nyerere of Tanzania, who famously stated in his 1972 paper, *Decentralisation*, that the developmental goals of the country were being compromised by overcentralization. "[I]t has gradually become obvious," he wrote, "that, in order to make a reality of our policies of socialism and self-reliance, the planning and control of development in this country must be exercised at local level to a much greater extent than at present. Our nation is too large for the people at the centre in Dar es Salaam always to understand local problems or to sense their urgency. When all the power remains at the centre, therefore, local problems can remain, and fester, while local people who are aware of them are prevented from using their initiative in finding solutions" (Nyerere 1972, 1).

Following Nyerere's guidance, Tanzania's solution was to abolish existing local government institutions in both the rural and urban areas, and to replace them with councils that combined both central government officials and local political representatives. Tanzania also took the decision in 1973 to move its capital and accompanying central government agencies to the town of Dodoma, away from the coast and close to the physical center of the country. Commentators soon noted that the official side dominated the proceedings of the new decentralized councils. And in spite of the extensive planning and building that took place in Dodoma, most civil servants stayed in Dar es Salaam, which also remained the commercial capital of the country. A centralizing trend also obtained in spite of decentralization policies in Ghana, Kenya, Uganda, Zambia, and Botswana in that little power—let alone finance and skilled professional staff—were given to representative local authorities for their own unrestricted use (Tordoff 1994). In Africa, this second "moment" dissipated its initial promise in the failures of large projects and the absence of finance. The end of this second phase of the decentralization story coincides with the beginnings of the structural adjustment period of the mid-1980s.

Other analysts who considered decentralization and local government in developing countries, were concerned with the degree to which already poorly equipped central governments could effectively deconcentrate functions and even programs to lower levels of the central government, given the very low levels of resources and experience available at the state/province and local government levels (Grindle 1980). This concern gave rise to an important conclusion: only governments that were strong at the center, both politically and administratively, could take the risk and find the resources to decentralize important programs or functions. Thus decentralization, in the opinion of many, had (paradoxically) to be accompanied by centralization—the two functions needed to be in a rough kind of balance for either to operate effectively.

In Asia, many of the same reasons as in Africa underpinned a brief flirtation with decentralization initiatives in the late 1960s and 1970s. While centralized planning was pervasive in the years after independence as a means of mobilizing and optimally utilizing scarce resources for major capital developments, a concern about increasing regional disparities and the expression of localized resistance to central government occasionally led to attempts to decentralize.

During the 1970s, these decentralizing initiatives were largely overcome by centralizing forces. In India, interest in decentralization gradually faded during this period, with emphasis shifting to creating organizations that could perform specialized development tasks. Decentralizing initiatives were further undercut during the mid to late 1970s because of political turbulence at the national level, and the imposition of an Emergency over the country from 1975 to 1977. In general, the Asian initiatives during this period (a) emanated from the central government, which attempted to retain control; and (b) involved very little popular participation at the local level. Writing in the early 1980s, one author noted that "in most Asian countries... little sympathy exists for devolution of authority to local governments" (Mathur 1983, 69).

As for Latin America during the 1960s and 1970s, this was a period of military *coups d'état* in a number of major countries, with the result that state systems that were already highly centralized through historical conditioning (Stein and Stein 1970) were reinforced with military might. Consolidation of authority at the center was more important than the devolution of power to localities. The general situation in Latin America whereby local governments had almost no power to tax or to administer social programs continued, even in a country not under military rule such as Mexico. An important exception to this rule was Colombia, where already in 1973 the share of local government in total public expenditures was 17 percent (Nickson 1995, 149). This figure rose only slightly in the next decade, settling at a level between 21 and 23 percent in the early 1990s (Bird and Fiszbein 1998, 176), a result of a series of important fiscal reforms begun during the 1980s. Another but more complex exception was Brazil where in 1985 there were 4,116 municipalities. Brazil's federal structure and local traditions seem to have shielded the municipalities from major reductions in their powers and taxation base during this period. While the proportion of central revenues transferred to the municipalities was reduced during the period 1968–75, mayors of many cities continued to be elected, and a limited degree of municipal autonomy obtained (Lordello de Mello 1991).

2.4. The Third Moment of Decentralization: 1980s to the Present

If the prospects for decentralization were dim for many countries as late as the early 1980s, by the late 1980s and early 1990s the situation had dramatically changed. Not only had a great number of states—both large and medium-sized—opted to undertake measures of decentralization from the center to local governments, there was also support within civil society for these measures. This support was a result of two major factors: the impressive growth of civil society organizations and movements within urban areas; and a concurrent "wave" of democratization and redemocratization that began to take place in the 1980s. Both of these trends have, in different ways, reinforced decentralization, but have, in a wide variety of countries, taken their own shape and dynamic. (In some countries, for example, there have been contrary trends toward "recentralization," though these scattered examples have not materially affected large cities [Wunsch 2001; Eaton and Dickovick 2004].) Since these trends have become a part of the experience of so many countries, decentralization initiatives have received substantially more social and political support in recent years than was the case with the earlier "moment" during the 1970s and early 1980s. The differential development of urban civil society in the developing world may be illustrated with the cases of Latin America and Africa.

3. Urban Civil Society in Latin America and Africa

During the 1960s and 1970s, the larger cities in many developing countries were the focus of increasingly intense conflicts between the public authorities and large numbers of the urban poor who could not afford the cost of shelter in planned areas with good roads, piped water, sewerage, electricity, and other infrastructural services. Partly as a result of the people's inability to afford the cost of planned (or "urbanized") areas, so-called squatter or popular settlements (variously named in different countries) developed on unserviced urban land. This land was usually marginal in terms of the quality of the site and the distance from major centers of employment and often compromised in terms of the legality of the land tenure rights of the new occupants. The social science literature of the time extensively investigated both the reasons for the growth of these settlements and the appalling living conditions many of them represented. These studies demonstrated that the massive increase in people living in the popular settlements was not a result of (nor did it result in) a challenge to the system of authority (Nelson 1979). Rather, the rise of spontaneous settlements represented marginal groups attempting to gain a foothold in the burgeoning urban economy, which could serve as a first step toward integration into the labor market and institutions of the larger society (Perlman 1976). Following this logic, a number of policy innovations—such as sites and services schemes and later squatter upgrading programs—were developed to respond to the need of the urban poor to gain entry, at minimal cost to the formal urban economy.

Latin America is one of the most urbanized continents of the developing world. Given the size of the urban presence, more attention than in other developing regions tended to be paid to the struggles of the urban poor to improve their conditions of life. Indeed, attempts by the urban poor to gain access to urban land and services were often conceptualized in Latin America as a component of what were called "urban social movements" (Hipsher 1996). The concept of social movement reflects broad-based, often multiclass, coordinated activity at the local level to make demands on the government (Tarrow 1998). These demands may be very specific (i.e. for water and services) or more general (i.e. for political or gender rights). At the same time, even though demands are being made, political parties and other specialized institutions are not the primary vehicles involved.

Lima, Peru from the early 1970s is a good example of these dynamics. A major element in the residential and commercial development of Lima was the building and establishment of informal, unplanned settlements on public land, land under disputed title, and on private land. Of some 136 settlements for which information was available in the mid-1970s, 41 were formed with explicit authorization from the government, 50 through an organized land invasion by groups of squatters, and 41 through gradual occupation (Collier 1976, ch. 3). Although the government resisted informal settlements over the years, those evicted from one area would eventually find space in another area, sometimes with the support of the government. By 1972, "a common way of getting a lot was to participate in an invasion and then get moved to a government-sponsored settlement. Invasions... continue to be a major means through which families acquire land in settlements" (Collier 1976, 115). As a case of how landless people organized to promote their interests, we have the well-known example of the "Pamplona" invasion. In 1971, a group of 80 to 100 families planned this event to coincide with meetings in Lima between the government of Peru and the Inter-American Development Bank. While a contingent of troops arrived to disperse the squatters—whose ranks had grown to some 9,000 families by the fifth day of the occupation—public opinion was such that they were eventually offered sites in another location named Villa el Salvador. By 1986, about 168,000 people lived in Villa el Salvador, most with electricity and over half with domestic water and sewerage. "Despite originally being a desert site, the area now has many trees and gardens, the main roads are paved and bus services link it to central Lima, some 20 kilometers away. Most of these improvements were made by the inhabitants and their organizations, not by government" (Hardoy and Satterthwaite 1989, 85). According to the municipality's website, their population has grown to 388,588 in 2005 (Villa El Salvador 2005).

As a general rule, national and local government agencies were either unable or unwilling to supply basic urban services to the rapidly growing popular settlements of Latin America—at least not at the pace and quality that the people demanded. To fill the gap between local needs and formal provision of services, a wide range of community organizations and self-help activities developed. In Mexico City, a well-known study of a small, peripheral shantytown that sprawled over the slopes of a ravine looked at the reciprocal social and kinship ties that supported the settlers even though their economic positions in the larger system were marginal. Aside from a dense network of extended family ties, the community of 176 households had four football teams, a medical center, and a number of temporary associations for specific purposes, often formed by small groups of neighbors (Lomnitz 1977).

These trends of self-help organization at the local level continued through the late 1970s and into the 1980s, which was the period during which NGOs (nongovernmental organizations) became a more prominent feature of civil society. NGOs as well as local community organizations (community-based organizations, or CBOs) gained further support from overseas aid agencies and foundations reluctant to assist authoritarian governments or government-dominated political parties. In many countries they were also supported by the Church. Regardless of the sources of their support, local organizations became very numerous in the 1980s, particularly in poor settlements. In Santiago, Chile, a survey found that 20 percent of the marginal urban population participated in popular organizations, 33 percent of which were involved with health problems. In the health area, some 673 self-help health organizations were operating at the community level alone, including 201 soup kitchens, 20 community kitchens, 223 cooperative buying organizations, 67 family garden organizations, 25 community bakeries, and 137 health groups. These organizations had 12,956 active members. Most of the members, as well as the leaders and managers of these organizations were women (Salinas and Solimano 1995). At the same time, there were literally thousands of NGOs operating in Chile during the period of military rule, which lasted from 1973 through 1989 (Loveman 1995).

The situation in Lima was similar. In Lima, one researcher reports, "the urban lower classes...had over the years created elaborate and enduring self-help mechanisms for which many of them contributed time, money, and effort. In the late 1980s Lima had an estimated eighteen hundred communal soup kitchens, serving approximately seventy thousand individuals daily, and some thirty-five hundred Vaso de Leche neighborhood committees delivering some 1 million glasses of milk a day." The same observer suggests that the number of kitchens may have doubled after the initial economic shocks of President Fujimori's adjustment policies in the early 1990s; in 1994 the USAID estimated that it was feeding one of three Peruvians (Dietz 1998, 253). These local groups were often related to international nongovernmental advocacy groups, or international NGOs, which proliferated in the 1980s and 1990s. The Union of International Associations shows that the number of nongovernmental social change organizations operating at the international level rose from 110 in 1953, to 141 in 1963 (19 percent increase), to 183 in 1973 (30 percent increase), to 348 in 1983 (90 percent increase), and to 631 in 1993 (representing an 81 percent increase) (based on Keck and Sikkink 1998, 11). These figures show a moderate growth in NGOs in the period up to the early seventies, followed by a very rapid growth thereafter.

By the 1990s, urban-based NGOs were very important participants in the decentralization story all over Latin America. In Mexico, for example, constitutional amendments enhancing the powers of states and municipalities began with a reform of Article 115 of the Constitution in 1983, strengthening the legal base of municipalities and making their functions and responsibilities ore explicit. But many issues were unresolved. While the story is complex, beginning in the 1980s (spurred on by civil society organizations established to deal with the government's failure to deal with the earthquake disaster of 1985), both local groups and regional and national networks began to grow in order to deal with local needs. A careful study counted 2,364 civic organizations across the country in 1995. By the year 2000 the figure had increased to 6,887. "At present," concludes Leticia Santín del Rio, "NGOs in Mexico form an integral part of all sphere of public and private life.... They coordinate participation in areas such as social assistance, social promotion, squatters' rights, human rights and democracy, legal advice, women, indigenous peoples, migrants and refugees, ecology, popular fronts, culture, civic education, and research and education institutes, among others.... They are fundamental actors in an evolving democratic system" (Santín del Rio 2004, 70–71).

Africa is one of the least urbanized parts of the developing world. In a predominantly rural continent, the voices and influence of urban civil society have been less influential on policy than in other more urbanized areas of the world. Nevertheless, in the period leading up to, and just following independence in the 1960s, trade unions, women's groups, and ethnic and regional associations played an active role in the establishment of new national and local government institutions. Many were active in the nationalist movements that brought independence, and continued to represent the positions of their members throughout the1960s. The influence and spread of these (often) urban groups was to be curtailed, however, as municipal and other local government institutions were either limited in their powers after independence, or were absorbed in one-party or no-party regimes. Except in South Africa which followed a different historical trajectory, the years of the 1960s and 1970s were a period of central government ascendancy and local government decline in much of Africa, both Anglophone and Francophone. As in other parts of the developing world, political initiatives came from the center, and a discourse of development planning—supported by international assistance—concentrated on large-scale formal projects, extensive state and parastatal employment, and widespread regulation of the economy

Beginning in the late 1970s and early 1980s, the system began to break down economically, as formal employment through government and import substitution-led industrialization reached its limits. The informal sector, in both urban and rural areas, grew dramatically in importance. If by the late 1970s, some 60 percent of the African urban population was operating in the informal sector (ILO 1985), the figure was much higher in the 1980s. A major trend in the last two decades has been the supplementation of formal sector jobs with informal activities on the part of a large proportion of public sector employees. In the cities, publicly provided urban services such as public transport, water supply, and garbage disposal, began seriously to deteriorate in the face of massive urban population expansion on the one hand, and tightened local budgets, on the other. As a result, growing numbers of low-income citizens were buying their water from private water vendors; paying more for private, but more accessible mass transport; and increasingly obtaining unserviced land and housing through the small-scale unregulated private market (Stren 1988).

The growth of informal sector employment on the one hand and the decline in urban services on the other, created new pathways for the development of civil society at the local level, at least in many of Africa's largest cities. According to a recent overview of the situation in African cities, "[t]he onset of the urban crisis in the mid-1980s... seems to have had a dramatic impact on the number and nature of associations.... Their role increasingly became centred on providing urban services that the state could not deliver (such as housing, water and sanitation) and catering for the more immediate needs of the expanding urban informal settlements through associations ranging from community security societies to religious and other spiritual associations" (Tostensen, Tvedten, and Vaa 2001, 22). Women have been particularly active in forming these associations, perhaps because their economic importance, through an expanded informal sector, has been enhanced. Swazi women in the city, for example, have organized savings groups, burial societies, wedding groups, and land and housing acquisition groups (Miles 2001, 66). A study of women's participation in informal economic activities in Dar es Salaam from the late 1980s through the early 1990s shows how, on a personal level, women confronted state harassment, networked with each other for support, and generally engaged in "everyday forms of resistance" in order to provide for their families during difficult times. The result of this spontaneous action was to affect, and to change, a number of important local and national government policies (Tripp 1997).

4. Democratization and Urban Governance

Reinforcing the tendency, in many countries, toward an increasingly active urban civil society has been a second major trend: democratization. Since the 1970s, we have witnessed a worldwide "wave" of democratization, according, at least, to Samuel Huntington's definition of democracy (as a system in which the "most powerful collective decision makers are selected through fair, honest, and periodic elections in which candidates freely compete for votes and in which virtually all the adult population is eligible to vote") (Huntington 1991, 7). Beginning in 1974 in Portugal, and eventually spreading outward, democratic reforms swept over more than 30 countries in both industrial and developing areas. This overall trend was particularly marked during the 1970s and early 1980s in Latin America, where democratic transitions took place in such major countries as Argentina, Bolivia, Brazil, Chile, Ecuador, and Peru, and in the late 1980s and early 1990s in the former Soviet Union and eastern Europe. The process continued during the 1990s although it seems to have stalled to some degree over the last decade.

As democratic forms and democratic practices have spread across many regions of the developing world, local municipal governance has been carried along by the tide of change. In eastern Europe and Latin America in particular, elected municipal councils have proliferated over the political landscape, bringing new forms and styles of governance to a large segment of the population. According to one estimate, democratically chosen executive and legislative officials are now found in more than 14,000 units of subnational government in Latin America (Campbell 2003, 4). All Latin American countries with the exception of Cuba now have elected mayors, for example.

The institutionalization of these trends toward decentralization—in cities as well as (to a lesser extent) in smaller towns and rural areas—has taken different forms in different countries. This is not the place to elaborate on these reforms, but among them are the Local Government Code of 1991 in the Philippines (which devolved significant powers from the national government to municipalities); the Seventy-Fourth Amendment to the Indian Constitution in 1992 (strengthening the finances of municipalities; giving them more independence from their state governments; and reserving one-third of all municipal council seats for women); a new Constitution for South Africa which, among other achievements, specifies a range of protected powers and governance responsibilities for local governments; and the upgrading of democratic institutions in Mexico City so that the former "head of government" in the Federal District is now elected, and the 16 subunits (*delegaciones*) have their own mayors and a range of new powers and functions.

Perhaps the most celebrated decentralization reforms took place in Brazil, following a new, postmilitary constitution that was proclaimed into law in 1988. That constitution "decentralized resources and authority over the provision of basic social services" (Wampler 2008, 25). This means that municipal services (such as basic education, health, water and sanitation, transport, and the like) now significantly affect the lives of all citizens. The constitution also created "devices" which both allow for, and even require voluntary local participation in many aspects of local governance. Throughout urban Brazil, by 2002 there were more than 10,000 health and social assistance councils, working alongside, and supporting, the work of formally elected bodies (Avritzer 2009, 14). The most well-known of these local institutions are the participatory budgeting processes which have been established in close to 200 Brazilian cities to give active public input to the investment budgeting part (about 15 percent overall) of the local government budget. In 2004, more than 300,000 people participated in these local budgeting processes in Brazil. The idea of local participatory budgeting has been taken up in Peru (as part of a national law) by over 800 municipalities (World Urban Forum 2006), as well as by many other cities around the world (Cabannes 2004).

While these, and other new powers are being consolidated at the municipal level in many countries, new fiscal arrangements have been made, and more collaborative relationships developed between the largest cities and their national governments. Although national governments are more likely to give powers and functions to municipalities than they are to offer the necessary fiscal powers to support these new powers (Falleti 2010), there is evidence that fiscal recalibration is gradually taking place. In Latin America, for example, subnational governments (municipalities in unitary states; and states/provinces and municipalities in federal states) managed 11.6 percent of all government expenditures in the early 1980s; by 2002 this figure had risen to 18.8 percent, more than a 50 percent increase (UCLG 2009, 174). The country with the most established and effective program of decentralization to the municipal level, Colombia, included an article in its new Constitution of 1991 explicitly stating that "There could not be a decentralization of responsibilities without the previous transfer of the necessary fiscal revenues to afford them" (Falleti 2010, 140–41).

The story we have told of decentralization over the decades illustrates a number of points. First of all, the current, or third "moment" of decentralization appears to be stronger, and more deeply entrenched than the earlier initiatives in the early 1960s and the 1970s and early 1980s. There are at least three reasons for this: greater experience with the reasons for failure in the earlier attempts; the increased interest of civil society groups in decentralized institutions, especially at the local level; and the spread of a culture of democracy (Chege 2005) throughout many areas of the developing world. Second, cities—and particular major cities—in the developing world have benefited enormously from this development, to the extent that their mayors can operate both locally and internationally with a lot more self-confidence than was the case before. This does not diminish their challenges at home—to improve services for their people, to reduce the incidence of poverty, and to increase participatory access to local projects and councils—but it definitely improves their resource base (both symbolic and material) and their political profile. Still—and this is the third point—decentralization remains somewhat of a mystery to researchers. As Philip Oxhorn puts it, "decentralization, economic liberalization, and democratic transition—are often intimately intertwined, yet it is not always clear how" (Oxhorn 2004, 4). In some countries decentralization is clearly related to democratization, and the opening of civil society, while in others (particularly the poorest countries) it is often initiated, and almost completely driven by elite needs from the center. In some countries decentralization appears to have been encouraged and even initiated from outside (Vilas 1996; Willis et al. 1999); but in others (perhaps most) it takes place as a result of purely local political calculations (Grindle 2000). In general, research on decentralization is not nearly as extensive as research on the parallel subjects of neoliberalization and democratization. But for cities, the subject cries out for more work and careful thought.

5. An Abbreviated Research Agenda

This chapter has focused on the relationship among four important variables: worldwide urbanization, the increasing political and economic influence of cities in the developing world, decentralization, and democratization (including the growth of civil society). The first is largely the terrain of demographers; but the next three are—and should be—developed much more by students of public administration and political science. Indeed, while we have numerous monographic studies of decentralization in one or more (usually at the most two or three) countries, or of democratic change in one country, we have few comparative studies of the same factors with respect to cities. There are numerous comparative studies of urban politics in developed societies, but very few in developing countries. While edited volumes on the theme of urban politics or urban governance in developing countries are valuable, more systematic monographs on multiple cities would be even more valuable in the development of the discipline.

Three major themes suggest themselves for further exploration. The first is the elaboration of what we can call a "culture of local governance" in the developing regions. By this I mean the elaboration of institutions of local government, including secure and reliable voting and party systems, transparency, and the involvement of citizens and civil society groups in the process of local government. This model includes the support of local government by higher levels of authority, and it includes the importance of good and responsible leadership. We have very few studies of local leaders, even though almost all successful cases of local development have some exceptional and dedicated leaders to thank for their results.

Second, we need to pay more attention to the manner by which cities operate politically in the larger world system. How do cities collaborate (or compete) with each other? How do they choose their proper "niche" within the larger system, and in light of this strategy, accommodate their policies to the needs of their citizens—many of whom require the most elementary services such as clean water and sanitary facilities, secure housing, health care, and basic employment. While most cities are adrift in a sea of international competition, how do—or should—they navigate these waters? A beginning is the Global City Indicators Facility (GCIF), which so far includes over 100 cities worldwide. This program provides an established set of city indicators allowing cities to compare themselves with each other and share knowledge together. Until this web-based facility was established, there was no existing international database of city services and quality of life indicators, to enable both cities and the scholarly community to make intelligent comparisons beyond almost purely demographic information.

Finally, there are many new and emerging players in the global politics of cities. One major—and heretofore little studied—group is young people. In this age of new information technology, how are young people participating in, and understanding, government and politics? How do they get their information about the immediate world in which they live? How do movements and new initiatives involving youth transfer themselves into the political arena? What are their challenges and issues? Similar questions might be proposed for another emerging group: the elderly. And in many cities of the developing world immigrants from other, more disadvantaged countries have challenges and issues of their own. Finally, there is a very large, and growing group, which overlaps with the others: the unemployed and those living in slums and working in the informal sector. How to understand all these voices, and to work toward what many scholars see as the goal of the "inclusive city"? The city is increasingly the space of many different voices and needs. How does politics express this emerging reality?

REFERENCES

Avritzer, Leonardo. 2009. *Participatory Institutions in Democratic Brazil.* Washington, DC and Baltimore: Woodrow Wilson Institute Press and the Johns Hopkins University Press.

Bird, Richard and Ariel Fiszbein. 1998. "Colombia: The Central Role of the Central Government in Fiscal Decentralization." In Richard M. Bird and Francois Vaillancourt, eds., *Fiscal Decentralization in Developing Countries.* Cambridge: Cambridge University Press.

Brugmann, Jeb. 2009. *Welcome to the Urban Revolution: How Cities are Changing the World.* Toronto: Viking.

Cabannes, Yves. 2004. "Participatory Budgeting: A Significant Contribution to Participatory Democracy." *Environment and Urbanization* 16(1): 27–46.

Cameron, Robert. 1999. *Democratisation of South African Local Government: A Tale of Three Cities.* Pretoria: J. L. van Schaik.

Campbell, Tim. 2003. *The Quiet Revolution: Decentralization and the Rise of Political Participation in Latin American Cities.* Pittsburgh: University of Pittsburgh Press.

Chege, Michael. 2005. "Democratic Governance in Africa at the Start of the Twenty-first Century: Lessons of Experience." In Leonardo A. Villalón and Peter VonDoepp, eds., *The Fate of Africa's Democratic Experiments: Elites and Institutions.* Bloomington: Indiana University Press.

Cities Alliance. 2006. *Guide to City Development Strategies: Improving Urban Performance* Washington, DC: Cities Alliance.

Collier, David. 1976. *Squatters and Oligarchs: Authoritarian Rule and Policy Change in Peru.* Baltimore: Johns Hopkins University Press.

Collin, Jean-Pierre and Mélanie Robertson, eds. 2007. *Governing Metropolises: Profiles of Issues and Experiments on Four Continents.* Quebec City: Lesw Presses de l'Université Laval.

Dietz, Henry. 1998. *Urban Poverty, Political Participation, and the State: Lima 1970–1990.* Pittsburgh: University of Pittsburgh Press.

Dillinger, William. 1994. *Decentralization and Its Implications for Urban Service Delivery.* Washington: World Bank, Urban Management Programme.

Dogan, Mattei and John D. Kasarda. 1988. "Introduction: How Giant Cities Will Multiply and Grow." In Mattei Dogan and John D. Kasarda, eds., *The Metropolis Era.* Vol. 1. *A World of Giant Cities.* Newbury Park, CA: Sage.

Duffy, H. 1995. *Competitive Cities: Succeeding in the Global Economy.* London: Chapman and Hall.

Eaton, Kent, and J. Tyler Dickovick. 2004. "The Politics of Re-Centralization in Argentina and Brazil." *Latin American Research Review* 39(1): 90–122.

Falleti, Tulia G. 2010. *Decentralization and Subnational Politics in Latin America.* Cambridge: Cambridge University Press.

Friedmann, John. 1995. "The World City Hypothesis." In Paul L. Knox and Peter J. Taylor, eds., *World Cities in a World-System.* Cambridge: Cambridge University Press.

Gold, John R. and Margaret M. Gold, eds. 2007. *Olympic Cities: City Agendas, Planning, and the World's Games, 1896–2012.* London: Routledge.

Grindle, Merilee, ed. 1980. *Politics and Policy Implementation in the Third World.* Princeton: Princeton University Press.

———. 2000. *Audacious Reforms: Institutional Invention and Democracy in Latin America.* Baltimore: Johns Hopkins University Press.

Hardoy, Jorge Enrique and David Satterthwaite. 1989. *Squatter Citizen: Life in the Urban Third World.* London: Earthscan.

Hiller, Harry H. 2000. "Mega-Events, Urban Boosterism and Growth Strategies: An Analysis of the Objectives and Legitimations of the Cape Town 2004 Olympic Bid." *International Journal of Urban and Regional Research* 24(2): 439–58.

Hipsher, Patricia.1996. "Democratization and the Decline of Urban Social Movements in Chile and Spain." *Comparative Politics* 28: 273–98.

Huntington, Samuel P. 1991. *The Third Wave: Democratization in the Late Twentieth Century.* Norman: University of Oklahoma Press.

ILO (International Labour Office). 1985. *Informal Sector in Africa.* Addis Ababa: Jobs and Skills Programme for Africa.

Isserman, Andrew M. 1977. "The Location Quotient Approach for Estimating Regional Economic Impacts." *Journal of the American Institute of Planners* 43(10): 33–41.

Kasfir, Nelson. 1983. "Designs and Dilemmas: An Overview of Decentralisation in Africa." In Philip Mawhood, ed., *Local Government in the Third World: The Experience of Tropical Africa.* Chichester: John Wiley.

Keck, Margaret E. and Kathryn Sikkink. 1998. *Activists Beyond Borders: Advocacy Networks in International Politics.* Ithaca: Cornell University Press.

Laquian, Aprodicio A. 2005. *Beyond Metropolis: The Planning and Governance of Asia's Mega-Urban Regions.* Baltimore: Johns Hopkins University Press.

Lefebvre, Henri. 2003. *The Urban Revolution* (translated from French by Robert Bonnono). Minneapolis: University of Minnesota Press.

Lipietz, Barbara. 2008. "Building a Vision for the Post-Apartheid City: What Role for Participation in Johannesburg's City Development Strategy?" *International Journal of Urban and Regional Research* 32(1): 135–63.

Lomnitz, Larissa. 1977. *Networks and Marginality*. New York: Academic Press.

Lordello de Mello, Diogo. 1991. "Brazil." In Samuel Humes, ed., *Local Governance and National Power*. Hertfordshire: Wheatsheaf Books.

Loveman, Brian. 1995. "Chilean NGOs: Forging a Role in the Transition to Democracy." In Charles A. Reilly, ed., *New Paths to Democratic Development in Latin America: The Rise of NGO-Municipal Collaboration*. Boulder, CO: Lynne Rienner.

Mathur, Kuldeep. 1983. "Administrative Decentralization in Asia." In G. Shabbir Cheema and Dennis A. Rondinelli, eds., *Decentralization and Development*. Beverly Hills, CA: Sage.

Mawhood, Philip, ed. 1983. *Local Government in the Third World: The Experience of Tropical Africa*. Chichester: John Wiley and Sons.

McCarney, Patricia L. and Richard E. Stren, eds. 2003. *Governance on the Ground: Innovations and Discontinuities in Cities of the Developing World*. Baltimore: Johns Hopkins University Press.

McDonald, David A. 2008. *World City Syndrome. Neoliberalism and Inequality in Cape Town*. New York: Routledge.

Miles, Miranda. 2001. "Women's Groups and Urban Poverty: The Swaziland Experience." In Arne Tostensen, Inge Tvedten, and Mariken Vaa, eds., *Associational Life in African CitiesL Popular Responses to the Urban Crisis*. Uppsala: Nordiska Afrikainstitutet.

Myers, David J. and Henry A. Dietz, eds. 2002. *Capital City Politics in Latin America: Democratization and Empowerment*. Boulder, CO: Lynne Rienner.

National Research Council. 2003. *Cities Transformed: Demographic Change and Its Implications in the Developing World*. Panel on Urban Population Dynamics, M. R. Montgomery, R. Stren, B. Cohen, and H.E. Reed, eds., Committee on Population, Division of Behavioral and Social Sciences and Education. Washington, DC: National Academies Press.

Nelson, Joan M. 1979. *Access to Power: Politics and the Urban Poor in Developing Nations*. Princeton: Princeton University Press.

Nickson, R. A. 1995. *Local Government in Latin America*. Boulder, CO: Lynne Rienner.

North, Douglass C. 1990. *Institutions, Institutional Change and Economic Performance*. Cambridge: Cambridge University Press.

Nyerere, Julius K. 1972. *Decentralisation*. Dar es Salaam: Government Printer.

Oxhorn, Philip. 2004. "Unravelling the Puzzle of Decentralization." In Philip Oxhorn, Joseph S. Tulchin, and Andrew D. Selee, eds. *Decentralization, Democratic Governance, and Civil Society in Comparative Perspective. Africa, Asia, and Latin America*. Washington, DC and Baltimore: Woodrow Wilson Center Press and Johns Hopkins University Press.

Parnell, Susan and Jenny Robinson. 2006. "Development and Urban Policy: Johannesburg's City Development Strategy." *Urban Studies* 43(2): 337–55.

Pasotti, Eleonora. 2010. *Political Branding in Cities: The Decline of Machine Politics in Bogotá, Naples, and Chicago*. Cambridge: Cambridge University Press.

Perlman, Janice. 1976. *The Myth of Marginality. Urban Poverty and Politics in Rio de Janeiro*. Berkeley and Los Angeles: University of California Press.

Pinheiro, Vinícius C. 2004. "The Politics of Social Security Reform in Brazil." In Kurt Weyland, ed., *Learning from Foreign Models in Latin American Policy Reform*. Washington, DC and Baltimore: Woodrow Wilson Center Press and Johns Hopkins University Press.

Ranking de Ciudades Latinoamericanas para la Atracción de Inversiones. Informe Oficial. 2010. Rosario University and IdN Consulting. April. Seen at http://www.urosario

.edu.co/competitividad/noticias/Destacadas/RANKING-DE-CIUDADES-LATINOAMERICANAS-PARA-LA-ATRAC/ on September 9, 2010.

Rao, Nirmala. 2007. *Cities in Transition: Growth, Change and Governance in Six Metropolitan Areas*. London: Routledge.

Robinson, Jennifer. 2006. *Ordinary Cities: Between Modernity and Development*. New York: Routledge.

Rojas, Eduardo, Juan R. Cuadrado-Roura, and José Miguel Fernández Güell, eds. 2008. *Governing the Metropolis: Principles and Cases*. Washington, DC and Cambridge, MA: Inter-American Development Bank and David Rockefeller Center for Latin American Studies, Harvard University.

Royer, C. 1995. "Foreword" to H. Duffy, *Competitive Cities: Succeeding in the Global Economy*. London: Chapman and Hall.

Salinas, Judith, and Giorgio Solimano.1995. "Chilean Health NGOs." In Charles A. Reilly, ed., *New Paths to Democratic Development in Latin America: The Rise of NGO-Municipal Collaboration*. Boulder, CO: Lynne Rienner.

Santín del Rio Leticia. 2004. "Decentralization and Civil Society in Mexico." In Philip Oxhorn, Joseph S. Tulchin, and Andrew D. Selee, eds., *Decentralization, Democratic Governance, and Civil Society in Comparative Perspective: Africa, Asia, and Latin America*. Washington, DC and Baltimore: Woodrow Wilson Center Press and Johns Hopkins University Press.

Sassen, Saskia. 2004. "Afterword" in Josef Gugler, ed., *World Cities Beyond the West: Globalization Development and Inequality*. Cambridge: Cambridge University Press.

Segbers, Klaus, ed. 2007. *The Making of Global City Regions. Johannesburg, Mumbai/ Bombay, São Paulo, and Shanghai*. Baltimore: Johns Hopkins University Press.

Slack, Enid and Rupak Chattopadhyay, eds. 2009. *Finance and Governance of Capital Cities in Federal Systems*. Montreal: McGill-Queen's University Press.

Stein, Stanley J. and Barbara H. Stein. 1970. *The Colonial Heritage of Latin America: Essays on Economic Dependence in Perspective*. Oxford: Oxford University Press.

Stren, Richard. 1988. "Urban Services in Africa: Public Management or Privatisation?" In Paul Cook and Colin Kirkpatrick, eds., *Privatisation in Less Developed Countries*. Sussex, UK: Wheatsheaf Books.

Stren, Richard and Dickson Eyoh. 2007. "Decentralization and Urban Development in West Africa: An Introduction." In Dickson Eyoh and Richard Stren, eds., *Decentralization and the Politics of Urban Development in West Africa/* Washington, DC: Woodrow Wilson International Center for Scholars, Comparative Urban Studies Project.

Tarrow, Sidney. 1998. *Power of Movement*. 2nd edi. Cambridge: Cambridge University Press.

Tordoff, William. 1994. "Decentralisation: Comparative Experience in Commonwealth Africa." *Journal of Modern African Studies* 32(4): 555–80.

Tostensen, Arne, Inge Tvedten, and Mariken Vaa, eds. 2001. *Associational Life in African Cities: Popular Responses to the Urban Crisis*. Uppsala: Nordiska Afrikainstitutet.

Tripp, Aili Mari. 1997. *Changing the Rules: The Politics of Liberalization and the Urban Informal Economy in Tanzania*. Berkeley: University of California Press.

UN-HABITAT. 2008. "Metropolitan Governance: Governing in a City of Cities." In *State of the World's Cities 2008/2009: Harmonious Cities*. London: Earthscan.

United Cities and Local Governments (UCLG). 2009. *Decentralization and Local Democracy in the World: First Global Report by United Cities and Local Governments*. Barcelona: United Cities and Local Governments.

United Nations. 2001. *World Urbanization Prospects: The 1999 Revision*. New York: Department of Economic and Social Affairs, Population Division, United Nations.

United Nations. 2006. *World Population Prospects: The 2006 Revision, Highlights.* New York: Department of Economic and Social Affairs, Population Division, United Nations.

United Nations. 2010. *World Urbanization Prospects: The 2009 Revision. Highlights.* New York: Department of Economic and Social Affairs, Population Division, United Nations.

United States Conference of Mayors. 2007. *U.S. Metro Economies: Gross Metropolitan Product with Housing Update* Lexington, MA: Global Insight. Seen online, July 1, 2007 at http://www.citymayors.com/statistics/richest-cities-2005.html.

Vilas, Carlos M. 1996. "Neoliberal Social Policy. Managing Poverty (Somehow)." *NACLA Report on the Americas* 29(6): 16–25.

Villa El Salvador (Municipality) 2005. *Resumen Ejecutivo.* Seen online, August 18, 2010 at http://www.munives.gob.pe/VillaElSalvador/Diagnostico/RESUMEN%20 EJECUTIVO.pdf.

Wampler, Brian. 2008. *Participatory Budgeting in Brazil: Contestation, Cooperation, and Accountability.* University Park: Pennsylvania State University Press.

Weyland, Kurt Gerhard. 2005. "Theories of Policy Diffusion: Lessons from Latin American Pension Reform." *World Politics* 57(2): 262–95.

Willis, Eliza, Christopher Garman, and Stephan Haggard. 1999. "The Politics of Decentralization in Latin America." *Latin American Research Review* 34(1): 7–56.

World Bank. 2006. *World Development Report 2007. Development and the Next Generation.* Washington: World Bank.

World Bank. 2009. *World Development Report 2010. Development and Climate Change* Washington: The World Bank.

World Urban Forum. 2006. "Participatory Budgeting: Building Participatory Democracy and/or Improving Municipal Finance." Networking event, Vancouver, June 21.

Wunsch, James S. 2001. "Decentralization, Local Governance and 'Recentralization' in Africa." *Public Administration and Development* 21: 277–88.

Zhang, Li and Simon Xiaobin Zhao. 2009. "City Branding and the Olympic Effect: A Case Study of Beijing." *Cities* 26: 245–54.

CHAPTER 29

THE WIRED CITY: A NEW FACE OF POWER? A CITIZEN PERSPECTIVE

HARALD BALDERSHEIM AND NORBERT KERSTING

1. The Promises: How Digitalization May Transform the City

The "wired city" is the "connected city." The higher levels of interconnectedness brought about by new information and communication technologies (ICTs) potentially transform urban politics and community life, much of it in democratically desirable ways but also in problematic ways. In the early stages of digitalization of politics and social life optimistic views, even utopian expectations, prevailed (e.g. Davis et al. 2002). Fairly soon, however, more discordant views were voiced. An early review of political impacts of ICTs was tellingly titled "Orwell in Athens" (Van de Donk, Snellen, and Tops). In one of his essays on "network society" the sociologist Manuel Castells predicted that the overall effects of ICTs would be to make democratically well functioning institutions more democratic and authoritarian institutions more authoritarian (Castells 2000). Studies of wired cities may take us back to the roots of research on urban politics—once more questioning the nature of community power.

The famous debate on "community power" evolved from one on who were actually making the important decisions to one on who could control the agenda of the city. To the proponents of the "second face of power" the latter was seen as the more fundamental form of local power (Bacharach and Baratz 1962). Digital channels of communications, with many-to-many formats, hold out promises of bringing citizens *en masse* into the process of agenda setting through partnerships with formal governing institutions. However, the emergence of digital divides as well as the spread of intensive electronic surveillance of public spaces in the city opens up more sinister prospects for urban politics. What is the digital face of community power going to look like?

Digitalization of city government and community life is an ongoing process without a clearly foreseeable end station. At an early stage (1960s) digitalization meant the city administration had acquired equipment for rapid processing of mass data, such as tax returns, census forms, or zoning regulations. The 1970s and 1980s saw the emergence of decision support systems that aided the decision-making of officials in various fields, for example, on how often roads should be surfaced, bulbs changed in street lights, or the distribution of social benefits. The 1990s was the breakthrough of the Internet helping cities in their communication with the public at large, while at the same time the Internet was a vast resource at the disposal of the same public for 24/7global communication. The 2000s have witnessed the growth of mobile technology (viz. the transformation of the cell phone) and social media (e.g. Facebook) connected to the Internet as the web 2.0 version with enhanced levels of interactivity is emerging. As we move on into the second decade of the 21st century *cloud* technology is the buzz word, meaning that applications can be downloaded from the web as they are needed; they no longer have to be installed on your local computer or your laptop. The precondition is of course that you are connected to the web anywhere (you might want to be). This is still a precondition that is far from fulfilled in many parts of the globe.

The promises of the wired city are that citizens through a variety of *digital channels* (cf. table 1) may

- find timely and relevant information on city politics and services when they need it, leading to *a better informed citizenry*
- identify political and administrative leaders who are responsible for decisions and services that affect the lives of citizens, leading to *more accountable and transparent city politics*
- access those leaders with queries and suggestions and also engage them in discussions on issues on the political agenda, leading to *more participatory politics*
- engage with other citizens for political and social purposes, for example, with the aim of influencing political decisions or the political agenda of the city or in other ways *enhancing community life*.

These are visions of the wired city that many cities today try to make a reality. How far have they come? The overall trend of technological development is allowing increasing levels of *interactivity* in communication between city authorities and citizens and in citizen-to-citizen contacts. The development from information retrieval to participatory applications as highlighted in table 1 is not only one of

Table 1. What Citizens May Expect from Wired Cities: Examples of Typical Goals and Technological Features Implemented in Wired Cities

Electronic applications for...	The city as...		
	Political arena	Service provider	Community
Information retrieval	More transparency through searchable electronic archives, webcasting of meetings	Easier access to city services through service catalogues, quality checks	Mutual citizen awareness through e-catalogues of civic groups
Communication	Better informed deliberations through web forums, issue-specific discussion groups	Better targeted services through e-complaints procedures, online satisfaction surveys	More civic interaction through online meetings
Participation	More extensive participation through i-voting, e-budgeting, e-consultation	More quality through interactive service provision	Enhancement of community life through networked social capital formation

increasing technological sophistication but also one that promises increasing levels of citizen empowerment. Illustrations and examples will be presented in the next sections.

The sections below provide examples and assessments of the efforts of cities in the areas indicated by the columns of table 1. Our outline of the wired city is presented in a citizen perspective. We focus on how digitalization may change relations between citizens and their city both in terms of political and community involvement. Outlines of digitalization of management processes, important though they are for the well-being of the city, do not figure very much in our presentation. Nor do we focus much on the back-office functions that are necessary to maintain a well-functioning digital interface with the public.

2. E-Democracy in the Urban Political Arena

Cities seek in a variety of ways to enhance local democracy through digitalization of political procedures (cf. Peart and Diaz 2008 for an overview of trends in North American and European local government). Fernando Mendez (2007) suggests that e-democracy should be viewed as a process rather than as a product or end-state. As a process it involves experimentation, trials, and errors with digital elements inserted into the procedures of governance throughout the political and administrative branches of government.

First, digitalization is seen as a means to improve the functioning of traditional representative democracy. In this respect, Internet voting is the most widely discussed and also the most hotly contested measure; Internet voting has been embraced in particular in countries with low levels of voter turnout (Kersting et al. 2004). Transparency and accountability may also be enhanced through digital measures. Cities strive to bring more information about city politics to citizens through measures such as webcasting or podcasting the meetings of city governing bodies, providing documents for meetings online ahead of meetings and minutes after meetings, in many cases in electronically archived and searchable formats; information supply may also be tailored to individual interest among citizens through electronic warning systems. *Second*, digitalization holds out the hope of higher levels of rationality in political decision-making through extended discourse through many-to-many channels of electronic communication. *Third*, digitalization has enabled a series of experiments in new forms of political participation, seeking to make political processes more responsive to citizen needs.

We shall briefly review some initiatives in these three fields and also some of the *problematiques* that they have entailed. Much scholarly attention has been devoted to prospects and problems engendered by e-voting, and we start the review with some urban examples and ensuing discussions in this field. Initiatives in the fields of e-discourse and e-participation are fewer in number, and the research coverage is more uneven; however, experiments in the cities of Bristol (UK) and Belo Horizonte (Brazil) are among the more renowned and well-documented ones.

3. E-VOTING

Electronic voting may take place through a variety of channels of communication. An important variable distinguishing the various systems is the level of control over the infrastructure exercised by the electoral authorities (see Kersting and Baldersheim 2004).

Consequently, electronic voting can be divided into four types as outlined in table 2.

- Voting computer: Electronic voting machines. Electoral computers are located in the polling station and can be completely controlled by the electoral authorities. Identification and authentification can be handled by the officials in the polling station through existing voter registers. External manipulation, for example by computer viruses, Trojan horses, or other service attacks is not possible because there is no external communication and the data are stored on the polling machine. So only an internal software bug can interfere with the electoral process.
- Kiosk voting: Here voters have the opportunity to use special computers situated in public rooms such as libraries, schools or shopping malls. Because the electoral process cannot be controlled by public authorities, special instruments for electronic authentification are necessary, for example a digital signature or smart card, finger prints, and so on.

Table 2. Channels of Electronic voting

Channel infrastructure controlled by electoral authority	Internet	Other electronic devices
Yes	Kiosk voting	Voting computer
No	Internet voting	SMS-text voting Telephone voting Interactive Digital Television voting

See also Gibson 2001; Pratchett et al. 2002.

- SMS-text voting/Telephone voting/Interactive Digital Television voting can be manipulated by computer viruses and so on. Also the privacy and secrecy of the vote is not controllable.
- Internet voting: Remote Internet voting at home or from the workplace entails further technical risks. Here, software programs or other instruments such as smart cards are required for identification and authentification. However, the social context cannot be readily controlled and problems regarding the secrecy of the vote may arise.

The main challenge of electronic voting is that of the attenuation of the secrecy of the vote inherent in Internet voting and other channels of communication that reduces or eliminates the control of electoral authorities over the voting process. These challenges are discussed in greater detail in the next section.

3.1. The Case of Geneva

Starting 2003 with nonbinding as well as binding pilot projects in cities in three different cantons, Geneva became one of the front-runners in i-voting with the objectives of increasing voter turnout especially among young people and covering also Swiss expatriates. In Geneva, electronic voter registration was already in place. Remote voting is not a novelty to the Swiss since in some elections more than 90 percent of the electorate make use of postal voting. In January 2003 the first Internet election was implemented in the suburb of Aniere. In this election 44 percent of the citizens voted via the Internet, 50 percent used postal voting, and only 6 percent went to the polling station to cast their ballot. However, such a high rate of i-voting is exceptional. In other local elections maximum of 10 percent of the voters used the Internet option. In a referendum in 2010 70 percent of the voters in the canton of Geneva supported the inclusion of the option of i-voting for cantonal and local elections in their cantonal constitution.

3.2. Prospects and Problems of Internet Voting

Of the potential transformations of democratic procedures engendered by ICTs that of Internet or online voting is the most controversial one (Kersting and Baldersheim 2004). Advocates see online voting as a much needed remedy against rising voter apathy while to opponents i-voting signals the end of democracy as we have known it. Table 3 outlines the most common arguments for and against online voting.

On the *pro* side arguments usually fielded emphasize political inclusion, efficiency, and transparency. I-voting is expected to lead to increased voter turnout because of the ease of casting the vote from one's home (or office, or summer house, or wherever one happens to be on Election Day). This form of voting is also expected to appeal in particular to young voters who tend otherwise to have low voting records. I-voting may also lead to efficiency gains since elections are less costly to

Table 3. Prospects and Threats of Internet Voting

Pros	Cons
Political inclusion (participation, turnout)	Political exclusion (digital divides)
Efficiency (cost reduction, effectiveness, etc.)	Legitimacy (technical problems, trust, etc.)
Transparency (voter information)	Identity (symbolism of voting)
	Secrecy (privacy, coercion, authentication, etc.)

conduct because votes can be more easily counted and outcomes calculated faster. Complicated voting procedures such as vote splitting, single transferable votes, and preference votes can be handled more easily. Transparency is not necessarily enhanced through online voting as such, but online elections are normally accompanied by various online features for voter information, such as web portals with candidate information, online debate and chat sites, and voter guidance features, for example, automated proximity scores.

Contra arguments include the problems of digital divides, voter trust, symbolism, and secrecy. Unequal access to digital technology, including the Internet, is a feature of all countries. There is a fear that e-democracy features will just empower those already politically active and powerful leaving behind segments of the population without access or expertise. The legitimacy problem means that if online elections could be proven to be tampered with, this could result in loss of trust in not only the electoral outcome at hand but also in election procedures and democracy in general (Krimmer 2006). A further problem of trust is that online voting leaves no paper trail, which makes recounting impossible.

Furthermore, to many voters turning up at the polling station in person and casting the vote in the presence of election officers are acts of great symbolic value, signifying citizen duty and patriotism as acts of identity and belonging. In the eyes of such voters online voting might reduce the value of voting and elections, perhaps even the value of democracy. Perhaps the most serious challenge to online voting is that of maintaining the secrecy of the vote. It is difficult to guarantee that voters have not been under undue pressure when casting their votes, say from their homes, places of work, or holiday resorts. The principle here is that in order to avoid undue pressure the voter should not be able to prove to others how he or she has in fact voted after the vote was cast. The traditional method of voting, casting the vote in a booth in a polling station under the eyes of election officers, ensures secrecy. One procedure suggested to get round this problem is to allow online voters to change their votes so that only the last vote counts. This of, course, only works if the voter is able to get away from whoever tries to control his or her vote.

As long as the problem of secrecy cannot be solved completely full-scale online voting is likely to be implemented only in countries where voting is seen as a national problem, such as the countries mentioned above. In other countries it may be used on an experimental scale or in elections of secondary importance.

4. More Rational and Responsive Governance?

4.1. Electronic Petitions in Bristol

With the New Labour government in the late 1990s British local government was seen as a laboratory for a number of reforms including e-participation and electronic voting. The city of Bristol implemented a broad range of instruments of e-democracy. In Bristol Internet subscriptions doubled between 1999 and 2009. By 2009 nearly two-thirds of families had Internet access. Although the well-known digital divide was not fully bridged and there were more users in the age group under 55, Bristol tried to overcome this gap by implementing around 14 street kiosks scattered around Bristol, by using large screen LED screens for information and by using Wi-Fi technology open for mobile phones. Half of the citizens with Internet access actually visited the city council's website.

Since 1998 a citizen panel is regarded as "the biggest think tank in town." Randomly selected citizens are invited to take part in a panel that is asked to respond to questionnaires up to four times a year (the questionnaires can be completed online or by paper through "snail-mail"). Because of selection through random sampling the panel provides statistically representative responses.

The City of Bristol has operated an e-petition system since January 2008. The system is included in the council's workflow process and allows the council officers to track and report on petitions in the different stages of the process. It is also possible to integrate other tools such as webcasting. Having no age restriction every citizen can submit a petition and become a "principal petitioner." Principal petitioners as well as supporters have to identify themselves, giving their names and (e-mail) addresses. A petition has to include a brief heading, a short statement covering the subject matter and may include additional information such as links to websites, photographs, and so forth. The application also includes options for e-debates related to petitions. Of course, only petitions relevant to the functions of the council and its powers are accepted. A petition may represent a new initiative or it may refer to or (dis-)approve of a council decision. The range of topics reaches from street lights in certain district to town planning projects of a shopping mall (pro and con).

Petitions may be rejected, recommended for clarification, and even restricted during politically sensitive periods such as election time. The principal petitioner decides when the number of signatures collected is sufficient. When submitted the petition is referred to an appropriate council officer, a committee, or councillor for consideration. At a later stage the petition is presented at a full council meeting or during public forums. Since the start in January 2008 around 80 petitions have been submitted. In early 2010 a dozen petitions were underway. Of these approximately 50 percent were pending submission to the council and 20 percent were closed because they were either withdrawn, or the council had agreed or disagreed.

4.2. Electronic Participatory Budgeting

Participatory budgeting (PB) was first implemented in the Brazilian city Porto Alegre in the late 1980s. From here it was exported to other Brazilian cities as well as to Europe and other parts of the world. A Brazilian city, Belo Horizonte, also developed an electronic version of participatory budgeting. Other cities that have experimented with electronic participatory budgeting include Northamptonshire, Maidstone, and Barnet (UK), Hamburg, Freiburg, Berlin-Lichternfelde, Leipzig (Germany), Rome, Bergamo, Parma Vimarcate (Italy), Albacete, Cordoba, Getafe, Jerez (Spain), Grigny (France). The process is often supported by applications such as video streaming and online voting.

Nevertheless, the process in 2006 in Belo Horizonte can still be seen as exceptional. One reason was the sheer volume of the budget to be decided upon—1.2 million US dollars for each district of the city. Traditional, "off-line" participatory budgeting in Brazil is normally divided into three main stages. All citizens above the age of 16 may express their priorities vis-à-vis the district assembly regarding a list of preselected of public works. The district assembly consists of neighborhood representatives. The assembly has beforehand visited sites in need of public works and then decided about a preselection of projects.

In 2006 digital participatory budgeting was tried for the first time. The idea was to modernize participatory budgeting, and to increase citizen participation by reducing costs (such as transport, time, etc.) and finally to include more projects of public works into the voting process. The citizens were allowed to vote for public works in their own district as well as in other districts. The participants could decide on important public works such as a new library, renovation of the main streets, a regeneration of the commercial center, public sport complexes, and so on. Official registration to obtain a voter identity certificate was obligatory.

The city administration presented the various projects through videos, texts, and pictures on its website (Peixoto 2009). The presentation also included an online forum with nine different threads for each district. Access was anonymous while a moderator function prevented misuse of this instrument. The debate attracted only 1,200 postings, but it was regarded as rational and thoughtful with a high level of argumentation (Peixoto 2009).

Altogether 173,000 voters participated, casting around 500,000 votes. Most of them concentrated on their own district and the majority cast only one vote. One-fifth of the voters made use of the full range of nine votes. To overcome the digital divide the city administration provided Internet access through a series of public voting points. A total of 187 voting points were set up. There is no indication that higher income groups dominated the participatory budgeting process. Few voters visited the website and most visitors only once, while 12 percent or 20,000 voters visited the site more often. The latter group made use of a range of options installed for the purpose of electronic participatory budgeting. One reason for the success was, beside the novelty factor, wide coverage by from local radio, television, and newspapers. The city administration campaigned to mobilize new social movements and also neighborhood associations, religious, groups, small local businesses, and other parts of civil society.

The rate of participation in electronic participatory budgeting was twice that of traditional participatory budgeting. Although the budget for e-PB was only 11 million—compared to 43 million US dollars allocated through the parallel traditional participatory budgeting process—10 percent of the population participated. The vote on the budget was a binding one, which probably contributed to the relatively high level of turnout. The extent of the voting period—42 days—may also have contributed to voter turnout and also the fact that Brazilian voters were used to voting machines that were introduced already in 2000.

Electronic initiatives and experiments such as those reviewed above are exceptional, however. Most surveys of city government initiatives and experiments in the field of e-democracy and civic engagement conclude that the overall picture is one of hesitancy and timidity in city hall, even in digitally advanced parts of the world such as the US or Scandinavia (cf., e.g., Mossberger and Jimenez 2010, Baldersheim and Ogard 2008, Haug 2007).

5. E-SERVICES

It is in the field of service management and service provision that cities have implemented the broadest range of electronic applications and where citizens most clearly may discern the electronic face of the city. What do cities actually do to provide citizens with services through electronic channels? Information about the spread of e-services may be garnered from a variety of sources, for example benchmarking surveys and awards that have been established to stimulate cities to develop or improve e-services. A good example of such a survey is that of the Center for Digital Government's report from the 2008 Digital Cities Survey of US cities. Table 4 outlines the core operations that citizens may perform through city websites as well as the range of services they may access through such operations.

The data in the table demonstrate that citizens may interact with the city authorities in four different ways: view and download information, submit questions and applications online, transact online (which usually means payments) or via IVR (interactive voice response). The subjects of those interactions will of course depend upon the range of services that cities are actually responsible for. The advantages of digital interaction to citizens are that they do not have to take time off from work or other activities to go to town hall during office hours to do their business with public authorities.

Cities have multiple objectives for offering e-services: cost-saving (especially in terms of staff) and becoming more user-friendly or business-friendly (and thus more competitive regarding business investments). Digitalized user-friendliness may include online surveys of user satisfaction, electronic complaints procedures, and tracking or online citizen juries for particular services.

Table 4. Survey of E-services and Types of E-interactions, US Cities, 2008 (percent)

Services	View and Download (Print & fill out)	Submit Online	Transact Online	Transact via IVR
Building permits	62	24	42	24
Public procurements — bids or RFPs	70	20	27	1
Parks and recreation services	45	23	54	6
Utility bills	19	17	63	24
Library card or materials renewal	15	17	50	8
Parking tickets or traffic citations	16	16	62	12
Tax filing and payment	51	25	17	9
City-owned property use tracking	28	11	15	1
Public facilities locator map	55	12	28	1
GIS maps on the Internet	44	22	42	1

Source: Center for Digital Government. 2008, 7.

Note: Transact means a secure end-to-end transaction that includes submission and payments as authorized; IVR = nteractive voice response.

The technical features of web portals may vary with regard to their user-friendliness: websites are scored for having for example aids for hearing- or sight-impaired persons, translation of material into foreign languages, security, and privacy features. The readability of information content is also assessed—high demands on literacy levels may exclude a substantial proportion of citizens. User-friendliness requires digitalized back-office functions that are not immediately visible to the general public, such as various types of "shareware" that make for better internal coordination and cooperation across administrative departments or even across levels of government. In recent years "green" policies are also promoted through online services and community-wide broadband coverage: when citizens can interact with town hall via the web there is less need to travel downtown and consequently less traffic and pollution; furthermore, people can monitor their energy consumption via the web and optimize it with a view to savings.

As the data in the box show, cities vary a lot with regard to the extent of digitalization of service provision. The top-ranking US digital cities in 2008 were found to be Aurora, Colo., Lincoln, Neb., Roanoke, Va., and Lynchburg, Va. in their respective size groups. Surveys of the qualities of the website features of cities have become popular undertakings, usually ranking cities in terms of quality of contents and levels of interactivity of web sites. A survey of the 70 largest US cities placed Denver, Charlotte, Boston, and Louisville on top (West 2003).

Other sources of information on innovations in e-services are the European Union's awards in the field of e-government and also its network of Digital Cities. In 2009 one of the categories of awards was "e-government empowering citizens" (www.epractice.eu/awards). The prize winner was the small Danish city of Gentofte while the other nominees were the city of Stockholm and the region of Catalonia. Gentofte won its award for its one-stop system for citizen access to a range of local and state services. Stockholm's contribution was a web-based Service Map that allows citizens to compare the performance of service units (e.g., schools, kindergartens, or nursing homes). Catalonia presented a communication system called C3CAT for coordinated interaction with citizens across departments in order to tailor services to citizen needs.

6. Community Informatics

May community life be enhanced through digital channels of communication? May erosion of social capital be reversed through electronic connectivity? Impacts of new media on the social life of cities were suggested already in the 1970s with the arrival of cable TV (Mandelbaum 1972). The days of one-way mass communication were claimed to be over. Telematics opened up opportunities for digital two-way interaction between broadcasters and their audiences, and in the wired neighborhood also between residents. Such visions remained largely dreams, however. The arrival of the Internet has revived those visions (Doheny-Farina 1996) and perhaps given them a more realistic foundation, at least in cities with high levels of broadband coverage (Albert 2008).

The City of Seattle provides a demonstration of digitally assisted promotion of community life. The basic tool is a dedicated community website operated by the city government. The website includes *inter alia* features such as lists of community groups, links to community associations, access to and training in the use of "community technologies," and blogging opportunities for community groups (www.cityofseattle.net/seattlecommunitiesonline/). However, it should also be pointed out that Seattle is an advanced case; although efforts vary a lot many cities just print lists of community groups on their websites, if they do anything at all in this field (Mossberger and Jiminez 2010). Consequently, the emergence of "wired cities," "smart communities," or "virtual communities" is also the result by "open government" policies, but also by initiatives outside the confines of urban governments and official websites (see e.g., Minneapolis).

A whole branch of informatics, *community informatics*, has emerged to help build the wired community (Gurstein 2007). Community informatics as a field of research has its own journal since 2003, appropriately titled the *Journal of Community Informatics*. It is also a movement as suggested by the existence of the World Foundation for Smart Communities, which defines a Smart Community as one "that has made a conscious effort to use information technology to transform life and work within its region in significant and fundamental, rather than incremental, ways. This transformation is beneficial to the community and attracts local participation and cooperation among community groups, government, business and education" (http://www.smartcommunities.org/concept.php, March 28, 2010).

The New York–based Intelligent Community Forum annually names the "Top 7 Intelligent Communities" around the world. The 2010 winners were Arlington (US), Dublin (US), Dundee (Scotland), Eindhoven (Netherlands), Ottawa (Canada), Suwon (South Korea), Tallin (Estonia) (http://www.intelligentcommunity.org/index.php?src=news&refno=433&category=Partner%20News, March 28, 2010). The indicators applied to describe intelligent communities include broadband connectivity, a knowledge workforce, digital inclusion policies, digital innovation strategies, and marketing and advocacy of the community. According to Albert et al. (2008) a "networked community has a physical presence in space and time, and people live there on a daily basis, but all their members are virtually connected to everyone else. In the 21st century, the common assumption is that the social and economic well being of communities is very much tied to networking."

Trends in electronic communication suggest, however, that the Internet as a communication platform may also serve to transform notions of community. In fact, the community of *place*, the neigbhorhood, may be challenged by emergent *virtual* communities based on shared interests and identities of people in places far apart. Applications such as Facebook or Twitter may sunder rather than unite the city as a territorial community. Your connectivity with friends in distant places may not do much to enhance community in the neighborhood where you happen to live.

7. An Emergent Research Agenda: Toward a New Face of Power?

7.1. Where Is Digitalization Taking Urban Politics and Community Life?

Some trends are clear; other developments are fuzzier. Many city operations are thoroughly digitalized, especially in the realms of city management and service provision. Citizens also enjoy an enhanced supply of information through digital channels, especially the Internet. Digital communication, furthermore, helps elected officers to stay more in touch with their voters. These developments will surely continue since cities have a lot to gain from them in terms of saving resources and manpower. They do not necessarily mean more citizen empowerment but certainly more citizen efficiency, which is also an achievement (Kotsiopoulos 2009).

Visions of more participatory politics, however, are realized only intermittently. Scattered experiments in electronic participation can be observed but experiences so far suggest that many hurdles must be overcome before they can become sustainable practices in cities. The interaction between standard, representative democracy and participatory democracy electronically sustained is an uneasy one. What is emerging in wired cities is a *blended democracy*—representative democracy as we have traditionally known it, *digitally enriched* with strands of participatory democracy. Consequently, a gap in terms of democratic development is opening up between cities that grasp the new technologies and cities that do not do so. Why some cities are more eager or more able than others to make use of digital technologies for democratic purposes is part of the new research agenda. However, the tensions inherent in blended democracy are also a part of the agenda.

7.2. A Research Agenda

The preceding sections have suggested ways in which digitalization is impacting on city politics, service provision, and community relations. Much research on the wiring of cities is of an accounting or benchmarking variety, that is, providing updated information on what cities actually do in the field of e-government and related areas, and trying to identify the most "advanced" cities (Janssen et al. 2004, Garson 2006). Because of the rapid and open-ended development of digital technologies this is, of course, no easy task. Organizations and websites are emerging offering snapshots of developments at regular intervals. In some cases data banks have been established that are also useful for research on "state of the art" in cities. Above reference has been made to some of these sources.

However, the field of local government has features (pinpointed by Peter John [2006] as "numerosity" and "propinquity") that enable research of a more general nature beyond providing updated versions of e-government accounts. Where are the frontiers of research on the wired city? Three issues in particular stand out: modeling digital innovation and transformation in city governance; the impacts of digital divides on city politics; and privacy and security challenges to citizens and community life.

What drives *digital innovation?* Why are some cities ahead of others in terms of e-governance? There is disagreement on how to approach the issue of technological innovation (Homburg 2008). Problem- or demand-driven models have only limited explanatory power. Overall, technological adoption is often supply-driven. Some models question the phenomenon of "adoption," arguing in favor of a "social shaping of technology" approach (Fountain 2001), which has become increasingly popular, acknowledging the role of local technology entrepreneurs and users in a continuous process of adoption and adaptation. Such an approach makes adoption an indeterminate and unpredictable process. However, this stance goes against another central finding of technology adoption: its path-dependent nature. E-innovation has been shown to be path-dependent in the sense that cities with an overall track record of innovation also tend to be front-runners in the field of e-government. And the front-runners tend to stay ahead (Haug 2007). As to transformative impacts in citizen-city government relations the easier access to information has been mentioned above and also a reduced need for citizens to travel to town hall to carry out transactions with city government officials. Deeper transformative impacts in political relations are harder to spot even in US cities with city government digitalization at an advanced stage and a digitally competent citizenry (Norris 2010). Consequently, better modeling of processes of e-innovation and their impacts in cities is one of the central research challenges of the field.

As digitalization of government operations was spreading through the 1990s so did worries about the emergence of *digital divides*, that is, groups of citizens being left behind because of unequal access to technology or lack of digital expertise (Servon 2002). One of the most influential books on the subject, *Digital Divide: Civic Engagement, Information Poverty and the Internet Worldwide,* by Pippa Norris (2001), highlighted digital divides not only between groups in particular countries but also on a global scale. Parts of, for example, Scandinavia and North America are hooked on to the web *en masse* while for example sub-Saharan Africa had an average Internet connection rate of about 3 percent of households in 2006. Some scholars have questioned the seriousness of the problem, however, arguing that the further spread of technology and access will make the problem disappear in due time (Compaine 2001). The "Post-PC Continent" Africa mobile phone technologies developed faster (see Kenya). Nevertheless, many cities have by now adopted policies to counteract the digital divide to ensure that "no citizens are left behind," as a slogan of the EU goes. The efficacy of such policies remains underresearched, however. Even in digitally advanced cities divides persist (Mossberger et al. 2006).

Digitalization entails serious challenges in terms of *privacy and security*. Nowhere is this more apparent than in cities. Through closed-circuit television (CCTV) spread over the city, citizens can be watched in numerous situations, from airports to government buildings, in shopping malls and parking lots, in hotels and housing estates. In the UK the CCTV User Group has estimated that there were in 2008 around 1.5 million CCTV cameras in city centers, stations, airports, major retail areas, and so forth. This figure did not include the smaller surveillance systems such as those that may be found in local corner shops (CCTV User Group 2008). An evaluation of CCTV in operation by local governments in Scotland found 2,149 cameras installed for the surveillance of public spaces, while guidelines regarding their use and data sharing were almost nonexistent (Bannister et al. 2009). "The small sisters"—credit cards, electronic tickets, and so on—tell tales about our shopping habits, travel routes, and much else. A thousand well-meant digital intrusions may accumulate into a minute record of citizens' daily lives that is fundamentally in conflict with the ideals of a liberal state. Furthermore, digitalization, normally intended to enhance the security of citizens, may actually threaten it when digital procedures break down or run amok. Recently, all trains throughout Norway came to a standstill for nearly four hours because a programming error caused a backup computer to be shut down instead of activating it when the main computer failed (Soerlie 2010). The spread of e-government has engendered a new form of terrorism—cyber terrorism, concentrated hacker attacks against government software and computers causing for example DoS (denial of service) or jamming government operations through overloading (Weimann 2006). Estonia, an avant-garde country in terms of e-government, is purported to have experienced such attacks in the wake of a conflict with Russia over war memorials in 2007. Research into the digital vulnerability of wired cities should be high on the agenda of urban researchers of the future.

The new face of power may not be unconditionally benign.

REFERENCES

Albert, S. R. 2008. "Defining the Networked Community Movement." *Journal of Community Informatics* 4(3). Downloaded February 21, 2010 from http://www.ci-journal.net/index.php/ciej/article/view/327/315.

Albert, S., D. Flournoy, and R. LeBrasseur. 2008. *Networked Communities: Strategies for Digital Collaboration*. Hershey, PA: IGI Global.

Bachrach, P. and M. Baratz 1962. "The Two Faces of Power." *American Political Science Review* 56:947–52.

Baldersheim, H. and M. Ogard. 2008. "Innovation in e-Government: Analysis of Municipal Web Pages in the Nordic Countries." *Information Polity* 14(3–4): 125–38.

Bannister, J., S. Mackenzie, and P. Norris. 2009. *Public Space CCTV in Scotland*. The Scottish Centre for Crime & Justice Research, Report No. 03/09.

Castells, M. 2000. *The Rise of the Network Society*. 2nd ed. Oxford: Blackwell Publishing.

CCTV User Group.2008. "How Many Cameras Are There?" http://www.cctvusergroup.com/art.php?art=94. Retrieved April 2, 2010.

Center for Digital Government. 2008. *Report from the 2008 Digital Cities Survey*. Executive summary.

Compaine, B. M., ed. 2001. *The Digital Divide: Facing a Crisis or Creating a Myth?* Cambridge, MA: MIT Press.

Davis, S., L. Elin, and G. Reeher. 2002. *Click on Democracy: The Internet's Power to Change Political Apathy into Civic Action*. Boulder, CO: Westview Press.

Doheny-Farina, S. 1996. *The Wired Neighborhood*. New Haven: Yale University Press.

Fountain, J. 2001. *Building the Virtual State*. Washington DC: Brookings Institution.

Garson, D. 2006. *Public Information Technology and E-Governance*. Sudbury: Jones and Bartlett.

Gibson, R. 2001. "Elections Online: Assessing Internet Voting in Light of the Arizona Democratic Primary." *Political Science Quarterly* 116(4): 561–83.

Gurstein, M. 2007. *What Is Community Informatics? (And Why Does It Matter)*. Milan: Polimetrica.

Haug, A. V. 2007. "Local Democracy Online: Driven by Crisis, Legitimacy, Resources, or Communication Gaps?" *Journal of Information Technology & Politics* 4(2): 79–99.

Homburg, V. 2008. *Understanding E-government: Information Systems in Public Administration*. London: Routledge.
Janssen, D., S. Rotthier, and K. Snijkers. 2004. "If You Measure It, They Will Score: An Assessment of International eGovernment Benchmarking." *Information Polity* 9(2): 121–30.
John, P. 2006. "Methodologies and Research Methods in Urban Political Science." In Baldersheim, H. and H. Wollmann, eds. *The Comparative Study of Local Government and Politics: Overview and Synthesis.* Opladen: Barbara Budrich Publishers.
Kersting, N. and H. Baldersheim eds. 2004. *Electronic Voting and Democracy: A Comparative Analysis*. London: Palgrave Macmillan.
Kersting, N., R. Leenes, and J. Svensson. 2004. "Adopting Internet Voting: Context Matters." N. Kersting and H. Baldersheim, eds.. *Electronic Voting and Democracy: A Comparative Analysis*. London: Palgrave Macmillan.
Kotsiopoulos, I. 2009. *Bringing Together and Accelerating eGovernment Research in the EU.* eDemocracy Report March 2009. Prepared for the ICT for Government and Public Services Unit DG Information Society and Media, European Commission.
Krimmer, R. 2006. "Electronic Voting 2006." *Proceedings of the 2nd Workshop on Electronic Voting P-86*. Bonn: LNI GI Series.
Mandelbaum, S. 1972. *Community and Communications.* New York: W. W. Norton.
Mendez, F. 2007. "E-Democratic Experimentation in Europe: The Case of e-Voting." International Conference on Direct Democracy in Latin America, March 14–15, Buenos Aires.
Mossberger, K., C. J. Tolbert, and M. Gilbert. 2006. "Race, Place, and Information Technology." *Urban Affairs Review* 41(5): 583–620.
Mossberger. K and B. Jimenez. 2010. "Can e-Government Promote Informed Citizenship and Civic Engagement? A Study of Local Government Websites in the U.S." *Explorations in e-Government and e-Goverance.* Selected Proceedings of the Second International Conference on e-Government & e-Governance, March 11–12 Antalya, Turkey, 2:29–43.
Norris, D. F. 2010. "e-Government, e-Transformation? Now? Soon? Ever?" *Explorations in e-Government and e-Governance.* Selected Proceedings of the Second International Conference on e-Government & e-Governance, March 11–12 Antalya, Turkey, 1:1–14.
Norris, P. (2001) *Digital Divide: Civic Engagement, Information Poverty and the Internet Worldwide.* Cambridge: Cambridge University Press.
Peart, M. and J. F. Diaz. 2008 "Taking Stock: Local e-Democracy in Europe and the USA." *International Journal of Electronic Governance* 1(4): 400–433.
Peixoto, T. 2009. "Beyond Theory: E-participatory Budgeting and Its Promises for e-Participation." *European Journal for ePractice* 7: 1–9.
Pratchett, L., S. Birch, S. Candy, B. Fairweather, S. Rogerson, V. Stone, B. Watt, M. Wingfield. 2002. *The Implementation of Electronic Voting in the UK*. London: Local Government Association.
Servon, L. 2002. *Bridging the Digital Divide: Technology, Community, and Public Policy.* Malden, MA: Blackwell.
Soerlie, E. 2010. "Togtrafikken stod stille i tre timer." *Aftenposten* (Oslo), March 30.
Van de Donk, W. B .H. J., I. Th. M. Snellen, and P. W Tops, eds. 1995. *Orwell in Athens: A Perspective on Informatization and Democracy*. Amsterdam: IOS Press.
Weimann, G. 2006. *Terror on the Internet: The New Arena, the New Challenges*. Washington, DC: United States Institute of Peace.
West, D. 2003. "Urban e-Government." Center for Public Policy, Brown University.

CHAPTER 30

SUBURBAN POLITICS

ERIC OLIVER

OVER the past century, a tremendous change has occurred in the types of places where most Americans live. At the end of the 19th century, most Americans were bifurcated between urban and rural places, being either crowded in large, dense cities or dispersed across small farms, villages, and towns. With the advent of railroads, streetcars, and automobiles, however, this pattern changed. The geography of large cities began to rapid expand outward, in some cases engulfing former rural communities but, more often than not, emerging from the creation of entirely new places. These new communities were often quite different from their predecessors: unlike rural towns, they could be densely populated and sometimes quite large; unlike large cities, these communities were often socially homogeneous and predominantly residential. These places are what we have come to know as suburbs.

Today, these suburbs contain a majority of Americans—over one in two currently live within a metropolitan area but outside of its central city. Yet despite the fact that a majority of Americans call a suburb home, we have little knowledge about the political life of these places. Most analyses of suburbs are based on anecdotes, stereotypes, or cultural criticisms that cast them in a negative light. Suburbanites, we are told, are alienated toward their neighbors and hostile toward government (Whyte 1956, Kunstler 1993). Suburban civic withdrawal threatens the well-being the American democracy (Putnam 2000, Suarez 1999). Suburbanites fight tax hikes, seek to exclude minorities, and focus primarily on a NIMBY style politics (McKenzie 1994). They are politically conservative and have enabled the rise of the Republican Party in national elections (McGirr 2001). Suburban politics, like suburban life, is allegedly parochial, reactionary, exclusionary, and xenophobic (see Mumford 1961, Jacobs 1961, Ehrenhalt 1996, Kunstler 1993, Langdon 1993).

Not only are such characterizations empirically baseless, they suffer from a number of fundamental conceptual problems. Take, for instance, the very idea of a suburb. In the United States, the term "suburb" generally refers to any place that is within what the U.S. Census Bureau designates as a metropolitan area but is not part of the central city or cities (many of America's largest metropolitan areas have several urban nodes, such as the San Francisco-Oakland–San Jose metropolitan area). The problem with this definition is that it obscures the terrific heterogeneity that exists across suburban areas. Consider the San Francisco Bay Area. This large metropolis contains over 100 different municipalities that exhibit a wide variety of sizes and forms, ranging from bucolic towns to gritty urban areas. Given this diversity, it is hard to see what academic Berkeley, residential Larkspur, impoverished Richmond, and industrial Daly City all have in common as suburbs that central cities like San Francisco or Oakland do not. This fact should give us pause before rushing to any negative generalizations. After all, how can one say that suburbs foster political conservatism when so many different places fall under the suburban rubric? One simply cannot make such a sweeping statement about the particular politics of an area if one cannot specify what makes that area particular to begin with.

In addition, most theories about local politics in the United States are not particularly well-suited for explaining suburban politics. The studies in this volume, for example, nearly all focus on large and relatively diverse cities and most theories of local politics reflect the particular this agenda. Debates about the role of elites versus pluralist influences (Banfield 1970, Dahl 1961, Polsby 1963, Wolfinger 1974), conceptions of urban regimes or growth machines (Stone 1989, Logan and Molotch 1987), and concerns with minority political incorporation (Browning et al. 1997, Karnig and Welch 1981, Welch and Bledsoe 1988) are all based on studies of large, dense, and heterogeneous communities. Yet because suburbs exhibit such a wide variety of forms, sizes, and institutional structures, it seems highly unlikely that characterizations of political life based on large cities are uniformly applicable. Even public choice theories that account for the large fragmentation within metropolitan areas (e.g., Peterson 1981, Tiebout 1956) have little to say about the internal dynamics within most suburban locales. Consequently, political scientists still lack any coherent theoretical framework for explaining the myriad layers of politics within most suburban areas.

Finally, there has been relatively little empirical research about politics in suburbia. Compared with the vast body of qualitative and quantitative studies of big city politics throughout the 20th century, the corpus of suburban research is quite emaciated and dated. Most empirical research consists of ethnographies conducted in the 1950s and 1960s or research that crudely dichotomizes people in either "city" or "suburban" categories and tries to examine their differences (e.g., Gainsborough 2001, Zikmund 1968). Given the small number of suburban places whose internal politics have actually been studied and the length of time since most research has taken place, it is simply impossible to know whether their findings still are valid or can be generalized to the country as a whole. For instance, were the active coffee klatches that sociologist Herbert Gans (1967) discovered in "Levittown" just a relic of the 1950s or even evident in other types of suburbs? American suburbs have simply not been very studied as places and their politics remains largely unexplored.

In short, there is much more we do not know about politics in American suburbs than we do and we need to tread with great caution when making any generalizations about suburban politics, negative or otherwise. Yet for researchers and students of American politics, this creates a terrific opportunity. In this chapter, I review what little we know about suburban politics and what we need to do to better understand them as political communities. I offer a new conceptual framework for understanding suburbs and their politics in the 21st century and, hopefully, identify areas ripe for further empirical investigation.

1. Defining Suburbia

The popular conception of suburbia is one that emerges from a host of cultural images that arose in the 1950s and continue to this day. This image consists of detached homes in quiet neighborhoods, with nuclear families attending to relatively benign domestic concerns. Depending on the source this image is alternatively positive (e.g., television programs like "Leave It to Beaver"), negative (e.g., films like "Revolutionary Road" or "American Beauty"), comical (e.g., "Desperate Housewives") or tragic (e.g., "Bowling for Columbine"). In reality, suburban life is much more complex and varied than any one of these conceptions. Largely, this is because of the diversity in suburban forms. America has been suburbanizing for well over a century and this transformation entails a number of different processes and types of places. There are streetcar and rail suburbs from the early 20th century, middle-class and working-class suburbs from the 1950s, and ex-urbs, postsuburbs, and edge cities from the past few decades. Some suburbs were created as solely residential enclaves while others are planned communities or retirement villages. Some suburbs grew around industrial facilities while others are oriented around leisure amenities like golf courses or marinas. This variety creates an enormous conceptual challenge in defining what exactly we mean by the term suburb.

In trying to tackle the problem of defining what a suburb is, it is important to keep two crucial factors in mind. First, it is probably unhelpful to think of suburbs as categorically different or subordinate to central cities. Although the term suburb literally means "beneath or inferior to" (sub) a "city" (urb), such a hierarchical relationship no longer really holds for most metropolitan areas. For example, in the United States, more people commute from one suburb to another than to a central city. Many big city residents work, shop, and play in suburbs and return home to the city at the end of the day. Many suburbs are now larger or more industrial than their nodal cities and, cumulatively, outmatch America's big cities in terms of population, employment, and government spending. Thus, rather than foist some irrelevant dichotomies upon these places, it probably makes more sense to simply consider all municipalities within metropolitan areas as equivalent units of analysis that can then be differentiated by crucial factors such as their population size, economic activity, or land use. This will yield much better analyses than seeing them in some position of super- and subordinance.

The other crucial aspect to understanding suburban politics is to understand that suburbs are first and foremost political creations. Political autonomy is the essence of suburbanization and the raison d'etre of suburban politics. Political boundaries are what separate Los Angeles from Santa Monica, Chicago from Oak Park, and Houston from Katy. These institutional boundaries not only divide the metropolis into separate political jurisdictions, they also create particular political constituencies and define the scope and agenda of political life. The political fragmentation generated by municipal and special district boundaries defines places as such, the issues they may or may not have to face, and the scope of conflict within their boundaries. The key to understanding suburban politics is not in differentiating whether a place is an edge city, streetcar suburb, or exurb, but rather the overall level of social and economic segregation and political fragmentation that arises from the institutional arrangements in the metropolis.

These facts force us to reconsider the traditional bifurcation of metropolitan places between city and suburb. Throughout most of the political science literature, metropolitan places are either labeled as a city (and thus subject to theories of urban politics) or suburbs (and not really understood at all). As noted above, the conceptualization is inadequate. A more sensible view differentiates metropolitan areas by their degree of institutional fragmentation. Metropolitan areas with a high degree of institutional fragmentation are likely to generate a much different set of political concerns and outcomes than those with a low level of fragmentation (Rusk 1993). In other words, suburbs of a largely unified and inclusive metropolitan area like Houston or Jacksonville are likely to have much different sets of political concerns than suburbs of a highly fragmented metropolitan area like Chicago. After gauging the extent of fragmentation in the metropolis, the politics within each incorporated place is likely to be affected by five central traits: population size, economic composition, racial composition, land use, and type of governing structure. Political life in central cities and suburbs is better differentiated by all of these characteristics than by any simple dichotomy. Indeed, one of the biggest effects of suburbanization has been to differentiate *all* metropolitan places along each of these dimensions.

Consider, for example, population size. After World War II, three-quarters of Americans lived either in rural areas or cities of over 100,000 in size. Today, most Americans live in municipalities under 100,000 in population within larger metropolitan areas. Population size not only differentiates suburbs, but also central cities. For example, central cities, as defined by the Census Bureau, range in population from 8 million people (New York) to just under 50,000 (Enid, Oklahoma). Suburbs also vary widely in their population sizes, ranging from tiny communities of under 500 residents like Golf, Illinois to enormous places like Garland, Texas with populations well above 100,000 residents.

With the growth of many smaller cities, metropolitan places have become increasingly differentiated by their economic composition. Although larger places tend to have cities with lower median household incomes than smaller ones, the income ranges among smaller places are quite great. For instance, most larger cities have a median household income somewhere between $40,000 and $60,000. Smaller places (most of which are commonly known as suburbs) have median household incomes that can fall below $30,000 a year (e.g. East St. Louis, Missouri) to over $200,000 (Atherton, California). This increasing diversity in income represents a tremendous change in the nature of local politics. When most urbanites lived in large cities, they lived in communities that had a wide variety of economic groups within their borders. Although rich and poor may have lived in separate neighborhoods, they still lived within the same city. Today, there are places comprised only of the rich (Scarsdale, New York) or only the poor (Camden, New Jersey). These income differences have the potential to make very different types of political questions: poor places face many challenges to simply funding basic services while more affluent ones may find themselves at odds over whether to reduce taxes or expand service provision.

Just as metropolitan places have become more economically differentiated, they have also become more racially diverse. The traditional view of suburbs is that they are largely white enclaves in opposition to racially-mixed central cities, a view that, until quite recently, was largely true. Forty years ago, over 97 percent of suburbs were almost entirely white while most large cities had high proportions of minorities. Although larger cities continue to have a higher proportion of nonwhites (and smaller cities a disproportionately high percentage of whites), smaller places on the outskirts of metropolitan areas have started to become more racially diverse as well. One in four African Americans now lives in a suburb and the fast-growing Latino and Asian American populations are increasingly suburbanizing. But rather than fostering integration, minority suburbanization has tended to replicate the racial segregation found in larger cities. In other words, even as African Americans and Latinos are becoming more suburbanized they are moving mostly to black and Latino suburbs rather than integrate into white suburbs.

The fourth way that places with American metropolitan areas can be differentiated is by their land usage. The traditional view of suburbs is as "bedroom communities," that is, places comprised largely of homes that surrounded the economic activity of the central city. This pattern has significantly changed in recent decades as suburbs began to host more commercial and industrial sites. So-called "edge cities" like Arlington, Virginia or Stamford, Connecticut have numerous buildings with vast amounts of commercial office space. Others small places hold manufacturing or industrial centers. Meanwhile, some very large places like Garland, Texas or Livonia, Michigan have relatively little commercial or industrial property. The diversity of land uses that used to be the sole characteristic of big cities is now evident across many suburban areas.

A fifth way to differentiate metropolitan places is by their political institutions. Historically, central cities were seen as dominated by machine style politics and political institutions that facilitated patronage, that is, mayor-council forms of government, district elections, and partisan ballots. Suburbs, on the other hand, had "reform style" institutions such as council-manager governments, at-large elections, and nonpartisan ballots. The expansion of metropolitan areas, particularly in the Sunbelt, has blurred this distinction. Many large, central cities now have "reform style" political practices such as nonpartisan elections or council-manager governments. Meanwhile, many smaller, suburban places, especially in the Northeast, have partisan elections and mayoral governments. Although the majority of medium-sized cities continue to have council-manager governments and most larger cities have mayors, cities and suburbs are no longer so neatly divided along institutional lines.

These institutional characteristics are important not simply because they define the types of governing arrangements within a particular community, but because they define the stakes of politics. Local governments in America (i.e., municipalities and special district governments) are differentiated not just by their types of institutions but by what their institutions do. Most local governments are quite limited in scope, that is, they have strictly defined institutional prerogatives and highly constrained powers. Unlike large cities that typically have very active municipal governments, most suburban municipalities only provide four or five basic services, usually fire and police protection, street maintenance, water and sewage treatment, and parks and libraries. In many metropolitan areas, these services are increasingly being provided by special district governments or counties, thus further limiting the scope of the local government (Berry 2009). Furthermore, unlike large cities, states, and the national government, suburban municipal governments tend to be relatively unbiased in the administration of these services, that is, they tend to provide a relatively even level of service provision, although this varies across states and regions (Oliver 2012).

Taking this all together, it is clear that any attempt to described suburban politics will depend on how a suburb is conceptualized. At a macro level, suburban politics can be understood relative to the amount of political fragmentation in the metropolis. Areas with higher degrees of fragmentation are likely to see more differentiation among their component governmental units and will experience different political conflicts than areas under the jurisdiction of a central governing body. At the micro level, it is important to transcend simple city-suburb dichotomies and instead compare places by the factors that have an impact on their politics: their size, income, racial composition, land use, and both the formal powers of their political institutions as well as the types and nature of their service provision. These characteristics are much more likely to have an important explanatory power than the crude fact of whether or not a place is in or outside of a central city. In other words, the politics of small, homogeneous places are going to be equally different from that of small, heterogeneous places as they will from large, homogeneous places. The next step, therefore, in understanding suburban politics is to understand how metropolitan fragmentation and differentiation along these characteristics influence the tenor of local politics.

2. The Politics of Metropolitan Fragmentation

At the macro level, suburbanization can be understood relative to the politics of the metropolitan area. Here the impact of suburbanization is partly a story of the role of institutions and the political cleavages they define. If the essence of suburbanization is the political fragmentation of a metropolis into various subunits, then a central part of suburban politics is what type of political dynamic that fragmentation creates. The flip side of this story is the attempt to unify metropolitan areas under one government. In looking at the literature over the past 50 years, political scientists are generally split about what impact political fragmentation has on the functioning of local democratic politics.

On one side are the critics of fragmentation. According to this view, the separation of metropolitan populations into various governmental units has several negative consequences including high levels of economic and racial segregation (Danielson 1976, Rusk 1993, Weiher 1991), allowing certain economic interests disproportionate political power (Burns 1994), hindering growth management and control (Caitlin 1997), promoting inefficiencies and replication in the distribution of public services (Wood 1959), and exacerbating the social problems of metropolitan areas including urban sprawl, traffic congestion, and concentrations of poverty (Dreier et al. 2004). For example, a metropolis divided among 50 suburbs will have to finance 50 separate police stations, fire stations, city halls, and so on, instead of just one. This replication of services makes costs in economies of scale as well as inhibiting coordination across units (Gullick 1962).

Moreover, fragmentation is alleged to have social costs as well. More often than not, fragmentation leaves central cities with disproportionate numbers of the poor who require more social services and provide less of a tax base to fund them. Through exclusionary zoning techniques (such as minimum lot sizes, banning multifamily dwellings, and minimum sizes on single family homes), high- and middle-income citizens can effectively exclude the poor from their communities (Danielson 1976). This economic segregation (and the racial segregation that typically accompanies it) generates inequalities in services, tax burdens, and in school financing (Rusk 1993).

One of the biggest policy consequences of political fragmentation in metropolitan areas is the increasing level of racial segregation in schools. By having either schools administered by suburban municipalities or having separate suburban school districts, political fragmentation creates tremendous differences in educational environments based on race. Nearly 50 years after the Supreme Court's opinion declaring racially segregated schools unconstitutional, most American schoolchildren remain in schools that are either predominantly white or predominantly minority. For example, 64 percent of African American children attend schools that are majority black and 30 percent attend schools that are over 90 percent black (Orfield, Eaton, and Jones 1997). Former Albuquerque mayor David Rusk argues that the solution to this problem is to allow central cities greater powers in annexing their surroundings. In his analysis of America's metropolitan areas, Rusk (1993) argues that those places with elastic central cities (cities with the ability to annex surrounding developed areas) have lower levels of racial and economic segregation and enjoy better fiscal health than their inelastic counterparts. Elastic cities like Houston, Atlanta, and Orlando are able to incorporate suburbs into their borders and are less constrained both fiscally and socially than inelastic cities like Boston, Cleveland, or Chicago which are effectively hemmed in by suburbs.

On the other side are those who see benefits from fragmentation (Ostrom et al. 1988, Schneider 1989). Most of these thinkers subscribe to a public choice view of local politics, an analytical framework derived from the field of economics. As first articulated by Tiebout (1956), public choice theorists begin with the assumption that individuals are rational actors, that is, that all human actions derive from individuals seeking to maximize the utility of their actions for their own personal gains. Using this assumption, public choice theorists speculate that citizens will seek to maximize the returns to their tax expenditures by choosing locales with a combination of the lowest tax rates and the highest levels of particular services they desire. In other words, citizens basically act as consumers of public services—senior citizens will seek towns with low taxes and senior centers, parents will move to places with better schools, businesses will seek towns with lower service fees, and so on. In the public choice world of high mobility and information, citizens "vote with their feet" for services and apply pressure to local leaders with a threat of exit. Local governments, eager to attract "ratables," those who will pay more in taxes than they require in services, such as businesses or wealthy residents, will seek efficiencies between their revenues and expenditures.

The political implications of fragmentation from a public choice perspective are best developed in Paul Peterson's *City Limits*. Peterson (1981) starts his analysis with the assumption that local governments both are interested in growth and are in competition with each other for taxable property investors. To attract these groups, Peterson suggests that localities will seek to cuts taxes by minimizing redistributive expenditures, the policies that transfer payments to groups who provide little in tax revenue such as the poor. Since most cities cannot maintain the high taxes necessary to finance redistributive policies such as welfare or housing assistance without losing their tax base to a nearby community, they will minimize such welfare spending. In short, suburban political fragmentation will cause a "race to the bottom" as communities compete for ideal taxpaying residents.

Although both analyses of fragmentation offer compelling logics, neither can offer empirical certainty. One the one hand, political consolidation might eliminate much of the exclusionary zoning, racial and economic segregation, and fiscal inequalities that exist across metropolitan areas in theory, but in practice researchers have not found any proof that consolidation promotes greater political or economic equality or provides greater economies of scale in the delivery of services (Keating 1995). Indeed, one problem with having a large unified government for an entire metropolis is that it further distances citizens from government (Berry et al. 1993, Oliver 2001). Under such a situation, the dynamics of big city politics, where wealthy groups exercise disproportionate power because of their small numbers and greater organizational capacity (Stone 1989) may hold. Political consolidation may eliminate the fragmentation that allows for high levels of economic and racial segregation, but it does not necessarily ensure greater equality in public services.

On the other hand, one may criticize the public choice celebrations of fragmentation as well. The public choice framework makes heroic assumptions about citizen mobility or information about localities and generally discounts the political process as an important determinant of policy. It is very unlikely that citizens act solely as consumers. Most citizens choose their residence because of work or family considerations and less because of some optimizing calculation between tax rates and municipal services. Moreover, local leaders, particularly in many suburban areas, are not simply concerned with growth or reducing taxes, particularly if their community has other amenities. There is mixed evidence that competition for localities actually provides more efficient local governments (Keating 1995).

Irrespective of whether one believes that fragmentation is harmful or beneficial, few metropolitan areas have succeeded in establishing more unified governments. Some metropolitan areas, like Phoenix, Arizona, are under one jurisdiction simply because they are dominated by an elastic central city that has been able to annex its surrounding areas. In most metropolitan areas, however, there are few formal institutions that have any significant governing power over the entire urban area. Outside of Miami-Dade County, Florida, Portland, Oregon, and Minneapolis–St. Paul, Minnesota, there are no metropolitan area governments with the ability to tax, zone, administer a range of services, and perform many of the same functions as municipalities. But does this mean America's metropolitan areas are simply collections of independent municipalities in fierce competition with each other? Not necessarily. Although metropolitan area governments may be very rare, in many American metropolitan areas alternative institutions have arisen to tackle metropolitan area problems.

The most common forms of metropolitan coordination are councils of government (COG). Arising largely from federal incentives for metropolitan planning that came in the 1960s, COGs are voluntary associations comprised of local governments including municipalities, counties, and special districts. These intergovernmental associations work to coordinate on service delivery such as sewage, solid waste disposal, roads, and water supplies across the municipalities that exist in the same region. Although COGs are useful in helping municipalities communicate and develop long-term plans, they are very weak as political units. Much like the United Nations, COGs depend upon the voluntary participation of their constituent members. Consequently, COGs rarely can impose decisions that would have adverse effects on any particular member or that municipality would leave. For example, if the Houston area COG decided to impose growth controls that would limit the ability of a suburb like Katy to develop its land, it is likely that Katy would simply remove itself from the COG and continue to do what it pleases. As institutions, COGs do little to actually govern a metropolitan area.[1]

1. One aspect of metropolitan area living, transportation, has become so important that a new type of regional institution has been created, the metropolitan planning organization (MPO). Federal legislation in the early 1990s required urban areas to create boards to design regional transportation plans and administer federal highway grants. Since regions that do not form these MPOs risk losing federal support for highways and transportations, most metropolitan areas have been quick to form them. Yet, like the COGs, the MPOs have little power to determine what the cities and counties within their jurisdiction actually do. Compliance among localities is voluntary and MPOs do not have the power to tax or zone or enforce compliance with the plans they derive. Given the experience with COGs, one might think that MPOs are nothing but paper tigers and real metropolitan governance is an illusory goal.

But as the case of Portland, Oregon demonstrates, simply having an organization dedicated to addressing metropolitan area issues is an important first step for the development of real institutions of metropolitan governance. Portland's Metro government, which originally evolved from a COG, coordinates zoning across all municipalities within the region, enforces a growth boundary that limits suburban sprawl, encourages urban redevelopment within the downtown, and coordinates transportation, solid waste disposal, and other vital services. What makes Portland's Metro unique is its ability to raise its own revenues through fees and voter-approved taxes and its independent authority to enforce land-use planning. With its regionally elected board, it is truly a metropolitan-area government.

In sum, the dynamics of metropolitan politics are determined by the extent to which its population is subdivided into separate governments. Metropolitan areas with less fragmentation or that are unified under a single metropolitan government are more likely to have political battles resembling larger cities, with a single institution being the focus of political struggle. The question of whether this style of governance is beneficial or harmful to the ideal practice of democratic governance remains open to debate. Metropolitan areas that are more politically divided among a large number of municipalities will experience a wider range of political conflicts spread over a larger number of sites. In these places, the focus of local politics will be more on mini-battles within each community. How such political battles play out, is the focus of the other level of analysis.

3. Local Politics in the Fragmented Metropolis

At the smallest level, suburban politics is also about the internal conflicts that occur within a particular community. Here, the evidence from political science is much less direct. As illustrated in the other chapters in this volume, the study of local politics in the United States has focused mostly on large cities and the traditional question first posed by Robert Dahl (1961) a half century ago of "Who governs?" Few studies have examined the internal dynamics of politics within suburbs. The question remains, therefore, as to whether the same groups and processes that typically dominate big city politics also rule in suburban areas.

Although these theories of local power are quite useful for explaining the political dynamics in large cities with ample commercial interests, their suitability for explaining suburban politics is questionable. Most theories of urban politics basically assume that a plurality of interests exists within a particular community and that communities are under pressure for economic growth. From these assumptions, most theories then strive to ascertain how well any one set of interests are represented or how much the growth pressure shapes the policymaking process.

However, for suburban politics, the presumption of either a difference in interests or of growth pressure is debatable, particularly in a community that is socially homogeneous or predominantly residential. In a place that is made up of only affluent, white homeowners or only poor minorities, we might expect less competition between interest groups and few arenas for developers to weave their political schemes. The question then arises, how well do these theories explain the dynamics of politics in suburban areas?

The answer to this question depends, in large part, on the social and institutional characteristics of the place. Take, for example, the trait of population size. Most larger places are typically more racially and economically diverse and are likely to have more mixed land-use types. Consequently, we should expect places with more than 100,000 in population to mimic the politics of larger cities, with the same types of political patterns: pressure for economic growth and development, the concerted efforts of economic interests preoccupied with commercial properties, and electoral politics defined by partisan and/or racial cues. Similarly, in places that are small but that have either mixed land uses or greater economic or racially diversity, we should find "big city" style electoral politics, dominated by organized and formal political groups. In short, if larger suburbs resemble large cities in their diversity, the patterns of democratic politics should be quite similar. In these instances, the politics surrounding growth regimes mentioned in research of Logan and Molotch (1987) or Stone (1989) will be evident.

Increasingly, however, suburban places of all sizes are becoming more distinctive from large cities. And the same traits that make suburban places distinctive can have a large impact on their politics. For example, one important way that suburban places are unique is in the singularity of their land usage, specifically among places that are comprised largely of homes. In residentially predominant bedroom suburbs, pressures for growth and economic development will be less acute. With fewer commercial interests seeking to extract rents from properties, the growth-oriented regimes often present in larger cities will not be evident.

But if the political fault lines that characterize large, urban settings are inapplicable for most other metropolitan places, then what exactly does shape politics in "suburbia"? From the limited research that has been conducted on suburban politics, some initial findings are beginning to emerge. For instance, the size and economic and racial composition of a community have all been identified as important determinants of whether people involve themselves in local affairs (Oliver 2001). Residents of places that are larger, very affluent, or economically and racially homogeneous are far less likely to participate in local civic activities than people in smaller, or more diverse communities. From this research, it appears that suburbanization by fragmenting and segregating American metropolitan areas, is having mixed implications for civic life in America.

Just as community diversity affects political participation, it is also important for shaping local politics. Because most suburban municipalities are socially homogeneous, have a narrow scope, and are relatively unbiased in their service provision, they have few of the permanent political divisions that exist on the nation or state level. They are what can be called "managerial democracies" (Oliver 2012). In managerial democracies, local politics and elections tend to focus on the managerial competence of incumbents. Local politicians tend to view themselves primarily in a "custodial" role, that is, local leaders are keenly attuned to their community's character and work as trustees for its future (Lewis and Neiman 2009).

These characterizations make suburban politics both easier and more difficult to describe. Take, for example, local elections. Almost all of our knowledge about how people vote is based on research concerning national elections. We know almost nothing about how and why people vote in local contests, particularly outside of central cities. Most research on local voting behavior derives either from case studies of individual locales (e.g., Ferman 1985, Hero and Beatty 1989, Kleppner 1985, Mollenkopf 1994, Shefter 1985, Sonenshein 1993), aggregate level analyses of voter turnout (Alford and Lee 1968, Monroe 1977), or focuses on the representation of women and minorities to local councils (e.g., Darcy et al. 1987, Engstrom and McDonald 1982, Svara 1991, Welch 1990).

But how do politics and elections work in managerial democracies? New research suggests they are quite different from not only national or state races, but from elections in large cities too. On the one hand, in managerial democracies, most incumbents run unopposed or win reelection when they do face an opponent (Oliver 2012). Much of this is due to the structure of the political domain: incumbents to local office enjoy success not simply from the political benefits of holding office but because there is usually not a highly motivated and well-organized opposition that is perpetually contesting their seats. Most localities are simply too small, limited in their services, and unbiased in how they distribute public resources to sustain long-standing political cleavages that characterize politics in larger democracies. When strong opposition groups do arise in local politics, they tend to be motivated by specific issues that are both parochial and temporal.

On the other hand, the absence of chronic political cleavages in most suburban localities also means that it is very difficult to predict when a certain issue, event, or personality is likely to animate an otherwise dormant constituency and motivate them to vote for someone new. It is very hard to foretell when a problematic issue becomes incendiary, it is unclear what makes a quality opponent suddenly decide to run for an office with little power or pay, and, as any politician can attest, it is impossible to foresee when some random comment mushrooms into a major political controversy. Ironically, the unpredictability of local politics also is exacerbated by the selective nature of the local electorate. Because "homevoters," that is, the homeowners and long-term residents who turn out in disproportionate numbers for local elections (Fischel 2005) are so attuned to local affairs and so personally connected to local politics, they are that much easier to mobilize around a specific issue. Local politics in a suburban "managerial democracy" may be mostly tranquil, but local voters are far from docile and it is difficult to anticipate when or why they will strike.

Of course, this description of local elections is not universal to all suburbs in America. Even the smallest and most unbiased suburb will occasionally have political divisions that fester over longer periods of time. Hard feelings over a minor political squabble may persist for years, particularly among those at the losing end of a political controversy. And because the actors in the local political drama are likely to know each other firsthand and run into each other as neighbors, the flames of resentment may continue to be stoked. There are also places where rapid demographic changes put long-standing political regimes at odds with their constituencies.

In sum, the key to understanding the dynamics of politics within a suburban place is to first identify what the social composition of that community is like. If it resembles a large city in its size, economic and racial diversity, and varied land-usage then presumably many of the existing theories developed in the urban politics literature will be applicable. But in places that are small or homogeneous or with unvaried land-usage, the internal dynamics of suburban politics tend to reflect a different type of politics. This is the politics of "managerial democracy" that tends to hinge on evaluations of incumbent performance relative to random exogenous shocks that occasionally jostle local politics.

4. Directions for Future Research

Scholars of local politics have not kept up with the changing demographics of the United States. Although most Americans now live in suburban areas, most political scientists concerned with local affairs continue to focus on the politics of large, central cities. As result, our knowledge of suburban politics is far behind what it should be. But at the same time, suburbanization is a prime topic for future research. The social, economic, and political diversity of suburban areas offers the conditions for natural experiments testing a wide range of hypotheses about local politics, particularly as America grows into the 21st century. This research could examine questions at the national, metropolitan, and local level.

For example, in the realm of national politics, new research suggests that suburban social contexts can shape their residents' political views (Gainsborough 2001), but the question remains whether this is a temporal effect or whether these trends will continue. As the major political parties orient themselves toward a suburban electorate, will suburban voters continue to divide along partisan lines? What also remains to be seen is how the suburban character of the electorate changes the political agenda within Congress. Is there more legislation aimed at suburban interests in Congress? Is this coming at the expense of rural or urban areas?

Similarly, the political impact of political fragmentation in the metropolitan area is also a topic needing further investigation. Many commentators argue for greater consolidation between cities and suburbs (Rusk 1993), but the politics of such consolidations are still uncertain. The political conditions under which political consolidation can occur are quite rare as resistance occurs from both suburbanites who want to protect their political autonomy and minorities in central cities afraid of losing political power (Owen and Wilburn 1985). Even smaller scale changes, like efforts to mandate "fair-share" low-income housing among affluent suburbs, meet fierce opposition (Kirp et al. 1995). The question remains as to how and where central cities and suburbs can coordinate more effectively and adopt mutually beneficial governing arrangements even without adopting formal institutional mechanisms of metropolitan governance.

Finally, the internal politics within most suburban places is still largely unknown. We have little knowledge about how the basic mechanisms of democratic governance operate in most homogeneous, suburban places. Does the managerial character of most American democracies favor certain groups above others? Does suburban "managerial democracy" inhibit or enhance the capacity of most Americans for meaningful self-governance? What differentiates people in a community where everyone has the same race, economic status, and land tenure? Are political battles in such a place the same as they are in a more diverse setting? Under what conditions are policy changes adopted in places that seem dedicated to preserving the status quo?

The key to answering these questions is to prioritize the social and institutional composition of a locality as a primary determinant of citizen attitudes and behavior. Individual-level differences in age, education, race, and gender are important in shaping local as well as national political attitudes, but they cannot fully explain how Americans understand local political life. The tremendous differentiation in places that has come as a by-product of suburbanization means that social contexts are becoming more important as determinants of citizen behavior. New studies of suburban politics need to focus on how social segregation and institutional arrangements reduce the capacity of municipal government for adjudicating conflict.

In addition to forming new theories that are more specific to these new suburban contexts, we also need better data to thoroughly test our assertions. In most research, there is no way to examine whether the extent of political conflict in a locality directly shapes citizens perceptions about the role and function of local government or their specific choices in local elections. Nor are there enough appropriately geo-coded survey data that sample from enough suburban locales. Most national level data either do not have enough respondents from suburbs or do not have proper geographic identifications. Most locally constructed surveys tend to be of large cities and do not have enough questions about issues, all vote choices, or on the role of government. One of the biggest challenges for researchers will be collecting data from a wide variety of locales that are easily comparable.

5. Conclusion

The transformation of America into a suburban nation offers many exciting challenges and opportunities for scholars of American politics. Suburbanization is changing the character of politics at the national, metropolitan, and local level. How these changes are occurring and what they mean for American democracy remain unclear. In short, with respect to suburban politics, there is a lot more that we do not know than we do. Much of our ignorance is due to the conceptual roadblocks presented by the diversity within suburban forms. It is impossible to determine what influence suburbs might have on national elections or how suburban voters might differ from city dwellers when so many different types of places get lumped together under one category. But this diversity need not be an impediment to understanding political life in the 21st-century metropolis. Suburbanization has created a greater systematic differentiation in American places, particularly with respect to their economic and racial composition and their land use. The key to understanding suburban politics remains in measuring how these differences affect the basic workings of democratic governance. Only once we compare how processes like voting, political participation, and policy formation differ in places comprised of only one social class or one type of land use from places that are more diverse can we begin to understand how the process of suburbanization is shaping the practice of American democracy.

REFERENCES

Alford, Robert, and Eugene C. Lee. 1968. "Voting Turnout in American Cities." *American Political Science Review* 62: 796–813.

Banfield, Edward C. 1970. *The Unheavenly City: The Nature and Future of Our Urban Crisis.* Boston: Little Brown.

Berry, Chris. 2009. *Imperfect Union: Representation and Taxation in Multi-level Governments.* New York: Cambridge University Press.

Berry, Jeffrey M., Kent E. Portney, and Ken Thomson. 1993. *The Rebirth of Urban Democracy.* Washington, DC: Brookings Institution.

Browning, Rufus, Dale Rogers Marshall, and David H. Tabb. 1997. *Racial Politics in American Cities.* 2nd ed. New York: Longman.

Burns, Nancy. 1994. *The Formation of American Local Governments.* New York: Oxford University Press.

Caitlin, Robert. 1997. *Land Use Planning, Environmental Protection, and Growth Management.* Chelsea, MI: Ann Arbor Press.

Dahl, Robert A. 1961. *Who Governs? Democracy and Power in an American City.* New Haven: Yale University Press.

Danielson, Michael. 1976. *The Politics of Exclusion.* New York: Columbia University Press.

Darcy, Robert, Susan Welch, and Janet Clark. 1987. *Women, Elections, and Representation.* New York: Longman.

Dreier, Peter, John Mollenkopf, and Todd Swanstrom. 2004. *Place Matters: Metropolitics for the 21st Century.* 2nd ed. Lawrence: University Press of Kansas.

Ehrenhalt, Alan. 1996. *The Lost City: Discovering the Forgotten Virtues of Community in the Chicago of the 1950s.* New York: Basic Books.

Engstrom, Richard, and Michael McDonald. 1982. "The Underrepresentation of Blacks on City Councils." *Journal of Politics* 44: 1088–105.

Ferman, Barbara. 1985. *Governing the Ungovernable City: Political Skill, Leadership, and the Modern Mayor.* Philadelphia: Temple University Press.

Fischel, William. 2005. *The Homevoter Hypothesis: How Home Values Influence Local Government Taxation, School Finance, and Land-Use Policies.* Cambridge, MA: Harvard University Press.

Gainsborough, Juliet. 2001. *Fenced Off: The Suburbanization of American Politics.* Washington, DC: Georgetown University Press.

Gans, Herbert J. 1967. *The Levittowners.* New York: Pantheon.

Gullick, Luther. 1962. *The Metropolitan Problem and American Ideas.* New York: Knopf.

Hero, Rodney, and Kathleen Beatty. 1989. "The Elections of Federico Pena as Mayor of Denver: Analysis and Implications," *Social Science Quarterly* 70: 300–310.

Jacobs, Jane. 1961. *The Death and Life of Great American Cities.* New York: Vintage.

Karnig, Albert, and Susan Welch. 1981. *Black Representation and Urban Policy.* Chicago: University of Chicago Press.

Keating, Michael. 1995. "Size, Efficiency and Democracy: Consolidation, Fragmentation and Public Choice." In David Judge, Gerry Stoker, and Harold Wolman, eds., *Theories of Urban Politics.* New York: Russell Sage Foundation.

Kirp, David, John Dwyer, and Larry Rosenthal. 1995. *Our Town: Race, Housing, and the Soul of Suburbia.* New Brunswick, NJ: Rutgers University Press.

Kleppner, Paul. 1985. *Chicago Divided: The Making of a Black Mayor.* DeKalb: Northern Illinois University Press.

Kunstler, James Howard. 1993. *The Geography of Nowhere: The Rise and Decline of America's Manmade Landscape.* New York: Simon and Schuster.

Langdon, Phillip. 1993. *A Better Place to Live: Reshaping the American Suburb.* Amherst: University of Massachusetts Press.

Lewis, Paul, and Max Neiman. 2009. *Custodians of Place: Governing the Growth and Development of Cities.* Washington, DC: Georgetown University Press.

Logan, John, and Harvey Molotch. 1987. *Urban Fortunes: The Political Economy of Place.* Berkeley: University of California Press.

McGirr, Lisa. 2001. *Suburban Warriors: The Origins of the New American Right.* Princeton: Princeton University Press.

McKenzie, Evan. 1994. *Privatopia: Homeowner Associations and the Rise of Residential Private Government.* New Haven: Yale University Press, 1994.

Mollenkopf, John. 1994. *A Phoenix in the Ashes: The Rise and Fall of the Koch Coalition in New York City Politics.* Princeton: Princeton University Press.

Monroe, Alan D. 1977. "Urbanism and Voter Turnout: A Note on Some Unexpected Findings." *American Journal of Political Science* 21: 71–78.

Mumford, Lewis. 1961. *The City in History.* New York: Harcourt, Brace, & World.

Oliver, J. Eric. 2001. *Democracy in Suburbia.* Princeton: Princeton University Press.

Oliver, J. Eric. 2012. *Local Elections and the Politics of Small-Scale Democracy.* Princeton: Princeton University Press.

Orfield, Gary, Susan Eaton, and Elaine Jones. 1997. *Dismantling Desegregation: The Quiet Reversal of Brown versus Board of Education.* New York: New Press.

Ostrom, Vincent, Robert Bish, and Elinor Ostrom. 1988. *Local Government in the United States.* San Francisco: Institute for Contemporary Studies.

Owen, C. James, and York Wilburn. 1985. *Governing Metropolitan Indianapolis: The Politics of Unigov.* Berkeley: University of California Press.

Peterson, Paul. 1981. *City Limits.* Chicago: University of Chicago Press.

Polsby, Nelson W. 1963. *Community Power and Political Theory.* New Haven: Yale University Press.

Putnam, Robert. 2000. *Bowling Alone.* New York: Simon Schuster.

Rusk, David. 1993. *Cities without Suburbs*. Washington, DC: Woodrow Wilson Center Press (distributed by Johns Hopkins University Press).
Schneider, Mark. 1989. *The Competitive City: The Political Economy of Suburbia*. Pittsburgh: University of Pittsburgh Press.
Shefter, Martin. 1985. *Political Crisis/Fiscal Crisis: The Collapse and Revival of New York City*. New York: Basic Books.
Sonenshein, Raphael. 1993. *Political in Black and White: Race and Power in Los Angeles*. Princeton: Princeton University Press.
Stone, Clarence. 1989. *Regime Politics: Governing Atlanta 1946–1988*. Lawrence: University Press of Kansas. Chicago: University of Chicago Press.
Suarez, Ray. 1999. *The Old Neighborhood: What We Lost in the Great Suburban Migration 1966–1999*. New York: Free Press.
Svara, James. 1991. *A Survey of America's City Councils: Continuity and Change*. Washington, DC: National League of Cities.
Tiebout, Charles M. 1956. "A Pure Theory of Local Expenditures." *Journal of Political Economy*. 44: 416–24.
Weiher, Gregory. 1991. *The Fractured Metropolis: Political Fragmentation and Metropolitan Segregation*. Albany: SUNY Press.
Welch, Susan. 1990. "The Impact of At-Large Elections on the Representation of Blacks and Hispanics." *Journal of Politics* 52: 1050–76.
Welch, Susan, and Timothy Bledsoe. 1988. *Urban Reform and Its Consequences: A Study in Representation*. Chicago : University of Chicago Press.
Whyte, William. 1956. *The Organization Man*. New York: Simon and Schuster.
Wolfinger, Raymond E. 1974. *The Politics of Progress*. Englewood Cliffs, NJ: Prentice-Hall.
Wood, Robert H. 1959. *Suburbia: Its People and Their Politics*. Boston: Houghton Mifflin.
Zikmund, Joseph II. 1968. "Suburban Voting in Presidential Elections." *Midwest Journal of Political Science* 2: 239–58.

CHAPTER 31

BUILDING METROPOLITAN INSTITUTIONS

CHRISTIAN LEFÈVRE AND MARGARET WEIR

1. Introduction

During the twentieth century, as cities across the globe began to spill beyond their old borders, new questions about how best to govern these complex and varied regional settlements emerged. At one pole of the debate, consolidationists argued that a single metropolitan government was needed to promote efficient and equitable development. At the other pole, public choice theorists and a large segment of the metropolitan population supported multiple governments as more effective in meeting the needs of the diverse populations and activities spread across metropolitan areas. Debate over these two perspectives—along with proposals that combine aspects of the two approaches—have surfaced regularly as policymakers seek to address a diverse menu of problems ranging from traffic congestion and concentrated poverty to economic competitiveness and global warming.

Despite the decades of debate in the U.S., major institutional reform of metropolitan areas has remained elusive. Local opposition overrode most efforts to create metropolitan governments; as a result most American metropolitan areas are governed by a broad array of local governments and functional special districts. Although Latin America and Africa have not enacted any significant metropolitan reforms, Canada and many European and East Asian countries implemented major institutional changes in the postwar decades. Among the most important are the establishment of the Tokyo Metropolitan Government in 1943, the Seoul Metropolitan Government in 1949, the metropolitan authority of Toronto in 1955 and Montreal in 1970, the Greater London Council in 1963, and the creation of metropolitan governments in all major British cities in the 1970s, the "communautés urbaines"[1] in France in the late 1960s. More recently other urban areas have experienced similar reforms, including Stuttgart in 1994, London in 1999, and Lisbon and Porto in the 1990s. However, despite these successes in establishing formal metropolitan institutions in specific urban areas only, most metropolitan areas in these continents do not possess their own area-wide government.

At the close of the twentieth century, stymied by the political obstacles standing in the way of new metropolitan governments, reformers in the United States began to promote the idea of regional governance. In contrast to earlier efforts at creating formal institutions, regional governance takes many forms, ranging from short-term collaboration among civic groups to standing forums of local governments. Elsewhere in the world, reformers experimented with more flexible modalities of institution building than those implemented in the earlier period.

While these new governance initiatives may have an impact in specific policy areas, such as public transportation, it is doubtful that they will significantly alter metropolitan arrangements more broadly. The recent metropolitan governance efforts do not address the major obstacles facing metropolitan institution building including the strength of local governments, the unwillingness of national states to seriously support metropolitan governance, and the lack of enthusiasm for metropolitan institutions in civil society.

2. One Government or Many?

For decades, the central argument about regional institution building pitted reformers, who advocated government consolidation, against public choice theorists, who favored multiple local governments as a superior approach. Drawing largely on the American case and on works carried out by the various Royal Commissions on Local Government in UK in the 1960s and 1970s, researchers marshaled empirical evidence on both sides of the debate (Keating 1995). Ultimately, however, the two perspectives rest on distinct sets of values, not easily reconciled by research findings. Moreover, the fate of reform rested in the hands of political processes that proved unwilling to support or unable to implement major metropolitan institutional reforms.

2.1. The Theoretical Debate

A classic statement of the reform perspective appeared in Victor Jones's 1942 book *Metropolitan Government* (Jones 1942). Jones argued that the primary problem

1. The French "Communautés urbaines" were established in 1966 for the four largest urban areas (Bordeaux, Lille, Lyon, Strasbourg). They are metropolitan authorities with significant responsibilities (public transport, water systems, planning, etc.).

facing metropolitan areas was the mismatch between the scale of urban problems and the scale of local government. A metropolitan area-wide perspective was needed to address key metropolitan problems, including transportation, zoning, parks and recreation, water, sewage, public health, and housing. Yet in most metropolitan areas, a multitude of local governments took charge of these functions. Because political fragmentation nurtured narrow localistic perspectives on metropolitan issues, it was both inefficient and undemocratic according to this perspective. Fragmentation created wasteful duplication and made it impossible to realize economies of scale. For many areas, it created disparities between their service needs and their financial ability to provide those services. Fragmentation also posed obstacles to democratic control: many residents were deeply affected by decisions made by jurisdictions in which they had no voice. According to Jones and a legion of good government advocates of the era, the best solution to all these problems was to consolidate the multiple localities into a single metropolitan government (Gulick 1957).

Public choice theorists disagreed. Instead, they argued that a system of multiple local governments would allow residents to choose the most desirable mix of taxes and services. The major theoretical statement of this argument is Charles Tiebout's 1956 article "A Pure Theory of Local Expenditures" (Tiebout 1956). For Tiebout, competition and choice were the central mechanisms that produced the greatest good for all. Competition among localities would spur local governments to provide the best services at the lowest cost to residents. Choice meant that residents who were dissatisfied with their local government could move to a different locality that provided a more attractive mix of taxes and services.

One of the central disputes between the two perspectives concerned the efficiency of these different governmental arrangements. Advocates of metropolitan consolidation argued that large political units were more efficient because they could realize economies of scale. They also pointed to the irrationality of fragmented government. For example, an influential book in the series of studies sponsored by the Ford Foundation in the 1950s, political scientist Robert Wood's *1400 Governments*, outlined the governmental arrangements set up to cope with postwar metropolitan growth (Wood 1961). Wood detailed the "defensive, unpremeditated, and parochial" responses of the bewildering array of general purpose governments—counties, cities, towns, villages, boroughs, and districts—charged with governing the New York metropolitan area.

Public choice analysts contend that large centralized governments are not more efficient and that a system of multiple local governments does not lead to the inefficiencies that its opponents suggest. Instead, they argue that competition among multiple units produces greater efficiency as jurisdictions eliminate waste and duplication in response to citizen preferences. In an early influential article, Ostrom, Tiebout, and Warren argued against making a priori judgments about the impact of fragmented versus centralized governmental forms (Ostrom, Tiebout, and Warren 1961). They posited that a "polycentric political system" with multiple governments produced benefits by allowing for variation in the scale of the political units appropriate to the function being performed. Single consolidated metropolitan government could not offer such variation in scale. Moreover, a system of multiple governments offered the flexibility that allowed smaller local governments to enter into a variety of cooperative arrangements and agreements for conflict resolution. In this way, they could operate interdependently while retaining the benefits of formal autonomy (Bish and Ostrom 1973).

Researchers have examined the impact of jurisdictional fragmentation on a range of issues related to efficiency, equality, and citizen satisfaction. Extensive quantitative research on the efficiency of different forms of metropolitan governance has produced mixed results: evidence supporting the public choice perspective shows that political fragmentation is related to lower government costs for labor-intensive services. However, for capital-intensive services, the research indicates that larger units are more cost effective (Altshuler et al. 1999; Foster 1997). Research assessing the impact of government form on income and racial segregation is more conclusive. There is wide agreement that jurisdictional fragmentation promotes racial segregation (Altshuler et al. 1999; Lowrey 2000; Powell 2002). Related research on fiscal disparities across political jurisdictions has shown that political fragmentation leaves some jurisdictions with a disproportionate share of needy populations (Pagano 1999).

The conflict over consolidation versus multiple governments is not simply one about which form of government is more efficient or equitable. The debate endures in part because advocates on opposing sides prioritize fundamentally distinct values. The public choice perspective places the highest premium on individual choice while reformers emphasize provision of collective goods.

In addition, these two perspectives diverge in their views about the appropriate size of democratic communities and about the nature of democratic engagement. Proponents of public choice praise the virtues of small communities, where like-minded residents engage in face-to-face interactions to solve problems in the ways they see fit. The ability of groups to form their own communities and to determine their boundaries is a central value in this perspective. In the United States, many advocates for enhanced minority power also support multiple smaller governments, on the grounds that minorities can more easily win office in such settings. By contrast, reformers who defend metropolitan governments point to "variety, disagreement, discussion, and debate" as the essence of the modern liberal polity (Wood 1958, 121). From this perspective, the clash of competing views in a common political arena provided the most likely path to the common good.

Outside the United States, notably in Europe, the debate was rarely so fierce. Most major countries were already very much in favor of consolidation or building new metropolitan governments. The debate, as we will see, centered much more on the modalities to implement reforms than on the content of reforms. Three major interrelated elements may explain the greater receptivity to metropolitan government in the European case. First, European local governments have generally fewer responsibilities and powers than those in the United States. In Europe (except in the early 1980s in the UK, the first years of Margaret Thatcher's government, which abolished metropolitan councils on the ground they were useless and not cost-effective)[2] national governments strongly supported local governmental consolidation and mergers and local governments had little power to block central government reform efforts. Second, European central governments are usually more directly involved in the government of urban areas than in the U.S. and they have been more willing to intervene in local matters. Finally, collective goods are more valued in Europe than in North America and consolidations, mergers, or "big" institutions are more legitimate.

2.2. The Politics of Metropolitan Reform, 1960–1990

The contrast between the United States and the rest of the world is evident in the political conflicts surrounding metropolitan reform throughout the twentieth century.

In the United States, reformers made little headway in creating metropolitan governments. The legal presumption of local control made it very difficult to erase existing political boundaries or to layer new general purpose governments over them. Although state governments enjoyed formal authority over land use, states had little political interest in using this power to create new metropolitan governments. Reflecting the high value placed on local autonomy, many states had ceded control over land use to localities in the first part of the twentieth century and most states had long placed only loose requirements on political incorporation (Briffault 1990). As a result, any movement toward metropolitan government required local approval. The most common form these efforts took were proposals to consolidate city and county governments. Reflecting popular preferences for smaller local governments, voters have rejected most such efforts, approving only 17.6 percent of these proposals since 1921 (Pagano 1999).

Throughout American history the preference for smaller local governments has also been linked to the racial and ethnic diversity of American society. The first independent suburbs in the late 1800s allowed the burgeoning Anglo-Saxon middle class to escape the increasingly immigrant city and the often-corrupt political machines that controlled city governments (Teaford 1979). In the postwar era, as African Americans left the South for cities, local government boundaries served as racial barriers. Postwar metropolitan areas in the United States grew into fragmented patchworks of many localities divided by race and income. However, despite Tiebout's argument, the existence of multiple local governments did not enhance the choices of all residents. Low-income urban residents—disproportionately minority—could not relocate to most suburbs, where housing costs were high and multifamily rental units were rare.

2. See for instance the 1983 Government White Paper "Streamlining the Cities: Government Proposals for Reorganising Local Government in Greater London and the Metropolitan Counties" which paved the way for the local government reform of 1986.

A handful of metropolitan areas in the United States took a different, more regional approach to government. Many large cities in the southwest—especially Texas—established lenient annexation laws that allowed the central cities to grow dramatically (Rusk 1993). In these regions, the city grew to encompass most of the metropolitan area, although by the 1990s, even these large cities had become surrounded by separate suburban governments. Only two metropolitan areas, the Minneapolis–St. Paul region of Minnesota and Portland, Oregon, succeeded in creating some form of metropolitan government during the 1960s and 1970s. In Minnesota's Twin Cities, the state legislature created an appointed Metropolitan Council in 1967 to oversee a wide range of metropolitan functions, including planning and policy development related to land use, sewage, transit, parks, and recreation. One of the Council's most significant accomplishments was its sponsorship of a 1971 tax-base sharing agreement among the seven counties in the region (Altshuler et al. 109–10). In Oregon, a 1973 state land use planning law required local governments to draw urban growth boundaries. Portland's Metropolitan Service District, an elected general purpose government, was initially created to carry out these planning functions but has since significantly increased its responsibilities. In each case, exceptional political circumstances facilitated the change: a coalition of rural and urban interests and a weak suburban building industry in Oregon; a tradition of good government in Minnesota; and a lack of racial diversity in both settings (Weir 2000a).

As proposals for general regional governments failed to win support in the United States, two less encompassing institutional alternatives emerged. The first were regional councils of government, created in the 1960s in response to federal government incentives designed to improve coordination of federal grants. But, with limited authority and voluntary membership, the regional councils had little impact on metropolitan development. More significant and enduring were special districts, which emerged as the most politically acceptable way to achieve regional coordination in the United States. By designating a single function to be carried out area-wide, special districts limit the infringements on local autonomy associated with consolidated government. But reliance on special districts introduces biases into regional decision-making. Because special districts are almost never created to serve social welfare functions, metropolitan regions with the greatest number of special districts spend disproportionately on developmental objectives rather than on social welfare (Foster 1997). Scholars have long criticized special districts as low-visibility political arenas with little democratic accountability.

In Europe, political conflict centered not on the desirability of formal institutional reform but rather on the modalities of such reform. Almost everywhere, institutional fragmentation was considered as the "metropolitan problem" (Sharpe 1995) to be combated. One solution was the merger of municipalities, which succeeded, at least in the non-Latin countries such as Germany, UK, Belgium, and the Scandinavian states. In these countries, the number of municipalities was significantly reduced in the 1960s and 1970s. In Germany, municipalities were reduced by two-thirds (from 24,000 to almost 8,000), in Denmark by almost four-fifths (from 1,300 to 280), in Sweden from 1,000 to 280, or in the Netherlands from 1,000 to 700. In Latin countries (France, Italy, Portugal, and Spain), mergers were not successful or even considered.

However, new metropolitan institutions were not created by reducing fragmentation through consolidation or mergers of municipalities, with the exception of Britain with the creation of the Greater London Council in 1963 and metropolitan councils in the 1970s. Outside Britain, consolidation almost exclusively concerned central cities, such as in all major German municipalities which became "kreisfreie Stadt," that is, which consolidated powers and resources of the central municipality and the "kreis," a sort of county. In these institutional processes, efforts to build institutions that would connect entire metropolitan areas were not considered, and remain off the agenda today. Indeed, metropolitan areas were not touched except in Spain (the Franco regime imposed some metropolitan corporations in Barcelona, Bilbao, and Valencia in the 1960s), in France (a few "communautés urbaines" in some large urban areas such as Bordeaux or Lyon), and in Canada (the establishment of "communautés urbaines" in Toronto and Montreal).

The 1980s were also a period of "counter-reforms," when many metropolitan authorities were abolished, including the Spanish metropolitan corporations, the metropolitan authorities of Copenhagen and Eindhoven, all English metropolitan councils (METS), London included. In Spain, the abolition of metropolitan corporations was largely due to the fact that they had been imposed by the Franco regime and thus were considered the symbol of the dictatorship. But it is also true that the newly created regions were afraid of these large metropolitan governments which could become political rivals. In the UK, English METS were abolished by the Thatcher government on the ground that these authorities were useless and costly, in a pure public choice argument.

As a consequence, most major North American and European metropolitan areas did not have true metropolitan government at the end of the twentieth century. For instance, in Europe, neither Barcelona, Berlin, Hamburg, Frankfurt, Milan, Munich, Naples, Paris, Rome, nor Zurich had metropolitan authorities. How can such a failure be explained?

The major reason for such a failure is to be found in the strong resistance and opposition of the local government systems. Although most European local governments do not enjoy formal autonomy comparable to that of their U.S. counterparts, they nevertheless benefit from significant political legitimacy. In some cases, such as France and Italy, they also have good access to national authorities. Their legitimacy stems from their long histories (most of the municipalities existed before central states) and a strong sense of belonging by their population. Local governments were thus able either to successfully oppose state laws regarding the establishment of metropolitan forms of government (such as in Italy in the 1980s and 1990s) or to "empty the laws of their content" when these laws were approved (such as in France in the 1970s and 1980s), by significantly limiting their effective impacts. For example, local political leaders in charge of metropolitan authorities usually agreed that those authorities should not impose anything on municipalities and should remain as weak as possible.

The opposition and resistance of local governments stemmed from the fear that these metropolitan authorities would become too strong and would impose their policies upon local governments in the long run. The fear of losing leadership over their own territory and of losing responsibilities and resources were among the most common arguments against metropolitan reforms. In addition, local leaders rejected institutional reforms because they were generally top-down, imposed by central governments, and "one size fits all"—requiring the same responsibilities, same political organization, same fiscal and financial resources—for all major urban areas whatever their specific features. These criticisms became more and more legitimate and successful as the decentralization process developed in the 1980s and 1990s in almost all European countries even in the most centralized ones such as the Netherlands and France.

3. Moving toward Regional Governance? 1990–2009

By the end of the twentieth century, disappointment with formal metropolitan governing institutions prompted new thinking about how to address metropolitan problems. Reformers began to promote the idea of regional governance: rather than seeking to build metropolitan governments, the new approach would promote innovative forms of regional engagement, drawing civil society and local governments into regional problem-solving networks. This approach envisions a bottom-up and incremental process of metropolitan institutional building. It also recasts the government role from one of top-down governing to that of facilitating new forms of civil society engagement with regional problem-solving.

In the United States, advocates of the new regionalism have championed goals related to the environment, economic growth, and equity, claiming that regional approaches can reduce the trade-offs among these objectives so that they become complementary rather than competing goals (Dreier, Mollenkopf, and Swanstrom 2001). Although differing strands of thought focus on business actors or community-based actors, much of the argument for the new regionalism rests on the premise that collaboration among diverse groups can produce region-wide benefits and that by engaging in collaboration, opposing interests can discover common goals.

In practice, the most widespread of the new regional institutions have been networks of civic groups. These include efforts of regional chambers of commerce to promote regional economic development in ways that capitalize on the unique strengths of the entire region (Peirce, Johnson, and Hall 1993; Dodge and Montgomery 1996). New regionalist initiatives often take the form of ad hoc collections of groups from public, private, and nonprofit sectors that collaborate to achieve specific regional goals, such as building regional infrastructure or cleaning up the environment (Foster 2001). There are also some examples of more enduring organizations that have emerged to provide forums for discussing regional problems, such as the Metropolitan Mayors' Caucus in Chicago. Although instances of collaborative regionalism abound, it remains unclear how such initiatives can be sustained and whether they can be deployed to achieve new goals once they achieve their initial objectives.

Despite the enthusiasm for collaborative regionalism, initiatives of this sort have thus far done little to address problems related to income and racial segregation within regions or fiscal disparities across local governments. A more political approach to regionalism argues that the way to address redistributive issues is to build coalitions among a subset of suburbs and the city on the basis of common interest. This perspective posits that some suburbs share objective interests with central cities around fiscal issues, the distribution of affordable housing, and growth management (Orfield 2002). In practice, such city-suburb coalitions have been difficult to organize. More successful have been the efforts of community-based regionalists, coalitions of community-based organizations that mobilize around a particular issue, seeking to ensure that some of the benefits of regional growth are shared by low-income communities (Pastor et al. 2009). One of the major tools used by these groups is the community benefits agreement, in which community organizations agree to support regional development projects in exchange for developers' commitments to provide some additional benefit, such as affordable housing or jobs, for neighborhood residents.

The increasing racial-ethnic and income diversity in American suburbs during the past decade suggests that some of the long-standing barriers to region-wide action on redistributive concerns may become less salient in the future. As many suburbs come to experience social and economic problems similar to those of the city and, as the needs of some urban and suburban populations begin to converge, it may be possible to build new coalitions to support region-wide problem solving.

In the United States, reforms in federal transportation policy constitute the most significant government efforts to promote regional thinking and action. Policy reforms in the early 1990s helped revive regional institutions by allocating new funds to Metropolitan Planning Organizations and delegating them the responsibility to plan regional transportation development. The reforms also sought to widen the scope of engagement in regional transportation decision-making by instituting requirements for community participation. Although the impact of the reforms fell far short of initial hopes that they would energize new regional coalitions, they have begun to create new networks engaged in transportation policy and in some places have strengthened institutions governing regional transportation decision-making (Weir, Rongerude, and Ansell 2009).

Indeed, for the past half century, federal policies—whether in the form of incentives or regulations—have been the most significant force encouraging regional cooperation. In the 1960s, several federal policies included requirements or incentives that aimed to promote coordinated action in metropolitan areas. These requirements were abandoned in the 1980s before they had much chance to change the way metropolitan areas operate. Many reformers currently see a renewal of such federal incentives as the best way to promote regional institution building. The federal role envisioned is one of promoting and prodding, not that of imposing institutions from above. Regional institutions are now connecting to new national purposes as well. Whereas the emphasis on efficiency and equity dominated earlier arguments about the need for regional institutions, today arguments center on their contribution to achieving national goals, such as reducing America's carbon footprint or promoting international economic competitiveness. With the creation of a new Office of Urban Policy in the White House under the Obama administration, there was optimism that the federal government would find new ways to promote regional cooperation. Yet, proved unable to provide meaningful coordination and quietly closed its doors after two years.

In Europe the situation has been rather similar with many experiences of metropolitan governance. However, in most cases, the final objective remains that of building a metropolitan institution or sets of institutions, the focus being more on the modalities to reach this objective (the process) than on the a priori content of the reform (the institutional output). At the same time—and in strong contrast with the U.S.—the 1990–2009 decades have remained a period of institutional reforms, most of which have not yet been implemented.

Almost every country in Europe has experienced either institutional reform or experiments aimed at building metropolitan arrangements that are stable and strong enough to address the major problems faced by the largest urban areas. Indeed, the list of such reforms is long. The 1990s began with the enactment of the Italian 142 Act, which created a new tier, the "Citta Metropolitana" (Metropolitan City) in all the 10 major urban areas of the country. In 1991, the Portuguese state voted to establish metropolitan authorities in Lisbon and Porto. In 1994, the German state Baden-Württemberg created the Verband Regio Stuttgart (VRS), the very first metropolitan authority in Germany. This was followed by a similar creation in Hannover in 1996. The same year, the proposal to merge the länder of Berlin and Brandeburg was put to vote but defeated. In 1995, a bill creating city-provinces in the largest Dutch urban regions was approved. In 1999, the French government approved a law creating new metropolitan governments in all areas over 500,000 people. The same year, the Italian government passed a new law to facilitate the establishment of Metropolitan Cities. In 1999, the Greater London Authority was established and its powers were reinforced by a new act in 2007. The same year, the Danish government created the Capital Region of Denmark (Region Hovestaden) for the Copenhagen area.

This profusion of institutional reforms and creations with various outcomes was not limited to Europe. In other parts of the world such as eastern Asia, southern Africa, and Latin America, several metropolitan areas have seen similar experiences (Seoul and Busan in the mid-1990s, Durban, Johannesburg, Cape Town in the early 2000s, Bogota in 1978, Quito in 1993, Caracas in 1999).

Despite this intense reform activity, outcomes have been disappointing. First of all, most institutional reforms, either as proposals or laws, have not been implemented. The Italian "Metropolitan Cities" remain a theoretical institution. They have been inserted in the national constitution but none has been established. The situation is similar with the Dutch city-provinces whose creation was blocked by negative referenda in Amsterdam and Rotterdam in 1995.

Second, even when institutional reforms have been implemented, the resulting "institutional product" has been weak. This is the case, for instance, of the metropolitan authority of Stuttgart (VRS) which has very few responsibilities, a weak budget, and almost no authority over local governments belonging to the metropolitan area. The same is true of the GLA, the metropolitan governments of Lisbon and Porto, and the Capital Region of Denmark. France remains a relative exception to this litany of failure because the important reforms of 1999 have permitted the establishment of strong metropolitan authorities. However, even here, success is limited because the territories do not cover the whole functional metropolitan areas.

Finally, in the few cases when metropolitan authorities have been established, it has been due to exceptional political and historical circumstances. Two examples illustrate this statement. The VRS in Stuttgart was created in 1994 by the State of Baden-Württemberg because of a political crisis which precipitated the construction of a "Grand Coalition" of the Socialist Party (SPD) and the Christian Democrats (CDU) at the state level. In the political negotiations, the SPD demanded the establishment of a kind of metropolitan authority which the CDU had to accept (Frenzel 2002). Since then, the Land (state) has continuously refused to grant any more power and resources to the VRS, which remains a very weak authority.

The Madrid Region (Autonomous Community of Madrid—CAM) is very likely one of the strongest metropolitan authorities in the world. It covers most of the metropolitan area, has important responsibilities and resources, and in many ways can be considered as a quasi-federated state. This situation is, however, the result of a distinctive political history. Indeed, the territory of the CAM is the political result of harsh negotiations between parties after the Franco regime ended in late 1970s. The issue was the territorial and political reorganization of Spain and the question of what to do with its capital. The urban area of Madrid could have been split up among the adjacent regions. Instead, a political trade-off gave Madrid the status of a political region (Rodriguez-Alvarez 2002). With urbanization and economic growth, this political region, the CAM, has de facto become a metropolitan authority.

In contrast to the limited impact of formal institutional reform, there has been considerable experimentation and innovation surrounding new efforts to promote metropolitan governance during the last two decades. In Europe, even though the effort to build metropolitan governments largely failed, the experiments with metropolitan governance have been many and are ongoing. We will simply focus on three of them as illustrative of three new conceptions and modalities for building metropolitan institutions.

3.1. Institutions as Processes

The 1990 act proposing Metropolitan Cities in Italy largely failed because it posited that metropolitan governments should be imposed by law and should be ready-made for all the largest urban areas, whatever their specific conditions. Taking this into account, in 1996, the Bologna area proposed to invert this logic. The Metropolitan City was presented as the outcome of a process which should be bottom-up. In addition, public policies at the metropolitan level were considered to be a first step, essential to create a "sense of necessity" to think metropolitan-wide, thus legitimizing the necessity for a metropolitan institution in a second step. In 1996, the various municipalities of the area and the Province of Bologna decided to set up a metropolitan conference to initiate a process leading to the establishment of a Metropolitan City of some kind. This process was embedded in a legal agreement, the Agreement for the Metropolitan City of Bologna—ACM. In addition to the constitution of the metropolitan conference, the ACM established a metropolitan secretariat within the central city of Bologna and the Province of Bologna, set up several metropolitan offices (joint offices of the municipalities and the Province to deal with metropolitan matters) and fixed a timetable for the whole process. The initial outcomes were encouraging: the launch of a metropolitan plan, several metropolitan public policies in the sectors of public transport, health, and development, and so on. Unfortunately, the process came to a stop when the political leaders of the municipality of Bologna were defeated in the 1999 municipal elections.

The Bologna experience was actively observed in Europe by those involved in the building of metropolitan authorities in other countries. It paved the way for new experiences such as those related to strategic planning as a process aiming at the creation of metropolitan government.

3.2. Strategic Planning and Institution Building

Barcelona was among the first European cities to innovate by producing a strategic plan in the late 1980s. Strategic planning has since been a way to manage the development of the city and further the metropolitan area with the first metropolitan strategic plan issued in the early 2000s. One indirect objective of Barcelona's strategic planning process is to build up a system of metropolitan governance that engages most of relevant players from the political, economic, social, and cultural spheres. In the medium term, this engagement may result in the creation of a metropolitan decision-making body. Following this model, the metropolitan area of Turin in Italy embarked on strategic planning in the late 1990s with an explicit aim of building a metropolitan-wide governance system with significant institutional ties which could take the form of a Metropolitan City according to the 142 Act. In 2000, most of the member municipalities set up a metropolitan conference with the Province to implement the first strategic plan and to discuss issues of metropolitan scope. In the mid-2000s, a second strategic plan was launched and in 2008, a new body, the "metropolitan table," was established with a reduced number of municipalities but these municipalities were "selected" because of their stronger political engagement in creating a decision-making body at the metropolitan level. Works of these structures (metropolitan conference and metropolitan table) have been substantiated by the various groups and committees formed during the elaboration of both strategic plans.

3.3. Involvement of Socioeconomic Actors

Engagement of civil society actors has been a leitmotiv in most European countries and elsewhere in the last 15 years, one strongly pushed by some central governments (United Kingdom, Netherlands), the European Union, and other international organizations (OECD 2001). By and large in Europe, there has been more rhetoric than practice in that matter (Lefèvre 2009). However such rhetoric has been omnipresent and in several cases has been put into practice. In France, the 1999 National Planning and Development Act established "councils of development" in all major urban areas. These councils are assemblies representing the social and economic forces of the metropolitan areas and are supposed to advise the existing metropolitan authorities. In many areas that have embarked on a strategic planning process, such as Barcelona, Manchester, or Turin, social and economic players are usually well represented in the various committees and advisory groups that are part of the sometimes very complex organizational structures which run them. But as a whole, civil society is not equally represented in the governance bodies at the metropolitan level. Generally speaking, economic actors are more involved and hold more important positions than civic or cultural groups (Jouve and Lefèvre 2006). This is specifically true in some countries like the UK, where the private sector occupies important decision-making positions such as in the Regional Development Agencies or in London. However, this situation is not confined to the British case and can be found in other European cities where, for instance, chambers of commerce or business associations hold key positions such as in Turin, Venice, Stuttgart, and Madrid.

In both the United States and Europe, proponents of regional governance have launched innovative activities that seek to build a new vision of the region and promote new connections among its members. But this process-oriented approach has been long on aspirations and short on accomplishments. In the United States, efforts at regional governance have emerged mainly as business campaigns to market the region. In Europe, experiments in regional collaboration have attracted more widespread interest on the part of local and state political actors. However, even the most promising experiments in Europe, such as that in Bologna, have been short-term and subject to reversal by political opponents. Moreover, the dominance of business organizations in both U.S. and European collaborations, raises serious questions about the democratic capacity of these experiments in regional governance.

4. Discussion

The meager results of efforts to create regional governments or to promote regional governance present classic examples of the challenges that confront institutional change. All forms of institutional analysis argue that institutions are hard to alter because entrenched constituencies have the incentive and the power to block change (Steinmo and Thelen 1992; Hall and Taylor 1996). Conflicts over regional governments and governance are centrally concerned with questions about what powers different governments should have over which set of decisions. For local governments, their residents, and organized interests within them regional institutions present a threat to valued local powers. In the United States, these include the power to control land use, to tax, and to spend. These powers mean that local jurisdictional boundaries can serve as powerful signals about the character and stability of communities (Weiher 1991). Regional institutions also threaten existing power relationships. Interests that can influence local decisions often fear that their power will be diluted by the creation of new regional decision-making arenas. In the United States, groups ranging from local property organizations to minority groups have opposed regional initiatives on these grounds (Weir 2000b; Powell 2002). In Europe, the situation is much the same. The fight against regional institution building has been essentially carried out by municipalities and provinces (counties) afraid of losing control over their own jurisdiction but also of having to obey the new regional entities. Given these inherent obstacles to change, institutional theories would predict that only in unusual instances where older constraints are lifted—such as in the case of Madrid in Spain's transition from authoritarianism—will strong regional institutions emerge.

Another model of institutional change, however, suggests that more incremental approaches might lead to the creation of regional institutions. Precisely because it is so difficult to abolish institutions, evolutionary approaches to institutional change suggest that layering a new institution on top of an older one can lead to significant transformation over time as the new institution gradually gains authority (Thelen 2004). The regional governance approach is similar to a strategy of institutional layering. Rather than posing a direct challenge to local governments, regional governance strategies seek to create new opportunities for regional interaction in order to consider issues of common concern. Such convening institutions have little direct authority and, as such, are unlikely to arouse much opposition. Yet, the hope is that through such collaboration, politicians and other groups may come to reassess their interests and find common ground. An initial aim of the collaboration is, therefore, to overcome "the defensive and parochial" stance of local governments that Wood identified in the early 1960s. In the longer run, advocates of regional collaboration see such shifts in interests as a step along the way to building more authoritative regional institutions.

In practice, however, the regional tables and strategic planning processes have rarely progressed toward establishing stronger regional institutions. In the United States, Metropolitan Planning Organizations, created by national transportation legislation in 1991, failed to gain strength over time, and instead found their authority eroded by local governments and national political actors (Weir, Rongerude, and Ansell 2009). Many European countries enacted measures to create regional institutions but these initiatives never resulted in subnational implementation. Such failures suggest that one of the persistent problems confronting regional institution building can be traced to the locally-rooted opposition identified in the earliest analyses of regional institutions.

The most ardent advocates of regional institutions remain planners, and occasionally politicians or business groups. They are animated by many of the same issues related to efficiency and long-term growth patterns that concerned the early "consolidationists" who advocated regional government. It has been much harder to build broad-based support among citizens and local political officials for addressing these long-term problems. Not surprisingly opposition is strongest to general-purpose regional institutions that could interfere with the benefits of fragmentation enjoyed by a majority of urban residents. Accordingly, in the United States, regionalism's greatest successes have been business-backed, project-specific efforts designed to improve the long-term economic viability of the region. Such initiatives often require access to higher levels of government for taxing and spending authority. For example, in the 1990s, business interests in Denver spearheaded a campaign to create a regional transportation system that first required building power at the state level. In Europe, examples of such regional successes are many in specific policy sectors such as public transport and planning but generally have not been backed by business interests but by senior governments such as national states (France, the Netherlands, Portugal) or regional (i.e. subnational) states (Spain, Germany).

The experience with regional institution building in Europe and the United States suggests some fruitful directions for future research. Perhaps most salient is the need to examine multilevel political and policy processes. Given the difficulty of creating general regional institutions, regional approaches are most likely to emerge in specific policy areas. The ability of groups to set the rules of the game at higher levels of government has always played a central role in shaping patterns of regional engagement (Sellers 2002). How those rules work in specific policy domains—especially related to infrastructure, housing, and social services—and the fate of efforts to change the rules are both critical questions for future research. Borrowing from theories of international relations, regional research should identify the power of actors to operate in multiple political arenas, with particular attention to the ways actors outside the region can use their influence to alter politics in the region (Keck and Sikkink 1998). These questions take research about regional institutions back to issues of power and the distribution of resources that became less prominent as the focus shifted to collaboration and governance in the 1990s.

5. Conclusion

Across the world, the tremendous growth of cities over the last century has raised questions about whether new encompassing forms of regional coordination are needed to promote efficiency, growth, and opportunity. The reemergence of these old questions indicates that the public choice model of fragmented government has continued to rouse dissatisfaction from those concerned with questions of efficiency and long-term patterns of metropolitan development. Yet the outcome of the most recent wave of regional institution building suggests that the power of local interests to block or contain regional institution building remains strong.

In these debates, the American bias in favor of local control has made it an outlier in failing to create formal metropolitan institutions. In other parts of the world, and in Europe in particular, central governments have succeeded in enacting top-down reforms intended to create metropolitan governing capabilities, but in most cases, the new institutions have not taken hold. Instead, in both Europe and America, bottom-up efforts at collaboration, incremental institutional building, and strategic planning characterize the contemporary process of building regional institutions. But moving from government to governance does not guarantee the success of metropolitan institution building. Unless there is a strong political leadership to carry the process forward and a political legitimacy of the metropolitan area, it is impossible to build enduring institutions at the metropolitan scale. Such conditions are not easily met because building new institutions is a conflictual process since it aims at establishing metropolitan areas as new political spaces (Boudreau and Keil 2004).

REFERENCES

Altshuler, A. et al. eds. 1999. *Governance and Opportunity in Metropolitan America.* Washington, DC: National Academy Press.

Bish, R. L. and V. Ostrom. 1973. *Understanding Urban Government: Metropolitan Reform Reconsidered.* Washington, DC: American Enterprise Institute.

Boudreau, J-A. and R. Keil. 2004. "In Search of a New Political Space? City-Regional Institution-Building and Social Activism in Toronto." Paper presented at the Annual Meeting of the Association of American Geographers, Philadelphia (March 15–19).

Briffault, R. 1990. "Our Localism: Part I The Structure of Local Government Law." *Columbia Law Review* 90(1):1–115.

Dodge, W. R. and K. Montgomery. 1996. *Shaping a Region's Future: A Guide to Strategic Decision Making for Regions.* Washington, DC: National League of Cities.

Dreier, P., J. Mollenkopf, and T. Swanstrom. 2001. *Place Matters: Metropolitics for the Twenty-first Century.* Lawrence: University Press of Kansas.

Foster, K. A. 1997. *The Political Economy of Special-Purpose Government.* Washington, DC: Georgetown University Press.

———. 2001. *Regionalism on Purpose.* Cambridge, MA: Lincoln Institute of Land Policy.

Frenzel, A. 2002. "Institutional Policy in a Federal State: The Creation of the Urban Region of Stuttgart." *In Search of Urban Gargantuas: The New Territories of Politics in Europe*, B. Jouve and C. Lefèvre, eds. Frank Cass: London.

Gulick, L. 1957. *Metro: Changing Problems and Lines of Attack*. Washington: Government Affairs Institute.

Hall, P. A. and R. C. R. Taylor. 1996. "Political Science and the Three New Institutionalisms." *Political Studies* 44:936–57.

Jones, V. 1942. *Metropolitan Government*. Chicago: University of Chicago Press.

Jouve, B. and C. Lefèvre. 2006. "The Organization of Government in European Metropolitan Areas." *Urban Public Economics Review* 6: 91–112.

Keating, M. 1995. "Size, Efficiency and Democracy: Consolidation, Fragmentation and Public Choice." *Theories of Urban Politics*, D. Judge, G. Stoker, and H. Wolman, eds. Thousand Oaks, CA: Sage.

Keck, M. and K. Sikkink. 1998. *Activists beyond Borders: Advocacy Networks in International Politics*. Ithaca, NY: Cornell University Press.

Lefèvre, C. 2009. *Gouverner les métropoles*. Paris: Dexia-LGDJ.

Lowrey, D. C. 2000. "A Transactions Costs Model of Metropolitan Governance: Allocation versus Redistribution in Urban America." *Journal of Public Administration Research and Theory* 10:49–78.

OECD 2001. *Cities for Citizens: Improving Metropolitan Governance*. Paris: OECD.

Ostrom, V., C. Tiebout, and R. Warren. 1961. "The Organization of Government in Metropolitan Areas: A Theoretical Inquiry." *American Political Science Review* 55:831–42.

Orfield, M. 2002. *American Metropolitics: The New Suburban Reality*. Washington, DC: Brookings Institution Press.

Pagano, M. A. 1999. "Metropolitan Limits: Intrametropolitan Disparities and Governance in U.S. Laboratories of Democracy." *Governance and Opportunity in Metropolitan America*, A. Altshuler et al., eds. Washington, DC: National Academy Press.

Pastor, M. Jr., C. Benner, and M. Matsuoka. 2009. *This Could Be the Start of Something Big*. Ithaca, NY: Cornell University Press.

Peirce, N. R., C. W. Johnson, and J. S. Hall. 1993. *Citistates: How Urban America Can Prosper in a Competitive World*. Washington, DC: Seven Locks Press.

Powell, J. 2002. "Sprawl, Fragmentation, and the Persistence of Racial Inequality: Limiting Civil Rights by Fragmenting Space." In *Urban Sprawl: Causes, Consequences and Policy Responses*, G. D. Squires, ed. Washington DC: Urban Institute Press.

Rodriguez-Alvarez, J. M. 2002. "Madrid: Le pilotage politique par la région." In *Métropoles ingouvernables: Les villles européennes entre globalisation et décentralisation*, B. Jouve and C. Lefèvre, eds. Elsevier: Paris.

Rusk, D. 1993. *Cities without Suburbs*. Washington, DC: Woodrow Wilson Center Press (distributed by Johns Hopkins University Press).

Sellers, J. 2002. *Governing from Below: Urban Regions and the Global Economy*. New York: Cambridge University Press.

Sharpe, L. J. 1995. *The Government of World Cities: The Future of the Metro Model*. Chichester: John Wiley & Sons.

Teaford, J. C. 1979. *City and Suburb: The Political Fragmentation of Metropolitan America, 1850–1970*. Baltimore: Johns Hopkins University Press.

Thelen, K. 2004. *How Institutions Evolve: The Political Economy of Skills in Germany, Britain, the United States, and Japan*. New York: Cambridge University Press.

Thelen, K. and S. Steinmo. 1992. "Historical Institutionalism in Comparative Politics." *Structuring Politics Historical Institutionalism in Comparative Analysis.* New York: Cambridge University Press.

Tiebout, C. M. 1956. "A Pure Theory of Local Expenditures." *Journal of Political Economy* 64(5):416–24.

Weiher, G. R. 1991. *The Fractured Metropolis: Political Fragmentation and Metropolitan Segregation.* Albany: State University of New York Press.

Weir, M. 2000a. "Coalition-building for Regionalism." In *Reflections on Regionalism,* B. J. Katz, ed. Washington, DC: Brookings Institution Press.

Weir, M.. 2000b. "Planning, Environmentalism, and Urban Poverty: The Political Failure of National Land Use Planning Legislation, 1970–1975." In *The American Planning Tradition: Culture and Policy,* R. Fishman, ed. Washington DC: Woodrow Wilson Center Press.

Weir, M., J. Rongerude, and C. Ansell. 2009. "Collaboration Is Not Enough: Virtuous Cycles of Reform in Transportation Policy." *Urban Affairs Review* 44(4):455–89.

Wood, R. C. 1958. "Metropolitan Government, 1975: An Extrapolation of Trends. The New Metropolis: Green Belts, Grass Roots or Gargantua?" *American Political Science Review* 52(1):108–22.

———. 1961. *1400 Governments: The Political Economy of the New York Metropolitan Region.* Cambridge, MA: Harvard University Press.

CHAPTER 32

EMERGING RESEARCH AGENDAS

SUSAN E. CLARKE

THERE is growing interest in comparative urban research, both conducted as systematic empirical comparisons as well as in analysis of themes, processes, and trajectories common to urban settings.[1] The development of information and communication technologies allowing quick access to data and information sources and reliable means of sharing research played an important role in encouraging comparative cross-national research. As a result, it now is more possible to think of a "comparative urban research agenda" than in the past when urban scholars turned to their own setting, with all its peculiarities, as a feasible and affordable research arena.

In the absence of significant funding for cross-national comparative urban research, until recently most comparative projects relied on the entrepreneurial efforts of individual scholars and the goodwill and internal subsidies provided by colleagues sharing this intellectual interest. The Fiscal Austerity and Urban Innovation (FAUI) project launched by Terry Clark in 1982 exemplifies these early efforts: the original U.S.-based survey was conducted by faculty and students using access to "free" phone

Initial version presented to the Political Studies Association Annual Conference, Edinburgh, March 2010. Many thanks to PSA participants, Karen Mossberger, and Peter John for helpful comments.

1. This is a common observation (see Robinson, 2011). I also draw on my experience as an editor of *Urban Affairs Review* (an interdisciplinary urban journal) since 2001 when we made an editorial commitment to increase the number of non-U.S. articles and authors published in the journal. The number of non-U.S. submissions and articles published in *UAR* has increased significantly, now averaging six per year.

services to conduct over 1,400 municipal interviews with mayors, council members, and administrators in all 50 states using a common research design and standardized protocol. Through panels at international conferences, this project disseminated to over 38 countries with the protocol being adjusted for local contexts. A database on 10,000 local governments is now available free of charge to any urban scholars interested in comparative analyses.[2] No central funding was involved although Clark estimates the various research teams have raised a total of about $20 million to cover their costs. Without Clark's enthusiasm and relentless promotion of FAUI's innovative decentralized research program, it is unlikely that the resources and networks for comparative urban research would have been available to this generation of scholars.

Decades later, the prospects for comparative urban research seem brighter and less arduous. Though still not abundant, funding is available through foundations and the EU along with some national funding agencies (the U.S. National Science Foundation remains notably chary of funding urban research, much less comparative urban research). And thanks to technological developments, "virtual" collaboration of international networks of scholars is feasible and familiar. During this same period, the salience of cities as an intellectual focus became greater as globalization and economic restructuring disrupted industrial urban hierarchies and challenged theoretical assumptions.

1. An Audacious Venture

We now appear to be in the midst of a similarly unsettling time, which makes the forthcoming *Oxford Handbook of Urban Politics* an especially timely and notable venture. Although not designed to be a comparative urban politics volume, the editors hoped to move beyond a U.S.-centric volume and encompass the perspectives of urban scholars in the UK, Canada, Europe, and elsewhere. The emphasis was on providing agenda-setting essays developed—where possible—by pairs of authors from different countries; as a result, the coverage is at least transatlantic and thematically comparative.[3] The chapter topics themselves reflect the evolution of urban research in the last decades, addressing issues that were not often of concern until recently. In this essay, I draw out some of the emerging themes evident in these chapters as the potential core for future urban research agendas that would be enriched by further comparative work.[4] Across chapters, there is notable concern

2. See the FAUI website: http://faui.uchicago.edu/about.html.

3. This audacious experiment involved matching of authors by the editors; in some instances, invited authors would suggest a colleague who met our cross-national criteria. There was also an effort to bring in junior scholars wherever possible.

4. Since these arguments are drawn from essays in this *Handbook*, quotations are drawn from the chapters being discussed and are not cited otherwise.

that many of the trends and changing conditions impacting cities—ranging from competition challenges to urban insecurity to sustainability rhetoric—contribute to depoliticization of fundamental governing questions. In addition, the recognition of complexity and differentiation brings an emphasis on the need for multilevel analysis: although cities may be the focal point for analysis and salient arena for policy strategies, the challenges shaping urban politics clearly emanate elsewhere even as they are shaped and structured by local political and social processes.

2. Emerging Themes

2.1. Power as the Core Concept

Although approaches to the study of power, and subsequent interpretations, have evolved over past decades, the concept of power remains the core feature of the study of urban politics. The concept of power links the study of local or urban politics to the broader study of political science; analyzing power at the local level offers a window on larger political dynamics as well as on the varying ways global and national forces intersect at the local level.

Stone weighs these possibilities while acknowledging that power remains an elusive and debated concept. Nevertheless, he argues that urbanists can productively approach power through a focus on agency and context. Drawing on Alan Harding's recent (2009) overview, Stone centers local power in collective, place-shaping decisions and asks who is included and excluded from these processes. Rather than focus on individual decisions, as in earlier community power studies, Stone emphasizes directionality and flow—what is the trajectory of decisions shaping place and how do we account for changes or modifications in this flow of decisions? To Stone, place-shaping choices are not narrowly concerned with economic development. Instead, they encompass education, crime, security, and other elements of local community. Similarly, he argues for a focus on efforts to orchestrate the relationships among actors rather than continued exercises to identify "who governs." As in other chapters in this volume, Stone directs the urban lens to the power dynamics shaping collective choice-making and place-shaping processes.

Baldersheim and Kersting update traditional views of power in their focus on digital technology as the new face of community power. As recent events in Cairo and Tripoli make clear, the wired city reduces the costs of mobilization and increases the potential for collective action. While digital divides remain important, new communication technologies overcome many of the traditional barriers to political action. Proximity becomes less relevant if technology digitally links citizens with each other. Instant and universally available information demands a reconsideration of our notions of transparency, accountability, and participation. And as Baldersheim and Kersting point out, this new face of power is not necessarily benign.

2.2. Every City a Competitive City

A central theme of the volume is the impact of globalization on urban politics. In contrast to an initial sense of "the death of distance," the prevalent viewpoint now highlights the resurgence of urban politics as cities are recognized as the engines of growth in postindustrial economies. This focus on urban vitality reflects the importance of specialized labor in knowledge economies—Reich's "symbolic analysts" and Florida's "creative class"—as well as the service workers needed to support these new economic networks and production processes. While these specialized labor groups can communicate and collaborate "virtually" in global networks, they also require locales that are attractive for work and lifestyle needs. Generally these are not the industrial cities dominant in the past (although some have made this transition) but new locations with the physical, social, cultural, and intangible amenities attractive to this sector.

As a result, there is a new global hierarchy of cities, with a general consensus that New York, Tokyo, and London are truly global cities. The other tiers of the hierarchy, however, are contested. This is due to the multiple schemas of global cities available, each using different criteria, but also because the salient factors of production that generated urban hierarchies in the past are not as obvious now. This more porous hierarchy is open to multiple locations who "believe" they are capable of capturing a position in this global hierarchy through local efforts at targeting specialized firms and providing amenities that are attractive. To many, this is encouraged by neoliberal strategies promoting competitiveness and often resulting in greater inequalities and weaker state roles.

Garcia and Judd contend that this openness and fluidity increases the imperative for every city to compete for investment. Not only do cities think they can and should compete, increasingly they must compete with other cities for private investment as central government support declines. As they note, this is a stark divergence from the historical context of most cities outside the U.S.: in contrast to American cities, most European cities and cities elsewhere rose as political, cultural, and administrative centers. Faced now with the need to compete, European cities in particular confront a new set of demands and dilemmas. Although every city may now be a competitive city, cultural differences persist: American cities continue to face these competitive challenges in the absence of any national policy framework while European cities do so structured by national and EU policies.

Yet as Kantor and Turok point out, within this intercity competition, "the pattern of strong and weak performing cities in Europe and North America" is not well-understood. They see this lack of an overarching theory or paradigm as positive to the extent that it encourages scholars to reach out to other fields and back to disciplinary mainstreams. One of the key reasons European and American scholarship differs on these issues is again cultural differences: "in western Europe, more centralized governmental conditions, the power of the public sector, and different civic traditions diminish the role of private elites in local development" whereas the American setting highlights the resources and legitimacy privileging private economic elites.

Garcia and Judd see common research questions generated by this new competitive reality: in the face of these challenges and the current economic crisis, are we likely to see greater intercity competition or new issues of social and environmental sustainability? If the latter, how do city leaders redirect their priorities toward issues of social and environmental sustainability, how do they influence their respective national government's priorities, and how do they balance competitive concerns and social justice? Indeed, they conclude by predicting that "the concept of the Just City is likely to become as important as the Competitive City in future research."

Seeing growth and decline as part of the same development continuum, Kantor and Turok argue for richer and more nuanced comparative analyses of the diverse institutional arrangements for economic development and their concrete effects on economic performance and social conditions. Special attention to the politics of decentralization in urban development is merited as this trend gains ground throughout the Western industrial world and, as Stren points out, in the less developed world as well. Finally, they highlight an issue only hinted at in Garcia and Judd's discussion of amenities and locational advantage: images and perceptions of cities—branding, if you will—are increasingly powerful even if they may often bear little relation to objective conditions.

Dowding and Feiock consider local competition and cooperation from a different standpoint—looking at cities in terms of service provision. This includes competition among service providers within a city and between jurisdictions within a metropolitan area. Their anticipation of increased cooperation stems from the very difficulties of maintaining the "pure conditions for competition" in the urban sphere—"the complex nature of the goods and services provided, the high search and exit, and noisy signals for public authorities from such market movements" ensure that "competition alone will not bring efficiency." In the absence of pure competition, there is a need for some form of local institutional collective action.

To Dowding and Feiock, the institutional collective action (ICA) framework offers a robust analytic strategy for understanding this complex system of cooperation and competition. By applying theories of individual collective action to institutional actors such as cities, counties, special districts, and partnerships, the ICA approach moves beyond the conventional focus on regional authorities or centralized consolidation as a way to solve collective action problems. Instead, we anticipate multiple types of cooperative systems—more or less self-organized—allowing more or less formal cooperation between and among local jurisdictions. This array of collaboration modes includes mechanisms for cooperation on economic development strategies, thus providing a trajectory from competition to cooperation that frames the competitive city viewpoint.

2.3. The Depoliticization of Poverty

Poverty is a constant and continuous theme in the urban literature. More recently, particularly in the European context, it is approached as social exclusion. This emphasis on social exclusion rather than income-based poverty measures recognizes the multiple dimensions of well-being; for policymakers, it raises the challenge of increasing well-being rather than increasing income alone through bureaucratic transfers. As Paugam contends (1995) poverty is a necessary but not sufficient condition for the creation of exclusion. This new poverty agenda has generated a host of innovative, often nonelectoral, institutional designs that bring many questions of efficiency, legitimacy, democratic accountability, and cross-sector collaboration to the urban research agenda. It also highlights the ways in which problem definitions structure policy solutions, in this instance leading to weak or misspecified policies and depoliticization of poverty.

While a social exclusion approach more accurately reflects the contextual nature of poverty and the diversity within poor and disadvantaged groups, Atkinson and Swanstrom contend that it also encourages "a depoliticized approach to poverty that obscures the underlying conflicts inherent in poverty policies." They trace this impact to the contested nature of the social exclusion concept itself. They also argue that social exclusion is difficult for policymakers to measure, often leading to indicators that fail to tap into the multiple dimensions of importance. Furthermore, the concept can obscure some of the hard political choices needed to reduce poverty and improve well-being. They note the familiar and common argument that "economic competitiveness depends on social cohesion, or inclusion" as an especially pernicious prescription that blurs the trade-offs necessary to truly confront poverty and exclusion.

The United States has been slow to consider social exclusion concepts although the Obama administration's recent initiative to revisit consumption-based poverty measures used in the U.S. since the 1960s signals the prospect of more relational measures. Instead of social exclusion, the recent policy focus is on poverty concentration in American cities (and increasingly, in suburbs). As Atkinson and Swanstrom note, this is somewhat similar to a social exclusion approach in that concentration of poverty is seen as disconnecting the poor from opportunities to become part of the mainstream economy (and society). This problem definition points to policies encouraging community development of poor neighborhoods or dispersion of the poor into areas with greater opportunity. Both have been tried in American cities, with ambiguous results. Both are criticized, especially dispersal strategies, for weakening the electoral and political clout of poor and minority communities.

Both the European and American experiences draw attention to the importance of the neighborhood context in which poverty occurs. Although still subject to challenge, as Horak and Blokland note, there is growing evidence that "neighborhood effects" matter. This is common ground for U.S. and European analyses in that neighborhoods are featured as providing opportunity structures that appear to intensify or ameliorate the disconnections facing the poor (Murie and Musterd

2004). In terms of research agendas, this recognition of neighborhood effects opens the poverty debate to noneconomic contextual factors and also to more multiscalar analyses. This is not an argument that poverty and social exclusion can be resolved at the neighborhood level. Rather there is a need for a better understanding of how forces playing out at multiple levels—global, national, regional, city, neighborhood—contribute to social exclusion. In the absence of such analyses, effective policy remains beyond our grasp.

2.4. The Formalization of Insecurity

Along with globalization, many cities face increased violence and even terrorism. This dark side of globalization is supported by the same technological developments that make communication and migration of people and jobs so viable. The inequalities rendered by these processes are apparent at every scale. Yet Body-Gendrot and Savitch claim that deprivation theory is not sufficient in explaining the incidence of urban collective violence occurring in disparate cities. Using Los Angeles 1992 and Paris 2005 as exemplars, they develop an interactive framework that analyzes the rioting in those cities in terms of mobilization potential, triggering events, preparations, regime stability, and political/bureaucratic response. This framework allows them to compare urban violence in these cities and to highlight the roles of the media, experts, and political elites in amplifying urban risks. It also allows them to address the counterfactual: why don't riots occur more often in situations where we might expect them? From this perspective, they argue the formalization of insecurity is becoming a unified and unifying trend across urban settings and a new focus for research.

Keil and Whitehead add to this agenda by recognizing the new paradigm of "ecological security" (Hodson and Marvin 2009) as an increasingly significant urban concern. As they put it, this introduces a politics of resilience rather than sustainability, given the realities of disasters and terrorism threatening cities with a series of "severe step changes" in unpredictable and unexpected ways. "Whereas sustainability highlights the importance of creating harmonious feedback between social, environmental, and economic systems, a politics of resilience openly recognizes that even if this goal were possible, the time for its potential achievement has long since passed most cities by." Yet the "high impact, low probability" nature of these ecological challenges means many local officials find it difficult to mobilize around resilience needs, much less create sustained and durable coalitions to prepare for events which may never happen (Clarke and Chenoweth 2006). While the media and political elites amplify the risks of urban terrorism, ecological risks are more contested and diffuse. Thus ecological security is perhaps as significant a threat but one facing more convoluted urban political processes. It would be interesting to test whether Body-Gendrot and Savitch's interactive framework—mobilization potential, triggering events, preparations, regime stability, and political/bureaucratic response—would be similarly insightful in analysis of ecological security.

2.5. The Reconfiguration of Identity-Based Politics

Marschall and Shah underscore the continuing centrality of racial and ethnic politics in American communities and its growing significance in European cities. But they also acknowledge that the landscape is changing as communities become more multicultural and diverse. Although in no way disputing the continued realities of stratification by racial, ethnic, gender, sexuality, class, disabilities, and other key distinctions, these identities often are being reconfigured at the local level. As cities become more diverse, we might expect an increase in identity-based politics as inequalities become more stark. Hero and Orr note Putnam's (2007) disturbing finding that the larger and more diverse the city, the lower the social capital. But in many ways, identities are increasingly destabilized as group identities intersect with other factors—such as social capital, class, education—that make mobilization and choice more strategic and less predictable. As Marschall and Shah document, the growth of multiracial cities—where no racial or ethnic group is large enough to be an electoral majority—in the U.S. is striking. A growing number of smaller towns as well as large cities, in every region of the U.S., are likely to be multiracial. Socio-spatial segregation and inequalities are persistent and, as Horak and Blokland note, appear to be increasing in some European cities.

But the differences *among* groups sharing an identity, rather than differences *between* identity groups may be the most critical in political terms.[5] Indeed, the Pew Center's findings (2007) that more than one-third of African-Americans doubt that the black population of the United States is any longer a single people is a reminder of these new realities. While ethnic or racial stratification will persist, future research agendas need to allow for more fluid categories, a hybridity that undermines conventional political expectations (Kasnitz et al. 2002).

Local political representation is contingent upon, but not determined by, these changing local conditions. Marschall and Shah emphasize that these conditions are mediated by local electoral structures and electoral patterns of minority representation. As they see it, researchers need to move beyond a focus on "crossover" voting to begin to untangle the coalitional politics underlying subnational political representation patterns. In American cities, electoral structures encourage "deracialized" electoral campaigns in order to mobilize sufficient electoral majorities; in European cities, with different electoral rules and structures, these may be less likely. But the common analytic thread is the question of whether, how, when, and where these changing conditions shape local politics—and, as Marschall and Shah ask, whether it makes a difference.

The conflation of race, ethnicity, and immigration status often obscures the political implications of these cross-group dynamics. Immigration trends underlie many of the analyses here but Garbaye and Mollenkopf highlight the low rates of electoral mobilization and local immigrant political representation in North

5. Drawn from Clarke (2008). Several chapters—Marschall and Shah, Horak and Blokland, Garbaye and Mollenkopf—also emphasize the importance of these relationships.

American and European cities. Their comparison of immigrant political incorporation in Los Angeles and New York City directs our attention to the importance of local political structures, dynamics, and histories in shaping immigrant access to decision-making power. Again, they call attention to differences in the degree and forms of local immigrant political incorporation within and between European countries and across the U.S. Like Marschall and Shah, they emphasize the role of electoral structures in supporting or suppressing local immigrant voice but they also document the importance of political parties and vigorous political competition in increasing immigrant access to power.

2.6. The Cultural Turn

In a rather uneven fashion, "the cultural turn" is emerging in urban political studies. Sharp and Brown argue that the "narrow focus on state-centered urban politics occludes extremely important politics across the realms of civil society, the home, and family" which are grounded in locales and communities. In recognizing the significance of this broader range of political activity, it is necessary to extend the empirical scope of urban political studies to encompass these salient issues. But this is a topic where U.S. and European differences are especially distinct. The "culture wars" that rage in American cities are less prevalent in European cities since many of the regulatory powers that set off these conflicts in American cities—siting of abortion clinics, same-sex marriage, regulation of pornography, siting of medical marijuana dispensaries, even gun control—are not local powers in Europe. Nevertheless, Sharp and Brown note that "urban cultural politics is increasingly taking the form of so-called 'quality-of-life' policies in which city government attempts to regulate allegedly antisocial behavior." In this sense, such quality-of-life policies are less constrained by allocation of public authority than by electoral pressures and public opinion and are likely to become more prevalent across cities.

The belated and uneven attention to cultural issues in part reflects this different allocation of powers and authority in diverse settings. But our current paradigms also limit such analyses. While regimes are, by definition, durable governing coalitions, Sharp and Brown remind us that "culture-war controversies tend to be explosive but episodic and the organized interests involved therein may not necessarily be continuously involved in other areas of local governance." Neither regime nor governance approaches are likely to be adequate analytic frameworks for understanding cultural conflicts.

This becomes more urgent when we recognize that immigration and changing demographic mixes in localities will bring religious and linguistic conflicts to the fore, independent of formal subnational structures. Many recent urban analyses, for example Garbaye (2006), address these contemporary dilemmas with similar critiques of our theoretical capacity to do so. To Sharp and Brown, "conflicts over traits like religion and language raise the importance of appreciating nationalism as a framework for understanding social and electoral cleavages in many world cities." Rather than an impasse or stalemate, they see increased study of cultural conflict and religion as likely to "reinvigorate *urban* political research by bringing urban scholarship into the discussions of morality issues and of religion and politics that mark other subfields of political science."

2.7. Urban Politics of Sustainability

Several authors identify issues of sustainability as a significant condition now facing city officials and a new priority on the urban research agenda. Even scholars not directly addressing sustainability matters see the growing concern with sustainability opening up new questions about intercity competition (Garcia and Judd), justice (Campbell and Fainstein), regional governance (Lefevre and Weir) and other major intellectual agendas. The new urgency on climate warming and sustainability is pushing urban scholars to see connections with their own work, rather than viewing sustainability as an isolated environmental concern. As Keil and Whitehead put it, even though a sustainability lens views the city in holistic, ecological terms, the sustainability "fix" has decidedly territorial connotations.

In Campbell and Fainstein's terms, sustainability provides normative criteria for evaluating urban justice through what Keil and Whitehead characterize as "a paradigm of urban development that recognizes the ecological costs of urban wealth creation, and the need for a more socially inclusive and energy restrained metropolitan future." It also raises questions about the conditions under which some cities choose to pursue more sustainable development practices—and whether these choices are actually reflected in more sustainable local outcomes.

Yet Keil and Whitehead contend that this holistic sustainable city vision also supports "the reformist depoliticization of urban policy" by acting as "a powerful consensual device for claiming and shaping space around a relatively narrow set of reformist agendas." In a provocative argument, they counter "the assumption that the sustainable city ideal represents a challenge to the political structures, economic imperatives, and environmental relations associated with neoliberal urbanization." Rather, they claim that the politics of sustainable city formation require more careful analysis of the "power dynamics that are shaping what types of sustainable cities are being built, and for whom such urban places are being created." In particular, they note that businesses take on a new role in urban economies—increasingly promising not only growth and efficiency but the ability to deliver the ecological technologies and green innovations city officials seek.

Keil and Whitehead cite the importance of Molotch's (1976) classic work on the growth machine thesis as integral to understanding the power dynamics in sustainable urban development. While they do not ultimately claim that antigrowth movements were precursors of sustainable development demands, they draw on Molotch's focus on business's and governments' mutual interests in growth to characterize the ways in which sustainability discourse now "cloaks" the growth machine. As a result, Keil and Whitehead warn that sustainability agendas can create a sense of well-being, social unity, and collective purpose while legitimating "politics as usual" in these uncertain times. Their skepticism extends to questioning whether cities proclaiming local sustainable development policies can be shown empirically to produce sustainability gains. Their critical assessment of sustainable urban development foregrounds the power relations implicit in sustainability agendas.

2.8. Weak Regional Institutional Building

Lefevre and Weir ask us to explain the failure of regional institution building in both the U.S. and Europe—as they see it, most major North American and European metropolitan areas did not have true metropolitan government at the end of the twentieth century. In their view, local resistance to regionalism is universal even if local autonomy varies. They recognize the continued efforts at regional institution building, particularly in Europe, but note there are few cases where metropolitan government is actually implemented. The U.S. is recognized as a true outlier, given traditions of local control, although they acknowledge innovative initiatives such as Metropolitan Planning Organizations for transit planning. But even in Europe, where regionalism is more likely to be appreciated as an efficient solution to fragmented authority and complex multilevel problems, Lefevre and Weir see little headway in carrying out the reforms of the past decade. Instead, they contend that "in both Europe and America, bottom-up efforts at collaboration, incremental institutional building, and strategic planning characterize the contemporary process of building regional institutions." To them, this is not the recipe for success—in particular, "moving from government to governance does not guarantee the success of metropolitan institution building." In the absence of political leadership and a sense of political legitimacy for the metropolitan area, Lefevre and Weir are not sanguine about the prospects of creating enduring institutions at the metropolitan scale.

Their critique is not aimed at the reform efforts themselves but at the need to better understand the multilevel politics involved. The regional research agenda, in Lefevre and Weir's perspective, must identify the actors in multiple political arenas—especially those outside the region—who can use their influence to alter politics in the region. In their view, this political focus on power and resources has been lost as the regional agenda became dominated by issues of collaboration and governance in the last decade. As a result, research on regional institution building with insufficient attention to politics cannot account for the continued failed reforms.

Keil and Whitehead echo this interpretation. They see this regionalization process as "more political than pragmatic" as new unelected regional elites and alliances "utilize the discursive promises of sustainable development and ecological modernization in order to gain strategic power over urban policy and key metropolitan resources." Similar to their argument on growth machines, the sustainability discourse can "cloak" regionalism initiatives in ways that distort and obscure the political struggles entailed.

Dowding and Feiock capture these tensions in their taxonomy of collaborative institutions: it arrays initiatives "according to whether the coordination mechanism relies primarily on political authority, legal or contractual arrangements, or social embeddedness and the extent to which the terms of a governance arrangement are subject to bargaining by individual members." By allowing decision making across local government units in a metropolitan area to be more integrated (Feiock 2004; 2009), these mechanisms introduce a variety of ways in which regional decision making and cooperation might be realized.

2.9. Is "Small" the New Big?[6]

In the shifting references to "local," "subnational," "urban," "communities," and "place" throughout this volume there is an implicit recognition that multiscalar politics are in play. This becomes explicit in Horak and Blokland's analysis of neighborhood politics in North America and Europe. While they find differences in central-local relations account for less socio-spatial inequalities in European cities, they also note that such inequalities are nevertheless increasingly evident. This is especially so where immigrant enclaves persist in many European cities. It also attends the growing presence of private, often gated, communities and partitioning of cities into distinct sectors noted by McKenzie (1994) as a global phenomenon. As a result, a growing set of European policy initiatives focus on the neighborhood as the scale at which to address poverty, social inclusion, and well-being. In many instances, these initiatives include efforts to increase the neighborhood's capacity to act as "a collective agent," in their terms; this could lead to more widespread neighborhood politics, as in the U.S. Yet they delineate a common tension between the goals of neighborhood agency and of reducing socio-spatial inequality in both American and European cities. More comparative cross-national work could test the many puzzles attendant to this renewed focus on neighborhoods, but Horak and Blokland also stress the need for more multilevel analyses that incorporate the historical trajectory of neighborhood experiences.

Suburban politics fit this scalar focus as well, even though some American suburbs are now larger, more dense, and more diverse than central cities. As Oliver argues, it is difficult to conceptualize and theorize suburban politics because it may well be that there is more variation within the "suburban" category than differences between "city" and "suburb." The many stereotypes and media portrayals of American suburbs belie actual trends toward the suburbanization of poverty, immigrant suburban settlement, and many other common decentralizing trends in the U.S., Canada, and Europe. Oliver's argument for an analytic framework mapping suburbs in terms of variation in population size, economic composition, racial composition, land use, and type of governing structure invites comparative research on the political consequences of these settlement patterns.

6. Denver, Colorado's Neighborhood Market Initiative proclaims "small is the new big" in emphasizing neighborhood business districts as an economic development strategy.

2.10. Prospects for the Just City

Many of the authors share a concern with the prospect for a more just city and the conditions under which it might be achieved. To name a few: Garcia and Judd ask whether greater intercity competition will push this issue off the agenda, Keil and Whitehead see justice as integral to sustainability but "cloaked" and displaced by sustainability rhetoric, Atkinson and Swanstrom highlight the depoliticization of poverty in social exclusion discourse. Campbell and Fainstein add to this debate with a direct assessment of values associated with a just city and the issues to be addressed.

Their analysis confirms the turn away from economic definitions of inequality to considerations of capacities and opportunities. But they note that the emphasis on participation and representation dominating the discourse on inequality is shifting to a focus on outcomes. To some extent, this reflects the rise of philosophical arguments emphasizing capabilities (Sen 1999; Nussbaum 2000) and also those underscoring the importance of spatial justice in Henri Lefebvre's concept of the "Right to the City." To Campbell and Fainstein, these views cause us to question whether just processes produce just outcomes—is there evidence that more inclusive processes necessarily produce just outcomes?

A view of urban justice, fitted to the realities of the urban context, considers this question of just process in terms of interest representation and participation but recognizes the substantive and spatial trade-offs involved. Campbell and Fainstein contend that a just city must attend to redistributive concerns as well as recognition needs. For example, the impact of immigration on U.S. and European cities means "the issue of recognition—whether ethnic groups should be acknowledged or pressed to assimilate—remains a political issue in both Europe and the United States." But they also point out that the extent to which local initiatives can be more or less just is shaped by important variations in service provisions, an argument reflected in Wolman's essay. So assessing urban justice, again, requires a contextualized and multiscalar approach.

In terms of a research agenda, Campbell and Fainstein identify three questions for scholars "concerned with the political economy of the just city." These include "the development of a set of normative criteria by which urban policy at various scales can be evaluated (see Fainstein 2009)," one that nests urban theory "within geographical and philosophical approaches to questions of justice" as they do in their essay. Also, they encourage more attention to "how normative concerns can be incorporated into social scientific analysis," particularly in relation to the framing of research questions. Similar to Atkinson and Swanstrom, they point out that framing the issue as "poverty" or "social exclusion" makes a difference. Both essays agree on the depoliticization of inequalities through the translation of current conceptualizations of poverty into policy prescriptions. In contrast to Atkinson and Swanstrom's emphasis on the fuzzy boundaries and weak measures of social exclusion, Campbell and Fainstein see social exclusion concepts as emphasizing individual choice, opportunity, and deficiencies with a concomitant move away from redistribution. In addition, they contend that the emphasis on levels and forms of participation dominating many political science and planning analyses diverts attention from redistributive patterns of actual policy choices. Finally, along with several other authors, Campbell and Fainstein see the global economic crisis of 2008–2009 as destabilizing many of the land development pressures at the heart of urban analyses, particularly in American cities, and potentially opening up opportunities for new housing initiatives. Although Keil and Whitehead provide a precautionary note, Campbell and Fainstein ask whether trends toward more sustainable cities offer the potential to link environmental and social justice concerns.

3. Rethinking Theories and Methods

Overall, these authors make a powerful case for an urban focus on contemporary politics. An urban lens ties down globalization trends to locales, forcing more precise analytic arguments. In particular, the recent global economic crisis vividly revealed the interdependence, complexity, and differentiation of local settings as they experienced and responded to these impacts. It is striking to note the emphasis on rhetoric and problem definitions that obscure the underlying conflicts in addressing urban poverty, insecurity, cultural differences, sustainability, and justice. As Stone puts it, the urban lens compels attention to context and agency in analyzing the power dynamics shaping collective choice-making and place-shaping processes.

In addition to these substantive themes, there is a consistent interest in enhancing the theories and methods available to address these new realities.

3.1. Turning to Governance

Two ongoing debates emerge across chapters: the viability of regime theory for comparative research and the utility of governance approaches. There are many other venues in which the regime debate is dissected (see Davies and Imbroscio 2009; Mossberger and Stoker 2001). Of interest here is the attention given to the relative merits of these approaches for addressing particular substantive concerns. Garcia and Judd, for example, highlight the ways in which variations in national and regional institutional contexts are important. The multiscalar institutional contexts in which European cities operate—especially the power of European institutions to steer local agendas through regulations and financing—make conventional understandings of regimes less useful since local coalitions and networks are more fluid and less durable. Given this variability, they argue that European scholars find governance approaches more useful because they conceptualize government in multiscalar institutional terms and anticipate multiple and shifting coalitions across scales, including state and nonstate actors (e.g. see John 2001).

To Peters and Pierre, both regime theory and urban governance approaches center on the necessary blending of public and private resources to get things done at the local level. Peters and Pierre define governance here as "the formulation and pursuit of collective goals at the local level of the political system." They are clear that "political institutions and elective office...play a leading if not dominant role in urban governance" but that these roles are changing significantly as are the processes and styles by which cities mobilize and coordinate resources. Specifically, the key change is in the role of government in governance—the process by which government steers and coordinates the actions of public institutions, market actors, and voluntary associations (see also Pierre 1999). Government is one of many actors seeking collaboration in the absence of hierarchy.

Davies and Trounstine's essay expands on this perspective, taking Kjaer's (2004) view that institutionalism grounds governance across the disciplines. From their perspective, there is an expansion of the institutional focus in the U.S. and UK to reflect the new forms of power (and depoliticization) noted here. As Davies and Trounstine point out, however, this common institutional focus leads in divergent directions with rational choice models more prevalent in the U.S. and sociological models more widespread in the UK.

Ejersbo and Svara sharpen this institutional focus with the contention that "cities cannot survive without a bureaucracy." Indeed, they argue that bureaucracies continue to do most of the work of the state and remain the "pivotal player" in local government. But bureaucracies evolve in response to changes in values, political resources, and information costs, new forms emerge—most notably New Public Management and New Governance—giving rise to more complex governance arrangements.

To Heinelt, the "inevitability" of governance raises participatory concerns and the need to reconceptualize citizenship. While Peters and Pierre recognize the normative dimension of governance arrangements, Heinelt specifically focuses on the democratic quality of governance arrangements. As governance processes create multiple "worlds of democratic action," achieving some consensus on the appropriateness of "rules in use" becomes essential.

Kübler and Pagano further complicate this turn toward governance with their argument that it is a multilevel phenomenon. As they point out we can no longer answer the classic question "who rules?" in a formalistic or institutional manner, even if we reference the nested nature of municipal authorities within intergovernmental systems. Rather research needs to take into account the horizontal and vertical structures of resources and influence that shape urban political circumstances.

3.2. Seeking Linkages

It is intriguing to note that U.S. scholars are more likely to advocate reaching out to other subfields as a means of integrating urban scholarship with the political science mainstream. This appears less of a concern to European researchers. The analyses of this perceived isolation of American urban scholarship are wide-ranging and sometimes startling: "Everything is Always Going to Hell: Urban Scholars as End-Times Prophets" (Judd 2005), and "Is Urban Politics a Black Hole?" (Sapotichne, Jones, and Wolfe 2007) are exemplars. One of the most obvious intellectual bridges is analysis of local elections and voter behavior. Clark and Krebs, however, acknowledge that such a focus is dogged by the persistent challenge that urban elections are irrelevant, second order contests. Given low local turnout and local electoral patterns that tend to parallel national voting choices, it is difficult to tease out the "local" dimension of local electoral politics. Furthermore, data on local elections allowing such analysis are not collected systematically and regularly in the U.S. Nevertheless, Clark and Krebs advocate for more comparative local election analyses while mindful of problems with measurement, functional equivalence, and the distinctive nonpartisan character of most U.S. local elections. They argue that the core question—what is the connection between issues, electoral success, and policy change in cities—is "badly understudied" yet amenable to comparative empirical research. As many city electorates become more diversified, these become increasingly important research issues.

While Copus, Wingfield, Steyvers and Reynaert focus more directly on partisan politics in the European setting, they also question conventional institutional assumptions. They begin with two visions of local government: nonpartisan, neutral, and technocratic, or partisan, partial, and ideological. Lack of comparable U.S. data on local partisan dynamics hampers analyses of these patterns in the U.S. But their comparisons of England and Belgium lead them to conclude that nonpartisanship provides openings to challenges to local governance by new parties and local civic society, although in the European context, the penetration of local politics by national parties seems to be the main story. In Europe as in the U.S., the continuing opportunistic pursuit by alternative groups of cracks and fissures in the local political terrain is the real dynamic for local political change. This complements Clark and Krebs' observation that many small parties presaging future national political change emerge in local electoral arenas, but remain understudied.

3.3. Finding Alternative Lenses for Comparative Research

While the debate on theories continues, there is near unanimous call for more diverse and more innovative urban research methods (see also Denters and Mossberger 2005). Wolman steps back from debates on large theoretical frameworks and argues for reconsidering some of the basic typologies in use. To Wolman, many of the shortcomings in urban research can be traced to measurement issues stemming from an inability to deal with counterfactuals—how do we measure what would have happened in the absence of policy? Wolman, along with Goldsmith, encourages shifting from comparing cities and countries based on typologies of central/local relations to typologies categorizing on the basis of allocations for specific functions. Since there are more variations within the central/local categories than between them, more precise grounds of budgetary allocations produce more useful categorizations of cities and the expectations we might have of them. In this sense, this responds to Campbell and Fainstein's agenda: the typology becomes a means of anticipating efforts at social justice given local limits.

Body-Gendrot and Savitch imply that more basic epistemological questions are at the root of methodological stalemates. They characterize their comparison of Los Angeles and Paris as guided by a "combination of chance, context, and causation." This seemingly whimsical approach is grounded in the work of political scientists and sociologists who are moving beyond positivist research strategies to conceptualize urban settings in interactive, interdependent, and configurational terms. This introduces a sense of a more contingent causation dynamic and is less likely to lead to prediction and falsification. But, as Body-Gendrot and Savitch's essay reveals, this might be more reflective of the complexities of the urban settings we are now dealing with.

Overall, the growing interest in comparative urban research raises intriguing and liberating questions of theory, methods, and measurement. Robinson (2011) notes that urban studies is an essentially comparative field but that scholars are "reluctant" to actually undertake comparative research. Indeed, she contends that conventional methods and weak theorization actually undermine many comparative efforts. Many of our assumptions about comparative research methods render cities "incommensurable" and "incomparable."

In a remarkable overview reaching beyond the transatlantic region to consider cities and politics in the developing world, Stren challenges this assertion. He argues for a focus on trends of worldwide urbanization, the increasing political and economic influence of cities in the developing world, decentralization, and democratization (including the growth of civil society). An analytic focus on decentralization trends offers one of the bridges to comparative analyses of developed and less developed areas. As Stren points out, decentralization is a plastic concept with multiple meanings and forms. Yet it appears to introduce a focus on local governance that demands more empirical analysis and comparative research. Goldsmith concurs but emphasizes the need for more empirical research on intergovernmental relations in developing countries that accounts for vertical and horizontal governance arrangements.

Kübler and Pagano advocate Seller's (2005) decentered strategy for such analysis. The research design would draw on large-N comparative analyses of urban politics and governance in various countries, in order to assess the generalizability of the findings generated by the comparative case studies approach now dominating the field. This requires investigating "the innumerable and undocumented" through mixed methods that bring together quantitative and qualitative research strategies.

To Mayer and Boudreau, more insightful comparative research—particularly moving beyond the North American and European regions—must move beyond highlighting "contrasts and similarities" to recognizing the gains from using "a different lens to shed light on a local process." From this perspective, a more international comparative urban research would be a flexible, interrogative practice that brings cities into "constantly shifting conversations with each other," as Robinson puts it (2011, 1). This necessarily involves a more nuanced understanding of contingent causality and a broader focus on configurations associated with multiple pathways to choices and outcomes. We hope to have moved that conversation forward.

REFERENCES

Bridge, Gary. 2005. *Reason in the City of Difference*. London: Routledge.

Clarke, Susan E. 2011. "Global cities, Metropolitan cultures, Multicultural politics." In Global Cities – Metropolitan Cultures: A Transatlantic Perspective Edited by Barbara Hahn, Meike Zwingenberger. Heidelberg: Universitätsverlag Winter.

Clarke, Susan E. and E. Chenoweth. 2006. "The Politics of Vulnerability: Constructing Local Performance Regimes for Homeland Security." Review of Policy Research 23(1): 95–114.

Davies, Jonathan S. and David Imbroscio. 2009. *Theories of Urban Politics*. London: Sage. 2nd ed.

——— (eds). 2009. *Critical Urban Studies: New Directions*. New York: SUNY Press.

Denters, Bas and Karen Mossberger. 2005. "Building Blocks for a Methodology for Comparative Urban Political Research." *Urban Affairs Review* 41: 550–71.

Feiock, Richard C. 2004. "Politics, Governance, and the Complexity of Local Land Use Regulation." *Urban Studies* 41(2): 363–77.

———. 2009. "Metropolitan Governance and Collective Action." *Urban Affairs Review* 44: 356–77.

Garbaye, Romain. 2006. *Getting Into Local Power: The Politics of Ethnic Minorities in British and French Cities*. London: Wiley-Blackwell.

Harding, Alan. 2009. "The History of Community Power." In Jonathan S. Davies and David L. Imbroscio, eds., *Theories of Urban Politics*. London: Sage. 2nd ed.

Hodson, M. and S. Marvin. 2009. "Urban Ecological Security: A New Urban Paradigm?" *International Journal of Urban and Regional Research* 40: 193–215.

John, Peter. 2001. *Local Governance in England and France*. London: Routledge.

Judd, Dennis. 2005. "Everything is Always Going to Hell: Urban Scholars as End-Times Prophets." *Urban Affairs Review* 40: 119–31.

Kasinitz, P., John Mollenkopf, and Mary C. Waters. 2002. "Becoming American/Becoming New Yorkers: Immigrant Incorporation in a Majority Minority City." *International Migration Review* 36(4): 1020–36.

Kjaer, A. M. 2004. *Governance*. Cambridge: Polity Press.

McKenzie, Evan. 1994. Privatopia: Homeowner Associations and the Rise Of Residential Private Government. New Haven: Yale University Press.

Molotch, Harvey. 1976. "The City as a Growth Machine: Toward a Political Economy of Place." *American Journal of Sociology* 82: 309–32.

Mossberger, Karen and Gerry Stoker. 2001. "The Evolution of Urban Regime Theory: The Challenge of Conceptualization." *Urban Affairs Review* 36: 810–35.

Murie, A. and S. Musterd. 2004. "Social Exclusion and Opportunity Structures in European Cities and Neighbourhoods." *Urban Studies* 41(8): 1441–59.

Nussbaum, Martha C. 2000. *Women and Human Development*. Cambridge: Cambridge University Press.

Paugam, Serge. 1995. "The Spiral of Precariousness: A Multidimensional Approach to the Process of Social Disqualification in France." In G. Room, ed., *Beyond the Threshold*. Bristol: Policy Press.

Pew Research Center. 2007. "Blacks See Growing Values Gap between Poor and Middle Class." November 13. http://pewsocialtrends.org/pubs/700/black-public-opinion. Last visited January 23, 2011.
Pierre, Jon. 1999. "Models of Urban Governance: The Institutional Dimension of Urban Politics." *Urban Affairs Review* 34: 372–96.
Putnam, Robert. 2007. "E Pluribus Unum: Diversity and Community in the Twenty-first Century: The 2006 Johan Skytte Prize Lecture." *Scandinavian Political Studies* 30: 137–74.
Robinson, Jennifer. 2011. "Cities in a World of Cities: The Comparative Gesture." *IJURR* 35: 1–23.
Sapotichne, Joshua, Bryan D. Jones, and Michelle Wolfe. 2007. "Is Urban Politics a Black Hole? Analyzing the Boundary Between Political Science and Urban Politics." *Urban Affairs Review* 43: 76–106.
Sen, Amartya K. 1999. *Development as Freedom.* New York: Oxford University Press.

Index

The manufacturer's authorised representative in the EU for product safety is Oxford University Press España S.A. of El Parque Empresarial San Fernando de Henares, Avenida de Castilla, 2 – 28830 Madrid (www.oup.es/en or product.safety@oup.com). OUP España S.A. also acts as importer into Spain of products made by the manufacturer.

Printed in the USA/Agawam, MA
June 27, 2025

889704.001

the study of

HISTORY

Bc

Commager, Henry Steele, 1902-

The study of history

the study of
HISTORY

Henry Steele Commager

Charles E. Merrill Publishing Co.
A Bell and Howell Company
Columbus, Ohio

International Standard Book Number: 0-675-09717-7

Library of Congress Catalog Card Number: 66-23542

5 6 7 8 9 10 11 12 13 14 15-76 75 74 73 72 71

Printed in the United States of America

To

ALLAN NEVINS

with

Gratitude

Admiration

and

Affection

Preface

History, it seems, is more self-conscious than other disciplines, the historian more introspective than his colleagues in other areas of study and research. For a century now, historians have been asking themselves, publicly and eloquently, what is the nature of history? what is the use of history? what is it we are about? until the matter has become something of a public scandal. Chemists, biologists, economists, engineers, economists and jurisprudents, are rarely assailed by comparable doubts; and if they are they tend to keep them to themselves.

Preoccupation with historical philosophy, historical criticism, historiography, is a relatively modern phenomenon, though there are of course antecedents stretching back to Plutarch or to St. Augustine. But it was not really until history became an academic subject—about a century ago—that such preoccupation became something of an obsession. Eighteenth century historians rarely questioned what it was they were engaged in. Giambattista Victo did, to be sure, but then he was generally ignored, but not Bolingbroke or Hume, Robertson or Gibbon, not Montesquieu or Voltaire, Muller or Raynal. They knew what history was—it was what they were writing. They knew what history was for, too; it was philosophy teaching by examples. Contrast with this self-confidence that long array of inaugural addresses by the Regius Professors of History at Oxford or Cambridge Universities, or the even more formidable series of annual addresses by the presidents of the American Historical Association, most of them confessing how troubled historians are about their profession.

The problem is not confined to that of identity or character; it has to do with function and method as well. Can history be impartial, can it be objective? Can it divorce itself from the tyranny of the present, of the nation, of the culture? Is the historian a judge—can he in fact avoid that function?—or is he a mere recorder, writing down "what actually happened"? Is it possible ever to know "what actually happened," possible to establish an historical "fact" as one establishes a fact in chemistry or biology? Is there such a thing as historical causation, and can the historian ever know the causes of things?

These questions are, in all likelihood, unanswerable and these problems insoluble, and I have not, here, attempted to answer the questions or to solve the problems. I have tried, rather, to do two things: first, to throw some light on the questions themselves, to show what use they have, if any, for the study of history; and, second, to help students and teachers to get on with the job of study and teaching and writing. To suggest that we cannot profitably study or write history until we have answered all of our questions about the nature and the function of history flies in the face of common sense. It is as if we should say that we cannot paint pictures until we know the meaning of art and of beauty, that we cannot build universities until we know with certainty what is education, or that we should hold up the machinery of law and the courts until we have answered ultimate questions about the nature of law and of justice. Experience and philosophy both admonish us that not only the pleasures and rewards but even the understanding of any great subject come pretty much out of study and practice.

Because we cannot answer ultimate questions, it does not follow that we cannot answer immediate questions. I have tried here to formulate some answers to more elementary questions about the nature and the uses of history. I have suggested that we approach history as one of a number of ways of looking at life and experience, just as philosophy, literature, art, politics, are ways of reflecting on life and experience. None of these answers ultimate questions—though philosophy sometimes tries to—and for that matter none guarantees to answer even immediate questions. Rightly studied, however, they illuminate our understanding and broaden our sympathies.

This book is not, then, yet another contribution to historical philosophy, nor a handbook on historical methodology, nor an essay on historiography. Nor have I attempted to review the various "philosophies" of history; the study of the philosophy of history seems to me to belong rather in the province of the philosopher than that of the historian, and I subscribe to G. M. Trevelyan's observation that philosophy is not something you take to history, it is, or should be, something you carry away from history.

H. S. C.
Amherst, 1966

Contents

The Nature of History

chapter one

The first thing to be said about History is that the word itself is ambiguous. It means two quite distinct things. It means the past and all that happened in the past. It means, too, the record of the past—all that men have said and written of the past, or, in the succinct words of Jacob Burckhardt, "what one age finds worthy of note in another." Sometimes it is said that these two things are in fact much the same: that the past exists only in our record of it, or our awareness of it, and that without such a record, there would be no meaningful past at all. Thus the great Italian philosopher-historian, Benedetto Croce, asserted that all history was contemporary history. There is, as we shall see, a germ of truth here. But this view is not so much wrong as confused and, in a sense, perverse. The past is not dependent on us for its existence, but exists in its own right. It happened even though historians failed to record it, just as the tree fell in the forest even though no one was there to hear the sound of its fall. History does not suddenly spring to life when some historian gets around to discovering it or recording it. The historian who clears up some puzzle about the past, or who discovers new material and fills in some gap in our knowledge of the past, does not in fact create the past, though he may recreate it. What happened, happened independently of him, and the consequences of whatever happened ensued independently of him. James Madison's *Notes on the Federal Convention*, for example, was not published until 1836; only then were historians able to penetrate into the very chamber of the Convention, to know, and to explain, what had occurred. Yet what had happened at the Convention—what delegates had said, for example—had in fact happened, and had made history. The consequences of the debates in the Convention did not wait upon the publication of Madison's *Notes.*

But if the debates in the Federal Convention were history, so was Madison's *Notes.* Just as what happened at the Convention had consequences, so the publication of the *Notes* fifty years later had consequences. It clothed with flesh and blood the skeleton of formal resolutions and conclusions with which historians had previously solaced themselves, and inaugurated both a more realistic and a more nationalistic interpretation of the Constitution.

What this suggests is that the historian, by discovering some lost ingredients in the past, or by illuminating dark areas of the past, can in a real way re-make the past. History is *there*—there in the fact that it did occur; there, too, in the conscious or the unconscious memories of men. The memory can be jogged, the consciousness can be stimulated, the image of the past can be changed. When the historian does these things he makes history.

History, then, is the past. History is also the memory of the past. Needless to say it is with the second of these meanings that we are concerned.

Let us consider history as memory.

For a people to be without history, or to be ignorant of its history, is as for a man to be without memory—condemned forever to make the same discoveries that have been made in the past, invent the same techniques, wrestle with the same problems, commit the same errors; and condemned, too, to forfeit the rich pleasures of recollection. Indeed, just as it is difficult to imagine history without civilization, so it is difficult to imagine civilization without history. As Frederic Harrison has written:

> Suppose that all knowledge of the gradual steps of civilization, of the slow process of perfecting the arts of life and the natural sciences, were blotted out; suppose all memory of the efforts and struggles of earlier generations, and of the deeds of great men, were gone; all the landmarks of history; all that has distinguished each country, race, or city in past times from others; all notion of what man had done or could do; of his many failures, of his successes, of his hopes; suppose for a moment all the books, all the traditions, all the buildings of past ages to vanish off the face of the earth, and with them the institutions of society, all political forms, all principles of politics, all systems of thought, all daily customs, all familiar arts; suppose the most deep-rooted and sacred of all our institutions gone; suppose that the family and home, property, and justice were strange ideas without meaning; that all the customs which surround each of us from birth to death were blotted out; suppose a race of men whose minds, by a paralytic stroke of fate, had suddenly been

deadened to every recollection, to whom the whole world was new. Can we imagine a condition of such utter helplessness, confusion, and misery? (*The Meaning of History and Other Historical Pieces,* New York, 1914, p. 5.)

Clearly the concept of history set forth here embraces rather more than most historians would claim: the total record of the past—literature, law, art, architecture, social institutions, religion, philosophy, all indeed that lives in and through the memory of man. We need not embrace this imperial definition of History in order to agree that man without memory would be bewildered and bereft. But memory, as we all know, is fitful and phantasmagoric. History is organized memory, and the organization is all-important. As organized memory, history takes almost innumerable forms, serves almost innumerable purposes. Let us consider some of the forms which it assumes and some of the purposes which it serves.

First, and if not most important, then most elementary, history is a story. That was its original character, and that has continued to be its most distinctive character. If history forgets or neglects to tell a story, it will inevitably forfeit much of its appeal and much of its authority as well. With the *Iliad* and the *Odyssey* story-telling and history are so inextricably co-mingled that we do not to this day know whether to classify them as literature or as history; they are of course both. "The Father of History," Herodotus, had a story to tell—the struggle between the Greeks and the Persians—and he told it with immense verve. So, too, his great successor Thucydides, who gave us the story of the Peloponnesian War. Livy and Tacitus, the greatest of the Roman historians, were both superb story-tellers, as are most of the leading modern historians, Voltaire and Gibbon, Carlyle and Macaulay, Prescott and Motley and Parkman. For, as Lord Macaulay wrote, "the art of history is the art of narration, the art of interesting the affections and presenting pictures to the imagination . . . by skillful selection and disposition without indulging in the license of invention."

Here we come to the second quality of history. History is a story, to be sure, but it is not a made-up story; history draws on and excites the imagination, but it is not a flight of the imagination. It is a story of what happened in the past, or what the historian is able to recover and reconstruct of what actually happened. In short, history is a *record.* It collects and organizes such facts as are available and relevant, provides some kind of framework for them, and lays down the guidelines for the presentation. It supplies order, harmony, direction, for what might otherwise be a chaotic assemblage of miscellaneous facts.

There are, to be sure, serious limitations on the record, as well as on the ability of history to organize the record; we have to accept this without getting too disturbed about it. First, the record is, and is bound to be, fragmentary and incomplete. That is particularly true of the several thousand years of history before the invention of the printing press, and of the history of many of the peoples who even after the mid-fifteenth century knew not the art of Gutenberg—the American Indians, for example, or the peoples of Africa, whose history is largely unrecorded. For much of modern history the record appears to be more nearly complete—witness the miles of filing cabinets in the Pentagon and elsewhere, crammed with documents from the Second World War. Yet even here, needless to say, the record is incomplete. How can we know what happened, during the war years, to each of the more than twelve million Americans in uniform, to say nothing of the forty million or fifty million men and women of other countries who fought in the war? How can we know what happened to the hundreds of millions of civilians who were involved in the war, as participants, as victims, or as spectators? The record is incomplete for another reason: the limitations on the time, the energies, the intelligence, and the practical and technical resources of historians. No individual historian, not even the largest committee of historians, can read all those miles of documents, all the newspapers, all the personal records of the combatants of all the countries involved in the Second World War.

The record is not only irremediably incomplete, it is also lopsided and biased. How can it be otherwise? Much of it is wholly fortuitous. Our knowledge of the past depends pretty much on what happened to be preserved, and what happened to be preserved is only a minute part of the total record, minute and indiscriminate. Much of the record has perished by fire and sword—from the burning of the Alexandrian Library to the bombings of World War II; much of it has been destroyed by fanaticism, religious or national; much of it has simply been lost: thus of the forty volumes of Polybius' *Histories* only five survived, of the 142 books of Livy's *History of Rome* only thirty-five have survived! There is no logic here, no pattern; what has survived is largely a matter of luck.

Largely—but not wholly; for what has survived—or rather what has failed to survive—is also to some degree a matter of power. Justice Holmes used to say that Truth was the majority vote of that nation which could lick all others. History, too, is in part the verdict of the nation which licks others. Over the centuries history has been written by the victors, not the vanquished. It is the Romans who have written the history of the Punic wars, not the Carthagenians; the Christians who recorded the triumph of Christianity over paganism, not the pagans; the Spaniards who told the story of the conquests of Mexico and Peru, not the Aztecs and the Incas. One of the less amiable traits of victors, in the past, has been the deliberate destruction of enemy records and the silencing—often by death—of enemy historians.

The record which has come down to us, then, is not only fragmentary and selective, it is also biased. To be biased is as human as to err. Everyone knows that bias enters into even the simplest statement of events. No two stories of a family quarrel are ever alike; how should we expect that a score of accounts of the Battle of Gettysburg, or of the beginnings of the First World War, should be alike? History is, after all, not something which exists independently of man; it is something that comes to us filtered through the mind and the imagination of men.

Of all this, later, when we consider some of the problems of history.

History as a record consists of three states, or processes, usually so skillfully blended that they appear to be a single one. The first is the collection of what are thought to be relevant facts; but remember, what seems relevant to one person will appear irrelevant to another. The second is the organization of these facts into some coherent pattern; but remember, no two patterns are ever quite alike. The third is the interpretation of the facts and of the pattern; and certainly no two interpretations are ever quite alike. Now, all of these processes flow into each other. The practiced historian is not ordinarily conscious of these separate steps any more than a skillful baseball player is conscious of the separate steps that go into a decision to strike at a ball. It is impossible to collect the facts in the first place without some theory of relationships among them; after all, what are you looking for? It is impossible to organize them into a pattern without some theory that dictates the pattern. And it is impossible to interpret them except on the basis of the material that has been selected and the pattern that has been drawn.

Neither collection nor organization is entirely under the control of the individual historian who is, in fact, wholly dependent on others for the material which he uses. No individual scholar can go very far in the collection of his material; mostly it has been done for him, over the years and the centuries, by earlier scholars; by archivists who have preserved manuscripts and records; by devoted librarians who have assembled manuscripts and books, organized them, classified them, and protected them; by government officials who have provided for the preservation of court or legislative or diplomatic records; and by editors who have organized these. Imagine trying to write on the history of modern Parliament without Hansard's *Debates;* imagine trying to write on the American constitutional system without the 375 or so volumes of the Supreme Court *Reports,* to say nothing of the thousands of volumes of lower court decisions; imagine trying to reconstruct the history of the

French in Canada without the *Jesuit Relations;* imagine trying to interpret Thomas Jefferson without the help of—nay without total dependence on—the devoted editors who have collected his papers and made them available to other scholars.

It is interpretation—the third step in the organization of the record—which is most nearly individual and which therefore makes the highest demands upon the historian. Industry will go far towards solving the first problem, that of collecting the materials; common sense and judgment will contribute much to the second, the organization of the materials. But intelligence of a high order is required for the interpretation of the facts. The greatest of historians, certainly in modern times, have been the interpreters; and all the major modern historians have tried to be interpreters—that is they tried to extract some meaning out of the inchoate raw materials of history, or to impose some philosophy upon it. Thus the great English historians: Clarendon and Gibbon and Hume, Macaulay and Froude and Lecky, Buckle and Freeman, Maitland and Lord Acton, and in our own day Namier and Butterfield, and Father David Knowles and Veronica Wedgwood, and Denis Brogan and Winston Churchill. Thus in France, Montesquieu and Voltaire and Michelet and Taine and Tocqueville and Aulard; thus in Germany, Niebuhr and Ranke, and von Sybel and Treitschke and Lamprecht, and Burckhardt, and more recently, Meinecke and Rothfels. Thus in the United States Francis Parkman and John Lothrop Motley, Henry Adams and Vernon Parrington, Lawrence Gipson, S. E. Morison, and Allan Nevins.

Yet while interpretation depends on the accumulation of facts and their skillful organization, even the most prodigious industry and the most painstaking analysis do not guarantee a profound interpretation. That requires judgment, originality, imagination, and art. And this brings us to the third form, or character, of history—history as art. As Arthur Schlesinger, Jr., has said:

> All the elements of artistic form are as organic in historical as in any other kind of literary composition. There are limits on the historian's capacity for invention, but there need be none on his capacity for insight. Written history, after all, is the application of an aesthetic vision to a welter of facts; and both the weight and the vitality of an historical work depend on the quality of the vision. ("The Historian as Artist.")

This is another way of saying that history is a branch of literature and that it serves some of the purposes and is governed by some of the principles of literature. Certainly most of the historical writing which we call great, and put into the category of the "classics," has literary distinction.

Literary history is not just a matter of fine writing. That can easily be overdone, and often is; the best style is plain and straightforward, as with Lincoln or Churchill in the realm of politics, or Trevelyan and Brogan among English historians, Douglas Freeman and Allan Nevins among American. Literary style is a matter rather of the tone, the color, the movement of the narrative; it is a matter of symmetry of structure, concentration of effort, architectural unity and harmony, and the imagination which suffuses the whole. Listen to an example from a master of literary style who was also a master of historical fact, Francis Parkman, calling to our attention one of the paradoxes of Franco-American history:

> The French dominion is a memory of the past; and when we invoke its departed shades, they rise upon us from their graves in strange, romantic guise. Again their ghostly camp-fires seem to burn, and the fitful light is cast around on lord and vassal and black-robed priest, mingled with wild forms of savage warriors, knit in close fellowship on the same stern errand. A boundless vision grows upon us: an untamed continent; vast wastes of forest verdure; mountains silent in primeval sleep; river, lake, and glimmering pool; wilderness oceans mingling with the sky. Such was the domain which France conquered for civilization. Plumed helmets gleamed in the shades of its forests, priestly vestments in its dens and fastnesses of ancient barbarism. Men steeped in antique learning, pale with the close breath of the cloister, here spent the noon and evening of their lives, ruled savage hordes with a mild parental sway, and stood serene before the direst shapes of death. Men of courtly nurture, heirs to the polish of a far-reaching ancestry, here, with their dauntless hardihood put to shame the boldest sons of toil. (*Pioneers of France in the New World,* preface.)

While it is true that unless history is reasonably accurate and fair it should not be read, it is equally true that unless history is well written it will not be read. "The world at large," writes Allan Nevins, himself a distinguished practitioner of literary history,

> will sooner forgive lack of scientific solidity than lack of literary charm. The great preservative in history, as in all else, is style. A book of consummate literary art may abound in passages of bad history, but nevertheless carry generation after generation before it. It is useless to protest that Lord Clarendon was far too biased on the English Civil War; he will be read for centuries by all who savor a close-packed, pithy, eloquent style, full of graphic sketches of men and events. Motley is unscientific in his treatment of Spanish misrule in the Netherlands, but the world will continue to read Motley. If an historian were compelled to take his choice, fame might urge him to select the winged pen, rather than the Aristotelian mind, to choose Apollo against Minerva; but he may

choose both. (*The Gateway to History,* Garden City, N.Y.: Doubleday & Company, Inc., 1962 ed., p. 379.)

Justice Holmes used to say, finely, that "life is painting a picture, not doing a sum." So we may say that writing history is painting a picture, not taking a photograph. It is not enough to give photographic exactness; not even a photograph by Brady carries the impact of a painting by Goya, the "Massacre" for example. It is not enough to compile statistics; if it were, the *Statistical Abstract of the United States* would be, each year, our best historical volume. It is not enough to pile up mountains of historical and social details; if it were, the raw materials of newspapers would suffice for historical literature. It is not enough to put together strings of episodes and anecdotes, no matter how dramatic; picture magazines which do this dull rather than excite the mind. History must rest on statistics, embrace details, exploit drama, but it should control all of these ingredients as an artist controls the ingredients of his materials and the elements of his subject—control them, master them, penetrate them with meaning and suffuse them with imagination.

Yet we must keep ever in mind that literary history, or history as literature, is not merely a matter of style—the winged word, the happy phrase, the brilliant epigram, the dramatist's art. The historian does not enroll, automatically, in the literary school when he writes well, nor suffer expulsion from that school when he writes in a flat or wooden style. Literary history is something more than a matter of style; it is something more than a matter of emphasis; it is a matter of philosophy.

The literary historian is primarily interested in recreating the past. He is, in a sense, a painter, and who can deny a Rembrandt, a Goya, a Longhi or Canaletto, a Reynolds, a George Catlin a place among historians? He is, in a sense, a dramatist, and who would deny Shakespeare or Molière or Holberg the title of historian? The literary historian employs his talents to conjure up what was once real and is now no more, and to excite the imagination of the beholder to see the past through his eyes. Like the painter, or the dramatist, he seeks to capture, for a moment, a brilliant, a famous, an endearing scene, to recreate a picturesque tableau, to paint a familiar portrait. He is Motley admitting us to the bedside of the dying Philip II of Spain; he is Prescott making us spectators of the bold attack across the causeway on Montezuma's great city; he is Michelet bringing us to our knees as we look on the tragic scene of the burning of the Maid of Orleans; he is Carlyle involving us in the heat of the battle of Rossbach.

All this is a far cry from the more prosaic and realistic purposes of the scientific historian. The gap between the literary and the scientific is not stylistic; it is deeper and more fundamental, a difference in the philosophy of history itself. The scientific historian is not really interested in recreating the past for its own sake, nor at pains to stir the imagination of the reader; indeed he is rather inclined to distrust the picturesque or the dramatic and even the individual. It is reason he wants to excite, not imagination, and as for the past he does not want to recreate it but to explain it. A great "technical" historian—Frederic Maitland, for example, who "turned the dust of archives into gold," or a Hastings Rashdall who made the medieval university as familiar as the contemporary, or Father Knowles, or S. E. Morison, can write with a style that sings and soars. But their primary purpose is not to stir the imagination but to solve problems. Was the "Mirror of Justices," upon which Lord Coke relied, authentic? How did St. Bernard triumph over the Cluniacs? Why did the students of medieval Bologna and Padua organize into Nations? Were the Puritans really hostile to music and the arts? Each of our historians has illuminated these problems with literary grace, but it was the problem that was important, not the grace.

Let us see how two distinguished historians, one "literary," the other "scientific," deal with the same situation. Here is Van Wyck Brooks, of all historians of American literature the most evocative, conjuring up for us the image of Nathaniel Hawthorne confronted by the spectacle of the New England Puritan in Rome:

> Was Hawthorne right in feeling that "it needs the native air" to give a writer's work reality? Rome had provided him with a fairy setting for the last of his own romances,—the last he was ever to finish,—the tale of Hilda, Miriam and Donatello, the dusky Miriam of the shrouded past and the delicate wood-anemone of the Western forest. This dance of Yankee girls and fauns and spectres was like a Pompeiian fresco or something immobilized on a Grecian urn. A bituminous light suffused it, as of an afternoon in the realm of shades. One caught in the shifting groups the magical, mythological grace of Poussin. One heard Mignon's song rising from the depths in the fitful measure of a wind-harp. Hawthorne had drawn enchantment from the Roman air; and yet, for all the spell of *The Marble Faun,* it was hardly comparable with *The Scarlet Letter* or *The House of the Seven Gables.* The orchidaceous existence of most of the exiles seemed to bear him out in his distrust. One could dream forever in these Roman gardens, under the cypress and ilex, while all one's mental muscles atrophied. Norton, with his acute social conscience, his sense of a mission at home, probed under the surface of Italian life. The repressive political system disturbed him, and he had understood, from his own observation, the sorrows of Petrarch, Dante and Alfieri, who had mourned over their country and its degradation. Norton's critical faculties were alert; he had ridiculed the old romantic guide-books and the cold and pretentious work of the German painters who were dominant in modern

> Rome. He had cared for the realities of Italian life, as Greenough and Margaret Fuller had cared before him. The others did not wish to care. It was to escape from the prose of existence that they had left America. If their writing lost all grip and bottom, was not this the reason and the explanation? (*The Flowering of New England*, New York: E. P. Dutton and Co., 1936, p. 477.)

Here is what Francis Matthiessen has to say in his brilliantly written interpretation of the *American Renaissance*:

> The danger of Brooks' impressionism is even more marked in the half paragraph which . . . is the only space he has left for *The Marble Faun*. When he says that Rome had provided Hawthorne with 'a fairy setting,' and speaks of 'the dusky Miriam of the shrouded past, the delicate wood-anemone of the Western forest,' the flower that he envisages has nothing to do with Hawthorne's maturely bitter fruit. . . . As a result of letting his attention be deflected from the work itself, he has made one of our few major artists seem less male and robust, much less concerned with important issues, than he was. Of all Hawthorne's heroines, Miriam leaves a impression least like the fragility Brooks describes. . . . Her quick response to Kenyon's statue of Cleopatra (which is Hawthorne's response to Story's) is owing to her feeling within herself the operation of qualities equally fierce and turbulent. . . She is more deeply involved in a background of ambiguous guilt than any other of Hawthorne's characters; and his method of conveying this should be observed as a final aspect of his tragic technique, since it leads directly into the practice of James and Eliot. (*American Renaissance*, New York: Oxford University Press, 1941, p. 352.)

The differences here go to the very heart of the problem of the nature of history. Why does the literary historian want to salvage, to resurrect, to recreate, the past? It is because he is interested in the past for its own sake, interested in the drama, the spectacle, the pageant, interested in the actors and actresses. His is the view expounded by George Macaulay Trevelyan: "It is not man's evolution but his attainment that is the greatest lesson of the past and the highest theme of history."

The scientific historian is not interested in history for its own sake. He studies it because it is part of the evolutionary process, and it is that process which concerns him. He behaves, as Herbert Butterfield observes, "as though only those things are worthy of attention which gain importance from the fact that they led to something else." Like a good scientist, the technical historian wants to solve problems.

If the scientific historian has done much to illuminate the processes of history, it is the literary historian who has done most to expand its boundaries. For if we are to conjure up the past, not only its drama and its heroisms but its everyday simplicities, we cannot ignore the commonplace. To be sure, literary historians do yield to the seduction of the dramatic—witness a Prescott or a Motley, or, in our own time, a Guedalla or a Rowse. But Carlyle—who was himself irresistibly tempted by the dramatic—warned against this a century ago: "Mournful it is to behold what the business called 'History' in these so enlightened and illuminated times, still continues to be. Can you gather from it . . . any dimmest shadow of an answer to that great question: how men lived and had their being?, were it but economically, as what wages they got and what they bought with them?" Carlyle did try to tell this, and so did his contemporary, John R. Green; somewhat later, so did the Dane Troels-Lund and the German Karl Lamprecht and the Frenchman Eli Halévy, and so did the American John Bach McMaster, who wrote clumsily enough. But we conclude as we began: "literary" history is not a matter of fine writing; it is a matter of the center of intellectual and historical gravity.

History is art; history is also philosophy. Lord Bolingbroke put it for all time when, drawing on the ancients, he defined History as "philosophy teaching by examples." So almost all the great historians have thought, from Thucydides to Toynbee. History was philosophy in the Old Testament stories; it was philosophy in Thucydides, Polybius, Plutarch, Livy, and Tacitus among the ancients. Most modern historians accepted the Bolingbroke dictum as a matter of course: Montesquieu in his *Spirit of the Laws* and *The Grandeur and Decadence of Rome,* Voltaire in the *Age of Louis XIV,* Gibbon in *The Decline and Fall of the Roman Empire,* the Abbé Raynal in his many-volumed *History of the Indies,* designed, really, as an "instrument of war" against the Church and the Empire, and David Hume in his *History of England.* It is only recently that historians have attempted to discard this traditional function of history, and without much success. For philosophy, ousted from the front door, creeps back in through the side door. The public still wants philosophy with its history, and it is no accident that the most popular historians of our time—H. G. Wells and Winston Churchill and Arnold Toynbee, Georg Brandes and Oswald Spengler, Benedetto Croce and André Malraux, Salvadore de Madariaga and Raymond Aron, all wrote history as philosophy.

Yet few historians have been philosophers in any formal sense. They have relied on history, most of them, to teach simple moral lessons: the superiority of Christianity over other religions; the dangers of infidelity; the triumph of virtue over vice, or, in more sophisticated times, the futility of religious intolerance, the wickedness of kings, the depravity of man and the necessity of restraints upon his passions, the rise and fall of empires and the causes thereof—these and other lessons equally simple and equally dubious.

No one can seriously question the claim of history to be story, record, literature, and philosophy. What of her claim—or the claim of some of her more infatuated disciples—to be a science? History is invariably embraced in that loose term, "the social sciences," but we do not know what that term really means. Are the social sciences in fact sciences at all, or is the word "science" used here rather in its original sense as "knowledge"?

It was the Victorians who first asserted that history was a science; that generation, so confident of its ability to create a science of man, embraced within this concept the science of society, economy, politics, law, and history. Thomas Buckle was sure that he had reduced history to a science by bringing it under the dominion of "one glorious principle of universal and undeviating regularity"—the law of Nature; while across the Channel August Comte announced that "History has now been for the first time systematically considered, and has been found, like other phenomena, subject to invariable laws." And at the turn of the century two Regius Professors at Cambridge University, Lord Acton and J. B. Bury, intimated that if history was not yet a science it would inevitably become one. No modern Regius Professors now speak in such confident tones, yet the habit of thinking and speaking of history as a science is deeply engrained.

Clearly history is not a science in the sense that chemistry or biology are sciences. It cannot submit its data to scientific experiments; it cannot repeat its own experiments; it cannot control its materials. Wanting these, it will be said that of course history is not a science in any useful sense of the word. Yet it is equally clear that history uses or aspires to use the scientific method. That is, it tests all things which can be tested, and holds fast to what it finds to be true, in so far as it is able to make any findings at all. But how does history "test" things? What are the techniques of testing? How does it know when it has arrived at "truth" or even when it has achieved agreement of "facts"? The chemist does not inject his personality, his beliefs and prejudices, into the chemicals which he uses in his experiments; how does the historian rid his materials of such foreign ingredients? Indeed can the term "scientific method" ever mean the same thing in history that it means in the exact sciences?

Should it perhaps give place to a more realistic term such as "critical method," and should "scientific" history yield to "technical" history?

For there is this further, and sobering, consideration that the scientific method is valid—if at all—only in what might be called the formal and somewhat elementary realms of history, never in the really fundamental realms. Thus we can prove—scientifically if you will—that John Wilkes Booth did in fact shoot President Lincoln in Ford's Theater in Washington, on the night of the fourteenth of April, 1865. So far so good—but how far, and how good? For beyond that our science does not take us. Why did Booth do it? Who, or what, was responsible for his action? What were the consequences of the act? These, the really interesting questions, cannot be answered scientifically; they can hardly be answered at all.

Disillusioned with the claims of scientific history, some modern historians settled for what we may call Technical History—a term coined by Professor Herbert Butterfield of Cambridge University. Let us not aspire too high, let us not try to formulate laws of history, let us not try to don the mantle of science! Let us rather take problems, one by one, as a biologist or a philologist takes problems one by one, the smaller the better, and works them out. If enough historians work tirelessly at enough problems, we may in time obtain a firm foundation upon which future historians can somehow rear the grand fabric of history.

The stigmata of technical history are by now sufficiently familiar. It distrusts the dramatic and prefers to catch history in a chemical solution, as it were, in a moment of arrested development, and to analyze it and dissect it. It eschews the narrative and turns instead to Problems, though it does not really believe that any problems can be finally solved. It detests generalizations and is revolted by Laws; it delights in the minute and the specific, and its characteristic form is the monograph. It has little interest in ideas and none at all in individuals, looking upon them as aberrations from some norm to be arrived at by the study of statistics, or distractions from the consideration of impersonal institutions. It is impatient with the notion of history as literature and rejects out of hand the idea of history as philosophy. And it has an irresistible fascination for the academic mind.

In all this, technical history has obvious association with modern developments in literature, art, criticism, and philosophy. In the second and third quarters of the twentieth century, literature too turned from its traditional concern with the narrative and the dramatic to the analytical and the descriptive, abandoned interest in plot and in characters and entangled itself instead with the impersonal, the subconscious, and the amorphous. "Let us record the atoms as they fall upon the mind in the order in which they fall," wrote Virginia Woolf. "Let us trace the pattern, however disconnected and incoherent in appearance, which each sight or incident scores upon the consciousness." Art, too, became increasingly abstract and impersonal, disdaining to tell a story and reluctant to present anything dramatic, heroic, or colorful: historical paintings and portraiture declined with historical narratives and biographies. Criticism addressed itself increasingly to the explanation of texts, while philosophy turned away from the great problems with which it had traditionally been preoccupied to problems of semantics. In the circumstances it was not surprising that the historian, bemused by the intricacies of technical history, should look with suspicion on history in the grand manner—history as narrative, as philosophy, as art—and settle for something that seemed to offer intellectual security.

The Varieties of History

chapter two

There are as many kinds of history as there are historians, and each historian writes his own kind of history. And, as the historical philosopher Carl Becker observed, there are innumerable historians because every man is "his own historian." In one sense that is undoubtedly true, for everyone who tells a story recalling his childhood, or writes a letter describing a trip abroad or a baseball game or an exhibition is, after a fashion, an historian. He is doing, in a crude fashion, what professional historians do in a more sophisticated fashion; he is summoning up the past from whatever evidence is at hand, organizing his material, and dressing it up with drama and with art; he is even interpreting it all. And when he puts himself in the center of his story, he is giving us autobiography as well. Yet just as we do not describe everyone who writes a letter as a "writer," or everyone who draws a picture as an "artist," so we should not describe everyone who records some past experience as an "historian." We do well to reserve the term for those who consciously undertake to reconstruct and present some segment of the past, and who do so with some semblance of craftsmanship, for more than private entertainment.

How is history to be told? No two histories are ever precisely alike, any more than any two poems or novels are precisely alike; if they were we should call it plagiarism. Yet over the centuries historians have worked out a number of patterns and these have come to be conventional, just as have patterns in poetry, music, or art. They are not fixed, or binding; there is room for variation and for experimentation (suggested, in our own day, by the film and television), and there is nothing either final or authoritative about the familiar patterns. But on the whole it is the traditional patterns, products of centuries of experience, that provide the best vehicles for history.

In a broad way these traditional patterns are the chronological, the geographical, the political, the cultural, the institutional, and the biographical. These are so familiar that they need little explanation or elaboration. The most elementary, and the most familiar, is the chronological, yet we speedily discover that even it presents problems. For where do you start? Start at the beginning, you may say, but that is not as easy as it sounds. There was a time, to be sure, when we could date the beginning with assurance: 4004 B.C., the date of the expulsion of Adam and Eve from the Garden of Eden. For centuries historians, as well as scientists, tried to fit their facts into this chronological strait-jacket; not really until the eighteenth century did they find a way to extricate themselves from it. In the past century or so history has been able to move back a few hundred thousand years into something vaguely called Pre-history, and properly to understand pre-history requires a knowledge of anthropology, paleontology, archeology, and many other things which few historians possess. Yet something is to be said for beginning if not at the outermost limits of pre-history, then with the Magdalenians who flourished in western Europe some ten to fifteen thousand years ago and who not only fashioned implements out of bone but left us the famous wall paintings in the caves of Lascaux in France and Altamira in Spain. If we prefer to leave this to the anthropologists, we are still confronted with the question of whether we start with "civilized" man in Mesopotamia about 3500 B.C., or in the Indus Valley, which boasted an advanced urban civilization some twenty-five hundred years before Christ, or perhaps with the Shang Dynasty of northern China, whose people had by that time already evolved a written language which was to endure until our own day.

The conventional thing is to begin with Egypt, Judea, Greece, and Rome. Here, after all, we can find the roots of our own civilization. And here, too, we can feel secure, for the territory has been surveyed, the guidelines and signposts all laid out. And how painless the transition to medieval history, traditionally dated from something called the fall of the Roman Empire and the transfer of the capital from Rome to Constantinople. Oddly enough, even with the recognition of that transfer Byzantine history was generally neglected; historically the center of gravity may have shifted eastwards, but most historians preferred to linger in the West, though they sometimes fell into the habit of calling these centuries of history the Dark Ages. With an almost audible sigh of relief, the historian struggled out of the medieval era into the twelfth century Renaissance, and then into that glorious Renaissance of the fourteenth to sixteenth centuries. This brilliant era was the threshold to Modern History which could be dated from the discovery of the New World, or from Luther's famous Theses, as you wished. From then on the going was easy.

It was all far too simple, this division into ancient, medieval, and modern; indeed it was almost arbitrary. Its most obvious defect was its parochialism: these divisions did not really apply to history but to the history of the European West; they blandly ignored Asia, Africa, and the Americas, and assumed that nothing really counted except Europe, and that what was valid for Europe was valid for the rest of the globe.

There were other drawbacks. To apply names to long periods of history is to imprison them in our own concepts and expect them to live up to these names and concepts; we forget that the names themselves are arbitrary and parochial. People who lived in Periclean Athens did not think of themselves as living in "ancient" times, nor did the inhabitants of Tours or of London in the eighth century think of themselves as Medieval People. To apply names, too, is to generalize; it is to suggest, if not to assume, that all who lived in the era of the Renaissance partook of what we now conclude to be the character of that era; that the Renaissance Man was to be found alike in Florence, in Upsala, in the forest of Bohemia or the bogs of Ireland. Then there is the further difficulty that the designation and study of history by periods or eras tends to encourage the fallacious belief in sharp demarcations in history, and to blur the fact that eras of history blend and overlap just as the years blend and overlap in the lives of individuals.

Granted all this, there remains convenience. To study anything—literature or art, zoology or mathematics, we have to impose some kind of order upon it, divide it up and parcel it out. As long as we are aware of its limitations, the chronological order is as valid as any other and perhaps more convenient than any other. And may we not assert, too, that if we confine ourselves to a particular country—Britain or the United States—or to a coherent group of peoples and nations, there is much to be said for chronological distinctions? The Elizabethan Age, for all its connections with the past and the future, did have a character of its own, and so too did the Puritan era and the era of the Restoration. The Revolution did in fact divide the colonial era from the national, in American experience, and Czarist Russia differed sufficiently from Communist Russia that we are justified in distinguishing the two eras and studying them separately. We need not subscribe to the fallacies of the Zeitgeist philosophy to concede that youth and age have their distinct characteristics.

There is, of course, a very different chronological approach to history—to begin with the present, and work back. This method has its points, especially with the young. It is the way most youngsters find out about their family history: they begin with their parents and grandparents, and work back as far as information or rumor will take them. It is the way lawyers habitually work, from the present case to immediate and then to more remote precedents. Thus we can study such institutions as the political party, the Presidency, the corporation, the labor union, the university, by tracing them back from their current character and conduct to their origins.

We tend, most of us, to look with misgivings on the writing of contemporary history, and therefore on this approach to history. The information is not yet available, we say, or it is impossible to achieve perspective so necessary to objectivity. True enough. Yet it is proper to remember that many of the greatest historians of the past wrote contemporary history. Thucydides lived through that Peloponnesian War whose history he relates; Tacitus wrote the history of his own times. Machiavelli's *History of Florence* is contemporary history, and Francesco Guicciardini's great *History of Italy* entirely so. Clarendon's *History of the Rebellion* is in part autobiographical; if Voltaire's *Age of Louis XIV* was not precisely contemporary history, Voltaire did live through twenty years of the Sun-King's reign. And who that reads the splendid pages of Winston Churchill's *World Crisis* or his *History of the Second World War* can doubt that in the hands of a master contemporary history can still be great history.

The geographical, like the chronological, organization of history has a kind of elementary simplicity about it that has long been irresistible to school teachers and writers of textbooks. The nineteenth century used to think of history as something that concerned only the European world, that is Europe, the Mediterranean, and the Americas. There was, to be sure, some fragmentary attention to the Near East at the time of Hammurabi and his Code, or of the Moslem conquest of North Africa and of Spain, or during the era of the Crusades. From time to time the Orient would be smuggled in—now with the story of the Chinese discovery of gunpowder, now with Marco Polo, now with Clive in India or the opening of Japan by Matthew Perry, or the Boxer Rebellion—how illuminating that the uprising of Chinese against Europeans should be called a "rebellion." Africa, too, swam occasionally over the historical horizon—certainly when Europeans began to raid the hapless continent for slaves or to carve it up into colonies.

All of this represented a curious kind of historical astigmatism. Eighteenth century historians—Voltaire, for example, and the Abbé Raynal—had seemed to break away from this European parochialism and "survey mankind from China to Peru," but even their gestures were artificial; clearly they were interested in the non-European parts of the globe only insofar as these may have impinged upon Europe. Only recently have historians generally abandoned the notion that history was something that happened to or affected the European world, and acknowledged that the non-European two-thirds of the globe is as important as the European one-third. Even yet this re-appraisal of history is only partial and fitful. The history that is studied in the schools is still the history of Europe; the history that is read by the public is almost wholly European—a term which, of course, embraces both the Americas, and the British Commonwealth. This deeply engrained habit of looking at Asia and Africa—and sometimes even Spanish America—as mere appendages to Europe illuminates and explains many of the difficulties in international political and cultural relations today.

Here again, however, there is some logic in the tradition and the habit of the organization of history along geographical lines. It is not only convenient, it is helpful, to deal with the Mediterranean world as something of a unit, to deal with Europe as a unit, to deal with the Americas as units. The history of all peoples is interconnected, but geography and climate—the environment—determined the course of history quite as much as inheritance, and the historian may properly make environment his starting point, and accept it as his framework. There is danger here, to be sure: Henry Thomas Buckle *(The History of Civilization in England)* made geography not only the beginning but the whole of his interpretation of history, and failed spectacularly to make out a persuasive case. But if we use geography as an organizing device rather than as a philosophical explanation, we will find it useful.

A third method of organizing history, and one which derives in part from the geographical, is the political—a form of organization particularly endemic since the rise of nationalism. Thus we almost instinctively organize our materials into the history of Rome or of France, of the United States or of the Confederacy. Sometimes, for convenience, we combine groups of nations: the British Commonwealth, for example, or Latin America, or Central Europe, or Scandinavia. This political approach to history is, needless to say, almost wholly a product of modern history, for the nation-state is itself modern. Of all forms of historical writing the political is the most convenient and the most popular; almost all history is now studied in a political framework and that framework is even used, retroactively, to embrace the histories of peoples who flourished long before the rise of nationalism or the organization of the political state. The political approach to history is the most convenient because historical materials are customarily organized along national lines and by political and administrative departments—in the publications of government, of courts, in military and naval records, and so forth, and in the collection and organization of archive and library materials. It is convenient, too, because it makes relatively few demands upon the linguistic talents of scholars. It is popular because it appeals irresistibly to national pride, connects itself dramatically with the interest and the practical concern of readers, and with all that is most familiar, from stories in the nursery to studies in the school-room, from politics to patriotic festivals.

In the circumstances it is not surprising that most modern historians have accepted E. A. Freeman's dictum that "History is past politics, past politics present history." Whatever the inadequacies of the political view, it can be said that a habit of history—it is too much to call anything so nearly instinctive a philosophy—which has given us such literary monuments as Macaulay's *History of England,* Michelet's glowing *History of France,* Johann Müller's eloquent *History of the Swiss Confederation,* Peter Münch's voluminous *History of the Norwegian People,* Henry Adams' brilliant *History of the United States During the Administration of Jefferson and Madison,* more than justifies itself. Whatever the limitations of national history, historians can, and do, overcome them and even turn them to advantage. Whether history written without nationalist preconceptions, or outside the nationalist framework, can improve on national history remains to be seen.

The student should keep in mind that the political approach to history is fraught with danger. It inculcates a narrow and parochial view of history, and tempts both historian and student to indulge in chauvinistic patriotism. It reads back into the past the artificial divisions of modern nationalism, and exaggerates the role of politics and diplomacy at the expense of other elements in history. By pouring everything into the political crucible, it melts down the rich ores of culture, religion, social and economic institutions into a single slab distinguished only by the political impress which is stamped upon it.

A fourth form, or pattern, of history is the cultural. It is not easy to define Cultural History. It is the history of the mind and character of a people, of the major ideas which appeared to dominate a society or an age, of the institutions with which we associate the conduct and faith of men. Probably no other form of history makes greater demands upon the scholar; probably none is more fascinating when those demands are satisfied. The requirements of cultural history are not satisfied—as some misguided historians appear to suppose—by a naked record of what was written, or painted, or composed, or built by a society during a particular era: during these years Mozart and Beethoven were composing sonatas, during these Kant and Kierkegaard thought deep thoughts, during these Renoir and Manet developed Impressionism—that sort of thing! No, the cultural historian is called upon to know, understand, and explain the ideas and interests of a whole generation, sometimes in many different societies, and to trace their manifestations in the whole fabric of history. As ideas are almost always cosmopolitan, he is required to cut across the barriers of nation and language and perhaps even of time as well. You can tell the story of the disputed election of 1876 in wholly isolated terms, but you cannot do justice to the Centennial Exposition of 1876 without bringing in romanticism, science, art, industry, and a dozen other subjects as well. The cultural historian is required to know the history of many countries, to be familiar with art, literature, philosophy, and science, and to be wise enough to fuse all these into a synthesis.

This is not easy, for where political history has, or appears to have, a certain simplicity and clarity of outline, cultural history is sprawling, distracted, and amorphous. What is it, after all? Is it anthropology, as in Frazer's famous *Golden Bough* or in Lewis Morgan's *Ancient Society*? Is it sociology as in the fourteen volumes on *Daily Life in the North in the Sixteenth Century* by the distinguished Danish historian, Troels-Lund, or in Charles Booth's monumental *Life and Labour in London*? Is it economics as in Rostovtzeff's *Economic History of Rome*? Is it religion as in Mandell Creighton's *History of the Popes* or the multi-volumed *History of the Papacy* by Ludwig von Pastor, or Anson Phelps Stokes' three immense volumes on *Church and State in the United States*? Is it art as in Jacob Burckhardt's *Renaissance in Italy* or Berenson's *Painters of the Northern Italian Renaissance* or Rewald's magisterial volumes on the *Impressionists* and the *Post-Impressionists*? Is it education, as in Rashdall's *History of Medieval Universities* or Sandys' *History of Classical Scholarship*? Is it law, as in Holdsworth's fifteen volumes on the *History of English Law* or Charles Warren's *Supreme Court in United States History*? Is it science as in Needham's *History of Science in China* or Lynn Thorndike's monumental *History of Magic and Experimental Science*? Is it military, even, as in Fortescue's *History of the British Army* or Oman's *History of the Peninsular Campaign* or Douglas Freeman's *R. E. Lee* and *Lee's Lieutenants*? Certainly it is literature, and cultural history has traditionally adopted literature as its most convenient vehicle: the examples here are too numerous to rehearse.

Some historians have been bold enough to try to put all of these things together, to provide a synthesis which embraces the whole thought and character of a society. Thus, for example, John Addington Symonds' seven volumes on the history of the *Renaissance in Italy,* thus Alfred Zimmern's luminous *Greek Commonwealth,* thus Paul Hazard's eloquent interpretation of *European Thought in the Eighteenth Century,* thus Werner Jaeger's magisterial study of Greek culture, *Paideia,* thus Vernon Parrington's controversial *Main Currents in American Thought,* which embraces almost every expression of thought except the philosophical.

All of these have in common an interest in ideas rather than in "events," and a resolution to cut across the barriers which divide politics, law, economics, society, philosophy, science, and art. These are admirable objectives, but they are difficult to realize. It is far easier to write a history of the Sherman Anti-Trust Act of 1890 than to trace the complex and elusive elements that explain German, English, and American Transcendentalism. But if the rigors and risks of intellectual history are great, so too are the rewards. It is gratifying to reflect that the writings of such cultural historians as Burkhardt, Symonds, Leslie Stephen, and Troels-Lund, now almost a century old, flourish with undiminished vigor and influence new generations.

The most interesting development in recent historical study has been the emergence of what we have come to call Cultural Anthropology—a study, or discipline—which has flourished especially in America. There are, to be sure, respectable antecedents: eighteenth century studies such as Voltaire's *History of the Morals and Customs of Nations* and Raynal's vast *History of the Indies* could both be classified as essays in cultural anthropology. So too could perhaps the greatest book ever written on America, Tocqueville's *Democracy in America* which, in a severely formal fashion, embraced most of the social and psychological characteristics now explored by the cultural anthropologists. Other nineteenth century cultural historians, too, borrowed heavily from anthropology: examples are Lewis Henry Morgan's pioneering *Ancient Society,* or Frazer's classic *Golden Bough,* or Wilhelm Grönbeck's neglected *Culture of the Teutons,* or Thorstein Veblen's epoch-making *Theory of the Leisure Class.* It is upon the work of such historians, and upon the writings of sociologists like Herbert Spencer and Lester Ward, that the new school of cultural anthropologists build. Perhaps their methods and techniques are more original than their ideas. To the highly civilized societies of America or Britain they apply the techniques originally developed for the study of primitive societies—the societies of Samoa or the Trobriand Islands or of the Pueblo Indians. With what they hope is scientific objectivity they turn their anthropological and sociological spotlights on the habits, customs, rites, and ceremonies of Middletown or Plainville, U.S.A., of Manchester, or Copenhagen, or the Vaucluse. They have little interest in the familiar subjects—politics or literature or philosophy or art—but address themselves rather to such matters as toilet training, dating patterns, the play and games of children, the sexual practices, eating habits, prestige concepts, and racial attitudes of adults.

Perhaps the chief value of all this to the historian was that it gave a new dimension to that familiar and traditional enterprise, the study of national character. The nineteenth century had been fascinated by this concept, and such books as Tocqueville's *Democracy in America* and Emerson's *English Traits* had given it respectability, while W. E. H. Lecky, the historian of eighteenth century Britain, had gone so far as to insist that national character was the only subject worthy of study. But as, increasingly, in the twentieth century, nationalism and race lent themselves willingly to the most evil purposes, historians became wary of generalization about national character, and eventually all but abandoned the notion that there was any such thing. After all, they said, men are more alike than they are different, and national traits are fortuitous rather than inherent; the whole idea of national character is romantic and probably pernicious.

Now, however, with the rise of the cultural anthropologists, the stone which the builders rejected became the cornerstone of the new history. As the historians hastened to abandon the field of cultural nationalism, the cultural anthropologists moved in. If there was no national character, there were national characteristics. Soon national character—and particularly the American character—was subjected to intensive statistical study by students of public opinion, child training, educational practices, class and caste, sports and games, popular culture and popular prejudices, language and idiom, and power struggles. And on the basis of their findings—so one of their spokesmen asserted—"the statistical prediction can safely be made that a hundred Americans will display certain defined characteristics more frequently than will a hundred Englishmen comparably distributed as to age, sex, social class, and vocation."

Cultural anthropology has a further contribution to make to history; it helps to democratize history. No one can deny that history is, and always has been, discriminatory and exclusive. It prefers to dwell with Monarchs rather than with their subjects, with Popes rather than rural vicars, with Generals rather than with privates, with Statesmen rather than civil servants, with Captains of Industry and Titans of Finance rather than workingmen and clerks. It delights in the spectacular, the dramatic, and the sensational—battles, crises, famines, natural catastrophes, heroic deeds, and foul crimes. The annals of the poor, we are assured, are short and simple; mostly they are non-existent.

As long as history depends on the written record, and the record that survives, all this is natural and almost inevitable, for the vast majority of mankind have left no records. The historian who wishes to find out how the great mass of plain people lived is forced to rely on such artifacts as happen to survive—tools, instruments, clothing, folk art and folk ballads, or on such records as have been made by churchmen or by officials—births, marriages, deaths, records of military service, the findings of courts, the statistics of the tax collector, and so forth; in modern times these miscellaneous records are supplemented by the newspaper. In the hands of skillful and imaginative historians like Troels-Lund who recreated *Daily Life in the North in the Sixteenth*

Century, or Ferdinand Gregorovius who traced the *History of the City of Rome in the Middle Ages,* such data come to life; but mostly historians have neglected them.

The cultural anthropologist is not, for the most part, interested in recreating the historical past, but the materials which he assembles and exploits do illuminate that past, for qualitatively, at least, his interests parallel those of the social historian. He is not concerned with the great and the powerful, the machinations of diplomats, the rhetoric of statesmen, the strategy of generals, except as these happen to illustrate popular traits. His interest is, by logical necessity, directed to the habits of play and courtship, of work and of worship, to family relationships, popular preferences in food and clothing, popular ideas of right and wrong. Because the commonplace generally has deep roots in the past, the data which the cultural anthropologist so carefully assembles from such miscellaneous sources becomes, sometimes retroactively, the data of history.

There is another form of history, one that parallels and contributes to all the others; history as biography. A large part of history has come down to us in the form of biography. Many of the most familiar stories of the Old Testament are biographical—the story of Joseph and his Brethren, for example, or of David and Naboth's Vineyard, or of Job. Plutarch was doubtless the greatest practitioner of history as biography, and his *Parallel Lives of the Greeks and the Romans,* as we know, deeply influenced the Founding Fathers. It was Thomas Carlyle who put the biographical theory of history most strongly:

> Universal history, the history of what man has accomplished in this world, is at bottom the History of the Great Men who have worked here. They were the leaders of men, these great ones, the modellers, patterns, and in a wide sense creators of whatsoever the general mass of men contrived to do or to attain. . . In all epochs of the world's history we shall find the Great Man to have been the indispensable saviour of his epoch;—the lightning, without which the fuel would never have burnt. (*On Heroes and Hero-Worship,* 1841, Lecture I.)

Though few modern historians have been willing to accept this extreme interpretation of the role of great men in history, many have written as if they would like to. English and American literature are peculiarly rich in biographies: Boswell's life of Dr. Johnson, for example, or Lockhart's many-volumed tribute to Sir Walter Scott, or James Anthony Froude's four volumes on Carlyle, or John Morley's solid monument to Gladstone and his slighter but more brilliant studies of Voltaire and Rousseau, or Winston Churchill's six volumes on his ancestor, the Duke of Marlborough, or George Macaulay Trevelyan's glowing story of Garibaldi, while in American literature such books as Beveridge's *John Marshall,* Douglas Freeman's *R. E. Lee,* Arthur Link's *Wilson,* Leon Edel's *Henry James* come to mind. Now, all these biographies have one thing in common: they are history as well as biography. They place their subject against a rich and elaborate historical background, relate him to the great historical ideas and events of his time, use him to illuminate the history of an age. They all belong to what we may call the Life and Times School, which contrasts sharply with the personal and psychological school which we associate with such writers as Lytton Strachey or Andre Maurois or the American, Gamaliel Bradford.

History never gets very far away from biography; even such austere subjects as law or science are illuminated by the biographical approach. Nothing, to be sure, quite comes up to Holdsworth's massive fifteen-volume *History of English Law,* but it is impossible to understand even the history of English law without knowing the men who made it and pronounced it: Lord Coke, Blackstone, Mansfield, Bentham, Brougham, Eldon, for example. It is even more futile to try to understand the history of American constitutional law without taking into account the personalities of John Marshall and Joseph Story, Justice Field and Justice Holmes, and it is no accident that American literature is particularly rich in judicial biographies. And while specialists can approach the history of science through the technical literature on that particular science, for the layman it is the biographical approach that is most rewarding. While the history of American science remains to be written, Americans are fortunate in a handful of first-rate biographies: Lynde Wheeler's *Willard Gibbs,* A. Hunter Dupree's *Asa Gray,* Brooke Hindle's *David Rittenhouse,* Wallace Stegner's biography of Major Powell, *West of the One Hundredth Meridian,* and Edwin Martin's *Thomas Jefferson, Scientist.*

For reasons easy to sympathize with, biography has always been the most popular form of history. It is pleasant to read, dramatic, and colorful; it personalizes and simplifies complex problems; it illustrates the promise of Longfellow's *Psalm of Life,* that

> Lives of great men all remind us,
> We can make our lives sublime,
> And, departing, leave behind us,
> Footprints on the sands of time.

It is for precisely these reasons that so many professional historians—particularly those who practice "technical" history—look upon biography with a deep suspicion. Nothing, said the great Lord Acton, "causes more error and unfairness in man's view of history, than the interest which is inspired by individual characters." And Lewis Namier, perhaps the most influential of modern British historians, insisted that the study of biography was a kind of historical kindergarten; the historian should not distract himself with the study of individual man, but address himself rather to those great forces of politics and the economy which determined the course of history or those great institutions where the influence of the individual was negligible.

Tackle any major problem in history and you will discover at once that you cannot understand it in isolation, but that you are involved in politics, international relations, science, technology, economics, psychology, and morals. If you want to understand James Fenimore Cooper's America you will find yourself inescapably involved in the history of romanticism, Indian ethnology, and the controversy over democracy, land laws and land policies, and a score of other matters. To understand the Supreme Court decisions in *Munn* versus *Illinois* requires some familiarity with the history of agriculture and of railroads in America, the politics of Supreme Court appointments, and the history of English as well as of American law. The fact is that men and women do not live in compartments labelled "politics" or "law" or "religion" or "economics"; they live in all of these simultaneously. The same people who write constitutions and draft laws also build houses, marry and raise families, work at machines, write books, go to church, and fight wars.

There is no danger of parochialism or of narrowness in history; properly studied each chapter of history opens out onto ever-new chapters. Nor can good history be neatly labelled and pigeon-holed. Is Parrington's *Main Currents in American Thought* history or literary criticism? Who cares? Where do you classify Leslie Stephen's *English Thought in the Eighteenth Century*? It is intellectual history; it is philosophy and theology as well. Turn to Morley's biographies of Voltaire and Diderot and Rousseau, and you are plunged into the very vortex of the most exciting intellectual controversies of modern times. If you wish to know Thomas Jefferson you are required to immerse yourself in all his interests: in politics and law, philosophy and religion, literature, art, and architecture, agriculture and gardening, history and natural history, anthropology and ethnology, education and libraries, and a dozen other things as well. History is as all-embracing as life itself and the mind of man.

The Study of History

chapter three

READING HISTORY

Does it make any difference what history we read? Justice Holmes once said that any subject is great when greatly pursued. A dull scholar can make even *Hamlet* or the Declaration of Independence dull, while a luminous mind like John Livingston Lowes can write a fascinating work, *The Road to Xanadu,* on the sources of Coleridge's poem, and a powerful mind like Walton Hamilton can write an original work on a single phrase of the Constitution—"commerce among the several states"—which throws new light on *The Power to Govern.* Admitting this, it still does make a difference what the scholar writes or the student reads. While, no doubt, all historical subjects are equal, some are more equal than others, and while all eras of history are interesting, as it turns out, the Renaissance, Elizabethan England, the French Revolution have a richness, a variety, a complexity which have excited students for generations, and that excitement has communicated itself in great literature.

This is, after all, the common sense of the matter. Doubtless every child is beautiful in the eyes of its mother, and we have on the authority of a hundred poets that every mistress is lovely in the eyes of her lover. The rest of the world, however, does not necessarily accept these verdicts, but abides by its own standards of beauty or virtue or interest. Certainly a biography of our old friends John Doe and Richard Roe is not as interesting as a biography of Abraham Lincoln or Robert E. Lee, and all the art in the world could not make it as interesting. No matter what genius an historian lavishes on a history of the Tariff of 1884, he cannot really make that subject as exciting as the history of the writing of the federal Constitution, nor is the history of Harrod's store, splendid as that London emporium doubtless is, quite in a class with the history of the Spanish Armada. It is no accident that almost all business biographies—purchased at no matter what cost—are failures, or that almost any book on Jefferson or Disraeli or Winston Churchill is interesting.

From this it follows that the argument for studying Periclean Athens or Renaissance Florence or the federal Constitution or the American Civil War is a circular one: for generations affluent minds have lavished their attention upon these and similar subjects, and the student can be sure, therefore, of a rich storehouse on which to draw. Just as we tend to study those areas of art which produced great artists—a Leonardo, a Raphael, a Michelangelo for example—or those chapters of the history of music which recount the careers of a Bach, a Haydn, a Mozart, a Beethoven, so we may be forgiven if we prefer to study those chapters of history which have produced or inspired the greatest historians.

For purposes of study, then, there are some preferred chapters of history. Study those chapters of history which, for one reason or another, have attracted first-rate minds and talents to their exposition. Study the history of ancient Greece because some of the greatest poets and dramatists and historians of all time recorded that history, and because for over two thousand years Greece has exercised an irresistible fascination over the minds of men. Study the Italian Renaissance because that study will take you to Florence, Siena, Rome, Milan, Venice, and because countless rich minds have been there before you and celebrated what they found: Cellini and Machiavelli and Castiglioni and Guicciardini, for example, among the contemporaries, and Jacob Burckhardt and John Addington Symonds and Ferdinand Schevill and Bernard Berenson among the moderns. Study the history of Puritanism or the making of the federal Constitution or the Jeffiersonian era because you will assure yourself of association with men of superior talents and characters, and because you will be guided, in turn, by historians who combine literary and scholarly talents of a high order. That cannot be said, for example, of the study of the Hayes or the Harrison or the Coolidge administrations.

A second rule for the study of history is equally elementary: read for pleasure and for intellectual excitement. History opens up new worlds, just as geological exploration and science open up new worlds. Needless to say history embraces both of these, so that through the pages of history we can share the excitement of discovery. The many volumes of the Hakluyt Society, in their enchanting light blue bindings, enable us to sail with Francis Drake and Martin Frobisher and Captain Cook to far quarters of the globe; through the pages of Beazley's great *Dawn of Modern Geography* we can share the excitement of the unfolding of the globe, the beginnings of cartography, the discovery of the compass and the astrolabe; with the greatest of all geographer-historians, Alexander von Humboldt, we can enter into a new *Kosmos.* Nowhere is the story of geographical discovery more exciting than in America; with Bernard De Voto we can follow *The Course of Empire* from Newfoundland to the Pacific; or we can concentrate on single chapters of that story by familiarizing ourselves with the exploits of the eccentric John Ledyard of Connecticut, or immersing ourselves in the *Journals* of the Lewis and Clark expedition. The history of science, still in its infancy, is no less exciting. Joseph Needham's volumes on *Science and Civilization in China*—Herbert Butterfield has called it the most important historical work of our generation—opens up new worlds to even the most sophisticated; and so does George Sarton's five-volume *Introduction to the History of Science.* If these seem too formidable there are fascinating interpretative studies such as Giedion's *Mechanization Takes Command,* or Loren Eiseley's brilliant recreation of *Darwin's Century* or Daniel Boorstin's *Lost World of Thomas Jefferson* or Lewis Mumford's critical *Technics and Civilization.*

History has depth as well as scope. It enables us to enter into the minds and characters of the great figures of the past with a degree of intimacy unimaginable for our own day or our own society. In this it is like compounding family history a thousand-fold; it permits us to know the pasts of other societies, even those which have been swept away by time such as the Etruscan, the Aztec, the Inca, the Viking. It plunges us into the most enthralling eras of human experience and enables us to know some of their greatest characters—a Leonardo, a Jefferson, a Goethe, a Lincoln—more intimately even than their friends and companions knew them. Through history we can follow them in their every deed and, through their letters, their journals and diaries—records rarely available in their own day—we can follow them almost in their every thought. This is one of the most gratifying of all rewards of history; perhaps only in great imaginative literature do we get anything comparable.

Every student of history can say to himself what Wordsworth said to Toussaint L'Ouverture—

> . . . thou hast great allies;
> Thy friends are exultations, agonies,
> And love, and man's unconquerable mind.

For history—and perhaps history alone—permits us to live with greatness.

The student of history can say, with Stephen Spender:

> I think continually of those who were truly great.
> . . . .
> The names of those who in their lives fought for life,
> Who wore at their hearts the fire's centre.
> Born of the sun, they travelled a short while towards the sun,
> And left the vivid air signed with their honour.

It is important then, in studying history, that we choose great companions. We would not willingly fritter away our lives on dull people, and there is no reason why we should fritter away our intellectual energies on the dull and the trivial. Concentration on the trivial makes for pedantry or for superficiality. Concentrate, then, on what historians have found to be significant. To be sure, historians are not infallible; to be sure, an original mind can often find drama and significance in what has long been neglected or deemed of no consequence. After you have become familiar with some of the great epochs of history, and some of the leading historians, it is time to do a bit of exploring on your own.

A third rule for reading history is to read systematically. Nothing is more time-consuming and, in the end, more surely calculated to consume interest as well, than to read miscellaneously and indiscriminately; that is like reading whatever magazine the air-line hostess happens to give us. In history, as in most matters, order, system, and discipline are essential. No one who flits from the piano to the violin to the flute without mastering any one of them will become a musician; no one who dabbles in French, German, Italian and Spanish without mastering one of them will become a linguist. The literature of history is almost infinitely voluminous: there are at least twenty thousand volumes dealing with the French Revolution and in all likelihood quite as many bearing on the American Civil War, and it requires the Folger Library of a quarter-million volumes to do justice to Shakespeare and his times. To "dip into" every era of history, or the history of every country, is to court lunacy.

What is wanted is system and seriousness. First, then, read solid works, not books made up of fluff and stuff. The butterfly technique—sipping at whatever is attractive—is the kind of self-indulgence which speedily leads to satiety. If you are interested in the American Civil War start with Douglas Freeman's four massive volumes on *R. E. Lee* and then go on to his three volumes on *Lee's Lieutenants.* By the time you have studied these, you should have a deep and ardent feeling for the War, and you should have too an awareness of having lived with a great man—and to have seen him through the eyes of another great man, Douglas Freeman. Then you can go on to other solid works—Allan Nevins' monumental *Ordeal of the Union,* for example, which carries you from the Compromise of 1850 to Appomattox in eight rich volumes, or Bruce Catton's dramatic recreation of life in the Union Army in his three volumes on the Army of the Potomac, or Sandburg's lyrical tribute to Lincoln—there are six sprawling volumes altogether. By then you will be able to appreciate Stephen Benet's epic poem, *John Brown's Body,* still in some ways the best evocation of the War. Historical novels, too, have a contribution to make, and there is no other chapter in our history that has attracted so many good novelists or inspired so many readable novels. You can immerse yourself in novels like De Forest's *Miss Ravenel's Conversion,* in Winston Churchill's *The Crisis,* or in more modern and more realistic recreations of the War like Evelyn Scott's *The Wave,* or McKinlay Kantor's *Andersonville.*

By this time you will perhaps have had your fill of secondary works and will want to turn to the sources themselves—the vast library of letters and diaries and memoirs bequeathed by participants, the lively accounts of journalists and travellers—not to mention the reports of the many artists—the immense mass of official papers and records, political, diplomatic, and military, far too voluminous for any one historian to master. To find your way through this labyrinth of source material would be a desperate task but for the happy fact that others have been there before you, have surveyed it and mapped it and marked out the paths.

You are not set adrift on a limitless sea of diplomacy: Owsley is there to guide you with his *King Cotton Diplomacy* and E. D. Adams with his two-volume study of *Great Britain and the American Civil War,* and a score of other scholars as well. You are not left to wander aimlessly through the records of the battle of Gettysburg; a dozen biographers, a score of military historians, are ready to provide guidance. You are not left to conjure up for yourself the causes for the defeat of the Confederacy; a hundred scholars have speculated on just that question, a hundred books provide not only the theories and explanations but notes and references which direct you to the source material and enable you to arrive at your own conclusions.

Or suppose it is Thomas Jefferson who has caught your fancy—there is no one more rewarding, no one who better fulfills the promises he holds out on first acquaintance. The literature here, too, is immense, and you will do well to begin with one of the many good biographies—that by the French-American scholar, Gilbert Chinard, for example, or the three fascinating volumes by Marie Kimball, or the still incomplete biography by Dumas Malone. Once you know what most interests you in Jefferson you will want to turn to his own astonishingly voluminous writings. There are two older editions of the writings, and one magnificent edition still under way—some seventeen volumes published—edited by the greatest of Jefferson scholars, Julian Boyd. Now you will be ready for some of the almost innumerable monographs dealing with particular aspects of the life of this versatile genius. There is, for example, Karl Lehmann's wide-ranging essay on *Thomas Jefferson, American Humanist,* or James Bryant Conant's lectures on *Jefferson and the Development of American Education,* or Edwin Martin's fascinating study of *Thomas Jefferson, Scientist,* or Fiske Kimball's authoritative book on *Thomas Jefferson, Architect,* or Edward Dumbauld's delightful *Thomas Jefferson, American Tourist.* If you want politics, there are the volumes which the incomparable Henry Adams devoted to Jefferson in his *History,* or the two volumes by the diplomat-historian Claude Bowers, *Jefferson and Hamilton* and *Jefferson in Power,* or C. M. Wiltse's *Jeffersonian Tradition in American Politics.* Charles A. Beard has investigated the *Economic Origins of Jeffersonian Democracy;* Leonard White has done a definitive job on the administrative side of the Jeffersonian years, *The Jeffersonians;* and Merril Petersen has traced the *Jeffersonian Image in the American Mind.*

But this is, in a sense, only the beginning. You cannot understand Jefferson in a vacuum; you must know his associates and disciples, you must know his intellectual companions and his philosophical antecedents; happily these are well worth knowing. James Madison was, for almost fifty years, Jefferson's disciple and friend—the friendship has been explored by Adrienne Koch in a book on the two men. You will want to read Irving Brant's six-volume biography of Madison and to read some of Madison's own essays and letters in the older edition by Gaillard Hunt or in the new edition of the *Papers* now under way. Albert Gallatin, too—the Swiss *philosophe* who cast in his lot with America and became, in time, Jefferson's Secretary of the Treasury—was a member of the Jeffersonian circle: you can read his life in a masterly biography by Henry Adams, and his *Writings* are edited, in three stout volumes, also by Adams. You can scarcely think of Jefferson without his life-long friend—and sometime antagonist—John Adams: they worked together for fifty years and died, dramatically, on the same day, precisely fifty years after the Declaration of Independence. To know Adams is almost as big a task, and almost as interesting, as knowing Jefferson. There are good biographies by Gilbert Chinard and Page Smith; there is an admirable study of Adams' political thought by Edward Handler, and Zoltan Haraszti has set forth his relation to the French *philosophes* in the ingenious *John Adams and the Prophets of Progress.* You will of course want to read Adams himself: the *Diary* and

Autobiography have already been republished, in four sumptuous volumes, and the correspondence and miscellaneous writings will soon be available in the new edition of the Adams papers edited by Lyman Butterfield. But to know Jefferson you must know not only his associates, but his intellectual and philosophical antecedents. Turn then to the five-volume catalogue of his wonderful library which Miss Millicent Sowerby has edited; to the elaborate annotations in Boyd's edition of the *Papers;* to the many monographs on Jefferson's French associates by Gilbert Chinard; and to studies of the Enlightenment by John Morley, Carl Becker, Ernst Cassirer, Paul Hazard, Basil Willey, and a score of other interpreters. By now you will realize that to do justice to Jefferson is the work not of a year but of a lifetime, but that is true of almost every really great or spacious subject.

A fourth rule in the study of history is always to work from the particular to the general, never from the general to the particular. General works—outlines of this or that, surveys of everything—are almost guaranteed to rot the brain. The method of history is the method of science—inductive, and empirical; it is the method of law—the case study; it is the method even of art—to start with the study of anatomy, with the mastery of paints, or of stone. Begin, then, with the particular—with an individual or an episode or an institution—and work from there to more general subjects. Are you interested in the United States Constitution? Start with the document itself, read the debates in the Federal Convention (they have been admirably edited by Max Farrand) and the debates in the ratifying conventions as well, the so-called *Elliot's Debates.* Read and re-read *The Federalist* papers, incomparably the most profound commentary on political philosophy and on constitutionalism written in this country: there are several good modern editions. Now you are ready to go on to constitutional history. A good book of documents will give you many of the essential laws, proclamations, presidential addresses, and judicial opinions. A good history of the Supreme Court—that by Charles Warren, though by now out of date, is unquestionably the best—and a few biographies such as Beveridge's voluminous *Marshall,* or Charles Fairman's *Justice Miller* or Alpheus Mason's *Chief Justice Stone* or Max Lerner's edition of the *Mind and Faith of Justice Holmes* will go a long way towards clarifying the intricacies and complexities of the constitutional system. Genuine scholarship would of course require that you immerse yourself in the decisions of the Supreme Court—the very stuff and substance of our constitutional law and history; there are some 375 volumes of these, and here you will clearly need expert guidance; fortunately, a score of case-books which bring together the leading decisions are at hand. By the time you have studied the Constitution and the Court intensively you will have familiarized yourself not only with the American constitutional system, but with most of the issues of American politics, economy, and society.

The average reader, it is fair to say, gets his sense of the past not through the writings of formal historians, but through the pages of fiction directly or, in recent times, translated into films and television dramas. This is natural enough; the story comes before history in the life of the race, as in the lives of individuals. Biblical stories came before Josephus' *History of the Jews,* and the *Iliad* and the *Odyssey* before either Herodotus or Thucydides, and it is not only children who have learned the history of England from the stories of King Arthur and his knights of the Round Table, or from Froissart or Chaucer, but their parents as well. Winston Churchill (who himself wrote an historical novel) said that he learned all of his English history from the plays of Shakespeare, and Francis Parkman's debt to Cooper's *Leatherstocking Tales* is notorious, while G. M. Trevelyan has paid handsome tribute to the influence of Walter Scott on his own historical writing. "Fiction is truth's elder sister," wrote Rudyard Kipling, with pardonable exaggeration. No one in the world knew what truth was till someone had told a story. So it is the oldest of the arts, the mother of history, biography, philosophy, and, of course, "politics."

Cooper and Scott, and Kipling, too, remind us that the historical novel is very much a nineteenth century invention. It began—there were of course antecedents—with Walter Scott and John Galt in Scotland, with Fenimore Cooper and William Gilmore Simms in America, with B. S. Ingemann in Denmark and Victor Hugo in France and Alessandro Manzoni in Italy. These were, for a generation and more, the most widely read of modern writers, providing the whole civilized world with stereotypes of historical characters and episodes. The historical novel spread from England throughout Europe, and became a standard expression of historical nationalism. Almost every major writer tried his hand at it: Thackeray and Bulwer-Lytton and George Eliot and Disraeli and even Dickens in England; Victor Hugo and Stendhal and Dumas and Flaubert in France; Gustav Freytag in Germany; Sienkiewicz in Poland; Manzoni in Italy; Pushkin, Turgenev, and Tolstoy in Russia; and in Spain Perez Galdos whose *Episodios Nacionales* filled no fewer than forty-six volumes.

Nowhere did the historical novel flourish more vigorously than in the United States. Almost all the major writers turned to history for their material: Irving, who was both an historian and a novelist, and his friend James Kirke Paulding, Cooper and Hawthorne and the almost forgotten De Forest and the prolific E. Marion Crawford, and the southerners Beverley Tucker and John Pendleton Kennedy and William Gilmore Simms; even the historians Motley and Parkman managed to squeeze in one historical novel apiece. Harriet Beecher Stowe gave us *The Minister's Wooing* and many other historical panels, and Howells did not fail to conjure up frontier Ohio, and Mark Twain, whom we do not ordinarily remember as an historical novelist, produced *The Prince and the Pauper* and *A Connecticut Yankee in King Arthur's Court.* One trait almost all of these had in common—as did most of the English historical novelists from Thackeray to Stevenson—is that they wrote for children, or wrote books which children took over and made their own. Teachers and scholars too commonly ignore the needs of children, forgetting that if they are to be attracted to the study of history their interests must be aroused and their sympathies enlisted, and forgetting that children want action, drama, adventure, heroes, and villains. These the historical novel offers them.

There are, in a broad way, two kinds of historical novels. There is the "costume piece"—the novel which quite deliberately seeks to recreate the past and to dramatize it; like a producer putting on an Elizabethan play, the author has to be sure to get all the "furniture" right—the clothing, the idiom, even the accent. Traditionally this kind of historical novel distorts history, leaving with the reader the impression that the past was a potpourri of fighting, derring-do, and non-stop romances by Scott or Dumas or Stevenson or John Buchan. But at its best this kind of historical fiction can be as faithful to history as a good many sober monographs, and can be, at the same time, great literature: Thackeray's *The Virginians,* Hawthorne's *Scarlet Letter,* Stendhal's *Charterhouse of Parma,* Tolstoy's *War and Peace,* Sigrid Undset's *Kristin Lavransdatter,* Thomas Mann's *Joseph and his Brethren,* and Lion Feuchtwanger's *Jew Süss* come readily to mind.

There is another and even more valuable genre of historical novel—the novel that is not deliberately "historical" at all, but that faithfully recreates a present which is or will be past, and which becomes, therefore, by virtue of its authenticity, an historical document. If we want to know what life was like in the comfortable upper classes of England during the Napoleonic wars we cannot do better than turn to the novels of Jane Austen—*Pride and Prejudice* or *Sense and Sensibility* or *Mansfield Park.* Is there anywhere a more faithful picture of Scotland during these same years than can be read in the salty pages of John Galt's *Annals of the Parish* or *The Entail*—unless it is possibly in the pages of Galt's contemporary, Susan Ferrier? Has anyone ever conjured up life in the London of the early nineteenth century more realistically than Dickens in *Nicholas Nickleby* or *Oliver Twist* or *Great Expectations*? What better way is there to understand the bourgeoisie of the Hansa towns than through Thomas Mann's *Buddenbrooks,* or of French provincial towns than in the pages of *Madame Bovary*? Selma Lagerlöv has given us eighteenth century Sweden in the marvellously picaresque *Saga of*

Gösta Berling and nineteenth century Sweden in *Jerusalem;* and Bjørnsen has done the same for Norway. Louis Couperus helps us to understand life in the crowded cities of modern Holland, and if we turn to Denmark we have no better guide than Martin Andersen-Nexö whose *Pelle the Conqueror* and *Ditte Girl Alive* recreate Copenhagen as Dickens recreated London. No sociological treatises conjure up life in the provincial towns of industrial England more faithfully than Arnold Bennett's Five Towns stories—*Clayhanger* and *Old Wives' Tale* and others; no historian of the class system illuminates it better than do Galsworthy in the *Forsyte Saga* or Frank Swinnerton in *Shops and Houses* or Virginia Woolf in *Day and Night.* Americans, too, can read their social history in works of fiction. William Dean Howells has some claim to be regarded as our most finished and comprehensive social historian, Howells who gives us the placid life of Boston and of the hinterland of New England, the Vermont countryside, the Ohio frontier and the turbulent life of New York City, and of the American abroad, and whose *Rise of Silas Lapham* is still in many ways the best portrayal of the American businessman in our literature. So it is with a host of others: the incomparable Henry James, foremost historian of the manners of the American leisure class and of the American expatriate, and most penetrating student of the American moral character; Edith Wharton with her sensitive feeling for the life of the upper classes of New York City and the Hudson Valley; Ellen Glasgow, who understood so fully what had happened to Virginia "after the War," and who explained it in a long series of novels carrying the history of Virginia from the Civil War to the twentieth century; Willa Cather, whose panels of life on the plains—*My Ántonia* and *O Pioneers* and *The Song of the Lark* and, best of all, *A Lost Lady*—are more realistic and penetrating than her formal historical novels. For a feeling of life on the farm in the years after the Civil War, and of the truth of the farm problem, we turn with confidence to Hamlin Garland's *Main Traveled Roads* or to Frank Norris' *The Octopus* or to Ole Rølvaag's wonderfully evocative *Giants in the Earth,* rather than to the formal histories; and the most penetrating accounts of the "revolt from the village" are, beyond doubt, such books as Sherwood Anderson's *Winesburg, Ohio* or Edgar Lee Masters' *Spoon River Anthology* or Sinclair Lewis' *Main Street.*

These observations apply with equal force to poetry and drama. Lord Tennyson's *Idylls of the King* and the plays of Hendrik Ibsen are historical documents of the first order; read with insight and with sympathy they will illuminate the Victorian mind, or the social history of Norway, as brightly as any formal historical treatises on these subjects.

WRITING HISTORY

So much for reading. What of the writing of history?

Let it be said at once that there is no mystery about writing history, nothing esoteric or cabalistic. There is no formula for historical writing. There are no special techniques or special requirements, except the technique of writing clearly and the requirements of honesty and common sense. It is useful to have special training, as it is useful to have special training for almost anything you wish to do well—driving a car, or cooking, or painting—but special training is by no means essential, and most of the great historians have been innocent of formal training. Professional history is, indeed, a very recent affair—it came in with "technical history" in the nineteenth century— and, except in Germany, the near-monopoly of historical writing by academicians is even more recent. Almost all the great historians of the past were men involved in one way or another in public affairs—Thucydides, Livy, Tacitus, Plutarch and, in modern times, Bolingbroke, Voltaire, Hume, Macaulay, Bancroft, Guizot, Grundtvig. Most of them, too, were amateurs, at least in the sense that they were not professional teachers: thus in the United States Bancroft, Prescott, Motley, Parkman, and Henry Adams. The amateur tradition is now almost a thing of the past, but it lingers on in Europe more tenaciously than in America: witness the contributions of such public figures as Croce, Madariaga, Malraux, De Gaulle, George Lukacs, and Winston Churchill.

Integrity, industry, imagination, and common sense—these are the important, indeed the essential, requirements. They are by no means familiar commonplace qualities. The requirement of integrity is of course implacable, in history as in all other forms of scholarship or science, and there is no need to elaborate upon it. Yet here, too, it must be admitted that standards of "integrity" are not universal, and that honest men differ on the nature of truth in history as in all other realms of thought. Perhaps it is sufficient to say that the historian must be honest according to his lights; that he should never consciously distort his evidence, even by literary artistry; that he should be ever on guard against religious, racial, class or national preconceptions; that he should try to see every problem from all possible points of view; that he should search diligently for all the evidence, and not be content until he has exhausted the available resources; that he should always remember that he is not God and that final judgment is not entrusted to him.

The requirement of industry, too, is elementary and rigorous. You need not, perhaps, emulate the great historian of ancient Rome, Theodore

Mommsen, who customarily worked eighteen hours a day and complained that on his wedding day he managed only twelve hours work, or that other German phenomenon, Leopold von Ranke, who kept working and writing well into his eighties, and who at the age of eighty-five launched a *History of the World,* seven volumes of which appeared in the next five years of his life. But, as with most things that are important, the writing of history requires patience, devotion, and indefatigable industry, much of it tiresome. You will have to accustom yourself to spending long hours and days tracking down some source which as often as not will prove quite useless, reading through newspapers or journals which as often as not yield only a scanty return, working patiently through ill-scrawled manuscripts in the hope, often vain, of hitting on something that is relevant to your inquiry, fighting your way stubbornly through the jungles of verbiage in the *Congressional Globe* or the *Reports* of royal commissions, or the decisions of courts. If you are going to come up with something that is new, original, fresh, and valuable, you cannot avoid these exercises; if you are not prepared for them, you will do well to abandon history for something less arduous.

As for imagination, that is in all likelihood something that cannot be cultivated; either you have it or you do not. If you do not have it you may be a worthy compiler of facts, a good analyst, a safe guide through the labyrinths of the past, but you will never be able to recreate that past, never set the blood coursing through the veins of your readers, or ideas tumbling over each other in their heads. As for "common sense"—alas it is by no means as common as the phrase implies. It is an all-inclusive term which embraces such disparate qualities as moderation, balance, judiciousness, critical intelligence, open-mindedness, tolerance, proportion, and good humor, and doubtless other qualities as well. Without it the most scholarly and interesting works misfire—for example as with William Crosskey's two learned volumes designed to prove that the Founding Fathers meant something quite different from what they said and wrote, or Otto Eisenschiml's elaborate proof that Secretary Stanton master-minded the plot to assassinate Lincoln, or Charles Tansill's well documented volumes designed to prove that Franklin Roosevelt instigated the Second World War, or—to take a more extreme example—those many volumes dedicated to the proposition that Lord Bacon or the Earl of Oxford, or somebody else wrote the plays hitherto attributed to Shakespeare.

Let us turn, then, to some practical considerations in the writing of history: first, the choice of a subject. That seems almost too elementary a matter to justify comment, but alas it is not. Again and again otherwise sensible neophyte historians come a cropper when they select a subject for their investigation. Here is where common sense comes in. Your subject should not be too ambitious, or too petty. It should not be too hackneyed, or too esoteric. It should be something you can manage within the time you have available, the time and the space. It should be something which has not been chewed up by generations of historians; at the same time it should not be something so strange and rare that it will be of interest only to you. Take care, too, that the materials you will need to use are not only available but available to you. Do not select some subject for which the materials are scanty and unreliable, or the essential documents inaccessible—some chapter in the history of the Secret Service, for example, or the CIA—or in the possession of a family which preserves them for its own purposes, or in the archives of Spain or Australia—unless indeed you happen to be bound for Spain or Australia. If you live in Montana do not select a subject which has to be studied in the files of eastern newspapers; if you live in New York City do not select a subject which has to be studied through materials scattered throughout a dozen western historical societies. If your command of languages is shaky, avoid subjects which require a knowledge of half a dozen foreign languages; if your eyesight is poor avoid subjects which are to be studied in seventeenth or eighteenth century manuscripts or—for that matter—in the manuscripts of Horace Greeley or Charles Sumner or others whose handwriting was notoriously indecipherable.

All of this is purely negative—this elimination of subjects that do not lend themselves to orderly treatment. There is one affirmative consideration equally basic and imperative: select a subject the way you would select a friend or, perhaps, a spouse. It is something you are going to live with for a long time, perhaps for years; select therefore a good companion for the journey. Ideally you should find a subject which so interests and excites you that you cannot resist it. On the whole it is desirable to choose a subject which enlists your sympathy, though that is by no means essential. You can write effectively about the Massacre of St. Bartholomew even though you disapprove in principle of religious intolerance; you can write perspicaciously of Hitler without approving of Nazism; yet it is perhaps best to avoid the first if you are of Huguenot descent and the second if you are Jewish.

For biographical subjects it is particularly important to find a figure who enlists your sympathy as well as your interest. As you would not want to live intimately with someone you heartily disliked, so you will not want to live on terms of intimacy with some historical character whom you heartily dislike. There are examples of biographers who have disliked—or come to dislike—their subject: Froude certainly appeared to dislike Carlyle—though in fact he did not—and Lytton Strachey had no use for his Eminent Victorians, while Paxton Hibbe scarcely tried to conceal his contempt for William Jennings Bryan. Bu these are exceptions. The best biographers confess admiration an sympathy for their subjects, and some of them deep personal affection–Boswell's famous biography of Dr. Johnson, for example, or Willia Dean Howells' tender interpretation, *My Mark Twain,* or George Ott Trevelyan's spirited biography of his uncle, *Lord Macaulay.*

Once you have found a sympathetic subject, and ascertained that there is something new to be said about it and that the materials on which to base your study are ample and readily available, you can get started. And from now on common sense really does take charge.

Even here there are some practical observations that are relevant. The first is this: do not waste time and energy in what is amiably called "reading around" a subject. Reading around, or reading for background, is more often than not an excuse for not getting on with the job: it is pleasant, it is edifying—and it is inexhaustible. A chemist concerned with a specific problem does not stop to "read around" chemistry; a lawyer dealing with a specific case does not "read around" the law. Plunge into the subject itself; get your problem by the throat and grapple with it. The closer you come to it, and the deeper your understanding of it, the more surely you will become familiar with all the surrounding landscape. Gradually everything will fall into place. That, after all, is the natural way: you come only gradually to know the background of a friend, and even children do not fill in the background of parents and grandparents until they themselves have children. In short, start with the particular, not with the general; read deeply in the history of the particular, and you will find that the general takes care of itself.

A second practical rule is to begin almost at once collecting the essential materials for your essay or monograph and organizing them into some coherent pattern. Granted you do not really know what is "essential," or just what the pattern is to be; the sooner you get started, the sooner you will find answers to these questions. Do not think you have to read everything, take notes on everything, track down every reference, look at every piece of manuscript before you begin to write. The sooner you begin the better, for only as you write will you discover the lacunae in your knowledge, and fill them.

There is a third practical consideration here that has to do with the compilation of your materials. For most purposes that means "taking notes"—that arduous and never-ending process which can, unless you are careful, become something of an opiate, a pleasant substitute for the real work of thinking and writing. Not long ago taking notes meant precisely that; the scholar painfully, and painstakingly, copied out mountains of passages which he hoped would one day prove useful, or hired someone to do it for him. Now all of that has changed; note-taking has been mechanized, like so many other things, and the happy researcher now sends his materials off to be Photostated, Xeroxed or microfilmed—all much better than in the bad old days. Now you can get ten times as much copied, nay a hundred times as much; now you can be sure of accuracy; now you can save time and go everywhere and see everything! Fortunate scholars; now we may expect them all to write twice as much as any former generation. How odd that they write only half as much!

We are all immensely indebted to modern techniques of mechanical reproduction, but do not be carried away by them to the point where you think that history itself has become mechanized. It is all very well to have machines do your copying for you, but remember that they cannot think for you. Something is to be said for doing things yourself—even for copying documents yourself. The great literary historian Van Wyck Brooks, author of the most interesting of literary histories of America, did all his own copying and, what is more, did it all by hand. He could, of course, have employed copyists, or bought himself a copying machine. He preferred to do his own work because he knew what every scholar comes to know: that if you copy things yourself, you remember them. He knew, too, another important lesson: that the by-product of copying is often more important than the product, namely the ideas you get as you go. No machine can get those ideas for you, and there is no substitute for the inspiration which comes from your own direct, fresh, and uncomplicated relation with your materials.

When it comes to writing history, keep in mind that there are almost as many ways of writing as there are historians. There is no formula; you will have to find your own formula. There is no pattern; you will have to work out your own pattern. But this is not to suggest that there are no models. There are models by the score. You will doubtless be influenced by them, just as a painter is influenced by Rembrandt or Goya, Whistler or Picasso. That does not mean that you can successfully adopt for your own the lordly style of a Gibbon, the rhetorical style of a Carlyle, the balanced cadences of a Macaulay, the strong masculine style of a Mahan, the brilliant style of a Parrington, the epigrammatic style of a Philip Guedalla, the allusive style of a Denis Brogan, the intimate style of a Paul Hazard. All of these are available, but in writing, as in other matters, the style reflects the man and your style must reflect you.

But style is not a single or a static thing; you will want to vary your style, to adapt it to the subject matter. You would not think of using the same pattern of organization, the same style of presentation, for all subjects, any more than you would clothe all men and women alike at all times. A style suitable, let us say, to a history of the Tariff of 1890 is not a good style for a history of the conquest of Peru or for a biography of Herman Melville. Each subject makes its own claim upon you; each one demands individual treatment. Practiced historians know this almost instinctively, and vary their styles, as do professional couturiers or photographers. Thomas Beer, for example—he was a novelist as well as an historian—used very different styles in his biography of *Stephen Crane* and his essay on *The Mauve Decade;* John Morley varied his style to suit the different requirements of *Voltaire* and of *Gladstone;* Henry Adams had one style for the *History* and a quite different one for the *Education,* more subtle, more allusive, though not more brilliant.

Some Problems of History

chapter four

LIMITATIONS ON THE HISTORIAN

"The historian," writes Veronica Wedgwood, "ought to be the humblest of men; he is faced a dozen times a day with the evidence of his own ignorance; he is perpetually confronted with his own humiliating inability to interpret his material correctly; he is, in a sense that no other writer is, in bondage to that material." In bondage! Most sophisticated historians would readily agree with this. They are ever conscious of the limitations and handicaps under which they work, and of the temptations and dangers to which they are exposed. But the public tends to overlook these limitations, and some historians are even innocent enough, or brash enough, to gloss over the difficulties inherent in their profession.

History is in fact far more complex and disorderly than the amateur suspects. To most laymen it is all simple and straightforward. What is it, he asks, that you want to know? Is it the writing of the Magna Carta, the consolidation of Germany under Bismarck, the triumph of Communism in China? Get your facts, put them together in some sensible order, and Presto! there is your history. The great historian Henry Adams has made the classic observation on this notion of history. "He had even published a dozen volumes of American history," he recalled, "for no other purpose than to satisfy himself whether, by the severest process of stating, with the least possible comment, such facts as seemed sure in such order as seemed rigorously consequent, he could fix for a familiar moment a necessary sequence of human movement." The result, he confessed, was failure. "Where he saw sequence other men saw something quite different, and no one saw the same unit of measure," and he concluded that "the sequence of men led to nothing and that the sequence of their society could lead no further, while the mere sequence of time was artificial, and the sequence of thought was chaos." (*The Education of Henry Adams,* Boston: Houghton Mifflin Company, 1918, p. 382.) So he abandoned history altogether and asserted, somewhat perversely, that any nine pages of his novel, *Esther,* were worth more than the nine volumes of his *History.* Posterity does not agree with this verdict, but that is another matter.

What, then, are some of these limitations which have discouraged so many historians, and which, Miss Wedgwood admonished us, should induce humility?

First, there are the many and sobering limitations on historical materials. There is, for example, the role of fortuity. The chemist or biologist can command whatever materials he needs for his experiments, but the historian works with what happens to come to hand. What we are permitted "to know" is not only but a small part of "what happened in history," but it is a miscellany which has come to us in large part by chance rather than by choice. What we can see of history is far less than what we can see of the iceberg; most of it, too, is buried and forever lost. It is lost because it was never compiled; it is lost because of the erosion of time—fire and water and weather and carelessness; it is lost because it was deliberately destroyed. How do we know that what has come down to us is either the most important or the most authentic representation of any chapter of past history?

Another limitation is that of distortion; the record of the past, as we have it, is monstrously lopsided. Thus we know a great deal of the history of some European peoples, and because this record is available we confuse it with History and write as if it embraced the whole of the past. It is not merely that the records for most non-European societies are non-existent or lost—the African, for example, or the American Indian or the Carthagenian—but that even where records are available—in China, or in India for example—western historians have not used them. This is easy to understand, but we should not call what we choose to interest ourselves in History, and formulate broad, even universal, generalizations on the basis of such fragmentary and arbitrary evidence.

The very fact that history is based so largely on the written record introduces a note of unbalance, and distorts our view. For what it inevitably means is that we exaggerate the role of the written record and of those peoples who did keep records at the expense of those who did not, or whose records are fitful and uninformative. Almost every historian has an unconscious bias in favor of the literary history-conscious, western European, and against the others: in favor of the Jews and against the Babylonians, in favor of the Greeks and against the Persians, in favor of the Romans and against the "barbarians." Even in highly sophisticated societies such as our own we must acknowledge a distortion induced by the charms of the written record. How much of American history has been colored by the fact that New Englanders have been more assiduous in keeping records and more effective in presenting them than, let us say, Virginians or Carolinians; Jamestown came before Plymouth, but every schoolboy knows, from poetry, fiction, and painting as well as from history, the story of the Pilgrims and the Puritans. The slave-owner was literate and articulate, the Negro slave illiterate and inarticulate; it was, until recently, the slave-owner's version of slavery which came down to us and which was widely accepted as history.

The seduction, or tyranny, of the written record introduces another element of distortion, namely, that what attracts the record-keeper and the historian is the dramatic, the spectacular, the bizarre, and the catastrophic. This has always been true, and it remains true today, as reference to any daily newspaper will make clear. The monkish chroniclers who bequeathed us so many records did not customarily record the daily routine of life, but only events which they considered out of the ordinary or miraculous: comets and earthquakes and plagues and wars; and millions of families have endorsed this view of history by recording in their family Bibles only births, marriages, and deaths. The historian too is attracted by whatever is dramatic or unusual or romantic; he writes the annals of the rich and the great; for the annals of the poor, as we know, are short and simple. How natural it is for us, how inevitable perhaps, to believe that history is, by its very nature, the record of what is dramatic and astonishing. A great statesman, a soldier, an explorer, we say "makes history"; or a particular people at a particular time—the Athenians of the fifth century B.C., or the French during their Revolution, "make history." This is, of course, nonsense; everybody makes history all the time, the Slave as well as the Master, the South Sea Islander as well as the Parisian. What we mean is that these people make the kind of history that appeals to us, that we happen to know about, and that we like to write about; it follows very easily that what appeals to us and what we write about is history.

Closely associated with the enchantment of the dramatic is the spell of the familiar. So accustomed are we to the formal patterns of history that it requires a convulsive effort for us to remember that these are not history's patterns, but ours. We have already considered the dangers latent in familiar chronological and regional patterns—the habit of dividing history into neat packets labelled Ancient, Medieval, and

Modern, or of carving up American history into Colonial, Revolutionary, Middle Period, and so forth. There is a further refinement on these divisions which is even more artificial, the habit of forcing history into the straitjackets of monarchical or presidential patterns. Thus we write of the Age of Louis XIV or of Napoleon, of the Jeffersonian era, or the era of Franklin D. Roosevelt.

Of all patterns which we have imposed upon history, it is the national which is the most powerful and the most pervasive, and perhaps the most mischievous. The limitations which nationalism imposes upon history go far beyond those of providing convenient but misleading patterns; we shall deal at greater length with these further limitations.

The parochialism of nationalism or of race is familiar, and most of us try to guard against it. We are less aware of and more vulnerable to another form of parochialism, the parochialism of time.

Present-mindedness is, perhaps, the most intractable of all the limitations on history—our instinctive habit of looking at the past through our own eyes, judging it by our own standards, recreating it in our own words or reading back into the language of the past our own meanings, assuming that whatever happened, happened in some "past" and forgetting that every past was once a present. As that wise counsellor, Frederic Maitland, reminds us:

> If we speak, we must speak with words; if we think we must think with thoughts. We are moderns, and our words and thoughts cannot but be modern. Perhaps . . . it is too late for us to be early English. Every thought will be too sharp, every word will imply too many contrasts. We must, it is to be feared, use many words and qualify our every statement until we have almost contradicted it. ("Township and Borough.")

It is probable that we are, to a large degree, helpless in this matter; try as we will we cannot "think ourselves back into a twilight," to use Maitland's wonderful phrase. We cannot really put ourselves inside the minds, or skins, of Cyrus, or Brutus, or Joan of Arc, or the Indian chief Pontiac. That we do try is a tribute to the rigor of our historical conscience, and a few great histories and biographies are monuments to the fact that we are not always unsuccessful, though in the nature of the case we are not permitted to know even this. But the difficulty of present-mindedness is really deeper. It is that we almost instinctively assume that the past was made just for us, that it is interesting only insofar as it caters to our current interests, and significant only when it has ostentatious consequences for us. How easily we fall into what might be called the fallacy of "quaintness"—the fallacy of supposing that Medieval People were medieval in their own eyes as well, or that Renaissance Man betrays us if he does not live up to our notion of what he should be, or that the Forefathers knew that they were Forefathers. How hard it is for us to realize that the past was as real to those who lived in it as the present is to us and that they no more lived for our edification than we live for the edification of distant future generations.

There is another danger implicit in present-mindedness, one, again, which we cannot, in the nature of things, escape, but against which we must everlastingly guard ourselves. That is what we may call the danger of the *fait accompli.* We know what happened in history and because we know it, we can never look back upon it with the eyes of innocence. We know that the Athenian expedition to Syracuse is going to fail; that Rome will humble Carthage, and the Roman Republic change into an empire; that the Moslems will eventually be driven out of western Europe, and that Christianity will triumph; that it is the English who will win the struggle for the American continent; that no matter how dark the outlook Washington will lead his ragged army to victory at Yorktown; that no matter how glittering the prospects, Robert E. Lee is headed for Appomattox. We are, all of us, in the position of the reader of mystery stories who reads the last chapter first. But we should remember that we do not know how our own history is going to come out, and neither did earlier generations of men.

Our inability to divorce ourselves from knowing how history is going to come out almost guarantees that our view of the past will be astigmatic. We inevitably read back into the past what we know occurred, and adopt a *post hoc propter hoc* attitude toward history. As Rome is bound to fall to the barbarian invaders we find explanations of that fall in the corruption and immorality of public life; as Britain is doomed to lose her American colonies, we accept Tom Paine's observation that it is absurd for a continent to belong to an island; as the Confederacy is predestined to defeat we confidently find the causes of that defeat. But if we adopt these positions, we render ourselves incapable of understanding the past in its own terms. As David Donald has said, historians are camp-followers of victorious armies. Knowing which side is going to win—the Romans, Christianity, the Union, the Atlantic powers—they instinctively ally themselves with the winning side; they look for explanations of what triumphed and ignore the evidence on the other side. Some of them see the hand of God, or of Progress, or of Evolution, in whatever triumphed and whatever failed.

Nothing, surely, is more fatal to the integrity of historical investigation than the doctrine of inevitability implicit in this attitude. For if whatever happened in history was inevitable, whether because it expressed the will of God or the force of evolution or of progress, then there is little point in conducting any investigation whatsoever into the causes or the consequences of things. *Felix qui potuit rerum cognoscere causas,* but if the causes of things are predestined, there is no happiness, and no value either. As Charles A. Beard warned us:

> If all human affairs were reduced to law, to a kind of terrestial mechanics, a chief end of the quest, that is, human control over human occurrences and actions, would itself become meaningless. Should mankind discover the law of its total historical unfolding, then it would be imprisoned in its own fate, and powerless to change it; the past, present and future would be revealed as fixed and beyond the reach of human choice and will. Men and women would be chained to their destinies as the stars and tides are to their routine. (*The Open Door at Home,* New York: The Macmillan Company, p. 14.)

But, as far as we know, the course of history is not predestined. Life has always been, as it is now, "a roar of bargain and of battle," and the intellectual challenge to understand the past is no less compelling than the challenge to understand the present and the future. There is, to be sure, one sobering difference here. If we understand the present we may be able to command it, but there is no way by which we can command the past.

THE TROUBLE WITH FACTS

These are some of the limitations on the historian. But there are limitations inherent in the facts of history, as well.

Poor, despised facts, they have a hard time. Nobody believes in them; nobody has any faith in them. With almost a single voice historians say that there are no facts, none that can be relied upon anyway; there are only some agreed-on assumptions which we choose to call facts so we can get on with the job. But do not be misled by them, do not take them seriously, or they will betray you. Facts are subjective, they exist in the mind of the historian, they change their character with each historian. The facts of the Franco-Prussian War are one thing to a French historian, another to a German; the facts about the creation of the state of Israel read very differently in the eyes of Jews and Arabs. Facts are like the Cheshire cat, in *Alice in Wonderland;* as we look at them they fade away, all but the grin.

What is the trouble with facts?

First, a paradox. There are too few facts, and there are too many. There are far too few facts about immense areas of past history. How little we know, after all, about most of mankind—about the people of Asia, of Africa, of pre-Columbian America; how little we know about lost people like the Carthaginians and the Etruscans, the early Celts and the Basques. How little we know about the remote past, as contrasted with the recent past. How do we dare reconstruct the ancient world with any assurance, when our knowledge is confined to small areas around the Mediterranean; yet we confidently call this Ancient History. How can we write with any assurance about the history of the American continents when—except for what ethnology and archeology may tell us—our knowledge embraces only five centuries out of a possible twenty-five thousand years? How little we know—even in modern times—of the lives of the poor, of those vast majorities of each generation about whom we have no reliable facts.

And, at the other end of the spectrum, we know almost too much about the modern history of the west—America, Britain, France, Germany, Italy in the nineteenth or twentieth centuries. We are overwhelmed by mountains of evidence; it accumulates faster than even computers can record it, and we still have to process the material from the computers. We do not and cannot have all the facts about the Second World War, but it is safe to conjecture that historians will never get through the miles of filing cases of historical records now resting in warehouses throughout the country. Inevitably our vision of the past is distorted by this disproportion in our evidence; inevitably we translate this disproportion into historical distortions.

We have already noted the role of caprice and fortuity in the historical record, and the influence of modern-mindedness and of subjectivity. There are still further limitations on "facts." There is for example the elementary consideration that we can rarely attain factual accuracy about the past, even about the recent past. The uninitiated take factual accuracy for granted in history as they take it for granted in chemistry or physics, but as soon as they try to reconstruct any chapter of past history they speedily discover that accuracy is unattainable. The science of statistics is new, and even such statistics as we have are rarely reliable. We do not know such fundamental things as the populations or the birth and death rates of ancient peoples; we do not know the numbers in armies or in battles, or the casualties in war. We do not know the value or the volume of farm production or of domestic industries or of trade. Even in modern history, statistics often fail us: we do not and probably cannot know with any accuracy the number of soldiers in the Union or the Confederate armies, or the losses, or the cost of the war; the ascertainable "facts" do not go very far in explaining why Britain did not intervene on the side of the Confederacy. Even so apparently elementary a matter as the total acreage of public lands granted by state and federal governments to American railroads has long been and still is a matter of conjecture and debate.

On these, and a hundred other important questions of history, we can only make educated guesses.

There are, to be sure, some matters about which we can be accurate and certain, but alas, these turn out to be matters of no great importance. We can be accurate about the succession of American Presidents, or of the kings of England or France, and we prefer an historian who knows that Buchanan succeeded Pierce, and not the other way around, and who can list the Richards and the Henrys, the Philips and the Louis in their proper order. This is too elementary to be helpful. We can be accurate about the dates of the Buchanan administration, but not about Buchanan's role in the coming of the Civil War; we can be accurate about the dates for Louis XVI, but there is no agreement on his contribution to the breakdown of the *ancien régime*.

Finally, the facts of history turn out to be not hard and objective but impalpable and subjective. Ranke and his successors taught us to rely on documents for our history; the documents, they were confident, would speak for themselves. Alas, they do not speak for themselves. They speak, rather, for us, and with a hundred different voices, usually raucous and clashing. They tell us not what actually happened but, more often than not, what we want to hear. Take, for example, the two most famous documents of American history—the Declaration of Independence and the federal Constitution. Even the textual history of the Declaration is an intricate affair, but look aside from the textual history to the political and philosophical. Here are the immortal words—their immortality, note, not inherent, but conferred upon them by later generations—what do they mean? What did Jefferson and the members of the Continental Congress mean when he wrote, and they endorsed, the statement that "all men are created equal"? What did he mean when he wrote, what did they mean when they endorsed, the sentiment that the "pursuit of happiness" is an unalienable right?

No two people read quite the same thing into these words. Certainly the generation of Thomas Jefferson (even the term "generation" is an artificial one, and if we accept Jefferson's own calculation of a generation as twenty years, he belonged to four!) and our own generation read different meanings into terms like "equality" and "happiness." Certainly, too, in our own day, men and women read different meanings into the word "happiness," and northerners and southerners, whites and Negroes, read different meanings into the term "equality." It requires a lifetime of study to understand these esoteric words, and after a lifetime of study different historians come up with very different explanations. Clearly this famous document does not speak for itself.

Contemplate, then, the Constitution of the United States, a document of some six thousand carefully chosen words, simple, lucid, logical. Does the Constitution speak for itself? Clearly it does not; if it did we should not need the 375 volumes of Supreme Court *Reports* to explain and interpret it, nor would learned and upright judges on the Supreme Court so frequently disagree about the meaning of such phrases as "commerce among the several states," "the executive power," "impair the obligation of contracts," "common defense and general welfare," "necessary and proper," and "due process of law."

Or take another kind of document: a painting. Does the meaning of the painting inhere in the painting itself? Not entirely. You can look at it and see a great deal which you have missed; an art historian or art critic can look at it through the eyes of history and see many things which escape the rest of us and some, perhaps, which were not in the mind of the artist when he painted the picture.

Take for example, the various paintings by Poussin on the theme *Et in Arcadia Ego,* which Edwin Panofsky has dealt with in a fascinating essay on that subject. To the onlooker it is a simple matter—shepherds and maidens stumbling on a tomb with that touching inscription are struck into sober contemplation by the realization that others before them had lived in Arcadia and now were dead and gone. But is that really what the paintings mean, or what the phrase and the concept originally meant? Not at all, says Panofsky. What they mean is not "I too have lived in Arcadia," but "Death, too, is in Arcadia." That reverses the moral of the pictures completely; it is no longer a reminder that every generation has known happiness, but a reminder that death is ever present, even in Arcadia. But hold, it is not that simple, either, for eighteenth century painters did in fact reverse the original meaning. Unwilling to contemplate the presence of death in Arcadia, they turned the whole thing into a pastoral scene, one designed to show that generation was linked to generation by happiness, not by death.

Contemplate another, and more familiar, artistic document: Emanuel Leutze's painting of "Washington Crossing the Delaware." Clearly this is not a contemporary record: there were no artists present to record that famous crossing. It was painted three-quarters of a century after the event; the river was the Rhine, not the Delaware, and Washington was Worthington Whittredge, a young American artist studying in Düsseldorf. The scene itself was a product of Leutze's romantic imagination. If Washington had stood up in that rowboat he would have fallen overboard; the flag was quite incorrect; and as the crossing was made before dawn of a winter night, neither Washington nor the sailors who rowed him would have been visible in the dark. But all that was of no importance. The painting had a life of its own. It was accepted with rapture as an authentic representation; it made its way at once into the minds and hearts of the American people; it has come to be, for all practical purposes, the authentic representation of the historic event. If it does not reproduce an historical fact it is, itself, an historical fact.

A document, then, may mean many things. Its meaning is to be understood in the light of its own contemporary history; it is to be understood in the light of the reason, temperament, and prejudices of the historian who uses it; it is to be arrived at and interpreted through the symbolism it communicates. Even that is not the end of it. For the historian has to communicate with each individual reader, and each one will read the document or the analysis in his own way, just as each individual looks at a Whistler painting or listens to a Mozart sonata in his own way.

The facts of history are fragmentary, elusive, and subjective. But that is true of most of these studies which engage the minds and the passions of men—art and letters, morals and ethics, even law and politics, as every judge and statesman knows. We must not expect things to be easier for the historian than they are for those many others who try somehow to reconcile the heritage of the past—its laws and principles and monuments—with the imaginations, the passions, the emotions, and the facts of their own time. It is not of history, but of the whole cargo of thought and character and habit that William Vaughn Moody wrote those moving lines:

> This earth is not the steadfast thing
> We landsmen build upon;
> From deep to deep she varies pace,
> And while she comes is gone.
> Beneath my feet I feel,
> Her smooth bulk heave and dip;
> With velvet plunge and soft upreel
> She swings and steadies to her keel
> Like a gallant, gallant ship.
>
> ("Gloucester Moors")

Yet though we admit the limitations and difficulties of history, item by item, if we take them too hard, we will find ourselves out of a job. If the limitations really are so severe, and the facts really are so elusive, we may be forced to give up history altogether. If we are to get on with the job, we must agree upon some kind of factual foundation or framework for our histories, if only that Washington was in fact the first President of the United States, or that the United States did in fact fight a war with Mexico which brought her Texas and California, or that Lincoln was in fact assassinated. For, treacherous as they no doubt are, facts are like syntax and grammar; we need them as a framework and a mechanism if we are to make ourselves clear. There is nothing sacred about grammar, and a wide latitude is permitted in its usage, but if we are perpetually to stop and question the authority of our grammar we will never finish what we are saying or writing.

Historians have, after all, surmounted the difficulties that crowd about them, and given us famous and affluent histories. Gibbon was aware of the difficulties, and Macaulay, Ranke and Mommsen, Maitland and Holdsworth, Parkman and Henry Adams, yet all of them managed to write histories which have enlarged the thoughts and lifted the spirits of generations of men. Let the young historian take to heart the lines of the Greek Anthology:

A shipwrecked sailor, buried on this coast
Bids you set sail;
Full many a gallant bark, when we were lost
Weathered the gale.

INTERPRETATION—AND BIAS

Let us admit at once that history is neither scientific nor mechanical, that the historian is human and therefore fallible, and that the ideal history, completely objective and dispassionate, is an illusion. There is bias in the choice of a subject, bias in the selection of material, bias in its organization and presentation, and, inevitably, bias in its interpretation. Consciously, or unconsciously, all historians are biased: they are creatures of their time, their race, their faith, their class, their country—creatures, and even prisoners.

Most historians strive manfully to avoid bias and achieve objectivity when they teach or write history, but there have always been some who out of defiance, or out of acquiescence to the inevitable, have accepted the fact of bias and tried to make a virtue of it. The famous German historian, Heinrich von Treitschke, represents the first attitude. Writing in 1865 he asserted that a "bloodless objectivity which does not say on which side is the narrator's heart, is the exact opposite of the true historical sense," and in his own many-volumed *History of Germany in the Nineteenth Century* he left no one in doubt about what side his heart was on, or his mind and his temper either. The American Charles A. Beard represents the second attitude. "Any selection and arrangement of facts," he said in his address on "History as an Act of Faith," "pertaining to any large area of History, either local or world, race or class, is controlled inexorably by the frame of reference in the mind of the selector or arranger." As long as this was true, he concluded, it was only honorable for the historian frankly to acknowledge his "frame of reference"—that is, his bias. And, as history is, inevitably, an instrument of propaganda, said Beard, let us take care that it is propaganda for good causes, for peace and progress, for justice and truth, and not for bad.

Pity the poor historian. He is the victim, the prisoner, of circumstances, of Nature and of human nature. Even St. Anthony was not exposed to so many temptations. Is he a modern man: then how will he ever understand medieval man? Is he a European: can he ever really understand and do justice to the world of Asia and of Africa—or even of America? Is he a white man: can he really understand the colored peoples who constitute three-quarters of the human race? Is he a Christian: can he do justice to those he has learned to designate pagans or heathens? Is he a Catholic: can he be fair to Protestants? Is he a Protestant: can he be fair to the Papacy and the Inquisition? Is he—and he almost certainly is—a member of the middle or the upper classes, literate and educated: can he really understand the point of view of the workingman and the peasant? Can a liberal like Macaulay do justice to the Stuarts? Can a Marxist like Albert Mathiez do justice to the *ancien régime*—or even to the Gironde? Can a Republican like Albert Beveridge understand Jefferson or a Democrat like Claude Bowers understand Hamilton or a New Dealer like Arthur Schlesinger, Jr., be fair to Herbert Hoover? Can a Georgia gentleman like Ulrich B. Phillips ever really understand slavery? Can a Negro Marxist like W. E. B. Du Bois write dispassionately of slaveholders or of southern Bourbons? Can an Englishman or an Irishman, a German or a Frenchman be expected to emancipate himself from his national predilections, and write history that gives no hint of national affiliations or loyalties?

It was the hope of Lord Acton that a new generation of historians could answer all these questions in the affirmative. When, in 1896, he launched the co-operative *Cambridge Modern History,* he told potential contributors that "we shall avoid the needless utterance of opinion or service of a cause. Contributors will understand that our Waterloo must satisfy French and English, Germans and Dutch alike; that nobody can tell, without examining the list of authors, where the Bishop of Oxford laid down the pen and whether Fairbairn or Gasquet, Liebermann or Harrison, took it up." But few historians have ever really managed to live up to these austere standards, and it is doubtful whether Acton did himself.

It is easy enough to discern bias in history, easy enough to recognize a great deal of what passes for history as propaganda of varying degrees of subtlety. Much of this propaganda does not rise to the dignity of history—the histories, put out by Nazi historians, designed to prove the superiority of the Aryan race and the virtue of Hitlerian Germany; the "new-think" put out by Communist historians to justify every turn and twist of Communist policy. But we should remember, too, that some of the most influential works of history have been propaganda: Clarendon's classic *History of the Rebellion,* for example, or the Abbé Raynal's *Philosophical History of the Indies*—an "instrument of war" against the Church—or Frederic Masson's adulatory but learned biography of Napoleon, or Henry Wilson's *Rise and Fall of the Slave Power in America.* In our own day we can readily discern elements of propaganda, or partisanship, in such major works as Charles A. Beard's studies of American foreign policy between the wars, or Parrington's brilliant *Main Currents of American Thought,* or Winston Churchill's *World Crisis,* but we do not really think the worse of them for that.

Actually partisanship often adds zest to historical writing; for partisanship is an expression of interest and excitement and passion, and these can stir the reader as judiciousness might not. Certainly Macaulay lives, while Stubbs and Gardiner are read only by the specialists; Motley's thrilling story of the *Rise of the Dutch Republic* has inspired generations of readers with enthusiasm for liberty and detestation of tyranny which cannot be wholly misguided; Parrington, for all his faults, excites an interest in American literature that no other historian or critic has been able to equal; Winston Churchill's splendid tributes to English courage had consequences to history that no other histories of this century could match. As that immaculate historian Lord Acton himself observed, "the strongest and most impressive personalities . . . project their own broad shadows upon their pages. This is a practice proper to great men, and a great man may be worth several immaculate historians."

Let us, then, not be too distressed that history is unscientific, partisan and hopelessly subjective; that it lends itself so readily to misrepresentation and even to propaganda; that it reflects, for better or for worse, the personality, the prejudices, the idiosyncrasies of historians. The subjectivity is inevitable; the partisanship is regrettable, but has compensations; the propaganda usually takes care of itself, for it carries with it a kind of built-in discount; the idiosyncrasy is almost always interesting. And let us remember, too, that nothing which deals with human beings can approach scientific objectivity, that there is no wholly impartial justice, no wholly impartial political, economic, or social theory, no impartial education.

There is one bias, one prejudice, one obsession, so pervasive and so powerful that it deserves special consideration: nationalism. History, which should be the most cosmopolitan of studies, most catholic in its sympathies, most ecumenical in its interests, has, in the past century and a half, become an instrument of nationalism.

Nationalism is, no doubt, the most powerful force in modern history, and it is scarcely surprising that it should have captured historiography and enslaved historians. The historian no longer writes in a universal language—Latin for example, or, in the eighteenth century, French—but in the national vernacular; he adapts his history to a national framework, depends on national archives and similar sources for materials, and almost inevitably expresses a national point of view. In the eighteenth century the ardors of nationalism were moderated by rationalism and cosmopolitanism, and if such books as Hume's *England,* Robertson's *Scotland* or Müller's *Switzerland* threw history a bit out of focus, they did no serious violence to historical truth. Very different was the nationalist history which came in, as on flood tide, with the French Revolution and Napoleon, and with modern, chauvinistic, nationalism. The new history reflected national interests, prejudices, and passions or, worse, stimulated them. It is a far cry from the cool rationalism of Robertson's *Scotland* to the romantic lyricism of Michelet's *France,* the savage chauvinism of Treitschke's *Germany,* the patriotic passion of Francis Palacky's *History of the Bohemian People,* or even the ardent enthusiasm of George Bancroft's *History of the United States.*

Nationalism, as we know it, is both recent and parochial. It was invented by western Europeans—British, French, Germans—and has flourished for less than 200 years. For historians to confuse it with universal history or—as some do—with the cosmic system, to read into it absolute values and absolute virtues, to identify themselves—and truth—passionately with one nation rather than another, is to betray history itself. It is to violate what should be the historical categorical imperative: never to subordinate the whole to the part, the permanent to the transient, the end to the means.

Overt bias, such as that which responds to nationalism, is easy to detect and not difficult to discount. There is a more subtle form of bias which is implicit in and all but inextricable from that present-mindedness which we considered earlier. This is sometimes called the problem of *nunc pro tunc*: the now for the then, the present for the past. What point of view should the historian adopt when he deals with the past, or with societies and civilizations very different from his own? Should he maintain his own standards and values, or should he try to adopt the standards and values of the peoples and the age with which he is concerned?

At first glance this problem seems easy enough: the right and proper thing to do is to adopt the measure and the standards of the era and the people we are trying to understand and to explain. How absurd, after all, to judge the Persians, or even the Egyptians or the Greeks, by the standards of modern England; how absurd to judge the American Indian by the standards of eighteenth century Europe; how misguided to apply our own artistic standards to ancient China or India, our intellectual and scientific standards to the Middle Ages. No, let us rather enter into the minds and the spirits of the people we are studying. So said Ranke, and all those who, after him, developed what it is fashionable to call Historicism. Let us so immerse ourselves in the past that we can see with their eyes, hear with their ears, think as they thought, and feel as they must have felt: only by emancipating ourselves from the present and re-entering into the past can we be true to history; only by this renunciation of our own personalities can we hope to recover the character of the past.

This ideal was hopefully advanced in a recent biography of the "Great American Preacher" Theodore Parker:

> I have tried to know and to feel what Parker and his friends knew and felt, to accept the limitations of their minds, and, perhaps, of their characters. I have tried to see men and measures with Parker's eyes, to react to the events of the time as he did, or as I think that he did. I have permitted Parker to act as he chose to act, to render such judgment as he wished to make, to love those friends whom he did love, and to disparage those persons whom he disliked, whether he was wise in all this, or unwise. Where he was vain I have not sought to rebuke his vanity, where he was inconsistent I have not thought it necessary to remark his inconsistency, where he was ungenerous I have not taken him to task, where he was violent I have not tried to abate his violence, where he was mistaken I have not attempted to set him right; all of these things he confessed in his own words and actions and they appear without my intervention. (H. S. Commager, *Theodore Parker,* Boston: Little, Brown and Company, 1936, preface.)

Douglas Freeman, the distinguished biographer of Robert E. Lee, attempted to achieve this goal by the somewhat mechanical method of limiting himself, quite rigorously, to knowing only what Lee knew, and writing entirely within that framework of knowledge or of ignorance. Still another method of recreating the past is that used by two masters of intellectual history, the American, Van Wyck Brooks, and the Frenchman, Paul Hazard; it is the technique of literary intimacy. Here is M. Hazard describing the adventurers of the eighteenth century:

> In those days no one would stop in one place. Here was Montesquieu, off on the search for political constitutions; Diderot, after holding out against the idea for a long time, at length made the journey to Russia. Then, one fine day, the youthful Goldsmith resolves to set out for the Continent, and set out he does, without a penny to his name, with no one to fall back on in case of need, and with no definite itinerary in view. However, off he goes, playing his flute at cottage doors in the hope of getting, maybe, a bowl of soup or a shake-down in a barn. Holberg says

> good-bye to Denmark, and takes to the road, relying on his fine voice, as Goldsmith on his flute-playing, to get him along. On he goes, from country to country, learns French in Paris, and teaches it at Oxford. He was not a man to be baulked by trifles. All these inquiring gentlemen, indeed, are as mobile as can be, and they are never satisfied, they've never seen enough. Exile brings them no repining. They don't mind knocking at strange doors, and the bread of the stranger leaves no bitterness in the mouth. Tossed by fate far beyond their native land, they profit by the occasion to improve their knowledge and shape their minds anew. Voltaire has no bad time of it in London. . . Nor does the Abbé Prévost fare so badly in Holland. Anyhow, that's where he sows his wild oats, and pretty plentifully, withal. . . . And Bolingbroke soon made himself at home as a noble lord of France, with his mansion and his ornamental gardens. He gathers a following about him, and wields the intellectual sceptre. Wincklemann finds his spiritual home in Italy. Look at the host of persecuted philosophers that crowded around Frederick in Berlin. No fugitives craving sanctuary, these; no more exiles; now we call them *cosmopolites*. (*European Thought in the Eighteenth Century,* London: Hollis and Carter, 1954, pp. 249–250.)

This is all admirable, but does it really enable us to recapture the past? We may believe that we can think as Theodore Parker thought, or know only what General Lee knew, or live and feel with the *philosophes,* but perhaps we delude ourselves.

For when we turn to the past and use the literature or the monuments of the past as a means of entering into its mind and spirit, how do we know that we have chosen correctly? The *philosophes* whom Hazard celebrates left an immense and entrancing literature, but did they really speak for France or for Germany in the eighteenth century? The Abolitionists of New England were incomparably articulate, but they were few in number and of feeble influence; they speak for themselves, to be sure, but do they speak for New England? We can, of course, confine ourselves to single individuals; we can spend a lifetime immersing ourselves in the writings of Jefferson or Edmund Burke or Napoleon until we come, at last, to think as these men thought. Ah, but do we? How does it happen that men who have in fact spent a lifetime with these great figures come up with such different reports?

We can doubtless do quite well in understanding the past—where the literature is voluminous, where the society is familiar, and where the past is recent. But what shall we say of the attempt to enter into the minds and thoughts of a distant or unfamiliar past—of the Spartans, for example, who differed so profoundly from the Athenians; of the Aztecs or the Incas whose records are fragmentary; of the Danes who invaded and harried England in the ninth century? Perhaps we can manage to understand Jefferson or Burke; can we manage to understand the Persian Cyrus, or Eric the Red?

There are many things to be said for accepting our limitations and looking at the past through the eyes of the present, but this is the most persuasive: no matter how hard we try, that is what we do anyway. We see the past through our own eyes, translate its language into our own, find interesting the things that interest us, and find significant the events that have had consequences for us. All this helps explain why each generation rewrites the history of the past: the view depends upon the point of view.

Consider, for example, the vicissitudes of the interpretation of Reconstruction by American historians.

Only half a century ago almost all students learned that after Appomattox the North imposed upon the stricken South a Punic peace, and they learned, too, that almost everything that happened—or failed to happen—thereafter could be blamed on the sins of Reconstruction. Through the tears that streamed from our sympathetic eyes we read that the federal government confiscated two billion dollars worth of slave property, that it imposed military rule upon the helpless South, that it forced—or tried to force—Negro equality upon a proud people long before the Negro was ready for equality or for anything; that it tolerated maladministration and corruption such as had never been known before in American history. In fact that generation of historians—the generation that ruled the roost during the first third of the twentieth century—was so ashamed of what the nation had done to the South that it almost apologized for fighting and winning the Civil War. Lee was the hero, not Grant, Confederate gray the stylish uniform, not Union blue, and everyone sang "Dixie Land." But now we look back on Reconstruction through very different eyes—or very different historical glasses. Now we regard it from the point of view of a generation that has lived through a war incomparably more savage and more destructive than the Civil War, and through peace-making incomparably more implacable than any that came in 1865. We have lost some of that innocence which still survived through the Victorian Age and into the new century, and lost our capacity to be surprised at ruthlessness, harshness, vindictiveness. Now when we look back at the American Civil War and Reconstruction it is with eyes that have seen what happened to the White Russians when the Bolsheviks won out; what happened to the Spanish Loyalists when Franco won out; what happened to the rebels first against Batista and then against Castro in Cuba; what happened to those desperate officers who tried to overthrow Hitler in 1944. And when we look at Reconstruction not from a provincial

American but from a world point of view we see that in all modern history no civil war was concluded with so little blood-letting or vindictiveness, and that in all modern history there is no example of magnanimity to compare with that which Lincoln and the national government displayed towards the defeated rebels. Now instead of writing the history of Reconstruction in terms of a Punic peace, we say rather that it was a magnanimous peace; instead of emphasizing the loss to slave-holders we emphasize the victory for Negro slaves; instead of deploring the establishment of military rule in the South we are astonished that the civil authority was so speedily restored and that the South was back in the Union—and even running it—within a few years. Instead of lamenting the fate of Jefferson Davis, languishing in prison for over a year, we note that after the greatest civil war of the century not one rebel lost his life, not one was proscribed, except briefly. And now, too, we re-examine—once again—the role of President Andrew Johnson, who first excited our reprobation and then our sympathies, and of the Radicals, who for a time excited our admiration, and then our contempt. We re-examine these in the light of recent developments in the position of the Negro in American life, and ask whether the Radical program might not have set the Negro question on the way to solution instead of leaving it for us to grapple with a century later. It would be presumptuous to say which of these points of view was the right one, for it is clear that there is no "right" point of view. What is clear is that, try how they will, historians see the past through the eyes of the present.

There is a final commentary on what is called Historicism. Even those who are most anxious to avoid imposing their own standards on the past and strive most sincerely to see the past in its own terms are tempted to make one exception to their principle. That is in the realm of moral judgment. Let us not force the past into the straitjacket of the present, they say, but at the same time let us not suspend the eternal rules of right and wrong.

And this brings us to the troublesome problem of moral judgment in history.

JUDGMENT IN HISTORY

To judge or not to judge, that is the historical question. Should the historian sit in judgment over the great drama of the past and the men and women who performed on that vast and crowded stage, exposing evil and celebrating virtue and damning and praising famous men? Or should he observe the historical processes with scientific detachment, and record them as automatically as a tape-recorder, rigorously excluding personal, national, or religious considerations? Is he competent to perform either of these functions—the function of the judge, or the function of the impartial reporter?

The problem is difficult and perhaps insoluble. It raises hard questions about the purpose of history, the duties and responsibilities of the scholar, the nature of historical judgment, and the distinctions, if any, between what might be called moral and secular judgment. It raises questions, too, about the competence of any historian to judge the past, and the sanctions, if any, behind such judgments as are rendered. And it requires us to weigh the dangers implicit in moral neutrality against those inherent in moral arrogance and intellectual parochialism.

Earlier generations of historians were not seriously troubled by this problem of judgment. The Greek historians, Herodotus and Thucydides, were surprisingly free from the urge to judge, but their successors in the ancient world took for granted that their function was to edify, to instruct, and to judge. Livy invited his readers to ponder the moral lessons taught by the history of Rome—as he presented it—and to observe how Rome rose to greatness through her virtues, and how the decay of these virtues brought ruin. Tacitus thought the highest function of history was to "rescue merit from oblivion," and "to hold out the reprobation of posterity as a warning and a rebuke to all base conduct." Plutarch, who wrote some sixty Moral Essays, compiled his famous *Parallel Lives* not to adorn a tale, but to point a moral, and succeeded beyond his farthest imagination.

Medieval historians knew perfectly well what were the moral standards to which history was obliged to conform, and knew, too, the penalties of non-conformity, for what was history but the working out of God's will with man? Even the great eighteenth century historians, Gibbon and Hume and Robertson, Rollin and Voltaire and Raynal, accepted Bolingbroke's aphorism that history was "philosophy teaching by examples," and they assumed that its lessons were moral and that it was the duty of the historian to point them. Only with the rise of "historicism" in the nineteenth century—there were antecedents, to be sure, in such historians as Machiavelli and Vico—did the question of the propriety and the validity of moral judgment come to the fore. Ranke, and his successors and disciples in almost every country, abjured moral judgment, or said that they did, and set themselves the task of simply recording what had happened, with a minimum of comment, and with neither ostentatious approval or disapproval. Theirs was the ideal which Henry Adams later found so futile: "To satisfy himself whether, by the severest process of stating, with the least possible comment, such facts as seemed sure, in such order as seemed rigorously consequent, he could fix for a familiar moment a necessary sequence of human movement." (*The Education of Henry Adams,* p. 382.)

There was bound to be a reaction away from this austere principle, especially as so few of its protagonists actually lived up to it. The Victorian era, which in Germany saw the triumph of historicism, was also the era of morality, of moral preaching in law and in economics, in politics and in history, as in art and in literature. It is difficult to know whether such historians as Froude in England, Michelet in France, Treitschke in Germany or Motley in America considered themselves primarily ethical leaders or historical scholars; in fact they did not distinguish sharply between the two roles. "The eternal truths and rights of things," said James Anthony Froude in his Inaugural Address as Rector of St. Andrews University, "exist independent of our thoughts or wishes, fixed as mathematics, inherent in the nature of man and the world."

To the American, John L. Motley, historian of the heroic struggle of the Dutch against the Spanish rulers, and of the creation of a United Netherlands, this was the story of the struggle of Protestantism against Catholicism, of the principle of liberty against the principle of tyranny. Motley did not hesitate to pronounce moral judgment; listen to his final verdict on Philip II of Spain:

> There have been few men known to history who have been able to accomplish by their own exertions so vast an amount of evil as the king who had just died. If Philip possessed a single virtue it has eluded the conscientious research of the writer of these pages. If there are vices—as possibly there are—from which he was exempt, it is because it is not permitted to human nature to attain perfection even in evil. The only plausible explanation—for palliation there is none—of his infamous career is that the man really believed himself not a king but a God. He was placed so high above his fellow creatures as, in good faith perhaps, to believe himself incapable of doing wrong; so that, whether indulging his passions or enforcing throughout the world his religious and political dogmas, he was ever conscious of embodying divine inspirations and elemental laws. When providing for the assassination of a monarch, or commanding the massacre of a townful of Protestants; when trampling on every oath by which a human being can bind himself when laying desolate with fire and sword during more than a generation the provinces which he had inherited as his private property or in carefully maintaining the flames of civil war in foreign kingdoms which he hoped to acquire; while maintaining over all Christendom a gigantic system of bribery, corruption and espionage . . . he ever felt that these base or bloody deeds were not crimes, but the simple will of the godhead of which he was a portion. (*United Netherlands,* New York, 1868, V, pp. 74–75.)

And, in case his readers might think that he had stepped out of his province in thus condemning the Spanish monarch, Motley added a word on the responsibility of the historian:

> When an humble malefactor is brought before an ordinary court of justice, it is not often, in any age or country, that he escapes the pillory or the gallows because, from his own point of view, his actions, instead of being criminal, have been commendable, and because the multitude and continuity of his offenses prove him to have been sincere. And because anointed monarchs are amenable to no human tribunal, save to that terrible assize which the People, bursting its chain from time to time in the course of the ages, sets up for the trial of its oppressors, and which is called Revolution, it is the more important for the great interests of humanity that before the judgment-seat of History a crown should be no protection to its wearer. There is no plea to the jurisdiction of history, if history be true to itself.
>
> As for the royal criminal called Philip II, his life is his arraignment, and these volumes will have been written in vain if a specification is now required. (*Ibid.*, p. 79.)

In a Carlyle or a Motley moral judgment was a form of self-indulgence. But there was more to it than this, there was high Duty! The clearest and most persuasive statement of the moral function of the historian came from Lord Acton himself. In 1895 Lord Acton was appointed Regius Professor of History at Cambridge University. In his Inaugural Address he exhorted his listeners, and all students of history,

> never to debase the moral currency or to lower the standards of rectitude, but to try others by the final maxim that governs your own lives, and to suffer no man and no cause to escape the undying penalty which history has the power to inflict on wrong. The plea in extenuation of guilt and mitigation of punishment is perpetual. At every step we are met by arguments which go to excuse, to palliate, to confound right and wrong and reduce the just man to the level of the reprobate. . . Opinions alter, manners change, creeds rise and fall, but the moral law is written on the tablets of eternity.

"We have the power," he concluded, ". . . to learn from undisguised and genuine records to look with remorse upon the past, and to the future with assured hope of better things; bearing this in mind, that if we lower our standard in History, we cannot uphold it in Church or State."

We cannot glibly ascribe Acton's philosophy to his Catholicism; he was, after all, not a very orthodox Catholic. Such diverse contemporary historians as Veronica Wedgwood, Isaiah Berlin, and Arnold Toynbee—none of them Catholic—all come out for the obligation, or the necessity, of moral judgment in history. Thus Miss Wedgwood, who has done so much to illuminate the great political and religious issues that stirred England in the seventeenth century, warns us against

> the confusion into which historians fall when they make allowances for "the standards of the age." Their intention is to understand and be just to the past, but the result in the long run may be unfair to the present, because this outlook steadily and stealthily fosters the conviction that nothing is good or bad in itself, but only in relation to its surroundings. . . The aspiration to understand and to forgive is noble and valid in personal relationships between the living but [she concludes] the application of the principle of . . . forgiveness to historical personages is a sentimental fallacy. (*Truth and Opinion,* New York: The Macmillan Company, 1965, pp. 48–49.)

Arnold Toynbee, who has concerned himself more consistently with the universal and the eternal than any other modern historian, has remained throughout his distinguished career a Christian moralist, ready to judge the quick and the dead; his assertion that the expulsion of the Arabs from Palestine by the Israelis was no less a crime than the Nazi murder of some six million Jews precipitated an international controversy.

All of this constitutes what might be called a moral argument in favor of moral judgment. The moral laws are universal and timeless; murder is always murder and betrayal is always betrayal, cruelty and intolerance are always the same, the historian cannot stand above the moral laws, or stand aside from them, but must acknowledge them and participate in them and apply them. If he does not, he will fail the cause of morality—and of History as well—and forfeit the confidence and respect of his peers.

There is, however, another and perhaps more persuasive argument for moral judgment in history, one that rests not so much on moral as on psychological grounds. It is this: that the historian cannot, in any event, help himself, and that he might as well acknowledge what is inherent and implicit in his condition. He is, after all, a creature of his time, his society, his faith. Even if he resolutely refrains from overt moral judgment, he will surely be guilty of covert judgment: his choice of subject, his selection of facts, his very vocabulary, will betray him. How much better, then, how much fairer and more honest, to acknowledge his position in advance; how much better to call his book—it is Charles A. Beard who makes the point—*An Economic Interpretation of the Constitution* rather than to fall back on a title like *The Making of the Constitution,* one which "does not advise the reader at the outset concerning the upshot to be expected." History is not a science, and the historian is not a scientist. "The supreme command," therefore, "is that he must cast off his servitude to the assumptions of natural science and return to his own subject matter—to history as actuality."

This is the argument, too, of the distinguished Oxford philosopher, Sir Isaiah Berlin, who sees in the passion for scientific impartiality yet another expression of the misguided and pernicious belief that history is a science. "The case against the notion of historical objectivity," he writes, "is like the case against international law, or international morality; that it does not exist." And he adds the warning that:

> Except on the assumption that history must deal with human beings purely as material objects in space, must, in short, be behaviourist—its method can scarcely be assimilated to the standards of an exact natural science. The invocation to historians to suppress even that minimal degree of moral or psychological evaluation which is necessarily involved in viewing human beings as creatures with purposes and motives . . . seems to me to rest upon a confusion of the aims and methods of the humane studies with those of natural science. It is one of the greatest and most destructive fallacies of the last hundred years. (*Historical Inevitability*, Oxford, Oxford University Press, 1954, pp. 52–53.)

But the stout champions of moral judgment do not have things all their own way. Not at all. Here comes a whole phalanx of historians with a formidable arsenal of counter-arguments.

First, while it is true that history tries to observe something like historical "due process," it cannot in the nature of the case do so. The past is not there to defend itself. We cannot recall the witnesses, put them on the stand, question and cross-examine them. It is difficult enough to render a moral verdict on anything so recent as, let us say, Hoover's dispersion of the "bonus army," or the conduct of the Vichy government, or the resort to the atomic weapon at Hiroshima; how much more difficult, then, to sit in judgment on the character of Alcibiades, the justification for the murder of Caesar, the conduct of the Norman invaders of England, or of the Spanish conquistadores.

Second, while technical judgment is essential, in the law, in the civil service, in the university, in athletics, if society is to function, such judgment does not pretend to be moral but professional. A university professor who permitted his moral views of a candidate to dictate his grades, a referee whose decisions were based on moral considerations, even a judge who allowed his private moral convictions to influence his decisions on questions of contracts, wills, liability, or bankruptcy proceedings, would be regarded as not only incompetent but expendable. There are reasonably clear standards for such practical judgments as society requires—laws, rules, tests—but as parents, psychiatrists, and priests so well know, moral judgments present questions of labyrinthine complexity even when all the relevant evidence appears to be available. Where history is concerned, the conduct of men or of nations in past centuries, all the relevant evidence is never available, and there are no universal standards. What the historian does, when he judges, is merely to identify his own "can't-help-but-believes" with eternal verities. Herodotus made this point twenty-five centuries ago: When Darius was upon the throne, he summoned

> into his presence the Hellenes at his court and asked them for what price they would consent to make a meal of their fathers when they died. The Hellenes replied that all the money in the World would not induce them to do such a thing, whereupon Darius summoned the Callatian Indians, who do eat their parents, and asked them (in the presence of the Hellenes, who were kept informed, through an interpreter, of the tenour of the conversation) for what price they would be willing to burn their fathers when they died. The Indians shrieked aloud and begged him not to pursue an unmentionable subject—a story which illustrates the habitual attitude of Mankind towards this question, and which, in my opinion, justifies Pindar's poetic aphorism that "Custom is king of all."

Justice Holmes made the point with even greater succinctness. "I prefer champagne to ditch-water," he said, "but I see no reason to suppose the cosmos does."

If history "tells us" anything, it tells us that standards, values, and principles have varied greatly from age to age and from society to society; indeed, that they have varied greatly from one generation to another within the same society. Popes chosen for their learning and their virtue were certain that morality required that they put down heresies with fire and sword, cruelty and torture; sixteenth century Europeans had no compunction about killing Indians, because the Indians had no souls; learned and upright Puritans readily sent witches to their death; and nineteenth century Christians in the American South regarded slavery as a blessing. The Hellenes of whom Herodotus tells us were no more shocked at the notion of eating their dead fathers than we are at Hellenic notions of love. Consider, for example, Plato's defense of a practice which most of our contemporaries regard not only as immoral but as pernicious, and which our military and civil authorities combat with sleepless zeal:

> I cannot say what greater benefit can fall to the lot of a young man than a virtuous lover and to the lover than a beloved youth. . . If then there were any means whereby a state or army could be formed of lovers and favorites, they would administer affairs better than all others, provided they abstain from all disgraceful deeds and compete with one another

in honest rivalry, and such men, together with others like them, though few in number, so to speak would conquer the world. (*Symposium*, p. 178.)

A problem which has confronted, and perplexed, American historians for a hundred years is slavery. Surely if anything is wrong, slavery is wrong. No social institution more deeply offends our moral sensibilities than this; no other collective experience induces in us a comparable sense of shame. Slavery, we are all agreed, corrupts alike the slave and the master; slavery corrupts the body politic, the poison still infects us.

This is the vocabulary of morality, and it is this vocabulary which we invoke, almost instinctively, whenever we discuss what was long euphemistically called the "peculiar institution."

Yet when we come to pronounce judgment on slavery we are met, at the very threshold, with the most intransigent consideration—that generation after generation of good, humane, Christian men and women not only accepted it, but considered it a blessing. What are we to say when confronted by the fact—a formidable body of evidence permits us to use that word—that our own forebears, only two or three generations back, embraced slavery, rejoiced in it, fought to defend it, and gave up their lives confident that they were dying in a good cause.

Clearly, we cannot fall back on the simple explanation that all these men and women—those who owned slaves and those who sustained the slave system—were bad. These beneficiaries of and defenders of slavery were neither better nor worse than their cousins north of the Mason and Dixon line who had managed to get rid of the "peculiar institution" one or two generations earlier; they were neither better nor worse than we are. Whatever may be said, on practical grounds, for the moral righteousness and self-righteousness of Abolitionists who fought slavery, it can be said that no comparable pressures weigh upon us as historians. It is absurd for us to pass moral judgment on slave-holders, absurd to indict a whole people or to banish a whole people to some historical purgatory where they can expiate their sins. Lincoln saw this, Lincoln who saw so much. The people of the North and the South, he said in his Second Inaugural Address, "read the same Bible and pray to the same God, and each invokes His aid against the other. It may seem strange that any men should dare to ask a just God's assistance in wringing their bread from the sweat of other men's faces. But let us judge not, that we be not judged."

We can agree now, most of us, that slavery was an unmitigated evil, but we cannot therefrom conclude that those who inherited it, were caught in it and by it, supported it and fought for it, were evil men. What we can say is that but for the grace of God, or the accident of history, we might ourselves have been caught up in slavery, and bound by it, and habituated to accepting it, just as our forebears were. What we can say is that if earlier generations—North and South alike—bore the burden and the guilt of slavery, we have born the burden, and the guilt, of racial discrimination, and that morally there is not much to choose between the two.

Clearly, different generations have different moral standards; it is a form of intellectual arrogance for us to impose ours upon the past. We do not accept ex post facto laws, bills of attainder, or guilt by association in our legal system; we should not apply these concepts or rules retroactively to the past. Far better to refrain from the folly and the vanity of moral righteousness about the past; far better to accept Lincoln's admonition to judge not, that we be not judged. The historian's task is not to judge, but to understand. How did it happen that men dedicated to carrying out the precepts of the Sermon on the Mount could send those who disagreed with them to the stake? How did it happen that men dedicated to the expansion of European civilization could carry fire and sword to the hapless inhabitants of the American continents? How did it happen that men and women who dearly loved their own children and whose daily lives were bound each to each with natural piety could bitterly oppose laws designed to protect little children from the awful burden of work in factory and mine? How did it happen that Christian men and women could look upon slavery as a blessing? How did it happen that a people who boasted a high civilization, who had produced Leibniz and Kant, Beethoven and Mozart, Goethe and Heine, Rilke and Thomas Mann, could stand by while six million Jews were done to death?

Tout comprendre, tout pardonner. But it does not follow that the historian who understands all forgives all. It is the historian's business to "understand"; it is not the historian's business either to condemn or to forgive. He is not God.

For here is a third argument against moral judgment in history—that the historian is not God. He is not called upon to judge the quick or the dead; indeed he is not called upon to judge. If he sets up as a judge he changes the whole pattern of his intellectual and professional role from one dedicated to objective inquiry to one devoted to prosecution or defense. As the distinguished historian of the Russian Revolution, E. H. Carr, observes, the attempt to erect standards of historical judgment "is itself unhistorical and contradicts the very essence of history. It provides a dogmatic answer to questions which the historian is bound, by his vocation, incessantly to ask. The historian who accepts answers in advance to these questions, goes to work with his eyes blindfolded, and, renounces his vocation."

The historian is not God; he is a man and like other men. He confesses most of the failings, responds to most of the pressures, succumbs to most of the temptations that afflict his fellow men. Consciously, or unconsciously, he is almost always taking sides. Can we really trust Carlyle on Cromwell, or Motley on Philip II, or Charles A. Beard on the causes of the Civil War or Vernon Parrington on John Marshall? Can we trust either Macaulay or Winston Churchill to write impartially about the Duke of Marlborough? Can we trust Lord Acton or Benedetto Croce on a subject so close to their hearts as the history of liberty? Clearly we cannot. The historian, like the judge, the priest, or the statesman, is a creature of his race, nationality, religion, class, of his inheritance and his education, and he can never emancipate himself from these formative influences and achieve Olympian impartiality. Where he undertakes to *judge* he does not even have the prop of professional training and traditions to sustain him, as he does when he records and reconstructs. His judgments are, therefore, as Herbert Butterfield has observed, but "pseudo-moral judgments, masquerading as moral ones, mixed and muddy affairs, part prejudice, part political animosity, with a dash of ethical flavoring wildly tossed into the concoction." And because not even a Ranke, not even a Mommsen, not even a Toynbee, can survey the whole of history, his forays into the past are bound to be haphazard and fortuitous as well. For purposes of reconstructing the past, that is not a fatal handicap; others will fill in the gaps. But for purposes of formulating a moral code and applying it systematically and impartially, it is a fatal handicap.

We may, then, accept the findings of the historian in matters of fact—always subject to subsequent revision, to be sure—but why should we accept his conclusions in matters of morality? "I beseech you in the bowels of Christ," wrote Oliver Cromwell in his Letter to the Church of Scotland, "think it possible you may be mistaken." Alas, the historians have so often been mistaken. Over the centuries they have stood ready to pronounce judgments which differ little from the tainted and tarnished judgments of statesmen, soldiers, and priests. Catholic historians have sustained the persecution of Protestant heretics, and Protestant historians looked with equanimity upon the persecution of Catholics. National historians have almost invariably defended and justified the conduct of their own nation and as regularly rendered judgment against the enemies of their nation; more, they have themselves provided the arguments for chauvinistic nationalism, imperialism, and militarism. No wonder that the chief professional preoccupation of the historian in our day is revision!

There is no special dispensation for the historian. He is not exempt from the prejudices, the ambitions, the vanities, the fears, that afflict his fellow men. When he dons his professional robes he is an impressive and sometimes a majestic figure; when he is persuaded to put on the robes of the moral judge, he is as naked as the unhappy Emperor of Hans Andersen's story.

We come then to a fourth consideration, practical rather than philosophical: the futility of moral judgment in history. Surely, say those who insist that the historian be a judge, it is proper that the historian reprobate the Inquisition and exalt tolerance, that he deplore slavery and celebrate freedom, that he execrate Hitler and Nazi genocide and rejoice in the triumph of the forces of liberation. But why should the historian go out of his way to condemn or to praise these things? The assumption behind this expectation is that the reader has no mind of his own, no moral standards, no capacity to exercise judgment; that he is incapable of distinguishing between slavery and freedom, persecution and tolerance, but depends upon the historian to do this for him. Are those mature enough to read serious histories really so obtuse that they cannot draw conclusions from the facts that are submitted to them? Is there really any danger that students will yearn for slavery or rejoice in the Inquisition or admire Philip II or Adolf Hitler if the historian does not bustle in and set them right? Alas, if the reader does not know that Hitler was a moral monster and that the murder of six million Jews was a moral outrage, nothing the historian can say will set him right; if he does not know in his bones that slavery corrupts both slave and master, nothing the historian can say will enlighten him. Is there not, indeed, some danger that if the historian continually usurps the role of judge, the reader may react against his judgments; that if the historian insists on treating his readers as morally incompetent, they may turn away from history altogether to some more mature form of literature?

There is a further consideration, which might be called a plea in abatement. It is this: that the problem of judgment may be trusted to take care of itself. No reader comes wholly unprepared to the contemplation of a chapter of history; he brings with him his own education, his own moral and philosophical outlook. Nor is the student ever confined to a single account of any important chapter of history. We can be confident that historians will differ in their interpretation of the past and that these differences will be available and familiar to readers. Errors will be corrected; wrong opinions will be set right. For every historian who defends British policy in Ireland there will be one to expose it and reprobate it; for every historian who paints slavery in sunlight terms, there will be one to expose its darkness and cruelty; for every historian who places responsibility for the First World War squarely at the door of the Germans, there will be one ready to make clear that it was the Russians or the French who were really to blame. Let the historian learn humility: the reader is not dependent upon him for the whole of his history; he is not dependent upon him for moral instruction.

That is what the great Italian historical philosopher Benedetto Croce meant when he wrote that "those who, on the plea of narrating history, bustle about as judges, condemning here and giving absolution there, because they think that this is the office of history, are generally recognized as devoid of historical sense."

One final observation is appropriate. We should not confuse moral with professional judgment. In the field of his professional competence the scholar has the same obligation as the judge, the teacher, the physician, the architect. The judge who pronounces sentence, the teacher who gives a grade, the physician who diagnoses an illness, the architect who condemns a building, is not indulging in moral but exercising professional judgment. So the historian who, after painstaking study of all available evidence, and after cleansing himself of all the perilous stuff which might distort his vision, concludes that Lee did right to surrender at Appomattox rather than fight it out in the west, that Roosevelt was not responsible for the attack on Pearl Harbor, that the conduct of the Crimean War was characterized by criminal folly, that the violation of Belgian neutrality in 1914 was an error of the first magnitude, that Cavour rather than Garibaldi deserves credit for Italian unification, that Shakespeare and not Bacon wrote *Hamlet*, that only the stone and not the inscription on the Kensington rune stone is genuine, and that the Protocols of Zion are forgeries, is performing his professional duty. He may be mistaken—but so may the judge, the teacher, the physician—that is a chance society takes. His judgments may have moral overtones—it is difficult to keep those out, and we have learned to discount them. But if it is exasperating to find a Carlyle or a Motley laying down the moral laws for us, it is equally exasperating to discover that when you lay all the scholarly investigators of a subject end to end, they do not reach a conclusion.

History as Law and as Philosophy

chapter five

THE USE OF HISTORY

We are all acquainted with the young man who earnestly assures us, with a mixture of vanity and zeal, that he has always "hated history." It is all dates, he tells us, or it is all a lot of rather tiresome problems—the problem of the "fall" of Rome, the problem of the French Revolution, the problem of Secession and Civil War. And it never gets you anywhere; you are no better off when you have finished than when you began.

Some of this attitude may be confidently set down to poor and uninspiring teaching—teaching which never challenged the interest nor excited the imagination of students. Some of it—perhaps a good deal—may be put down to the same kind of uninspired teaching embodied in textbooks in which the authors try to please everybody, avoid the "controversial," ignore the dramatic, concentrate on problems which are never solved or whose solution is of no interest, and, like so many of the novels and dramas of our time, eschew narrative and leave out heroes and villains. Some of it can be ascribed to the individual himself; his inability to respond imaginatively to the drama of the past. In all likelihood he is one of those of whom Wordsworth wrote:

> A primrose by the river's brim,
> A yellow primrose was to him,
> And it was nothing more.

But after we have done all this explaining, there remains a stubborn residuum of intelligent and open-minded students who still find nothing to nourish them in history. They may agree with Gibbon that history is "the register of the follies and misfortunes of mankind," or with Napoleon that it is a "lie agreed upon," or with Carlyle that it is "a great dust-heap," and they do not stop to read those marvellous volumes in which Gibbon recorded the "follies and misfortunes" of man, or discover how Carlyle proved that history was charged with life and passion, nor are they excited by the challenge to separate truth from lies about Napoleon himself.

What are we to say to all this? Why should the young study history? Why should their elders read history, or write it?

That is a question which recurs again and again: What use is history? Let us admit at once that in a practical way history has no use, let us concede that it is not good for anything that can be weighed, measured, or counted. It will not solve problems; it will not guarantee us against the errors of the past; it will not show nations how to avoid wars, or how to win them; it will not provide scientific explanations of depressions or keys to prosperity; it will not contribute in any overt way to progress.

But the same can be said, of course, of many other things which society values and which men cherish. What use, after all, is a Mozart sonata or a painting by Renoir, or a statue by Milles? What use is the cathedral of Siena or the rose windows of Chartres or a novel by Flaubert or a sonnet by Wordsworth? What use, for that matter, are a great many mundane things which society takes for granted and on which it lavishes thought and effort: a baseball game, for example, or a rose garden, or a brocade dress, or a bottle of port?

Happily, a civilized society does not devote all of its thought and effort to things whose usefulness can be statistically demonstrated. There are other criteria than that of usefulness, and other meanings to the term "useful" than those acknowledged by the Thomas Gradgrinds of this world.

History, we can confidently assert, is useful in the sense that art and music, poetry and flowers, religion and philosophy are useful. Without it—as without these—life would be poorer and meaner; without it we should be denied some of those intellectual and moral experiences which give meaning and richness to life. Surely it is no accident that the study of history has been the solace of many of the noblest minds of every generation.

The first and doubtless the richest pleasure of history is that it adds new dimensions to life itself, enormously extending our perspective and enlarging our experience. It permits us to enter vicariously into the past, to project our vision back over thousands of years and enlarge it to embrace all the races of mankind. Through the pages of history we can hear Pericles deliver his Funeral Oration, look with wonder as Scipio and Hannibal lock forces in that desperate field of Zama, trek with the Crusaders to the Holy Land, sail with Columbus past the gates of Hercules and to a new world, sit with Diderot as he edits the Encyclopédie, share the life of Goethe and Schiller at the little court of Weimar, stand and listen to those stirring debates in those dusty prairie towns which sent Douglas to the Senate and Lincoln to the White House, share the agony of General Lee as he surrenders the Army of Northern Virginia at McLean's Court House, stand beside Winston Churchill as he rallies the people of Britain to their finest hour. History supplies to us all those elements which Henry James thought essential to the life of the mind: density, variety, intricacy, richness, in the pattern of thought and of action, and with it "the sense of the past."

This immense enlargement of experience means, of course, that history provides us with great companions on our journey through life. This is so familiar a consideration that it needs no elaboration. Wherever the historian or biographer has been, he has given new depth and range to our associations. We have but to take down the books and we are admitted to the confidence of Voltaire and Rousseau, Johnson and Boswell, Thomas Jefferson and John Adams, Justice Holmes and William James. We can know them with more of an intimacy than their contemporaries knew them, for we can read their letters, journals and diaries. This is not just one of the pleasures of history, it is one of the indispensable pleasures of life.

A third, and familiar, pleasure of history is the experience of identifying the present with the past, and thus adding a new dimension to places and events. It was Macaulay who observed that "the pleasure of History is analogous in many respects to that produced by foreign travel. The student is transported into a new state of society. He sees new fashions. He hears new modes of expression. His mind is enlarged by contemplating the wide diversities of laws, of morals, and of manners." George Macaulay Trevelyan—himself a grand-nephew of Macaulay—has conjured up this pleasure for us in one of his most glowing passages:

> Places, like books, have an interest or a beauty of association, as well as an absolute or aesthetic beauty. The garden front of St. John's, Oxford, is beautiful to everyone; but for the lover of history its outward charm is blent with the intimate feelings of his own mind, with images of that same college as it was during the Great Civil War. Given over to the use of a Court whose days of royalty were numbered, its walks and quadrangles were filled, as the end came near, with men and women learning to accept sorrow as their lot through life, the ambitious abandoning hope of power, the wealthy hardening themselves to embrace poverty, those who loved England preparing to sail for foreign shores, and lovers

> to be parted forever. There they strolled through the garden, as the hopeless evenings fell, listening, at the end of all, while the siege guns broke the silence with ominous iteration. Behind the cannon on those low hills to northward were ranked the inexorable men who came to lay their hands on all this beauty, hoping to change it to strength and sterner virtue. And this was the curse of the victors, not to die, but to live, and almost to lose their awful faith in God, when they saw the Restoration, not of the old gaiety, that was too gay for them, and the old loyalty that was too loyal for them, but of corruption and selfishness that had neither country nor king. The sound of the Roundhead cannon has long ago died away, but still the silence of the garden is heavy with unalterable fate, brooding over besiegers and besieged, in such haste to destroy each other and permit only the vile to survive. St. John's College is not mere stone and mortar, tastefully compiled, but an appropriate and mournful witness between those who see it now and those by whom it once was seen. (*Clio, A Muse and Other Essays,* New York, 1913, p. 26.)

Everyone who has visited historic towns, in the Old World or the New, knows that when he looks at them through the eyes of history they cease to be museum pieces and pulse with life and with vigor. Nestling between its ancient hills, bisected by the gleaming Arno, its domes and towers piercing the skies, Florence is beautiful to the eyes of even the purblind. But how it springs into life when we people its piazzas and narrow streets with the men and women of the past: when we conjure up the spectacle of Savonarola burned at the stake in the great Piazza de la Signoria where the mighty David now stands; Bruneleschi erecting the giant Duomo; Ghiberti carving the great bronze doors of the Baptistry, a lifetime work, this; Giotto and Fra Filippo Lippi and Raphael and Leonardo and Michelangelo painting those pictures which now hang in such lavish profusion from the glittering walls of the Uffizi and the Pitti palaces; Machiavelli pondering the history of the condottieri while he writes the *Prince,* and Galileo seeing a new universe through his telescope and opening up a new universe of the mind as well. Did ever a city boast a comparable galaxy of genius; did ever a city publish itself more generously in its monuments, or impress itself more richly on the eye and on the mind?

Nor is it only the great centers of art and letters, like Florence or Venice or Salzburg, that take on new dimensions when seen through the eyes of history; the same miracle transforms even the most modest of towns. Henry James observed, somewhat condescendingly, that Emerson had "dwelt for fifty years within the undecorated walls of his youth"; but to Emerson those rooms were redolent of the past, as was the little village of Concord. And as for Hawthorne, how, wrote James, could he have found materials for his stories, living where he did, where "the coldness, the thinness, the blankness . . . present themselves so vividly that our foremost feeling is that of compassion for a romancer looking for subjects in such a field." But Hawthorne himself looked out of his attic window on a Salem rich in history and tradition and found in it the ingredients for *The Scarlet Letter* and *The House of Seven Gables,* and a dozen other stories that are a precious part of our literature.

Consider the little town of Salem in Massachusetts, now no more than a suburb of Boston. It is a lovely town in its own right, there by the sea and the rocks, its handsome old houses still standing sedately along Chestnut and Federal Streets. As we look at it through the eyes of history we conjure up a straggling village busy with fishing and with theological disputes and remember that Roger Williams preached here those heresies which brought him banishment from the Bay Colony, and so too Mistress Anne Hutchinson. We look at Gallows Hill and recall the dark and terrifying story of Salem witchcraft which haunted Nathaniel Hawthorne, who grew up here, and whose spirit still broods over the town. We recreate it in its heyday, when its captains sailed all the waters of the globe and its flag was thought to be the flag of an independent nation, and the spoils and rewards of the China trade glittered in every drawing room. For at the turn of the century Salem was like one of the famous city states of Italy—Florence or Venice or Pisa. It had its own architects, like Samuel McIntyre who built the stately mansions of the sea captains and the merchant princes, mansions which still stand; its own preachers, like the famous William Bentley of the East Church, reputed to be the most learned man in America; its own jurists, like Samuel Putnam and Samuel Sewall who became Chief Justices of the Commonwealth, and Joseph Story who joined the Supreme Court of the United States at thirty-two. Samuel Bowditch was a boy here, watching the sailing ships come in to India Wharf and learning celestial mathematics and navigation from a library which had been captured from a British ship during the War for Independence; he sailed on a Salem merchantman, and grew up to write the *Practical Navigator.* So was George Crowninshield who built the magnificent Cleopatra's Barge and sailed it through the Mediterranean, and the dour Timothy Pickering who lived in the oldest house in town—which still stands—and grew up to be the most reactionary politician in the country; so too the astonishing Benjamin Thompson who grew up to be Count Rumford of the Holy Roman Empire and to live in state in Munich and found the Royal Institution in London, and so too William Prescott who played as a boy along India Wharf and Derby Wharf, and swam in the cold waters of the harbor and picnicked on Hog Island, and who became the historian of Mexico and of Peru.—Then another generation, and Salem entered its long decline, its harbors silted up and its wharfs falling into decay and grass growing up between the cobblestones of its ancient streets, while the paint peeled off the proud McIntyre houses. It is all there—in Nathaniel Hawthorne's stories, in the reminiscences of Joseph Story and Rufus Choate, in the historical romances by Joseph Hergesheimer and Esther Forbes, so faithful to the spirit and the reality of the old town—all there for us to recapture through the pages of history.

Needless to say, all this makes great demands upon the imagination, the imagination of the historian and of the student alike. "At bottom," George Macaulay Trevelyan has said, "the appeal of history is imaginative," and he gives us, as an example of this, one of Carlyle's recreations of the past—it is in his essay on Boswell's Johnson:

> Rough Samuel and sleek wheedling James *were,* and *are not.* Their Life and whole personal Environment has melted into air. The Mitre Tavern still stands in Fleet Street; but where now is its scot-and-lot paying, beef-and-ale loving, cocked-hatted, pot-bellied Landlord; its rosy-faced assiduous Landlady, with all her shining brass-pans, waxed tables, well-filled larder-shelves; her cooks and bootjacks, and errand boys and watery-mouthed hangers-on? Gone! Gone! The becking Waiter, who, with wreathed smiles, was wont to spread for Samuel and Bozzy their supper of the gods, has long since pocketed his last sixpence; and vanished, sixpences and all, like a ghost at cock-crowing. The Bottles they drank out of are all broken, the Chairs they sat on all rotted and burnt; the very Knives and Forks they ate with have rusted to the heart, and become brown oxide of iron, and mingled with the indiscriminate clay. All, all has vanished; in very deed and truth, like that baseless fabric of Prospero's air-vision. Of the Mitre Tavern nothing but the bare walls remain there; of London, of England, of the World, nothing but the bare walls remain; and these also decaying (were they of adamant), only slower. The mysterious River of Existence rushes on; a new Billow thereof has arrived, and lashes wildly as ever round the old embankments; but the former Billow with its loud, mad eddyings, where is it?—Where?—
>
> Now this *Book* of Boswell's, this is precisely a revocation of the edict of Destiny; so that Time shall not utterly, not so soon by several centuries, have dominion over us. (*Critical Essays,* p. 4.)

A dangerous thing, this, for once we introduce the element of imagination we imperil the integrity of the historical record. Yet how can we possibly exclude it? What is history, after all, without imagination? Imagination comes to our aid at every moment; it is what permits us to clothe the bare bones of history with life. It throws a glow over the most impersonal, the dullest, of the data of history. It infuses even a statistical table with color and life: who can read the statistics of the population growth of the western territories and states of the United States in the nineteenth century without seeing, in his mind's eye, the Conestoga wagon, and the canal boats on the Erie Canal, the railroad puffing its way across the Appalachians, weather-beaten men with their wives and children and cattle, beating out a trail to Oregon or to the Mormon utopia at the Great Salt Lake?

Imagination brings home to us that the names in the history books represent real people, that the decisions which were made involved the same fears and hopes and uncertainties and courage as those which we ourselves make, that Latimer at the stake and Lord Nelson at Trafalgar suffered the same agonies and exaltations which we ourselves experience, that to a man like Robert E. Lee the decision to stay with his state was no abstract "problem" of secession, but just such a spiritual and moral crisis as would plunge us into despair if we confronted it today. Alas, many historians are like the preacher of whom Emerson writes:

> A snow-storm was falling around us. The snow-storm was real, the preacher merely spectral, and the eye felt the sad contrast in looking at him, and then, out of the window behind him into the beautiful meteor of the snow. He had lived in vain. He had no one word intimating that he had laughed or wept, was married or in love, had been commended, or cheated, or chagrined. If he had ever lived and acted, we were none the wiser for it. The capital secret of his profession, namely to convert life into truth, he had not learned. . . This man had ploughed and planted and talked and bought and sold; he had read books; he had eaten and drunken; his head aches, his heart throbs; he smiles and suffers; yet was there not a surmise, a hint, in all the discourse, that he had ever lived at all. (Divinity School Address, July 15, 1838.)

It might be thought that imagination like—let us say—an ear for music, is something you either have or have not. If you have it, well and good; if not, there is nothing to be done about it. But the imagination, like a taste for music, or for painting, can be cultivated. How can the historical imagination be cultivated? It can be cultivated through drama and poetry. Shakespeare suffused the stuff of history with his glorious imagination; no wonder Winston Churchill said that he had learned all of his English history out of Shakespeare! How history comes alive in the novels of Walter Scott—such varied historians as Prescott and Carlyle and Trevelyan have acknowledged his inspiration. With what insight does Wordsworth read its moral lessons, in the sonnet "On the Extinction of the Venetian Republic," for example, or in "To Toussaint L'Ouverture," or in *The Prelude*. Imagination can be cultivated, too, by the study of art and architecture. Who can wander through the National Portrait Gallery in London and not feel stirred by the spectacle of these men and women who have made England; how exhilarating to visit such great Palladian palaces as the Villa Rotonda and the Villa Malcontenta outside Vicenza, and to see Jefferson's Monticello emerge out of these models.

This does not exhaust the pleasures of history; they are, indeed, inexhaustible. We may, without too gross an impropriety paraphrase Dr. Johnson's observation on London, that anyone who is tired of history is tired of life.

Can we go beyond the pleasures of history to Laws of History, or even to the Philosophy of History? That all depends on what you mean by "laws" and by "philosophy."

CAUSATION IN HISTORY

One of the liveliest pleasures of history is that, more continuously and more persuasively than almost any other study, it nourishes and enlists the reflective faculties. Nowhere are those faculties more busily engaged than in seeking for causes.

"Happy is he who knows the causes of things." But if this is true then it can be said that historians are forever pursuing happiness, but never quite attaining it. The search for the causes of things is, and has long been, the chief preoccupation of thoughtful historians. No self-respecting modern historian is content merely with recording what happened; he wants to explain why it happened. Of all problems of history, causation is the most urgent, the most fascinating, and the most baffling.

Why did history turn out the way it did? Why were the Chinese ahead of the West in civilization; why did civilization flourish so spectacularly in Greece at a time when most of Europe was lost in what we think of as barbarism; why were Europeans so far in advance of Americans for so many centuries? Why did the Roman Empire "decline and fall"; why were the Moslems able to conquer so much of Europe, and why did Moslem power ebb? What explains the amazing vitality of the Vikings and then of the Norsemen who swarmed over seas and over land, and carried their culture to the shores of Ireland and France and Sicily, and then fell back into obscurity? How did it happen that a little fog-bound island off the north coast of Europe came to be one of the greatest of world powers, and that the English language—of all unlikely languages—came to be spoken from London to Singapore and from Toronto to the Cape of Good Hope? Why did the American colonies break away from the Mother Country, and why were they successful in their revolution; why did the Southern States break away from the American Union and why was their revolution unsuccessful? Why did British America become two great countries, while Latin America fragmented into more than twenty? Why do only English-speaking peoples have a two-party system while all others have a one- or a multi-party system? What caused the two great wars of the twentieth century; what explains the spread and the triumphs of Communism? How explain the change in styles, from classical to romantic, from romantic to modern? How explain the change in moral standards from age to age—the changing attitude towards slavery, for example, or towards child labor, or towards sex?

For over two thousand years philosophers and historians have tried to answer these and similar questions about the course of history, though it is only in the last two or three centuries that the inquiry has been both open-minded and independent. Socrates, in one of the most famous of his discourses, asserted the validity of inquiry: "That we shall be better and braver and less helpless if we think that we ought to enquire than we should have been if we indulged in the idle fancy that there was no knowing and no use in seeking to know what we do not know—that is a theme upon which I am ready to fight in word and deed to the utmost of my power."

Yet most ancient historians did, in fact, indulge in something very like "idle fancy." The great Greek and Roman historians rarely inquired into the causes of things; it was enough for them that whatever happened was bound to happen, that it was all in the hands of the gods or of fate:

> The things men looked for cometh not,
> And a path there is where no man thought–
> So hath it fallen here.

Even so great an historian as Thucydides does not seek the deeper causes of the Peloponnesian War or the defeat of Athens, nor does a moralist like Plutarch inquire into the explanation for the virtues and the vices which he describes.

Christian historians, too, had an easy time of it. Everything that happened in history, from the sparrow that fell to the earth to the fall of empires, had a cause: it was all the working out of a divine plan. St. Augustine had made this clear, once and for all, in *The City of God,* and thereafter it was accepted without serious question. It is hard for us to realize, now, how this simplistic theory dominated historical thinking for more than a thousand years, how it persisted, even, well past the Renaissance and Reformation and down to the Age of Reason. Thus it was in the seventeenth century that the great French historian, Jacques Bossuet prepared his *Discourses on Universal History* to demonstrate that the whole course of history was but the working out of a divine plan which happened, also, to be the plan of the Catholic popes. And at almost the same time, Bossuet's American contemporary, Edward Johnson, explained the planting of the Bay Colony under the title *The Wonder-Working Providence of Sion's Saviour in New England.* Or consider the great debate over the meaning and the explanation of America which raged from the fifteenth to the eighteenth centuries. How explain the New World? How explain its primitive state, the backwardness of its native races, the absence of organized society, or government? Every historian and philosopher who addressed himself to this problem started with the Flood, postulating for the New World a later Flood or a greater Flood or a series of Floods; all, too, with few exceptions, took for granted that mankind in every continent was descended from a common set of ancestors, Adam and Eve.

The mental habit of ascribing historical events, great and small, to the caprice of the gods or to the inscrutable will of God, persisted even into the eighteenth century: thus the popularity of cyclical theories of history or of what might be called the "ebb and flow" theory, as illustrated by *The Grandeur and Decadence of Rome,* or the *Decline and Fall of the Roman Empire, Westward the Star of Empire,* and other books with titles of a like nature. So, too, did the habit of acknowledging the authority of impersonal law, only now it was secular, not divine law, now it was "the law of Nature" as well as of "Nature's God." This was the Newtonian theory applied to the affairs of men, and it had the immense advantage of making history not only a secular but a rational affair. Soon all the historians and philosophers were explaining history in terms of Nature, and in one way or another this has persisted down to our own time. The eighteenth century concept of Nature and Nature's law was, however, very different from ours: Nature was orderly, rational, and, in a curious way, anthropocentric. The universe, as men knew it, was ruled by Law that operated harmoniously and implacably, like some great mechanism; as men were part of the universe, they, too, were subject to universal law. Oddly enough this did not turn out to be deterministic in any malign sense. For the laws which controlled the universe were harmonious and rational. That meant that they applied to society and government as well as to the courses of the stars or the ebb and flow of the tides, and it meant that they could be apprehended and adopted by the reason of man. If men could but conform to these laws of Nature instead of ignoring them or flouting them, the miseries and agonies that had so long afflicted man would disappear, and peace, prosperity, and progress would usher in a millenium.

Curiously enough, though the faith in Reason evaporated, reliance on Force persisted in a more sophisticated form down to our own time. Montesquieu had argued the importance of "climate" in history—a term which he used much as we would use the term "environment," and since his day climate or geography has been one of the most popular of all explanations of history. The Abbé Raynal used it to explain the backwardness of the Americas; and after him a host of scholars and scientists as diverse as Alexander von Humboldt and Henry T. Buckle, Richard Green and Friedrich Raetzel, Frederick Jackson Turner and Brooks Adams celebrated the predominant role of climate and geography in guiding the destinies of man. But climate and geography were by no means the only impersonal forces which won the allegiance of historians. Karl Marx founded a school of history, and not of history alone, which interpreted most of the activities and ideas of men in terms of economic interests and forces. Admiral Mahan worshipped sea power as a kind of brooding omniscience in history; Henry Adams insisted quite simply on force—first—and for many centuries—the force of religion, then, in modern times, coal, steam, and electricity as symbolized in the dynamo. "The historians' business," wrote Henry Adams, "was to follow the track of energy" wherever it led, and that is what he did, until he came at last to radium and to atomic power. "Power leaped from every atom, and enough of it to supply the stellar universe showed itself running to waste at every pore of matter. Man could no longer hold it off. Forces grasped his wrist and flung him about as though he had hold of a live wire." (*The Education of Henry Adams,* p. 494.)

The "forces of the stellar universe" were impersonal and aimless; if history was indeed controlled by such forces, there was no possibility of reducing it to law—just what Adams concluded when he somewhat perversely hit upon the law of the dissipation of energy as the sovereign law of history. But the eighteenth century had invented and the nineteenth had perfected a new and more benign force. Progress was the new idea and the new force; progress first within the framework of Natural Law and then within the framework of Evolution. Turgot had announced it in a memorable address in 1750; the Encyclopaedists had embraced it, and with Condorcet it became well-nigh official. We are all children of the Age of Progress, all heirs to the belief that

> through the ages one increasing purpose runs,
> And the thoughts of men are widened with the process of the suns,
> (Tennyson, "Locksley Hall")

and it is unnecessary to elaborate upon anything so familiar.

The doctrine of progress was confirmed by faith rather than by observation, and sometimes—as Voltaire made clear in *Candide* or Dr. Johnson in *Rasselas*—faith gave way to scepticism. It lacked historical support—had there really been progress in the oldest societies such as China or Egypt or Greece?—and it lacked scientific support, as well. How fortunate, then, that the doctrine of evolution appeared to provide it with the strongest scientific support, at least the doctrine of evolution according to Herbert Spencer. For Spencer made clear that the great, transcendent laws of organic evolution which regulated the animal world, regulated the world of man as well. As evolution assured the survival of the fittest in the world of Nature, so it guaranteed that man, too, would progress towards perfection by the elimination of all imperfections. "Progress is not an accident," said Spencer, "but a necessity. It is a part of Nature." And his American disciple, John Fiske, wrote raptly that "The creation of Man is the goal towards which Nature tended from the beginning. Not the production of any higher creature, but the perfecting of Humanity, is to be the glorious consummation of Nature's long and tedious work."

All this was gratifying enough, but as an explanation of history it was not very helpful. For to be told, when we ask why Rome declined, or why the Spanish Armada foundered, or why the Confederacy lost the Civil War, that it was all in harmony with the law of Progress, or that it was part of Evolution, leaves us pretty much where we were in the beginning. Granted Progress, granted Evolution, why should they manifest themselves in one way rather than in another? Was the decline of the Roman Empire progress? Is it certain that Britain and not Spain was destined to be the beneficiary of the evolutionary process?

No, the search for an explanation could not be satisfied that easily. If we were to explain the past, if we were to predict the future, we needed something at once more rigorous and more specific than the windy doctrine of progress or the impersonal doctrine of evolution. Mathematics, biology, chemistry, physics, these things had provided laws which explained so much that had heretofore been mysterious; surely history, too, could provide laws which would explain the past and illuminate the future. So said Auguste Comte, in France, who worked out an elaborate scheme of the social sciences; so said Herbert Spencer in England, who created a science of society on the basis of biology and anthropology and psychology; so said the American John Fiske whose *Outlines of Cosmic Philosophy* drew on the whole body of social and philosophical thought to find the laws which regulated the moral world, and whose many histories proved that these laws had operated in America from the beginning. Other social sciences boasted laws—Malthus' law of population growth, Gresham's law in economics, Ferdinand LaSalle's law of wages, Henry Buckle's law of geography, which was "one glorious principle of universal and undeviating regularity"—why should not history, too, have her laws?

LAWS IN HISTORY

"Four out of five students who are living today," wrote Henry Adams some sixty years ago,

> have, in the course of their work, felt that they stood on the brink of a great generalization that would reduce history under a law as clear as the laws which govern the material world. . . He seemed to have it, as the Spanish say, in his ink stand. Scores of times he must have dropped his pen to think how one short step, one sudden inspiration, would show all human knowledge; how in these thickest forests of history, one corner turned, one faint trail struck, would bring him on the high road of science.

Alas, when Adams himself hit on a law—it was the law of entropy, or the degradation of energy—it did not clear a way through thickest forests, but put up a permanent barrier to further historical research. Twenty years later Edward P. Cheyney sounded the same note:

> I look forward [he said in his Presidential Address to the American Historical Association in 1923] to some future meeting of this Association when the search for the laws of History and their application will have become the principal part of their procedure. . . The most conspicuous part on the program will be assigned to some gifted young historical thinker who, quite properly disregarding the earlier and crude efforts of his predecessors, will propound and demonstrate to the satisfaction of all his colleagues, some new and far-reaching law or laws of history.

Alas, again, for human hopes; forty years later the sessions of the Historical Association were given over almost exclusively to "technical history," and philosophical speculations were looked upon with disfavor.

Professor Cheyney himself propounded six "laws of history" and it may be useful to recite them, for they reveal, as well as anything of their kind, some of the difficulties inherent in the formulation of such laws. They are: 1. The law of continuity; 2. The law of mutability; 3. The law of interdependence; 4. The law of democracy; 5. The law of the necessity for free consent; 6. The law of moral progress. Now it can be said of these—as of almost every attempt to formulate laws of history—that either they do not deal with history, but with life in general, or that they are not laws but expressions of hope and of faith. Take, for example, Cheyney's law of continuity. If this means that we have constructed an historical chronology and that in this chronology one event appears to follow another, then it is valid but meaningless. If it means that everything that happens grows out of some antecedent cause which we can discover, then it is not so. The voyages of Columbus and the discovery of America doubtless grew out of a complex of antecedent causes which yield a logical pattern, but can it be said that the destruction of the Aztec and the Inca empires grew out of recognizable causes and followed a pattern which the natives of Mexico and Peru would have regarded as logical? Scholars who trace the history of Negro slavery in America construct a neat and logical pattern which almost makes us think that slavery was inevitable, but is there a comparable logic which would persuade Africans kidnapped and transported to America that slavery was inevitable for them? One major trouble with the principle of continuity and of causation is that it assumes a single line of continuity, a single chain of causes, instead of a hundred or a thousand.

Or consider Cheyney's law of mutability: that nothing is permanent in history. But that is not a law of history, it is a law of life, and poets and moralists had proclaimed it more than two thousand years before Cheyney took it over for history. What is important—and what the historian wants to know—is that some things appear to be more permanent than others. Which seem to be more permanent, and why? To this urgent question the law of mutability says nothing. It is as if we should submit, as a "law" of history, that all men are mortal and that all flesh is grass.

And what of Cheyney's other laws—democracy, liberty, morality? Clearly these are the formulations of a Victorian liberal. How many Chinese or Russian historians would subscribe to the "law" of democracy; how many American Negroes would subscribe to the "law" of liberty; how many German Jews would endorse the "law" of moral progress, or for that matter how many of the survivors of Hiroshima or of Dresden?

Confronted by the seemingly insuperable difficulty of formulating laws or solving the problems of causation, some historians have thrown in the sponge, as it were, and taken refuge in the principle of fortuity. Thus H. A. L. Fisher, whose *History of Europe* is something of a classic, confessed in his preface to that work that:

> One intellectual excitement has been denied me. Men wiser and more learned than I have discovered in history a plot, a rhythm, a predetermined pattern. These harmonies are concealed from me. I can see only one emergency following upon another as wave follows upon wave; only one great fact with respect to which, since it is unique, there can be no generalizations; only one safe rule for the historian: that he should recognize in the development of human destinies the play of the contingent and the unforeseen. (Preface to *A History of Europe*, Boston: Houghton Mifflin Company, 1935–36.)

In its most unsophisticated form this becomes the "Cleopatra's nose" theory of history first stated by no other than Blaise Pascal: "Had Cleopatra's nose been shorter, the whole face of the earth would have been different." Voltaire embraced the same theory, and so too did his friend Frederick the Great: "The older one becomes, the more clearly one sees that King Hazard fashions three-fourths of the events in this miserable world."

"The passion for tidiness," Arthur Schlesinger, Jr., has written, "is the historian's occupational disease." It is, indeed, though we should add in all fairness that it is a kind of historical necessity, as well. Organization always does some violence to the stream of thought or the chaos of conduct that is life—the organization of melody into music, the organization of color into painting, the organization of inspiration into poetry, and of ideas into philosophy, and the organization of facts into history. Granted that history is a record of disorderly conduct; it does not follow that it is to be reported in a disorderely fashion, and it is the mark of a great judge that he is able to bring order and coherence out of conflicting evidence and arguments. History is a jangle of accidents, blunders, surprises and absurdities, and so is our knowledge of it, but if we are to report it at all we must impose some order upon it. Literature is able to compensate for this necessity by falling back on the "stream of consciousness" technique, but history cannot do this.

The danger is that in tidying up history the historian will convey the impression (he may even convince himself!) that everything was tidy from the beginning. A battle, for example, is often a nightmare of blunder and confusion; then the historian comes along and tidies it all up, tells us just how the battle was planned, how the center struck at this moment and the left flank moved in next, how the artillery joined in, or the cavalry charged, and there is your victory, all nicely explained. Or he looks back upon a diplomatic incident, or upon an election, and explains it all very neatly, leaving out all the contingencies, all the unforeseen events, all the hesitations and fears and confusions. He presents us with the logic of some historical *fait accompli*—the Monroe Doctrine, or the Open Door policy, or Truman's Point Four, and we can indeed see how logical it all was; then we learn—as we have recently learned of Point Four, that it was all a series of accidents, and that far from being a deliberate policy it came even to President Truman himself as a happy surprise.

But while we must avoid assuming that history is a kind of chess game with every gambit logical and planned, we must avoid, equally, the other extreme, that of ascribing everything to accident or luck; we must avoid giving too much prominence to untidiness and disorder. For disorder is, in a sense, itself orderly; it is at once a principle of life and a rule of life. Birth is a very disorderly business, but we forget the disorder (or assume that it is taken for granted) and celebrate the birthday. The whole of life is disorderly—our growing-up, our education, our falling in love, our jobs or careers, our relations with friends or enemies. Our societies are disorderly—physically disorderly in their cities, institutionally disorderly in their economies, their politics, their social relationships. Intelligence tries to bring order out of all of this, and thereby to decrease the disorder, or to master it. So, too, in history, the intelligence of the historian is directed to bringing some order out of the chaos of the past.

And there is, too, a further and consoling consideration, that though accidents often change the pace or the pattern of history, they rarely change it in any fundamental way. For the sophisticated historian remembers what is, after all, the common sense of the matter, that there are always enough accidents to go around, and that accidents tend to cancel out, just as the sophisticated spectator at a football game knows that there are enough fumbles to go around and that a particular fumble rarely changes the course of a game, or of a season of games. It is immature and almost perverse to assign too much importance to what we denominate the accidents of history. The wind scattered the Spanish Armada and helped the English destroy it, but that was not the reason why Spain failed to conquer England; Spain had never conquered England, wind or no wind, nor had any other power. Washington surprised the Hessians at Trenton on Christmas of 1776, and the American cause looked up; but that was not the reason the Americans finally won their independence. Even had the Hessians repulsed Washington's ragged troops the Americans would, in all likelihood, have won sooner or later. A Federal soldier picked up Lee's plan of battle for Antietam and took it to McClellan; that was not the reason Lee lost the battle of Antietam or the Confederacy lost the war. Even had Lee won the battle of Antietam it is highly improbable that the Confederacy would have won the war. President Wilson suffered a fateful breakdown on his train outside Wichita, Kansas, in the midst of his crusade for the ratification of the League of Nations, and the League was defeated. But that is not the reason that the Senate rejected the League or that the Republicans won the election of 1920; these things would have come about in any event, regardless of the fate of President Wilson.

Yet in every one of these instances, and in a hundred others which we could readily conjure up, fortuity did play a part, and an important part. It changed things; it meant that some men who might have lived, died; it meant that some battles had to be fought over again; it meant that what we call the course of history was slowed up or speeded up or temporarily deflected.

May we not conclude that fortuity itself is predictable, and that the mature historian takes it into account in his explanations, just as the wise general or statesman takes it into account in his calculations? An earthquake, a drought, the discovery of a new continent, or of gold and silver mines, an epidemic, an assassination, all of these are in a sense fortuitous, yet all of them are in a sense normal, as well, for such as these recur in the history of every country and every century.

Perhaps the most useful lesson the student of history can learn is to avoid oversimplification, and to accept the notion of multiple causation or to resign himself to the fact that as yet we do not know enough to explain the causes of things. To yearn for a single, and usually simple, explanation of the chaotic materials of the past, to search for a single thread in that most tangled of all tangled skeins, is a sign of immaturity. More, it is a practice which encourages dangerous intellectual habits, for it leads, almost inevitably, to a simplistic view of the present as well as of the past. Any historian who invites us to accept some single explanation of the great events of the past excites our distrust; all too often such men find the explanation of prodigious events in some fortuitous occurrence, in some lurid conspiracy, or in some naive observation of character. They tell us that for want of a nail a kingdom was lost; they explain the Reformation in terms of Luther's desire to marry, or the Spanish conquest of Mexico in terms of Cortez' mistress, or the "loss" of China by reference to traitors in the United States Department of State! They are those men of maxims against whom George Eliot has warned us:

> All people of strong, broad sense have an instinctive repugnance to men of maxims; because such people early discover that the mysterious complexity of our life is not to be embraced by maxims, and that to lace ourselves up in formulas of that sort is to repress all the divine promptings and inspirations that spring from a growing insight and sympathy. And the man of maxims is the popular representative of the minds that are guided in their moral judgments solely by general rules, thinking that these will lead them to justice by ready-made patent method, without the trouble of exerting patience, discrimination, impartiality, without any care to assure themselves whether they have the insight that comes from a hardly-earned estimate of temptation, or from a life vivid and intense enough to have created a wide fellow-feeling with all that is human.

THE PHILOSOPHY OF HISTORY

We come then, at the end, to the Philosophy of History. The term itself is ambiguous. It may mean either one of two things, or both of them. It may mean the philosophy which the student brings to the study and the interpretation of history and to which he confidently expects history to conform. Or it may mean, more simply, the philosophy which the student finds in history, and to which he himself will, perchance, conform.

The term Philosophy of History is a formal and even a forbidding one. It conjures up for us those system makers and systems of the past, and of the present, too, who organized full scale philosophies of history and demanded that history shoulder arms and march to its commands: an Augustine who proved that history was the working out of the will of God with man, a Hegel with his mystical sense of history as the history of freedom culminating in the present, a Condorcet who saw all history as a serried panorama of progress, a Karl Marx with his iron laws of history as a record of the struggle for material ends, a John Fiske with his assurance that history was progressive evolution, a Henry Adams imposing an irrelevant law of thermodynamics on the reluctant stuff of history, a Benedetto Croce with his magisterial principle that all history is contemporary history and must be recaptured and realized by each historian for himself, an Arnold Toynbee with his theory of the rise and dispersion of civilizations.

As we contemplate these and many other philosophies of history we are forced to conclude that the effort to compress the incalculably vast, infinitely complex, and wantonly elusive stuff of history into any single framework, or to express it in any single formula, is doomed to futility. This conclusion in turn suggests not so much that men have failed to solve the enigma of history as that there is no solution and possibly no enigma. Who are we, after all, to impose our will upon history? Who are we to require that it embrace our theories, dance to our tunes, march to our commands? Certainly nothing in the record of historical philosophy encourages us to believe that we can ever find some meaning in history upon which all sound men will agree.

Indeed the very multiplicity of historical philosophies and the inability of the most profound historians to agree on the meaning of history suggest that the philosophies are dictated not by history itself, but by circumstances, or by the temperament and the training of the historical philosophers.

All of this is entirely natural. After all, philosophers and saints have been brooding over the relation of man to God for thousands of years without arriving at a common religion. Philosophers and statesmen have been working out political theories for over two thousand years without arriving at one on which any large portion of mankind voluntarily agrees. Philosophers and teachers have been considering the nature of education for centuries, but we have not yet arrived at any generally accepted philosophy of education. Why should we expect an authoritative philosophy of history when we still lack authoritative philosophies of religion, politics, or education?

If the deductive approach to the philosophy of history is unprofitable, let us turn to the inductive. G. M. Trevelyan has well said that philosophy is not something you take to history, it is something you carry away from history. If we cannot impose our philosophical patterns upon history, let us see if history can impose philosophical lessons upon us.

This is, to be sure, a manner of speech. There is no such thing as "history" in the abstract, something which works out lessons and proceeds to impose them upon her disciples. What we mean when we say that "history" imposes its lessons is that after prolonged study and profound consideration of some chapter of history, the historian, like the educator, or the jurisprudent, or the political philosopher, may draw some general conclusions about its meaning, its purposes, and its value. Such considerations will have no scientific validity; they will have only the authority which may attach itself to the character and the reputation of the historian. But that is true in every non-scientific domain. If, over the years and centuries, learned and sagacious scholars from many different societies arrive at some common generalizations, may we not be justified in according these some degree of respect?

So, at least, men have thought in the past. "The great errors of the age are very useful," wrote Voltaire. "One cannot remind oneself too often of crimes and disasters. These, no matter what people say, can be forestalled. The history of the tyrant Christiern can prevent a nation from giving absolute power to a tyrant, and the undoing of Charles XII at Pultawa will warn a generation not to plunge too deeply into the Ukraine without supplies." That is combining the serious and the frivolous with a vengeance, but it suggests how the liveliest mind of the eighteenth century turned to history, and wrote it, too. Certainly the American Founding Fathers thought the study of history profitable. All of them were immersed in history, especially in the history of the ancient world; almost all of them wrote history. They drew with confidence on the history of the past to justify independence, to guide them along the paths of federalism, to provide examples for their every experiment in politics and government, to illuminate the problem of the reconciliation of liberty and order. The debates in the Federal Convention of 1787, the debates in the ratifying conventions, *The Federalist* papers—these are one continuous historical commentary. And so, too, the private letters of John Adams, Madison, Jefferson, Hamilton, Washington—it was always history they turned to, for examples and illustrations and morals. Nor were the resources of history exhausted with the ratification of the Constitution. Washington drew upon history when he warned his fellow countrymen against the baleful influence of factions and parties; Jefferson called upon it when he denounced the Alien and Sedition Acts and celebrated the long record of freedom from governmental tyranny; Calhoun invoked it to vindicate States' Rights, and Webster, in that eloquent appeal for a Union one and inseparable, which still has the power to quicken our heart-beats. Lincoln reviewed the history of the nation in his First Inaugural Address to prove that "the nation came before the states," and he began his Gettysburg Address with a reminder of what had happened four score and seven years ago—. A hundred other examples flood into our minds; it is sufficient to recall one of the most fateful. Winston Churchill, an historian as well as a maker of history, tells us that when at Chequers he heard the news of the attack on Pearl Harbor, he knew that Britain was saved. "I had studied the American Civil War, fought out to the last desperate inch . . . I went to bed and slept the sleep of the saved."

We have quoted before what is probably the most familiar of all definitions of History: "philosophy teaching by examples." The phrase is Bolingbroke's, but Dionysius of Halicarnassus said the same thing two thousand years ago, and fifteen centuries later, Sir Walter Raleigh, who was an historian as well as an explorer, wrote that "the end and scope of all history" is "to teach us by examples of times past such wisdom as may guide our desires and actions." No definition is more hackneyed; perhaps none is more acceptable.

Very well, then; if history is philosophy teaching by examples, what does it teach?

Candor forces us to confess that it teaches pretty much what historians or, more commonly, those who are in power, want taught. All too often, over the centuries, history has been the camp-follower of victorious armies, the champion of successful parties, the apologist of dominant classes, the protagonist of established religions. Indeed, so widespread is the exploitation of history for personal, partisan, religious, class, or national purposes, that we cannot but have some sympathy with Napoleon's remark that "history is a lie agreed upon," or with Matthew Arnold's reference to "that huge Mississippi of falsehood called history," or speculate how applicable to history is Justice Holme's sardonic definition of Truth: "the majority vote of that nation that can lick all others." How sobering it is that in almost every major war both sides have invoked history with complete assurance that it will respond. Over the years history has been made to do service for almost every cause. The rich and the powerful on both sides of the Atlantic invoked the history of the French Revolution to damn all popular reforms and protect their privileges. Southern planters used the history of Greece and Rome to prove that slavery was a beneficent institution, and essential to a high civilization. Hitler prostituted history to prove the superiority of the Aryans over all other races. The Chinese Communists today rewrite history to prove that the white races have always exploited the yellow. Even in smaller matters politicians do not hesitate to summon up history to vindicate their arguments: that inflation always leads to ruin, or that centralization inevitably leads to tyranny, or that socialization destroys initiative, or that the majority have a peculiar proclivity for injustice.

If this were the whole story, we might well conclude that the study of history was at best an idle self-indulgence, and at worst corrupting; a number of critics have come to just that conclusion—Nietzsche and Verlaine among them. Happily it is not the whole story. History has other and more benevolent uses. It can, and does, provide mankind with memory. It does fire the imagination, broaden intellectual horizons, and deepen sympathies. It does summon up a great cloud of witnesses from the past to instruct and edify each new generation. It does encourage each generation to believe that it can build upon the past and perhaps progress into the future. And it does inculcate moral precepts.

What moral precepts? History provides perspective. It reminds us that time is indeed long and our own life fleeting; that for thousands of years each generation has thought that it was the end and the object of history; that men have known crises before, and wars, and turmoils, and triumph and tragedy, and have survived; that those issues and problems which loom so large on our horizons may not even be visible on the larger horizon of history; and that the cloud-capp'd towers, the gorgeous palaces, the solemn temples, which to us seem the very wonders of the world, may dissolve and leave not a rack behind.

Because history gives us a larger perspective, it moderates our instinctive and pervasive parochialism, a parochialism of both time and space, a parochialism which is moral as well as social or political. It teaches us that the world is large, miscellaneous, and haphazard, not subject to our fiat or to our desires. It tells us that one people and then another, one nation and then another, one civilization and then another has moved to the center of the historical stage, and claimed for itself the principal role, and then moved into the shadows. It admonishes us that our habits and interests, our standards and values, have no cosmic validity; that we cannot impose our will upon history, or bestride history like some Colossus. It teaches therefore modesty and humility.

Along with these precepts history enjoins patience—patience with the long struggle of men to conquer Nature, to organize government and society, to cope with the thousand problems that glare and glower upon them ceaselessly through time. It teaches patience with the errors of men, the mischief of their enterprises, the failures of their institutions, the frustrations of their hopes and ambitions. It teaches patience too with our own contemporaries, patience with those who, in the words of Jefferson describing the French Revolution, "seek through blood and slaughter their long-lost liberties"; patience with those who are just now emerging out of centuries of darkness and deprivation and are trying to catch up, in one convulsive leap, with the peoples of the western world; patience with those who do not accept or adopt our ways of thinking or adopt our institutions; patience with experiments that seem misguided and even pernicious. It counsels us to be patient with the unfathomable processes of history, the unexpected, the unforeseen, the unfamiliar; with change that never comes the way we want it to come; with problems that are never solved the way we would solve them, or that are simply transformed into new problems equally insoluble. It teaches us patience with all of this, but impatience with all those simplifications which do violence to the mysterious complexity, the subtlety, the richness and density and intricacy of the historical process.

History teaches tolerance—tolerance with different faiths, different loyalties, different cultures, different ideas and ideals. It instructs us that over the centuries there have been so many of these, so many faiths, so many cultures, so many nations, so many parties, so many philosophies, that each people has been guilty of supposing, "Lo we are the people and all wisdom dies with us"; that each sect, each party, has indulged in the vanity of believing that it, somehow, represented the larger purposes of history and the will of God. It teaches tolerance of alien peoples and opposing interests, and of ideas which, in the words of Justice Holmes, we think "loathsome and fraught with death." It teaches, therefore, the necessity of freedom—freedom for inquiry, freedom for heterodoxy and dissent—for it makes clear that freedom is the only method mankind has thus far found for avoiding error and discovering truth.

History assures us that man is neither the creature of iron laws over which he has no control nor the victim of chance and fortuity. Man need not sink beneath some secular determinism, nor need he acquiesce in the notion that day after day the wind of history bloweth where it listeth, and that he is the sport of vagrant historical winds. For history tells us that if men are not masters of their fate, neither are they the victims of fate. It reminds us, by a thousand stirring examples, that the individual counts, that character counts. It makes clear that it was the genius of Mohammed that revitalized the Arab world, that it was the moral power of the Maid of Orleans which united the French against the English; that the iron will of Cromwell was essential to the triumph of the Puritan cause; that it was Washington who made possible the American victory in the Revolutionary War, that Mahatma Gandhi was the driving force behind Indian independence and nationhood, and that without Winston Churchill's eloquence and resolution, England might have gone under before help could have arrived from across the sea.

And does not history tell us, too, that it is not only the character of the individual but of a whole people that counts? "What kind of a people do they think we are?" cried Churchill at a famous moment in history, and may we not say that it was because Hitler and his supporters were ignorant and contemptuous of history that they failed so fatefully to understand what kind of people the British were. The character of a people counts, and makes a difference—in the long nightmare struggle of the Dutch against their Spanish overlords, in the bulldog tenacity of the British against the Napoleonic imperium, in the passionate patriotism and courage of the Swiss, in the courage, the prudence, the industry, the wisdom of the Norwegians in surviving through Nazi tyranny and rebuilding their shattered nation after liberation.

And history reminds us, too, that character is to be read not only in manifestations of courage and power, but in things of the mind and the spirit as well. We do not turn to the histories of ancient Athens, of Renaissance Florence and Siena, of Elizabethan England or colonial Virginia or nineteenth century Denmark because they recount great deeds of courage or mighty strokes of power, but because they provide us with refreshment of the mind and the spirit. History admonishes us that the tests of happiness, of greatness, and of power are not everywhere or always the same, and that in the long run what we turn to are not the triumphs of wealth and of might but of the mind and the spirit of man.

It is not given us to know the causes of things, but the search for causes is itself an affluent enterprise, one which enlarges the mind and quickens the sympathies of all who engage in it. No laws of history command authority, but the study of those manifold forces which ceaselessly play upon history deepens our understanding and brings magnanimity to our judgment. No philosophy encompasses or explains the trackless course of history, but to those who study it with sympathy and understanding and imagination history teaches philosophy. *Esto perpetuo.*

Bibliography

Acton, Lord. *Essays on Freedom and Power,* ed. by Gertrude Himmelfarb. Boston: Beacon Press, 1948.

Ausubel, Herman. *Historians and Their Craft: A Study of the Presidential Addresses to the American Historical Association, 1884–1945.* New York: Columbia University Press, 1952.

———, *et al. Some Modern Historians of Britain, Essays in Honor of R. L. Schuyler.* New York: Holt, Rinehart & Winston, Inc., 1951.

Barraclough, Geoffrey. *History in a Changing World.* New York: Oxford University Press, 1955.

Barzun, Jacques and Graff, Henry A. *The Modern Researcher.* New York: Harcourt, Brace & World, Inc., 1957.

Bassett, John Spencer. *The Middle Group of American Historians.* New York: The Macmillan Company, 1917.

Beard, Charles A. *The Economic Basis of Politics.* New York: Random House, Inc., 1957.

Becker, Carl. *Everyman His Own Historian.* New York: Appleton-Century-Crofts, 1935.

Berlin, Isaiah. *Historical Inevitability.* New York: Oxford University Press, 1954.

Bloch, Marc. *The Historian's Craft.* New York: Alfred A. Knopf, Inc., 1953.

Bowen, Catherine Drinker. *Adventures of a Biographer.* Boston: Atlantic-Little, Brown, 1959.

Bury, J. B. *The Ancient Greek Historians.* New York: The Macmillan Company, 1909.

———. *The Idea of Progress.* New York: The Macmillan Company, 1932.

Butterfield, Herbert. *The Englishman and His History.* Cambridge: Cambridge University Press, 1944.

———. *History and Human Relations.* London: Collins, 1951.

———. *Man on His Past: The Study of the History of Historical Scholarship.* Cambridge: Cambridge University Press, 1954.

Carr, Edward Hallett. *What Is History?* New York: Alfred A. Knopf, Inc., 1962.

Cassirer, Ernst. *The Philosophy of the Enlightenment.* Boston: Beacon Press, 1951.

Cheyney, Edward P. *Law in History and Other Essays.* New York: Alfred A. Knopf, Inc., 1927.

Collingwood, R. G. *The Idea of History.* Oxford: Clarendon Press, 1946.

Dilthey, Wilhelm. *Pattern and Meaning in History.* New York: Harper & Row, Publishers, 1961.

Dunning, William A. *Truth in History and Other Essays,* intro. by J. G. DeRoulhac Hamilton. New York: Columbia University Press, 1937.

Flint, Robert. *History of the Philosophy of History.* Edinburgh and London: William Blackwood and Sons, 1893.

Gardiner, Patrick, ed. *Theories of History: Readings from Classical and Contemporary Sources.* New York: Free Press of Glencoe, Inc., 1959.

Geyl, Pieter. *Debates with Historians.* Cleveland: The World Publishing Co., 1958.

———. *Encounters in History.* New York: Meridian Books, Inc., 1961.

Gooch, G. P. *History and Historians in the Nineteenth Century,* 2nd ed. New York: David McKay Co., Inc., 1952.

Gottschalk, Louis. *Generalization in the Writing of History.* Chicago: The University of Chicago Press, 1963.

———. *Understanding History.* New York: Alfred A. Knopf, Inc., 1950.

Harrison, Frederic. *The Meaning of History.* New York: The Macmillan Company, 1908.

Hexter, J. H. *Reappraisals in History.* Evanston, Ill.: Northwestern University Press, 1961.

Hughes, H. Stuart. *History as Art and as Science.* New York: Harper & Row, Publishers, 1964.

Hutchinson, William T., ed. *The Marcus W. Jernegan Essays in American Historiography.* Chicago: University of Chicago Press, 1937.

Kent, Sherman. *Writing History.* New York: Appleton-Century-Crofts, 1941.

Kichan, Lionel. *Action on History.* London: Deutsch, 1954.

Klibansky, Raymond and Paton, H. J., eds. *Philosophy and History.* New York, Evanston, and London: Harper & Row, Publishers, 1963.

Knowles, David. *The Historian and Character.* Cambridge: Cambridge University Press, 1963.

Kraus, Michael. *A History of American History.* New York: Farrar and Rinehart, 1937.

Laistner, M. L. W. *The Greater Roman Historians.* Berkeley: University of California Press, 1947.

Leisy, Ernest E. *The American Historical Novel.* Norman, Okla.: University of Oklahoma Press, 1950.

Levin, David. *History as Romantic Art: Bancroft, Prescott, Motley, and Parkman.* Stanford, Calif.: Stanford University Press, 1959.

Lovejoy, Arthur O. *Essays in the History of Ideas.* Baltimore: Johns Hopkins Press, 1948.

Malin, James. *The Contriving Brain and the Skillful Hand in the United States: Something About History and the Philosophy of History.* Lawrence, Kan.: University of Kansas Press, 1955.

———. *Essays on Historiography.* Lawrence, Kan.: University of Kansas Press, 1946.

———. *On the Nature of History: Essays about History and Dissidence.* Lawrence, Kan.: University of Kansas Press, 1954.

Meyerhoff, Hans. *The Philosophy of History in Our Time: An Anthology Selected and Edited by Hans Meyerhoff.* Garden City, N. Y.: Doubleday & Company, Inc., 1959.

Morison, Samuel Eliot. *Vistas of History.* New York: Alfred A. Knopf, Inc., 1964.

Muller, Herbert J. *The Uses of the Past.* New York: Columbia University Press, 1952.

Namier, L. B. *Avenues of History.* London: Hamish Hamilton, 1952.

Neff, Emery. *The Poetry of History.* New York: Columbia University Press, 1947.

Nevins, Allan. *The Gateway to History.* Garden City, N. Y.: Doubleday & Company, Inc., 1962.

———, "Not Capulets, Not Montagus," *American Historical Review,* LXV (1960), 253–271.

Niebuhr, Reinhold. *The Irony of American History.* New York: Charles Scribner's Sons, 1952.

Nietzsche, Frederick. *The Use and Abuse of History.* New York: Liberal Arts Press, 1949.

Pares, Richard. *The Historian's Business and Other Essays,* ed. by R. A. and Elisabeth Humphreys. New York: Oxford University Press, 1961.

Popper, Karl. *The Poverty of Historicism.* Boston: Beacon Press, 1957.

Renier, Gustaf J. *History, Its Purpose and Method.* Boston: Beacon Press, 1950.

Rowse, A. L. *The Use of History.* New York: The Macmillan Co., 1947.

Salmon, Lucy M. *Why Is History Rewritten?* intro. by Edward P. Cheney. New York: Oxford University Press, 1929.

Schevill, Ferdinand. *Six Historians.* Chicago: University of Chicago Press, 1956.

Smith, Page. *The Historian and History.* New York: Alfred A. Knopf, Inc., 1964.

Stern, Fritz, ed. *Varieties of History.* New York: Meridian Books, Inc., 1956.

Strayer, Joseph R., ed. *The Interpretation of History.* Princeton, N. J.: Princeton University Press, 1943.

Strout, Cushing. *The Pragmatic Revolt in American History: Carl Becker and Charles Beard.* New Haven, Conn.: Yale University Press, 1958.

Teggart, Frederick J. *The Processes of History.* New Haven, Conn.: Yale University Press, 1918.

———. *Prolegomena to History: The Relation of History to Literature, Philosophy, and Science.* Berkeley: University of California Press, 1916.

———. *Theory and Processes of History.* Berkeley: University of California Press, 1941.

Thompson, J. W. *A History of Historical Writing.* New York: The Macmillan Company, 1942. 2 vols.

Trevelyan, George Macaulay. *Clio, A Muse and Other Essays.* London: Longmans, Green, 1913. 2nd ed., 1930.

———. *An Autobiography and Other Essays.* London: 1949.

Wedgwood, C. V. *The Sense of the Past.* New York: Columbia University Press, 1957.

———. *Truth and Opinion.* London: Collins; New York: The Macmillan Company, 1960.

Weiss, Paul. *History, Written and Lived.* Carbondale, Ill.: Southern Illinois University Press, 1962.

Wish, Harvey. *The American Historian.* New York: Oxford University Press, 1960.

———, ed. *American Historians, A Selection.* New York: Oxford University Press, 1962.

Index
